GREAT FOREIGN
LANGUAGE WRITERS

Great Writers series

Poets (in English)

Novelists (in English)

Dramatists (in English)

Foreign Language Writers

GREAT FOREIGN
LANGUAGE WRITERS

EDITED BY
James Vinson and Daniel Kirkpatrick

ST MARTIN'S PRESS
NEW YORK

© St. Martin's Press 1984

All rights reserved. For information, write:
St. Martin's Press, Inc., 175 Fifth Avenue, New York, N.Y. 10010
Printed in the United States of America
First published in the United States of America in 1984

Library of Congress Catalog Card Number 83-40552

ISBN 0-312-34585-2

CONTENTS

7128504

EDITOR'S NOTE

The selection of writers included in this book is based on the recommendations of the advisers listed on page ix.

The entry for each writer consists of a biography, a complete list of separately published books, a selected list of published bibliographies and critical studies on the writer, and a signed critical essay.

In the biographies, details of education, military service, and marriage(s) are generally given before the usual chronological summary of the life of the writer; awards and honours are given last.

The Publications section is meant to include all book publications, including translations into English, though as a rule broadsheets, single sermons and lectures, minor pamphlets, exhibition catalogues, etc., are omitted. Under the heading Collections, we have listed the most recent collections of the complete works; on-going editions are indicated by a dash after the date of publication; often a general selection from the writer's works is included.

Titles are given in modern spelling; often the titles are "short." The date given is that of the first book publication, which often followed the first periodical or anthology publication by some time. No attempt has been made to indicate which works were published anonymously or pseudonymously, or which works of fiction were published in more than one volume. Reprints of books (including facsimile editions) and revivals of plays are not listed unless a revision of title is involved.

In the essays, short references to critical remarks refer to items cited in the Publications section or in the Critical Studies section. Introductions, memoirs, editorial matter, etc., in works cited in the Publications section are not repeated in the Critical Studies.

We would like to thank the advisers and contributors for their patience and help.

ADVISERS

A. James Arnold
William Arrowsmith
Thomas G. Bergin
Gordon Brotherston
Ruby Cohn
Wallace Fowlie
Michael Freeman
Janet Garton
Igor Hájek
Peter Hutchinson

Harry Levin
Earl Miner
Jerzy Peterkiewicz
Christopher R. Pike
Dušan Puvačić
Olga Ragusa
James Russell Stamm
Robert M. Torrance
Daniel Weissbort

CONTRIBUTORS

Hans Christian Andersen
J.K. Anderson
A. James Arnold
Peter Avery
K.P. Bahadur
D.R. Shackleton Bailey
David M. Bain
Barry Baldwin
Alan Bance
Gabrielle Barfoot
John Barsby
Roderick Beaton
Thomas G. Bergin
Binghong Lu
Patrick Brady
Gerard J. Brault
S.H. Braund
Gordon Brotherston
A.W. Bulloch
Mary Ann Caws
Andrea C. Cervi
C. Chadwick
Ruby Cohn
Michael Collie
Desmond J. Conacher
David Constantine
Ray Cooke
Neil Cornwell
C.D.N. Costa
Sally McMullen (Croft)
G.P. Cubbin
Santiago Daydi-Tolson
René de Costa
Ken Dowden

Sam Driver
John Dunkley
Herman Ermolaev
Nancy Kanach Fehsenfeld
John Fletcher
A.P. Foulkes
Wallace Fowlie
Michael Freeman
Frank J. Frost
Janet Garton
Margaret Gibson
Nahum N. Glatzer
Sander M. Goldberg
George Gömöri
Roger Green
Claire E. Gruzelier
Oscar A. Haac
David T. Haberly
David M. Halperin
P.T. Harries
John Hart
Thomas R. Hart
E.C. Hawkesworth
Lois Boe Hyslop
Regina Janes
Lewis Jillings
W.J.S. Kirton
Charles Klopp
Linn Bratteteig Konrad
David Konstan
Maurice Marc LaBelle
F.J. Lamport
Ladislaus Löb
Gregory L. Lucente

David S. Luft
Haydn T. Mason
Gita May
Patrick McCarthy
Keith McMahon
Gary B. Miles
John Douglas Minyard
Masao Miyoshi
Matthew Mizenko
Kenneth Muir
Frank J. Nisetich
Cecil Parrott
Alan K.G. Paterson
Christopher R. Pike
Donald Peter Alexander Pirie
Gordon Pocock
Valentina Polukhina
Charles A. Porter
Dušan Puvačić
Olga Ragusa
Judy Rawson
J.H. Reid
Robert Reid
John H. Reilly
Barbara Reynolds
Norma Rinsler
Michael Robinson
Eamonn Rodgers
Hugh Rorrison
Shoichi Saeki
William Merritt Sale III
Jeffrey L. Sammons
N.K. Sandars
Barbara Saunders
Barry P. Scherr

Irene Scobbie
Mary Scott
Edward Seidensticker
Ruth Sharman
Barnett Shaw
David Sices
G. Singh
C.N. Smith
J. Kelley Sowards
James Russell Stamm
C.C. Stathatos
Mary E. Stewart
Alexander Stillmark
Ian C. Storey
Arrigo V. Subiotto
Henry W. Sullivan
Helena Szépe
Myron Taylor
Philip Thody
David Thomas
Judith Thurman
Hugo J. Verani
Maïr Verthuy
Albert H. Wallace
George Walsh
David Welsh
Kenneth S. Whitton
A.J. Woodman
M.J. Woods
James B. Woodward
A. Colin Wright
Barbara Wright
Elizabeth Wright
John D. Yohannan
Howard T. Young

GREAT FOREIGN
LANGUAGE WRITERS

Arthur Adamov
Aeschylus
S.Y. Agnon
Anna Akhmatova
Vittorio Alfieri
Hans Christian Andersen
Ivo Andrić
Guillaume Apollinaire
Apollonius of Rhodes
Apuleius
Ludovico Ariosto
Aristophanes
Antonin Artaud
St. Augustine
Marcus Aurelius

Isaak Babel
Honoré de Balzac
Basho
Charles Baudelaire
Beaumarchais
Andrey Bely
Bhagavad Gita
Bible
Alexander Blok
Giovanni Boccaccio
Boethius
Nicolas Boileau
Heinrich Böll
Jorge Luis Borges
Bertolt Brecht
André Breton
Hermann Broch
Georg Büchner
Mikhail Bulgakov

Pedro Calderón de la Barca
Callimachus
Luís de Camoës
Albert Camus
Elias Canetti
Karel Capek
Alejo Carpentier
Catullus
C.P. Cavafy
Guido Cavalcanti
Paul Celan
Louis-Ferdinand Céline
Miguel de Cervantes
Chateaubriand
Anton Chekhov
Chin P'ing Mei
Chrétien de Troyes
Cicero
Paul Claudel

Jean Cocteau
Colette
Pierre Corneille

Gabriele D'Annunzio
Dante Alighieri
Rubén Darío
Dazai Osamu
Denis Diderot
Isak Dinesen
Fyodor Dostoevsky
Dream of the Red Chamber
Joachim Du Bellay
Alexandre Dumas, père
Friedrich Dürrenmatt

Desiderius Erasmus
Euripides

Gustave Flaubert
Theodor Fontane
Max Frisch

Federico García Lorca
Jean Genet
André Gide
Gilgamesh
Jean Giraudoux
Johann Wolfgang von Goethe
Nikolai Gogol
Carlo Goldoni
Witold Gombrowicz
Ivan Goncharov
Luis de Góngora
Maxim Gorky
Gottfried von Strassburg
Günter Grass
Franz Grillparzer
Hans Jakob Christoffel von Grimmelshausen

Hafiz
Knut Hamsun
Jaroslav Hašek
Gerhart Hauptmann
Friedrich Hebbel
Heinrich Heine
Herodotus
Hesiod
Hermann Hesse
E.T.A. Hoffmann
Hugo von Hofmannsthal
Ludvig Holberg
Friedrich Hölderlin
Homer
Horace

3

Ödön von Horváth
Victor Hugo

Henrik Ibsen
Gyula Illyés
Eugène Ionesco

Alfred Jarry
Juan Ramón Jiménez
Saint John of the Cross
Juvenal

Franz Kafka
Kawabata Yasunari
Nikos Kazantzakis
Gottfried Keller
Velimir Khlebnikov
Heinrich von Kleist
Jan Kochanowski
Miroslav Krleža

Choderlos de Laclos
Madame de Lafayette
Jean de La Fontaine
Jules Laforgue
Pär Lagerkvist
Selma Lagerlöf
Lazarillo de Tormes
Giacomo Leopardi
Mikhail Lermontov
Gotthold Ephraim Lessing
Li Po
Livy
Lucian
Lucretius
Lu Hsun
Martin Luther

Joaquim Maria Machado de Assis
Niccolò Machiavelli
Maurice Maeterlinck
Mahabharata
Stéphane Mallarmé
André Malraux
Osip Mandelstam
Thomas Mann
Alessandro Manzoni
Marivaux
Martial
Guy de Maupassant
François Mauriac
Vladimir Mayakovsky
Menander
Adam Mickiewicz
Mishima Yukio

Molière
Michel de Montaigne
Eugenio Montale
Murasaki Shikibu
Robert Musil
Alfred de Musset

Natsume Soseki
Pablo Neruda
Gérard de Nerval
Nibelungenlied
Novalis

Omar Khayyam
Ovid

Pier Paolo Pasolini
Boris Pasternak
Cesare Pavese
Octavio Paz
Benito Pérez Galdós
Fernando Pessoa
Petrarch
Petronius
Pindar
Luigi Pirandello
Plato
Plautus
Plutarch
Abbé Prévost
Marcel Proust
Alexander Pushkin

Raymond Queneau

François Rabelais
Jean Racine
Ramayana
Rainer Maria Rilke
Arthur Rimbaud
Alain Robbe-Grillet
Fernando de Rojas
Song of Roland
Pierre de Ronsard
Romance of the Rose
Jean-Jacques Rousseau
Gabrielle Roy

Marquis de Sade
Saint-John Perse
George Sand
Sappho
Jean-Paul Sartre
Friedrich von Schiller
Arthur Schnitzler

Bruno Schulz
George Seferis
Seneca
Henryk Sienkiewicz
Angelos Sikelianos
Ignazio Silone
Alexander Solzhenitsyn
Sophocles
Stendhal
Adalbert Stifter
August Strindberg
Snorri Sturluson
Italo Svevo

Tacitus
Tanizaki Jun'ichiro
Torquato Tasso
Terence
Theocritus
Thousand and One Nights
Thucydides
Tirso de Molina
Leo Tolstoy
Georg Trakl
Marina Tsvetayeva
Tu Fu
Ivan Turgenev

Miguel de Unamuno

Sigrid Undset
Giuseppe Ungaretti
Upanishads

Paul Valéry
César Vallejo
The Vedas
Lope de Vega Carpio
Giovanni Verga
Paul Verlaine
Gil Vicente
Alfred de Vigny
François Villon
Virgil
Elio Vittorini
Voltaire

Walther von der Vogelweide
Water Margin
Frank Wedekind
Peter Weiss
Stanislaw Witkiewicz
Wolfram von Eschenbach

Xenophon

Evgeny Zamyatin
Émile Zola

ADAMOV, Arthur. Born in Kislovodsk, Russia, 23 August 1908; lived abroad after 1912. Educated at Rosset School, Geneva; French lycée, Mainz, Germany, 1922-24; Lycée Lakanal, Paris, 1924-27. Married Jacqueline Trehet in 1961. Translator and writer in Paris: Editor, *Discontinuité* in late 1920's, and *L'Heure Nouvelle*, 1945-47. *Died 15 March 1970.*

PUBLICATIONS

Plays

La Parodie (produced 1952). With *L'Invasion*, 1950.
L'Invasion (produced 1950). With *La Parodie*, 1950; as *The Invasion*, 1968.
La grande et la petite manoeuvre (produced 1950). 1950.
Le Sens de la marche (produced 1953). 1953.
Tous contre tous (produced 1953). 1953.
Le Professeur Taranne (produced 1953). 1953; as *Professor Taranne*, in *Two Plays*, 1962.
Comme nous avons été (produced 1954). In *La Nouvelle Nouvelle Revue Française 1*, 1953; as *As We Were*, in *Evergreen Review 4*, 1957.
Théâtre I-IV. 1953-68.
Le Ping-Pong (produced 1955). 1955; as *Ping Pong*, 1959.
Les Retrouvailles. 1955.
Paolo Paoli (produced 1957). 1957; translated as *Paolo Paoli*, 1959.
Les Âmes mortes (produced 1960). 1960.
Le Printemps 71 (produced 1963). 1961.
La Politique des restes (produced 1963). 1967.
M. Le Modéré (produced 1968). In *Théâtre IV*, 1968.
Off Limits (produced 1969). 1969.
Si l'été revenait. 1970.

Radio Play: *En fiacre*, 1959.

Fiction

Je...ils.... 1969.

Other

L'Aveu. 1946.
Auguste Strindberg, dramaturge, with Maurice Gravier. 1955.
Théâtre de société. 1958.
Ici et maintenant. 1964.
L'Homme et l'enfant. 1968.

Editor, *Le Commune de Paris.* 1959.

Translator, *Le Moi et l'inconscient*, by Jung. 1938.
Translator, with Marie Geringer, *Le Livre de la pauvrété et de la mort*, by Rilke. 1941.
Translator, with Marthe Robert, *Théâtre complet*, by Büchner. 1953.
Translator, *Crime et châtiment*, by Dostoevsky. 1956.
Translator, *Les Aventures de Tchitchikov*, by Gogol. 1956.
Translator, *La Mère, Vassa Geleznova*, and *Les petits bourgeois*, by Gorky. 3 vols., 1958.

Translator, *Théâtre*, by Chekhov. 1958.
Translator, *Le Père*, by Strindberg. 1958.
Translator, *Le Revisor*, by Gogol. 1958.
Translator, *Oblomov*, by Goncharov. 1959.
Translator, *Cinq récits*, by Gogol. 1961.
Translator, with Claude Sebisch, *Le Théâtre politique*, by Erwin Piscator. 1962.
Translator, *Les Ennemis*, by Gorky. 1970.
Translator, with Jacqueline Autrusseau, *La grande muraille*, by Max Frisch. 1973.

*

Bibliography: *Adamov* by David Bradby, 1975.

Critical Studies: *Regards sur le théâtre de Adamov* by Samia Assad Chahine, 1961; *Adamov* by John H. Reilly, 1974; *The Theatre of Adamov* by John J. McCann, 1975.

*   *   *

When Arthur Adamov first began writing for the French stage in the late 1940's and early 1950's, he was considered, along with Samuel Beckett and Eugène Ionesco, one of the most promising dramatists of the burgeoning movement of the theatre of the absurd. Similar to these two playwrights, Adamov wanted to free himself from the normal constraints of dramatic construction, eliminating the traditional concepts of characterization, action, and even time and place, if need be.

He differed from Beckett and Ionesco, however, to the extent that he used the stage as a means of expressing the enormous fears and obsessions that plagued him. For Adamov, the theatre became a personal cry of anguish, a form of catharsis, a way of attempting to liberate himself from his private demons. Essentially, the Russian-born playwright revealed his feelings of injustice and his sense of persecution and victimization in his works. In his first play, *La Parodie* (The Parody), the dramatist communicated the solitude, futility, and frustration of living. The two central characters are the victims of life's horrors: the one, identified only by the initial "N.," is crushed by a car, his body swept away by the sanitation department; the other, The Employee, ends up in prison, blind. In one of his most successful works, *Professor Taranne*, based on a dream of Adamov's, Professor Taranne finds himself in a nightmarish situation in which he has been accused by some children of indecent exposure on a beach. By the end of the play, unable to convince anyone of his innocence, he slowly begins to undress, thereby performing the very act with which he had been charged.

At this stage in his writing, Adamov's expression of his personal visions of terror had much in common with the Surrealist movement as well as with the theories of the Theatre of Cruelty espoused by Antonin Artaud. During the 1950's, however, the writer took an unusual step—he rejected all of his previous theatre: "I already saw in the 'avant-garde' an easy escape, a diversion from the real problems, the words 'absurd theatre' already irritated me. Life was not absurd—only difficult, very difficult." Having achieved some limited control of his personal obsessions, he was now able to develop his political and social concerns. Much of his drama of that period, like *Paolo Paoli* and *Le Printemps 71* (Spring 71), had strongly Marxist overtones and reflected the alienation effect experienced in the works of Bertolt Brecht. Another important play of this genre, *Le Ping-Pong*, is an impressive examination of two men's obsession with a simple pinball machine and the disastrous results when they are swept up into the capitalist world of big business.

Yet, finally, while Adamov may have planned to write politically committed theatre, he was basically still dealing with the sense of victimization and injustice that had always pursued him. Probably because of this, his theatre, while often highly acclaimed, never went on to achieve the popularity with the public of a Beckett or an Ionesco—it was too private, too personal to attain universal appeal. Interestingly enough, Adamov's most successful writing may have been his very first, *L'Aveu* (The Confession). Written between 1938 and 1943, *L'Aveu* is a series of ruthlessly honest journals in which the writer recounted directly the difficulties of existence. In the journals, the most personal form of expression, Adamov may have found his best means of communication.

—John H. Reilly

AESCHYLUS. Born in Eleusis, 525 or 524 B.C. Fought in the Battle of Marathon, 490, and probably at Artemisium and Salamis, 480. Wrote over 90 plays (we have the titles of 70): won his first playwriting prize in 484, 12 subsequent prizes, and some posthumously; also acted in his plays; visited Sicily to produce plays for Hieron I of Syracuse, soon after the foundation of the city of Aetna, 476, and again in 456. *Died in 456 B.C.*

PUBLICATIONS

Collections

[*Works*], edited by Denys Page. 1972; also edited by Ulrich von Wilamowitz-Moellendorf, 1914, and Gilbert Murray (includes translations), 1955.
Complete Greek Tragedies 1, edited by Richmond Lattimore and David Grene. 1959; also translated by H.W. Smyth (Loeb edition), 2 vols., 1922-26.
Die Fragmente der Tragödien, edited by Hans Joachim Mette. 1959.

Plays

Persae (produced 472). Edited by H.D. Broadhead, 1960; as *The Persians*, translated by S.G. Benardete, in *Complete Greek Tragedies 1*, 1959; also translated by A.J. Podlecki, 1970, and Janet Lembke and C.J. Herington, 1981.
Septem contra Thebas (produced 467). As *The Seven Against Thebes*, translated by David Grene, in *Complete Greek Tragedies 1*, 1959; also translated by Peter Arnott, 1968, Christopher M. Dawson, 1970, and Anthony Hecht and Helen H. Bacon, 1974.
Supplices (produced 466-59). Edited by H. Friis Johansen, 1970; as *The Suppliant Maidens*, translated by S.G. Benardete, in *Complete Greek Tragedies 1*, 1959; as *The Suppliants*, translated by Janet Lembke, 1975.
Oresteia (trilogy; produced 458). As *The Oresteia*, translated by Richmond Lattimore, in *Complete Greek Tragedies 1*, 1959; also translated by Philip Vellacott, 1956, Michael Townsend, 1966, Douglas Young, 1974, Robert Fagles, 1976, Robert Lowell, 1978, and Tony Harrison, 1981; as *The Orestes Plays*, translated by Paul Roche, 1963; as *The House of Atreus*, translated by John Lewin, 1966.
Agamemnon, edited by E. Fränkel (includes prose translation). 1950; also edited by John Dewar Denniston and Denys Page, 1957; translated by Louis MacNeice, 1936, Anthony Holden, 1969, and H. Lloyd-Jones, 1970.
Choephoroi (The Libation-Bearers), translated by H. Lloyd-Jones, 1970.
Eumenides (The Furies), translated by H. Lloyd-Jones, 1970.
Prometheus Vinctus (produced after 456). Edited by Mark Griffith, 1983; as *Prome-*

theus Bound, translated by David Grene, in *Complete Greek Tragedies 1*, 1959; also translated by Rex Warner, 1947, W.B. Anderson, 1963, Paul Roche, 1964, Peter Arnott, 1968, and James Scully and C.J. Herington, 1975.

*

Critical Studies: *Aeschylus, The Creator of Tragedy* by Gilbert Murray, 1940; *The Style of Aeschylus* F.R. Earp, 1948; *The Harmony of Aeschylus* by E.T. Owen, 1952; *In Praise of Prometheus: Humanism and Rationalism in Aeschylean Thought* by Leon Golden, 1966; *Aeschylus and Athens: Study in the Social Origins of Drama* by G.D. Thomson, 1966; *The Political Background of Aeschylean Tragedy* by A.J. Podlecki, 1966; *The Oresteia: A Study in Language and Structure* by Anne Lebeck, 1971; *Aeschylus: A Collection of Critical Essays* edited by Marsh H. McCall, Jr., 1972; *Aeschylean Metaphors for Intellectual Activity* by D. Sansome, 1975; *Aeschylean Drama* by Michael Gagarin, 1976; *The Stagecraft of Aeschylus* by Oliver Taplin, 1977; *Aeschylus: Prometheus Bound: A Literary Commentary* by Desmond J. Conacher, 1980; *The Art of Aeschylus* by Thomas G. Rosenmeyer, 1982; *Studies in Aeschylus* by R.P. Winnington-Ingram, 1983.

* * *

Aeschylus was the first of the three famous poets (Sophocles and Euripides are the other two) who, from antiquity onwards, have been celebrated as the great tragic dramatists of ancient Greece. In accordance with the conventions of the tragic festivals at Athens, Aeschylus based most of his plays (an exception will be noted below) on ancient myths, dating back to the Mycenaean Age at the dawn of Greek civilization; however, like the other Greek tragic poets, he invested this legendary (and, occasionally, historical) material with new, often contempo-rary, meanings of his own. Whether from choice, or due to a convention of early Greek tragedy, Aeschylus composed most of his tragedies in the form of connected trilogies. (Three tragedies, not necessarily related in subject matter, followed by a semi-comic satyr-play, remained the normal requirement for those competing in the tragic festivals throughout the Classical period.) A brief survey of his extant plays will illustrate the wide-ranging material (theological, ethical, and, in the loftiest sense of the term, political) of his themes, most of which as we shall see are well suited, by the grandeur of their dramatic conceptions, to the trilogic form of composition.

The Persians, Aeschylus's earliest extant tragedy (and the earliest Greek tragedy which we possess), is exceptional in that it is *not* part of a connected trilogy. It is of particular interest also because it is the only extant Greek tragedy based on historical, not mythological, material. *The Persians* is, however, by no means mere "dramatized history." Rather, in his treatment of the recent defeat of the Persian despot Xerxes and his Persian fleet by the Athenians at Salamis, Aeschylus "mythologizes" history to present a striking illustration of the tragic theme of *koros, hybris, atê*: excessive confidence in wealth and power, leading to an act of outrage (in this case, that of Xerxes overstepping the divinely ordained limits of his rule), which brings down the swift retribution of the gods. To present his material in tragic rather than in "historical" terms, the poet takes certain bold liberties with the factual material and employs typically Aeschylean touches of symbolism (such as the striking image of "the yoke of the sea," constraining the great sea-god Poseidon, for Xerxes's bridge of boats across "the sacred Hellespont") to stress the overreaching ambition of the Persian King.

In *The Seven Against Thebes* Aeschylus brings to a tragic conclusion (the lost plays *Laius* and *Oedipus* were the preceding plays of this trilogy) the treatment of another of his favourite themes: the working-out of a family curse, inevitably fulfilled by the gods through the "free" decisions of one of its doomed heroic victims.

In the *Oresteia*, Aeschylus's only extant trilogy, the poet combines, in magnificent fashion, both of the above two themes, that of a family curse and that of divine vengeance for a deed of hybristic outrage. In the first play, the *Agamemnon*, Agamemnon suffers (by the murderous hand of his Queen, Clytemnestra) both for the outrageous deed of his father, Atreus, against the children of his brother Thyestes, and for his own sacrifice ("impious, unholy and polluting," however "necessitous") of his daughter, Iphigenia, in order to obtain favourable winds for his great assault on Troy. In the trilogy sequel, Orestes and Electra, loyal children of King Agamemnon, continue the sequence of "blood-for-blood" by murdering, at the god Apollo's command, the usurpers, Clytemnestra (their mother) and her paramour, Aegisthus. Only in the third play, the *Eumenides*, is the curse on the family, and the attendant blood-feud, resolved. In this play, Orestes takes refuge from Clytemnestra's avenging Furies (the Chorus in the play), first at Apollo's Oracle at Delphi and then at Athens. Here the goddess Athena institutes a human court of justice (the Areopagus, which was a celebrated Athenian institution of some political importance in Aeschylus's time), in which Orestes (and all homicides thereafter) will be tried. Orestes is acquitted by Athena's casting vote and the Chorus of Furies, exactors of the old "blood-for-blood justice," are persuaded by Athena, daughter of Olympian Zeus, to become beneficent, though still awe-inspiring guardians, supporting the new order of justice which Athena has instituted.

This brief review of the *Oresteia* highlights another feature of Aeschylean thought and dramatic structure which some scholars (most notably C.J. Herington in "The Last Phase," *Arion 4*, 1965) believe was typical of the trilogies (the Danaid and the Prometheus trilogies as well as the *Oresteia*) composed in the final period of the poet's career. Thus, in the Danaid trilogy (only the first play of which, *The Suppliant Maidens*, survives) a violent sequence of forced marriage and murderous requital appears to have been "resolved" by the decision of one bride (out of the fifty sworn to slay their violent suitors) who chooses love instead of further bloodshed. As in the *Eumenides*, a goddess (in this case Aphrodite, as a fragment of the final play reveals) appears as a champion of this fruitful resolution.

Finally, the Prometheus trilogy seems to have presented a comparable sequence of tragic action leading to a positive finale. (The *Prometheus Bound* was probably the first play in the trilogy; we have only fragmentary knowledge of *Prometheus Unbound* and *Prometheus the Firebearer*, and the Aeschylean authorship of even the extant *Prometheus Bound* has been doubted by some scholars; see especially Mark Griffith, *The Authenticity of Prometheus Bound*, 1977.) This time the struggle is between Prometheus, divine champion of men, bestower of fire and all the human arts, and Zeus, man's would-be destroyer, here presented as a harsh and tyrannical new god, only recently established as lord of the Universe. That Zeus, the god of power and order, needs Promethean intelligence and foresight is established on the literal level by the fact that only Prometheus has the secret knowledge which can prevent Zeus falling from power. And that intelligence and foresight are unavailing when suppressed by power, is demonstrated by the noble martyrdom of the enchained Prometheus, whose heroic defiance ends (in the finale of *Prometheus Bound*) in his further punishment in the lowest depths of Tartaros. Again the fragments of the trilogy (and other external evidence) suffice to indicate its probable *denouement*. Prometheus and Zeus are ultimately reconciled by their mutual needs. Zeus, saved by Prometheus's foreknowledge, continues to reign supreme over a less troubled universe, and Prometheus, his "cause" now vindicated, is re-established, under Zeus, as the bestower of the civilizing gift of fire (hence the third title, *Prometheus the Firebearer*) to men. Once again, if this symbolic interpretation of the evidence be sound, we find that the sequence of suffering presented in the trilogy ends in a triumphant resolution.

In this brief survey of the extant themes of Aeschylean tragedy, it has not been possible to do justice to the impressive dramatic structure of his plays and to the grandeur of his choral odes which, particularly in the *Oresteia*, are an integral part of that structure. While it is true, as Aristotle believed, that the plot is the soul of tragedy, in Aeschylus, the plots are simple, both "action" and "characterization" being kept to the minimum necessary to expound, in compelling dramatic form, the recurrent and meaningful patterns of tragic experience.

—Desmond J. Conacher

AGNON, S.Y. Pseudonym for Shmuel Yosef Halesi Czaczkes. Born in Buczacz, Galicia, Austria-Hungary (now Poland), 17 July 1888. Studied in private schools; Baron Hirsch School. Married Esther Marx in 1919; one daughter and one son. Lived in Palestine, 1907-13: first secretary of Jewish Court in Jaffa, and Secretary of the National Jewish Council; Lecturer and tutor in Germany, 1913-24; in Palestine again from 1924. Fellow, Bar Ilan University. Recipient: Bialik Prize, 1934, 1954; Hakhnasat Kala, 1937; Ussishkin Prize, 1950; Israel Prize, 1954, 1958; Nobel Prize for Literature, 1966. D.H.L.: Jewish Theological Seminary of America, 1936; Ph.D.: Hebrew University, Jerusalem, 1959. President, Mekitzei Nirdamim, 1950. Member, Hebrew Language Academy. *Died 17 February 1970.*

PUBLICATIONS

Fiction

> *Givat ha-Hol* [The Hill of Sand]. 1920.
> *Be-Sod Yesharim* [Among the Pious]. 1921.
> *Me-Hamat ha-Metsik* [From the Wrath of the Oppressor]. 1921.
> *Al Kapot ha-Man'ul* [Upon the Handles of the Lock]. 1922.
> *Polin* [Poland]. 1925.
> *Ma'aseh rabi Gadiel ha-Tinok* [The Tale of Little Reb Gadiel]. 1925.
> *Sipur ha-Shanin ha-Tovot.* 1927.
> *Agadat ha-Sofer* [The Tale of the Scribe]. 1929.
> *Kol Sipurav* [Collected Fiction]:
>> 1-2. *Hakhnasath Kallah.* 1931; as *The Bridal Canopy*, 1937.
>> 3. *Me-Az une-Ata* [From Then and from Now]. 1931.
>> 4. *Sippurei Ahavim* [Love Stories]. 1931.
>> 5. *Sippur Pashut* [A Simple Story]. 1935.
>> 6. *Be-Shuva u-ve-Nahat* [In Peace and Tranquillity]. 1935.
>> 7. *Ore-ah Nata Lalun.* 1939; as *A Guest for the Night*, 1968.
>> 8. *Elu-va-Elu* [These and Those]. 1941.
>> 9. *Tmol Shilshom* [The Day Before Yesterday]. 1945; section published as *Kelev Hutsot*, 1950.
>> 10. *Samukh ve-Nireh.* 1951.
>> 11. *Ad Heinah* [Until Now]. 1952.
> *Bi-levav Yamim.* 1935; as *In the Heart of the Seas*, 1948.
> *Sefer, Sofer ve-Sipur.* 1938.
> *Shevu'ath Emunim.* 1943; as *The Betrothed*, in *Two Tales*, 1966.
> *Kol Sipurav*, revised edition (includes additional volume *Al Kapot ha-Man'ul*). 8 vols., 1953-62.
> *Tehilla* (in English). 1956.
> *Two Tales: The Betrothed, Edo and Enam.* 1966.
> *Twenty-One Stories*, edited by Nahum N. Glatzer, 1970; as *(Selection)*, 1977.
> *Shira* [Song]. 1971.
> *Pit'chey d'varim.* 1977.

Other

> *Miatsmi el Atsmi* [From Me to Me]. 1976.

> Editor, with Ahron Eliasberg, *Das Buch von den polnischen Juden.* 1916.
> Editor, *Yamim Nora'im.* 1938; as *Days of Awe, Being a Treasury of Traditions, Legends, and Learned Commentaries...*, 1948.

Editor, *Atem re'item.* 1959.
Editor, *Sifrehem shel Tsadikim.* 1961.

*

Bibliography: *Agnon: Eine Bibliographie seiner Werke* by Werner Martin, 1980.

Critical Studies: *Nostalgia and Nightmare: A Study in the Fiction of Agnon* (includes bibliography) by Arnold J. Band, 1968; *The Fiction of Agnon* by Baruch Hochman, 1970; *Agnon* by Harold Fisch, 1975.

* * *

S.Y. Agnon was a man of two worlds: the world of his ancestors' Judaic tradition and the realm of modernity. Some literary critics attempt to point to a harmony of the two, others insist on the radical difference and inconsistency between the two.

The province of tradition comprised the daily prayers and the celebration of the Sabbath, the lighting of the candles by the mother with its songs, hymns, special food, and parental blessings; the feasts such as the Passover, celebrating the Exodus from Egypt; the most holy Day of Atonement, a fast day and a season of forgiveness; the rabbi's home, the synagogue, and the House of Study; the spirit of neighborliness and mutual help; the occasions of birth, circumcision, marriage, and death. The learned men were honored and the youth encouraged to emulate them. The language of everyday was Yiddish, a mixture of Hebrew, German, Polish (or Russian), while Hebrew was reserved for prayer and the sacred texts; God was exalted for his majesty and goodness and the Messiah expected to redeem Israel and the world.

Agnon grew up in this world. Though the 19-year-old young man left his native Buczacz, Galicia, in 1907, the memories of the "old home" were strong and vivid enough to sustain his creative imagination for years to come. He portrays this culture in, e.g., the novel *The Bridal Canopy* and the short story "Agadat ha-Sofer" (The Tale of the Scribe). Agnon was aware of the breakdown of this culture; thus a tragic element enters both the novels and the short stories: in "The Tale of the Scribe" both the humble and saintly scribe and his pious, chaste wife, as well as the sacred scroll, perish in a conflagration.

Answering some critics' contention that Agnon adheres to a style patterned after the Jewish folktale and the homiletic mode of the ancient Midrash, he wrote a series of pieces in a strictly modern, expressionistic form; collected they appeared as "Sefer ha-Maasim" (Book of Deeds), in 1932 and later. Here cause and effect do not apply, neither the consequence of time, life and death, dream and reality: the narrator forgets his address, misses the post office and the last bus; he takes part in a memorial meeting for an important person, and returning home he finds that person waiting for him. Both the reader and the critic had to realize that Agnon was not confined to any one style; also, he chose his particular mode for he believed this mode to be most readily and universally understood by the Hebrew reader. Also, the stories evidenced that the writer was indeed a man of the Western world and that the problems of the Jewish people and those of the world at large meet and cross. At this point Agnon and Franz Kafka used a related language, symbols and metaphors. The motif of love appears throughout Agnon's works. His last novel, *Shira* (Song), places love in the center; here love is a fiercely passionate, secular, abysmal force.

—Nahum N. Glatzer

AKHMATOVA, Anna. Born Anna Andreyevna Gorenko in Bolshoy Fontan, near Odessa, 23 June 1889. Educated at girls gymnasium, Tsarskoye Selo; Smolny Institute, St. Petersburg; gymnasium and law school, Kiev; also studied literature in St. Petersburg. Married Nikolai G. Gumilyov in 1910 (divorced, 1918), one son. Recipient: Taormina Prize, 1964. D.Litt.: Oxford University, 1965. *Died 5 March 1966.*

PUBLICATIONS

Collections

Sochineniya, edited by Gleb Struve and Boris Filippov. 2 vols., 1965-68.
Stikhi i proza (selections), edited by B.G. Druian. 1977.
Stikhi, perepiska, vospominaniya, ikongrafiya, edited by Ellendea Proffer. 1977.

Verse

Vecher [Evening]. 1912.
Chotki [The Rosary]. 1913.
U samogo moria [At the Very Edge of the Sea]. 1914.
Belaya staya [The White Flock]. 1917.
Skrizhal sbornik [Ecstasy Collection]. 1921.
Podorozhnik [Plantain]. 1921.
Anno Domini MCMXXI. 1922.
Forty-Seven Love Poems, translated by Natalie Doddington. 1927.
Stikhi [Poems]. 1940.
Iz shesti knig [From Six Books]. 1940.
Izbrannoe [Selection]. 1943.
Izbrannye stikhi [Selected Poems]. 1946.
Stikhotvoreniya 1909-1957, edited by A.A. Surkov. 1958; revised edition, 1965.
Poema bez geroya: Triptikh. 1960; as *Poem Without a Hero*, 1973.
Stikhi 1909-1960. 1961.
50 Stikhotvorenii. 1963.
Rekviem: Tsikl stikhotvorenii. 1964; as *Requiem*, with *Poem Without a Hero*, translated by D.M. Thomas, 1976.
Beg vremeni [Race of Time]. 1965.
Selected Poems, translated by Richard McKane. 1969.
Poems, edited by Stanley Kunitz and Max Hayward. 1973.
Selected Poems, edited by Walter Arndt. 1976.
Way of All the Earth, translated by D.M. Thomas. 1979.
Poems (selection), translated by Lyn Coffin. 1983.
Three Russian Women Poets (with Bella Akhmadulina and Tsvetayeva), translated by Mary Maddock. 1983.

Other

Translator, *Koreyskaya klassicheskaya poeziya* [Korean Classical Poetry], edited by A.A. Kholodovich. 1956.
Translator, with Vera Potapova, *Lirika drevnevo egipta* [Ancient Egyptian Lyrics]. 1965.
Translator, *Golosa poetov* [Voices of the Poets]. 1965.
Translator, *Klassicheskaya poeziya vostoka* [Classical Poetry of the East]. 1969.

*

Critical Studies: *The Theme of Time in the Poetry of Akhmatova* by Kees Verheul, 1971; *Akhmatova* by Sam Driver, 1972; *Anna Akhmatova: A Poetic Pilgrimage* by Amanda Haight, 1976; *Akhmatova's Petersburg* by Sharon Leiter, 1983.

*   *   *

Anna Akhmatova occupies a position unique in the history of modern Russian poetry. An established poet before the Revolution, she continued her active creative life well into the mid-1960's, and after the death of Pasternak, Akhmatova was the last remaining major link with what had been one of the great ages of Russian poetry.

Her early career was closely associated with Acmeism, a poetic movement which defined itself in opposition to Russian Symbolism, stressing craftsmanship in poetry and affirming the significance of this phenomenal world in contradistinction to the abstract "Other World" of the Symbolists. Akhmatova's early work was perceived as exemplary for the new movement, and achieved a remarkable popular and critical success. The reading public welcomed the clarity, accessibility, and almost conversational style of her brief, fragile love lyrics, especially after the mystifications and abstractions of the symbolists. The critics recognized and appreciated Akhmatova's innovations, her technical accomplishment, and the extraordinary compactness of her verse. By the publication of the sixth book in 1922, an "Akhmatova style" in Russian poetry was widely recognized.

As a matter of conscious artistic choice, Akhmatova limited her early themes in large part to love, to poetry, and to her homeland. Settings for the predominant love theme are typically drawn from what has traditionally been thought of as the woman's world: home, interiors, garden, details of decor and dress. Simple enough in themselves, the images evolve in sum into a complex symbolic system. The otherwise spare and laconic poems are enriched, moreover, by a matrix of images drawn from Russia's cultural history: folk motifs, the old patriarchal life, Orthodoxy, the great cities of Russia. Related to this matrix, and just below the surface of the worldly love lyrics, are the old Orthodox themes of conscience and remorse, sin and retribution, repentance and self-abnegation. It is such themes which developed in the later major works to an extraordinary power and dignity.

Although Akhmatova maintained a remarkable stylistic consistency throughout her career, it was as early as 1924 that her beloved friend and fellow-poet Mandelstam noted a "sharp break" in Akhmatova's work: "The voice of self-abnegation grows stronger in Akhmatova's poetry, and at present her poetry approaches becoming one of the symbols of the greatness of Russia." Mandelstam's words were prophetic for Akhmatova's longer works like "Requiem," "Poem Without a Hero," and the "Northern Elegies."

In the dark years of official disfavor and persecution which followed her former husband's execution, Akhmatova continued to write, but except for a brief respite during World War II she was not permitted to publish any original poetry. Many of her poems were lost in those tragic years; during the worst of them, many were burned by the poet herself. For a long time, Akhmatova did not dare even to set new poems to paper: the more important ones were committed to memory by her friends and thus preserved.

As works from this period began to appear in the 1950's, it was clear that Akhmatova had undergone an amazing growth and development. The poet emerges as a preserver and continuator of a poetic culture older and broader than the one of her current reality. In the longer works, the poet stands also as conscience and judge for a society suffering under the cataclysms of wars and revolution. "Requiem" is an epic lament for a Russia in the grip of the Stalinist Terror. "Poem Without a Hero" is a retrospective of Akhmatova's own world from the Petersburg in 1913 to the nightmare of World War II and beyond. It is her judgment on an age and also her retribution for her own suffering. By the time she added the last touches to the poem in 1962, Akhmatova had become for Russian poetry the very symbol of moral rectitude and artistic integrity in the face of intolerable personal hardship and official persecution. Along with some of the shorter poems, these masterworks stand as tribute to one of the great Russian poets of this century.

—Sam Driver

ALFIERI, Vittorio. Born in Asti, Italy, 16 January 1749. Educated at Royal Academy, Turin, 1759-66. Served as an ensign (resigned commission, 1774). Began lifelong relationship with Luisa Stolberg D'Albany, 1777. *Died 8 October 1803.*

PUBLICATIONS

Collections

Opere, edited by Luigi Fassò and others. 35 vols., 1951— .
Opere I, edited by Mario Fabini and Arnaldo DiBenedetto. 1977.

Plays

Tragedie. 1783; augmented edition, 1789.
Tragedie. 6 vols., 1787-89; edited by U. Brilli, 1961.
The Tragedies, translated by Charles Lloyd. 3 vols., 1815; augmented edition, edited by E.A. Bowring, 2 vols., 1876.

Verse

L'America libera: Odi. 1784; as *America the Free: Five Odes*, 1975.
Parigi sbastigliata. 1789.
Rime. 1789.
L'Etruria vendicata. 1800.

Other

La virtù sconoscuita: Dialogo. 1786.
Della tirannide. 1789; as *Of Tyranny*, 1961.
Del principe e delle lettere. 1795; edited by Luigi Rosso, 1943; as *The Prince and Letters*, 1972.
Il misogallo: prose e rime. 1799.
Vita. 1806; as *Memoirs*, 1810, revised edition, 1961.

Translator, *Panegirico a Trajano*, by Pliny. 1787.
Translator, [Works], by Sallust. 1826.

*

Critical Studies: *Alfieri: Forerunner of Italian Nationalism* by Gaudens Megaro, 1930; *Alfieri: A Biography* by C.R.D. Miller, 1936; *Ritratto dell'Alfieri* by Mario Fubini, 1967; *Saggi alfieriani* by Walter Binni, 1969.

*   *   *

"A truly remarkable individual," Vittorio Alfieri was called by his contemporary Alessandro Verri, a judgment anyone will concur in who reads the *Memoirs* without being waylaid, as earlier critics were, by doubts as to their reliability. From 1775, after having spent six restless years in intellectually stimulating European travels and three years in frivolous aristocratic pursuits in Turin, Alfieri turned to literature, and henceforth his life was intensely and single-mindedly devoted to his studies and his writing. His major public objective was to give Italy tragedy, the genre it lacked almost completely and which had recently been brought to new splendor in France. To achieve this he had to master a language which, as a French-speaker since birth, was virtually foreign to him. The project came to fruition in 19 tragedies (23, if the first one, rejected by him, and the so-called posthumous ones are added), their range, according to George Steiner, "an index to the romantic imagination." The style he forged for himself was unique, a radical departure from the melodious, often sing-song verses for which Italian lyric poetry, thanks to the Arcadia and Metastasio, was famous. "Mi trovan duro?.... Taccia ho d'oscuro?" (They find me difficult/harsh?.... I have the reputation of being obscure?), he asked in an epigram dated 30 July 1783, harbinger of his repeated efforts at self-clarification.

Alfieri's tragedies have been variously classified: chronologically by periods treated, as Greek, Roman and modern; by themes, as tragedies of love, freedom, royal ambition, familial affections, and inner struggle; or again, as those in which fate predominates, those built on the contrast between liberty and servitude, and those in which the tyrant triumphs over his victims. But no doubt the best comprehensive commentary on his work—which he approaches both diachronically and synchronically—is his own self-exegesis: in his answer written to the critic Calsabigi in 1783, in his "Parere dell'autore su le presenti tragedie" (The Author's Opinions on the Present Tragedies) prepared for the 1789 Paris edition, repeatedly in the *Memoirs*, and indirectly but forcefully in *The Prince and Letters*. What distinguishes Alfieri's perception of his originality is his self-knowledge: his grounding the impulse that led him to tragedy in his passionate reaction to great deeds (such as those recorded in Plutarch's *Lives*) and his desire to emulate them in the only arena—art—in which he felt his times gave him freedom to act; and secondly, his intimate understanding of the stubborn determination needed to vanquish the difficulties of a genre which he conceived of as exceptionally concentrated and concise, making no allowances for even such normal procedures in drama as the use of secondary characters and episodic actions. Basing himself on the distinctions of classical theories of rhetoric between *inventio, dispositio,* and *elocutio* (the selection of a subject, its distribution into its component parts or acts and scenes, its expression, which in his case meant the turning it into verses), he detailed the various stages through which each of his tragedies passed, incidentally leaving an analysis of composition, a blue print for the construction of a text, which continues to be valid even today. The unity he achieves is not given; it is arrived at. But in a circular movement that goes back to the moment of "inspiration"—the *impulso naturale,* the *bollore di cuore e di mente* (the natural impulse, the excitement of heart and mind), so eloquently described in *The Prince and Letters,*—he ends up by giving its due to the inescapable coherence of content and form in great art.

From the point of view of *inventio* (or originality), Alfieri thought of his tragedies as falling into two groups: the few "new" ones (on subjects never before treated in tragic form) and the majority, in which he strove to "make something new out of something old." Among the first group are two of his recognized masterpieces, *Saul* and *Mirra,* both of which depart from the model most frequently associated with Alfieri, the unmasker of arbitrary power and its trappings as analyzed in the treatise *Of Tyranny.* In the dramatization of the struggle between the aged Biblical king and the young David, in which the accent falls on the human rather than regal destiny of the "tyrant" condemned to fearful solitude, even the usual norms of neo-classical tragedy are broken by the insertion into the text of David's songs (passages that remind us that Alfieri was also a great lyric poet, in the tradition of Petrarch). In his retelling on stage of Ovid's story of the incestuous love of Mirra for her father, Alfieri defies the rules of *bienséance* and creates a work of the utmost dramatic tension as the hapless protagonist—no more than a young girl—is again and again on the verge of revealing a secret (to which the spectator who knows his classics is privy), whose ultimate telling spells self-imposed death.

—Olga Ragusa

ALL MEN ARE BROTHERS. *See* **WATER MARGIN.**

ANDERSEN, Hans Christian. Born in Odense, Denmark, 2 April 1805. Educated at schools in Odense to age 14; alone in Copenhagen, and patronized by various benefactors: loosely associated with the singing and dancing schools at Royal Theater, 1819-22; attended Slagelse grammar school, 1822-26, and Elsinore grammar school, 1826-27; tutored 'n Copenhagen by L.C. Müller, 1827-28; completed *examen artium*, 1828. Free-lance writer from 1828: royal grant for travel, 1833, 1834, and pension from Frederick VI, 1838; given title of Professor, 1851; Privy Councillor, 1874. Knight of Red Eagle (Prussia), 1845; Order of the Danneborg, 1846; Knight of the Northern Star (Sweden), 1848; Order of the White Falcon (Weimar), 1848. *Died 4 August 1875.*

PUBLICATIONS

Collections

Samlede Skrifter [Collected Writings]. 33 vols., 1853-79; 2nd ed, 15 vols., 1876-80.
Collected Writings. 10 vols., 1870-71.
Romaner og Rejseskildringer, edited by H. Topsøe-Jensen. 7 vols., 1941-44.

Fiction

Improvisatoren. 1835; as The Improvisatore; or, Life in Italy, 1845.
Eventyr: Fortalte for Børn [Fairy Tales for Children]. 6 vols., 1835-42; Nye Eventyr [New Fairy Tales], 4 vols., 1843-47; edited by Erik Dal and Erling Nielsen, 1963—.

O.T. 1836; as *O.T.; or, Life in Denmark*, with *Only a Fiddler*, 1845.
Kun en Spillemand. 1837; as *Only a Fiddler*, with *O.T.*, 1845.
Billedbog uden Billeder [Picture Book Without Pictures]. 2 vols., 1838-40; as *Tales the Moon Can Tell*, 1955.
Eventyr og Historier [Tales and Stories]. 1839; *Nye Eventyr og Historier*, 6 vols., 1858-67; edited by Hans Brix and Anker Jensen, 5 vols., 1918-20.
De to Baronesser. 1848; as *The Two Baronesses*, 1848.
A Poet's Day Dreams. 1853.
To Be, or Not to Be? 1857.
Later Tales. 1869.
Lykke-Peer [Lucky Peer]. 1870.
Complete Fairy Tales and Stories, translated by Erik Haugaard. 1974.
Samlede eventyr og historier, edited by Erik Dal. 5 vols., 1975.

Verse

Digte. 1830.
Samlede digte [Collected Poems]. 1833.
Seven Poems. 1955.

Plays

Kjaerlighed paa Nicolai Taarn [Love on St. Nicholas Tower] (produced 1829). 1829.
Skibet, from a play by Scribe. 1831.
Bruden fra Lammermoor, music by Ivar Bredal, from the novel *The Bride of Lammermoor* by Scott (produced 1832). 1832.
Ravnen [The Raven], music by J.P.E. Hartmann, from a play by Gozzi (produced 1832). 1832.
Agnete og Havmanden [Agnete and the Merman], music by Nils V. Gade, from Andersen's poem (produced 1833). 1834.
Festen paa Kenilworth [The Festival at Kenilworth], music by C.E.F. Weyse, from the novel *Kenilworth* by Scott (produced 1836).
Skilles og [Parting and Meeting] (produced 1836). In *Det Kongelige Theaters Repertoire*, n.d.
Den Usynlige paa Sprogø [The Invisible Man on Sprogø] (produced 1839).
Mulatten [The Mulatto], from a story by Fanny Reybaud (produced 1840). 1840.
Mikkels Kjaerligheds Historier i Paris [Mikkel's Parisian Love Stories] (produced 1840).
Maurerpigen [The Moorish Girl] (produced 1840). 1840.
En Comedie i det Grønne [Country Comedy], from a play by Dorvigny (produced 1840).
Fuglen i Paeretraeet [The Bird in the Pear Tree] (produced 1842).
Kongen Drømmer [Dreams of the King] (produced 1844). 1844.
Dronningen paa 16 aar, from a play by Bayard. 1844.
Lykkens Blomst [The Blossom of Happiness] (produced 1845). 1847.
Den nye Barselstue [The New Maternity Ward] (produced 1845). 1850.
Herr Rasmussen (produced 1846). Edited by E. Agerholm, 1913.
Liden Kirsten [Little Kirsten], music by J.P.E. Hartmann, from the story by Andersen (produced 1846). 1847.
Kunstens Dannevirke [The Bulwark of Art] (produced 1848). 1848.
En Nat i Roskilde [A Night in Roskilde], from a play by C. Warin and C.E. Lefevre (produced 1848). 1850.
Brylluppet ved Como-Søen [The Wedding at Lake Como], music by Franz Gläser, from a novel by Manzoni (produced 1849). 1849.
Meer end Perler og Guld [More Than Pearls and Gold], from a play by Ferdinand Raimund (produced 1849). 1849.

Ole Lukøie [Old Shuteye] (produced 1850). 1850.
Hyldemoer [Mother Elder] (produced 1851). 1851.
Nøkken [The Nix], music by Franz Gläser (produced 1853). 1853.
Paa Langebro [On the Bridge] (produced 1864).
Han er ikke født [He Is Not Well-Born] (produced 1864). 1864.
Da Spanierne var her [When the Spaniards Were Here] (produced 1865). 1865.

Other

Ungdoms-Forsøg [Youthful Attempts]. 1822.
Fodreise fra Holmens Canal til Ostpynten af Amager i 1828 og 1829 [A Walking Trip from Holmen's Canal to Amager]. 1829.
Skyggebilleder af en Reise til Harzen. 1831; as *Rambles in the Romantic Regions of the Harz Mountains*, 1848.
En Digters Bazar. 1842; as *A Poet's Bazaar*, 1846.
Das Märchen meines Lebens ohne Dichtung (in collected German edition). 1847; as *The True Story of My Life*, 1847; as *Mit eget Eventyr uden Digtning*, edited by H. Topsøe-Jensen, 1942.
I Sverrig. 1851; as *Pictures of Sweden*, 1851; as *In Sweden*, 1851.
Mit Livs Eventyr. 1855; revised edition, 1859, 1877; edited by H. Topsøe-Jensen, 1951; as *The Story of My Life*, 1871; as *The Fairy Tale of My Life*, 1954.
I Spanien. 1863; as *In Spain, and A Visit to Portugal*, 1864.
Breve, edited by C.S.A. Bille and N. Bøgh. 2 vols., 1878.
Briefwechsel mit den Grossherzog Carl Alexander von Sachsen-Weimar-Eisenach, edited by Emil Jonas. 1887.
Correspondence with the Late Grand-Duke of Saxe-Weimar, Charles Dickens, etc., edited by Frederick Crawford. 1891.
Optegnelsesbog, edited by Julius Clausen. 1926.
Breve til Therese og Martin R. Henriques 1860-75, edited by H. Topsøe-Jensen. 1932.
Brevveksling med Edvard og Henriette Collin, edited by H. Topsøe-Jensen. 6 vols., 1933-37.
Brevveksling med Jonas Collin den Aeldre og andre Medlemmer af det Collinske Hus, edited by H. Topsøe-Jensen. 3 vols., 1945-48.
Romerske Dagbøger, edited by Paul V. Rubow and H. Topsøe-Jensen. 1947.
Brevveksling, with Horace E. Scudder, edited by Jean Hersholt. 1948; as *The Andersen-Scudder Letters*, 1949.
Reise fra Kjøbenhavn til Rhinen, edited by H. Topsøe-Jensen. 1955.
Brevveksling, with Henriette Wulff, edited by H. Topsøe-Jensen. 3 vols., 1959-60.
Breve til Mathias Weber, edited by Arne Portman. 1961.
Levnedsbog 1805-1831 [The Book of Life], edited by H. Topsøe-Jensen. 1962.
Breve til Carl B. Lorck, edited by H. Tøpsoe-Jensen. 1969.
Dagbøger 1825-75 [Diary], edited by Kåre Olsen and H. Topsøe-Jensen. 1971—.
Tegninger til Otto Zinck, edited by Kjeld Heltoft. 2 vols., 1972.
Rom Dagbogsnotater og tegninger, edited by H. Topsøe-Jensen. 1980.
Album, edited by Kåre Olsen and others. 3 vols., 1980.

*

Bibliography: *Andersen Bibliografi 1822-1875* by B.F. Nielsen, 1942; *Andersen Litteraturen 1875-1968* by Aage Jørgensen, 1970, supplement, 1973.

Critical Studies: *Andersen and the Romantic Theatre* by Frederick J. Marker, 1971; *Andersen and His World* by Reginald Spink, 1972; *Andersen: The Story of His Life and Work* by Elias Bredsdorff, 1975.

*   *   *

The fame of Hans Christian Andersen—H.C. Andersen to his fellow country-men and Hans Andersen to countless readers outside Denmark—is founded on paradox. Although he was—and is—a very distinctly Danish author he was anything but parochial. Well-read, well-informed about the cultural and scientific developments of his time, and well-travelled—some of Andersen's travel-books still deserve attention, e.g., *En Digters Bazar* (*A Poet's Bazaar*)—he made a name for himself both in his own country and internationally as a novelist during his own life-time. And yet, as the physicist H.C. Ørsted told a sceptical Andersen, if his novels made him famous, his fairy tales would make him immortal.

Andersen's first love was the theatre, but in spite of his many works for the stage—of which *Mulatten* (The Mulatto) was the most significant—he was more at home in the free form of the novel than in the conventionally more disciplined forms of lyric and drama. His first novel, *Improvisatoren* (The Improvisatore), soon became popular abroad because of its perceptive descriptions of the colourful Italian life and landscapes. Like much of Andersen's work, including the fairy tales, it had its roots in his own experience, and aspects of his own childhood among the lower classes formed part of the next two novels, *O.T.* and *Kun en Spillemand* (Only a Fiddler). He described his life directly in his autobiography, *Mit Livs Eventyr* (The Fairy Tale of My Life).

If the novel had given him greater freedom, it was only in the shorter form of the fairy tale, which did not demand control of long plots or complex characterization, that he found his true medium. Andersen's first tales were published in 1835. That they gave him a name as a children's writer is no coincidence: the earliest among his 156 tales were written for children, and until 1843 his published collections carried the subtitle "Told for Children." As he gained confidence and inceasingly wrote original stories—in fact only a minority, e.g., "Fyrtøjet" (The Tinder Box), 1835, derive from traditional folk tales—he abandoned that subtitle and increasingly addressed himself to a grown-up audience. Stories like "Historien om en Moder" (Story of a Mother), 1848, can be understood but not fully appreciated by children. Andersen's great achievement was to develop the form of the folk tale into original, mature art in a way which has not been surpassed, and he did so partly by creating a new literary language which was essentially that of spoken narration, free of abstractions, concrete and deceptively simple. His best tales reveal his keen sense of observation of human behaviour and his deep understanding of the major issues of human existence, told with humour and sympathy.

—Hans Christian Andersen

ANDRIĆ, Ivo.   Born in Trávnik, Bosnia, Austria-Hungary (now Yugoslavia), 10 October 1892.   Educated at schools in Višegrad and Sarajevo; University of Zagreb; Vienna University; University of Krakow; Graz University, Ph.D. 1923. Married Milica Babić in 1959 (died, 1968). Member of Mlada Bosna (Young Bosnia) and imprisoned for three years during World War I; in the Yugoslav diplomatic service, 1919-41: in Rome, Geneva, Madrid, Bucharest, Trieste, Graz, Belgrade, and, as Ambassador to Germany, Berlin; full-time writer, 1941-49; representative from Bosnia, Yugoslav parliament, 1949-55. Member of the Editorial Board,

ANDRIĆ

Književni jug [The Literary South]. President, Federation of Writers of Yugoslavia, 1946-51. Recipient: Yugoslav Government Prize, 1956; Nobel Prize for Literature, 1961. Honorary Doctorate: University of Krakow, 1964. Member, Serbian Academy. *Died 13 March 1975.*

PUBLICATIONS

Collections

Sabrana djela [Collected Works], edited by Risto Trifković and others. 17 vols., 1982.

Fiction

Pripovetke [Stories]. 3 vols., 1924-36.
Gospodjica. 1945; as *The Woman from Sarajevo,* 1965.
Travnička hronika. 1945; as *Bosnian Story,* 1958; as *Bosnian Chronicle,* 1963.
Na Drini ćuprija. 1945; as *The Bridge on the Drina,* 1959.
Prica o vezirovam slonu. 1948; as *The Vizier's Elephant: Three Novellas,* 1962.
Nove pripovetke [New Stories]. 1949.
Prica o kmeta Simanu. 1950.
Novele. 1951.
Pod grabicem: Pripovetke o zivotu bosanskog sela. 1952.
Prokleta avlija. 1954; as *Devil's Yard,* 1962.
Izbor. 1961.
Ljubav u Kasabi. 1963.
Anikina vremena. 1967.
The Pasha's Concubine and Other Tales. 1968.

Verse

Ex ponto. 1918.
Nemiri [Anxieties]. 1919.

Other

Panorama: Pripovetke [Panorama: Stories] (juvenile). 1958.
Lica. 1960.
Kula i druge pripovetke [Children's Stories]. 1970.
Goya. 1972.

*

Bibliography: *Andrić: Bibliografija dela, prevoda, i literature 1911-1970,* 1974.

Critical Studies: "The French in *The Chronicle of Travnik*" by Ante Kadić, in *California Slavic Studies 1,* 1960; "The Work of Andrić" by E.D. Goy, in *Slavonic and East European Review 41,* 1963; "The Later Stories of Andrić" by Thomas Eekman, in *Slavonic and East European Review 48,* 1970; *Andrić: A Bridge Between East and West* by E.C. Hawkesworth, 1984.

*　　*　　*

The work for which Ivo Andrić is probably best known outside Yugoslavia is *The Bridge on the Drina*, a chronicle of the life of the small Bosnian town of Višegrad over several centuries. This rich fusion of legend and history is given shape by the central symbol of the bridge, linking East and West, past and future, and instilling in the townspeople a sense of harmony and the endurance of life despite individual transience.

The major part of Andrić's fiction—five novels and six volumes of short stories—is set in his native Bosnia and informed by a detailed knowledge of this region of the Balkans under Ottoman and, later, Habsburg rule. This precise setting in time and space is an essential feature of Andrić's work but it has proved an obstacle to his reception in some countries, despite the fact that he has been extensively translated. There has been a tendency not to look beyond the "exotic" setting in this "remote" corner of Europe. Andrić focuses his attention on Bosnia because it represents a particularly varied concentration of cultures: an indigenous population of both Catholic and Orthodox Christians, a large Moslem community, Jews and Gypsies. Bosnia also represents a crossroads between East and West, visited by Ottoman dignitaries and European merchants, diplomats, and administrators. It serves consequently as a microcosm of both the variety of human life and the arbitrary divisions and antagonisms between men.

A detailed exploration of this clash of cultures is offered by *Bosnian Story* in which the French and Austrian consuls and the Turkish vizier confront and, when international politics permit, console each other in this harsh and hostile land. Andrić exploits this setting to reveal universal patterns of behaviour and experience, drawing on legend, myth, archetype, and symbol. The complement of the symbol of the bridge in Andrić's work is that of its opposite, the prison, suggesting all the constraints which compel an individual to seek some way out of the fundamental laws of human existence. The image is most fully developed in the short novel, or novella, *Devil's Yard*, in which the prison inmates "escape" by telling stories. It is perhaps in the shorter prose forms that Andrić excels and the best of his stories offer a vivid, intensely suggestive and often disturbing image or anecdote, rich in meanings and associations.

Andrić also wrote verse intermittently throughout his life. More characteristic, however, are his prose reflections, jottings prompted by experiences of all kinds. Selections of these were published posthumously in his Collected Works as *Znakovi pored puta* (Signs by the Roadside) and *Sveske* (Notebooks), providing insight into the fine and subtle mind of this otherwise very private man. Parallels may be drawn between Andrić's work and that of Thomas Mann, Conrad, and Henry James. He was an avid reader and himself spoke of a sense of affinity with a wide variety of writers from Camus and Goethe to Marcus Aurelius.

—E.C. Hawkesworth

APOLLINAIRE, Guillaume. Born Guillaume Apollinaris de Kostrowitzky in Rome, 26 August 1880. Educated in Monte Carlo, Cannes, and Nice. Served in World War I, 1914-16: invalided out. Married Jacqueline Kolb in 1918. Tutor in Germany, 1901-02; free-lance writer and critic in Paris: Editor, *Le Festin d'Esope* and *La Revue Immoraliste*; helped organize cubist room at Salon des Indépendants, 1911, and wrote manifesto on Futurism; Editor, *Soirées de Paris*. Died 9 November 1918.

PUBLICATIONS

Collections

Oeuvres complètes, edited by Michel Décaudin.   4 vols., 1965-66.
Oeuvres en prose, edited by Michel Décaudin.   1977.

Verse

Le Bestiare; ou, Cortège d'Orphée. 1911; translated as *Le Bestiare*, 1977.
Alcools. 1913; edited by Tristan Tzara, 1953, and Garnet Rees, 1975; translated as *Alcools*, 1964.
Case d'armons. 1915.
Vitam impendere amori. 1917.
Calligrammes. 1918.
Le Cortège priapique. 1925.
Julie; ou, La Rose. 1927.
Le Condor et le morpion. 1931.
Ombre de mon amour. 1947; revised edition, as *Poèmes à Lou*, 1955.
Le Guetteur mélancolique. 1952.
Tendre comme le souvenir. 1952.
Selected Poems, edited by Oliver Bernard. 1956.

Plays

Les Mamelles de Tirésias (produced 1917). 1918.
Couleur du temps (produced 1918). 1949.
Casanova. 1952.
La Température, with André Salmon (produced 1975). In *Oeuvres en prose*, 1977.

Fiction

Les Mémoires d'un jeune Don Juan. 1907.
Les Onze Mille Verges. 1907; translated as *The Debauched Hospodar*, 1958; as *Les Onze Mille Verges*, 1979.
L'Enchanteur pourrissant. 1909.
L'Hérésiarque et cie. 1910; selection, as *Contes choisis*, 1922; as *The Heresiarch and Company*, 1965.
La Fin de Babylone. 1914.
Les Trois Don Juan. 1915.
Le Poète assassiné. 1916; edited by Michel Décaudin, 1959; as *The Assassinated Poet*, 1923.
La Femme assise. 1920.
Les Épingles: Contes. 1928.
Que faire? 1950.
The Wandering Jew and Other Stories. 1965.

Other

Méditations esthétiques: Les Peintres cubistes. 1913; edited by Leroy C. Breunig and J.-Cl. Chevalier, 1965; as *The Cubist Painters: Aesthetic Meditations 1913*, 1949.
Le Flâneur des deux rives. 1918.
Il y a. 1925.
Anecdotiques. 1926.
Contemporains pittoresques. 1929.
Oeuvres érotiques complètes (verse and prose). 3 vols., 1934.
L'Esprit nouveau et les poètes. 1946.
Lettres à sa marraine. 1948.
Selected Writings, edited by Roger Shattuck. 1950.

Chroniques d'art, edited by Leroy C. Breunig.   1961; as *On Art*, 1972.
Correspondance, with André Level, edited by Brigitte Level.   1976.

Editor, *Chronique des grands siècles de la France*.   1912.

*

Critical Studies: *Apollinaire* by Marcel Adéma, 1954; *The Evolution of Apollinaire's Politics 1901-1914* by Francis J. Carmody, 1963; *Apollinaire, Poet among Painters* by Francis Steegmuller, 1963; *Apollinaire* by Margaret Davies, 1964; *Apollinaire* by Scott Bates, 1967; *Apollinaire* by Leroy C. Breunig, 1969; *The Drama of Self in Apollinaire's Alcools* by Richard Howard Stamelman, 1975; *Apollinaire* by Roger Little, 1976; *Apollinaire as an Art Critic* by Harry E. Buckley, 1981; *The Creative Vision of Apollinaire* by David Berry, 1982.

*   *   *

Guillaume Apollinaire's culture was eclectic. He preferred the Latin of the mystics to that of Virgil, heretical theologians to St. Thomas, Italian story tellers of the Renaissance to Dante, The Kabbala to the Bible. In contrast to his learning, his heart was simple and limpid. At the publication of *Alcools* in 1913, Georges Duhamel called Apollinaire a peddler with the mingled characteristics of a Levantine Jew, a South American, a Polish gentleman, and an Italian porter. To these roles might be added that of the innocent hero, part braggart, part simpleton, who discovered in war the brotherhood of man, and revealed to his many friends one of the truly noble, truly good souls of his age.

His poetry is composed of influences, readings, memories, echoes of many poets, from Villon to Verlaine and Jarry. But his voice is also bare and personal. The story of his life was the effort he made to guard secrets and mysteries, and to create for his friends and his public a character whom they would love and yet not know too intimately. The buffoonery of his character, his endless anecdotes and pranks, permitted him to conceal or disguise the nostalgia and sadness and even perhaps the tragedy of his life. But the poetry of Guillaume Apollinaire is not mask and deceit. It is fantasy in the deepest sense of the word. It is lawful fantasy: its images rightfully conceal and communicate at the same time the emotions he had experienced.

His poetic fantasy was, first, that of revolt, by which he always remained precious and close to the surrealists. He broke with the familiar patterns of thought, with the poetic clichés and literariness of the parnassians and symbolists, and with the familiar units and rules of syntax. His poetry comes together in a great freedom of composition, as if he allowed the images and emotions to compose themselves. In his poetry, phantoms, wanderers, mythic characters bearing sonorous names, appear and disappear as the laws of syntax and prosody do.

It was appropriate that Apollinaire, coming after the highly self-conscious and studied literary school of symbolism, would, in rebellion against such artifice, seek to return to the most primitive sources of lyricism. His adventure, if we were to extract such a subject from his work, would closely resemble Gide's adventure: the lessons on freedom and gratuitousness and individual morality, which were being formulated at the same time. Apollinaire thus prolongs the lesson of Rimbaud and Mallarmé, in considering poetic activity as a secret means of knowledge, self-knowledge and world-knowledge.

All the opposites are joined and harmonized in his poetry: fire and water, day and night, the bookish and the popular, the libertine and the sorrowing lover. All the myths are in his verses, in close company with pure inventions. He calls upon his immediate knowledge of cities and ports, of unscrupulous *voyous* and popular songs, in order to speak in his tone of prophet and discoverer. His universe is one of chance and naivety, of a certain childlike candor which the surrealists will later try to reconstruct. He is the first to use a facile exoticism and eroticism which today is found in American films and jazz music. But in his most facile songs, as in "Le Musicien de Saint-Merry," he is able to generate a delicate irony from the shifts in tone.

There is a record of Apollinaire's voice reciting "Le Pont Mirabeau," which contains his most persistent theme: the passing and change of sentiments, and the poet's own stability.

> Vienne la nuit sonne l'heure
> Les jours s'en vont je demeure

The chance meetings in the world and their dissolutions bear relationship with the chance meetings of words in a poem. Apollinaire is first a poet of regret, of delicate nostalgia, and then, in a very mysterious way, he is the poet of resurrection and exaltation. His memory of the dead makes them into constant presences. "Vendémiaire," the long poem that ends *Alcools*, is a striking evocation of Paris and of all the myths of poetic preservation, of Orpheus and of Icarus who tried to possess the world. The wine of the universe brought contentment to "oceans animals plants cities destinies and singing stars." The poem also contains accents of sorrow and Apollinaire's familiar reference to the sadness of children with their salt tears that taste of the ocean. But it is at the same time a poem on hope and one of the most stirring of the century.

The contrast between Apollinaire's erudition, nourished on pornography, magic, popular literature, encyclopedias, and his total simplicity as a song writer, explains to some degree the profound irony pervading all of his poetry. His appearance, at the beginning of the 20th century, coincided with many new aesthetic preoccupations to which he brought his own inventiveness and speculative inquiry. His work joined with that of Max Jacob, Picasso, Braque, Derain, Matisse in a series of fantasies and works of art that have gone far in shaping modern sensitivity. A farcical festive air presided over many of the modes of art which were given the names of cubism, fauvism, Negro art, cosmopolitanism, erotology. Apollinaire himself was responsible for the term "surrealism." He literally became a prophet in his support of aesthetic innovations that were to become the accepted forms of the future. His articles on painting place him second to Baudelaire among the aestheticians of modern France.

The lesson Apollinaire teaches about poetry is the most important in France since Rimbaud's. ("La Chanson du Mal-Aimé" has become for our age what "Le Lac" and "Tristesse d'Olympio" were for the 19th century.) His poetry does not try to fathom the supernatural, but simply to state the incomprehensibleness of the ordinary and the commonplace. Every human expression he saw became sphinx-like for him, and every word he overheard resembled a sibyl's utterance. Nascent language it would seem to be, as the poet, performing his earliest role of demiurge, calls the world to be born again by naming it.

—Wallace Fowlie

APOLLONIUS of Rhodes (Apollonius Rhodius).   Born in Alexandria; exact dates unknown, but active during first half of 3rd century B.C., and possibly later. Held post of Director (*prostates*) of the Museum Library at Alexandria, and was tutor to the royal family; traditionally supposed to have quarrelled with Callimachus and retired to Rhodes, but evidence for this is flimsy. In addition to various poems, of which only the *Argonautica* survives, wrote scholarly works on Homer, Hesiod and Archilochus, now lost.

PUBLICATIONS

Argonautica, edited by H. Fränkel. 1961; also edited by F. Vian, (included French translation), 3 vols., 1974-81; as *The Tale of the Argonauts*, translated by A.S. Way, 1901; also translated by R.C. Seaton, as *Argonautica* (in prose), 1912, and by E.V. Rieu, as *The Voyage of the Argo* (in prose), 1959.

*

Critical Studies: *Hellenistic Poetry* by A. Körte, 1929; *Epic and Romance in the "Argonautica" of Apollonius* by C.R. Beye, 1982.

*   *   *

The only work of Apollonius which survives is the epic *Argonautica*, written in hexameters, the traditional epic metre, with the high archaic language and style of the Homeric poems. After the *Iliad* and *Odyssey* the *Argonautica* is the most important epic from the ancient Greek world, and it was soon recognised as such; Vergil's *Aeneid* was profoundly influenced by it (behind Vergil's Dido, for instance, stand Apollonius's Hypsipyle and Medea). Early history of the work is uncertain. The Greek biographical tradition (which usually contains much palpably fictitious material) reports that the *Argonautica* was at first badly received in Alexandria and suggests that Apollonius was at odds with his "teacher" Callimachus, the most important scholar and poet of the Hellenistic period, who radically changed the course of Greek poetry, but only amid great controversy; to what extent the *Argonautica* was considered by Apollonius's contemporaries more traditional than avant-garde is no longer known, but there are many cross-references between the poems of Callimachus and the *Argonautica*, and Apollonius's poem is thoroughly modernistic in tone and style.

Superficially the *Argonautica* could seem to be an orthodox work aiming for a place in the mainstream tradition of heroic epic (though of literate, not oral, composition), and it has often been so regarded; modern critics who view it in this way generally contrast the *Argonautica* with what they see as the straightforward heroic world of the Homeric poems and conclude that Apollonius's work is an interesting failure. However, the *Iliad* and *Odyssey* are far from simplistic in outlook, and recent scholarship on Hellenistic poetry suggests that the *Argonautica* is a complex and original poem which successfully reworked the old epic form and reflects the troubled and introspective mentality of 3rd century Alexandria.

The *Argonautica* can appear to be an episodic, disjointed work with many characteristically Hellenistic "travelogue" features (it touches often on matters of ethnography, geography, anthropology, etc.); but in fact the poem is a remarkable whole. The work's perspective is established not through narrative directness, or through imagery or symbolism, but by a process of reversal often thought of as "irony" in the 20th century: the familiar is taken for granted and suppressed in favour of the less familiar, and what is important is most often expressed indirectly and at a secondary level. The result can be enigmatic but genuinely disturbing, and an effective way of conveying a pessimistic vision of a fragile and fragmented world. First, the story of the voyage of Jason and the Argonauts to Colchis in the distant parts of the Black Sea to capture the Golden Fleece, and of the difficult but crucial passion of the local princess Medea for Jason, was an ancient one, and Apollonius assumes that his audience do not need to have it retold in all its details; Jason's subsequent abandonment of Medea, for example, is nowhere recounted openly (the poem even ends just before the Argonauts reach home), but the whole poem broods on the issues of commitment, trust, and deception. Secondly, Apollonius takes for granted a familiarity with the two monumental epics which preceded his own, and, by using the *Iliad* and *Odyssey* as "archetypal" reference points against which the Argonauts and their various encounters are juxtaposed and interpreted, he creates a multiplicity of dimensions and a kind of commentary to his *Argonautica*; thus Medea does not appear until Book 3 (the poem consists in four long "books"), but the most substantial episode of Book 1, the Argonauts' visit to the strange island of Lemnos with its all-female population, turns out to be diagnostic for Colchis. Although Jason's affair with the Lemnian queen Hypsipyle seems idle and affectless on the surface of the narrative, once Apollonius's references to Homer are recognised and Hypsipyle is considered as a figure reminiscent of Nausicaa and Circe, and Jason as an Odysseus or even Agamemnon, the real issues of ambivalence, pressure of circumstance, and expedient compromise begin to emerge. These are the issues which underlie the whole poem, whether in the exotic account of the outward journey of Books 1 and 2, the pathology of Medea's awful passion and conflict in Book 3, or the alienated return home through the strange, semi-mythical half-real world of the Adriatic and north Africa in Book 4.

—A.W. Bulloch

APULEIUS.   Born in Madaura, province of Africa (now M'Daourouch, Algeria), c. 123-125 A.D.   Educated in Carthage, Athens, and Rome. Married Aemilia Pudentilla; possibly had a son called Faustinus. Lived in Oea (now Tripoli) where he married; acquitted of a charge of magic at nearby Sabratha; later lived in Carthage, where his success in public speaking led to various honours, including a statue and the important priesthood of Asclepius.   *Died later than 163 A.D.* (probably much later).

PUBLICATIONS

Collections

[*Works*], edited by R. Helm and P. Thomas.   3 vols., 1907-31.

Fiction

Metamorphoses, edited by D.S. Robertson.   1940-45; also edited by C. Giarratano, revised by P. Frassinetti, 1960; as *The Golden Ass*, translated by W. Adlington, 1566 (this edition revised by S. Gaselee, 1915), by Robert Graves, 1950, and by Jack Lindsay, 1960.

Other

Apologia, Florida, edited (with French translation) by P. Vallette.   2nd edition, 1960.
Philosophica (includes *De deo Socratis, De dogmate Platonis, De Mundo*), edited (with French translation) by J. Beaujeu.   1973.

*

Bibliography: *Ad Apulei Madaurensis Metamorphoseon librum primum commentarius exegeticus* by M. Molt (Dissertation, Groningen) 1938; "The Scholarship on Apuleius since 1938" by C.C. Schlam, in *Classical World 64*, 1971.

Critical Studies: *Apuleius and His Influence* by E.H. Haight, 1927; *The Ancient Romances* by B.E. Perry, 1967; *Aspects of the Ancient Romance and Its Heritage: Essays on Apuleius, Petronius, and the Greek Romances* by Alexander Scobie, 1969; *The Roman Novel: The "Satyricon" of Petronius and the "Metamorphoses" of Apuleius* by P.G. Walsh, 1970; *Aspects of the Golden Ass* edited by B.L. Hijmans, Jr., and R. Th. van der Paardt, 1978; *Apuleius and the Golden Ass* by James Tatum, 1979.

*　　*　　*

Apuleius is best understood as a performer. He regularly gave public speeches before the large crowds they attracted in his age, and his written work too reflects a concern to use style and knowledge to capture and maintain an audience's attention.

The *Florida*, a collection of the most "florid" parts of his public speeches, displays a man supremely confident before his admiring audience. He speaks with authority on a multitude of subjects, from Alexander the Great to parrots, though usually in a philosophical or cultural key. His style is as luxuriant as his subjects: in defiance of the careful, if at times precious, styles of the Golden and Silver Ages of Latin literature before him, his own style overflows with archaism, colloquialism, neologism, particularly if it will add to the rhythm, balance, music, or patterning. His style not only exemplifies the new tendencies of the age, but pushes them to an extreme.

Public speakers such as Apuleius considered they had a duty to educate, and some fulfilled this duty through a sort of popularising philosophy. Apuleius had pretensions to being a Platonist philosopher, and there survive works ascribed to him which expound the philosophy of Plato as understood in his time. Most Apuleian is the energetic showpiece *On the God of Socrates*, which analyses the way in which an intermediary spirit connects us with God and which, for instance, memorably depicts the human condition in 19 successive epithets! Otherwise, these philosophical works are more disappointing and sometimes just translate minor Greek works, although the translations seem to have proved useful to Greekless readers, if one may judge by the example of St. Augustine.

Once, Apuleius *needed* to deliver a speech, to defend himself against the charge of winning the rich widow Pudentilla's affections by magic. The *Apologia* (or *On Magic*) is the only surviving classical Latin law-court speech not by Cicero, and, at least in its published form, displays the style of the *Florida* and a wicked sense of humour which we meet again in his novel.

The *Metamorphoses*, or *Golden Ass* as it has generally been known, is Apuleius's sole surviving novel (novels were in any case rare, late, and unprestigious in Greek and Roman literature), and is what Apuleius means to us today. He takes a Greek short story and lengthens it to five times its original size by inserting stories (unlikely to be his own invention), thus making a Latin novel of some 250 modern pages. The Greek tale told how Lucius, dabbling in magic, was accidentally turned into an ass and underwent various adventures before being restored. Apuleius enriches the simple style of the original, producing something not easily translated into modern English. The inserted stories—of magic, brigands, and adultery—are related with verve and humour. Apuleius is interested too in psychological portrayal, though not in psychological development as in the modern novel; rather, the mind is as promising a subject for a description as is a brigands' camp or a god's garden.

The longest inserted tale, the celebrated story of *Cupid and Psyche*, is different. Its magical tone stands in stark contrast to the rumbustiousness of most of the novel. It adds, too, problems of interpretation: it is like a folk-tale, and thought by many to *be* a folk-tale; but it is difficult to deny some connection with the Platonic doctrine that Soul (*Psyche*) reaches its divine target through an intermediary spirit, Love (*Cupid*). The ending of the novel too, where Apuleius's hero is saved by initiation in the rites of the Egyptian goddess Isis, is thought by some to be a mere show of seriousness to finish, but by others to be the climax of a novel all along about the dangers of worldly vices.

We know nothing of the initial reception of the novel; and something of our assessment must depend on the precise interpretation adopted. But the extraordinary energy of the work is

APULEIUS

undeniable, as is the success of the frame-and-insertion structure in maintaining an unflagging interest. It displays many contrasts, from the flippant to the gruesome, from realism to make-believe, from bawdiness to extravagant piety. In character development it has the limitations of all ancient novels and most ancient thought. Its style has offended purists, but may be more validly criticised for unrelievedly trying too hard. Apuleius seems self-indulgent, but, more accurately, is preoccupied with dazzling his audience, an aim in which, as a professional, he generally succeeds.

—Ken Dowden

ARABIAN NIGHTS. *See* **THOUSAND AND ONE NIGHTS.**

ARIOSTO, Ludovico. Born in Reggio Emilio, Ferrara territory, 8 September 1474. Studied in the law faculty, University of Ferrara, 1489-94. Married Alessandra Benucci Strozzi in late 1520's; two earlier illegitimate children. Took a court post during the political unrest of the 1490's; captain of the garrison, Canossa, 1502-03; courtier, diplomat, and writer in service of Cardinal Ippolito d'Este until 1517; in service of Alfonso d'Este the Duke of Ferrara, 1518-33; Commissario of the Garfagnana, 1522-25. *Died 6 July 1533.*

PUBLICATIONS

Verse

> *Orlando Furioso.* 1515 (40 cantos); revised version, 1521; 3rd edition, 1532 (46 cantos); additional *Cinque Canti* published in 1545 edition; edited by S. Debenedetti and Cesare Segre, 1960; edited by Segre, 1976; translated as *Orlando Furioso*, 1591; as *The Frenzy of Orlando*, translated by Barbara Reynolds, 2 vols., 1975.
> *Satire.* 1534; as *Seven Planets Governing Italy*, 1611; as *The Satires*, 1976 .
> *Two Satires.* 1977.

Plays

> *Cassaria* (produced 1508). 1509 or 1510; revised version, in verse (produced 1531), 1546; as *The Coffer*, in *The Comedies*, 1975.
> *I suppositi* (produced 1509). 1509 or 1510; revised version, in verse, 1525; as *The Pretenders*, in *The Comedies*, 1975.

La lena (produced 1528).   1533 or 1536; edited by Guido Davico Bonino, 1976; as *Lena*, in *The Comedies*, 1976.
Il negromante (produced 1529).   1535; as *The Necromancer*, in *The Comedies*, 1975.
La scholastica, completed by Gabriele Ariosto.   1547; as *The Students*, in *The Comedies*, 1975.
Le Commedie, edited by Michele Catalano.   2 vols., 1933.
The Comedies (includes *The Coffer* [prose and verse versions], *The Pretenders*, *The Necromancer*, *Lena*, *The Students*), edited by Edmond M. Beame and Leonard G. Sbrocchi.   1975.

Other

Opere Minori, edited by Cesare Segre.   1954.
Lettere, edited by A. Stella.   1965.

*

Critical Studies: *The King of the Court Poets, Ariosto* by E.G. Gardner, 1906; *The Figure of the Poet in the Renaissance Epic* by R.M. Durling, 1965; *Ariosto: A Preface to the "Orlando Furioso"* by C.P. Brand, 1974; *Names on the Trees: Ariosto into Art* by Rennselaer W. Lee, 1977; *Ariosto and the Classical Simile* by Kristen Olson Murtaugh, 1980.

*   *   *

Ariosto's masterpiece, *Orlando Furioso*, is the culmination of a long tradition. Beginning in the 11th century with the Old French epic, *La Chanson de Roland* (The Song of Roland), it continued in Italy (as elsewhere) in a series of extravagant romances, both oral and written. The legends, relating to Charlemagne and his paladins in their defence of Christendom against the Muslims, became part of folklore, as may be seen in Sicily where puppet masters in Palermo still perform the stories and where the sides of donkey carts are painted with colourful scenes of combat.

In the 15th century Luigi Pulci of Florence wrote an elaborate version of Roland's (Orlando's) adventures. This was *Il Morgante*, a poem in rhymed octaves, much admired by Byron, who translated the first canto. Pulci was followed by Matteo Boiardo of Ferrara, who complicated the story still further with oriental elements and combined it with episodes and characters drawn from the Arthurian cycle. Boiardo's poem, also in rhymed octaves, was entitled *Orlando Innamorato* (Roland in Love). In 1494, when the French invaded Italy, he felt unable to continue and laid down his pen. Violent events had irrupted into his world of fantasy and destroyed it.

A generation later Ariosto undertook to complete Boiardo's poem. The result was his *Orlando Furioso* (Roland Driven Mad by Love). In Ariosto's hands chivalrous romance becomes romantic epic. To the themes of war, chivalry, and love, already in Boiardo, Ariosto added history, from mythological antiquity down to contemporary times, from the Fall of Troy to the Sack of Rome. The factual is rendered poetic; the poetic acquires the solemnity of historical fact. It is this which converts romance into epic. Epic also is the intensity with which Ariosto visualizes and communicates his world. His descriptions of beauty, chivalry, noble achievement, violence, and evil are on a scale that exceeds life. Yet the work is far from solemn throughout. The legacy of exuberant exaggeration, rollicking humour, suspense and wilful complexity, inherited from the conventions of the *cantastorie* (narrators who recited the tales in public), as well as from Pulci and Boiardo, enriches and varies the 46 cantos. Ariosto's octaves justly deserve the epithet of "golden."

To 16th-century critics the *Orlando Furioso* appeared to lack unity, and the stories it contained were dismissed as unworthy of the attention of serious-minded men of letters. Ariosto has also been condemned for his adulation of the House of Este, the rulers of Ferrara and his patrons. Such criticisms, still voiced in modern times, can be answered. On the charge of adulation it can be said that Ariosto's praise of Ferrara and of the Estense dynasty was in the tradition of works of praise (encomia), which had the warrant of Aristotle and also of Erasmus, who held that the most efficacious way of correcting a prince was to present him, in the guise of flattery, with an ideal picture of himself. This may have been Ariosto's intention in those octaves which lavish praise on Duke Alfonso and his brother, Cardinal Ippolito, to whom he dedicated the poem. But the praise was not all flattery. There was much to admire in the achievements of the Dukes of Ferrara and in the world of beauty they created. Furthermore, what Ariosto thought worthy of condemnation he condemned: the use of gunfire in battle, for instance (in which Duke Alfonso was a pioneer), and the neglect of poets by their patrons.

The charge of disunity in the *Orlando Furioso* is based on assumptions which are not relevant to the nature of Ariosto's art. The poem is composed not of homogeneous elements arranged with predictable symmetry, but of vastly disparate material, controlled and balanced with apparent nonchalance but, in reality, with subtle skill. Thematic unity resides in the concept of Europe as the civilizing force both of antiquity and of the newly enlarged Christian world. The contemporary danger of Turkish power is imaged in the menace of the Muslims in the time of Charlemagne; and Charles V, on his election as Emperor, may have been seen by Ariosto, as his poem progressed, to be a natural symbol of that other Charles, the 8th-century head of Christendom.

Ariosto takes up the story at the point where Agramante, king of the Moors, and Marsilio, the Saracen king of Spain, have invaded France. Orlando has escorted the princess Angelica from the Far East to the Pyrenees and is at once caught up in the war. Angelica was introduced into the story by Boiardo to serve, with her dazzling beauty, as a distraction to Christian and Muslim knights alike. Orlando and his cousin, Rinaldo, both love her and their rivalry is a danger to the Christian side. Angelica, unmoved by the adoration she inspires, eventually falls in love with a wounded Moorish soldier, whom she nurses back to health and marries. The discovery of this causes Orlando to lose his wits and supernatural aid is required before he can be brought back to sanity.

In constructing this sequel to Boiardo's poem Ariosto had three main tasks: to bring the war to a close, to disentangle both Orlando and Rinaldo from their infatuation for Angelica, and to enable Rinaldo's sister, Bradamante, to marry a noble warrior, Ruggiero, who, though fighting for the Infidel, is, as he discovers, of Christian origin. From their union is destined to descend the illustrious line of the House of Este. All three tasks are accomplished and all the minor stories left unfinished by Boiardo are likewise brought to a conclusion. The *Orlando Furioso* is, however, far more than an appendix to the *Innamorato*. It is an original work in its own right, dazzling in the *bravura* of its execution.

Ariosto's other works include *capitoli* (burlesques), satires, and five comedies on the models of Plautus and Terence, whose plays were then fashionable in Ferrara. Ariosto had acted in the court theatre in his youth and during his last years he was director of theatrical entertainments. His *Orlando Furioso* is itself rather like a huge theatrical production, of which the author is also the stage-manager and property-man.

—Barbara Reynolds

ARISTOPHANES. Born in Athens, certainly after 457 B.C., and possibly as late as 445. May have lived or owned property on Aigina; his son, Araros, produced two of his plays, and also wrote plays of his own. Won at least four prizes at the Great Dionysia and Lenaia festivals;

besides the 11 surviving plays, 32 other titles, some possibly alternative titles, and nearly 1000 fragments survive. Served on the *boule* (the Athenian Senate) in the early fourth century. *Died c. 385 B.C.*

PUBLICATIONS

Collections

> [*Comedies*], edited by F.W. Hall and W.M. Geldart.   2 vols., 1901-02; also edited by J. van Leeuwen, 1893-1906, and B.B. Rogers 1902-1915.
> [*Comedies*], translated in *Complete Plays*, edited by Moses Hadas.   1962; also translated by David Barrett and Alan H. Sommerstein, 3 vols., 1964-1977, and by Patric Dickinson, 2 vols., 1970.

Plays

> *Acharneis* (produced 425).   Edited by W. Rennie, 1909, and by Alan H. Sommerstein, 1980; as *The Acharnians*, translated by Douglass Parker, 1973.
> *Hippeis* (produced 424).   Edited by R.H. Neil, 1901 and by Alan H. Sommerstein, 1981; as *The Knights*, translated by Kenneth McLeish, 1979.
> *Nephelai* (produced 423, partially revised 420-417).   Edited by K.J. Dover, 1968, and by Alan H. Sommerstein, 1982; as *The Clouds*, translated by William Arrowsmith, 1962, and Kenneth McLeish, 1979.
> *Sphekes* (produced 422).   Edited by Douglas M. MacDowell, 1971; as *The Wasps*, translated by Douglass Parker, 1962.
> *Eirene* (produced 421).   Edited by Maurice Platnauer, 1964; as *The Peace* translated by Doros Alastos, 1953.
> *Ornithes* (produced 414).   Edited by W.W. Merry, 1904; as *The Birds*, translated by William Arrowsmith, 1961, and Kenneth McLeish, 1970.
> *Lysistrate* (produced 411).   As *Lysistrata*, translated by Jack Lindsay, 1925, Charles T. Murphy, 1944, Dudley Fitts, 1955, and Douglass Parker, 1970.
> *Thesmophoriazousai* [Women Celebrating the Thesmophoria] (produced 411).   As *Ladies' Day*, translated by Dudley Fitts, 1959; as *The Poet and the Women*, translated by David Barrrett, 1964.
> *Batrachoi* (produced 405).   Edited by W.B. Stanford, 1963; as *The Frogs*, translated by Dudley Fitts, 1957, Richmond Lattimore, 1962, and Kenneth McLeish, 1970.
> *Ekklesiazousai* (produced c. 392).   Edited by R.G. Ussher, 1973; as *Women in Parliament*, translated by Jack Lindsay, 1929; as *The Congresswomen*, translated by Douglass Parker, 1973; as *Women in Power*, translated by Kenneth McLeish, 1979.
> *Ploutos* (produced 388).   As *Plutus*, translated by William Rann Kennedy, 1912.

Critical Studies: *Aristophanes: A Study* by Gilbert Murray, 1933; "Aristophanes and Politics" by A.W. Gomme, in *Classical Review*, 1938; *The People of Aristophanes: A Sociology of Old Attic Comedy* by Victor Ehrenberg, 1962; *Aristophanes: His Plays and His Influence* by L.E. Lord, 1963; *Aristophanes and the Comic Hero* by C.H. Whitman, 1964; "The Political Opinions of Aristophanes," Appendix XXIX of *The Origins of the Peloponnesian War* by G.E.M. de Ste. Croix, 1972; *Aristophanic Comedy* by K.J. Dover, 1972; *The Stage of Aristophanes* by C.W. Dearden, 1976; *Aristophanes* by R.G. Ussher, 1979; *Aristophanes: Essays in Interpretation* edited by Jeffrey Henderson, 1981; *Aristophanic Poetry* by Carroll Moulton, 1981.

*   *   *

ARISTOPHANES

Aristophanes is the best-known (and only surviving) exponent of Old Attic Comedy, an art form which, like its older sister Tragedy, was performed as part of the artistic competitions at the civic festivals at Athens in honour of the god Dionysos. Aristophanes appears to have been typical of this dramatic form, which enjoyed its high point c. 440-400 B.C., the years of the age of Perikles and the flourishing of the vigorous democracy at Athens. Old Comedy was very much a child of that democracy. In the widest and best sense of the word, his comedy was *political (polis* = city-state), as his plays are concerned essentially with Athens of his day, which supplied him with his inspiration, his themes and issues, his jokes, characters, and personalities. Firmly anchored in the social milieu of 5th-century Athens, his work exhibits a unique mixture of humours, ranging from political satire to obscenity and bowel humour, from sophisticated parody to slapstick, from fantastic comedy to personal abuse. His comedy is without parallel or successors in Western literature.

Aristophanes is neither a master of comic plot (the "comedy of errors" on which so much subsequent comedy is based) nor a creator of comedy of character interaction. Rather the kernel of an Aristophanic play is the establishment of a fantastic idea, a grand scheme, the more outrageous the better, whose implementation and consequences form the action ("plot" is not a term useful in Aristophanic criticism). Examples include *Acharnians* where the hero (whose name means "Just City") forms his own personal peace-treaty with the Spartan enemy, or *Lysistrata* in which the wives of Greece agree on a "sex-strike" to force their men to end the war and occupy the Athenian *akropolis* to reinforce their plot. This *grande idée* is explained and developed in a series of more or less formal structural features, e.g., *parodos*—the formal entry of the chorus (as in tragedy, an integral and expected part of the drama) which provided either an on-stage audience or the opposition; *agon*—a formally constructed debate in which the great idea was contested or explained; the *parabasis*—in which the chorus spoke directly to the audience in an equally formal structure, often for the comedian himself; and the *episodes*—a series of loosely connected scenes in which the consequences of the great idea are worked out. No play is "typical," although *Wasps* and *Birds* come closest. In his later plays, Aristophanes begins to employ a freer use of the traditional format; *Thesmophoriazousai*, in particular, most resembles a comedy as we understand it.

Space does not allow for individual discussion of the comedies. In the 11 extant plays (of the 40 presented 427-c. 385), we can see from the variety of topics how all aspects of Athenian life were fair game for comedy. Three are the so-called "peace plays," *Acharnians*, *Peace*, and *Lysistrata*, from which it is clear that Aristophanes was not himself a pacifist, but an ardent opponent of *this* war, the Peloponnesian War (431-04). *Acharnians*, with its unparalleled identification of the protagonist with the comic hero and its open hostility to Athens's war policy and its proponents, is worthy of attention. *Knights* and *Wasps* are both largely concerned with politics and the demagogues, especially Kleon whose distinctive political style and policies are subjected to a sweeping and at times coarse caricature in *Knights*. *Wasps*, a humorous satire on the jury system and Kleon's manipulation of it, features Philokleon, perhaps the most appealing rogue in all comedy. Philosophy and literature form the themes of *Clouds* and *Thesmophoriazousai*, the former containing the controversial portrait of Sokrates as a sophistic charlatan which contributed to his condemnation in 399. *Lysistrata*, *Thesmophoriazousai*, and *Ekklesiazousai* form the "women's plays"; the latter portrays the seizure by women of the government at Athens and the institution of a communistic regime very much like Plato's ideal Republic. *Lysistrata*, with its themes of "Women's Liberation" and "Make love, not war!," has become the favourite of modern audiences.

Two plays, *Birds* and *Frogs*, stand out as Aristophanes's masterpieces. *Birds* features two Athenians who flee Athens and all its woes; after taking refuge with the birds they join with them in founding the now famous city, Cloudcuckooland, and in the end displace the Olympian gods as the rulers of the universe. *Frogs* shows Dionysos, god of drama, descending to the underworld to bring back Euripides, the recently deceased and controversial tragedian. After some very amusing adventures, Dionysos ends up judging a hilarious contest for the throne of tragedy between Euripides and Aeschylus, the old master, in which Dionysos eventually judges Aeschylus the victor and returns with him to Athens "to save the city." Produced in the months preceding Athens's defeat, this comedy with its mingling of political, literary, and religious themes provides a poignant farewell to Athens's greatness.

Critical discussion has focussed on the motives of the comedian. In a landmark article A.W. Gomme argued that no serious political purpose was to be found in Aristophanes; his *forte* was a brilliant, revolutionary comedy. De Ste. Croix argued in return that although creation of comedy was his first concern, a consistent political stance may be ascertained, that of a "conservative," but neither oligarchic nor radical democrat. His opposition to the demagogues, especially Kleon, is clear, as is his hostility to the war with Sparta. The end of *Knights* and *Lysistrata* reveals an affection for the glorious days of Athens of the previous generations, the glory of the triumphs of the Persian Wars. Similarly, despite his obvious intellectual affinities with Euripides, he chooses Aeschylus in the end; technical ability yields to the moral purpose of art. Yet Aristophanes is no anti-intellectual; his caricature of Sokrates is more humorous than satirical, and his appreciation of Euripides is clear. Similarly, in his treatment of the individuals made fun of in his plays—personal abuse (*to onomasti komodein*) has fascinated critics, both ancient and modern—commentators have tried to find a personal motive behind the jokes. Here too comedy must take precedence over motive. Only with Kleon and the demagogues can we detect any hint of malice. For the most part we should regard Aristophanes as what he himself claimed to be, a superb creator of imaginative and fantastic comedy.

—Ian C. Storey

ARTAUD, Antonin (Marie Joseph).   Born in Marseilles, France, 4 September 1896. Served in the French military: medical discharge, 1916. Hospitalized frequently, 1916-20; Co-Editor, *Demain*, 1920-21, and *Le Bilboquet*, 1923; actor and designer for Lugné-Poë, Charles Dullin, and Georges Pitoeff theatre companies, Paris, 1921-24; actor in films by Abel Gance, Carl Dreyer, and others, 1924-35; Director, Bureau of Surrealist Research, 1925, and Editor of 3rd issue of *La Révolution Surréaliste*, 1925; Founder, with Roger Vitrac and Robert Aron, Théâtre Alfred Jarry, Paris, 1926, and Théâtre de la Cruauté, 1933; lecturer on theatre, the Sorbonne, Paris, 1928, 1931, 1933; confined, 1937-46, primarily in Rodez Asylum. Drawings exhibited: Loeb Gallery, 1947. Recipient: Sainte-Beuve prize, 1948. *Died 4 March 1948.*

PUBLICATIONS

Collections

> *Oeuvres complètes.*   16 vols., 1956-81; revised edition, 1970—.
> *Collected Works.*   4 vols., 1968-75.

Plays

> *Les Cenci* (produced 1935).   In *Oeuvres complètes 4*, 1967; as *The Cenci*, 1970.
> *Pour en finir avec le jugement de Dieu.*   1948; as *To Have Done with the Judgment of God*, in *Selected Writings*, 1976.

Verse

Tric-trac du ciel. 1923.
Artaud le mômo. 1947; as *Artaud the Momo*, 1976.
Ci-gîtt, précedé de la culture indienne. 1947.

Other

Le Pese-nerfs. 1925; with *Fragments d'un journal d'enfer*, 1927.
L'Ombilic des limbes. 1927.
Correspondance, with Jacques Rivière. 1927.
L'Art et la mort. 1929.
Le Théâtre Alfred Jarry et l'hostilité public, with Roger Vitrac. 1930.
Le Théâtre de la cruauté. 1933.
Héliogabale; ou, L'Anarchiste couronné. 1934.
Le Théâtre de Séraphin. 1936.
Les Nouvelles Révélations de l'être. 1937.
Le Théâtre et son double. 1938; as *The Theatre and Its Double*, 1958.
D'Un Voyage au pays de Tarahumaras (essays and letters). 1945.
Lettres de Rodez. 1946.
Van Gogh, Le suicidé de la société. 1947.
Supplément aux Lettres de Rodez suivi de Coleridge le traître. 1949.
Lettres contre la Cabbale. 1949.
Lettres à Jean-Louis Barrault. 1952.
La Vie et mort de Satan le feu. 1953; as *The Death of Satan and Other Mystical Writings*, 1974.
Les Tarahumaras (letters and essays). 1955; as *The Peyote Dance*, 1976.
Galapagos, Les Îles du bout du monde (travel). 1955.
Autre chose que l'enfant beau. 1957.
Voici un endroit. 1958.
Mexico. 1962.
Lettres à Anaïs Nin. 1965.
Artaud Anthology, edited by Jack Hirschman. 1965.
Poète noir et autres textes/ Black Poet and Other Texts, edited by Paul Zweig. 1966.
Lettres à Génica Athanasiou. 1969.
Selected Writings, edited by Susan Sontag. 1976.
Nouvelles écrits de Rodez. 1977.
Lettres à Anie Besnard. 1978.

Translator, *Le Moine*, by Matthew Gregory Lewis. 1931.
Translator, with Bernard Steele, *Crime passionel*, by Ludwig Lewisohn. 1932.

*

Bibliography: in *Artaud et le théâtre* by Alan Virmaux, 1970.

Critical Studies: *The Dramatic Concepts of Artaud* by Eric Sellin, 1968; *Artaud: Poet Without Words* by Naomi Greene, 1970; *Artaud: Man of Vision* by Bettina Knapp, 1971; *Artaud* by Martin Esslin, 1976; *Artaud and After* by Ronald Hayman, 1977; *Artaud* by Julia F. Costich, 1978.

*   *   *

Paradox envelops Antonin Artaud. The man who wished to de-emphasize words in theater—"No more masterpieces!"—has written 16 volumes of words. A theater prophet who valued performance far above theory, Artaud's productions were limited to a few sporadic efforts of his Alfred Jarry Theater and seventeen performances of *The Cenci* as Theater of Cruelty; in contrast, Gallimard publishers printed 100,000 copies of *The Theatre and Its Double*, his 1938 collection of manifestoes and letters which has had wide influence. A strikingly handsome film actor, Artaud drew self-portraits when he was ill and haggard. Plagued with illness all his life, Artaud undertook to cure what he saw as a sick civilization. After nine years of neglect in asylums, he became a cult figure in postwar Paris, during the last two years of his life. After his death, Artaud inspired two divergent movements: 1) the experimental theater groups of the 1960's, particularly in the United States; 2) the "human science" intellectuals of that same decade, particularly in France.

Artaud's writing takes many forms—fiction, drama, essays, diatribes, production plans, poems, and letters that sometimes read like soliloquies to be declaimed. All his writing is seared by his flaming self-consciousness; he flaunted his suffering with inimitable intensity. Up until the time of his incarceration—1937—Artaud espoused theater as an instrument of civilizational catharsis, and he equates theater with plague, alchemy, metaphysics, and cruelty—doubles all. At Rodez Asylum and later, however, his long poems and essays lacerate to scourge. With sound play, obscenity, neologisms, occult and fantastic reference, Artaud inveighs against Western materialism; as *poète maudit* he curses the familiar scenes of modern life. His passion—utterance and suffering—has inspired theatermen like Jean-Louis Barrault, Roger Blin, Peter Brook; and thinkers like Gilles Deleuze, Jacques Derrida, and Susan Sontag. Less read than read about, Artaud is only recently being studied as writer rather than martyr.

—Ruby Cohn

ASSIS, Joaquim Maria Machado de. *See* **MACHADO DE ASSIS, Joaquim Maria.**

AUGUSTINE, St. (Aurelius Augustinus). Born in Tagaste (now Souk Ahras, Algeria), 13 November 354 A.D. Reared as a Christian; educated in Tagaste and Carthage. Had a son by his concubine. Taught rhetoric in Tagaste, 1 year, Carthage, 8 years, Rome, 383-84, and Milan, 384-86, where he met the bishop Ambrose; after a period of Manichaeism, turned to Neoplatonism; converted to Christianity, 386: baptized by Ambrose, 387; returned to Tagaste, 388; ordained as a priest in Hippo Regius (now Annada, Algeria), 391, and became its bishop, 396-430: during this period, had to deal with Donatist schism, Pelagian heresy, and Vandal invasions. *Died 28 August 430 A.D..*

PUBLICATIONS

Collections

[*Works*], in *Patrologia Latina*, vols. 22-47; translations in *The Fathers of the Church, Ancient Christian Writers, Library of Christian Classics 6-8*, and *Nicene and Post-Nicene Fathers of the Christian Church*.
Basic Writings, edited by Whitney J. Oates. 2 vols., 1948.
An Augustine Reader, edited by John J. O'Meara. 1973.

Works

Confessiones, edited by M. Skutella, revised by H. Juergens and W. Schaub. 1969; as *Confessions*, translated by F.J. Sheed, 1943, R.S. Pine-Coffin, 1961, and Rex Warner, 1963.

De civitate Dei, edited and translated by G.E. McCracken (Loeb edition), 7 vols., 1957-72; also translated as *The City of God*, in *Fathers of the Church*.

De doctrina Christiana, edited by H.J. Vogels. 1930; as *Christian Instruction*, in *Fathers of the Church*.

De trinitate, edited by M.F. Sciacca. 1973; as *On the Trinity*, in *Nicene and Post-Nicene Fathers of the Christian Church*.

Selected Sermons, edited and translated by Quincy Howe. 1966.

Epistolae, edited by L. Carrozzi. 1974; as *Letters*, in *Fathers of the Church*; as *Select Letters* (Loeb edition), 1930.

De sermone Domini in monte, translated as *Commentary on the Lord's Sermon on the Mount*, in *Fathers of the Church*.

Soliloquia, translated as *Soliloquies*, 1910.

Enarrationes in Psalmos, translated as *On the Psalms*, in *Ancient Christian Writers*, 1960— .

Tractatus in Joannis Evangelium, translated as *Homilies on the Gospel of John*, in *Nicene and Post-Nicene Fathers of the Christian Church*.

Tractatus in Epistolam Joannis ad Parthos, translated as *Homilies on St. John's Epistle*, in *Library of Christian Classics*.

De vera religione, translated as *Of True Religion*, in *Library of Christian Classics*.

De libero arbitrio, translated as *On Free Will*, in *Library of Christian Classics*.

De baptismo, contra Donatistas, translated as *On Baptism, Against the Donatists*, in *Nicene and Post-Nicene Fathers of the Christian Church*.

Contra litteras Petiliani, translated as *Answers to Letters of Petilian*, in *Nicene and Post-Nicene Fathers of the Christian Church*.

De spiritu et littera, translated as *The Spirit and the Letter*, in *Library of Christian Classics*.

De natura et gratia, translated as *On Nature and Grace*, in *Nicene and Post-Nicene Fathers of the Christian Church*.

De gratia et Christi et de peccato originali, translated as *On the Grace of Christ and on Original Sin*, in *Nicene and Post-Nicene Fathers of the Christian Church*.

Regula, translated as *The Rule of St. Augustine*. 1942.

De beata vita, edited by Michael Schmaus. 1931; as *The Happy Life*, 1939.

De Genesi ad literam [Literal Commentary on Genesis], edited and translated by John Hammond Taylor. 1948.

De dialectica, edited by Jan Pinborg, translated by B. Darrell Jackson. 1975.

*

Bibliography: in *Revue des études augustiniennes*, 1956— ; *Repertoire bibliographiques de saint Augustin 1950-1960* by T.J. van Bavel, 1963; *Fichier augustinien*, 4 vols., 1972; *Bibliographia Augustiniana* by Carl Andresen, 1973; *Augustinian Bibliography 1970-1980* by Terry L. Miethe, 1982.

Critical Studies: *St. Augustine's Philosophy of Beauty* by Emmanuel Chapman, 1939; *The City of God* by J.H.S. Burleigh, 1949; *A Companion to the Study of St. Augustine* edited by R.W. Battenhouse, 1955; *St. Augustine and His Influence Through the Ages* by H.I. Marrou, 1957; *The Christian Philosophy of St. Augustine* by Etienne Gilson, 1960; *St. Augustine the Bishop* by F. van der Meer, 1961; *St. Augustine of Hippo: Life and Controversies* by Gerald Bonner, 1963; *Augustine of Hippo*, 1967, and *Religion and Society in the Age of St. Augustine*, 1972, both by P.R.L. Brown; *St. Augustine's Confessions: The Odyssey of a Soul*, 1969, and *Art and the Christian Intelligence in St. Augustine*, 1980, both by R.J. O'Connell; *Augustine: A Collection of Critical Essays* edited by R.A. Markus, 1972; *The Problem of Self-Love in St. Augustine* by Oliver O'Donovan, 1980; *The Young Augustine: An Introduction to the "Confessions" of St. Augustine* by John J. O'Meara, 1980.

*　　*　　*

Augustine's works are characterised by their number and their variety. When he came to edit them at the end of his life he had 93 on his library shelves, not including vast numbers of letters and sermons as well as the numerous abandoned projects that littered his life. His writings chart the stages of his personal development, from ambitious young career-maker to international religious thinker and controversialist: he described himself as one who writes because he has made progress and who makes progress—by writing.

Augustine received the traditional late classical education in rhetoric, the influence of which is apparent in his love of sophisticated wordplay, paradox and contrast, vivid similes and verbal fireworks. His works show a precision in choice of words, a phenomenal memory for, and telling use of, both classical and scriptural quotations, and a mastery of dry irony and sarcasm. The abstract quality of his mind prevented him from dwelling on landscape or nature but he was attracted by light, faces, music, and above all by the rhythms of speech. Augustine addressed in different capacities a diverse range of audiences, and varied his style accordingly. Thus he composed the monumental and learned *City of God*, with its expansive, orderly argumentation and sweeping periodic style; powerful, demagogic sermons with lapses into common parlance, the better to communicate with his congregation; letters to personal friends, officials of church and state, and a correspondence with Jerome notable for its tone of courteously veiled rancour; and outright ecclesiastical propaganda such as *De agone Christiano (On the Christian's Conflict)*, written in deliberately simple Latin, and the literature attacking the Donatists, full of colloquialisms and popular jingles. Augustine was the only major Latin philosopher who never properly learned Greek, but he turned this seeming deficiency to advantage and ended by replacing the largely Greek culture of the contemporary church with his own works of scholarship, such as *On the Trinity* and his commentary on *Genesis*. Much of his philosophy was merely garnered from Cicero and translations of the Neo-Platonists, but with it Augustine transformed the shape of Latin Christianity.

Augustine's talents lie chiefly in self-justification and dialectic, and this is nowhere clearer than in *The Confessions*. This work, and the *Soliloquies*, which preceded it, were startling innovations with their welding of classical and religious language and ideas and their ferocious self-analysis. *The Confessions* is not autobiography in the usual sense—Augustine wholly ignores such details as the number of his family, the name of the friend whose death caused him to flee to Carthage or of his faithful concubine who bore his son—rather it is an account of the emotional evolution of a relentless seeker after Truth and Perfection, an anatomy of the most well-documented conversion of antiquity. It is also the therapeutic self-reassessment of a man entering middle age and seeking to interpret his past from the only-too-present viewpoint of a bishop of a provincial town on the frontiers of a collapsing empire. The public aspect of these preoccupations emerges in his polemical works against ecclesiastical opponents—Donatists, Pelagius, and Bishop Julian.

The climax of Augustine's career was the move outwards from himself and his community to address no less a task than the transformation of the secular pagan state. In *De doctrina Christiana* he sought to strip the pagan gods and the empire itself of centuries of mystique. Finally, in *City of God*, an outline for a theology of history depicting two cities—earthly and divine, of unbelief and of faith—Augustine exploited the resources given him by his education in the old tradition to transform it into a vehicle for the new.

—Claire E. Gruzelier

AURELIUS (Antoninus), Marcus. Born Marcus Annius Verus in Rome, 26 April 121 A.D. Married Annia Galeria Faustina in 145 (died, 176); one daughter and one son. Gained favor of Emperor Hadrian, who made him a Salian priest at age of 8, supervised his education, and arranged his marriage; adopted (as Marcus Aelius Aurelius Verus Caesar) by emperor designate Antoninus Pius in 138: quaestor in 139, consul with Antoninus Pius in 140, and also in 145 and 161; tribunicia potestas and proconsular imperium, the main formal powers of emperorship, conferred on him in 147; abandoned study of rhetoric about this time, and began study of philosophy; succeeded Antoninus Pius as emperor in 161, and elevated his fellow-consul for that year, Lucius Verus, to joint authority with himself (Verus died in 169); negotiated with German tribes in Aquileia, 168; fought the Marcomanni and Quadi, two Danube tribes, 170-74; visited Syria and Egypt to settle revolts, 175-76; raised his son Commodus to rank of Augustus, 177; fought the Marcomanni, 177-78. *Died 17 March 180 A.D.*

PUBLICATIONS

Prose

Meditations, edited by A.S.L. Farquharson. 2 vols., 1944 (includes translation); also translated by C.R. Haines, 1930 (Loeb edition), and Maxwell Staniforth, 1964.
Letters, edited by L. Pepe. 1957.

*

Critical Studies: *Marcus Aurelius: His Life and His World* by A.S.L. Farquharson, edited by D.A. Rees, 1951; *Marcus Aurelius* by Anthony Birley, 1966.

*　　*　　*

Marcus Aurelius's writings are unusual in the extant literature of the ancient world in being almost wholly personal documents, not intended for publication. He was a prolific letter writer, sometimes dispatching three notes to a friend in a single day, and there are about 200 letters still surviving. Many of these are preserved in the correspondence of Fronto, his tutor, for whom he shows great affection and concern. They date from between 139 and 166, when Fronto died, and shed passing illumination upon Marcus's youthful enthusiasms, family concerns, and personal habits.

But his major work is that "breviary for contemplatives" which we call *The Meditations*, but should more correctly be translated (from the Greek) as *To Himself*. It consists of 12 books of unsystematic private reflections, addressed to himself in the second person like a dialogue, which lends itself to being sipped from time to time rather than drunk off in a draught. Historians concerned with facts are disappointed in their perusal of *The Meditations* since Marcus makes little reference, except incidentally, to external events, and the books are consequently hard to date, beyond saying that they were largely written on campaign in the last 10 years of his life. The present arrangement of the books is possibly not his own and certainly not chronological, since the first book, a summing up of all he owes to his family, friends, and associates, appears to have been written last. The manner of transmission is also uncertain—whether his notebooks were entrusted to his secretary's care or found among his papers after his death is not known—but there is little trace of organized editing since the work often progresses in a disconnected fashion from one topic to another and is full of repetitions and loose ends.

It is written in Greek, the language of upper-class, educated men. However, Marcus abandoned rhetoric early in life, and his style, while being slightly old-fashioned and awkward, is plain and unadorned—an index of its private nature, but also of the character of the writer. He has a talent for epigrammatic brevity, and often resorts to quick enumeration of points as they occur to him, or even preserves straight lists of quotations from his reading of philosophers and poets. He has a quick eye for natural detail, such as the cracks in a loaf of baked bread or the way a sunbeam streams into a dark room, and his writing is full of brief, vivid similes showing an acute observation of the everyday scene like army surgeons' instruments, a fire burning a pile of rubbish, lotions and poultices for the sick, scuffling puppies, or fights in the arena. His comparisons are all drawn from war, dancing, wrestling, eating—the common occupations of life within his personal experience—and he employs certain predictable, recurring images: life as a road, time as a river, reason as a helmsman, the sphere as perfection.

Marcus is not notable as an original thinker; he modestly considered scholarship and philosophy far above him. His attitude is mainly Stoic: a belief in calm acceptance of one's lot, a view of the world as a unified organism constantly changing and of the life spirit returning after death to the universal fire; but he read widely among different schools of philosophy and made his own choice influenced by his personal experience, transmuting pure Stoicism into an individual code for living, a code that in many ways prefigures Christianity.

The Meditations is a kind of spiritual last will and testament—the thoughts of an ill and aging man aware of the increasing nearness of death and taking stock of what life has taught him: to accept himself, making a conscious effort to improve his failings, striving to assimilate the bad things that happen to good people as part of a universal plan of nature; to bear pain gracefully in the belief that there is a reason for suffering; to face the world with fortitude and his fellow man with understanding; to see man in his correct perspective in relation to the great universe as a transient piece of nothingness, so as to be able to accept approaching death as a small change and another of the processes of nature which is the universal lot of mankind.

Marcus has often been accused of being a moral prig and a humbug, but it is obvious from his writings that he was a genuinely good man of sincere and sensitive character, conscious of his duties as emperor and military leader, who endured many personal griefs and public misfortunes and ended with a realistic, if melancholy, view of life—that one may not be rewarded for service or affection to others, but one does not cease to act according to personal canons of rightness because of this.

—Claire E. Gruzelier

BABEL, Isaak (Emmanuilovich). Born in Odessa, 1 July 1894. Educated in Nikolayev; Nicholas I Commercial School, Odessa, 1905-11; Institute of Financial and Business Studies, Kiev, later in Saratov, 1911-15, graduated 1915. Served in the army, 1917-18. Married Eugenia Gronfein in 1919; one daughter; also one daughter by Antonina Pirozhkova. In St. Petersburg from 1918: worked on Gorky's magazine *New Life*, 1918; editor, Ukrainian State Publishing House, 1919-20; news service correspondent with First Cavalry on the Polish campaign, 1920, and correspondent for Tiflis newspaper in Caucasus; in Moscow from 1923; secretary of the village soviet at Molodenovo, 1930; out of favor in the 1930's, and arrested, 1939. *Died (allegedly) 17 March 1941.*

PUBLICATIONS

Collections

Izbrannoye. 1957; another edition, 1966.
Collected Stories, edited by Walter Morison. 1955.
Destvo i drugie rasskazy [Childhood and Other Stories], edited by Efraim Sicher. 1979.

Fiction

> *Rasskazy* [Stories].   1925.
> *Konarmiya.*   1926; as *Red Cavalry*, 1929.
> *Bluzhdaiushchiye zvezdy: Rasskaz diya kino* [Wandering Stars: A Cine-Story].   1926.
> *Istoriya moey golubyatni* [The Story of My Dovecot].   1926.
> *Benya Krik: Kinopovest.*   1926; as *Benia Krik: A Film-Novel*, 1935.
> *Korol'* [The King].   1926.
> *Odesskie rasskazy* [Odessa Stories].   1931.
> *Benya Krik, The Gangster, and Other Stories*, edited by A. Yarmolinsky.   1948.
> *Lyubka the Cossack and Other Stories*, edited by Andrew R. MacAndrew.   1963.
> *The Lonely Years 1925-29: Unpublished Stories and Private Correspondence*, edited by
>   Nathalie Babel, 1964.
> *You Must Know Everything: Stories 1915-1937*, edited by Nathalie Babel.   1969.
> *The Forgotten Prose*, edited by Nicholas Stroud.   1978; as *Zabytyy Babel*, 1979.

Plays

> *Zakat* (produced 1927).   1928; as *Sunset*, in *Noonday 3*, 1960.
> *Mariya* (produced 1964).   1935; as *Marya*, in *Three Soviet Plays*, edited by Michael
>   Glenny, 1966.

*

Critical Studies: *Babel* by Richard W. Hallett, 1972; *The Art of Babel* by Patricia Carden, 1972; *Babel, Russian Master of the Short Story* by James R. Falen, 1974; *An Investigation of Composition and Theme in Babel's Literary Cycle "Konarmija"* by Ragna Grøngaard, 1979; *Babel's Red Cavalry* by Carol Luplow, 1982; *Metaphor in Babel's Short Stories* by Danuta Mendelson, 1982; "Art as Metaphor, Epiphany, and Aesthetic Statement: The Short Stories of Babel," in *Modern Language Review*, 1982, and "The Road to a Red Cavalry: Myth and Mythology in the Works of Babel," in *Slavonic and East European Review*, 1982, both by Efraim Sicher.

*   *   *

Isaak Babel is, along with Zamyatin and Olesha, an outstanding exponent of short prose of the decade or so in which, following 1917, modernist experimentation flourished in Soviet Russian fiction.

Babel's work is notable for its treatment of Jewish and revolutionary themes and for its cultivation of the "cycle" form: an open-ended series of short stories, linked by theme, character, setting, and imagery, with additions being made at will—e.g., that of "Argamak" (1931) to *Red Cavalry* (1926), with "The Kiss" (1937) and further (unwritten) stories possibly being intended for the same sequence.

Red Cavalry, Babel's best known work, deals by unusual techniques of snapshot and montage (Babel enjoyed close associations with the film industry) with the fortunes of Budyonny's First Cavalry in the Polish campaign of 1920. A series of 35 "miniatures" examines the nature and ethics of personal and revolutionary violence, portraying a Jewish intellectual's quest for true fraternity amid Cossack fellow soldiers and assorted Jews, Poles, and peasants. Violence, sex, art, and nature are treated in rhythmic prose and striking images. Ambiguity, paradox and polarity, and the use of subsidiary narrators are key devices. Actions and perceptions are presented subjectively in an interplay of varied points of view underlined by use of metaphor; interpretations and judgements are left to the reader.

Other, less complete, main cycles ("definitively" ordered by Sicher in his 1979 edition) are set in the Jewish "Moldavanka" of Odessa. *Odesskie rasskazy* (Odessa Stories) features the exploits of Benia Krik (modelled on the real Mishka-Yaponchik), while the "early childhood" series, to have been collected under the title "The Story of my Dovecot," concentrate on Jewish upbringing amid the pogroms of 1905.

The degree of overall unity varies, as much for biographical as for artistic reasons. *Red Cavalry*, with its clear time span and largely sequential plot development, can be viewed as an episodic modernist novel (Mendelson, 1982) or as "a twentieth-century version of a Renaissance novella cycle" (Lowe, 1982). Important "independent" stories are "Line and Colour" (1923) and "Guy de Maupassant" (1932). However, the all-pervading presence of a purportedly autobiographical or obviously Babelian narrator suggests the possibility of considering Babel's short fictional *oeuvre* as a unit—a single collective "super-cycle."

Compression, to achieve a close organic unity of form and content, is the essence of Babel's compositional method. Plays and film scenarios apart, few of Babel's stories exceed ten pages. "A truly cautious master" (Mendelson), Babel re-worked his stories tirelessly, pruning every spare word, tightening paragraphing and punctuation. The resulting language is frequently called "a collision of styles"; words and their associations are foregrounded rather than the ideas behind them, while Babel's constant switches in modes of narrative discourse create a calculated role for the reader.

Babel seems again neglected in the Soviet Union, no edition of his works having appeared there since 1966. However, recent western studies (notably by Mendelson and Sicher) have advanced Babel criticism onto promising new ground.

—Neil Cornwell

BALZAC, Honoré de. Born in Tours, France, 20 May 1799. Educated at pension Le Guay-Pinel, Tours, 1804-07; Collège de Vendome, 1807-13; L'Institution Lepître, Paris, 1815; L'Institution Ganzer et Beuzelin, Paris, 1815-16; attended law lectures, the Sorbonne, Paris, Baccalaureat of Law 1819. Married Mme. Hanska (Eve Rzewuska) in 1850. Clerk for M. Guillonnet de Merville, 1816-18, and M. Passez, 1818-19; then writer, editor, magazine writer: obtained printer's license, 1826-28; owner, *La Chronique de Paris*, 1835-36; Editor, *La Revue Parisienne*, 1840. President, Société des Gens de Lettres, 1839. Chevalier, Legion of Honor, 1845. *Died 18 August 1850.*

PUBLICATIONS

Collections

Oeuvres complètes, edited by Marcel Bouteron and Henri Longnon.   40 vols., 1912-40.
La Comédie humaine, edited by Marcel Bouteron.   11 vols., 1951-58; revised edition, edited by Pierre-George Castex and Pierre Citron, 1976—.

The Human Comedy, edited by George Saintsbury. 40 vols., 1895-98.
Works. 1901.

Fiction

L'Héritage de Birague, with Le Poitevin de Saint-Alme and Etienne Arago. 1822.
Jean-Louis; ou, La Fille trouvée, with Le Poitevin de Saint-Alme. 1822.
Clotilde de Lusignan; ou, Le beau juif. 1822.
Le Centenaire; ou, Les Deux Beringheld. 1822; as *Le Sorcier*, in *Oeuvres complètes de Horace de Saint-Aubin*, 1837.
Le Vicaire des Ardennes. 1822.
La Dernière Fée; ou, La Nouvelle Lampe merveilleuse. 1823.
Annette et le criminel. 1824.
Wann-Chlore. 1825; as *Jane la pâle*, in *Oeuvres complètes*, 1836.
Le Dernier Chouan; ou, Le Bretagne au 1800. 1829; revised edition, as *Les Chouans; ou, Le Bretagne en 1799*, 1834; as *Le Chouan*, 1838; as *The Chouans*, 1893.
Mémoires pour servir à l'histoire de la révolution française, with Lheritier de l'Ain. 1829.
La Physiologie du mariage; ou, Méditations de philosophie éclectique. 1829; as *The Physiology of Marriage*, 1904.
Scènes de la vie privée. 1830; augmented edition, 1832.
Le Peau de chagrin. 1831; edited by S. de Sasy, 1974; as *The Magic Skin*, 1888; as *The Wild Ass's Skin*, in *Human Comedy*, 1895-98.
Romans et contes philosophiques. 1831.
Contes bruns, with Philarète Chasles and Charles Rabou. 1832.
Les Salmigondis: Contes de toutes les coleurs. 1832; as *La Comtesse à deux maris*, in *Scènes de la vie privée*, 1835; as *Le Colonel Chabert*, in *Comédie humaine*, 1844.
Les Cent Contes Drolatiques. 3 (of an intended 10) vols., 1832-37; *Quatrième dixain* (fragments), 1925; translated as *Contes drolatiques*, 1874.
Nouveaux contes philosophiques. 1832.
Le Médecin de campagne. 1833; excerpt, as *Histoire de Napoléon*, 1833; edited by Patrick Barthier, 1974.
Études de moeurs au XIXe siècle. 12 vols., 1833-37; includes reprints and the following new works:
    La Fleur des pois. 1834.
    La Recherche de l'absolu. 1834; as *Balthazar; or, Science and Love*, 1859; as *The Alchemist*, 1861; as *The Quest of the Absolute*, in *Human Comedy*, 1895-98; as *The Tragedy of a Genius*, 1912.
    Eugénie Grandet. 1833; translated as *Eugenie Grandet*, 1859.
    La Femme abandonnée. 1833.
    La Grenadière. 1833.
    L'illustre Gaudissart. 1833.
    La Vieille Fille. 1837.
    Illusions perdues (part 1: *Les deux poètes*). 1837.
    Les Marana. 1834.
    Histoire des treize. 1834-35; as *History of the Thirteen*, 1974; translated in part as *The Mystery of the Rue Soly*, 1894, *The Girl with the Golden Eyes*, 1928, and *The Duchess of Langeais*, 1946.
Le Père Goriot. 1835; translated as *Pere Goriot*, 1886.
Le Livre mystique (includes *Louis Lambert* and *Séraphita*). 1835; translated as *Louis Lambert* and *Seraphita*, 2 vols., 1889.
Études philosophiques. 20 vols., 1835-40; includes reprints and the following new works:
    Un Drame au bord de la mer. 1835.

Melmoth réconcilié. 1836.
L'Interdiction. 1836.
La Messe de l'Athée. 1837.
Facino cane. 1837.
Les Martyrs ignorés. 1837.
Le Secret des Ruggieri. 1837.
L'Enfant maudit. 1837.
Une Passion dans le désert. 1837.
Le Lys dans la vallée. 1836; as *The Lily of the Valley*, 1891.
L'Excommuniée, with Auguste de Belloy, in *Oeuvres complètes de Horace de Saint-Aubin.* 1837.
La Femme supérieure. 1837; as *Les Employés*, 1865; as *Bureaucracy*, 1889.
Histoire de César Birotteau. 1838; as *History of the Grandeur and Downfall of Cesar Birotteau*, 1860; as *The Bankrupt*, 1959.
Le Femme supérieure, La Maison Nucingen, La Torpille. 1838.
Les Rivalités en province. 1838; as *Le Cabinet des antiques* (includes *Gamara*), 1839; as *The Jealousies of a Country Town*, in *Human Comedy*, 1895-98.
Gambara; Adieu. 1839; translated as *Gambara*, in *Human Comedy*, 1895-98.
Une Fille d'Eve (includes *Massimilla Doni*). 1839; as *A Daughter of Eve* and *Massimilla Doni*, in *Human Comedy*, 1895-98.
Un Grand Homme de province à Paris (Illusions perdues 2). 1839; as *A Great Man of the Provinces in Paris*, 1893.
Beatrix; ou, Les Amours forcées. 1839; edited by Madeleine Fergeaud, 1979; translated as *Beatrix*, 1895.
Pierrette. 1840; translated as *Pierrette*, 1892.
Physiologie de l'employé. 1841.
Physiologie du rentier de Paris et de province, with Arnould Frémy. 1841.
Le Curé de village. 1841; as *The Country Parson*, in *Human Comedy*, 1895-98.
Oeuvres complètes: La Comédie humaine. 20 vols., 1842-53; includes reprints and the following new works:
Albert Savarus. 1842; translated as *Albert Savarus*, 1892.
Autre étude de femme. 1842.
Illusions perdues (part 3). 1843; parts 1 and 3 translated as *Lost Illusions*, 1893.
Esquisse d'homme d'affaires; Gaudissart II; Les Comédiens sans le savoir. 1846.
Un Épisode sous la terreur; L'Envers de l'histoire contemporain; Z; Marcas. 1846; *L'Envers...* translated as *Love*, 1893.
Ursule Mirouët. 1842; translated as *Ursula*, 1891.
Scènes de la vie privée et publique des animaux. 1842.
Mémoires de deux jeunes mariées. 1842; as *Memoirs of Two Young Married Women*, 1894.
Une Tenebreuse Affaire. 1842; edited by René Guise, 1973; as *The Gondreville Mystery*, 1898; as *A Murky Business*, 1972.
Les Deux Frères. 1842; as *Un Ménage de garçon en province*, in *Comédie humaine*, 1843; as *La Rabouilleuse*, in *Oeuvres complètes*, 1912; edited by René Guise, 1972; as *The Two Brothers*, 1887; as *A Bachelor's Establishment*, in *Human Comedy*, 1895-98; as *The Black Sheep*, 1970.
Un Début dans la vie (includes *La fausse maîtresse*). 1844.
Catherine de Médicis expliquée; Le Martyr calviniste. 1845; translated as *Catherine de' Medici*, 1894.
Honorine (includes *Un Prince de la Bohème*). 1845.
Splendeurs et misères des courtisanes: Esther. 1845; as *A Harlot's Progress*, in *Human Comedy*, 1895-98; as *A Harlot High and Low*, 1970.
La Lune de miel. 1845.
Petites misères de la vie conjugale. 1845-46; as *The Petty Annoyances of Married Life*,

1861.
Un Drame dans les prisons. 1847.
Le Provincial à Paris (includes *Gillette, Le Rentier, El Verdugo*). 1847.
Les Parents pauvres (includes *La Cousine Bette* and *Le Cousin Pons*). 1847-48; as *Poor Relations*, 1880; as *Cousin Pons*, 1886; as *Cousin Betty*, 1888.
La Dernière Incarnation de Vautrin. 1848.
Le Député d'Arcis, completed by Charles Rabou. 1854; as *The Deputy of Arcis*, 1896.
Les Paysans, completed by Mme. Balzac. 1855; as *Sons of the Soil*, 1890; as *The Peasantry*, in *Human Comedy*, 1895-98.
Les Petits Bourgeois, completed by Charles Rabou. 1856; as *The Lesser Bourgeoisie*, 1896; as *The Middle Classes*, 1898.
Sténie; ou, Les Erreurs philosophiques, edited by A. Prioult. 1936.
La Femme auteur et autres fragments inédits, edited by le Vicomte de Lovenjoul. 1950.
Mademoiselle du Vissard, edited by Pierre-George Castex. 1950.
Selected Short Stories. 1977.

Plays

Vautrin (produced 1840). 1840; translated as *Vautrin*, in *Works*, 1901.
Les Ressources de Quinola (produced 1842). 1842; as *The Resources of Quinola*, in *Works*, 1901.
Paméla Giraud (produced 1843). 1843; translated as *Pamela Giraud*, in *Works*, 1901.
La Marâtre (produced 1848). 1848; as *The Stepmother*, in *Works*, 1901.
Le Faiseur (produced 1849). 1851; translated as *Mercadet*, in *Works*, 1901.
L'École des ménages, edited by le Vicomte de Lovenjoul (produced 1910). 1907.

Other

Du droit d'ainesse. 1824.
Histoire impartiale des Jésuites. 1824.
Code des gens honnêtes; ou, L'Art de ne pas être dupe des fripons. 1825.
Mémoires de Mme. la Duchesse d'Abrantes, with the duchess. vol. 1 only, 1831.
Maximes et pensées de Napoléon. 1838.
Traité de la vie élégante. 1853.
Lettres à l'etrangère (to Mme. Hanska). 4 vols., 1899-1950.
Cahiers balzaciens, edited by Marcel Bouteron. 8 vols., 1927-28.
Le Catéchisme social, edited by Bernard Guyon. 1933.
Traité de la prière, edited by Philippe Bertault. 1942.
Journaux à la mer, edited by Louis Jaffard. 1949.
Correspondance, edited by Roger Pierrot. 5 vols., 1960-68.

Editor, *Oeuvres complètes*, by La Fontaine. 1826.
Editor, *Oeuvres complètes*, by Molière. 1826.

*

Bibliography: *A Balzac Bibliography* and *Index* by W. Hobart Royce, 1929-30.

Critical Studies: *Balzac and the Novel* by Samuel G.A. Rogers, 1953; *Balzac: A Biography*, 1957, and *Balzac's Comédie Humaine*, 1959, both by Herbert J. Hunt; *Balzac the European* by Edward J. Oliver, 1959; *Prometheus: The Life of Balzac* by André Maurois, 1965; *Balzac: An Interpretation of the Comédie Humaine* by F.W.J. Hemmings, 1967; *The Hero as Failure: Balzac and the Rubempré Cycle* by Bernard N. Schilling, 1968; *Balzac* by V.S. Pritchett, 1973;

Balzac's Comedy of Words by Martin Kanes, 1975; Balzac's Recurring Characters by Anthony Pugh, 1975; Balzac Criticism in France (1850-1900) by David Bellos, 1976; Balzac: Fiction and Melodrama by Christopher Prendergast, 1978; Balzac: Illusions Perdues by Donald Adamson, 1981; Balzac and His Reader by Mary Susan McCarthy, 1983.

*   *   *

Honoré de Balzac's first sustained piece of writing was Cromwell, a still-born historical tragedy in verse. Towards the end of his career he turned to drama once again, and it was probably not solely the need to raise some cash in a hurry that impelled him to do so. La Marâtre (The Stepmother), for instance, was well received by the critics in 1848, and after initial difficulties when first produced, the five-act melodrama Vautrin was a popular success at the Théâtre Porte-Saint-Martin two years later. Yet though Balzac remained fascinated all life long by the drama of his age whose emphatic acting styles and tempestuous emotionality left their distinctive stamp on his style and imagination, it was not in the theatre that he was destined to make his mark. Instead we must look to his three sets of quasi-Rabelaisian Contes drolatiques (Droll Tales), published between 1832 and 1837, and to his towering achievement, the teeming fictional world of La Comédie humaine, the creation of a lifetime devoted to writing, a work which though never carried through to completion encompasses upwards of 80 novels and tales.

The sheer scope of the enterprise is deeply impressive, even within the context of the enormous output of vast novels in the 19th century, and the audacity of transmuting the title of Dante's epic has been allowed to pass unchallenged, even though there are few obvious connections. A reliable census of Balzac's fictional world has established that it is peopled by over two thousand named characters. Nearly all are sharply individualised, by sex and, equally strongly, by social class, by temperament, appearance, mannerism, and speech habits. Many appear only fleetingly, but others are developed very fully, dominating the scene on occasion or else present as more or less shadowy background figures to events in which they do not play the primary role. A number of these characters, like some in Dickens and Dostoevsky, have made such an impact on the general consciousness that they have come to be regarded as having a status similar to that of historical personages, possessing individuality that seemingly transcends fiction. For a setting Balzac usually, though not exclusively, chose the period in French history just before the time at which he was writing. His characters stand before the backdrop of the French Revolution and the Empire, of the Restoration and the July Monarchy, an era of political turmoil and social upheaval which placed ordinary people under exceptional pressure and allowed unusual opportunities for outstanding individuals to develop their personalities to the full.

Balzac had a considerable number of major novels to his name before the grand conception of La Comédie humaine dawned on him. Les Chouans (The Chouans) of 1829 reflected the current fashion for historical romance. That same year La Physiologie du mariage (The Physiology of Marriage) though not important in itself, marked the crucial decision to use the novel for the study of social conditions in relation to the individual. Eugénie Grandet (1833) and Le Père Goriot (1835), two of Balzac's most popular novels, are evidence that he had indeed struck a rich vein, with observation and imagination combined in nice proportion. But in the early 1830's he also began to perceive the possibility, indeed the necessity, of thinking not in terms of single novels but of sets of what he liked to think of as fictionalised studies of 19th-century French society. Slowly the idea crystallised, and in 1842 Balzac was ready to present his views, in somewhat oracular tones, in his famous Preface to the Comédie humaine. In it he acknowledged his debt to Walter Scott who had raised the status of the novel by using it for the serious investigation of society in former times. The influences bearing on Balzac are not, however, just literary. He invokes the name of famous naturalists such as G.-L. Leclerc de Buffon and Geoffroy de Saint-Hilaire, and of mystical thinkers like Charles Bonnet, Emanuel Swedenborg, and L.-C. de Saint-Martin. What Balzac sought and found in their writings was some sort of corroboration of his intuitions of the unity of observed creation. In the rich variety of human life as he witnessed it there could, he believed, be perceived the working out of a single vital principle. His object became to present individual human beings as the products of the social forces bearing in on them just as biology was attempting to relate specialization and variation to environmental factors.

The pretension to using fiction as a tool for scientific analysis or even just demonstration is, of course, inadmissible, and despite Balzac's efforts to make his examination of society as comprehensive as possible and his mapping out *La Comédie humaine* as "studies" of various aspects, the procedure inevitably lacks compelling experimental rigour. Though Balzac felt obliged to return to some of his earlier novels and make some changes, critics have, however, been ready to accept that the unifying vision emerged from the fiction, as a scientific observation might, and was not something deliberately imposed after the event. As early as 1834 Balzac had begun to employ the device of making the same character reappear in different novels, and the tendency to bring out patterns of continuity becomes more and more marked from then on. *La Comédie humaine* is not a serial novel or the chronicle of a family, but something more complex; it is a fictional world in which individual destinies may be best appreciated in wider perspectives. In his descriptions Balzac revealed himself as an observer of exceptional acumen. Yet to hail him primarily as a recorder of the life of his times is to diminish his achievement. Though *La Comédie humaine* represented a major step in the direction of Realism, Balzac is too much of a visionary to be thought of as a Realist. His prose style sometimes lacks elegance, and credibility is occasionally taxed by emotionality and improbability. These excesses are, it seems, inseparable from the vigour and vitality of his vision of human nature and the inescapable conflicts between the demonic forces that spur on mankind and the constraints of religion and the monarchy that alone may hold them in check.

Balzac's rank as a novelist was in question throughout his life. Only towards the end of the 19th century was it generally recognised that his importance, both as an observer and as an imaginative visionary, decisively outweighed a degree of inelegance in execution and of coarseness in sensibility.

—C.N. Smith

BASHO. Pseudonym for Matsuo Munefusa. Born at Ueno, near Kyoto, Japan, in 1644. In service to a local lord of samurai status, and studied poetry with him until his death in 1666; then led an unsettled life: in Tokyo after 1672; from 1680, lived in a recluse's hut near Tokyo, and took his name from banana (*basho*) tree; his travels were described in verse and prose in journals and diaries; collections of his works appeared from 1684. *Died early autumn 1694.*

PUBLICATIONS

Collections

Zenshu [Complete Works], general editor Komiya Toyotaka. 10 vols., 1959-69.

Verse and Prose in English translation

Haiku (includes about 250 verses by Basho), translated by R.H. Blyth. 4 vols., 1949-52.
"Basho's Journey to Sarashina," translated by Donald Keene, in *Transactions of the Asiatic Society of Japan*, December 1957.

"Basho's Journey of 1684," translated by Donald Keene, in *Asia Major*, December 1959.
The Narrow Road to the Deep North and Other Travel Sketches, translated by Nobuyuki Yuasa. 1966.
Back Roads to Far Towns: Basho's Oku-no-hosomichi, translated by Cid Corman and Kamaike Susumu. 1968.
A Haiku Journey: Basho's The Narrow Road to the Deep North, translated by Dorothy Britton. 1974.
The Monkey's Straw Raincoat and Other Poetry of the Basho School, translated by Earl Miner and Hiroko Odagiri. 1981.

*

Critical Studies: *An Introduction to Haiku*, by H.G. Henderson, 1958; *Zeami, Basho, Yeats, Pound: A Study in Japanese and English Poetics*, 1965, and *Basho*, 1970, both by Makoto Ueda.

* * *

Basho is recognised as one of Japan's greatest literary figures. He transformed haiku from a somewhat frivolous pastime into a serious art form and he remains to this day its greatest exponent. He was in addition a seminal critic and teacher. Though he himself produced only a few works of criticism, many of his critical opinions and comments are preserved in the voluminous notes and accounts of his pupils, particularly Mukai Kyorai and Hattori Doho. Such is the importance of his critical precepts and the example of his poetry that no writer of haiku from his time to the present has been able to escape his influence.

In Basho's own day the haiku was regarded not as a form in itself but as the first stanza of a longer poem consisting of up to a hundred linked stanzas written by two or more poets taking turns. Much of Basho's effort was given to this type of composition, known as *renku* or *haikai no renga*, and it was in this field that he showed his greatest superiority, for he was an unrivalled master at the subleties of linking stanzas and controlling the changes of pace, mood and theme, which are the essence of this extremely demanding form.

Basho was also a skilled prose writer. He was as meticulous in his prose as in his verse and virtually forged a new style in which he integrated prose and poetry to an extent never before achieved. In addition to his few critical commentaries, he produced *haibun*, which are short occasional essays written in the haiku spirit, and travel journals. His *Essay on the Unreal Dwelling (Genjuan no ki)* is a moving apologia for his life and is generally considered the finest *haibun* ever written. His travel journal *The Narrow Road to the Deep North (Oku no hosomichi)* is his most famous work and one of the masterpieces of Japanese literature, in which he displays his mastery of prose style together with a sure command of form and the highest skill at reshaping events into art.

The greatness of Basho lies not only in his technique but in the depth of his probing of life. To him art was a way of life, a search for religious truth, which was to be found in nature: and this search led to continuous development, giving his work a variety that can appeal to all types of reader. Following his move to Edo, he changed from refined and often artificial wit to genuine humour in more mundane subjects; and on settling at his Basho hermitage he continued this trend towards greater simplicity, objectivity and description, creating a genuine style of his own. The years of his wanderings saw his creative peak in the style of *sabi* ("loneliness"), in which nature, usually in its most insignificant forms, is shown quietly fulfilling its often bleak destiny. In his final years he turned to *karumi* ("lightness"), an obscure term that seems to imply a more contented attitude of acceptance and less tension within a poem. To some, this step was retrograde, but however it is judged, it shows Basho developing and striving to the end to perfect his art in the light of his philosophy of life.

—P.T. Harries

BAUDELAIRE

BAUDELAIRE, Charles (Pierre). Born in Paris, 9 April 1821. Educated at boarding schools in Lyons and Paris; École Louis-le-Grand, Paris, expelled 1839; law student, University of Paris, 1839-41. After 1842, was able to live on an inheritance from his father; art critic and translator; publication of *Les Fleurs du mal* led to a trial for indecency, and 6 poems were suppressed. *Died 31 August 1867.*

PUBLICATIONS

Collections

Oeuvres complètes: Les Fleurs du mal; Curiosités esthétiques; L'Art romantique; Petits poèmes en prose, Les Paradis artificiels, La Fanfarlo, Le Jeune Enchanteur, foreword by Théophile Gautier. 4 vols., 1868-69.
Oeuvres complètes, edited by Jacques Crepet and Claude Pichois. 19 vols., 1922-53.
Oeuvres complètes, edited by Claude Pichois. 2 vols., 1975-77.

Verse

Les Fleurs du mal. 1861; revised edition, 1861, 1868 (in *Oeuvres complètes*); as *Flowers of Evil,* 1909; also translated by Richard Howard, 1982.
Les Épaves. 1866.
Le Parnasse contemporain (includes "Les Nouvelles Fleurs du mal"). 1866.
Petits poèmes en prose. 1869; as *Paris Spleen,* 1869.
Vers retrouvés. 1929.
Selected Verse, translated by Francis Scarfe. 1961.
Selected Poems, translated by Joanna Richardson. 1975.

Other

Salon de 1845. 1845; edited by André Ferran, 1933.
Salon de 1846. 1846; edited by David Kelley, 1975.
Théophile Gautier. 1859.
Les Paradis artificiels: Opium et haschisch. 1860.
Richard Wagner et Tannhäuser à Paris. 1861.
Le Peintre de la vie moderne. 1863.
L'Oeuvre et la vie d' Eugène Delacroix. 1863.
Journaux intimes. 1920; as *Intimate Journals,* 1930.
Selected Critical Studies, edited by D. Parmee. 1949.
The Mirror of Art: Critical Studies, edited by J. Mayne. 1955.
Baudelaire: A Self-Portrait (selected letters), edited by Lois Boe and F.E. Hyslop. 1957.
Baudelaire as a Literary Critic, edited by Lois Boe and F.E. Hyslop. 1964.
The Painter of Modern Life and Other Essays, edited by J. Mayne. 1964.
Art in Paris 1845-1862: Salons and Other Exhibitions, edited by J. Mayne. 1965.
Edgar Allan Poe, sa vie et ses ouvrages, edited by W.T. Bandy. 1973.
Correspondance, edited by Claude Pichois and Jean Ziegler. 2 vols., 1973.

Translator, *Histoires extraordinaires, Nouvelles histoires extraordinaires, Aventures d'Arthur Gordon Pym, Euréka, Histoires grotesques et sérieuses,* by Edgar Allan Poe. 5 vols., 1856-65.

*

Bibliography: *Baudelaire et la critique française 1868-1917* by A.E. Carter, 1963, supplemented by W.T. Bandy, 1953, and P.M. Trotman, 1971; *Baudelaire Criticism 1950-1967* by R.T. Cargo, 1968.

Critical Studies: *Baudelaire the Critic* by Margaret Gilman, 1943; *Baudelaire* by P. Mansell Jones, 1952; *Baudelaire: A Study of His Poetry* by Martin Turnell, 1953; *Baudelaire: Les Fleurs du Mal* by Alison Fairlie, 1960; *Baudelaire's Tragic Hero* by D.J. Mossop, 1961; *Baudelaire: A Collection of Critical Essays* edited by Henri Peyre, 1962; *Baudelaire* by M.A. Ruff, 1966; *Baudelaire and Nature* by F.W. Leakey, 1969; *Baudelaire as a Love Poet and Other Essays* edited by Lois Boe Hyslop, 1969, and *Baudelaire, Man of His Time* by Hyslop, 1980; *Baudelaire: A Lyric Poet in the Era of Capitalism* by Walter Benjamin, 1973; *Baudelaire, Prince of Clouds* by Alex de Jonge, 1976; *Baudelaire's Literary Criticism* by Rosemary Lloyd, 1981; *Baudelaire the Damned: A Biography* by F.W.J. Hemmings, 1982.

*   *   *

Poet, critic, translator, Charles Baudelaire, though largely ignored in his own time, is today considered one of the giants of the 19th century. His translations of five volumes of Poe's tales, in addition to his three essays on the American writer, are mainly responsible for Poe's fame in France and in all Europe. His essays on art and literature and his article on Wagner make him one of the greatest critics of the 19th century. And finally his volume of verse *Les Fleurs du mal* and his *Petits poèmes en prose* have earned him the title of our first modern poet as well as one of the finest of city poets.

Baudelaire is often called "the father of modern criticism" and "the first aesthetician of his age," not so much because of his value judgments of individual artists and writers as because of the ideas and principles he articulated. If his essays on art are usually considered superior to those on literature, it is mainly because demands of publishers often made it necessary for him to discuss a number of minor writers, while laws of censorship forced him to resort to irony, parody, and pastiche in order to express unpopular opinions.

Except during the Revolutionary period, when for a short time he adopted a more utilitarian conception of art, Baudelaire, like Flaubert, believed that the goal of art was beauty—beauty which, when "purified by art," could be derived from even ugliness, evil, and horror. That is why, in an unfinished epilogue intended for the second edition of *Les Fleurs du mal*, he could say to the city of Paris: "You have given me your mud and I have turned it into gold."

Baudelaire's personal conception of beauty, as noted in his *Journaux intimes*, was much like that of Poe. Though he was obviously influenced by the American writer, even to the point of extensively plagiarizing him in his three Poe essays, recent investigation has proved that what he found in Poe's literary doctrine was a confirmation of his own poetic practice as well as an affirmation of aesthetic principles he had already espoused.

Like Poe, Baudelaire prefers a beauty tinged with melancholy, regret, and sadness. Like Poe also, he insists on the importance of the bizarre or strange—"an artless, unpremeditated, unconscious strangeness," as he wrote in his *Exposition universelle*. In his 1857 essay on Poe, he even agrees that "the principle of poetry is...human aspiration toward a superior beauty"—a definition less characteristic of his poetry than his observation that "every lyric poet by virtue of his nature inevitably effects a return to the lost Eden." In his verse, Baudelaire himself often made that return, whether to the Eden of his childhood or to that of tropical seas and skies and of happiness he had known with his dark-skinned mistress.

With Delacroix, whose art he never ceased to glorify and whose opinions he frequently cited, Baudelaire believed that every age and every nation possesses its own particular beauty. In addition to its eternal or absolute element, all beauty, he maintained, must necessarily contain this particular or transitory element which, for him, was really synonymous with modernity. It was his emphasis on modernity—his call for "the heroism of modern life" and his belief that Parisian life was "rich in poetic and marvelous subjects"—that did much to change the course of both literature and painting and is often reflected in his own best verse.

Baudelaire was violently opposed to the servile imitation of nature as practiced by the

Realists. For him, as for Delacroix, nature was a dictionary whose hieroglyphics he sought to interpret. Imagination, the "queen of all faculties," alone permits the poet to discover in the vast storehouse of nature the symbols, analogies, and correspondences that can transform reality into the poet's vision of reality.

Baudelaire's chief claim to fame is his volume of verse known as *Les Fleurs du mal* in which can be seen a strange amalgam of old and new. Classic in its clarity, discipline, and reliance on traditional forms, Romantic in its subjectivity, its spirit of revolt, and its macabre elements, *Les Fleurs du mal* is also considered a distant forerunner of Surrealism in its use of dreams, myths, and fantasies. Far more important, however, is the fact that, by its use of suggestion as opposed to description and narration, it anticipates Symbolism and opens the door to modern poetry.

The unifying theme running throughout the six sections of *Les Fleurs du mal* is that of the human condition, of the conflict between good and evil, spleen and ideal, dream and reality. Obsessed with a belief in original sin and in the duality of man and using his own personal experiences as raw material, Baudelaire examined the spiritual problems of his age with a probing, almost brutal self-analysis. Unlike the Romantics, however, he saw himself not as unique but closely akin to the reader, whom he addresses in his introductory poem as "hypocritical reader, my counter-part, my brother."

One of Baudelaire's most important innovations is his use of correspondences. Although in his essays he speaks of the transcendental correspondences between the visible and invisible worlds, it is the synesthetic correspondences between colors, sounds, and perfumes that he employs in both his poetry and prose. Even more characteristic is his use of the correspondences between exterior nature and his own inner world. By finding symbols in outer reality that correspond to and suggest his inner thoughts and feelings, he often succeeds in creating what he himself called "a suggestive magic...containing the world exterior to the artist and the artist himself"—a suggestive magic leaving a "lacuna" to be filled by the reader. Such use of the symbol not only allowed him to exteriorize his idea or mood, by giving concrete form to the abstract, but also helped him achieve what he termed an "indispensable obscurity" that stops short of being hermetic.

Almost as important as his use of suggestion is Baudelaire's use of the cityscape to replace the nature description of the Romantics. Although the city is never described, its sounds are almost everywhere heard, and its presence everywhere felt. Both *Les Fleurs du mal* and the *Petits poèmes en prose* are permeated with the omnipresence of the city, if only through choice of imagery or through implication.

In style, Baudelaire introduced a number of innovations that have since been adopted by most modern poets. As a result of his emphasis on suggestion, the image, no longer merely peripheral, often becomes the very essence of the poem. His tendency to introduce a prosaic or even crude image in the midst of an otherwise highly poetic style as well as his remarkable ability to treat sordid reality without losing poetic elevation have been widely imitated. Equally characteristic are his musical sonorities, his subtle and suggestive rhythms, his frequent use of monologue or dialogue to achieve dramatic effect, and his mingling of the grand manner with a quiet, subdued, and conversational tone.

—Lois Boe Hyslop

BEAUMARCHAIS.　Born Pierre-Augustin Caron, in Paris, 24 January 1732.　Educated at Ecole d'Alfort to age 13, then apprenticed to his clock-maker father. Married 1) Madeleine-

Catherine Franquet in 1756 (died, 1757); 2) Geneviève-Madeleine Warebled in 1768 (died, 1770), one son; 3) Marie-Thérèse Willermawlas in 1786, one daughter. Clockmaker: his work recognized by Academy of Sciences, 1754, and popular at court; bought title of Clerk Controller in Royal Household, 1755; took name Beaumarchais from first wife's estate; also a harpist (improved the pedal system): gave lessons and organized concerts at court; bought title of Secretaire du Roi, 1761 (and consequently made a nobleman, 1761), and Lt.-General of hunting in the Varenne du Louvre, 1761; visited Spain, 1764-66; involved in several spectacular court cases in 1770's; government agent, 1774-75, and responsible for aid to American insurgents, 1775; involved in founding the Bureau de Legislation Dramatique (later Société des Auteurs et Compositeurs Dramatiques), 1777; arrested, 1792, but took refuge in London, Holland, and Germany until 1796. *Died 17-18 May 1799.*

PUBLICATIONS

Collections

> *Oeuvres complètes*, edited by Edouard Fournier. 1876.
> *Théâtres, Lettres relatives à son théâtre*, edited by Maurice Allem and Paul Courant. 1957.
> *Oeuvres complètes*, edited by Albert Demazière. 1973.

Plays

> *Colin et Colette, Les Bottle de sept lieues, Les Députés de la Halle, Léandre Marchand d'Agnus, Jean Bête à la foire* (farces: produced 1760-75). In *Théâtre*, 1957.
> *Eugénie* (produced 1767). 1767; as *The School for Rakes*, 1769.
> *Les Deux Amis; ou, Le Négociant de Lyon* (produced 1770). 1770; as *The Two Friends*, 1800.
> *Le Barbier de Séville; ou, La Précaution inutile* (produced 1775). 1775; as *The Barber of Seville*, 1776.
> *La Folle Journée; ou, Le Mariage de Figaro* (produced 1783). 1785; as *The Follies of a Day; or, The Marriage of Figaro*, 1785.
> *Tarare*, music by Antonio Salieri (produced 1787; revised version, produced 1790). 1790; as *Axur, King of Ormus*, 1813.
> *L'Autre Tartuffe; ou, La Mère coupable* (produced 1792). 1794; as *Frailty and Hypocrisy*, 1804; as *A Mother's Guilt*, in *The Complete Figaro Plays*, 1983.

Other

> *Mémoires contre M. Goëzman.* 1775.
> *Mémoires*, edited by J. Ravenal. 4 vols., 1830.
> *Lettres inédites*, edited by Gilbert Chinard. 1929.
> *Correspondance*, edited by Brian N. Morton. 1969—.

*

Bibliography: *Bibliographie des oeuvres de Beaumarchais* by H. Cordier, 1883.

Critical Studies: *Beaumarchais* by G. Lemaitre, 1949; *The Comic Style of Beaumarchais* by J.B. Ratermanis and W.R. Irwin, 1961; *The Real Figaro: The Extraordinary Career of Caron de Beaumarchais* by Cynthia Cox, 1962; *Beaumarchais: Le Barbier de Seville* by Robert

Niklaus, 1968; *A Critical Commentary on Beaumarchais's "Le Mariage de Figaro"* by Anthony Pugh, 1968; *Beaumarchais* by Joseph Sungolowski, 1974; *Beaumarchais: The Man Who Was Figaro* by Frédéric Grendel, 1977.

* * *

The creator of Figaro, perhaps the best known of all French fictional characters, was a highly successful businessman who smuggled arms to the American rebels of 1776, published a complete edition of the works of Voltaire between 1783 and 1790, and founded one of the first organizations to protect authors' rights, *La Société des Auteurs Dramatiques* (Society of Dramatic Authors), in 1777. The readiness of Figaro to defy his master Almaviva verbally in *La Barbier de Séville* (*The Barber of Seville*) and to intrigue against him in *Le Mariage de Figaro* (*The Marriage of Figaro*) was thus not the expression of any personal resentment on Beaumarchais's part towards a society which had not allowed him to prosper. It was much more the statement of a general need for the hierarchical, unjust, and inefficient society of the late 18th century to change so that other men of talent could more easily rise, as Beaumarchais himself had done, from being sons of watch-makers to becoming successful businessmen and even purchasing patents or nobility. Both Beaumarchais's plays about Figaro have been turned into operas, the first by Rossini and the second by Mozart, and the musical genius of *Le Nozze de Figaro* inevitably makes a straight performance of the original play seem a little tame. Both plays are saved less by the plot, which is unoriginal in *Le Barbier de Séville* and not always easy to follow in *Le Mariage de Figaro*, than by the character of Figaro himself, with his ready wit, verbal dexterity, and indomitable ingenuity. In this respect, he represents the archetypal Frenchman as the French would like to see themselves, mercifully free from the tendency to sentimental moralising that makes its way into *Le Mariage de Figaro* with the character of Marcelline, and inspired other, unperformable plays, such as *Le Mère coupable* (*A Mother's Guilt*). For Beaumarchais was also a man of his time in that he shared the opinion of Denis Diderot about the need for serious plays which dealt in a serious manner with the sexual and other problems of the middle class. It is this rather than any Oedipal impulses which explains the presence of Marcelline as Figaro's mother in *Le Mariage de Figaro*, and there is an interesting contrast with the lack of conviction which she carries for the modern audiences and the much more genuine affection which links Figaro to Suzanne. In the history of the theatre, Beaumarchais stands as the first successful practitioner of a comic style deriving its appeal from rapidity of action, vivacity of dialogue, and complexity of intrigue. Sociologically, he provides a comment on his society by exploiting the paradox that it is the social inferior, Figaro, who far exceeds his official master, Almaviva, in wit and intelligence, and can thus be seen as an ancestor to the Jeeves/Bertie Wooster relationship in P.G. Wodehouse.

—Philip Thody

BELY, Andrey. Pseudonym for Boris Nikolayevich Bugaev. Born in Moscow, 26 October 1880. Educated at gymnasium, Polivanov, 1891-99; studied science, then philology, then philosophy, University of Moscow, 1899-1906. Married 1) Asya Turgeneva, c. 1910 (separated, 1914); 2) K.N. Vasil'eva in 1924; 3rd marriage in 1931. Associate Editor, *Scales*, 1907-09; associated with the publishers Musaget, 1909; traveled abroad, studying with Rudolf Steiner, 1910-16; lecturer in Moscow and St. Petersburg; in Berlin, 1921-23: Editor, *Epopeya*, 1922-23. *Died 7/8 January 1934.*

Collections

Stikhotvoreniya i poemy, edited by T. Yu. Khmel'nitskaya. 1966.

Verse

Zoloto v lazuri [Gold in Azure]. 1904.
Pepel [Ashes]. 1908.
Urna [The Urn]. 1909.
Christos voskres [Christ Is Arisen]. 1918.
Pervoye svidanie. 1921; as *The First Encounter*, 1979.
Posle razluki: Berlinsky pesennik [After the Parting: A Berlin Songbook]. 1922.
Stikhi o Rossii [Verses about Russia]. 1922.
Vozvrashchen'e na rodinu [Returning Home]. 1922.
Stikhotvoreniya [Selected Poems]. 1923.
Stikhotvoreniya [Selected Poems]. 1940.

Fiction

Serebryany golub'. 1909; as *The Silver Dove*, 1974.
Peterburg. 1916; translated as *St. Petersburg*, 1959; complete version, as *Petersburg*, 1978.
Kotik Letayev. 1922; translated as *Kotik Letaev*, 1971.
Moskva. 1926.
Kreshchony kitayets [The Baptized Chinaman]. 1927.
Maski [Masks]. 1933.
Complete Short Stories, edited by Ronald E. Peterson. 1979.

Other

Simfoniya (2-aya, dramaticheskaya) [Symphony (Second, Dramatic)]. 1902.
Severnaya simfoniya (1-aya, geroicheskaya) [Northern Symphony (First, Heroic)]. 1903.
Vozvrat: III-ia simfoniya [The Return: 3rd Symphony]. 1904.
Kubok meteley: Chetvortaya simfoniya [A Goblet of Blizzards: Fourth Symphony]. 1908.
Lug zelony [The Green Meadow]. 1910.
Simvolizm [Symbolism]. 1911.
Arabeski [Arabesques]. 1911.
Tragediya tvorchestva: Dostoevsky i Tolstoy. 1911.
Revolyutsiya i kul'tura [Revolution and Culture]. 1917.
Rudolf Steiner i Gete v mirovozzrenii sovremenosti [Rudolf Steiner and Goethe from a Contemporary Point of View]. 1917.
Na perevale [At the Divide]. 3 vols., 1918-20.
Korolevna i rytsari [The Princess and the Knights]. 1919.
Zapiski chudaka [Notes of an Eccentric]. 1922.
Glossolalia: Poema o zvuke [Glossolalia: Poem about Sound]. 1922.
Putevye zametki: Sitsiliya i Tunis [Travel Notes: Sicily and Tunis]. 1922.
Poesiya slova: Pushkin, Tyutchev, Baratynsky, V. Ivanov, A. Blok [Poetry of the Word]. 1922.
Odna iz obiteley tsarstva teney [In the Kingdom of the Shades]. 1924.

Veter s Kavkaza [A Wind from the Caucasus]. 1928.
Ritm kak dialektika i "Medny vsadnik" [Rhythm as Dialectic and "The Bronze Horseman"]. 1929.
Na rubezhe dvukh stoletiy [On the Brink of Two Centuries]. 1930.
Nachalo veka [The Turn of the Century]. 1933.
Masterstvo Gogolya [The Art of Gogol]. 1934.
Mezhdu dvukh revolyutsii [Between Two Revolutions]. 1934.
Vospominaniya A.A. Bloke [Reminiscences of A.A. Blok]. 1964.

*

Critical Studies: *The Frenzied Poets: Bely and the Russian Symbolists* by Oleg Maslennikov, 1952; *Bely*, 1972, and *Bely: A Critical Study of the Novels*, 1983, both by J.D. Elsworth; *The Apocalyptic Symbolism of Bely* by S.D. Cioran, 1973; *Bely: The "Symphonies"* by Anton Kovač, 1976; *The Poetic World of Bely* by Boris Christa, 1977; *Bely: His Life and Works* by K. Mochulsky, 1977; *Bely: A Critical Review* edited by G. Janecek, 1978; *Bely's Short Prose* by Ronald E. Peterson, 1980; *Word and Music in the Novels of Bely* by Ada Steinberg, 1982.

*　　　*　　　*

Andrey Bely, Russia's greatest modernist writer and a leading poet of that most remarkable period of Russian intellectual history which is called the Silver Age, was also a theorist of Symbolism, a pioneer in the structural method of literary analysis, and, according to Bryusov and later Pasternak, "the most interesting man in Russia." Before he became A. Bely (1901), he considered himself a philosopher, a follower of the mystical philosopher Solovyov, a scientist, and a composer, regarding himself as "simply a person who is searching."

In his search to find new forms of art, he wanted to fuse art with music and religion, "to escape into a primitive phase of culture, into rhythm and gesture..." ("About Myself as a Writer"). He maintained that life reveals itself only through creative activity which is "unanalysible, integral and omnipotent." It is only expressible in symbolic images which envelop the idea. In the process of cognitive symbolisation the Symbol becomes reality, it can run ahead, depicting the future. He claimed that he had foreseen in his novels people and historical events, such as Rasputin in *The Silver Dove*, the downfall of tsarist Petersburg in *Petersburg*, and the fascist conspiracy in his projected novel *Germany*. Symbolism for Bely was a way of thinking, writing, and living. The Bely-Bryusov-Petrovskaya weird and grotesque triangle, and Bely's dramatic affair with Blok's wife, conformed to the Symbolist doctrine that life and art should be unitary. The principal hero of his novels is a philosophising eccentric, a madman-artist "whose only art is the creation of himself." Even the choice of the colour white (bely) for his pseudonym was to be significant. White is a recurrent symbol in his poetry: it stands for the snowstorm, that vast elemental force, and for life itself. Sounds and colours always had for Bely a mystical significance. As Bely himself tells us, the subjects of his first four books "were drawn from musical leitmotifs, and I called them not stories or novels but *Symphonies*."

Bely believed that, in moving towards music, a work of art becomes more profound. All his prose has distinct rhythmical qualities. The story *Kreshchony Kitayets*, for example, was composed from the sounds of Schumann's *Kreisleriana*. The regular beat, the pause for breath are supposed to express a deep secret rhythm of the spirit. In poetry, too, phonetic structure is often more important than meaning. Words with similar consonants clutch at one another, cling to each other, echoing his favourite images of wind and storm. He deliberately obliterated all discourse from his poetry. There are hardly any developments of thought; instead Bely repeats certain images pointing to a central theme. His poetry is, however, inferior to his prose. He saw rhythm as a "principle which unites poetry with prose." He called his last novel, *Maski*, a "lyrical epic poem." He often thought of himself more as a theoretician than as a poet. He devoted many years (from 1902 to 1910, and again from 1918 to 1921) to the development of the theory of Symbolism. He gave many public lectures, wrote hundreds of essays, which were collected in the most complex book, *Simvolizm*; he also conducted seminars and research work in the field of prosody. Only in 1924 did he return to literature completely, and he then began to fall into obscurity.

Like Blok, he saw the October Revolution as the birth of a new cosmical world. But Russia, risen anew, failed to appreciate him. In 1921, after Blok's death, he left Russia for Berlin only to find out that "the Russian émigré is as alien to me as the Bolsheviks." The two people he wanted to be with most, Asya Turgeneva and Rudolf Steiner, didn't need him. Bitterly disenchanted, exhausted and sick, he came back to Moscow: "I returned to my grave...all journals, all publishing houses are closed to me." After Trotsky's merciless attack, stating that Bely's novels "poison your very existence," he appealed to Stalin (1931), and compromised with his conscience by becoming a Marxist. In the Soviet Russia of today he remains a controversial writer, too modernist for the literary officials, too incomprehensible for the reading public. In the West his works have always been praised "without being understood or read," as the translators of *Petersburg* put it. Although Nabokov included *Petersburg* among the four "greatest masterpieces of twentieth century prose," Bely never achieved such enormous popularity as Joyce, Kafka, and Proust. Like them he did his best to destroy the simplicity of forms, but it was precisely his linguistic experiments that cut him off from the foreign reader.

—Valentina Polukhina

BHAGAVAD GITA.   Anonymous work of c. 200 B.C. inserted into the *Mahabharata, q.v.*

PUBLICATIONS

> *Shrimadbhagavad Gita* (Sanskrit text, English translation, and commentary), edited by R.N. Narayanaswami.   1936; also edited by K.K. Bhattacharya, 1972, and Tulsiramaswami, 1977; translated by Swami Prabhavananda and Christopher Isherwood, 1945, Juan Mascaro, 1962, P. Lal, 1965, and Kees W. Bolle, 1979.

*

Critical Studies: *The Bhagavadgita* by L.D. Barnett, 1905; *Essays on the Gita* by Shri Aurobindo, 1928; *The Bhagavad Gita* by Douglas P. Hill, 1928; *The Bhagavadgita* by F. Edgerton, 1944; *Talks on the Gita* by A.V. Bhave, 1960.

*   *   *

The *Bhagavad Gita* (*Gita* for short) is just an episode in Vyasa's *Mahabharata*, but it has achieved even more fame. Most devout Hindus recite a few lines of it daily in their homes. The *Gita* is really a dialogue between Arjuna, the Pandava hero, and Krishna, his divine charioteer, to dispel his hesitation and gloom in having to kill his own kinsmen to get an empire.

Krishna tells Arjuna that death is really of no consequence for it means only rebirth in another form. The immortal soul never dies. And even if you do not believe in the soul's immortality and reincarnation, Krishna tells him, "you should still not grieve. For it is certain that death is inevitable and controlled by destiny. So why worry about what *has* to happen, and of which you are merely the instrument?" Krishna goes on to explain how one can achieve emancipation. It can be either by knowledge, or by perfect devotion to god, or by desireless works. Thus the *Gita* is a kind of philosophical synthesis. It is also a practical guide to human conduct, and favours renunciation. A man should do his own work and not bother about that of another. And work should be done to perfection, for it is a kind of yoga. It is the man at the top who should set the standard in conduct, for the others lower down follow his example. The wise man makes no distinction between a learned person, a cow, an elephant, a pariah, and even a dog. He is kind to them all. All works should be desireless, and one should act according to his conscience without expecting any reward or fearing any punishment. "Your right is to works alone," Krishna tells Arjuna "not to its fruit. Nor should you be enamoured of inaction."

Apart from its unrivalled philosophy, the *Gita* is also a literary work. The Sanskrit of its verses is simpler in structure than that of other Hindu works on philosophy. It has more flow and smoothness. It has a mixed metre, the *upajati*, some lines being in the *indravajra* and others in the *upendravajra* form. Both of these have eleven syllables each. The poet uses language to suit the occasion, as for example the musical stanzas of Arjuna's prayer to the Lord when he disclosed his cosmic form. Death is a mere "change of clothes." Enjoyments come to a calm man yet leave him undisturbed, as rivers entering the sea. The mind of the yogi is like "a light in a sheltered place." Passion, anger, and greed are "the triple gates of hell." Creation is like the huge spreading Indian fig tree. Its roots are the Primal Being, its stems the creator, its leaves the scriptures, and its branches the living creatures with all their frailties. One is urged to fell this tree with the formidable axe of dispassion.

The keynote of the *Gita* is renunciation, and it strongly advocates self-control and the relinquishment of all sense pleasures—even the thought of them. But it is against ascetics who torture their bodies, calling them "fiends." The *Vedas* are not discarded by it, but it considers them merely aids to emancipation, and "like a tank flooded with water" when the goal is achieved. The universality of the *Gita* lies in its complete freedom from all dogma. After propounding his doctrine, Krishna tells Arjuna, "Don't take my word for it. Reflect on what I have told you and do as you like." In fact Krishna goes to the extent of saying, "They are also my devotees, who with faith worship other gods." The *Gita* is undiluted philosophy expressed in layman's language, and effectively reconciles the various views of Indian schools of philosophy. It undoubtedly holds a high place in the immortal literature of the world.

—K.P. Bahadur

BIBLE. Compilation of Hebrew and Greek texts. *Old Testament* collects Hebrew prose and verse works dating from c. 900-100 B.C.: Pentateuch, the first five books canonized c. 400 B.C.; The Former Prophets, principally historical works, canonized c. 200 B.C.; and the miscellaneous Writings gradually canonized individually to c. 90 A.D. *New Testament* collects Greek prose writings from c. 50-100 A.D.: letters of Paul, other letters, the three synoptic gospels (Matthew, Mark, Luke), and the Johannine writings. Non-canonical works of both periods are collected into Old and New Testament Apocrypha.

PUBLICATIONS (translations)

Bible, translated by Wyclif, 1380(?); Tyndale, 1525-26 (New Testament), 1530 (Pentateuch); Coverdale, 1535; Rheims-Douai version (Roman Catholic), 1582-1610; King

James Version, 1611; Revised Standard Version, 1946-52; New English Bible, 1961-70; and many others; annotated editions include *The Interpreter's Bible*, edited by George Buttrick and others, 1952-57, *The Oxford Annotated Bible* edited by Herbert C. May and Bruce M. Metzger, 1962, and *The Jerusalem Bible*, 1966.

*

Critical Studies: *The Old Testament in Modern Research* by Herbert F. Hahn, 1954, revised bibliographical essay by Horace D. Hummel, 1970; *The New Testament Background: Selected Documents* edited by C.K. Barrett, 1956; *History of the Bible in English* by F.C. Bruce, 1961, revised edition, 1970, 1979; *The Interpreter's Dictionary of the Bible* edited by George Buttrick, 4 vols., 1962, supplementary volume edited by Keith Crim, 1976; *The Cambridge History of the Bible* edited by P.R. Ackroyd, C.F. Evans, G.W.H. Lampe, and S.L. Greenslade, 3 vols., 1963-70, and *Cambridge Bible Commentary* edited by Ackroyd, A.R.C. Leaney, and J.W. Parker, n.d.; *The Anchor Bible*, 1964— ; *Irony in the Old Testament* by Edwin M. Good, 1965; *The Old Testament: An Introduction* by Otto Eissfeldt, revised edition, 1965; *The Art of the Biblical Story* by Shimon Bar-Efrat, 1979; *The Art of Biblical Narrative* by Robert Alter, 1981.

* * *

Literally, Bible simply means "book" and "scriptures" denotes "writings." Yet these most general of terms have come to be applied to one work of literature. To reach such a position of eminence this collection of writings had to meet the competition of all other writings. First written and collected by an unimportant and politically insignificant desert tribe, their library has become the basic charter of western civilization. Every word has been set to music, often many times. The world's greatest artists and poets have found their inspiration in its pages. Thomas Aquinas and Thomas Babington Macaulay were among those who knew the work by heart. Its language has shaped the rhetoric and poetic style of many nations in many eras. Does this work deserve the literary eminence it has gained? Originally the product of religious experience, it became in turn the producer of religious experience. Expressed first in Hebrew, then in Greek, finally in Latin and all the other languages through translations, the derivative translations have themselves become great literary productions in their own cultures.

The Psalms must rank as the world's favorite poems. Musical in their origin, they have inspired the greatest of composers to set their texts. Attributed to David but drawn from eclectic sources, they may well be the world's earliest poems. The names of the original deities were silently excised, the collectors of the hymns sensing the truth of the religious experience behind the false gods. The subject range of the poems is enormous—from joy to the deepest grief. The entire range of the human religious experience finds expression in these pages.

Most ancient cultures have produced accounts of creation, but the Biblical account has been the most popular and the most influential. Adam and Eve became the progenitors of all of humanity, not just of the Jewish people. No other story puts at its center such an account of human fallibility. The power of evil to seduce is fully recognized in the Fall of Man, but yet there is the promise of final salvation. Many medieval poems began with the words "In the beginning God created," this becoming the bedrock axiom on which an assurance of life's meaning might be based. The Garden was one of the earliest afirmations of the centrality of sexuality to the human experience.

Of even greater significance has been the story of Egyptian bondage. Other peoples celebrated their victories, Israel affirmed its defeat and bondage. In its Egyptian sufferings the people found their historical identity and their greatness. Throughout history all oppressed peoples have cried "Let my people go." The Egyptian Pharaoh has replaced all other images of the tyrant in the world's literature. God was affirmed to be on the side of the victim, not on the side of the victor. Even when they were delivered out of Egypt, they still had to wander for forty years in the wilderness before they could enter the promised land. The framework established by these experiences has been normative for later ages. The American slaves knew themselves to be in Egypt. Their own Psalms (spirituals) affirmed the Jewish experience to be theirs as well.

They looked for the Jordan which they might cross to reach their "land of milk and honey." They too hoped to reach the heavenly city, Jerusalem the Golden, which replaced Plato's ideal city as the goal of human striving. Jehovah was on the side of the slaves, not the masters. So there was the assurance of ultimate deliverance, and of the achievement of justice.

The Book of Job, the most Greek of the Jewish collection, has expressed the message of all classical tragedy, that suffering comes to the good as to the wicked. But the good achieve wisdom through their suffering. And that in the tragic experiences one can discern a divine purpose.

But not just the obviously literary books deserve attention. From the beginning the Bible was an historical work of great importance. The last events of history were prophecies contained in the earliest human experiences. The world has had many prophets, but the Jewish prophets were unique in their ability to discern the eternal purpose in the transient historical moment. Christian apologists simply continued the kind of historical thinking and patterning that had always been implicit in the Jewish writings.

The Bible has given the world many "notable images of vices and virtues," Philip Sidney's "right discerning note to know a poet by." The greatest creations have been the figures of good: Abraham, Joseph, Moses, Noah, Joshua. But two of these images have caught the imagination of the world, David and Jesus.

David has become the world's image of human perfection. It is that ideal that Michelangelo captured and expressed in his statue. The young man about to battle Goliath is symbol of the fragile goodness of this world that is quite adequate to the defeat of the world's most monstrous evils. David is the eternal affirmation of the justice that will raise the underdog to victory. The courage of the gallant young warrior in "the wars of truth" finds expression in calm assurance, not in the rage of Achilles. It is the courage of faith and knowledge, not of simple strength. But David is the poet as well as the warrior, the singer of psalms, the man as adept at the harp as at the sling. And he is also the figure of the priest. He is, as Michelangelo portrays him, Plato's ideal philosopher king caught in stone rather than in words. Goliath, like other figures of evil, is treated with derision. Those who rebel against good are laughable, to be held in scorn.

No other figure in the world's literature has proven a rival to the Jesus of the Gospel accounts. Indeed a new literary form had to be created to express so radically new an idea of virtue. In the earliest gospel account, that of Mark, one sees the miracle of an unlettered author fighting through limitations of language to express an ultimate vision of truth. The greatest lessons of history were in the gospels found in the life of the humblest carpenter from Nazareth. For the earliest compilers of the gospels, the teachings were less important than the life, the ethics were addenda to the history. Roman grandeur was confronted by a man who had died the death of a slave, on a cross. And yet the peace that the angels had celebrated at his birth was affirmed, rightly, to be of greater significance than that *pax romana* achieved by Augustus, the figure whose decree sent Mary and Joseph to Bethlehem to be taxed. The hopes of Virgil's Messianic Eclogues were to be fulfilled in Jerusalem, not in Rome. A story so unlikely to have any appeal to humanity has instead proven to be "the greatest story ever told."

Finally the last things. All of the earlier treatments of eschatology are summed up in Revelation. The book has become the treasure trove for the world's most radical thinkers and dreamers. Those who labor to change human society speak in the language of John. They hope to reach the New Jerusalem, and find the assurance of ultimate success that gives them hope. Jerusalem has replaced Athens as the image of the ideal city, the native land of the world's pilgrims. While they might never live to reach the promised land, they have at least known that the cities of this world cannot be their final home. In this great truth the writings of Plato and of the Bible become one.

—Myron Taylor

BLIXEN, Karen. *See* **DINESEN, Isak.**

BLOK, Alexander (Alexandrovich). Born in St. Petersburg, 28 November 1880. Educated at Vvedensky School, St. Petersburg, 1891-99; studied law, 1899-1901, and philology, 1901-06, University of St. Petersburg. Married Lyubov Dmitrievna Mendeleyeva in 1903. Writer from 1906; served behind the lines in 1916; later had government jobs: verbatim reporter, Extraordinary Investigating Commission, 1917-18; on various cultural committees after 1918: in Theatrical Department of People's Commissariat for Education (and Chairman of Repertory Section), 1918-19, and involved with Gorky's World Literature publishing house, 1918-21; adviser, Union of Practitioners of Literature as an Art, 1919; Chairman of Directorate of Bolshoi Theatre, 1919-21. *Died 7 August 1921.*

PUBLICATIONS

Collections

> *Sobraniye sochineniy.* 7 vols. (of 9 planned), 1922-23; edited by V.N. Orlov and others, 8 vols., 1960-65 (includes diaries and letters); edited by S.A. Nebolsin, 6 vols., 1971 (includes notebooks).

Verse

> *Stikhi o Prekrasnoy Dame* [Verses about the Most Beautiful Lady]. 1905.
> *Nechayannaya radost'* [Unexpected Joy]. 1907.
> *Snezhnaya maska* [The Snow Mask]. 1907.
> *Zemlya v snegu* [The Earth in Snow]. 1908.
> *Nochnye chasy* [The Night Watches]. 1911.
> *Sobraniye stikhotvoreniy* [Collected Poems]. 3 vols., 1911-12.
> *Stikhi o Rossii* [Poems about Russia]. 1915.
> *Solov'iny sad* [The Nightingale Garden]. 1918.
> *Dvenadtsat; Skify* [The Twelve; The Scythians]. 1918.
> *Yamby: Sovremennye stikhi (1907-1914)* [Iambs: Contemporary Poems]. 1919.
> *Za gran'yu proshlykh dney* [Beyond the Bounds of Days Gone By]. 1920.
> *Sedoye utro* [The Grey Morning]. 1920.
> *Stikhotvoreniya* [Poems]. 1921.
> *Selected Poems,* edited by James B. Woodward. 1968.
> *Selected Poems,* edited by Avril Pyman. 1972.
> *Selected Poems,* translated by Alex Miller. 1981.

Plays

> *Balaganchik* (produced 1906). In *Liricheskiye dramy,* 1908; as *The Puppet Show,* 1963.
> *Liricheskiye dramy.* 1908.

Neznakomka [The Stranger] (produced 1914). In *Liricheskiye dramy*, 1908.
Pesnya sud'by [The Song of Fate]. 1919.
Teatr, edited by P.P. Gromova. 1981.

Other

Skazki: Stikhi dlya detey [Fairy Tales: Poems for Children]. 1913.
Krugly god: Stikhotvoreniya dlya detey [All the Year Round: Poems for Children]. 1913.
Sobraniye stikhotvoreniy i teatr [Collected Poems and Plays]. 4 vols., 1916.
Rossiya i intelligentsiya (1907-1918) [Russia and the Intelligentsia]. 1918; revised edition, 1919.
Katilina. 1919.
Otrocheskiye stikhi; Avtobiografiya [Adolescent Poems; Autobiography]. 1923.
An Anthology of Essays and Memoirs, edited by Lucy Vogel. 1982.

Editor, *Posledhiye dni imperatorskoy vlasti* [The Last Days of the Imperial Regime].- 1921.

*

Bibliography: *Blok* by N. Ashukin, 1923; in *O Bloke* by E. Blyum and V. Goltsev, 1929; by E. Kolpakova and others, in *Vilnyussky gosudarstvenny pedagogichesky Institut 6*, 1959; by Avril Pyman, in *Blokovsky Sbornik 1*, 1964, and in *Selected Poems*, 1972; by P.E. Pomirchiy, in *Blokovsky Sbornik 2*, 1972.

Critical Studies: *Blok, Prophet of Revolution* by C.H. Kisch, 1960; *Blok: Between Image and Idea* by F.D. Reeve, 1962; *Blok: A Study in Rhythm and Metre* by R. Kemball, 1965; *Blok: The Journey to Italy* by Lucy Vogel, 1973; *The Poet and the Revolution: Blok's "The Twelve"* by Sergei Hackel, 1975; *Listening to the Wind: An Introduction to Blok* by James Forsyth, 1977; *The Life of Blok* by Avril Pyman, 2 vols., 1979-80; *The Life of Blok* by Vladimir Orlov-Hamayun, 1981; *Blok as Man and Poet* by Kornei Chukovsky, 1982; *Blok* by Konstantin Mochulsky, 1983.

*   *   *

Alexander Blok is Russia's last great romantic poet and one of her most charismatic personalities. Blok's legend began when he discovered his great theme of the Eternal Feminine—this myth-making Symbolists' ideal, which they saw as the link between the earthly and the divine. His first book of poems, *Stikhi o Prekasnoy Dame*, comprised 800 "romantic hymns to one woman," his future wife Lyubov Mendeleyeva. These, the most immaterial, rarified lyrics in Russian literature, are "poems of praise," "heavenly songs" to idealistic Beauty. Blok believed that the world was created according to absolute Beauty. The ecstatic vision of the Beautiful Lady appeared in Blok's poetry in various incarnations representing the spirit of harmony. It became the Symbolists' Symbol of Symbols and "passions' game." B. Eikhenbaum called Blok a "dictator of feelings," saying that Blok always lived in the "aura of those emotions which he himself aroused." Blok, indeed, "went from cult to cult" (Mandelstam), from the Beautiful Lady and "The Unknown Lady" through "The Snow Mask" and "Carmen" to Russia and the Revolution. He tried to find the truth through intensely lived emotional experiences, and his poetry mirrored his inner life which was essentially dualistic. "I am afraid of my two-faced soul," he confessed, "and carefully bury its demonic and fierce visage in shining armour." He was torn between his apocalyptical predictions and hope for the future harmony, between the music of the spheres and the tumult-rhythms of the coming social upheavals.

Russia, as the theme of his life, also troubled him with her two faces: beautiful and hungry, great and drunken. The dissonance between vision and reality constitutes Blok's tragedy: "The love and hate I have within me—no one could endure." He found irony as the best weapon to deal with discontent and despair. He ridiculed the mysticism in his dramatic trilogy *The Puppet Show*, *Korol' na Ploshchadi* (The King in the Square, in *Liricheskiye dramy*), and *Neznakomka*. Blok shed the mysticism by 1906 but wanted to stay in touch with the infinite, having the capacity to hear the music of the "world's orchestra."

Music was the "essence of the world" for Blok. He built his metaphysical system on the conception of the "spirit of music": "There are...two times, two dimensions," he wrote in his essay "The Downfall of Humanism," "one historical, chronological, the other immeasurable and musical." Unlike Bely, Blok was never a theorist or a thinker. He possessed enormous sensitivity and an impeccable ear, but not a great intellect. Blok's strictly poetic achievement has usually been exaggerated. As Mandelstam said: "In literary matters Blok was an enlightened conservative. He was exceedingly cautious with everything concerning style, metrics or imagery: not one overt break with the past." Harmony between the ear and the eye led him to use symbols of an auditory nature, elemental sounds, the wild howl of violins, the tune of the wind, the harps and strings of a blizzard. He incorporated the lilting rhythms of gypsy songs, their uneven beat and abrupt alternations of fire and melancholy. Many of his best lyrics are a curious transposition of gypsy tunes into the moods, forms, and vocabularies of modern Symbolism. The predominance of the musical over the discursive and the logical was a feature of his poetry as much as of his character.

Blok dreamt all his life about creating a musical poem which would reflect this antimusical world. He realized his dream in the poem "The Twelve," which he wrote in two days. Here chaos and music almost fuse. The imagery of snow-storms formed the background of the birth of the new world. Twelve Red soldiers, spreading terror and death, became twelve apostles with Christ as their invisible leader. In the Revolution Blok saw a new manifestation of the spirit of Music. But it was too loud for Blok's hypersensitive ear: soon after "The Twelve" and "The Scythians" (1918) he ceased to "hear." "I have not heard any new sounds for a long time; they have all vanished for me and probably for all of us...it would be blasphemous and deceitful to try deliberately to call them back into our soundless space," he told Chukovsky, and he ceased writing poetry. Not all Blok's friends shared his belief that the time had come for the intellectuals to sacrifice themselves under the wheels of the "troika." Hostility toward Blok was inevitable. He was told to his face that "he had outlived his time and was inwardly dead"—a fact with which, Pasternak told us, he calmly agreed. Russia's last poet-nobleman with Decembrist blood in his veins was out of time. It was unfortunate for Blok that greater poets followed him so quickly. For them, however, Blok, as a man and a poet, became a Symbol, a "monument of the beginning of the century" and the "tragic tenor of the epoch" (Akhmatova).

—Valentina Polukhina

BOCCACCIO, Giovanni. Born in Florence or Certaldo, in 1313. Apprentice in his father's banking business, Naples, 1327-31; studied canon law, 1331-36. Worked in banking in Naples until 1341; returned to Florence in 1341 and was there during the Black Death, 1348; met Petrarch in 1350 and thereafter devoted himself to humanistic scholarship; took minor clerical orders, 1357; active in Florentine public life, and went on several diplomatic missions in the 1350's and 1360's; lectured on Dante in Florence, 1373-74. *Died 21 December 1375.*

PUBLICATIONS

Collections

> *Opere latine minori,* edited by A.F. Massèra. 1928.
> *Opere,* edited by Vittore Branca and others. 12 vols., 1964.
> *Opere minori in volgare,* edited by Mario Marti. 4 vols., 1969-72.

Fiction

> *Il filocolo,* edited by A.E. Quaglio. 1967; translated in part as *Thirteen Questions of Love,* edited by Harry Carter, 1974.
> *Elegia de Madonna Fiammetta,* edited by Mario Marti, in *Opere minori 3.* 1971; as *Amorous Fiammetta,* 1587.
> *Decameron,* edited by Vittore Branca. 1976; translated as *The Decameron,* 1620; also translated by Harry McWilliam, 1972, Mark Musa and Peter E. Bondanella, 1977, and John Payne (revised edition by Charles S. Singleton), 1984.

Play

> *L'ameto,* èdited by A.E. Quaglio, in *Opere 2.* 1964.

Verse

> *Il ninfale fiesolano,* edited by Armando Balduino. 1974; as *The Nymph of Fiesole,* translated by Daniel J. Donno, 1960; also translated as *Nymphs of Fiesole,* translated by Joseph Tusiani, 1971.
> *L'amorosa visione,* edited by Vittore Branca, in *Opere.* 1964.
> *La caccia di Diana,* edited by Vittore Branca. 1958.
> *Rime,* edited by Vittore Branca. 1958.
> *Il Teseida,* edited by Alberto Limentani, in *Opere 2.* 1964; as *The Book of Theseus,* translated by Bernadette Marie McCoy, 1974.
> *Il filostrato,* edited by Vittore Branca, in *Opere 2.* 1964; as *The Filostrato,* 1929; as *Il Filostrato: The Story of the Love of Troilo,* 1934.

Other

> *Le lettere,* edited by Francesco Corazzini. 1877.
> *Il commento alla Divina Commedia e altri scritti intorno a Dante,* edited by Domenico Guerri. 4 vols., 1918-26.
> *De genealogia deorum gentilium* [The Genealogies of the Gentile Gods], edited by Vincenzo Romano. 1951; section translated as *Boccaccio on Poetry,* 1930.

De claris mulieribus, as *Concerning Famous Women.* 1930.
Trattatello in laude di Dante, edited by Pier Giorgio Ricci. 1974; translated in *The Early Lives of Dante*, 1904.
De casibus virorum illustrium, abridged as *The Fates of Illustrious Men.* 1965.
Il corbaccio, edited by Tauno Nurmeela. 1968; as *The Corbaccio*, edited by Anthony K. Cassell, 1975.

*

Bibliography: *Boccacciana: Bibliografia delle edizione i degla scritti critici 1939-1974* by Enzo Esposito, 1976.

Critical Studies: *Boccaccio: A Biographical Study* by E. Hutton, 1910; *Boccaccio in England from Chaucer to Tennyson* by Herbert G. Wright, 1957; *Nature and Love in the Middle Ages: An Essay on the Cultural Context of the Decameron* by Aldo D. Scaglione, 1963; *An Anatomy of Boccaccio's Style* by Marga Cottini-Jones, 1968; *Nature and Reason in the Decameron* by Robert Hastings, 1975; *The Writer as Liar: Narrative Technique in the "Decameron"* by Guido Almansi, 1975; *Critical Perspectives on the Decameron* edited by Robert S. Dombrowski, 1976; *Boccaccio: The Man and His Works* by Vittore Branca, 1976; *Boccaccio's Two Venuses* by Robert Hollander, 1977; *Studies on Petrarch and Boccaccio* by Ernest H. Wilkins, 1978; *Boccaccio* by Thomas G. Bergin, 1981; *Five Frames for the Decameron: Communication and Social Systems in the Cornice* by Joy Hambuechen Potter, 1982.

*   *   *

Boccaccio's literary production is characterized by an unusual versatility; his work, both in prose and verse, contains a variety of genres, many of which were pioneer ventures, destined to exercise a powerful influence on succeeding generations. His essay in the field of narrative in verse was *La caccia di Diana*, an allegory of love, designed, it would seem, to memorialize the glamorous ladies of the Neapolitan court. It is a very "Dantean" composition, written in *terza rima* and with numerous echoes of the *Divine Comedy*; it is a trifle but a well-constructed trifle. Of the same period is the *Filocolo*, a prose romance of Byzantine stamp composed, the author tells us, in honor of his "Fiammetta," the Neapolitan siren who charmed and betrayed him. Called by some critics "the first prose romance in European literature," the *Filocolo* is long and digressive; although the central characters are of royal blood, the peripatetic plot anticipates the picaresque. For all its rhetoric and prolixity the narrative is well told and the characters in the main believable. This cumbrous initiative was followed by the *Filostrato*, telling in *ottava rima* of the ill-starred love of the Trojan prince Troiolo for the faithless Criseida. It is a skillfully planned composition, set forth with economy, and successful in its depiction of characters; the romantic prince is artfully paired with the worldly Pandaro, his friend and counselor. *Il Teseida*, which followed a few years later, is, for all its Greek title and background, essentially a medieval work; the "epic" is actually a love story. All of these early productions reflect the feudal tastes of the Neapolitan court.

A change of inspiration becomes evident in the works written after the return to Tuscany in 1341. The *Ameto* is a moralizing allegory, combining prose and verse (as had Dante's *Vita nuova*) yet the use of "frame" to serve as a background for moralizing tales (paradoxically erotic in tone) points to the *Decameron*. In the *Amorosa visione* (a somewhat confused allegory) the presence of Dante is even more patent. *Elegia di Madonna*, which follows, is by contrast, original and strikingly "modern"—one might say timeless. The abandoned Fiammetta, who tells in her own words (in prose) of her misplaced obsession for a false lover, though somewhat prolix, wins our sympathy. In one sense the *Fiammetta* is a reversion, for the background is Naples. Truly Tuscan, on the other hand, is the charming idyll *Il ninfale fiesolano*. With winning simplicity in *ottava rima* of unpretentious construction, the story is told of a simple shepherd and his beloved "nymph of Diana" who is in effect a simple *contadina*.

The Decameron, Boccaccio's masterpiece, marks a new departure in the author's trajectory. We deal no more with Trojan princes or even woodland nymphs—we have left Naples for good, and allegory has no part in the author's intention (though it must be conceded that in the flight of the narrators of the "frame" from the plague-stricken city one can argue some implications regarding the relation of art to its subject matter). The essential feature of *The Decameron* is realism; the world of the tales is the world of here and now. The demographic range is wide: it includes not only lords and princes but merchants, bankers, doctors, scholars, peasants, priests, monks—and a surprising number of women. A token of the feministic thrust of the work may be seen in the fact that seven of the ten "frame characters" or narrators are women. All of the actors in this extensive comedy are deftly presented, with sympathetic tolerance for their motivation and participant relish in their adventures, vicissitudes, and resourceful stratagems. If the work is without didactic intent—"Boccaccio doesn't want to teach us anything," the Italian critic Umberto Bosco has justly observed—yet the nature of its substance carries its own implications. *The Decameron* is democratic, feminist, and *au fond* optimistic. No doubt heaven is our destination but life can be joyous too, given a certain amount of wit and adaptability. Only in the last day does a kind of medievalism creep in, as the author sets before us a series of *exempla*, signifying sundry abstract virtues. Yet the narratives told even on that day are set forth with skill and verve and without undue lingering on their moralizing purpose; Griselda, for example, may seem an absurdly morbid creature (as in fact she does to some of the frame characters), but her story is told with a *brio* that compels the reader's attention. As entertaining today as when it was written, Boccaccio's great work both reflects and inspires a new appreciation of the human pilgrimage.

Save for the *Corbaccio*, a violent misogynistic satire, *The Decameron* is the last work of a creative nature to issue from Boccaccio's pen—and the last work in the vernacular as well. Moved by the example of Petrarch, he put aside fiction and turned to exercises in erudition, notably the massive compilation of the *Genealogies of the Gods*, an encyclopedia that would serve scholars for generations to come, and the catalogue of rivers, lakes, and mountains, both composed in Latin, as were his *Eclogues (Buccolicum Carmen)*, patently in imitation of his revered master. After *The Decameron*, too, a certain inner spiritual change is apparent in the hitherto worldly Boccaccio; he took holy orders, and although the instinct for story-telling was still strong—witness the *Life of Dante* and *De claris mulieribus (Concerning Famous Women)*—it was clearly affected by his new outlook on life. A letter suggests even a repudiation of *The Decameron*. His last work, and one of importance to Dantists, was his exposition of the *Divine Comedy*, a series of lectures given in Florence, never properly edited by the lecturer.

Many of Boccaccio's creative works are seminal: the *Teseida* foreshadows the Renaissance epic, the *Filostrato* has left a trail of progeny ranging from Chaucer through Shakespeare to Christopher Morley. The *Ninfale fiesolano* has 15th-century echoes. And *The Decameron* has had many imitators. Boccaccio's contributions to the literature of the Western world is of impressive and all but unique dimensions.

—Thomas G. Bergin

BOETHIUS (Anicius Manlius Severinus Boethius).   Born, probably in Rome, c. 480 A.D. Married to Rusticiana; two sons. Consul under the Ostrogothic King Theodoric, 510; head of government and court services (*magister officiorum*), 520; accused of treason, practicing magic, and sacrilege: sentence ratified by the Senate, and he was imprisoned near Pavia, 522.

Also a Hellenist: translator (with commentary) of works of Aristotle, Plato, and Porphyry. *Died (executed) in 524 A.D.*

PUBLICATIONS

Collections

[*Works*], edited by J.P. Migne, in *Patrologia Latina 63-64.* 2 vols., 1847.
The Theological Tractates and The Consolation of Philosophy, edited by S.J. Tester (includes translation; Loeb edition).   1973; *Opera theologica* also edited by R. Peiper, 1871.

Works

De consolatione philosophiae (prose and verse), edited by Ludwig Bieler.   1957; as *The Consolation of Philosophy*, translated by Richard Green, 1963; also translated by V.E. Watts, 1969.
De divisione, edited by Paulus Maria de Loe.   1913.
De syllogismus hypotheticus, edited by Luca Obertello.   1969.
De topicis differentiis, translated by Eleonore Stump.   1978.
De arithmetica, De musica, edited by G. Friedlein.   1867.
In Ciceronis topica commentarium, edited by J.G. Baiter.   1833.
[*Commentaries on Porphyry*], edited by G. Schepss and S. Brandt.   1906; translated by E.W. Warren,   1975.
[*Commentaries on De interpretatione*], edited by C. Meiser.   1877-80.

Translator, *Categoriae, De interpretatione, Analytica priora, Topica, Elenchi sophistici*, by Aristotle, edited by Lorenzo Minio-Paluello, in *Aristoteles Latinus.*   1961—.

*

Critical Studies: *The Tradition of Boethius: A Study of His Importance in Mediaeval Culture* by Howard R. Patch, 1935; *Boethius: Some Aspects of His Times and Works* by Helen M. Barrett, 1940; *Poetic Diction in the Old English Meters of Boethius* by Allan A. Metcalf, 1973; *Boethian Fictions: Narratives in the Medieval French* by Richard A. Dwyer, 1976; *Boethius and the Liberal Arts* edited by Michael Masi, 1981; *Boethius: His Life, Thought, and Influence* edited by Margaret Gibson, 1981; *Boethius: The Consolations of Music, Logic, Theology, and Philosophy* by Henry Chadwick, 1981.

*   *   *

As a member of the Roman senatorial class, which still kept its identity in the barbarian Italy of c.500 A.D., Boethius expected to hold political and ceremonial office: he was consul and (fatally) *magister officiorum*, the dispenser of patronage at Theodoric's court in Ravenna. But most of his time was his own. He lived in his townhouse and his country estates immersed in his books—and entertaining his friends: see Sidonius Apollinaris's letters and poems on the life of "senatorial ease" in Roman Gaul in the later 5th century. It was for these friends and proteges of his own family and class that Boethius wrote his literary and scholarly works. He was no schoolmaster, no compiler of encyclopaedias, dependent on an unknown popular audience.

Boethius's interest in language and the structure of argument is seen in his many studies of logic and rhetoric. He translated some key texts from the Greek, and much of his analysis derived from Greek writers and teachers in the universities of Athens and Alexandria. These translations gave readers who knew only Latin access to mainstream philosophical discussion. In the same way Boethius's highly technical writing on mathematics and musical theory made Greek thought available to a Roman audience. That is the context for his "papers"—they are too brief to be called books—on Christian doctrine: Boethius's careful definitions have a solid basis in Greek philosophy.

His masterpiece, *The Consolation of Philosophy*, is his most readable and literary work. He had been informed on by his enemies and faced almost certain death. Could he face it? He argues through issue after conflicting issue, still the practised logician: but now he himself is a term in the problem. Why me? Why do the wicked prosper? Doesn't God care? Can God care? His partner in the argument is the Lady Philosophy, who is the traditional literary, mathematical, and philosophical learning to which he has devoted most of his life. Later readers thought of her as the Wisdom of the Old Testament: "Wisdom hath builded her house, she hath hewn out her seven pillars." But Boethius is not so easily brought into line. His argument with himself in *The Consolation of Philosophy* reaches the point of an omniscient God, who is fully in control of the universe. Because it is an argument—rather than, e.g., a vision or a confession—it *can* go no further. *The Consolation of Philosophy* stops short of the Christianity in which Boethius, judging by his theological papers (above), was an informed believer.

Boethius was killed in 524. His books seem to have lain undisturbed until approximately the time of Charlemagne (c.800), when Alcuin and succeeding medieval scholars with little or no Greek read and transcribed and discussed this treasury of material on argument and on mathematics. Above all they welcomed the *Consolation*, in which the great questions of justice, chance, and freedom were analysed by the man who, in a changed intellectual climate, was now regarded as "Boethius, the Christian philosopher."

—Margaret Gibson

BOILEAU (-Despréaux), Nicolas. Born in Paris, 1 November 1636. Educated at Collège d'Harcourt, Paris, 1643-48; Collège de Beauvais, Paris, 1648-52; studied law, 1652-56: admitted to the bar 1656. Writer from 1657: slowly achieved a reputation; friend of Molière, Racine, La Fontaine; favored by the court from 1674: Historiographer to the king (with Racine), 1677. Member, French Academy, 1684. *Died 13 March 1711.*

PUBLICATIONS

Collections

Oeuvres complètes, edited by Charles-H. Boudhors. 7 vols., 1932-43.
Oeuvres complètes, edited by Françoise Escal. 1966.
Works, translated by Nicholas Rowe. 3 vols., 1711-13.

Verse

Satires (12). 1666-1711; edited by A. Adam, 1941; translated as *Satires*, 1904.
Épîtres (12). 1670-98; edited by A. Cahen, 1937.

Oeuvres diverses.   1674; augmented edition, 1683.
L'Art poétique, in *Oeuvres diverses.*   1674; edited by V. Delaporte, 3 vols., 1888.
Le Lutrin.   1674-83; translated by Nicholas Rowe, 1708.

Other

L'Arrêt Burlesque.   1671.
On Longinus, edited by John Ozell.   1972.

Translator, *Traité du sublime*, by Longinus, in *Oeuvres diverses.*   1674.

*

Critical Studies: *Boileau and the Classical Critics in England* by Alexander F.B. Clark, 1925; *Racine and the "Art Poétique" of Boileau* by Sister M. Haley, 1938; *Boileau and Longinus* by Jules Brody, 1958; *Pour le commentaire linguistique de l'Art poétique* by John Orr, 1963; *Boileau* by Julian Eugene White, Jr., 1969; *Boileau and the Nature of Neo-Classicism* by Gordon Pocock, 1980.

*   *   *

Although Boileau's fame has rested as much on his reputation as high-priest of French Classicism as on his poetry, it is doubtful whether he added much to the critical ideas of his day, or significantly influenced his contemporaries.

His literary personality is complex. His iconoclasm comes out strongly in his early satires, and remains in his later work, even when he was in favour at Court. His early series of *Satires* (I-IX) are concerned with literary and social themes. In his social satires (I, III, IV, V, VI, and VIII), he often paints with representational detail, but his comic exuberance lifts them well beyond realism. In the literary satires, he is less a critic of specific authors than a creator of startling images of poetry at war with dunces. The best of his satires (especially VII and IX) are dramatic in method. They bring together with kaleidoscopic brilliance wit, word-play, eloquence, and straight-speaking, leading the reader to heightened awareness of his responses which transcends the often banal content. The first series of *Epistles* (I-IX) are frequently plainer and more didactic, but even those addressed to Louis XIV (the *Discourse to the King*, *Epistles I*, *IV*, and *VIII*) mix humour with seriousness. *Epistles VII* and *IX*, on literary themes, express poignantly Boileau's sense of the high role of poetry, and its vulnerability in the face of ignorance and barbarism.

His verse *Art Poétique* (*Art of Poetry*) is on the surface an assertion of the Classical demand for rationalism and craftsmanship, with summaries of the neo-Aristotelian rules for different kinds of poem. More fundamentally, however, it demonstrates again Boileau's use of verbal dexterity (it is full of puns) to dramatise the effect of good and bad poetry on the reader. The mock-heroic *Le Lutrin* (*The Lectern*) is in lighter vein, but dazzles by its mixture of comedy with genuine grandeur.

His later works show a slackening of verve. The best are the long *Satire X* (*On Women*) in which some of the portraits recapture his earlier mordant vigour, and *Epistles X* and *XI*, in which he skilfully represents himself as a man of honest but endearing simplicity. The last works, much concerned with theological disputes, are clumsily written and hectoring in tone.

Boileau's lyrics have little merit. His ambitious *Ode on the Capture of Namur* fails to accommodate in lyric form his mixture of grandiloquence and satire. Of his prose, the early *Arrêt Burlesque* (*Mock Edict*) is the liveliest, with its exuberant satire on official hostility to new ideas. His translation of Longinus, with his *Remarks* and *Reflections* on it and his 1701 preface to his works, gave him the opportunity to assert again the moral and aesthetic dignity of poetry, against what he saw as the triviality and decadence of his contemporaries. Of his work as Historiographer to Louis XIV (a post he shared with Racine) only a few occasional pieces remain. His surviving letters, mainly from his old age, display his passionate and quirky temperament.

—Gordon Pocock

BÖLL, Heinrich (Theodor). Born in Cologne, Germany 21 December 1917. Educated at gymnasium, Cologne; University of Cologne. Served in the German army, 1939-45; prisoner of war, 1945. Married Annemarie Cech in 1942; three sons. Joiner in his father's shop, then apprentice in the book trade before the war; full-time writer since 1947: Co-Editor, *Labyrinth*, 1960-61, and *L*, since 1976. Recipient: Bundesverband der Deutschen Industrie grant; Rene Schickele prize; Gruppe 47 prize, 1951; Tribune de Paris prize, 1953; Prix du Meilleur Roman Étranger, 1955; Heydt prize, 1958; Bavarian Academy of Fine Arts award, 1958; Nordrhein-Westfalen prize, 1959; Veillon prize, 1960; Siehe-Heydt prize; Cologne prize, 1961; Elba prize, 1965; Georg Büchner prize, 1967; Nobel Prize for Literature, 1972. Honorary degrees: Aston University, Birmingham, 1973; Brunel University, Uxbridge, Middlesex, 1973; Trinity College, Dublin, 1973. Lives in Cologne, Germany.

PUBLICATIONS

Fiction

> *Der Zug war pünktlich.* 1949; as *The Train Was on Time*, 1956.
> *Wanderer, kommst du nach Spa....* 1950; as *Traveller, If You Come to Spa*, 1956.
> *Die schwarzen Schafe.* 1951.
> *Wo warst du, Adam?* 1951; as *Adam, Where Art Thou?*, 1955; as *And Where Were You Adam?*, 1974.
> *Nicht nur zur Weihnachtszeit.* 1952.
> *Und sagte kein einziges Wort.* 1953; as *Acquainted with the Night*, 1954; as *And Never Said a Word*, 1978.
> *Haus ohne Hüter.* 1954; as *Tomorrow and Yesterday*, 1957; as *The Unguarded House*, 1957.
> *Das Brot der frühen Jahre.* 1955; as *The Bread of Our Early Years*, 1957; as *The Bread of Those Early Years*, 1976.
> *So ward Abend und Morgen.* 1955.
> *Unberechenbare Gäste: Heitere Erzählungen.* 1956.
> *Im Tal der donnernden Hufe.* 1957.
> *Doktor Murkes gesammeltes Schweigen und andere Satiren.* 1958.
> *Der Mann mit den Messern.* 1958.
> *Die Waage der Baleks und andere Erzählungen.* 1958.
> *Der Bahnhof von Zimpren.* 1959.
> *Billard um Halbzehn.* 1959; as *Billiards at Half Past Nine*, 1961.
> *Als der Krieg ausbrach, Als der Krieg zu Ende war.* 1962.
> *Ansichten eines Clowns.* 1963; as *The Clown*, 1965.
> *Entfernung von der Truppe.* 1964.

Absent Without Leave (2 novellas). 1965.
Ende einer Dienstfahrt. 1966; as *End of a Mission*, 1967.
Eighteen Stories. 1966.
Absent Without Leave and Other Stories. 1967.
Geschichten aus zwölf Jahren. 1969.
Children Are Civilians Too. 1970.
Gruppenbild mit Dame. 1971; as *Group Portrait with Lady*, 1973.
Der Mann mit den Messern: Erzählungen (selection). 1972.
Die verlorene Ehre der Katharina Blum. 1974; as *The Lost Honor of Katharina Blum*, 1975.
Berichte zur Gesinnungslage der Nation. 1975.
Fürsorgliche Belagerung. 1979; as *The Safety Net*, 1982.
Du fährst zu oft nach Heidelberg. 1979.
Gesammelte Erzählungen. 2 vols., 1981.

Plays

Die Brücke von Berczaba (broadcast, 1952). In *Zauberei auf dem Sender und andere Hörspiele*, 1962.
Der Heilige und der Räuber (broadcast, 1953). In *Hörspielbuch des Nordwestdeutschen und Süddeutschen Rundfunks 4*, 1953; as *Mönch und Räuber*, in *Erzählungen, Hörspiele, Aufsätze*, 1961.
Zum Tee bei Dr. Borsig (broadcast, 1955). In *Erzählungen, Hörspiele, Aufsätze*, 1961.
Eine Stunde Aufenthalt (broadcast, 1957). In *Erzählungen, Hörspiele, Aufsätze*, 1961.
Die Spurlosen (broadcast, 1957). 1957.
Bilanz (broadcast, 1957). 1961.
Klopfzeichen (broadcast, 1960). With *Bilanz*, 1961.
Ein Schluck Erde (produced, 1961). 1962.
Zum Tee bei Dr. Borsig (includes *Mönch und Räuber, Eine Stunde Aufenthalt, Bilanz, Die Spurlosen, Klopfzeichen, Sprechanlage, Konzert für vier Stimmen*). 1964.
Hausfriedensbruch (broadcast, 1969). 1969.
Aussatz (produced, 1970). With *Hausfriedensbruch*, 1969.

Radio Plays: *Die Brücke von Berczaba*, 1952; *Ein Tag wie sonst*, 1953; *Der Heilige und der Räuber*, 1953; *Zum Tee bei Dr. Borsig*, 1955; *Anita und das Existenzminimum*, 1955, revised version, as *Ich habe nichts gegen Tiere*, 1958; *Die Spurlosen*, 1957; *Bilanz*, 1957; *Eine Stunde Aufenthalt*, 1957; *Die Stunde der Wahrheit*, 1958; *Klopfzeichen*, 1960; *Hausfriedensbruch*, 1969.

Verse

Gedichte. 1972.

Other

Irisches Tagebuch. 1957; as *Irish Journal*, 1967.
Im Ruhrgebiet, photographs by Karl Hargesheimer. 1958.
Unter Krahnenbäumen, photographs by Karl Hargesheimer. 1958.
Menschen am Rhein, photographs by Karl Hargesheimer. 1960.
Brief an einen jungen Katholiken. 1961.
Erzählungen, Hörspiele, Aufsätze. 1961.
Assisi. 1962.

Hierzulande. 1963.
Frankfurter Vorlesungen. 1966.
Aufsätze, Kritiken, Reden 1952-1967. 1967.
Leben im Zustand des Frevels. 1969.
Neue politische und literarische Schriften. 1973.
Politische Meditationen zu Glück und Vergeblichkeit, with Dorothee Sölle. 1973.
Drei Tage in März, with Christian Linder. 1975.
Der Lorbeer ist immer noch bitter: Literarische Schriften. 1976.
Briefe zur Verteidigung der Republik, with Freimut Duve and Klaus Staeck. 1977.
Einmischung erwünscht: Schriften zur Zeit. 1977.
Werke, edited by Bernd Balzer. 10 vols., 1977-78.
Missing Persons and Other Essays. 1977.
Querschnitte: Aus Interviews, Aufsätzen, und Reden, edited by Viktor Böll and Renate Matthaei. 1977.
Gefahren von falschen Brüdern: Politische Schriften. 1980.
Warum haben wir aufeinander geschossen?, with Lew Kopelew. 1981.
Was soll aus dem Jungen bloss werden?. 1981.
Vermintes Gelände. 1982.

Editor, with Erich Kock, *Unfertig ist der Mensch.* 1967.

Translator, with Annemarie Böll:

Kein Name bei den Leuten [No Name in the Street], by Kay Cicellis. 1953.
Ein unordentlicher Mensch, by Adriaan Morriën. 1955.
Tod einer Stadt [Death of a Town], by Kay Cicellis. 1956.
Weihnachtsabend in San Cristobal [The Saintmaker's Christmas Eve], by Paul Horgan. 1956.
Zur Ruhe kam der Baum des Menschen nie [The Tree of Man], by Patrick White. 1957.
Der Teufel in der Wüste [The Devil in the Desert], by Paul Horgan. 1958.
Die Geisel [The Hostage], by Brendan Behan. 1958.
Der Mann von Morgen früh [The Quare Fellow], by Brendan Behan. 1958.
Ein Wahrer Held [The Playboy of the Western World], by J.M. Synge. 1960.
Die Boote fahren nicht mehr aus [The Islandman], by Tomás O'Crohan. 1960.
Eine Rose zur Weihnachtszeit [One Red Rose for Christmas], by Paul Horgan. 1960.
Der Gehilfe [The Assistant], by Bernard Malamud. 1960.
Kurz vor dem Krieg gegen die Eskimos, by J.D. Salinger. 1961.
Das Zauberfass [The Magic Barrel], by Bernard Malamud. 1962.
Der Fänger im Roggen [The Catcher in the Rye], by J.D. Salinger. 1962.
Ein Gutshaus in Irland [The Big House], by Brendan Behan, in *Stücke.* 1962.
Franny und Zooey, by J.D. Salinger. 1963.
Die Insel der Pferde [The Island of Horses], by Eilís Dillon. 1964.
Hebt den Dachbalken hoch, Zimmerleute; Seymour wird vorgestellt [Raise High the Roof Beam, Carpenters; Seymour: An Introduction], by J.D. Salinger. 1965.
Caesar und Cleopatra, by G.B. Shaw. 1965.
Der Spanner [The Scarperer], by Brendan Behan. 1966.
Die Insel des grossen John [The Coriander], by Eilís Dillon. 1966.
Das harte Leben [The Hard Life], by Flann O'Brien. 1966.
Neun Erzählungen [Nine Stories], by J.D. Salinger. 1966.
Die schwarzen Füchse [A Family of Foxes], by Eilís Dillon. 1967.
Die Irrfahrt der Santa Maria [The Cruise of the Santa Maria], by Eilís Dillon. 1968.
Die Springflut [The Sea Wall], by Eilís Dillon. 1969.
Seehunde SOS [The Seals], by Eilís Dillon. 1970.
Erwachen in Mississippi [Coming of Age in Mississippi], by Anne Moody. 1970.

Candida, Der Kaiser von Amerika, Mensch und Übermensch [Candida, The King of America, Man and Superman], by G.B. Shaw. 1970.
Handbuch des Revolutionärs, by G.B. Shaw. 1972.

*

Bibliography: *Der Schriftsteller Böll: Ein biographisch-bibliographischer Abriss* edited by Werner Lenging, 5th edition, 1977; *Böll in America 1954-1970* by Ray Lewis White, 1979.

Critical Studies: *Böll, Teller of Tales: A Study of His Works and Characters* by Wilhelm Johannes Schwartz, 1969; *A Student's Guide to Böll* by Enid Macpherson, 1972; *Böll: Withdrawal and Re-Emergence* by J.H. Reid, 1973; *The Major Works of Böll: A Critical Commentary* by Erhard Friedrichsmeyer, 1974; *The Writer and Society: Studies in the Fiction of Günter Grass and Böll* by Charlotte W. Ghurye, 1976; *The Imagery in Böll's Novels* by Thor Prodaniuk, 1979; *Böll* by Robert C. Conard, 1981.

*   *   *

More consistently than any of his contemporaries Heinrich Böll has documented the development of the Federal Republic since its inception. In doing so he has achieved the remarkable feat of becoming a best-selling author who is under constant attack from the popular press. His works are invariably provocative and the subject of critical disagreement in both academic and non-academic circles. Abroad he has a solid reputation as "the good German" who has unambiguously condemned fascism and the less appealing features of the land of the Economic Miracle. Sales of his books in Eastern Europe are considerable and in the Soviet Union he is one of the best-known Western writers.

Implicit in all his works is the theme of the individual under threat from impersonal forces of all kinds. In *Adam, Where Art Thou?* and *End of a Mission* it is the war machine; in *Acquainted with the Night* and *The Clown* it is the Roman Catholic Church; in *Group Portrait with Lady* it is big business; in *The Lost Honour of Katharina Blum* and *The Safety Net* it is the unholy empire of press and industry working hand in hand with the police. His standpoint is that of a left-wing humanism tinged with a strong element of non-conformist, anti-clerical Catholicism. He has been publicly involved in all the important issues of the day. His particular literary strength lies in satire, the medium most suited to his conception of a literature which must in content be socially committed and in technique "exaggerate" ("Second Wuppertal Speech," 1960), test the limits to artistic freedom by "going too far" ("The freedom of art," 1966); it also relates to his notable sense of humour allied to his eye for the significant, absurd detail. Thus his most memorable writings include those on the broadcaster who collects "silences," the family which celebrates Christmas all the year round, and the man who is employed to defeat the packaging industry by *unpacking* goods for the customer.

Böll is essentially a writer of prose fiction—his few excursions into other genres have been failures. He has experimented in a moderate way with narrative techniques. In the 1950's his favourite form was the short story, that genre peculiarly suited to existentialist statement. His novels of these years are marked by a pre-occupation with the phenomenon of time and make extensive play with fluctuating narrative perspectives. *Billiards at Half-Past Nine* comes closest to the *nouveau roman* of the day. In the more politically charged atmosphere of the 1960's and later, his writing became deliberately more casual and direct, although the ironic play with the convention of a first-person biographer-narrator in *Group Portrait with Lady* betrays a continued concern for questions of form. It is interesting therefore that *The Safety Net* reverts to the peculiar narrative economy of the earlier works with its condensation of narrated time and its use of multiple limited points of view.

—J.H. Reid

BORGES, Jorge Luis. Born in Buenos Aires, Argentina 24 August 1899. Educated at Collège de Genève, Switzerland; Cambridge University. Married. Co-Founding Editor, *Proa*, 1924-26, and *Sur*, 1931; also associated with *Prisma*; Literary adviser, Emecé Editores, Buenos Aires. Municipal librarian, Buenos Aires, 1939-43; Director, National Library, 1955-73; Professor of English Literature, University of Buenos Aires, 1955-70. Norton Professor of Poetry, Harvard University, Cambridge, Massachusetts; Visiting Lecturer, University of Oklahoma, Norman, 1969. President, Argentine Writers Society, 1950-53. Recipient: Buenos Aires Municipal Prize, 1928; Argentine Writers Society prize, 1945; National Prize for Literature, 1957; Prix Formentor, 1961; Ingram Merrill Award, 1966; Bienal Foundation Inter-American Prize, 1970; Alfonso Reyes Prize, 1973. D.Litt.: Oxford University, 1971; Ph.D.: University of Jerusalem, 1971. Member, Argentine National Academy; Uruguayan Academy of Letters. Honorary Fellow, Modern Language Association (USA), 1961. Member, Legion of Honor. Honorary K.B.E. (Knight Commander, Order of the British Empire). Lives in Buenos Aires, Argentina.

PUBLICATIONS

Fiction

Historia universal de la infamia. 1935; as *A Universal History of Infamy*, 1971.
El jardín de senderos que se bifurcan. 1942.
Seis problemas para don Isidro Parido (with Adolfo Bioy Casares, as H. Bustos Domecq). 1942; as *Six Problems for Don Isidro Parodi*, 1981.
Ficciones (1935-1944). 1944; augmented edition, 1956; translated as *Ficciones*, 1962; as *Fictions*, 1965.
Dos fantasías memorables, with Adolfo Bioy Casares. 1946.
Un modelo para la muerte, with Adolfo Bioy Casares. 1946.
El Aleph. 1949; as *The Aleph and Other Stories 1933-1969*, 1970.
La muerte y la brújala. 1951.
Los orilleros; El paraíso de los creyentes, with Adolfo Bioy Casares. 1955.
Crónicas de Bustos Domecq, with Adolfo Bioy Casares. 1967; as *Chronicles of Bustos Domecq*, 1979.
El informe de Brodie. 1970; as *Dr. Brodie's Report*, 1972.
El congreso. 1970; as *The Congress*, 1974.
El libro de arena. 1975; as *The Book of Sand*, 1977.

Verse

Fervor de Buenos Aires. 1923.
Luna de enfrente. 1925.
Cuaderno San Martín. 1929.
Poemas 1922-1943. 1943.
Poemas 1923-1958. 1958.
El hacedor. 1960; as *Dreamtigers*, 1963.
Obra poética 1923-1964. 1964.
Para las seis cuerdas. 1965; revised edition, 1970.
Obra poética 1923-1967. 1967.
Obra poética. 5 vols., 1969-72.
Elegio de la sombra. 1969; as *In Praise of Darkness*, 1974.
El otro, el mismo. 1969.
El oro de los tigres. 1972.
Selected Poems 1923-1967, edited by Norman Thomas di Giovanni. 1972.

Obra poética 1923-1976.   1978.

Other

Inquisiciones.   1925.
El tamaño de mi esperanza.   1926.
El idioma de los Argentinos.   1928; augmented edition, as *El lengaje de Buenos Aires*, with José Edmundo Clements, 1963.
Evaristo Carriego.   1930.
Discusión.   1932.
Las Kennigar.   1933.
Historia de la eternidad.   1936; augmented edition, 1953.
Nueva refutación del tiempo.   1947.
Aspectos de la literatura gauchesca.   1950.
Antiguas literaturas germánicas, with Delia Ingenieros.   1951.
Otras inquisiciones 1937-1952.   1952; as *Other Inquisitions 1937-1952*, 1964.
El "Martín Fierro," with Margarita Guerrero.   1953.
Obras completas.   10 vols., 1953-60.
Leopoldo Lugones, with Betina Edelberg.   1955.
Manual de zoología fantástica, with Margarita Guerrero.   1957; revised edition, as *El libro de los seres imaginarios*, 1967; as *The Imaginary Zoo*, 1969; revised edition, as *The Book of Imaginary Beings*, 1969.
Labyrinthe.   1960; as *Labyrinths: Selected Stories and Other Writings*, edited by Donald A. Yates and James E. Irby, 1962.
Antología personal.   1961; as *A Personal Anthology*, edited by Anthony Kerrigan, 1968.
The Spanish Language in South America: A Literary Problem; El Gaucho Martín Fierro (lectures).   1964.
Introducción a la literatura inglesa, with María Esther Vázquez.   1965; as *An Introduction to English Literature*, 1974.
Literaturas germánicas medievales, with María Esther Vázquez.   1966.
Introducción a la literatura norteamericana, with Esther Zemborain de Torres.   1967; as *An Introduction to American Literature*, 1971.
Nueva antología personal.   1968.
Conversations with Borges, by Richard Burgin.   1968.
Borges on Writing, edited by Norman Thomas di Giovanni, Daniel Halpern, and Frank MacShane.   1973.
Obras completas, edited by Carlos V. Frías.   1974.
Prólogos.   1975.

Editor, with Pedro Henriques Ureña, *Antología clásica de la literatura argentina.*   1937.
Editor, with Silvana Ocampo and Adolfo Bioy Casares, *Antología de la literatura fantástica.*   1940.
Editor, with Silvana Ocampo and Adolfo Bioy Casares, *Antología poética argentina.*   1941.
Editor, with Adolfo Bioy Casares, *Los mejores cuentos policiales.*   2 vols., 1943-51.
Editor, with Silvina Bullrich Palenque, *El Campadrito: Su destino, sus barrios, su música.*   1945.
Editor, with Adolfo Bioy Casares, *Prosa y verso*, by Francisco de Quevedo.   1948.
Editor, and translator with Adolfo Bioy Casares, *Poesía gauchesca.*   2 vols., 1955.
Editor, with Adolfo Bioy Casares, *Cuentos breves y extraordinarios.*   1955; as *Extraordinary Tales*, 1971.
Editor, with Adolfo Bioy Casares, *Libro del cielo y del infierno.*   1960.
Editor, *Paulino Lucero, Aniceto y gallo, Santos Vega*, by Hilario Ascasubi.   1960.
Editor, *Macedonia Fernández* (selection).   1961.

Editor, *Páginas de historia y de autobiografía*, by Edward Gibbon. 1961.
Editor, *Prosa y poesía*, by Almafuerte. 1962.
Editor, *Versos*, by Evaristo Carriego. 1963.

Translator, *La metamorfosis*, by Kafka. 1938.
Translator, *Bartleby*, by Herman Melville. 1944.
Translator, *De los héroes; Hombres representativos*, by Carlyle and Emerson. 1949.

*

Bibliography: *Borges: Bibliografía total 1923-1973* by Horacio Jorge Becco, 1973.

Critical Studies: *Borges, The Labyrinth Maker* by Ana Marie Barrenchea, 1965; *The Narrow Act: Borges Art of Illusion* by Ronald J. Christ, 1969; *Borges* by Martin S. Stabb, 1970; *Prose for Borges* edited by Charles Newman and Mary Kinzie, 1974; *Borges: Ficciones* by Donald Leslie Shaw, 1976; *Paper Tigers: The Ideal Fictions of Borges* by John Sturrock, 1977; *Borges: Sources and Illumination* by Giovanni De Garayalde, 1978; *Borges and His Fiction* by Gene H. Bell-Villada, 1981.

*   *   *

Borges is one of the most influential living writers. His lasting contribution to world literature is to be found in his short-stories. *Fictions* and *The Aleph* collect his classic tales, the ones that secured his place among the masters of world literature and became the cornerstone of the new Spanish-American narrative. It is in these two books, along with the essays of *Other Inquisitions* and the texts (prose, poetry, fragments) of *Dreamtigers* where the synthesis of his literary art can be found. In later books of short-stories, such as *Dr. Brodie's Report*, he turns to simplicity, to straightforward storytelling. *The Book of Sand*, however, his most recent collection of short stories, continue creative lines developed early. The recurrent aesthetic and philosophical concerns of his writing (time, the identity of the self, human destiny, eternity, infinite multiplicity, the double, the mirages of reality) remain the predominant themes, but the rigorous verbal precision of his celebrated stories becomes a freer, simpler, and more direct prose.

Borges's narrative develops within a tradition that has been called fantastic literature. Borges himself highlights the four basic procedures of fantastic fiction: the work of art within the work of art, the contamination of reality by dream, travels through time, and the use of the double. These procedures, along with his favorite devices and symbols (the labyrinth, mirrors, symmetry, plurality and multiplicity, infinite bifurcations, the cyclical nature of reality), contribute to reveal the essential unreality of all human constructions. His stories problemize man's relation with the world and convey a deep and disquieting uneasiness. Borges's fictions are a lengthy interrogation (philosophical, theological, metaphysical) without a possible answer, a terrifying questioning of the problematic and illusory nature of reality, of the existence itself of the universe. The anguish caused by the implacable destiny of humanity haunted by the passing of time and by the dissolution of the image of the self is a basic motif of all his writing.

Borges founds an imaginary universe based on intellectual premises (Idealism is a guiding principle of his fiction), discovers in literature a coherent order in contrast with the chaos of the world, but his fictions always end up by being a terrifying duplication of our chaotic universe. Incapable of comprehending reality, he writes self-reflective, involuted, ironic, or *ludic* stories, that become continuous dialogues with nothingness, where reality and dream are undistinguishable.

Borges's technical control, the evocative and allusive strength of his prose, the verbal rigor, the subtle conceptual irony, the lucid exercise of intelligence, and the power to create a world of his own, distinguishable from any other, are lasting contributions of his prose. He proposes that literature be, above all, literature, and that fiction accept, in the words of Rodríguez Monegal, "deliberately and explicitly its character of fiction, of verbal artifice."

Borges's writing can be seen, in short, as an elaborate way to justify life through art. His inexhaustible imagination justifies, aesthetically, his reason for being. Borges finds in the creative act and in the invention of ideal worlds a provisory salvation. He creates his own reality in order to erase the inscrutable chaos of the world. "Unreality is the condition of art," he writes in "The Secret Miracle," and in "Examination of the Work of Herbert Quain" he "affirmed that of the many joys that literature can provide, the highest is invention." Borges's skepticism with the elusive and inexplicable universe becomes elaborately constructed fictions, games that mirror life but undermine all facile assumptions.

—Hugo J. Verani

BRECHT, Bertolt. Born Eugen Berthold Friedrich Brecht in Augsburg, Germany, 10 February 1898. Educated at elementary school, 1904-08, and gymnasium, Augsburg, 1908-17; University of Munich, 1917-18, 1919. Served as medical orderly during World War I. Married 1) Marianne Zoff in 1922 (divorced 1927), one daughter; 2) the actress Helene Weigel in 1929, one son and one daughter; also had one son by Paula Banholzer. Drama critic, *Der Volkswille*, Augsburg, 1919-21; dramaturg, Munich Kammerspiele, 1920-24; in Berlin, 1924-33: dramaturg, Deutsches Theater; left Germany 1933: in Denmark, 1933-39: Editor, with Lion Feuchtwanger and Willi Bredel, *Das Wort*, 1936-39; in Sweden, 1939-40, Finland, 1940-41, United States, 1941-47, Switzerland, 1947-49; became Austrian citizen, 1950; in East Berlin after 1949: artistic adviser, Berliner Ensemble (directed by his wife), 1949-56. Recipient: Kleist Prize, 1922; Stalin Peace Prize, 1954. *Died 14 August 1956.*

PUBLICATIONS

Collections

Gesammelte Werke (*Stücke, Gedichte, Prosa,* and *Schriften*). 20 vols., 1967.
Plays, Poetry, and Prose, edited by John Willett and Ralph Manheim. 1970— ; the UK and USA versions of this collection have a slightly different arrangement.

Plays

Baal (produced 1923). 1922; edited by Dieter Schmidt, 1968; translated as *Baal*, 1964.
Trommeln in der Nacht (produced 1922). 1923, as *Drums in the Night*, 1966.
Im Dickicht der Städte (as *Im Dickicht*, produced 1923; revised version, produced 1927). 1927; edited by Gisela E. Bahr, 1968; as *In the Swamp*, in *Seven Plays*, 1961; as *Jungle of Cities*, 1966.
Leben Eduards des Zweiten von England, with Lion Feuchtwanger, from a play by Marlowe (produced 1924). 1924; edited by Reinhold Grimm, 1968; translated as *Edward II*, 1966.
Die Kleinbürgerhochzeit (as *Die Hochzeit,* produced 1926). 1966; as *A Respectable Wedding,* in *Plays,* 1970.

Mann ist Mann, Das Elephantenkalb (produced 1926). 1927; as *A Man's a Man, The Elephant Calf*, 1964.

Kalkutta 4 Mai, with Lion Feuchtwanger, from the play *Warren Hastings, Gouverneur von Indien* by Feuchtwanger, in *Drei Angelsächsische Stücke*. 1927; as *Warren Hastings*, in *Two Anglo-Saxon Plays*, 1929.

Die Dreigroschenoper, music by Kurt Weill, from the play *The Beggar's Opera* by John Gay (produced 1928). 1929; as *The Threepenny Opera*, in *From the Modern Repertoire*, edited by Eric Bentley, 1958.

Happy End, with Elisabeth Hauptmann, music by Kurt Weill (produced 1929).

Der Flug der Lindberghs, music by Kurt Weill and Paul Hindemith (produced 1929). 1929.

Aufstieg und Fall der Stadt Mahagonny, music by Kurt Weill (produced 1930). 1929; as *The Rise and Fall of the City of Mahagonny*, 1976.

Das Badener Lehrstück vom Einverständnis, music by Paul Hindemith (produced 1929). 1930; as *The Didactic Play of Baden-Baden on Consent*, in *Tulane Drama Review*, May 1960.

Der Jasager, music by Kurt Weill (produced 1930). 1930; edited by Peter Szondi, 1966.

Die Massnahme, music by Hanns Eisler (produced 1930). 1931; edited by Reiner Steinweg, 1972; as *The Measures Taken*, in *The Jewish Wife and Other Short Plays*, 1965.

Versuche 1-7, 9-15. 14 vols., 1930-57.

Die heilige Johanna der Schlachthöfe (broadcast, 1932; produced 1959). 1932; edited by Gisela E. Bahr, 1971; as *St. Joan of the Stockyards*, in *From the Modern Repertoire*, edited by Eric Bentley, 1956.

Die Mutter, music by Hanns Eisler, from the novel by Gorky (produced 1932). 1933; edited by W. Hecht, 1969; as *The Mother*, 1965.

Die Sieben Todsünden der Kleinbürger, music by Kurt Weill (produced 1933). 1959; as *The Seven Deadly Sins of the Petty Bourgeoisie*, in *Plays*, 1979.

Die Rundköpfe und die Spitzköpfe, music by Hanns Eisler (produced 1936). In *Gesammelte Werke 2*, 1938; as *Roundheads and Peakheads*, 1966.

Furcht und Elend des Dritten Reiches (produced 1937). 1945; as *The Private Life of the Master Race*, 1944.

Die Gewehre der Frau Carrar (produced 1937). 1937; as *The Guns of Carrar*, 1971.

Die Ausnahme und die Regel, music by Paul Dessau (produced 1947). In *Gesammelte Werke 2*, 1938; as *The Exception and the Rule*, in *The Jewish Wife and Other Short Plays*, 1965.

Die Horatier und die Kuriatier, music by Kurt Schwän (produced 1958). In *Gesammelte Werke 2*, 1938, as *The Horatians and the Curatians*, in *Accent*, 1947.

Das Verhör des Lukullus (broadcast, 1940; revised version, music by Paul Dessau, produced 1951). 1951; as *The Trial of Lucullus*, 1943.

Mutter Courage und ihre Kinder (produced 1941). 1949; edited by W. Hecht, 1964; as *Mother Courage and Her Children*, in *Seven Plays*, 1961.

Der gute Mensch von Sezuan (produced 1943). 1953; edited by W. Hecht, 1968; as *The Good Woman of Setzuan*, in *Parables for the Theatre*, 1948.

Galileo (produced 1943; revised version, with Charles Laughton, produced 1947; revised version, as *Leben des Galilei*, produced 1955). 1955; edited by W. Hecht, 1963; as *The Life of Galileo*, 1960.

Der kaukasische Kreidekreis (produced 1947). 1949; as *The Caucasian Chalk Circle*, in *Parables for the Theatre*, 1948.

Herr Puntila und sein Knecht Matti (produced 1948). 1948; as *Mr. Puntila and His Man Matti*, 1977.

Die Antigone des Sophokles (produced 1948). 1955.

Der Hofmeister, from a play by Jacob Lenz (produced 1950). 1953.

Herrnburger Bericht, music by Paul Dessau (produced 1951). 1951.

Coriolan (produced 1951-52). 1959.

Der Prozess der Jeanne d'Arc zu Rouen 1431, from a play by Anna Seghers (produced 1952). In *Gesammelte Werke 6*, 1967.

Don Juan, from the play by Molière (produced 1953). In *Gesammelte Werke 6*, 1967.

Die Gesichte der Simone Machard, with Lion Feuchtwanger (produced 1957). 1956; as *The Visions of Simone Machard*, 1965.

Die Tage des Kommune (produced 1956). 1957; as *The Days of the Commune*, in *Dunster Drama Review*, 1971.

Pauken und Trompeten, with Elisabeth Hauptmann and Benno Besson, music by Rudolf Wagner-Regeny, from the play *The Recruiting Officer* by Farquhar (produced 1956). In *Gesammelte Werke 6*, 1967; as *Trumpets and Drums*, 1963.

Der Aufhaltsame Aufstieg des Arturo Ui (produced 1958). 1957; as *The Resistible Rise of Arturo Ui*, 1976.

Schweik im zweiten Weltkrieg (produced 1957). In *Gesamtausgabe 10*, 1957; edited by Herbert Knust, 1974; as *Schweyk in the Second World War*, in *Plays*, 1976.

Plays, edited by Eric Bentley. 1961— .

Der Brotladen (produced 1967). 1969.

Kuhle Wampe: Protokoll des Films und Materialien, edited by W. Gersch and W. Hecht. 1969.

Screenplays: *Kuhle Wampe*, with others, 1932; *Hangmen Also Die*, with John Wexley and Fritz Lang, 1943.

Fiction

Der Dreigroschenroman. 1934; as *A Penny for the Poor*, 1937; as *The Threepenny Novel*, 1956.

Kalendergeschichten. 1948; as *Tales from the Calendar*, 1961.

Short Stories 1921-1946. 1983.

Verse

Taschenpostille. 1926.

Hauspostille. 1927; as *Manual of Piety*, 1966.

Svendborger Gedichte. 1939.

Selected Poems. 1947.

Die Erziehung der Hirse. 1951.

Hundert Gedichte. 1951.

Gedichte. 1955.

Gedichte und Lieder. 1956.

Selected Poems, translated by H.R. Hays. 1959.

Poems on the Theatre, translated by John Berger and Anna Bostock. 1961.

Poems 1913-1956. 3 vols., 1976.

Gedichte aus dem Nachlass, edited by Herta Ramthun. 2 vols., 1983.

Other

Gesammelte Werke. 2 vols., 1938.

Theaterarbeit. 1952.

Gesammelte Werke. 40 vols., 1953— .

Kriegsfibel. 1955.

Schriften zum Theater. 1957; as *Brecht on Theater*, edited by John Willett, 1964.

Dialoge aus dem Messingkauf. 1964; as *The Messingkauf Dialogues*, 1965.
Arbeitsjournal, edited by Werner Hecht. 2 vols., 1973.
Autobiographische Aufzeichungen 1920-1954, Tagebücher 1920-22, edited by Herta Ramthun. 1975; *Tagebücher* translated as *Diaries*, 1979.
Briefe, edited by Günter Glaeser. 2 vols., 1981.

Translator, with Margarete Steffin, *Die Kindheit*, by Martin Andersen-Nexoe. 1945.

*

Bibliography: in *Sinn und Form*, 1957; *Brecht-Bibliographie* by Gerhard Seidel, 1975— .

Critical Studies: *Brecht: A Choice of Evils*, 1959, revised edition, 1980, and *Brecht*, 1969, both by Martin Esslin; *The Theatre of Brecht*, 1959, revised edition, 1977, and *Brecht in Context*, 1983, both by John Willett; *Brecht: A Collection of Critical Essays* edited by Peter Demetz, 1962; *Brecht: His Life, His Art, and His Times* by Frederic Ewen, 1970; *The Essential Brecht* by John Fuegi, 1972; *Understanding Brecht* by Walter Benjamin, 1973; *Brecht Chronicle*, 1975, and *Brecht: A Biography*, 1979, both by Klaus Völker; *Brecht the Dramatist* by Ronald Gray, 1976; *Towards Utopia: A Study of Brecht* by Keith Dickson, 1978; *The Brecht Commentaries* by Eric Bentley, 1981; *Brecht in Perspective* edited by Graham Bartram and Anthony Waine, 1982.

*   *   *

Bertolt Brecht is the single most innovative and influential force in 20th-century theatre. He wrote some three dozen plays, and these, together with his theories and productions, prose and verse, are all of a unity, generated by and contributing to a coherent and rational philosophy of man and society. This philosophy is essentially political in the widest sense, defining theatre as the depiction in artistic terms of the interaction of individuals in social situations, affecting each other's lives. Brecht was not satisfied with illusory depiction—the mimetic reproduction of the world, he was a realist who aimed at illuminating his audience's perception of society. He sought to articulate the underlying, objective "truth" of a situation, to explain how "what is" comes about. Such a view rested on the conviction that all human actions are explicable in terms of the workings of society, that "the fate of a man is determined by other men."

For most of his life Brecht was a Marxist. He endeavoured to assimilate into drama the investigative methods and findings of the "new" sciences of sociological, political, and economic analysis, and tried to evolve for the theatre a strategy of writing, acting, and production that would render it adequate to its role in the contemporary world. This he called "epic" theatre because of its fundamental rejection of the primacy of illusion and emotion, and its emphasis on the "narrative," reflective stance of the historian.

In his early plays after the First World War Brecht showed a predilection for the rejects of society, victims of the grinding capitalism of the bourgeois world. The "beaten hero," as Walter Benjamin called him, reflected the imbalance of overwhelming economic forces and individual powerlessness. *Baal* showed an asocial hero in an asocial world; *Jungle of the Cities* provided a model of the isolated individual's struggle for survival in a capitalist structure; and the dismantling and reassembly of the hero in *A Man's a Man* thematized the manipulation of human beings by exploitative powers. During the period of his systematic study of Marxism after 1926 Brecht evolved from a rebellious to a disciplined supporter of the working-class struggle. The idiosyncratic "learning plays" like *The Measures Taken* and *The Exception and the Rule* are milestones in Brecht's developing conception of the function of theatre in a social context, offering openly didactic Marxist studies in models of (political) action. Even the apparently innocuous entertainment of *The Threepenny Opera*—audiences have long been captivated by Kurt Weill's catchy tunes—masked a virulent attack on the bandit morality of bourgeois capitalism.

On the accession to power of the Nazi regime in 1933 Brecht immediately went into exile. This caesura paradoxically signalled the start of his most productive period, an astounding output of major plays, theoretical essays, prose writing, and a stream of poetry from 1933 to 1945. It is symptomatic of Brecht's single-mindedness, perseverance, and vision that at this time, driven as he was from one country to another and almost entirely deprived of a German-speaking public—Denmark, Finland, and the U.S.A. were his major staging-posts— he created a handful of plays that were to establish his truly international reputation: *Mother Courage, Galileo, The Good Woman of Setzuan, Herr Puntila and His Servant Matti, The Caucasian Chalk Circle*. To some extent these plays compromise with the traditional"Aristotelian" drama from which Brecht had earlier dissociated himself so vehemently. They rely partly for their effect—and certainly for their popularity—on full-bodied characters caught in the classical dilemmas of dramatic heroes. Yet Brecht does ascribe the emotionally absorbing contradictions of human behaviour to the dialectics of society and its distorting, brutalizing effects on human personality.

The Nazis provided Brecht with a precise and concrete target in place of formless, anonymous capitalism of Marxist theory and rhetoric, for he saw the actual fascist regime in Germany as a manifestation of "the most naked, shameless, oppressive and deceitful form of capitalism." His literary attacks on this virulent menace range from the sober documented realism of *The Private Life of the Master Race*, culled from newspaper items and information leaking from inside Germany, to the gangster satire of *The Resistible Rise of Arturo Ui*, and a range of vitriolic, elegiac, admonishing, hopeful poems.

After the Second World War Brecht eventually made his way back to Europe, settling in East Berlin in 1949. Here he was afforded every facility as the most prized cultural figure in the German Democratic Republic; supported by generous subsidies, he founded the world-renowned Berliner Ensemble with his wife, the actress Helene Weigel. Under Brecht's direction this theatre company established a wide-ranging repertoire, including Brecht's own plays as well as his free adaptations of many classics, such as Shakespeare's *Coriolanus* and Molière's *Don Juan*. Brecht also had the freedom and complete control of theatrical resources to try out, alter, and refine his ideas on epic writing, acting, and production. It was largely in these years until his death in 1956 that Brecht's dramatic style and theories were disseminated throughout the world to establish him as the focal point of 20th-century theatre.

The most important element in Brecht's theories was the celebrated "alienation effect" (*Verfremdungseffekt*), a term he used to describe the technique of "distancing" the audience from the play. The purpose of this was to enable the spectator to retain a detached, dispassionate, critical view of the events being enacted on stage, and not to be totally absorbed emotionally with a consequent loss of rational judgement. Brecht demanded that an alienating depiction should be "one that allows the object to be recognized but at the same time makes it appear unfamiliar"; it requires "a technique of taking the human social incidents to be portrayed and labelling them as something striking, something that calls for explanation, and is not to be taken for granted, not just natural. The object of this 'effect' is to allow the spectator to criticize constructively from a social point of view." Alienation, Brecht found, could be induced in many ways. Hence his free borrowing and parodying of other writers, his liberal use of music and songs (along with all the other "sister arts" of theatre), his exploitation of full lighting, placards, masks, "montage" and cinematic techniques—all to break the "atmosphere" of the stage and prevent the mystification of the spectator. By these means Brecht tried to reflect in the dialogue, structure, and production of individual scenes and whole plays the inconsistencies, ironical illogicalities, and dialectical contradictions of history and of individuals. His purpose was to foster insight into the workings of society and open the way to progress by emancipating men's thinking from the rigidities of tradition.

—Arrigo V. Subiotto

BRETON, André (Robert). Born in Tinchebray, France, 19 February 1896. Educated at Collège Chaptal, Paris, 1906-12; Faculté de Médecine, Paris, 1913-15. Served as medical assistant in army psychiatric centers, 1915-19, and medical director of École de Pilotage, Poitiers, 1939-40. Married 1) Simone Kahn in 1921 (divorced); 2) Jacqueline Lamba in 1934 (divorced), one daughter; 3) Elisa Bindhoff in 1945. Founding Editor, *Littérature*, 1919-24; founded Bureau of Surrealist Research, 1924; Editor, *La Révolution Surréaliste*, 1925-29, *Le Surréalisme au Service de la Révolution*, 1930-33, and *Minotaure*, 1933-39; broadcaster, Voice of America, 1942-45; Editor, *VVV*, 1942-44; Director, Galerie à l'Étoile Scellée, 1952-54; Editor, *Le Surréalisme Même*, 1956-57. Organized exhibitions of surrealist art from 1936. *Died 28 September 1966.*

PUBLICATIONS

Verse

Mont de piété. 1919.
Les Champs magnétiques, with Philippe Soupault. 1920.
Clair de terre. 1923.
Ralentir travaux, with René Char and Paul Éluard. 1930.
L'Union libre. 1931.
Le Révolver à cheveux blancs. 1932.
L'Air de l'eau. 1934.
Le Château étoilé. 1937.
Fata morgana. 1941; translated as *Fata Morgana*, 1969.
Les États-Généraux. 1943.
Pleine marge. 1943.
Young Cherry Trees Secured Against Hares, translated by Edouard Roditi. 1946.
Ode à Charles Fourier. 1947; as *Ode to Charles Fourier*, translated by Kenneth White, 1969.
Martinique charmeuse de serpents. 1948.
Poèmes. 1948.
Au regard des divinités. 1949.
Constellations. 1959.
Le là. 1961.
Selected Poems, translated by Kenneth White. 1969.
Poems, translated by Jean-Pierre Cauvin and Mary Ann Caws. 1983.

Other

Manifeste du surréalisme; Poissonsoluble. 1924; augmented edition, 1929.
Les Pas perdus. 1924.
Légitime défense. 1926.
Introduction au discours sur le peu de réalité. 1927.
Le Surréalisme et la peinture. 1928; augmented edition, 1965; as *Surrealism and Painting*, 1972.
Nadja. 1928; revised edition, 1963; translated as *Nadja*, 1960.
Second manifeste du surréalisme. 1930.
L'Immaculée Conception, with Paul Éluard. 1930.
Misère de la poésie: "L'Affaire Aragon" devant l'opinion publique. 1932.
Les Vases communicants. 1932.
Point du jour. 1934; revised edition, 1970.
Qu'est-ce que le surréalisme? 1934; as *What Is Surrealism?*, 1936.

Position politique du surréalisme. 1935.
Notes sur la poésie, with Paul Éluard. 1936.
L'Amour fou. 1937.
Arcane 17. 1944; augmented edition, 1947.
Situation du surréalisme entre les deux guerres. 1945.
Yves Tanguy (bilingual edition). 1946.
Les Manifestes du surréalisme. 1947; revised edition, 1955, 1962; complete edition, 1972;
    as *Manifestoes of Surrealism*, 1974.
La Lampe dans l'horloge. 1948.
Flagrant délit: Rimbaud devant la conjuration de l'imposture et du truquage. 1949.
Entretiens 1913-1952. 1952; revised edition, 1973.
La Clé des champs. 1953.
Toyen, with Jindrich Heisler and Benjamin Péret. 1953.
Adieu ne plaise. 1954.
Farouche à quatre feuilles, with others. 1954.
L'Art magique, with Gérard Legrand. 1957.
Pierre Moliner: Un Film de Raymond Borde. 1964.
Perspective cavalière, edited by Marguerite Bonnet. 1970.

Editor, *Trajectoire du rêve.* 1938.
Editor, with Paul Éluard, *Dictionnaire abrégé du surréalisme.* 1938.
Editor, *Anthologie de l'humour noir.* 1940 (?); augmented edition, 1950.

*

Bibliography: *Breton: A Bibliography* by Michael Sheringham, 1972.

Critical Studies: *Surrealism and the Literary Imagination: A Study of Breton and Bachelard*, 1966, *The Poetry of Dada and Surrealism*, 1970, and *Breton*, 1971, all by Mary Ann Caws; *Breton, Arbiter of Surrealism* by Clifford Browder, 1967; *Breton, Magus of Surrealism* by Anna E. Balakian, 1971; *Breton and the First Principles of Surrealism* by Franklin Rosemont, 1978.

*   *   *

Founder of the surrealist movement, André Breton was one of the 20th century's great writers; his highly poetic prose, even more than his poems, bears witness to a magnetic power of language as the equivalent of thought.

Believing that we can remake the world by our imagination as it is activated by and through our words, Breton was able to persuade, by those words, a whole generation of thinkers and artists to pay attention to their inner gifts and intuitions as they could be seen not only to respond to the world outside but even to discover in that world "an answer to a question we were not conscious of having." By what he called the law of objective chance, it comes about that the inner and the outer experiences mingle in an ongoing constant communion he compared to the scientific experiment of "Communicating Vessels." Like the mingling of day and night, life and death, up and down, the two contraries are held in balance and provide the dynamism of the activated images which make over, for us, what we live by, "the unacceptable human condition."

Surrealism is, then, by the vision of Breton, turned towards a positive future possibility; surrealist sight insists—with the Zen master Bashô—that, instead of, for example, removing the wings from a dragonfly and calling it a red pepper, we add wings to the pepper to have it become that dragonfly. The attitude is characteristic of the entire movement, whose comportment Breton repeatedly defined as "lyric."

In his own works, Breton stressed the overwhelming power and frightening effect of love (*L'amour fou, Mad Love*) as it participates in the a-rational mystery of complete surprise.

Walking along the garbage peelings on the streets of the marketplace at midnight, wondering whether it is not too late to turn back, the narrator and the poet are one with the observer of that love itself, always to be kept as marvelous, safe from the "null and void moments" which go to make up an ordinary life.

Nadja, Breton's quite unordinary heroine, herself mad, is no more adapted to "real" life than were the alchemists, with whom Breton feels such a bond—they aimed at transmuting our own base metal into our highest or golden selves. The impulse towards the arcane (*Arcane 17*) in no way rules out an openness to the simple everyday things; nor does madness invalidate the love of the marvelous, that child-like expectation of the next moment, this "disponibilité" or openness to chance which infuses surrealist writing and thinking at its best.

Nor was Breton separated from dailiness: against the worst of it, he insisted that art had to stand up, "for the problem is no longer, as it used to be, whether a canvas can hold its own in a wheat field, but whether it can stand up against the daily paper, open or closed, which is a jungle." Art has to stand good against famine, against reality, and against what people have done and thought.

Surrealism, as Breton conceived it, was directed against habit and against the predictable: the famous experiments in automatic writing, made to unleash the dams of imagination as the surrealist manifestoes point out, provocatively, worked towards this end, as did the images in the poems, upsetting to "normal" ways of seeing. But always the style and the vision of Breton went far past the limits of any experiment, and worked together to—as he put it—"prevent the paths of desire from being overgrown."

In a time of despair and uncaring, Breton may be read as resolutely turned towards what he perceived as just, with an ardor we cannot help but perceive as genuine, and with a poetic temperament which is all too rare.

—Mary Ann Caws

BROCH, Hermann. Born in Vienna, 1 November 1886. Trained as an engineer in Vienna and Mülhausen. Administrator for Austrian Red Cross during World War I. Managed family's factory in Teesdorf, 1907-28; then writer: detained briefly by Nazis, 1938; then settled in New York. Involved in refugee work; lecturer, Yale University, New Haven, Connecticut. Recipient: Guggenheim Fellowship, 1941. Member, American Academy, 1942. *Died 31 May 1951.*

PUBLICATIONS

Collections

    Gesammelte Werke, edited by Felix Stössinger and others. 10 vols., 1953-61.
    Kommentierte Werkausgabe, edited by Paul Michael Lützeler. 1974— .

Fiction

    Die Schlafwandler: translated as *The Sleepwalkers*. 1932.
    Pasenow; oder, Die Romantik—1888. 1931.

Esch; oder, Die Anarchie—1903. 1931.
Hugenau; oder, Die Sachlichkeit—1918. 1932.
Die unbekannte Grösse. 1933; as *The Unknown Quantity*, 1935.
Der Tod des Vergil. 1945; as *The Death of Vergil*, 1945.
Die Schuldlosen. 1950; as *The Guiltless*, 1974.
Der Versucher, edited by Felix Stössinger, in *Gesammelte Werke*. 1953.
Bergroman, edited by Frank Kress and Hans Albert Maier. 4 vols., 1969.

Other

Zur Universitätsreform, edited by Götz Wienold. 1969.
Briefwechsel 1930-1951, with Daniel Brody, edited by Bertold Hack and Marietta
    Kleiss. 1971.
Völkerbund-Resolution, edited by Paul Michael Lützeler. 1973.

*

Critical Studies: *Broch* by Theodore Ziolkowski, 1964; *The Sleepwalkers: Elucidations of Broch's Trilogy* by Dorrit C. Cohn, 1966; *The Novels of Broch* by Malcolm R. Simpson, 1977.

*   *   *

At the age of 42, Hermann Broch gave up a distinguished career in industry to devote himself to writing. His first major work, the trilogy *The Sleepwalkers* (1931-32) is set in Germany between 1880 and 1918. It depicts a society in crisis: the old social and political order is breaking up, traditional ethical and religious tenets are being challenged. People, left without moral guidance, seem like sleepwalkers, only dimly aware of their course of action.

The first novel of the trilogy, *The Romantic*, portrays the symptoms of decline among the aristocracy; in the second part, *The Anarchist*, a bookkeeper, failing in his search for justice, turns against society. The last novel, *The Realist*, set during the revolution of 1918, shows how the total disregard for moral values leads to betrayal and murder.

In the course of writing, Broch began to experiment with new modes of narration. His essay "James Joyce and the Present" (1936) is a tribute to Joyce and to the modern novel in general. It also reveals much about Broch's own thoughts about art. He rejects the purely aesthetic point of view as "Kitsch," arguing that as science promotes man's material well-being, art should set standards for his ethical conduct. The main theme of Broch's works is a plea for a re-evaluation of moral values without which he thought the political and social decay of modern society could not be prevented.

Besides being a prolific essayist, Broch wrote plays and poems which, however, do not seem to measure up to his accomplishments as a novelist.

Knowing Broch's earlier dedication to modern narrative techniques, it comes somewhat as a surprise that in his next major work, *Bergroman* (which went through three versions), he returned to the traditional form of the novel. The narrator is an old country doctor who witnesses with horror and some fascination how a charlatan is able to gain, at least for a short time, control over the minds of his villagers.

The Death of Vergil, considered by many critics to be Broch's greatest achievement, depicts in the form of inner monologue Vergil's visions and dreams during the last eighteen hours before his death.

Broch's last work, the short story cycle *The Guiltless*, is essentially a reworking of earlier published material. *The Death of Vergil*, therefore, remains, as Broch had wished it to be, his true farewell as a writer.

—Helena Szépe

BÜCHNER, Georg. Born in Goddelau, 17 October 1813. Educated at Carl Weitershausen's school, 1822-25; Gymnasium, Darmstadt, 1825-31; studied medicine at University of Strasbourg, 1831-33, and University of Giessen, 1833-34; studied biology: received doctorate from University of Zurich, 1836. Lecturer in biology, University of Zurich, 1836-37. *Died 19 February 1837.*

PUBLICATIONS

Collections

  Nachgelassene Schriften, edited by Ludwig Büchner. 1850.
  Sämtliche Werke, edited by K. Franzos. 1879.
  Sämtliche Werke und Briefe, edited by Werner R. Lehmann. 2 vols., 1967-71.
  Plays, translated by Victor Price. 1971; also translated by Michael Hamburger, 1972.

Plays

  Dantons Tod (produced 1902). 1835; as *Danton's Death,* translated by Stephen Spender
    and Goronwy Rees, 1958; also translated by James Maxwell, 1961, and Howard
    Brenton, 1982.
  Leonce und Lena (produced 1895). In *Mosaik, Novellen, und Skizzen,* edited by K.
    Gutzkow, 1842; as *Leonce and Lena,* translated by Eric Bentley, in *From the Modern
    Repertoire 3,* 1956.
  Woyzeck (produced 1913). As *Wozzeck,* in *Sämtliche Werke,* 1879; as *Woyzeck,*
    translated by John MacKendrick, 1979.

*

Bibliography: *Das Büchner Schrifttum bis 1965* by Werner Schlick, 1968; "Kommentierte Bibliographie zu Büchner" by Gerhard P. Knapp, in *Text und Kritik Sonderbank Büchner,* 1979.

Critical Studies: *Büchner* by Arthur Knight, 1951; *Büchner* by H. Lindenberger, 1964; *Satire, Caricature, and Perspectivism in the Works of Büchner* by Henry J. Schmidt, 1970; *Büchner* by Ronald Hauser, 1974; *The Drama of Revolt: A Critical Study of Büchner* by Maurice B. Benn, 1976; *Büchner and the Birth of Modern Drama* by David G. Richards, 1977; *Büchner* by William C. Reeve, 1979; *Büchner* by Julian Hilton, 1982; *Büchner's "Dantons Tod": A Reappraisal* by Dorothy James, 1982.

*   *   *

Georg Büchner died in 1837 at the age of 23 with only one play, *Danton's Death,* in print and that in a bowdlerized version. His *Woyzeck* was not performed until the centenary of his birth. Yet he is now acknowledged to be a crucial link in the chain of innovative German drama which stretches from J.M.R. Lenz through Büchner, Frank Wedekind, the Expressionists, and Bertolt Brecht to the present day. In a wider context he is recognised as a seminal figure in the history of modern drama.

At Giessen University Büchner was a republican activist and co-editor of *Der hessische Landbote,* an inflammatory pamphlet exposing the exploitative taxation which kept the aristocracy in Hesse in luxury. This led to a warrant being issued for his arrest, and he had to flee the country and complete his studies in Strasbourg. It was while he was in hiding on the way that he wrote *Danton's Death,* which broke with the idealist drama of Schiller and tried to present history "as it really happened." He revealed the bloody and bawdy side of revolution, showing the clash between Robespierre's ideological asceticism ("Virtue is the strength... terror the weapon of the Republic") and Danton's liberal hedonism as a mere phase in the inexorable, inscrutable cycle of history. It is a powerful but bleak piece of writing, in which the masses feature mainly as rabble, and it is so poised that left and right wing interpreters have struggled in vain for half a century to make it their own. *Leonce and Lena* is an ironic, satirical variant of the romantic comedy, set among the blasé and inane aristocrats of the lands of Pipi and Popo.

Büchner left his most important work, *Woyzeck*, unfinished, with only vague indications of possible endings. It is a study of social victimisation. The passive, plebeian hero, Woyzeck, is a common soldier who acts as barber to his Captain and as dietetic guinea-pig to a demented physician in order to support his mistress and child. She succumbs haplessly to the crude blandishments of the virile Drum-major, and Woyzeck, hounded by imaginary voices, stabs her to death. The fragment, of which there are several drafts, ends with Woyzeck wading into a pond to recover the murder weapon he has thrown away, but the play would not have ended there. Büchner based it on the controversial case of a murderer who was executed in Leipzig in 1824 after two years of medical examinations to determine whether he was responsible for his actions, and here, as in *Danton's Death*, historically authentic speeches are woven seamlessly into the dialogue. Büchner presents a *crime passionel* in which degradation, debility, sexuality, love, and Christian conscience weave an intricate, compelling pattern which, one is tempted to say, positively benefits from being incomplete. Its 24 brief scenes, which add up to a longish one-act play, are the model for the *montages* of short scenes that are characteristic of Expressionism and Epic Theatre. Like Danton and Robespierre, Woyzeck is a puppet with an inscrutable controller. Inside themselves, Büchner's more positive characters see an abyss. Büchner was a humane pessimist to whom human life seemed locked in the grip of events. He has the unblinking vision of the moderns, and he provides his suffering characters, no matter what their station, with a voice that is natural and authentic, and at the same time universal and poetic.

—Hugh Rorrison

BULGAKOV, Mikhail (Afanas'evich). Born in Kiev, 3 May 1891. Educated at First Kiev High School, 1900-09; Medical Faculty, Kiev University, 1909-16, doctor's degree 1916. Served as doctor in front-line and district hospitals, 1916-18. Married 1) Tatyana Nikolayevna Lappa in 1913; 2) Lyubov' Yevgeni'evna Belozerskaya in 1924; 3) Yelena Serge'evna Shilovskaya in 1932. Doctor in Kiev, 1918-19, but abandoned medicine in 1920; organized a "sub-department of the arts," Vladikavkaz, 1920-21; in Moscow from 1921: journalist, with jobs for various groups and papers; associated with the Moscow Art Theatre from 1925: producer, 1930-36; librettist and consultant, Bolshoi Theatre, 1936-40. *Died 10 March 1940.*

PUBLICATIONS

Collections

P'esy. 1962; revised edition, as *Dramy i komedii*, 1965.

Izbrannaya proza. 1966.
Sobraniye sochineniy, edited by Ellendea Proffer. 1982—.

Fiction

D'yavoliada: Rasskazy. 1925; as *Diaboliad and Other Stories,* edited by Ellendea and Carl Proffer, 1972.
Rasskazy [Stories]. 1926.
Dni Turbinykh (Belaya gvardiya). 2 vols., 1927-29; as *Day of the Turbins,* 1934; as *The White Guard,* 1971.
Rokovyye yaytsa. 1928.
Zapiski yunogo vracha. 1963; augmented edition, as *A Country Doctor's Notebook,* 1975.
Teatralny roman, in *Izbrannaya proza.* 1966; as *Black Snow: A Theatrical Novel,* 1967.
Master i Margarita. 1967; complete version, 1969; as *The Master and Margarita,* 1967; complete version, 1967.
Sobach'e serdtsa. 1969; as *The Heart of a Dog,* 1968.

Plays

Dni Turbinykh, from his novel (produced 1926). With *Poslednie dni (Pushkin),* 1955; as *Days of the Turbins,* in *Early Plays,* edited by Ellendea Proffer, 1972; as *The White Guard,* 1979.
Zoykina kvartira (produced 1926). Edited by Ellendea Proffer, 1971; as *Zoia's Apartment,* in *Early Plays,* edited by Proffer, 1972.
Bagrovy ostrov (produced 1928). In *P'esy,* 1971; as *The Crimson Island,* in *Early Plays,* edited by Ellendea Proffer, 1972.
Myortvye dushi [Dead Souls], from the novel by Gogol (produced 1932). With *Ivan Vasil'evich,* 1964.
Kabala sviatosh (as *Mol'er,* produced 1936). In *P'esy,* 1962; as *A Cabal of Hypocrites,* in *Early Plays,* edited by Ellendea Proffer, 1972; as *Molière,* 1983.
Skupoy, from *L'Avare* by Molière, in *Polnoye sobraniye sochiniy 4,* by Molière. 1939.
Don Kikhot, from the novel by Cervantes (produced 1940). In *P'esy,* 1962.
Posledniye dni (Pushkin) (produced 1943). With *Dni Turbinykh,* 1955; as *The Last Days (Pushkin),* in *Russian Literature Triquarterly 15,* 1976.
Rakhel, edited by Margarita Aliger, music by R.M. Glier (broadcast 1943; produced 1947). Edited by A. Colin Wright, in *Novy zhurnal 108,* September 1972.
Beg (produced 1957). In *P'esy,* 1962; as *Flight,* 1970; as *On the Run,* 1972.
Ivan Vasil'evich (produced 1966). With *Myortvye dushi,* 1964.
Poloumnyi Zhurden, from *Le Bourgeois Gentilhomme* by Molière (produced 1972). In *Dramy i komedii,* 1965.
Adam i Eva, in *P'esy.* 1971; as *Adam and Eve,* in *Russian Literature Triquarterly 1,* Fall 1971.
Minin i Pozharski, edited by A. Colin Wright, in *Russian Literature Triquarterly 15,* 1976.
Voina i mir [War and Peace], from the novel by Tolstoy, edited by A. Colin Wright, in *Canadian-American Slavic Studies 15,* Summer-Fall 1981.

Other

Rokovye yaytsa. 1925.
Zhizn' gospodina de Mol'era. 1962; as *The Life of Monsieur de Molière,* 1970.

*

Bibliography: *An International Bibliography of Works by and about Bulgakov* by Ellendea Proffer, 1976.

Critical Studies: *Bulgakov's "The Master and Margarita": The Text as a Cipher* by Elena N. Mahlow, 1975; *The Master and Margarita: A Comedy of Victory* by Lesley Milne, 1977; *Bulgakov: Life and Interpretations* by A. Colin Wright, 1978; "Bulgakov Issue" of *Canadian-American Slavic Studies 15*, Summer-Fall 1981.

*   *   *

Mikhail Bulgakov is today one of the best-loved writers in the Soviet Union, although "official" attitudes towards him remain tolerant rather than acclamatory. His principal claim to fame rests on his masterpiece *The Master and Margarita*, his only creation widely known outside his country but arguably one of the major works of world literature of the 20th century. Published 25 years after his death, it combines an account of the devil's visiting Moscow in the 1930's with an unorthodox interpretation of Christ before Pilate in ancient Jerusalem: this presented through a "novel" written by the book's hero. As well as being fantasy, satire, comedy, mystery, and romance, it is a work of considerable philosophical depth, drawing equally on biblical and apocryphal sources and on the Faust tradition. Its basic postulates are that "Jesus existed," that "Manuscripts don't burn"—a belief in the enduring nature of art—and that "Everything will turn out right. That's what the world is built on": an extraordinary metaphysical optimism for a man whose life was characterized by recurring disappointment.

Before the publication of *The Master and Margarita*, Bulgakov had been remembered virtually for only one play. (In the oppressive post-war years of Stalinism his name was not mentioned at all.) The performance in 1926 of *Days of the Turbins*, a loose adaptation for the Moscow Art Theatre of his novel *The White Guard* (which had been published only in part), was a major theatrical event in that—despite the necessary changes to make it more politically acceptable—it portrayed with sensitivity the problems of a "white" family in Kiev during the upheavals that followed the Revolution. Withdrawn in 1929, as well as two further plays (*Zoia's Apartment*, a surrealistic tragi-farce, and *The Crimson Island*, a satiric allegory on the Revolution), *Days of the Turbins* was restaged in 1933 with Stalin's approval. Another play, *Flight*, with its psychological study of a white general in the Civil War, was not performed in Bulgakov's lifetime.

Bulgakov began his career as a doctor, and his experiences in a country hospital during the years of the First World War became the basis for a number of humorous stories which may be seen as self-satire (later published as *A Country Doctor's Notebook*). He then abandoned medicine for literature and supported himself in journalism, writing feuilletons which, although of little literary value, provide an interesting picture of Russian life in the 1920's. He published several satirical stories, although the one best known in the West, *Heart of a Dog*, with its bitter criticism of the new communist society, has never appeared in the Soviet Union.

In 1930, after an unsuccessful appeal to Stalin to be allowed to leave the country, Bulgakov was found employment with the Moscow Art Theatre, which led ultimately to his (uncompleted) satire *Theatrical Romance* (or *Black Snow*) including a humorous portrait of Stanislavsky in his later years. The failure of his major play *Molière*, in which he treated the French dramatist as a fallible human being instead of the "great man" Stanislavsky demanded, led to his resignation from the Theatre. His stage version of Gogol's *Dead Souls* enjoyed a modest success, as did too, posthumously, an adaptation of Cervantes's *Don Quixote* and a play about Pushkin, but other plays, film scenarios, and opera libretti written in the 1930's remained unknown until more recently. His last years were devoted to a major effort to complete *The Master and Margarita* before his death.

—A. Colin Wright

CALDERÓN de la Barca, Pedro.   Born in Madrid, 17 January 1600.   Educated at the Jesuit Colegio Imperial; studied canon law at the University of Alcalá, 1614-15, and University of Salamanca, 1615-c.1621, no degree. Entered the household of the Constable of Castille, Don Bernardino Fernández de Velasco, 1621; began writing plays for the court from 1623; entered order of St. James, 1637; served in the campaign against the Catalans, 1640-42; served in the household of the Duke of Alba from 1645; became a priest in 1651, but continued to write plays for religious occasions; Chaplain of the Chapel of Reyes Nuevos, Toledo, from 1653, but lived in Madrid after 1657: Honorary Chaplain to the King, 1663. *Died 25 May 1681.*

PUBLICATIONS

Collections

Comedias, edited by Joseph Calderón.   4 vols., 1636-72; edited by J. de Vera Tassis, 9 vols., 1685-91.
Autos sacramentales.   1677.
Poesias, edited by Adolfo de Castro Cadiz.   1845.
Obras escogidas.   1940.
Obra lírica, edited by M. de Montoliu.   1943.
Obras completas:
   1.   *Dramas*, edited by Luis Astrana Marín.   1959.
   2.   *Comedias*, edited by Angel Valbuena Briones.   1956.
   3.   *Autos sacramentales*, edited by Angel Valbuena Prat.   1959.
Tragedias, edited by Francisco Ruiz Ramón.   3 vols., 1967-69.

Plays (selection)

A María el corazón, edited by Giacomo Vaifro Sabatelli (with *La hidalga del Valle*).   1962.
A secreto agravio, secreta vengenza, edited by Edward Nagy.   1966; in *Tragedias 2*, 1968; translated by Edwin Honig as *Secret Vengeance for Secret Insult*, in *Four Plays*, 1961.
El alcalde de Zalamea, edited by Peter N. Dunn.   1966; translated as *The Mayor of Zalamea* by E. Fitzgerald in *Eight Dramas*, 1906, and Edwin Honig in *Four Plays*, 1961.
Amar después de la muerta, translated by Roy Campbell as *Love after Death*, in *Classic Theatre 3*, edited by Eric Bentley, 1960.
La aurora en Copacabana, edited by Antonio Pages Larraya.   1956.
La cabellos de Absalón, edited by Helmy Fuad Giacoman.   1968; in *Tragedias 3*, 1969.
Cada uno para si, edited by José M. Ruano de la Haza.   1982.
Casa con dos puertas malas es de guardar, edited by G.T. Northrup, in *Three Plays*.   1926; translated by Kenneth Muir as *A House with Two Doors Is Difficult to Guard*, in *Tulane Drama Review*, 1963.
Celos aún de aire matan, edited by J. Subirá.   1933; translated by M. Stroud, as *Even Baseless Jealousy Can Kill*, 1981.
La cena de Baltazar, in *Tragedias 3*.   1969.
La dama duende, edited by José Luis Alonso.   1966; translated by Edwin Honig as *The Phantom Lady*, in *Four Plays*, 1961.
La desdicha de la voz, edited by Gwynne Edwards.   1970.
La devoción de la cruz, edited by Sidney F. Wexler.   1966; in *Tragedias 3*, 1969; translated by Edwin Honig as *The Devotion of the Cross*, in *Four Plays*, 1961.
Dicha y desdicha del nombre, translated by Kenneth Muir as *The Advantages and Disadvantages of a Name*, in *Four Comedies*, 1980.
La divina Filotea, edited by José Carlos de Torres Martínez, in *Segismundo 3*.   1967.

Eco y Narciso, edited by Charles V. Aubrun. 1961.
En esta vida todo es verdad y todo mentira, edited by D.W. Cruickshank. 1971.
La estatua de Prometeo, edited by Charles V. Aubrun. 1961.
El gran duque de Gandía, edited by Václav Cerný. 1963.
El gran teatro del mundo, edited by Eugenio Frutos Cortes. 1958; translated by G.W. Brandt as *The Great Stage of the World*, 1976.
Guardate del agua mansa, translated by E. Fitzgerald as *Beware of Smooth Water*, in *Eight Dramas*, 1906.
La hidalga del Valle, edited by Giacomo Vaifro Sabatelli (with *A María el corazón*). 1962.
La hija del aire, edited by Gwynne Edwards. 1970.
Luis Pérez el gallego, translated by E. Fitzgerald as *Gil Pérez the Galician*, in *Eight Dramas*, 1906.
El magico prodigioso, edited by Alexander A. Parker and Malveena McKendrick. 1972; translated by B.W. Wardropper as *The Wonderworking Magician*, 1982.
El mayor monstruo los celos, in *Tragedias 1*. 1967.
El medico de su honra, edited by C.A. Jones. 1961; in *Tragedias 2*, 1968; translated by Roy Campbell as *The Surgeon of His Honour*, 1960.
Nadia fie su secreto, translated by E. Fitzgerald as *Keep Your Own Secret*, in *Eight Dramas*, 1906.
No hay burlas con el amor, edited by I. Arrellano. 1981.
No hay cosa como callar, edited by Angel Valbuena Briones, in *Comedias de capa y espada 2*. 1954.
No hay más fortuna que Dios, edited by Alexander A. Parker. 1949.
No hay que creer ni en la verdad, edited by Václav Cerný. 1968.
No siempre lo peor es cierto, edited by Luis G. Villaverde and Lucile Farinas. 1977; translated by Kenneth Muir as *The Worst Is Not Always Certain*, in *Four Comedies*, 1980.
Peor está que estaba, translated by Kenneth Muir as *From Bad to Worse*, in *Four Comedies*, 1980.
El pintor de su deshonra, edited by Manuel Ruiz Lagos. 1969; translated by E. Fitzgerald as *The Painter of His Own Dishonour*, in *Eight Dramas*, 1906.
El pleito matrimonial del cuerpo y el alma, edited by Manfred Engelbert. 1969.
El postrer duelo de España, edited by Guy Rossetti. 1979.
El principe constante, edited by Alexander A. Parker. 1975.
El secreto a voces, edited by José M. de Osma. 1938; translated by Kenneth Muir as *The Secret Spoken Aloud*, in *Four Comedies*, 1980.
El sitio de Bredá, edited by Johanna R. Schrek. 1957.
Las tres justicias en una, translated by E. Fitzgerald as *Three Judgments at a Blow*, in *Eight Dramas*, 1960.
El verdadero dios Pan, edited by José M. de Osma. 1949.
La vida es sueño, edited by A.E. Sloman. 1961; also edited by Everett W. Hesse, 1978; translated by Roy Campbell as *Life's a Dream*, in *Classic Theatre 3*, edited by Eric Bentley, 1960.

Verse

Psalle et sile, edited by Leopoldo Trenor. 1936.

Other

Obras menores, edited by A. Pérez Gómez. 1969.

*

Bibliography: *A Chronology of the Plays of Calderón de la Barca* by H.W. Bilborn, 1928; *Bibliografía tematica de estudios sobre el teatro español antiguo* by Warren T. McCready, 1966; *Calderón de la Barca Studies 1951-69* by Jack H. Parker and Arthur M. Fox, 1971.

Critical Studies: *The Allegorical and Metaphorical Language in the Autos Sacramentales de Calderón* by F. de S. MacGarry, 1937; *The Allegorical Drama of Calderón* by Alexander A. Parker, 1943; *The Dramatic Craftsmanship of Calderón: His Use of Earlier Plays* by A.E. Sloman, 1958; *Critical Essays on the Theatre of Calderón* edited by B.W. Wardropper, 1965; *A Literary History of Spain: The Golden Age: Drama* by Edward M. Wilson and Duncan Moir, 1971; *Calderón and the Seizures of Honor* by Edwin Honig, 1972; *Calderón de la Barca: Imagery, Rhetoric, and Drama* by John V. Bryans, 1977; *The Prison and the Labyrinth: Studies in Calderonian Tragedy* by Gwynne Edwards, 1978; *On Calderón* by James E. Maraniss, 1978; *Spanish and English Literature of the 16th and 17th Centuries* by Edward M. Wilson, 1980; *Critical Perspectives on Calderón de la Barca* edited by Frederick A. De Armas and others, 1981; *Calderón in the German Lands and the Low Countries: His Reception and Influence 1654-1780* by Henry W. Sullivan, 1983.

*   *   *

Don Pedro Calderón de la Barca, one of the two greatest dramatists of the Spanish Golden Age, was extremely prolific, and his work was of many different kinds. Although he was not ordained until he was over fifty, his plays are frequently religious in spirit, and many of them are directly doctrinal. In particular he wrote more than seventy one-act allegorical dramas which Shelley, although an atheist, called "incomparable autos." They resemble, but are greatly superior to, English Morality plays; and, like the Mystery cycles, they were performed on wagons in the open air. The best known of the *autos*, outside Spain, is *The Great Stage of the World* in which representative human beings are put into the world to perform their allotted parts on the stage of life. Calderón sometimes rewrote his secular plays as allegories: there is, for example, an *auto* of *Life's a Dream* and another based on *El mayor encanto Amor*, dramatising the story of Ulysses and Circe.

Several of Calderón's full-length plays, written for performance in the public theatres of Madrid, have religious themes. It is arguable that *The Wonderworking Magician* is the finest religious play in any language; and *El principe constante*, in which the phantom of the martyred prince leads the Portuguese army to victory, and *Devotion of the Cross*, which ends in the miraculous resurrection and repentance of a scoundrel, are among Calderón's most admired plays. When he wrote about *Henry VIII* in *La cisma de Inglaterra*, he concentrated, in a way Shakespeare did not, on the religious issue. His most famous play, *Life's a Dream*, is directly didactic, demonstrating that the pursuit of fame or wealth is foolish, that we ought to overcome our passions, and set our hearts on eternal things. Segismundo, returned to prison, is made to believe that he has only dreamed that he was a prince with absolute power; but when he is released again he decides to behave morally instead of selfishly.

Several of Calderón's important plays are marriage tragedies, demonstrating the disastrous effects of the code of honour under which husbands were expected to kill their wives on the mere suspicion of infidelity. In two of these plays the wives are innocent; and in a third the imprudent wife has been compelled to marry a man she does not love. In *The Surgeon of His Honour* a husband has his wife bled to death; in *Secret Vengeance for Secret Insult* another deluded husband murders both his wife and her lover; and in *The Painter of His Own Dishonour* Juan Roca kills the innocent wife whom he still loves. Calderón contrasts the honour code with Christian ethics, most obviously in the first of these plays, but the husbands are regarded as mistaken rather than evil: one is provided by the King with another wife, another, tortured with remorse, is allowed to go free; the third seeks to die in battle. Othello, who commits suicide when he discovers that Desdemona was innocent, provides an illuminating contrast. A modern reader has to make an effort of imagination to put himself in the place of the original audience; but it is important to note that the cruelty of the code is criticised by a number of sympathetic characters, even by those who conform to it in practice.

One of the most popular of Calderón's dramas, *The Mayor of Zalamea*, contrasts two conceptions of honour: that of the aristocratic rapist who prefers to die rather than marry the woman he has wronged, and that of her father, the Mayor, who believes that his own honour can be redeemed by the marriage of the rapist to his daughter or, failing that, by his execution. The King, who arrives opportunely, commends the justice of the execution, although the man should properly have been given a court martial.

Calderón also wrote a large number of love comedies—cloak and sword plays, as they are often called. These have ingenious plots, witty dialogue, charming poetry, comic jealousy, sword fights, confusion over identity, humorous servants, and romantic love-making. The heroes, fashionable gallants, are, as Goethe complained, often indistinguishable; but the heroines, whether unjustly suspected of unchastity or gay flouters of convention, are expertly characterised. In a male-dominated society, with rigid notions of female propriety, they can obtain the husbands of their choice only by refusing to conform. One of the two heroines of *Mañanas de abril y mayo* finally persuades her jealous lover to trust her, and not to insist on a proof of her innocence; the other one exposes, and refuses to marry, a conceited philanderer. Marcela, in *A House with Two Doors Is Difficult to Guard*, secures a husband by meeting her brother's guest clandestinely; Angela in *The Phantom Lady* uses a concealed door to obtain access to a guest's room; and the lovers in *The Secret Spoken Aloud* communicate with each other in public by use of an ingenious code.

These comedies often have an element of satire, as of the affected Beatriz in *No hay burlas con el amor*. Other plays in this genre raise more serious issues: *The Advantages and Disadvantages of a Name* contains an attempted murder and an attempted rape; and *No hay cosa como callar* begins with a rape and ends, years later, with the marriage of the rapist to his victim.

In his later years Calderón wrote mainly for the Court theatres, and here he made use of elaborate scenery, spectacle, and music. The plays were often on classical and mythological subjects, and usually didactic.

There were adaptations of some of Calderón's plays in France and England during the second half of the 17th century; but if one compares, for example, Wycherley's *Love in a Wood* with *Mañanas de abril y mayo*, Calderón's plots are submerged in several others; the tone is vulgarised; the rake is rewarded with a bride; and undistinguished prose is substituted for the delicate verse of the original.

—Kenneth Muir

CALLIMACHUS. Born in Cyrene; active during first half of 3rd century B.C. and until at least 246 B.C. Said to have been a school-teacher in an Alexandria suburb before working at the royal Library and Museum at Alexandria; once believed to have been Librarian, but apparently never held that post, though he was responsible for compiling the main bio-bibliographical reference catalogue (*Pinaces*) from which is derived much of the information we have today about ancient Greek writers and their works. Traditionally supposed to have quarrelled with Apollonius of Rhodes, but evidence for this is poor, though he does seem to have been involved in numerous literary enmities. The scholars Eratosthenes and Aristophanes of Byzantium were among his pupils.

CALLIMACHUS

PUBLICATIONS

Collections

[*Works*], edited by R. Pfeiffer. 2 vols., 1949-53; supplemented by P. Parsons and H. Lloyd-Jones, in *Supplementum Hellenisticum* (*Texte und Kommentare 11*), 1983; translated by A.W. and G.R. Mari (Loeb edition), 1921, and C.A. Trypanis (Loeb edition), 1958; selection translated by R.A. Furness, 1931; "Hymn to Athena" translated in *Callimachus: The Fifth Hymn* by A.W. Bulloch, 1984.

*

Critical Studies: *The Discovery of the Mind* by Bruno Snell, 1953; *History of Classical Scholarship from the Beginnings to the End of the Hellenistic Age* by R. Pfeiffer, 1968; *Cambridge History of Classical Literature I: Greek Literature* edited by P.E. Easterling and B.M.W. Knox, 1984.

* * *

Callimachus was the most brilliant intellectual and poet of his time, and, although an extremely controversial figure, had a more radical influence on the course of Greek (and Roman) poetry than almost any other writer except Homer. He wrote prolifically, but few of his works now survive (or they are known only in fragmentary form), and we have to gauge Callimachus's importance from his effect on other writers. Yet his vivacious, penetrating, and rather quixotic intelligence shows through in almost every line that we have. He was said to have written more than 800 works altogether, and was one of the very few who was equally scholar and poet, in both activity and achievement.

His research involved compilation and classification of data rather than speculative thinking; he wrote scarcely anything of a philosophical or historical nature, and although some of his works have titles such as *On Birds*, or *On Winds*, these were surveys rather than scientific enquiries based on independent observation. But his work was of fundamental importance in another way: he lived at a point in history when modern scholarship was just beginning to evolve, and in a place where the resources to conduct that scholarship were being assembled for the first time; the principles of philosophical and scientific enquiry were laid down in Athens by Plato and Aristotle, and their pupils, but the idea of a body of *knowledge*, and its collection and transmission, came to maturity in 3rd-century Alexandria. Callimachus played a key part in the evolution of the principles and standards of true, energetic scholarship, and was one of its most important practitioners; many of the great intellectuals of the next generation were his pupils. His most important work, the *Pinaces*, the reference catalogue to the Library, consisted of 120 books, and was the first of its kind and exemplary: it classified the works of all Greek writers of any importance and attempted to provide all the basic information that a reader might need (biography, contents, authenticity, etc.). In effect the *Pinaces* was the first encyclopedia in western culture.

As a poet Callimachus was equally vigorous and idiosyncratic. He thought that he diagnosed muddle and mediocrity in the mainstream of contemporary Greek poetry, and set a premium in his own work on originality and refreshment of the language. Late in his career Callimachus published a collection of his poetry, and for it wrote a preface, in verse, expounding the critical principles which had guided him as a writer ("The Prologue" to the *Aetia*). He claimed to have avoided the trite, uninspired, hackneyed, "high" manner which was popular at the time and to have been uncompromisingly unorthodox and original, even if that took him "along a narrower path." He set a premium on concision and clarity; he was fascinated by language and words, and set out, almost ideologically, to transform the linguistic material of poetry. Like any Greek poet he was thoroughly imbued with Homer, but was too great a writer to think that Homer needed to be overthrown: he advocated passionately the creation of a "fine," spare, even elegant style, with none of the inflation of unthinking traditionality. Poetry had to be wrought, and writing was the result of work. Despite being a court poet, dependent on, and gratefully acknowledging, the support of royal patronage, he was a non-conformist, an experimenter, at times an iconoclast, and seems always to have been controversial and involved in fierce argument and criticism. He had a perpetual sense of the odd or bizarre. Thus it was the mundane dimensions of what were supposed to be the ideal realms that intrigued him: what were the practicalities of being a hero, and what are the day-to-day effects when man encounters god? His gods are often children and his men involved in pursuing their own odd rituals, and although he represents religious passion with sympathetic insight, he suggests that the only real meaning comes from the limited warmth of human friendship, not from the spiritual or the sublime.

His most important work was the *Aetia* (*Origins* or *Causes*), an eccentrically learned work in 4,000-6,000 lines, which mixed strange and wonderful stories into an episodic, almost picaresque narrative of religious rituals and practices: the length was epic, but the style and concerns crankily different, with off-beat accounts, bizarre humour, unpredictable climaxes, and intricate but razor-sharp language. Narrative poetry was never the same again. The *Hecale* was an inverted epic, nominally "about" Theseus's defeat of the bull of Marathon, but mostly comprising an account of his stay overnight, during a rain-storm, in the hut of a solitary peasant-woman. His thirteen *Iambi* were mostly social satire, with some personal invective, directed at the foibles of human ambitions and drives. None of these works survives in full, but we do possess the complete text of six "hymns." All are difficult but fine texts, superficially dealing with the myths and rituals connected with some of the principal Olympian deities, with some recognition of the semi-divine power of his royal patrons; but their overall effect is to convey, behind a brilliant, edgy, and often entertaining manner, that traditional religion is puzzling and disturbing. All is not, in fact, right with the world. Callimachus also wrote epigrams which are taut, wry, witty, and pungent, and among the very best in the long history of the genre.

Callimachus changed the course of Greek poetry: writers who saw themselves as "mainstream" thereafter were deeply influenced by both his style and outlook, and for poets rebelling against their own traditions he was the archetypal avant-garde non-conformist.

—A.W. Bulloch

CAMÕES, Luís (Vas) de. Born, probably in Lisbon, in 1524 or 1525. May have been educated at Coimbra University. Served as a soldier in the Centa, and may have lost an eye in combat; went to India as a soldier, 1533; stayed for a year or two in East Africa, and possibly went to Macao and Goa; returned to Lisbon, 1569; received a small pension from the king. *Died in 1580 (?).*

PUBLICATIONS

Collections

Obras completas, edited by Hernâni Cidade. 5 vols., 1946-47.
Obra completa, edited by Antônio Salgado Junior. 1963.

Verse

Os Lusíadas.   1572; edited by Frank Pierce, 1973; as *The Lusiad*, translated by Richard
Fanshaw, 1655; also translated by J.J. Aubertin, 1878, Richard Burton, 1880, Leonard
Bacon, 1950, and William C. Atkinson, 1952.
Rhythmas.   1595, as *The Lyricks*, translated by Richard Burton, 2 vols., 1884.
Rimas, edited by Alvaro J. da Costa Pimpão.   1953.

Plays

Auto dos Enfatriões, from a play by Plautus, in *Autos e comedias portuguesas.*   1587.
Auto de Filodemo, in *Autos e comedias portuguesas.*   1587.
El Rei-Seleuco, in *Rimas.*   1645.

*

Critical Studies: *Camões* by A.F.G. Bell, 1923; *From Vergil to Milton* by C.M. Bowra, 1945;
Camões and the Epic of the Lusiads by H.H.Hart, 1962; *Camoens and His Epic: A Historic,
Geographic, and Cultural Background* by W. Freitas, 1963; *History and Heroes in the Lusiads*
by Colin Michael O'Halloran, 1974.

*   *   *

Camões's most important work is his epic poem, *The Lusiads*, which deals with Vasco da
Gama's successful attempt to discover a sea route to India. Camões's poem owes a great deal to
classical epic, and especially to Virgil's *Aeneid*. Gama is not, however, the protagonist of
Camões's poem, as Aeneas is of Virgil's. For much of the poem he is not an actor at all but a
narrator, and the story he tells is not just that of his own voyage, like the account of his
adventures that Aeneas gives Dido, but embraces the whole history of Portugal from its
legendary beginnings right down to Camões's own day.
The Lusiads offers abundant evidence of Camões's mastery of the sublime style which he
inherited from Virgil. Like Virgil, Camões is fond of complex sentences, full of subordinate
clauses, but, again like Virgil, his predilection for elaborate patterns of subordination does not
keep him from being a superb storyteller. On the contrary, we can say of him, as C.S. Lewis says
of Milton, that he "avoids discontinuity by avoidance of what grammarians call the simple
sentence" and that he "compensates for the complexity of his syntax by the simplicity of the
broad imaginative effects beneath it and the perfect rightness of their sequence."
The Lusiads is not merely a faithful imitation of an admired model. Perhaps the most striking
feature of the poem is the way it combines repeated reminders that it belongs to the noblest of
the established literary kinds, the epic, with daring innovations. Camões repeatedly acknowledges Homer and Virgil as his models but he insists just as firmly on the differences which
separate his work from theirs. The most important is that the story he tells is true. Many
passages of the poem follow closely the accounts given by the great Portuguese historians of
Asia who were Camões's contemporaries, most notably João de Barros. Camões repeatedly
asserts that the real achievements of the Portuguese rival and even outdo the fictional ones
attributed to Odysseus and Aeneas. It is because he has a greater subject than the ancient epic
poets that his poem may hope to surpass theirs. Camões stresses not only the truthfulness of his
account but also its exemplary character. He believes, like Dryden, that "the design of [the
heroic poem] is to form the mind to heroic virtue by example." Camões's conception of heroic
virtue is, however, one that many modern readers find hard to accept; *The Lusiads* can serve as
a magnificent example of Wallace Stevens's assertion that "poetry is a cemetery of nobilities."
Another obstacle for many modern readers is Camões's readiness to evoke the hand of God to
explain the course of historical events, a readiness that he shares with many 16th-century
historians.

Much of the poem is, of course, invention, not historical reporting. 16th-century poets saw the marvelous as an indispensable element in poetry, and Camões supplies it in his mythological frame-story which pits Venus against Bacchus, one aiding Gama and the other opposing him. For many readers the most memorable episodes in the poem are those which spring from Camões's imagination, often sparked, of course, by his memories of classical poetry: the giant Adamastor, for example, a personification of the Cape of Good Hope, who represents the hostile forces of nature which the Portuguese must confront on their voyages of discovery, or the Isle of Love, where Venus and her nymphs offer Gama and his men an erotic romp on their return voyage to Portugal.

The Lusiads is an extremely personal poem. Just how personal is difficult to appreciate without some familiarity with Camões's lyrics, which elaborate many of the motifs touched on in the epic, most notably a note of melancholy which has much in common with the Virgilian *lacrimae rerum*. The lyrics are not autobiographical poetry; they do not deal directly with the experiences of the poet's life but rather with their emotional effect on him. For this reason, and because so little is known with certainty about Camões's life, they have often served as points of departure for arbitrary and incompatible biographical interpretations. Like *The Lusiads*, Camões's lyrics offer an astonishing fusion of tradition and innovation. He is a master of both the principal currents which flow into 16th-century Portuguese poetry, one deriving from the 15th-century *cancioneiros* (songbooks, though the poems in them were not always intended to be sung) and the other from the love-poetry of Petrarch and his 16th-century Spanish followers, notably Garcilaso de la Vega. Camões sometimes combines elements of both traditions in a single poem, just as he sometimes combines traditional materials with an intensely individual development presumably drawn from his own lived experience. An outstanding example is the long poem "Sôbolos rios," which begins as a paraphrase of Psalm 137 ("By the waters of Babylon...") and turns into a moving meditation on the poet's own life, expressed with incomparable grace in an inimitably personal style which nevertheless is firmly rooted in the tradition of the songbooks.

Camões's three plays turn aside from the classical comedies and tragedies of Francisco de Sá de Miranda and António Ferreira and return to the tradition established by Gil Vicente, though with important differences, most notably Camões's choice, in two of the three, of subjects drawn from classical antiquity. The apparent amorality of Camões's theater also sets it apart from that of Gil Vicente. The prose passages in the *Auto de Filodemo*, like Camões's letters, show a mastery of language comparable to that of his lyrics or of *The Lusiads*, though both style and subject matter are entirely different. In the plays and letters we often encounter a playful and mocking Camões quite unlike the despairing lover of some of the lyrics or the inspired bard of *The Lusiads*.

—Thomas R. Hart

CAMUS, Albert. Born in Mondovi, Algeria, 7 November 1913. Educated at the University of Algiers, graduated 1936. Married 1) Simone Hié in 1933 (divorced); 2) Francine Faure in 1940 (died, 1979), twin son and daughter. Worked as meteorologist, ship-broker's clerk, automobile parts salesman, clerk in the automobile registry division of the prefecture, actor and amateur theatre producer, Algiers, 1935-39; staff member, *Alger-Républicain*, 1938-39, and editor, *Soir-Républicain*, 1939-40, both Algiers; sub-editor for lay-out, *Paris-Soir*, 1940; teacher, Oran, Algeria, 1940-42; convalescent in central France, 1942-43; joined Resistance in

CAMUS

Lyons region, 1943; journalist, Paris, 1943-45; reader, and editor of Espoir series, Gallimard, publishers, Paris, 1943-60; Co-Founding Editor, *Combat*, 1945-47. Recipient: Critics Prize (France), 1947; Nobel Prize for Literature, 1957. *Died 4 January 1960.*

PUBLICATIONS

Collections

Théâtre, récits, nouvelles; Essais, edited by Roger Quilliot.   2 vols., 1962-65.

Fiction

L'Étranger.   1942; as *The Stranger*, 1946; as *The Outsider*, 1946.
La Peste.   1947; as *The Plague*, 1948.
La Chute.   1956; as *The Fall*, 1957.
L'Exil et le royaume.   1957; as *Exile and the Kingdom*, 1958.
La Mort heureuse.   1971; as *A Happy Death*, 1973.

Plays

Le Malentendu (produced 1944).   With *Caligula*, 1944; as *Cross Purpose*, with *Caligula*, 1947.
Caligula (produced 1945).   With *Le Malentendu*, 1944; 1941 version (produced 1983), 1984; translated as *Caligula*, with *Cross Purpose*, 1947.
L'État de siège (produced 1948).   1948; as *State of Siege*, in *Caligula and Three Other Plays*, 1958.
Les Justes (produced 1949).   1950; as *The Just Assassins*, in *Caligula and Three Other Plays*, 1958.
La Dévotion à la croix, from a play by Calderón (produced 1953).   1953.
Les Esprits, from a work by Pierre de Larivey (produced 1953).   1953.
Un Cas intéressant, from a work by Dino Buzzati (produced 1955).   1955.
Requiem pour une nonne, from a work by William Faulkner (produced 1956).   1956.
Le Chevalier d'Olmedo, from the play by Lope de Vega (produced 1957).   1957.
Les Possédés, from a novel by Dostoevsky (produced 1959).   1959; as *The Possessed*, 1960.

Other

L'Envers et L'endroit.   1937.
Noces.   1939.
Le Mythe de Sisyphe.   1942; as *The Myth of Sisyphus and Other Essays*, 1955.
Lettres à un ami allemand.   1945.
L'Existence.   1945.
Le Minotaure; ou, La Halte d'Oran.   1950.
Actuelles 1-3: Chroniques 1944-1948, Chroniques 1948-1953, Chronique algérienne 1939-1958.   3 vols., 1950-58.
L'Homme révolté.   1951; as *The Rebel: An Essay on Man in Revolt*, 1954.
L'Été.   1954.
Réflexions sur la guillotine, in *Réflexions sur la peine capitale*, with Arthur Koestler.   1957; as *Reflections on the Guillotine*, 1960.

Discours de Suède.   1958; as *Speech of Acceptance upon the Award of the Nobel Prize for Literature*, 1958.
Resistance, Rebellion, and Death (selection).   1961.
Méditation sur le théâtre et la vie.   1961.
Carnets: Mai 1935-fevrier 1942.   1962; translated as *Carnets 1935-1942*, 1963; as *Notebooks 1935-1942*, 1963.
Lettre à Bernanos.   1963.
Carnets: Janvier 1942-mars 1951.   1964; as *Notebooks 1942-1951*, 1970.
Lyrical and Critical Essays, edited by Philip Thody.   1968.
Le Combat d'Albert Camus, edited by Norman Stokle. 1970.
Selected Essays and Notebooks, edited by Philip Thody. 1970.
Le premier Camus.   1973; as *Youthful Writings*, 1976.
Journaux de voyage, edited by Roger Quilliot.   1978.
Fragments d'un combat 1938-1940: Alger-Républicain, Le Soir-Républicain, edited by Jacqueline Lévi-Valensi and André Abbou.   1978.
Correspondance 1932-1960, with Jean Grenier, edited by Marguerite Dobrenn.   1981.

Translator, *Le dernière fleur*, by James Thurber.   1952.

*

Bibliography: *Camus: A Bibliography* by Robert F. Roeming, 1968; by R. Gay-Crosier, in *A Critical Bibliography of French Literature 6*, 1980.

Critical Studies: *Camus* by Philip Thody, 1962; *Camus: A Collection of Critical Essays* edited by Germaine Bree, 1962, and *Camus* by Bree, 1964, revised edition, 1972; *Camus: The Artist in the Arena* by Emmett Parker, 1965; *Camus* by Phillip H. Rhein, 1969; *Camus* by Conor Cruise O'Brien, 1970; *The Theatre of Camus* by Edward Freeman, 1971; *Camus: The Invincible Summer* by Albert Maquet, 1972; *The Unique Creation of Camus* by Donald Lazere, 1973; *Camus: A Biography* by Herbert R. Lottman, 1979; *Camus' Imperial Vision* by Anthony Rizzuto, 1981; *Camus: A Critical Study of His Life and Work* by Patrick McCarthy, 1982.

*   *   *

Although French critics on the right and the left have proclaimed Albert Camus *passé* for every imaginable reason, he has remained the best-selling author of France's largest and most prestigious literary publisher, Gallimard. In 1971, eleven years after his death at the age of 46, the publication of an early novel that Camus had had the good sense to abandon stimulated sales that pushed the French edition of *A Happy Death* to the top of the best-seller list within a few weeks. This is but one belated aspect of the paradox of Camus's career and reputation as a writer. When he was selected in 1957 to receive the Nobel Prize for Literature, he was, at 44, the youngest literary laureate but one, Rudyard Kipling having received the prize at 42. He himself stated publicly at the time that he would have voted for Malraux.

Camus is exceptional among French writers, the majority of whom have come from comfortable middle-class origins even in recent times. He was reared in Algiers by his mother, an illiterate charwoman. His first writings published in Paris catapulted him to a literary celebrity for which he was ill prepared. The climate of the immediate postwar period, combined with his position as a popular editorial writer for the Resistance newspaper *Combat*, rapidly created an aura about Camus that he had not sought and that was to cause him considerable difficulty a decade later.

In the first important review of *The Stranger*, Jean-Paul Sartre was struck by the contemporaneity of this objective, apparently dispassionate, non-novel. An essay on the notion of the Absurd, entitled *The Myth of Sisyphus*, has been taken by many readers since Sartre to be the theory of which *The Stranger* is the illustration. Camus's Absurd is a description of a state more familiar to some English-speaking readers as a variety of contemporary thought posited on the death of God. It owes a great deal to such thinkers as Pascal, Kierkegaard, Dostoevsky, and Nietzsche. Camus was at pains to point out that there were, in his view, few points of contact between the Absurd and Sartrean existentialism, a distinction that readers, critics, and historians have tended to honour in the breach. The third piece in this cycle is *Caligula*, which remains the most important and the most popular of his plays.

Camus's view of his own career involved cycles of trilogies. The cycle of the Absurd antedates his experience of the war in the Resistance. It was essentially complete by 1941, and in 1942 he began work on the cycle of Revolt which owed a great deal more to the war than did its predecessor. Once again the trilogy included a novel, *The Plague*, an essay, *The Rebel*, and a play, *The Just Assassins*. *The Rebel* was attacked in *Les Temps Modernes*, a pro-Communist magazine edited by Sartre. The subsequent polemic caused Camus to break with Sartre and to become disgusted with left-wing intellectuals. Several works written after this experience testify to a deepened awareness of human motivation, resulting in a more complex and satisfying style. The most substantial of these is *The Fall*. During the 1950's Camus turned progressively to the theatre for both solace and stimulation. At the time of his death he was preparing a third cycle, to be called Nemesis, and had begun a novel entitled *Le Premier Homme* (The First Man). He left interesting *Notebooks*, in two volumes, and an important collection of journalistic writings, *Actuelles*. *Noces*, an early work, is written in a fine lyrical prose.

—A. James Arnold

CANETTI, Elias. Born in Russe, Bulgaria, 25 July 1905. Educated at schools in England, Austria, Switzerland, and Germany; University of Vienna, Ph.D. 1929. Married Venetia Toubner-Calderon in 1934 (died, 1963). Full-time writer; resident of England since 1938. Recipient: Dichterpreis, Vienna, 1966; Deutsche Kritikpreis, 1967; Grosser Osterreichischer Staatspreis, 1968; Georg Büchner Prize, 1972; Hebbel Prize, 1980; Nobel Prize for Literature, 1981. Lives in London, England.

PUBLICATIONS

Fiction

Die Blendung. 1936; translated as *Auto-da-Fe*, 1946; as *The Tower of Babel*, 1947.

Plays

Hochzeit (produced 1965). 1932.
Komödie der Eitelkeit (produced 1965). 1950; as *Comedy of Vanities*, with *Life-Terms*, 1982.
Die Befristeten (produced 1967). In *Dramen*, 1964; as *Life-Terms*, with *Comedy of Vanities*, 1982.
Dramen. 1964.

Other

Fritz Wotruba. 1955.
Masse und Macht. 1960; as *Crowds and Power,* 1962.
Welt im Kopf (selection), edited by Erich Fried. 1962.
Aufzeichnungen 1942-1948. 1965.
Die Stimmen von Marrakesch: Aufzeichnungen nach einer Reise. 1967; as *The Voices of Marrakesh,* 1978.
Die andere Prozess: Kafkas Briefe an Felice. 1969; as *Kafka's Other Trial: The Letters to Felice,* 1974.
Alle vergeudete Verchrung: Aufzeichnungen 1949-1960. 1970.
Die gespaltene Zukunft: Aufsätze und Gespräche. 1972.
Macht und Überleben: Drei Essays. 1972.
Die Provinz des Menschen: Aufzeichnungen 1942-1972. 1973; as *The Human Province,* 1978.
Der Ohrenzeuge: 50 Charaktere. 1974; as *Earwitness: Fifty Characters,* 1979.
Das Gewissen der Worte: Essays. 1975; as *The Conscience of Words,* 1979.
Der Beruf des Dichters. 1976.
Die gerettete Zunge: Geschichte einer Jugend. 1977; as *The Tongue Set Free,* 1979.
Die Fackel im Ohr: Lebensgeschichte 1921-1931. 1980; as *The Torch in My Ear,* 1982.

*

Critical Studies: *Canetti: Stationen zum Werk* by Alfons-M. Bischoff, 1973; *Kopf und Welt: Canettis Roman "Die Blendung"* by D.G.J. Roberts, 1975; *Canetti* by Dagmar Barnouw, 1979.

*   *   *

Elias Canetti has never been widely known in Britain, although he came to live here in 1938. Since 1981, when he won the Nobel Prize for Literature, the contemporary relevance of his work has once again attracted attention. A reticent man, Canetti has dedicated his life to the study of a single theme: the behaviour of the individual within the mass and the power struggle associated with this conflict.

The works for which he is most famous are his first novel, *Auto da Fé,* and a study of the behaviour of the mass, *Crowds and Power.* His autobiographies of recent years, *The Tongue Set Free* and *The Torch in My Ear,* have underlined the origins of and inspiration for his lifetime's work. His dramas and essays, too, reflect a preoccupation with hallucination, political pressure, linguistic ambiguity, and the destructive power of the masses.

The events of most outstanding significance for Canetti in the formation of his interest in crowd psychology and the hypnotic power of the masses were the awaited arrival of a comet in Rustschuk, the sinking of the Titanic, the fire at the Law Courts in Vienna in 1927, and an experience in Vienna's Alserstrasse in the winter of 1924-25. These powerful emotional experiences are linked in Canetti's mind and work by images of great energy, of blood, of a rushing sound, and of fire. Fire is frequently seen as a magnetic driving force and is associated with the uncontrolled rhythm of the masses. These symbols recur in Canetti's work. Sight and blindness, insight and illusion are related themes. In *Auto da Fé* the central character, Kien, who becomes increasingly deluded by his world of books, eventually perishes in a fire with them. Canetti is always at pains to point out the contrasts and similarities between a character's external appearance, his environment, and his use of language. Each character, e.g., the man of books, the collector, the spend-thrift, has "fixed ideas" which stand out because reality is portrayed as fragmented, communication as very partial. Canetti distances himself from the suggestiveness of his characters, and yet he has clearly been closely involved with the experience of each of them. Attempts at communication between these different kinds of people are often portrayed as grotesque, leading only to an intensification of individual isolation.

Despite themes which are characteristic of a period of social and political upheaval, Canetti's style is serene, controlled, and lucid, almost part of another era and tradition. His work reflects self-assurance and composure. Its stylistic poise and balance based on an authoritative use of language, rich in imagery, set him apart from many younger contemporary writers. Nevertheless, his subject matter is complex and his vision powerful—a confidence in one's own destiny, a respect for the experience of others, and a resistance to illusion, manipulation, and death.

—Barbara Saunders

CAPEK, Karel. Born in Malé Svatoňovice, Bohemia, 9 January 1890; brother of the writer Josef Capek. Educated at the universities of Prague, Berlin, and Paris; Charles University, Prague, Ph.D. in philosophy 1915. Married the actress Olga Scheinpflugova in 1935. Journalist, *Lidové noviny*; stage director at Vinohrady Theatre, Prague, 1921-23. *Died 25 December 1938.*

PUBLICATIONS

Collections

Spisy bratří [Collected Works]. 51 vols., 1928-47.

Fiction

Zářivé hlubiny [The Luminous Depths], with Josef Capek. 1916.
Boží muka [Wayside Crosses]. 1917.
Krakonošova zahrada [The Garden of Krakonos], with Josef Capek. 1918.
Trapné povídky. 1921; as *Money and Other Stories*, 1929.
Továrna na Absolutno. 1922; as *The Absolute at Large*, 1927.
Krakatit. 1924; translated as *Krakatit*, 1925; as *An Atomic Fantasy*, 1948.
Povídky z jedné kapsy [Tales from One Pocket], *Povídky z druhé kapsy* [Tales from the Other Pocket]. 2 vols., 1929; translated in part as *Tales from Two Pockets*, 1932.
Apokryfy; Kniha apokryfu. 2 vols., 1932-45; as *Apocryphal Stories*, 1949.
Hordubal. 1933; translated as *Hordubal*, 1934.
Povětrón. 1934; as *Meteor*, 1935.
Obyčejný život. 1934; as *An Ordinary Life*, 1936.
Válka s mloky. 1936; as *War with the Newts*, 1937.
První parta. 1937; as *The First Rescue Party*, 1939.
Život a dílo skladatele Foltýna. 1939; as *The Cheat*, 1941.

Plays

Lásky hra osudná [The Fateful Game of Love], with Josef Capek (produced 1930). 1910.
Loupežník [The Brigand] (produced 1920). 1920.
R.U.R. (produced 1921). 1920; as *R.U.R. (Rossum's Universal Robots)*, 1923.
Ze života hmyzu, with Josef Capek (produced 1922). 1921; as *And So ad Infinitivum*

(The Life of the Insects): An Entomological Review, 1923; as *The Insect Play*, 1923; as *The World We live In (The Insect Comedy)*, 1933.
Věc Makropulos (produced 1922).   1922; as *The Macropulos Secret*, 1925.
Adam Stvořitel, with Josef Capek (produced 1927).   1927; as *Adam the Creator*, 1929.
Bílá nemoc (produced 1937).   1937; as *Power and Glory*, 1938.
Matka (produced 1938).   1938; as *The Mother*, 1939.

Other

Pragmatismus; čili, Filosofie praktického života.   1918.
Kritika slov.   1920.
Italské listy.   1923; as *Letters from Italy*, 1929.
Anglické listy.   1924; as *Letters from England*, 1925.
O nejbližšich věcech.   1925; as *Intimate Things*, 1935.
Jak vzniká divadelní hra a pruvodce po zákulisí.   1925; as *How a Play Is Produced*, 1928.
Skandální afera Josefa Holouška.   1927.
Hovory s T.G. Masarykem.   3 vols., 1928-35; as *President Masaryk Tells His Story*, 1934, and *Masaryk on Thought and Life*, 1938.
Zahradníkuv rok.   1929; as *The Gardener's Year*, 1931.
Výlet do Spanél.   1930; as *Letters from Spain*, 1932.
Minda; čili, Ochova psu.   1930; as *Minda; or, On Breeding Dogs*, 1940.
Devatero pohádek.   1932; as *Fairy Tales*, 1933.
Obrazky z Holandska.   1932; as *Letters from Holland*, 1933.
O věcech obecných; čili, Zoon politikos.   1932.
Dasěnka.   1933; translated as *Dashenka*, 1940.
Legenda o člověku zahradníkovi.   1935.
Cesta na sever.   1936; as *Travels in the North*, 1939.
Jak se co dělá.   1938; as *How They Do It*, 1945.
Kalendář.   1940.
O lidech.   1940.
Vzrušené tance.   1946.
Bajky a prdpovídky [Fables and Would-Be Tales].   1946.
Sedm rozhlásku.   1946.
Ratolest a vavřín.   1947.
In Praise of Newspapers and Other Essays on the Margin of Literature.   1951.
Obrázky z domova.   1953.
Sloupkový ambit.   1957.
Poznámky o tvorbě.   1959.
Na břehu dnu.   1966.
Divadelníkem proti své vuli.   1968.
V zajetí slov.   1969.
Cteni o T.G. Masarykovi.   1969.
Místo pro Janathana!   1970.
Listy Olze 1920-38.   1971.
Drobty pod stolem doby.   1975.
Dopisy ze Zasuvky [Letters Out of a Drawer] (letters to Vera Hruzová), edited by Jiří Opelik.   1980.

*

Critical Studies: *Capek* by William E. Harkins, 1962; *Capek: An Essay* by Alexander Matuska, 1964.

*   *   *

Karel Capek sprang into world fame with his play *R.U.R.* about the production and commercial exploitation of semi-human automata. It gave the English language a new word— "robot." He and his brother followed this up with *The Insect Play*, where the jungle law of the insect world was portrayed as a reflection of the amorality of human society. Later plays included *The Macropulos Secret* (best known today in Janáček's operatic version) about a woman who was the victim of an experiment to prolong life, in which Capek, unlike Shaw, reached the comforting conclusion that our existing life span is about right.

Although Capek was a gifted playwright, his best work did not lie in the theatre. The world publicity he received for his plays with their sensational themes obscured the merit of his more philosophical works like his "Trilogy" (*Hordubal, Meteor,* and *Ordinary Life*), his series of short stories (*Tales from Two Pockets,* etc.) and his feuilletons, which were admirably suited to his particular genius. His delightful travel books, some of which he illustrated himself, achieved popularity in the countries he was describing.

In his "Trilogy" Capek expresses his relativist view of life by showing that human personality is compounded of many disparate elements, some hidden and others only rarely coming to the surface. The Ukrainian peasant Hordubal is murdered by his wife and her paramour, but at the trial it is clear that facts and motives are impossible for outsiders to determine. In *Meteor* three people make conflicting but plausible conjectures about the past history of an unknown airman who has been brought into a hospital unconscious, while in *An Ordinary Life* a man finds in retrospect that he has had not one personality but several. Capek adopts the same approach in his last, unfinished novel, *Cheat*.

In his brilliant "Pocket" tales Capek shows himself to be a master of short story writing, following the example of Chesterton, just as his "Utopian" plays and novels show the influence of H.G. Wells.

Less successful was his satirical fantasy *The Absolute at Large*, which tells how the discovery of the power of electrons and their application in a factory lead to overproduction and unemployment (including not "butter mountains" but all other "mountains" from tacks to rolls of paper) and release "fall-out" in the form of widespread religious hysteria; *Krakatit*, a half-mystical and strongly erotic story of the struggle of foreign powers to obtain the secret of an atomic bomb; and *The First Rescue Party*, a social realist novel about working-class heroism during an accident in a coal mine. His novel *War with the Newts*—an extension of the theme in *R.U.R.*—was particularly topical at the time as it reflected the alarm felt at the power of the Nazi system and the threat of Hitler's aggression.

Capek's writings are the product of his highly original imagination and deep philosophical thought. They are strongly influenced by his preoccupation with epistemology. His novels and plays are full of thought-provoking ideas and intriguing situations but lack fully rounded characters. He has continued to maintain his hold over the Czech reading public in spite of (or perhaps because of) his close identification with the officially rejected "Masaryk Republic," but his work is today less well-known abroad, perhaps because many of the problems he ventilated so imaginatively have been overtaken or are seen today in a more modern light. The failure of existing English translations to match his highly individual literary style has proved an additional handicap to full appreciation of his talents. He had great faith in the West, and the Munich "betrayal" robbed him of his will to live. ("It's not so bad. They haven't sold us out, only given us away" [*Fables*]). He died on Christmas Day 1938 at the age of 48.

—Cecil Parrott

CARPENTIER (y Valmont), Alejo. Born in Havana, Cuba, 26 December 1904. Educated at the University of Havana. Married Andrea Esteban. Journalist, Havana, 1921-24; Editor, *Carteles* magazine, Havana, 1924-28; Director, Foniric Studios, Paris, 1928-39; writer and producer, CMZ radio station, Havana, 1939-41; Professor of the History of Music, Conservatorio Nacional, Havana, 1941-43; lived in Haiti, Europe, the United States, and South America, 1943-59; Director, Cuban Publishing House, Havana, 1960-67; Cultural Attaché, Cuban Embassy, Paris, from 1967. Columnist, *El National*, Caracas; Editor, *Imam*, Paris. *Died 24 April 1980.*

PUBLICATIONS

Fiction

¡*Écue-yamba-Ó!*   1933.
Viaje a la semilla.   1944.
El reino de este mundo.   1949; as *The Kingdom of This World*, 1957.
Los pasos perdidos.   1953; as *The Lost Steps*, 1956.
El acoso.   1956.
Guerra del tiempo: Tres relatos y una novela: El Camino de Santiago, Viaje a la semilla, Semejante a la noche, y El acoso.   1958.
El siglo de las luces.   1962; as *Explosion in a Cathedral*, 1963.
El derecho de asilo, Dibujos de Marcel Berges.   1972.
Los convidados de plata.   1972.
Concierto barroco.   1974.
El recurso del método.   1974; as *Reasons of State*, 1976.
Cuentos.   1977.
La consagración de la primavera.   1979.
El arpa y la sombra.   1979.

Plays

Yamba-O, music by M.F. Gaillard (produced 1928).
La passion noire, music by M.F. Gaillard (produced 1932).

Verse

Dos poemas afrocubanos, music by A. Garcia Caturla.   1929.
Poèmes des Antilles, music by M.F.Gaillard.   1929.

Other

La música en Cuba.   1946.
Tientos y diferencias: Ensayos.   1964.
Literatura y consciencia política en América Latina.   1969.
La ciudad de las columnas, photographs by Paolo Gasparini.   1970.
Letra y solfa.   1976.
Crónicas.   1976.
Bajo el Signo de la Cibeles: Crónicas sobre España y los españoles, edited by Julio Rodríguez Puértolasi.   1979.
La novela latinoamericana en vísperas de un nuevo siglo y otros ensayos.   1981.

*

Bibliography: *Carpentier: 45 años de trabajo intelectual*, 1966.

Critical Studies: *Three Authors of Alienation: Bombal, Onetti, Carpentier* by M. Ian Adams, 1975; *Major Cuban Novelists* by Raymond D. Souza, 1976; *Carpentier: The Pilgrim at Home* by Roberto González Echevarría, 1977; *Carpentier and His Early Works* by Frank Janney, 1981.

*   *   *

Musicologist, journalist, critic, leader in the Afro-Cuban and vanguardia movements in Cuba in the 1920's, associate of the surrealists in Paris in the 1930's, Alejo Carpentier gave to 20th-century Latin-American letters an important critical concept and a distinctive vision of American identity through history. In the prologue to *The Kingdom of This World*, Carpentier proposed that there exists a "marvelous American reality" ("lo real maravilloso americano"). A conflation of the vocabulary of surrealism ("marvelous") and the primitivism of the Afro-Cuban movement, the term has, along with "magic realism," been used to justify and to describe the element of the fantastic so prominent in much Latin American writing this century. (Among the authors significantly influenced by Carpentier's precept and practice is the Colombian Gabriel García Márquez.) Almost as soon as he had elaborated the concept, however, Carpentier turned in his own work from the marvelous as the impossible and folkloric to the marvelous as the real, perceived by a modern, alienated eye, struck by the incongruity and irreality of what it really sees.

His early works include the first history of Cuban music, a scenario for an Afro-Cuban ballet, poems on Afro-Cuban themes, and a novel, *Écue-Yamba-Ó!*, that followed a contemporary rural black into the city and through the rites of the santería and ñañigo cults. His second novel was a product of his middle age, and in it he began the turn from the primitive as the essentially American to the paradoxical synthesis of times, peoples, cultures, styles, simultaneously primitive and sophisticated, European, African, and Indian that constitutes Carpentier's America. While his fictions remained conventional in structure, over time he elaborated an allusive, witty, ornately encrusted style, heterogeneous and baroque, itself both original and a synthesis.

Set in Haiti during the period of the French revolution, *The Kingdom of This World* juxtaposed the effete high culture of Europeans with the primitive powers of their black slaves. Such folkloric impossibilities as taking animal shapes parallel cyclic political metamorphoses in which a black revolution re-enacts and intensifies the white oppression violently thrown off and is in its turn violently replaced by the oppressive rule of mulattoes. In *The Lost Steps* Carpentier sent a modern protagonist on a search for primitive musical instruments from inauthentic, synthetic Paris through a Latin American city in the grip of a civil war that seemed a quarrel "between the Guelphs and the Ghibellines" to the upper reaches of the Orinoco, a journey still further back in time, to "the roots of life." In part a parable of Carpentier's own efforts to discover the essential America, the project of modern man's finding himself by losing himself in the primitive is doomed: the journey cannot be made twice.

Thereafter, Carpentier embraced his distinctive vision of Latin America as a place and a history split between its American realities and its European origins and consciousness. A volume of short stories, obsessed with origins, returns, and time, four novels and a fragment, all of the first order, complete an oeuvre distinguished by a paradoxical habit of seeing things twice, as past and as present, a multiplication of illusions with artifice as the nature of man, fallen into history, committed to "Adam's task of naming things." *Explosion in a Cathedral* returned to the Caribbean to chart once again the betrayals of the French revolution, but this time from the perspective of the creole bourgeoisie. *Reasons of State* set an exemplary dictator amid real and fictive personages in Paris, 1913, and followed him back and forth across the Atlantic, never fully at home on either side, until his death, downed and out in comfortable, homesick Parisian exile, sometime in the 1940's, with a brief epilogue dated 1972. *Concierto barroco* reached an apotheosis of heterogeneous synthesis as a Mexican and his black servant give Vivaldi a topic for an opera, *Montezuma*, and as the trumpet in Handel's *Messiah* becomes the trumpet of Louis Armstrong, a glorious concert of incongruities in which all is transformed, but nothing is lost. It is a final, fitting paradox that Carpentier, still writing at 76, should have died while at work on a novel celebrating a triumph of the Cuban revolution—in Paris.

—Regina Janes

CATULLUS (Gaius Valerius Catullus). Born c. 84 B.C. Father a citizen of Verona; lived in Rome, and probably had a villa near Tivoli; also owned property at Sirmio (now Sirmione); friend of Cicero and other important men; accompanied C. Memmius Gemellus on visit to Bithynia, Asia Minor, 57-56. *Died c. 54 B.C.*

PUBLICATIONS

[Verse], edited by R.A.B. Mynors, revised edition. 1972; also edited by H. Bardon, 1973, D.F.S. Thomson, 1978, and G.P. Goold (with translation), 1983; commentary by R. Ellis, 2nd edition, 1889, E.T. Merrill, 1893, C.J. Fordyce (in part), 1961, and Kenneth Quinn, 1970; translated by Jack Lindsay, 1929, Horace Gregory, 1931, Frank Copley, 1957, R.A. Swanson, 1959, C.H. Sisson, 1966, Peter Whigham, 1966, Reney Myers and Robert J. Ormsby, 1972, James Michie, 1972, and Frederic Raphael and Kenneth McLeish, 1978.

*

Bibliography: *A Bibliography to Catullus* by Hermann Harrauer, 1979.

Critical Studies: *Catullus and His Influence* by K.P. Harrington, 1923; *Catullus in English Poetry* by E.S. Duckett, 1925; *Catullus and the Traditions of Ancient Poetry* by E.A. Havelock, 1939, revised edition, 1967; *Catullus in Strange and Distant Britain* by J.A.S. McPeek, 1939; *The Catullan Revolution*, 1959, revised edition, 1969, and *Catullus: An Interpretation*, 1973, both by Kenneth Quinn, and *Approaches to Catullus* edited by Quinn, 1972; *Enarratio Catulliana* by C. Witke, 1968; *Catullan Questions* by Timothy P. Wiseman, 1969; *Style and Tradition in Catullus* by David O. Ross, Jr., 1969; *Studies in Catullan Verse* by Julia W. Loomis, 1972; *Interpreting Catullus* by G.P. Goold, 1974; *Catullan Self-Revelation* by E. Adler, 1981; *Catullus' "Passer": The Arrangement of the Book of Polymetric Poems* by M.B. Skinner, 1981; *Sexuality in Catullus* by Brian Arkins, 1982; *Three Classical Poets: Sappho, Catullus, and Juvenal* by Richard Jenkyns, 1982.

*   *   *

Catullus's poems are traditionally divided into three distinct groups: the short polymetric poems (1-60), the long poems (61-68), and the epigrams (69-116). Whether this arrangement, and that of the poems within each group, were Catullus's own work is much disputed; some, for example, believe that he intended 65-116 as a group, since they are all written in elegiacs. At present, the weight of scholarly opinion favours the view that at least the majority of the polymetrics were arranged in their present order by the poet, though some interference by a later editor is generally accepted to be evident.

Two types of poem, by virtue of their frequency, dominate the polymetrics and epigrams. First, there are roughly 3 dozen poems of invective (e.g., 28-29, 39, 69, 71, 94), which very often employ obscene language (incest is a recurrent theme) and of which several are often directed at a single target (thus 74, 88-91, 116 against one Gellius). Second, and most famously, there are between 2 dozen and 30 poems which relate to Catullus's love-affair with Lesbia (the exact number is uncertain because she is named explicitly in only 13). This woman (for "Lesbia" is a pseudonym) is usually identified with Clodia, the wife of Q. Metellus Celer who was consul in 60 B.C. and died the following year.

These two main types of poem are interspersed with a refreshing variety of others: e.g., poems on homecoming (4, 9, 31, 46), homosexual love (e.g., 15, 48, 81, 99), his dead brother (101) and the death of a friend's wife (96), and literature (e.g., 35, 50, 95); there are mock hymns (36, 44) and a real hymn (34); and there is vers de société (e.g., 10, 12-13, 25, 55, 84, 103), sometimes of a risqué nature (e.g., 6, 32, 56, 110). As for the group of long poems, there are two on weddings (61-62); one (63) on the fanatical cult of the goddess Cybele, depicting the self-castration of her devotee Attis; an epyllion (miniature epic) on the marriage of Peleus and Thetis (64); a translation into Latin of Callimachus's "Lock of Berenice" (66), together with its epistolary introduction in verse (65); a dialogue with a door (67); another verse letter, on the death of his brother (68A); and an elegy which combines the themes of his brother's death and his love for Lesbia with a complicated series of mythological illustrations (68B) (these last two are written as a single poem in the MSS and are still so regarded by many scholars). Of these long poems, 63 is one of the most remarkable poems in Latin on account of its theme; 64 is the only epyllion which survives from the literature of the late republic and early empire; and 68B is the forerunner of the poetry of Propertius, Tibullus, and Ovid. On these grounds alone, Catullus's work would be significant; but his principal achievement lies elsewhere.

Such long poems as 64, 68, and 68B are characterised above all by the *doctrina* (learning, scholarship) which was dear to the other *noui poetae* (new poets) of Catullus's generation and which was inspired by the work of the Greek librarian-poet Callimachus (fl. 250 B.C.). Until fairly recently it was often thought that there were, so to speak, "two Catulluses": the scholar-poet of the long poems, whose obscure and allusive verse was very much an acquired taste; and the simple poet of the polymetrics and epigrams, whose direct and passionate language had impressed centuries of readers. Yet this myth has been exploded by more recent scholarship, which has shown that learning, allusiveness, and technical refinement are not restricted to the long poems but permeate much of the other poetry too. Indeed it is precisely in the area where *doctrina* interacts with the portrayal of emotion that Catullus holds most fascination for the reader who knows Latin and Greek and is prepared to put his knowledge to good use. For it is by no means easy fully to appreciate the poetry written by Callimachus and his followers, and many of Catullus's polymetrics and epigrams require considerable effort for their understanding. Six examples, which appear to reflect his love-affair from its beginning to its end, will make this clear.

Poem 51 is an expression of Catullus's love for Lesbia, yet the poem is a translation and adaptation of a famous poem by Sappho (31); and the fact that Catullus has troubled to clarify the meaning of his exemplar (line 4) suggests that he expected his readers, including Lesbia, to be aware of the problems raised by Sappho's poem and to notice his own view of their solution. Poems 7 and 70 each has a "twin" (5 and 72 respectively), which suggests that all four poems reflect episodes in the poet's affair and are thus heavily biographical; yet 7 is full of learned allusion to the life and works of Callimachus, quite apart from treating us to a virtuoso display of oral imagery, while 70 is actually an adaptation of an epigram by Callimachus (25), which Catullus has completely transformed. 85 is a two-line epigram of deceptive simplicity; yet its first three words (*Odi et amo*, "I hate and love") recall a theme which echoes back to the beginnings of Greek personal poetry, and the remainder of the couplet is a superb example of the arrangement and suggestiveness of apparently simple words. 8 and 11 reflect the end of the affair, with all its bitterness; yet the former seems inspired by a soliloquy from the comic playwright Menander (*The Girl from Samos*, 325-356), and in the latter (lines 7-9) Catullus finds time to demonstrate his knowledge of the vernacular name for Egypt, of the original name for the Nile, and of the etymology of the word "Alps" (we must remember that Callimachus's most famous work was entitled *Origins* and that another work dealt with the foundations of islands and cities and their changes of name).

To the modern reader, these and countless other instances of *doctrina* may seem strange; but it is vital to appreciate that they in no way detract from, but rather enhance, the conviction with which Catullus expresses himself. He has achieved that fusion of form and emotion which many believe to be the quintessence of poetry and which has made his work everlastingly memorable.

—A.J. Woodman

CAVAFY, C(onstantine) P(etrou).   Born in Alexandria, Egypt, 29 April 1863. Spent several years in England as a child, and lived in Constantinople, 1882-85; otherwise lived in Alexandria. Issued one private pamphlet of his verse in 1904, and thereafter compiled notebooks of verse for distributing to friends. *Died 29 April 1933.*

PUBLICATIONS

Verse

Poiemata, edited by Alexander Singopoulos.   1935; as *Poems*, translated by John Mavrogordato, 1951; as *Complete Poems*, translated by Rae Dalven, 1961, and by Edmund Keeley and Philip Sherrard, 1975.
Anecdota poiemata 1882-1923 [Unpublished Poems], edited by G.P. Savidis, 1968; translated in part as *Passions and Ancient Days: Twenty One New Poems*, translated by Edmund Keeley and G.P. Savidis, 1972.

Other

Peza [Prose], edited by G. Papoutsakis.   1963.
Anecdota Peza [Unpublished Prose], edited by M. Peridis.   1963.
Epistoles ston Mario Valano, edited by E.N. Moschou.   1979.

*

Critical Studies: *Cavafy* by Peter Bien, 1964; *Cavafy: A Critical Biography* by Robert Liddell, 1974; *Cavafy's Alexandria: Study of a Myth in Progress* by Edmund Keeley, 1976; "A Concise Introduction to Cavafy" by Marguerite Yourcenar, in *Shenandoah 32*, no. 1, 1980; "Cavafy Issue" of *Journal of the Hellenic Diaspora 10*, 1983.

*   *   *

Solemnly asked his opinion of his own work, Cavafy towards the end of his life is said to have replied, "Cavafy in my opinion is an ultra-modern poet, a poet of future generations." History has proved him right, but the tone of the reply also reveals an important ingredient of the unique poetic voice that is Cavafy's: a gentle mockery of all pretension, even that of the poet interviewed about his own work, and a light-hearted concealment of his true self at the very moment when he appears about to lay his cards on the table. "Cavafy," he says, not "I," as if "Cavafy" were someone different.

Cavafy's poetry is distinguished by many subtle forms of irony, and also by an intriguing self-effacement in poems which purport to tell of personal experience and feeling. The subject matter of his poems is equally unusual. Approximately half of his output that he published in his lifetime (consisting of 154 fairly short poems) and a similar proportion of those published posthumously, are devoted to subjects taken from Greek history, chiefly between 340 B.C. and 1453 A.D., while the remainder deal more or less explicitly with homosexual encounters against a backdrop of contemporary Alexandria.

Cavafy's uniqueness has posed a problem for critics, for whom he continues to exercise a profound fascination. To many his erotic poetry is a disreputable appendage to more "sublime" poetry dedicated to the Greek past, but Cavafy's uncompromisingly "historical" treatment of that past has also disconcerted many. And those critics who have not chosen to ignore the erotic poems have been hard put to it to identify the source of powerful emotion, felt by many readers, in response to poems from which all reference to love is lacking, and the sordidness and triviality of the sexual encounters evoked are freely confessed.

The common denominator between Cavafy's two principal preoccupations, the distant Greek past and contemporary homosexual experiences, is Time, which plays a major role in both types of poem. Often it appears that the true subject of the erotic poems is not the experience described so much as its loss to the passage of time. Time takes away and alienates all real experience, but through art the poet can sometimes regain it in the creation of a poem, though what is regained is both more and less than the original. More, because, as the poet frankly says in several of these poems, he is free to touch up reality in the imaginative act of writing; less, because, no matter how "perfect" an experience can become thus imaginatively recreated, it is only imaginary, the real thing remains lost to the past. This sense of "lost to the past" is central, too, to Cavafy's historical poems, in which he juxtaposes vivid pictures of flesh-and-blood, fallible human beings with a chillingly historical sense of how remote they are, and how futile are these people's preoccupations now.

In their treatment of time, *all* Cavafy's poems can be said to belong to his third type, into which he once said his work could be divided, namely "philosophical" poetry.

—Roderick Beaton

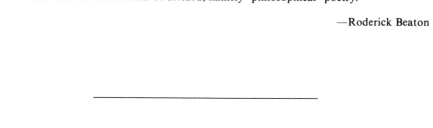

CAVALCANTI, Guido. Born in Florence, c. 1255; member of a Guelph merchant family. Engaged to Bice, a member of the Ghibelline family, in 1267. Guelph guarantor for a peace settlement, 1280; member of the general council of the commune, 1284 and 1290; banished for leading the white faction and confined to Sarzana, 1300. Friend of Dante whose *Vita nuova* was dedicated to him. *Died 29 August 1300.*

PUBLICATIONS

Verse

Rime, edited by Guido Favati. 1957; also edited by Marcello Ciccuto, 1978; translated by Dante Gabriel Rossetti, in *The Early Italian Poets*, 1861, revised edition, as *Dante and His Circle*, 1874; translated by Ezra Pound as *The Sonnets and Ballate*, 1912.

*

Critical Studies: *Cavalcanti's Theory of Love: The "Canzone d'Amore" and Other Related Problems* by J.E. Shaw, 1949; "Cavalcanti" by Ezra Pound, in *Literary Essays*, 1954; *Medieval Latin and the Rise of the European Love Lyric* by Peter Dronke, 2 vols., 1968; "Pound and Cavalcanti" by G. Singh, in *Essays in Honour of J.H. Whitfield*, 1975.

*   *   *

Cavalcanti's merit as a lyricist has never been overshadowed by the genius of his close friend Dante. A *Dolce Stil Novo* poet, he imposed on the conventions of that school his own particular individuality and moulded them to suit his own taste and poetic exigency. Ezra Pound, the creator of modern poetry, singled him out as an inspiration in his own poetry, and as an embodiment of something authentically modern. He put Cavalcanti in the same category as Sappho and Theocritus—poets who have sung, "not all the modes of life, but some of them, unsurpassedly; those who in their chosen or fated field have bowed to no one." What characterizes Cavalcanti's lyricism as such is the dramatic intensity of his passions and the consequent precision and individuality of diction in which it is couched, together with the conceptual depth and subtlety of his content. If, as Pound said, "no psychologist of emotions is more keen in his understanding, more precise in his expression" than Cavalcanti, it is both because he conveys the feelings, intuitions, and convictions of a highly individual mind and because of his use of a singularly concrete and specific language with no trace of conventional poeticalities.

Cavalcanti's concept of love too—love being the leitmotif of the *Dolce Stil Novo* school of poetry—is significantly different from that of a contemporary poet like Guinicelli, in that it is conceived more in earthly and sensuous terms than in mystical and transcendental ones, and the language Cavalcanti uses to describe or characterize it is direct and graphic rather than symbolic or abstract. And this in spite of the fact that he brought to bear on his treatment of love all his philosophic learning and intellectual curiosity, so that his similes, metaphors, and descriptions, even though they might at times appear to be arid and prosaic, always embody a definite concept or meaning as well as a fineness of perception. Apropos of this, Pound's evaluative comparison between Cavalcanti and Petrarch, or between Cavalcanti and Dante, is worth quoting. After noting how Cavalcanti "thought in accurate terms" and how his phrases "correspond to definite sensations undergone," Pound goes on to argue that in Guido "the 'figure', the strong metaphoric or 'picturesque' expression is there with purpose to convey or to interpret a definite meaning. In Petrarch it is ornament, the prettiest ornament he could find, but not an irreplaceable ornament, or one that he couldn't have used just about as well somewhere else." Pound's comparison between Cavalcanti and Dante too is equally illuminating—Dante "qui était diablement dans les idées reçues," Cavalcanti more independent and unconventional; Dante willing "to take on any sort of holy and orthodox furniture," Cavalcanti "eclectic," swallowing "none of his authors whole"; lastly, "Dante himself never wrote more poignantly, or with greater intensity than Cavalcanti...a spirit more imperious, more passionate, less likely to give ear to sophistries; his literary relation to Dante is not unlike Marlowe's to Shakespeare" (though, Pound himself adds, "such comparisons are always unsafe").

—G. Singh

CELAN

CELAN, Paul. Pseudonym for Paul Ancel. Born in Czernowitz, Bukovina, 23 November 1920. Educated at the Czernowitz Gymnasium; École de Médecine, Tours, France, 1938-39; University of Czernowitz, 1939-41; studied for a License-ès-Lettres in Paris, 1950. Married Gisèle Lestrange in 1952. In a forced labor camp during World War II; settled in Paris in 1948: language teacher and translator. Recipient: Bremen Literary Prize, 1958; Georg Büchner Prize, 1960; Nordrhein-Westfalen Prize, 1964. *Died* (suicide) *20 April 1970.*

PUBLICATIONS

Collections

Gedichte. 2 vols., 1975.

Verse

Der Sand aus den Urnen. 1948.
Mohn und Gedächtnis. 1952.
Von Schwelle zu Schwelle. 1955.
Sprachgitter. 1959.
Die Neimandsrose. 1963.
Atemwende. 1967.
Totnauberg. 1968.
Fadensonnen. 1968.
Lichtzwang. 1970.
Speech-Grille and Selected Poems, translated by Joachim Neugroschel. 1971.
Schneepart. 1971.
Selected Poems, translated by Michael Hamburger and Christopher Middleton. 1972.
Zeitgehoft: Späte Gedichte aus dem Nachlass. 1976.
Poems (bilingual edition), translated by Michael Hamburger. 1980.

Other

Edgar Jené und der Traum von Traume. 1948.
Der Meridian. 1961.

Translator (into Romanian), *Taranii,* by Chekhov. 1946.
Translator (into Romanian), *Un eroual timpalu,* by Lermontov. 1946.
Translator (into Romanian), *Chestinnea Rusa,* by Konstantin Simonov. 1947.
Translator, *Lehre vom Zerfall,* by E.M. Cioran. 1953.
Translator, *Die Zwölf,* by Blok. 1958.
Translator, *Das trunkene Schiff,* by Rimbaud. 1958.
Translator, *Gedichte,* by Mandelstam. 1959.
Translator, *Die junge Parze,* by Valéry. 1960.
Translator, *Gedichte,* by Essenin. 1961.
Translator, *Im Bereich einer Nacht,* by Jean Cayrol. 1961.
Translator, *Maigret und die schrecklichen Kinder; Hier irrt Maigret,* by Simenon. 1963.
Translator, *Dichtungen,* by Henri Michaux. 1966.
Translator, *Einundzwanzig Sonette,* by Shakespeare. 1967.
Translator, *Gedichte,* by Jules Supervielle. 1968.
Translator, *Vakante Glut: Gedichte,* by André du Bouchet. 1968.
Translator, *Das verheissene Land,* by Ungaretti. 1968.

*

Critical Studies: *Zur Lyrik Celans* by P.H. Neumann, 1968; *Über Celan* edited by Dietlind Meinecke, 1970, revised edition, 1973; *Celan* by Jerry Glenn, 1973; *Celans Poetik* by Gerhard Buhr, 1976; "Celan Issue" of *Text +Kritik 53-54* edited by H.L. Arnold, 1977.

*   *   *

Paul Celan is arguably the most important poet writing in German in the period after 1945. His poetry met with early and widespread recognition, although critics have always found difficulty in reconciling its manifestly superior stature—it has an immediate and haunting appeal—with its considerable resistance to interpretation.

Celan's complex poetic idiom is rooted in the Jewish-Hasidic mystical tradition of his ancestors, as also in the heritage of European Symbolism. The uncompromisingly reflexive nature of his language—as elusive as it is allusive—has, however, less in common with the hermeticism of Mallarmé's art, than with the extreme tendency towards internalisation that characterised the work of Hölderlin, Trakl, and Rilke.

Celan's poetry is a profoundly serious response to the darkest period of modern history, and a statement, too, of its own invalidity in such an age of crisis. One cannot afford to overlook the significance of Celan's position as a Jew writing in German after the Nazi holocaust; the poet's parents were among the millions who are mourned in countless of his poems. The most famous of these—"Todesfuge" (Death Fugue), in *Mohn und Gedächtnis* (Poppy and Memory)—superbly illustrates his ability to fuse the historically specific with the universal; to term his poetry political is indeed to underestimate its power and relevance, for, above all, the fate of the Jew in the Diaspora is for Celan a metaphor for the existential condition of humanity as a whole.

Acutely aware of the chasm dividing individual perception from the generalities of speech, which can convey but a "darkling splinterecho" of a distorted, fragmented reality, Celan's poetic voice withdraws into extreme semantic privacy. The metaphor of the "Sprachgitter" (Speech-Grille)—title of one poem and the collection in which it stands—is applicable to his poetry as a whole. Representing language as a complex framework which obstructs man's relation to reality, it is also a metaphor for the net of words and associations with which we attempt to capture that reality. Such paradox is central to Celan's art—cf. the title of his early collection *Mohn und Gedächtnis* (Poppy and Memory). As the bars of the grille delimit and connect empty spaces, so Celan used language to circumscribe the silent interstices between words. He was constantly preoccupied with the poem's precarious, marginal existence "on the verge of falling silent." However, his poetry remains essentially dialogic (between man and woman, Man and God, Life and Death—the situation is rarely fully defined), and this communicative quality constitutes a dimension of hope.

Celan's work does not allow of easy division into "phases": from the flowing rhythms and surrealistic imagery of *Mohn und Gedächtnis* it developed steadily towards increasing concentration and fragmentation, while continuing to draw and elaborate on a wide range of recurring metaphors and highly expressive neologisms, and making intricate use of repetition, allusion, antithesis, and paradox. The same features mark Celan's prose poem "Gespräch im Gebirg" (Conversation in the Mountains) (in *Neue Rundschau 71*, no. 2, 1960), which directly complements his theoretical discussion of his art in *Der Meridian* (Meridian).

—Andrea C. Cervi

CELESTINA, The. *See* **ROJAS, Fernando de.**

CÉLINE, Louis-Ferdinand. Pseudonym for Louis-Ferdinand Destouches. Born in Cour-
bevoie, France 27 May 1894. Educated at a school in Paris; Diepholz Volkschule in Germany, 1908; a school in Rochester, Kent, 1909; worked as a clerk in a silk shop, an errand boy in
Paris and Nice, and for a goldsmith while studying for his baccalaureate; Rennes Medical
School, 1919-24, qualified as doctor 1924. Married 1) Edith Follet in 1919 (divorced, 1928), one
daughter; 2) Lucette Almanzoe in 1943. Served in the French cavalry, 1912-15: sergeant;
military medal; worked in French passport office, London, 1915; worked as ship's doctor,
1939-40. Practicing doctor: in Rennes, then with League of Nations, in Geneva and abroad, to
1928; in Paris, privately to 1931, then in municipal clinic to 1939; in Bezons 1940-44, Germany,
1944-45, and Denmark, 1945; imprisoned in Denmark, 1945-47; returned to France in 1950:
found guilty of collaboration with Germany during World War II, and sentenced to 1 year in
prison: pardoned in 1951; then lived in Meudon, near Paris. Recipient: Priz Renaudot, 1933.
Died 1 July 1961.

PUBLICATIONS

Collections

  Oeuvres complètes, edited by Henri Godard. 2 vols., 1962-74.
  Oeuvres, edited by Jean Ducourneau. 5 vols., 1966-69.

Fiction

  Voyage au bout de la nuit. 1932; revised edition, 1952; as *Journey to the End of the
    Night,* 1934; revised edition, 1983.
  Mort à crédit. 1936; as *Death on the Installment Plan,* 1938.
  Guignol's Band. 1944; translated as *Guignol's Band,* 1950.
  Féerie pour une autre fois. 1952.
  Normance. 1954.
  D'un château à l'autre. 1957; as *Castle to Castle,* 1968.
  Nord. 1960; as *North,* 1972.
  Le Pont de Londres. 1963.
  Rigadon. 1969; translated as *Rigadoon,* 1974.

Plays

  L'Église. 1933.
  Ballets, sans musique, sans personne, sans rien (includes *La Naissance d'une fée* and
    Voyou Paul, Pauvre Virginie). 1959.
  Progrès. 1978.

114

Other

La Quinine en therapeutique. 1925.
Mea Culpa, suivi de La Vie et l'oeuvre de Semmelweis. 1936; as *Mea Culpa and the Life and Work of Semmelweis,* 1937.
Bagatelles pour un massacre. 1937.
L'École des cadavres. 1938.
Les beaux draps. 1941.
A l'agité du bocal. 1948.
Foudres et flèches. 1948.
Casse-pipe. 1949.
Scandale aux abysses. 1950.
Entretiens avec le Professor Y. 1955.
Cahiers. 1976— .

*

Critical Studies: *Céline* by David Hayman, 1965; *Céline and His Vision* 1967, and *Voyeur Voyant: A Portrait of Céline,* 1971, both by Erika Ostrovsky; *Céline: The Novel as Delirium* by Allen Thiher, 1972; *Céline, Man of Hate* by Bettina Knapp, 1974; *Céline* by Patrick McCarthy, 1975; *Céline* by David O'Connell, 1976; *Céline* by Merlin Thomas, 1979.

*   *   *

Louis-Ferdinand Céline emerged as a great writer in 1932 with his first novel, *Journey to the End of the Night.* Although the early pages, which depict the carnage of the First World War and hallucinatory journeys to Africa and America, are more brilliant and were responsible for the book's immediate success, the second half of the book may be of greater significance. The doctor-hero, Bardamu, undertakes a quest to understand and absorb the suffering of modern life, which allows Céline to demonstrate not merely the collapse of traditional values but the inadequacy of traditional fiction with its reliance on plot, rounded characters, and familiar language.

So in *Death on the Installment Plan* he dismembers his sentences and introduces a tide of Parisian slang which is meant more as a lyrical than as a realistic device. This novel reverses the conventional view of childhood in order to depict the pain the child undergoes as he awakens to his surroundings, and the broken rhythms, the slang, and the obscenity permit Céline to render the child's world with great immediacy.

Obsessed with his own nightmares and convinced that another world war was imminent, Céline then wrote his pamphlets *Bagatelles pour un massacre* (Bagatelles for a Massacre) and *L'École des cadavres* (School for Corpses). Although their message is appalling, they are an integral part of his work and cannot be ignored. The solution to Hitler's threat is, Céline maintains, appeasement and the author of all the world's evil is the Jew. Whereas evil in Céline's novels is not so easily explained away for it is inherent in the human condition, here it is personified in the figure of the Jew. During the Occupation Céline remained in France and continued to publish and, while in no sense a leading collaborator, he certainly helped the cause of anti-semitism.

For this reason his work was banned at the Liberation, was afterwards long neglected and has only in the last 15 years been widely read. His later novels are generally considered to be less good than the early ones, but one of them, *Féerie pour une autre fois* (Fairytale for Another Time), is a fascinating work which is an investigation both of the Second World War and of artistic creation itself. Céline attempts to incorporate into the novel other arts like painting and film while giving pride of place to the ballet. Art is depicted as making and unmaking the universe, and its demonic, destructive quality is emphasized, although the role of the ballet-dancer is to restore harmony. In this novel Céline created a multiple work of art that is not governed by a single point of view and invites many different readings.

The only one of his later novels to be appreciated in his lifetime was *Castle to Castle*, a satire of the collaborators and a good example of Céline's black humour. In general Céline was the voice of the 1930's and 1940's who sought to express with a novel intensity the violence of his age. But he was also a consummate artist whose experiments with the language and structure of novels have influenced contemporary writers, both French and foreign.

—Patrick McCarthy

CERVANTES (Saavedra), Miguel de. Born in Alcala de Henares, 29 September 1547. Studied in Valladolid, and probably in Seville and Madrid. Married Catalina de Salazar y Palacios in 1584; had one daughter by Ana Franca de Rojas. Entered the service of Cardinal Acquaviva in Italy, 1569; soldier by 1570: participated in naval battle of Lepanto, 1571: wounded; later expeditions to Corfu, Navarino, and Tunis, then in garrisons at Palermo and Naples to 1575; imprisoned by Turks, 1575-80: ransomed, 1580; back in Spain, tax collector and purchasing agent (excommunicated briefly in 1587 for commercial zeal); bankruptcy and two short prison terms (1597, 1602) indicate his financial difficulties; lived in Madrid after c. 1606. *Died 23 April 1616.*

PUBLICATIONS

Collections

Obras completas, edited by R. Schevill and A. Benilla y San Martin.　16 vols., 1914-41.
Obras completas, edited by Angel Valbuena Prat.　2 vols., 1967.
Complete Works, edited by James Fitzmaurice-Kelly.　1901-03.
The Portable Cervantes, edited and translated by Samuel Putnam.　1947.

Fiction

La Galatea.　1585; translated as *La Galatea*, 1867.
El ingenioso hidalgo Don Quixote de la Mancha.　2 vols., 1605-15; edited by Francisco Rodríguez Marín, 8 vols., 1911; as *Don Quixote*, translated by Thomas Shelton, 1612, Samuel Putnam, 1949, and J.M. Cohen, 1950.
Novelas ejemplares.　1613; as *Exemplary Novels*, translated by C.A. Jones, 1972.
Los trabajos de Persiles y Sigismunda.　1617; as *The Travels of Persiles and Sigismunda*, 1619.

Plays

Ocho comedias y ocho entremeses nuevos.　1615.
La Numancia, El trato de argel (with *Viage al Parnaso*).　1784.
Entremeses, edited by Miguel Herrero Garcia.　1945.
Interludes, translated by Edwin Honig.　1964.

Verse

El viage al Parnaso. 1614.

*

Bibliography: *Cervantes: A Bibliography* by R.L. Grismer, 1946.

Critical Studies: *Cervantes in Arcadia* by J.B Trend, 1954; *Don Quixote's Profession* by Mark Van Doren, 1958; *Don Quixote: An Introductory Essay in Psychology* by Salvador de Mandariaga, 1961; *Cervantes's Theory of the Novel* by Edward C. Riley, 1962; *Cervantes and the Art of Fiction* by George D. Trotter, 1965; *Cervantes: A Collection of Critical Essays* edited by L. Nelson, Jr., 1969; *Cervantes, The Man and the Genius* by Francisco Navarro y Ledesma, 1973; *The Romantic Approach to Don Quixote* by Anthony Close, 1978; *Cervantes: A Biography* by William Byron, 1978; *Cervantes and the Humanist Vision: A Study of Four Exemplary Novels* by Alban K. Forcione, 1982.

*   *   *

Biographers and critics of Miguel de Cervantes have been no less fascinated by his remarkable life and personality than by the quality of his literary work. Few of our great geniuses have been more stringently treated by luck or fortune, and fewer still have born life's ill will with greater magnanimity and creative resignation. Cervantes suffered, precisely in the period which for most men offers the opportunity to build a foundation for their future lives, the most arduous fate that might befall a Spaniard of his times: five years of imprisonment and slavery under the Moors in Algeria, from the age of 28 to 33. His heroism as a soldier in the battle of Lepanto and other encounters with the Turks had been rewarded with highly laudatory letters of recommendation. On the basis of these commendations, his captors set a correspondingly high price for his ransom.

When this was finally achieved, and he returned to Spain, he found that his exploits were not to be rewarded with favoritism in the Court. He was a valiant but minor hero of battles now forgotten. The wounded veteran, now well into the fourth decade of his life, decided to pursue a literary career and very consciously modeled his early works on currently popular genres. The pastoral novel was enjoying vogue, and his first novel, *La Galatea*, was cast in that mode. Few read the work today, but it was certainly among the best of the Spanish mannerist style and represented fertile possibilities to this new author, who prided himself on his elegant prose style, his gift for dialogue and plot, and his ability as a poet. *La Galatea* was an ample showcase for these talents, and to the end of his life the author promised a continuation of the novel, but it was never written.

Cervantes proved to be an untalented literary businessman. He was never able to make his living by the pen, although most of his works had moderate success for the period, and translations and pirated editions, while they brought him no income, established his name quite firmly in the literary world. He was forced to seek his livelihood with commissions as a tax collector and purchasing agent for the Spanish government. Through bad management or actual misappropriation, he was twice imprisoned—a popular conjecture is that he wrote the early chapters of *Don Quixote* in the infamous dungeons of Seville—and he was briefly excommunicated for expropriating grain from Church stores.

While pursuing such minor bureaucratic and commercial occupations, Cervantes seems never to have stopped writing—poetry, plays, short comedies, some works of prose. Much of his early work is lost, but it is doubtful that it would have added much of value to the Cervantine corpus we have. The writer did not prize very highly the forgotten plays and poetry that he refers to in passing, and he had little success even with those works which were produced. Better dramatic writers than he—especially Lope de Vega—had "run off with the monarchy of the theatre," and his poetry, he admitted ruefully, was never of the highest quality.

Cervantes's talent lay above all in narration, in the novel, a genre which was just achieving solidity and definition at the beginning of the 17th century. He claims in the prologue to his *Exemplary Novels* that he is the first to "novelize" in Castilian, a boast that is only partly true. The *novella* was well established in Italy and had been introduced to Spain at least half a century earlier in the form of very short narrative pieces taken from a variety of sources, and Mateo Alemán, his contemporary, had intercalated *novelas* in his picaresque work *Gusmán de Alfarache* (1599; 1604). But it is true that Cervantes brought wholly new dimensions to the form in terms of giving each of the twelve tales autonomy and a much broader development of plot and character.

El ingenioso hidalgo Don Quixote de la Mancha, which began as a parody of the popular books of chivalry, was his superb creation. The immense body of critical examination and eulogy stresses his perspectivism, his ability to create character, contrast, and believable dialogue; his comprehensive knowledge of his own time and of the currents of the age, and the tone of optimistic good humor and moral clarity which characterizes his treatment of the society of his time. *Don Quixote* is frequently referred to as the first modern novel, and very rightly so. It is the first extensive work of narrative fiction conceived on a grand scale which engages the reader with basic human questions of integrity, folly, social honesty, moralistic delusion, idealism, practical interest, basic concepts of justice, and the strengths and weaknesses of our best resolve. It is certainly the first work of western literature to offer the reader a world view and, as well as telling him an involved and entertaining story, invites him to think about life and experience in very broad terms.

The first part of *Don Quixote* (1605) had very wide success, but Cervantes had sold his rights to the book for a ridiculously small sum of money. He had begun the promised second part of the novel when a plagiarist published a spurious continuation (1614), probably based on an incomplete manuscript which Cervantes had allowed to circulate in the literary court of Madrid. The real identity of the plagiarist is still unknown, but the apocryphal work, not entirely without merit, is decidedly inferior to the first part of *Don Quixote* or to Cervantes's own continuation (1615). The authentic second part abandons much of the parodic quality with which the novel had begun, to enquire more deeply into the nature of human consciousness, faith in ourselves and beyond ourselves, and the moral perspectives by which we live. Most critics have seen more conceptual depth in the second part, but it is the first which continues to be more widely read and which forms the basis for our English adaptation of the word "quixotic."

Cervantes was a writer totally, perhaps obsessively, committed to his craft, and it is with the urgency of impending death that he completed his last novel, *The Travels of Persiles and Sigismunda*, a rambling account of adventures, separations, reunions, and recognitions, a form rare in Spanish Golden Age literature: the Byzantine novel. He had long planned the work, and had extravagant hopes for its success. Aware that his time was mercilessly short, Cervantes was forced to write the last chapters hurriedly. Perhaps the last strokes of his pen were the lines of the dedicatory prologue to the Count of Lemos, which quote an ancient poem which begins, "puesto ya el pie en el estribo"—"with one foot already placed in death's stirrup." This last book was not a success either in popular or critical terms, although many later Cervantists have sought to find value in the work.

Cervantes must be read and reread in his masterpieces, not sought in his minor works, where so many flaws are overwhelmingly evident to the most ingenuous and tolerant eye. These great works are half a dozen of the *Exemplary Novels* and, above all in western literature of the 17th century, the two parts of *Don Quixote*, where the incredible mind of Cervantes lays bare the human soul in all of its possibilities for good, for hope, and for imaginative moral creation.

—James Russell Stamm

CHATEAUBRIAND, François René August, Vicomte de. Born in Saint-Malo, France, 4 September 1768. Attended schools in Saint-Malo and Dol, 1777-81; Collège de Rennes, 1781-83; Collège de Dinan, 1783-84. Married Céleste Buisson de la Vigne in 1792. Entered the army, 1786; visited America, 1791-92; served in the Prussian army briefly, 1792; taught French in Beccles and Bungay, Suffolk, 1792-1800; returned to France and joined state service: Secretary to Embassy in Rome, 1802; appointed Chargé d'Affaires to Swiss canton of Valais, 1804, but resigned, 1804; appointed Minister of Interior of Government in exile, 1815, and Ambassador to Sweden (not taken up); honorary Minister of State, 1815-16; made Peer of France, 1815, and President of Electoral College of Orleans, 1815; Envoy Extraordinary to Berlin, 1820; Ambassador to London, 1822; attended Congress of Verona, 1822; Minister of Foreign Affairs, 1822; Ambassador to Rome, 1828. Editor, *Le Mercure*, 1800's. Many women friends, especially Mme. Récamier. Member, French Academy, 1815. *Died 4 July 1848.*

PUBLICATIONS

Collections

Oeuvres complètes. 31 vols., 1826-31, and later revised editions.
Oeuvres romanesques et voyages, edited by Maurice Regard. 2 vols., 1969.

Fiction

Atala; ou, Les Amours de deux savages dans le désert. 1801; edited by J.M. Gautier, 1973; translated as *Atala*, 1802.
René; ou, Les Effets des passions. 1802; edited by Armand Weil, 1947; edited by J.M. Gautier, 1970; as *René: A Tale*, 1813.
Les Martyrs; ou, Le Triomphe de la religion chrétienne. 1809; original version edited by B. d'Andlau, 1951; as *The Two Martyrs*, 1819; as *The Martyrs*, 1859.
Les Aventures du dernier Abencérage, in *Oeuvres complètes.* 1826; as *The Last of the Abencérages*, 1826.
Les Natchez. 1827; edited by G. Chinard, 1932; as *The Natchez*, 1827.

Other

Essai historique, politique, et moral sur les révolutions anciennes et modernes. 1797; edited by Maurice Regard, 1978.
Génie du christianisme; ou, Beautés de la religion chrétienne. 5 vols., 1802; edited by Maurice Regard, 1978; as *The Beauties of Christianity*, 3 vols., 1813; as *The Genius of Christianity*, 1856.
Itinéraire de Paris à Jérusalem et de Jérusalem à Paris. 3 vols., 1811; as *Travels in Greece, Palestine, Egypt, and Barbary*, 2 vols., 1812.
De Buonaparte et des Bourbons. 1814.
Réflexions politiques. 1814; as *Political Reflections*, 1814.
Mélanges de politique. 2 vols., 1816.
De la monarchie selon la charte. 1816; as *The Monarchy According to the Charter*, 1816.
Mémoires, lettres, et pièces authentiques touchant la vie et la mort du duc de Berry. 1820.
Maison de France; ou, Recueil de pièces relatives à la légitimité et à la famille royale. 2 vols., 1825.
Voyage en Amerique, Voyage en Italie. 2 vols., 1827; as *Travels in America and Italy*, 2 vols., 1828.

Mélanges et poésies. 1828.
Études ou discours historiques sur la chute de l'empire romain, la naissance et les progrès du christianisme, et l'invasion des barbares. 4 vols., 1831.
Mémoires sur la captivité de Mme. la duchesse de Berry. 1833.
La Vie de Rancé. 1844; edited by Fernand Letessier, 1955.
Les Mémoires d'outre-tombe. 12 vols., 1849-50; edited by Maurice Levaillant and Georges Moulinier, 2 vols., 1951; translated as *Memoirs,* 3 vols., 1848; complete version, 1902; selections edited by Robert Baldick, 1961.
Souvenirs d'enfance et de jeunesse. 1874.
Correspondance générale, edited by Louis Thomas. 5 vols., 1912-24.
Le Roman de l'occitanienne et de Chateaubriand (letters). 1925.
Lettres à la comtesse de Castellane. 1927.
Lettres à Mme. Récamier pendant son ambassade à Rome, edited by Emm. Beau de Loménie. 1929.
Lettres à Mme. Récamier, edited by Maurice Levaillant. 1951.
Mémoires de ma vie: Manuscript de 1826, edited by J.M. Gautier. 1976.
Correspondance générale, edited by Pierre Riberette. 1977— .

Translator, *Le Paradis perdu,* by Milton. 2 vols., 1836.

*

Critical Studies: Société Chateaubriand *Bulletin,* 1930— ; *Chateaubriand, Poet, Statesman, and Lover* by Andre Maurois, 1938; *Chateaubriand: A Biography* by Joan Evans, 1939; *Chateaubriand* by Friedrich Sieburg, 1961; *Chateaubriand* by Richard Switzer, 1971; *Chateaubriand: A Biography* by George D. Painter, vol. 1, 1977; *Chateaubriand: Composition, Imagination, and Poetry* by Charles A. Porter, 1978.

*   *   *

Chateaubriand's dozen and a half major works and copious tracts, discourses, and parliamentary opinions appeared during that most political half-century beginning with the Revolution and ending with the fall of the July Monarchy. His most original narratives portray the emotions and yearnings of the Romantic self amid historical European landscapes or against the background of the North American wilderness. In his vigorous and wide-ranging polemical writings he argues the Christian and royalist cause with sarcasm and an idealistic vision. His major literary distinction has been as a stylist.

Not all Chateaubriand's narrative writings are frankly autobiographical. The figure of the brooding, proud, aristocratic European in the post-Revolutionary world, partially discernable in the American Indian brave, Chactas of *Atala* and *Les Natchez,* appears more clearly as the protagonist of Chateaubriand's best-known story, *René,* confession of a self-exiled Frenchman in the American forest in the early 18th century. The life of the 17th-century Trappist serves in the late *Vie de Rancé* as the locus of curious digressions about both Chateaubriand and 17th-century France. *L'Itinéraire de Paris à Jérusalem* is Chateaubriand's first autobiographical book. His most important work, composed and often refashioned over 30 years into the 1840's, is his autobiography, *Les Mémoires d'Outre-Tombe.*

Much of the charm of Chateaubriand's narratives comes from evocative descriptions and the metaphors and complex rhythms of his prose. His descriptions of America in the "Indian" works, and of his childhood Brittany, Rome, the Near East in the autobiographical writings, present a nearly seamless web of memories of earlier travel accounts, his own personal observation, and, no doubt, brilliant invention: scholars will continue to differ over how much of the America he described he ever actually saw. His descriptive prose, characterized by visual detail and suggestive, often exotic names, is arranged in rhythmically ordered sentences and chapters. His polemical writings scan more like oratory; there too nouns and figures of speech focus the meaning. The château de Chambord, with all its chimneys, is personified in the *Vie de*

Rancé as "une femme dont le vent aurait soufflé en l'air la chevelure" (a woman with wind-blown hair); in 1815 in Louis XVIII's antechamber he sees a "vision infernale": Talleyrand supported by Fouché "le vice appuyé sur le bras du crime" (vice leaning on crime's arm).

The force of his narratives stems from their subtle analysis of the difficulties of modern life: how to be both an aristocrat and a leader in the new democratic world, appreciate the beauties of religion in the age of science, live true to one's own sensibilities without shirking one's duties toward others. Unfortunately the autobiography—though not the autobiographical fictions—is weakened by Chateaubriand's determination to hide almost everything intimate, including his many passionate liaisons. The strength of the polemical writings lies in their juxtaposition of noble themes—fidelity, honor, national pride—with a quick, savage denunciation of posturing and opportunism.

Abundance characterizes his rhetoric; his writing displays ease and vigor in invention, high color, passion and sentiment. Admiration, anger, scorn, enthusiasm animate sometimes flowing, sometimes cadenced and elaborate prose. The criticism though often harsh is never mean, the praise though sentimental is grand, and the ever-present portrait of the self is pompous, often insincere, indiscreetly long—and lucid, probing, subtle, and finally very moving.

—Charles A. Porter

CHEKHOV, Anton (Pavlovich). Born in Taganrog, 17 January 1860. Educated at a school for Greek boys, Taganrog, 1867-68; Taganrog grammar school, 1868-79; Moscow University Medical School, 1879-84, graduated as doctor 1884. Married the actress Olga Knipper in 1901. Practicing doctor in Moscow, 1884-92, Melikhovo, 1892-99, and in Yalta after 1899. Free-lance writer while still in medical school, especially for humorous magazines, and later for serious ones. Recipient: Pushkin Prize, 1888. Member, Imperial Academy of Sciences, 1900 (resigned, 1902). *Died 2 July 1904.*

PUBLICATIONS

Collections

Polnoye sobraniye sochineniy i pisem [Complete Works and Letters], edited by S.D. Balukhaty and others. 20 vols., 1944-51; a new edition, 30 vols., 1974—.
The Oxford Chekhov, edited by Ronald Hingley. 9 vols., 1964-80; excerpts as *Seven Stories,* 1974, and *Eleven Stories,* 1975.

Plays

Ivanov (produced 1887; revised version, produced 1889). In *P'esy,* 1897; translated as *Ivanov,* in *Plays 1,* 1912.
Lebedinaya pesnya (produced 1888). In *P'esy,* 1897; as *Swan Song,* in *Plays 1,* 1912.
Medved' (produced 1888). 1888; as *The Bear,* 1909; as *The Boor,* 1915.
Leshy (produced 1889). 1890; as *The Wood Demon,* 1926.

Predlozheniye (produced 1889).   1889; as *A Marriage Proposal*, 1914.
Svad'ba (produced 1890).   1889; as *The Wedding*, in *Plays 2*, 1916.
Dyadya Vanya (produced 1896).   In *P'esy*, 1897; as *Uncle Vanya*, in *Plays 1*, 1912.
Chayka (produced 1896).   In *P'esy*, 1897; revised version (produced 1898), 1904; as *The Seagull*, in *Plays 1*, 1912.
Tri sestry (produced 1901).   1901; as *The Three Sisters*, in *Plays 2*, 1916.
Vishnyovy sad (produced 1904).   1904; as *The Cherry Orchard*, 1908.
Neizdannaya p'esa, edited by N.F. Belchikov.   1923; as *That Worthless Fellow Platonov*, 1930; as *Don Juan (in the Russian Manner)*, 1952; as *Platonov*, 1964.

Fiction

Pyostrye rasskazy [Motley Tales].   1886; revised edition, 1891.
V sumerkakh [In the Twilight].   1887.
Nevinnye rechi [Innocent Tales].   1887.
Rasskazy [Tales].   1889.
Khmurye lyudi [Gloomy People].   1890.
Duel [The Duel].   1892.
Palata No. 6 [Ward No. 6].   1893.
Tales (translated by Constance Garnett).   13 vols., 1916-22.
The Unknown Chekhov: Stories and Other Writings Hitherto Untranslated, edited by A. Yarmolinsky.   1954.
Early Stories.   1960.
Chuckle with Chekhov: A Selection of Early Stories.   1975.
The Early Stories 1883-1888, edited by Patrick Miles and Harvey Pitcher.   1983.

Other

Ostrov Sakhalin [Sakhalin Island].   1895.
Sobraniye sochineniy.   11 vols., 1899-1906.
Pis'ma [Letters].   1909; *Sobraniye pis'ma*, 1910; *Pis'ma*, 1912-16, and later editions.
Zapisnye knizhki.   1914; as *The Note-Books*, 1921.
Letters to Olga Knipper.   1925.
Literary and Theatrical Reminiscences, edited by S.S. Koteliansky.   1927.
Personal Papers.   1948.
Letters, edited by Simon Karlinsky.   1973.

*

Bibliography: *Chekhov in English: A List of Works by and about Him* edited by Anna Heifetz and A. Yarmolinsky, 1949; *The Chekhov Centennial: Chekhov in English: A Selective List of Works by and about Him 1949-60* by Rissa Yachnin, 1960.

Critical Studies: *Chekhov: A Biographical and Critical Study*, 1950, and *A New Life of Chekhov*, 1976, both by Ronald Hingley; *Chekhov: A Biography* by Ernest J. Simmons, 1962; *The Breaking String: The Plays of Anton Chekhov* by Maurice Valency, 1966; *Chekhov and His Prose* by Thomas Winner, 1966; *Chekhov: A Collection of Critical Essays* edited by Robert Louis Jackson, 1967; *Chekhov in Performance: A Commentary on the Major Plays* by J.L. Styan, 1971; *The Chekhov Play: A New Interpretation* by Harvey Pitcher, 1973; *Chekhov: The Evolution of His Art* by Donald Rayfield, 1975; *Chekhov: A Study of the Major Stories and Plays* by B. Hahn, 1977; *Chekhov* by Irina Kirk, 1981; *Chekhov: The Critical Heritage* edited by Victor Emeljanow, 1981; *Chekhov and the Vaudeville: A Study of Chekhov's One-Act Plays* by Vera Gottlieb, 1982; *Chekhov: A Study of the Four Major Plays* by Richard Peace, 1983.

*   *   *

The leading exponent of the short story and the drama in modern Russian literature, which is otherwise dominated by poetry and the novel, Chekhov began to write for money while he was a medical student. The majority of his early comic stories are characterised by the muddles and confusions of life. They portray overweening Russian respect for authority and hilarious conflicts between the sexes and the generations, in which the expected "triggers" of social occasions, chance meetings, love entanglements and relatives, children and animals rarely fail to appear. Nevertheless, the best of these stories already illustrate the serious aspects of Chekhov's vision. "The Death of a Clerk" is a reworking of Gogolian menace. "Daughter of Albion," "The Upheaval," and "Sleepy" all explore the relationship between master and servant. None of these is actually funny: the first two reveal the humiliation of servants, while the third is an early demonstration of Chekhov's ability to conjure horror out of commonplace situations, as the exhausted girl servant unemotionally smothers her masters' crying baby. Chekhov's medical training, to be evident later in the illnesses which afflict many of his characters, influences his study of adolescence, "Volodya," with its themes of corruption, sexuality, and suicide. In stories such as "The Huntsman," "Happiness," and "The Steppe" Chekhov showed his ability to describe the natural settings and atmosphere of rural Russia, featuring within them episodic moments of communication between man and his world or between men themselves against a background of silence, emptiness, and timelessness.

Later, the comic element in Chekhov ceases to be the framework of an attitude to life and becomes instead the sometimes relieving, always revealing observation, a perception of the continuity of life and of man's remarkable ability to endure it. In the stories of 1888-96 the still young Chekhov captures the loss of momentum in middle age ("A Dreary Story"). The grim "Ward Number Six" and "The Black Monk" study psychological alienation, while other stories explore sexual relations. A wife's abuse of a weak, loving husband in "The Butterfly" is complemented by the wife's triumph over her husband in "The Order of St. Anne." In "The Artist's Story" romance itself is shown to be imbued with misunderstanding, potential disaster, and the loss of opportunity. The most positive story of this period is undoubtedly "The Student," in which myth and beauty inspire a moment of communication against the background of an atmospherically evoked rural evening and the passage of centuries.

In Chekhov's last years stories of loneliness and isolation reveal fear of life ("A Hard Case"), the sadness of missed opportunities for happiness ("Concerning Love"), and estrangement ("The Bishop"). Chekhov also exposes the suffocating power of bourgeois self-satisfaction, materialism, and philistinism that is contained in the one Russian word *poshlost'*: this is what overcomes the vitality of Startsev in "Ionych" and what permeates the life of Olga Semenovna in "The Darling." In "A Case History" the gentry shelter helplessly from the world of peasant-workers and alien factories, while "The Peasants" and "In the Hollow" take us to the primitive world of the peasant and the kulak. Here materialism and greed emerge as violent weapons by which the strong abuse the weak. One of Chekhov's last stories is perhaps his best creation, "The Lady with a Dog": for once, a story of mature love, of genuine communication and self-sacrifice, in which the characters respect each other enough to face their uncertain future consciously and courageously.

Chekhov's "vaudevilles," his comic one-act plays (such as *The Bear* and *A Marriage Proposal*), are mainly dramatised encounters, in which human feelings and follies undermine the solemnity of social occasions and rituals. Here, as in the major plays, dialogue and the revelation of character and atmosphere predominate over event. The major plays themselves, the foundation of Chekhov's Western reputation, give dramatic form to the themes of the later stories. The way in which history overtakes the gentry is illustrated in Chekhov's bewildered central characters as they confront their own failure, the success of others, and the new strangeness of the world beyond their estates. Characters "in mourning for their lives" immerse themselves in nostalgia, petty rivalries, games, and hopeless dreaming or planning, while the forces of *poshlost'* and social change threaten their way of life and their future. The pathos and bathos of the unloved pervade *The Seagull*, while *Uncle Vanya* traces the erosion of hopes and dreams by age and failure. The despair of provincial life is all too evident in *The Three Sisters*, but this play also shows how the characters' own self-indulgences and self-delusions frustrate their yearning for "Moscow." Finally, in *The Cherry Orchard*, the axes are being sharpened not just for trees, but for the softer material of a self-obsessed gentry that has lost the will to resist.

Chekhov does not abandon plot altogether, but he creates a startling division between the extreme events of his plays, whether on or off stage (suicide, duel, attempted murder, fire, and death), and the spelling-out through stage direction, dialogue, and sub-text of the ironies of man's hopes and fears. The atmosphere created by the chartacters' inertia, the sounds of their surroundings, and their own silences resonates at one moment with amusement, affectation, and confusion and at the next with bitterness, recrimination, and loss. Chekhov's integration of these resonances into frameworks of "everyday life" was a major dramatic innovation, one which was not accomplished without difficulty or with complete success. The balance between laughter and tears is sometimes too precarious in these plays, the relationship between exposition and natural discourse too artificial. Nevertheless, they are dramatic masterpieces, which have been of most significant influence on 20th-century Western drama.

Throughout, Chekhov preserved his humanity and his practical activity. Continuing to practice frequently as a doctor, he made a remarkable journey in 1890 across Siberia to visit the penal colony on Sakhalin Island, later producing an extensive account of conditions there, and in 1892 he helped in famine relief (as did Tolstoy). Although he was not devoid of the prejudices and shortcomings of his age, the simplicity, modesty, and gentle but firm truthfulness of Chekhov's vision mark him out among modern Russian writers.

—Christopher R. Pike

CHIN P'ING MEI (*Golden Lotus*).

PUBLICATIONS

Fiction

Chin P'ing Mei tz'uhua.   21 vols., 1933; reprinted, 1963.
The Golden Lotus, translated by Clement Egerton.   4 vols., 1939.
Chin P'ing Mei: The Adventurous History of Hsi Men and His Six Wives, translated by Bernard Miall from a German version.   1939.

*

Critical Studies: *The Classic Chinese Novel* by C.T. Hsia, 1968.

*   *   *

The dating and authorship of the *Chin P'ing Mei*, or *Golden Lotus*, are a mystery. The novel's first known circulation was in manuscript form and goes back to the 1590's, its first printing to about 1617. The author was perhaps a well-known literary figure but kept his name secret because of the erotic contents of the work. He seems to have written his novel over an extended period of time, and, because of certain glaring inconsistencies, not even to have finished it. It may safely be said that he wrote in the second half of the 16th century (though some scholars say earlier), the beginning of an especially productive period in the history of Chinese fiction.

Golden Lotus, of one hundred chapters, is about a wealthy but un-educated merchant named Hsi-men Ch'ing whose main activities consist of celebrating with friends and sleeping with concubines, courtesans, and other people's wives (his name may be translated as "Celebrations at the Gate of Death"). The novel starts with an episode of adultery (lifted from another important 16th-century novel, *Water Margin*) in which he and his paramour, P'an Chin-lien (her name translates as Golden Lotus), poison her husband in order to bring her into the Hsi-men household. After this he steals yet another man's wife, Li P'ing-er, whom he then favors over the jealous and insatiable P'an Chin-lien. Li Ping-er's status soon rises when she bears him his first son, but she and the son die within a year, mainly due to the plotting of P'an Chin-lien. The inconsolable Hsi-men Ch'ing enters the last stretch of his life. Having already obtained a marvelous aphrodisiac from a Buddhist monk, he has been all along expanding the sphere of his sexual activities. But after Li P'ing-er's death he gradually allows both sexual and financial powers to drain away, and finally dies when P'an Chin-lien accidentally gives him a lethal overdose of the aphrodisiac. The last quarter of the novel tells of the decline of his estate, the dispersal or death of its members, and the survival of his main wife Yueh-niang and his only son by her, Hsiao-ko, who is Hsi-men's reincarnation and who ends by becoming a monk.

Golden Lotus is unique among other novels of the period because of the fact that its story matter is largely the creation of a single author. To be sure, the novel absorbs many sources (including current popular song, drama, and short story, not to mention the initial episode from *Water Margin*), which are at times quoted verbatim; but it is common for the Chinese novel to do so. For that matter, the reader of *Golden Lotus* should not expect a high degree of uniformity in style, plot sequence, or characterization. Scene changes are often extremely abrupt. The author uses diverse styles and language. Character types seem redundant with one another and individual characters seem inconsistent within themselves.

But upon close examination the novel betrays an astounding degree of unity and organization, particularly if one is attuned to certain generic features of Chinese fiction and discursive prose. Most important of these features are the techniques of interlocking patterns of recurrence and alternation. In the 16th century such compositional techniques were central to prose theory and criticism and were reflected in both structural and imagistic layers of the text. In the *Golden Lotus*, for example, on a simple structural level, the novel consists of a first half in which the narrative world is steadily filled-in and a second in which it is emptied. In addition, polar images of heat and cold frequently accompany scenes of prosperity and decline, or sexual frenzy and frustration or depletion. At times a cold figure is used as an ironic comment on an otherwise hot scene. Recurrence with variation is also common, a notable example of which is the image of the woman on top of the man. At the beginning of the novel, when P'an Chin-lien has poisoned her husband, she smothers him with a blanket while straddling his body. Later she is astride the semi-conscious Hsi-men Ch'ing when she gives him his fatal overdose of the aphrodisiac. Finally, at the end, after P'an is dead, her maid Ch'un-mei (who continues in her footsteps) dies of sexual exhaustion while in the superior position.

Golden Lotus is most renowned as a pornographic novel and has been therefore censored throughout its history. But despite such a reputation there are in fact relatively few scenes which portray sex in a positive way. Sexuality is essentially the scene of a battle in which opponents attempt to score gains and recover losses. On a large scale, this battle is symbolic of all social struggle depicted in the book. It is remarkable that this novel took advantage of eroticism at such an early point in the history of Chinese vernacular fiction, especially since to this day (in contrast to the West) eroticism has been absent from all great Chinese art.

—Keith McMahon

CHRÉTIEN de TROYES

CHRÉTIEN de Troyes. Almost nothing is known of his life; because of dedications of his works, it is commonly assumed that he knew or served Countess Marie de Champagne at her court in Troyes and Philip of Alsace, Count of Flanders; works were probably written in the 1170's and 1180's.

PUBLICATIONS

Collections

Sämtliche Werke, edited by Wendelin Foerster. 4 vols., 1884-99.
Arthurian Romances (includes translations of *Erec and Énide, Cligès, Yvain, Lancelot*), translated by W.W. Comfort, edited by D.D.R. Owen. 1975.

Verse

Philomena, edited by C. de Boer. 1909.
Erec et Énide, edited by Mario Roques. 1952.
Cligès, edited by Alexandre Micha. 1957.
Yvain [*Le Chevalier du Lion*], edited by Mario Roques. 1960.
Lancelot [*Le Chevalier de la charrette*], edited by Mario Roques. 1958.
Conte du Graal [*Perceval*], edited by William Roach. 1956; translated as *Perceval* by Nigel Bryant, 1982.

*

Critical Studies: *Arthurian Tradition and Chrétien de Troyes* by Roger Sherman Loomis, 1949; *The Portrait in Twelfth-Century French Literature: An Example of the Stylistic Original-ity of Chrétien de Troyes* by Alice M. Colby, 1965; *Aesthetic Distance in Chrétien de Troyes* by Peter Haidu, 1968; *Chrétien de Troyes* by Urban T. Holmes, 1970; *Chrétien Studies* by Z.P. Zaddy, 1972; *The Creation of the First Arthurian Romance: A Quest* by Claude A. Luttrell, 1974; *The Craft of Chrétien de Troyes: An Essay on Narrative Art* by Norris J. Lacy, 1980; *Chrétien de Troyes: A Study of the Arthurian Romances* by Leslie T. Topsfield, 1981; *Love and Marriage in Chrétien de Troyes* by Peter S. Noble, 1982.

*   *   *

Chrétien de Troyes brought the nascent romance form to one of its highest points and gave Arthurian characters and situations their courtly cast. Some of his early works—adaptations of Ovid and a version of the Tristan story—have not survived; others are of doubtful attribution or of marginal interest (the *Philomena*, the *Guillaume d'Angleterre*, and two short lyrical poems); on the other hand, his five major romances have earned him great critical acclaim. A product of the revival of interest in the classics, notably Ovid, and of the vogue of Celtic tales and of courtly love, these compositions written in octosyllabic rhymed couplets are among the most sophisticated literary creaions of the Twelfth Century Renaissance. Chrétien was encouraged and probably supported for a while by Countess Marie of Champagne, daughter of King Louis VII of France and Eleanor of Aquitaine.

Erec and Énide (c. 1170) is the first full-blown account of King Arthur and the knights of the Round Table. After Erec weds the fair Énide, he becomes so enamored of her that he loses interest in chivalry. Prodded into taking up arms again by his bride's hasty words, the hero forces her to accompany him on a series of perilous adventures in the course of which he proves his valor and Énide her loyalty and devotion to him.

Cligès (c. 1176) appears to have been modeled in part on Thomas's *Tristan* whose heroine Chrétien criticized. Unlike Isolt, Fenice refuses to become involved with two lovers simultane-

126

ously. With the aid of magic potions, she prevents her husband from consummating their marriage, then, after feigning death, flees with Cligés to an idyllic hideaway. When the husband succumbs, the lovers are finally free to marry. In this romance, Chrétien developed the soliloquy as a means of analyzing love's torments.

There is some evidence that Chrétien worked alternately on his next two romances in the late 1170's.

Lancelot; or, The Knight of the Cart is perhaps the author's best-known story. Held hostage by the evil Meleagant, Queen Guenevere is rescued by her secret lover Lancelot who must first overcome several obstacles and, above all, suffer the humiliation of mounting a cart driven by a dwarf. Guenevere is a haughty and demanding mistress who makes her lover give in to all her caprices; Lancelot is a model of chivalry and courtesy for whom love-service has many of the characteristics of religious devotion and even mysticism.

Yvain; or, The Knight of the Lion recounts the adventures of a hero who weds the widow of a man he has slain. Though passionately in love with his bride, Yvain becomes so preoccupied with tourneying that she is soon out of his mind. The two are eventually reconciled after Yvain expiates his fault.

Perceval; or, The Story of the Grail (1181 or later) is about a naive young man who, after receiving training in chivalry and courtesy at King Arthur's court, happens upon a mysterious castle whose host is the Fisher King. There he witnesses a curious procession that includes a bleeding lance and a grail. Perceval fails to inquire about the significance of these objects and must then face the consequences. Medieval continuators gave a Christian interpretation to this story and some scholars believe Chrétien intended to provide this kind of explanation. However, the poem was left unfinished and constitutes one of the most fascinating literary conundrums of all time.

—Gerard J. Brault

CICERO (Marcus Tullius Cicero). Born in Arpinum (now Arpino), 3 January 106 B.C. Educated in Rome, and studied rhetoric and oratory in Athens and Rhodes, 79-77. Served in the army of Pompeius Strabo, 89. Married 1) Terentia in 80 (divorced, 47), one daughter and one son; 2) Publilia (divorced, 45). Lawyer: first appearance in courts, 81: usually appeared for the defense, but his prosecution of Verres (70) is his most famous case. Financial administrator (*quaestor*), western Sicily, 75; judicial officer (*praetor*), 66; consul, 63: exposed Catiline's conspiracy to carry out uprisings in Italy and arson in Rome; declared an exile by Clodius in 58, and lived in Thessalonica and Illyricum, but recalled with help of Pompey, 57; reluctantly allied himself with triumvirate of Pompey, Caesar, and Crassus, 56, and retired from public life until 51; elected augur of the college of diviners, 53; governor of Cilicia, Asia Minor, 51-50; allied with Pompey in civil war, 49-48: after Pompey's defeat Cicero's safety was guaranteed by Caesar; after Caesar's assassination, 44, supported general amnesty (delivered 14 Philippic orations against Antony, 44-43); the triumvirate of Octavian, Antony, and Lepidus put Cicero on the execution list, 43, and he was captured and killed. *Died 7 December 43 B.C.*

CICERO

PUBLICATIONS

Collections

[*Works*], edited by C.F.W. Mueller. 1884-1917; also edited by K. Simbeck and others, 1923— ; translation (in Loeb edition), 28 vols., 1912-58 (new translation, 1977—).

Works

[*Letters*], edited by R.Y. Tyrrell and L.C. Purser. 7 vols., 1899-1918; *Letters* (selection) translated by L.P. Wilkinson, 1949; *Selected Letters* translated by D.R. Shackleton Bailey, 1980.
Epistulae ad Atticum: Letters to Atticus, edited by D.R. Shackleton Bailey (includes translation). 7 vols., 1965-70; also edited by W.S. Watt, 2 vols., 1961-65.
Epistulae ad familiares [Letters to His Friends], edited by D.R. Shackleton Bailey. 2 vols., 1977; also edited by W.S. Watt, 1982; translated by Bailey, 1978.
Epistulae ad Quintum fratrum et M. Brutus, edited by D.R. Shackleton Bailey. 1980; also edited by W.S. Watt, 1958; translated by Bailey, 1978.
Pro M. Caello, edited by R.G. Austin. 1960.
Philippics I-II, edited by J.D. Denniston. 1939.
In Vatinium, edited by L.F. Pocock. 1926.
De domo sua, edited by R.G. Nisbet. 1939.
In Pisonem, edited by R.G. Nisbet. 1961.
De oratore, edited by A.S. Wilkins. 1892.
Orator, edited by J.E. Sandys. 1885.
Brutus, edited by A.E. Douglas. 1966; also edited by H. Malcovati, 1963; translated by H.M. Poteat, 1950.
Academica, edited by J.S. Reid. 1885.
De finibus, edited by J.N. Madvid. 3rd edition, 1876; Books I-II edited by J.S. Reid, 1925.
De natura deorum, edited by A.S. Pease. 2 vols., 1955-58; as *On the Nature of the Gods*, translated by H.M. Poteat, 1950; also translated by H.C.P. McGregor, 1972.
De republica, as *On the Commonwealth*, translated by G.H. Sabine and S.B. Smith, 1929; *Res Publica* (selections), translated by W.K. Lacey and Harry G. Edinger, 1974.
De officiis, edited by P. Fedeli. 1965; as *On Duties*, translated by H.M. Poteat, 1950; also translated by John Higginbotham, 1967, and Harry G. Edinger, 1974.
De senectute, edited by Leonard Huxley, revised edition. 1923; as *On Old Age*, translated by Frank Copley, 1967.
Laelius, edited by Frank Stock, revised edition. 1930; as *On Friendship*, translated by Frank Copley, 1967.
Tusculanae disputationes, edited by T.W. Dougan and R.M. Henry. 1905-34.
[*Poems*], edited by W.W. Ewbank. 1933.
De divinatione, edited by A.S. Pease. 1920-23; as *On Divination*, translated by H.M. Poteat, 1950.
Selected Works, translated by Michael Grant. 1960; revised edition, 1971.
The Caesarian Orations, translated by G.J. Acheson. 1965.
Nine Orations and the Dream of Scipio, translated by P. Bovie. 1967.
Selected Political Speeches, translated by Michael Grant. 1969; revised edition, 1973.
On the Good Life (selections), translated by Michael Grant. 1971.
Murder Trials (selected orations), translated by Michael Grant. 1975.

*

Critical Studies: *Cicero and the Roman Republic* by Frank R. Crowell, 1948; *The Humanism of Cicero* by H.A.K. Hunt, 1954; *Cicero* by T.A. Dorey, 1965; *Cicero the Statesman* by Richard E. Smith, 1966; *Cicero* by D.R. Shackleton Bailey, 1971; *Cicero: A Political Biography* by David Stockton, 1971; *Cicero and the State Religion* by R.J. Goar, 1972; *Cicero and Rome* by David Taylor, 1973; *Cicero: A Portrait* by Elizabeth Rawson, 1975; *Cicero and the End of the Roman Republic* edited by W.K. Lacey, 1978; *Cicero: The Ascending Years* by Thomas N. Mitchell, 1979.

*   *   *

Cicero was one of the most prolific and versatile of Latin authors, but his literary reputation has varied more than most. In antiquity he was generally accepted as the prince of Roman orators, though sometimes with reservations. In the Middle Ages, when his speeches and letters were almost forgotten, the less technical of his philosophical works became vastly popular and influential. Petrarch was his devout admirer, and among the humanists of the Renaissance his Latin style was a fetish. The 18th century found him congenial, the 19th less so.

In the 20th the most valuable part of Cicero's literary legacy seems to be the part he never intended to leave: his private correspondence. It was published at intervals after his death, apparently with scarcely any editing. The first extant letter was written when Cicero was 38 and they continue in uneven flow down to within a few months of his death. Many were to his closest intimates, his brother and his life-long friend, Pomponius Atticus. They take us behind the political and domestic scenes, and thanks to them the colorful history of the last two decades of the Roman Republic is more than a bare chronicle of events. The famous names—Pompey, Cato, Crassus, Julius Caesar—come to life, and Cicero's own complex personality gets ample exposure. Incidentally, they show him as a master of vivid narrative and description in a colloquial style very different from that of his publications. Nothing in the remains of Greco-Roman literature takes us so close to an individual and a society.

The speeches, too, offer much of this kind of interest and some of them, like the letters, are an important source of information about the speaker and his times. Covering a period of nearly forty years, almost the whole of Cicero's public career, they range from legalistic pleas on behalf of obscure clients to grand occasions when Cicero held forth to the Senate or the People in its assemblies on great political issues. To a modern eye the faults of his eloquence are all too often all too plain: inflation, false pathos, egotism, verbosity, and what Theodor Mommsen called a dreadful barrenness of thought. Even so, a receptive reader may let himself be swept along with the tide of impeccably constructed periods, especially if he can read the Latin aloud. Not seldom there is more, as the rhetorical drive of the *Catilines*, the genuine pathos of the *Fourteenth Philippic*, or the brilliant badinage in the defence of Murena. As for Cicero's prose style, even Mommsen admired it. It was his most creative achievement.

Cicero was not an original thinker, but like many educated Romans of his time he was much interested in Greek philosophy. Late in life he conceived the plan to present it, at least its more recent developments, in Latin form. The result was a rapidly produced series of metaphysical and moral treatises based on Greek sources. As literature, the gem of the collection is the little tract on Old Age, perhaps Cicero's one unqualified artistic success. Another attractive piece, on friendship, characteristically tells us nothing about the actualities of Roman *amicitia*, as Cicero knew them from his own experience. Even the works on rhetoric have this second-hand quality, except the *Brutus*, a survey of Roman orators which often reads like a catalogue but contains some highly interesting sketches of speakers whom Cicero had heard and personally known.

Cicero also wrote poetry, mostly in his youth. It had a considerable vogue, until Catullus and the "New Poets" brought their fresh inspiration. Posterity would have none of it, and enough survives to show that posterity was right. Even the advance in verse technique as compared with the remnants of earlier writing need not have been due to Cicero.

—D.R. Shackleton Bailey

CLAUDEL, Paul (Louis Charles Marie). Born in Villeneuve-sur-Fère, France, 6 August 1868. Educated at schools in Bar-le-Duc, 1870-75, Nogent-sur-Seine, 1876-79, and Wassy-sur-Blaise, 1879-81; Lycée Louis-le-Grand, Paris, 1882-85; law school, and École des Sciences Politiques. Married Reine Sainte-Marie-Perrin in 1906; five children. In the French diplomatic service from 1890: commercial department, Paris, 1890-92, New York, 1893, Boston, 1894, China, 1894-1909, Prague, 1909-11, Frankfurt, 1911-14, Berlin, 1914, Rome and Brazil during World War I; Ambassador to Japan, 1921-25, to the United States, 1926-33, and to Belgium, 1933-35: retired 1935; served in the Ministry of Propaganda during World War II. Member of the French Academy, 1946. *Died 23 February 1955.*

PUBLICATIONS

Collections

[Works]:

> *Théâtre*, edited by Jacques Madaule and Jacques Petit. 2 vols., 1956; revised edition, 1965-67.
> *Oeuvres poétiques*, edited by Stanislas Fumet. 1957.
> *Oeuvres en prose*, edited by Jacques Petit and Charles Galperine. 1965.
> *Journal*, edited by Jacques Petit and François Varillon. 2 vols., 1968-69.

Plays

> *Tête d'or.* 1890; revised version (produced 1924), in *L'Arbre*, 1901; translated as *Tete-d'or*, 1919.
> *La Ville.* 1893; revised version (produced 1931), in *L'Arbre*, 1901; edited by Jacques Petit, 1967; as *The City*, 1920.
> *L'Agamemnon*, from the play by Aeschylus (produced 1963). 1896.
> *L'Échange* (produced 1914). In *L'Arbre*, 1901; revised version (produced, 1951), 1954.
> *Le Jeune Fille Violaine*, in *L'Arbre*. 1901; revised version, as *L'Annonce faite à Marie* (produced 1912), 1912; revised version (produced, 1948), 1948; as *The Tidings Brought to Mary*, 1916.
> *Le Repos du septième jour* (produced 1928). In *L'Arbre*, 1901.
> *Partage de midi* (produced 1921). 1906; revised version (produced 1948), 1914, 1949; as *Break of Noon*, 1960.
> *L'Otage* (produced 1913). 1911; edited by Jean-Pierre Kempf, 1977; as *The Hostage*, 1917.
> *Protée*, in *Deux poèmes d'été.* 1914; revised version (produced 1929), in *Deux farces lyriques*, 1927.
> *La Nuit de Noël 1914.* 1915.
> *La Pain dur* (produced 1941-43). 1918; edited by Jacques Petit, 1975, as *Crusts*, in *Three Plays*, 1945.
> *L'Ours et la lune* (produced 1948). 1919.
> *Le Père humilié* (produced 1928). 1920; as *The Humiliation of the Father*, in *Three Plays*, 1945.
> *Les Choéphores*, from the play by Aeschylus (produced 1935). 1920.
> *Les Eumenides*, from the play by Aeschylus (produced 1949). 1920.
> *L'Homme et son désir*, music by Darius Milhaud (ballet; produced 1921). In *Le Livre de Christophe Colomb*, 1929.
> *La Femme et son ombre* (produced 1923). In *Le Livre de Christophe Colomb*, 1929.
> *Sous le rempart d'Athènes*, music by Germaine Taillefer (produced 1927). 1928.

Le Livre de Christophe Colomb, music by Darius Milhaud (produced 1930). 1929; as *The Book of Christopher Columbus*, 1930.
Le Soulier de satin. 1929; revised version (produced 1943), 1944; as *The Satin Slipper*, 1931.
Jeanne d'Arc au bucher, music by Arthur Honegger (produced 1938). 1939.
L'Histoire de Tobie et de Sara (produced 1947). 1947.
La Sagesse; ou, La Parabole du Festin, music by Darius Milhaud (broadcast, 1946; produced, 1950). 1939.
L'Endormie. 1947.

Verse

Vers d'exile. 1895.
Connaissance du temps. 1904.
Cinq grandes odes. 1910; as *Five Great Odes*, 1967.
Cette heure qui est entre le printemps et l'été. 1913; as *La Cantate à trois voix*, 1931.
Corona benignitatis anni dei. 1915; as *Coronal*, 1943.
Trois poèmes de guerre. 1915; as *Three Poems of the War*, 1919.
Autres poèmes durant la guerre. 1916.
Poèmes et paroles durant la guerre. 1916.
La Messe là-bas. 1919.
Poèmes de guerre. 1922.
Feuilles de saints. 1925.
Écoute, ma fille. 1934.
La Légende de Prakriti. 1934.
Poèmes et paroles durant la guerre de trente ans. 1945.
Visages radieux. 1946.
Paul Claudel répond les psaumes. 1948; as *Psaumes: Traductions 1918-1959*, edited by Renée Nantet and Jacques Petit, 1966.
Sainte Agnès et poèmes inédites. 1963.

Other

Connaissance de l'est. 1900; augmented edition, 1907; edited by Gilbert Gadoffre, 1973; as *The East I Know*, 1914.
Art poétique. 1907; as *Poetic Art*, 1948.
Correspondance 1907-1914, with Jacques Rivière. 1926; as *Letters to a Doubter*, 1929.
Positions et propositions. 2 vols., 1928-34.
L'Oiseau noir dans le soleil levant. 1929.
Ways and Crossways. 1933.
Introduction à la peinture hollandais. 1935.
Conversations dans le Loir-et-Cher. 1935.
Toi, qui es-tu? Tu quis es? 1936.
Figures et paraboles. 1936; edited by Andrée Hirschi, 1974.
Vitraux des cathédrales de France. 1937.
L'Aventure de Sophie. 1937.
Un Poète regarde la croix. 1938; as *Poet Before the Cross*, 1958.
L'Epée et le miroir. 1939.
Contacts et circonstances. 1940.
La Rose et le rosaire. 1946.
L'Oeil écoute. 1946; as *The Eye Listens*, 1950.
Chine, photographs by Hélène Hoppenot. 1946.
Présence et prophétie. 1947.

Lord, Teach Us to Pray. 1947.
Sous le signe du dragon. 1948.
Paul Claudel interroge la Cantique des Cantiques. 1948.
Accompagnements. 1949.
Correspondance 1899-1926, with André Gide, edited by Robert Mallet. 1949; as *Correspondence*, 1952.
Emmaüs. 1950.
L'Evangile d'Isaïe. 1951.
Correspondance 1904-1938, with André Saurès. 1951.
Paul Claudel interroge l'Apocalypse. 1952.
Mémoires improvisés, edited by Jean Amrouche. 1954.
J'aime la Bible. 1955.
Correspondance 1918-1953, with Darius Milhaud, edited by Jacques Petit. 1961.
I Believe in God: A Commentary on the Apostles Creed, edited by Agnes du Sarment. 1965.
Au milieu des vitraux de l'Apocalypse, edited by Pierre Claudel and Jacques Petit. 1966.
Mes idées sur le théâtre, edited by Jacques Petit and Jean-Pierre Kempf. 1966.
Correspondance 1908-1914, with Louis Massignon, edited by Michel Malicet. 1973.
Correspondance, with Jean-Louis Barrault, edited by Michel Lioure. 1974.
Chroniques du Journal de Clichy, with François Mauriac (includes Claudel-Fontaine correspondence), edited by François Morlot and Jean Touzot. 1978.

Translator, *Poèmes*, by Coventry Patmore. 1912.

*

Bibliography: *Bibliographie des oeuvres de Claudel* by Jacques Petit, 1973.

Critical Studies: *The Double Image: Mutations of Christian Mythology in the Work of Four French Catholic Writers* by Rayner Heppenstall, 1947; *The Poetic Drama of Claudel* by Joseph Chiari, 1954; *The Theme of Beatrice in the Plays of Claudel* by Ernest Beaumont, 1954; *Claudel* by Wallace Fowlie, 1957; *Claudel: A Reappraisal* edited by Richard Griffiths, 1963; *Claudel and Aeschylus* by William H. Matheson, 1965; *The Inner Stage: An Essay on the Conflict of Vocations in the Early Works of Claudel* by Richard Berchan, 1966; *Claudel et l'univers chinois* by Gilbert Gadoffre, 1968; *Claudel* by Harold A. Waters, 1970; *Claudel and Saint-John Perse* by Ruth N. Horry, 1971; *Claudel's Immortal Heroes: A Choice of Deaths* by Harold Watson, 1971; *The Prince and the Genie: A Study of Rimbaud's Influence on Claudel* by John A. MacCombie, 1972; *Two Against Time: A Study of the Very Present Worlds of Claudel and Charles Péguy* by Joy Nachod Humes, 1978; *In/stability: The Shape and Space of Claudel's Art* by Lynne L. Gelber, 1980.

*   *   *

Despite the high praise of Charles Du Bos, who called him the greatest genius of the west, and despite the judgment of Jacques Madaule, who compared him to Dante, Claudel's place in literature and in Catholic thought is still vigorously disputed. At the time of his death, in his middle eighties, he appeared as belligerent as ever, having maintained to the end not only his full powers as a writer but also his violent temper and his animosities. His detractors are still legion and his admirers come from many varying quarters differing widely in their religious, political, and aesthetic beliefs.

During his last year at the Lycée Louis-le-Grand, he read Baudelaire and Verlaine, but the first major revelation to Claudel of both a literary and spiritual order was to to be Rimbaud. He has described in a passage justly celebrated and justly disputed the profound effect which the reading of *Les Illuminations* had on him. He first came upon some of the prose poems in the July issue of *La Vogue* of 1886. To him it meant release from what he called the hideous world of Taine, Renan, and other Molochs of the 19th century. "J'avais la révélation du surnaturel," he wrote to Jacques Rivière.

After a spiritual experience on Christmas, 1886, in Notre-Dame, Claudel began to study the Bible, the history of the Church and its liturgy, and discovered that what he had once valued as poetry was indissolubly associated with religion. He attended Mallarmé's Tuesday evening gatherings and learned from the master of symbolism to look at the universe as if it were a text to be deciphered. To Rimbaud's doctrine on the power of poetic language and to Mallarmé's doctrine on the symbolism of the universe Claudel added the gigantic synthesis of Aquinas and the religious interpretation of metaphorical language.

Taken as a whole, Paul Claudel's work is praise to God and praise to His creation. It does not reflect the exaltation of a mystic but is rather the expression of the natural joy of a man who has found an order in the universe and believes in a certain relationship between this world and the next. In whatever he wrote—poems, letters, plays, essays, Biblical exegesis—he steadfastly explored the central drama of the human soul engaged in its adventure with eternity. His dramas are not a combination of the comic and the tragic; they are works of one piece and one texture—simultaneously dramatic speech and poetry.

The French literary mind has been predominantly analytical in each century. Claudel's mind is more inclined toward the creation of a synthesis. His fundamental preoccupations are more metaphysical than is usual in French writers who tend to psychological and moralistic preoccupations. Moreover, the seeming bluntness of his style, its vehemence, its violence, separates his work from the central tradition of the French literary style. Claudel believes that at our birth we enter into a secret pact with all beings and all objects. The poet's mission is that of pointing out our relationship with all the realities of the world.

—Wallace Fowlie

COCTEAU, Jean (Maurice Eugène Clément). Born in Maisons-Laffitte, France, 5 July 1889. Educated at the Lycée Condorcet, Paris, and privately. Writer, artist, journalist, film writer and director; co-founder, *Shéhérazade* magazine; contributor, *Paris-Midi*, 1919, and *Ce Soir*, 1937-38. President, Jazz Academy; Honorary President, Cannes Film Festival. Recipient: Louions-Delluc Prize, 1946; Avant-garde Film Grand Prize, 1950. D. Litt.: Oxford University, 1956. Member, French Academy, 1955; and Royal Academy of Belgium; Honorary Member, American Academy and German Academy. Commander, Legion of Honor, 1961. *Died 11 October 1963.*

PUBLICATIONS

Plays

> *Les Mariés de la Tour Eiffel* (produced 1921). 1924; as *The Eiffel Tower Wedding Party*, in *The Infernal Machine and Other Plays*, 1963.
> *Antigone* (produced 1922; revised version, music by Arthur Honegger, produced 1927). 1927; translated as *Antigone*, in *Four Plays*, 1962.
> *Roméo et Juliette*, from the play by Shakespeare (produced 1924). 1926.
> *Orphée* (produced 1926). 1927; translated as *Orpheus*, 1933.

Le Pauvre Matelot, music by Milhaud (produced 1927). 1927.
Oedipus Rex, music by Stravinsky (produced 1927). 1949.
Oedipe-Roi (produced 1937). 1928.
La Voix humaine (produced 1930). 1930; as *The Human Voice*, 1951.
La Machine infernale (produced 1934). 1934; as *The Infernal Machine*, 1936.
Les Chevaliers de la table ronde (produced 1937). 1937; as *The Knights of the Round Table*, 1963.
Les Parents terribles (produced 1938). 1938; edited by R.K. Totton, 1972; as *Intimate Relations*, 1962.
Les Monstres sacrés (produced 1940). 1940; as *The Holy Terrors*, 1962.
La Machine à écrire (produced 1941). 1941; as *The Typewriter*, 1947.
Renaud et Arminde (produced 1943). 1943.
L'Aigle a deux têtes (produced 1946). 1946; as *The Eagle Has Two Heads*, 1948.
Ruy Blas (screenplay). 1947.
Le Sang d'un poète (screenplay). 1948; as *The Blood of a Poet*, 1949.
Un Tramway nommé désir, from the play by Tennessee Williams (produced 1949). 1949.
Théâtre de poche (includes scenarios, sketches, and radio works). 1949.
Orphée (screenplay). 1951; translated as *Orphée*, in *Three Screenplays*, 1972.
Bacchus (produced 1951). 1952; translated as *Bacchus*, in *The Infernal Machine and Other Plays*, 1963.
La Belle et la bête (screenplay). 1958; translated as *La Belle et la bête*, in *Three Screenplays*, 1972.
Cher Menteur, from the play by Jerome Kilty (produced 1960). 1960.
Le Testament d'Orphée (screenplay). 1961; as *The Testament of Orpheus*, in *Two Screenplays*, 1968.
L'Impromptu du Palais-Royal. 1962.
L'Eternel Retour (screenplay), translated as *L'eternel retour*, in *Three Screenplays*. 1972.

Screenplays: *Le Sang d'un poète*, 1930; *La Comédie du bonheur*, 1940; *Le Baron fantôme*, with Serge de Poligny, 1943; *L'Eternel Retour*, 1943; *Les Dames du Bois du Boulogne*, with Robert Bresson, 1945; *La Belle et la bête*, 1946; *Ruy Blas*, 1947; *L'Aigle a deux têtes*, 1948; *Les Parents terribles*, 1948; *Noces de sable*, 1949; *Les Enfants terribles*, 1950; *Orphée*, 1950; *La Villa Santo-Sospiro*, 1952; *La Corona Negra*, 1952; *Le Testament d'Orphée*, 1960; *La Princesse de Clèves*, 1961; *Thomas l'imposteur*, 1965.

Ballet scenarios: *Le Dieu bleu*, 1912; *Parade*, 1917; *Le Boeuf sur le toit*, 1920; *Le Train bleu*, 1924; *Le Jeune Homme et la mort*, 1946; *La Dame à la licorne*, 1953; *Le Poète et sa muse*, 1959.

Fiction

Le Potomak. 1919; revised edition, 1934.
Le Grand Écart. 1923; as *The Grand Ecart*, 1925; as *The Miscreant*, 1958.
Thomas l'imposteur. 1923; as *Thomas the Imposter*, 1925; as *The Imposter*, 1957.
Les Enfants terribles. 1929; translated as *Enfants Terribles*, 1930; as *Children of the Game*, 1955; as *The Holy Terrors*, 1957.
Le Fantôme de Marseille. 1936.
Le Fin du Potomak. 1940.
Deux travestis. 1947.

Verse

La Lampe d'Aladin. 1909.

Le Prince frivole. 1910.
La Danse de Sophocle. 1912.
Le Cap de bonne-espérance. 1919.
Ode à Picasso. 1919.
Discours du grand sommeil. 1920.
Escales, with André Lhote. 1920.
Poésies 1917-20. 1920.
Vocabulaire. 1922.
Plain-chant. 1923.
La Rose de François. 1923.
Poésie 1916-23. 1924.
Cri écrit. 1925.
Prière mutilée. 1925.
L'Ange Heurtebise. 1926.
Opéra: Oeuvres poétiques 1925-27. 1927.
Morceaux choisis. 1932.
Mythologie. 1934.
Allégories. 1941.
Les Poèmes allemands. 1944.
Léone. 1945; translated as *Leoun*, 1960.
La Crucifixion. 1946.
Poèmes. 1948.
Le Chiffre. 1952.
Appogiatures. 1953.
Dentelle d'éternité. 1953.
Clair-obscur. 1954.
Poèmes 1916-1955. 1956.
Gondole des morts. 1959.
Cérémonial espagnol du phénix; La Partie d'echecs. 1961.
Le Requiem. 1961.
Faire-part. 1969.

Other

Le Coq et l'Arlequin: Notes autour de la musique. 1918; as *Cock and Harlequin*, 1921.
Dans le ciel de la patrie. 1918.
Carte blanche. 1920.
La Noce massacrée. 1921.
Le Secret professionnel. 1922.
Dessins. 1923.
Picasso. 1923.
Ferat. 1924.
Le Mystère de l'oiseleur. 1925.
Lettre à Jacques Maritain. 1926.
Le Rappel à l'ordre. 1926; as *A Call to Order*, 1926.
Maison de santé: Dessins. 1926.
Le Mystère laïc. 1928.
Le Livre blanc. 1928; as *The White Paper*, 1957.
Un Entrevue sur la critique avec Maurice Rouzaud. 1929.
25 Dessins d'un dormeur. 1929.
Essai de critique indirecte. 1932.
Opium. 1932; translated as *Opium*, 1932.
Portraits-souvenir 1900-1914. 1935; as *Paris Album 1900-1914*, 1956.
60 Dessins pour "Les Enfants terribles." 1935.

Mon premier voyage: Tour du monde en 80 jours. 1936; as *Round the World Again in Eighty Days*, 1937.
Enigme. 1939.
Dessins en marge du texte des "Chevaliers de la table ronde." 1941.
Le Greco. 1943.
Serge Lifar à l'opéra. 1944.
Portrait de Mounet-Sully. 1945.
La Belle et la bête: Journal d'un film. 1946; as *Diary of a Film*, 1950.
Poésie critique. 1946.
La Difficulté d'être. 1947; as *The Difficulty of Being*, 1966.
Le Foyer des artistes. 1947.
Oeuvres complètes. 10 vols., 1947-50.
Art and Faith: Letters Between Jacques Maritain and Cocteau. 1948.
Drôle de ménage. 1948.
Reines de France. 1948.
Lettre aux Américains. 1949.
Maalesh: Journal d'une tournée de théâtre. 1949; as *Maalesh: A Theatrical Tour in the Middle-East*, 1956.
Dufy. 1949.
Orson Welles, with André Bazin. 1950.
Modigliani. 1950.
Jean Marais. 1951.
Entretiens autour de cinématographe, edited by André Fraigneau. 1951; revised edition, edited by André Bernard and Claude Gauteur, 1973; as *On Film*, 1954.
Journal d'un inconnu. 1952; as *The Hand of a Stranger*, 1956.
Gide vivant, with Julien Green. 1952.
La Nappe du Catalan. 1952.
Aux confins de la Chine. 1955.
Lettre sur la poésie. 1955.
Le Dragon des mets. 1955.
Journals, edited by Wallace Fowlie. 1956.
Adieu à Mistinguett. 1956.
L'Art est un sport. 1956.
Impression: Arts de la rue. 1956.
Cocteau chez les sirènes, edited by Jean Dauven. 1956.
Témoignage. 1956.
Entretiens sur la musée de Dresde, with Louis Aragon. 1957; as *Conversations in the Dresden Gallery*, 1983.
Erik Satie. 1957.
La Chapelle Saint-Pierre, Villefranche-sur-Mer. 1957.
La Corrida du premier mai. 1957.
Comme un miel noir (in French and English). 1958.
Paraprosodies, précédés de 7 dialogues. 1958.
La Salle des mariages, Hôtel de Ville de Menton. 1958.
La Canne blanche. 1959.
Poésie critique: Monologues. 1960.
Notes sur "Le Testament d'Orphée." 1960.
Le Cordon ombilical: Souvenirs. 1962.
Hommage. 1962.
Anna de Noailles oui et non. 1963.
Adieux d'Antonio Ordonez. 1963.
La Mesangère. 1963.
Entretien avec Roger Stéphane. 1964.
Entretien avec André Fraigneau. 1965.

Pégase. 1965.
My Contemporaries, edited by Margaret Crosland. 1967.
Entre Radiguet et Picasso. 1967.
Professional Secrets: An Autobiography, edited by Robert Phelps. 1970.
Lettres à André Gide, edited by Jean-Jacques Kihm. 1970.
Cocteau's World (selections), edited by Margaret Crosland. 1972.
Cocteau, Poète graphique, edited by Pierre Chanel. 1975.
Lettres à Milorad, edited by Milorad. 1975.

Editor, *Almanach du théâtre et du cinéma.* 1949.
Editor, *Choix de lettres de Max Jacob à Jean Cocteau 1919-1944.* 1949.
Editor, *Amadeo Modigliani: Quinze dessins.* 1960.

*

Critical Studies: *Cocteau* by Margaret Crosland, 1956; *Scandal and Parade: The Theatre of Cocteau* by N. Oxenhandler, 1957; *Cocteau: The History of a Poet's Age* by Wallace Fowlie, 1966; *Cocteau: The Man and the Mirror* by Elizabeth Sprigge and Jean-Jacques Kihm, 1968; *An Impersonation of Angels: A Biography of Cocteau* by Frederick Brown, 1968; *Cocteau: A Biography* by Francis Steegmuller, 1970; *Cocteau* by Bettina Knapp, 1970; *The Esthetic of Cocteau* by Lydia Crowson, 1978.

*   *   *

Precociously Jean Cocteau published his first volume of verse at the age of 19. A small public flattered him and applauded the facile brilliance of the poems. Between 1917 and 1919, with three very different works, Cocteau became a public figure. *Parade,* of 1917, a ballet performed in Rome, was an early experiment with the theater. *Le Coq et l'Arlequin* (1918), a manifesto against the disciples of Debussy and Wagner, revealed his interest in aesthetics and his powers of a critic. *Le Cap de Bonne-espérance* (1919), a volume of war poems, placed him in the ranks of the best young poets. Poetry was the mark of all three works, and the principle which was thereafter to direct the varied activities of Cocteau.

His sentence is swift and seemingly lucid, but the content is mysterious and enigmatical. Cocteau's style became a manner of expressing complicated matters with discerning simplicity. The poems of *Vocabulaire* (1922) contained the key words of his poetic experience, symbols and characters projected out of his imagination that were to form in time his mythology—episodes, myths, and characters charged with the duty of narrating the poet's drama. Kidnappers, sailors, angels, and cyclists appear and disappear as if searching for their poet.

The play *Orphée* performed in Paris in 1926 by Georges and Ludmilla Pitoëff, was his first work to reach a fairly wide public. In *Orphée,* the poet appears to be the combined characters of Orpheus and Angel Heurtebise. The action of the play is both familiar and esoteric; in it Orpheus is both poet and hierophant, both husband and priest.

Les Enfants terribles was written in three weeks and published in 1929. This book has now become a classic, both as a novel belonging to the central tradition of the short French novel, and as a document of historical-psychological significance in the study it offers of the type of adolescent referred to in the title. The intertwined destinies of brother and sister, Paul and Elisabeth, with the dark forbidding figure of Dargelos behind them, provide an unusual picture of adolescence in its actions and speech and games.

The theme of Cocteau's first film, *Le Sang d'un poète* (1932), was an idea close to the romantics a century earlier, in which the poet writes with his own blood. Much later, in the film *Orphée* Cocteau developed this lesson of the poet and borrowed from *Le Sang d'un poète* and his play *Orphée.* These films are two esoteric poems for the screen.

In his plays, as in *La Machine infernale* (1934), on the Oedipus theme, Cocteau presented experimentations on the stage with the enthusiasm of a dramatist enamoured of the theater and of the idea of a spectacle. Between the death of Apollinaire in 1918 and his own death in 1963, Cocteau occupied an active position in all the domains of French art.

—Wallace Fowlie

COLETTE, (Sidonie-Gabrielle). Born in Saint-Saveur en Puisaye, France, 28 January 1873. Educated at local school to age 16. Married 1) the writer Henry Gauthier-Villars ("Willy") in 1893 (divorced, 1910); 2) Henry de Jouvenal in 1912 (divorced, 1925), one daughter; 3) Maurice Goudeket in 1935. Actress and revue performer, 1906-27; columnist, 1910-19, and literary editor, 1919-24, *Le Matin*; drama critic, *La Revue de Paris*, 1929, *Le Journal*, 1934-39, *L'Eclair*, and *Le Petit Parisien*; operated a beauty clinic, Paris, 1932-33. Recipient: City of Paris Grand Médaille, 1953. Member, Belgian Royal Academy, 1936; Member, 1945, and President, 1949, Goncourt Academy; Honorary Member, American Academy, 1953. Chevalier, 1920, Officer, 1928, Commander, 1936, and Grand Officer, 1953, Legion of Honor. *Died 3 August 1954.*

PUBLICATIONS

Fiction

> *Claudine à l'école*, with Willy. 1900; as *Claudine at School*, 1930.
> *Claudine à Paris*, with Willy. 1901; as *Claudine in Paris*, 1931; as *Young Lady of Paris*, 1931.
> *Claudine en ménage*, with Willy. 1902; as *The Indulgent Husband*, 1935; as *Claudine Married*, 1960.
> *Claudine s'en va*, with Willy. 1903; as *The Innocent Wife*, 1934; as *Claudine and Annie*, 1962.
> *Minne; Les Egarements de Minne.* 2 vols., 1903-05; revised version, as *L'Ingénue libertine*, 1909; as *The Gentle Libertine*, 1931.
> *Le Retraite sentimentale.* 1907; as *Retreat from Love*, 1974.
> *Les Vrilles de la vigne.* 1908.
> *La Vagabonde.* 1911; as *The Vagrant*, 1912; as *Renée la vagabonde*, 1931; as *The Vagabond*, 1954.
> *L'Entrave.* 1913; as *Recaptured*, 1931; as *The Shackle*, 1963.
> *Les Enfants dans les ruines.* 1917.
> *Dans la foule.* 1918.
> *Mitsou; ou, Comment l'esprit vient aux filles.* 1918; as *Mitsou; or, How Girls Grow Wise*, 1930.
> *La Chambre éclairée.* 1920.
> *Chéri.* 1920; translated as *Chéri*, 1929.
> *Le Blé en herbe.* 1923; as *The Ripening Corn*, 1931; as *Ripening Seed*, 1959.
> *La Femme cachée.* 1924.
> *Quatre saisons.* 1925.
> *Le Fin de Chéri.* 1926; as *The Last of Chéri*, 1932.
> *La Naissance du jour.* 1928; as *A Lesson in Love*, 1932; as *Morning Glory*, 1932; as

Break of Day, 1961.
La Seconde. 1929; as *The Other One*, 1931; as *Fanny and Jane*, 1931.
Paradises terrestres. 1932.
La Chatte. 1933; as *The Cat*, 1936; as *Saha the Cat*, 1936.
Duo. 1934; translated as *Duo*, 1935; as *The Married Lover*, 1935.
Bella-Vista. 1937.
Le Toutounier. 1939; as *The Toutounier*, with *Duo*, 1976.
Chambre d'hôtel. 1940.
Julie de Carneilhan. 1941; translated as *Julie de Carneilhan*, 1952.
Le Képi. 1943.
Gigi et autres nouvelles. 1944; translated as *Gigi*, 1953.
Stories. 1958.
Collected Stories, edited by Robert Phelps. 1983.

Plays

En camerades (produced 1909). In *Oeuvres complètes 15*, 1950.
Claudine, music by Rodolphe Berger, from the novel by Colette (produced 1910). 1910.
Chéri, with Léopold Marchand, from the novel by Colette (produced 1921). 1922; translated as *Cheri*, 1959.
La Vagabonde, with Léopold Marchand, from the novel by Colette (produced 1923). 1923.
L'Enfant et les sortilèges, music by Maurice Ravel (produced 1925). 1925; as *The Boy and the Magic*, 1964.
La Décapitée (ballet scenario), in *Mes Cahiers*. 1941.
Gigi, with Anita Loos, from the story by Colette (produced 1951). 1952; in French, 1954.
Jeune filles en uniform, Lac aux dames, Divine (screenplays), in *Au Cinéma*. 1975.

Screenplays: *La Vagabonde*, 1917, remake, 1931; *La Femme cachée*, 1919; *Jeunes filles en uniform* (French dialogue for German film *Mädchen in Uniform*), 1932; *Lac aux dames*, 1934; *Divine*, 1935.

Other

Dialogues de bêtes. 1904; augmented edition, as *Sept dialogues de bêtes*, 1905; as *Douze dialogues de bêtes*, 1930; as *Barks and Purrs*, 1913.
L'Envers du music-hall. 1913; as *Music-Hall Sidelights*, 1957.
Prrou, Poucette, et quelques autres. 1913; revised edition, as *La Paix chez les bêtes*, 1916; translated in *Creatures Great and Small*, 1951.
Les Heures longues 1914-1917. 1917.
La Maison de Claudine. 1922; as *The Mother of Claudine*, 1937; as *My Mother's House*, 1953.
Le Voyage égoïste. 1922.
Rêverie du nouvel an. 1923.
Aventures quotidiennes. 1924.
Renée Vivien. 1928.
Sido. 1929; translated as *Sido*, 1953.
Histoires pour Bel-Gazou. 1930.
La Treille Muscate. 1932.
Prisons et paradis. 1932.
Ces plaisirs. 1932; as *Le Pur et l'impur*, 1941; as *These Pleasures*, 1934; as *The Pure and the Impure*, 1934.
La Jumelle noire. 4 vols., 1934-38.

Mes apprentissages.   1936; as *My Apprenticeships*, 1957.
Chats.   1936.
Splendeur des papillons.   1937.
Mes cahiers.   1941.
Journal à rebours.   1941; in *Looking Backwards*, 1975.
De ma fenêtre.   1942; augmented edition, as *Paris de ma fenêtre*, 1944; in *Looking Backwards*, 1975.
De la patte à l'aile.   1943.
Flore et Pomone.   1943.
Nudités.   1943.
Broderie ancienne.   1944.
Trois...six...neuf.   1944.
Belles Saisons.   1945; as *Belles Saisons: A Colette Scrapbook*, edited by Robert Phelps, 1978.
Une Amitié inattendue (correspondence with Francis Jammes), edited by Robert Mallet.   1945.
L'Étoile vesper.   1946; as *The Evening Star: Recollections*, 1973.
Pour un herbier.   1948; as *For a Flower Album*, 1959.
Oeuvres complètes.   15 vols., 1948-50.
Trait pour trait.   1949.
Journal intermittent.   1949.
Le Fanal bleu.   1949; as *The Blue Lantern*, 1963.
La Fleur de l'âge.   1949.
En pays connu.   1949.
Chats de Colette.   1949.
Creatures Great and Small.   1951.
Paysages et portraits.   1958.
Lettres à Hélène Picard, edited by Claude Pichois.   1958.
Lettres à Marguerite Moréno, edited by Claude Pichois.   1959.
Lettres de la vagabonde, edited by Claude Pichois and Roberte Forbin.   1961.
Lettres au petit corsaire, edited by Claude Pichois and Roberte Forbin.   1963.
Earthly Paradise: An Autobiography Drawn from Her Lifetime of Writing, edited by Robert Phelps.   1966.
Places (miscellany; in English).   1970.
Contes de mille et un matins.   1970; as *The Thousand and One Mornings*, 1973.
Journey for Myself: Selfish Memoirs (selection).   1971.
Lettres à ses pairs, edited by Claude Pichois and Roberte Forbin.   1973.
Au Cinéma, edited by Alain and Odette Virmaux.   1975.
Letters from Colette, edited by Robert Phelps.   1980.

*

Critical Studies: *Madame Colette: A Provincial in Paris* by Margaret Crosland, 1952; *Colette* by Elaine Marks, 1961; *Colette* by Margaret Davies, 1961; *Colette* by R.D. Cottrell, 1974; *Colette: A Taste for Life* by Yvonne Mitchell, 1975; *Colette: Free and Fettered* by Michèle Sarde, 1981; *Colette: The Woman, The Writer* edited by Erica M. Eisinger and Mari McCarty, 1981; *Colette* by Joanna Richardson, 1983.

*   *   *

If French literature, like English literature, had a number of women writers of the first rank, then Colette would rate as a distinctly minor figure; but since the number of French women writers who achieved prominence before the beginning of the present century can be reckoned on the fingers of one hand, she is a person of some significance. In common with others, such as Madame de Staël and George Sand, she counts for more than a strict evaluation of her purely literary merit would suggest. She stands, as they do, for feminism in a culture which until recently was dominated by men.

As one might expect, she began her literary career under the tutelage of a man, her husband Willy, and her first novels were written in collaboration with him and were published under his name. But the partnership was not a happy one, and after their divorce she branched out on her own. She wrote many more books, and survived into the second half of the 20th century, but she is essentially a *fin de siècle* writer who captures with great finesse and depth of perception the particular world which we call the *belle époque*: middle-class society in France (especially Paris) before 1914. She is particularly adept at exploring human relationships, such as the tragic love of a young man for a woman of fifty in *Chéri* and *The Last of Chéri*, or a husband's destructive jealousy of his wife in *Duo*, but she also writes with great sensitivity about children (in, for instance, *Claudine at School*, her first book) and about nature, especially animals. This is not to imply, however, that she is a sentimental writer, quite the reverse: there are a toughness and sharpness in her analysis of her characters' moods and whims which is firmly in the great French tradition of psychological precision inaugurated by Madame de Lafayette and continued by Constant and Stendhal. At her best she sustains comparison with these illustrious forebears in her unclouded perception of the ravages of love.

But her books, fine as some of them are, constitute only a part of her legacy. Like George Sand nearly a century earlier she worked hard as a professional woman of letters, and even, after her divorce from Willy, plunged for a time into the gruelling life of a professional actress and performer. This was a brave and original thing to do then, but it is characteristic of the lack of pretentiousness and of the no-nonsense attitude manifested in her fiction. Since she had to earn her own living after the break with Willy, she put her talents to good use. Unsentimental in her attitudes as in her art, she accepted that if she was to be free and independent she had to raise income by her own unaided efforts. Like Simone de Beauvoir, who is perhaps more of an intellectual though not necessarily more intelligent, she may in the last analysis be a minor writer only, but there is no doubt that she is a great woman, a figure of whom women of today can be proud. In spite of knowing great personal unhappiness in her younger days, she lived to become one of most famous and honoured writers of her generation, and this, in a male-dominated society, is no small achievement.

—John Fletcher

CORNEILLE, Pierre. Born in Rouen, France, June 1609; elder brother of the writer Thomas Corneille. Educated in Jesuit college, Rouen, 1615-22; studied law, 1622-24, licensed lawyer, 1624. Married Marie de Lampérière in 1641; seven children. Member of the Rouen Parlement, 1629-50: held offices as King's advocate in water and forests court and in Rouen port Admiralty court. Lived in Paris after 1662. *Died 1 October 1684.*

PUBLICATIONS

Collections

Oeuvres, edited by Charles Marty-Leaveaux. 12 vols., 1862-68.

Oeuvres complètes, edited by A. Stegman. 1963.
Oeuvres complètes, edited by Georges Couton. 1980— .

Plays

Mélite; ou, Les Fausses Lettres (produced 1629-30). 1633; translated as *Melite*, 1776.
Clitandre; ou, L'Innocence delivrée (produced 1630-31). 1632.
La Veuve; ou, Le Traitre trahi (produced 1631-32). 1634.
La Galerie du Palais; ou, L'Amie rivale (produced 1632-33). 1637; edited by Milorad R. Margitic, 1981.
La Suivante (produced 1633-34). 1637; edited by Milorad R. Margitic, 1978.
La Place Royale; ou, L'amoureux extravagant (produced 1633-34). 1637.
Médée (produced 1635). 1639; edited by André de Leyssac, 1978.
La Comédie des Tuileries, with others (produced 1635). 1638.
L'Illusion comique (produced 1635-36). 1639; as *The Theatrical Illusion*, 1975.
Le Cid (produced 1637). 1637; translated as *The Cid*, 1637.
L'Aveugle de Smyrne, with others (produced 1637). 1638.
Horace (produced 1640). 1641; translated as *Horatius*, 1656.
Cinna (produced 1640-41). 1643; as *Cinna's Conspiracy*, 1713.
Polyeucte, Martyr (produced 1642-43). 1643; translated as *Polyeuctes*, 1655.
La Mort de Pompée (produced 1643-44). 1644; as *Pompey the Great*, 1664.
Le Menteur (produced 1643-44). 1644; as *The Mistaken Beauty; or, The Liar*, 1685; as *The Lying Lover*, 1717.
Oeuvres (plays). 1644; and later editions.
La Suite du Menteur (produced 1644-45). 1645.
Rodogune, Princesse des Parthes (produced 1644-45). 1645; translated as *Rodogune*, 1765.
Théodore, vierge et martyre (produced 1645-46). 1646 or 1647.
Héraclius, Empereur d'Orient (produced 1646-47). 1647; as *Heraclius, Emperor of the East*, 1664.
Andromède (produced 1649-50). 1650.
Don Sanche d'Aragon (produced 1649-50). 1650.
Nicomède (produced 1651). 1651; translated as *Nicomede*, 1671.
Pertharite, Roi des Lombards (produced 1651-52). 1653.
Oedipe (produced 1659). 1659.
Le Toison d'Or (produced 1660). 1661.
Sertorius (produced 1662). 1662.
Sophonisbe (produced 1663). 1663.
Othon (produced 1664). 1665.
Agésilas (produced 1666). 1666.
Attila, Roi des Huns (produced 1667). 1667.
Tite et Bérénice (produced 1670). 1671.
Psyché, with Molière and Quinault, music by Lully (produced 1671). 1671.
Pulchérie (produced 1672). 1673.
Suréna, Général des Parthes (produced 1674). 1675; translated as *Surenas*, 1969.

Other

Oeuvres diverses. 1738.
Writings on the Theatre, edited by H.T. Barnwell. 1965.

Translator, *L'Imitation de Jésus-Christ*, by Thomas à Kempis. 1651.
Translator, *Louanges de la Sainte Vierge*, by St. Bonaventure. 1665.

Translator, *L'Office de la Sainte Vierge*. 1670.

*

Critical Studies: *The Classical Moment: Studies of Corneille, Molière, and Racine* by Martin Turnell, 1947; *Corneille: His Heroes and Their Worlds* by Robert J. Nelson, 1963, and *Corneille and Racine* edited by Nelson, 1966; *Corneille* by P.J. Yarrow, 1963; *The Cornelian Hero* by Albert West, 1963; *The Criticism of Cornelian Tragedy* by Herbert Fogel, 1967; *Corneille* by Claude K. Abraham, 1972; *Corneille and Racine: Problems of Tragic Form* by Gordon Pocock, 1973; *Corneille: Horace* by R.C. Knight, 1981; *The Tragic Drama of Corneille and Racine* by H.T. Barnwell, 1982.

*   *   *

Corneille is the earliest of the great French Classical playwrights. "Cornelian" has become an adjective to describe qualities of grandeur, heroism, and the subordination of passion to duty which are apparent in many of his plays.

His production is in fact very various. He shows a constant desire to astound—by extreme gestures and situations, by complication, surprise, verbal display, variety. As a poet, his great gift is for emphatic and weighty eloquence, admirably suited to his "Cornelian" moments. But his range is wide—tenderness, lyricism, irony, with a talent (not only in his comedies) for realistic dialogue and repartee. His changes of tone and delight in verbal ingenuity have often led to complaints of bathos and bad taste, but can be seen as indications of his breadth and daring. He shows a fascination with human behaviour in bizarre and confused situations, and especially with the complexity of moral decisions, sometimes reflecting contemporary events and controversies. This fascination is most memorably focussed on the hero's struggle to fulfil the demands of his "gloire" (literally "honour" or "reputation," but in Corneille's best work a subtle concept involving self-realisation at a high moral level). There is also a sense of the complexity of life in a more obvious way. Even in his loftiest plays there is an awareness of the self-seeking, even comical, elements which accompany and oppose or corrupt the heroic impulse. In many of his works, this shades into irony and a disabused realism.

Corneille's early plays are mainly comedies on the intrigues of young lovers. They are best read in the original versions, before Corneille toned them down. Free in form, with a mixture of realism and fantasy, they show a Baroque concern with illusion and the falsity of appearances, especially in the play-within-a-play-within-a-play of *L'Illusion comique*. Despite their often frank realism and comedy, deeper themes emerge: real or assumed madness and real grief at a supposed death (*Mélite*); misery caused by a young man's rejection of love in order to preserve his freedom (*La Place Royale*—King's Square); the bitterness of a woman at her social status (*La Suivante*—The Waiting-Woman). *Clitandre*, though labelled a tragedy, is a romantic comedy. *Médée* signals Corneille's approach to tragedy. It sets the selfish triviality of Jason and the Court against the lonely figure of Medea, who asserts her identity by a terrible revenge.

Le Cid shows the crisis in the hero's life when he has to kill the father of his beloved Chimène in order to fulfil his heroic destiny, and she, to match his integrity, has to seek his death. Although Corneille blurs the ending, the poignancy and dramatic boldness of the situations, together with the lyricism and energy of the verse, make this his most accessible play. *Horace*, the first play within the strict unities (though Corneille, as often, has difficulty in unifying his action), shows the hero isolating himself in his destiny, which leads him both to save his country and murder his sister. Corneille resolves the crisis ambiguously, showing the hero both glorious and flawed. *Cinna* is perhaps his most unified achievement. In a shifting drama of love and political intrigue, it focusses on the effort of the Emperor Augustus to transcend his past and convert by forgiveness those who have conspired against him. *Polyeucte* deals with a clash between Christianity and Paganism in the Roman Empire, and shows how the heroic Polyeucte, in seeking martyrdom, brings to Christianity not only his passionate wife but also his cynical father-in-law. Powerful in structure, characterisation, and verse, it is often regarded as his masterpiece though some have found the ending unconvincing.

Corneille's later plays only intermittently achieve this level. Until the failure of *Pertharite*, he produced a series of very varied plays—tragedies, plays with music and spectacular effects, and *comédies héroïques* (plays with noble characters, but less serious than tragedies). The best are the comedy *Le Menteur* (*The Liar*) and the tragedy *Nicomède*, a play of complex ironies showing the hero triumphing (largely through the efforts of others) over the hostility of Rome and the intrigues of his stepmother, who dominates his realistic and weak father. *Rodogune* and *Héraclius*, both tragedies, are more typical, in their schematic characterisation, exciting plots, and melodramatic verve.

The plays after Corneille's return to the theatre in 1659 are uneven, but in some ways his most interesting. The heroic mode of his masterpieces and the melodrama of his middle plays give way to a subtle blend of political and psychological intrigue, with flashes of both grandeur and comedy. The finest are *Sertorius*, dramatising the clash of personal and political ambitions in the civil wars of the Roman Republic, and *Suréna*, his last play. *Suréna*, with its atmosphere of ambiguity and menace, has an emotional and tragic resonance rare in Corneille.

As well as various prefatory pieces, Corneille wrote the substantial critical *Discourses* and critiques (*Examens*) of individual plays prefixed to each volume of his 1660 *Works*. Although not very illuminating on individual plays, they show his difficulties with the contemporary critical concern for verisimilitude and moral utility in poetry. He stresses pleasure as the aim of drama, and historical truth as an aid to credibility.

Apart from some lively personal pieces, his non-dramatic poetry is of little interest.

—Gordon Pocock

D'ANNUNZIO, Gabriele. Born in Pescara, Italy, 12 March 1863. Educated at a secondary school, Prato, 1874-81; University of Rome, 1881. Served in the Italian Infantry, Navy, and Air Force during World War I: injury led to loss of sight of one eye. Married Duchess Maria Hardouin di Gallese in 1883, three children; had romance with the actress Eleonora Duse, 1895-1904. Staff member, *Tribuna*, Rome, in the 1880's; elected to Chamber of Deputies, 1897-1900 (defeated, 1900); lived in Tuscany, 1899-1910; forced by debts to live in France, 1910-15; after the Treaty of Versailles, seized Fiume with other patriots and held the city, 1919-20; supported the Fascists: granted a title by Mussolini. *Died 1 March 1938.*

Publications

Collections

    Tutte le opere, edited by Angelo Sodini. 49 vols., 1927-36.
    Tutte le opere, edited by Egidio Bianchetti. 10 vols., 1939-50.
    Poesie, Teatro, Prose, edited by Mario Praz. 1966.

Verse

    Primo vere. 1879; revised edition, 1880.
    Canto novo. 1882.

Intermezzo di rime. 1883.
San Pantaleone. 1886.
Isaotta Guttadàuro ed altre poesie. 1886; revised edition, as *L'Isottèo, La Chimera*, 1890.
Elegie romane 1887-1891. 1892.
Odi navali. 1893.
L'Allegoria dell' autunno. 1895.
La canzone di Garibaldi. 1901.
Laudi del cielo, del mare, della terra, e degli eroi: Anno 1903—Maia; Anno 1904—Elettra, Alcyone; Libro IV—Merope. 3 vols., 1903-12.
L'orazione e la canzone in morte di Giosuè Carducci. 1907.
Canto novo. 1907.
Le città del silenzio. 1926.
Poesia, edited by Federico Roncoroni. 1978.

Plays

Sogno d'un mattino di primavera (produced 1897). 1897; as *The Dream of a Spring Morning*, 1911.
La città morta (produced 1898). 1898; as *The Dead City*, 1900.
La Gioconda (produced 1899). 1898; translated as *Gioconda*, 1901.
Sogno di un tramonto d'autunno (produced 1905). 1898; as *The Dream of an Autumn Sunset*, 1903.
La gloria (produced 1899). 1899.
Francesca da Rimini (produced 1901). 1901; revised version, music by Riccardo Zandonai (produced 1914), 1914; translated as *Francesca da Rimini*, 1902.
La figlia di Iorio (produced 1904). 1904; revised version, music by Alberto Franchetti (produced 1906), 1906; as *The Daughter of Jorio*, 1907.
La fiaccola sotto il moggio (produced 1905). 1905.
Più che l'amore (produced 1906). 1907.
La nave (produced 1908). 1908; translated as *La Nave*, 1919.
Fedra (produced 1909). 1909.
Le Martyre de Saint Sébastien, music by Debussy (produced 1911). 1911.
Il ferro (produced 1913). 1914; as *The Honeysuckle*, 1911.
Parisina, music by Mascagni. 1913.
La pisanelle (produced 1913). In *Tutte le opere*, 1935.
Cabiria. 1914.

Screenplay: *La crociata degli innocenti*, 1911.

Fiction

Terra vergine (short stories). 1882.
Il libro delle vergine. 1884.
Il piacere. 1889; as *The Child of Pleasure*, 1898.
L'innocente. 1892; as *The Intruder*, 1898; as *The Victim*, 1915.
Giovanni Episcopo. 1892; as *Episcopo and Company*, 1896.
Trionfo della morte. 1894; as *The Triumph of Death*, 1896.
Le vergini delle rocce. 1896; as *The Maidens of the Rocks*, 1898; as *The Virgins of the Rocks*, 1899.
Il fuoco. 1900; as *The Flame of Life*, 1900; as *The Flame*, 1906.
Le Novelle della Pescare. 1902; as *Tales of My Native Town*, 1920.
Forse che sì, forse che no. 1910.
La leda senza cigno. 1916.

D'ANNUNZIO

Bibliography: *D'Annunzio Abroad: A Bibliographical Essay* by Joseph G. Fucilla and Joseph M. Carrière, 2 vols., 1935-37; *Bibliografia critica di d'Annunzio* by Mario Vecchioni, 1970; *Bibliografia della critica dannunziana nei periodici italiani dal 1880 al 1938* by Anna Baldazzi, 1977.

Critical Studies: *D'Annunzio* by Tom Antongini, 1938; *D'Annunzio: The Poet as Superman* by Anthony Rhodes, 1959; *D'Annunzio in France: A Study in Cultural Relations* by Giovanni Gullace, 1966; *D'Annunzio* by Philippe Julian, 1973; *The First Duce: D'Annunzio at Fiume* by Michael A. Ledeen, 1977.

*　　*　　*

The grounds for regarding D'Annunzio as a major 20th-century Italian poet are aptly summed up by Montale: "D'Annunzio experimented or touched upon all the linguistic and prosodic possibilities of our time.... Not to have learned anything from him would be a very bad sign." Yet Montale as well as Ungaretti and Saba reacted against him, just as D'Annunzio had reacted against the poetic tradition represented by Carducci and Pascoli. D'Annunzio's metrical and linguistic innovations altered expression and reflected a new sensibility. He was a prolific writer (in French and in Italian): his first book of poems, *Primo Vere*, came out in 1879 and his last, *Teneo te, Africa* (in *Tutte le opere*), in 1936. In between he published several important books of lyrics; *Alcyone*—the third of four books (*Maia, Elettra*, and *Merope* are the others) in the cycle of poems called *Laudi del cielo, del mare, della terra, e degli eroi* (Praises of the skies, the sea, the earth, and the heroes)—offers a synthesis between his naturalistic creed and rhythmic mastery and control, and is deservedly regarded as his most inspired and most successful book of lyrics.

The characteristic qualities of D'Annunzio's best work are exuberant naturalism, plastic and pictorial talent, rhythmic, metric, and imagistic skill, mastery over landscape in depicting which D'Annunzio brings out and fuses into one "physicality" and "sensuousness" as well as profound inwardness and spirituality.

But with such qualities, there co-existed in D'Annunzio's work certain defects and weaknesses, such as a self-indulgent dilettantism in dealing with things that are not rooted in the poet's life and experience; a kind of moral as well as impressionistic exhibitionism not redeemed by the vitality and concreteness of a fully realized experience; and a rhetorical, musical, and aesthetic artifice which aims at and at times achieves a kind of perfection which is hollow and unconvincing.

D'Annunzio also wrote novels and plays. Of the former those most indicative of his powers as a decadent aesthete are *The Child of Pleasure, The Virgins of the Rocks, The Flame of Life*, and *Forse che sì forse che no*; and of the latter *The Dead City, Gioconda, Francesca da Rimini*, and the best-known, *The Daughter of Jorio*, are the most characteristic. Both in the plays and the novels one underlying theme is the Nietzschean myth of the superman; another is the cult of sensuality.

—G. Singh

DANTE Alighieri. Born in Florence, in 1265, probably late May. Details of his education are conjectural, but he was raised as a gentleman and was an avid student of philosophy and poetry. Served the Guelphs as a mounted soldier in 1289. Married Gemma di Maretto Donati in 1294 (affianced, 1283); four children. Involved in Florentine civic affairs: served on people's council, 1295-96, and other councils, 1296 and 1297, and diplomatic missions; one of the six priors of the city, 1300; while on a mission to Rome in 1301 his party was defeated in Florence and he was exiled: sought refuge at courts of various Ghibelline lords in northern Italy: in San Godenzo in 1302, Forli in 1303, then in Verona; in his later years he refused a conditional amnesty and probably spent time in Lucca, Mantua, Verona, and Ravenna. *Died 13 September 1321.*

PUBLICATIONS

Collections

The Latin Works. 1904.
Opere, edited by Michele Barbi and others.   2 vols., 1921-22; 2nd edition, 1960.
The Portable Dante, edited by Paolo Milano.   1947.

Verse

La Vita Nuova, edited by Michele Barbi, in *Opere*.   1960; translated by D.G. Rossetti, in *The Early Italian Poets*, 1861, and by Mark Musa, 1962.
Rime, edited by Michele Barbi and F. Maggini.   1965; translated by Patrick S. Diehl, 1979.
Eclogae latinae, edited by E. Pistelli, in *Opere*.   1960; translated by W. Brewer, 1927.
Commedia, edited by Giorgio Petrocchi.   4 vols., 1966-67; also edited (with translation) by Charles S. Singleton, 6 vols., 1970-75; as *Divine Comedy*, translated by H.W. Longfellow, 1867, Laurence Binyon, 1933-46, L.G. White, 1948, Dorothy L. Sayers and Barbara Reynolds, 1949-62, and John Ciardi, 1954-70; translated into prose by J. Carlyle, T. Okey, and P. Wicksteed, 1899-1901.
Lyric Poetry, edited by Kenelm Foster and Patrick Boyde.   2 vols., 1967.

Other

Il Convivio, edited by G. Busnelli and G. Vandelli.   1964; as *The Banquet*, 1909.
De Vulgari Eloquentia, edited by A. Marigo, revised by P.G. Ricci.   1957; translated in *Latin Works*, 1904.
De Monarchia, edited by E. Rostagno, in *Opere*.   1960; as *On World-Government*, edited by H.W. Schneider, 1957.
Epistolae: The Letters, edited and translated by Paget Toynbee.   1920; revised edition, edited by C.G. Hardie, 1966.
Questio de aqua et de terra, edited by E. Pistelli, in *Opere*.   1960; translated in *Latin Works*, 1904.
Literary Criticism, edited by Robert S. Haller.   1973.

*

Critical Studies: *An Essay on the Vita Nuova*, 1949, and *Dante Studies 1-2*, 1954-58, all by Charles S. Singleton; *Dante the Philosopher* by Étienne Gilson, 1952; *Dante as a Political Thinker* by A. Passerin d'Entrèves, 1952; *Dante's Drama of the Mind: A Modern Reading of the Purgatorio*, 1953, and *Dante*, 1966, both by Francis Fergusson; *Introductory Papers on Dante*, 1954, and *Further Papers on Dante*, 1957, both by Dorothy L. Sayers; *Structure and Thought in the Paradiso* by Joseph Mazzeo, 1958; *The Ladder of Vision: A Study of Dante's*

Comedy by Irma Brandeis, 1960; *Dante, Poet of the Secular World* by Erich Auerbach, 1961; *Dante* by Thomas G. Bergin, 1965, as *An Approach to Dante*, 1965; *Dante and His World* by T.C. Chubb, 1966; *Enciclopedia dantesca*, 5 vols., 1970-75; *Dante's Epic Journeys* by D. Thompson, 1974; *The Two Dantes and Other Studies* by Kenelm Foster, 1977; *Dante the Maker* by William Anderson, 1980; *Dante* by G. Holmes, 1980.

*   *   *

The city in which Dante was born and where he spent the first 38 years of his life was in his time already an important cultural center as well as the focus of conflicting political forces. Having cast off its feudal allegiance it was a self-governing community, administered by its own citizens under the direction of a prosperous bourgeoisie. Although Dante's father was not a prominent figure in the life of the city (he was perhaps a money lender) the poet claimed to be descended from the aristocracy and he was in his youth sufficiently well endowed to enable him to study painting, music, and letters (according to Boccaccio) and, it seems likely, to spend a year at the University of Bologna. Florence already possessed a literary tradition; Dante readily acknowledged his indebtedness to Brunetto Latini, author of the allegorizing *Tesoretto*, and to the poet Guido Cavalcanti (slightly older than Dante) who had brought a speculative element into the love lyric of the Provençal tradition. Dante's literary production in fact begins with lyrics in the Cavalcanti style. Dante's first notable work, however, was the *Vita Nuova*, an account of his idealistic love for Beatrice Portinari, composed after her death. It is a carefully constructed composition of unique and original character: prose is interspersed with verse, serving to provide a narrative line between the lyrics and also to illuminate their meaning by exegesis of a scholastic tone. The combination of realism and suggestion of hidden meanings as well as the calculated design of the little book give the reader a foretaste of the *Comedy*. The poet's immersion in politics following the death of Beatrice and his subsequent banishment and disillusionment altered the course of both his reading and his writing; he turned from the quasi-mystic devotion to Beatrice (and Revelation) to the study of philosophy; this shift is documented in the *Convivio*, a long, digressive work, dealing with philosophical, ethical, and even political matters, revealing a new area of study: Aristotle, Boethius, and Virgil are authorities of recurrent reference. As in the *Vita Nuova* prose is used to explicate poems but in the *Convivio* the prose element is far greater. Another area of his studies after his exile is disclosed by the *De Vulgari Eloquentia*, written in Latin, a pioneering exercise in linguistic studies in which the author attempts to define the characteristics of true Italian speech. The all but obsessive interest in political matters, a natural concomitant of his exile, is the motivation for his *Monarchia* and his impassioned *Epistolae*. These Latin items of his canon were composed in all likelihood in the years of Henry VII's effort to reassert Imperial supremacy in Italy and probably when the writing of the *Comedy* was already in progress.

For his "minor works" alone—all original and significant—Dante would be accounted a major figure in Italian—and even European—literary history, but it is the *Comedy* which has given him a unique and enduring pre-eminence. In the context of the times it is surprising that a work of such epic dimensions should not have been written in Latin—and, according to Boccaccio, Dante at first thought of using that tongue. The choice of the vernacular for his masterpiece was of crucial importance in the development of Italian literature, but the greatness of the work makes even such a determinant role merely incidental.

The prestige of the poem has long endured. Through the centuries immediately following its composition it maintained its eminence and survived through the less appreciative climate of the 17th and 18th centuries, gathering new vitality in the 19th and growing in popularity and esteem over the past two hundred years. The scope of its attraction has been uniquely vast, rivalling that of the Homeric poems; through the years it has consistently won wide readership and critical attention in all nations of the old world and the new. It has charmed "the man in the street" and fascinated intellectuals. For the English-speaking world, one eloquent statistic may be cited: there have been no fewer than 47 translations of the poem into English (not counting partial versions) and more are in course of preparation.

There are many reasons for such persistent vitality just as there are many facets and levels of meaning in the work itself. For Dante, according to his letter to Can Grande, the literal substance of the poem is simply an account of the state of souls after death, with allegorical implications below the surface. But the mode of depiction is not simply expositional; it is cast in narrative form. And it is a story compellingly told, in which the protagonist, the author himself, describes his pilgrimage through the Christian realms of the after-life, Hell, Purgatory, and Heaven. These are kingdoms of fancy, to be sure, in which the author is free to invent backgrounds, scenes, and events. But these kingdoms are populated by characters drawn not from inventive fancy but from the narrator's own acquaintance, whether in experience or in his readings, and they are set forth with convincing realism. The essential ingredients for assuring the reader's interest—movement, suspense, recognition—are present from beginning to end as the pilgrim-narrator moves from one circle of Hell, one terrace of Purgatory, or one circling Heaven to another with surprises for himself and his reader at every passage. In all of these realms the wayfarer has a companion and guide (Virgil or Beatrice) to instruct and advise him but with the tactical function also of giving life to the narrative through dialog, more effective than simple narrational exposition in providing dramatic movement. No writer of fiction has planned his art with greater care or shrewdness. But the *Comedy* is more than fiction. The characters, including the narrator, have suggestive symbolic dimensions, allusive and often challengingly ambiguous. As the story unrolls the reader becomes aware that the realms of fancy or theological postulate are also provinces of the world we live in, depicted with a perception fortified by learning and a commitment born of faith and hope. It is our world that we recognize behind the veil, with all its faltering waywardness, penitential meditation, and yearning for salvation and exaltation. The wayfarer too is not simply a 14th-century Florentine exile; he is everyman, and he speaks for all of us. We are his fellow pilgrims sub specie aeternitatis.

The substance of the poem is given strength and beauty by rare technical artistry. The *Comedy* is a masterful design, with carefully planned and harmonious proportions; all of the *cantiche* are of approximately the same length, and the dimensions of each canto also bear witness to the "fren dell'arte." *Terza rima* itself, with its syllogistic construction and its subliminal trinitarian implications, has also the practical uses of linkage and invitation to memorization. The poet makes skillful use, too, of such devices as alliteration, assonance, and even deft repetition. His imagery is remarkable for its variety—animals, plants, trees, flowers mingle with historical allusions and numerological and mathematical figures in the embroidery of the poem. Some of these are lost in translation but a good translation—and there have been many such—can convey much of this accidental charm into another tongue.

So many, rich, and varied are the threads of which the cloth of the *Comedy* is woven that the nature of the work defies simple definition. It has been called "a personal epic," it is assuredly a confessional autobiography. It is likewise a patient and lucid exposition of orthodox dogma and an encyclopedia as well. At the same time it may be seen as a great love poem, for Beatrice is the motivation and the goal of the pilgrimage; furthermore each great division ends with the same word, suggesting a vast "canzone" of three great stanzas. Or we may see the *Comedy* as a "synthesis of medieval learning," which, at least incidentally, it is. But it is also a synthesis of the aspirations, sensibilities, and ultimate destiny of mankind. It is, most deeply, a statement of affirmation, set forth in terms of a certain time and place and contingent circumstance but valid for all times. Matter, manner, and message are blended not only with exceptional craftsmanship but with commitment and conviction. Aesthetically irresistible, the story of the extra-terrestrial pilgrimage is also on a deeper level reassuring and inspirational.

—Thomas G. Bergin

DARÍO, Rubén. Pseudonym for Felíx Rubén García Sarmiento. Born in Metapa, Nicaragua, 18 January 1867. Married 1) Rafaela Contrera in 1890 (died, 1892), one son; 2) Francisca Sánchez, one son. Journalist from age 14: worked on papers in Santiago, Valparaiso, and Buenos Aires; then correspondent for Latin American papers in various parts of Latin America as well as in Paris and Madrid; also served Guatemala in various diplomatic and representative functions. *Died 6 February 1916.*

PUBLICATIONS

Collections

> *Obras completas.* 22 vols., 1917-20.
> *Obras completas*, edited by Alberto Ghiraldo and Andrés González-Blanco. 21 vols., 1923-29.

Verse

> *Epístolas y poemas.* 1885.
> *Abrojos.* 1887.
> *Las rosas andinas: Rimas y contra-rimas*, with Rubén Rubí. 1888.
> *Azul.* 1888; revised edition, 1890.
> *Rimas.* 1889.
> *Prosas profanas y otros poemas.* 1896; revised edition, 1901; as *Prosas Profanas and Other Poems*, 1922.
> *Cantos de vida y esperanza, Los cisnes, y otros poemas.* 1905.
> *El canto errante.* 1907.
> *Poema del otoño y otros poemas.* 1910.
> *Canto a la Argentina y otros poemas.* 1914.
> *Obra poética.* 4 vols., 1914-16.
> *Eleven Poems*, translated by Thomas Walsh and Salomon de la Selva. 1916.
> *Sol del domingo: Poesías ineditas.* 1917.
> *Poesías completas*, edited by Alfonso Méndez Plancarte. 1952; revised edition, edited by Antonio Oliver Belmás, 2 vols., 1967.

Fiction

> *Emelina*, with Eduardo Poirier. 1887.
> *Edelmira*, edited by Francisco Contreras. 1926(?).

Other

> *A. de Gilbert.* 1890.
> *Los raros.* 1893.
> *Castelar.* 1899.
> *Peregrinaciones.* 1901.
> *España contemporánea.* 1901.
> *La caravana pasa.* 1902.
> *Tierras solares.* 1904.
> *Opiniones.* 1906.
> *Parisiana.* 1907.

El viaje a Nicaragua.　1909.
Blanco.　1911.
Letras.　1911.
Todo al vuelo.　1912.
Autobiografía.　1912.
La casa de las ideas.　1916.
La vida de Rubén Darío, escrita por el mismo.　1916.
El mundo de los sueños: Prosas póstumas.　1917.
Cartas: Epistolario inedito, edited by Dictino Álvarez Hernández.　1963.
Escritos dispersos, edited by Pedro Luis Barcia.　2 vols., 1968-73.

*

Bibliography: *A Bibliography of Darío* by Henry Grattan Doyle, 1935; *Darío: A Selective Classified and Annotated Bibliography* by Hensley C. Woodbridge, 1975.

Critical Studies: *Poet-Errant: A Biography of Darío* by Charles D. Watland, 1965; *Cuadrivio* (on Darío, Lopez Verlarde, Pessoa, Cernuda) by Octavio Paz, 1965; *Darío and the Pythagorean Tradition* by Raymond Skyrme, 1975.

*　　*　　*

Throughout the Spanish-speaking literary world Rubén Darío is known as the great innovator, the poet who transformed the prosody of that language. At the turn of the century he emerged as the leader of the movement known as "Modernismo," and as the first American writer seriously to influence the literary conventions of metropolitan Spain.

His first important collection, *Azul...,* shows an obvious allegiance to 19th-century French poetry, from Hugo through the Parnassians to the Symbolists and Verlaine, otherwise evident in the sketches collected in *Los raros;* in fact the coda of *Azul...,* "Échos," is actually written in French. The core of the book is a "lyrical year," in which the four seasons are experienced in terms less appropriate to the poet's native Nicaragua than to a Europe whose culture dazzled Darío from the start of his career. Nonetheless there are characteristic American notes in the sonnets to Caupolican, the Mapuche hero of Chile, and to the poet Salvador Díaz Mirón, a fellow Modernist whom Darío had known in Mexico and whose "unfettered" verses are said to resound like a herd of American buffalo.

Usually thought of as his most decadent and precious collection, *Prosas profanas* is by any account his least American in terms of overt theme and subject matter, despite, that is, his famous invocation of Palenque and Utatlan, Moctezuma and the Inca, in the introduction. For example, the past evoked in the section "Recreaciones arqueológicas" definitely belongs to the classic Mediterranean, also the backdrop for the extensive "Coloquio de los centauros," with its Pythagoreanism. Elsewhere in this collection Darío turns to the Cid and medieval Spain, much as Ezra Pound (triumphant in London not long after Darío was in Madrid) turned to medieval England. Indeed, this parallel helps us to focus on what is a new cosmopolitanism in the poetry of Darío and the Spanish language in general. Associated repeatedly with Buenos Aires, where Darío began the collection, this cosmopolitanism is most fully expressed in the poem "Divagación," a spiralling journey through cultures and time.

From a technical point of view, *Prosas profanas* announces spectacular innovations in prosody, notably in the syncopation of the alexandrine, which continue to be used to great effect in Darío's three subsequent collections *Cantos de vida y esperanza, El canto errante,* and *Poema del otoño,* though less so in the somewhat stentorian *Canto a la Argentina,* the last collection published in his lifetime. (In his nomadic career, he left a good deal of work uncollected). Typical of the more sombre agility of his later period are the Nocturnes in *Cantos de vida,* notably the arresting alexandrine that opens the second: "Los que auscultasteis el corazón de la noche." The alexandrine is also the verse form chosen by Darío in *El canto errante* for his "Epístola a Madame Lugones," she being the wife of another fellow Modernist, the Argentinian Leopoldo Lugones. Remarkable for its colloquialism, its shifts of mood and tone, as well as its technical virtuosity, this poem has received brilliant elucidation in "El caracol y la sirena," Octavio Paz's indispensable vindication of Darío as the father not just of Modernist but of modern poetry in Spanish.

—Gordon Brotherston

DAZAI, Osamu. Pseudonym for Tsushima Shuji. Born in Kanagi, Japan, 19 June 1909. Educated in Kanagi grade school; middle school in Aomori City; Higher school in Hirosaki, 1927-30; University of Tokyo, 1930. Married 1) Oyama Hatsuyo in 1931; 2) Ishihara Michiko in 1939. Journalist and writer: illness, drinking, and drugs led to several suicide attempts. *Died 13 June 1948*.

PUBLICATIONS

Collections

Zenshu [Works].   12 vols., 1955-56; revised edition, 1967-68, 1979.

Fiction

Bannen [The Declining Years].   1936.
Doke No Hana [The Flower of Buffoonery].   1937.
Dasu Gemaine [Das Gemeine].   1940.
Hashire Merosu [Run Melos].   1940.
Shin Hamuretto [The New Hamlet].   1941.
Kojiki Gakusei [Beggar-Student].   1941.
Kakekomi Uttae [The Indictment].   1941.
Seigi to Bisho [Justice and Smile].   1942.
Udaijin Sanetomo [Lord Sanetomo].   1943.
Tsugaru.   1944.
Shinshaku Shokoku Banashi [A Retelling of the Tales from the Province].   1945.
Otogi Zoshi [A Collection of Fairy Tales].   1945.
Pandora no Hako [Pandora's Box].   1946.
Shayo.   1947; as *The Declining Sun*, 1950; as *The Setting Sun*, 1956.
Biyon No Tsuma [Villon's Wife].   1947.
Ningen Shikkaku.   1948; as *No Longer Human*, 1953.

Other

Fugaku Hyakkei [One Hundred Views of Mt. Fuji].   1940.
Tokyo Hakkei [Eight Views of Tokyo].   1941.
Human Lost (in Japanese).   1941.

*

Critical Studies: *Landscapes and Portraits* by Donald Keene, 1971; *Accomplices of Silence: The Modern Japanese Novel* by Masao Miyoshi, 1974; *Dazai* by James A. O'Brien, 1975; *Modern Japanese Writers and the Nature of Literature* by Makoto Ueda, 1976.

* * *

Though he is regarded as one of the greatest stylists of modern Japanese literature, Dazai Osamu's masterpiece was his life itself. Virtually all his works were reflections of that life. For Dazai, fiction was ultimately a lie, and in his often nostalgic quest for sincerity he strove to strip bare the authorial self and let it speak directly to the reader. In this respect, Dazai can be associated with the autobiographical strain in modern Japanese fiction, the *watakushi-shosetsu* or "I-novel." The practitioners of this form felt that reality could only be portrayed through the unmediated perspective of the author, presented as the first-person narrator in the text. This mode coincided with traditional tendencies to view literature as a mode of self-expression and to hold a somewhat skeptical attitude towards "objective" reality.

Dazai consciously conceived of his life as art, as the subject matter of his writings. Dazai the man became "Dazai" the text, and his works represented various readings of that text. The Dazai persona was that of the sensitive but cynical dissolute, the sloppy drunk who arouses more pity than disgust. It was characterized by an all-too-human weakness that was designed to elicit compassion, the highest virtue. Born to a wealthy landholding family, Dazai developed a rebellious streak that he briefly tried to channel into political activism, but it seems that he could not even believe in Communism. Distrusting virtually all social institutions, he lived a scandalous life. Hypocrisy, arrogance, and pretension are denounced everywhere in his works, while simplicity, sincerity, and honesty are praised. In Dazai's literary world, consciousness is the curse that keeps one from living a true life. While idealizing simple people who live day-to-day in an un-self-conscious manner, Dazai found himself irresistibly drawn to despair and death.

Many of Dazai's writings are in the "I-novel" vein. Such works as *Tokyo Hakkei*, *Fugaku Hyakkei*, and *Tsugaru* are first-person narratives by the archetypal "Dazai" character. In *Shin Hamuretto*, *Otogi Zoshi*, and similar works, old literary works are retold in a uniquely Dazaiesque manner, irreverent yet profoundly human. Dazai's most accomplished works of fiction—the short story "Villon's Wife" and the novels *The Setting Sun* and *No Longer Human*—appeared shortly after the end of the Second World War. Taken together, the works present a deep and multi-faceted composite image of the "Dazai" persona. *The Setting Sun*, Dazai's most famous work, has been praised for its portrayal of the desolation and hope of postwar Japan. Yet although one of the central characters, Kazuko, appears to have made an existentialist decision at the end, even her resolve is cloaked in ambiguity.

If Dazai's oeuvre suffers from its narrowly-drawn subject, it nevertheless contains some of the most beautiful prose in 20th-century Japanese literature. Due to his basic love of humanity, Dazai possessed an extraordinary sensitivity to the rhythm and flow of speech which was revealed in a limpid, entertaining, and often humorous literary style that makes his works a joy to read, and must account for some of the popularity he maintains among Japanese readers to this day.

—Matthew Mizenko

DIDEROT, Denis.   Born in Langres, France, 5 October 1713.   Educated in a Jesuit school in Langres, 1723-28; in Paris from 1728: master of arts from University of Paris, 1732; studied with a lawyer, 1732-34. Married Antoinette Champion in 1743; two daughters and two sons. Tutor, and free-lance writer and translator from 1734; imprisoned briefly in 1749 for *Lettre sur les aveugles*; commissioned by the publisher Le Breton to edit the Encyclopédie, which appeared from 1751 to 1772: also a major contributor; writer for F.M. Grimm's private periodical *Correspondance Littéraire* from 1759; patronized by Catherine the Great from 1765, and visited Russia, 1773-74. Member, Prussian Royal Academy, 1751; Foreign Member, Russian Academy of Sciences, 1773. *Died 31 July 1784*.

Publications

Collections

> *Oeuvres complètes*, edited by Jean Assezat and Maurice Tourneux.   20 vols., 1875-77.
> *Oeuvres complètes* (chronological edition), edited by Roger Lewinter.   15 vols., 1969-73.
> *Oeuvres complètes*, edited by H. Dieckmann, Jean Varloot, and Jacques Proust.   1975—.
> *The Irresistible Diderot* (selections), edited by John Hope Mason.   1982.

Fiction

> *Les Bijoux indiscrets*.   1748; as *The Indiscreet Toys*, 1749.
> *Contes moraux et nouvelles idylles*, with Salomon Gessner, edited by J.-H. Meister.   1773.
> *Jacques le fataliste et son maître*.   1796; edited by Simone Lecointre and Jean Le Galliot, 1976; as *James the Fatalist and His Master*, 1797.
> *La Religieuse*.   1796; edited by Robert Mauzi, 1972; as *The Nun*, 1797.
> *Le Neveu de Rameau*.   1821; edited by Jean Fabre, 1950; as *Rameau's Nephew*, 1897.
> *Récits*, edited by Ph. Van Tieghem.   1959.
> *Oeuvres romanesques*, edited by Henri Bénac.   1962.

Plays

> *Le Fils naturel; ou, Les Épreuves de la vertu* (produced 1757).   1757; as *Dorval; or, The Test of Virtue*, 1767.
> *Le Père de famille* (produced 1759).   1758; as *The Father*, 1770; as *The Family Picture*, 1781.
> *Est-il bon est-il méchant?* (produced 1913).   1784.
> *Le Joueur*, from the play *The Gamester* by Edward Moore.   1819.

Other

> *Pensées philosophiques*.   1746; as *Philosophical Thoughts*, in *Early Philosophical Works*, 1916.
> *Mémoires sur différens sujets de mathématiques*.   1748.
> *Lettre sur les aveugles*.   1749; as *An Essay on Blindness*, 1750.
> *Lettre sur les sourds et muets*.   1751; edited by Paul Hugo Meyer, 1965; as *Letter on the Deaf and Dumb*, in *Early Philosophical Works*, 1916.
> *Pensées sur l'interprétation de la nature*.   1753.
> *Leçons de clavecin et principes d'harmonie*.   1771.
> *Oeuvres philosophiques*.   6 vols., 1772.

Essai sur Sénèque.   1778; revised edition, as *Essai sur les règnes de Claude et de Néron*, 1782.
Essai sur la peinture.   1795.
Supplément au voyage de Bouganville.   1796; edited by Herbert Dieckmann, 1955.
Mémoires, correspondances, et ouvrages inédits.   4 vols., 1830-31.
Mémoires pour Cathérine II.   1899; edited by Paul Verniere, 1966.
Observations sur la Nakaz.   1920.
Dialogues (in English).   1927.
Lettres à Sophie Volland, edited by André Babelon.   1938; as *Letters to Sophie Volland*, 1972.
Correspondance, edited by Georges Roth.   16 vols., 1955-70.
Oeuvres philosophiques, edited by Paul Vernière.   1956.
Salons, edited by Jean Séznec and Jean Adhémar.   4 vols., 1957-67.
Oeuvres esthétiques, edited by Paul Vernière.   1959.
Le Rêve de d'Alembert, edited by Jean Varloot.   1962.
Oeuvres politiques, edited by Paul Vernière.   1963.
Rameau's Nephew and Other Works, edited by R.H. Bowen.   1964.
Éléments de physiologie, edited by Jean Mayer.   1964.
Encyclopedia: Selections, edited by Nelly S. Hoyt and Thomas Cassirer.   1965; another selection edited by Stephen Gendzier, 1967.
Selected Writings, edited by Lester G. Crocker.   1966.

Editor, and contributor, *Encyclopédie; ou, Dictionnaire raisonné des sciences, des arts, et des métiers, par une société de gens de lettres.*   17 vols., 1751-65; *Recueil de planches*, 11 vols., 1762-72.

Translator, *Histoire de Grèce*, by Temple Stanyan.   3 vols., 1743.
Translator, *Principes de la philosophie morale*, by Shaftesbury.   1745; revised edition, as *Philosophie morale réduite à ses principes*, 1751.
Translator, with Marc-Antoine Eidous and François-Vincent Toussaint, *Dictionnaire universel de médecine*, by Robert James.   6 vols., 1746-48.
Translator, *Les Oeuvres de Shaftesbury.*   3 vols., 1769.

*

Bibliography: *Bibliographie de Diderot* by Frederick A. Spear, 1980.

Critical Studies: *Diderot Studies*, 1949— ; *Diderot's Determined Fatalist* by J. Robert Loy, 1950; *The Embattled Philosopher: A Biography of Diderot*, 1954, revised edition, 1966, and *Diderot's Chaotic Order*, 1974, both by Lester G. Crocker; *Essays on the "Encyclopédie" of Diderot and d'Alembert* by John Lough, 1968; *Diderot the Satirist: "Le Neveu de Rameau" and Related Works* by Donal O'Gorman, 1971; *Diderot* by Arthur M. Wilson, 1972; *Diderot's Politics* by Anthony Strugnell, 1973; *Diderot and the Art of Dialogue* by Carol Sherman, 1976; *Diderot: La Religieuse* by Vivienne Mylne, 1981; *Diderot* by Peter France, 1983.

*   *   *

Diderot is best remembered as the general editor of the *Encyclopedia* and as one of its main contributors. The project absorbed most of his energies from 1750-72. Conceived initially as a translation of Chambers *Cyclopaedia*, the *Encyclopedia* developed into an overview of world knowledge and was intended to illustrate its inherent harmony and order. In Diderot's hands the work became an organ of radical and anti-reactionary propaganda; hence publication was from time to time impeded by the French authorities. Technology figures largely in the text and in the accompanying plates, and the work also contains numerous articles on ethical, philosophical, and aesthetic topics. Though produced in a society still dominated by the Roman

Catholic Church, the *Encyclopedia* reflects its editor's hostility to religious authority, and, while many of the contributors were priests, Diderot contrived to incorporate heterodox or "dangerous" views in seemingly minor articles to which the reader is directed by cross-references given in the more prominent, orthodox ones. The *Encyclopedia* encapsulates the spirit of the French Enlightenment and is its most noteworthy product.

From early adherence to a deism derived from the English deists (principally Shaftesbury), Diderot moved to an openly atheistic viewpoint in the *Letter on the Blind* of 1749, which earned him a brief spell in the Vincennes prison. In his novel *The Nun*, which was not in general circulation in his lifetime, Diderot uses a protagonist forced to take the veil against her will in order to explore the pernicious effects on nuns of life in the convent, separated as it is from normal society. A film based on the novel, directed by Jacques Rivette, was banned in France in 1966 and released in the U.K. in the following year. Among his other novels, the best known is the picaresque *Jacques the Fatalist*, partially inspired by *Tristram Shandy*. As well as being a rather ambivalent examination of philosophical determinism, this novel is notable for the strikingly modern way in which Diderot engages the active participation of the reader in the unfolding of the episodes, through authorial harangues, questions, puzzles, alternative versions, and ascribed reactions. Both *Jacques...* and *The Nun* are perfectly accessible to the modern reader.

Diderot was a polymath very familiar with the scientific trends of his day. He was especially fascinated by discoveries in the biological sciences of the 1740's and 1750's onwards and, in works which include *On the Interpretation of Nature*, the *Dialogue between D'Alembert and Diderot*, *D'Alembert's Dream* and the *Elements of Physiology*, developed theories of the cellular structure of matter and of animal adaptation which prefigured the work of Lamarck and Darwin.

While intellectually a philosophical materialist and a determinist, believing that individual character was principally the product of heredity, Diderot thought man was generally susceptible to modification by environmental influences. He ascribed most of the evil he saw around him to the baleful influence of European (especially French) society, but his attempts, in works like his *Supplement to Bougainville's Voyage*, to develop a moral code based on "natural" principles were doomed to failure by the impossibility of formulating a definition of nature which could underpin social morality.

Like a number of his contemporaries, he clung in his published works to the belief that only the virtuous man can know true happiness and that even apparently prospering evil-doers suffer in their conscience. However, *Rameau's Nephew*, a polythematic dialogue which he began in 1761 and polished over the next 20 years without ever attempting to publish it, casts doubts on this view. In the belief that the theatre could serve to further ethical progress—and that both the writer and the State could exploit it in this way—he wrote three very detailed treatises on dramatic art, which Lessing admired, and three original plays (discounting adaptations) which fail to match the dynamism of the theoretical works.

In his *Salons*, written for readers unable actually to see the pictures described, he proves himself a judicious and sensitive art critic and was the first to interest himself in the technical processes ancillary to painting.

—John Dunkley

DINESEN, Isak. Pseudonym for Karen Christentze Blixen, née Dinesen. Born in Rungsted, Denmark, 17 April 1885. Educated privately; studied art at Academy of Art, Copenhagen, 1902-06, in Paris, 1910, and in Rome. Married Baron Bror Blixen-Finecke in 1914 (divorced, 1921). Managed a coffee plantation near Nairobi, Kenya, with her husband, 1913-21, and alone, 1921-31; lived in Rungsted after 1931. Recipient: Holberg Medal, 1949; Ingenio e Arti Medal, 1950; Nathansen Memorial Fund Award, 1951; Golden Laurels, 1952; Hans Christian Andersen Prize, 1955; Danish Critics Prize, 1957. Founding Member, Danish Academy, 1960; Honorary Member, American Academy 1957; Corresponding Member, Bavarian Accademy of Fine Arts. *Died 7 September 1962.*

PUBLICATIONS

Collections

Mindeudgave. 7 vols., 1964.

Fiction

Syv fantastiske Fortaellinger. 1935; as *Seven Gothic Tales*, 1934.
Vinter Eventyr. 1942; as *Winter's Tales*, 1942.
Gengaeldeslens Veje (as Pierre Andrezel). 1944; as *The Angelic Avengers*, 1946.
Kardinalens Tredie Historie [The Cardinal's Third Tale]. 1952.
Babettes Gaestebud [Babette's Feast]. 1955.
Sidste Fortaellinger. 1957; as *Last Tales*, 1957.
Skaebne-Anekdoter. 1958; as *Anecdotes of Destiny*, 1958.
Ehrengard. 1963; translated as *Ehrengard*, 1963.
Efterladte Fortaellinger, edited by Frans Lasson. 1975; as *Carnival: Entertainments and Posthumous Tales*, 1977.

Play

Sandhedens Haevn: En Marionetkomedie (produced 1936). 1960; as *The Revenge of Truth: A Marionette Comedy*, in *"Isak Dinesen" and Karen Blixen*, by Donald Hannah, 1971.

Other

Den afrikanske Farm. 1937; as *Out of Africa*, 1937.
Om restkrivning: Politiken 23-24 marts 1938. 1949.
Farah. 1950.
Daguerrotypier (radio talks). 1951.
Omkring den nye Lov on Dyreforsøg [The New Law on Vivisection]. 1952.
En Baaetale med 14 Aars Forsinkelse [A Bonfire Speech 14 Years Later]. 1953.
Spøgelseshestene. 1955.
Skygger paa Graesset. 1960; as *Shadows on the Grass*, 1960.
On Mottoes of My Life. 1960.
Osceola, edited by Clara Svendsen. 1962.
Essays. 1965.
Breve fra Afrika 1914-31, edited by Frans Lasson. 2 vols., 1978; as *Letters from Africa*, 1981.

DINESEN

Daguerrotypes and Other Essays. 1979.

*

Bibliography: *Dinesen: A Bibliography* by Liselotte Henriksen, 1977; supplement in *Blixeni-ana 1979*, 1979.

Critical Studies: *The World of Dinesen* by Eric O. Johannesson, 1961; *Dinesen: A Memorial* edited by Clara Svendsen, 1964; *The Gayety of Vision: A Study of Dinesen's Art* by Robert Langbaum, 1965; *Titania: the Biography of Dinesen* by Parmenia Migel, 1967; *The Life and Destiny of Blixen* by Clara Svendsen and Frans Lasson, 1970; *"Isak Dinesen" and Karen Blixen: The Mask and the Reality* by Donald Hannah, 1971; *Dinesen: The Life of a Storyteller* by Judith Thurman, 1982.

*   *   *

Isak Dinesen liked to disclaim the complex erudition of her tales and to speak of herself as a "storyteller," a Scheherazade, whose mission was simply to "entertain" people. Entertain them she did, with leisurely and urbane philosophical discourse, painterly descriptions of nature, a wry and refined eroticism, and in narratives as intricate and polished as Chinese boxes, that took her years of reworking to perfect. But the lightness of her tone and the preciousness of her surfaces have tended to obscure her scope of vision, which is that of a major and highly original writer.

In Denmark, Dinesen was accused of decadence and an indifference to social issues. These were charges deserved, perhaps, by Baroness Karen Blixen, who cultivated a sybilline persona and liked to *épater les bourgeois*, not to mention *les socialistes*. But Dinesen, the storyteller, was a passionate and rather pure-hearted immoralist, rather than a decadent. The erotic daredevils and demonic heroes of Romantic literature had given her her first glimpse of emotional freedom, and she perceived the attempt to spare oneself repression, at whatever price, as heroic and ennobling. This was the lion hunt, the great gesture, the daring fantasy, the mortal sin. Steeped in the Either/Or, and a fierce partisan of the Either, she had to believe there *was* a price. In Marxist terms, her heroes may be decadents; in Freudian terms they may be perverts of one stripe or another; but in Dinesen's terms they are *dreamers*—planted in the soil of life like a coffee tree with a bent taproot. "That tree will never thrive," she wrote, "nor bear fruit, but will flower more richly than the others."

Dinesen did, of course, "neglect social issues." Her choice of form—the tale, rather than the novel or the short story—was a way of taking sides with the past against her contemporaries, although she was also never without a keen sense of irony about her own absurd position, in modern Denmark, as the defender of a way of life that had vanished, to general applause. She set her tales a hundred years in the past, defining her period as "the last great phase of aristocratic culture," and aware that it was also the first great phase of bourgeois culture, when wealth was shifting from the land to the cities and to currency; when the feudal world, with all its certainties and its inequities, the one inseparable from the other, was dissolving. By taking such a distance, she was able to gain clarity and a certain imaginative freedom. She was also better able to describe the tension between her own aristocratic idealism and the materialism that had triumphed over it. And she was able to understand the nature of a certain kind of Fall: the loss that occurs to a culture or to a child when values that have once been absolute become relative.

Dinesen's work does, despite its great literary sophistication, have a common ground with the old tales, which she defined as Nemesis: "the thread in the course of events that is determined by the psychic assumptions of a person." By psychic assumptions, she meant the scenarios that we absorb from our family and our culture, the patterns we unconsciously repeat. Like the old storytellers, but also like Mann, Joyce, or Yeats, Dinesen is interested in the points at which the individual and the typical, psychology and culture, intersect as *myth*, and she works with myth in an innovative modern way. The climax of a Dinesen tale comes at the moment that the hero, and the reader, recognize how the forces that have been shaping the events of the story have also shaped their perception of it: history from without, desire from within.

Isak Dinesen stands at the end of a long cultural process, looking back ironically and self-ironically upon it. She sums up the Romantic tradition as she carries it forward. Perhaps her vision could only belong to a writer who took up her pen at the age of forty-six, when she had lost everything of importance to her, except the thing with the greatest value of all: experience itself.

—Judith Thurman

DOSTOEVSKY, Fyodor (Mikhaylovich). Born in Moscow, 30 October 1821. Educated at home to age 12; Chermak's School Moscow; Army Chief Engineering Academy, St. Petersburg, 1838-43: commissioned as ensign, 1839, as 2nd Lieutenant, 1842, graduated 1843 as War Ministry draftsman; resigned 1844. Married 1) Mariya Dmitriyevna Isayeva in 1857 (died, 1864), one step-son; 2) Anna Grigorevna Snitkina in 1867, two daughters and two sons. Writer; political involvement caused his arrest, 1849, and imprisonment in Omsk, 1850-54; exiled as soldier at Semipalatinsk, 1854: corporal, 1855, ensign, 1856, resigned as 2nd Lieutenant for health reasons, and exile ended, 1859; Editor, *Time*, 1861-63; took over *Epoch* on his brother's death, 1864-65; in Western Europe, 1867-71; Editor, *Citizen*, 1873-74. *Died 28 January 1881.*

PUBLICATIONS

Collections

    Novels, translated by Constance Garnett. 12 vols., 1912-20.
    Sobraniye Sochineniy, edited by Leonid Grossman. 10 vols., 1956-58.
    Polnoye sobraniye sochineniy. 1972— .

Fiction

    Bednye Lyudi. 1846; as *Poor Folk*, 1887.
    Dvoynik. 1846; as *The Double*, in *Novels*, 1917.
    Zapiski iz podpol'ya. 1864; as *Letters from the Underworld*, 1915; as *Notes from Underground*, in *Novels*, 1918.
    Igrok. 1866; as *The Gambler*, 1887.
    Prestupleniye i nakazaniye. 1867; as *Crime and Punishment*, 1886.
    Idiot. 1869; as *The Idiot*, 1887.
    Vechny muzh. 1870; as *The Permanent Husband*, 1888; as *The Eternal Husband*, 1917.
    Besy. 1872; as *The Possessed*, 1913; as *The Devils*, 1953.
    Podrostok. 1875; as *A Raw Youth*, 1916.
    Brat'ya Karamazovy. 1880; as *The Brothers Karamazov*, 1912.

Other

> *Zapiski iz myortvovo doma.* 1861-62; as *Buried Alive; or, Ten Years of Penal Servitude in Siberia*, 1881; as *The House of the Dead*, 1911.
> *Dnevnik pisatelya.* 1876-81; as *The Diary of a Writer*, 1949.
> *Pis'ma k zhene*, edited by V.F. Pereverzev. 1926; as *Letters to His Wife*, 1930.
> *Occasional Writings.* 1961.
> *The Notebooks for "The Idiot"* [*"Crime and Punishment," "The Possessed," "A Raw Youth," "The Brothers Karamazov"*], edited by Edward Wasiolek. 5 vols., 1967-71.

*

Bibliography: *Dostoevsky, Bibliografiya proizvedeniy Dostoevskogo i literatury o nyom 1917-65* edited by A.A. Belkin, A.S. Dolinin, and V.V. Kozhinov, 1968; "Dostoevsky Studies in Great Britain: A Bibliographical Survey" by Garth M. Terry in *New Essays on Dostoevsky* edited by Malcolm V. Jones and Garth M. Terry, 1983.

Critical Studies: *Dostoevsky: His Life and Art* by A. Yarmolinsky, 1957; *Dostoevsky in Russian Literary Criticism 1846-1954* by Vladimir Seduro, 1957; *Dostoevsky* by David Magarshak, 1961; *Dostoevsky: A Collection of Critical Essays* edited by Rene Wellek, 1962; *The Undiscovered Dostoevsky*, 1962, and *Dostoevsky: His Life and Work*, 1978, both by Ronald Hingley; *Problems of Dostoevsky's Poetics* by Mikhail M. Bakhtin, 1963; *Dostoevsky: The Major Fiction* by Edward Wasiolek, 1964; *Dostoevsky's Quest for Form* by Robert Louis Jackson, 1966; *Dostoevsky: His Life and Work* by Konstantin Mochulsky, 1967; *Dostoevsky: An Examination of the Major Novels* by Richard Peace, 1971; *Dostoevsky: The Seeds of Revolt 1821-1848* and *The Years of Ordeal 1850-1859* by Joseph Frank, 2 vols., 1976-83; *Dostoevsky* by Malcolm V. Jones, 1976, and *New Essays on Dostoevsky* edited by Jones and Garth M. Terry, 1983; *A Dostoevsky Dictionary* by Richard Chapple, 1983.

*   *   *

The darkness of Dostoevsky's life—a murdered father, epilepsy, near-execution and exile, debt, compulsive gambling, estrangement from friends, and a tormented sexuality—reflects the rapidly overheating Russian society of the later 19th century. So does his literature. His early work, including *Poor Folk*, *The Double*, and "White Nights," surfaces in a post-Gogolian "civic realism," with a compassion for the little man, but this feature is quickly overshadowed by his characteristic and seminal perceptions of the paranoia, deception, emptiness, and illusion of modern urban life. In the score of years following his penal servitude and exile for "socialist" activities (1849-59) Dostoevsky produced a series of works of lasting significance for 20th-century literature. The Underground Man (central character of *Notes from Underground*) is a determining prelude to most of the later heroes: a frustrated modern man, adrift in a moral void. Estranged from the roots of land, tradition, and faith, he attempts to establish, if only negatively, his own identity and dignity against the palliatives and platitudes of authority on the one hand and the serious, but dangerous appeal of "rationalism" on the other. Rationalism, in Dostoevsky's view, came to embrace utilitarianism, materialism, socialism, and the temporal power of Roman Catholicism. Throughout his work Dostoevsky seeks to counteract rationalism by appeal to the intuitive Christian faith which he sees embodied, however imperfectly, in the beliefs of the Russian people.

The conflicting interplay between the rationalist analysis of existence and the natural response to life is pursued in stronger terms in the characters and plots of the major novels. In *Crime and Punishment* Raskolnikov's espousal of a "rational" superman morality results only in the squalid murder of a pawnbroker, followed by Raskolnikov's own self-torment which eventually leads him to an unconvincing "salvation." In *The Idiot* Prince Myshkin's passive beauty and his all too perceptive innocence stimulate, rather than reconcile, the perverse impulses of his society. In *The Possessed* (also known as *The Devils*), a Messianic, anti-revolutionary novel, Stavrogin's unique strength and individuality is sapped to suicide by disillusionment with ideologies, causes, and beliefs. Finally, in *The Brothers Karamazov* the Karamazov family, beset by jealousy, pride, and hatred, disintegrates into parricide, a crisis which tests the extremes of Christianity and atheism. It is only in this last novel that Dostoevsky's attempt to give a positive depiction of active Christian love (in the persons of Father Zossima and Alyosha Karamazov) is artistically successful, although even here it often fails to match the power of Ivan Karamazov's reasoned objections to "God's world."

Dostoevsky's heroes are strong but divided personalities, engaged in intimate and frequently mortal debate with themselves, their "doubles," and the reader over the moral basis of their actions. His murder-centred plots are a visionary, fantastic, and mythically structured reworking of the sensational and extremist life observed in his journalism. The polarised themes of reason and unreason, faith and unbelief, moral freedom and moral slavery frame the tension of modern man, a tension which finds a precarious resolution in the vision of Christ, Dostoevsky's moral-aesthetic ideal. His journal chronicle *The Diary of a Writer* portrays these issues in the form of justification of tradition, discussion of psychology and education, and nationalistic, reactionary vaunting of the Russian destiny over a corrupt Europe.

The essence of Dostoevsky's work is dialogue. Vladimir Nabokov, a noted critic of Dostoevsky's otherwise largely undisputed reputation, describes him as a writer who "seems to have been chosen by the destiny of Russian letters to become Russia's greatest playwright," but who "took the wrong turning and wrote novels" (*Lectures on Russian Literature*, 1982). Those novels are constantly destabilised by narrators, chroniclers, and a host of narrating characters who run amok through authorial corridors. Mikhail Bakhtin's identification of this dialogic structure as "polyphony" (in his *Problems of Dostoevsky's Poetics*, 1963) has been revolutionary to the understanding of Dostoevsky and highly influential in the development of modern structuralism. Dostoevsky creates from his settings of fateful threshold and crowded room, grubby town and fantastic city the fragmented universe inherited by the 20th-century novel. Nothing in Dostoevsky's work is single, whole, or certain, but his imperfective vision looks forward with a desperate hope for perfection.

—Christopher R. Pike

DREAM OF THE RED CHAMBER. Novel of the 18th century, written by Ts'ao Hsueh-ch'in (born c. 1715-16; died 1763), about whom little is known. He probably completed the first 80 chapters of the novel; the later 40 chapters were probably "edited" or revised by others.

PUBLICATIONS

Fiction

Hung-lou meng pa-shih hui chiao-pen, edited by Yu P'ing-po. 1958; also edited by Hu Shih, 2 vols., 1961, and by Gao E, 3 vols., 1982; as *The Dream of the Red Chamber*, translated by Wang Chi-Chen, 1929, and by Florence and Isabel McHugh (from a German translation), 1958; as *The Story of the Stone*, translated by David Hawkes, 5 vols., 1973— .

DREAM OF THE RED CHAMBER

Critical Studies: *On "The Red Chamber Dream"* by Wu Shih-ch'ang, 1961; *The Classic Chinese Novel* by C.T. Hsia, 1968; *The Dream of the Red Chamber: A Critical Study* by Jeanne Knoerle, 1972; *New Interpretations of the Dream of the Red Chamber* by Klaus-Peter Koepping and Lam Mai Sing, 1973; *Masks of Fiction in the Dream of the Red Chamber* by Lucien Miller, 1975; *Archetype and Allegory in the Dream of the Red Chamber* by Andrew Henry Plaks, 1976.

*   *   *

Dream of the Red Chamber is perhaps the most beloved and widely read traditional Chinese novel. It appears to have been written some time before 1763 by a man named Ts'ao Hsueh-ch'in, the impoverished grandson of Ts'ao Yin, a notable political and literary figure of the early Ch'ing dynasty and the K'ang-hsi Emperor's trusted servant. For several decades the book circulated in an 80-chapter manuscript version under the title *Story of the Stone*. The first printed edition, in 120 chapters, appeared in 1792, with prefaces by Kao O and Ch'eng Wei-yuan, who claimed to have pieced together various old manuscript fragments in order to complete the earlier version. The exact proportion of mere editing to actual creation *de novo* in their edition is still the subject of debate, as is the literary merit of the last 40 chapters. However, this version soon supplanted the earlier one, and it was not until the early 20th century that the old manuscripts came to light. Their accompanying commentary, mostly by a friend of the author known to us as Chih-yen chai ("Red Inkstone"), has allowed us not only to trace the evolution of the text itself, but to glimpse some of the historical persons and events behind the novel. The book clearly incorporates certain features of the Ts'ao family history as Ts'ao Hsueh-ch'in experienced it.

On this level, *Dream of the Red Chamber* is the story of the fictional Chia family's fall from wealth and position. As the novel opens, their splendor is already said to be waning. Yet they are still dazzlingly wealthy and powerful: the junior and senior branches of the family, four generations of them and scores of servants and dependents, live in vast and elegant adjoining mansions in the imperial capital. Their fortunes, moreover, appear in some ways to be on the rise. When their daughter is made an imperial concubine, the family spares no expense to build a magnificent garden in which to entertain her—though only for a few brief hours—as befits her rank. Throughout the account of the garden's construction which leads up to the elaborate reception itself, there is a note of sadness for the fragility of worldly splendor—a note which recurs more and more insistently through the slow-moving idyll of garden life which takes up the novel's inner 80 chapters, until the imperial concubine's untimely death heralds the family's final precipitous fall from imperial favor and the confiscation of their estate.

Dream of the Red Chamber is also the story of the boy Pao-yü's initiation into the mysteries of love and loss. Pao-yü—whose name, "Precious Jade," refers to the magic jade he bore in his mouth at birth, the "stone" of the novel's fantastic frame-tale—is tenderly solicitous of the girl cousins and maids who live with him in the family garden. Most of all Pao-yü loves his cousin Tai-yü, who is equally devoted to him, though they quarrel constantly. Tai-yü's fragile health, her acerbic tongue, and her morose and solitary turn of mind lead the elder Chias to marry Pao-yü, instead, to an equally beautiful and talented cousin who is in every other way Tai-yü's opposite: Hsüeh Pao-ch'ai. Having been deceived into thinking that she is Tai-yü, Pao-yü marries the veiled Pao-ch'ai at the very moment of Tai-yü's death. Already in ill health from the loss of his magic jade, and deeply grieved by Tai-yü's death and the trick that has been played on him, Pao-yü eventually has a dream which parallels his dream-initiation into love near the novel's beginning. At last he begins to understand the connection between that first cryptic dream and the sorrowful events of his own recent life. In the end, his accumulated grief and disillusionment lead him to leave his family for the life of a Buddhist mendicant.

And so at one stroke the Chias lose both their fortune and their heir-apparent. Their fall, though, is not a sudden blow of fate, but the delayed consequence of their own corrupt machinations. Very early in the novel their high position at court saves their relative Hsüeh P'an from prosecution for murder. Later, their ambitious and scheming daughter-in-law, Wang Hsi-feng, embarks on a spiralling scheme of illegal loansharking; her abuse of the family's influence causes the deaths of several people and plays an important part in the Chia's disgrace and financial ruin. Some of the Chia family men are wastrels with a penchant for bribery and extortion; others are sexual profligates whose tastes run to incest. Though these dark details impinge only very gradually on the garden enclave where Pao-yü and his cousins practice poetry, calligraphy, and other elegant and scholarly arts, multiplying signs of decay eventually suggest that even the garden-dwellers are not immune to the corrupt passions of the world outside.

Most critics agree that *Dream of the Red Chamber* is unsurpassed in the tradition of the Chinese novel for its magisterial portrayal of literati culture and for its subtle depiction of interior states. Beyond these rather obvious points, however, there is little unanimity. Throughout its history the novel has been the object of a wide variety of interpretive schemes, some of them quite fanciful. It both invites and frustrates interpretation: the text is replete with erudite puns, riddles, and complex patterns of word and image which hinge on the ambiguous relation between the "real" and the "illusory." Its multitude of subplots and the sheer vastness of its scale also ensure that any neatly consistent reading will fail to do it justice. Any reading, though, must take into account the centrality of the garden, which in the long course of the novel lapses from its original perfection to become a haunted, weed-grown wilderness. It is in this central image that Pao-yü's story and the larger story of his family's fall are fused. Like Pao-yü's perfect and unattainable love and his family's visions of splendor, the garden is an expression of the unquenchable human longing for riches, honor, beauty, and pleasure, and of the loss and dissolution which are the inevitable consequence of that longing.

—Mary Scott

DU BELLAY, Joachim. Born at the Château de la Turmelière, Liré, France, probably in 1522. Studied law at the University of Poitiers, c. 1545. Took minor clerical orders; writer by 1547: at Collège de Coqueret, Paris, with Ronsard and other writers; lived in Rome in the service of his relation, cardinal Jean Du Bellay, 1553-57. *Died 1 January 1560.*

PUBLICATIONS

Collections

Oeuvres poétiques, edited by Henri Chamard. 6 vols., 1907-31; revised by Yvonne Bellenger, 1982— .

Verse

L'Olive. 1549; augmented edition, 1550.
Antérotique. 1549.
Vers lyriques. 1549.
Recueil de poésie. 1549; augmented edition, 1553.
Oeuvres. 1552.
Hymnes. 2 vols., 1555-56.

Premier livre des antiquités de Rome. 1558; as *Ruins of Rome,* translated by Edmund Spenser, in *Complaints,* 1591.
Les Regrets et autres oeuvres poétiques. 1558.
Divers jeux rustiques. 1558.
Poemata (in Latin). 1558.
Discours sur le sacre du treschrétien roi François I. 1558.
Ample discours au roi. 1567.
Oeuvres françaises, edited by Guillaume Aubert and Jean Morel. 1568.
Xenia. 1569.

Other

La Défence et illustration de la langue française. 1549; as *The Defense and Illustration of the French Language,* 1939.
Lettres, edited by Pierre de Nolhac. 1883.

*

Bibliography: *Du Bellay: A Bibliography* by Margaret B. Wells, 1974.

Critical Studies: *The Platonism of Du Bellay* by R.V. Merrill, 1925; *Histoire de la Pléiade* by Henri Chamard, 4 vols., 1939-40; *Du Bellay in Rome* by Gladys Dickinson, 1960; *Du Bellay* by Louis C. Keating, 1971; *Spenser, Ronsard, and Du Bellay: A Renaissance Comparison* by Alfred W. Satterthwaite, 1972; *The Chaste Muse: A Study of Du Bellay's Poetry* by Dorothy Gabe Coleman, 1980; *Trials of Desire: Renaissance Defenses of Poetry* by Margaret W. Ferguson, 1983.

*   *   *

It was perhaps inevitable that Joachim Du Bellay should be overshadowed both in and after his lifetime by his friend and contemporary, Ronsard. Yet the fact remains that he is the author of some of the finest and best-known sonnets in the French language. These are for the most part to be found among the 191 sonnets of the *Regrets* which, a mixture of elegy and satire, owe their inspiration to his progressive disenchantment with his life as a minor diplomat in Rome. Other, less famous, sonnets in the same collection are delightfully sharp sketches of Roman life in the 1550's and in particular of the intrigues of the Papal court.

However, it was not just this personal frustration which triggered off Du Bellay's disillusionment. He seems to have been by temperament a melancholy man and as early as 1549 had written a "Chant du desesperé." Compared to Ronsard he was something of a lightweight intellectually, but he can appear more sensitive, and certainly more vulnerable. He seems indeed to have been a sick man (or at the very least a chronic hypochondriac) much of his life, which fact makes it all the more surprising that he should adopt the aggressive posture of a young man in a hurry in the first major publication to carry his name, the *Defence and Illustration of the French Language* published in 1549. This short work quickly established itself as the manifesto of the "Brigade" which had gathered around Ronsard, but later developments cast doubt on the extent to which Du Bellay himself subscribed to the views he expounded. In fact, parts of this "defence" of the French language were cribbed from an Italian treatise by Sperone Speroni (1542). Du Bellay seems concerned above all with demolishing the achievements of his predecessors among the French poets, whom he compares unfavourably with the Greek and Roman masters and with the Italians such as Petrarch. He soon outgrew his theories: his *Olive* is a Petrarchist *canzoniere* but within a few years he would be claiming that he had forgotten the art of "petrarchizing," and one of the main planks of his work—the admonition against writing in Latin—is similarly forgotten in the mid 1550's when he set about composing his *Poemata*. In the *Regrets* he even renounces the *imitatio* which was supposed to raise the level of French poetry by a close imitation of Greek and Roman models. Du Bellay claims in this collection that he will write only what his "passion" dictates, thereby suggesting that he will restrict himself to his own personal misfortunes, without reference to illustrious examples or personal glory. Such disclaimers are perhaps more apparent than real. Certainly, in the 32 sonnets in the *Ruins* he sought to universalize his sense of bewilderment at the change of fortune of this once great city, victim of its own hubris.

But it is above all to the *Regrets* that the non-specialist poetry lover will wish to return again and again. In this sequence of sonnets Du Bellay emerges as one of the great poets of nostalgia, for a far-away country and for the illusions of youth; a poet, too, of solitude who peoples his poems, mysteriously, with absences, and who turns his back both on the ambitions of his youth and on the meagre consolation of immortality through verse.

—Michael Freeman

DUMAS, père, Alexandre (Davy de la Pailleterie). Born in Villers-Cotterêts, 24 July 1802. Attended local school. Married Ida Ferrier in 1840 (separated, 1844; died, 1861); had one son, the writer Alexandre Dumas, fils, by Catharine Labay, a daughter by Mélanie Serre, a son by Anna Bauër, and a daughter by Emilie Cordier. Articled at age 14 to a solicitor in Villers-Cotterêts, and one in Crépy, until 1822; employed in the secretariat of the Duc d'Orléans, 1822-29, and entered literary circle of Charles Nodier: Librarian, Palais Royal, 1829; successful playwright, then historical novelist (often revising and polishing works written first by someone else); Co-Founder, Théâtre Historique, Paris, 1847-50; friend of Garibaldi; director of Excavations and Museums, Naples, 1860-61, and Editor, *L'Indipendente*, Naples, 1860-64; also editor (and copious contributor), *La France Nouvelle,* 1848, *Le Mois,* 1848-50, *La Liberté,* 1848, *Le Mousquetaire,* 1853-57, 1866-67, *Le Monte-Cristo,* 1857-60, 1862, *Journal de Jeudi,* 1860, *Le D'Artagnan,* 1868, and *Théâtre Journal,* 1868-69. Chevalier, Legion of Honor, 1837; Order of Isabella the Catholic (Belgium); Cross of Gustavus Vasa (Sweden); Order of St. John of Jerusalem. *Died 5 December 1870.*

<small>PUBLICATIONS</small>

Collections

    Oeuvres complètes. 286 vols., 1848-1900.
    Théâtre complet. 15 vols., 1863-74.

Fiction

    Nouvelles contemporains. 1826.
    Souvenirs d'Antony. 1835; as *The Reminiscences of Antony,* 1905.
    Guelfes et Gibelins. 1836; translated as *Guelphs and Ghibellines,* 1905.
    Isabelle de Bavière. 1836; as *Isabel of Bavaria,* 1846.
    La Main droite du Sire de Giac. 1838; as *The King's Favorite,* 1906.
    Le Capitaine Paul. 1838; as *Captain Paul,* 1848; as *Paul Jones,* 1889.

La Salle d'Armes (includes *Pauline, Pascal Bruno, Murat*). 1838; translated as *Pascal Bruno*, 1837, and *The Sicilian Bandit*, 1859; as *Pauline*, 1844.

Acté. 1839; translated as *Acté*, 1904.

Les Crimes célèbres, with others. 1839-40; as *Celebrated Crimes*, 1896.

La Comtesse de Salisbury. 1839.

Monseigneur Gaston Phoebus. 1839.

Mémoires d'un maître d'armes. 1840; as *The Fencing-Master*, 1850.

Aventures de John Davys. 1840.

Maître Adam le Calabrais. 1840.

Othon l'archer. 1840; as *Otho the Archer*, 1860.

Praxède. 1841.

La Chasse au Chastre. 1841; as *The Bird of Fate*, 1906.

Aventures de Lyderic. 1842; as *Lyderic, Count of Flanders*, 1903; as *Adventures of Lyderic*, 1981.

Jehanne la Pucelle. 1842; as *Joan the Heroic Maiden*, 1847.

Albine. 1843; as *Le Château d'Eppstein*, 1844; as *The Spectre Mother*, 1864; as *The Castle of Eppstein*, 1903.

Le Chevalier d'Harmental, with Auguste Maquet. 1843; as *The Chateau d'Harmental*, 1856; as *The Orange Plume*, 1860; as *The Conspirators*, 1910.

Georges. 1843; as *George*, 1846.

Ascanio. 1843-44; translated as *Francis I*, 1849; as *Ascanio*, 1861.

Le Comte de Monte-Cristo, with Auguste Maquet. 1844-45; as *The Count of Monte Cristo*, 1846.

Amaury. 1844; translated as *Amaury*, 1854.

Une Âme à naître [*Histoire d'une âme*]. 1844.

Cécile. 1844; as *La Robe de noces*, 1844; translated as *Cecile*, 1904.

Fernande. 1844; translated as *Fernande*, 1904.

Une Fille du régent, with Auguste Maquet. 1844; as *The Regent's Daughter*, 1847.

Les Frères corses. 1844; as *The Corsican Brothers*, 1880.

Les Trois Mousquetaires, with Auguste Maquet. 1844; as *The Three Musketeers*, 1846.

Trois Maîtres (on Michelangelo, Titian, and Raphael). 1844.

Gabriel Lambert. 1844; as *The Galley Slave*, 1849; as *Gabriel Lambert*, 1904.

Invraisemblance [*Histoire d'un mort*]. 1844.

Sylvandire, with Auguste Maquet. 1844; as *The Disputed Inheritance*, 1847; as *Beau Tancrede*, 1861; as *Sylvandire*, 1907.

La Guerre des femmes, with Auguste Maquet. 1845-46; translated as *Nanon*, 1847; as *The War of Women*, 1895.

La Reine Margot, with Auguste Maquet. 1845; translated as *Margaret de Navarre*, 1845; as *Marguerite de Valois*, 1846; as *Queen Margot*, 1885.

Vingt ans après, with Auguste Maquet. 1845; as *Twenty Years After*, 1846; as *Cromwell and Mazarin*, 1847.

La Dame de Monsoreau, with Auguste Maquet. 1846; as *Chicot the Jester*, 1857; translated as *La Dame de Monsoreau*, 1894; as *Diane*, 1901.

Mémoires d'un médecin: Joseph Balsamo. 1846-48; as *Memoirs of a Physician*, 1847.

Le Chevalier de Maison-Rouge, with Auguste Maquet. 1846; translated as *Marie Antoinette*, 1846; as *Chateau-Rouge*, 1859; as *The Chevalier de Maison-Rouge*, 1895.

Le Bâtard de Mauléon, with Auguste Maquet. 1846; as *The Bastard of Mauleon*, 1849; as *The Half Brothers*, 1858; as *Agenor de Mauleon*, 1897.

Les Quarante-cinq, with Auguste Maquet. 1848; as *The Forty-Five Guardsmen*, 1847.

Le Vicomte de Bragelonne; ou, Dix ans plus tard, with Auguste Maquet. 1848-50; as *The Vicomte de Bragelonne*, 1857; as *The Man in the Iron Mask*, 1893.

Les Mille et un fantômes. 1848-51; as *Tales of the Supernatural* [*Strange Adventures, Terror*], 1907-09.

Le Collier de la Reine, with Auguste Maquet. 1849-50; as *The Queen's Necklace*, 1855.

Le Trou de l'enfer. 1850-51; as *The Mouth of Hell*, 1906.
La Tulipe noire. 1850; as *Rosa; or, The Black Tulip*, 1854.
La Colombe. 1851; as *The Dove*, 1906.
Dieu dispose. 1851-52; as *God's Will Be Done*, 1909.
La Comtesse de Charny. 1852-55; as *The Countess of Charny*, 1858.
Un Gil-Blas en Californie. 1852; as *A Gil Blas in California*, 1933.
Isaac Laquedem. 1852-53.
Conscience l'innocent. 1852; as *The Conscript*, n.d.; as *Conscience*, 1905.
Olympe de Clèves. 1852; translated as *Olympe de Cleves*, 1894.
Emmanuel Philibert. 1852-54; as *Le Page du duc de Savoie*, 1855; translated as *Emmanuel Philibert*, 1854; as *The Page of the Duke of Savoy*, 1861.
Ange Pitou. 1853; as *Taking the Bastille*, n.d.; translated as *Ange Pitou*, 1907.
Le Pasteur d'Ashbourne. 1853.
El Salteador. 1854; as *The Brigand*, 1897.
Ingénue. 1854; translated as *Ingenue*, 1855.
Les Mohicans de Paris; Salvator le Commissionnaire, with Paul Bocage. 1854-59; as *The Mohicans of Paris*, 1875.
Catherine Blum. 1854; as *The Foresters*, 1854; translated as *Catherine Blum*, 1861.
Les Compagnons de Jéhu. 1857; as *Roland of Montreval*, 1860; as *The Company of Jehu*, 1894.
Charles le téméraire. 1857; as *Charles the Bold*, 1860.
Le Meneur de loups. 1857; as *The Wolf Leader*, 1904.
Black. 1858; translated as *Black*, 1895.
Le Capitaine Richard. 1858; as *The Twin Captains*, 1861; as *The Young Captain*, 1870.
Herminie. 1858.
L'Horoscope. 1858; as *The Horoscope*, 1897.
Les Louves de Machecoul. 1859; as *The Last Vendee*, 1894; as *The She Wolves of Machecoul*, 1895.
Ammalet Beg. 1859; as *Sultanetta*, in *Tales of the Caucasus*, 1895.
La Boule de neige. 1859; as *The Ball of Snow*, in *Tales of the Caucasus*, 1895.
L'Histoire d'un Cabanon et d'un chalet. 1859; as *Monsieur Coumbes*, 1860; as *Le Fils de Forçat*, 1864; as *The Convict's Son*, 1905.
La Princesse Flora. 1859.
Jane. 1859; translated as *Jane*, with *Crop-Ear Jacquot*, 1903.
Le Chasseur de Sauvagine. 1859; as *The Wild Duck Shooter*, 1906.
Le Médecin de Java. 1859(?); as *L'Île de feu*, 1870; as *Doctor Basilius*, 1860.
Madame de Chamblay, 1859; translated as *Mme. de Chamblay*, n.d.
Une Aventure d'amour. 1860.
Le Père la Ruine, with de Cherville. 1860; translated as *Père la Ruine*, 1905.
La Maison de glace. 1860; as *The Russian Gipsy*, 1860.
Jacquot sans oreilles. 1860; as *Crop-Ear Jacquot*, with *Jane*, 1903.
Les Drames galants, La Marquise d'Escoman. 1860.
Une Nuit à Florence. 1861.
La San-Felice [*Emma Lyonna*]. 1864-65; as *The Lovely Lady Hamilton*, 1903; as *The Neapolitan Lovers; Love and Liberty*, 1916-18.
La Pêche aux filets. 1864.
Les Souvenirs d'une favorite (on Lady Hamilton). 1865.
Le Comte de Moret. 1866; as *The Count of Moret*, 1868.
La Terreur prussienne. 1867; as *The Prussian Terror*, 1915.
Les Blancs et les bleus. 1867-68; as *The Polish Spy*, 1869; as *The First Republic*, 1894; as *The Whites and the Blues*, 1895.
Les Hommes de fer. 1867.
Parisiens et provinciaux, with de Cherville. 1868.
Création et rédemption: Le Docteur mystérieux, La Fille du marquis. 1872.

Plays

La Chasse et l'amour, with Adolphe de Leuven and Pierre-Joseph Rousseau (produced 1825).
La Noce et l'enterrement, with E.H. Lassagne (produced 1826).
Henri III et sa cour (produced 1829). 1829.
Christine (produced 1830). 1830.
Antony (produced 1831). 1831.
Napoléon Bonaparte (produced 1831). 1831.
Richard Darlington, with Dinaux (produced 1831). 1832.
Charles VII chez ses grands vassaux (produced 1831). 1831.
La Tour de Nesle, from play by Frédéric Gaillardet (produced 1832). 1832.
Térésa, with Anicet Bourgeois (produced 1832). 1832.
Le Fils de l'émigré, with Anicet Bourgeois (produced 1832).
Le Mari de la veuve, with Anicet Bourgeois and Eugène Durieu (produced 1832). 1832.
Angèle, with Anicet Bourgeois (produced 1833). 1834.
La Venitienne, with Anicet Bourgeois (produced 1834). 1834.
Catherine Howard (produced 1834). 1834; translated as *Catherine Howard*, 1859.
Cromwell et Charles Ier, with Cordellier Delanoue (produced 1835). 1835.
Don Juan de Marana (produced 1836). 1836.
Kean; ou, Désordre et genre, with Théaulon (produced 1836). 1836; translated as *Edmund Kean*, 1847.
Le Marquis de Brunoy, with others (produced 1836). 1836.
Caligula (produced 1837). 1838.
Piquillo, with Gérard de Nerval, music by Hippolyte Monpou (produced 1837). 1837.
Paul Jones (produced 1838). 1838.
Mademoiselle de Belle-Isle (produced 1839). 1839; as *The Lady of Belle Isle*, 1872; as *The Great Lover*, 1979.
Bathilde, with Auguste Maquet (produced 1839). 1839.
L'Alchimiste, with Gérard de Nerval (produced 1839). 1839.
Léo Burckart, with Gérard de Nerval (produced 1839). 1839.
Jarvis l'honnête homme, with Charles Lafont (produced 1840). 1840.
Un Mariage sous Louis XV (produced 1841). 1841; as *A Marriage of Convenience*, 1899.
Jeannic le Breton; ou, Le Gérant responsable, with Eugène Bourgeois (produced 1841). 1842.
Le Séducteur et le mari, with Charles Lafont (produced 1842). 1842.
Halifax, with Adolphe d'Ennery (produced 1842). 1842.
Lorenzino (produced 1842). 1842.
Les Demoiselles de Saint-Cyr (produced 1843). 1843; as *The Ladies of Saint-Cyr*, 1870.
Le Laird de Dumbicky, with Adolphe de Leuven and Léon Lhérie (produced 1843). 1844.
Louise Bernard, with Adolphe de Leuven and Léon Lhérie (produced 1843). 1843.
Le Garde-Forestier, with Adolphe de Leuven and Léon Lhérie (produced 1845). 1845.
Un Conte de fées, with Adolphe de Leuven and Léon Lhérie (produced 1845). 1845.
Sylvandire, with Adolphe de Leuven and Léon Lhérie, from the novel by Dumas and Maquet (produced 1845). 1845.
Les Mousquetaires, with Auguste Maquet, from their novel *Vingt ans après* (produced 1845). 1845.
Une Fille du régent, from the novel by Dumas and Maquet (produced 1846). 1846.
Echec et Mat, with Octave Feuillet and Paul Bocage (produced 1846). 1846.
Intrigue et amour, from a play by Schiller (produced 1847). Published in *Théâtre complet*, 1864.
Hamlet, with Paul Meurice, from the play by Shakespeare (produced 1847). 1848.
La Reine Margot, with Auguste Maquet, from their novel (produced 1847) 1847.

Le Chevalier de Maison-Rouge, with Auguste Maquet, from their novel (produced 1847). 1847; as *The Chevalier de Maison-Rouge*, 1859.

Catalina, with Auguste Maquet (produced 1848). 1848.

Monte-Cristo, parts 1-2, with Auguste Maquet, from their novel *Le Comte de Monte-Cristo* (produced 1848). 2 vols., 1848.

Le Cachemire vert, with Eugène Nus (produced 1849). 1850.

Le Comte Hermann (produced 1849). 1849.

La Jeunesse des Mousquetaires, with Auguste Maquet, from their novel *Les Trois Mousquetaires* (produced 1849). 1849; as *The Three Musketeers*, 1855; as *The Musketeers*, 1898.

Le Chevalier d'Harmental, with Auguste Maquet, from their novel (produced 1849). 1849.

La Guerre des femmes, with Auguste Maquet, from their novel (produced 1849). 1849.

Le Connétable de Bourbon; ou, L'Italie au seizième siècle, with Eugène Grangé and Xavier de Montépin (produced 1849). 1849.

Le Testament de César, with Jules Lacroix (produced 1849). 1849.

Trois entr'actes pour L'Amour médecin (produced 1850). 1850.

La Chasse au Chastre, from his own novel (produced 1850). 1850.

Les Chevalier du Lansquenet, with Eugène Grangé and Xavier de Montépin (produced 1850). 1850.

Urbain Grandier, with Auguste Maquet (produced 1850). 1850.

Le Vingt-quatre fevrier (produced 1850). 1850.

La Barrière de Clichy (produced 1851). 1851.

Le Vampire, with Auguste Maquet (produced 1851). 1851.

Le Comte de Morcerf; Villefort, with Auguste Maquet, from their novel *Le Comte de Monte-Cristo* (produced 1851). 2 vols., 1851.

La Jeunesse de Louis XIV (produced 1854). 1854; as *Young King Louis*, 1979.

Le Marbrier, with Paul Bocage (produced 1854). 1854.

Romulus (produced 1854). 1854; translated as *Romulus*, 1969.

La Conscience (produced 1854). 1854.

L'Orestie (produced 1856). 1856.

La Tour Saint-Jacques, with Xavier de Montépin (produced 1856). 1856.

Le Verrou de la reine (produced 1856). Published in *Théâtre complet*, 1865.

L'Invitation à la valse (produced 1857). 1857; as *Childhood's Dreams*, 1881.

La Bacchante (Thais), with Adolphe de Leuven and A. de Beauplan, music by Eugène Gautier (produced 1858).

L'Honneur est satisfait (produced 1858). 1858.

Les Forestiers, from his novel *Catherine Blum* (produced 1858). In *Théâtre complet 13*, 1865.

L'Envers d'une conspiration (produced 1860). 1860.

Le Roman d'Elvire, with Adolphe de Leuven, music by Ambroise Thomas (produced 1860). 1860.

Le Gentilhomme de la montagne, from his novel *El Salteador* (produced 1860). 1860.

La Dame de Monsoreau, with Auguste Maquet, from their novel (produced 1860). 1860.

Le Prisonnier de la Bastille: Fin des Mousquetaires, with Auguste Maquet, from their novel *Le Vicomte de Bragelonne* (produced 1861). 1861.

Les Mohicans de Paris, from the novel by Dumas and Bocage (produced 1864). 1864.

Gabriel Lambert, with Amédée de Jallais, from the novel by Dumas (produced 1866; as *Gabriel le Faussaire*, produced 1868). 1866.

Madame de Chamblay, from his own novel (produced 1868). 1869.

Les Blancs et les bleus, from his own novel (produced 1869). 1874.

Ivanhoë; Fiesque de Lavagna. 1974.

Other

La Vendée et Madame. 1833; as *The Duchess of Berri in La Vendée*, 1833.

Gaule et France. 1833.

Impressions de Voyage: En Suisse. 5 vols., 1833-37; as *Adventures in Switzerland*, 1960.

Quinze jours à Sinaï. 2 vols., 1839.

Napoléon. 1840; translated as *Napoleon*, 1894.

Le Capitaine Pamphile (juvenile). 1840; as *Captain Pamphile*, 1850.

Les Stuarts. 2 vols., 1840.

Excursions sur les bords du Rhin. 3 vols., 1841.

Une Année à Florence. 2 vols., 1841.

Midi de la France. 3 vols., 1841.

Le Speronare. 4 vols., 1842; as *The Speronara*, 1902.

Le Capitaine Arena. 2 vols., 1842.

Le Corricolo. 4 vols., 1843.

La Villa Palmieri. 2 vols., 1843.

Filles, lorettes, et courtisanes. 1843.

Louis XIV et son siècle. 2 vols., 1844-45.

Histoire d'un casse-noisette (juvenile). 2 vols., 1845; as *The Story of a Nutcracker*, 1846; as *The Nutcracker of Nuremberg*, 1930.

La Bouillie de la Comtesse Berthe (juvenile). 1845; as *Good Lady Bertha's Honey Broth*, 1846; as *The Honey Feast*, 1980.

Italiens et Flamands. 1845.

Les Médicis. 2 vols., 1845.

De Paris à Cadix. 5 vols., 1848; as *Adventures in Spain*, 1959.

Le Véloce; ou, Tanger, Alger, et Tunis. 4 vols., 1848-51; as *Tales of Algeria*, 1868; as *Adventures in Algeria*, 1959.

Louis XV et sa cour. 4 vols., 1849.

La Régence. 2 vols., 1849.

Montevideo; ou, Une Nouvelle Troie. 1850.

Histoire de Louis XVI et la révolution. 3 vols., 1850-51.

Mémoires de Talma. 3 vols., 1850.

Le Drame de '93. 7 vols., 1851-52.

Les Drames de la mer. 2 vols., 1852.

Histoire de Louis-Philippe. 1852; as *The Last King; or, The New France*, 1915.

Mes Mémoires. 22 vols., 1852-54; annotated edition, 5 vols., 1954-68; selections as *Memoirs*, 2 vols., 1890; as *My Memoirs*, 6 vols., 1907-09.

Une Vie d'artiste. 2 vols., 1854; as *A Life's Ambition*, 1924.

La Jeunesse de Pierrot (juvenile). 1854; as *When Pierrot Was Young*, 1975.

La Dernière Année de Marie Dorval. 1855.

Isabel Constant. 2 vols., 1855.

Les Grands Hommes en robe de chambre: Henri IV, Louis XIII, et Richelieu; César. 12 vols., 1856-57.

L'Homme aux contes (juvenile). 1857.

Le Lièvre de mon grand-père (juvenile), with de Cherville. 1857.

Marianna. 1859.

Les Baleiniers, with Felix Meynard. 3 vols., 1860.

Le Caucase. 1859; as *Adventures in Caucasia*, 1962.

L'Art et les artistes contemporains au salon de 1859. 1859.

Contes pour les grands et les petits enfants (juvenile). 2 vols., 1859.

Causeries. 2 vols., 1860.

La Route de Varennes. 1860.

Les Garibaldiens: Révolution de Sicile et du Naples. 1861; as *The Garibaldians in Sicily*, 1861; complete version, as *On Board the "Emma": Adventures with Garibaldi's "Thousand" in Sicily*, edited by R.S. Garnett, 1929.

Bric-à-brac. 2 vols., 1861.

Les Morts vont vites. 2 vols., 1861.

Le Pape devant les évangiles. 1861.

I Borboni di Napoli.   10 vols., 1862-64.
Impressions de voyage: En Russie, 4 vols.   1865; as *Voyage en Russie,* edited by Jacques
   Suffel, 1960; excerpts as *Celebrated Crimes of the Russian Court,* 1906; as *Adventures
   in Czarist Russia,* 1960.
Bouts-rimés.   1865.
Étude sur "Hamlet" et sur William Shakespeare.   1867.
Histoire de mes bêtes.   1868; as *My Pets,* 1909; as *Adventures with My Pets,* 1960.
Souvenirs dramatiques.   2 vols., 1868.
Le Grand Dictionnaire de cuisine.   1873; as *Dictionary of Cuisine,* 1958; selection as
   Dumas on Food, 1978.
Propos d'art et de cuisine.   1877.
The Dumas Fairy Tale Book, edited by H.A. Spurr.   1924.

Editor, *Un Pays inconnu.*   1845.
Editor, *Pierre précieuse,* by Saphir.   1854.
Editor, *L'Arabie heureuse.*   1855.
Editor, *Le Journal de Madame Giovanni.*   4 vols., 1856; as *The Journal of Madame
   Giovanni,* 1944.
Editor, *Pèlerinage de Hadji-abd-el-Hamid-Bey (à la Mecque).*   6 vols., 1856-57.

Translator, *Mémoires de Garibaldi.*   2 vols., 1860; revised edition, 5 vols., 1860-61; 3
   vols., 1861; as *Garibaldi: An Autobiography,* 1860; revised edition, as *The Memoirs of
   Garibaldi,* 1931.

*

Bibliography: *A Bibliography of Alexandre Dumas Père* by F.W. Reed, 1933; *Dumas père:
Works Published in French. Works Translated into English* by Douglas Munro, 2 vols.,
1978-81.

Critical Studies: *Alexandre Dumas Père* by Richard S. Stowe, 1976; *The King of Romance: A
Portrait of Alexandre Dumas* by F.W.J. Hemmings, 1979; *Alexandre Dumas* by Michael Ross,
1981.

Victor Hugo said: "No popularity of this century has surpassed that of Alexandre Dumas.
The name of Alexandre Dumas is more than French...it is universal. Alexandre Dumas
seduces, fascinates, interests, amuses, teaches." Dumas was too large in scope, too dynamic,
too overpowering to be judged merely by the 40 years in which he dominated every field of
writing in France. Just as with Shakespeare, it will take many years to evaluate him properly.
   Sardou called Dumas the greatest theatrical craftsman of the century. From 1829 until 1868
he had at least one play on the boards, often two or three, and in 1849, five. He inaugurated the
Romantic movement with his play *Henri III* in 1829. His *Antony,* in 1831, was the first modern
romantic play, and imitations are in the hundreds. An 1833 trip to Switzerland started Dumas
on another type of writing—travel impressions, but a new kind of travelogue that was as
interesting as a novel.
   In 1844, his novel *The Three Musketeers* was the literary sensation of the century. Within ten
years he had covered most of the history of France in his novels, and also turned out other gems
such as *The Count of Monte-Cristo, The Black Tulip,* and *The Corsican Brothers.* He also
wrote purely historical works such as *Gaule et France, Louis XIV, Napoleon,* and many
others, probably the least boring history books ever written.
   Dumas had collaborators on many of his novels, but their work consisted of research and
planning; Dumas rewrote everything in his own hand. Critics have been amazed at his

enormous output, but this was a man who could entertain a group of people for hours with facts and anecdotes drawn from the deep well of his memory; this was a man who could write 14 hours a day with scarcely a single erasure or reference. Whatever he heard or read remained in his fertile brain—history, mythology, swordsmanship, geography, names, dates. At a gathering, he was describing the battle of Waterloo in great detail when he was interrupted by a pompous general who said: "But it wasn't like that; I was there!" "I'm sorry, general," replied Dumas, "but you were not paying attention to what was going on." Dumas often had an entire novel or play in his head before he ever put it on paper. One of his finest plays, *Mademoiselle de Belle Isle*, which had 500 performances, was recited for the committee of the Comédie-Française, and was accepted by acclamation before one word of it had ever been written.

Dumas has had his detractors, mostly writers who were jealous of his great popularity. He was often slighted in histories of French literature. His son, Alexandre Dumas fils, became a playwright, and for a decade or more almost eclipsed his father. But time works in favor of Dumas père. Except for *Camille*, his son's plays are virtually forgotten, even in France, but the father's works are being reprinted constantly, and more than three hundred films have been made from his novels, his plays, and his life.

Dumas père was a master story-teller. His style, as Robert Louis Stevenson said, "is light as a whipped trifle, strong as silk." Dumas will survive. Two hundred years from now, you can be sure that at any given moment, someone, in some far-off place, will be reading *The Three Musketeers* or *The Count Of Monte-Cristo* in one of the dozens of languages into which Dumas has been translated.

—Barnett Shaw

DÜRRENMATT, Friedrich. Born in Konolfingen bei Bern, Switzerland, 5 January 1921. Educated at Grosshöchstetten school; Freies Gymnasium and Humboldtianum, Bern; University of Zurich, one term; University of Bern. Married Lotti Geissler in 1946; one son and two daughters. Writer: drama critic, *Die Weltwoche*, Zurich, 1951, and co-owner, *Zürcher Sonntags-Journal*, 1969-71; also stage and television director: co-director, Basel Theaters, 1968-69. Recipient: Radio Play Prize (Berlin), 1957; Italia Prize, for radio play, 1958; Schiller Prize (Mannheim), 1959; New York Drama Critics Circle Award, 1959; Schiller Prize (Switzerland), 1960; Grillparzer Prize, 1968; Kanton of Bern prize, 1969; Welsh Arts Council International Writers Prize, 1976; Buber-Rosenzweig Medal, 1977; Austrian State Award, 1983. Honorary doctorate: Temple University, Philadelphia, 1969; Hebrew University, Jerusalem, 1977; University of Nice, 1977; University of Neuchatel, 1981. Honorary Fellow, Modern Language Association (USA). Lives in Neuchatel, Switzerland.

PUBLICATIONS

Plays

    Es steht geschrieben (produced, 1947). 1947; revised version, as *Die Wiedertäfer* (produced, 1967), 1969.
    Der Blinde (produced, 1948). 1960.

Romulus der Grosse (produced, 1949).   1956; revised version (produced, 1957), 1958; translated as *Romulus*, 1962.
Die Ehe des Herrn Mississippi (produced, 1952).   1952; revised version, 1957; film versions, 1961; as *The Marriage of Mr. Mississippi*, 1966.
Ein Engel kommt nach Babylon (produced, 1953).   1954; revised version, 1958; as *An Angel Comes to Babylon*, with *Romulus the Great*, 1964.
Der Besuch der alten Dame (produced, 1956).   1956; film version, 1963; as *The Visit*, 1958.
Nächtliches Gespräch mit einem verachteten Menschen (radio play).   1957; as *Conversation at Night with a Despised Character*, n.d.
Komödien I-III.   3 vols., 1957-70.
Das Unternehmen der Wega (radio play).   1958.
Frank V, music by Paul Burkhard (produced, 1959).   1960.
Der Prozess um des Esels Schatten (radio play).   1959.
Stranitzky und der Nationalheld (radio play).   1959.
Abendstunde im Spätherbst (radio play; also produced on stage, 1959).   1959; as *Episode on an Autumn Evening*, n.d.; as *Incident at Twilight*, in *Postwar German Theatre*, edited by Michael Benedikt and George E. Wellwarth, 1968.
Der Doppelgänger (radio play).   1960.
Herkules und der Stall des Augias (radio play; also produced on stage, 1963).   1960; as *Hercules and the Augean Stables*, n.d.
Die Panne (radio play).   1961; revised version, 1979; as *The Deadly Game*, 1966.
Gesammelte Hörspiele (includes *Abendstunde im Spätherbst, Der Doppelgänger, Herkules und der Stall des Augias, Nächtliches Gespräch mit einem verachteten Menschen, Die Panne, Der Prozess um des Esels Schatten, Stranitzky und der Nationalheld, Das Unternehmen der Wega*).   1961.
Die Physiker (produced, 1962).   1962; television version, 1963; as *The Physicists*, 1963.
Der Meteor (produced, 1966).   1966; as *The Meteor*, 1973.
König Johann, from the play by Shakespeare (produced, 1968).   1968.
Play Strindberg: Totentanz nach August Strindberg (produced, 1969).   1969; as *Play Strindberg: The Dance of Death*, 1972.
Titus Andronicus, from the play by Shakespeare (produced, 1970).   1970.
Porträt eines Planeten (produced, 1970; revised version, produced, 1971).   1970.
Urfaust, from the play by Goethe (produced, 1970).   1980.
Der Mitmacher (produced, 1973).   1973.
Die Frist (produced, 1977).   1977.
Achterloo (produced, 1983).   1984.

Screenplay: *Es geschah am hellichten Tag* (*It Happened in Broad Daylight*), 1960.

Fiction

Pilatus.   1949.
Der Nihilist.   1950.
Der Richter und sein Henker.   1952; as *The Judge and His Hangman*, 1954.
Die Stadt.   1952.
Der Verdacht.   1953; as *The Quarry*, 1961.
Grieche sucht Griechin.   1955; as *Once a Greek...*, 1965.
Das Versprechen: Requiem auf den Kriminalroman.   1958; as *The Pledge*, 1959.
Die Panne: Eine noch mögliche Geschichte.   1960; as *Traps*, 1960; as *A Dangerous Game*, 1960.
Der Sturz.   1971.

Other

Theaterprobleme. 1955; as *Problems on the Theatre*, with *The Marriage of Mr. Mississippi*, 1966.
Der Rest ist Dank (addresses), with Werner Weber. 1961.
Die Heimat im Plakat: Ein Buch für Schweizer Kinder. 1963.
Theater-Schriften und Reden, edited by Elisabeth Brock-Sulzer. 2 vols., 1966-72; translated in part as *Writings on Theatre and Drama*, edited by H.M. Waidson, 1976.
Monstervortrag über Gerechtigkeit und Recht. 1968.
Sätze aus Amerika. 1970.
Zusammenhänge: Essay über Israel. 1976.
Gespräch mit Heinz Ludwig Arnold. 1976.
Der Mitmacher: Ein Komplex. 1976.
Frankfurter Rede. 1977.
Lesebuch. 1978.
Bilder und Zeichnungen, edited by Christian Strich. 1978.
Albert Einstein: Ein Vortrag. 1979.
Werkausgabe. 30 vols., 1980.
Stoffe 1-3: Winterkrieg in Tibet, Mondfinsternis, Der Rebell. 1981.
Plays and Essays, edited by Volkmar Sander. 1982.

*

Critical Studies: *Dürrenmatt* by Murray B. Peppard, 1969; *Dürrenmatt* by Armin Arnold, 1972; *Dürrenmatt: A Study in Plays, Prose, and Theory* by Timo Tiusanen, 1977; *Dürrenmatt: A Study of His Plays* by Urs Jenny, 1978; *The Theatre of Dürrenmatt: A Study in the Possibility of Freedom* by Kenneth S. Whitton, 1980.

* * *

Born in Switzerland in 1921, Friedrich Dürrenmatt has occupied a major place among writers in German since the *succès de scandale* of his first play, *Es steht geschrieben*, in Zurich in 1947.

His witty, provocative, grotesque caricatures of his fellow human-beings seemed to mirror the chaotic post-World War II conditions and ensured his plays and prose works a permanent place in the best-seller lists. Dürrenmatt wrote of the human condition, of the shifting moral values in government and politics, of the loosening of familial and societal bonds, and of the despair of "the little man," suffering at the hands of well-organized, tyrannical bureaucracies. His shafted barbs of humour were directed at the "bringing-down," a true *reductio ad absurdum*, of the pompous and the entrepreneurial, the over-rich and the over-powerful.

His vehicle was "die Komödie," not the light-hearted, frothy social comedy of the western world, of Molière to Noel Coward, but that savage, grotesque, satirical comedy deriving ultimately from the satires of Aristophanes, and often presented in the farcical form of the mediaeval "commedia dell'arte." Dürrenmatt's reputation will rest on his two great international stage successes, *The Visit* and *The Physicists*, presented throughout the world, and on his short novels, e.g., *The Judge and His Hangman* and *A Dangerous Game*, which have been studied in schools and universities worldwide.

The Visit deserves its phenomenal success because of the brilliant simplicity of what Dürrenmatt calls the "Einfall," that "germ-idea" which lies behind and illuminates a play— here philosophically effective and scenically and dramatically masterly: an aged grotesque, Clare Zachanassian, once driven out of her little village because she had been made pregnant by the village shop-keeper, Alfred Ill, returns to seek revenge. Now the richest woman in the world, she will give the ailing village "eine Milliarde" (a billion) if one of them will kill Alfred. The hypocrisy of the villagers as they declare their firm resolve to stand by Alfred (now in the running for Mayor) and at the same time crowd into his shop to buy goods on credit in anticipation of the flood of gold, has been taken to be a symbolical attack on the then prevailing western capitalist values—but Dürrenmatt has never flailed one side alone. In *The Physicists*, Möbius, the brilliant scientist who has fled into an asylum to bury with him his potentially dangerous, revolutionary discovery, finds that his two "fellow-patients" are in fact USA and Soviet agents bent on extracting his secrets.

Dürrenmatt attacked both sides of the Curtain again later in two biting prose works, *The Fall*, a story about "a" Politburo, and *Sätze aus Amerika*, written after a visit to the States to receive a doctorate which showed that his target was the laming and cruel bureaucratization and the denial of freedom to *all* sorts and conditions of men.

In his gradual withdrawal from the stage, Dürrenmatt has busied himself with political and philosophical treatises—he was one of the few Europeans to support Israel in the Yom Kippur war—and with his grotesque paintings. Dürrenmatt's withdrawal from the public gaze may well turn out to be more than temporary; but even if it is, he will have left his mark on European letters as a witty scourge of Man's inhumanity to Man.

—Kenneth S. Whitton

ERASMUS, Desiderius.   Born in Rotterdam, probably 27/28 October 1467.   Educated at a school in Gouda, age 4-9; at Deventer, 1478-93; a seminary at 's Hertogenbosch; entered monastery of Canons Regular of St. Augustine, Steyn, 1487: ordained priest, 1492; released from monastic confinement, and entered secretarial service of Bishop of Cambrai, 1493-95; studied at College of Montaigue, Paris, 1495-99, 1500-01, became Doctor of Divinity, University of Turin, 1506; in England, 1499, 1505-06, 1509-14 (lectured on Greek in Cambridge), 1515, 1516, 1517; in Italy, 1506-09; and other travels; lived in Louvain, 1517-21; in Basel, 1521-29: general editor of John Froben's press; in Freiburg, 1529-35; in Basel again, 1535-36: declined offer of becoming a Cardinal. *Died 12 July 1536.*

PUBLICATIONS

Collections

> *Opera omnia*, edited by Jean Leclerc.   10 Vols., 1703-06.
> *Opera omnia*, edited by J.H. Waszink and others.   1969—.
> *The Essential Erasmus*, edited by John Dolan.   1964.
> *Essential Works*, edited by W.T.H. Jackson.   1965.
> *Collected Works* (in English).   1974—.

Works

> *Adagia*.   1500, and later augmented editions; as *Proverbs or Adages*, translated by Richard Taverner, 1569; as *Adages*, translated by Margaret Mann Phillips, annotated by R.A.B. Mynors, in *Collected Works*, 1982—.
> *Enchiridion militis Christiani*.   1503; as *The Manual of the Christian Knight*, translated

by William Tyndale, 1533; also translated by Raymond Himelick, 1963, and Anne M. O'Donnell, 1981.

Encomium moriae. 1511; revised edition, 1514; as *The Praise of Folly,* edited and translated by Hoyt Hudson, 1941, and Clarence H. Miller, 1979; also translated by Thomas Chaloner, 1549, and Betty Radice, 1971.

De ratione studii. 1512; revised edition, 1514; edited by Jean-Claude Margolin, in *Opera omnia,* 1971; as *A Method of Study,* translated by Brian McGregor, in *Collected Works,* 1978.

De copia. 1512; revised edition, 1514; as *On Copia,* translated by Betty I. Knott, in *Collected Works,* 1978.

Institutio principis Christiani. 1516; as *The Education of a Christian Prince,* translated by Lester K. Born, 1936.

Colloquia familiaria. 1518, and later augmented editions; edited by L.-E. Halkin, F. Bierlaire, and R. Hoven, in *Opera omnia,* 1972; as *The Colloquies,* edited and translated by Craig R. Thompson, 1965.

De libero arbitro. 1524; edited by J. Walter, 1910; as *Discourse on the Freedom of the Will,* edited and translated by Ernest F. Winter, 1961.

Dialogus Ciceronianus. 1528; edited by Pierre Mesnard, in *Opera omnia,* 1971; as *Ciceronianus,* edited and translated by Izora Scott, 1908.

Opus epistolarum, edited by P.S. Allen and others. 12 vols., 1906-58; as *The Epistles,* edited and translated by Francis M. Nichols, 3 vols., 1901; as *Correspondence,* translation of Allen's edition by R.A.B. Mynors and D.F.S. Thomson, annotated by Wallace K. Ferguson, James K. McConica, and Peter G. Bietenholz, in *Collected Works,* 1974— (6 vols. to 1982).

The Poems, edited by Cornelis Reedijk. 1956.

Erasmus and Cambridge: The Cambridge Letters, edited by H.C. Porter. 1963.

Christian Humanism and the Reformation: Selected Writings, edited by John C. Olin. 1965.

Erasmus and Fisher: Their Correspondence 1511-1524, edited by Jean Rouschausse. 1968.

Erasmus and His Age: Selected Letters, edited by Hans J. Hillerbrand. 1970.

Editor and translator, *Novum instrumentum* [New Testament]. 1516; revised edition, 1527. (translated into Latin)

Translator, with Thomas More, *Lucian.* 1506. (translated into Latin)

Translator, *Hecuba, Iphigenia in Aulide,* by Euripides. 1506. (translated into Latin)

Also edited works by Ambrose, Aristotle, Augustine, Basil, Cato, Chrysostom, Cicero, Cyprian, Hilary, Irenaeus, Jerome, Lactantius, Origen, Plutarch, Pseudo-Arnobius, Seneca, and others.

*

Critical Studies: *Erasmus and the Northern Renaissance,* 1949, and *The Adages of Erasmus,* 1964, both by Margaret Mann Phillips; *Thomas More and Erasmus* by Ernest E. Reynolds, 1965; *Erasmus and Luther* by Rosemary D. Jones, 1968; *Twentieth Century Interpretations of The Praise of Folly* edited by Kathleen Williams, 1969; *Erasmus of Christendom* by Roland H. Bainton, 1969; *Erasmus of Rotterdam,* 1971, and *Essays on the Work of Erasmus,* 1978, both edited by Richard L. DeMolen; *Erasmus: The Growth of a Mind* by James D. Tracy, 1972; *Desiderius Erasmus* by J. Kelley Sowards, 1975; *Six Essays on Erasmus* by John C. Olin, 1979; *Ecstasy and The Praise of Folly* by M.A Screech, 1980; *Le Neveu de Rameau and The Praise of Folly: Literary Cognates* by Apostolos P. Kouidos, 1981.

*   *   *

Desiderius Erasmus of Rotterdam was the most famous man of letters of early 16th-century Europe, a figure who dominated the intellectual world of his time as clearly as Petrarch, Voltaire, or Goethe did theirs. He was acclaimed "the Prince of humanists." He was the leading biblical scholar of his time, the editor of the first modern critical text of the Greek New Testament. He was an advocate of educational reform and an author of textbooks and educational tracts. He was a passionate advocate of peace. And, perhaps most important of all, he was one of the most tireless advocates of religious reform in the age of the Reformation. The titles of his books run into the hundreds. But his most famous works were his satirical books, especially the *Praise of Folly* and the *Colloquies*.

The *Praise of Folly*, Erasmus's single best-known book, is a complex multi-layered general satire. It is a satire of the outworn classical form of the oration of praise, a parody of such worthy abstractions as Dame Philosophy or The Seven Liberal Arts—in this case the goddess Folly. Folly, arising before the court of mankind, intends to praise herself, since no one else will praise her. She proves with impeccable logic that all important actions and accomplishments are owing to her influence. She claims all manner and conditions of men, from kings and nobles and wealthy merchants to calamity-ridden and tormented teachers of grammar, even husbands and wives, parents and children. But Folly also claims theologians with their pride of learning and endless hair-splitting definitions: monks with their empty formalism and self-serving piety; and the powerful, cynical rulers of the church, including the popes, the vicars of Christ so unlike him in every way. Then Folly claims that true Christians are the greatest of fools, that no people behave more foolishly, giving away their goods, overlooking wrongs and injuries, forgiving their enemies. And finally, Folly argues, Christ himself became something like a fool to cure the folly of mankind by the foolishness of the cross.

The serious religious-reforming purpose of the *Praise of Folly* is equally clearly expressed in the other major satiric work of Erasmus, the *Colloquies*. This was probably the most-often printed of Erasmus's books in his lifetime. It began as a series of brief and simple Latin conversational exercises for students which proved to be so popular that Erasmus prepared expanded editions through the 1520's and early 1530's, adding many new colloquies. Most of these were little satiric dialogues directed at the targets of his reforming efforts—corrupt monks and ignorant priests, the excesses of the veneration of saints and relics and pilgrimages; the senseless preference for the formalities of religion to the neglect of its spirit; and his hatred of war. Several of the colloquies—*Charon, The Shipwreck, The Pilgrimage for Religion's Sake, The Abbot and the Learned Lady, Exorcism or the Specter*—can be compared with the best satiric writing of the 16th century.

—J. Kelley Sowards

EURIPIDES. Born in 480 or 485 B.C. Married to Melito; three sons. Held a local priesthood at Phlya; not prominent politically, but did go on an embassy to Syracuse; also went to the court of Archelaus in Macedonia, c. 408; first competed in the Dionysia in 455: won four prizes during his lifetime, and one posthumously; 80 play titles are known. *Died before February-March 406 B.C.*

PUBLICATIONS

Collections

[*Plays*], edited by Gilbert Murray.   3 vols., 1901-13; also edited by James Diggle, 1982—.
Complete Greek Tragedies, edited by David Grene and Richmond Lattimore.   1959; also translated by A.S. Way (Loeb edition), 4 vols., 1912.

Plays

Alcestis (produced 438).   Edited by A.M. Dale, 1954; also edited by Antonius Garzya, 1980; as *Alcestis*, translated by Richmond Lattimore, in *Complete Greek Tragedies*, 1959; also translated by Richard Aldington, 1930, Philip Vellacott, 1953, Alistair Elliot, 1965, C.R. Beye, 1973, and William Arrowsmith, 1974.

Medea (produced 431).   Edited by Denys Page, 1938; also edited by Alan Elliott, 1969; as *Medea*, translated by Rex Warner, in *Complete Greek Tragedies*, 1959; also translated by Philip Vellacott, 1963, Michael Townsend, 1966, and Kenneth McLeish, 1970.

Heracleidae (produced c. 430-28).   Edited by Antonius Garzya, 1972; as *Children of Heracles*, translated by Ralph Gladstone, in *Complete Greek Tragedies*, 1959; also translated by Philip Vellacott, 1972, and Henry Taylor and Robert A. Brooks, 1981.

Hippolytus (produced 428).   Edited by W.S. Barrett, 1964; as *Hippolytus*, translated by David Grene, in *Complete Greek Tragedies*, 1959; also translated by Rex Warner, 1949, Philip Vellacott, 1953, and Robert Bagg, 1974.

Andromache (produced c. 426-25).   Edited by P.T. Stevens, 1971; also edited by Antonius Garzya, 1978; as *Andromache*, translated by John Frederick Nims, in *Complete Greek Tragedies*, 1959; also translated by L.R. Lind, 1957, and Philip Vellacott, 1972.

Hecuba (produced 424).   Edited by Stephen G. Daitz, 1973; also edited by Michael Tierney, 1946; as *Hecuba*, translated by William Arrowsmith, in *Complete Greek Tragedies*, 1959; also translated by Peter Arnott, 1969; as *Hecabe*, translated by Philip Vellacott, 1963.

Supplices (produced c. 423-22).   Edited by Christopher Collard, 2 vols., 1975; as *The Suppliant Women*, translated by Frank Jones, in *Complete Greek Tragedies*, 1959; also translated by Philip Vellacott, 1972; as *The Suppliants*, translated by L.R. Lind, 1957.

Electra (produced c. 422-416).   Edited by J.D. Denniston, 1939; as *Electra*, translated by Emily Townsend Vermeule, in *Complete Greek Tragedies*, 1959; also translated by Moses Hadas, 1950, and Philip Vellacott, 1963.

Heracles (produced c. 417-15).   Edited by Godfrey W. Bond, 1981; as *Heracles*, translated by William Arrowsmith, in *Complete Greek Tragedies*, 1959; also translated by Philip Vellacott, 1963; as *The Madness of Heracles*, translated by Peter Arnott, 1969.

Troades (produced 415).   Edited by K.H. Lee, 1976; as *The Trojan Women*, translated by Richmond Lattimore, in *Complete Greek Tragedies*, 1959; also translated by Neil Curry, 1966; as *The Women of Troy*, translated by Philip Vellacott, 1954.

Iphigeneia Taurica (produced c. 414-13).   Edited by Maurice Platnauer, 1938; as *Iphigenia in Tauris*, translated by Witter Bynner, in *Complete Greek Tragedies*, 1959; also translated by Philip Vellacott, 1953, and Richmond Lattimore, 1974.

Ion (produced c. 414-13).   Edited by Werner Biehl, 1979; also edited by A.S. Owen, 1939;

as *Ion*, translated by Ronald Frederick Willetts, in *Complete Greek Tragedies*, 1959; also translated by H.D., 1937, Philip Vellacott, 1954, and A.P. Burnet, 1970.

Helena (produced 412). Edited by A.Y. Campbell, 1950; also edited by A.M. Dale, 1967, and Richard Kannicht, 1969; as *Helen*, translated by Richmond Lattimore, in *Complete Greek Tragedies*, 1959; also translated by Rex Warner, 1951, Philip Vellacott, 1954, and Neil Curry, 1981.

Phoenissae (produced c. 412-08). As *The Phoenician Women*, translated by Elizabeth Wychoff, in *Complete Greek Tragedies*, 1959; also translated by Philip Vellacott, 1972, and Peter Burian and Brian Swann, 1981.

Orestes (produced 408). Edited by Werner Biehl, 1975; as *Orestes*, translated by William Arrowsmith, in *Complete Greek Tragedies*, 1959; also translated by Philip Vellacott, 1972.

Bacchae (produced c. 405). Edited by E.R. Dodds, 1960; also edited by E. Christian Kopff, 1982; as *The Bacchae*, translated by William Arrowsmith, in *Complete Greek Tragedies*, 1959; also translated by Philip Vellacott, 1954, Henry Birkhead, 1957, G.S. Kirk, 1970, and Neil Curry, 1981.

Iphigeneia Aulidensis, completed by another writer (produced c. 405). As *Iphigenia in Aulis*, translated by Charles R. Walker, in *Complete Greek Tragedies*, 1959; also translated by Philip Vellacott, 1972, Kenneth Cavander, 1973, and W.S. Merwin and George E. Dimock, Jr., 1978.

Rhesus (possibly not by Euripides). As *Rhesus*, translated by Richmond Lattimore, in *Complete Greek Tragedies*, 1959; also translated by Richard Emil Braun, 1978.

Cyclops, edited by Jacqueline Duchemin. 1945; also edited by R.G. Ussher, 1978; as *Cyclops*, translated by William Arrowsmith, in *Complete Greek Tragedies*, 1959; also translated by Roger Lancelyn Green, in *Two Satyr Plays*, 1957.

Hypsipyle (fragmentary), edited by Godfrey W. Bond. 1969.

Phaethon (fragmentary), edited by James Diggle. 1970.

*

Critical Studies: *The Drama of Euripides* by G.M.A. Grube, 1941; *Euripides and His Age* by Gilbert Murray, revised edition, 1946; *Essays on Euripidean Drama* by G. Norwood, 1954; *The Political Plays of Euripides*, 1955, revised edition, 1963, and *An Inquiry into the Transmission of the Plays of Euripides*, 1966, both by Gunther Zuntz; *Euripides* by W.N. Bates, 1961; *Euripides and His Influence* by F.L. Lucas, 1963; *Euripidean Drama: Myth, Theme, and Structure* by Desmond J. Conacher, 1967; *The Tragedies of Euripides* by T.B.L. Webster, 1967; *Euripides: A Collection of Critical Essays* edited by Erich Segal, 1968; *The Imagery of Euripides* by S.A. Barlow, 1970; *Catastrophe Survived: Euripides' Plays of Mixed Reversal* by A.P. Burnett, 1971; *Ironic Drama: A Study of Euripides; Method and Meaning* by Philip Vellacott, 1975; *Studies on the Text of Euripides* by James Diggle, 1981.

* * *

Euripides was the youngest of the famous tragedians of 5th-century Athens; he is regarded by some as responsible for a break-down in the lofty spirit of Greek tragedy from which it never recovered; by others as introducing a new and enduring humanism, a sense of the pathos of the human condition, which expressed more powerfully than that of his predecessors the tragic realities of life.

To some degree, perhaps, the impression of contrast which the Euripidean corpus of plays provides with that of Aeschylus and Sophocles may be due to the fact we possess a greater number of his plays (18 or 19 as compared with seven of each of the other two) and so a wider variety of Euripidean themes. However, this explanation of "the difference" is, at best, a very partial one, for all of Euripides's plays betray, to a greater or lesser degree, a distinctly new tragic style and approach to traditional myth.

These "new directions" of Euripidean tragedy are in part traceable to two major influences, those of the Sophistic movement and of the Peloponnesian War, both of which appear to have affected Euripides more than they did his elder contemporary Sophocles. The Sophists (the first professional teachers in Greece) imbued Euripides with their rationalistic way of looking at traditional beliefs and values and strongly influenced his dramatic style by the rhetorical emphasis of their teaching. In a very different way, Euripides's tragic outlook was also affected by certain dire events of the Peloponnesian War and of their effects on Athenian morale and policy.

As I have implied above, Euripides was something of an iconoclast, a "reducer" of the ancient mythological tradition on which the plot material of Greek tragedy was, by convention, based. Thus he tended to reinterpret and reformulate the tales of arbitrary, often vengeful "anthropomorphic" gods and of heroes from a remote and glorious past in ways which related them more closely to recognizable human experience. In a few plays, such as the *Hippolytus* and the *Bacchae* (which I shall call "the mythological tragedies") these anthropomorphic gods still play a major role, but even here, though they are presented physically as dramatically real personages in the tragedies, they clearly symbolize mysterious forces governing the emotional and irrational areas of human experience. Thus, in the *Hippolytus*, Aphrodite, goddess of sexual passion, declares that she will take vengeance on the hero for his refusal to do her honour. However, the actual action of the play (once the intentions of the goddess have been expressed in the Prologue) is worked out in essentially human terms: the catastrophe comes about from the conflict between the woman-hating Hippolytus and his step-mother Phaedra, the unwilling victim of guilty love for him. Here the poet makes it clear that it is the excess of Hippolytus's scorn for sex and his failure to understand the power of sexual passion that leads to his destruction. So, too, in the *Bacchae* King Pentheus, the puritanical rationalist, suffers for suppressing in his state the mystical ecstasy and emotional release brought by the communal singing, drinking, and dancing of Dionysian worship.

In other, quite different plays of Euripides, such as the *Medea* and the *Electra*, the catastrophe occurs as a result of the destructive power of hate and vengeance within the soul of the individual tragic figure. Here the mythological dimension is notably less marked, since no divine figure is needed to represent the actively destructive power now embodied in the tragic personality itself. The *Medea* is perhaps the most powerful example of this kind of Euripidean tragedy which presents in psychologically "realistic" terms the destructive power of passion. Medea, who loves her children, slays them in order to be avenged on her faithless husband Jason. "My passion is stronger than my reason!" she exclaims at the climax of her struggle between mother-love and vengeful fury: a very Euripidean expression of what this poet felt to be one of the mainsprings of human tragedies. Other plays which I would describe (despite certain supernatural overtones) as psychologically "realistic" human tragedies are the *Electra* and the *Hecuba* (in which the same power of vengeful hatred, in very different circumstances, corrupts and destroys noble tragic figures) and (apart from its melodramatic finale) the *Orestes*, which studies the effects of guilt and social rejection on the condemned matricide Orestes.

"Tragedies of War and (in the broadest sense) of Politics" might be selected as the label (with all the inadequacies which such labelling entails) for a third group of Euripidean tragedies. Here the issues are almost exclusively human and social, and the tragic situations arise, not from any divine vengeance (however "symbolically" understood) or from individual human passions, but from man's more impersonal inhumanity to his fellow men. In *The Suppliant Women* and *Children of Heracles*, "just wars" are fought by legendary Athenian kings on behalf of just such victims of human cruelty but in each case the plays end with an ironic undermining of the noble purpose of the war or else of the just pretensions of the suppliants themselves. In *The Trojan Women* and the *Hecuba* (which belongs as well in this group as in the preceding one), we witness the destructive results of war's cruelties on the helpless survivors of the defeated: in the one case, collectively, on the women and children of the slain Trojan heroes, in the other, individually, on the tragic (and initially noble) figure of the Trojan Queen. Again the setting is in the mythological past, but the themes are universal and, *mutatis mutandis*, apply in some respects all too tellingly to certain historical circumstances and events of Euripides's own day.

Another group of Euripidean plays, very different from the sombre "war plays," comprise such plays as *Ion, Helen*, and *Iphigenia in Tauris*, which have been variously described by modern critics as "tragi-comedy," "romantic tragedy," and (here some would include the *Orestes*) "melodrama." Of these, the *Helen* is, perhaps, at the furthest remove from traditional Greek Tragedy. Euripides bases this play on a variant version of the Trojan War myth according to which Helen spent the Trojan War secretly hidden away in Egypt while the goddess Hera caused a wraith of Helen to be substituted (and mistaken) for the real Helen of Troy. The plot includes a highly comic "recognition scene" (in which shipwrecked Menelaus, returning from Troy with the wraith, has great difficulty in recognizing his "real," and somewhat indignant, wife) and an ingenious and exciting "escape" sequence, in which Helen and Menelaus outwit the wicked Egyptian King and escape over the seas to Sparta with the King's ship and generous provisions of arms and supplies. In this and similar plays the poet seems to be taking traditional myth rather less seriously than in the more properly "tragic" plays and to adopt a satirical tone (not always absent even in the most "serious" tragedies) concerning the more improbable and anthropomorphic treatments of the gods. However, even in these less tragic plays, there are sometimes serious overtones: the Trojan War, the Chorus reminds us in the *Helen*, was fought for a wraith: perhaps all wars, including the war currently ruining the poet's own beloved city, could be avoided if men allowed words and reasoning (*logoi*) instead of bloody strife (*eris*) to settle their differences.

This brief account inevitably fails to do justice to the great variety in the Euripidean treatment of human experience and human folly. If the reader has been left with the wrong impression that, in questioning traditional mythology, Euripides rejects the super-natural element in that experience, he should read the *Bacchae*, one of the last, and surely the most terrifying, of Euripides's extant tragedies. Here he will discover, with King Pentheus, what sort of fate awaits those scorning the timeless and universal powers ("even stronger than a god, if that were possible", as we are reminded of Aphrodite in the *Hippolytus*) which Euripides recognized as dominating certain crucial areas in the life of man.

—Desmond J. Conacher

FLAUBERT, Gustave. Born in Rouen, France, 12 December 1821. Educated at Collège Royal de Rouen, 1831-39; École de Droit, Paris, 1841-45. Lived with his family at Croisset, near Rouen, after 1845 until his death; spent winters in Paris after 1856; visited Egypt and the Near East, 1849-51; publication of *Madame Bovary*, 1857, led to unsuccessful prosecution for indecency. State pension, 1879. Chevalier, Legion of Honor, 1866. *Died 8 May 1880.*

PUBLICATIONS

Collections

Oeuvres complètes (includes correspondence). 35 vols., 1926-54.
Oeuvres, edited by A. Thibaudet and R. Dumesnil. 2 vols., 1946-48.
Complete Works. 10 vols., 1926.

Fiction

Madame Bovary.   1857; translated as *Madame Bovary*, 1881.
Salammbô.   1862; translated as *Salammbô*, 1886.
L'Education sentimentale.   1869; as *Sentimental Education*, 1896.
La Tentation de Saint Antoine.   1874; as *The Temptation of Saint Anthony*, 1895.
Trois contes.   1877; edited by S. de Sasy, 1973; as *Stories*, 1903.
Bouvard et Pécuchet.   1881; edited by Alberto Cento, 1964; as *Bouvard and Pecuchet*,
   1896; reprinted in part as *Dictionnaire des idées reçues*, edited by Lea Caminiti, 1966; as
   The Dictionary of Accepted Ideas, 1954.
Le première Education sentimentale.   1963; as *The First Sentimental Education*, 1972.
Le second volume de Bouvard et Pécuchet, edited by Geneviève Bollème.   1966.

Plays

Le Candidat (produced 1874).   1874.
Le Château des coeurs, with Louis Bouilhet and Charles d'Osmoy (produced 1874).   In
   Oeuvres complètes, 1910.

Other

Par les champs et par les grèves.   1886.
Mémoires d'un fou.   1901.
Souvenirs, notes, et pensées intimes, edited by L. Chevally-Sabatier.   1965; as *Intimate
   Notebook 1840-1841*, edited by Francis Steegmuller, 1967.
November, edited by Francis Steegmuller.   1966.
Flaubert in Egypt, edited by Francis Steegmuller.   1972.
Correspondance, edited by Jean Bruneau.   2 vols., 1973-80.
Letters, edited by Francis Steegmuller.   2 vols., 1980-82.
Correspondance, with George Sand, edited by Alphonse Jacobs.   1981.

Editor, *Dernières chansons*, by Louis Bouilhet.   1872.

*

Bibliography: *Bibliographie de Flaubert* by D.L. Demorest and R. Dumesnil, 1947.

Critical Studies: *Flaubert and Madame Bovary* by Francis Steegmuller, 1947; *Flaubert and the Art of Realism* by Anthony Thorlby, 1956; *On Reading Flaubert* by Margaret G. Tillett, 1961; *Flaubert: A Collection of Critical Essays* edited by Raymond D. Giraud, 1964; *The Novels of Flaubert* by Victor Brombert, 1966; *Madame Bovary and the Critics* edited by Benjamin F. Bart, 1966, and *Flaubert* by Bart, 1967; *Flaubert* by Stratton Buck, 1966; *Flaubert* by Enid Starkie, 2 vols., 1967-71; *The Greatness of Flaubert* by Maurice Nadeau, 1972; *Sartre and Flaubert* by Hazel E. Barnes, 1981; *The Family Idiot: Flaubert 1821-1857* by Jean-Paul Sartre, 1981— ; *Flaubert and the Historical Novel* by Anne Green, 1982.

*   *   *

Gustave Flaubert's best and best-known novel, *Madame Bovary*, marked a turning point in the history of the European novel. For the first time, an ordinary, middle to lower-middle-class woman occupied the central place in a detailed study of how dull everyday life could be in a small town, and the romantic myth that true love could be found in successfully consummated adultery was convincingly presented as a total illusion. In the wider history of fiction, Emma Bovary resembles Cervantes's Don Quixote (1614) in that she is a person who tries to live her life in terms of ideas derived from books but fails, and she also, perhaps more significantly, represents the first version of the "miserable married woman" who recurs in Tolstoy's *Anna Karenina* (1873), in the Irene of Galsworthy's *Forsyte Saga* (1906-28), in François Mauriac's *Thérèse Desqueyroux* (1927), and even—though here the problem finds a satisfactory solution—in D.H. Lawrence's *Lady Chatterley's Lover*. Like her fictional successors, Emma is married to a worthy but dull man, and the fact that she is, for all her self-centeredness and folly, by far the most enterprising and interesting character in the novel does enable *Madame Bovary* to be interpreted nowadays as a not entirely unsympathetic account of the problems to which the Women's Movement seeks to find a solution. Such an interpretation would, however, have excited only ridicule from Flaubert himself.

As his other novels, especially *L'Education Sentimentale*, show, and as his voluminous *Correspondance* confirms, Flaubert was an unremitting pessimist who did not believe that human beings either could achieve happiness or deserved to do so. For him, the only activity deserving any consideration was the construction of perfect works of art, and it was to this that he devoted the whole of his life. He rewrote incessantly, spending sometimes a week on one paragraph, and it took him five years to complete *Madame Bovary*. It is consequently slightly surprising that the heroine of what is otherwise rightly regarded as a masterpiece of realism should have eyes that are blue on one page but black on another, and the modern French critics who profess to admire Flaubert do so because of his mastery of form. His other novels, especially the exotic *Salammbô* and *La Tentation de Saint Antoine*, have a less immediate appeal to the modern reader, though the various versions through which the latter book passed between 1848 and 1874 make it the work on which Flaubert spent most time. Flaubert's attitude of caustic superiority to the modern world joined with an obsession with stupidity to produce *Bouvard et Pécuchet*, unpublished in his life-time, as well as the shorter and more amusing *Dictionnaire des idées reçues*. Although he was himself of impeccably middle-class origins, and adopted a very middle-class life-style, he contributed greatly to the growth of the now universal custom in France whereby imaginative writers have only contempt for the members of the middle-class who buy and read their books.

His literary influence showed itself in the 19th century principally in the development of the realist movement with Zola and Maupassant, and in the 20th in the self-styled "nouveaux romanciers" of the 1950's. Thus Alain Robbe-Grillet saw in Flaubert a writer with a comparable interest to his own in the minute description of inanimate physical objects, and tended to pay less attention to the concern for pitiless psychological analysis which led to Flaubert being shown, in his life-time, in a cartoon depicting him as a surgeon in a blood-stained apron holding up the dissected heart of the unhappy Emma Bovary.

There is general unanimity among critics of all tendencies to admire the long short stories in *Trois contes* as undisputed masterpieces; one of them, "Un Coeur simple," an account of how a servant woman devotes herself entirely to the welfare of others is indeed a masterpiece of a kind. It is certainly the work in which Flaubert shows something of the sympathy for his own creations which traditionally characterises the novelist, and in which the hatred of normal humanity which so often informs his work gives way to a more charitable vision of our limitations. Those who consider singleness of purpose in the pursuit of aesthetic perfection will admire the hermit-like existence which Flaubert imposed upon himself, and detach themselves from Jean-Paul Sartre's view that Flaubert, like the other 19th-century French writers who retired to their "ivory tower," is to be held responsible for the massacres which followed the Commune of 1871 because they did not write a single line to protest against them. Those who admire the vigour and even the vulgarity of a Dickens or a Balzac, or who share the sympathy with ordinary life which so often shows itself in Tolstoy, will speculate more on the paradox of how a man who disliked human beings so much managed to write novels at all. The subtitle of *Madame Bovary* is "Moeurs de Province" (Customs of the Provinces), and this draws attention to the character of the local pharmacist Homais, the embodiment of all that Flaubert most disliked in the optimism and enthusiasm for scientific progress which were so marked a feature of mid-19th-century France.

—Philip Thody

FONTANE, Theodor. Born Henri Théodore Fontane in Neuruppin, 30 December 1819. Educated at Gymnasium, Neuruppin, 1832-33; Gewerbeschule K.F. Klödens, Berlin, 1833-36. Military service, 1844. Married Emilie Rouanet-Kummer in 1850; three sons and one daughter. Pharmacist: apprenticed in Berlin, 1836-40, and worked in Leipzig, Dresden, and Berlin, 1841-49; then free-lance writer: worked for Prussian government press bureau; London correspondent for Berlin papers, 1855-59; editor for London affairs, *Kreuzzeitung*, 1860-70; theatre critic, *Vossische Zeitung*, 1870-89. Recipient: Schiller Prize (Prussia), 1891. *Died 20 September 1898.*

PUBLICATIONS

Collections

Sämtliche Werke, edited by Edgar Gross and others. 24 vols., 1959-75.
Werke, Schriften, und Briefe, edited by Walter Keitel and Helmuth Nürnberger. 1962— .
Romane und Erzählungen, edited by Peter Goldammer and others. 8 vols., 1969.

Fiction

Vor dem Sturm. 1878.
Grete Minde. 1880.
Ellernklipp. 1881.
L'Adultera. 1882; as *The Woman Taken in Adultery*, 1979.
Schach von Wuthenow. 1883; as *A Man of Honor*, 1975.
Graf Petöfy. 1884.
Unterm Birnbaum. 1885.
Cecile. 1887.
Irrungen, Wirrungen. 1888; as *Trials and Tribulations*, 1917; as *A Suitable Match*, 1968.
Quitt. 1890.
Stine. 1890; translated as *Stine*, 1977.
Unwiederbringlich. 1891; as *Beyond Recall*, 1964.
Frau Jenny Treibel. 1892; translated as *Frau Jenny Treibel*, 1976.
Effi Briest. 1895; translated as *Effi Briest*, 1967.
Die Poggenpuhls. 1896; as *The Poggenpuhl Family*, 1979.
Der Stechlin. 1899.
Mathilde Möhring. 1906.

Verse

Von der schönen Rosamunde. 1850.

Männer und Helden. 1850.
Gedichte. 2 vols., 1851-75.
Balladen. 1861.

Other

Ein Sommer in London. 1854.
Aus England. 1860.
Jenseit des Tweed. 1860; as *Across the Tweed,* 1965.
Wanderungen durch die Mark Brandenburg. 4 vols., 1862-82.
Kriegsgefangen. 1871.
Aus den Tagen der Okkupation. 1872.
Christian Friedrich Scherenberg und der literarische Berlin von 1840 bis 1860. 1885.
Fünf Schlösser. 1889.
Meine Kinderjahre. 1894.
Von Zwanzig bis Dreissig. 1898.
Aus dem Nachlass, edited by Joseph Ettlinger. 1908.
Journeys to England in Victoria's Early Days 1844-1859. 1939.
Briefe, edited by Kurt Schreinert. 4 vols., 1968-71.
Briefwechsel, with Paul Heyse, edited by Gotthard Erler. 1972.
Briefwechsel, with Theodor Storm, edited by Jacob Steiner. 1981.

*

Critical Studies: *Formen des Realismus* by Peter Demetz, 1964; *The Gentle Critic: Fontane and German Politics 1848-98* by Joachim Remak, 1964; *Fontane: An Introduction to the Man and His Work* by A.R. Robinson, 1976; *The Preparation of the Future: Techniques of Anticipation in the Novels of Fontane and Thomas Mann* by Gertrude Michielsen, 1978; *Some Aspects of Balladesque Art and Their Relevance for the Novels of Fontane* by R. Geoffrey Lackey, 1979; *Supernatural and Irrational Elements in the Works of Fontane* by Helen Elizabeth Chambers, 1980; *The Berlin Novels of Fontane* by Henry Garland, 1980; *Fontane: The Major Novels* by Alan F. Bance, 1982.

*   *   *

It was as a writer of ballads that Theodor Fontane first made his way in the literary world, and it was on the ballad, and on his historical researches, *Wanderungen durch die Mark Brandenburg,* that Fontane's reputation rested for most of his own lifetime. He emerged as a novelist only in his late fifties, with the historical novel *Vor dem Sturm,* on the mood of Prussia on the eve of the Wars of Liberation against Napoleon.

Fontane is typically concerned here to present large-scale events through the details of everyday life, and this predilection for the actual conditions of life (albeit within a limited social range) is somewhat un-German. In fact, Fontane and Heinrich Heine were perhaps the only two 19th-century writers of rank to grapple closely with the political reality of their country. The author himself thought his wealth of topical references would render him unreadable in the next century (yet Ernst Jünger was sustained by the love story *A Suitable Match* in the trenches of the First World War). Everything Fontane writes is in a sense political, and yet everything is conveyed through the intimate medium of a private fate. Thus his novella on the decadent state of Prussian society in the era of its defeat at Napoleon's hands in 1806 reveals the nature of the times through the character of an individual, the Prussian officer Schach von Wuthenow (after whom the story is named), a vacillating conformist. Fontane's highly developed handling of conversation is the most praised quality of his art, and it especially offers him scope for revealing the link between private existence and the public totality of an epoch. His preference for reticence and discretion as a narrator has allowed him to be read as an apologist for the accommodations required of the individual in society. But he is at heart a romantic, who knows, however, that individuals only exist within the given of their society and cannot transcend it. Yet it is *through* these individuals that Fontane must convey his sense of an alternative world, and he does so often through female characters who possess a mysterious natural attraction, and whose potential the world stifles or leaves unrealized. The most poetic expression of this confrontation of nature and society is the figure of Effi Briest in Fontane's best-known novel; and yet this book more than any other makes clear that society is known and understood only through individuals who are products of their society and cannot stand outside it. His last novel, *Der Stechlin*, is a serene and yet politically astute analysis of the tension between reified "facts"—the facts of self-interest and power politics which became a dominant fetish in Wilhelm II's materialistic Second Reich—and the possibility of change. Fontane's life-long attraction to England, prominent in *Der Stechlin*, was precisely to do with the contrast between English political culture and Prussia's difficulty in evolving social structures commensurate with the dynamic forces of its modernization.

—Alan F. Bance

FRISCH, Max (Rudolf). Born in Zurich, Switzerland, 15 May 1911. Educated at the University of Zurich, 1931-33; Zurich Institute of Technology, diploma in architecture 1940. Served in the Swiss Army, 1939-45. Married Gertrud Anna Constance von Meyenburg in 1942 (divorced, 1959); two daughters and one son. Free-lance journalist after 1933; architect in Zurich, 1945-54; then full-time writer. Recipient: Raabe Prize, 1954; Schleussner Schüller Prize, for radio play, 1955; Büchner Prize, 1958; Zurich Prize, 1958; Veillon Prize, 1958; Nordrhein-Westfalen Prize, 1962; Jerusalem Prize, 1965; Schiller Prize (Baden-Württemberg), 1965; Schiller Prize (Switzerland), 1974; German Book Trade Freedom Prize, 1976. Honorary doctorate: University of Marburg, 1962; Bard College, Annandale-on-Hudson, New York, 1980; City University of New York, 1982. Honorary Member, American Academy, 1974. Lives in Berzona, Switzerland.

PUBLICATIONS

Plays

> *Nun singen sie wieder: Versuch eines Requiems* (produced, 1945).   1946.
> *Santa Cruz* (produced, 1946).   1947.
> *Die chinesische Mauer* (produced, 1946).   1947; revised version, 1955; as *The Chinese Wall*, 1961.
> *Als der Krieg zu Ende war* (produced, 1948).   1949; as *When the War Was Over*, in *Three Plays*, 1967.
> *Graf Öderland* (produced, 1951).   1951; as *Count Oderland*, in *Three Plays*, 1962.
> *Don Juan; oder, Die Liebe zur Geometrie* (produced, 1953).   1953; translated as *Don Juan*, in *Three Plays*, 1967.
> *Rip van Winkle*, from the story by Washington Irving (broadcast, 1953).   1969.
> *Biedermann und die Brandstifter* (broadcast, 1953; produced on stage, 1958).   1958; as *The Fire Raisers*, 1962; as *The Firebugs*, 1963.
> *Die grosse Wut des Philipp Hotz* (produced, 1958).   1958; as *The Great Fury of Philipp*

Hotz, in *Three Plays*, 1967.
Andorra (produced, 1961). 1962; translated as *Andorra*, in *Three Plays*, 1962.
Stücke. 2 vols., 1962.
Zurich Transit (televised, 1966). 1966.
Biografie (produced, 1968). 1967; as *Biography*, 1969.
Triptychon. 1978; as *Triptych*, 1981.

Radio Plays: *Rip van Winkle*, 1953; *Biedermann und die Brandstifter*, 1953.

Television Play: *Zurich Transit*, 1966.

Fiction

Jürg Reinhart: Eine sommerliche Schicksalsfahrt. 1934.
Antwort aus der Stille: Eine Erzählung aus den Bergen. 1937.
J'adore ce qui me brûle; oder, Die Schwierigen. 1943.
Bin; oder, Die Reise nach Peking. 1945.
Marion und die Marionotten: Ein Fragment. 1946.
Stiller. 1954; as *I'm Not Stiller*, 1958.
Homo Faber. 1957; translated as *Homo Faber*, 1959.
Mein Name sei Gantenbein. 1964; as *A Wilderness of Mirrors*, 1965; as *Gantenbein*, 1982.
Wilhelm Tell für die Schule. 1971.
Montauk. 1975; translated as *Montauk*, 1976.
Der Mensch erscheint im Holozän. 1979; as *Man in the Holocene*, 1980.
Blaubart. 1982; as *Bluebeard*, 1983.

Other

Blätter aus dem Brotsack. 1940.
Tagebuch mit Marion. 1947; revised edition, as *Tagebuch 1946-1949*, 1950; as *Sketch-book 1946-1949*, 1977.
Achtung: Die Schweiz. 1955.
Ausgewählte Prosa. 1961.
Öffentlichkeit als Partner. 1967.
Tagebuch 1966-1971. 1972; as *Sketchbook 1966-1971*, 1974.
Dienstbüchlein. 1974.
Stich-Worte (selection), edited by Uwe Johnson. 1975.
Gesammelte Werke. 12 vols., 1976.
Kritik, Thesen, Analysen. 1977.

*

Critical Studies: *Frisch* by Ulrich Weisstein, 1967; *The Novels of Frisch* by Michael Butler, 1976; *The Dramatic Works of Frisch* by Gertrud Bauer Pickar, 1977; *Frisch: His Work and Its Swiss Background* by Malcolm Pender, 1979; *Gombrowicz and Frisch: Aspects of the Literary Diary* by Alex Kurczaba, 1980.

*   *   *

Max Frisch has attained wide popularity both as a novelist and dramatist. His central theme from his very earliest works has always been the individual's longing to discover and realize his "true" self, but the works themselves encompass a rich variety of emphases, moods, and styles. The early novels such as *Jürg Reinhart* derive from the German Bildungsroman tradition (novel of development), but in the immediate post-war years Frisch began to experiment much more with genre and form. *Bin; oder, Die Reise nach Peking*, for example, is a whimsical reflection on unfulfilled longing, while a drama like *Nun singen sie wieder* uses almost surrealistic pictures to capture the conflict of egotism and humanitarian feeling in war. Some dramas like *Santa Cruz* or *Count Oderland* are quasi-mythical presentations of the problem of marrying personal dream to social reality, but though Brechtian in structure they lack Brecht's imaginative clarity. Nevertheless, it is in this period that Frisch's major leitmotif emerges, the concept of "image-making"—the imposition of arbitrary labels, social, racial, psychological, upon our fellows.

In the late 1950's and 1960's Frisch began to produce the works upon which his international reputation is really founded. *The Fire Raisers* and *Andorra*, for example, have become stage classics, the former a satirical attack upon middle-class concern for the "right image," the latter a powerful critique of the destructive effect on others of the images we create of them through fear, self-interest, or convenience. Both plays have a tellingly spare structure, and *Andorra* is a particularly fascinating mix of emotive visual symbolism and distancing effects.

Inventive formal structure is also the hallmark of *I'm Not Stiller*, perhaps Frisch's finest work to date. This novel combines sheer entertainment in the constant question-mark held over the main figure's identity, with a probing investigation into the meaning of "identity." Frisch logically abandons omniscient narration and allows Stiller to reflect his own complex self, a battle-ground between the images others would impose, those inherent in language itself, and those fashioned by the self even in moments of apparent existential insight. The novel's wonderful intricacy forces the reader to reassess his own modes of judgement. And the same is true of Frisch's subsequent novels. *Homo Faber* is an attack upon the complacent belief that technology rules the world. Faber's neat image of a calculable, controllable reality is shattered by age, emotion, and the incursion of his own unacknowledged past, the loss of simplicity revealed in his tortuous account. *Gantenbein* also captures the complexity of personality, in a delightfully comic interplay of "experimental" identities.

In his later works Frisch has tended to use shorter forms, but again with great variety, from sophisticated comedy in *Biography*, through painful confession in *Montauk* to scurrilous wit in *Bluebeard*. All these, like his diaries, show Frisch as concerned as ever over the limits and possibilities of self: what perhaps characterizes the later work is a lighter touch, with a profounder scepticism, than ever before.

—Mary E. Stewart

GALDÓS, Benito Pérez.   *See* PÉREZ GALDÓS, Benito.

GARCÍA LORCA, Federico. Born in Fuentevaqueros, Spain, 5 June 1898. Educated at Colegio del Sagrado Corazón de Jesús, Granada; also studied piano at Granada conservatory; Residencia de Estudiantes, Madrid, 1919-29; Columbia University, New York, 1929-30. Editor, *El Gallo*, 1928; director of itinerant theatre group, La Barraca, in the 1930's. Arrested and shot almost immediately after Franco's troops began uprising. *Died 18/19 August 1936.*

PUBLICATIONS

Collections

Obras completas, edited by Arturo del Hoyo. 2 vols., 1973.

Plays

El maleficio de la mariposa (produced 1920). In *Obras completas*, 1954; as *The Butterfly's Evil Spell*, in *Five Plays*, 1963.
Los títeres de Cachiporra (produced 1923). 1949; as *The Billy-Club Puppets*, in *Five Plays*, 1963.
Mariana Pineda (produced 1927). 1928.
La zapatera prodigiosa (produced 1930; revised version, produced 1933). In *Obras completas*, 1938; as *The Shoemaker's Prodigious Wife*, in *Five Plays*, 1963.
El amor de Don Perlimpín (produced 1933). In *Obras completas*, 1938; as *The Love of Don Perlimpín*, in *Five Plays*, 1963.
Bodas de sangre (produced 1933). 1935; as *Blood Wedding*, in *III Tragedies*, 1947.
Yerma (produced 1934). 1937; translated as *Yerma*, in *III Tragedies*, 1947.
Doña Rosita la soltera (produced 1935). In *Obras completas*, 1938; as *Doña Rosita the Spinster*, in *Five Plays*, 1963.
El "retablillo" de Don Cristóbal (produced 1935). In *Obras completas*, 1938.
Así que pasen cinco años (produced 1945). In *Obras completas*, 1938.
La casa de Bernarda Alba (produced 1945). 1945; translated as *Bernarda Alba*, in *III Tragedies*, 1947.
El público y Comédia sin título: Dos obras teatrales póstumas, edited by R. Martínez Nadal. 1978; as *The Public, and Play Without a Title: Two Posthumous Plays*, 1983.

Verse

Libro de poemas. 1921.
Canciones. 1927; as *Canciones*, translated by Philip Cummings, edited by Daniel Eisenberg, 1976.
Primer romancero gitano. 1928; as *Gypsy Ballads*, translated by Rolfe Humphries, 1963.
Poema del canto jondo. 1931.
Oda a Walt Whitman. 1933.
Llanto por la muerte de Ignacio Sánchez Mejías. 1935.
Primeras canciones. 1936.
Lament for the Death of a Bullfighter and Other Poems, translated by A.L. Lloyd, 1937.
Poems, translated by Stephen Spender and J.L. Gili. 1939.
Poeta en Nueva York. 1940; as *Poet in New York*, translated by Rolfe Humphries, 1940; also translated by Ben Belitt, 1955.
[Selection], translated by J.L. Gili. 1960.
Lorca and Jiménez, translated by Robert Bly. 1973.

GARCÍA LORCA

Divan and Other Writings, translated by Edwin Honig. 1974.
Poesía I, edited by Miguel Garcia-Posada. 1980.

Other

Deep Song and Other Prose, edited by Christopher Maurer. 1980.
Selected Letters, edited and translated by David Gershator. 1983.

*

Bibliography: *García Lorca: A Selectively Annotated Bibliography of Criticism* by Francesca Colecchia, 1980.

Critical Studies: *Lorca: The Poet and His People* by Arturo Barea, 1945; *Lorca and the Spanish Poetic Tradition* by J.B. Trend, 1956; *Lorca: A Collection of Critical Essays* edited by Manuel Durán, 1962; *The Theatre of García Lorca* by Robert Lima, 1963; *García Lorca* by Edwin Honig, 1963; *García Lorca* by Carl W. Cobb, 1967; *The Symbolic World of García Lorca*, 1972, and *Psyche and Symbol in the Theatre of García Lorca*, 1974, both by Rupert Allen; *The Death of Lorca* by Ian Gibson, 1973, revised edition, as *The Assassination of García Lorca*, 1979; *The Comic Spirit of García Lorca* by Virginia Higginbotham, 1976; *García Lorca, Playwright and Poet* by Mildred Adams, 1977; *Lorca: The Theatre Beneath the Sands* by Gwynne Edwards, 1980.

*   *   *

Lorca has come to be one of the most widely read and admired authors who have written in Spanish in the 20th century. His execution by fascists at the outbreak of the Spanish Civil War abruptly brought his name into world focus, but since then his work as a poet and playwright has endured the test of political notoriety and has continued to prosper on the strength of its intrinsic worth.

Leonardo, the protagonist of *Blood Wedding*, one of Lorca's most famous plays, defends adulterous love in these terms: "The fault is not mine/The fault belongs to the earth." A case could readily be made to substantiate the point of view that all of Lorca's protagonists, including the poet-narrator himself, struggle in the grip of telluric passions. Smugglers, gypsies, suppressed women, and ultimately the poet have but one goal: to exult, by means of startling metaphors fashioned against the backdrop of Andalusia, their pain and grief at the indifference of society and the silence of death. In a celebrated lecture, Lorca pointed to the Andalusian *duende* (goblin) as the embodiment of dark and dangerous feelings. In Lorca's canon, the greatest crime is to stifle the expression of these emotions and the greatest fear is the total tranquility of death.

By emphasizing the demonic inspiration of his verse, Lorca placed himself in the tradition of those who believe in the Platonic seizure, or in Housman's shivers down the spine. A master of details of form, he, nevertheless, insisted that the totality of the poem was something over which he had no control. "If it is true," he once said, "that I am a poet through the grace of God (or the devil), I have also gotten where I am by virtue of work and technical skill, without having the slightest notion of what a poem is."

Constantly requested to read his poetry aloud (which he did with great effect), Lorca had all the appearances of a latter-day bard. His strong sense of the oral tradition led him at times to display indifference toward the printed word. Many poems circulated among friends, or survived in the intimacy of small public readings before they became fixed between the covers of books.

Childhood memories of playing in meadows with crumpled purple mountains in the distance, such is Lorca's own characterization of his first book of verse *Libro de poemas* (Book of Poems). Graceful combinations of humor, irony, and whimsy bestow a tone notably lacking in most of the subsequent poetry. A strong sense of mystery and magic, however, pervade this Andalusian pastoral. Like Yeats, Lorca was interested in "the little folk" and longed to learn the secret of the ancient fairy who first heard the grass grow.

In *Poema del canto jondo* (Poem of the Deep Song), Lorca sought to capture in verse the impact of the heady, monotonous, and pathetic chant that had been introduced into Spain from oriental sources. He personifies the *cante*, turns it into a baleful, dark-haired woman, attributes cosmic powers to it (the shout of the singer causes olive groves to tremble and even silence quivers), and finally makes it an expression of elemental grief. By now, the characteristics of Lorca's modernism have become clear: using an acute sense of local culture (Andalusia), he will express in bold metaphorical terms the loneliness, grief, and frustration of the human predicament.

The *Gypsy Ballads* raises the persecuted gypsies of Spain to the level of poetry by inventing a mythology for them. In doing so, Lorca went back beyond the Greek and Roman myths and intuited a primitive mythology in which there is a close relationship between man and cosmic reality. The moon opens the book by stealing away a gypsy boy, and under her influence, the fortunes of the gypsies wax and wane. The wind attempts to rape a gypsy girl, and all of nature reacts in sympathy to her plight. By skillfully employing the eight-syllable line and the strong dramatic dialogue form of the old Spanish *romance* (ballad), Lorca demonstrates once again his ability to meld traditional elements into his modern outlook. The bedazzling, sometimes disturbing metaphors of this popular book have still not worn thin.

Seeking to step aside from the success accorded him in Madrid, Lorca went to New York in the summer of 1929. His sensitivities, developed in an agrarian and conservative European region, were overwhelmed by the vast concreteness of New York, its technological power, and the festering racial prejudice. *Poet in New York*, making use of a modified form of surrealism, is a description of the collapse of his personal world and the painful process of picking up the pieces again. In terms of its denunciation of modern civilization, it is often compared to *The Waste Land*. Lorca's outraged feeling of social justice and his sympathy for the underdog comes through loud and clear. The section on Harlem, with its forecast of violence between blacks and whites, has turned out to be remarkably prescient. The death of a bullfighter friend inspired *Lament for the Death of a Bullfighter*, considered by many critics to be one of the most impressive of modern elegies.

Aside from the playfulness and sense of humor sporadically present in the early verse, the register of Lorca's poetic voice is intense, dark, and somber. Passionate descriptions rather than philosophical reflections mark his work. Once again, his regional background plays a role, for the *andaluz*, he once remarked, is either asleep in the dust or shouting at the stars.

Lorca's plays have been performed around the world. *Blood Wedding*, *Yerma*, and *The House of Bernarda Alba* all deal with the theme of sexual repression. The violent punishment of adultery, the tortures of sterility imposed by environment as well as nature, and the oppressiveness of a matriarchal family, respectively, are powerfully handled in these three plays. The first two make extensive use of poetry, earning Lorca the reputation among modern dramatists of being one of the most successful in using poetry on the stage.

—Howard T. Young

GENET, Jean.   Born in Paris, 19 December 1910; abandoned by his parents, and reared by foster parents in Le Morvan. In reformatory, Mettray, 1926-29, and lived the life of a criminal in several countries until 1942; began writing during term in Fresnes Prison. Lives in Paris, France.

PUBLICATIONS

Fiction

Notre-Dame des Fleurs.   1944; revised edition, in *Oeuvres complètes 2*, 1951; as *Our Lady of the Flowers*, 1949; as *Gutter in the Sky*, 1956.
Miracle de la rose.   1946; revised edition, in *Oeuvres complètes 2*, 1951; as *Miracle of the Rose*, 1965.
Pompes funèbres.   1947; revised edition, in *Oeuvres complètes 3*, 1953; as *Funeral Rites*, 1969.
Querelle de Brest.   1947; revised edition, in *Oeuvres complètes 3*, 1953; as *Querelle of Brest*, 1966.

Plays

Les Bonnes (produced, 1946; revised version, produced, 1954).   1954; as *The Maids*, with *Deathwatch*, 1954.
'Adame Miroir (ballet scenario), music by Milhaud.   1948.
Haute surveillance (produced, 1949).   1949; as *Deathwatch*, with *The Maids*, 1954.
Le Balcon (produced, 1956).   1956; revised version, 1956; 1961; as *The Balcony*, 1957.
Les Nègres (produced, 1959).   1958; as *The Blacks*, 1960.
Les Paravents (produced, 1961).   1961; as *The Screens*, 1962.

Screenplays: *Un Chant d'amour*, 1950; *Goubbiah*, 1955; *Mademoiselle*, 1966.

Verse

Chants secrets.   1947.
La Galère.   1947.
Poèmes.   1948; revised edition, 1966.
Poems.   1980.
Treasures of the Night: Collected Poems, translated by Steven Finch.   1981.

Other

Journal du voleur.   1949; as *The Thief's Journal*, 1954.
L'Enfant criminel, 'Adame Miroir.   1949.
Oeuvres complètes.   4 vols., 1951-68.
Lettres à Roger Blin.   1966; as *Letters to Roger Blin: Reflections on the Theatre*, 1969.
May Day Speech.   1970.
Reflections on the Theatre and Other Writings.   1972.

*

Bibliography: *Genet and His Critics: An Annotated Bibliography 1943-1980* by Richard C. Webb, 1982.

Critical Studies: *Saint-Genet, Actor and Martyr* by Jean-Paul Sartre, 1963; *The Imagination of Genet* by Joseph H. McMahon, 1963; *Genet* by Tom F. Driver, 1966; *Genet* by Bettina Knapp, 1968; *Genet: A Study of His Novels and Plays* by Philip Thody, 1968; *The Visions of Genet* by Richard N. Coe, 1968, and *The Theatre of Genet: A Casebook* edited by Coe, 1970;

Profane Play, Ritual, and Genet: A Study of His Drama by Lewis T. Cetta, 1974; *Genet: A Collection of Critical Essays* edited by Peter Brooks and Joseph Halpern, 1979; *Genet* by Jeannette Savona, 1983.

*   *   *

When Jean-Paul Sartre published his long study, *Saint-Genet, Actor and Martyr*, in 1952, many readers came to Genet through Sartre's evaluation and sympathy. The book proposed that Genet be classified among the greatest French writers of the century. At every step of the way, Genet has known what he was doing. Hence Sartre's term to designate him *comédien* or actor. And Genet never failed to acknowledge the condition imposed upon him by society when he was young; hence the second term in the title of *martyr*.

One day the parallels will be studied that exist between Rimbaud's revolt against his condition in the world, and Genet's submission to his fate. A world only half-seen by Rimbaud in episodes of *Une Saison en enfer* is raucously dramatized in Genet's first novel *Notre-Dame des Fleurs*. Extravagant in every sense, this late adolescent world of Montmartre, engendered by the early adolescent world in the prisons of Mettray and Fontevrault, is the *légende dorée* of Jean Genet, in which existence is a cult, a ceremony of evil where the male is female. Death in violence obsesses the minds of the tough heroes of Genet (*les durs*: Bulkaen, Pilorge, Harcamone), and martyrdom obsesses the minds of the effeminate (Divine and Notre-Dame). The guillotine is the symbol of the male and of his greatest glory.

The central drama in his books is always the struggle between the man in authority and the man to whom he is attracted. The psychological varieties of this struggle are many. Each of the novels and each of the plays is a different world in which the same drama unfolds. *Querelle de Brest* is the ship: naval officers and sailors. *Pompes funèbres* is the Occupation: Nazi officers and young Frenchmen of the capital. *Notre-Dames des Fleurs* is Montmartre, with its world of male prostitutes and pimps. *Miracle de la rose* is the prison, with the notorious convicts and slaves.

The play *Haute surveillance* (*Deathwatch*) is also the prison cell with the intricate hierarchy of criminals where those standing under the death sentence exert the greatest power and prestige over those with lesser sentences. *Les Bonnes (The Maids)* is the household, where in the absence of the mistress one of the maids plays her part. *Les Nègres (The Blacks)* is the world of colonialism: the conflict between whites and blacks. It is much more than a satire on colonialism. The oppression from which the blacks suffer is so hostile, so incomprehensible, as to be easily the oppression of mankind. The hostility which Genet persistently celebrates throughout all his work, in his opulent language, is the strangely distorted love joining the saint and the criminal, the guard and the prisoner, the policeman and the thief, the master and the slave, the white and the black.

—Wallace Fowlie

GIDE, André (Paul-Guillaume).   Born in Paris, 22 November 1869.   Educated at École Alsacienne, Paris, 1878-80; Lycée in Montpellier, 1881; boarder at M. Henri Bauer, 1883-85, and at M. Jacob Keller, 1886-87; École Alsacienne, 1887; École Henri IV: baccalauréat, 1890. Married Madeleine Rondeaux in 1895 (died, 1938); had one daughter by Elisabeth van Bysselberghe. Mayor of a Normandy commune, 1896; juror in Rouen, 1912; special envoy of

Colonial Ministry on trip to Africa, 1925-26. Helped found *Nouvelle Revue Française*, 1909. Recipient: Nobel Prize for Literature, 1947. Ph.D.: Oxford University. Honorary Member, American Academy, 1950. *Died 19 February 1951*.

PUBLICATIONS

Fiction

Les Cahiers d'André Walter. 1891; as *The White Notebook*, 1965; as *The Notebook of Andre Walter*, 1968.
La Tentative Amoureuse. 1893.
Le Voyage d'Urien. 1893; as *Urien's Voyage*, 1964.
Paludes. 1895; as *Marshlands*, 1953.
Les Nourritures terrestres. 1897; as *Fruits of the Earth*, 1949.
Le Prométhée mal enchaîné. 1899; as *Prometheus Misbound*, with *Marshlands*, 1953.
L'Immoraliste. 1902; as *The Immoralist*, 1930.
Le Retour de l'enfant prodigue. 1907.
La Porte étroite. 1909; as *Strait Is the Gate*, 1924.
Isabelle. 1911; as *Isabelle*, in *Two Symphonies*, 1931.
Les Caves du Vatican. 1914; as *The Vatican Swindle*, 1925; as *Lafcadio's Adventures*, 1927; as *The Vatican Cellars*, 1952.
La Symphonie pastorale. 1919; as *The Pastoral Symphony*, in *Two Symphonies*, 1931.
Les Faux-monnayeurs. 1926; as *The Counterfeiters*, 1927; as *The Coiners*, 1950.
L'École des femmes. 1929; as *The School for Wives*, 1929.
Deux récits. 1938.
Thésée. 1946, translated as *Theseus*, 1948.

Plays

Philoctète (produced 1919). 1899; as *Philoctetes*, in *My Theatre*, 1951.
Le Roi Candaule (produced 1901). 1901; as *King Candaules*, in *My Theatre*, 1951.
Saül (produced 1922). 1903; as *Saul*, in *My Theatre*,1951.
Le Retour de l'enfant prodigue (produced 1928). 1909.
Bethsabé. 1912; as *Bathsheba*, in *My Theatre*, 1951.
Antoine et Cléopatre, from the play by Shakespeare (produced 1920). In *Théâtre complet*, 1949.
Amal; ou, La Lettre du roi, from the play by Tagore (produced 1928). 1922.
Robert: Supplément a l'école des femmes (produced 1946). 1930; as *Robert; ou, L'Intérêt général*, 1949.
Oedipe (produced 1931). 1931; as *Oedipus*, in *Two Legends*, 1950.
Les Caves du Vatican, from his own novel (produced 1933). 1950.
Perséphone, music by Igor Stravinsky (produced 1934). 1934; edited by Patrick Pollard, 1977; translated as *Persephone*, 1949.
Geneviève. 1936.
Le treizième arbre (produced 1939). In *Théâtre*, 1942.
Hamlet, from the play by Shakespeare (produced 1946). In *Théâtre complet*, 1949.
Le Procès, with Jean-Louis Barrault, from the novel by Kafka (produced 1947). 1947; translated as *The Trial*, 1950.
Théâtre complet. 8 vols., 1947-49.

Verse

Les Poésies d'André Walter.   1892.

Other

Le Traité du Narcisse.   1891.
Réflexions sur quelques points de littérature et de morale.   1897.
Feuilles de route 1895-1896.   1899.
Philoctète, suivi de Le Traité du Narcisse, La Tentative amoureuse, El Hadj.   1899.
De l'influence en littérature.   1900.
Lettres à Angèle (1898-1899).   1900.
Les Limites de l'art.   1901.
De l'importance du public.   1903.
Prétextes.   1903.
Amyntas.   1906.
Dostoïevsky d'après sa correspondance.   1908.
Oscar Wilde.   1910; translated as *Oscar Wilde*, 1951.
Charles-Louis Philippe.   1911.
C.R.D.N.   1911.
Nouveaux prétextes.   1911.
Souvenirs de la cour d'assises.   1914; as *Recollections of the Assize Court*, 1941.
Corydon.   1920; translated as *Corydon*, 1950.
Si le grain ne meurt.   2 vols., 1920-21; as *If It Die...*, 1935.
Numquid et tu...?   1922; translated in *Journal*, 1952.
Dostoïevsky.   1923; translated as *Dostoevsky*, 1925.
Incidences.   1924.
Caractères.   1925.
Le Journal des faux-monnayeurs.   1926.
Dindiki.   1927.
Émile Verhaeren.   1927.
Joseph Conrad.   1927.
Voyage au Congo.   1927.
Le Retour du Tchad, suivi du Voyage au Congo, Carnets de route.   1928; as *Travels in the Congo*, 1930.
Essai sur Montaigne.   1929; translated as *Montaigne*, 1929.
Un Esprit non prévenu.   1929.
Lettres.   1930.
L'Affaire Redureau, suivie de Faits divers.   1930.
Le Sequestrée de Poitiers.   1930.
Jacques Rivière.   1931.
Divers.   1931.
Oeuvres complètes, edited by Louis Martin-Chauffier.   15 vols., 1932-39; *Index*, 1954.
Les nouvelles nourritures.   1935; in *Fruits of the Earth*, 1949.
Retour de l'U.R.S.S.   1936; *Retouches*, 1937; as *Return from the U.S.S.R.*, 1937.
Journal 1889-1939.   1939; *1939-1942*, 1946; *1942-1949*, 1950; translated as *Journal 1889-1949*, 1952.
Découvrons Henri Michaux.   1941.
Attendu que.   1943.
Interviews imaginaires.   1943; as *Imaginary Interviews*, 1944.
Jeunesse.   1945.
Lettres à Christian Beck.   1946.
Souvenirs littératures et problèmes actuels.   1946.

Et nunc manet in te. 1947; as *The Secret Drama of My Life*, 1951; as *Madeleine*, 1952.
Paul Valéry. 1947.
Poétique. 1947.
Correspondance 1893-1938, with Francis Jammes, edited by Robert Mallet. 1948.
Notes sur Chopin. 1948; as *Notes on Chopin*, 1949.
Préfaces. 1948.
Rencontres. 1948.
Correspondance 1899-1926, with Paul Claudel, edited by Robert Mallet. 1949; as *Correspondence*, 1952.
Feuillets d'automne. 1949.
Lettres, with Charles du Bos. 1950.
Littérature engagée, edited by Yvonne Davet. 1950.
Égypte 1939. 1951.
Ainsi soit-il; ou, Les Jeux sont faits. 1952; as *So Be It; or, The Chips Are Down*, 1960.
Correspondance 1909-1926, with Rainer Maria Rilke, edited by Renée Lang. 1952.
Lettres à un sculpteur (Simone Marye). 1952.
Correspondance 1890-1942, with Paul Valéry, edited by Robert Mallet. 1955.
Lettres au Docteur Willy Schuermans (1920-1928). 1955.
Correspondance inédite, with Rilke and Verhaeren, edited by C. Bronne. 1955; as *Self-Portraits: The Gide-Valéry Letters*, 1966.
Correspondance, with Marcel Jouhandeau. 1958.
Romans, récits, et soties; Oeuvres lyriques. 1958.
Correspondance 1905-1912, with Charles Péguy, edited by Alfred Saffrey. 1958.
Correspondence 1904-1928, with Edmund Gosse, edited by Linette F. Brugmans. 1960.
Correspondance 1908-1920, with André Suarès, edited by Sidney D. Braun. 1963.
Correspondance 1911-1931, with Arnold Bennett, edited by Linette F. Brugmans. 1964.
Correspondance 1909-1951, with André Rouveyre, edited by Claude Martin. 1967.
Correspondance 1913-1951, with Roger Martin du Gard, edited by Jean Delay. 2 vols., 1968.
Lettres, with Jean Cocteau, edited by Jean-Jacques Kihm. 1970.
Correspondance 1912-1950, with François Mauriac, edited by Jacqueline Morton. 1971.
Correspondance, with Charles Brunard. 1974.
Correspondance, with Jules Romains, edited by Claude Martin. 1976.
Correspondance 1897-1944, with Henri Ghéon, edited by Jean Tipy. 2 vols., 1976.
Correspondance 1892-1939, with Jacques-Émile Blanche, edited by Georges-Paul Collet. 1979.
Correspondance, with Dorothy Bussy, edited by Jean Lambert. 2 vols., 1979-81; as *Selected Letters*, edited by Richard Tedeschi, 1983.

Editor, *The Living Thoughts of Montaigne.* 1939.
Editor, *Anthologie de la poésie française.* 1949.

Translator, *Typhon*, by Conrad. 1918.
Translator, with J. Schiffrin, *Nouvelles; Récits*, by Pushkin. 2 vols., 1929-35.
Translator, *Arden of Faversham*, in *Le Théâtre élizabethain.* 1933.
Translator, *Prométhée*, by Goethe. 1951.

*

Bibliography: *Bibliographie des écrits de Gide* by Arnold Naville, 1949, supplement, 1953.

Critical Studies: *Gide*, 1951, and *Gide: A Critical Biography*, 1968, both by George D. Painter; *Gide* by Enid Starkie, 1953; *The Theatre of Gide* by J.C. McLaren, 1953; *Gide and the Hound of Heaven* by H. March, 1953; *Portrait of Gide* by Justin O'Brien, 1953; *Gide* by Albert Guerard, 1963, revised edition, 1969; *Gide: His Life and Work* by Wallace Fowlie, 1965; *Gide:*

The Evolution of an Aesthetic by Vinio Rossi, 1967; *Gide and the Greek Myth* by H. Watson-Williams, 1967; *Gide* by Thomas Cordle, 1969; *Gide* by G.W. Ireland, 1970; *Gide: A Collection of Critical Essays* edited by David Littlejohn, 1970; *Gide and the Art of Autobiography* by C.D.E. Tolton, 1975.

*   *   *

By the end of his life, Gide had received the official sign of consecration, the recognition of his century, that he was one of its major writers. The Nobel prize, awarded to him in 1947, indicated that his work had attained a degree of accepted universality. The miracle was that Gide had become a "classical" writer by the time of his death while remaining a "dangerous" writer. This man who invented for his age the term "restlessness" (*inquiétude*) ended his life in a seeming calm and resignation. A tone of affirmation, a marked denial of God, and a belief in the void of death provided a different portrait of Gide that has been added to the long series of self-portraits his books had already fashioned.

The vast work of Gide is, in a sense, a written confession, initiated by a need to communicate what he felt to be true about himself. He knew that he possessed nothing of the anguish of a Pascal. That trait he left to Mauriac, and accepted for himself the characteristics of a Montaigne—of a wavering and diverse mind, as Montaigne had described himself: *esprit ondoyant et divers*. He remained at all times the writer who profited from every kind of experience, important or trivial.

Marc Allégret's film *Avec André Gide* opens with a few solemn pictures of the funeral at Cuverville and Gide's own reading of the opening pages of his autobiography *Si le grain ne meurt*. There are pictures showing the two contrasting family origins of Gide: Normandy and Languedoc, the north and the south, the Catholic and the Protestant background. The landscape pictures of Algeria and Tunisia provide a documentation for many of his works, from the earliest, such as *Les Nourritures terrestres* to his *Journal* in 1941-42. Among the most curious episodes are the trip to the Congo, the walk with Valéry, the home of his daughter Catherine in Brignoles, the speech made in Moscow in the presence of Stalin, the visit with Roger Martin du Gard in Bellème.

A genius is a man who considers passionately what other men do not see. In the tradition of French letters, Montaigne was pre-eminently this type of genius, seizing every occasion of pleasure, every meeting, for the subject matter of his writing. The art of both the 16th-century essayist and the 20th-century moralist is based upon an indefatigable curiosity and a relentless critical spirit. Gide's enthusiasm for whatever came within his vision was usually followed by an admirable detachment from it. Once the conquest was made, he refused to be subjugated by it, to be dominated by his conquest. The image of the Minotaur's labyrinth, elaborated in his last important book, *Thésée*, represents any body of doctrine that might constrict or imprison the thinking powers of a man. The problem for Theseus, as it was for Gide, was that of surpassing his adventures. The one moral error to be avoided at all cost was immobility, fixation. The meaning of Gide's celebrated word *disponibilité* seems to be the power of remaining dissatisfied, capable of change and growth.

From his avid curiosity about everything, whether it was the coloration of a leaf or the first book of a new author, his ideas were engendered. In the manifold forms of attentiveness with which his life seems to have been spent, there were no traces of misanthropy, of pessimism, of class prejudice, or of fatuous satisfaction with self. From a nature that accepted all contradictions—a will to freedom as well as a sense of destiny, good as well as evil—Gide's mind grew into one of the most critical of our age, a mind of infinite subtlety and unexpected boldness.

Gide began writing about 1890, at a moment of great peacefulness in Europe, and continued to write during the next 60 years. He remained a constant and fervent witness to every ominous development in Europe and the world, from the period in which a religion of science and a rational vision of the universe dominated Europe to the mid-century of deep unrest.

There is little doubt that Gide hoped to compose a new gospel. With his favorite themes of adolescence, revolt, escape, the gratuitous act, he was able to upset the convictions of his readers, particularly his youthful readers, without creating in them feelings of terror or dismay. He tried to write in all the genres because he was unwilling to restrict himself to any one form and because each book, once it was well under way, became irksome to him; he would finish it off quickly in order to move on to a newer work. He had planned, for example, several further chapters for *Les Faux-monnayeurs*, but when he wrote the sentence, "Je suis bien curieux de connaître Caloub," it appeared to him such an admirable final sentence that he felt freed from continuing farther.

Whenever Christianity appeared to him in the form of a system, of a body of principles, he refused to accept it. His was an attitude of detachment and adventure, which permitted him the practice of what has been so often called his "sincerity." Problems of ethics worried Gide far more than religion. He was more concerned with justice than salvation. His knowledge of the Bible and his love for the Gospels always gave hope to his Catholic friends (Claudel, Jammes, DuBos, Ghéon, Copeau) that he would finally submit.

What appears as conformity to the world's law was seriously castigated in *Les Nourritures* and in *L'Immoraliste*. And yet the very difficulty involved in living within a new freedom provided the moral problem of most of his subsequent books, such as *Les Caves du Vatican*, *Les Faux-monnayeurs*, *Thésée*. For the expression of human freedom, for its power and its peril, Gide created massive formulas that have returned, only slightly modified, in the writings of Sartre and Camus and René Char. His long life was one of self-examination, of courage in liberating himself in such experiences as his African visits, communism, Catholicism. Gide developed one need—that of doubting everything—and one obligation—that of never doubting himself.

—Wallace Fowlie

GILGAMESH, Epic of.

PUBLICATIONS

Verse

An Old Babylonian Version of the Epic of Gilgamesh, edited by M. Jastrow and A.T. Clay. 1920.
The Gilgamesh Epic and Old Testament Parallels, edited by A. Heidel. 2nd edition, 1949.
Ancient Near Eastern Texts Relating to the New Testament, edited by J.B. Pritchard, translations by S.N. Kramer (Sumerian) and A. Speiser (Akkadian). 1950; 3rd edition, 1969.
The Epic of Gilgamesh, translated by N.K. Sandars. 1960; revised edition, 1972.

*

Critical Studies: *History Begins at Sumer*, 1956, and *The Sumerians: Their History, Culture, and Character*, 1964, both by S.N. Kramer; *Gilgamesh et sa légende* edited by P. Garelli, 1960; *The Bible and the Ancient Near East: Essays in Honour of W.F. Albright*, 1961; *The Treasures of Darkness* by T. Jacobsen, 1976; *Das Gilgamesh-Epos* edited by K. Oberhuber, 1977.

* * *

Gilgamesh is the oldest surviving literary epic. In its most complete form it is a compilation of the 7th century B.C. written in Akkadian (Old Semitic) on 12 tablets in the cuneiform script. This is a synthesis of older versions, the earliest written in the non-semitic Sumerian language of Mesopotamia in the early second millennium B.C. and probably based on oral traditions of the third millennium. Other versions and fragments come from Hittite Anatolia, Syria, and Egypt. The 7th-century tablets were found at Nineveh in the library of Ashurbanipal, King of Assyria, by A.H. Layard in the 1840's; the first translation was attempted in 1872 by George Smith of the British Museum. Since then much fresh material has come to light and many translations have been made.

Gilgamesh was an historical king of Uruk, a city state in southern Iraq, who probably lived in the early third millennium B.C. From then until the fall of Nineveh in 612 he was remembered as a mighty hero throughout the Middle East. According to the epic tradition Gilgamesh was two parts god and one part man, inheriting from his mother, a minor goddess, beauty, strength, and ambition, and from his father mortality. As a young king he oppressed the people till they complained to the gods who sent him a companion Enkidu, who is uncivilised "natural" man, and with whom he first fights, then forms a deep friendship. Together they go to the "Cedar Mountain" where they kill its monster guardian Humbaba, bringing back cedar-wood and a famous name. Gilgamesh is then wooed by the capricious goddess of love and war, Ishtar (Inanna in Sumerian). He rejects her and in revenge the goddess sends the "Bull of Heaven" to revenge the land. The two friends kill the bull but Enkidu falls sick and dies. Gilgamesh mourns his friend and in dispair he sets out to find Utnapishtim the "Far Away," the Akkadian Noah, who alone survived the flood, to learn from him the secret of immortality. After much wandering in the wilderness he reaches the waters of death which he crosses with the help of the ferryman; but Utnapishtim gives him little comfort, though he recounts the story of the Flood (Tablet XI) which in the Sumerian is a separate account. Gilgamesh obtains a plant of "Eternal Youth," but it is stolen from him by a snake which promptly sheds its skin, so he returns to Uruk alone and empty-handed.

The diction of the Assyrian version is a loose rhythmic verse with four (in earlier versions two) beats to the line. The language is unadorned, with many repetitions but also with striking and memorable expressions. The over-riding theme of the epic is the contrast between human aspirations and the reality of loss and of death. Gilgamesh is a hero with whom it is possible to feel sympathy and human understanding in spite of the great age of the epic:

> Gilgamesh answered her, "And why should not my cheeks be starved and my face drawn? Despair is in my heart and my face is the face of one who has made a long journey, it was burned with heat and with cold. Why should I not wander over the pastures in search of the wind? My friend, my younger brother, he who hunted the wild ass of the wilderness and the panther of the plains, my friend, my younger brother who seized and killed the Bull of Heaven and overthrew Humbaba in the cedar forest, my friend who was very dear to me and who endured dangers beside me, Enkidu my brother, whom I loved, the end of mortality has overtaken him. I wept for him seven days and nights till the worm fastened on him. Because of my brother I am afraid of death, because of my brother I stray through the wilderness and cannot rest."

—N.K. Sandars

GIRAUDOUX, Jean (Hippolyte). Born in Bellac, France, 29 October 1882. Educated at a school in Pellevoisin; Lycée, Chateauroux, 1893-1900; Lycée Lakanal, Paris, 1900-02; École Normale Supérieure, Paris, 1903-05. Military service, 1902-03; served in World War I; wounded twice; Legion of Honor; High Commissioner for Information, 1939-40. Married in 1918; one son. In French diplomatic service from 1910: at Ministry of Foreign Affairs, 1911: mission to Russia and the East; head of "Service des oeuvres françaises à l'étranger," 1920; Secretary to Embassy in Berlin, 1924; Chief Government Press Officer, 1924; in Turkey, 1926. *Died 31 January 1944.*

PUBLICATIONS

Collections

>   *Théâtre complet.* 16 vols., 1945-53.
>   *Oeuvre romanesque; Oeuvres littéraires diverses.* 3 vols., 1955-58.

Plays

>   *Siegfried* (produced 1928). 1928; translated as *Siegfried*, 1930.
>   *Amphitryon 38* (produced 1929). 1929; translated as *Amphitryon 38*, 1938.
>   *Judith* (produced 1931). 1931; translated as *Judith*, in *Drama 1*, 1963.
>   *Intermezzo* (produced 1933). 1933; edited by Colette Weil, 1975; as *The Enchanted*, 1950.
>   *Tessa*, from the play *The Constant Nymph* by Margaret Kennedy and Basil Dean (produced 1934). In *Théâtre 2*, 1958.
>   *La fin de Siegfried.* 1934.
>   *Supplément au voyage de Cook* (produced 1935). 1937; as *The Virtuous Island*, 1956.
>   *La Guerre de Troie n'aura pas lieu* (produced 1935). 1935; as *Tiger at the Gates*, 1955; as *The Trojan War Will Not Take Place*, 1983.
>   *Electre* (produced 1937). 1937; translated as *Electra*, 1957.
>   *L'Impromptu du Paris* (produced 1937). 1937.
>   *Cantique des cantiques* (produced 1938). 1939.
>   *Ondine* (produced 1939). 1939; translated as *Ondine*, 1954.
>   *L'Apollon de Bellac* (as *L'Apollon de Marsac*, produced 1942). In *Théâtre 4*, 1959.
>   *Sodome et Gomorrhe* (produced 1943). 1943.
>   *Le Film de Béthanie: Texte du "Les Anges du péché,"* with R.-L. Bruckberger and Robert Bresson. 1944.
>   *La Folle de Chaillot* (produced 1945). 1945; as *The Madwoman of Chaillot*, 1949.
>   *Pour Lucrèce* (produced 1953). 1954; as *Duel of Angels*, 1958.
>   *Les Gracques*, edited by R.M. Albérès and Jean-Pierre Giraudoux. 1958.

>   Screenplay: *Les Anges du péché*, with R.-L. Bruckberger and Robert Bresson, 1943.

Fiction

>   *Provinciales.* 1909.
>   *Simon le pathétique.* 1918.
>   *Adorable Clio.* 1920.
>   *Suzanne et le Pacifique.* 1921; as *Suzanne and the Pacific*, 1923.
>   *Siegfried et le Limousin.* 1922.
>   *Juliette au pays des hommes.* 1924.

Bella.   1926; translated as *Bella*, 1927.
Eglantine.   1927.
Les aventures de Jérôme Bardini.   1930.
Combat avec l'ange.   1934.
L'École des indifférents.   1934.
Choix des élues.   1938.
Les Contes d'un matin.   1952.
La Menteuse.   1958; as *Lying Woman*, 1972.

Other

Retour d'Alsace, août 1914.   1916.
Lectures pour une ombre.   1917.
Amica America.   1919.
Elpénor.   1919.
Visite chez le prince.   1924.
Le Sport.   1928.
Racine.   1930; translated as *Racine*, 1938.
Fugues sur Siegfried.   1930.
La France sentimentale.   1932.
Fontrages au Niagara.   1932.
De pleins pouvoirs à sans pouvoirs.   1935.
Les cinq tentations de La Fontaine.   1938.
Le Futur armistice.   1939.
Pleins pouvoirs.   1939.
Littérature.   1941.
Sans pouvoirs.   1946.
Pour une politique urbaine.   1947.
La Française et la France.   1951.
Visitations.   1952.
Portugal, suivi de Combat avec l'image.   1958.
Or dans le nuit: Chroniques et préfaces littératures 1910-1943.   1969.
Carnets des Dardanelles, edited by Jacques Body.   1969.
Souvenir de deux existences.   1975.

*

Critical Studies: *Giraudoux* by Donald Inskip, 1958; *Giraudoux: His Life and Works* by Laurence LeSage, 1959; *Giraudoux: Three Faces of Destiny* by Robert Cohen, 1968; *Giraudoux: La Guerre de Troie n'aura pas lieu* by Roy A. Lewis, 1971; *Precious Irony: The Theatre of Giraudoux* by Paul A. Mankin, 1971; *Giraudoux* by Chris Marker, 1978.

*   *   *

Jean Giraudoux's theatre dominated the French stage in the period between the two World Wars. When he first began writing his plays in the late 1920's, his stylistic inventiveness, his witty sense of the incongruity of life, and his search for purity made Giraudoux's work unique and individual. Since then, his fame has been world-wide and there have been numerous translations and productions of his theatre in English and in other languages.

What makes this even more extraordinary is that the dramatist did not begin writing for the stage until he was 46 years old. Before that time, he had achieved some renown, although on a minor scale, as a novelist. Such works as *Suzanne and the Pacific* and *Juliette au pays des hommes* (Juliette in the Land of Men) gave him a reputation as a writer of complex and subtle novels that were limited to only a very small public. Indeed, it is only in recent years that his fiction has begun to receive greater recognition.

The presentation of his first play, *Siegfried* (1928), catapulted Giraudoux from the ranks of the minor novelists to the forefront of the French theatre movement. This startling success with both audiences and critics was to last throughout his lifetime and beyond, as some of his new works were not presented until after his death, including one of his most popular, *The Madwoman of Chaillot*. At first glance, the fanciful creativity and the unusual turn of mind of the writer would seem ill-suited to the more restrictive demands of the stage. Several factors, however, played a role in his achievement. Certainly, Louis Jouvet, the director-actor who formed a close collaboration with Giraudoux and who directed most of his plays, was one of the principal reasons that the dramatist established himself so easily. Another important element was evidently Giraudoux's major theme—man's search for a purity and an ideal beyond the imperfections of reality, a theme that touched a sensitive nerve in the public of the 1930's. It found its expression in whimsical comedies like *Amphitryon 38* and *Intermezzo* in which the central characters flirt with the attractiveness of the unknown, only to accept a compromise with the appeal of everyday reality. And the theme also appears in a more concrete form in *Tiger at the Gates* in which the characters debate the issue of peace and war. In the final analysis, however, it can be argued that the real reason for Giraudoux's appeal was his style—his elegant, civilized, witty account of life in its diverse aspects. The writer's special use of metaphors and symbols, his ironic view of reality, and his sense of the spontaneous and the unexpected were basically responsible for the singular universe that enchanted and delighted his public.

Jean Giraudoux is no longer the major force in French drama that he once was. The contemporary theatre has taken a number of new directions in recent years, passing from the theatre of the absurd of a Eugène Ionesco or a Samuel Beckett to a theatre in which the director assumes the prominent role, the writer and his words becoming only one part of the whole. Giraudoux's plays, based upon dialogue and discussion, hold language in high esteem. As a result, he could seem less current today. Nevertheless, his imaginative views of man and man's role in the universe and his creative use of language are likely to endure and he should remain one of the major French playwrights of the 20th century.

—John H. Reilly

GOETHE, Johann Wolfgang von. Born in Frankfurt, 28 August 1749. Studied law at Leipzig University, 1765-68, and drawing with Adam Oeser; after a period of illness, resumed his studies in Strasbourg, 1770-71, Licentiate in Law 1771. Lived with Christiane Vulpius from 1788; married her in 1806 (died, 1816); one son. Practiced law in Frankfurt, 1771-72, and Wetzlar, 1772; then writer: contributor, *Frankfurter Gelehrte Anzeigen*, 1772-73; at invitation of Duke Karl August, joined the small court of Weimar in 1775: Member of the Council, 1776, President, War Commission, 1779, Director of Roads and Services, 1779, granted degree of nobility, 1782, took over much of the financial affairs of the court; after a visit to Italy, 1786-88, released from day-to-day government business: general supervisor for arts and sciences, 1788, and Director of the Court Theatres, 1791-1817. Editor of a variety of yearbooks and magazines, including, with Schiller, *Xenien*, 1796-97; with J.H. Meyer, *Die Propyläen*, 1798-1800; *Kunst und Altertum*, 1816-32; and *Zur Naturwissenschaft*, 1817-24. Chancellor of the University of Jena. *Died 22 March 1832.*

Collections

Schriften. 8 vols., 1787-90; later editions, as *Werke*, 13 vols., 1806-10, etc.; 69 vols., 1826-42.
Werke [Sophie or Weimar Edition]. 134 vols., 1887-1919.
Sämtliche Werke [Jubiläumsausgabe], edited by Eduard von der Hellen. 40 vols., 1902-07.
Werke [Hamburg Edition], edited by Erich Trunz and others. 14 vols., 1948-69.
Gedenkausgabe der Werke, Briefe, and Gespräche, edited by Ernst Beutler. 27 vols., 1948-71.
Complete Works [Bohn Standard Library]. 14 vols., 1848-90.

Plays

Götz von Berlichingen mit der eisernen Hand (produced 1774). 1772; as *Goetz of Berlichingen with the Iron Hand*, translated by Walter Scott, 1799; as *Ironhand*, translated by John Arden, 1965; as *Götz von Berlichingen*, translated by Charles E. Passage, in *Plays*, 1980.
Clavigo. 1774.
Götter, Helden, und Wieland. 1774.
Erwin und Elmire, music by Jean André (produced 1775). 1775; revised version, in *Schriften 5*, 1788.
Stella. 1776; revised version (produced 1806), in *Werke 6*, 1816.
Claudine von Villa Bella (produced 1780). 1776; revised version (produced 1789), in *Schriften 5*, 1788.
Die Geschwister (produced 1776). In *Schriften 1*, 1787.
Die Mitschuldigen (produced 1777). In *Schriften 2*, 1787; as *Fellow Culprits*, in *Plays*, 1980.
Lila, music by Sigmund von Seckendorff (produced 1777). In *Schriften*, 1790.
Das Jahrmarktsfest zu Plundersweilern (produced 1778). In *Schriften 6*, 1790.
Der Triumph der Empfindsamkeit (produced 1778). In *Schriften 4*, 1787; revised version, as *Proserpina*, music by Karl Eberwein (produced 1915), in *Werke*, 1808.
Die Laune des Verliebten (produced 1779). In *Werke 4*, 1806; as *The Lover's Whim*, in *Plays*, 1980.
Iphigenie (produced 1779; revised version, in verse, as *Iphigenie auf Tauris*, produced 1802). In *Schriften 3*, 1787; translated as *Iphigenia in Tauris*, 1793; also translated by Charles E. Passage, in *Plays*, 1980.
Die Vögel, from the play by Aristophanes (produced 1780). 1787.
Jery und Bätely, music by Sigmund von Seckendorff (produced 1780). 1790.
Die Fischerin, music by Corona Schröter (producer 1782). 1782.
Egmont (produced 1784). 1788; as *Egmont*, translated by F.J. Lamport, in *Five German Tragedies*, 1969; also translated by Charles E. Passage, in *Plays*, 1980.
Torquato Tasso (produced 1807). In *Schriften 6*, 1790; as *Torquato Tasso*, translated by Charles E. Passage, in *Plays*, 1980.
Der Gross-Cophta (produced 1791). 1792.
Der Bürgergeneral (produced 1793). 1793.
Mahomet, from the play by Voltaire (produced 1799). 1802.
Paläophron und Neoterpe (produced 1800; revised version, produced 1803). In *Werke*, 1808.
Tancred, from the play by Voltaire (produced 1801). 1802.

Die natürliche Tochter (produced 1803).   1803.
Faust, part 1 (produced 1819).   In *Gesamtausgabe*, 1808; part 2, 1833; translated as
Faustus, 1821; numerous subsequent translations.
Romeo und Juliet, from the play by Shakespeare (produced 1812).
Des Epimenides Erwachen (produced 1815).   1815.
Plays, translated by Charles E. Passage.   1980.

Verse

Neue Lieder mit Melodien, music by Bernhard Breitkopf.   1770.
Gedichte, in *Schriften 8*.   1789; and subsequent editions.
Römische Elegien.   1789; as *Roman Elegies*, 1977.
Reineke Fuchs.   1794; as *Reynard the Fox*, 1886.
Hermann und Dorothea.   1798; as *Herman and Dorothea*, 1801.
West-östlicher Divan.   1819.
Selected Verse (bilingual edition), edited by David Luke.   1964.
Selected Poems (bilingual edition), edited by Christopher Middleton.   1983.

Fiction

Die Leiden des jungen Werthers.   1774; revised edition, 1787; as *The Sorrows of Werter*,
1780; and subsequent translations.
Wilhelm Meisters Lehrjahre [and *Wanderjahre*].   1795-1821; as *Wilhelm Meister's
Apprenticeship* [and *Travels*], 1824-27; also translated by H.M. Waidson, 1977-79.
Die Wahlverwandtschaften.   1809; as *Elective Affinities*, in *Works*; as *Kindred by
Choice*, 1960; as *Elective Affinities*, translated by R.J. Hollingdale, 1971.
Novelle.   1826.

Other

Beiträge zur Optik.   1790.
Versuch die Metamorphose der Pflanzen zu erklären.   1790.
Winckelmann und sein Jahrhundert.   1805.
Zur Farbenlehre.   1810.
Aus meinem Leben: Dichtung und Wahrheit.   4 vols., 1811-33.
Italienische Reise.   1816-17; as *Travels in Italy*, 1849; as *Italian Journey*, translated by
W.H. Auden and Elizabeth Meyer, 1962.
Tag- und Jahreshefte, in *Werke 31-32*.   1830; translated as *Annals*, 1901.
Gespräche mit Goethe, by Johann Peter Eckermann.   1836; edited by Fritz Bergemann,
1955; as *Conversations with Goethe*, 1839.
Correspondence with Goethe, by Carlyle.   1887.
Die Schriften zur Naturwissenschaft.   1947—.
Amtliche Schriften, edited by Willy Flach and Helma Dahl.   3 vols., 1950-72.
Gespräche, edited by W.F. and F. von Biedermann, revised by Wolfgang Herwig.   3
vols., 1965-72.
Goethe on Art, edited by John Gage.   1980.

*

Bibliography: *Goethe-Bibliographie* by Hans Pyritz, Heinz Nicolai, and Gerhard Burckhardt,
1954; supplement, 1968.

Critical Studies: *A Study of Goethe* by Barker Fairley, 1947; *Goethe's Major Plays* by Ronald Peacock, 1959; *Goethe, Poet and Thinker* by E. Wilkinson and L.A. Willoughby, 1962; *Goethe: His Life and Times* by Richard Friedenthal, 1965; *Goethe and the Drama* by Ronald D. Miller, 1966; *A Student's Guide to Goethe* by F.J. Lamport, 1971; *Goethe and the Novel* by E.A. Blackall, 1976; *Goethe: Portrait of the Artist* by Ilse Graham, 1977; *Goethe and the Weimar Theatre* by Marvin Carlson, 1978; *The Classical Centre: Goethe and Weimar 1775-1832* by T.J. Reed, 1980; *Goethe's Faust: The Making of Part I* by John Gearey, 1981; *Goethe's Narrative Fiction* edited by William J. Lillyman, 1983.

*   *   *

Goethe is the dominant figure in the history of modern German literature, whose works established in all the principal genres, models, or norms which have dominated succeeding generations (whether they have sought to follow or emulate, or to rebel against them). His creative life is customarily divided into three principal periods. The first embraces his youth and early manhood and coincides with (or, indeed, determines) the rise and fall of the "Sturm und Drang" movement in German literature. The second comprises his maturity and middle age, from the Italian journey of 1786 through the years of his collaboration with Schiller and their joint attempt to establish a "classical" German literature; the third, the last quarter-century of his life, after Schiller's death, in which he appears as an increasingly solitary figure. Goethe himself spoke of the Italian journey as a "rebirth," of the death of Schiller as "the loss of half of myself." In each of these phases Goethe made contributions of the highest rank and importance to German lyric and dramatic poetry and prose fiction.

Goethe's literary beginnings were more or less conventional, but in 1770 his own characteristic individuality was liberated by his meeting with the critic Herder. Herder introduced him to new ideas of spontaneous creation and inspiration and of national character in literature, to the beauties of folk-song and of other "unsophisticated" forms free of the rules and precepts of continental neo-classicism, such as the plays of Shakespeare. Before he was 25, Goethe had effectively created models for the whole European romantic movement: with the exuberant outpourings of his lyrical poetry on the themes of nature, love, individuality, genius, and creativity; with the sprawling, shapeless, but powerful pseudo-Shakespearian historical drama *Götz von Berlichingen* and the as yet unfinished and unpublished *Faust*; not least with the tragic, "confessional" epistolary novel *Werther*, which established his European reputation at a stroke—somewhat to his subsequent chagrin. But it was to the reputation thus earned that he owed his appointment to the court of the young Duke Karl August of Weimar, with whom he soon established a close relationship.

Before long, court life began to impose its restraints on the hitherto unfettered genius, and the idealistic spiritual drama *Iphigenia in Tauris* exhibits a highly "classical" formal balance and discipline appropriate to its content and message, even in its original prose version (only after the journey to Italy was it recast in polished blank verse). In the lyric poetry written in the aftermath of the Italian journey Goethe carries this formal "classicism" to the extent of writing almost exclusively in the ancient Greek and Latin metres, hexameter and elegiac distich. This poetry is also concerned with balance and harmony, with a wholeness of all aspects of human life, of art and nature, of intellect, emotion, and sensuality. In respect of the last-named, however, it marks the overcoming of courtly restraint: the *Roman Elegies* celebrate a ripe sense of sexual fulfilment quite different from the youthful "romantic" passion of the earlier poetry. But that the Romantic spirit was still alive in the classical Goethe is demonstrated above all by the poetic drama *Torquato Tasso*, which introduces into European literature that quintessentially Romantic figure, the lonely artist tragically at odds with society.

A fragment of *Faust* was published in 1790, but it was during the period of his collaboration with Schiller that Goethe was able to create an over-all design for the work—now conceived not as the tragedy of a heaven-storming genius, but as a celebration of universal human striving. The first of its two parts was completed in 1805, the year of Schiller's death. The novel *Wilhelm Meister's Apprenticeship* was another recasting of an earlier project. Originally concerned with

Wilhelm's "theatrical mission," typical of the attempts of earlier generations of German writers to create a national dramatic literature, it is now extended to embrace the much wider theme of his "apprenticeship" to life, of his development and growth into a complete human being, into some sort of modern equivalent (with all the necessary limitation that that implies) of the *kalokagathos* of classical antiquity. The novel is the prototype of the "Bildungsroman" which has represented the apogee of the novel form to many German writers, from the Romantics, Goethe's immediate successors, to Thomas Mann, Hesse, and even Grass in the 20th century.

Despite or indeed because of their self-consciously "classical" and exemplary character, many of the works of Goethe's middle period have often been felt to lack the vigour and immediacy of his earlier writing: many readers have found in their balance and restraint a certain blandness or evasiveness. In the works of his old age these very qualities are, paradoxically, intensified into a uniquely personal obliquity and ironical allusiveness, particularly in the Second Part of *Faust* and in the novels *Wilhelm Meister's Years of Travel* (the sequel to the *Apprenticeship*) and *Die Wahlverwandtschaften* (*Elective Affinities*). But much of his late lyrical poetry is of a mysterious, luminous simplicity, and there is direct expression of powerful emotion in the love-poems of the *West-östlicher Divan* and in the "Marienbad Elegy."

The chief ever-present theme of all Goethe's work is nature, with its all-pervading harmonies, its universal laws of metamorphosis, of evolution, of permanence in change, of death and rebirth. Man, both as an individual and in his social and political life, is seen essentially as part of this natural order. Goethe devoted much effort to scientific work. His anti-Newtonian theory of light and colours has found little favour, but his work in geology and biology, in comparative anatomy, and in plant and animal morphology still commands respect. He was profoundly drawn to evolutionary theories of geological and of human development—which made him politically a conservative, an enemy of the French Revolution and of all arbitrary violence. Despite the many upheavals he witnessed in his long life, he remained essentially an optimist: despite the tragedy that has accompanied his strivings, his Faust is ultimately—untraditionally and un-Romantically—redeemed.

—F.J. Lamport

GOGOL (Yanovsky), Nikolai (Vasil'evich). Born in Sorochintsy, 19 March 1809. Educated at Nezhin high school, 1821-28. Civil servant, 1828-31; history teacher, Patriotic Institute, St. Petersburg, and private tutor, 1831-34; assistant lecturer in history, University of St. Petersburg, 1834-36; in Western Europe, 1836-39, 1842-48. *Died 21 February 1852.*

PUBLICATIONS

Collections

Works, translated by Constance Garnett. 6 vols., 1922-27.
Polnoye sobraniye sochineniy. 14 vols., 1937-52.

Fiction

Vechera na khutore bliz Dikanki [Evenings on a Farm near Dikanka]. 1831-32.
Mirgorod. 1835; as *Mirgorod, Being a Continuation of Evenings in a Village near Dikanka*, 1928.

Arabeski. 1835; as *Arabesques*, 1982.
Myortvye dushi. 1842; as *Home Life in Russia*, 1854; as *Tchitchikoff's Journeys*, 1886; as *Dead Souls*, 1887.
Cossack Tales. 1860.
St. John's Eve and Other Stories from "Evenings at the Farm" and "St. Petersburg Stories." 1886.
Taras Bulba, also St. John's Eve and Other Stories. 1887.

Plays

Revizor (produced 1836). 1836; as *The Inspector-General*, 1892; as *The Government Inspector*, in *Works*, 1927.
Zhenitba (produced 1842). 1841; as *The Marriage*, in *Works*, 1927.
Igroki. 1842; as *The Gamblers*, in *Works*, 1927.

Other

Sochineniya. 2 vols., 1842.
Vybrannye mesta iz perepiski s druz'yami [Selected Passages from Correspondence with Friends]. 1847.
Meditations on the Divine Liturgy. 1913; as *The Divine Liturgy of the Russian Orthodox Church*, 1960.
The Theatre of Gogol: Plays and Selected Writings, edited by Milton Ehre. 1980.

*

Critical Studies: *Gogol* by Vladimir Nabokov, 1944; *Gogol as a Short Story Writer* by F.C. Driessen, 1965; *Gogol: His Life and Works* by Vsevolod Setchkarev, 1965; *Gogol: The Biography of a Divided Soul* by Henri Troyat, 1974; *Gogol from the Twentieth Century* edited by Robert A. Maguire, 1976; *The Sexual Labyrinth of Gogol* by Simon Karlinsky, 1976; *Through Gogol's Looking Glass: Reverse Vision, False Focus, and Precarious Logic* by William Woodin Rowe, 1976; *Gogol's Dead Souls*, 1978, and *The Symbolic Art of Gogol: Essays on His Short Fiction*, 1982, both by James B. Woodward; *The Creation of Gogol* by Donald Fanger, 1979; *The Enigma of Gogol* by Richard Peace, 1981.

*   *   *

The contribution of Nikolai Gogol to the remarkable renaissance of Russian literature in the 19th century is exceeded only by that of Pushkin. With his three volumes of stories and his novel *Dead Souls* he not only ensured that the prose genres would predominate till the advent of Symbolism; he also effected with his subject-matter, themes, and character-types and his highly complex style the enormous expansion of the range of Russian literature and the Russian literary language without which the major works of his successors, particularly Dostoevsky, could hardly have been written. In addition, his fiction and plays laid the foundations of Russian satire, and his central concern with the themes of guilt and redemption and with the contradictions and fragmentation of society marked the transition from a disinterested to a committed art, to the conception of art as service and a spur to action, which has given modern Russian literature its characteristic sense of engagement.

But although Gogol's influence on the development of the modern Russian literary tradition was far-reaching, his works represent a totally unique body of writing which differs from that tradition in numerous fundamental respects. Herein lies the first of the many paradoxes with which they confront the reader. Thus neither of the two most conspicuous elements of that tradition, realism and penetrating psychological analysis, can be readily ascribed to Gogol's own art, in which the boundaries between the real, the supernatural, and the grotesque are always likely to dissolve, and the inner man is usually seen only through the props of his portrait. Similarly his elaborate style, in which extremes converge and a sentence or simile can encompass a paragraph or page, remained an inimitable testimony to the uniqueness of his genius.

The transition from his first two volumes of stories, *Evenings on a Farm near Dikanka* and *Mirgorod*, to his uncompleted novel conveys the impression of a complex evolution. In seven of the eight tales of *Evenings on a Farm near Dikanka* he drew extensively on his intimate knowledge of the Ukrainian folklore tradition, responding both to the contemporary vogue for exotic regionalism and to the taste for Gothic horror stories whetted by such German romantic writers as Hoffmann and Tieck. The result is a bizarre mixture of the mundane and the supernatural, the comic and the horrific, which immediately established contrast as the central feature of Gogol's art. But the most striking contrast of all is created by the volume's penultimate story "Ivan Fyodorovich Shpon'ka and His Aunt" in which the scene is abruptly switched to the Russian provinces of the 1820's and detailed characterisation replaces tortuous plots. The story presents the first intriguing foretaste of the manner and preoccupations of the later novelist.

In the four works which comprise the volume *Mirgorod* the Ukrainian setting is retained, and the particular forms of contrast here serve significantly to clarify the underlying theme of Gogol's Ukrainian tales. The four works are essentially parodies of four literary genres—the idyll ("Old-World Landowners"), the heroic epic ("Taras Bul'ba"), the folktale ("Viy"), and the comic tale ("The Tale of How Ivan Ivanovich Quarrelled with Ivan Nikiforovich")—which in combination express a powerful lament on the social and moral decline of Gogol's native land. In each case the reader's expectations are abruptly confounded by the intrusion of unfamiliar elements which evoke a pervasive sense of degeneration, aberration, and debilitating betrayal. Love yields to habit, heroism to inertia, and the appetites and senses replace honour and duty as the ultimate arbiters of human conduct. Greeted with wide acclaim, the four works are the first major embodiments of the theme to which Gogol's art was thereafter to be devoted—the theme of moral decline, of the emasculation and perversion of the human spirit.

On moving to St. Petersburg Gogol soon found congenial material for the further development of this theme in the dehumanising world of the capital's bureaucracy in which he spent himself a few wretched months. The most celebrated of his so-called "Petersburg tales"—"The Overcoat" and "The Diary of a Madman"—were the fruits of this experience. Here again a disconcerting effect is produced by the coexistence of contrasting elements—in this case compassion for the depersonalised "little man" and detached, ironic scorn both for his abject surrender of his human dignity and for his belated, grotesque attempts to restore it. At the same time these and other stories in Gogol's third volume—"The Nevsky Prospect," "The Portrait," and especially "The Nose"—make abundantly clear the umbilical connection between his deceptive, nightmarish St. Petersburg and the folk-tale world of his Ukrainian tales. Again comedy and horror, the real and the fantastic are inseparably fused, and the devil and the witch retain their prominent roles, now clothed anew in the elegant attire of dignitaries, generals, and imperious ladies.

It was in the play *The Government Inspector* and the novel *Dead Souls*, however, that the contrasting elements of Gogol's art combined to produce two of the masterpieces of world literature. Selecting the vacuous Khlestakov and the acquisitive Chichikov as his itinerant heroes and employing in both works the simple plot device of confronting them with the senior citizens of the provincial towns in which they briefly alight, he was able to bring his unique gifts as humorist and satirist and his mature art of portraiture to bear on the task which he had now come to believe he was called on to perform: to expose the limitless extent of human folly and corruption and to infect his readers with his personal craving for moral rebirth. But the appearance of Part One of the projected three-part novel in 1842 marked the death of Gogol the artist. Only fragments of Part Two have survived, together with his collection of essays *Selected Passages from Correspondence with Friends*, to illuminate the agonies that he experienced in exchanging his role as a castigator of evil for that of a guilt-ridden instrument of divine revelation. The struggle continued for ten long years before his body succumbed to the fate of his art.

—James B. Woodward

GOLDEN LOTUS. *See* **CHIN P'ING MEI.**

GOLDONI, Carlo. Born in Venice, 25 February 1707. Educated in Venice; at a Jesuit school in Perugia; with Domenicans in Rimini; studied law at Papal College in Pavia, 1723-25. Married Nicoletta Conio in 1736. Assistant to his physician father in Chioggia, 1721-23, and in other towns; clerk in criminal court, Chioggia, 1728-29, and Feltre, 1729-30; passed law examinations in Padua in 1731, and called to the Venetian bar, 1732; wrote plays for amateur companies as early as 1729-30, and for Giuseppe Imer's company, 1734-44, beginning with bare scenarios and gradually working towards completely written scripts; lawyer in Pisa, 1744-47; associated with Medebec acting company, 1748-53, and with San Luca Theatre, 1753-62, both in Venice (in Rome, 1757-58); with the Italian Comedy theatre in Paris, 1762-64; Italian tutor to the daughter of Louis XV, Princess Adelaide, 1764-65, and to royal children, 1768-80, in Versailles; in Paris after 1780. Wrote plays in both Italian and Venetian dialect, and some plays in French; also wrote librettos for cantatas and operas. *Died 6 February 1793.*

PUBLICATIONS

Collections

> *Opere complete.* 39 vols., 1907-54.
> *Tutte le opere* (includes letters), edited by Giuseppe Ortolani. 14 vols., 1935-56.
> *Opere*, edited by Filippo Zampieri. 1954.

Plays (selection)

> *L'amore artigiano*, music by Florian Gassman, translated as *L'amore artigiano*. 1778.
> *L'Avare fastueux*, as *The Spendthrift Miser*, in *Comedies*. 1892.

L'avaro, edited by Antonio Marenduzzo. 1946.

Le baruffe chiozzote, edited by Carlo Pedretti. 1978; as *The Squabbles of Chioggia*, in *Drama 15*, 1914; as *It Happened in Venice*, 1965.

La bottega del caffe, edited by Gianni Di Stefano. 1967; as *The Coffee House*, 1925.

Le Bourru bienfaisant, edited by Gerolamo Bottoni, as *Il burboro benefico*. 1964; as *The Times*, 1780; as *The Beneficent Bear*, in *Comedies*, 1892.

Il bugiardo, edited by Pietro Azzarone. 1967; as *The Liar*, 1922.

La buona famiglia, edited by Polisseno Fegejo. 1942.

La buona figliuola, music by Egidio Duni, as *The Accomplished Maid*, 1767.

Il campiello, edited by Luigi Lunari. 1975; translated as *Il Campiello*, 1976.

La casa nova, edited by Antonia Veronese Arslan. 1969; as *The Superior Residence*, in *Four Comedies*, 1968.

Il cavaliere e la dama, edited by Nicola Mangini. 1964.

Un curioso accidente, as *A Curious Mishap*, in *Comedies*. 1892.

Le donne curiose, edited by Ettore Allodoli. 1960.

Le donne gelose, as *The Good-Humoured Ladies*. 1922.

I due gemelli veneziani, edited by Guido Davico Bonino. 1975; as *The Venetian Twins*, in *Four Comedies*, 1968.

La famiglia dell'antiquario, edited by Pietro Azzarone. 1961.

La figlia obbediente, as *The Good Girl*, in *Four Comedies*. 1922.

Il filosofo di campagna, as *The Wedding Ring*. 1773.

L'impresario delle Smirne, as *The Impressario from Smyrna*, in *Four Comedies*. 1922.

Gl'innamorati, edited by Andrea Sangiuolo. 1965.

La locandiera, edited by Gian Piero Brunetta. 1967; translated as *La Locandiera (The Mistress of the Inn)*, 1912; as *Mine Hostess*, 1928; as *Mirandolina*, in *Four Comedies*, 1968.

L'osteria della posta, edited by Antonio Marenduzzo. 1935; as *The Post-Inn*, in *The Drama 5*, edited by A. Bates, 1902.

Il padre di famiglia, as *The Father of a Family*. 1757.

La Pamela, from the novel by Richardson, edited by Carmine Montella. 1968; as *Pamela*, 1756.

I pettegolezzi della donne, edited by Antonio Marenduzzo. 1942.

I rusteghi, edited by Guido Davico Bonino. 1970; as *The Boors*, in *Three Comedies*, 1961.

Il servitore di due padroni, edited by Eugenio Levi. 1957; as *Arlecchino servitore di due padroni*, edited by Carlo Pedretti, 1979; as *The Servant of Two Masters*, 1928.

Le smanie della villeggiatura, edited by Edgardo Maddalena. 1963.

Il teatro comico, edited by Gerolamo Bottoni. 1926; as *The Comic Theatre*, 1969.

La vedova scaltra, edited by Avancinio Avancini. 1935; as *The Artful Widow*, in *Four Comedies*, 1968.

Il ventaglio, edited by Luigi Squarzina. 1979; as *The Fan*, in *Comedies*, 1892.

La villeggiatura, edited by Manlio Dazzi. 1954.

Other

Mémoires, pour servir à l'histoire de sa vie, et à celle de son théâtre. 3 vols., 1787; as *Memoirs*, 2 vols., 1814.

On Play-Writing, edited by F.C.L. van Steenderen. 1919.

*

Bibliography: *Saggio di una bibliografia delle opere intorno a Goldoni (1793-1907)* by A. Della Torre, 1908; *Bibliografia goldoniana 1908-1957* by Nicola Mangini, 1961.

Critical Studies: *Goldoni* by H.C. Chatfield-Taylor , 1913; *Goldoni* by Heinz Riedt, 1974; *A Servant of Many Masters: The life and Times of Goldoni* by Timothy Holme, 1976; *Language and Dialect in Ruzante and Goldoni* by Linda L. Carroll, 1981.

*   *   *

Goldoni's career as a dramatist can be easily plotted in terms of his relationship to the historical development of the drama in Italy. And in fact he is usually presented in such terms.

In the first half of the 18th century, Italian comedy was essentially that of the *commedia dell'arte* (as opposed to the erudite comedy based on classical models). The plays were not written out, but a scenario was prepared around which the players improvised. All the characters were conventional, and in Venice four of the players still wore the *commedia dell'arte* masks: a miserly old man (Pantalone); a pretentious old man called the Doctor, usually learned and absurd; and two "zany" servants, one lively and simple (Arlecchino), one clever and roguish (Brighella). The masks themselves instantly revealed to the audience the players' characters; other characters—various servants, banal lovers—might be the basis of the simple plot, but the masked characters were the leading players. The "creative" element of each play was centered on the ingenuity of the stage business and the verbal dexterity of the permanent company members. (Many of these practices are shown in Goldoni's play *The Comic Theatre*.)

Goldoni, a youthful enthusiast for the theatre, slid into this theatrical world almost by accident, if his *Memoirs* are to be believed. After an early involvement with a touring company, he became a lawyer, married, and set up a law practice in Pisa. A play he had earlier written out in complete form became a success in Venice, and he was approached by the "Pantalone" character of the Medebac company to write some more plays for them. Goldoni agreed, but insisted on a written text, gradually ensuring that natural speech replaced the exaggerated and obscene dialogue formerly used, and, most revolutionary of all, he insisted that the masks be abandoned. (The success of one of his first plays, *The Venetian Twins*, lay in having a leading actor play both twin brothers—one a clever romantic hero, the other a simple country boy—so that the mask would have become a liability rather than an aid.)

His "new" plays proved so successful that he was gradually able to bring about these changes in the next 15 years of play-writing in Venice. (His interest in these "reforms" is clear only from the prefaces he wrote for editions of his plays: he wrote no theoretical works.)

That his plays did not represent a complete break with the past is obvious from the way in which many of his leading characters are based on the conventional *commedia dell'arte* characters: Pantalone usually reappears in the guise of a hard-up nobleman, always on the look-out for a free meal or a present (for instance, the Count in both *Mirandolina* and *The Fan*); the Doctor is also often placed among the aristocracy, as a pretentious or "literary" man; comic servants are still well-employed, since the plots *do* spring from mistaken identity or trivial misunderstandings—but such a character as Fabrizio, the servant of Mirandolina, is complex, with doubts concerning his position and a past that acts on his character; and other servants or working-class characters are often full of individuality as well as zest.

The most interesting transformation in his characterizations—those in his romantic heroines—leads to the other major point to be made about Goldoni: his amiability and good nature, based on a perception of the world that is missing from the earlier comedy. The timid conventional heroine has become a sensible and intelligent girl, if not well educated at least aware of her own dignity and worth, and not averse to fighting for her right to choose her own mate. Many of the plays have such a girl: usually she is concerned in overturning the prejudices of the father (or uncle or brother) who is in charge of arranging her marriage (often to a fool or fortune-hunter). The most exaggerated heroine of this type is Mirandolina, who has no older person to protect her, and in her heart is committed to marriage with her servant and childhood friend, Fabrizio. Before this happens, however, she has to fend off the advances of the men who have fallen for her obvious charm and efficiency (she runs an inn), and even to prove to herself that she is in charge of her own fate by wilfully making a woman-hater staying at the inn fall in love with her. This plot would sound bitter if it were not so funny—no one is harmed by the intrigue; in fact, all the male characters learn something about themselves from the experience.

This interest in the naturalness of love and marriage—and in the natural relations of people in a social group—also led Goldoni often to center his plays on a milieu—a shop or an inn, a small village or a square in a city—where no single character emerges as an obvious hero or heroine, and where the good will and acceptance of the outcome of the story seem to be the end in view; there is usually a liberated spokesman for the group—often a woman. Examples of this sort of play are *Il campiello*, *The Boors*, *The Squabbles of Chioggia*, and *The Fan*. *The Superior Residence*, though involving only two families in an apartment house in Venice, and with a smaller cast, also promotes good nature, lack of pretentions, and the value of simple love.

Goldoni's plays are not deep, and his *Memoirs* reflect this lack of theoretical or intellectual interest, but his characters, like those of Marivaux, are human and often complex, and his plots are arranged to bring out this complexity rather than to submerge it in a conventional framework.

—George Walsh

GOMBROWICZ, Witold. Born in Maloszyce, Poland, 4 August 1904. Educated at Warsaw University, 1922-27, degree in law 1927; studied philosophy and economics in Paris, 1927-29. Married Marie Labrosse in 1969. Bank employee, Argentina, 1939-63; Ford Foundation Fellow, Berlin, 1963-64; lived in Vence, France, 1964-69. Recipient: International Literary Prize, 1967. *Died 25 July 1969.*

PUBLICATIONS

Collections

Dziela zebrane (Collected Works). 11 vols., 1969-77.

Fiction

Pamietnik z okresu dojrzewania [Memoir from Adolescence]. 1933.
Ferdydurke. 1937; translated as *Ferdydurke*, 1961.
Trans-Atlantyk [Trans-Atlantic]. With *Ślub*, 1953.
Bakakaj (selections). 1957.
Pornografia. 1960; translated as *Pornografia*, 1966.
Kosmos. 1965; as *Cosmos*, 1966.
Opetani. 1973; as *Possessed; or, The Secret of Myslotch*, 1980.

Plays

Iwona, Ksiezniczka Burgunda (produced 1957). 1935; as *Princess Ivona*, 1969; as *Ivona,*

Princess of Burgundy, 1969.
Ślub (produced 1963). 1947; as *The Marriage*, 1969.
Operetka (produced 1969). 1966; as *Operetta*, 1971.
Historia [History] (unfinished). 1975.

Other

Dziennik 1953-1966 [Journal]. 3 vols., 1957-66.
Entretiens avec Gombrowicz, edited by Dominique de Roux. 1968; as *A Kind of Testament*, 1973.
Wspomnienia polskie [Polish Reminiscences]. 1977.

*

Critical Studies: *Gombrowicz* (in French) by Dominique de Roux, 1971; *Gombrowicz* by Ewa M. Thompson, 1979; *Gombrowicz and Frisch: Aspects of the Literary Diary* by Alex Kurczaba, 1980.

*   *   *

Witold Gombrowicz is one of the most original Polish writers of the 20th century. His first book *Pamietnik z okresu dojrzewania* (Memoir from Adolescence), a collection of grotesque short stories, already established his obsessive themes which he was to pursue in later years. These can be described as a desire for sexual domination and / or submission, and the manipulation (sexual and intellectual) of others. In *Ferdydurke*, his first and most striking novel, all these themes are woven into the plot which shows the adventures of Joey, a thirty-year-old man forced back into the immaturity of adolescence by a determined schoolteacher. *Ferdydurke* is a parody of traditional Polish and fashionable Western values which are displayed and then effectively discredited in three different domains of life: at school, in the "progressive" household of an engineer, and in the old-fashioned manor-house. The conclusion of the very entertaining novel is that however much we may try to break out of the prison of Form, there is no escape from play-acting.

In 1939 Gombrowicz visited Argentina and after the outbreak of the Second World War decided to stay there, so it was this country that became the backdrop to his next novel *Trans-Atlantyk*. It depicts a conflict between the old and new generation of Polish emigrés in Argentina, the author acting as a narrator-chronicler of a fairly trivial quarrel which he tells with the panache of Polish memoirs from the Baroque period. What Gombrowicz really questions in this novel is the relevance of the Polish national myth. He continues to investigate this and other controversial issues in the three volumes of his *Dziennik* (Journal) which has been called an "autobiographical novel" as well as a running commentary on the philosophical, cultural, and political problems of the day. Gombrowicz's Journal exhibits the same sharp wit and far-reaching skepticism to traditional values as his novels, but it also lays bare the author's obsessions, complexes, and narcissistic tendencies. These reappear in a less striking form in the novels *Pornografia* and *Kosmos*, which are both essays on the possibilities and limits of psychological manipulation—of the young by the old, and the normal by the obsessed.

Gombrowicz was also a playwright; indeed, his first international successes were due to the production of his plays in Paris and in Germany in the 1960's. There are altogether four plays by Gombrowicz, one of which, the amusing but perhaps too ambitious *Historia*, was left unfinished. The earliest play, *Iwona, Ksiezniczka Burgunda* (*Princess Ivona*), is a "tragifarce." It takes place in a mythical kingdom where the young heir to the throne plans but eventually fails to marry the singularly ugly and unpleasant girl whom he chose in a moment of malicious whim. Ivona acts as a catalyst of suppressed guilt for everyone, so in the end she has to be eliminated in the name of state interests. There are pseudo-Shakespearean undertones in the excellent *Ślub*, which, on one level, is the story of human beings shaping each other through words, gestures, and acts of homage or defiance, while on another level it is the tragedy of overstrained human will. The sacralization of certain symbols can force society into their temporary acceptance, but not even the most charismatic figure can "give himself" a wedding which would restore the lost innocence of a fallen bride. *Operetka* (*Operetta*) is a bizarre tragi-comedy which through the parody of this "idiotic art form" (Gombrowicz) manages to convey a philosophical and historiosophic message. Although its starting-point is the striving of an over-formalized society towards "nakedness" (i.e., freedom), anarchy and totalitarianism are alternative "forms" also to be experienced. While Gombrowicz's savage parody of the past hundred years of European history brings the play very close to the theatre of the absurd, it nevertheless ends on an optimistic note, hailing "nudity eternally youthful" and "youth eternally nude," that expresses faith in the mysterious self-regenerating forces of mankind.

—George Gömöri

GONCHAROV, Ivan (Aleksandrovich). Born in Simbirsk (now Ulyanovsk), 18 June 1812. Educated at local boarding school, 1820-22; Moscow Commercial School, 1822-31; University of Moscow, 1831-34. Civil servant in St. Petersburg from 1834: secretary to Admiral Pityatin on trip to Far East, 1852-55; official censor, St. Petersburg, 1856-60, and member of the committee of review of Russian censorship groups, 1863-67; retired from civil service as Actual Councilor of State, 1867. *Died 27 September 1891.*

PUBLICATIONS

Collections

Povesti i ocherki, edited by B.M. Engelgardt. 1937.
Sobraniye sochineniy. 8 vols., 1952-55.

Fiction

Obyknovennaya istoriya. 1848; as *A Common Story*, 1894; as *The Same Old Story*, 1957.
Oblomov. 1859; translated as *Oblomov*, 1929.
Obryv. 1870; as *The Precipice*, 1916.

Other

Russkie v Yaponii v kontse 1853 i v nachale 1854 godov [Russians in Japan in the End of 1853 and the Beginning of 1854]. 1855; revised edition, as *Fregat Pallada*, 1858; as *The Frigate Pallas: Notes on a Journey*, 1965.
Literaturno-kriticheskiye stat'i i pis'ma [Literary Critical Articles and Letters], edited by A.P. Rybasova. 1938.

*

Bibliography: *Bibliografiya Goncharova 1832-1964* by A.D. Alekseev, 1968.

Critical Studies: *Goncharov* by Janko Lavrin, 1954; *Goncharov* by Alexandra and Sverre Lyngstad, 1971; *Oblomov and His Creator: The Life and Art of Goncharov* by Milton Ehre, 1973; *Goncharov: His Life and His Works* by V. Setchkarev, 1974.

*   *   *

Oblomov, Goncharov's best known novel, so dwarfs his other fiction that, in the West, at least, he tends to be known for this work alone. This is regrettable because, for all its uniqueness, it is still arguable that *Oblomov* achieves its fullest resonance against the background of its predecessor, *A Common Story*, and its successor, *The Precipice*.

All three novels are concerned with the confrontation between the rising pragmatism of the mid-19th century and the comparatively established norms of romantic idealism. *A Common Story* explores the relationship between Alexander Aduyev, a young idealist dreaming of love and literary success and his uncle who has become reconciled to the uninspiring realities of the world. Somewhat too schematically, perhaps, Goncharov plots the course of Aduyev's disenchantment to its issue: assimilation to the uncle's viewpoint. In *The Precipice* the ineffective Raysky, another idealist, vies with a nihilist for the heroine's hand. Although the nihilist manages to seduce her both he and Raysky are ultimately rejected in favour of Tushin, a solid, commonsensical neighbour of the heroine.

The triumph of the pragmatic outlook is also an essential feature of *Oblomov*. Stolz, the half-German friend of the eponymous hero, attempts to awaken the latter from his torpid inactivity, urging him to use his talents in the real world before it is too late. Encouraged by the practical Stolz and by the heroine, Olga, with whom he has an affair, Oblomov makes some progress in extricating himself from the mire before succumbing once more to the temptations of inertia. Oblomov dies of a stroke and Stolz marries the heroine. Oblomov's slothful attachment to his bed, his almost symbiotic relationship with his aged servant Zakhar and his addiction to comfort are generally seen as satirised characteristics of the declining Russian landed gentry of the mid-19th century. Stolz embodies the entrepreneurial class which will oust the aristocracy unless it adapts.

However, the status of *Oblomov* as a world classic derives from the fact that Oblomov, like Hamlet (whose indecisiveness he shares) transcends his *chronotopos* to personify a universal human predicament. Oblomov is the passive romantic who instinctively resists every incursion from the real world of disturbing activity. This passivity is represented in the novel as something akin to sleep, and, like sleep, is solaced by dreaming.

"Oblomov's Dream," a pivotal section of the novel, was published separately in 1849. It offers an idyllic vision of the hero's rural childhood which has so fatefully shaped his later life. The dream is not just a representation of the past but an abiding subconscious reality which continues to exert a stultifying influence on Oblomov's will. Such is its fatally soothing power that, after his brief awakening by Olga and Stolz, Oblomov is unable to resist his landlady's adult reconstruction of the old childhood comforts.

The use of dream, both for subliminal analysis and as a means of representing contradictions inherent in the romantic outlook, makes *Oblomov* a profoundly psychological novel. It is Goncharov's achievement to have successfully grafted psychological portrayal on to the Gogolian stock of external characterisation. To this extent *Oblomov* may be held to anticipate the great novels of Tolstoy and Dostoyevsky and must be assigned a crucial role in the development of the Russian novel.

—Robert Reid

GÓNGORA (y Argote), Luis de. Born in Córdoba, Spain, 11 July 1561. Educated at Jesuit school in Córdoba; University of Salamanca, 1576-80, no degree. Took minor orders at university, and deacon's orders, 1586: prebendary of Córdoba Cathedral, 1586-1617: undertook various business trips for the Cathedral; ordained priest, 1517, and royal chaplain in Madrid, 1617-25. *Died 23 May 1627.*

PUBLICATIONS

Collections

> *Obras en verso del Homero español,* edited by Juan López de Vicuña. 1627; edited by Dámaso Alonso, 1963.
> *Todas las obras,* edited by Gonzalo de Hozes y Córdoba. 1633.
> *Obras completas,* edited by Juan and Isabel Millé y Giménez. 1972.

Verse

> *Soledades,* edited by Dámaso Alonso. 1927; revised edition, 1956; as *The Solitudes,* translated by Edward M. Wilson, 1931; also translated by Gilbert F. Cunningham, 1968.
> *Góngora y el "Polifemo,"* edited by Dámaso Alonso. 1960; revised edition, 2 vols., 1961; as *Polyphemus and Galatea,* translated by Gilbert F. Cunningham, 1977.
> *Romance de "Angelica y Medoro,"* edited by Dámaso Alonso. 1962.
> *Sonetos completos,* edited by Biruté Ciplijauskaite. 1969.

*

Critical Studies: *The Metaphors of Góngora* by E.J. Gates, 1933; *Góngora* by D.W. and V.R. Foster, 1973; *Góngora: Polyphemus and Galatea: A Study in the Interpretation of a Baroque Poem* (includes text and translation by Gilbert F. Cunningham) by Alexander A. Parker, 1977; *The Poet and the Natural World in the Age of Góngora* by M.J. Woods, 1978; *Aspects of Góngora's "Soledades"* by John R. Beverley, 1980; *The Sonnets of Góngora* by R.P. Calcraft, 1980.

*   *   *

Góngora was a remarkable poet who made a significant contribution in a variety of poetic fields, expanding the range of poetry by his conception of the ballad as a more sophisticated, artistically balanced form than was traditional, by his promotion of the burlesque as a valid artistic form, and, in the case of his most famous major poem, *The Solitudes,* by creating a work which not only did not fit into any recognized genre, but also had a dazzling stylistic novelty.

Having already acquired a reputation as a writer of fine sonnets and ballads from the publication of a number of his poems in a general anthology in 1605, Góngora in his native Andalusía dreamed of making a career for himself at the court in Madrid. Hence in 1614 copies of his *Solitudes* and his *Polyphemus and Galatea,* major poems he had recently completed, were being circulated at court and caused a major literary controversy which centered upon the original and exceptionally difficult style in which they were written. There was a spate of letters, pamphlets, and poems attacking and defending Góngora. Although he never achieved the patronage he sought, he attracted many imitators, and detailed explanatory commentaries of his works were published later in the century.

The features of Góngora's style attracting comment were his use of neologisms (so-called *cultismos*), his liberties with syntax, particularly word-order, and frequency and complexity of his metaphors. But it is misleading to portray Góngora's novelty as merely stylistic, a question of mode of expression rather than of what was being said. Thematically, the major poems give a novel prominence to the world of nature. With his *Polyphemus and Galatea*, which re-tells the story found in Ovid's *Metamorphoses* of the giant Polyphemus's love for Galatea and his enraged killing of her lover, Acis, despite the importance which Góngora gives the rural Sicilian setting we still have basically a narrative poem. But in his *Solitudes*, of which there are two of an originally planned four, the second being unfinished, we have basically a descriptive poem, which is in itself a novelty. Góngora shows the hospitality offered by a rustic community to a shipwrecked young courtier, presenting their way of life and the environment in which they live in an enthusiastic way. When we consider Góngora's use of metaphor as a means of presenting this positive vision, again it is clear that we are dealing with a mode of thought, not merely one of speech. It is through metaphor that he draws attention to surprising patterns and relationships in the world, inviting us to wonder at them. Hence, when he calls the sea "a Lybia of waves," he invites us to consider the parallels between desert and sea, their common vastness and inhospitability, dunes mirroring waves, and at the same time surprises us by describing the extremely wet in terms of the extremely dry. Through his exploration of relationships Góngora reveals himself as a major exponent of wit.

—M.J. Woods

GORKY, Maxim. Pseudonym for Alexey Maximovich Peshkov. Born in Nizhny Novgorod, now Gorky, 16 March 1868. Educated in parish school, Nizhny Novgorod; Kumavino elementary school, 1877-78. Married Ekaterina Pavlovna Volzhina in 1896 (separated); one son and one daughter. Apprenticed to a shoemaker at age 12; then draughtsman's clerk and cook's boy on a Volga steamer; from 1888, associated with revolutionary politics: first arrest, 1889; travelled on foot through much of Russia; member of publishing cooperative Knowledge, and Literary Editor, *Life*, St. Petersburg, from 1899; in the USA, 1906, and Capri, 1906-13; set up revolutionary propaganda school, 1909; returned to Russia after general amnesty, 1913: editor, *Chronicles* magazine, 1915-17, and newspaper *New Life*, 1917-18; established publishing house World Literature; involved in Petrograd Workers and Soldiers Soviet, and in writers and scholars conditions generally; left Russia in 1921: Editor, *Dialogue*, Berlin, 1923-25, and in Sorrento during most of 1924-31; returned to Russia in 1931: Editor, *Literary Apprenticeship* magazine, 1933. Recipient: Order of Lenin, 1932. Gorky Literary Institute established in his honor. *Died 18 June 1936.*

PUBLICATIONS

Collections

Polnoye sobraniye sochineniy: Khudozhestvennaya literatura. 25 vols., 1968-76.
Collected Works. 10 vols., 1978-79.

Plays

Na dne (produced 1902).   1903; as *A Night's Lodging*, 1905; as *The Lower Depths*, 1912; as *Submerged*, 1914; as *At the Bottom*, 1930.

Meshchane (produced 1902).   1902; as *The Smug Citizens*, 1906; as *The Courageous One*, 1958; as *The Petty Bourgeois*, in *Collected Works 4*, 1979.

Dachniki (produced 1904).   1904; as *Summerfolk*, 1975.

Varvary.   1905; as *Barbarians*, in *Seven Plays*, 1945.

Deti solntsa.   1905; as *Children of the Sun*, 1912.

Vragi (produced 1907).   1906; as *Enemies*, in *Seven Plays*, 1945.

Vassa Zheleznova (produced 1911).   1910; revised version, 1935; translated as *Vassa Zheleznova*, in *Seven Plays*, 1945.

Vstrecha [The Meeting].   1910.

Chudaki.   1910; as *Queer People*, in *Seven Plays*, 1945.

Zykovy.   1913; as *The Zykovs*, in *Seven Plays*, 1945.

Starik.   1915; as *The Judge*, 1924; as *The Old Man*, 1956.

Somov i drugiye [*Somov and the Others*].   1931.

Yegor Bulychov i drugiye (produced 1932).   1932; as *Yegor Bulichoff and Others*, in *The Last Plays*, 1937.

Dostigayev i drugiye (produced 1934).   1933; as *Dostigaeff and the Others*, in *The Last Plays*, 1937.

Seven Plays.   1945.

Fiction

Ocherki i rasskazy.   3 vols., 1898-99; as *Tales*, 1902.

Foma Gordeyev.   1899; translated as *Foma Gordeyev*, 1902; as *The Man Who Was Afraid*,   1905; as *Foma*, 1945.

Troye.   1900; as *Three of Them*, 1902; as *Three Men*, 1902; as *The Three*, 1958.

Orloff and His Wife: Tales of the Barefoot Brigade.   1901.

The Outcasts and Other Stories.   1902.

Twenty-Six Men and a Girl and Other Stories.   1902.

Mat'.   1906; as *Mother*, 1907; as *Comrades*, 1907.

Zhizn nenuzhnovo cheloveka.   1907-08; as *The Spy: The Story of a Superfluous Man*, 1908; as *The Life of a Useless Man*, 1971.

Ispoved'.   1908; as *A Confession*, 1909.

Gorodok Okurov [Okurov City].   1909.

Leto [Summer].   1909.

Zhizn' Matveya Kozhemyakina.   1910-11; as *The Life of Matvei Kozhemyakin*, 1959.

Tales of Two Countries.   1914.

Zhizn' Klima Samgina.   1925-36; as *The Bystander*, *The Magnet*, *Other Fires*, and *The Spectre*, 4 vols., 1938.

Delo Artamonovykh.   1925; as *Decadence*, 1927; as *The Artamanov Business*, 1948; as *The Artamanovs*, 1952.

Unrequited Love and Other Stories.   1949.

Verse

Pesnya o Burevestnike.   1901.

Chelovek.   1902.

Devushka i smert'.   1917.

Other

A.P. Chekhov. 1905; as *Anton Tchekhov: Fragments of Recollections,* 1921.
Detstvo, V lyudakh, Moi universitety. 1913-22; as *My Childhood, In the World* [*My Apprenticeship*]*, My University Days* [*My Universities*]*,* 1915-23; as *Autobiography* 1949.
Vospominaniya o Tolstom. 1919; as *Reminiscences of Tolstoy,* 1920.
Revolyutsiya i kul'tura [Revolution and Culture]. 1920.
O russkom krestyanstve [On the Russian Peasantry]. 1922.
Vospominaniya [Reminiscences]. 1923.
Zametki iz dnevnika. 1924; as *Fragments from My Diary,* 1924.
V.I. Lenin. 1924; translated as *V.I. Lenin,* 1931; as *Days with Lenin,* 1933.
Reminiscences of Leonid Andreyev. 1928.
O literature. 1933; revised edition, 1935, 1955; as *On Literature: Selected Articles,* 1958.
Literature and Life: A Selection from the Writings. 1946.
History of the Civil War in the USSR, volume 2: The Great Proletarian Revolution, October-November 1917. 1947.
F.I. Chaliapin. 2 vols., 1957-58; as *Chaliapin: An Autobiography,* edited by Nina Froud and James Hanley, 1967.
Nesvoyevremennye mysli. 1971; as *Untimely Thoughts,* edited and translated by Herman Ermolaev, 1968.

*

Critical Studies: *Maxim Gorky and His Russia* by Alexander Kaun, 1931; *Maxim Gorky: Romantic Realist and Conservative Revolutionary* by Richard Hare, 1962; *Stormy Petrel: The Life and Work of Maxim Gorky* by Dan Levin, 1965; *Gorky: His Literary Development and Influence on Soviet Intellectual Life* by I. Weil, 1966; *The Bridge and the Abyss: The Troubled Friendship of Maxim Gorky and V.I. Lenin* by Bertram D. Wolfe, 1967; *Maxim Gorky, The Writer: An Interpretation* by F.M. Borras, 1967.

*   *   *

Within the Soviet Union Maxim Gorky is revered as the founder of socialist realism, the father of Soviet literature, and one of the greatest 20th-century writers. Critical attitudes towards him in the West are less unanimous. Virtually all would agree, though, that he is one writer for whom it is difficult to separate the literary and non-literary achievements. Before the revolution he was active both politically, as a supporter of revolutionary causes, and, among his fellow writers, as a leader of the so-called "critical realists" and the organizer of various publishing enterprises. After the revolution his political connections enabled him to protect, aid, and encourage an entire generation of writers, at the same time that he was again instrumental in establishing major publication projects, some of which continue to the present day.

As a writer Gorky introduced or at least popularized many topics that had largely been ignored by 19th-century Russian writers. He drew upon his own experiences to depict the vagrants and social outcasts who were the main characters in many of his early stories, while his upbringing provided the material for graphic descriptions of Russia's merchant class and its emergent capitalists, many of whom, especially in the provinces, retained the superstitions and habits instilled by peasant backgrounds. His particular talent lay in his descriptive skills. He created unforgettable portraits of his main characters and also brought out vividly the most mundane details of their everyday lives. That ability, along with the exotic quality of his subject matter, was sufficient to ensure the near-instant fame that he achieved. On the other hand, his fiction was occasionally marred by faults that he never completely overcame: a political tendentiousness that sometimes led to exaggeration and overly broad generalizations, the appearance of florid passages and lack of simplicity in his style, and difficulty in creating narratives with sufficient drama and cohesiveness to serve as vehicles for the characters he created.

This last feature of his writing perhaps explains why he achieved mixed success with his novels and plays but had more consistent results with his short stories and, particularly, his autobiographical writings and memoirs. In early stories such as "Chelkash" (1894) and "Konovalov" (1896) the single vagrant figure predominates and is sufficient to hold the reader's interest throughout. Further, since Gorky's vagrants turn out to originate from widely divergent classes, they possess sufficient variety so that the stories as a group do not become repetitive. Also notable among his stories is "Twenty-Six Men and a Girl" (1899), in which Gorky offers a concise and powerful treatment of a theme that was to be important for much of his subsequent work: the need for many people, especially those who have virtually nothing, to create illusions to sustain themselves, and the ease with which those illusions may be destroyed. The novels too are most notable for their central figures, as well as for the social milieu that Gorky depicts with his customary skill and knowledge. In this genre, though, Gorky's problems with narrative are particularly telling. Typical is *Foma Gordeyev* (1899), in which the title character rejects the merchant-class society into which he is born, and *Mother* (1906), which passionately describes the birth of a revolutionary consciousness in the mother of an imprisoned worker and which is regarded by Soviet critics as a model work for what became known as socialist realism. In both instances the introduction of fascinating characters dominates the first third or so of the work, but the action then becomes diffuse until the concluding pages.

Remarkably, Gorky created his best play with only his second effort as a dramatist, *The Lower Depths* (1902). The play lacks any single predominant figure, but its collection of castoffs, who seem to be refugees from several of his early stories, offers originality and dramatic interaction that more than compensate for the lack of a strong plot. In other plays of this type the static quality of Gorky's writing tends to undercut his efforts, though he still succeeds in those plays that are dominated by a strong figure, such as *Yegor Bulichoff and the Others* (1932). In recent years Gorky's plays have enjoyed renewed interest in both England and America, with stagings of both these works as well as *Summerfolk* (1904) and *Enemies* (1906). However, Gorky's best writing occurred when he was writing directly about himself or about those whom he knew intimately. At such moments he was able to give full vent to his descriptive abilities at the same time that the necessity to invent a plot was removed. The brilliant portrayal of his grandparents in his *Childhood* and the skillful capturing of the complexities and contradictions exhibited by a great writer in his memoir devoted to Tolstoy are typical of the qualities that make Gorky's autobiography and various reminiscences his major contributions to world literature.

—Barry P. Scherr

GOTTFRIED von Strassburg. Active in Alsace, possibly at the episcopal court in Strasbourg, in the generation around 1200.

PUBLICATIONS

Verse

Tristan, edited by Friedrich Ranke. 1930; as *Tristan und Isolde*, edited by Reinhold Bechstein, revised by P.F. Ganz, 1978; as *Tristan and Isolde*, translated by Edwin H. Zeydel, 1948; as *Tristan*, translated by A.T. Hatto, 1960; a shortened version, as *The Story of Tristan and Iseult*, translated by Jessie L. Weston, 1899.

*

Bibliography: *Bibliographie zu Gottfried* by Hans H. Steinhoff, 1971.

Critical Studies: *Gottfried* by Michael S. Bates, 1971; *A History of Tristan Scholarship* by Rosemary Picozzi, 1971; *The Anatomy of Love: The "Tristan" of Gottfried* by W.T.H. Jackson, 1971; *The Poetics of Conversion: Number Symbolism and Alchemy in Gottfried's "Tristan"* by Susan L. Clark and Julian N. Wasserman, 1977; *Medieval Humanism in Gottfried's Tristan und Isolde* by C. Stephen Jaeger, 1977.

*　　　*　　　*

In the flourishing of courtly literature in Germany around 1200 Gottfried von Strassburg must be counted among the most profound narrative poets, and certainly the most enigmatic. Of his life nothing is known but his name and designation; he did work in Alsace, but his social position, whether aristocratic or bourgeois, cannot be determined, nor any patron identified. His chivalric romance *Tristan*, the supreme poetic account of the ill-fated lovers Tristan and Isolde at the court of Mark, king of Cornwall, remains incomplete, and breaks off (probably because of Gottfried's death) at v. 19 1548. Running through this romance are complex strands of reflection and commentary on matters literary, social, ethical, and religious which render difficult any unitary interpretation according to customary categories.

Tristan, a romance in rhymed couplets, shows Gottfried's sovereign command of Latin poetics and vernacular narrative techniques alike, and the stylistic richness of its verbal figures matches the dialectic artistry with which the story unfolds its model of a love-force which transforms human existence.

Contemporary literary references indicate that the romance was composed between 1200 and 1220. It is recorded in a strong, early tradition from the 13th century, with 11 manuscripts complete (to the break-off point) and 16 fragments. Later poets (Ulrich von Türheim and Heinrich von Freiberg) wrote continuations.

The tragic love of Tristan's parents anticipates the entanglements of his own love for Isolde, his queen and wife of his uncle, when the two, joined by mischance through a love potion, feel driven to abuse the bonds of court and society in order to nurture their illicit love. After episodes of mounting hazard and bold deception Tristan flees the court and succumbs to the charms of another Isolde. The many episodes are linked in a tectonic pattern of analogies and contrasts which reflect the mystical, paradoxical power of the love that dominates the romance. While presenting essentially the adventure-sequences familiar in diverse European Tristan-texts since the late 12th century, Gottfried claims to follow specifically the account of Thomas of Brittany (between 1155 and 1190), and insists on the authenticity of his source as guarantee of the moral truth and validity of his work in contrast to that of disreputable minstrels. Such professional polemic underlies, too, his important literary review of contemporary German courtly poets (including Wolfram von Eschenbach and Walther von der Vogelweide).

Indeed, high ideals are Gottfried's constant concern. In numerous reflective passages he probes chivalric aristocratic society, its military ethos and its values and use of religion (in, for example, a critique of trial by ordeal), and postulates through allegory (in the introduction and the Cave of Lovers) a mystical community of *edele herzen* ("noble hearts") who embody the power of this fateful love. Gottfried addresses himself to this elite audience of "noble hearts" who alone are culturally and ethically worthy of the love which is depicted in the romance as an ennobling force. This passionate love, absolute and compulsive, is in flagrant conflict with the normal standards of law, religion, and ethics. Through its dialectic of *liebe unde leit* ("the joy and suffering of love"), this love force raises the exceptional individual to an autonomy beyond the social constraints which encompass human beings in medieval courtly society, but leads finally to self-loss and death. Gottfried's romance is perhaps the most radical exploration of the potential of the individual in medieval literature.

—Lewis Jillings

GRASS, Günter (Wilhelm). Born in Danzig (now Gdansk, Poland), 16 October 1927. Educated at volkschule and gymnasium, Danzig; trained as stone mason and sculptor; attended Academy of Art, Dusseldorf, 1948-49, and State Academy of Fine Arts, Berlin, 1953-55. Served in World War II: prisoner of war. Married 1) Anna Margareta Schwarz in 1954, three sons and one daughter; 2) Ute Grunert in 1979. worked as farm laborer, miner, apprentice stonecutter, jazz musician; speechwriter for Willy Brandt when Mayor of West Berlin; writer-in-residence, Columbia University, New York, 1966; also artist and illustrator; Co-Editor, *L*, since 1976, and the publishing house Verlages L'80, since 1980. Recipient: Gruppe 47 prize, 1959; Berlin Critics prize, 1960; Bremen Prize, 1960 (withdrawn); Prix du Meilleur Livre Etranger, 1962; Georg Büchner Prize, 1965; Fontane Prize, 1968; Theodor Heuss Prize, 1969; Mondello Prize (Palermo), 1977; International Literature Prize, 1978; Alexander Majkowski Medal, 1978; Vienna Literature Prize, 1980; Feltrinelli Prize, 1982. Honorary doctorate: Kenyon College, Gambier, Ohio, 1965; Harvard University, Cambridge, Massachusetts, 1976. Member, 1963, and since 1983, President, Academy of Art, Berlin; Member, American Academy of Arts and Sciences. Lives in Berlin, Germany.

PUBLICATIONS

Fiction

> *Die Blechtrommel.* 1959; as *The Tin Drum*, 1962.
> *Katz und Maus.* 1961; as *Cat and Mouse*, 1963.
> *Hundejahre.* 1963; as *Dog Years*, 1965.
> *Örtlich betäubt.* 1969; as *Local Anaesthetic*, 1969.
> *Aus dem Tagebuch einer Schnecke.* 1972; as *From the Diary of a Snail*, 1973.
> *Der Butt.* 1977; as *The Flounder*, 1978.
> *Das Treffen in Telgte.* 1979; as *The Meeting at Telgte*, 1981.
> *Kopfgeburten; oder, Die Deutschen sterben aus.* 1980; as *Headbirths; or, The Germans Are Dying Out*, 1982.

Plays

> *Noch zehn Minuten bis Buffalo* (produced, 1954). In *Theaterspiele*, 1970; as *Only Ten Minutes to Buffalo*, in *Four Plays*, 1967.
> *Hochwasser* (produced, 1957). 1963; as *Flood*, in *Four Plays*, 1967.
> *Onkel, Onkel* (produced, 1958). 1965; as *Onkel, Onkel*, in *Four Plays*, 1967.

Die bösen Köche (produced, 1961). In *Theaterspiele*, 1970; as *The Wicked Cooks*, in *Four Plays*, 1967.
Die Plebejer proben den Aufstand (produced, 1966). 1966; as *The Plebeians Rehearse the Uprising*, 1966.
Four Plays (includes *Flood; Onkel, Onkel; Only Ten Minutes to Buffalo; The Wicked Cooks*). 1967.
Davor (produced, 1969). In *Theaterspiele*, 1970; as *Max*, 1972.
Theaterspiele. 1970.
Die Blechtrommel als Film, with Volker Schlöndorff. 1979.

Screenplay: *Katz und Maus*, 1967.

Ballet Scenarios: *Stoffreste*, 1957; *Die Vogelscheuchen*, 1970.

Verse

Die Vorzüge der Windhühner. 1956.
Gleisdreieck. 1960.
Selected Poems, translated by Michael Hamburger and Christopher Middleton. 1966.
Ausgefragt. 1967; as *New Poems*, translated by Michael Hamburger, 1968.
Poems, translated by Michael Hamburger and Christopher Middleton. 1969; as *Selected Poems*, 1980.
Gesammelte Gedichte. 1971.
Mariazuehren/Inmarypraise. 1973.
Liebe geprüft. 1974.
Mit Sophie in die pilze Gegangen. 1976.
In the Egg and Other Poems, translated by Michael Hamburger and Christopher Middleton. 1977.
Als vom Butt nur die Gräte geblieben war. 1977.

Other

O Susanna: Ein Jazzbilderbuch: Blues, Balladen, Spirituals, Jazz. 1959.
Die Ballerina. 1963.
Dich singe ich, Demokratie (pamphlets). 6 vols., 1965.
Briefe über die Grenze; Versuch eines Ost-West Dialogs, with Pavel Kohout. 1968.
Über meinen Lehrer Döblin und andere Vorträge. 1968.
Ausgewählte Texte, Abbildungen, Faksimiles, Bio-Bibliographie, edited by Theodor Wieser. 1968; as *Porträt und Poesie*, 1968.
Der Fall Axel C. Springer am Beispiel Arnold Zweig. 1968.
Über das Selbstverständliche: Politische Schriften. 1969; translated in part as *Speak Out! Speeches, Open Letters, Commentaries*, 1969.
Die Schweinekopfsülze. 1969.
Originalgraphik. 1970.
Dokumente zur politischen Wirkung, edited by Heinz Ludwig Arnold and Franz Josef Görtz. 1971.
Der Bürger und seine Stimme. 1974.
Denkzettel: Politische Reden und Aufsätze 1965-76. 1978.
Aufsätze zur Literatur. 1980.
Zeichnungen und Texte 1954-1977. 1982; as *Drawings and Words 1954-1977*, 1983.

Illustrator, *Ein Ort für Zufälle*, by Ingeborg Buchmann. 1965.

*

GRASS

Bibliography: *Grass: A Bibliography 1955-1975* by P. O'Neill, 1976; *Grass in America: The Early Years* edited by Ray Lewis White, 1981.

Critical Studies: *Grass: A Critical Essay* by Norris W. Yates, 1967; *Grass* by W. Gordon Cunliffe, 1969; *Grass* by Kurt Lothar Tank, 1969; *A Grass Symposium* edited by A. Leslie Willson, 1971; *Grass* by Irene Leonard, 1974; *A Mythic Journey: Grass's Tin Drum* by Edward Diller, 1974; *Grass* by Keith Miles, 1975; *The "Danzig Trilogy" of Grass* by John Reddick, 1975; *Grass: The Writer in a Pluralist Society* by Michael Hollington, 1980.

* * *

Günter Grass has shown in his novels that he is one of the most acute observers and critics of West Germany. After beginning in the 1950's with short prose pieces, poems, and plays in the then dominant "absurd" style, he made a dramatic impact on the literary scene with *The Tin Drum, Cat and Mouse*, and *Dog Years*. These were later named the Danzig Trilogy after Grass's native city which, detached and distant like Joyce's Dublin, became the prism through which he conveyed his vision of the world about him. In Danzig, with its mixed German and Polish population, the Second World War began. The city was a paradigmatic setting for the gradual growth of Nazism amid the banality of the petty bourgeoisie, and symbolised the lost homelands from which millions of Germans would be forever exiled after 1945. In this picaresque trilogy Grass, with great zest and wide-ranging scope, imaginatively investigated both recent German history—the monstrous crimes of the Nazis, the acquiescence and coward-ice of the ordinary citizen; and contemporary post-war reality—the suppression of guilt, economic reconstruction and the return to affluence and complacency, the loss of moral values. Inevitably Grass became identified with the new generation of critical realists, which included Heinrich Böll and Martin Walser, who implacably satirized the faults and errors of their fellow-countrymen and untiringly reminded them of the guilty involvement in Nazi Germany they were eager to forget.

Grass's sense of social justice and his contentious nature took him into the political arena where he threw his authority and weight behind the Social Democratic Party in the general elections of the 1960's. His personal friend Willy Brandt became Chancellor in 1969 and Grass's fiery, hard-hitting campaign speeches, open letters, and commentaries were variously pub-lished in *Über das Selbstverständliche* (*Speak Out!*) and *Der Bürger und seine Stimme*. The creative work accompanying this intense activity was also coloured by Grass's political commitment; the play *Davor* and the novel *Local Anaesthetic* thematize the dominant preoccupations of intellectual and public life, namely the war in Vietnam and radical student protest in German universities. Though imbued with socialist ideas Grass stopped short of violence and destruction, advocating reform rather than revolution, practical measures for eradicating injustice rather than ideological posturings.

The anti-ideological scepticism of Grass's political stance is articulated in the novel *From the Diary of a Snail*, which charts the author's reflections on his active participation in the election campaign of 1969 as well as telling the fictional story of the teacher Ott, "nicknamed Doubt," who resisted the Nazis and clandestinely helped the persecuted Jews to the best of his ability. During the mid-1970's Grass seemed to be out of tune with the more extreme progressive forces in Germany and his literary talents appeared to lie dormant and inactive. In fact this proved to be the period of gestation of another epic masterpiece. *The Flounder* incorporates so many autobiographical details that the blurring of the distinction between author and narrator already initiated in *From the Diary of a Snail* is here completed. *The Flounder* is a complemen-tary piece to the Danzig Trilogy; where the latter focusses on the enormities of contemporary events, *The Flounder* embraces in its narrative structure the whole sweep of German social and political history. The perennial human endeavour to ascribe progress and meaning to historical process as well as the more topical question of feminism and the secular domination of women by men are central themes given expression by Grass.

In his most recent "fictional" work, *Headbirths; or, The Germans Are Dying Out*, Grass displayed his political persona once more, thematizing the massive and urgent problems facing the industrialised nations: energy crisis, the threat of nuclear war, a declining birth-rate, the Third World. Yet, despite all his concern as a citizen with the struggles of the real world, Grass's faith in the significance of literature and the aesthetic dimension still shines through; he maintains that even in the most catastrophic destruction of civilisation "a hand holding a pen would reach up out of the rubble."

—Arrigo V. Subiotto

GRILLPARZER, Franz. Born in Vienna, 15 January 1791. Educated at Anna-Gymnasium, Vienna, 1800-07; studied law at University of Vienna, 1807-11. Tutor in law studies to nephew of Graf von Seilern, 1812; unpaid assistant in court library, 1813; civil servant from 1814: appointed Theaterdichter, 1818; Archive Director, 1832: retired 1856, as Hofrat; created a member of the Herrenhaus, 1861. Founder-Member, Austrian Academy of Sciences, 1847. Honorary Doctorate: University of Leipzig, 1859. *Died 21 January 1872.*

PUBLICATIONS

Collections

Sämtliche Werke, edited by August Sauer and Reinhold Backmann. 42 vols., 1909-48.
Sämtliche Werke, edited by Peter Frank and Karl Pörnbacher. 4 vols., 1964-70.

Plays

Die Ahnfrau (produced 1817). 1817.
Sappho (produced 1818). 1819; translated as *Sappho*, 1820.
Das Goldene Vlies (trilogy; produced 1821). 1822; translated as *Medea*, 1879; as *The Golden Fleece*, 1942; as *The Guest-Friend* and *The Argonauts*, 2 vols., 1947.
König Ottokars Glück und Ende (produced 1825). 1825; as *King Ottokar, His Rise and Fall*, 1932.
Ein treuer Diener seines Herrn (produced 1828). 1830; as *A Faithful Servant of His Master*, 1941.
Des Meeres und der Liebe Wellen (produced 1831). 1839; edited by E.E. Pabst, 1967; edited by Mark Ward, 1981; as *Hero and Leander*, 1938; as *The Waves of Sea and Love*, 1969.
Melusina, music by Konradin Kreutzer (produced 1833). 1833.
Der Traum ein Leben (produced 1834). 1840; edited by W.E. Yuill, 1955; as *A Dream Is Life*, 1946.
Weh dem, der lügt (produced 1838). 1840; as *Thou Shalt Not Lie*, 1939.
Esther (produced 1868). In *Gesamtausgabe*, 1872; translated as *Esther*, with *The Jewess of Toledo*, 1953.
Ein Bruderzwist in Habsburg (produced 1872). In *Gesamtausgabe*, 1872; edited by

Bruce Thompson, 1982; as *Family Strife in Hapsburg*, 1940.
Die Jüdin von Toledo (produced 1872). In *Gesamtausgabe*, 1872; as *The Jewess of Toledo*, with *Esther*, 1953.
Libussa (produced 1874). In *Gesamtausgabe*, 1872; translated as *Libussa*, 1941.

Other

Gespräche und Charakteristiken seiner Persönlichkeit durch die Zeitgenossen, edited by August Sauer. 6 vols., 1904-16; supplementary vol. edited by Reinhold Backmann, 1941.
Tagebücher und Reiseberichte, edited by Klaus Geissler. 1981.

*

Critical Studies: *Grillparzer, Lessing, and Goethe in the Perspective of European Literature* by Fred. O. Nolte, 1938; *Grillparzer: A Critical Biography* (vol. 1 only) by Douglas Yates, 1946; *The Inspiration Motif in the Works of Grillparzer* by Gisela Stein, 1955; *The Plays of Grillparzer* by George A. Wells, 1969; *Grillparzer* by W.E. Yates, 1972; *A Sense of Irony: An Examination of the Tragedies of Grillparzer*, 1976, and *Grillparzer*, 1981, both by Bruce Thompson, and *Essays on Grillparzer* edited by Thompson and Mark Ward, 1978; *Grillparzer's Aesthetic Theory* by W.N.B. Mullan, 1979.

*   *   *

Nothing ever went right for Franz Grillparzer, a fact he viewed with grim satisfaction. He was the archetypal Viennese grumbler, and a wealth of anecdote testifies to his melancholy and his crusty hypochondria. At 81, still beset by a conflict between literature and marriage, he died in the arms of his "eternal betrothed" Katharina Fröhlich, to whom he had been engaged for 50 years.

Grillparzer's writing is rooted in the rich cultural heritage of the multi-lingual Hapsburg Empire. As a child he marvelled at the musical fantasies and magical transformations of Viennese popular theatre in which the spectacular visual effects of the baroque survived in a naive form. His comedy *Thou Shalt Not Lie*, in which a cook's boy rescues a Frankish bishop's nephew from the heathen Germans, barely, but humorously, managing not to perjure himself in the process, uses the fun and wealth of incident of popular comedy to make a moral point. *A Dream Is Life* translates the hero into a dream to live out his ambitions then brings him back to renounce the life of action because of the inevitable guilt it involves.

Grillparzer was, however, drawn to the more austere world of German Classicism, and even visited Goethe in Weimar, with disastrous results for his always parlous self-confidence. He set three plays in the ancient world. *Sappho*, in which the heroine forsakes poetry for a young lover and commits suicide when he abandons her, and *Hero and Leander*, in which a novice priestess forsakes religion, only to have her lover drown in the Hellespont when the High Priest extinguishes the lamp she has lit to guide him, are lyrical, tragic verse dramas of the conflict between the spirit and the flesh. In *The Golden Fleece* there is a foretaste of Strindberg's sexual psychology in the clash of the exotic alien Medea with her husband Jason in his sophisticated Greek homeland, but the tame sagacity of Grillparzer's conclusion underlines the gap between Biedermeier Vienna and the tragic ferocity of Greece.

Grillparzer's finest achievements were his historical dramas in verse. He was a rationalist and a liberal whom the nationalism of the mid-century turned into a conservative. *King Ottokar, His Rise and Fall* celebrates the first Hapsburg Holy Roman Emperor, Rudolf I. *A Faithful Servant of His Master*, on the theme of loyalty, is set in Hungary. *Libussa* dramatises the legendary founding of Prague in Bohemia. The best of these Austrian dramas is *Family Strife in Hapsburg* which unites Grillparzer's main themes in the drama of the self-abnegating, intellectual Emperor Rudolf II who struggles in vain to prevent the Reformation from splitting his empire. It was a plea for a supra-national concept, and took on a new meaning when the empire was broken up in 1918. *King Ottokar*, with Ottokar von Horneck's hymn to Austria, is staged at the Burgtheater in Vienna on days of public celebration. But the Austrian national dramatist's complex language has defied translation and even in Germany his plays have never shown the power to move and entertain which Austrian actors can readily extract from them.

—Hugh Rorrison

GRIMMELSHAUSEN, Hans Jakob Christoffel von. Born in Gelnhausen in 1621; family fled to Hanau, 1634, after Gelnhausen was plundered in Thirty Years War. Married Katharina Henninger in 1649. In the Kaiser's army after 1637: garrison soldier in Offenburg, 1639, clerk, 1645, then secretary, 1648, in regimental office; steward for the von Schauenburg family in Gaisbach bei Oberkirch, 1649; innkeeper in Gaisbach, 1657; steward for Dr. Küeller, 1662; innkeeper, 1665; mayor of Renchen, 1667; temporary soldier, 1675. *Died in 1676.*

PUBLICATIONS

Works

> *Der Abenteuerliche Simplicissimus Teutsch und Continuatio*, edited by Rolf Tarot. 1967; as *The Adventurous Simplicissimus*, 1912; as *Simplicissimus the Vagabond*, 1924; as *The Adventures of a Simpleton*, 1962.
> *Dietwalts und Amelindens anmutige Lieb- und Leidsbeschreibung*, edited by Rolf Tarot. 1967.
> *Trutz Simplex; oder,...Lebensbeschreibung der Erzbetrügerin und Landstörzerin Courasche*, edited by Wolfgang Bender. 1967; as *Mother Courage*, 1965.
> *Des durchleuchtigen Prinzen Proximi...und Lympidae Liebs-Geschicht-Erzählung*, edited by Franz Günter Sieveke. 1967.
> *Des vortrefflich keuschen Josephs in Ägypten Lebensbeschreibung samt des Musai Lebenslauf*, edited by Wolfgang Bender. 1968.
> *Simplicianischer Zweiköpfiger Ratio Status*, edited by Rolf Tarot. 1968.
> *Der seltsame Springinsfeld*, edited by Franz Günter Sieveke. 1969; as *The Singular Life Story of Heedless Hopalong*, 1981.
> *Satyrischer Pilgram*, edited by Wolfgang Bender. 1970.
> *Das wunderbarliche Vogelnest*, edited by Rolf Tarot. 1970.
> *Die verkehrte Welt*, edited by Franz Günter Sieveke. 1973.
> *Kleinere Schriften (Beernhäuter, Gauckeltasche, Stolze Melcher, Bart-Krieg, Galgen-Männlin, etc.)*, edited by Rolf Tarot. 1973.
> *Ratstübel Plutonis*, edited by Wolfgang Bender. 1975.
> *Teutscher Michel und Ewigwährender Kalender*, edited by Rolf Tarot. 1976.

*

Bibliography: *Grimmelshausen-Bibliographie 1666-1972* by Italo Michele Battafarano, 1975.

GRIMMELSHAUSEN

Critical Studies: *Grimmelshausen* by Kenneth C. Hayens, 1932; *Grimmelshausen* by Kenneth Negus, 1974; *Grimmelshausen in Selbstzeugnissen und Bilddokumenten* by Curt Hohoff, 1978; *The Nature of Realism in Grimmelshausen's Simplicissimus Cycle of Novels* by R.P.T. Aylett, 1982.

* * *

Reading Grimmelshausen we feel ourselves to be in the immediate company of a narrator; stories are told—to fictional listeners and to us—and much of the material rings like first-hand truth. But the narrative voices have to be listened to critically; they are continually ironized and relativized by other perspectives offered in the text. The text itself supplies its own commentary—from the perspective of the narrator's old age, for example—or we ourselves, among the listeners, are encouraged to comment.

Grimmelshausen is a great realist. He worked in a genre, the picaresque, marvellously suited to his times, his purposes, and his gifts. The picaresque novel, imported from Spain in the service of the Counter-Reformation by Aegidus Albertinus, is realistic and anti-heroic. In Spain it flourished during the Moorish Wars, and the Thirty Years War makes up all of Grimmelshausen's world. The picaro is a delinquent, and he lives in delinquent times. In times of licensed immorality he lives his immoral life.

War is depicted truthfully by Grimmelshausen, as pointless and horrible. He repeatedly mocks the lying heroic tradition. War is the licence, under arbitrary creeds and slogans, to commit atrocities. War is seen from the true, the lowest point of view: from among the dead, for example, as the scavengers come round. We learn most, to our greatest horror, quite incidentally. What happens to an officer's mistress when he tires of her? She is given to the stable boys; a detail, Grimmelshausen implies, too ordinary to dwell on. War is continually rendered strange; it has to be, or we should not see it for what it is, so accustomed have we become.

Grimmelshausen works to the important Baroque principle of "mögliche Realität" ("possible reality"). More happens to his heroes than really could; he accumulates around them an implausible number of truthful incidents. For realism is not an end in itself; it serves an urgent moral and religious purpose. Man must be shown as he is, as he really lives, in order that he may change. All human life is precarious and war only accentuates that fact; and in war man behaves according to his nature, which is greedy, cruel, and selfish. Much of Baroque literature rests on a simple antithesis: the World or God. To be in the world is to be apart from God. The ordinary state of the world, for Grimmelshausen, is war. What the child last sees of the world as he enters the forest is his family home pillaged and its inhabitants raped or tortured; and what he first sees when he leaves the forest is again torture. That is the world.

Simplicissimus passes, without plausible inner motivation, through the predetermined stages of a religious and ethical career. He begins life in brute ignorance; in the forest with the hermit (his true father) he acquires *sancta simplicitas*; leaving the forest he is for a time a holy fool (Christianity in such a world appearing necessarily foolish); then, as court fool, he becomes a knowing social critic. Next, for most of the book, he lives not as a critic of the world but as its exemplar, as a worldling. Finally, with only nominal motivation, he leaves the world to resume his innocent hermit's state. He undergoes an exemplary dis-illusioning, an *Enttäuschung*.

Grimmelshausen's books are still, as he intended them, amusing and instructive. They are enjoyable and affirmative in their exuberance of language and invention; and salutary in their truthful exposure of man living badly.

—David Constantine

HAFIZ (Shams al-Din Muhammad Hafiz).   Born in Shiraz, Persia, in 1325/26.   Studied Islamic literature and mastered Arabic (the name Hafiz indicates one who has memorized the *Koran*). Patronized by Shah Abu Ishaq-i Inju, 1341-53, by Shah Shuja, 1358-68/69, and Muzaffarid Shah Mansur in late 1380's; lectured on theology, and wrote commentaries on religious classics. Little is known of his private life. *Died 1389/90.*

PUBLICATIONS

Verse

> *Die Lieder des Hafis* (Persian text), edited by Hermann Brockhaus.   3 vols., 1854-63.
> *Der Diwan des grossen lyrischen Dichters Hafis* (Persian and German texts), edited by Vincenz von Rosenzweig-Schwannau.   3 vols., 1858-64.
> *Divan-e-Hafez* (Persian text), edited by Mohammed Qazvini and Qasem Ghani.   1941.
> *Diwan-i-Hafiz*, translated (into English prose) by H. Wilberforce-Clarke.   3 vols., 1891; *The Poems*, translated (into English verse) by John Payne, 3 vols., 1901; selections in English translation include *Poems from the Divan* by G. Bell, 2nd edition, 1928, *Hafiz in Quatrains* by C.K. Street, 1946, *Fifty Poems* by A.J. Arberry, 1947, and *Poetical Horoscope or Odes* by A. Aryanpur, 1965.

*

Bibliography: *Towards a Hafiz Bibliography* by Henri Broms, 1969.

Critical Studies: *A Literary History of Persia* by Edward G. Browne, 1928; *Classical Persian Literature* by A.J. Arberry, 1958; *History of Iranian Literature* by Jan Rypka, edited by Karl Jahn, 1968; "Hafez" by G.M. Wickens, in *Encyclopedia of Islam*, revised edition, 1971; *Unity in the Ghazals of Hafez* by Michael C. Hillmann, 1976.

*   *   *

Even in his lifetime, the fame of Hafiz had extended beyond his homeland—eastward to India and westward to other portions of the Islamic realm. In the first centuries after his death, it was still Islam's taste for Persian poetry that nourished his reputation; but in the last two or three centuries, when the East and the West have impacted upon each other, Hafiz has become truly a world poet, read in many languages, both Eastern and Western.

Not all readers will agree with Ralph Waldo Emerson (who read him in German translation) that Hafiz ranks with Shakespeare as the type of the true poet; or with John Payne (who translated him into English verse) that he is, along with Shakespeare and Dante, one of the three greatest poets of the world; but there is a consensus that he is "the Prince of Persian poets" and the fullest flowering of the lyric gift in a nation famed for its poetry. Regarding the substance of his poetic thought, however, there is again considerable difference of opinion.

His compatriots and fellow Moslems have for the most part accepted his native reputation as *Lishan-al-ghaib* (The Tongue of the Hidden); that is, as a mystical poet of the Sufi school, whose allusions to love, wine, roses, and revelry signify spiritual concepts. A few Westerners, too, are so inclined—e.g., the philosopher Hegel—but the majority of his European and American readers have had different views. Sir William Jones, who in the late 18th century practically discovered Hafiz to the West, regarded him as "the Persian Anacreon." Goethe, whose *West-östlicher Divan* was composed in emulation of the *Divan* of Hafiz, was disposed to stress the poet's joy in love and life, as suited the taste of the Romantic age. Emerson, who learned from Hafiz to take deeper poetic drafts than his Puritan heritage allowed, believed the poet's wine stood for intellectual libertion rather than for the divine afflatus on the one hand or [Thomas] "Moore's best Port" on the other. The English Victorians, reflecting their own anxieties over faith and doubt, heard in Hafiz the voice of weeping and loud lament; and the fin de siècle hedonists and skeptics saw in him a latter day Omar Khayyam. In this century, A.J. Arberry has described him as a philosophical nihilist propounding the gospel of Unreason.

Unfortunately, the *ghazal* form in which Hafiz wrote (and which, in the opinion of G.M. Wickens, he took "so far beyond the work of his predecessors that he practically cut off all succession") does not lend itself to easy translation. It has variously been likened to the ode and the sonnet, and, by Arberry, to the late sonatas of Beethoven. The "wonderful inconsecutiveness" of the Persian *ghazal* (in Emerson's phrase) has led Arberry, Wickens, and Hillmann to seek in the form a kind of organic unity that is quite unlike the linear and dramatic continuity characteristic of Western poetry. Some hint of the suggestive ambiguity of Hafiz, and of his mellifluous music, might be gleaned from the following couplet:

> Hameh kass tálib-i-yárand, che hushyár che mast
> Hameh já kháneh-i-ishk ast, che masjid che kunasht.
> (Everyone is desirous of the Friend, what is sober what is drunk?
> Every place is the house of love, what is temple what is mosque?)

—John D. Yohannan

HAMSUN, Knut. Pseudonym for Knut Pedersen. Born in Lom, Norway, 4 August 1859. Married twice; four children. Apprenticed to a shoemaker in Bodö; then a road worker and wanderer for 10 years; in the United States, 1882-84, 1886-88: streetcar conductor in Chicago, farmhand in North Dakota, and secretary and lecturer in Minneapolis; lived several years in Paris in early 1890's; writer after 1890, and after 1911 farmer in Hamarøy, later near Grimstad; openly supported Quisling's pro-German party during World War II: indicted, fined, and briefly confined to a mental institution after the war. Recipient: Nobel Prize for Literature, 1920. *Died 19 February 1952.*

PUBLICATIONS

Collections

Samlede Verker [Collected Works]. 15 vols., 1954.

Fiction

Den gaadefulde [The Mysterious One]. 1877.
Bjørger. 1878.
Sult. 1890; as *Hunger*, 1899.
Mysterier. 1892; as *Mysteries*, 1927.
Ny Jord. 1893; as *Shallow Soil*, 1914.
Redaktør Lynge [Editor Lynge]. 1893.
Pan. 1894; translated as *Pan*, 1920.
Siesta. 1897.
Victoria. 1898; translated as *Victoria*, 1923.
Kratskrog [Brushwood]. 1903.

Svaermere. 1904; as *Mothwise*,1921; as *Dreamers*, 1921.
Stridende Liv [Struggling Life]. 1905.
Under Høststjaernen. 1906; as *Autumn*, in *Wanderers*, 1922; as *Under the Autumn Stars*, in *The Wanderer*, 1975.
Benoni. 1908; translated as *Benoni*, 1926.
Rosa. 1908; translated as *Rosa*, 1926.
En Vandrer spiller med Sordin. 1909; as *With Muted Strings*, in *Wanderers*, 1922; as *On Muted Strings*, in *The Wanderer*, 1975.
Den sidste Glaede. 1912; as *Look Back on Happiness*, 1940.
Børn av Tiden. 1913; as *Children of the Age*, 1924.
Segelfoss By. 1915; as *Segelfoss Town*, 1925.
Markens Grøde. 1917; as *The Growth of the Soil*, 1920.
Konerne ved Vandposten. 1920; as *The Women at the Pump*, 1928.
Siste Kapitel. 1923; as *Chapter the Last*, 1929.
Landstrykere. 1927; as *Vagabonds*, 1931; as *Wayfarers*, 1980.
August. 1930; translated as *August*, 1932.
Men Livet lever. 1933; as *The Road Leads On*, 1934.
Ringen sluttet. 1936; as *The Ring Is Closed*, 1937.
Paa gjengrodde Stier. 1949; as *On Overgrown Paths*, 1968.

Plays

Ved rigets port (produced 1896). 1895.
Livets Spil [The Game of Life] (produced 1896). 1896.
Aftenrøde [Evening Glow] (produced 1898). 1898.
Munken Vendt (produced 1926). 1902.
Dronning Tamara [Queen Tamara] (produced 1903). 1903.
Livet i vold (produced 1910). 1910, as *In the Grip of Life*, 1924.

Verse

Det vilde Kor [The Wild Choir]. 1904

Other

Fra det moderne Amerikas aandsliv. 1889; as *The Cultural Life of Modern America*, edited by Barbara Gordon Morgridge, 1969.
I Aeventyrland [In the Land of Fairy Tales]. 1903.
Sproget i fare [Language in Danger]. 1918.
Artikler, edited by Francis Bull. 1939.
Paa Turné [On Tour]. 1960.
Brev til Marie [Letters to Marie], edited by Tore Hamsun. 1970.

*

Bibliography: *Hamsun: En bibliografi* by Arvid Østby, 1972.

Critical Studies: *Hamsun* by Hanna Astrup Larsen, 1922; *Hamsun* (in Norwegian) by Tore Hamsun, 1959; *Six Scandinavian Novelists* by Alrik Gustafson, 1966; *Konflikt og visjon* by Rolf Nyboe Nettum, 1970; "Critical Attitudes to Hamsun 1890-1969" by Ronald Popperwell, in *Scandinavica 9*, 1970; *The Hero in Scandinavian Literature* edited by John M. Weinstock and Robert T. Rovinsky, 1975.

*　　*　　*

Knut Hamsun burst upon Norwegian literature in 1890 with a series of lectures attacking the Realist writers, including Ibsen; he appealed instead for a new kind of writing, which he called "psychological literature." His first novel, *Sult (Hunger)*, published in the same year, embodies his theories. It is the story of a mind—a lively, fantastic, creative mind which ever and again rises irrepressibly above the vicissitudes of a mundane bodily existence. "The unconscious life of the soul" is the centre of focus; the starving artist pacing the streets of Christiania is not an occasion for an attack on social injustice but a creator of a vibrant inner world.

Inspired, often unstable visionaries are the heroes of Hamsun's other early novels: *Mysterier (Mysteries)*, *Pan* and *Victoria*. With these novels Hamsun became the first Modernist writer in Scandinavia, reflecting the turbulent inner conflict of modern man; Nietzsche and Dostoevsky were among his antecedents. The interplay of instinct and impulse, the celebration of spontaneity over sober reflection and nature over civilization give his heroes a quixotic air of inconsistency which made his contemporaries dismiss them as "erratic." His prose style is equally innovative, and has proved inimitable—though many have since tried to imitate it. There is a lyrical intensity in his phrasing which makes whole chapters of *Pan* and *Victoria* read like prose poems; the rhythms are incantatory, the mood is ecstatic. The novels are hymns to love—but it is a self-destructive, impossible love which bars the way to its own fulfillment and mocks at its own despair.

Hamsun's heroes grew older as he himself grew old; and the exuberance of youth gave way to a more disillusioned world-weariness. Social issues, which he had previously dismissed, also preoccupied him increasingly. In *Børn av Tiden (Children of the Age)* and *Segelfoss By (Segelfoss Town)* he attacked the decadence of modern capitalist society and the emergent workers' movements. *Markens Grøde (The Growth of the Soil)*, for which he was awarded the Nobel prize in 1920, celebrated instead his ideal, the noble peasant who rejects the softness of city ways and chooses the harsh, unremitting struggle of the pioneering farming life.

Nostalgia for a lost patriarchal era and dislike of modern industrial society were among the factors which led Hamsun towards the end of his long life to support Hitler; a fateful choice for which his countrymen have still not forgiven him. However, the best of his writing is not marred by his political blindness. In his final trilogy, *Landstrykere (Wayfarers)*, *August*, and *Men Livet lever (The Road Leads On)*, the vitality of his inventiveness and the suppleness of his style are undiminished. August, the central character, is Hamsun's last great adventurer and orchestrator of humanity's dreams—though his stock is running low, and the chill winds of old age and bankruptcy are felt with increasing keenness. But like his creator, he is dogged to the end, and the rich gallery of characters around him is depicted with discerning clarity and a fine sense of life's ironies.

—Janet Garton

HASEK, Jaroslav. Born in Prague, Bohemia, 30 April 1883. Educated at St. Stephen's School, 1891-93; Imperial and Royal Junior Gymnasium, 1893-97, expelled; Czechoslavonic Commercial Academy, 1899-1902. Married Jarmila Mayerová in 1910 (separated 1912), one son; bigamous marriage with Shura Lvova in 1920. Worked for a chemist in late 1890's; wrote stories and sketches for several humorous and political magazines from 1901; also wrote and performed cabaret sketches; clerk, Insurance Bank of Slavie, 1902-03; jailed for anarchist rioting, 1907; Editor, *Svět zvířat* [Animal World], 1909-10; Assistant Editor, *Czech Word*, 1911; conscripted, 1915; captured by the Russians: allowed to work for Czech forces in Russia, and staff member, *Cechoslovan*, Kiev, 1916-18; after a propaganda battle, 1917-18, left Czech group and entered political department of the Siberian Army: Editor, *Our Path* (later *Red Arrow*), 1919, *Red Europe*, 1919, and other propaganda journals in Russia and Siberia; sent to Czechoslovakia to do propaganda work, 1920; lived in Lipnice from 1921. *Died 3 January 1923.*

PUBLICATIONS

Collections

  Spisy [Works]. 16 vols., 1955-68.

Fiction

  Dobrý voják Svejk a jiné podivné historky [The Good Soldier Svejk and Other Strange Stories]. 1912.
  Trampoty para Tenkráta [The Tribulations of Mr. That-Time]. 1912.
  Pruvodčí cizincu a jiné satiry [The Tourists' Guide and Other Satires from Home]. 1913.
  Muj obchod se psy [My Trade with Dogs]. 1915.
  Dobrý voják Svejk v zajetí [The Good Soldier Svejk in Captivity]. 1917.
  [Two Dozen Stories]. 1920.
  Pepíček Nový a jiné historky [Pepíček Nový and Other Stories]. 1921.
  Osudy dobrého vojáka Svejk za světové války [The Good Soldier Svejk and His Fortunes in the World War]. 4 vols., 1921-23; as *The Good Soldier Schweik*, 1930; complete version, 1973.
  Tři muži se žralokem a jiné poučné historky [Three Men and a Shark and Other Instructive Stories]. 1921.
  Mírová Konference [The Peace Conference]. 1922.
  The Red Commissar, Including Further Adventures of the Good Soldier Svejk and Other Stories. 1981.

*

Bibliography: *Bibliografie Haška* by Boris Mědílek, 1983.

Critical Studies: *The Bad Bohemian: The Life of Hašek*, 1978, and *Hašek: A Study of Svejk and the Short Stories*, 1982, both by Cecil Parrott.

*   *   *

Jaroslav Hašek wrote his one and only novel, *Good Soldier Svejk*, in 1921 and 1922, at the very end of his adventurous and chequered life, and left it unfinished at his death. It has been translated into countless languages and is now far better known in the world than any other Czech book—a development which he could never have foreseen. At first the Czech literary "establishment" dismissed the book as unliterary, and it was only when it was translated into German in 1926 and presented by Erwin Piscator in dramatised form at the famous Theater Am Nollendorfplatz in Berlin in 1928 that it achieved European fame.

When it was published in final form in 1923, it anticipated by several years the wave of popular war books which appeared at the end of the decade, like *All Quiet on the Western*

Front and others. But whereas the authors of such books mostly dwelt on the horror and suffering of war and their disillusionment with it, Hašek, to quote the perceptive judgement of a contemporary Czech writer, Ivan Olbracht, "stood above it" and "just laughed at it." Olbracht went on to say that he had read several war novels and even written one himself, but none of them showed up the World War "in all its infamy, idiocy and inhumanity" so vividly as Hašek's.

Hašek found the material for his novel during the one year he spent in the Austrian army on the way to the Eastern Front. Most of its leading characters are modelled on the officers, N.C.O.'s, and men of the regiment he served in. He had already invented the character of "The Good Soldier" in 1911, when he wrote five short stories about him, but in his final novel Svejk had become a much rounder and more enigmatic figure. Was he an idiot or only pretending to be one? In consequence of this ambiguity Svejk was caught up in the political struggles between Left and Right in the young republic. The Left wanted to see him as a revolutionary, while the Right condemned him as a dodger and a threat to national morale. While most other readers of the book would laugh aloud at Svejk's misadventures, Czechoslovakia's leading critic, F.X. Salda, saw their tragic side. For all its comedy, he wrote, it was a desperately sad book, because in it the individual was fighting against a giant power, against the War.

Hašek himself would have been greatly surprised to know that his book had given rise to such discussions, because he just dictated it as it came into his head—sometimes in the middle of a pub bar—with nothing but a map to go on. He filled the pages of his book with a vast array of fascinating types, whom he involved more often than not in ludicrous situations. He had a Dickensian gift for describing character, although unlike Dickens he did not dwell on their appearance but rather on their actions and manner of speech. He was particularly successful in reproducing the conversations of ordinary men and the anecdotes they tell. And he described in a masterly fashion the scrapes they got into and the idiotic ideas they had, saying under his breath, "Lord, what fools these mortals be." The book is as much a condemnation of the Austrian Army as it is of the War. Its generals are shown either as inept fuddy-duddies or potential hangmen. (Hašek was of course free for the first time to say exactly what he thought of the Monarchy, as it no longer existed.)

In writing his novel Hašek drew on his long experience in contributing short stories and feuilletons to the Czech press, which are said to have amounted to over 1200. He wrote them for Prague dailies before the War, for the Czech Legion's newspaper in Kiev during it, and Soviet journals in Siberia after it was over. He wrote easily, but carelessly. He once described a feuilleton as "something which can be read in the morning at breakfast, when a man is still yawning, and in the afternoon, when after lunch he lies agreeably stretched out on a soft sofa, a kind of writing in which one can skip half a column without missing it." His short stories prove his inexhaustible ingenuity in inventing comic situations, but as the newspapers he contributed to seldom allowed him more than a little over a thousand words they almost all suffer from compression and sometimes end with the point only half made. His best stories are the Bugulma tales, which he published in Prague on his return from Russia after the War, and which recount his experiences as deputy-commandant of a little town beyond the Volga. Although in these he ridicules Soviet petty officials, he is more indulgent to them than he is to Austrians or indeed to his own people.

In the years before the War Hašek acquired something of a reputation as a popular entertainer, when he helped to create a mock political party and posed as its candidate in the national elections. People flocked to hear his improvised speeches, in which he mercilessly pilloried the activities of the Czech political parties. When the elections were over he sat down and wrote up the "annals" of his "party" and ascribed to its members various imaginary exploits, but much of what he wrote was too personal and defamatory to be published at the time and only found its way into print as late as 1963.

None of Hašek's flamboyant posturings as electioneering agent, speaker at Anarchist rallies, or cabaret entertainer earned him much respect, and his lampoons and tomfoolery alienated many who might otherwise have helped him. By the time war broke out Prague had become rather too hot for him, and he no doubt joined up with a certain feeling of relief. But it can be said of him that he added another dimension to conventional humorous writing by acting and actually living his stories. All his experiences, whether lived or written, bore fruit later, when he drew on them for his one great novel.

—Cecil Parrott

HAUPTMANN, Gerhart (Johann Robert). Born in Ober-Salzbrunn, 15 November 1862. Educated at a school in Breslau; studied sculpture at Royal College of Art, Breslau, 1880-82; also studied at University of Jena, 1882-83. Married 1) Marie Thienemann in 1884 (divorced), three sons; 2) Margarete Marschalk in 1905, one son. Sculptor in Rome, 1883-84; also worked as actor in Berlin, before becoming a full-time writer. Recipient: Grillparzer Prize, 1896, 1899, 1905; Goethebünde Schiller Prize, 1905; Nobel Prize for Literature, 1912; Goethe Prize (Frankfurt), 1932. Honorary degrees: Oxford University, 1905; University of Leipzig, 1909; University of Prague, 1921; Columbia University, New York, 1932. Ordre pour le Mérite, 1922. *Died 8 June 1946.*

PUBLICATIONS

Collections

> *Sämtliche Werke*, edited by Hans-Egon Hass.   10 vols., 1962-70.
> *Dramatic Works*.   9 vols., 1913-29.

Plays

> *Vor Sonnenaufgang* (produced 1889).   1889; as *Before Dawn*, 1909.
> *Das Friedenfest* (produced 1890).   1890; as *The Coming of Peace*, 1900; as *The Reconciliation*, in *Dramatic Works*, 1914.
> *Einsame Menschen* (produced 1891).   1891; as *Lonely Lives*, 1898.
> *Die Weber* (produced 1893).   1892; as *The Weavers*, 1899.
> *Kollege Crampton* (produced 1892).   1892; as *Colleague Crampton*, in *Dramatic Works*, 1914.
> *Der Biberpelz* (produced 1893).   1893; as *The Beaver Coat*, 1912.
> *Hanneles Himmelfahrt* (produced 1893).   1893; translated as *Hannele*, 1894.
> *Florian Geyer* (produced 1896).   1896; translated as *Florian Geyer*, in *Dramatic Works*, 1929.
> *Die versunkene Glocke* (produced 1896).   1896; as *The Sunken Bell*, 1898.
> *Fuhrmann Henschel* (produced 1898).   1898; as *Drayman Henschel*, in *Dramatic Works*, 1913.
> *Schluck und Jau* (produced 1900).   1900; as *Schluck and Jau*, in *Dramatic Works*, 1919.
> *Michael Kramer* (produced 1900).   1900; translated as *Michael Kramer*, in *Dramatic Works*, 1914.

Der rote Hahn (produced 1901). 1901; as *The Conflagration*, in *Dramatic Works*, 1913.

Die arme Heinrich (produced 1902). 1902; as *Henry of Auë*, in *Dramatic Works*, 1914.

Rose Bernd (produced 1903). 1903; translated as *Rose Bernd*, in *Dramatic Works*, 1913.

Elga (produced 1905). 1905; translated as *Elga*, in *Dramatic Works*, 1919.

Und Pippa tanzt! (produced 1906). 1906; as *And Pippa Dances*, 1907.

Die Jungfrau vom Bischofsberg (produced 1907). 1907; as *Maidens of the Mount*, in *Dramatic Works*, 1919.

Kaiser Karls Geisel (produced 1908). 1908; as *Charlemagne's Hostage*, in *Dramatic Works*, 1919.

Griselda (produced 1909). 1909; translated as *Griselda*, in *Dramatic Works*, 1919.

Die Ratten (produced 1911). 1911; as *The Rats*, in *Dramatic Works*, 1913.

Gabriel Schillings Flucht (produced 1912). 1912; as *Gabriel Schilling's Flight*, in *Dramatic Works*, 1919.

Festspiel in deutschen Reimen (produced 1913). 1913; as *Commemoration Masque*, in *Dramatic Works*, 1919.

Der Bogen des Odysseus (produced 1914). 1914; as *The Bow of Ulysses*, in *Dramatic Works*, 1919.

Winterballade (produced 1917). 1917; as *A Winter Ballad*, in *Dramatic Works*, 1925.

Der weisse Heiland (produced 1920). 1920; as *The White Savior*, in *Dramatic Works*, 1925.

Indipohdi (produced 1920). 1920; translated as *Indipohdi*, in *Dramatic Works*, 1925.

Peter Bauer (produced 1921). 1921.

Veland. 1925; translated as *Veland*, in *Dramatic Works*, 1929.

Dorothea Angermann (produced 1926). 1926.

Spuk: Die Schwarze Maske; Hexenritt (produced 1928). 1929.

Vor Sonnenuntergang (produced 1932). 1932.

Die goldene Harfe (produced 1933). 1933.

Hamlet in Wittenberg (produced 1935). 1935.

Ulrich von Lichtenstein (produced 1939). 1939.

Die Tochter der Kathedrale (produced 1939). 1939.

Atridentetralogie: Iphigenie in Aulis, Agamemnons Tod, Elektra, Iphigenie in Delphi (produced 1940-44). 4 vols., 1941-48.

Magnus Garbe (produced 1942). 1942.

Die Finsternisse. 1947.

Herbert Engelmann, completed by Carl Zuckmayer (produced 1952). 1952.

Fiction

Fasching. 1887.

Bahnwärter Thiel. 1888.

Der Apostel. 1890.

Der Narr in Christo, Emanuel Quint. 1910; as *The Fool in Christ, Emanuel Quint*, 1911.

Atlantis. 1912; translated as *Atlantis*, 1912.

Lohengrin. 1913.

Parsival. 1914.

Der Ketzer von Soana. 1918; as *The Heretic of Soana*, 1923.

Phantom. 1922; translated as *Phantom*, 1923.

Die Insel der grossen Mutter. 1924; as *The Island of the Great Mother*, 1925.

Wanda. 1928.

Buch der Leidenschaft. 1930.

Die Hochzeit auf Buchenhorst. 1931.

Das Meerwunder. 1934.

Im Wirbel der Berufung. 1936.

Der Schuss im Park. 1939.

Das Märchen. 1941.
Mignon. 1944.

Verse

Promethidenlos. 1885.
Das bunte Buch. 1888.
Anna. 1921.
Die blaue Blume. 1924.
Till Eulenspiegel. 1928.
Ährenlese. 1939.
Der grosse Traum. 1942.
Neue Gedichte. 1946.

Other

Griechischer Frühling. 1908.
Ausblicke. 1922.
Gesammelte Werke. 12 vols., 1922.
Um Volk und Geist. 1932.
Gespräche, edited by Josef Chapiro. 1932.
Das Abenteuer meiner Jugend. 1937.
Diarium 1917 bis 1933, edited by Martin Machatzke. 1980.

*

Critical Studies: *The Death Problem in the life and Works of Hauptmann* by Frederick A. Klemm, 1939; *Hauptmann* by Hugh F. Garten, 1954; *Hauptmann: His Life and Work* by C.F.W. Behl, 1956; *Hauptmann: The Prose Plays* by Margaret Sinden, 1957; *Witness of Deceit: Hauptmann as a Critic of Society* by L.R. Shaw, 1958; *Hauptmann: Centenary Lectures* edited by K.G. Knight and F. Norman, 1964; *The Image of the Primitive Giant in the Works of Hauptmann* by Carolyn Thomas Sussère, 1979.

*　　　*　　　*

Gerhart Hauptmann's reputation as the leading representative of German naturalism has tended to obscure the fact that he enjoyed a period of literary creativity which lasted for more than 60 years. Apart from Goethe, few German writers have succeeded in bequeathing a life's work of such astonishing variety, richness, and breadth. From naturalism to neo-romanticism to 20th-century mysticism and neo-classicism, there are few literary movements between 1880 and 1940 which failed to influence Hauptmann or indeed to be influenced by him.

Hauptmann's plays, ranging from the crude but powerful *Before Dawn* (1889) to the deeply pessimistic recasting of antique sources in the *Atriden* tetralogy (1940-44), are remarkable for the easy assurance with which the author displays his mastery of diverse registers, themes, styles, and genres. The raucous naturalism of his earliest work was tempered in 1891 by the performance in Berlin of *Lonely Lives,* a poignant middle-class tragedy which, in its probing analysis of the roles ascribed by society to women, has lost none of its topicality. Realism re-emerged in *The Weavers,* a moving account of the ill-fated uprising of the Silesian weavers in 1844, in the comedies *The Beaver Coat* and *The Conflagration,* and in the tightly knit dialect tragedy *Drayman Henschel.* Even in this early period Hauptmann was not willing to accept the dictates of naturalism in any doctrinaire sense, for in *Hanneles* the techniques of realism are employed as a means of making visual the delirious dreams and mental states of a dying child. Hannele's hallucinations, which express the reality of her wretched childhood and at once represent a flight from it, symbolise Hauptmann's own deepening interest in the workings of the imagination and its relationship to the human capacity to apprehend reality in mythical and poetic ways. This development is carried much further in the dramatic fairy-tale *The Sunken Bell*, and in a more realistic framework it is evident in the father/son conflict portrayed in the artist tragedy *Michael Kramer*. The subtlest and most magical expression of this thematic material is the drama *And Pippa Dances*, a work which owes much to Hauptmann's intensive study of the myths and legends of his native Silesia.

Hauptmann's works of prose fiction reflect in both theme and style the main trends discernible in his development as a dramatist. And similarly, the earlier naturalistic stories such as *Fasching* and *Bahnwärter Thiel* have had a greater impact than the mythological and symbolic works of the later period (*The Fool in Christ, Emanuel Quint, The Heretic of Soana*, and *The Island of the Great Mother*). Narratives such as *Bahnwärter Thiel* reveal even more clearly than the naturalistic plays, however, that Hauptmann was transcending naturalism in those very works which explored its themes and its expressive possibilities. The story certainly abounds in fashionable literary touches: the low social position of Thiel, the second-by-second description of trains appearing on the horizon and disappearing in the distance, the realistic "close-up" of a spade turning over the soil, and so on. At the same time, the narrative penetrates beyond realism to suggest the existence of realities and levels of perception which can be grasped only through symbol and myth. The train which kills Thiel's son and destroys Thiel is depicted on one level with all the photographic detail and meticulous accuracy which one expects to find in late 19th-century fiction; on a different level, the level at which the train's headlights transform the falling rain into droplets of blood, the train comes to symbolize the unpredictable and chaotic forces of destruction which, in Hauptmann's fictional world, are never very far from surface reality, however rational and well ordered it might appear.

—A.P. Foulkes

HEBBEL, (Christian) Friedrich. Born in Wesselburen, Holstein, Denmark (now Germany), 18 March 1813. Educated in a dame's school, 1817-19; primary school, Wesselburen, 1819-25; servant and clerk for local official, 1827-35; in Hamburg a group of benefactors supported him in his studies, and helped send him to University of Heidelberg, 1836; doctorate, University of Erlangen, 1844. Married Christine Enghaus in 1846, two children; also had two sons by Elise Lensing. Free-lance writer in Munich, 1836-39, Hamburg, 1839-43; travel allowance from the Danish king allowed him to live in Paris, 1843-44, and Rome, 1844-45; lived in Vienna from 1845. Honorary Court Librarian, Weimar, 1863. Recipient: Schiller Prize, 1863. *Died 13 December 1863.*

PUBLICATIONS

Collections

Sämtliche Werke, edited by Richard Maria Werner. 27 vols., 1904-22.
Werke, edited by Gerhard Fricke, Werner Keller, and Karl Pörnbacher. 5 vols., 1963-67.

Plays

>*Judith* (produced 1840).   1840; translated as *Judith*, 1914.
>*Genoveva* (produced 1849).   1843.
>*Maria Magdalena* (produced 1846).   1844; translated as *Maria Magdalena*, 1914.
>*Der Diamant* (produced 1852).   1847.
>*Julia* (produced 1903).   1848.
>*Herodes und Mariamne* (produced 1849).   1850; as *Herod and Mariamne*, 1914.
>*Der Rubin* (produced 1849).   1851.
>*Michel Angelo* (produced 1861).   1851.
>*Ein Trauerspiel in Sizilien* (produced 1907).   1851.
>*Agnes Bernauer* (produced 1852).   1852; translated as *Agnes Bernauer*, in *Poet Lore*, 1909.
>*Gyges und sein Ring* (produced 1889).   1856; as *Gyges and His Ring*, 1914.
>*Die Nibelungen* (produced 1861).   2 vols., 1862; as *The Nibelungs*, 1921.
>*Ein Steinwurf*.   1883.

Fiction

>*Erzählungen und Novellen*.   1855.

Verse

>*Gedichte*.   1842.
>*Neue Gedichte*.   1848.
>*Gedichte*.   1857.
>*Mutter und Kind*.   1859.

Other

>*Mein Wort über das Drama!*   1843.
>*Über den Stil des Dramas*.   1857.
>*Neue Hebbel-Briefe*, edited by Anni Meetz.   1963.
>*Der einsame Weg* (diaries), edited by Klaus Geissler.   1966.

*

Bibliography: *Hebbel-Bibliographie 1910-1970* by Ulrich H. Gerlach, 1973.

Critical Studies: *Hebbel: A Study of His Life and Work* by Edna Purdie, 1932; *Motivation in the Drama of Hebbel* by William F. Oechler, 1948; *Hebbel's Conception of Movement in the Absolute and History*, 1952, and *Hebbel*, 1968, both by Sten G. Flygt; *Hebbel as a Critic of His Own Works* by Ulrich H. Gerlach, 1972; *Hebbel's Prose Tragedies* by Mary Garland, 1973.

*   *   *

Poised between the fading beliefs of philosophical idealism and the positivism that came to replace them in the mid-19th century, Friedrich Hebbel sought to compromise between the literature of metaphysical ideas associated with German Classicism and the new Realism in European literature. While he also wrote stories, poems, and comedies, he is remembered today for a number of tragedies, based mostly on history or legend, written in prose or blank verse, and inclining towards the traditional "closed" form. As a "poetic realist" he defined drama as "the art of mixing the general and the specific so that the law all living things obey never appears naked and is never completely missed" ("Schiller und Körner"). Self-taught and self-made, touchy but ruthless, arrogant yet depressive, suffering considerable poverty and humiliation until he achieved fame in his fifth and last decade, and inflicting pain on others—particularly Elise Lensing, a seamstress who kept him for ten years and bore him two sons before he abandoned her to marry the successful actress Christine Enghaus—Hebbel felt that "All life is a struggle of the individual against the universe" (*Diaries*, September 1840). Individuals, as he explains in his treatise *Mein Wort über das Drama*, are obliged by their very nature to incur the guilt—existential rather than moral—of self-assertion, for which they must be destroyed: the destruction occurs through conflicts with other individuals, but it serves the universal order, which itself changes in the process. These views, which owe much to the philosophy of Hegel and Schelling, are at the centre of Hebbel's world-picture and his theory of tragedy.

In all of Hebbel's major tragedies the recurrent clash of overbearing heroes and victimised heroines reflects both his personal experiences and his Kantian maxim, "To use a human being as a means to an end: the worst sin" (*Diaries*, May? 1839). While his greatest artistic asset is his ability to create powerful conflicts involving the sado-masochistic battle of the sexes, he often weakens the impact of his acute psychological insights by imposing on them his notion of a superhuman dialectic, as he does in such otherwise impressive plays as *Judith, Herod and Mariamne*, and *Gyges and His Ring*. There are, however, two instances where he avoids abstruse speculation. In *Agnes Bernauer*, a historical tragedy set in the 15th century—in which a barber's daughter marries the son of a ruler, who has her assassinated to prevent a war of succession—Hebbel's conservative suggestion that the citizen must always be sacrificed to the state may raise liberal objections, but his handling of the conflict of love and politics links human reality with abstract thought in a dramatically convincing manner. In *Maria Magdalena* any abstract thought that may be present is entirely transformed into concrete drama. Set in Hebbel's own time, this play—as he argues in his renowned preface—represents a significant innovation in the development of domestic tragedy by deriving the decisive conflict no longer from the opposition of the bourgeoisie and the aristocracy but from the prejudices of the petty bourgeoisie itself. The tragedy of the pregnant joiner's daughter, who is driven to suicide by her treacherous seducer and her censorious father, combines the compelling portrayal of characters and circumstances with merciless social criticism to produce not only Hebbel's masterpiece but one of the outstanding works of European Realism as a whole.

—Ladislaus Löb

HEINE, Heinrich. Born Harry Heine in Düsseldorf, probably 13 December 1797; baptized as protestant, Christian Johann Heinrich Heine, 1825. Educated in a dame's school for 2 years; Hebrew school; Catholic schools, 1804-14; business school, 1814-15; apprenticed to a banking house and to a grocery dealer, Frankfurt, 1815; worked in his uncle Salomon's bank, Hamburg, 1816, and was set up in a cloth business, 1818-19; studied law at universities of Bonn, 1819-20, Göttingen, 1820-21, Berlin, 1821-24, Göttingen, 1824-25, Doctor of Law 1825. Married Crescence Eugenie Mirat in 1841. Writer: in Lüneberg and Hamburg, 1825-27; Co-Editor, *Neue Allgemeine Politische Annalen*, Munich, 1827-28; Italy, 1828; Hamburg and Berlin, 1829-31; in Paris from 1831: correspondent for Augsburg *Allgemeine Zeitung*; ill after 1845, and bed-ridden after 1848. *Died 17 February 1856.*

PUBLICATIONS

Collections

Sämtliche Werke, edited by Ernst Elster. 7 vols., 1887-90.
Sämtliche Schriften, edited by Klaus Briegleb and others. 7 vols., 1968-76.
Säkularausgabe: Werke, Briefwechsel, Lebenszeugnisse. 1970— .
Historisch-kritische Gesamtausgabe der Werke, edited by Manfred Windfuhr. 1973— .
Works. 16 vols., 1905.

Verse

Gedichte. 1822.
Tragödien nebst einem lyrischen Intermezzo (includes the plays *Almansor* and *William Ratcliff*). 1823.
Buch der Lieder. 1827; revised edition, 1844; as *Book of Songs*, 1856.
Neue Gedichte. 1844; revised edition, 1851; as *New Poems*, 1910.
Deutschland: Ein Wintermärchen. 1844; as *Germany: A Winter's Tale*, 1944.
Atta Troll: Ein Sommernachtstraum. 1847; as *Atta Troll and Other Poems*, 1876.
Romanzero. 1851; translated as *Romancero*, 1905.
Paradox and Poet: The Poems, translated by Louis Untermeyer. 1937.
Complete Poems, translated by Hal Draper. 1982.

Other

Reisebilder (*Die Harzreise*; *Ideen: Das Buch Le Grand*; *Reise von München nach Genua*, *Die Bäden von Lucca*; *Die Stadt Lucca, Englische Fragmente*). 4 vols., 1826-31; as *Pictures of Travel*, 1855.
Französische Zustände. 1833; as *French Affairs*, 1889.
Der Salon. 4 vols., 1834-40.
Die Romantische Schule. 1836; as *The Romantic School*, 1882.
Shakespeares Mädchen und Frauen. 1839; as *Heine on Shakespeare*, 1895.
Ludwig Börne: Eine Denkschrift. 1840; as *Ludwig Börne: Portrait of a Revolutionist*, 1881.
Der Doktor Faust (ballet scenario). 1851; as *Doctor Faust: A Dance Poem*, 1947.
Vermischte Schriften (includes *Gedichte, Lutezia*). 3 vols., 1854.
Memoiren und neugesammelte Gedichte, Prosa, und Briefe, edited by Eduard Engel. 1884; as *Memoirs*, 1884.
Poetry and Prose, edited by Frederic Ewen. 1948.
Briefe, edited by Friedrich Hirth. 6 vols., 1950-51.
The Sword and the Flame (selected prose), edited by Alfred Werner. 1960.
Begegnungen mit Heine: Berichte der Zeitgenossen, edited by Michael Werner. 2 vols., 1973.
Selected Works, translated by Helen M. Mustard and Max Knight. 1973.

*

Bibliography: *Heine-Bibliographie* by Gottfried Wilhelm and Eberhard Galley, 2 vols., 1960; supplement by Siegfried Seifert, 1968; *Heine: A Selected Critical Bibliography of the Secondary Literature 1956-1980* by Jeffrey L. Sammons, 1982.

Critical Studies: *Judaic Lore in Heine* by Israel Tabak, 1948; *Heine: An Interpretation* by

HEINE

Barker Fairley, 1954; *Heine: Two Studies of His Thought and Feeling*, 1956, and *The Early Love Poetry of Heine*, 1962, both by William Rose; *Heine: Buch der Lieder*, 1960, *Heine, The Tragic Satirist*, 1962, *Heine's Shakespeare*, 1970, and *Heine's Jewish Comedy*, 1983, all by S.S. Prawer; *Heine* by Laura Hofrichter, 1963; *The Exile of Gods* by A.E. Sandor, 1967; *Heine, The Elusive Poet*, 1969, and *Heine: A Modern Biography*, 1979, both by Jeffrey L. Sammons; *Heine: Poetry and Politics* by Nigel Reeves, 1974; *Heine's Reception of German Grecophilia* by Robert C. Holub, 1981; *Heine* by Hanna Spencer, 1982.

*   *   *

Heinrich Heine is the most widely read or, perhaps one should say, *heard*, poet to have written in the German language. His poetry has been carried around the world, in his own phrase, "on wings of song," in more than three thousand musical settings. It can be difficult to apprehend the poetry accurately through all that music, which in some cases re-Romanticizes and resentimentalizes it. For Heine had an exceptionally tense relationship to poetry, including his own. Through much of his career he was a more reactive than strikingly original poet. While he had a great lyrical gift, genuinely fueled by an experience of unrequited love that became virtually archetypal for him, he doubted the relevance of poetry and its traditional materials in his politically and socially stressed post-Romantic environment. Thus, from within, he undermined the tradition with his bitterly accusatory tone directed toward the beloved, with abrasive irony and jarring stylistic dissonances, with ingenious dexterity and a visible manipulation of poetic devices that exposes them as fictions, ultimately with studied salaciousness and fiercely aggressive political verse. Not until *Romanzero* in 1851 did he find a genuinely original, mid-19th-century style, a bleak, ironically serious verse composed in the suffering of his "mattress-grave." With all his misgivings, however, he regarded the poetic vocation as one of high dignity and by mid-life he had doubtless achieved his ambition to succeed Goethe as the major living poet in the German language.

With his prose *Pictures of Travel* beginning in the mid-1820's he developed greater originality of form. With sparkling wit, they weld together essay and fiction, imaginative autobiographical reminiscence and acute contemporary observation, high and low comedy and sardonic social criticism. Though he pretends to easy-going free association, as though setting down the first thing that came into his head, they are, like all of his writing, meticulously formulated and ordered. The comedy and wit, as always with Heine, have a seriously committed purpose. For he lived in gloomily repressive times and was determined to take up arms against the reactionary political order of the neo-feudal Metternichian system, under whose heavy-handed censorship he suffered unremittingly. He came to subsume political and cultural phenomena under a dichotomy of "spiritualism" versus "sensualism" or, in his later vocabulary, "Nazarenism" versus "Hellenism." What he perceived in the repressive order was a denial of gratification and plenitude, a reservation of aristocratic luxuries and erotic liberty to the privileged few, while the mass of people were kept in superstitious ignorance, compensated for their deprivation by promises of mythical joys in the other world. Since he regarded religion and especially Christianity as part of this conspiracy, he attacked religious institutions and Christian doctrine with an explicitness unparalleled in his generation.

Heine's at first voluntary, then involuntary exile in France beginning in 1831 was initially motivated by his interest in the Saint-Simonian movement, which for a time he thought congruent with his own vision of emancipation and sensualism. He reported on France in two series of newspaper articles in 1830-32 and 1840-43, published in book form as *French Affairs* (1833) and *Lutezia* (1854). He covers not only political and public events but also music, theater, art, and the common life of the people. It was a report on the painting exhibition of 1831 that gave the title to a four-volume collection of essays, fiction, and poetry, *Der Salon*. At the same time he endeavored to explain Germany to France in terms of a secret revolutionary doctrine of sensualism, in a book directed against Madame de Staël and bearing her title *De l'Allemagne*; it appeared in two parts in German, as *Zur Geschichte der Religion und Philosophie in Deutschland* (*On the History of Religion and Philosophy in Germany*) in *Salon II*

(1834), and *The Romantic School* (1836). Heine's views, despite all their vigor and forthrightness, were complex and sometimes gave an impression of capriciousness because of his contradictory commitments. He insisted that he was a democrat, but the commanding figure of his heroic imagination was the conquerer Napoleon and he sometimes claimed to be a monarchist; he championed the proletariat against the dominant order and yet feared a barbarian destruction of cultural and civilized values; and he turned against his liberal and radical contemporaries because he suspected them of nationalism, which he always strongly opposed, and of puritanical spiritualism. Thus in 1840 he greatly damaged his reputation with an ill-considered book directed against the deceased spokesman of the German dissidents, Ludwig Börne, and then exhibited the opposing vectors of his outlook in two contrasting mock-epic poems, *Atta Troll: A Midsummer Night's Dream*, which spoofs the radical poets of his time, and *Germany: A Winter's Tale*, a tough satire on German conditions. The latter, considered the greatest of German political poems, was written during his months of friendship with the young Karl Marx and is the chief product of his most radical phase. With the collapse of his health into painful paralysis, he became more thoughtful and discouraged, and also underwent a religious reversal, though not abandoning his habits of irony, independence, and impudence. He occupied himself with his memoirs, a segment of which appeared as *Geständnisse (Confessions)* in 1854; the remainder was suppressed by his relatives, with whom he had had a violent public feud over his uncle's inheritance, and was not published until 28 years after his death.

Few writers in literature have had such an embattled reputation as Heine; he has been scorned by nationalists, conservatives, and anti-Semites, and for a long time his reputation was stronger outside Germany. During the current era of his rehabilitation it is sometimes forgotten how much he was himself responsible for the hostility of his public and posterity; he scoffed at their cherished values and his career was often marked by ethical carelessness. But he lucidly drew into himself and exposed with ultimate sincerity the critical dilemmas of his time, and he stands as not only one of the wittiest but also one of the most penetrating writers in European letters.

—Jeffrey L. Sammons

HERODOTUS. Born 484 B.C. (traditional date). Possibly related to the ruling family of Halicarnassus, Asia Minor; moved to Samos during civil strife, c. 460; travelled and lectured in Greece, including Athens, and settled in the Athenian colony of Thurii in South Italy (founded 444-43); also travelled in South Italy, Egypt, the Near East and Babylon, Scythia and the Black Sea, and the North Aegean. *Died in 420 B.C.* (traditional date).

PUBLICATIONS

[*History*], edited by Carl Hude. 2 vols., 1927; also edited by P.E Legrand, 1932-54; as *The History*, translated by George Rawlinson, 1858-60 (this translation edited by A.W. Lawrence, 1935, and abridged by W.G. Forrest, 1966); also translated by A.D. Godley, 1920-24, Enoch Powell, 1949, Aubrey de Selincourt, 1954, and H. Carter, 1962.

*

HERODOTUS

Critical Studies: *The World of Herodotus* by Aubrey de Selincourt, 1962; *Form and Thought in Herodotus* by H.R. Immerwahr, 1966; *Herodotus: An Interpretative Essay* by C.W. Fornara, 1971; *Herodotus, Father of History* by J.L. Myres, 1971; *The Histories of Herodotus: An Analysis of the Formal Structure* by H. Wood, 1972; *The Interrelation of Speech and Action in the Histories of Herodotus* by Paavo Hohti, 1976; *The Travels of Herodotus* by R.P. Lister, 1979; *Herodotus and Greek History* by John Hart, 1982; *Past and Process in Herodotus and Thucydides* by Virginia J. Hunter, 1982.

*   *   *

Herodotus is traditionally styled "Father of History," and rightly so: he invented it. There were before him a few local chronicles and geographical studies, which have entirely perished; no one had essayed a great and significant theme, nor assembled masses of material from diverse sources and organized them into a coherent whole. As there is no reason to think that those lost works were of any great literary merit, Herodotus is also entitled to be regarded as a pioneer of artistic prose composition.

And yet there is nothing primitive or unsophisticated about Herodotus. He aims to record for posterity the great deeds of men, and his chosen vehicle is the conflict between the Greeks and the Persians that reached its climax with Xerxes's defeat by the Greeks in 480-79 B.C. His handling of that tremendous theme shows a remarkable sense of planning and design: the first half of the work is devoted to the rise of Persia to her greatest extent; the second, by a smoothly negotiated transition, to her wars against the Greeks. The story unfolds in no crude annalistic way: instead it proceeds by a mixture of narrative and digression. The digressions are sometimes little more than footnotes; equally often they are substantial chapters, carefully designed to explain the background to the main narrative, while spacing out its climactic points. Some of these are miniature narratives themselves; others are extended essays in ethnology or sociology, such as the full-length study of Egypt (Book II).

Herodotus understands the broad tides of history, making it clear that Persia's aggression was motivated by imperialist expansion; equally he is good on the grand strategy of the combatants in 480-79—such non-narrative issues being conveyed through direct speech put into the mouths of his characters. He is noticeably weaker on detailed military tactics, however, and tends to personalize the causes of lesser events. He does not gloss over the failings of the Greeks at war—their occasional loss of nerve, the inter-allied bickerings; war itself he hates, despite the glorious exploits associated with it.

Accepting the Homeric picture of man's relationship with the gods, he emphasizes the role of oracles in Greek life, and often quotes oracular texts, many authentic, some spurious. His "theological" passages, such as the story of Xerxes's cabinet meeting (VII), teach the lesson that man cannot escape his destiny, and that the gods are envious of excessive prosperity in mortals. This pessimistic view informs his whole work, which is tinged with sadness and pity for human suffering; yet this is lightened by passages of irresistible sparkle and humour—Aristagoras's appeal to Sprata (V), "Hippocleides doesn't care" (VI), and dozens of others. His Greek is unmannered and effortless, resembling an educated man's friendly conversation.

Herodotus was a man of broad sympathies. His travels furnished him with a wide variety of oral sources, and enabled him to appreciate the "barbarian" point of view; but he was equally at home with the Athenian nobility, some of whose family history he records. His interests include poetry (he quotes from Pindar, Simonides, and many others), the visual arts, and medicine. But above all, he is concerned with humanity, and, like Homer, describes man's behaviour as he finds it: heroism, generosity, foresight, loyalty, vindictiveness, xenophobia, cowardice, treachery, corruption, paranoia, sacrilege—all these, and more, are exemplified many times over in his pages. But what sets Herodotus apart from most other ancient historians is his conviction that history is more than war, politics, and diplomacy. Today, students of social and cultural history can regard Herodotus as their truest ancestor.

—John Hart

HESIOD. Fl. c. 700 B.C. According to the poet himself, he lived in Ascra in Boeotia, and tended sheep on Mt. Helicon; won a tripod at the funeral games of Amphidamas in Chalcis. Said to have died in Locri or Orchomenus.

PUBLICATIONS

Collections

[*Works*], edited by Friedrich Solmsen, R. Merkelbach, and M.L. West. 1970, revised edition, 1983; translated by Hugh G. Evelyn-White (Loeb edition), 1936; also translated by Richmond Lattimore, 1959, and R.M. Fraser, 1983; as *The Essential Hesiod*, translated by C.J. Rowe, 1978.

Verse

Theogonia, edited by M.L. West. 1966; as *Theogony*, translated by N.O. Brown, 1953, and Dorothea Wender, 1973.
Opera et dies, edited by M.L. West. 1978; as *Works and Days*, translated by Dorothea Wender, 1973.

*

Critical Studies: *Hesiod and Aeschylus* by Friedrich Solmsen, 1949; *The World of Hesiod: A Study of the Greek Middle Ages c. 900-700 B.C.* by A.R. Burn, 1966; *Hesiod and the Near East* by Peter Walcot, 1966; *The Language of Hesiod in Its Traditional Context* by G.P. Edwards, 1971; *The Winged Word: A Study in the Technique of Ancient Greek Oral Composition as Seen Principally Through Hesiod's "Works and Days"* by B. Peabody, 1975; *Hesiod and the Language of Poetry* by Pietro Pucci, 1976; *Hesiod and Parmenides* by M.E. Pelikaan-Engel, 1977; *Theogony, Works and Days, Shield* by Apostolos N. Athanassakis, 1983.

*   *   *

Antiquity attributed a number of poems to Hesiod: besides *Theogony* and *Works and Days*, the only ones which are both nearly intact and probably genuine, there is a fragmentary *Catalogue of Famous Women*, a spurious *Shield of Heracles*, and some others of which we know little more than the titles.

The *Theogony* begins with a prayer-song celebrating the Muses, recounting their encounter with the poet on the foothills of Helicon, and invoking their power to fill him with true song. They—and he—start with a cosmogony. Chaos, the primal chasm, came first into being, then Earth, the Underworld, and Eros, sexual desire, the primal energy from which further creation flowed. Once he has established that primordial being is a unity, and material if also divine, the poet interests himself mainly in the emergence of the various gods, and the generations of their rulers. First in power were nature gods, Earth and Heaven; then came Cronus and the Titans, who ruled by force and violence; these were replaced by Zeus and the Olympians, the present regime, characterized by intelligence as well as power, and a deathless being which transcends nature. The shift in power from Earth and Sky is accomplished by a savage fulfilment of the Freudian Oedipal wish: the boy Cronus, at the instigation of his mother Earth, castrates his father Heaven and takes his throne. The triumph of Zeus over Cronus is different, a triumph of practical intelligence. Cronus is deceived by his mother Earth into swallowing a stone when he intended to devour his son Zeus. Zeus had the sense to free the spirits of lightning and thunder, who armed him with weapons to crush Cronus and the Titans, weapons he still uses. Mental agility will keep Zeus in power: warned that his first wife Metis (Intelligence) is to give birth to

Athena, her father's equal in strength and wisdom, and a son destined to rule, Zeus swallows Metis and procures her power for himself: Athena is born from his head, and the son is never conceived.

A myth is needed to illustrate the quality of intelligence which rules the world, and Hesiod adapts *Prometheus*. The hero first tricks Zeus into granting humans the better share of sacrifices. Zeus does not undo, but rather compensates, by withholding fire from mortals. Prometheus steals the fire; again Zeus compensates, fashioning the first woman, regarded by Hesiod as a mixed blessing at best. Divine retribution is creative rather than destructive, a balancing which achieves a kind of justice.

If the cosmos began as a unity, it is a unity no longer: the trascendent has seemingly emerged from primal matter and become Olympian. But Olympus is not born, any more than it was present at the beginning: its becoming is as mysterious as its super-natural being. Though beyond nature, it is somehow above us; occasionally called Heaven, it is in fact a place beyond the sky. At the other pole lies Tartarus, the Underworld, where the defeated Titans dwell, along with Night, Sleep and Death. Above Tartarus is a chasm, perhaps identical with primordial Chaos; then comes the natural world and the monsters "beyond the sea," such as the Gorgons, Echidna, and the defunct Medusa.

The *Theogony*'s suggestion of a close connection among Zeus, Earth, and Justice is developed into an elaborate theodicy in the *Works and Days*. The premises are, not unexpectedly, questionable; but the argument is highly rational. Zeus is a just god, who rewards the good and punishes the wicked. The good, in this Iron age of ours, are those who honor the goddess good Strife, competition; the wicked are worshippers of bad Strife—battle, disputation, and theft legal and illegal. Strife (Eris) is thus the energy of human purposes, just as Sexual Desire (Eros) is the energy of the *Theogony*. We all desire wealth, but it must be acquired justly, through good strife, else the gods will destroy us, our offspring, our cities. And this means that we must work. It was not always thus: as the myths of Prometheus-Pandora and of the Decadence from the Golden Age reveal, Zeus has punished human arrogance by hiding our livelihood. But the life of hard work is not a mere avoidance of evil, rather a fulfilment of justice, an honorable response to the act of a just Zeus. Hesiod's paradigm for work is the life of the farmer, who struggles to be in harmony with Zeus, Heaven and Earth, divinities of Olympus and of Nature. This life is depicted in the imperative mood: "Now plough, now sow, now reap," a device which combines description with prudential—and moral—imperative. The poem ends with a superstitious Catalogue of Good and Bad Days for doing things, which many scholars have adjudged spurious. But the bulk of the poem is a well thought out and logical vindication of a life of honorable competition in harmony with nature and a just God.

The style of Hesiod is the oral-epic style of Homer. Whether Hesiod utilized writing is not known, but he probably shaped and reshaped his poems for many years. Their final form is somewhat, but probably not radically, different from what we read. Catalogue poetry such as the *Theogony*, didactic verse such as the *Works and Days*, will have its wearisome moments for moderns. But—to name only a sample—the opening portions of both poems, and the description of Zeus's battle with the Titans and of the Underworld in the *Theogony* are exceedingly powerful reflections of apocalyptic inspiration.

—William Merritt Sale

HESSE, Hermann. Born in Calw, Württemberg, 2 July 1877. Educated at Basel Mission; Rector Otto Bauer's Latin school, Göppingen, 1890-91; Protestant Seminary, Maulbronn, 1891-92; Cannstatt Gymnasium, 1892-93. Volunteer Worker, as editor of books and magazines for prisoners of war in Switzerland during World War I. Married 1) Marie Bernoulli in 1904 (divorced, 1923), three sons; 2) Ruth Wenger in 1924 (divorced, 1927); 3) Ninon Auslander Boldin in 1931. Clock factory apprentice, Calw, 1894-95; apprentice, 1895-98, then assistant, 1898-99, Heckenhauer Bookshop, Tübingen; worked for bookdealers in Basel, 1899-1903; free-lance writer from 1903: Editor, *März*, 1907-15; Co-Editor, *Vivos Voco*, 1919-20; also editor of publishers' book series in 1910's and 1920's; regular contributor to *Carona* and *Bonniers Litterära Magasin* in 1930's. Lived in Gaienhofen, Germany, 1904-12, near Bern, Switzerland, 1912-19, and Montagnola, Switzerland, 1919-62. Recipient: Bauernfeldpreis (Vienna), 1904; Fontane Prize (refused), 1919; Keller Prize, 1936; Nobel Prize for Literature, 1946; Goethe Prize, 1946; Wilhelm Raabe Prize, 1950; German Book Trade Peace Prize, 1955. Honorary doctorate: University of Bern, 1947. *Died 9 August 1962.*

Pᴜʙʟɪᴄᴀᴛɪᴏɴꜱ

Collections

Gesammelte Werke. 12 vols., 1970; supplement, 2 vols., 1972.

Fiction

Peter Camenzind. 1904; translated as *Peter Camenzind,* 1961.
Unterm Rad. 1906; as *The Prodigy,* 1957; as *Beneath the Wheel,* 1968.
Diesseits: Erzählungen. 1907; revised edition, 1930.
Nachbarn: Erzählungen. 1908.
Gertrud. 1910; as *Gertrude and I,* 1915; as *Gertrude,* 1955.
Umwege: Erzählungen. 1912.
Anton Schievelbeyns ohn-freywillige Reise nacher Ost-Indien. 1914.
Der Hausierer. 1914.
Rosshalde. 1914; translated as *Rosshalde,* 1970.
Knulp: Drei Geschichten aus dem Leben Knulps. 1915; as *Knulp:Three Tales from the Life of Knulp,* 1971.
Am Weg. 1915.
Schön ist die Jugend: Zwei Erzählungen. 1916.
Hans Dierlamms Lehrzeit. 1916.
Alte Geschichten: Zwei Erzählungen. 1918.
Zwei Märchen. 1919; revised edition, 1946, 1955; as *Strange News from Another Star and Other Tales,* 1972.
Demian: Geschichte einer Jugend. 1919; translated as *Demian,* 1965.
Im Pressel'schen Gartenhaus. 1920.
Klingsors Letzter Sommer: Erzählungen. 1920; as *Klingsor's Last Summer,* 1970.
Siddhartha: Eine indische Dichtung. 1922; translated as *Siddhartha,* 1951.
Psychologia balnearia; oder, Glossen eines Badener Kurgastes. 1924; as *Kurgast,* 1925.
Die Verlogung: Erzählungen. 1924.
Der Steppenwolf. 1927; translated as *Steppenwolf,* 1929.
Narziss und Goldmund. 1930; as *Death and the Lover,* 1932; as *Goldmund,* 1959; as *Narcissus and Goldmund,* 1968.
Die Morgenlandfahrt. 1932; as *The Journey to the East,* 1956.
Kleine Welt: Erzählungen. 1933.

Fabulierbuch: Erzählungen. 1935.
Das Glasperlenspiel. 1943; as *Magister Ludi,* 1949; as *The Glass Bead Game,* 1969.
Der Pfirsichbaum und andere Erzählungen. 1945.
Traumfährte: Neue Erzählungen und Märchen. 1945.
Berthold: Ein Romanfragment. 1945.
Glück (collection). 1952.
Zwei jugendliche Erzählungen. 1957.
Freunde: Erzählungen. 1957.
Geheimnisse: Letzte Erzählungen. 1964.
Erwin. 1965.
Aus Kinderzeiten und andere Erzählungen. 1968.
Stories of Five Decades, edited by Theodore Ziolkowski. 1972.
Die Erzählungen. 2 vols., 1973.

Verse

Romantische Lieder. 1899.
Hinterlassene Schriften und Gedichte. 1901.
Gedichte. 1902.
Unterwegs. 1911.
Musik des Einsamen: Neue Gedichte. 1915.
Gedichte des Malers. 1920.
Ausgewählte Gedichte. 1921.
Trost der Nacht: Neue Gedichte. 1929.
Vom Baum des Lebens: Ausgewählte Gedichte. 1934.
Das Haus der Träume. 1936.
Stunden im Garten: Eine Idylle. 1936.
Neue Gedichte. 1937.
Die Gedichte. 1942.
Der Blütenzweig: Eine Auswahl aus den Gedichten. 1945.
Bericht an die Freunde: Letzte Gedichte. 1961.
Die späten Gedichte. 1963.
Poems, translated by James Wright. 1970.
Hours in the Garden and Other Poems, translated by R. Lesser. 1979.

Other

Eine Stunde hinter Mitternacht. 1899.
Boccaccio. 1904.
Franz von Assisi. 1904.
Aus Indien: Aufzeichnungen von einer indische Reise. 1913.
Zum Sieg. 1915.
Brief ins Feld. 1916.
Zarathustras Wiederkehr: Ein Wort an die deutsche Jugend. 1919.
Kleiner Garten: Erlebnisse und Dichtungen. 1919.
Wanderung: Aufzeichnungen. 1920; as *Wandering: Notes and Sketches,* 1972.
Blick ins Chaos: Drei Aufsätze. 1920; as *In Sight of Chaos,* 1923.
Elf Aquarelle aus dem Tessin. 1921.
Sinclairs Notizbuch. 1923.
Erinnerung an Lektüre. 1925.
Bilderbuch: Schilderungen. 1926.
Die schwere Weg. 1927.
Die Nürnberger Reise. 1927.

Betrachtungen. 1928.
Krisis: Ein Stück Tagebuch. 1928; translated as *Crisis,* 1975.
Eine Bibliothek der Weltliteratur. 1929; revised edition, 1957.
Zum Gedächtnis unseres Vaters, with Adele Hesse. 1930.
Gedenkblätter. 1937.
Aus der Kindheit der heiligen Franz von Assisi. 1938.
Der Novalis: Aus den Papieren eines Altmodischen. 1940.
Kleine Betrachtungen: Sechs Aufsätze. 1941.
Dank an Goethe. 1946.
Der Europäer. 1946.
Krieg und Frieden: Betrachtungen zu Krieg und Politik seit dem Jahr 1914. 1946; revised edition, 1949; as *If the War Goes On...: Reflections on War and Politics,* 1971.
Stufen der Menschwerdung. 1947.
Frühe Prosa. 1948.
Berg und See: Zwei Landschaftsstudien. 1948.
Gerbersau. 2 vols., 1949.
Aus vielen Jahren. 1949.
Späte Prosa. 1951.
Briefe. 1951; revised edition, 1959, 1964.
Eine Handvoll Briefe. 1951.
Über das Alter. 1954.
Briefe, with Romain Rolland. 1954.
Aquarelle aus dem Tessin. 1955.
Beschwörungen: Späte Prosa, Neue Folge. 1955.
Abendwolken: Zwei Aufsätze. 1956.
Aus einem Tagebuch des Jahres 1920. 1960.
Aerzte: Ein paar Erinnerungen. 1963.
Prosa aus dem Nachlass, edited by Ninon Hesse. 1965.
Neue deutscher Bücher. 1965.
Kindheit und Jugend vor Neunzehnhundert, edited by Ninon Hesse. 1966.
Briefwechsel, with Thomas Mann, edited by Anni Carlsson. 1968; revised edition, 1975; as *Letters,* 1975.
Briefwechsel 1945-1959, with Peter Suhrkamp, edited by Siegfried Unseld. 1969.
Politische Betrachtungen. 1970.
Beschreibung einer Landschaft. 1971.
Lektüre für Minuten, edited by Volker Michels. 1971; as *Reflections,* 1974.
Meine Glaube, edited by Siegfried Unseld. 1971; as *My Belief,* 1974.
Zwei Autorenporträts in Briefen 1897 bis 1900: Hesse—Helene Voigt-Diederichs. 1971.
Eigensinn: Autobiographische Schriften, edited by Siegfried Unseld. 1972; as *Autobiographical Writings,* edited by Theodore Ziolkowski, 1972.
Briefwechsel aus der Nähe, with Karl Kerenyi, edited by Magda Kerenyi. 1972.
Die Kunst des Müsiggangs: Kurze Prosa aus dem Nachlass, edited by Volker Michels. 1973.
Gesammelte Briefe, edited by Ursula and Volker Michels. 1973—.
Briefwechsel, with R.J. Humm, edited by Ursula and Volker Michels. 1977.
Briefwechsel 1924-1934, with Heinrich Wiegand, edited by Klaus Pezold. 1978.

*

Bibliography: *Hesse: Biography and Bibliography* by Joseph Mileck, 2 vols., 1977.

Critical Studies: *Faith from the Abyss: Hesse's Way from Romanticism to Modernity* by Ernst Rose, 1965; *The Novels of Hesse,* 1965, and *Hesse,* 1966, both by Theodore Ziolkowski, and *Hesse: A Collection of Critical Essays,* edited by Ziolkowski, 1973; *Hesse: His Mind and Art* by Mark Boulby, 1966; *Hesse* by G.W Field, 1970; *Hesse: An Illustrated Biography* by Bernhard Zeller, 1971; *Hesse* by Edwin F. Basebeer, 1972; *Hesse's Futuristic Idealism* by

Roger C. Norton, 1973; *Hesse, The Man Who Sought and Found Himself* by Walter Sorrell, 1974; *Hesse: A Pictorial Biography* by Volker Michels, 1975; *Hesse: His Life and Art* by Joseph Mileck, 1978.

* * *

Hermann Hesse's work has roots in many areas of culture, especially German Romanticism and Eastern religious philosophy. It has always appealed particularly to the young because of its recurrent stress—already perhaps implied in these sources—on breaking barriers, on the individual's need to emancipate itself from all ties and follow its own star. In his first major work, *Demian*, Hesse employs striking Old Testament and gnostic symbolism, reminiscent of Expressionism's emotive simplicity, to depict his typical hero: the man who learns to accept and so channel the unconventional, even a-moral, complexity of his soul. A heady optimism attaches to his "rebirth," which then becomes tempered over the years. Already in *Siddhartha*, another stylised but gentler picture of the search for self, this is so. The new Eastern idiom indicates a new depth of understanding: the goal of self-overcoming is attainable but the search is lifelong. Perhaps the most remarkable aspect of this novel is its beautifully sustained imagery and simplicity of style. It is here that Hesse first shows himself a master of the German language: it flows with wonderful euphony, and elsewhere—as in *Klingsor's Last Summer*—can attain a splendidly rich sensuousness.

Hesse's next major work was *Steppenwolf*, perhaps his best-known novel but one marked by deep pessimism. It is a remarkable portrayal in strong visual, almost psychedelic images of the agonising simultaneity of violent oppositions in one and the same personality, for whom life becomes a battle between the longing for simple security and the painful awareness of inner division. The novel's most extraordinary feature is perhaps its ruthless honesty: where in earlier works the less "acceptable" aspects of personality are portrayed as sensuality or Nietzschean will-power, here the depths of degradation are plumbed from aggressive sexuality to bestial destructiveness. It also raises interesting aesthetic questions about the presentation of simultaneity in epic form, which Hesse returns to in *Nürnberger Reise*.

Surprisingly, Hesse's next novel *Narcissus and Goldmund* lacks all such complexity; set in medieval times, it tells an allegorical tale of two friends, artist and intellectual, and their different processes of self-discovery. While charming in its narrative simplicity, it lacks conviction at a deeper level, especially when compared with Hesse's great novel *The Glass Bead Game*. This summation of all Hesse's inspiration from Goethe to the Orient projects the theme of personal multiplicity onto a cultural plane, and explores the grandiose possibility of harmonising all knowledge, only to raise many profound questions about the relationship between intellect and practical activity, insight and realization, harmony and extremism, culture and barbarism, stasis and progress.

In addition to these major works Hesse produced many short stories, autobiographical sketches, and essays of great delicacy and perceptive insight into himself and his age. His poetry, while lacking the originality of his prose, still has the power to charm by its romantic sensitivity to nature and inwardness of imagery. Some of it has indeed been set to music, notably by Richard Strauss (*Four Last Songs*).

—Mary E. Stewart

HOFFMANN, E(rnst) T(heodore) A(madeus). Born Ernst Theodore Wilhelm Hoffmann in Königsberg, 24 January 1776. Educated at Burgschule, Königsberg, 1782-92; studied law at University of Königsberg, 1792-95. Married Maria Thekla Michalina Rorer-Trzynska in 1802; one daughter. In legal civil service: posts in Glogau, 1796-98, Berlin, 1798-1800, Posen, 1800-02, Plozk, 1802-04, Warsaw, 1804-08, and, after Napoleon's defeat, Berlin, 1814-22. Also a composer: Kappellmeister, 1808-09, house composer and designer, 1810-12, Bamberg Theatre, and conductor for Sekonda Company, Leipzig and Dresden, 1813-14; composer of operas, and editor of musical works by Beethoven, Mozart, Gluck, and others, 1809-21. *Died 25 June 1822.*

PUBLICATIONS

Collections

> *Werke*, edited by Georg Ellinger. 15 vols., 1927.
> *Sämtliche Werke*, edited by Walter Müller-Seidel and others. 5 vols., 1960-65.

Fiction

> *Fantasiestücke in Callots manier.* 4 vols., 1814-15.
> *Die Elixiere des Teufels.* 1815-16.
> *Nachtstücke.* 2 vols., 1817.
> *Seltsame Leiden eines Theater-Direktors.* 1819.
> *Klein Zaches genannt Zinnober.* 1819.
> *Die Serapions-Brüder: Gesammelte Erzählungen und Märchen.* 4 vols., 1819-21; as *The Serapion Brethren*, 1886-92.
> *Lebens-Ansichten des Katers Murr.* 1820-22.
> *Prinzessen Brambilla.* 1821.
> *Meister Floh.* 1822.
> *Die Letzten Erzählungen.* 2 vols., 1825.
> *Tales*, edited by Christopher Lazare. 1960.
> *Tales*, translated by James Kirkup. 1966.
> *Tales*, edited by R.J. Hollingdale. 1982.

Play

> *Die Maske*, edited by Friedrich Schnapp. 1923.

Verse

> *Poetische Werke*, edited by Gerhard Seidel. 6 vols., 1958.

Other

> *Die Vision auf dem Schlachtfelde bei Dresden.* 1814.
> *Briefwechsel*, edited by Hans von Müller and Friedrich Schnapp. 3 vols, 1967-69.
> *Selected Writings*, edited by Leonard J. Kent and Elizabeth C. Knight. 2 vols., 1969.
> *Tagebücher*, edited by Friedrich Schnapp. 1971.
> *Juristische Arbeiten*, edited by Friedrich Schnapp. 1973.

*

Bibliography: *Hoffmann: Bibliographie* by Gerhard Salomon, 1963.

Critical Studies: *Hoffmann, Author of the Tales* by H. Hewett-Taylor, 1948; *Hoffmann* by Ronald Taylor, 1963; *Hoffmann's Other World: The Romantic Author and His "New Mythology"* by Kenneth Negus, 1965; *Music: The Medium of the Metaphysical in Hoffmann* by Pauline Watts, 1972; *The Shattered Self: Hoffmann's Tragic Vision* by Horst S. Daemmrich, 1973; *Hoffmann and the Rhetoric of Terror* by Elizabeth Wright, 1978; *Spellbound: Studies on Mesmerism and Literature* by Maria M. Tatar, 1978; *Baudelaire et Hoffmann* by Rosemary Lloyd, 1979; *Mysticism and Sexuality: Hoffmann* by James M. McGlathery, 1981.

*   *   *

Hoffmann is one of the few authors belonging to German Romanticism who has attained international status. As an exponent of "black Romanticism," as it is called in Europe, he was hailed by Baudelaire and scorned by Sir Walter Scott for his preoccupation with the grotesque and the bizarre. He managed to combine this trait with, on the one hand, the most astringent satire, criticizing the injustices of his day in *Master Flea*, and on the other hand, with a modern concern regarding a writer's identity in *The Life and Opinions of Tomcat Murr*.

He made the best possible use of the literary conventions of his day, such as the popular Gothic novel, the epistolary novel, and the short story or novella. He was a diarist, a keen letter-writer; like most of his fellow-Romanticists he constantly reflected on what he did and on how and why he did it. Interspersed with his fictional writings he developed a theory of representation which accounts for the artist's fascination and concern with subjective phenomena, what he called his "inner world," and he argued that the persuasiveness of the artist's vision depended on his ability to project this world accurately into the external. But it also depended on a reader, playfully addressed by the narrator as "dear reader," and placed within the fictional world of the novel, an example of Romantic irony whereby the artist asserted his supremacy. This reader was expected to suspend disbelief and to open himself up to the experience offered by the novels and stories.

Hoffmann's modernity rests in the powerful description of this inner world, later systematically examined by Freud's new science of the mind, a science not like the physical sciences but like the human ones, depending on interpretation of subjective phenomena. One of Freud's key essays, "The Uncanny," uses one of Hoffmann's stories, "The Sandman," in order to capture a certain kind of aesthetic experience. Hoffmann was himself interested in parapsychological phenomena of all kinds, being well acquainted with the work of Anton Mesmer, who played a key role in the history of medicine and psychoanalysis. Hoffmann wrote a number of stories about strange characters, hypnotized and possessed by powerful and threatening figures.

A major theme in Hoffmann's work is that of the divided self, now almost a cliché of Hoffmann scholarship. Whereas in Goethe's *Faust* this can be seen as a benign split, in Hoffmann's work it is usually catastrophic, a prime instance being *The Elixirs of the Devil*, though it sometimes resolves itself ironically, as in *The Golden Pot*, or satirically, as in *Princess Brambilla*. The split is between the hero's desire to belong to the world of art and music, and his desire to partake of the pleasures and security of the life of an average citizen. These dual desires manifest themselves in a simultaneous love for two different women, an idealized figure, usually connected with the world of art and music, and a domestic figure who promises the joys of marriage. This precarious stance also parallels the situation in Hoffmann's life, where he simultaneously maintained a satisfactory marriage and an unconsummated but passionate love for an erstwhile music pupil, from the days when he earned his living by giving music lessons. He was similarly divided in his profession, earning his living in one sphere and following his bent in another, the career of civil servant later replacing that of music teacher.

Those who do not recognize him as an author may be acquainted with him as the inspiration behind Offenbach's opera *The Tales of Hoffmann* and Delibes's ballet *Coppélia*.

—Elizabeth Wright

HOFMANNSTHAL, Hugo (Laurenz August Hofmann, Edler) von. Born in Vienna, 1 February 1874. Educated at Akademischen Gymnasium, Vienna, 1884-92; studied law, 1892-94; and romantic philology: dissertation on Pléiade poets, 1897, and habilitation work on Hugo, 1900-01, University of Vienna. Served with 6th Dragoon Regiment in Göding, 1894-95. Married Gertrud Schlesinger in 1901; one daughter, two sons. Writer: Editor, Österreichische Bibliothek, 1915-17; founder, with Max Reinhardt, Salzburg Festival, 1919. *Died 15 July 1929.*

PUBLICATIONS

Collections

> *Gesammelte Werke in Einzelausgaben,* edited by Herbert Steiner. 15 vols., 1945-59.
> *Selected Writings: Prose, Plays and Libretti, Poems and Verse Plays.* 3 vols., 1952-63.

Plays

> *Gestern.* 1896.
> *Der weisse Fächer* (produced 1897). 1907.
> *Der Abenteurer und die Sängerin* (produced 1898). 1899; revised version, 1909.
> *Die Frau im Fenster* (produced 1898). In *Theater in Versen,* 1899.
> *Theater in Versen.* 1899.
> *Die Hochzeit der Sobeide* (as *Sobeide, Abenteurer,* produced 1899). 1899; as *The Marriage of Zobeide,* in *Selected Writings,* 1961.
> *Das Bergwerk zu Falun,* from a story by E.T.A. Hoffmann (produced 1899). 1933; as *The Mine at Falun,* in *Selected Writings,* 1961.
> *Der Kaiser und die Hexe* (produced 1900). 1900; as *The Emperor and the Witch,* in *Selected Writings,* 1961.
> *Der Thor und der Tod* (produced 1908). 1900; as *Death and the Fool,* 1914.
> *Der Tod der Tizian.* 1901; as *The Death of Titian,* 1920.
> *Elektra* (produced 1903). 1904; revised version, music by Strauss (produced 1909), 1908; translated as *Electra,* in *Selected Writings,* 1963.
> *Das kleine Welttheater; oder, Die Glücklichen.* 1903; as *The Little Theatre of the World,* in *Selected Writings,* 1961.
> *Das Gerettete Venedig,* from the play *Venice Preserved* by Otway (produced 1905). 1905.
> *Ödipus und die Sphinx* (produced 1905). 1906.
> *Kleine Dramen.* 2 vols., 1906-07.
> *Vorspiele.* 1908.
> *Christinas Heimreise* (produced 1910). 1910.
> *König Ödipus,* from the play by Sophocles (produced 1910). 1910.
> *Alkestis,* from the play by Euripides, music by Egon Wellesz (produced 1924). 1911.
> *Der Rosenkavalier,* music by Strauss (produced 1911). 1911; edited by Willi Schuh, 1971; as *The Cavalier of the Rose,* in *Selected Writings,* 1963.
> *Jedermann: Das Spiel von Sterben des reichen Mannes* (produced 1911). 1911; as *The Salzburg Everyman,* 1930.
> *Ariadne auf Naxos,* music by Strauss (produced 1912). 1912; revised version (produced 1916), 1916; as *Ariadne on Naxos,* 1912.
> *Josephs Legende* (ballet scenario), with Harry Graf Kessler, music by Strauss (produced 1914). 1914.
> *Die Frau ohne Schatten,* music by Strauss (produced 1919). 1916.
> *Die Lästigen,* from a play by Molière (produced 1916).
> *Der Bürger als Edelmann,* from a play by Molière. 1918.
> *Lucidor.* 1919.

Dame Kobold, from a play by Calderón. 1920.
Der Schwierige (produced 1921). 1921; as *The Difficult Man*, in *Selected Writings*, 1963.
Das Salzburger Grosse Welttheater, from a play by Calderón (produced 1922). 1922.
Die grüne Flöte (ballet scenario). 1923.
Prima Ballerina (ballet scenario). 1923(?).
Florindo. 1923.
Der Unbestechliche (produced 1923). With *Der Schwierige*, 1958.
Die Ruinen von Athen. 1925.
Der Turm, from a play by Calderón. 1925; revised version (produced 1928), 1927; as *The Tower*, in *Selected Writings*, 1963.
Die ägyptische Helena, music by Strauss (produced 1928). 1928.
Semiramis: Die Beiden Götter. 1933.
Arabella, music by Strauss (produced 1933). 1933; translated as *Arabella*, in *Selected Writings*, 1963.
Dramatische Entwürfe aus dem Nachlass, edited by Heinrich Zimmer. 1936.
Danae; oder, Die Vernunftheirat. 1952.

Fiction

Prinz Eugen der edle Ritter. 1905.
Das Märchen der 672. Nacht und andere Erzählungen. 1905.
Die Frau ohne Schatten. 1919.
Andreas; oder, Die Vereinigten. 1932; as *Andreas; or, The United*, 1936.

Verse

Ausgewählte Gedichte. 1903.
Die gesammelten Gedichte. 1907.
Die Gedichte und kleinen Dramen. 1911.
Lyrical Poems, translated by Charles Wharton Stork. 1918.
Gedichte. 1922.
Nachlese der Gedichte. 1934.

Other

Stüdie über die Entwickelung des Dichters Victor Hugo. 1901; as *Versuch über Victor Hugo*, 1925.
Unterhaltungen über literarische Gegenstände. 1904.
Victor Hugo. 1904.
Die prosaischen Schriften gesammelt. 2 vols., 1907; 3rd vol., 1917.
Hesperus: Ein Jahrbuch, with Rudolf Borchardt and Rudolf Alexander Schröder. 1909.
Grete Wiesenthal in Amor und Psyche und Das Fremde Mädchen. 1911.
Die Wege und die Begegnungen. 1913.
Rodauner Nachtrage. 3 vols., 1918.
Reden und Aufsätze. 1921.
Buch der Freunde. 1922; edited by Ernst Zinn, 1965.
Gesammelte Werke. 6 vols., 1924; revised edition, 3 vols., 1934.
Augenblicke in Griechenland. 1924.
Früheste Prosastücke. 1926.
Grillparzers politisches Vermächtnis. 1926.
Loris: Die Prosa des Jungen Hoffmansthals. 1930.

Die Berührung der Sphären. 1931.
Briefe. 2 vols., 1935-37.
Briefwechsel, with Anton Wildgans, edited by Joseph A. von Bradish. 1935.
Briefwechsel, with Stefan George, edited by Robert Boehringer. 1938; revised edition, 1953.
Briefwechsel, with Richard Strauss, edited by Franz and Alice Strauss. 1952; revised edition, edited by Willi Schuh, 1954; as *Correspondence,* 1961.
Briefe der Freundschaft, with Eberhard von Bodenhausen, edited by Dora von Bodenhausen. 1953.
Briefwechsel, with Rudolf Borchardt, edited by Marie Luise Borchardt and Herbert Steiner. 1954.
Briefwechsel, with Carl J. Burckhardt, edited by Burckhardt. 1956.
Sylvia in "Stern," edited by Martin Stern. 1959.
Briefwechsel, with Arthur Schnitzler, edited by Theresa Nickl and Heinrich Schnitzler. 1964.
Briefwechsel, with Helene von Nostitz, edited by Oswalt von Nostitz. 1965.
Briefwechsel, with Edgar Karl von Bebenburg, edited by Mary E. Gilbert. 1966.
Briefwechsel, with Max Rycher, Samuel and Hedwig Fischer, Oscar Bie, and Moritz Heimann, edited by Claudia Mertz-Rycher and others. 1973.
Briefwechsel, with Ottonie Gräfin Degenfeld, edited by Marie Therese Miller-Degenfeld. 1974.
Briefwechsel 1899-1925, with Rainer Maria Rilke, edited by Rudolf Hirsch and Ingeborg Schnack. 1978.
Briefwechsel, with Max Mell, edited by Margret Dietrich and Heinz Kindermann, 1982.
Briefwechsel, with Ria Schmujlow-Claasen. 1982.

*

Bibliography: *Hofmannsthal: Bibliographie des Schrifttums 1892-1963* by Horst Weber, 1961.

Critical Studies: *Hofmannsthal* by Hans Hammelmann, 1957; *Hofmannsthal's Festival Dramas* by B. Coughlin, 1964; *Hofmannsthal: Three Essays* by Michael Hamburger, 1972; *Hofmannsthal and the French Symbolist Tradition* by Steven P. Sondrup, 1976; *Hofmannsthal* by Lowell A. Bangerter, 1977; *The Banal Object: Theme and Thematics in Proust, Rilke, Hofmannsthal, and Sartre* by Naomi Segal, 1981.

*　　*　　*

Hugo von Hofmannsthal is chiefly remembered as the successful librettist who partnered Richard Strauss. Their operas, including the famous *Der Rosenkavalier,* are lively and powerful, rich in register and motif.

Hofmannsthal's fame, however, neither begins nor ends with Strauss. He had enjoyed some 15 years of precocious celebrity before their collaboration began. His schoolboy lyrics established his reputation as one of the foremost young poets in Vienna. Even his earliest works, among them *Gestern* ("Yesterday"), *Death and the Fool,* and *The Marriage of Zobeide,* reveal his remarkable insight into some of the questions most crucial to man: the passing of time, the problem of death, the dangers of excessive aestheticism, the role of women in society. His range, even in the 1890's, is vast.

The turn of the century brought a change of style. There were several reasons for this change. One, metaphysical, reason prompting him to abandon his lyrical mode is expressed in the fictitious *Chandos-Letter* of 1902. A more immediate reason can be found in his desire to stage his dramas more successfully. They made good reading, but as theatre they were indicted by critics as "lukewarm" and "boring." Hofmannsthal began to write with a specific theatre in mind, that of Max Reinhardt in Berlin. He made increasing use of stage technology in order to enhance the sensuous impact of his works. Lighting, music, the rhythms of movement are all incorporated into the text, as the stage directions of the powerfully visual *Elektra* demonstrate.

Further factors influencing Hofmannsthal's change of style include the literary trend of "anti-erotic" writers such as Wilde, Strindberg, and Wedekind, and also the writings of Freud. Their influence shows most overtly in the so-called "Greek" plays, *Elektra* and *Oedipus and the Sphinx*, where Hofmannsthal probes the depths of sexual antagonism, repression, and perversion—a radical departure from his Sophocleian model. Greek myth is here used to underline the most primitive aspects of human behaviour. Hofmannsthal was to return to the symbolic world of myth in his operas *Ariadne on Naxos* and *Die Ägyptische Helena*, explaining in his late essay on the latter work that mythological opera was the only form in which the "atmosphere of the present" could be expressed adequately.

Hofmannsthal had already explored other possible modes of expression. Moving away from the "armchair playlets" of the 1890's, and the Greek plays of 1903 and 1905, he wrote his *Everyman*, and *The Great Salzburg Theatre of the World*, expressing fundamental human truths in the universalising form of the medieval mystery play. Social satires, such as *The Difficult Man*, again treat universal themes, but this time in the context of modern Austria. Yet another mode is the magical setting of *Die Frau ohne Schatten*, and of *The Tower* which, with its oblique references to politics and its background of language scepticism, constitutes one of Hofmannsthal's most difficult plays.

The range and density of Hofmannsthal's poems and plays, essays and correspondence, account for the continuing interest in these works today.

—Sally McMullen (Croft)

HOLBERG, Ludvig. Born in Bergen, 3 December 1684. Studied at school and university in Bergen; University of Copenhagen, 1702-04; traveled in Holland and Germany, 1704-06; traveled in England, and studied in Oxford and London, 1706-08; tutor in Germany, 1708-09; at Borch's College, Copenhagen, 1709-14; appointed unpaid associate professor at University of Copenhagen, 1714; but spent the time of the appointment traveling in Low Countries, Paris, and Rome, 1714-16; Professor of Metaphysics, 1717, Professor of Latin, 1720, Member of the University Council, 1720, Professor of History and Geography, 1730, and University Bursar (*quaestor*), 1737-51, University of Copenhagen. Wrote for the newly organized Danish Theatre in Copenhagen, especially 1722-28 and, after a lapse during the reign of Christian VI, from 1747. Made a baron, 1747. *Died 28 January 1754.*

PUBLICATIONS

Collections

Samlede Skrifter, edited by Carl S. Petersen. 18 vols., 1913-62.

Verse

Peder Paars. 2 vols., 1719-20; translated in part as *Peder Paars*, 1862; complete version, 1962.
Opuscula latina. 2 vols., 1737-43.
Mindre poetiske skrifter. 1746.

Plays (selection)

Comedier. 3 vols., 1723-25; revised edition, as *Den danske skue: Plads*, 5 vols., 1731-54; these collections include all the plays cited below.
Diderich Menchenschreck, as *Captain Bombastes Thunderton*, in *Three Comedies*, 1912; as *Diderich the Terrible*, in *Seven One-Act Plays*, 1950.
Erasmus Montanus, translated as *Erasmus Montanus*, 1885.
Den forvandlede Brudgom, as *The Changed Bridegroom*, in *Seven One-Act Plays*, 1950.
Henrik og Pernille, translated as *Heinrich and Pernille*, in *Three Comedies*, 1912.
Jeppe paa Bjerget, as *Jeppe of the Hill*, in *Comedies*, 1914.
Julestuen, as *The Christmas Party*, in *Seven One-Act Plays*, 1950.
Kilderejsen, as *The Healing Spring*, in *Three Comedies*, 1957.
Mascarade, translated as *Masquerade*, in *Four Plays*, 1946.
Mester Gert Westphaler, as *The Talkative Barber*, in *Seven One-Act Plays*, 1950.
Den pantsatte bondedreng, as *The Peasant in Pawn*, in *Seven One-Act Plays*, 1950; as *The Transformed Peasant*, in *Three Comedies*, 1957.
Den politiske Kandestøber, as *The Blue-Apron Statesman*, 1885; as *The Political Tinker*, in *Comedies*, 1914.
Det arabiske Pulver, as *The Arabian Powder*, in *Seven One-Act Plays*, 1950.
Sganarels reyse til det Philosophiske Land, as *Sganarel's Journey to the Land of the Philosophers*, in *Seven One-Act Plays*, 1950.
Den Stundelose, as *Scatterbrains*, in *Three Comedies*, 1912; as *The Fussy Man*, in *Four Plays*, 1946.
De usynlige, as *The Masked Ladies*, in *Four Plays*, 1946.
Den Voegelsindede, as *The Weathercock*, in *Four Plays*, 1946.

Fiction

Nicolai Klimii iter subterraneum [Niels Klim] (in Latin). 1741; as *A Journey to the World Under-Ground*, 1742; as *Niels Klim's Journey Under the Ground*, 1845.

Other

Introduction til de formemste Europaeiske Rigers Historier. 1711; revised edition, 1728.
Introduction til Natur-og Folke-Retten [Introduction to Natural Law]. 1715; revised edition, 1734.
Epistola ad virum perillustrem. 1728.
Dannemarks og Norges Beskrivelse. 1729; translated in part as *The History of Norway*, 1817.
Dannemarks Riges Historie [History of the Kingdom of Denmark]. 1732-35.
Synopsis Historiae Universalis. 1733; as *An Introduction to Universal History*, 1755.
Bergens Beskrivelse [Description of Bergen]. 1737.
Almindelig Kirkehistorie [General Church History]. 1738.
Heltehistorier [Achievements of Great Men]. 1739.
Jødiske Historie [History of the Jews]. 2 vols., 1742.
Moralske tanker [Moral Thoughts]. 1744; edited by F.J. Billeskov Jansen, 1943.
Heltindehistorier [Comparative History of Famous Women]. 1745.
Epistler. 2 vols., 1748-54; edited by F.J. Billeskov Jansen, 8 vols., 1944-54; translated in part as *Selected Essays*, edited by P.M. Mitchell, 1955.
Moralske Fabler [Moral Fables]. 1751.
Remarques sur quelques positions qui se trouvent dans l'Esprit des loi (written in French). 1753.

Memoirs (translation based on various sections of works). 1827; edited by Stewart E.
   Fraser, 1970.
Memoirer, edited by F.J. Billeskov Jansen. 1943.

Translator, *Herodiani historie*. 1746.

                                    *

Critical Studies: *The Comedies of Holberg* by Oscar James Campbell, Jr., 1914; *Holberg* by
F.J. Billeskov Jansen, 1974.

                          *   *   *

When Holberg wrote his first comedies in 1722, there was effectively no tradition of
playwriting in Scandinavia to which he could turn for inspiration. He was at the time a
much-travelled scholar, recently appointed to the Chair of Metaphysics at the University of
Copenhagen. He felt a deep sympathy with the rationalist, conservative ethos of French
neo-classicism, and it was accordingly to the work of Molière that he looked for dramatic
inspiration. Between 1722 and 1723, he wrote some 15 comedies, all of which, in the best of
neo-classic traditions, brilliantly satirise socially deviant behaviour in a way that is both
entertaining and yet unmistakably didactic. Holberg uses the weapons of ridicule and irony to
highlight the folly of characters such as the feckless peasant in *Jeppe of the Hill*, the know-all
amateur politician in *The Political Tinker* and the pretentious undergraduate from peasant
stock in *Erasmus Montanus*. Like Molière, Holberg felt an obvious sympathy for his unfortunate victims, never losing sight of the transparently human qualities of even his most outrageous fools. This gives his plays, underneath the satiric thrust, a feeling of warmth, at times
almost endearment.

Holberg was a precise observer of human behaviour, and his plays faithfully reflect the
unsophisticated earthiness of peasant and middle-class culture in 18th-century Denmark.
Despite the classical framework, his plays are manifestly Danish in sprit and texture. (Which
may explain why so few of them have been performed in England.) This is as true of the
boasting warrior plays modelled on Plautus, such as *Diderich the Terrible* or *Jacob von Tyboe*,
as it is of plays like *The Fuss-Pot* or *The Weathercock*, modelled on *Le Malade imaginaire* by
Molière.

Holberg had begun his literary career with a mock epic poem in 1720 called *Peder Paars*.
Based on the *Aeneid*, it follows the mock heroic journey of Peder Paars between two Danish
provincial towns, Kallundborg and Aarhus. His comedies were written in 1722 at the invitation
of a French actor called Montaigu who was given a licence to set up the first public theatre in
Copenhagen with Danish actors. After the theatre went bankrupt in 1727, Holberg concentrated on his academic duties, publishing a number of important historical works. In 1740, he
wrote a long satirical novel in the style of Swift called *Niels Klim's Journey to the World
Underground* and, in 1744, published a collection of essays called *Moral Thoughts*, similar in
tone to those of Addison in *The Spectator*.

When a new theatre was established in Copenhagen in 1748, with the official title of The
Theatre Royal, Holberg wrote a set of six new comedies to celebrate the occasion. However,
these late plays lack the charm and appeal of his early work. His satiric, neo-classic approach to
comedy was out of tune with an age that was increasingly embracing the liberal, sentimental
values of English and French writers. By now a Baron and a conservative pillar of the
establishment, Holberg, in 1748, found himself writing for a culture that no longer existed.
However, his fame as the founding father of Danish comedy was beyond question. And still
today, his plays occupy an important and much-loved place on the repertoire of The Theatre
Royal in Copenhagen.

—David Thomas

HÖLDERLIN, (Johann Christian) Friedrich. Born in Lauffen, 20 March 1770. Educated at Latin school, Nürtingen, 1774-84; theological seminary, Denkendorff, 1784-86, and Maulbronn, 1786-88; Tübingen Seminary, 1788-93, Master of Philosophy, 1790. Tutor to son of Charlotte von Kalb, in Waltershausen, 1793-94, and in Weimar, 1794-95; lived in Jena, 1795; tutor to son of Herr Gontard, Frankfurt, 1795-98; tutor in house of Herr Honzenbach, Hauptweil, Switzerland, 1801, and of a German official in Bordeaux, 1801-02. Mentally ill after 1805: confined first in clinic in Tübingen, 1806-07, and privately after 1807.

PUBLICATIONS

Collections

Sämtliche Werke, edited by Friedrich Beissner.   6 vols., 1943-61.
Sämtliche Werke und Briefe, edited by Günter Mieth.   4 vols., 1970.
Sämtliche Werke, edited by D.E. Sattler.   1976— .

Verse

Selected Poems, translated by J.B. Leishman.   1944.
(Selection), translated by Michael Hamburger.   1952.
Alcaic Poems, translated by Elizabeth Henderson.   1962.
Poems and Fragments, translated by Michael Hamburger.   1966; revised edition, 1980.
Selected Poems (with *Selected Poems* by Mörike), translated by Christopher Middleton. 1972.

Fiction

Hyperion; oder, Der Eremit in Griechenland.   2 vols., 1797-99; translated as *Hyperion*, 1965.

*

Critical Studies: *Hölderlin* by Ronald Peacock, 1938; *Hölderlin* by L.S. Salzberger, 1952; *A Study of Hölderlin* by R.D. Miller, 1958; *Hölderlin's Hyperion: A Critical Reading* by Walter Silz, 1969; *The Young Hölderlin* by Roy C. Shelton, 1973; *Hölderlin's Major Poetry* by Richard Ungar, 1975; *Hölderlin and Goethe* by Eudo C. Mason, 1975; *Hölderlin and Greek Literature* by R.B. Harrison, 1975; *The Significance of Locality in the Poetry of Hölderlin* by David Constantine, 1979.

*   *   *

Poetry—"this most innocent of occupations"—was Friedrich Hölderlin's vocation, and he had from the start the highest ambitions in it. His models as a young man were Pindar, Klopstock, and, closer to home, Schiller—whom he adulated, to his own detriment. He shared with his companions at school and in the *Stift* (several of them highly gifted) a passion for liberty excited by events in France, and a belief that poetry might, in its manner, serve the revolutionary cause. The regime in Württemberg, especially as it touched the students in Tübingen, was oppressive, and poetry served as a medium of revolt. The language of Hölderlin's early poems is often very violent; they depict the beleaguering of the Good, in whatever definition, by the forces of Wrong—of injustice, tyranny, philistinism, etc. In the Tübingen Hymns these oppositions are expressed in abstract terms, and the poetry suffers accordingly.

Hölderlin was educated for the Church but avoided entry into it by taking the customary house-tutor jobs. In the second of these, in Frankfurt, he met and fell in love with Susette Gontard. Through her he found his own true poetic voice; Frankfurt, in a late fragment, he called "the navel of the earth." His first poems for her, whom he addressed as Diotima, are marvellously expressive of love and joy; thereafter, as social circumstances oppressed the lovers, he turned to lament and the determined celebration of the Good he was losing. The loss of Susette confirmed him in his elegiac character.

Hölderlin had been working on the novel *Hyperion* before he met Susette (she had read fragments of it in Schiller's *Thalia*), but meeting her he continued it as their book. "Forgive me that Diotima dies," he wrote. Hyperion, the modern Greek fighting for the recovery of the Hellenic Ideal in the abortive rising of 1770, sees his ideals founder in the bitterest fashion; his attempt to realize them costs him Diotima too. There is almost a will to failure in the book; as though the hero pushes the foreboding that will fail to its ultimate proof, and salvages his ideals out of a wretched reality into the spirit.

Forced to quit the Gontard household Hölderlin held out in nearby Homburg for as long as he could. There he schooled himself for his greatest poetry. He translated Pindar literally, to learn what his own German language might do; he reflected on the nature and practice of poetry, especially the crucial question of how form might express the spirit without imprisoning or travestying it. Further, he worked at the drama *Empedokles*; but having written extensive notes and attempted three versions, he abandoned the work. Attractive though the idea was and although much of the poetry, especially that of the second version, has an exciting vitality, in essence the conception itself was undramatic and could not have been executed satisfactorily.

The world of Hölderlin's mature poetry, of the great hymns and elegies, is conceived in very concrete terms: it can be mapped, it has two poles—Greece and Hesperia—and numerous renowned features—rivers, mountains, islands, and cities. It incorporates a simple idea (deriving from Herder but also from contemporary Pietist beliefs): that the Spirit of Civilization, having flourished in the East and most splendidly in Periclean Athens, will alight and flourish now north of the Alps, in Germany. The Revolutionary Wars, and the momentousness attaching to the turn of the century, inclined the determinedly optimistic Hölderlin to believe in such a renaissance. In his cosmology we inhabit an Age of Night—initiated by Christ, the last of the Greek gods. We are benighted, and await the new daylight; the poet's task is to encourage us not to despair. This benighted age is characterized by restlessness and wandering; an ideal homeland (Hölderlin's childhood Swabia) is a focus of longing. These are not so much ideas or beliefs as poetic images of immense persuasive power; they express certain readily identifiable conditions: alienation, loss, nostalgia. The theme of Hölderlin's poetry is, *in nuce*: love in absence—how to survive and continue to hold to ideals in times of their manifest absence.

It will not do, when reading Hölderlin, simply to abstract the above adumbrated scheme. That is paraphrase. Instead we have to attend to the rhythms of his poetry, which are very subtle. Contradictions (inclination to despair, insistence on hope, longing for the past, assertion of a better future) are expressed less in statement than in rhythm, in the running of the verse itself against the exact constraints of form. His handling of hexameters and the elegiac couplet is infinitely finer than Goethe's or Schiller's. There is a movement of tones in Hölderlin's verse, there are oscillations of feeling, shifts, transitions through discord and harmony. In a sense, the poems do not end; their constituent emotions have been so finely rendered that we feel them to be still in play. There is no neat conclusion, as of a logical argument. There could not be. The spirit resists such finality. In this manner, in what he himself called a "loving conflict," Hölderlin's poetry serves the cause of perpetual renewal, of revolt against oppression, deadness, and despair of whatever kind.

After the time in Bordeaux, after the death of Susette Gontard, Hölderlin's poetic world expanded and disintegrated. It is much to be regretted that his mind, because of illness, could not compose the terrific richness of his last creative years. There are moments of vision unlike any others in his poetry, of an intense sensuousness and particularity.

During his years in the tower, half his life, Hölderlin wrote, very often to order, rhyming stanzas on the view through his window of the Neckar and the fields and hills beyond; or, less successfully, on abstract topics. These last poems are very moving, sometimes in their own flat simplicity (*tension* being a hallmark of the mature poetry) but often, alas, only as documents.

Nobody nowadays would be likely, as earlier generations did, to disregard anything Hölderlin wrote on the grounds of his presumed insanity. In his life and in all his work he is a poet for our times. He confronts us with benightedness, and demonstrates the spirit's will to survive.

—David Constantine

HOMER. Nothing is known of his life: possibly 8th century B.C.; generally thought to have come from Ionia in Asia Minor, specifically Chios or Smyrna; ancient tradition that he was blind may be true.

Publications

Verse

Iliad, edited by Thomas W. Allen. 1931; also edited by W. Leaf, 1900-02; as *The Iliad*, translated by Richmond Lattimore, 1951; also translated by E. Rees, 1977, and, as *The Anger of Achilles*, by Robert Graves, 1959; translated into prose by A.T. Murray (Loeb edition), 1924-25, W.H.D. Rouse, 1938, and E.V. Rieu, 1950.

Odyssey, edited by Thomas W. Allen. 1906; also edited by W.B. Stanford, 1959; as *The Odyssey*, translated by Richmond Lattimore, 1967; also translated by Robert Fitzgerald, 1962, Albert Cook, 1973, E. Rees, 1977, and Walter Shewring, 1980; translated into prose by A.T. Murray (Loeb edition), 1919, T.E. Lawrence, 1932, W.H.D. Rouse, 1938, and E.V. Rieu, 1946.

*

Bibliography: *A Bibliography of Homeric Scholarship 1930-1970* by D.W. Packard, 1973.

Critical Studies: *The Composition of Homer's Odyssey* by W.J. Woodhouse, 1930; *Homer and the Monuments* by H.L. Lorimer, 1950; *The World of Odysseus* by M.I. Finley, 1954; *From Mycenae to Homer* by T.B.L. Webster, 1958; *History and the Homeric Iliad* by Denys Page, 1959; *The Songs of Homer*, 1962 (as *Homer and the Epic*, 1965), and *The Language and Background of Homer*, 1965, both by G.S. Kirk; *A Companion to Homer* edited by A.J.B. Wace and F.H. Stubbings, 1962; *Essays on the Odyssey: Selected Modern Criticism* edited by C.H. Taylor, 1963; *Homer: A Collection of Critical Essays* edited by George Steiner and Robert Fagles, 1963; *The Flexibility of the Homeric Formula*, 1968, and *Homer*, 1969, both by J.B. Hainsworth; *Homer's Odyssey: A Critical Handbook* edited by C.E. Nelson, 1969; *Nature and Culture in the Iliad: The Tragedy of Hector* by J.M. Redfield, 1975; *Essays on the Iliad: Selected Modern Criticism* edited by J. Wright, 1978; *Approaches to Homer* edited by Carl A. Rubeno and Cynthia W. Shelmerdine, 1983.

*   *   *

The *Iliad* and *Odyssey* come at the end of a 500-year-long tradition of oral epic, and parts of them—phrases, lines, perhaps even passages—must have been composed at the beginning of this tradition, when the city of Troy fell to the Achaean armies commanded by King Agamemnon of Mycenae. The oral epic style is a formulaic style, and most of the verses contain formulae: half-lines consisting of a noun plus an adjective, adverb, verb, or another noun, repeated exactly throughout the poem; whole lines stating a recurring fact, such as the coming of dawn; and a few passages of several lines describing, e.g., the preparation and eating of a meal. The formulae exist in order to insure that the improvising oral poet can keep his metre from breaking down.

Such poetry and its audiences are not offended by repetitions that serve metrical needs, nor by epithets that are otiose or even slightly inappropriate: Achilles is "swift-footed," whether running, standing, or seated. Repetition weakens the adjective, not so as to render it meaningless, but to make it seem part of the name. Repeated adjectives never, or very rarely, mean the wrong thing, but they need hardly be the *mot juste*.

The oral-formulaic style did not evolve in order that poems of the length of the *Iliad* be composed, and the Homeric compositions are extraordinary achievements even as craftworks. It is quite possible, even probable, that they were composed with the aid of writing: perhaps they were dictated, perhaps the poet learned how to write. That they were preserved orally is of course possible, but in that case what we read undoubtedly suffered distortion during oral transmission. Since most Homeric critics prefer to talk about a text assumed to go back to the 7th or 8th centuries, criticism cannot safely rest its analyses on one or two passages; or if it does, it must recognize that it is analyzing a text that may well not be Homer's. Granted this caveat, it is safe to look on each poem as a unity, not an editorial amalgamation of long passages previously existing. Whether one poet composed both poems cannot be decided.

The theme of the *Iliad* is the Wrath of Achilles, directed first at Agamemnon, who robbed Achilles of his battle-prize Briseis, and then at Hector, who killed Achilles's beloved companion Patroclus. The young Achilles had dedicated himself to the heroic code, the most attractive concept of values in his Achaean society. To be a hero is to be publicly recognized for one's valour on the battlefield, in combat fought no further from the enemy than a spear's throw. Such recognition is symbolized by the battle-prize, awarded by the troops or by Agamemnon after a city is sacked. To take away one's prize is to shatter one's honour, and Achilles is quite justified in withdrawing from battle. Agamemnon, his cause seriously threatened by Achilles's absence, sends an embassy offering vast recompense. Achilles, still in the grip of his wrath, has by now come to question the value of heroism: life and love seem more important, and the pleas of Odysseus—representing Agamemnon—and of Achilles's old teacher Phoenix, are turned aside. Ajax's brilliant appeal to Achilles's love for his comrades has better luck. Achilles agrees with him intellectually, though he is still too angry to rejoin the battle. But he does allow his companion Patroclus to lead his troops back to fight; when Hector kills Patroclus, Achilles conceives a blind hatred for Hector which is not satisfied even by Hector's death. Priam comes seeking his son's body, offering the ransom appropriate to the heroic code, and more importantly basing his appeal on the love between father and son. To this common human value Achilles responds, and the Wrath comes to an end.

Achilles's movement from heroism to love is interlaced with the poet's exploration of other perceptions of value and of the conflicts such differing perceptions create. Agamemnon, at least initially, believes himself justified by his superior power: his ability to field the most troops. Odysseus is the professional soldier who most honours success: never to return from war empty-handed. The Achaeans and their codes are essentially military; the Trojans are more diverse. We never forget that their city was once at peace, and prosperous. One of the king's sons, Paris, is a skilled bowman in battle, but has no interest in war; he values beauty, and is not only the consort of Helen, but was the architect of his own palace. The shipbuilder Phereclus, no great warrior, is nonetheless eminent enough to merit a pedigree. The individual Achaean nations are under the absolute command of their kings, while Troy is loosely governed by a council of elders dominated, but hardly dictated to by Priam's family. Corresponding to such institutional looseness is a moral pluralism: unlike his brother Paris, Hector values heroism, while their father Priam is broadly tolerant, kindly, and sympathetic. Troy's acceptance of diversity is the reason for its destruction: it does not force Paris to return the stolen Helen, nor Hector to re-enter his city and shun the duel with Achilles. Achaean society will always put the military goal first, while the Trojans will sacrifice national security to preserve individual freedom of choice. This is Troy's tragedy, played against Achilles's finding value in love, at the price of losing his friend and becoming forever alienated spiritually from his own society. Homer's vision is pessimistic, but affirmative: human life has more ill than good, but it has value, in heroism and in love.

The *Odyssey* moves in very different worlds. Odysseus, returning from the Trojan War, is thrust into a fairyland world inhabited by the one-eyed giant Cyclops, the witch Circe, the seductive Sirens, the inexorable Scylla and Charybdis. Reluctant, fascinated, curious, self-indulgent, Odysseus pits himself against the temptations and dangers of this world with considerable personal success, but with the loss of his entire army. His various adventures usually have a ready symbolic interpretation: the Sirens represent the danger of losing one's soul to the power of great art; Scylla and Charybdis, the need to choose to surrender a part to save the whole; Calypso, the surrender of one's humanity to a world without death or domestic responsibility, Odysseus visits the underworld and hears from Achilles how any kind of life is preferable to non-existence. Despite this gloomy prospect, and despite the lure of the beauty of Calypso and her island, Odysseus chooses to be a mortal, a human being, and to go home.

Before this picture of the temptations of sensuality, adventure, and escape from the human lot, Homer places a "Telemachy" revealing how desperately Odysseus is needed at home in Ithaca. His wife Penelope, not knowing if her husband is alive, is besieged by suitors: though anxious to remain faithful, she cannot afford to reject a second marriage out of hand. Her son Telemachus is beginning to grow up in this hostile world: he acts creditably enough, but clearly requires a father's help. Odysseus's household—in Greek, his *oikos*, the fundamental unit of Ithacan society—is being consumed by the suitors, and pleas to fellow-citizens receive no effective response. The last half of the poem describes Odysseus's return to Ithaca, where he reclaims his household and restores order. Husband and wife reunite in their wedding-bed; and it appears at this moment that the destiny of humanity, male and female, is essentially domestic, and that ultimate fulfillment lies in establishing and maintaining the *oikos*.

Yet the poem's vision is larger than this. Odysseus must some day journey to an inland place and there dedicate his oar to Poseidon, thus placating the hostile god of the sea. Only then can he return to Ithaca. The life of Odysseus, as of Penelope, is defined by two movements: one is a struggle to attain domestic stability; the other is the fascination offered by the adventures and challenges along the way.

—William Merritt Sale

HORACE (Quintus Horatius Flaccus).   Born in Venusia (now Venosa), Apulia, 8 December 65 B.C.   Educated in Rome and Athens, c. 46. Joined Brutus's army in Athens, 44, and probably accompanied him to Asia Minor, then fought at the battle of Philippi, 42; returned to Italy, 41, and became treasury clerk, c. 39; in Maecenas's circle, and given a farm in the Sabine country; friend of Virgil. *Died 27 November 8 B.C.*

HORACE

PUBLICATIONS

Collections

[*Works*], edited by E.C. Wickham and H.W. Garrod. 1912; also edited by Friedrich
Klinger, 3rd edition, 1959; translated by C.E. Bennett and H.R. Fairclough, 1927-29.
The Essential Horace, translated by Burton Raffel. 1983.

Verse

Odes: commentary by P. Shorey and G.J. Laing, 2nd edition, 1910, Kenneth Quinn, 1980,
R.G.M. Nisbet and M. Hubbard (Books 1-2), 1970-78, and Gordon Williams (Book 3),
1969; translated by J.B. Leishman (in *Translating Horace*), 1956, Joseph P. Clancy,
1960, Helen Rowe Henze, 1961, James Michie, 1964, and W.G. Shepherd (includes
Epodes), 1983.
Satires and Epistles: commentary by E.P. Morris, 1909-11; translated by S.P. Bovie,
1959; *Satires*: commentary by A. Palmer, 4th edition, 1891; translated by Niall Rudd,
1973, revised edition, 1979; *Epistles*: commentary by A.S. Wilkins, 1892, and C.O.
Brink (Book 2), 1982; *Ars Poetica* [Art of Poetry; one of the epistles] edited by C.O.
Brink, 1971.
Ad Pyrrham (*Odes* 1.5): several hundred translations, mostly into English, edited by R.
Storrs. 1959.

*

Critical Studies: *Horace and His Influence* by G. Showerman, 1922; *Horace: A New Interpretation* by A.Y. Campbell, 1924; *Horace and His Lyric Poetry* by L.P. Wilkinson, 1945, revised
edition, 1968; *Horace* by E. Fraenkel, 1957; *The Structure of Horace's Odes* by Neville E.
Collinge, 1961; *The Odes of Horace: A Critical Study* by Steele Commager, 1962; *Horace* by J.
Perret, 1964; *The Satires of Horace* by Niall Rudd, 1966; *Reading Horace* by David A. West,
1967; *Horace* by Kenneth J. Reckford, 1969; *Word, Sound, and Image in the Odes of Horace*
by M.O. Lee, 1969; *The Epodes of Horace* by R.W. Carrubba, 1969; *Studies in Horace's First
Book of Epistles* by M.J. McGann, 1969; *Horace* by Gordon Williams, 1972; *Horace* edited by
C.D.N. Costa, 1973; *Horace and Callimachean Aesthetics* by J.V. Cody, 1976; *Profile of
Horace* by D.R. Shackleton Bailey, 1982; *The Golden Plectrum: Sexual Symbolism in
Horace's Odes* by R. Minadeo, 1982.

*   *   *

Horace's achievement is to have mastered two completely different types of poetry, each of
which is remarkable for its originality and each of which has endeared itself to generations of
readers.
The first type is his hexameter poetry. In 36/35 B.C. Horace published *Satires 1*, a collection
of ten poems written in the manner of Lucilius (a Roman landowner and littérateur of the late
2nd century B.C.) and described by Horace himself as *sermones* (conversation pieces). Lucilius
had been famous for his invective and biting wit; but though Horace subjects certain individuals to intermittent mockery throughout his collection, and though the first three satires deal
with such moral questions as discontent and adultery, the book as a whole is hardly satirical at
all in our sense of the word. Among the matters described or discussed are literary criticism (4,
10), a journey from Rome to Brundisium (5), and the poet's own life and his relationship with
his patron Maecenas (6). Several representative features are combined brilliantly in satire 9, in
which Horace describes how, on a walk through Rome, he was pursued by a stranger claiming
to be a poet and hoping for an introduction to Maecenas. The satire, which begins with an

allusion to Lucilius, is almost wholly taken up with dialogue, in which the pest's importunity is matched by Horace's politeness, the latter's irony by the former's insensitivity. Since both protagonists are poets, the satire resembles the traditional form of the literary *agon* (contest); yet the pest unwittingly presents his own work in terms which, as the reader well knows, Horace (and Maecenas) can only regard with contempt. Further wit is displayed by means of epic motifs and military imagery, which are used throughout to suggest that the combatants are a pair of Homeric heroes; yet this language is entirely belied by the appalling behaviour of the pest, by whom Horace is nevertheless characteristically worsted until the very last moment, when he is rescued by the surprise intervention of a third party. The rescue itself is expressed in language which is again borrowed from Lucilius. The whole poem exhibits a confident combination of humour and humanity, and in the dialogue form the resources of metre and language are exploited to the full. Yet underneath the wit Horace has a serious message for his readers about admission to Maecenas's circle and hence, by implication, to the entourage of Octavian (the future emperor Augustus) himself.

A second book of *Satires*, containing 8 poems, followed in 30 B.C., and ten years later Horace published twenty more hexameter poems which are known as *Epistles 1*. Finally, he published three very long letters, the first two of which are collectively known as *Epistles 2*: to Augustus, to Florus, and to the Pisones (the *Ars Poetica, Art of Poetry*). Although the *Satires* and *Epistles* are conventionally distinguished by their titles, and though the latter display some epistolographical features which are naturally absent from the former, there is little otherwise to distinguish the two sets of poems. Since the verse letter had no significant analogue in Greek, and satire no analogue at all (cf. Quintilian 10.1.93), Horace in these works has produced a body of poetry which for its principal inspiration owes virtually nothing to the world of Greece. In this his poetry differs fundamentally both from that of other Roman poets, almost all of whom wrote in rivalry of Greek genres, and from the rest of the poetry which he wrote himself.

At the same time as he was engaged with *Satires 1*, Horace was also writing iambic poetry in the manner of the early Greek iambist Archilochus. Iambics were traditionally associated with invective and disillusionment, and Horace's *Epodes* (as the 17 poems, published around 30 B.C., are known) include examples of this type (e.g., 2, 4, 8, 10, 12); but there is a wider range of subjects too, e.g., civil war (7, 16), the battle of Actium (1, 9), life (13), and love (11, 14, 15). Thus the *Epodes* have affinities not only with the satires but also with Horace's second major achievement, the three books of *Odes* which he published in 23 B.C. These 88 poems, all written in lyric metres, cover an enormous variety of subject-matter: famous examples are, in Book 1, 4 (spring), 5 (the flirtatious Pyrrha, this being one of the most translated poems in Latin), 9 (Mt. Soracte), and 37 (Cleopatra); in Book 2, 3 and 14 (death); and in Book 3, 1 (ambition), 29 (life), and 30 (the immortality of the *Odes*). These three books represent Horace's attempt at producing a substantial collection of Latin lyric poetry which would be a cultural adornment of Augustan Rome and which would rival the lyrics written by the Greek monodists Sappho and Alcaeus. Characteristic in many ways is 2.7, in which Horace welcomes back to Italy a friend with whom he served on the republican side at the battle of Philippi many years before. Metaphor is used with striking originality to contrast the old soldiers' periods of enforced idleness with their bursts of frenzied activity, their comradely carousing with their defeat on the field of battle. Whereas his friend was sucked away by the tides of war, Horace had a fortunate escape: ever conscious of the imminence of death, Horace presents his escape in epic terms; but there is no hint of self-congratulation, for he has already described his own part in the battle ignominiously, symbolised by his abandoned shield. This last is a motif found in several archaic Greek poets, including Alcaeus; Horace thus aligns his experience with theirs and underscores his poetic relationship with them. Now that his friend has returned to Italy, tellingly evoked by its sky and native gods, Horace conveys his delight by the detailed preparations he is making for their renewed carousings; and though the poet seems proud to have fought alongside Brutus, the reader is subtly reminded that his friend's return, and Horace's own prosperity, are due to the clemency and beneficence of the victor. This ode, in its linguistic brilliance, its feeling for friends and home, its blending of pride and understatement and of literature and life, illustrates much that is outstanding in Horace's lyric work.

There can be no question that Horace's achievement in the *Odes* was triumphantly successful. Official recognition of that success came when he was commissioned by the emperor to write the *Carmen Saeculare* (Secular Hymn) for the important Secular Games of 17 B.C.; and the emperor also requested poems celebrating the military exploits of his step-sons: these poems duly appear (4, 14) in Book 4 of the *Odes*, which was published separately about 13 B.C.

In metre and form the *Odes* could hardly be more different from the *Satires* and *Epistles*; yet all are recognisably written by the same poet, all have certain features in common, and all evince a concern for the same subjects. Horace is one of the few great classical writers whom readers easily convince themselves that they know intimately; yet his remarkable habit of partly revealing and partly concealing his personality means that, while throughout his different types of poetry the common link is provided by the poet himself, one person's Horace is never the next person's, and the "real Horace" is a source of endless fascination. Horace similarly tantalises us in his manner of expression. Common features of his hexameter and lyric works are the wit and subtlety of their argumentation; yet his unrivalled facility with words means that apparently key sentences can look both forwards and backwards in such a way that his effortless transitions provide constant delight to the reader who, after much labour, thinks he has worked them out. Similarly ambivalent are Horace's favourite topics. He can combine support for the emperor's efforts at moral rearmament with hedonistic recommendations to drink and make love before the summons of death, he can profess to prefer light poetry to grand and at the same time produce the noblest of political poems. Horace's work has that capacity for constantly surprising the reader which we associate with great art; yet nothing could be more familiar than the many famous lines which he wrote and which are among the most memorable statements ever uttered about the human condition.

—A.J. Woodman

HORVÁTH, Ödön (Josef) von. Born in Fiume, 9 December 1901. Educated at Episcopal School, Budapest, 1909-13; Wilhelmsgymnasium and Realschule, Munich, 1913-16; school in Pressburg, 1916; Realgymnasium, Vienna, 1916-19; University of Munich, 1919-22. Married Maria Elsner in 1933 (divorced, 1934). Writer; involved in politics from an early age; left Germany and became Hungarian citizen, 1934. Recipient: Kleist Prize, 1931. *Died 7 June 1938.*

PUBLICATIONS

Collections

Stücke, edited by Traugott Krischke. 1961.
Gesammelte Werke, edited by Traugott Krischke, Walter Huder, and Dieter Hildebrandt. 4 vols., 1970; also edition in 8 vols., 1972.

Plays

Revolte auf Cote 3018 (produced 1927). 1927; as *Die Bergbahn* (produced 1929), 1928.

Zur schönen Aussicht (produced 1969). 1927.
Sladek; oder, Die schwarze Armee. 1928; revised version, as *Sladek, der schwarze Reichswehrmann* (produced 1929), 1929.
Rund um den Kongress (produced 1959). 1929.
Italienische Nacht (produced 1931). 1930.
Geschichten aus dem Wiener Wald (produced 1931). 1931; as *Tales from the Vienna Woods*, 1977.
Kasimir und Karoline (produced 1932). 1932; edited by Traugott Krischke, 1973.
Glaube, Liebe, Hoffnung (produced 1936). 1932; edited by Traugott Krischke, 1973.
Die Unbekannte aus der Seine (produced 1949). 1933.
Hin und Her (produced 1934). In *Gesammelte Werke*, 1970.
Mit dem Kopf durch die Wand (produced 1935). 1935.
Figaro lässt sich scheiden (produced 1937). 1959.
Der jüngste Tag (produced 1937). 1955.
Ein Dorf ohne Männer, from a novel by Koloman van Mikszath (produced 1937). In *Gesammelte Werke*, 1970.
Himmelwärts (produced 1950). In *Gesammelte Werke*, 1970.
Don Juan kommt aus dem Krieg (produced 1952). In *Stücke*, 1961; as *Don Juan Comes Back from the War*, 1978.
Pompeji (produced 1959). In *Stücke*, 1961.

Fiction

Der ewige Spiesser. 1930.
Ein Kind unserer Zeit; Jugend ohne Gott. 2 vols., 1938; as *Zeitalter der Fische*, 1953; as *A Child of Our Time*, 1938; as *The Age of the Fish*, 1939.

*

Critical Studies: *Materialien zu Horváth* edited by Traugott Krischke, 1970, and *Horváth: Ein Lesebuch* by Krischke, 1978; *Über Horváth* (includes bibliography) edited by Dieter Hildebrandt and Traugott Krischke, 1972; *Symposium on Horváth* published by Austrian Institute, London, 1977; *Horváth Studies: Close Readings of Six Plays* by Krishna Winston, 1977.

*　　*　　*

Ödön von Horváth, the most representative dramatist of the Weimar Republic, saw himself as "a faithful chronicler" of his times. His plays portray the "gigantic struggle between the individual and society, that eternal slaughter in which there is to be no peace" (Randbemerkung, Marginal Comment). His characters are conceived as representative "creatures of an ailing age." His plays are divided between the genres of comedy, dialect theatre, and period drama yet they anticipate the theatre of the absurd in their mixture of the comic, the tragic, and the gruesome. Though he adopted the naive, established conventions of Austrian popular theatre in a conscious attempt to revitalize that tradition, his plays are ironic-realistic portrayals of the contemporary historical scene, set in the years 1925-37 against a background of inflation, unemployment, political extremism, and the rise of Fascism. The chosen social milieu is almost exclusively that of the petit-bourgeois in Vienna and Munich whose typical life-style, ideology, and speech habits are sharply set in focus.

The critical irony which pervades Horváth's plays results largely from his subtle handling of dialogue. The use of unreflective speech, the pretentious jargon and clichés of the semi-educated, as the principal key both to individual psychology and to the consciousness of a class is a dramatic device which Horváth developed and perfected. His "attempted synthesis between irony and realism," in his own words, produces a form of theatre which combines life-like representation with critical distancing. Though a kind of "alienation," in theatrical terms, is achieved by subversive and ironic use of dialect and stereotyped language, what distinguishes Horváth from Brecht is the avoidance of dialectical debate and of didacticism.

In Horváth not action but the word is the principal carrier of drama, and he insisted on a stylized manner of performance. Dialogue is used with a fine sense of its force, ambiguities, and psychological implications. "Demaskierung des Bewusstseins" (the unmasking of consciousness) is Horváth's phrase for his technique of allowing characters involuntarily to reveal their inner natures, intentions, and thought through the words they use. The conflict between appearance and reality, pretence and truth is thus dramatically enacted. The social dimension is at the same time manifested, since the conventions of language used by the classes portrayed are equally subject to critical scrutiny. The menacing political reality behind an apparently harmless facade is best exemplified in *Geschichten aus dem Wiener Wald* (*Tales from the Vienna Woods*), which presents a suspect image of "the old honest true golden Viennese heart" compounded of sentimentalism, kitsch, and brutality. A number of other plays (*Glaube, Liebe, Hoffnung, Kasimir und Karoline, Die Unbekannte aus der Seine, Hin und Her*) portray the cold indifference of a bureaucratized society which exploits and ultimately destroys the individual. Yet tragic intensity is always held in check by a dramatist who chooses to explore the darker side of existence within the sordidness, pettiness, and banalities of life.

Deprived of a stage for his plays, the exiled Horváth latterly turned to prose and wrote three short novels. These depict the stark realities of the contemporary prevalent influence of "Neue Sachlichkeit" (the New Functionalism).

—Alexander Stillmark

HUGO, Victor (Marie). Born in Besançon, France, 26 February 1802. Educated at Cordier and Decotte's school, Paris, 1814-18. Married Adèle Foucher in 1822 (died, 1868); three sons and two daughters; lived with Juliette Drouet from 1868 (she had been his mistress from 1833; she died, 1883). Editor, with his two brothers, *Le Conservateur littéraire*, 1819-21; involved in politics: founded newspaper *L'Événement* (later *L'Événement du Peuple*), 1848; elected to assembly, but exiled in 1851, first in Brussels, then in Jersey and Guernsey to 1870, and intermittently after that; visited France, 1870-71; deputy at Bordeaux Assembly, 1871; defeated in 1872 election because of his tolerance of Communards; elected to Senate, 1876. Chevalier, Legion of Honor, 1825; Member, French Academy, 1841. Became Vicomte Hugo, 1845. *Died 22 May 1885*.

PUBLICATIONS

Collections

Oeuvres complètes, edited by Jean Massin. 18 vols., 1967-70.

Fiction

Han d'Islande. 1823; as *Han of Iceland*, 1825; as *The Demon Dwarf*, 1847; as *The Outlaw of Iceland*, 1885.

Bug-Jargal. 1826; as *The Slave King*, 1833; as *The Noble Rival*, 1845; as *Jargal*, 1866.
Le Dernier Jour d'un condamné. 1829; as *The Last Day of a Condemned*, 1840.
Notre-Dame de Paris. 1831; edited by Jacques Seebacher and Yves Gohin, 1975; as *The Hunchback of Notre-Dame*, 1833; as *La Esmeralda*, 1844.
Les Misérables. 1862; translated as *Les Misérables*, 1862.
Les Travailleurs de la mer. 1866; edited by Jacques Seebacher and Yves Gohin, 1975; as *Toilers of the Sea*, 1866.
L'Homme qui rit. 1869; as *By Order of the King*, 1870; as *The Laughing Man*, 1887.
Quatre-Vingt-Treize. 1874; as *Ninety-Three*, 1874.
Novels. 28 vols., 1895.
Romans, edited by Henri Guillemin. 3 vols., 1963.

Plays

Amy Robsart, from *Kenilworth* by Scott (produced 1827).
Cromwell. 1827; edited by Annie Ubersfeld, 1968.
Marion Delorme (produced 1831). 1829; as *The King's Edict*, 1872.
Hernani (produced 1830). 1830; translated as *Hernani*, 1830.
Le Roi s'amuse (produced 1832). 1832; translated as *Le Roi s'Amuse*, 1843.
Marie Tudor (produced 1833). 1833.
Lucrèce Borgia (produced 1833). 1833; translated as *Lucretia Borgia*, 1847.
Angelo, Tyran de Padoue (produced 1835). 1835; translated as *Angelo*, 1855(?).
La Esméralda, music by Louise Bertin, from *Notre-Dame de Paris* by Hugo (produced 1836). 1836.
Ruy Blas (produced 1838). 1838; edited by Annie Ubersfeld, 2 vols., 1971-72; translated as *Ruy Blas*, 1860(?).
Les Burgraves (produced 1843). 1843.
Torquemada. 1882.
Théâtre en liberté. 1886.
Théâtre complet, edited by Roland Purnal. 2 vols., 1963-64.

Verse

Odes et poésies diverses. 1822.
Nouvelles Odes. 1824.
Odes et ballades. 1826; edited by Pierre Albouy, 1980.
Les Orientales. 1829; edited by Pierre Albouy, 1981.
Les Feuilles d'automne. 1831; edited by Pierre Albouy, 1981.
Les Chants du crépuscule. 1835; as *Songs of Twilight*, 1836.
Les Voix intérieures. 1837.
Les Rayons et les ombres. 1840.
Le Rhin. 1842; as *Excursions along the Banks of the Rhine*, 1843.
Les Châtiments. 1853; edited by P.J. Yarrow, 1975, and René Journet, 1977.
Les Contemplations. 1856; edited by Pierre Albouy, 1973.
La Légende des siècles. 3 vols., 1859-83; edited by André Dumas, 1974.
Les Chansons des rues et des bois. 1865.
L'Année terrible. 1872.
L'Art d'être grand-père. 1877.
Le Pape. 1878.
La Pitié suprême. 1879.
Religions et religion. 1880.
L'Ane. 1880; edited by Pierre Albouy, 1966.
Les Quatre vents de l'esprit. 1881.

La Fin de Satan. 1886.
Toute la lyre. 2 vols., 1888-93.
Dieu. 1891; edited by René Journet and Guy Robert, 3 vols., 1969.
Oeuvres poétiques, edited by Pierre Albouy. 1964—.
Poésies, edited by Bernard Leuilliot. 3 vols., 1972.
The Distance, The Shadows: Selected Poems, translated by Harry Guest. 1981.

Other

Littérature et philosophie mêlées. 1834; edited by Anthony R.W. James, 1976.
Lettres sur le Rhin. 1846.
Napoléon le Petit. 1852; as *Napoleon the Little,* 1852.
Dessins de Hugo (art). 1862; edited by J. Sergent, 1955.
L'Archipel de la Manche. 1863.
Hugo raconté par un témoin de sa vie. 1863.
William Shakespeare. 1864; translated as *William Shakespeare,* 1864.
Actes et paroles. 3 vols., 1875-76.
Choses vues. 2 vols., 1887-1900; edited by Hubert Juin, 4 vols., 1972; translated in part
    as *Things Seen,* 1887; revised edition, edited by David Kimber, 1964.
Alpes et Pyrénées. 1890; as *The Alps and Pyrenees,* 1896.
France et Belgique. 1892; edited by Claude Gély, 1974.
Les Années funestes. 1896.
Memoirs. 1899.
Post-scriptum de ma vie. 1901; edited by Henri Guillemin, 1961; as *Hugo's Intellectual
    Biography,* 1907.
Dernière gerbe. 1902.
Océan, Tas de Pierres. 1942.
Correspondance. 4 vols., 1947-52.
Pierres: Vers et prose, edited by Henri Guillemin. 1951.
Carnets intimes, edited by Henri Guillemin. 1953.
Journal 1830-1848, edited by Henri Guillemin. 1954.
Hugo dessinateur, edited by Roger Cornaille and Georges Herscher. 1963.
Lettres à Juliette Drouet 1833-1883, edited by Jean Gaudon. 1964.
Correspondance, with Pierre-Jules Hetzel, edited by Sheila Gaudon. 1979—.

*

Bibliography: *Hugo's Drama: An Annotated Bibliography 1900-1980* by Ruth Lestha Doyle, 1981.

Critical Studies: *The Career of Hugo,* 1945, and *The Perilous Quest: Image, Myth, and Prophecy in the Narratives of Hugo,* 1968, both by Elliott M. Grant; *Hugo,* 1956, and *Hugo and His World,* 1966, both by André Maurois; *A Stage for Poets: Studies in the Theatre of Hugo and Musset* by Charles Affron, 1971; *Hugo* by John Porter Houston, 1974; *Hugo: A Biography* by Samuel Edwards, 1975; *The Medievalism of Hugo* by Patricia A. Ward, 1975; *Hugo* by Joanna Richardson, 1976; *"Les Contemplations" of Hugo: An Allegory of the Creative Process* by Suzanne Nash, 1977; *Hugo: Philosophy and Poetry* by Henri Peyre, 1980.

*   *   *

When Gide was asked to name France's greatest poet, his reply was "Victor Hugo, hélas!," a response expressing Hugo's undeniable stature and a concomitant embarrassment on the part of a mature Frenchman in acknowledging such a fact. Hugo spanned the 19th century, and dealt in his works with all the major issues central to individuals, society, literature, politics, and religion through this period of violent and frequent change. Along with the published novels, plays, poems, and essays go more volumes of fragments, ideas, images, word-associations, rhymes, all scribbled on whatever piece of paper was at hand. His output is monumental, indeed he himself referred to it as a single edifice in which individual works were merely stones. Given such a proliferation it is perhaps natural that among the marks of genius there should also be much that is trite, oversimplified, and self-indulgent.

The main explanation for this apparent paradox is that Hugo was a great primitive, who approached his subjects with intensity, simplicity, and an unshakeable confidence in the validity of his own vision. All his writings were informed by the belief that creation was a composite of forces of good and evil and this dualism provides both the structural security of his works, which deal invariably with conflicting opposites, and the richness of an imagery whose prism translates everything into a battle between light and darkness. His attempts thus to categorize and render accessible the mysterious absolutes that are the dynamics of existence take account also of another omnipresent sensation, that of vertigo. It is the feeling, absorbed during childhood and adolescence from the traumas of Imperial and Restoration society and shared by an entire generation, that the fragile hold on faith, reason, or any human construct may dissolve and leave only "le gouffre." It is not a distortion to describe the fundamental Hugolian experience as a play of day and night on the edge of an abyss.

His philosophy, intuited early and evolved and refined through the middle years, placed man at the centre of an axis stretching between God and stones. Once again the condition is that of antithesis which seeks synthesis. Matter is evil, its very weight and substance separating it from spirit, and therefore God. Original sin is literally a fall and only by a progressively greater awareness of and recourse to things of the spirit may the prison of matter by breached and the soul released back towards its source. More than any other writer Hugo was aware of his Messianic role in such a context. With sometimes disarming and sometimes infuriating conceit he places himself above his fellow-mortals to act as a visionary, a gifted intermediary between God and his creatures. Writing was the manipulation of material things to reveal spiritual truths, an interface between concrete and abstract, and Hugo recognized the importance of the fact that "In the beginning was the word...." Words to him were simultaneously "things" and "mysterious wanderers of the soul," the black and literal object on the page was the envelope of a spreading transcendent truth, and thus the ingredients and processes of artistic creativity mirrored those of Creation itself.

He began writing his poetry in a climate of dissatisfaction. Although his earliest works expressed conventional attitudes to Church and King and execrated Napoleon, the recognition that the Ancien Régime was stifling progress quickly began to break the moulds of poetry as well as those of belief. A collection of poems like *Les Orientales* demonstrates the true Romantic revolution of lyric poetry. The forms are new, the rhythms daring and mysterious, the subject-matter exotic, and Hugo's contemporaries acknowledged the fact that their literary generation had found its leader. He himself claimed later in life to have "dislocated" the alexandrine, liberated French versification, and revolutionized poetic vocabulary, a boast entirely validated by the collections of the 1820's and 1830's. The works are those of a man totally involved in the moods and movements of his times. Enforced exile, however, removed him from the literary barricades and allowed time for reflection, or more properly contemplation. In the Channel Islands, his own exile, the death of his daughter, his "crimes" and his sexuality are examined and, through the alchemy of the poetic process, transformed into a strong, single affirmation of divine purpose. *Les Contemplations* is a masterpiece, containing poems brilliant in themselves and yet also important as components within the deliberate architecture of an overall poetic narrative. The conviction at which he arrives in the making of this work provides the basis for the great epic collections of his middle and later years, the gigantic stories of myth, creation, history which continue his exploration of verse, image, and language through poetic registers more varied than those of any of the poets who had preceded him.

His pre-eminence extended to the world of the theatre. The preface to his play *Cromwell* became the manifesto of the French Romantics, not because its ideas were particularly new, but because the power of Hugo's rhetoric gave it coherence and force. Its main original contribution to the debate between Classical and Romantic adherents was the theory of the grotesque. This proposed not, as is sometimes mistakenly suggested, that emphasis should fall only on the ugly and misshapen, but that art should mix extremes of the beautiful and the grotesque in order to convey a more complete picture of the world than that which had been proposed by the Classical imitators with their ideals of beauty. His own plays adopted the morality of popular melodrama, and criticism of them has always been directed at their "unreality" and the fact that he created only stereotypes. Hugo himself, however, never claimed verisimilitude, and if the plays are experienced as dramatic poems, then character, like symbol and image, is seen to be a constituent part of an artistic whole which conveys its meanings through the totality of its impact rather than from the activities of some of its parts; when Hernani confronts Don Salluste it is not merely a young man facing an old one, it is the whole tangle of Ancien Régime, the Restoration's desire to perpetuate it and the frustrating and inexpressible need of the new generation to be liberated from both.

It is easy also to offer facile criticisms of his novels. Indeed the earliest are in themselves Gothic parodies, the hero of one making meals of human flesh washed down with sea-water drunk from his son's skull. His linguistic facility, however, and the vast imagination of the visionary produced the great evocation of medieval Paris clutched around the cathedral in *The Hunchback of Notre Dame*, the socio-political tapestry of *Les Misérables* which contains enough themes and sub-plots to fill several novels, and the mysticism of *Toilers of the Sea* in which the central character defeats wind and waves, and Hugo reminds the reader that reality consists of more than just conscious imaginings. The prose is as sonorous as the poetry and in all the works the great unifying tendency of the visionary is the controlling factor.

Hugo's work is monolithic. In it the Romantics, the Symbolists, and even the Surrealists found examples of their own desired effects. It is inhabited by monsters, Gods, and men, sprawling, digressing, and yet simultaneously rendering accessible the moods and movements of the human spirit in its own time and beyond.

—W.J.S Kirton

IBSEN, Henrik (Johan). Born in Skien, Norway, 20 March 1828. Educated at local schools, and a private school in Skien; attended the University of Oslo, 1850-51. Married Suzannah Thoresen in 1858; one son; also had one son by Else Jonsdatter. Pharmacist's assistant in Grimstad, 1844-50; drama critic, *Manden*, later *Andhrimner*, 1851; house poet, Norwegian Theatre, Bergen, 1851-57; director, Norwegian Theatre, Oslo, 1857-62; consultant, Christiania Theatre, 1863; lived in Italy, 1864-68, Dresden, 1868-75, Munich, 1875-78, Rome, 1878-85, Munich, 1885-91, Oslo, 1891-1906. Government pension, 1866. Doctor of Letters, Uppsala University, 1877. *Died 23 May 1906.*

PUBLICATIONS

Collections

Samlede verker (includes letters), edited by Francis Bull, Halvdan Kogt, and Didrik Arup

Seip. 21 vols., 1928-58.
Collected Works, edited by William Archer. 12 vols., 1906-12.
The Oxford Ibsen, edited by J.W. McFarlane. 8 vols., 1960-77.

Plays

Catalina (produced 1882). 1850; as *Cataline*, in *Early Plays*, 1921.
Kjaempehøjen (produced 1850). 1902; as *The Warrior's Barrow*, in *Early Plays*, 1921.
Sankthansnatten (produced 1852). 1909; as *St. John's Night*, in *The Oxford Ibsen 1*, 1970.
Fru Inger til Østråt (produced 1855). 1857; revised edition, 1874; as *Lady Inger of Ostraat*, in *Prose Dramas*, 1890.
Gildet pa Solhaug (produced 1856). 1856; as *The Feast at Solhaug*, in *Collected Works*, 1908.
Olaf Liljekrans (produced 1857). 1898; translated as *Olaf Liljekrans*, in *Early Plays*, 1921.
Haermaendene på Helgeland (produced 1858). 1857; as *The Vikings at Helgeland*, in *Prose Dramas*, 1890.
Kjaerlighedens komedie (produced 1873). 1862; as *Love's Comedy*, 1900.
Kongs-Emnerne (produced 1864). 1863; as *The Pretenders*, in *Prose Dramas*, 1890.
Brand (produced in part, 1866; complete version, 1885). 1866; translated as *Brand*, 1906.
Peer Gynt (produced 1876). 1867; translated as *Peer Gynt*, 1892.
De unges forbund (produced 1869). 1869; as *The League of Youth*, in *Prose Dramas*, 1890.
Kejser og Galilaeer (produced in part 1896). 1873; as *The Emperor and the Galilean*, 1876.
Samfundets støtter (produced 1877). 1877; as *The Pillars of Society*, 1888.
Et dukkehjem (produced 1879). 1879; translated as *Nora*, 1880; as *A Doll's House*, in *Prose Dramas*, 1890.
Gengangere (produced 1881). 1881; as *Ghosts*, in *The Pillars of Society and Other Plays*, 1888.
En folkefiende (produced 1883). 1882; as *An Enemy of the People*, in *The Pillars of Society and Other Plays*, 1888.
Vildanden (produced 1885). 1884; as *The Wild Duck*, in *Prose Dramas*, 1890.
Rosmersholm (produced 1887). 1886; translated as *Rosmersholm*, in *Prose Dramas*, 1890.
Fruen fra havet (produced 1889). 1888; as *The Lady from the Sea*, in *Prose Dramas*, 1890.
Hedda Gabler (produced 1891). 1890; translated as *Hedda Gabler*, in *Prose Dramas*, 1890.
Bygmester Solness (produced 1893). 1892; as *The Master Builder*, 1893.
Lille Eyolf (produced 1895). 1894; as *Little Eyolf*, in *Collected Works*, 1907.
John Gabriel Borkman (produced 1897). 1896; translated as *John Gabriel Borkman*, in *Collected Works*, 1907.
Når vi døde vågner (produced 1900). 1899; as *When We Dead Awaken*, in *Collected Works*, 1907.

Verse

Digte [Verse]. 1871; augmented edition, 1875.
Lyrical Poems, translated by R.A. Streatfeild. 1902.
On the Heights. 1910.
Lyrics and Poems, translated by F.E. Garrett. 1912.

Terje Viken, translated by M. Michelet and G.R. Vowles. 1918.

Other

Correspondence, edited by Mary Morrison. 1905.
Episke Brand (fragment), edited by Karl Larsen. 1907.
Speeches and New Letters, edited by Lee M. Hollander. 1911.
Letters and Speeches, edited by Evert Sprinchorn. 1965.
Brevveksling med Christiania Theater 1878-1899, edited by Øyvind Anker. 1965.
Brev 1845-1905, edited by Øyvind Anker. 1979.

*

Bibliography: *Ibsen 1828-1928* by H. Pettersen, 1928; *Ibsen Bibliography 1928-1957* by I. Tedford, 1961; *Ibsen Årbok* [Ibsen Yearbook], 1954— .

Critical Studies: *The Quintessence of Ibsenism* by G.B. Shaw, 1913; *Ibsen the Norwegian* by M.C. Bradbrook, 1946, revised edition, 1966; *Ibsen: The Intellectual Background*, 1946, and *A Study of Six Plays by Ibsen*, 1950, both by Brian W. Downs; *Ibsen's Dramatic Method*, 1952, and *Ibsen: A Critical Study*, 1973, both by John Northam; *The Drama of Ibsen and Strindberg* by F.L. Lucas, 1962; *Ibsen* by Michael Meyer, 3 vols., 1967-71; *Ibsen: A Critical Anthology* edited by J.W. McFarlane, 1970; *Ibsen: The Critical Heritage* edited by Michael Egan, 1972; *Ibsen: The Man and His Work* by Edward Beyer, 1978; *Ibsen and the Theatre: The Dramatist in Production* edited by Errol Durbach, 1980, and *Ibsen the Romantic* by Durbach, 1982; *Ibsen: The Open Vision* by John Chamberlain, 1982; *Ibsen* by David Thomas, 1983.

*　　*　　*

"Anyone who wants to understand me must know Norway," Henrik Ibsen once remarked. This most European of Norwegian dramatists, still played regularly to packed houses the world over, often to theatre-goers ignorant of his nationality, insisted upon the importance of his national heritage. There was much about Norway which irritated and depressed him—to such an extent that he spent 27 of his most creative years (1864-91) abroad, in Italy and Germany— yet his plays, almost without exception, are set in the land he had rejected. Trolls and hobgoblins, Viking legends, brooding fjord landscapes and deep sunless valleys, snow and ice and extreme cold and light, hectic summer nights—these permeate the lives and form the personalities of the characters in his plays.

Yet even before he left Norway, Ibsen was well versed in European theatrical tradition. After an inauspicious and poverty-stricken beginning, he was appointed theatre director in Bergen (1851-57), then Christiania (the old Oslo, 1857-62). The European stage at this period was dominated by French salon comedies, the "well made play" written by dramatists such as Eugène Scribe; and it was largely these which Ibsen directed.

Most of Ibsen's early works are historical dramas, often in verse, which combine tales of Norway's heroic, half-legendary past with the techniques of Scribean drama: a complicated intrigue, involving convoluted misunderstanding and mistaken identity, and a neat tying-off of ends in conclusion (*Lady Inger of Ostraat, The Feast at Solhaug*). They are lofty in style, with a tendency to melodrama; it was not until Ibsen turned to depiction of contemporary society in colloquial modern prose that he found his natural medium.

Before that, however, he had written the two vast and sprawling verse dramas *Brand* and *Peer Gynt*. They were "reading dramas," not intended for the stage—and could not be staged realistically; they required not only an enormous cast but (for *Brand*) whole mountain ranges, storms and avalanches, and (for *Peer Gynt*) a removal across several continents, shipwreck, and a multitude of supernatural and monstrous creatures. It was not until Ibsen had achieved success with his prose dramas that they were accepted into theatre repertoires. Nowadays, however, they are among the most frequently performed of the plays.

At the centre of each play is a loner, a man ostracised by his fellow men. Brand is a fanatical priest who demands unquestioning submission to his stern Jehovah, and destroys his family and finally himself in his obsessive devotion to his call. Peer Gynt is his antithesis, a man who stands for nothing, taking the line of least resistance throughout his life; yet both die equally unsure that they have achieved anything.

This pattern of antitheses—exposing the deficiencies of one extreme standpoint in one play and then those of its polar opposite in another—was to repeat itself in many of Ibsen's later plays. Ibsen's protagonists feel driven to take a stand: the lofty claims of the ideal clash with the more sordid compromise of the real, the egotistical drive for success and fame with the gentler values of love and friendship.

It was with the "social" dramas of his next period (from *Pillars of Society* to *The Wild Duck*) that Ibsen won an international reputation and established himself as a European dramatist. Initially the success was often one of scandal rather than acclaim; for Ibsen wrote about such subjects, and in such a way, that polite society was outraged. The slamming of the door at the end of *A Doll's House*, which announces Nora's abandonment of husband and children, and her determination to find self-fulfillment on her own terms, aroused furious condemnation. *Ghosts*, with its frank treatment of debauchery, illegitimacy, and syphilis, was banned and reviled. "An open drain," the *Daily Telegraph* called it. Posterity, however, has discovered that it was neither lubricity nor frankness which was the truly revolutionary aspect of these plays; it was rather Ibsen's determination to challenge social convention and hypocrisy, which barred the way to individual self-realization.

Ibsen read few books; but he did read newspapers—and his reading is reflected not only in his involvement in contemporary debates but in the language and style of his plays. His actors were not required to strike heroic poses and indulge in elevated conceits, but to talk to each other in the contemporary language of everyday life. Acting traditions had to change before Ibsen's ideas could be realised.

From 1877 Ibsen's plays are entirely in prose, and the centre of interest narrows to a small group of people, frequently a family within the four walls of their home, a refuge which grows more and more like a prison as the conflict intensifies. The mainspring of the action is often the revelation of a guilty secret, a past misdeed which returns to haunt the present and disrupt the fragile security which has been erected over its concealment. The end is often death or despair (*Ghosts*, *The Wild Duck*, *Rosmersholm*); with the relentlessness of Greek tragedy, the characters are doomed by their own acts even as they struggle to escape. It is but rarely that they find the strength to take charge of their own fates, as in *The Lady from the Sea*, where understanding and tolerance break the vicious spiral of mutual destructiveness.

Ibsen's late plays puzzled critics and audiences; they found them obscure and disturbing. In the 1890's he began to depart from the familiar realistic form and to move towards a more experimental, modernistic drama. Complex images or symbols dominate the play, like the tower in *The Master Builder* or the iron mountains in *John Gabriel Borkman*; strange, surreal characters appear; the protagonists are groping uncertainly for the meaning of life. In Ibsen's last play, *When We Dead Awaken*, the artist and his muse disappear into the apocalypse hand in hand.

Ibsen wrote not just in one dramatic form but in many. There are few European dramatists since his day who do not owe something to his tightly controlled form and his sense of theatre.

—Janet Garton

ILLYÉS

ILLYÉS, Gyula. Born in Rácegrespuszta, Hungary, 2 November 1902. Educated in Budapest, 1916-19; at the Sorbonne, Paris, in the 1920's. Married Flóra Kozmutza; one daughter. Forced to leave Hungary in 1921 because of leftist activity; lived in Paris until 1926, then returned to Hungary; contributor from 1928 and Editor, with Mihály Babits, 1937-41, *Nyugat* [West]; Founding Editor, *Magyar Csillag* [Hungarian Star], 1941-44; Editor, *Válasz* [The Answer], 1946-48. Co-Founder, 1939, and parliamentary representative from 1945, National Peasant Party. Vice President, International P.E.N., from 1970. Recipient: Baumgarten Prize, 4 times in the 1930's; Kossuth Prize, 1948, 1953, 1970; International Grand Prize for Poetry, 1965. Commander, Order of Arts and Letters (France), 1974. *Died 14 April 1983.*

PUBLICATIONS

Collections

Munkái [Works]. 1969—

Verse

Nehéz föld [Heavy Earth]. 1928.
Három öreg [Three Old Men]. 1931.
Sarjúrendek [Swaths of Hay]. 1931.
Hősökről beszélek [I Speak of Heroes]. 1933.
Ifjúság [Youth]. 1934.
Szálló egek alatt [Under a Moving Sky]. 1935.
Rend a romokban [Order upon Ruins]. 1937.
Külön világban [In a Separate World]. 1939.
Összegyűjtött versei [Collected Poems]. 1940.
Válogatott versek [Selected Verse]. 1943.
Egy év [A Single Year]. 1945.
Összes versei [Complete Poems]. 3 vols., 1947.
Szembenézve [Face to Face]. 1947.
Tizenkét nap Bulgáriában [Twelve Days in Bulgaria]. 1947.
Két kéz [Two Hands]. 1950.
Válogatott versei [Selected Verses]. 1952.
A csodafurulyás juhász [The Shepherd and His Miraculous Flute]. 1954.
Kézfogások [Handclasps]. 1956.
Új versek [New Poems]. 1961.
Nem volt elég... [It Was Not Enough]. 1962.
Nyitott ajtó [Open Door]. 1963.
Dőlt vitorla [With Tilted Sail]. 1965.
Poharaim [My Cups]. 1967.
A Tribute to Illyés, edited by Thomas Kabdebo and Paul Tabori. 1968.
Fekete-fehér [Black-White]. 1968.
Selected Poems, edited by Thomas Kabdebo and Paul Tabori. 1971.
Abbahagyott versek [Unfinished Poems]. 1971.
Teremteni: Összegyűjtött versek 1946-1968 [To Create: Collected Poems]. 1972.
Haza a magasban: összergyűjtött versek 1920-1945 [Homeland in the Heights: Collected Poems]. 1972.
Minden lehet: Új versek [Everything Is Possible: New Poems]. 1973.
Különös testamentum [A Strange Testament]. 1977.
Közügy [Public Matter]. 1981.

Konok kikelet [Stubborn Springtime]. 1981.
A semmi közelit [The Approach of Nothingness]. 1983.

Plays

A tű foka [The Eye of the Needle]. 1944.
Lélekbúvár [Psychiatrist]. 1948.
Tűz-víz [Fire-Water]. 1952; revised version as *Fáklyaláng* [Torchbearers], 1953.
Ozorai példa [The Example of Ozora]. 1952.
Tűvé-tevők [Turning the House Upside Down]. 1953.
Dózsa György [George Dozsa]. 1954.
Malom a Séden [Mill on the Séd]. 1960.
Bolhabál [Flea Dance]. 1962.
Különc [The Eccentric]. 1963.
Kegyenc [The Minion], from a play by László Teleki. 1963.
Az éden elvesztése: Oratórium [The Loss of Eden: An Oratorio]. 1967.
Drámák [Plays]. 2 vols., 1969.
Tiszták [The Pure Ones]. 1969.
Testvérek [Brothers]. 1972.
Bál a pusztán; Bölcsek a fán [Ball at the Ranch; Wise Men on the Tree]. 1972.
Ujabb drámak [More Recent Plays]. 1974.
Dániel az övei közt [Daniel among His Own People]. 1976.

Fiction

Puszták népe. 1936; as *People from the Puszta,* 1967.
Kora tavasz [Early Spring]. 1941.
Húnok Párizsban [Huns in Paris]. 1946.
Két férfi [Two Men]. 1950.
Kháron ladikján [In Charon's Boat]. 1969.
Once upon a Time: Forty Hungarian Folk-tales. 1970.

Other

Oroszország [Russia]. 1934.
Petöfi (biography). 1936; translated as *Petöfi,* 1974.
Magyarok [Hungarians]. 1938.
Ki a magyar? [The Hungarian—Who Is He?]. 1939.
Lélek és kenyér [Soul and Bread], with Flora Kozmutza. 1939.
Csizma az asztalon [Boots on the Table]. 1941.
Mint a darvak [Like Cranes]. 1942.
Honfoglalók között [Among the New Masters]. 1945.
Kiáltvány a parasztság művelődése ügyében! [Manifesto about the Education of the Peasantry]. 1946.
Franciaországi változások [Changes in France]. 1947.
Ebéd a kastélyban [Lunch in the Castle]. 1962.
Ingyen lakoma: Tanulmányok, vallomások [A Free Feast: Studies, Confessions]. 2 vols., 1964.
Hajszálgyökerek [Capillary Roots]. 1971.
Itt elned kell [You Have to Live Here]. 1976.
Beatrice aprodjai [The Pages of Beatrice]. 1978.

*

ILLYÉS

Critical Studies: *Az ismeretlen Illyés* [The Unknown Illyes] by László Gara, 1965; "The Seventy Years of Illyés" by Miklós Beladi, in *New Hungarian Quarterly 48*, 1972.

*   *   *

Gyula Illyés was a poet first and foremost, although he created works of importance in practically all literary genres. Born into a poor family on a manorial estate in western Hungary, he remained loyal to the cause of the underprivileged throughout his life, though in old age he was regarded by many as the most forceful literary representative of the whole Hungarian nation. His early poetry was influenced by French surrealism and the constructivism of Lajos Kassák but soon after his return to Hungary from Paris in 1926 he found his own distinctive voice. While in his epic poems he followed the traditions of popular realism, his lyrical verse was characterised by a supple syntax, admirable intellectual vigour, and sharp psychological introspection. In some pre-war poems such as "The Wonder Castle" Illyés foretold the collapse of the anachronistic social system of Hungary based on entrenched class-privilege; to the Second World War he reacted with the lyrical diary *Egy év* (A Single Year) and with the rousing condemnation of the poem "It was not enough." Among his post-war collections probably *Kézfogások* (Handclasps) and *Dölt vitorla* (With Tilted Sail) were the most accomplished. Outside Hungary he will be best remembered for the powerful "A Sentence for Tyranny" (English version by Vernon Watkins), a long litany of unfreedom told through a succession of poetic metaphors including this stanza:

> Where seek tyranny? Think again:
> Everyone is a link in the chain;
> Of tyranny's stench you are not free:
> You yourself are tyranny.

A Socialist since his youth, Illyés was bitterly disappointedat the un-Socialist manner in which most Communist regimes in Central East Europe suppressed and forcibly tried to assimilate their Hungarian national minorities. His solidarity with fellow-Hungarians outside the borders of Hungary was expressed in a number of poems as well as essays; for example he wrote an introduction to Kálmán Janics's book on the persecution of the Hungarian ethnic minority in Czechoslovakia after 1945. Illyés was a master of the essay and published several collections of essays before and after the Second World War, *Hajszálgyökerek* (Capillary Roots) being the most comprehensive. He also wrote two autobiographical novels as well as an objective though cautious travelogue about Soviet Russia (following his visit there in 1934), but his most memorable prose works were probably *People from the Puszta*, which first focused attention on the semi-Asiatic living conditions of the Hungarian agrarian proletariat, and the short biography of the 19th-century revolutionary poet *Petőfi*. The genuine radicalism and uncompromising character of Sándor Petőfi exerted a great attraction on the less passionate but no less committed Illyés; like Petőfi he also believed that a politically active literature can promote the democratization of society.

Illyés the playwright was particularly fertile in the 1950's and 1960's when he wrote a cycle of historical plays tackling national issues. Both *Fáklyaláng* (Torchbearers) and *Ozorai példa* (The Example of Ozora) are about events of the war of independence which followed the Hungarian revolution of 1848. Later the character of László Teleki, a far-sighted but tragic political figure of the Kossuth emigration, captured Illyés's imagination and he wrote *Különc* (The Eccentric) about him, while another play entitled *Kegyenc* (The Minion) is the adaptation of a play by Teleki on a Roman theme, showing that it is impossible to serve tyranny without being dehumanized in the process. Of Illyés's later plays probably *Tiszták* (The Pure Ones) is the most interesting with its tale of moral conflict among the Cathar believers just before the fall of Monségur. By and large, Illyés's comedies are less successful than his dramas, though even the best plays suffer from an overdose of noble rhetoric and from too much concentration on national issues.

Apart from Hungary where since 1956 his standing has been exceptionally high, Illyés was better known in France than anywhere else in Europe; many French poets translated his work which he repaid by translating French poetry into Hungarian and editing in 1942 an excellent anthology *A Francia Irodalom Kincsesháza* (The Treasure-House of French Literature.)

—George Gömöri

IONESCO, Eugène. Born in Slatina, Romania, 26 November 1912; grew up in France. Educated at the University of Bucharest, graduated 1936; the Sorbonne, agrégation de lettres. Married Rodica Burileanu in 1936; one daughter. Taught French in Bucharest from age 18; worked as a proofreader in Paris, 1938; then free-lance writer. Recipient: Tours Festival Prize, for film, 1959; Italia Prize, 1963; Society of Authors theatre prize (France), 1966; National Grand Prize for Theatre, 1969; Monaco Grand Prize, 1969; Austrian State Prize for European Literature, 1970; Jerusalem Prize, 1973. Honorary doctorate: New York University, 1971; universities of Louvain, Warwick, Tel Aviv. Chevalier, Legion of Honor, 1970. Member, French Academy, 1971. Lives in Paris.

PUBLICATIONS

Plays

> *La Cantatrice chauve* (produced 1950). In *Théâtre I*, 1954; as *The Bald Soprano*, in *Plays I*, 1958.
> *La Leçon* (produced 1951). In *Théâtre I*, 1954; as *The Lesson*, in *Plays I*, 1958.
> *Les Chaises* (produced 1952). In *Théâtre I*, 1954; as *The Chairs*, in *Plays I*, 1958.
> *Sept petits sketches* (*Les Grandes Chaleurs, Le connaissez-vous?, Le Rhume onirique, La Jeune Fille à marier, Le Maître, La Nièce-Épouse, Le Salon de l'automobile*) (produced 1953). *La Jeune Fille à marier* included in *Théâtre II*, 1958, as *Maid to Marry*, in *Plays III*, 1960; *Le Maître* included in *Théâtre II*, 1958, as *The Leader*, in *Plays IV*, 1960; *La Nièce-Épouse* translated as *The Niece-Wife*, in *Ionesco* by Richard N. Coe, 1971; *Le Salon de l'automobile* included in *Théâtre IV*, 1966, as *The Motor Show* in *Plays V*, 1963.
> *Victimes du devoir* (produced 1953). In *Théâtre I*, 1954; as *Victims of Duty*, in *Plays II*, 1958.
> *Théâtre I* (*La Cantatrice chauve; La Leçon; Jacques, ou, La Soumission; Les Chaises; Victimes du devoir; Amédée, ou, Comment s'en debarrasser*). 1954.
> *Amédée; ou, Comment s'en débarrasser* (produced 1954). In *Théâtre I*, 1954; as *Amedee*, in *Plays II*, 1958.
> *Jacques; ou, La Soumission* (produced 1955). In *Théâtre I*, 1954; as *Jack*, in *Plays I*, 1958.
> *Le Nouveau Locataire* (produced 1955). In *Théâtre II*, 1958; as *The New Tenant*, in *Plays II*, 1958.
> *Le Tableau* (produced 1955). In *Théâtre III*, 1963; as *The Picture*, in *Plays VII*, 1968.
> *L'Impromptu de l'Alma; ou, Le Caméléon du berger* (produced 1956). In *Théâtre II*, 1958; as *Improvisation; or, The Shepherd's Chameleon*, in *Plays III*, 1960.

279

L'Avenir est dans les oeufs; ou, Il faut tout pour faire un monde (produced 1957). In *Théâtre II*, 1958; as *The Future Is in Eggs; or, It Takes All Sorts to Make a World*, in *Plays IV*, 1960.

Impromptu pour la Duchesse de Windsor (produced 1957).

Plays I (The Chairs; The Bald Soprano; The Lesson; Jack, or, Obedience). 1958; as *Four Plays*, 1958.

Théâtre II (L'Impromptu de l'Alma, ou, Le Caméléon du berger; Tueur sans gages; Le Nouveau Locataire; L'Avenir est dans les oeufs, ou, Il faut tout pour faire un monde; Le Maître; La Jeune Fille à marier). 1958.

Tueur sans gages (produced 1959). Included in *Théâtre II*, 1958; as *The Killer*, in *Plays III*, 1960.

Plays II (Amedee, or, How to Get Rid of It; The New Tenant; Victims of Duty). 1958.

Rhinocéros (produced 1959). In *Théâtre III*, 1963; translated as *Rhinoceros*, in *Plays IV*, 1960.

Scène à quatre (produced 1959). In *Théâtre III*, 1963; as *Foursome*, in *Plays V*, 1963.

Apprendre à marcher (ballet scenario; produced 1960). In *Théâtre IV*, 1966; as *Learning to Walk*, in *Plays IX*, 1973.

Plays III (The Killer; Improvisation, or, The Shepherd's Chameleon; Maid to Marry). 1960.

Plays IV (Rhinoceros; The Leader; The Future Is in Eggs, or, It Takes All Sorts to Make a World). 1960.

Délire à deux (produced 1962). In *Théâtre III*, 1963; as *Frenzy for Two*, in *Plays VI*, 1965.

Le Roi se meurt (produced 1962). 1963; as *Exit the King*, 1963.

Le Piéton de l'air (produced 1962). In *Théâtre III*, 1963; as *A Stroll in the Air*, in *Plays VI*, 1965.

Théâtre III (Rhinocéros; Le Piéton de l'air; Délire à deux; Le Tableau; Scène à quatre; Les Salutations; La Colère). 1963.

Plays V (Exit the King, The Motor Show, Foursome). 1963.

Les Salutations (produced 1970). In *Théâtre III*, 1963; as *Salutations*, in *Plays VII*, 1968.

La Soif et la faim (produced 1964). In *Théâtre IV*, 1966; as *Hunger and Thirst*, in *Plays VII*, 1968.

La Lacune (produced 1965). In *Théâtre IV*, 1966.

Plays VI (A Stroll in the Air, Frenzy for Two). 1965.

Pour préparer un oeuf dur (produced 1966). In *Théâtre IV*, 1966.

Théâtre IV (Le Roi se meurt, La Soif et la faim; La Lacune; Le Salon de l'automobile; L'Oeuf dur; Pour préparer un oeuf dur; Le Jeune Homme à marier; Apprendre à marcher). 1966.

Plays VII (Hunger and Thirst, The Picture, Anger, Salutations). 1968.

Jeux de massacre (produced 1970). 1970; as *Killing Game*, 1974.

Plays VIII (Here Comes a Chopper, The Oversight, The Foot of the Wall). 1971.

Macbett (produced 1972). 1972; translated as *Macbett*, in *Plays IX*, 1973.

Plays IX (Macbett, The Mire, Learning to Walk). 1973.

Ce formidable bordel (produced 1973). 1973.

Théâtre V (Jeux de massacre, Macbett, La Vase, Exercices de conversation et de diction françaises pour étudiants américains). 1974.

L'Homme aux valises (produced 1975). 1975; as *Man with Bags*, 1977; as *The Man with the Luggage*, in *Plays XI*, 1979.

A Hell of a Mess. 1975.

Plays X (Oh What a Bloody Circus, The Hard-Boiled Egg). 1976.

Plays XI (The Man with the Luggage, The Duel, Double Act). 1979.

Théâtre VII (Voyages chez les morts: Thèmes et variations). 1981; as *Plays XII (Journey among the Dead)*. 1983.

Screenplays: "La Colère" episode in *Les Sept Péchés capitaux*, 1962; *Monsieur Tête* (animated film), 1970.

Ballet Scenarios: for Television, with Fleming Flindt: *La Leçon*, 1963; *Le Jeune Homme à marier*, 1965; *The Triumph of Death*, 1971.

Fiction

> *La Photo du Colonel.* 1962; as *The Colonel's Photograph*, 1967.
> *Le Solitaire.* 1973; as *The Hermit*, 1974.

Other

> *Elegii pentru fiinti mici.* 1931.
> *Nu!* 1934.
> *Notes et contre-notes.* 1962; revised edition, 1966; as *Notes and Counter-Notes*, 1964.
> *Entretiens avec Claude Bonnefoy.* 1966; as *Conversations with Ionesco*, 1970.
> *Journal en miettes.* 1967; as *Fragments of a Journal*, 1968.
> *Présent passé, passé présent.* 1968; as *Present Past, Past Present*, 1971.
> *Conte pour enfants.* 4 vols., 1969-75; as *Story for Children*, 1968-75.
> *Découvertes*, illustrated by the author. 1969.
> *Mise en train: Première année de français*, with Michael Benamou. 1969.
> *Monsieur Tête* (animated film text). 1970.
> *Discours de réception à l'Académie française....* 1971.
> *Entre la vie et la rêve: Entretiens avec Claude Bonnefoy.* 1977.
> *Antidotes.* 1977.
> *Un Homme en question.* 1979.
> *Le Noir et le blanc.* 1980.
> *Hugoliade.* 1982.

*

Bibliography: *Ionesco: A Bibliography* by Griffith R. Hughes and Ruth Bury, 1974; *Bibliographie et index thématique des études sur Ionesco* by Wolfgang Leiner, 1980.

Critical Studies: *Ionesco* by Richard N. Coe, 1961; revised edition, 1971; *Ionesco* by Leonard C. Pronko, 1965; *Ionesco and Genet* by Josephine Jacobsen and William Randolph Mueller, 1968; *Brecht and Ionesco: Commitment in Context* by J.H. Wulbern, 1971; *Ionesco* by Ronald Hayman, 1972; *Ionesco* by Allan Lewis, 1972; *Ionesco: A Collection of Critical Essays* edited by Rose C. Lamont, 1973, and *The Two Faces of Ionesco* edited by Lamont and M.J. Friedman, 1978.

*   *   *

Like some other members of the new drama movement which burst on the French stage in the early 1950s, such as Beckett and Adamov, Eugène Ionesco was a foreigner and so an outsider. His first play, *The Bald Soprano*, created a sensation when it was put on in a small theatre in Paris, and the so-called "theatre of the absurd" was suddenly born. At least, not quite suddenly; there had been a few lone forerunners, but they had remained without much of a following. Ionesco's dazzling comedy about a couple who discover, after a long and increasingly zany conversation, that they are man and wife, changed all that. It came like a bolt from the blue, not surprisingly, since it was not based on anything which had gone before in the theatre, but on the eminently actable exchanges on a Linguaphone record which Ionesco had bought in an attempt to teach himself English conversation. That simple initial stroke of genius—to perceive theatricality where no one else had thought to look for it—launched Ionesco on a controversial but lucrative career which has brought him many honours. *The Lesson*, his next play, is a superb piece of theatre, in which a girl's private lesson turns into ritual rape and murder as the tutor "assaults" her with words which pour unstoppably from his lips. *The Chairs* is also concerned with proliferation, something of an Ionesco trade mark: in this case chairs fill the stage as an elderly couple welcome an invisible audience to listen to the wisdom of an orator who turns out to be dumb. In *Victims of Duty* one character is stuffed with food he does not want and another dies a "victim of duty" in a black comedy which disturbs and amuses the audience simultaneously. This gift—of treating serious matters with unsettling levity—is exercised to perfection in *Amedee*, perhaps Ionesco's finest work. Amedee is host to a corpse which he cannot rid his flat of (hence the subtitle "how to get rid of it"); indeed, it starts instead to grow, and mushrooms spring up from his floors. Hilariously incapable of disposing of the suffocating nuisance, Amedee (who, it is revealed, is a failed playwright) floats away from it all to the consternation of his long-suffering wife and the dismay of a passing policeman, who laments the loss to literature of such a promising writer.

There is a unique charm about the early plays that disappears when later on the writing becomes more didactic and less dramatically inventive. The recent works have been put on in major theatres by prestige companies but the critics' reaction has been mixed. This should not however detract from the magnitude of the achievement represented by the sheer theatrical inventiveness of the early work; besides, Ionesco is not merely a playwright. His meditations on the art of theatre, collected in *Notes and Counter-Notes*, are a major contribution to the theory of drama; he is also a poet, a short story writer of some power, and a charming autobiographer and essayist; altogether a fine, if not perhaps a great writer.

—John Fletcher

JARRY, Alfred.   Born in Laval, France, 8 September 1873.   Educated at schools in Saint-Brieuc, 1879-88, and Rennes, 1888-91; Lycée Henri IV, Paris, 1891-93. Military service, 1895. Writer: Co-Founding Director, with Rémy de Gourmont, *L'Ymagier*, 1894-95; publisher, *Perhinderion*, 1896. *Died 1 November 1907.*

PUBLICATIONS

Collections

    Oeuvres poetiques complètes, edited by Henri Parisot.   1945.
    Oeuvres complètes, edited by René Massat.   8 vols., 1948.
    Oeuvres complètes, edited by Michel Arrivé.   1972— .

Plays

    César-Antéchrist.   1895.

Tout Ubu, edited by Maurice Saillet.   1964; as *Ubu*, edited by Noël Arnaud and Henri Bordillon, 1980; as *The Ubu Plays*, 1968.
    Ubu roi (produced 1896).   1896; translated as *Ubu roi*, 1951.
    Ubu enchaîné (produced 1937).   1900; as *Enslaved*, 1953.
    Ubu cocu.   1944; as *Ubu Cuckolded*, 1965.
Le Moutardier du pape.   1907; as *La Papesse Jeanne*, edited by Marc Voline, 1981.
Pantagruel, with Eugène Demolder, music by Claude Terrasse.   1911.
Les Silènes, from a play by Christian Grabbe, edited by Pascal Pia.   1926.
L'Objet aimé.   1953.

Fiction

    Les Jours et les nuits.   1897.
    L'Amour en visites.   1898.
    L'Amour absolu.   1899; edited by Noël Arnaud and Henri Bordillon, 1980.
    Messaline.   1900; as *The Garden of Priapus*, 1936.
    Le Surmâle.   1902; as *The Supermale*, 1968.
    Les Gestes et opinions du docteur Faustroll, Pataphysicien.   1911; edited by Noël Arnaud and Henri Bordillon, 1980.
    La Dragonne, completed by Charlotte Jarry.   1943.

Verse

    La Revanche de la nuit, edited by Maurice Saillet.   1949.

Other

    Les Minutes de sable, mémorial (miscellany).   1894.
    Spéculations.   1911.
    Selected Works, edited by Roger Shattuck and Simon Watson Taylor.   1965.
    Le Manoir enchanté et quatre autres oeuvres inédites, edited by Noël Arnaud.   1974.

Other works have been issued in *Cahiers* and *Dossiers* of the Collège de 'Pataphysique, since 1950.

*

Critical Studies: *The Banquet Years: The Arts in France 1885-1918* by Roger Shattuck, 1959, revised edition, 1968; *Jarry: D'Ubu roi au Docteur Faustroll* by Noël Arnaud, 1974; *Jarry: Nihilism and the Theatre of the Absurd* by Maurice Marc LaBelle, 1980; *Jarry, dramaturge* by Henri Behar, 1980.

*   *   *

Alfred Jarry was a product of Romanticism and symbolism as well as of the disasters of the Franco-Prussian War and the Paris Commune. Consequently, he willingly became part of a cadre of creators who rejected traditional esthetic views and dared to experiment with new forms and ideas.

An uncompromising nihilist and pessimist, Jarry concluded that there was no hope of success or progress. One of the principal obstacles to cultural advancement is the omnipotent bourgeois, whom Jarry depicts as bepaunched, obsessed with money, egocentric, hypocritical, intellectually superficial, ignorant of humanism, and supportive of traditional and suppressive morality.

Jarry also hated christianity, and he delighted in ridiculing its theology in order to expose its grotesque irrationality. He also scoffed at the christian concept of an organized and benevolent universe; to Jarry, the cosmos is clearly absurd if not homicidal.

Ridicule, sarcasm, and vituperation are integral parts of Jarry's most devastating literary and philosophical weapon, his humor. He remains one of the foremost exponents of "black humor."

In his masterpiece, *King Ubu*, considered the progenitor of the "theater of the absurd," as well as in his letters and essays which concern this play, Jarry asked profound questions about the nature and function of the theater. He was especially insightful in his experiments in stage architecture, decor, costumes, voice, and "depersonalization" of performers. His rejection of Aristotle's *Poetics* was a liberating influence on modern drama, and his use of scatological expressions and symbols signaled that dramatists would no longer be bound by "decent" language.

Jarry is rightly associated with Baudelaire, Lautréamont, and Rimbaud as one of the illustrious "black angels of literature." He was indeed an original and revolutionary creator.

—Maurice M. LaBelle

JIMÉNEZ (Mantecón), Juan Ramón. Born in Moguer, Spain, 23 December 1881. Educated at a Jesuit school in Cadiz, 1891-96; University of Seville, 1896. Married Zenobia Camprubí Aymar in 1916 (died, 1956). In sanatoriums, 1901-05, then a writer: settled in Madrid, 1912, but left Spain in 1936; traveled and taught in Puerto Rico, Cuba, North Carolina, and Florida, 1939-42, Washington D.C., 1942-51; faculty member, University of Puerto Rico, Río Piedras, 1951-58. Recipient: Nobel Prize for Literature, 1956. *Died 29 May 1958.*

PUBLICATIONS

Collections

    Libros de poesía, edited by Agustin Caballero. 1957.
    Primeros libros de poesía, edited by Francisco Garfias. 1960.

Verse

    Almas de violeta. 1900.
    Ninfeas. 1900.
    Rimas. 1902.
    Arias tristes. 1903.
    Jardines lejanos. 1904.
    Elegías. 3 vols., 1908-10.
    Olvidanzas. 1909; edited by Francisco Garfias, 1968.
    Baladas de primavera. 1910.

La soledad sonora. 1911.
Pastorales. 1911.
Poemas mágicos y dolientes. 1911.
Melancolía. 1912.
Laberinto. 1913.
Estío. 1916.
Sonetos espirituales. 1917.
Diario de un poeta recién casado. 1917; revised edition, as *Diario de poeta y mar,* 1948, 1955.
Poesías escogidas. 1917.
Eternidades. 1918.
Piedra y cielo. 1919.
Segunda antología poética. 1922.
Poesía. 1923.
Belleza. 1923.
Canción. 1936.
Voces de mi copla. 1945.
La estación total. 1946.
Romances de Coral Gables. 1948.
Animal de fondo. 1949.
Fifty Spanish Poems, translated by J.B. Trend. 1950.
Tercera antología poética 1898-1953. 1957.
Three Hundred Poems 1903-1953, translated by Eloise Roach. 1962.
Lorca and Jiménez, translated by Robert Bly. 1973.
Jiménez and Machado, translated by J.B. Trend and J.L. Gili. 1974.
Leyenda, edited by A. Sánchez Romeralo. 1978.

Other

Platero y yo: Elegía andaluza. 1914; as *Platero and I,* 1956.
Conferencias I: Política poética. 1936.
Ciego ante ciegos. 1938.
Españoles de tres mundos. 1942.
El zaratán. 1946.
Selected Writings, translated by H.R. Hays. 1957.
Olvidos de Granada. 1960.
Cuadernos, edited by Francisco Garfias. 1960.
La corriente infinita. 1961.
El trabajo gustoso. 1961.
Cartas, edited by Francisco Garfias. 1962.
Primeras prosas, edited by Francisco Garfias. 1962.
Estética y ética estética. 1967.
Libros de prosa. 1969— .

Translator, with Z. Camprubí de Jiménez, *Jinetes hacia el mar,* by J.M. Synge. 1920.

*

Critical Studies: *The Religious Instinct in the Poetry of Jiménez* by Leo R. Cole, 1967; *Jiménez* by Donald F. Fogelquist, 1976; *Jiménez: The Modernist Apprenticeship 1895-1900* by Richard A. Cardwell, 1977; *The Line in the Margin: Jiménez and His Readings in Blake, Shelley, and Yeats* by H.T. Young, 1980.

*   *   *

Juvenile filter of a highly sentimental form of fin de siècle decadence in his first two books published in 1900, Juan Ramón Jiménez quickly grew more constrained and became a sensitive transmitter and adapter of Verlaine's style of symbolism, as well as a continuer of Bécquer in such works as *Rimas* (Rhymes) and *Arias tristes* (Sad Airs). This early lyrical stage led eventually to the triumph of the *Diario de un poeta recién casado* (Diary of a Newly Married Poet). Written as a result of its author's wedding in New York to Zenobia Camprubí Aymar, a Puerto Rican educated in America and Spain, the book exerted enormous influence on subsequent Hispanic poetry. It stands between the towers of Bécquer's *Rimas* (1871) and Lorca's *Romancero gitano* (*Gypsy Ballads*, 1928) as one of the indisputable landmarks of the modern Spanish lyric.

Leaving aside the prose descriptions of New York, Boston, and Philadelphia, the style of the *Diario* is lucid, stripped down to a minimum of adjectives and expressed in an unrhymed and brief free verse form. The imagists had introduced *vers libre* to the United States at about that time, and Jiménez reacted with a version he called *verso desnudo* (naked verse), a short stanza that had considerable impact on younger poets.

In the *Diario* the characteristic mature tone of Jiménez is set. Highly self-referential but less hermetic than Mallarmé, he began in this book a long series of poems that continue in *Eternidades* (Eternities) and *Belleza* (Beauty). They record epiphanies that express the manifold aspects of a mind perceiving the indifferent beauty of the world. Pebbles and petals on the one hand and the sea and sidereal distances on the other were among the fragments of his surroundings that Jiménez sought to appraise, reconnoiter, and finally to possess.

However, for many readers, he is the author of only one book: *Platero and I*. It is a pastoral prose poem that reveals many layers of meaning and nuance as the somberly clad poet-narrator, with his Nazarene beard, rides the donkey Platero through the village of Moguer and out into the countryside. The book also contains astute observations on the poor and oppressed.

Jiménez returned to the United States at the outbreak of the Spanish Civil War in 1936. The flat open land of the Florida Everglades inspired the much admired "Espacio" (Space). An audacious experiment with form, "Espacio" turns discourse into an examination of the possibilities of language. Contingency, the confluence of past and present, memory, spiritual versus carnal love, destiny and mortality are its themes.

Animal de fondo (Enduring Animal) celebrates the encounter with a humanistic god. Like Blake, he discovered the divinity of the creative consciousness, which seemed to him a god within and without, desiring and desired. On this note of apodictic humanism, with "all the clouds ablaze," the best of Jiménez's work concludes.

Except for the uneven early books, his work, although repetitive and unduly extensive— thirty books and a mass of unpublished material—sustains a remarkably high quality. He was a scrupulous self-critic and devoted much time to revising and rewriting large amounts of his poetry.

—Howard T. Young

JOHN OF THE CROSS,Saint (San Juan de la Cruz).   Born Juan de Yepes y Álvarez, in Fontiveros, Spain, in 1542. Boarded at an orphanage by his widowed mother; studied at Jesuit college, Medina del Campo, 1559-63; took the habit as Fray Juan de Santa Matía; attended Carmelite College of San Andrés, University of Salamanca, 1564-68; ordained, 1567. Joined

St. Teresa's reformed Discalced Order of Carmel in a priory at Duruelo, near Fontiveros, as San Juan de la Cruz, 1568-70, then at Mancera, 1570; rector of a new Carmelist college at University of Alcalá, 1571-72; confessor at convent in Ávila, 1572-77; controversy over reformation of the Carmelite order caused him to be confined in conventual prison in Toledo, 1577-78, because of his reforming attitudes; escaped to a nearby convent; at El Calvario hermitage near convent at Beas de Segura, 1578-79; rector of new Carmelite college at Baeza, 1579-82; prior of Los Mártires, Granada, 1582-88; prior at Segovia, 1588-91; out of favor with head of Discalced Order, and made a simple friar at Priory of La Peñuda, 1591. Beatified, 1675; Canonized, 1726. *Died 14 December 1591.*

PUBLICATIONS

Vida y obras completas, edited by Crisógono de Jesús, Matías del Niño, and Lucinio Ruano. 1946; 6th edition, 1972.
Complete Works, edited and translated by E. Allison Peers. 3 vols., 1934-35; poems also translated by Roy Campbell, 1951, John Frederick Nims, 1959, revised edition, 1968, Kieran Kavanaugh and Otilio Rodríguez, 1964, and Willis Barnstone, 1968.

*

Bibliography: *Bibliografia di S. Juan de la Cruz* by Pier P. Ottonello, 1966.

Critical Studies: *St. John of the Cross and Other Lectures and Addresses,* 1946, and *Handbook to the Life and Times of Saint Teresa and Saint John of the Cross,* 1954, both by E. Allison Peers; *Medieval Mystical Tradition and Saint John of the Cross* by a Benedictine of Stanbrook Abbey, 1954; *San Juan de la Cruz, Saint John of the Cross* by Bernardo Giovate, 1971; *St. John of the Cross: His Life and Poetry* by Gerald Brenan, 1973; *St. John of the Cross: Poems* by Margaret Wilson, 1975; *The Poet and the Mystic: A Study of the Cántico Espiritual of San Juan de la Cruz* by Colin P. Thompson, 1977.

*   *   *

The 22 poems of St. John of the Cross must certainly constitute one of the briefest opuses of any major poet, but, since the 1880's, they have exerted a significant influence on the course of European and American poetry. In his conviction that words provide, at best, only indirect access to experience and that meaning does not exist on a one-to-one basis but, instead, spills over from the play of rhetorical devices (see the 1584 prologue to "The Spiritual Canticle"), St. John anticipated the basic symbolist tenet of indirect expression as expounded by Mallarmé and Valéry (the latter acknowledged the importance to him of St. John). The highly polished lyrical quality of his lines in Spanish inspired Bécquer, whose work represents a transition from romanticism to symbolism, and found a worthy follower in the leading Spanish symbolist poet Juan Ramón Jiménez. St. John's presence may be discovered in "East Coker," the first of T.S. Eliot's *Four Quartets,* and the image "dark night of the soul" has gained much currency among modern writers.

The major theme of St. John's poetry is a description of the various stages of development that the soul undergoes in its efforts to become unified with God. In St. John's hands, this mystical undertaking achieves one of the highest levels of lyricism known to western poetry. Delicate alliteration and simple diction endow the poems with pellucid beauty. St. John chose to recount the story of divine love by having recourse to the symbols and devices used to portray human love, and this accounts for the strong but refined sensuality that characterizes his work. "The Dark Night," "The Spiritual Canticle," "The Living Flame of Love," and "Although by Night," to mention only some of the better-known poems, are nourished by three distinct sources: the pastoral tradition, exemplified in Spanish by Garcilaso de la Vega; the ballads (*romances*); and the Bible, above all, "The Song of Songs." St. John drew heavily from Solomon's adaptation of eastern nuptial songs to limn the marriage between the soul and God.

Part of the modern attraction of these poems is that they lend themselves so readily to multiple levels of meaning. "The Dark Night" is, at once, great amorous verse, a biographical description of escape from prison, and an allegory of mystical experience.

St. John left assiduously detailed comments on these poems. *Ascent of Mount Carmel* and *Dark Night of the Soul* do not get beyond the first 11 lines of the last named poem. The glosses on *The Spiritual Canticle* and *The Living Flame of Love* are complete. Written within the hermeneutic tradition of the Counter-Reformation, these commentaries, except for scattered moments, display none of the consummate literary talent of the poetry. Such is the disparity that it is almost as if one were reading two different authors. *Sayings of Light and Love*, a collection of aphorisms, and, incidentally, the only autograph of his work extant, displays many pleasant paradoxes, but hardly surpasses any other such miscellany. Clearly, it was only as a lyrical poet that he excelled.

—Howard T. Young

JUVENAL (Decimus Junius Juvenalis).   Born, possibly in Aquinum, c. 50-65 A.D. or perhaps later. Possibly became army officer, and then began career in administrative service of the emperor Domitian. *Died after 130 A.D.*

PUBLICATIONS

[*Satires*], edited by W.V. Clausen (with Persius's satires).   1959; *14 Satires* edited by J.D. Duff, 1970; also edited by Paolo Frassinetti and Lucia Di Salvo (with Persius's satires), 1979, and John Ferguson, 1979; translated by Rolfe Humphries, 1958, Hubert Creekmore, 1963, Jerome Mazzaro, 1965, Peter Green, 1967, Charles Plumb, 1968, and Steven Robinson, 1983.

*

Critical Studies: *Juvenal the Satirist* by Gilbert Highet, 1954; *Irony in Juvenal* by Alba Claudia Romano, 1979; *A Commentary on the Satires of Juvenal* by E. Courtney, 1980; *Three Classical Poets: Sappho, Catullus, and Juvenal* by Richard Jenkyns, 1982; *Essays on Roman Satire* by William S. Anderson, 1982.

*   *   *

Juvenal's entire oeuvre comprises 16 *Satires* in hexameters. They were published in five separate books during the reigns of the emperors Trajan and Hadrian.

In his first book (*Satires* 1-5) Juvenal adopts an indignant *persona*, following the convention of using a first-person mouthpiece expressing views not necessarily attributable to the poet himself. The angry man whose voice we hear in Book I was a type familiar to the Romans from philosophical works, e.g., of Seneca. As suits the angry man, the poems have the appearance of being a jumbled and excited outburst. Yet there is order behind the façade of disorder: Juvenal has arranged the poems in an alternating sequence featuring the patron-client relationship perverted by mercenary preoccupations (*Satires* 1, 3, and 5) and the corrupt nobility as a canker at the heart of Roman society (*Satires* 2 and 4). The satiric technique invites us to agree with the angry rantings *and* to ridicule the angry man for his narrow-minded, petty, and vicious obsessions. The high epic tone adopted ought to dignify the attack on society but the intrusion of mundane and crude words and ideas deflates the pretensions of the angry *persona*. The "angry" approach proved to be Juvenal's most important legacy to and influence on later European satire.

The angry stance is maintained in Book II (*Satire* 6), a huge attack of epic proportions and unparalleled length in Roman satire on women. The angry man reveals himself as utterly unreasonable (e.g., he cannot stand even a perfect woman!) and hence absurd.

Juvenal has now exhausted the "angry" approach and in his remaining three Books he adopts an ironic and detached *persona*. In the three poems of Book III Juvenal applies this new approach to the main themes of Book I, patrons and clients (*Satires* 7 and 9) and the nobility (*Satire* 8).

The poems of Books IV and V feature a wide variety of topics: men's prayers (*Satire* 10), a simple meal (*Satire* 11), true and false friendship (*Satire* 12); anger and vengeance (*Satire* 13), parents' bad examples to their children (*Satire* 14), the quality of humanness (*Satire* 15), the advantages of the soldier's life (*Satire* 16: incomplete). These poems are reminiscent of Horace's satire, sharing his interest in friendship and moderation and his double-edged ironic approach. At the same time, Juvenal's abandonment of the early angry *persona* emerges clearly from *Satire* 13 where anger is explicitly condemned.

Complementing the variety of the *Satires*, there are characteristic features present throughout Juvenal's work. The *Satires* constantly reflect the rhetorical nature of Roman education. Rhetoric is Juvenal's idiom which he exploits brilliantly to produce many memorable epigrammatic phrases. He is clearly steeped in Roman literature: the poems are packed with literary allusions, and throughout Juvenal shows his debt to his predecessors in the genre, Lucilius, Horace, and Persius. In every poem, Juvenal's powers of vivid visualisation are evident. He prefers to depict vice in the concrete rather than the abstract, ranging from brief vignettes of crooks or perverts sumptuously dressed to extended descriptions, for example of a subhuman act of cannibalism.

Finally, Juvenal's essential satiric technique may perhaps be encapsulated in the word "surprise." Throughout his poems, Juvenal springs on his audience surprise after surprise, showing his great fund of wit and humour. On a large scale, it is impossible to predict the direction or proportions of a poem: Juvenal often links two unconnected topics to create surprise. On a smaller scale, he often saves for the end of a section or sentence or line a surprise word or idea: deflating, pompous, witty, funny, or absurd. Particularly powerful are pithy juxtapositions like "princess whore" and "muleteer consul." All such surprises were highly effective in the original context of oral recitation. In short, Juvenal exemplifies Feinberg's definition of satire as "the playfully critical distortion of the familiar."

—S.H. Braund

KAFKA, Franz. Born in Prague, 3 July 1883. Educated at Staatsgymnasium, Prague; German University, Prague, 1901-06; qualified in law: unpaid work in law courts, 1906-07. Worked for Assicurazioni Generali insurance company, 1907-08; Workers Accident Insurance Institute, 1908-22: retired because of tuberculosis. *Died 3 June 1924.*

PUBLICATIONS

Collections

> *Gesammelte Werke*, edited by Max Brod and others. 11 vols., 1950— .
> *Schriften, Tagebücher, Briefe*, edited by Nahum N. Glatzer and others. 1983— .

Fiction

> *Betrachtung.* 1913.
> *Die Verwandlung.* 1915.
> *Der Heizer.* 1916.
> *Das Urteil.* 1916.
> *In der Strafkolonie.* 1919.
> *Ein Landarzt.* 1919.
> *Ein Hungerkünstler.* 1924.
> *Der Prozess.* 1925; as *The Trial*, 1937.
> *Das Schloss.* 1926; as *The Castle*, 1930.
> *Amerika.* 1927; original version, as *Der Verschollene*, edited by Jost Schillemeit, 1983; translated as *Amerika*, 1949.
> *Beim Bau der chinesischen Mauer.* 1931.
> *Wedding Preparations in the Country and Other Stories.* 1953.
> *Dearest Father: Stories and Other Writings.* 1954.
> *Metamorphosis and Other Stories.* 1961.
> *Sämtliche Erzählungen*, edited by Paul Raabe. 1970.
> *Complete Stories*, edited by Nahum N. Glatzer. 1971.
> *Shorter Works*, edited by Malcolm Pasley. 1973.

Other

> *Tagebücher 1910-23.* 1951; as *Diaries*, edited by Max Brod, 2 vols., 1948-49.
> *Briefe an Milena*, edited by Willy Haas. 1951; as *Letters to Milena*, 1953.
> *Briefe 1902-24.* 1958.
> *Briefe an Felice*, edited by Erich Heller and Jürgen Born. 1967; as *Letters to Felice*, 1973.
> *Briefe an Ottila und die Familie*, edited by Klaus Wagenbach and Hartmut Binder. 1975.

*

Bibliography: *A Kafka Bibliography 1908-76* by Angel Flores, 1976.

Critical Studies: *The Kafka Problem* edited by Angel Flores, 1946, and *The Kafka Debate* by Flores, 1976; *Kafka's Castle*, 1956, and *Kafka*, 1973, both by Ronald Gray, and *Kafka: A Collection of Critical Essays* edited by Gray, 1962; *Kafka: Parable and Paradox* by Heinz Politzer, 1962; *The Reluctant Pessimist: A Study of Kafka* by A.P. Foulkes, 1967; *Kafka* by Anthony Thorlby, 1972; *Kafka: A Collection of Criticism* edited by Leo Hamalian, 1974; *Kafka: Literature as Corrective Punishment* by Franz Kuna, 1974, and *On Kafka* edited by

Kuna, 1976; *Kafka* by Meno Spann, 1976; *The World of Kafka* by J.P. Stern, 1980; *K: A Biography of Kafka* by Ronald Hayman, 1981; *Kafka: Geometrician of Metaphor* by Henry Sussman, 1981; *Kafka of Prague* by Jiri Grusa, 1983.

*　　*　　*

If one were to judge the worth of an author solely according to the amount of critical commentary which his works have generated, then there is no doubt that Kafka has already earned his place beside Shakespeare, Goethe, and Cervantes. The primary attraction and challenge for the critic lie in the strange and enigmatic quality of the fiction, its disturbing capacity to invite and yet to resist interpretation, and at the same time the intuitive belief of many readers that they are being addressed by a writer who has managed to capture in words the very essence of 20th-century experience and *Angst*. Kafka's stories, moreover, possess a degree of semantic openness which makes it possible to re-express many of his narrated scenes and images within the interpretative schemes which have come to dominate modern thought, be they derived from political systems, theological concerns, psychoanalysis, or philosophy. Nor is it difficult, once such an interpretation has been put forward, to "corroborate" it by referring to events in the author's life or indeed to more general cultural factors which helped shape early 20th-century views of the individual's relationship to society, to his own unconscious self, or to the Divine. And finally, the lack of specificity characteristic of Kafka's fiction can be resolved into conceptual systems derived from the author's non-fictional writings, for the critic has at his disposal a considerable collection of posthumously published letters, diaries, fragments, and conversations.

There is some evidence, when we consider Kafka's work in its chronological entirety, that the author was increasingly concerned to forestall the kind of criticism which might attempt to view his fictional creations as referring in a straightforward way to events, localities, or people outside the narratives. In the three novels this process is apparent in the progressive disappearance of all references to actual topographical entities as well as in the names of the three main protagonists, Karl Rossmann, Josef K, and K. Some of the later short stories, told through the first-person mental associations of shadowy animal narrators, carry this stylistic device to the point that the reader is deprived of almost any familiar landmark which might indicate a concealed meaning waiting to be discovered.

Kafka's earliest novel *Amerika* (first published in 1927) has attracted less critical attention than his later works, and is regarded by some as an only partially successful attempt to satirize the institutions of the New World by recounting them from the perspective of Karl Rossmann, a young European who has been packed off to America by his parents after he is seduced by a servant girl. The bizarre adventures which befall Karl certainly possess a Chaplin-like quality, and significantly they provide us with one of Kafka's few overt examples of social criticism, for the episodic narrative is a reversal of the Horatio Alger, poor-boy-makes-good myth; Karl, despite his unfailing optimism and his determination to succeed, is slowly destroyed by the very system of values in which he has faith. The novel is fragmentary and unfinished, and a final interpretation would have to speculate on the possible ending. Max Brod, Kafka's biographer and confidant, insisted that the novel was to end "on a note of reconciliation," but this is thrown into doubt by a diary entry (30 September 1915) in which Kafka stated that the "innocent" Rossmann, just like the "guilty" K, was to meet his death.

Der Prozess and *Das Schloss*, translated respectively as *The Trial* and *The Castle*, are also fragmentary, and *The Castle*, like *Amerika*, remained without an ending. The two later novels have in common a number of thematic similarities, and to a much greater extent than *Amerika* they portray the singular and oppressive dreamlike sequences which have enriched many of the world's languages with the phrase "it's like something out of Kafka." Reflecting the two sides of Kafka's aphorism, according to which, "He who seeks, will not find; he who does not seek will be found," the two novels suggest the existence of aloof and inscrutable authorities which can reach out to destroy, as in *The Trial*, or which will withdraw into a state of total inaccessibility as in *The Castle*. In each case the authorities are represented by a lower hierarchy of pompous officials and libertine servants, and they have additionally given rise to a vast body of anecdotal and superstitious lore designed to divine their intentions in order that one may either cooperate with them or thwart their will. The diversity of opinion typical of Kafka interpretation is strikingly evident in the interpretations of these two novels. They have been seen as the vain struggle of the individual seeking to comprehend the faceless bureaucracies which govern him, as depictions of the alienated Jew in a hostile Christian world, as grotesque fictive transmutations of Kafka's obsession with his father's power, and as parables on humanity's eternal but fruitless striving for the Absolute. Before embracing any one of these interpretations, the reader might do well to heed the words of advice offered to Josef K by the prison chaplain in *The Trial*: "You mustn't pay too much attention to opinions. The words are unchangeable, and the opinions are often just an expression of despair about that."

According to Max Brod, Kafka "thought in pictures and he spoke in pictures." This tendency to pictorialize inner thoughts and feelings, to lend visual form to the subjective and the abstract, is a feature which Kafka's writings share with dreams, and it can be seen as one of the guiding structural principles of the short stories and of the literary experimentation published in the volume *Wedding Preparations in the Country*. On the surface Kafka's short pieces treat a remarkable variety of themes and situations, including the father-son conflict in "The Judgment," the transformation of a commercial traveller into a monstrous insect in "The Metamorphosis," the horrifying method of execution described in "In the Penal Colony," and the self-imposed death by starvation depicted in "A Hunger Artist." There are stories narrated both by and about animals, and pieces concerning themselves with circus riders, country doctors, mysterious hunters, Ulysses, and the Emperor of China. A unifying stylistic factor behind this thematic diversity is the fact that each story can be interpreted as the manifest portrayal of certain inner experiences and states of mind which recur constantly in Kafka's fiction. This does not mean of course that the stories should be regarded simply as variations to be reduced to the same theme, for each work contributes uniquely through its imagery and structure to the thematic aspect which it embodies. Nor should it be forgotten that the fiction, even though Kafka himself once described it as "the representation of my inner life," has been received as significant and compelling by countless readers who have related it to their own experience of the 20th century.

—A.P. Foulkes

KAWABATA Yasunari. Born in Osaka, Japan, 11 June 1899. Educated at Ibaragi Middle School, 1915-17, and First Higher School 1917-20, Ibaragi; Tokyo Imperial University, 1920-24, degree in Japanese literature 1924. Married Hideko; one daughter. Writer and journalist: helped found *Bungei Jidai* magazine, 1924, and Kamakura Bunko, publishers, Kamakura, later in Tokyo, 1945. Author-in-Residence, University of Hawaii, Honolulu, 1969. Chairman, 1948, and Vice-President, 1959-69, Japan P.E.N. Recipient: Bungei Konwa Kai prize, 1937; Kikuchi Kan Prize, 1944; Geijutsuin-sho prize, 1952; Japan Academy of Arts prize, 1952; Noma Literary Prize, 1954; Goethe Medal (Frankfurt), 1959; Prix du Meilleur Livre Etranger, 1961; Nobel Prize for Literature, 1968. Member, Japan Academy of Arts, 1954. First Class Order of the Rising Sun, 1972. *Died 16 April 1972.*

PUBLICATIONS

Collections

Zenshu. 19 vols., 1969-74.

Fiction

Kanjo shushoku [Sentimental Decoration]. 1926.
Tenohira no shosetsu [Stories on the Palm]. 1926.
Izu no odoriko [The Izu Dancer]. 1926.
Asakusa kurenaidan [The Red Gang of Asakusa]. 1930.
Jojoka [Lyrical Feelings]. 1934.
Kinju [Of Birds and Beasts]. 1935.
Hana no warutsu [The Flower Waltz]. 1936.
Yukiguni. 1937; revised edition, 1948; as *Snow Country*, 1957.
Aisuru hitotachi [Lovers]. 1941.
Utsukushii tabi [Beautiful Travel]. 1947.
Otome no minato [Sea-Port with a Girl]. 1948.
Shiroi mangetsu [White Full-Moon]. 1948.
Maihime [The Dancer]. 1951.
Sembazuru. 1952; as *Thousand Cranes*, 1959.
Hi mo tsuki mo [Days and Months]. 1953.
Suigetsu [The Moon on the Water]. 1953.
Yama no oto. 1954; as *The Sound of the Mountain*, 1970.
Go sei-gen kidan. 1954; as *The Master of Go*, 1972.
Mizuumi. 1955; as *The Lake*, 1974.
Onna de aru koto [To Be a Woman]. 1956-58.
Nemureru bijo [House of the Sleeping Beauties]. 1961.
The Izu Dancer and Others. 1964.
Kata-ude [One Arm]. 1965.
Utsukushisa to kanashimi to. 1965; as *Beauty and Sadness*, 1975.
Sakuhin sen [Selected Works]. 1968.
House of the Sleeping Beauties and Other Stories. 1969.
Tampopo [Dandelion]. 1972.

Other

Bunsho [Prose Style]. 1942.
Zenshu [Collected Works]. 16 vols., 1948-54; revised edition, 12 vols., 1959-61.
Aishu [Sorrow] (stories and essays). 1949.
Asakusa monogatari [Asakusa Story]. 1950.
Shosetsu no kenkyu [Studies of the Novel]. 1953.
Tokyo no hito [The People of Tokyo]. 4 vols., 1955.
Who's Who among Japanese Writers, with Aono Suekichi. 1957.
Koto [Kyoto]. 1962.
Senshu [Selected Works], edited by Yoshiyuki Junnosuke. 1968.
Utsukushii nihon no watakushi; Japan, The Beautiful, and Myself (Nobel Prize lecture). 1969.
Shosetsu nyumon [Introduction to the Novel]. 1970.

*

Critical Studies: *Accomplices of Silence: The Modern Japanese Novel* by Masao Miyoshi, 1974; *The Search for Authenticity in Modern Japanese Literature* by Hisaaki Yamanouchi, 1978; *The Moon in the Water: Understanding Tanizaki, Kawabata, and Mishima* by Gwenn Boardman Petersen, 1979.

*　　*　　*

Japan's only Nobel laureate in literature so far, Kawabata is perhaps better known than any other recent writer of his country. His standing at home, however, may not be quite so unchallenged: a large number of critics might mention more intellectual and ideological writers as truly representative of the modern Japanese tradition.

Kawabata's reputation rests on the subtly evocative images that continually startle the reader with clarity and brilliance. When successful—as in *Snow Country, The Sound of the Mountain*, or *The House of the Sleeping Beauties*—the images serve to add dimensions to the straight-forward narrative flow. They suspend the plot, deflect the causal expectation, and open up new spaces for meaning. The narrative vibrates with the fullness of sensory perception that reaches out toward what remains untold. When overcharged, however, the images tend to turn inert. In *Thousand Cranes* or *Beauty and Sadness*, for instance, flashes after flashes of images light up aimlessly, as if prettiness were the tale's sole objective. The result is an ostentatious display in the manner of airline posters. Kawabata is never completely free from such pitfalls.

Kawabata's dependence on visualization must be explained by the fact that he is essentially a short-story writer. By this it is not meant that he principally wrote short stories—though he in fact did write a great many—but that his "novels" were nearly always accumulated short stories. His longer works grew out of assembled modules, each managing to remain flexible and open-ended like individual verse-stanzas in a *renga* (linked poem). That is, his narrative is generated by spatialization and detemporalization of acts and events. Hence it is not causal but casual: it intersects time and offers the still moments pictorially. Neither psychological nor sociological, Kawabata's narrative is antithetical to novelistic representation and is likewise resistant to novelistic analysis. His characters are often unfulfilled swift sketches, and his plots are series of unconnected tableaux vivants. Both are embedded among the beauties of background. In the Kawabata territory, scenery is serious.

Although sensitive to popular demands, Kawabata had a streak of stubbornness that saved as well as damned him. During the second world war, he was reluctant to play an active role in the militarist programs, spending his time quietly reading the nation's classics. In the postwar years when most intellectuals switched their allegiance to Western humanism, Kawabata kept recalling Japan's traditional heritage. Later, when Mishima Yukio's self-destructive histrionics was increasingly antagonizing Japan's literary establishment, Kawabata steadfastly stood with the younger writer. His uncharacteristic involvement in municipal politics just before his own suicide, too, seems inseparable from his attachment to his nationalist friend.

It would be a mistake to latch on to Kawabata's art as the quintessence of the famed "Japanese lyricism." And yet one recalls even now how solacing and encouraging the sensitive images in his work were to the war-ravaged Japanese in those dark postwar years. Kawabata is thus remembered despite his refusal to propose any particular reflection or recommendation in his art.

—Masao Miyoshi

KAZANTZAKIS, Nikos. Born in Heraklion, Crete, 18 February 1883. Educated at French School of Holy Cross, Naxos, 1897-99; gymnasium, Heraklion, 1899-1902; University of Athens, 1902-06, degree in law; studied in Paris, Germany, and Italy, 1906-10. Married Eleni Samios (second wife) in 1945. Writer and traveler; director general of Ministry of Public Welfare, 1919-20; Cabinet Minister without Portfolio, 1945; served in Unesco's Department of Translations of the Classics, 1947-48. Recipient: Lenin Peace Prize. *Died 26 October 1957.*

PUBLICATIONS

Fiction

Ophis kai Krino. 1906; as *Serpent and Lily*, 1980.
Toda Raba (written in French). 1934; translated as *Toda Raba*, 1964.
Vios kai Politeia tou Alexi Zorba. 1946; as *Zorba the Greek*, 1952.
O Kapetan Michalis. 1953; as *Freedom or Death*, 1955; as *Freedom and Death*, 1956.
O Christos Xanastavronetai. 1954; as *The Greek Passion*, 1954; as *Christ Recrucified*, 1954.
O Teleftaios Peirasmos. 1955; as *The Last Temptation of Christ*, 1960.
O Ftochoulis tou Theou. 1956; as *Saint Francis*, 1962; as *God's Pauper*, 1962.
Le Jardin des rochers (written in French). 1959; as *The Rock Garden*, 1963.
Aderfofades. 1963; as *The Fratricides*, 1964.

Plays

O Protomastoras. 1910.
Niceforos Fokas. 1927.
Christos. 1928.
Odysseas. 1928.
Melissa. 1939; translated as *Melissa*, in *Three Plays*, 1956.
Ioulianos. 1945.
O Kapodistrias. 1946.
Theatro: Tragodies (includes *Prometheas, Kouros, Odysseas, Melissa, Christos, Ioulianos, Niceforos Fokas, Konstantinos o Paleaologos, O Kapodistrias, Christoforos Kolomvos, Sodoma kai Gomorra, Voudos*). 3 vols., 1955-56; *Kouros* and *Christoforos Kolomvos* translated as *Kouros* and *Christopher Columbus*, in *Three Plays*, 1969; *Voudos* translated as *Buddha*, 1983.

Verse

Odyseia. 1938; as *The Odyssey: A Modern Sequel*, translated by Kimon Friar, 1958.
Tertsines. 1960.

Other

O Freiderikos Nitse [Friedrich Nietzsche]. 1909.
Salvatores Dei: Askitiki. 1927; revised edition, 1945; as *The Saviors of God: Spiritual Exercises*, 1960.
Taxidevontas (travel). 1927.
Te eida set Rousia. 2 vols., 1928; as *Taxidevontas: Rousia*, 1956.

Historia tes Rosikes logotechnias.   2 vols., 1930.
Taxidevontas: Ispania.   1937; as *Spain*, 1963.
O Morias.   1937; as *Journey to the Morea*, 1965; as *Travels in Greece*, 1966.
Taxidevontas II: Iaponia, Kina.   1938; as *Japan-China*, 1963; as *Travels in China and Japan*, 1964.
Taxidevontas III: Anglia.   1941; as *England*, 1965.
Epistoles pros te Galateia.   1958.
Anafora ston Greco.   1961; as *Report to Greco*, 1965.
Tetrakosia grammata tou Kazantzakis sto Prevelaki (letters).   1965.
Journeying: Travels in Italy, Egypt, Sinai, Jerusalem, and Cyprus.   1975.
Alexander the Great (juvenile).   1982.

Translated *The Divine Comedy* by Dante, *Faust* by Goethe, *Iliad* by Homer, several Platonic dialogues, *The Birth of Tragedy* and *Thus Spake Zarathustra* by Nietzsche, *The Prince* by Machiavelli, *Conversations with Goethe* by Eckermann, *Origin of Species* by Darwin, *On Laughter* by Bergson, and other works, including many books for children.

*

Bibliography: *Kazantzakis bibliografi* by G.K. Katsimpales, 1958; "Kazantzakis in America: A Bibliography of Translations and Comment" by Sandra A. Parker, in *Bulletin of Bibliography* 25, 1968.

Critical Studies: *Kazantzakis and His Odyssey* by Pandelis Prevelakis, 1961; *Kazantzakis: A Biography Based on His Letters*, 1968, and *Kazantzakis*, 1970, both by Helen Kazantzakis; *Kazantzakis*, 1972, and *Kazantzakis and the Linguistic Revolution in Greek Literature*, 1972, both by Peter Bien; *Kazantzakis: The Politics of Salvation* by James F. Lea, 1979; *The Cretan Glance: The World and Art of Kazantzakis* by Morton P. Levitt, 1980.

*   *   *

Nikos Kazantzakis was an insatiable traveller, internally and externally. He visited many countries. He read a vast amount of books. He calls to mind Wordsworth's lines about Newton: "a mind for ever/voyaging through strange seas of thought, alone" (*Prelude* III, 62-3). No wonder he took as the hero of his epic (*Odyssey*, 1938) a timeless, intellectual Odysseus.

This ploy enabled him, in the course of 33,333 lines of great virtuosity, to explore again various answers to the human predicament which he had already considered in travel books, in the slim but significant *Spiritual Exercises*, and in several plays of unrelieved seriousness.

These answers include the philosophy of Nietzsche and Bergson, Communism (which he had seen at first hand on visits to Russia in the 1920's), the idea of Christ (rather than any particular form of Christianity), Buddhism, anarchy, nihilism, and so on. In the end they are all found wanting.

Kazantzakis makes his Odysseus exclaim (II, 960): "Hail, my soul, whose homeland has always been the journey!" It is really the poet himself who is speaking. Kazantzakis's world-outlook was too all-encompassing for him to be contained by any one literal homeland, even though his Cretan origins were tremendously important to him.

Kazantzakis was for ever moving on, from one country to another, from one creed to another. But, apart from the journey, there was one "homeland" to which he always remained loyal: "The demotic language is our homeland," he wrote in *England*. He loved natural, spoken Greek passionately. His *Odyssey* is not only a hymn to the spirit of man, it is also a hymn to the Greek language.

If Kazantzakis had died in 1938, aged 55, he would probably be known only to a few researchers. The plays "smell of the ink-well," as the Greeks say. The travel books are charming, but slight. The *Odyssey* is too vast, rambling, and daunting. There the case would rest.

But on the island of Aegina, during the German occupation, between 1941 and 1943,

Kazantzakis wrote his novel *The Life and Times of Alexis Zorbas*, known in English as *Zorba the Greek*. In *Zorba* he exclaims: "if only I could do that, remain silent until the abstract idea reaches its highest point and becomes fable"—which is exactly what he did.

He managed, in his remaining fifteen or so years, in five major novels (*Freedom and Death, Christ Recrucified, The Last Temptation, St. Francis, The Fratricides*) and one autobiographical masterpiece (*Report to (El) Greco*), to rework, as fables, all the themes which had preoccupied him for years with, for the first time, humanity and humour.

Among Kazantzakis's papers was found a note which said: "Major work—the *Odyssey*. Everything else—spin-offs." It might be more accurate to say that his real Odyssey was his lifelong search for the meaning of existence, and that *all* his works, including the enormous epic, were spin-offs from that.

—Roger Green

KELLER, Gottfried. Born in Zurich, 19 July 1819. Educated at Armenschule zum Brunnenturm; Landknabeninstitut, to age 13; Industrieschule, 1832-33; studied painting with Peter Steiger, 1834, and Rudolf Meyer, 1837; Munich Academy, 1840-42. Gave up art for writing in Zurich, 1842: government grant to study at University of Heidelberg, 1848-50, and University of Berlin, 1850-55; Cantonal Secretary (Staatschreiber), 1861-76. Honorary doctorate: University of Zurich, 1869. Honorary Citizen, Zurich, 1878. Member, Order of Maximilian (Bavaria), 1876. *Died 15 July 1890.*

PUBLICATIONS

Collections

   Sämtliche Werke, edited by Jonas Fränkel and Carl Helbling.   24 vols., 1926-54.

Fiction

   Der grüne Heinrich.   1853-55; revised edition, 1880; as *Green Henry*, 1960.
   Die Leute von Seldwyla.   1856-74; as *The People of Seldwyla*, with *Seven Legends*, 1929.
   Sieben Legenden.   1872; edited by K. Reichert, 1965; as *Seven Legends*, with *The People of Seldwyla*, 1929.
   Züricher Novellen.   1877.
   Das Sinngedicht.   1881.
   Martin Salander.   1886; translated as *Martin Salander*, 1963.
   Clothes Maketh Man and Other Swiss Stories.   1894.

Verse

   Gedichte.   1846.
   Neue Gedichte.   1852.

Gesammelte Gedichte. 1883.

Other

Gesammelte Briefe, edited by Carl Helbling. 4 vols., 1950-54.
Briefwechsel, with Hermann Hettner, edited by Jürgen Jahn. 1964.

*

Bibliography: *Keller Bibliographie 1844-1934* by Charles C. Zippermann, 1935.

Critical Studies: *The Cyclical Method of Composition in Keller's "Sinngedicht"* by Priscilla M. Kramer, 1939; *Keller: Kleides machen Leute* by B.A. Rowley, 1960; *Keller: Life and Works* by J.M. Lindsay, 1968; *Light and Darkness in Keller's "Der grüne Heinrich"* by Lucie Karcic, 1976.

*   *   *

Gottfried Keller, together with Jeremias Gotthelf and Conrad Ferdinand Meyer, is today generally regarded as one of the three pillars of 19th-century Swiss-German literature. His poems are no longer widely read, and he is remembered chiefly for his novel *Green Henry*, his four collections of short stories, and the correspondence he conducted with writers such as Theodor Storm and Paul Heyse. His reputation was slow to establish itself even in the German-speaking countries, and outside Germany his works have never attracted a readership which truly reflected Keller's standing as a master story-teller and an acute but humane observer of human passion and folly.

Green Henry, conceived as a novel of education ("Bildungsroman") within a German tradition which stretches from the medieval *Parzifal* to Thomas Mann's *Magic Mountain* and beyond, depicts in sympathetic and at times painful detail the early life of Heinrich Lee, a young Swiss who is torn between the compulsion to be an artist and the demands of domestic and civic duty. Partly autobiographical, the novel portrays a number of scenes and situations familiar to Keller, ranging from the small Swiss village to student life in Munich. The descriptions of Heinrich's early childhood, his thought on religion, his encounters at school, above all his ability to project an inner poetic vision onto events and experiences, reveal strikingly Keller's powers of psychological observation and his capacity to bring out the symbolic and the significant in his treatment of everyday and indeed mundane occurrences. The second version of the novel lacks the lyrical spontaneity and exuberance of the first; it is provided with a more conciliatory ending and is altogether more measured and distanced in tone and style. It no doubt reflects Keller's own mature view that to renounce art for the sake of duty was not of necessity a tragic choice.

Keller's ability to transcend the surface meaning of events and human actions, and to attribute to them a more universal significance, is even more clearly evident in his collections of stories and short novels, especially in *The People of Seldwyla* and the cycle of *Züricher Novellen*. The two groups of Seldwyla tales take as their fictional milieu a small town described by Keller as being "situated somewhere in Switzerland, surrounded by the same old city walls and towers as it was three hundred years ago." The narratives which revolve around this setting display a playful inventiveness and a sharp eye for incongruity and pretence. With humour and gentle irony they lay bare the realities underlying the seemingly placid exterior of peasant and bourgeois life in 19th-century Switzerland, and in doing so they illuminate and clarify the reader's understanding of the perennial conflicts deriving from personal and social relationships.

Literary history tends to assign Keller and his writings to the period of "poetic realism," a movement which some modern critics would disparage as a manifestation of political quiescence produced both for and by the German bourgeoisie. Such generalisations can on occasion be useful, but they would do scant justice to stories like "Romeo und Julia auf dem Dorf" and

"Der Landvogt von Greifensee" which, quite apart from their artistic perfection as narrative structures, touch upon the most basic contradictions which appear whenever individual conscience and consciousness seek to define themselves within systems of social values and traditional beliefs.

—A.P. Foulkes

KHLEBNIKOV, Velimir.   Born Viktor Vladimirovich Khlebnikov near Tundutovo, Astrakhan province, 28 October 1885.   Educated at Kazan 3rd Gymnasium, 1898-1903; studied mathematics and natural sciences at University of Kazan, 1903-08; studied biology and Slavic languages, University of St. Petersburg, 1909-11. Writer, associated with Futurist and other literary groups; served in Tsarist army, 1916-17; wandering poet, travelled across Russia: arrested by Whites in Kharkov, then by Reds, 1919; worked in Caucasus propaganda bureau (Rosta) in Baku, 1920; lecturer in Revolutionary Army headquarters in Persia, 1921; night watchman in Rosta office in Pyatigorsk, 1921. *Died 28 June 1922.*

PUBLICATIONS

Collections

> *Stikhi* [Poems].   1923.
> *Sobraniye proizvedeniy*, edited by Yury Tynyanov and Nikolai Stepanov.   5 vols., 1928-33.
> *Neizdannye proizvedenii* [Unpublished Works], edited by N. Khardziev and T. Grits.   1940.
> *Stikhotvoreniya i poemy*, edited by Nikolai Stepanov.   1960.
> *Sobraniye sochineniy*.   4 vols., 1968-72.
> *Snake Train: Poetry and Prose*, edited by Gary Kern.   1976.

Works

> *Uchitel' i uchenik* [Teacher and Pupil].   1912.
> *Igra v adu*.   1912.
> *Ryav! Perchatki 1908-1914* [Roar! The Gauntlets].   1913.
> *Izbornik stikhov 1907-1914* [Selected Poems].   1914.
> *Tvoreniya (1906-1908)* [Creations].   1914.
> *Bitvy 1915-1917: Novoye ucheniye o voyne* [Battles: The New Teaching about War].   1915.
> *Vremya mera mira* [Time the Measure of the World].   1916.
> *Truba marsian*.   1916.
> *Oshibka smerti* [Death's Mistake] (produced 1920).   1916.
> *Ladomir* [Goodworld].   1920.
> *Noch' v okope*.   1921.
> *Vestnik*.   2 vols., 1922.

Zangezi. 1922.
Otryvok iz dosok sud'by [Fragment from the Boards of Destiny]. 3 vols., 1922-23.
Nastoiashchee. 1926.
Vsem: Nochnoi bal. 1927.
Zverinets. 1930.

*

Critical Studies: *The Longer Poems of Khlebnikov*, 1961, and *Russian Futurism: A History*, 1968, both by Vladimir Markov; *Khlebnikov and Carnival: An Analysis of the Poem "Poet"* by Barbara Lonnqvist, 1979; *Xlebnikov's Shorter Poems: A Key to the Coinages* by Ronald Vroon, 1983.

*   *   *

When the Russian Futurists "slapped the face of public taste" it was largely with the gauntlet of Khlebnikov's work that they administered the blow. His experimentation with the Russian language and his ingenious neologisms helped to earn the Futurists the notoriety they were seeking. His work on the word was an embodiment of the Futurist aesthetic stance. He placed the word at the centre of attention, showed how it could develop according to an inner logic. A fossilised literary language came alive at his touch.

The Futurists proclaimed Khlebnikov "King of Russian Poetry." He could not, however, summon the regal presence or stentorian tones of such as Mayakovsky. Although the Futurists toured Russia, Khlebnikov did not take part. He seemed to have a pathological inability to perform in public. Yet, Russian Futurism without Khlebnikov would have been an empty shell.

Nevertheless, Khlebnikov's association with the Futurists was somewhat double-edged. Their tendency to publicise those of his works which reflected the movement's iconoclastic interests led to him acquiring a reputation as a poet of gibberish. This is a grave misjudgement. Despite his espousal of the "self-developed" word, Khlebnikov was a keen seeker after meaning. Even his transrational language (*zaum'*) was designed not to destroy meaning but to enhance it.

Khlebnikov's preoccupation with language should not be stressed unduly. His work reveals a considerable concern for the world as well as the word. Social and ideological motivations provided a major inspiration for his writing. Many works reflect militant pan-Slavist and revolutionary sentiments. He was opposed to western influence and looked towards the folk art of the Russian and Slavic peoples. He also directed his gaze eastwards towards India, Persia, and Central Asia.

After the outbreak of World War I Khlebnikov directed his poetic militancy against war. This campaign soon intermingled with a general assault on the arbitrary nature of fate. He became increasingly preoccupied with numerological theories aimed at discovering the laws of time. By practical prophecy he wished to make man the master of his destiny, to make him capable of directing his passage through the centuries like a ship along the Volga. This utopian element finds expression in much of his work. However, running parallel to it is a vivid awareness of the conflict and disaster constantly threatening mankind. Convinced that events unfolded according to some determinable and rational schema, Khlebnikov proclaimed that "measure" had come to replace faith. Yet there is something irrational about his faith in "measure." His mathematical formulas can appear as incantational as his verse.

As well as his "experimental" works Khlebnikov was an author of long poems with an unusual epic sweep, of short lyric verse with surprising depth, of prose, and of drama. Above all he was a visionary, and it is this vision coupled with an acute sensitivity towards the world which makes some of his works among the best in Russian literature.

—Ray Cooke

KLEIST, (Bernd) Heinrich (Wilhelm) von. Born in Frankfurt an der Oder, 18 October 1777. Entered the army in 1792, but resigned his commission in 1799 to be a writer and student: at University of Frankfurt, 1799. Wanderer: in Paris, Switzerland, Berlin; civil service post in Königsberg, 1805; Editor, *Phöbus*, Dresden, 1808, and *Berliner Abendblätter*, 1808-11. Suffered many nervous breakdowns. *Died (suicide) 21 November 1811.*

PUBLICATIONS

Collections

> *Hinterlassene Schriften*, edited by Ludwig Tieck. 1821.
> *Gesammelte Schriften*, edited by Ludwig Tieck. 3 vols., 1826.
> *Werke*, edited by Erich Schmidt and others. 5 vols., 1904-05; revised edition, 7 vols., 1936-38.
> *Sämtliche Werke und Briefe*, edited by Helmut Sembdner. 2 vols., 1961.

Plays

> *Die Familie Schroffenstein* (produced 1804). 1803; as *The Feud of the Schroffensteins*, 1916.
> *Amphitryon* (produced 1899). 1807; translated as *Amphitryon*, 1974.
> *Der zerbrochene Krug* (produced 1808). 1811; as *The Broken Pitcher*, 1961.
> *Penthesilea* (produced 1876). 1808; translated as *Penthesilea*, in *The Classic Theater*, edited by Eric Bentley, 1959.
> *Das Käthchen von Heilbronn* (produced 1810). 1810; translated in *Fiction and Fantasy of German Literature* by F.E. Pierce, 1927.
> *Prinz Friedrich von Homburg* (produced 1821). In *Hinterlassene Schriften*, 1821; as *The Prince of Homburg*, in *The Classic Theater*, edited by Eric Bentley, 1959.
> *Die Hermannsschlacht* (produced 1839). In *Hinterlassene Schriften*, 1821.
> *Robert Guiskard* (unfinished; produced 1901). In *Gesammelte Schriften*, 1826.

Fiction

> *Erzählungen.* 2 vols., 1810-11.
> *The Marquise of O. and Other Stories*, translated by Martin Greenberg. 1960.

Other

> *Lebensspuren: Dokumente und Berichte der Zeitgenossen*, edited by Helmut Sembdner. 1964.

*

Critical Studies: *Reason and Energy* by Michael Hamburger, 1957; *Kleist's Dramas* by E.L. Stahl, 1961; *Kleist: Studies in His Work and Literary Character* by Walter Silz, 1961; *Kleist: A Study in Tragedy and Anxiety* by John Gearey, 1968; *Kleist's Prinz Friedrich von Homburg*, 1970, and *Kleist*, 1979, both by J.M. Ellis; *From Lessing to Hauptmann: Studies in German Drama* by Ladislaus Löb, 1974; *Kleist and the Tragic Ideal* by H.M. Brown, 1977; *The Stories of Kleist* by Denys Dyer, 1977; *Kleist: Word into Flesh: A Poet's Quest for the Symbol* by Ilse Graham, 1977; *Kleist: A Biography* by Joachim Maass, 1983; *Desire's Sway: The Plays and Stories of Kleist* by James M. McGlathery, 1983.

*   *   *

Throughout his short life Heinrich von Kleist was bedevilled by contradictions and misfortunes. Prussian aristocrat by birth and maladjusted poet by temperament, brilliantly gifted yet deeply neurotic, he was torn between pedantry and passion, sensitivity and violence, furious ambition and a paralysing sense of failure. His obsessive striving for absolute certainties was confounded by doubts. His uncompromising search for fulfilment through love, friendship, nature, nation, or art foundered on external obstacles and on his own instability. Some moments of euphoria apart, his dominant mood was despair, leading to an early suicide. It is suitably ironic that, ignored for a century, he should now be considered one of Germany's greatest writers.

Kleist shared the subjectivism and spiritualism of the Romantic age: unlike the Romantics, he incorporated, rather than suppressed, the recalcitrance of objective reality in his writing. Anticipating psychoanalysis, alienated, sceptical about communication, and rejecting traditional philosophical, moral, and social assumptions in his treatment of existential issues, he seems strikingly modern.

Kleist's central problem—documented in his correspondence and occasional essays—was that of knowledge. At first he sought happiness through both Enlightenment rationalism and Rousseauesque sensibility, but he was shattered when the ideas of Kant confirmed his suspicion that the intellect was "unable to decide whether what we call truth is truly the truth, or only appears so to us" (letter of 22 March 1801). He continued to commend "feeling," and he claimed (notably in "Über das Marionettentheater") that the pristine grace of an unthinking condition, which was upset by reflection, would be regained in a divine state of infinite awareness; but basically he believed that emotion, in its inconstancy, was as unreliable as reason. Consequently he concluded that, since men could not make any informed choices or recognise any providential purpose, human freedom was an illusion and fate synonymous with chance. His creative works explore these dilemmas from a variety of angles.

Kleist's first play, *The Feud of the Schroffensteins*, is a gothic melodrama in which the trust of the young lovers proves helpless against the accidents, errors, and enmities that destroy them. His next two plays mix hope and anxiety: in the neo-classically based *Amphitryon* the tragicomedy of Jupiter impersonating the title hero to seduce his wife, alongside the farcical impersonation of the servant Sosias by Mercury, raises vexing questions about personal identity, the fallibility of perception, and the bewildering quality of love; in *The Broken Pitcher*, a rural comedy with mythical overtones, the truth emerges as the judge Adam convicts himself of his advances to the virtuous Eve, but her fiancé's distrustfulness almost causes disaster. Two subsequent plays, as Kleist noted, are complementary: in *Penthesilea*, a tragedy on Greek legend, the inefficacy of the intellect is compounded by the ambivalence of emotion as the Amazon queen, after many misunderstandings, slaughters the warrior Achilles in a paroxysm of love-hate and wills herself to death; in *Das Käthchen von Heilbronn*, a medievalising romance, undivided love and inner assurance prevail as the devoted heroine, supported by suprasensory promises, conquers the reluctant hero against all reasonable expectation. Kleist's vaguely historical last play, *The Prince of Homburg*, is also his greatest. The development of the Prince, who disobeys orders but wins a battle and after agonies of fear welcomes the death penalty but is rehabilitated and married, recalls German Classicism by apparently reconciling subjective inclination and objective duty. But again misconceptions abound, the Elector's crucial decisions are inconsistent, and the ending completes the Prince's initial somnambulistic fantasy of love and glory. Destiny, even when most benevolent, remains arbitrary, and a happy outcome is literally declared "a dream."

Kleist's collected stories were published in his last two years: five are commonly regarded as the most important. In "The Earthquake in Chile" a young couple is lynched in a resurgence of religious hysteria after an interlude of idyllic peace following the collapse of the city. In "The Engagement in Santo Domingo" the hero, misinterpreting the heroine's attempt to save his life during a colonial uprising, kills her, and, on learning the truth, himself. In "The Marquise of O—" the conundrum of the celibate but pregnant heroine is resolved by the confession of her eventual husband, who raped her while she was unconscious. In "The Duel" the champion's belief in his lady's innocence is vindicated when he recovers from the near-fatal wounds he sustained in the trial by ordeal, while the villain, whose alibi rested on delusion, dies of a slight injury. In "Michael Kohlhaas," Kleist's greatest story, a righteous horsedealer in pursuit of justice becomes a fanatically revengeful outlaw when he is denied a fair legal hearing, and triumphs, with supernatural aid, at the very moment of his execution when his grievances are redressed and his enemies punished. The positive values of love, trust, and intuitive confidence thus thrive in some cases and perish in others. In all cases, however, deceptive appearances, intellectual fallacies, and emotional disturbances, allied with strange coincidences and baffling incongruities, reiterate Kleist's view of the irrationality and mystery of existence.

Kleist's style, which is highly original though not deliberately experimental, is marked above all else by ambiguity, irony, and paradox. His characters, faced with surprising situations, locked in fierce conflicts or painful isolation, and driven by forces they can neither understand nor control, represent extreme impulses rather than normal human behaviour. His superbly timed actions replace conventional linearity with cyclic recurrences, sudden reversals, abrupt contrasts, and complex symbolic variations on a relatively limited number of enigmatic themes. His restraint from authorial comment and analytical explanation, his shifting perspectives, his insistence on accurate detail in the midst of upheaval and confusion invest his subjective concerns with a semblance of objectivity and provide solid realistic foundations for his surrealistic visions. His language—oscillating between mathematical precision and extravagant rhetoric, laconic matter-of-factness and lyricism, amplification and explosive compression; revelling in bold metaphors, puns, equivocations, and inexorable question-and-answer sequences; checking long periods with encapsulated elucidations, qualifications, and counter-statements, before rushing headlong to their conclusion; and breaking down into speechless gestures, blushing and fainting, when words fail—conveys his experience directly through its form, instead of discussing it in abstract conceptual terms. It is this masterly use of all the dramatic, narrative and linguistic devices at his disposal that enables Kleist to impose aesthetic order on a world of chaos and to shape the perplexities of a tortured individual into generally valid art.

—Ladislaus Löb

KOCHANOWSKI, Jan. Born in Sycyna, Poland, in 1530. Educated at Cracow Academy, 1544-49; University of Padua, 1550's. Married Dorota Podlodowska; six daughters. Courtier: secretary to King Zygmunt, 1560-68; retired to estate in Czarnolas, 1570. *Died 22 August 1584.*

PUBLICATIONS

Collections

Dziela wszystkie [Complete Works]. 4 vols., 1884-97.
Dziela polskie [Polish Works], edited by Julian Krzyzanowski. 1960.

Verse

Zuzanna [Susanna]. 1562.
Szachy [A Game of Chess]. 1562 (?).
Zgoda [Concord]. 1564.
Satyr; albo, Dziki maz [The Satyr; or, The Wild Man]. 1564.
Psalterz Dawidów [Psalms of David]. 1579.
Treny. 1580; as *Laments,* 1920.
Lyricorum libellus. 1580.
Fraszki [Trifles]. 1584.
Pieśni [Songs]. 1586.
Poems, edited by G.R. Noyes. 1928.

Play

Odprawa posłów greckich (produced 1578). 1578; as *The Dismissal of the Greek Envoys,* 1918.

*

Bibliography: *Bibliografia dziel Jana Kochanowskiego: wiek XVI-XVII* by Kazimierz Piekarski, 1934.

*   *   *

Jan Kochanowski's reputation outside the Polish cultural sphere is small, and his significance in European terms is difficult to assess, though his works are of an ingenuity and civilization that compete with the best among his international contemporaries.

His début was as a cosmopolitan poet taking advantage of the medium of progressive humanist culture, Neo-Latin. The erudite and inventive Virgilian verse of his early work, widely circulated in manuscript after 1550, was published much later as the *Lyricorum libellus* in 1580. Well known among the small cultured élite of the Polish-Lithuanian Commonwealth's few courts, Kochanowski was patronized by both courtiers and clerics, eventually securing himself the position of Royal Secretary for most of the 1560's. It was in this milieu that he switched to his native idiom, in which he wrote first the vignettes of humorous verse in the anthology entitled *Fraszki,* which satirize contemporary society and its mores.

Kochanowski soon advanced to a combination of the sophisticated style of Neo-Latin verse and its Classical models and genres with Polish vocabulary and syntax in the *Pieśni* (again, known widely, but published posthumously in 1586) closely modelled on Horace's *Odes.* In these highly polished "songs," he set the stylistic and thematic standards for almost two centuries. His subjects range from subtle (and not so subtle) panegyric dedicated to court patrons, through hymns on the beauty of Creation, to the erotic and melancholic, pastoral and religious. While some are artful paraphrases from Horace, most are entirely original, and stand as a testament of the achievements of the "Augustan" Golden Age under the sophisticated Zygmunt August (1548-72). The *Pieśni* are a fusing of two cultures (Roman and Sarmatian), two languages (Latin and Polish), and two poets (Horace the Master, and Kochanowski the Apprentice).

Towards 1570, however, for reasons that are unclear, Kochanowski had severed his dependence on court favour, and retired with his new wife to his estate at Czarnolas, evoked so lyrically in the "Pieśń świetojańska o Sobótce" (published with *Pieśni*). Despite irregular commissions from his earlier patrons, such as his experimental Euripidean tragedy in Polish, *The Dismissal of the Greek Envoys,* in this idyllic environment he concentrated on his true "vocation," a versified paraphrase of the Psalter in Polish. This huge work, the *Psalterz Dawidów,* is another blending, of Biblical, Classical Latin, and Polish vernacular ingredients. His version surpassed all others in originality, beauty, and popularity. On all levels it is the culmination of his life's work.

The last five years of the poet's life were overshadowed by the deaths of court friends, relatives, and in particular his own children. A record of the struggle between faith and despair following the death of his three-year-old daughter Orszula, entitled the *Laments*, was published in 1580. It contains a cycle of contemplative lyrics on the implications of Orszula's demise and his sense of loss. Once again there is the combination of contrasting elements: the Classical and Biblical, the philosophical and personal, the lyrical and dramatic, all focused by the factual event that inspired the cycle. Together they transform these laments from a conventional exercise into an extraordinarily honest psychological document, revealing much of the mentality of 16th-century man.

With the exception of some secondary political and panegyric verse, Kochanowski's sublime poetry is not the product of a provincial. Singlehandedly he extended the Polish language's limits in all directions. The *Laments* are his last word, a personal legacy of the potential of Christian humanism, after which the poet abandoned his artificial lute for the rewards of David's faith.

—Donald Peter Alexander Pirie

KRLEZA, Miroslav. Born in Zagreb, 7 July 1893. Educated at Lucoviceum military academy, Budapest. Served in the Servian Army, 1912: suspected of spying, expelled from Serbia and arrested by the Austrians; served in the Austrian Army during World War I. Married Bela Kangrga. Member of Communist Party from 1918: expelled, 1939; rehabilitated by Tito, 1952; founded the periodicals *Plamen* [Flame], 1919, *Književna republika* [Literary Republic], 1923-27, *Danas* [Today], 1934, *Pečat* [Seal], 1939-40, and *Republika*, 1945-46; from 1952, Director, Lexicographic Institute, Zagreb; Editor, *Pomorska enciklopedija*, 1954-64, *Enciklopedija Jugoslavije*, 1955-71, and *Enciklopedija Leksikografskog savoda*, 1955-64. Deputy, Yugoslav National Assembly. President, Yugoslav Writers Union; Vice President, Yugoslav Academy of Science and Art. *Died 29 December 1981.*

PUBLICATIONS

Collections

   Sabrana djela [Collected Works]. 27 vols., 1953-72.

Fiction

   Hrvatska rapsodija [Croatian Rhapsody]. 1918.
   Tri kavalira gospodice Melanije [Three Suitors of Miss Melania]. 1920.

Magyar királyi honvéd novela [Short Story on the Royal Hungarian Homeguards]. 1921.
Hrvatski bog Mars [The Croatian God Mars]. 1922.
Novele. 1923.
Vražji otok [Devil's Island]. 1924.
Povratak Filipa Latinovicza. 1932; as *The Return of Philip Latinovicz*, 1959.
Hiljadu i jedna smrt [A Thousand and One Deaths]. 1933.
Novele. 1937.
Na rubu pameti. 1938; as *On the Edge of Reason*, 1976.
Banket u Blitvi [Banquet in Blitva]. 3 vols., 1938-56.
Tri domobrana [Three Homeguards]. 1950.
Zastave [Banners]. 5 vols., 1967— .
The Cricket Beneath the Waterfall and Other Stories. 1972.
Baraka pet be i druge novele (collection). 1976.

Plays

Golgota [Golgotha] (produced 1922). 1926.
Vučjak (produced 1922). 1923.
Michelangelo Buonarroti (produced 1925).
Adam i Eva [Adam and Eve] (produced 1925).
Gospoda Glembajevi [The Glembays] (produced 1929). 1928.
U agoniji [In Agony] (produced 1928; revised version produced 1959). 1931.
Leda (produced 1930).
Legende [Legends] (includes 6 plays). 1933.
U logoru [In the Camp] (produced 1937). With *Vučjak*, 1934.
Maskerata [Masquerade] (produced 1955).
Kraljevo [The Kermess] (produced 1955).
Kristofor Kolumbo (produced 1955).
Aretej; ili, Legenda o Svetoj Ancili [Aretheus; or, The Legend of St. Ancilla] (produced 1959). 1962.
Saloma [Salome] (produced 1963).
Put u raj [Journey to Paradise] (produced 1973).

Verse

Pan. 1917.
Tri simfonije [Three Symphonies]. 1917.
Pjesme 1-3 [Poems]. 3 vols., 1918-19.
Lirika [Lyrics]. 1919.
Knjiga pjesama [A Book of Poems]. 1931.
Knjiga lirike [A Book of Lyrics]. 1932.
Balade Petrice Kerempuha [Ballads of Petrica Kerempuh]. 1936— .
Pjesme u tmini [Poems in Darkness]. 1937.

Other

Izlet u Rusiju [Excursion to Russia]. 1926.
Eseji [Essays]. 1932.
Moj obračun s njima [My Squaring of Accounts]. 1932.
Podravski motivi [Motifs of Podravina]. 1933.
Evropa danas [Europe Today]. 1935.
Deset krvavih godina [Ten Years in Blood]. 1937.

Eppur si muove.   1938.
Knjiga proze [A Book of Prose].   1938.
Dijalektički antibarbarus [A Dialectical Antibarbarian].   1939.
Knjiga studija i putopisa [A Book of Studies and Travels].   1939.
Goya.   1948.
O Marinu Držiću [On Marin Držić].   1949.
Zlato i srebro Zadra [The Gold and Silver of Zadar].   1951.
Djetinjstvo u Agramu godine 1902-1903 [Childhood in Agram].   1952.
Kalendar jedne bitke 1942 [Almanac of a 1942 Battle].   1953.
Kalendar jedne parlamentarne komedije [Almanac of a Parliamentary Comedy].   1953.
O Erasmu Rotterdamskom [On Erasmus of Rotterdam].   1953.
Davni dani [Long Bygone Days].   1956.
Eseji [Essays].   6 vols., 1961-67.
Razgovori s Miroslavom Krležom [Conversations with Miroslav Krleza].   1969.
99 varijacija lexicographica [99 Lexicographic Variations].   1972.
Djetinjstvo 1902-1903 i drugi zapisi [Childhood and Other Pieces].   1972.
Dnevnik [Diary].   1977.
Tito 1892-1937-1977, with Edvard Kardelj.   1977.

Editor, with others, *Danas* [Today].   2 vols., 1971.

*

Bibliography: *Bibliografia djela Miroslava Krleže* by T. Jakić, 1953; *Literatura o Miroslavu Krleži 1914-1963* by D. Kapetanić, 1967.

*   *   *

Miroslav Krleža was the most dominant figure in contemporary literature of Croatia, a small country which is today one of the six republics of Yugoslavia. As the writer of novels, short stories, poems, essays, journals, travelogues, polemics, and memoirs, and as the editor of a series of leftist literary journals, he had a considerable influence on his contemporaries. His search for an enlightened humanism brought him to communism after the collapse of the Austro-Hungarian empire, but he was never an obedient Party member who marched uncritically following the Party policy. His criticism of the marxist dogmatism and of the notion of socialist realism in the arts as well as his outspoken demands "for freedom of artistic expression, for the simultaneous existence of differing schools and styles, for liberty of choice and independence of moral and political convictions," left their lasting mark on the cultural climate of post-Second World War Yugoslavia.

Krleža began his literary career as a poet celebrating in pagan terms the triumph of life over the powers of darkness, mysticism, and death. However, World War I brought a dramatic change in his outlook. His war poems evoke in a series of striking expressionistic images the idea of the futility of life and the absurdity of death and have as their underlying theme one of Krleža's favourite notions, that of the supremacy of stupidity over reason in human life. The same theme of dehumanization caused by the horrors of the war is central to his collection of short stories *Hrvatski bog Mars* (The Croatian God Mars), in which the useless squandering of lives of the Croats enlisted to fight for Austria in the war of 1914-18 is depicted in a dramatic and memorable narrative.

The poetry he continued to write in the 1920's and 1930's shows an increased social awareness and concerns itself primarily with the themes of social protest. The peak of his career as a poet was reached by the publication of his *Balade Petrice Kerempuha* (Ballads of Petrica Kerempuh), a collection of poems written in the dialect of north-western Croatia, used by the writers of the 17th and the 18th centuries. It is a unique satirical saga of Croatian history. Although overshadowed with suffering, injustice, blood and a symbol of gallows, the Croatian past is approached without any romantic illusions and rather treated in a bitter but mocking tone of Rabelaisian laughter.

In his youthful plays, published in a collection entitled *Legende* (Legends), Krleža uses historical figures and themes as means of handling underlying themes of his time. His reputation as a dramatist was established with the piece *Golgota* (Golgotha), a socialist play set in a shipyard, and enhanced with two anti-war plays, *Vučjak* and *U logoru* (In the Camp). The best known, and the best, of his plays make up his Glembay trilogy, *Gospoda Glembajevi* (The Glembays), *U agoniji* (In Agony) and *Leda*, which constitute an organic unity with the short stories of the same cycle. The plays and the short stories combine to portray the rise and the decline of a rich Croatian family against the background of the agony of a dying civilization (the Austro-Hungarian empire). Ibsenian in character and scope, these plays were written in the best vein of psychological realism.

Povratak Filipa Latinovicza (*The Return of Philip Latinovicz*) is the most popular of his four novels. It tells a story of an expatriate artist who, in a moment of personal and creative crisis, returns to his native Panonia to establish his paternity. But his pilgrimage turns into a quest of his own identity and a scathing portrayal of provincial decadence and his struggle to confront it. *Na rubu pameti* (*On the Edge of Reason*) is a novel of a model citizen who falls from society's grace after speaking out his mind. Abandoned both by his family and his friends, persecuted and jailed, put into an asylum, he finishes as a lonely and desperate man listening in his hotel room to the discordant and meaningless sounds coming from the radio. Krleža's two other novels provide an imaginative and critical portrait of both Yugoslavia and Europe in the first decades of the 20th century, and make some major political, social, and psychological statements about the predicament of modern man. *Banket u Blitvi* (Banquet in Blitva) shows Krleža as a political satirist at his best. It is a political-allegorical novel with various references to those European countries (including his own) where, after the World War I, people were deprived of their freedoms and democratic rights by military dictatorships. The vivid and dramatic story of a struggle between a dictator and a courageous political idealist is interspersed with typical Krleža polemics, soliloquies, and conversations with the intention of showing the amoral nature of politics in general. *Zastave* (Banners) spans the period between 1912 and 1922 in Croatian and Yugoslav history. The novel is built around one of Krleža's recurring themes, that of the conflict between a father, a loyal and acquiescent servant of the Establishment, and his only son, the embittered, freedom-loving rebel. Their precarious relations are designed to bring out a psychological and ideological drama caused by the disillusionments of the two generations in the political upheavals of the early 20th century.

Alongside the best of Krleža's creative writing may be set the best of his non-fiction prose: essays which reflect his vast reading and his moral and intellectual integrity; the two books of memoirs, *Djetinjstvo u Agramu* (Childhood in Agram) and *Davni dani* (Long Bygone Days); the account of his visit to the USSR in 1925, *Izlet u Rusiju* (Excursion to Russia); and, finally, his writings and annotations for the Yugoslav Encyclopaedia, of which he was the spiritus movens and the editor-in-chief.

—Dušan Puvačić

LACLOS, (Pierre Antoine Francois) Choderlos de. Born in Amiens, France, 18 October 1741. Married Marie-Soulange Duperré in 1786. Educated at École d'Artillerie de la Fère,

1759-63: 2nd Lieutenant, 1762: served in Toul, 1763-66, Strasbourg, 1766-69, Grenoble, 1769-75, Besançon, 1775-76, Valence, 1776-78, l'Île d'Aix, 1778-88: Captain; left the army for a brief period as politician: Editor, *Journal des Amis de la Constitution*, 1790-91; rejoined army as Maréchal de camp, 1792; general of the artillery in the army of Naples, 1800. *Died 5 September 1803.*

PUBLICATIONS

Collections

Oeuvres complètes, edited by Maurice Allem.   1944; revised edition, edited by Laurent Versani, 1979.

Fiction

Les Liaisons dangereuses.   1782; edited by René Pomeau, 1981; as *Dangerous Connections*, 1784; as *Dangerous Acquaintances*, 1924.

Play

Ernestine, music by Saint-Georges, from a novel by Mme. Riccoboni (produced 1777).

Verse

Poésies, edited by Arthur Symons and Louis Thomas.   1908.

Other

Lettre à MM. de l'Académie française.   1786.
La Galerie des États-Généraux, with others.   1789.
La Galerie des dames françaises.   1789.
Causes secrètes de la révolution.   1795.
De l'education des femmes, edited by Edouard Champion.   1903.
Lettres inédites, edited by Louis de Chauvigny.   1904.

*

Critical Studies: *Laclos and the Epistolary Novel* by Dorothy R. Thelander, 1963; *The Novel of Worldliness: Crébillon, Marivaux, Laclos, and Stendhal* by Peter P. Brooks, 1969; *Laclos: Les Liaisons dangereuses* by Philip Thody, 1970; *Critical Approaches to Les Liaisons dangereuses* edited by Lloyd R. Free, 1978.

*   *   *

Choderlos de Laclos is a man of one book, *Les Liaisons dangereuses (Dangerous Acquaintances)*, an impeccably constructed epistolary novel describing and analysing the sexual immorality which is said to have characterised certain members of the French aristocracy in the years immediately preceding the Revolution of 1789. But the novel is not the endorsement of promiscuity which it was considered to be in the 19th century, any more than it is the transference into fiction of Laclos's own exploits and world view, or a realistic novel in the sense of one based on actual events. Indeed, recent historical research has revealed how the principal male character, le Vicomte de Valmont, far from being drawn from life, served rather as a model to would-be seducers who wished to follow his example after reading the novel. Laclos himself, unlike Valmont, was a very minor nobleman, whose dislike of the top aristocracy of the day may well have stemmed from the slowness with which, as a professional soldier, he obtained promotion in the artillery in the *Ancien régime*. *Les Liaisons dangereuses* can thus be seen as a socially committed novel written by a man sympathetic to the revolutionary and moralistic views of Jean-Jacques Rousseau, and intended to show, by contrast, the superiority of the more modest but increasingly self-confident middle-class. Laclos's own marriage, to a girl who was 17 when he married her at the age of 45, was a very happy one. Indeed, a letter exists, written to her while he was on active service with the Revolutionary armies in the 1790's, telling her of his ambition to write a novel proving that "true happiness can be found only in the Family."

The plot of *Les Liaisons dangereuses* can certainly be interpreted as a criticism of how Valmont and his female accomplice, la Marquise de Merteuil, behave in their sexual relationships to other people and to each other, and it is also possible to see the extremely intelligent and somewhat terrifying Marquise as a very conscious warning of how feminism can go sour. For Laclos, as an essay published long after his death revealed, held views on the equality of women and men which are advanced even by modern standards ("Learn," he wrote, "that one escapes from slavery only by a great revolution"), and Madame de Merteuil is the strongest willed, the most intellectual, the most interesting, and the least successful of all French fictional heroines. *Les Liaisons dangereuses* is nevertheless too complex and ambiguous a novel to be interpreted in only one light. It deserves its place as the best novel written in France in the 18th century, and one of the best studies of evil, of sexual aggression and of the lust for power ever published. There is also an intriguing contrast between the perfection of its formal finish and the endlessly interesting questions to which it gives rise.

—Philip Thody

LAFAYETTE, Madame de. Born Marie-Madeleine Pioche de la Vergne, in Paris, in 1634. Married François, comte de Lafayette, in 1655 (died 1683), two sons. Grew up in Paris, and after a period of life in her husband's chateau of Nades, lived in Paris after 1659; friend of Henriette d'Angleterre, wife of Louis XIV's brother, of Mme. de Sévigné, and the duc de La Rochefoucauld. *Died 25 May 1693.*

PUBLICATIONS

Collections

> *Oeuvres*, edited by Robert Lejeune. 3 vols., 1925-30.
> *Romans et nouvelles*, edited by Emile Magne. 1958.

Fiction

> *La Princesse de Montpensier.* 1662; as *The Princess Monpensier*, 1805.

Zaïde. 1669-70; as *Zayde: A Spanish History*, 1678.
La Princesse de Clèves. 1678; edited by Emile Magne, 1950; edited by Peter H. Nurse, 1971; as *The Princess of Cleves*, 1679.
La Comtesse de Tende. 1724.

Other

Histoire d'Henriette d'Angleterre. 1720; edited by Gilbert Sigaux, 1965; as *Fatal Gallantry*, 1722.
Mémoires de la cour de France. 1731; edited by Gilbert Sigaux, 1965.
Correspondance, edited by A. Beaunier. 2 vols., 1942.

*

Bibliography: *Madame de Lafayette: A Selected Critical Bibliography* by James W. Scott, 1974.

Critical Studies: *Moral Perspective in "La Princesse de Clèves"* by Helen Kaps, 1968; *Madame de Lafayette* by Stirling Haig, 1970; *Classical Voices: Studies of Corneille, Racine, Moliere, Madame de Lafayette* by Peter H. Nurse, 1971; *Madame de Lafayette and "La Princesse de Clèves"* by Janet Raitt, 1971; *La Princesse de Clèves: The Tension of Elegance* by Barbara R. Woshinsky, 1973.

*   *   *

As a member of the nobility, Madame de Lafayette was an amateur writer, and was reluctant to admit authorship of her novels. Indeed, she wrote them to a certain extent in collaboration with male friends, particularly Gilles Ménage and La Rochefoucauld. But they are unquestionably her creation and bear the stamp of her particular if somewhat narrowly focussed genius. Her works have survived because one of them, *The Princess of Cleves*, ranks among the finest psychological novels ever written. Her other books, however, are of interest only to the literary historian.

She left four works of fiction. All are variations on the same theme, a love story in the form of a pseudo-historical romance. *La Comtesse de Tende* is a slight novella about an adulterous wife, the countess of the title, who nobly repents before her death. *Zaïde* is a "Spanish history" very much in the taste of the time, replete with digressions, adventures, and discourses on the finer points of amorous activity, and needless to say describes love's tribulations at generous length. *The Princess Monpensier* is a more solid effort, which argues, as does the Comtesse de Tende's story, that women can be sure of attaining happiness only if both prudence and virtue govern their actions; but they find that rather difficult, and most of them allow men to make a mess of their lives.

A somewhat mechanistic psychology allied with a platitudinous morality considerably reduces the interest of these works for the modern reader. It is all the more remarkable, then, that using the same ingredients Madame de Lafayette produced one novel which is a masterpiece. *The Princess of Cleves* is set a century earlier than the time in which she was writing (the material is lifted, with some changes as was her wont, from the candid memoirs of Pierre de Brantôme). It tells of a beautiful young woman who arrives at the French court and is soon married to the Prince of Clèves. She likes and respects him, but feels no sexual attraction for him. When the Duc de Nemours appears at court, however, this handsome and seductive creature steals her heart. For a long time she conceals her violent feelings from Nemours, and indeed from everyone else except her own stern mother, but eventually she betrays herself when she experiences acute jealousy over a love letter which she assumes (wrongly) has been sent to Nemours by another woman. When her mother dies she turns for comfort to exactly the wrong person: her husband. Her famous "avowal" of her feelings for a rival poisons his life, and he dies not long afterwards of a broken heart. She is now, paradoxically, free to marry the man she loves, but to the reader's surprise she decides not to do so. This is partly out of remorse at having precipitated her husband's death, but mainly because she fears Nemours will be unfaithful to her once he has made her his wife. So she sacrifices her love on the altar of her peace of mind, and dies not long afterwards, an unattached and virtuous woman. This early blow for feminism, coupled with precise insight into the painful ecstacies of erotic attraction, has ensured the survival of this at first sight unlikely classic.

—John Fletcher

LA FONTAINE, Jean de. Born in Château-Thierry, France, 8 July 1621. Married Marie Héricart in 1647 (separated, 1658). Succeeded his father as Maîtres des Eaux et Forêts of the Duchy of Château-Thierry; possibly licensed to practice as a lawyer; writer in Paris: patronized by Fouquet and others, especially Mme. de la Sablière. Member, French Academy, 1684. *Died 13 March 1695.*

PUBLICATIONS

Collections

Oeuvres complètes, edited by H. de Regnier. 11 vols., 1883-92.
Oeuvres: Fables, contes, et nouvelles; Oeuvres diverses, edited by René Groos, Jacques Schiffrin, and Pierre Clarac. 2 vols., 1942-54.

Verse

Elégie aux nymphes de Vaux. 1661.
Nouvelles en vers. 1665.
Contes et nouvelles en vers (4 parts). 4 vols., 1665-74; augmented edition, 1686; edited by Jacqueline Zeugschmitt, 2 vols., 1972.
Fables (12 parts). 3 vols., 1668-69; augmented edition, 1693; translated as Fables, 1804; also translated by Edward Marsh, 1931, Marianne Moore, 1954, and Reginald Jarman, 1962.
Fables nouvelles et autres poésies. 1671.
Poème du Quinquina et autres ouvrages en vers. 1682.

Fiction

Les Amours de Psyché et de Cupidon. 1669; as The Loves of Cupid and Psyche, 1744.

Plays

L'Eunuque, from the play by Terence. 1654.

Les Rieurs de Beau-Richard (ballet; produced 1659-60?).   In *Oeuvres*, 1827.
Astrée, music by Pascal Colasse (produced 1691).   1691.

Other

Voyage en Limousin.   1663.
Ouvrages de prose et de poésie, with Abbé François de Maucroix.   2 vols., 1685.
Oeuvres posthumes.   1696.

*

Critical Studies: *Young La Fontaine* by P. Wadsworth, 1952; *La Fontaine* by M. Sutherland, 1953; *La Fontaine: Fables* by Odette de Mourgues, 1960; *La Fontaine, Poet and Counterpoet* by Margaret O. Guiton, 1961; *The Style of La Fontaine's Fables* by Jean Dominique Biard, 1966; *The Esthetics of Negligence: La Fontaine's Contes* by John C. Lapp, 1971; *La Fontaine and His Friends: A Biography* by Agnes Ethel MacKay, 1972.

*   *   *

La Fontaine stands out as the one French writer of the 17th century to have written sympathetically about animals and the natural world, and the one poet in the classical period to have combined a deep respect for form with a readiness and ability to experiment in different types of versification. His two collections of *Fables* continue to make him probably the most frequently read and quoted of all French poets, and he is probably the only great French writer to be equally appreciated by children and by adults. His first book of *Fables* was written for the instruction of the Dauphin, the future Louis XIV, and offers a view of the world which contains a greater awareness of *Realpolitik* than the nobler elements in the concept of Christian monarchy. Thus when, in "La Génisse, la chèvre, et la brebis en société avec le lion" (The Heifer, the Goat, and the Sheep in company with the Lion), the animals prepare to share out the spoils, the lion—the King of Beasts—takes the largest share on the indisputable grounds that he is called Lion and is the strongest. One of the best known fables, "Le Loup et l'Agneau" (The Wolf and the Lamb) demonstrates the truth that might is right, and the qualities needed to succeed, or even to survive, in the social world depicted in La Fontaine's animal allegories are exactly those which Hobbes considered inseparable from the State of Nature. For it is indeed the war of all against all in which the cardinal virtues are force and fraud, and the human beings who make an appearance in this world tend to be on the same moral level as the animals who represent the various ranks in the extremely hierarchical society which La Fontaine knew. When a bird is wounded in a fight and lands in a field, a child casually throws a stone to kill it, thus illustrating the pre-Rousseauist view of children as "an age without pity." Only perhaps by adopting an attitude of suspicion, humility, and self-effacement can those at the bottom end of the social spectrum survive, and it is clear that La Fontaine had no vision of a society in which a King or any other kind of ruler might act or intervene to improve the lot of his subjects.

Most of the actual stories, of course, are traditional, coming down from Aesop and Phaedra, and the almost unremitting pessimism which is the quality that most strikes the modern reader may well have been more axiomatic and therefore less surprising for La Fontaine's contemporaries. This pessimism is also occasionally relieved by fables such as "Les Deux Amis" (The Two Friends), showing as it does an idealised vision of friendship, and is prevented from making a really deep emotional impact by the humour of versification and characterisation which run through all the *Fables*. La Fontaine excels in matching verbal rhythms to the physical features of the animals he describes, writing about mice in short, neat, light, precise lines, and about bears and lions in more ponderous and self-important tones. You can see his animals moving as you read or listen to the *Fables*, and visualize the French countryside against which the action takes place.

In his lifetime, and by connoisseurs since the 17th century, La Fontaine was also known as the author of a number of *Contes et nouvelles en vers* (Tales and Short Stories in Verse), whose agreeably pagan inspiration gave way to a more orthodox Christian sensibility in the "Recueil de Poésies Chrétiennes" (Collection of Christian Poetry) in 1671. It is traditional in France to refer to the author of the *Fables* as "le bon La Fontaine," a reference more to his genial disposition than to the view of humanity running through his work.

—Philip Thody

LAFORGUE, Jules.   Born in Montevideo, Uruguay, 29 August 1860.   Educated at Tarbes, 1866-76; Lycée Condorcet, Paris, 1876-77. Married Leah Lee in 1886. French reader to Empress Augusta of Germany, in Berlin and travelling, 1881-86. *Died 21 August 1887.*

PUBLICATIONS

Collections

    Oeuvres complètes, edited by G. Jean-Aubry.   6 vols., 1922-30.
    Poésies complètes, edited by Pascal Pia.   2 vols., 1979.

Verse

    Les Complaintes.   1885; edited by Michael Collie, 1977; edited by Pierre Reboul, 1981.
    L'Imitation de Notre-Dame la Lune.   1886; edited by Pierre Reboul, 1981.
    Le Concile féerique.   1886.
    Les Derniers Vers.   1890; edited by Michael Collie and J.M. L'Heureux, 1965; as *The Last Poems*, edited by Madeleine Betts, 1973.
    Poésies complètes.   1894.
    Poems, translated by P. Terry.   1958.

Fiction

    Moralités légendaires.   1887; edited by Daniel Grojnowski, 1980.

Other

    Lettres à un ami 1880-86.   1941.
    Stéphane Vassiliew.   1946.
    Selected Writings, edited by William Jay Smith.   1956.

    Translator, *Oeuvres choisies*, by Walt Whitman.   1918.

*

Critical Studies: *Laforgue and the Ironic Inheritance* by Warren Ramsey, 1953, and *Laforgue: Essays on a Poet's Life and Work* edited by Ramsey, 1969; *Laforgue*, 1963, and *Laforgue*, 1977, both by Michael Collie; *Looking for Laforgue: An Informal Biography* by David Arkell, 1979.

*   *   *

Jules Laforgue helped liberate and rejuvenate French prosody by means of a series of bold, iconoclastic, but highly original verse experiments which had the effect of establishing free verse as a legitimate and viable poetic mode not only in France, but also in Britain and the United States. Though disguised as a dilettante, Laforgue was devoted to literature; though a fashionable dandy, he worked through the night and in a short career was extremely productive. His early poems, *Le Sanglot de la terre*, he himself suppressed, realizing they were derivative, tendentious, verbally flat, and technically uninspired. Two other volumes, *L'Imitation de Notre-Dame la Lune* and *Le Concile féerique*, are distinctly modish and lightweight, though some of the Pierrot poems in the first of these show a pleasing cleverness in the dramatization of the clown's anguish. Laforgue's reputation, however, rests chiefly on two volumes of great historical as well as intrinsic importance: *Les Complaintes* and *Les Derniers Vers*.

In these two volumes he challenged, not just traditional, middle-class ideas about institutions such as marriage and the church, but also the stability of language itself. Standard usage and normal meanings are in both books ironically subverted by puns and neologisms; by disruptive, unconventional rhymes; by a vigorous, but controlled disturbance of metrical expectation; and by the invention, or at least adoption of new forms. A reader brought up on Lamartine and Hugo could only be shocked by Laforgue's rejection of traditional poetic rhetoric. The witty poems in *Les Complaintes* are remarkably inventive, superbly sophisticated verbal confections presented in the demotic guise of reworked street tunes and popular ballads, confections, one can say, because of their artificiality and high-spiritedness, but nonetheless in many cases brilliantly imaginative as well (e.g., "Complainte du pauvre Chevalier-errant" and "Complainte d'une Convalescence en Mai"). The twelve poems of *Les Derniers Vers* constitute a further advance in lexical and prosodic experimentation. Influenced, as he acknowledged himself, both by the theory of Impressionist painting and by the music of Wagner, Laforgue wrote a set of free-verse tone poems whose emphasis and impact were artistic, in the *fin-de-siècle* art-for-art's-sake sense, rather than moral. He had interested himself in anything that was different, modern, untraditional: photography, for example, and contemporary sculpture. In Paris he had seen the work of Monet, Sisley, and Pissarro. In Germany he had heard the music of Wagner. He had read about these, and other artists in *avant-garde* journals like *la Vogue* and *la Revue Wagnérienne*. He had studied and translated Whitman. Thoroughly imbued with a nihilistic, but technically innovative, modern spirit, he proceeded right at the end of his short life to produce *Les Derniers Vers*, the poetic *tour-de-force* that first established free-verse as an exciting extension of what was possible in French, and then later exerted a strong influence on English and American writers, most notably T.S. Eliot.

Laforgue's nihilism was that of the late 19th-century *flâneur* whose mind, like Ibsen's, was dominated by the imagined reality of biological determinism. In that post-Darwinian intellectual climate no man acted freely; all men were helpless pawns in a meaningless biological game; women were despised because seemingly ignorant of their merely sexual role; and the individual's only hope of personal integrity was not to participate in other people's normal activities. Experience was a kaleidoscope of impressions; nothing whatsoever could be trusted absolutely. In highly crafted poems like "Dimanches," "Solo de Lune," and "L'Hiver qui vient" Laforgue gave expression to the sensations of disbelief, the psychology of alienation, the loneliness in a world where "il n'y a plus de raison" and where the subjunctive and the conditional must necessarily have greater appeal than either the present or the future tense. "J'eusse été le modèle des époux," said Laforgue; "your heart would have responded/Gaily" said T.S. Eliot some years later in imitation of him. Whatever one may think, ultimately, about Laforgue's tantalizing amalgam of irony and sentiment—his cynicism fretted with nostalgia—there seems no doubt that the poems of *Les Derniers Vers* are one of the landmarks of 19th-century French poetry, marking the point at which freedom from conventional rhetoric had been fully achieved.

The same ironic, nihilist sensibility was given expression in a collection called *Moralités légendaires*. Laforgue amused himself by giving popular stories or myths an extravagantly anti-romantic treatment, negating the idealism of the original and poking fun at out-moded heroism. The flippancy and ebullience of these stories can still be enjoyed, as can their affected decadent prose, even though the underlying tone is remorselessly negative. Nor need one be too severe in judging these nihilistic contrivances; Laforgue died at the age of 27, with his great talent denied its full expression.

—Michael Collie

LAGERKVIST, Pär (Fabian). Born in Växjo, Sweden, 23 May 1891. Educated at the University of Uppsala, 1911-12. Married 1) Karen Dagmar Johanne Sørensen in 1918 (divorced, 1925); 2) Elaine Luella Hallberg in 1925. Theatre critic, *Svenska Dagbladet*, Stockholm, 1919. Recipient: Samfundet De Nio prize, 1928; Bellman Prize, 1945; Saint-Beuve Prize, 1946; Foreign Book Prize (France), 1951; Nobel Prize for Literature, 1951. Honorary degree: University of Gothenburg, 1941. Member, Swedish Academy of Literature, 1940. *Died 11 July 1974.*

PUBLICATIONS

Fiction

Människor [People]. 1912.
Två sagor om livet [Two Tales about Life]. 1913.
Järn och människor [Iron and People]. 1915.
Det eviga leendet. 1920; as *The Eternal Smile,* 1934.
Onda sagor [Evil Tales]. 1924.
Kämpande ande [Struggling Spirit]. 1930; translated in part as *Masquerade of Souls,* 1954.
Bödeln. 1933; as *The Hangman,* in *Guest of Reality,* 1936.
I den tiden [In That Time]. 1935.
Dvärgen. 1944; as *The Dwarf,* 1945.
Barabbas. 1950; translated as *Barabbas,* 1951.
The Eternal Smile and Other Stories. 1954.
The Marriage Feast and Other Stories. 1955.
Sibyllan. 1956; as *The Sibyl,* 1958.
Pilgrimen. 1966.
  Ahasverus' död. 1960; as *The Death of Ahasuerus,* 1962.
  Pilgrim på havet. 1962; as *Pilgrim at Sea,* 1964.
  Det heliga landet. 1964; as *The Holy Land,* 1966.
Mariamne. 1967; as *Herod and Mariamne,* 1968.

Plays

Sista Mänskan [The Last Man]. 1917.
Teater: Den svåra stunden; Modern teater: Synpunkter och angrepp [The Difficult Hour; Points of View and Attack] (produced 1918). 1918; essay and play translated in *Modern Theatre*, 1966.
Himlens hemlighet (produced 1921). In *Kaos*, 1919; as *The Secret of Heaven*, in *Modern Theatre*, 1966.
Den osynlige [The Invisible One] (produced 1924). 1923.
Gäst hos verkligheten. 1925; as *Guest of Reality*, 1936.
Han som fick leva om sitt liv (produced 1928). 1928; as *The Man Who Lived His Life Over*, in *Five Scandinavian Plays*, 1971.
Konungen (produced 1950). 1932; as *The King*, in *Modern Theatre*, 1966.
Bödeln, from his own novel (produced 1934). In *Dramatik*, 1946; as *The Hangman*, in *Modern Theatre*, 1966.
Mannen utan själ (produced 1938). 1936; as *The Man Without a Soul*, in *Scandinavian Plays of the Twentieth Century 1*, 1944.
Seger i mörker [Victory in Darkness] (produced 1940). 1939.
Midsommardröm i fattighuset (produced 1941). 1941; as *Midsummer Dream in the Workhouse*, 1953.
Dramatik. 1946.
Den vises sten (produced 1948). 1947; as *The Philosopher's Stone*, in *Modern Theatre*, 1966.
Låt människan leva (produced 1949). 1949; as *Let Man Live*, in *Scandinavian Plays of the Twentieth Century 3*, 1951.
Barabbas, from his own novel (produced 1953). 1953.
Modern Theatre: Seven Plays and an Essay. 1966.

Verse

Motiv [Motifs]. 1914.
Ångest [Anguish]. 1916.
Den lyckliges väg [Happy Road]. 1921.
Hjärtats sånger [Songs of the Heart]. 1926.
Vid lägereld [By the Campfire]. 1932.
Genius. 1937.
Sång och strid [Song and Battle]. 1940.
Dikter [Verse]. 1941; revised edition, 1958, 1974.
Hemmet och stjärnan [The Home and the Stars]. 1942.
Aftonland. 1953; as *Evening Land*, translated by W.H. Auden and Leif Sjöberg, 1975.
Valda dikter [Selected Poems]. 1967.

Other

Ordkonst och bildkonst [Word Art and Picture Art]. 1913.
Kaos [Chaos]. 1919.
Det besegrade livet [The Conquered Life]. 1927.
Skrifter [Writings]. 3 vols., 1932.
Den knutna näven [The Clenched Fist]. 1934.
Den befriade människan [Liberated Man]. 1939.
Prosa. 5 vols., 1945; revised edition, 1949.
Antecknat [Noted] (diary), edited by Elin Lagerkvist. 1977.

*

Critical Studies: *Lagerkvist: An Introduction* by Irene Scobbie, 1963, and "Lagerkvist," in *Essays on Swedish Literature from 1880 to the Present Day* edited by Scobbie, 1978; *Lagerkvist: A Critical Essay* by Winston Weathers, 1968; Lagerkvist Supplement, in *Scandinavica*, 1971; *Lagerkvist* by Robert Spector, 1973; *Lagerkvist* by Leif Sjöberg, 1976; *Lagerkvist in America* by Ray Lewis White, 1979.

*   *   *

As lyric poet, dramatist, satirist, and novelist Pär Lagerkvist was an innovator and one of Sweden's most influential writers of the 20th century. The autobiographical prose work *Guest of Reality* shows his deep affection for his pious parents and a yearning for a faith but an inability to accept their god. The resultant spiritual void and a fevered reaction to the bloodshed of World War I led to an overwhelming *Angst* conveyed in his poems *Ångest*, and the plays *Sista Mänskan, Den svåra stunden*, and *The Secret of Heaven*, in which he emerged as Sweden's leading Expressionist writer. The prose fantasy *The Eternal Smile* reflects a newly found resignation, an appreciation of the beauty of the world and a tentative belief in humanity. Two of his best cycles of poems included in *Hjärtats sånger* also suggest an inner harmony. This was dispelled as totalitarian regimes took control in Europe. In 1933 Lagerkvist published *The Hangman* where the role of the symbolic central character is examined in a medieval and then contemporary setting. Modern man's propensity for evil clearly surpasses the superstitious crudities of the Middle Ages. A further powerful symbol of evil is the title figure in *The Dwarf*, a masterly novel in diary form set in an Italian Renaisssance court. We all have a dwarf within us which when unleashed exults in destruction. The dwarf is in chains in the final chapter but is certain of eventual release.

In *Barabbas*, largely instrumental in his winning the Nobel Prize, Lagerkvist makes the biblical robber and insurgent an existentialist figure searching for a belief. Born into a world of violence and hatred he cannot accept the Christian message but having met Christ he cannot shake off his influence. Afraid of death, unable to believe in an after-life, he remains a lonely, moving representative of modern man. Man's relation to God is explored further in a series of symbolic novels. For the Pythia in *The Sibyl* the god can be both wonderful and terrible but her life without him would have been nothing; the Wandering Jew in *The Death of Ahasuerus* bears God's course and achieves death only by turning his back on religion; in *Pilgrim at Sea* and *The Holy Land* the struggling pilgrim finally finds reconciliation with God and man. In *Herod and Mariamne* evil in man is embodied in the symbolic figure of Herod. It is a desolate book, for Herod has Mariamne the Good killed, but it ends in hope—the Magi have found their way to a new-born babe.

Lagerkvist's last cycle of poems, *Evening Land*, contains beautifully expressed reminiscences and an indication of his unsolved paradox: "The non-existing god/he has set my soul in flames." In his early twenties Lagerkvist wrote numerous articles on Cubism and other forms of modern art. He subsequently endeavoured to apply the cubist's method of composition to his creative writing. Even at its most feverishly inspired his work is carefully constructed, his novels particularly having an almost architectural structure.

—Irene Scobbie

LAGERLÖF, Selma (Ottiliana Lovisa). Born at Mårbacka, Värmland, Sweden, 20 November 1858. Lame from age 3, and educated at home; studied at Teachers Seminary, Stockholm, 1880. Taught in a school in Landskrona until 1895, then writer: lived in Falun and, after she bought back her birthplace, Mårbacka. Recipient: *Idun* magazine prize, 1895; traveling fellowship, 1895; Swedish Academy Gold Medal, 1904; Nobel Prize for Literature, 1909. Ph.D.: Uppsala University, 1907. Member, Swedish Academy, 1914. *Died 16 March 1940.*

PUBLICATIONS

Collections

Skrifter. 12 vols., 1949-56.

Fiction

Gösta Berlings Saga. 1891; translated as *Gösta Berling's Saga,* 1898; as *The Story of Gösta Berling,* 1898.
Osynliga länkar: Berättelser. 1894; as *Invisible Links,* 1899.
Antikrists mirakler. 1897; as *The Miracles of Antichrist,* 1899.
Drottningar i Kungahälla jämte andra berättelser. 1899; as *The Queens of Kungahälla and Other Sketches,* 1917.
En herrgårdssägen. 1899; as *From a Swedish Homestead,* 1901.
Jerusalem I-II. 1901-02; translated as *Jerusalem* and *The Holy City,* 2 vols., 1903-18.
Herr Arnes Penningar. 1903; as *Herr Arne's Hoard,* 1923.
Legender: Berattade [Legends: Stories]. 3 vols., 1904.
Kristuslegender. 1904; as *Christ Legends,* 1908.
En saga om en saga och andra sagor. 1908; as *The Girl from the Marsh Croft,* 1911.
Meli. 1909.
Liljecronas hem. 1911; as *Liliecrona's Home,* 1913.
Körkarlen. 1912; as *The Soul Shall Bear Witness,* 1921.
Astrid och andra berättelser [Astrid and Other Stories]. 1914.
Kejsarn av Portugallien. 1914; as *The Emperor of Portugallia,* 1916.
Silvergruvan och andra berättelser [The Silver Mine and Other Stories]. 1915.
Troll och människor [Trolls and Humans]. 1915.
Kavaljersnoveller. 1918.
Bandlyst. 1918; as *The Outcast,* 1920.
Legender i urval [Selected Legends]. 1922.
The Tale of a Manor and Other Sketches. 1922.
The Ring of the Löwenskölds. 3 vols., 1931.
   1. *Löwensköldska ringen.* 1925; as *The General's Ring,* 1928.
   2. *Charlotte Löwensköld.* 1925; translated as *Charlotte Löwensköld,* 1927.
   3. *Anna Svärd.* 1928; translated as *Anna Svärd,* 1931.
Mors porträtt och andra berättelser [Portrait of Mors and Other Stories]. 1930.
Julberättelser [Christmas Stories]. 1938.

Plays

Fritiofs saga, music by E. Andree. 1899.
Stormyrtösen [Girl from the Marshes], with Bernt Fredgren, from a story by Lagerlof. 1913.

Dunungen. 1914.
Vinterballaden [Winter Ballad], from the play by Gerhart Hauptmann. 1919.
The Lighting of the Christmas Tree. 1921.
Kejsarn av Portugallien, with Poul Knudsen, from the novel by Lagerlöf. 1939.

Other

Nils Holgerssons underbara resa (juvenile). 1906-07; as *The Wonderful* [and *Further*] *Adventures of Nils*, 1907-11.
Mårbacka:
   1. Mårbacka. 1922; translated as *Mårbacka*, 1924.
   2. Ett barns memoarer. 1930; as *Memories of My Childhood*, 1934.
   3. Dagbok. 1932; as *Diary*, 1936.
Höst: Berättelser och tal. 1933; as *Harvest: Tales and Essays*, 1935.
Från skilda tider: Efterlämnade skrifter [Posthumous Works], edited by Nils Afzelius. 2 vols., 1943-45.
Brev 1871-1940 [Letters], edited by Ying Toijer-Nilsson. 2 vols., 1967-69.

*

Bibliography: *Lagerlöfs bibliografi originalskrifter* by Nils Afzelius, 1975.

Critical Studies: *Lagerlöf* by H.A. Larsen, 1936; *Fact and Fiction in the Autobiographical Works of Lagerlöf* by Folkerdina Stientje de Vrieze, 1958; *Lagerlöf* (in Swedish) by Carl O. Zamore, 1958; *Six Scandinavian Novelists* by Alrik Gustafson, 1966; *Lagerlöf* by Walter A. Berendsohn, 1968; *Lagerlöf: Herrn Arnes Penningar* by Brita Green, 1977.

*   *   *

Selma Lagerlöf's childhood at Mårbacka offered a rich store of old Värmland traditions but the realistic mode of writing in the 1880's was alien to her temperament and material. Witnessing the sale of Mårbacka in 1888, she resolved to eschew current fashion and write "in the Mårbacka manner." *Gösta Berling's Saga* was completed in 1891. The handsome, Byronic defrocked parson joins 12 "cavaliers" who are to run Ekeby estate for a year provided they live only for beauty and pleasure. There is much merrymaking, but Lagerlöf could not wholly accept a *carpe diem* philosophy and ends by eulogising hard work. This novel introduces typical Lagerlöfian themes: guilt and atonement; the saving qualities of a woman's selfless love; how to combine happiness with goodness. Having betrayed his calling Gösta must purge his guilt; the magnificent Margareta Celsing, the major's wife, has broken two Commandments and accepts banishment until she has expiated her sin. The supernatural is introduced when the cavaliers sell their souls to the Mephistophelian Sintram, while the elements are used both to heighten effect and to force characters' course of action. The style ranges from rhetoric and *Sturm und Drang* tempestuousness to textbook prose but the book bears the stamp of genius.
    In *The Tale of a Manor* Lagerlöf successfully fuses Beauty and the Beast with a Dalarna legend. Fear of losing his estate threatens Gunnar Hede's sanity but a young girl's unselfish love saves him. Within the framework of symbolic folk-tale Lagerlöf produces a valid psychological study of schizophrenia.
    On a visit to Palestine in 1900 Lagerlöf discovered a settlement of Dalarna peasants and this inspired the novel *Jerusalem* at the heart of which are the Ingmarssons representing such sterling qualities as loyalty to one's province, an innate sense of justice, simple faith, and moral courage. The powerful stylised characterisation and the epic scope of the novel show the influence of the Icelandic saga. Acknowledged as her masterpiece, *Jerusalem* won universal acclaim. The supernatural, merely suggested in *Jerusalem*, is a major element in *Herr Arne's Hoard* where a murdered girl's ghost is instrumental in bringing the murderers of Herr Arne's

household to justice. Commissioned to write a school text book Lagerlöf, influenced partly by Kipling's *Jungle Book*, wrote *The Wonderful Adventures of Nils*, in which Sweden's geography, flora, and fauna become part of a tale about a boy's magic journey on a goose's back.

World War I had a debilitating effect, and although Lagerlöf subsequently wrote autobiographies centred on Mårbacka and completed the Löwensköld trilogy her creative genius was spent. Her greatest gift was that of a storyteller. She refashioned local oral tradition into powerful universal prose works reflecting her instinctive understanding of the human heart and conscience. Her attitude to miracles and religion is ambivalent but her innate sense of justice and natural order ultimately restores harmony in her works. There is nothing facile in such happy endings, however, for they are achieved by personal sacrifice and a supreme effort to overcome destructive elements in human nature.

—Irene Scobbie

LAZARILLO de Tormes. Anonymous Spanish work.

PUBLICATIONS

La vida de Lazarillo de Tormes y de sus fortunas y adversidades.   1554; edited by R.O. Jones, 1963; translated as *Lazarillo de Tormes*, 1586; also translated by Michael Apert, in *Two Spanish Picaresque Novels*, 1969; as *Blind Man's Boy*, translated by J.M. Cohen, 1962.

*

Critical Studies: *Lazarillo de Tormes: A Critical Guide* by Alan David Deyermond, 1975; *Language and Society in "La Vida de Lazarillo de Tormes"* by Harry Sieber, 1978; *The Spanish Picaresque Novel* by P.N. Dunn, 1979.

*   *   *

Lazarillo de Tormes, a short novel in autobiographical form, tells of the career of the young miller's son, Lazarillo, in the service of a variety of masters, who are satirically portrayed, and of his eventual acquisition of the post of town-crier and his marriage to a servant girl, at the suggestion of an archpriest whose mistress she is reputed to be.

Lazarillo's father is imprisoned for theft, and dies in exile. His widowed mother's lover, by whom she has a child, is also caught stealing to provide for the household. Lazarillo's personal struggle for survival begins when his mother entrusts him to an itinerant blind man seeking a guide. The lad is forced to find ingenious stratagems for filching food from this sharp-witted master, and from the miserly priest he serves next. Under the impoverished hidalgo we meet in Chapter Three, we find Lazarillo begging in order to keep both himself and his master, who, though not mean, is too proud to work, and has nothing to give. After a spell with a worldly friar and a fraudulent pardoner who stages a fake miracle, Lazarillo saves some money as a water-seller, buys some second-hand clothes which have the remnants of stylishness, tries the job of constable's assistant, which he finds too dangerous, and finally, "with the assistance of friends and gentlemen," is made town-crier, a post with wide-ranging duties, including auctioneering and officially accompanying convicted criminals to the gallows or the stocks to announce publicly their crimes. His clients include the archpriest, whose wine he auctions. Despite the gossip about his wife, which the archpriest advises him to ignore, he declares himself well contented with his achievements.

This book has always been popular, particularly for its ironic portrayal of Lazarillo's masters, the portrait of the poor hidalgo who is ridiculously sensitive on matters of honour being the most carefully developed. But its true subtlety reveals itself in the ambiguity surrounding the presentation of the character of Lazarillo himself. Much turns upon whether we take Lazarillo's comments about himself as made in all innocence, or whether we see him as being deliberately ironic, and capable of laughing at himself and teasing his audience. For example, does he genuinely imagine that his new clothes are impressive when at the same time he objectively describes how shabby they are? Again, when he says his wife is as good as any in Toledo, is this a naive statement of her innocence, or a barbed comment about the moral standards of Toledan women? In a foreword, Lazarillo indicates that he is writing in response to somebody who has asked him to recount "the matter" ("el caso"). We are left in the dark until the end of the book, when we learn that the inquirer is a friend of the archpriest. Perhaps he wishes to know about the set-up between Lazarillo, his wife, and the archpriest. If so, is Lazarillo so full of self-importance that he is blind to the irrelevance of most of his life story to the inquirer, or is he teasing his audience, one of the idle rich he despises? The ironic reading is an attractive one.

—M.J. Woods

LEOPARDI, Giacomo. Born in Recanati, 29 June 1798; became a Count on his father's death. Educated at home by tutors; studied privately until 1822. Lived in Rome, 1822-23; advisor, A.F. Stella, publishers, Milan, 1825-28; lived in Bologna, Florence, and Pisa, and in Naples from 1833. *Died 14 June 1837.*

PUBLICATIONS

Collections

Opere, edited by Antonio Ranieri. 6 vols., 1845-49.
Tutte le opere, edited by Francesco Flora. 5 vols., 1937-49.
Tutte le opere, edited by Walter Binni and Enrico Ghidetti. 2 vols., 1969.
A Leopardi Reader, edited by Ottavio M. Casale. 1981.

Verse

Canzoni. 1819.

Canzone ad Angelo Mai. 1820.

Versi. 1824.

Versi, edited by Pietro Brigherti. 1826.

I canti. 1831; revised edition, 1835; edited by I. Sanesi, 1943, Francesco Flora, 1949, and Mario Fubini, 1970; translated by J.H. Whitfield as *Canti,* 1962.

I Paralipomeni della Batracomiomachia. 1842; as *The War of the Mice and the Crabs,* edited and translated by Ernesto G. Caserta, 1976.

The Poems, translated by Francis H. Cliffe. 1893.

The Poems ("Canti"), translated by J.M. Morrison. 1900.

The Poems (bilingual edition), edited by Geoffrey L. Bickersteth. 1923.

(Selections), translated by R.C. Trevelyan. 1941.

Poems, translated by John Heath-Stubbs. 1946.

Poems, translated by J.-P. Barricelli. 1963.

Canti, paralipomeni, poesie varie, traduzioni, poetiche, e versi puerili, edited by C. Muscetta and G. Savoca. 1968.

Other

Operette morali. 1827; revised edition, 1836; edited by Cesare Galimberti, 1978; as *Essays and Dialogues,* 1882; as *Operette Morali* (bilingual edition), edited by Giovanni del Cecchetti, 1983.

Opere inedite, edited by Giuseppe Cugnoni. 2 vols., 1878-80.

Pensieri di varia filosofia e di bella letteratura ["Lo Zibaldone"]. 7 vols., 1898-1900; edited by Anna Maria Moroni, 2 vols., 1972.

Epistolario, edited by F. Moroncini and others. 7 vols., 1934-41.

Selected Prose and Poetry, edited by Iris Origo and John Heath-Stubbs. 1966.

Poems and Prose, edited by Angel Flores. 1966.

Entro dipinta gabbia, edited by Maria Corti. 1972.

Lettere, edited by Sergio and Raffaella Solmi. 1977.

Pensieri, edited by W.S. Di Piero. 1981.

Editor, *Rime,* by Petrarch. 1826.

Editor, *Crestomazia italiana: prosa, poesia,* 2 vols., 1827-28.

*

Bibliography: *Bibliografia leopardiani,* 3 vols., 1931-53; *Bibliografia analitica leopardiani,* 2 vols., 1963-73.

Critical Studies: *Leopardi: A Biography* by Iris Origo, 1935, revised edition, as *Leopardi: A Study in Solitude,* 1953; *Leopardi* by J.H. Whitfield, 1954; *Leopardi and the Theory of Poetry* by G. Singh, 1964; *The Artifice of Reality: Poetic Style in Wordsworth, Foscolo, Keats, and Leopardi* by Karl Kroeber, 1964; *Night and the Sublime in Leopardi* by Nicolas James Parella, 1970; *Leopardi: The Unheeded Voice* by Giovanni Carsaniga, 1977.

* * *

No Italian poet—not even Dante—exemplifies with such vigour and convincingness as Leopardi the validity of Coleridge's dictum that a great poet is also a profound philosopher. The union between poetry and first-hand thought—critical as well as philosophical, analytical as well as exploratory—gives Leopardi's style and language an unmistakably personal timbre which is at the same time a hall-mark of universality. A contemporary of the English Romantic poets, Leopardi was not "romantic" as they were; in fact, as his essay "Discorso di un italiano intorno alla poesia romantica" shows, he adopted a polemical attitude to Romanticism, as he conceived it; and although a contemporary of Goethe and Hölderlin, he wasn't "Classical" in the way they were. Similarly, although he was a precursor of poetic modernity (like Baudelaire), Leopardi's art is as different in ethos and temperament from Baudelaire's as it is from Byron's, Keats's, or Shelley's. Moreover, although he was saturated—few poets more—in classical literature and classical learning, his poetry is conspicuously free from the weight of such learning. Ill-health and growing blindness as well as frustration in love dogged him all his life, but he managed to rise above these, transforming his joy and pain, and the vicissitudes of his uneventful but emotionally rich life, into material for poetic and philosophic contemplation which is at once rapt and deliberate, cool and impassioned. Hence his poetry, even at its most lyrical, is at bottom philosophical, and his style and diction, even at their most charged, have about them a philosophic detachment and serenity. In fact, Leopardi may be said to have created a new poetic genre in Italian—the philosophic lyric—through which he interfused, to borrow Eliot's words, the man who suffers and the artist who creates.

Leopardi's poetic genius finds its supreme manifestation in the *Canti*, just as his analytical and speculative powers do theirs in his *Operette morali*. *Epistolario*, on the other hand, is a richly human document of the psychological and autobiographical side of Leopardi's personality, and *Zibaldone*—a monumental miscellany of notes, comments, and reflections—is a mine of literary and philological erudition and encyclopaedic culture rolled into one. Binding all these works as well as underlying them is a singularly gifted mind—at once creative and critical, learned and inventive, cultivated and inquisitive—with an unsurpassed mastery over prose and verse style.

The English critics, together with Sainte-Beuve, were the first to recognize and critically comment on these qualities of Leopardi's art and personality. "A man of acknowledged genius and irreproachable character," wrote Henry Crabb Robinson after meeting Leopardi in Florence in 1830-31. "There have been," observed H.G. Lewes, apropos of Leopardi's patriotic odes, "no more piercing, manly, vigorous strains than those which vibrate in the organ-peal of patriotism sent forth by Leopardi." And as a poet of despair, Lewes went on, "we know of no equal to Leopardi.... His grief is so real and so profound that it is inexhaustible in expression, to say nothing of the beauty in which he embalms it." According to Gladstone, too, Leopardi applies to his work, "with a power rarely equalled, all the resources of thought and passion, all that his introspective habit had taught him...and he unites to a very peculiar grace a masculine energy and even majesty of expression which is not surpassed...in the whole range of poetry." And as far as Leopardi's mastery over form and style is concerned, here is Matthew Arnold's testimony: Leopardi "has the very qualities which we have found wanting in Byron; he has the sense for form and style, the passion for just expression, the sure and firm touch of the true artist...he has a far wider culture than Wordsworth, more mental lucidity, more freedom from illusions as to the real character of the established fact and of reigning conventions; above all, this Italian, with his pure and sure touch, with his fineness of perception, is far more of the artist [than Wordsworth]." But besides being that of a stylist and an artist of such calibre, Leopardi's poetry has something perpetually modern about it, as has his theory of poetry. Leopardi jotted down his reflections on and discoursed about the nature of poetry, style, poetic inspiration, the language of poetry—in fact no poet in the history of Italian literature has occupied himself with the theory of poetry as much as Leopardi, and, indeed, as Maurice Bowra remarks, "few men have given so much hard thought to the matter"—by virtue of which he may be regarded as a worthy peer of Goethe, Wordsworth, and Coleridge. Moreover, certain aspects of Leopardi's poetics—and Poetry—are startlingly modern and anticipate the development of 20th-century poetry.

For although Leopardi's poetry treats of themes which are conventional—love, death, youth, nature, memory, the transience of life, etc.—what comes out of his treatment of such themes is of the very essence of modernity—modernity of thought as well as of style. And if his poetry has a philosophic basis to it, it is not because it expounds a particular philosophy, or is inspired by or tied up with philosophic ideas as such. The fulcrum of the union between poetry and philosophy in Leopardi is his perception of the truth about life as he saw it and of the illusions one needed in order to be able to bear it, since "human kind cannot bear very much reality."

Thus Leopardi's pessimism, in the *Canti* no less than in *Operette morali*, is not so much a poetic creed based on emotional or imaginative grounds as a mixture of closely argued conclusions as well as personal convictions regarding the nature of life and human destiny which the poet-philosopher has the courage to look unflinchingly in the face and at the same time embrace what his own experience of life forced upon him and what his knowledge as well as observation of the world and of man in society taught him. From his very early life Leopardi was filled with what he himself calls "the infinite desire to know precisely," and this desire never abandoned him. His explorations of reality were conveyed in accents of matchless lyricism which served him to cover "the nudity of things." Leopardi's art was admired not only by a modern poet like Pound—"Leopardi splendid, and the only author since Dante who need trouble you," Pound wrote to Iris Berry—but also by a modern philosopher like Bertrand Russell. In a letter to me Russell said that he found Leopardi's poetry and philosophy "the most beautiful expression of what should be the creed of a scientist," and considered "La ginestra" as expressing "more effectively than any other poem known to me my views about the universe and the human passions."

—G. Singh

LERMONTOV, Mikhail (Yur'evich). Born in Moscow, 2-3 October 1814. Educated at School for the Nobility, 1828-30; University of Moscow, 1830-32; Junker School, St. Petersburg, 1832-34: Cavalry cornet in Regiment of Life Guards Hussars; exiled to the Caucasus for poems on Pushkin's death, 1835-38; because of a duel, again exiled, to Tenginsky Infantry Regiment on Black Sea, 1840-41. *Died (in duel) 15 July 1841.*

PUBLICATIONS

Collections

Sochineniya v shesti tomakh. 6 vols., 1954-57.
Izbraniye sochineniy. 4 vols., 1958-59.

Fiction

Geroy nashevo vremeni. 1840; as *Sketches of Russian Life in the Caucasus*, 1853; as *A Hero of Our Times*, 1854; as *The Heart of a Russian*, 1912.

Play

Maskarad. 1842.

Verse

Pesnya pro tsarya Ivana Vasil'evicha. 1837; as *A Song about Tsar Ivan Vasilyevich*, 1929.

325

Mtsyri.   1840; as *The Circassian Boy*, 1875.
Demon.   1842; as *The Demon*, 1875.
Selected Poetry.   1965.
Selected Works.   1976.
Major Poetical Works, edited and translated by Anatoly Liberman.   1983.
Narrative Poems by Pushkin and Lermontov, translated by Charles Johnston.   1983.

*

Critical Studies: *Lermontov* by Janko Lavrin, 1959; *Lermontov* by John Mersereau, Jr., 1962; *Lermontov: Tragedy in the Caucasus* by Laurence Kelly, 1977; *An Essay on Lermontov's "A Hero of Our Times"* by C.J.G. Turner, 1978; *Lermontov: A Study in Literary-Historical Evaluation* by B.M. Eikhenbaum, 1981; *Lermontov* by John Garrard, 1982.

*   *   *

Lermontov is often thought of as Pushkin's successor in the role of Russian national poet. Lermontov was profoundly influenced by Pushkin but an equally potent and more visible influence was that of Byron. Whereas Pushkin's ingrained classical instincts allowed him to assimilate classical influences (often ironically) without wholly succumbing to romantic style, Lermontov must be regarded as a full-blooded representative of the romantic movement.

During his short life Lermontov attempted most literary genres but was chiefly a lyric and narrative poet. His drama is less memorable but his single prose work of note, *A Hero of Our Times*, is one of the most original and influential of Russian novels.

Lermontov's lyrics are often highly subjective and reflect the isolation of the post-Decembrist poet and the search for inner consolation which eluded Lermontov more than his contemporary, Tyutchev. Lermontov also uses lyric poetry as a means of expressing his metaphysic, often symbolically. Inanimate objects in juxtaposition (a rock and a cloud; a dead leaf floating in a river) or in isolation (a mountain peak; a solitary tree) are used in an almost Ovidian way to convey the tragic helplessness of particular aspects of the human condition. Ineluctable fate is a brooding presence throughout Lermontov's work: in the short poem "Angel" (1831), the human soul is conceived as pre-existing physical birth, birth itself being the forcible removal of the soul from a state of heavenly bliss to bodily imprisonment and exile among the world's miseries.

Fate, however, is not to be accepted blindly. Lermontov's most memorable creations are those in which Sisyphus-like characters struggle heroically against insuperable forces. Early in his literary career Lermontov became fascinated by the demonic personality, which, though shunned by God, is nevertheless capable of love and passion. As well as several lyrics on this theme, Lermontov produced, in successive drafts, a narrative poem called *The Demon* in which a demon, expelled from heaven, seeks redemption through the love of a Georgian girl but is eventually thwarted by God. Undemonic, but equally heroic, the hero of *The Circassian Boy* is a young postulant of Circassian origin. He is brought up in a Georgian monastery, and his one wish is to return to his home in the Caucasus but, after an ill-fated attempt to escape, he is brought back to the monastery and dies.

A Caucasian setting and demonic exertion of the will against fate also dominate *A Hero of Our Times*. This work, generally thought to be Lermontov's greatest, is sometimes said by critics to show that, by the end of his life, Lermontov was forsaking romanticism in favour of realism. Certainly Lermontov takes great pains to motivate his novel, i.e., to suggest that it has as its initial impulse a documentary rather than a fictional intention. But the hero himself is still an embittered representative of the Byronic tradition and, though at times self-deprecating, is never a vehicle for parodying or diminishing that tradition. The most remarkable feature of *A Hero of Our Times* is its architecture: five structurally autonomous but thematically inter-meshed first-person narratives create the illusion of a living, multi-dimensional hero who makes himself known to the reader by the gradual accumulation of psychological detail rather than by the consecutive unfolding of plot. Lermontov's prose style in the novel, remarkably simple but capable of sustaining impressive passages of natural description, influenced later writers, particularly short-story writers such as Chekhov. The character of Pechorin, the hero, has come to epitomise "the superfluous man," the disillusioned internal exile who figures so largely in the 19th-century Russian novel.

—Robert Reid

LESSING, Gotthold Ephraim.   Born in Kamenz, 23 January 1729.   Educated at school of St. Afron, Meissen, 1741-46; studied theology, then medicine, at University of Leipzig, 1746-48; University of Wittenberg, 1748, 1751-52, Master of Arts 1752. Married Eva König in 1776 (died, 1778); one son. Writer from 1748 in Berlin: Editor, with Christlob Mylius, *Beiträge zur Historie und Aufnahme des Theaters*, 1750; Editor, *Theatralische Bibliothek*, 1754-58, and *Briefe die neueste Literatur betreffend* (*Literaturbriefe*), 1759; official secretary to General Bogislaw von Tauentzien, Breslau, 1760-65; resident adviser to the National Theatre in Hamburg, 1767-68; Librarian to the Duke of Brunswick, Wolfenbüttel, 1770-81. Member, Academy of Mannheim, 1776. *Died 15 February 1781.*

PUBLICATIONS

Collections

> *Sämtliche Schriften*, edited by Karl Lachmann, revised by Franz Muncker.   23 vols., 1886-1924.
> *Werke*, edited by Julius Petersen and Waldemar von Olshausen.   25 vols., 1925; supplement, 5 vols., 1929-35.
> *Werke*, edited by H.G. Göpfert and others.   8 vols., 1970-79.

Plays

> *Der junge Gelehrte*, with others (produced 1748).   In *Schriften*, 1754.
> *Die alte Jungfer.*   1749.
> *Miss Sara Sampson* (produced 1755).   In *Schriften*, 1755; edited by K. Eibl, 1971.
> *Philotas* (produced 1774).   1759.
> *Lustspiele.*   2 vols., 1767.
> *Minna von Barnhelm* (produced 1767).   In *Lustspiele*, 1767; edited by D. Hildebrandt, 1969; as *The Disbanded Officer*, 1786; as *The School for Honor*, 1789; as *Minna von Barnhelm*, 1805; also translated by K.J. Northcott, 1972.
> *Trauerspiele.*   1772.
> *Emilia Galotti* (produced 1772).   In *Trauerspiele*, 1772; translated as *Emilia Galotti*, 1800; also translated by F.J. Lamport, in *Five German Tragedies*, 1969.
> *Nathan der Weise* (produced 1783).   1779; edited by P. Demetz, 1966; as *Nathan the Wise*, 1868; also translated by W.A. Steel, with *Laocoon* and *Minna von Barnhelm*, 1930.

Other

Schriften.   6 vols., 1753-55; revised edition, 1771.
Fabeln.   1759; revised edition, 1777; as *Fables*, 1829.
Laokoon; oder, Über die Grenzen der Malerei und Poesie.   1766; as *Laocoon; or, The Limits of Poetry and Painting*, 1853; and subsequent translations.
Briefe, antiquarischen Inhalts.   2 vols., 1768.
Berengarius Turonensis.   1770.
Zur Geschichte und Literatur[so-called *Wolfenbütteler Beiträge*].   1773-81.
Anti-Goeze, 1-11.   1778.
Ernst und Falk.   1778-81; as *Ernst and Falk*, 1854-72; as *Masonic Dialogues*, 1927.
Die Erziehung des Menschengeschlechts.   1780; edited by Louis Ferdinand Helbig, 1980; as *The Education of the Human Race*, 1858; also translated by H. Chadwick, in *Lessing's Theological Writings*, 1956.
Theologischer Nachlass, edited by K.G. Lessing.   1784.
Theatralischer Nachlass, edited by K.G. Lessing.   2 vols., 1784-86.
Literarischer Nachlass, edited by K.G. Lessing.   3 vols., 1793-95.
Hamburgische Dramaturgie (1767-69), edited by O. Mann.   1958.
Lessing im Gespräch, edited by Richard Daunicht.   1971.
Briefwechsel über das Trauerspiel, edited by J. Schulte-Sasse.   1972.
Briefe aus Wolfenbüttel, edited by Günter Schulz.   1975.
Meine liebste Madam: Briefwechsel, with Eva König, edited by Günter and Ursula Schulz.   1979.

*

Bibliography: *Lessing-Bibliographie* by S. Seifert, 1973.

Critical Studies: *Lessing, The Founder of Modern German Literature* by H.B. Garland, 1939, revised edition, 1962; *Lessing and the Enlightenment* by Henry E. Allison, 1966; *Lessing and the Language of Comedy* by M.M. Metzger, 1966; *Lessing* by F.A. Brown, 1971; *Lessing's Theology* by L.P. Wessell, 1977; *Lessing and the Drama* by F.J. Lamport, 1981.

*   *   *

Lessing is the principal literary figure of the German Enlightenment and founder of the modern German drama. Intended to follow his father into the Lutheran ministry, he made his literary debut while still a theological student with a number of comedies, for the most part conventional but in some cases (*Die Juden, Der Freigeist*) touching upon serious matters of intellectual controversy and humanitarian concern. By the time he was 25 he had also established a reputation as a trenchant critic and essayist on a wide range of topics. But the series of works upon which his lasting reputation rests begins with *Miss Sara Sampson*. This "domestic" or "middle-class" tragedy was the first successful attempt in German, indeed in European drama, at the serious and in some measure "realistic" depiction of ordinary contemporary characters, situations, and issues. This vein is continued in *Minna von Barnhelm*, a comedy of love and reconciliation in the aftermath of the Seven Years' War, and the tragedy *Emilia Galotti*, a powerful amalgam of social and psychological conflict with a strong (if only implicit) note of political criticism. These works paved the way for the realistic social drama which was only to develop fully in the 19th century. Less successful was the laconic *Philotas*, a tragedy of patriotic fanaticism in a neo-classical setting. Lessing admired the Greeks, and in *Laocoon* praised Greek art as the supreme expression of the human spirit, while attacking what he saw as perversions of the true classical tradition; similarly in the *Hamburg Dramaturgy* he sought to liberate the German drama from any dependence on the neo-classic style of 17th-century France. *Laocoon* also seeks to delimit the proper spheres of the various arts, attacking the doctrine "ut pictura poesis" and maintaining that while the scope of the visual arts is limited to beauty, poetry and literature should depict actions.

In the 1770's Lessing's interests returned largely to theology. Beginning with the defence of various so-called heretics and of the rights of freedom of conscience, of intellectual inquiry, and of expression, he proceeded to a number of searching examinations of the concept of religious truth. Truth itself becomes increasingly elusive, increasingly relative, but Lessing holds fast to the belief in an ultimately benevolent Providence and in the supreme importance of ethical conduct in man. This faith is proclaimed in his last play, *Nathan the Wise*: here Lessing abandons his earlier realism for a kind of symbolic fairy-tale, in which Christian, Moslem, and Jew are ultimately revealed as members of one family. His final treatise, *The Education of the Human Race*, traces the course of human history as a dialectic between human reason and divine revelation, between developing human autonomy and a transcendent providential plan.

By his own and succeeding generations, Lessing has been regarded above all as a liberator, a champion of humanity, and an unrelenting critic of intolerance and pretension. His major plays are still successfully performed today; his critical writings are models of supple and incisive German prose.

—F.J. Lamport

LI PO. Born in 701; brought up in Szechwan province, China. Spent a few years as a Taoist hermit in his teens, and trained as a knight-errant before the age of 25; then began a life of wandering: summoned to court, and retained as a sort of court poet, 742-45; entered service of Prince Lin, 16th son of the Emperor, 757, but banished after Lin's defeat in a bid for the throne, 759. Had four wives. *Died in 762.*

PUBLICATIONS

Verse

Works, translated by Shigeyoshi Obata.   1922.
Poems (with Tu Fu), translated by Arthur Cooper.   1973.
Li T'ai-po chüan-chi [Complete Works].   3 vols., 1977.

*

Critical Studies: *The Poetry and Career of Li Po* by Arthur Waley, 1950; *The Genius of Li Po* by Wong Siu-kit, 1974.

*   *   *

No poet, except Tu Fu, holds so preeminent a position as Li Po among the Chinese classical poets since the T'ang dynasty. Li Po was highly praised by the poets of his time and earned the title "celestial poet." His poems, especially because of their exuberant and romantic style, were not only admired and imitated by the poets of the past but are also widely read by one generation after another. His poems have always been a must for learners of Chinese literature or for family libraries in China.

He was born of a wealthy family and lived an extravagant life when he was young. At the age of 26 he left his native place and travelled over almost the entire country and became a poor wanderer. His love for the beauty of nature and his legendary experiences contributed a great deal to the enduring themes and style of his poems. In many poems he described the beautiful landscape of the swift Yellow River, the precipitous mountains, and the long and wide Yangtze River. Some of these poems, such as "Looking at the Falls of Lushan Mountain from a Distance," rank as masterpieces through the ages.

He was a patriot, and his poems express his love for the country and sympathy with the sufferings of the common people. He condemned the evil war in his verse: "White bones are piling up like hills, Why should the people suffer?" Failing to fulfill his wish to save the common people and help the country out of great difficulties, he nevertheless severely criticized and mocked the debauched and treacherous court officials in his poems, while, on the other hand, he revealed his personal anguish and melancholy. From time to time he found escape from his worldly trouble in retirement and indulgence in wine. As he was unsatisfied with life, he expressed in his poems his wish to withdraw from human society and seek happiness by living in seclusion. For him wine was indispensable. He said point-blank in "The Song of Wine": "I wish to drink myself drunk, never to become sober again."

Among other poems, "I Miss My Husband When Spring Comes," "Lovesick," and "The Crows Caw in the Evening" are expressive of faithful love and the grief of lovers separated by long military service. Elsewhere he showed his sympathy with women forsaken by their husbands.

Li Po learned from his predecessors and from the folk songs and ballads (*yueh-fu* poetry). He inherited the tradition of Chinese poetry but developed his own style which is characterized by his brilliant imagination, exquisite but not ornate language, delicate, vivid, and yet natural descriptions. As far as aesthetic value is concerned, in the history of Chinese literature there is hardly any classic poet of later generations who could equal him.

—Binghong Lu

LIVY (Titus Livius).   Born in Patavium (now Padua), in 59 or 64 B.C. Had one daughter and one son. Settled in Rome, c. 29; came to know the emperor Augustus, and supervised the studies of the future emperor Claudius. *Died 17 or 12 A.D.*

PUBLICATIONS

[*History*], edited by W. Weissenborn, revised by Müller and Heraeus.   1887-1908; books 21-22 re-edited by T.A. Dorey, 1971, and books 26-27 by P.G. Walsh, 1982; books 1-10 and 21-35 edited by R.M. Ogilvie, C.F. Walters, A.H. McDonald, and others, 1919-74; also edited by J. Bayet and P. Jal, 1947—; commentary on books 1-5 by R.M. Ogilvie, 1965, on books 31-33 by J. Briscoe, 1973, and on books 34-37 by J. Briscoe, 1981; translated (in Loeb edition), 14 vols., 1919-59; *The Early History of Rome* (books 1-5) translated by Aubrey de Selincourt, 1960; *Rome and Italy* (books 6-10) translated by Betty Radice, 1982; *The War with Hannibal* (books 21-30) translated by Aubrey de Selincourt, 1965; *Rome and the Mediterranean* (books 31-45) translated by Henry Bettenson, 1976.

*

Critical Studies: *Constancy in Livy's Latinity* by K. Gries, 1947; *God and Fate in Livy* by I. Kajanto, 1957; *Livy: His Historical Aims and Methods*, 1961, and *Livy*, 1974, both by P.G. Walsh; *Livy* edited by T.A. Dorey, 1971; *Livy: The Composition of His History* by T.J. Luce, 1977; *The Prose Rhythms of Sallust and Livy* by Hans Aili, 1979; *A Historiographical Study of Livy, Books VI-X* by J.P. Lipovsky, 1981.

* * *

Although the tradition of Roman historical writing goes back to the third century B.C., Cicero was still able to complain in the mid-50's (*On the Orator* 2.53, 63-4) that the earlier Roman historians had no pretensions to literary embellishment and were unable to tell a properly constructed story; he wished that they had brought to their works an elegant style and not regarded brevity as the only stylistic virtue. But it was more than 20 years before a historian set out to eclipse the writers whom Cicero had criticised, and to produce the great historical work for which Cicero had called. That historian was Livy.

Livy's original plan was immensely ambitious: to tell the story of Rome from its legendary foundation to the death of Cicero (43 B.C.) in 120 volumes. In his preface to the work, almost certainly written before the end of the civil wars (49-31 B.C.), Livy expresses dismay at his own times and relishes the prospect of being able to escape from them by reliving the past in his history (cf. 43.13.2). It may therefore be inferred that he saw Roman history in terms of decline, thus following a tradition of Roman historiography already established in the second century B.C. according to which the course of Roman history was seen as undergoing progressive degeneration. At the same time, however, Livy intended to lay before his readers examples, drawn from history, of the kind of behaviour which they should imitate and avoid (preface 10): evidently he did not exclude the possibility of Rome's recovering from the nadir epitomised by contemporary society.

Unfortunately only 35 of Livy's 120 volumes have survived (1-10, 21-45), but the flavour of his work can be appreciated in a story such as Tarquin's rape of Lucretia. The story is divided, like a miniature play, into 4 "acts" (1.57, 58-59.2, 59.3-13, 60.1-3), each of which is subdivided into individual "scenes"; the action is brought before the reader's eyes by means of judiciously selected detail and the use of direct speech at crucial moments; the pathos of the episode is further underlined by effective repetitions of word and phrase; and the whole drama is designed to praise Lucretia's *pudicitia* (chastity) and condemn Tarquin's *uis*, *libido*, and *superbia* (violence, lust, arrogance). Livy's achievement in this and many other passages can be gauged where we are able to compare his work with that of a predecessor. Thus Claudius Quadrigarius, writing 50 years earlier, described how Manlius Torquatus and Valerius Corvinus acquired their *cognomina* ("surnames"); but his accounts are brief and crude, written in an unambitious and inelegant style. Livy (7.9-10, 26) has expanded the episodes with a wealth of circumstantial detail and expressed them in a "periodic" style that is the historian's counterpart of the oratorical period of Cicero. Here, no less than in his long and patriotic treatment of the struggle against Hannibal (Books 21-30), Livy convinces the reader that he is witnessing one of the glorious episodes of Rome's past history, written in an appropriately elevated style.

No doubt Livy originally intended these earlier and glorious periods of Rome's history to emphasise by contrast the degeneration which had set in subsequently and which was epitomised by the civil wars of his own lifetime; but at some unknown point he decided to extend the scope of his work by almost 35 years, bringing the history down to 9 B.C. This decision radically affected the whole perspective of the work. No longer did the latest years of his history afford an unhappy comparison with the past: since the extra 22 volumes (of which none survives) now took him mid-way through Augustus' reign, his revised plan meant that the latest years of his history now actually challenged the past in glory. The explanation for Livy's change of mind presumably rests with the emperor himself, with whom the historian, as tutor to the future emperor Claudius, was on personal terms and whom he came to see as the saviour of Rome. As a result, the 142 volumes of the completed enterprise constituted a monumental testimony to a nation's inherent greatness and its remarkable capacity for survival.

—A.J. Woodman

LOPE DE VEGA.   *See* **VEGA, Lope de.**

LORCA, Federico García.   *See* **GARCÍA LORCA, Federico.**

LORRIS, Guillaume de.   *See* **ROSE, Romance of the.**

LUCIAN.   Born in Samosata, Syria (now Samsat, Turkey), c. 120 A.D. Probably not a Greek. Married; one son. Apprenticed to a sculptor; then received an education in rhetoric, and became a pleader, then a traveling lecturer, practicing Sophistic rhetoric in Gaul; moved to Athens about age 40; may have accompanied the Emperor Verus to Antioch in 162; chief court usher (*archistator*) with the Roman administration in Alexandria in early 170's. *Died after 180 A.D.*

PUBLICATIONS

Verse

[*Works*], edited by M.D. Macleod. 3 vols. (of 4), 1972-80; also edited by J. Sommerbrodt, 5 vols., 1886-99, and Nils Nilén, 1906-23 (incomplete); translated by A.M. Harmon and others (Loeb edition), 8 vols., 1913-67; *Satirical Sketches* translated by Paul Turner, 1961, *Selected Satires* by Lionel Casson, 1962, and *Selected Works* by B.P. Reardon, 1965.

*

Critical Studies: *Lucian, Satirist and Artist* by F.G. Allinson, 1926; *The Translations of Lucian by Erasmus and Thomas More* by C.R. Thompson, 1940; *Literary Quotation and Allusion in Lucian* by F.W. Householder, 1941; *Lucien écrivain* by J. Bompaire, 1957; *Studies in Lucian* by Barry Baldwin, 1973; *Studies in Lucian's Comic Fiction* by Graham Anderson, 1976; *Ben Jonson and the Lucianic Tradition* by Douglas Duncan, 1979; *Lucian and His Influence in Europe* by Christopher Robinson, 1979.

*   *   *

Literal-minded Byzantines saw Lucian as an Anti-Christ; Lord Macaulay dubbed him the Voltaire of antiquity. He deserves neither title. Lucian is best regarded as a journalist-cum-intellectual, unscrupulously versatile like the hero of Kingsley Amis's *I Like It Here*, albeit more prolific.

Least popular now are his occasional pieces on various rhetorical themes. One or two deserve attention, notably his essay on Slander which describes a Greek painting that inspired Botticelli's *La Calunnia*. Lucian is one of a relatively small number of ancient writers on art, which should commend him to modern counterparts.

As is ever the case with intellectuals, Lucian was frequently embroiled in controversies; several pamphlets commemorate these in vicious terms. Their contemporary bite has naturally staled, but two stand out. The *Peregrinus* lambastes its eponymous villain who, after flirting with Christianity and Cynicism, immolated himself at the Olympic Games—a media event by any standard! Some mild comments on Christian credulity earned Lucian a place on the Catholic index of Forbidden Books. But Christians get a better press in his *Alexander* where, along with the Epicureans and Lucian himself, they oppose a trendy religious charlatan not unlike certain television evangelists.

Lucian was also capable of liking, and turned out some admiring obituaries, notably the *Demonax*, commemorating a witty philosopher and preserving a large collection of his jokes that would-be comedians might find worth pillaging.

Hypocrisy is not uniquely English. Having pilloried the alleged philistinism of rich Romans, Lucian was later obliged to backtrack upon accepting appointment to the imperial civil service. His *Apology* shows him wriggling on the horns of a dilemma of his own making. A Muggeridgian situation!

Lucian also tried his hand at verse. Fifty or so epigrams attributed to him in the Greek Anthology are unremarkable. But his *Goddess Gout* is a delicious parody of Greek drama, comparable to Housman's immortal *Fragment of a Greek Tragedy*.

Perhaps most congenial is the *True Story*, at one level a parody of travellers' tall tales, but also enjoyable as early science fiction with monsters and adventures worthy of *Dr. Who* and *Star Wars*. However, Lucian himself prized his satirical dialogues, a genre he revived and perfected. Some of these pass social comments on wealth and poverty that might endear him to the modern left, but which were politically safe in his own relatively enlightened age—Lucian was no martyr. His main targets are the absurdities of mythology, also the illogical and often hypocritical representatives of the philosophical schools. Typical pieces include *Descent into Hell, Dialogues of the Dead, Philosophies for Sale*—all much imitated in later times.

Many scholars dismiss Lucian as a flogger of dead horses, a criticism not totally unjust in that few educated people then took myth as literal truth. Yet the objects of his ridicule *were* still the official gods of Rome. Compare contemporary Christianity: the churches are half-empty, and intellectuals scoff at fundamentalist beliefs, but the masses, although not conventionally religious, tend to profess belief in a god and resent "clever" attacks on orthodox piety. Viewed thus, Lucian's squibs have genuine point.

Lucian was no deep thinker, and had no obvious influence on his own times. His fame was in the future. He was a professional entertainer in a crowded and competitive field, and it is probably fair to suppose that *his* works survived because they were superior in elegance and wit to those that did not.

—Barry Baldwin

LUCRETIUS (Titus Lucretius Carus). Born c. 99-94 B.C. His work is dedicated to C. Memmius Gemellus, the friend of Catullus and Cinna; otherwise nothing is known of his life. *Died c. 55 B.C.*

Publications

Verse

De Rerum Natura, edited by K. Müller. 1975; also edited by Cyril Bailey (includes translation), 1947, revised edition, 1977, Joseph Martin, 1953, William Ellery Leonard and Stanley Barney Smith, 1961, Alfred Ernout, 2 vols., 1964-66, and W.H.D. Rouse, revised by M.F. Smith, 1975; as *On the Nature of Things*, translated by R.C. Trevelyan, 1937, J.H. Maitland, 1965, Rolfe Humphries (as *The Way Things Are*), 1968, C.H. Sisson (as *The Poem on Nature*), 1976, and Frank Copley, 1977; also translated in prose by Ronald Latham, 1951, R. Geer, 1965, and M.F. Smith, 1969.

*

Bibliography: *A Bibliography of Lucretius* by Cosmo A. Gordon, 1962.

Critical Studies: *Lucretius* by E.E. Sykes, 1936; *Lucretius's Imagery* by G.J. Sullwood, 1958; *Philosophy of Poetry: The Genius of Lucretius* by Henri Bergson, 1959; *Lucretius* edited by Donald R. Dudley, 1965; *The Imagery and Poetry of Lucretius* by David A. West, 1969; *The Lyre of Science: Form and Meaning in Lucretius's De Rerum Natura* by Richard Minadeo, 1969; *Epicurean Political Philosophy: The De Rerum Natura of Lucretius* by James Hunt

Nichols, 1976; *Lucretius* by E.J. Kenney, 1977; *Mode and Value in the De Rerum Natura: A Study in Lucretius's Metrical Language* by John Douglas Minyard, 1978; *Lucretius and Epicurus* by Diskin Clay, 1983.

*   *   *

The *De Rerum Natura* (*On the Nature of Things*) is Lucretius's only work, and ranks with Dante's *Divine Comedy* as one of the two most important Western philosophical poems. In form and conception it is the most extraordinary and original poem in either of the Classical literatures. Lucretius's ambition was to refound poetry on principles acceptable to the post-mythological age and independent of the ideals of the Classical community. To this end, he incorporated the Epicurean system into the domain of Roman poetry, even though Epicurus had forbidden poetic expression in philosophical discourse, and both united and re-evaluated all the major traditions of the literary heritage in the frame of one poem. The audacity of his enterprise, which is closely related to but not to be confused with contemporary interest in Empedocles and scientific poetry, has yet to be appreciated in the accounts of Greek and Roman literature.

Epicurus developed his ideas at the end of the 4th century B.C. in response to the crisis of independent civic life and its values in the Hellenic world. The height of what is good in life, he said, was pleasure, by which he meant sustained peace of mind, free from every disruption, including fear of the gods and of punishment in the Underworld. Participation in the conflicts of civic life (politics) brings disturbance of mind and is thus the enemy of peaceful pleasure. The most peacefully pleasurable human relationship is genuine but moderate friendship. To explain the way the world really works and so make peace of mind possible, Epicurus created his physics, in which every event is the result of the mechanical interaction of atoms within void, the only two fundamental categories of reality. All things are mortal, including the soul, so there is no existence after death. The gods exist but have no contact with human beings. There is no divine plan at work in the world. We can know this by reasoning from sense perceptions. All sense perceptions are true, but, because analysis of them can be mistaken, Epicurus set out the rule for their correct interpretation in his "Canonic." Epicureanism replaced the civic account of reality, pattern of life, and standard of value. This put it in conflict also with the other major philosophical schools, as the only radical rejection of the entire communal tradition.

In the first century B.C., Rome recapitulated the crisis in civic life to which Epicurus had reacted. As previously in Greek history, Epicureanism was one of the possible responses, and, indeed, the late Republic was the only period of real prominence for Epicureanism in Rome's intellectual life. Lucretius gave form to this prominence in the *De Rerum Natura*.

The Proem (verses 1-148) to the first book sets out the intellectual and cultural position of the whole poem. Religion and piety, instead of being mutually validating and interdependent categories, as they were in Roman tradition, are placed in conflict in the narrative of Agamemnon's sacrifice of his daughter Iphianassa. Rearranging his audience's perception of the structure of reality in this fashion, and declaring that true knowledge comes from the intellectual triumph of a Greek man, not Rome's tradition, Lucretius urges rejection of the false piety of the old religion and adoption of the new and true piety of Epicurus.

Later in this proem, Lucretius calls up Homer (as the founder of Greek literature) and the poet Ennius (Homer's successor as the real founder of Roman literature) to praise their poetic talent but ridicule their notions of an Underworld and a life after death. He will also, in verses 714-781 of Book 1, praise the talent of the philosophical poet Empedocles, while rejecting his views. In these remarks, Lucretius suggests the ambition he declares openly at Book 1, verses 921-950 (the last 25 of which are repeated as Book 2, verses 1-25): to follow in the literary line of these three great artists of epic verse, but to correct their false ideas and so create an entirely new kind of poetry, placed on the right path to truth by Epicureanism, every aspect of which he will touch with art. Asserting no originality in philosophy, claiming only to imitate, not to rival, Epicurus (Book 3, verses 3-6), he does declare total originality in poetry, in the insight that Epicureanism needs a poetic dimension, if it is to be accepted, and that literature needs Epicurean content, if it is to be acceptable. The poetry will lead the reader to adopt the philosophy because the philosophy will make poetry tell the truth. This directly contradicts the view of Epicurus, for whom poetry led to error. This contradiction, and his union of the warring traditions of poetry and post-Socratic philosophy, from which poetry had been banned by Plato and Aristotle, as well as Epicurus, defined Lucretius's originality as a poet and audacity as an Epicurean, revealing an astounding self-confidence and cultural scope. It also explains the significance of the fact that his poem reflects every important literary interest and tendency of its own period.

Each of the remaining five books begins, like the first, with a proem which typically involves praise of Epicurus, condemnation of civic virtue, proclamation of the poet's mission and ideals, description of the blessings of true philosophy, and a résumé of the contents of the book to follow. In Books 1 and 2, the proems are followed by a narration of the basic structure of reality. These books provide the necessary foundation of understanding for developing the ethical thrust of the poem. Indeed, the end of Book 2 draws conclusions closer to the observed reality of actual human life, and the proems to Books 1 and 2 have already forecast the ethical dimension.

Each of the four remaining books both opens with a proem ethical in aim and closes with a satire on some aspect of human life. Satire depends upon a grasp of the standard of criticism to which it is referred, if an audience is to perceive it as satire and understand its point. The audience need not agree with the standard, but it must know what it is. Lucretius controlled the thrust of his satire by anchoring its origin in an Epicurean narrative. Otherwise, his specifically Epicurean criticisms would have been unintelligible, and the more general satire, drawn from the commonplaces of Hellenistic thought, would have lacked specifically Epicurean point.

Book 3 describes the nature and mortality of the soul, which establishes the foundation for the diatribe against fear of death and punishment in the Underworld and against the follies of civic life, which are caused by ignorance of the nature of the soul. The diatribe against the passion and literature of love and the concluding positive advice on sex and procreation in Book 4 flow naturally from the description of sensation and human psychology which precedes them. The account of the origin and growth of the universe sets the stage in Book 5 for the narration of the origin of human life and the history of human culture. In this historical satire, Lucretius narrates the stages by which the follies of contemporary life, described here and in the diatribes at the ends of Books 3 and 4, arose through deviations from the life according to nature. In Book 6, the picture of the real status of those natural phenomena that impinge most directly and obviously on human life gives the context for the satire on Athens during the Great Plague. This civic satire follows naturally also on the general historical narrative of Book 5, narrowing it down to focus on one great event in the history of the greatest of the old-style cities. Here, at the poem's end, the Epicurean picture of reality and the satires on civic virtue coalesce in the decription of the helplessness of the old-time understanding of the world at the point of its severest testing. The old religion and the civic life it held together and justified are in final intellectual and moral ruin.

In subject, then, the *De Rerum Natura* is Epicurean (philosophy), in literary kind Empedoclean (philosophical epic), in tone Hesiodic (didactic), and in method and mode Homeric (formulaic narrative). It is highly idiosyncratic, allusive, and difficult in style, the product of the noble education and aimed at the noble audience. It is, nevertheless, unfinished in detail throughout and at its end. However satisfying the close of the poem is thematically and structurally, stylistically it has not been given closure. Indeed, the poem does not end, it simply stops. The belief that Lucretius died before completing his work is clearly true. It is, however, just as clear that the poem exhibits firm principles of coherence for unifying its various elements and that stylistically the chief of these principles are Homeric.

Lucretius recreates the Homeric effect and cohesion by the deployment of a vast system of personally created formulas, which extend the rhythm of the narrative line to the verbal level, giving clear identity to the line and a regular rhythm to the narration by causing it to unfold again and again according to the same pattern of formulas. The repeated assertions at the same places in the structure of the versed language that we are seeing the unrolling of the structure of right reason are reassuring and persuasive, whether or not they are logically convincing. The reader begins to feel, before he begins to believe, that this is the way things really are. The waves of assertion become gradually tides of plausibility, then, of truth. The appeal Lucretius makes is to feeling more than to reason, to the feelings in which his ideas were born and which he associates with his relation of these ideas to one another. This conjunction of feeling and idea produces the final fusion of Epicureanism and the poetic tradition that constitutes Lucretius's attempt to save poetry for philosophy and philosophy for poetry, and it is here we find his positive and original contribution to the European literary mind.

—John Douglas Minyard

LU HSUN. Pseudonym for Chou Shu-jen. Born in Shao-hsing, Chekiang province, China, in 1881. Educated at Kiangnan Naval Academy, Nanking, 1898-99; School of Railways and Mines, Nanking, 1899-1902; studied Japanese language in Japan, 1902-04, and medicine at Sendai Provincial Medical School, Japan, 1904-06; continued private studies in Japan, 1906-09. Teacher in Shao-hsing, 1910-11; served in the Ministry of Education, Peking, 1912-26, and taught Chinese literature at National Peking University, 1920-26; taught at Amoy University, 1926, and University of Canton, 1927; then lived in international settlement of Shanghai: Editor, *Pen-liu* [The Torrent], 1928, and *I-wen* [Translation], 1934; also a translator of Japanese and western works, and a draftsman/designer. *Died 19 October 1936.*

PUBLICATIONS

Collections

    Lu Hsün hsien-shang ch'uan-chi [Complete Works]. 20 vols., 1938; supplements edited by T'ang T'ao, 2 vols., 1942-52.
    Selected Works. 4 vols., 1956-60.

Fiction

    Na Han [Call to Arms]. 1923.
    P'ang-huang [Wandering]. 1926.
    Ku-shih hsin-pien. 1935; as *Old Tales Retold*, 1961.
    Ah Q and Others: Selected Stories. 1941.
    Selected Stories. 1954.
    Wild Grass (prose poems). 1974.

Other

    Chung-kuo hsiao-shuo shih-lueh. 1924; as *A Brief History of Chinese Fiction*, 1959.

LU HSUN

Silent China: Selected Writings, edited by Gladys Yang.   1973.
Dawn Blossoms Plucked at Dusk.   1976.

*

Critical Studies: Lu Hsün and the New Culture Movement of Modern China by Huang
Sung-k'ang, 1957; Gate of Darkness by T.A. Hsia, 1974; The Social Thought of Lu Hsün by
Pearl Hsia Chen, 1976; Lu Hsün's Vision of Reality by William A. Lyell, 1976; The Style of Lu
Hsun by Raymond S.W. Hsu, 1980.

*   *   *

Lu Hsun, whose real name was Chou Shu-jen, has been regarded as one of the greatest
modern Chinese writers. The first to compose Western-style fiction, he was also in the vanguard
of the colloquial language movement starting in 1918. A communist sympathizer from about
1929, he died in 1936 before the revolution, and has since been praised as a cultural hero in the
Peoples' Republic of China.
   He decided upon a writing career after formative experiences during his studies in Japan
from 1902 to 1909. From the start his goal was polemical in nature, to take China to task for its
excessive traditionalism and its refusal to adjust to the modern world. But he produced only
mediocre essays and one story in the classical language until 1918, when he wrote the first
Western-style story in China, "The Diary of a Madman." After a piece by Gogol, the story is
about a man who concludes that all around him intend to kill and eat him, and that such
cannibalism is an inevitable result of hypocritical moral teachings of ancient Chinese history.
   "The Diary of a Madman" and other stories were published in a collection called Call to
Arms (Na Han) in 1923. Of these the most famous is "The True Story of Ah Q," which has
received international acclaim. The character of Ah Q is the composite of all weak and lowly
qualities of the Chinese national character, especially at the time in history when China was
pathetically subservient to nations of greater physical and moral strength. He is the epitome of
the individual who lacks self-knowledge, a condition which leads to absurd acts of self-abuse
and accomodation to the external world. Although Ah Q is a composite and symbolic
character, each detail of his behavior, however grotesque or absurd, might as well be taken as a
representation of what Lu Hsun saw in actual life—for example, Ah Q's attempt to outdo
someone else by searching his own body for lice and cracking them loudly between his teeth.
   Wandering (P'ang-huang) is Lu Hsun's second story collection, published in 1926. In general
it is bleaker in tone than Call to Arms and is more mature and incisive, as Lu Hsun himself
asserted. As in all his works, the themes are topical and deal with various traditional evils.
However, the stories in Wandering are rarely lost on moral or polemical points and show how
Lu Hsun has mastered a technique of stark and essential portrayal. "Regret for the Past," for
example, is a concise and ironic story of a "modern" love affair. It begins with a period of idyllic
attachment but then evolves to a state in which that beginning becomes history, only to be
reinvoked in the form of a sort of sustaining ritual. It ends when neither can any longer play
their original roles.
   Lu Hsun's stories have rightly been compared to those of James Joyce's Dubliners, and also
resemble the 19th-century fiction of a Gogol or a Dostoevsky. His characters are mostly petty
but nevertheless real and sympathetic individuals who are caught in a general condition of
apathy, brutality, superstition, and hypocrisy.
   In addition to writing stories, Lu Hsun also composed a volume of prose poetry, Wild Grass,
and a volume of childhood memories, Dawn Blossoms Plucked at Dusk. After 1926 he mainly
wrote polemical essays, his only stories being those of Old Tales Retold (1935), in which he
satirically revised the accounts of various ancient heroes. In his essays, besides repeatedly
attacking wrong-headed contemporaries, he also seeks to expose what he sees as an accumulated and collective national lethargy. He views the Chinese nation as a "dish of loose sand" in
which individuals are separate and "oblivious to each other's sufferings" ("Silent China," 1927).
Moreover, hierarchy is so ingrained that, as he literally demonstrates in Ah Q, "a hand cannot

help but look down upon a foot" (his preface to the Russian translation of "The True Story of Ah Q," 1925). Lu Hsun must be counted among the sharpest and most highly conscious critics and defenders of China that modern times have witnessed.

—Keith McMahon

LUTHER, Martin. Born in Eisleben, Thuringia, 10 November 1483. Educated at the University of Erfurt, B.A. 1502, M.A. 1505; entered Augustinian monastery, Erfurt, 1505; installed as professor of moral philosophy, University of Wittenberg, 1508: Doctor of Theology 1512. Married Katherine von Bora in 1525; three sons and three daughters. Visited Rome, 1511; published 95 Theses against the sale of indulgences, 1517, and thereafter drawn into Reformation controversies: excommunicated, 1520, outlawed, 1521, after appearing at Imperial Diet of Worms; spent most of the remainder of his life in Wittenberg, teaching, preaching, writing, and overseeing the emergence of reformed, Lutheran churches. *Died 18 February 1546.*

PUBLICATIONS

Werke (Weimar Edition), edited by J.C.F. Knaake and others. 110 vols., 1883— .
Works (American Edition), edited by Jaroslav Pelikan and Helmut T. Lehmann. 55 vols., 1955— .
Luther: Selections from His Writings, edited by J. Dillenberger. 1961.

*

Bibliography: by Mark U. Edwards, in *Reformation Europe: A Guide to Research* edited by Steven Ozment, 1982.

Critical Studies: *Here I Stand: A Life of Luther* by Roland Bainton, 1950; *Luther: An Introduction to His Thought* by Gerhard Ebeling, 1970; *The German Nation and Luther* by A.G. Dickens, 1974; "Luther and Literacy," in *Publications of the Modern Language Association of America 91*, 1976, and *Luther: An Experiment in Biography*, 1980, both by H.G. Haile.

*   *   *

Martin Luther used to be credited with creating almost single-handed a national unified German language; nowadays it is acknowledged that he made few innovations of syntax or phonology, but did, however, succeed in reinforcing trends in the language decisively. His home territory—Saxony and Thuringia—was the dialect area of East Central German, which embraced features of diverse dialects from the old German "heartlands" in northwest and southwest; moreover it straddled the linguistic boundary between Lower and Upper (north and south) German dialects. Luther employed the synthetic scribal language of the Saxon chancellory, an official language which was by assimilation comprehensible in most of the German territories. He began his translation of the Bible in 1522 in order to promote his theological principle of the priesthood of all believers by making the Scriptures accessible in the vernacular to all estates of men, and revised the work constantly up to his death. In his Bible Luther imbued the stilted official language with the colour, idiom, flexibility—in short: life—of spoken German. His aim was to translate faithfully the matter of Scripture, but in keeping with the inherent principles of the German language: to write what he "heard," from "the mother in the house, the child in the street, the man in the market place." In particular, his striking innovations of vocabulary gave his German Bible a unifying cultural significance for the nation comparable to that of the King James Bible in England.

Luther always regarded his writing and teaching as forms of preaching, in continuation of the saving work of God, the supreme poet. Trained in scholastic and humanistic studies alike, he used of them merely the skills which aided his "preaching." Equally fluent in Latin and German, he employed the vernacular increasingly after 1515 to impart his Reformation precepts to the people, setting clarity and simplicity as goals. He was no systematic theologian: his writings have the character of dialogue or polemic (often virulent) about them; most of his main ideas were formulated in response to an adversary. His thinking is strongly antithetical, he worked in terms of polar opposites: Letter and Spirit, Faith and Works, Freedom and Bondage, God and Man. His output was prolific: for thirty years after 1516 he published almost one title per fortnight. Especially in the period 1520-25 he gave articulated theoretical foundation to traditional national grievances; his tract *An den Christlichen Adel deutscher Nation* (To the Christian Rulers of Germany) (1520) ran to 13 editions within five months. Of his Bible translation over half a million whole or part-Bibles were sold (for a population of 15 million). His oeuvre includes devotional works, prayers and *ars moriendi* books of comfort for the dying, tracts on catechism and sacraments, about 2000 sermons, hundreds of letters, programmatic tracts on matters of ecclesiastical and social controversy, and exegesis. The outer form of his writings is usually simple, the language clear, often crude. Frequently, however, as in *Von der Freyheyt eyniss Christen menschen* (The Freedom of a Christian) (1520), plain and direct language couches a profoundly logical dialectical argument in which the precepts of classical rhetoric are deployed. Literature, in the sense of the written word being read and taken seriously by a significant proportion of the population, was virtually brought into existence by Luther. Almost single-handed during the Reformation he created public opinion as an effective power in the land.

Luther's hymns are possibly the most powerful manifestation of his theology, and it is a major achievement of his Reformation that the vernacular hymn has so central a role in Church worship; Luther's love of music—he composed several tunes himself—contrasts with the stance of other reformers (Zwingli, Calvin). He wrote hymns as part of his vernacular liturgy, prompted by his arch-rival, the radical Thomas Müntzer; of the 36, some 30 survive in current hymnals. For Luther hymns lent unity, and—memorable for being set to music—implanted theological principles in the minds of the congregation. Luther drew heavily on traditions; most hymns are adaptations, of biblical or sacramental material: "Christ unser Herr zum Jordan kam" (Christ our Lord to Jordan came), "Aus tieffer Not. De Profundis" (Out of the Depths, o Lord). Others derive from Latin hymns: "Mitten wyr ym leben sind" (In the midst of life we are in death) from the antiphonal "Media vita in morte sumus," while a few spring from German folksongs: "Vom himel hoch da kom ich her" (From Heaven above) adapts an old traveller's song as children's Nativity story. The most famous, "Ein feste burg" (A safe stronghold), portrays in pugnacious monosyllables and stark antitheses the cosmic battle between man and devil in which impotent man is saved by alliance with Christ alone in faith and trust: truths central to Luther's Reformation breakthrough.

—Lewis Jillings

MACHADO de Assis, Joaquim Maria. Born in Rio de Janeiro, 21 June 1839. Married Carolina de Novaes in 1869 (died, 1904). Journalist from age 15: proofreader, typesetter, writer and editor; Editor and columnist, *Diário do Rio de Janeiro*, and *A Semana Ilustrada*, 1860-75. Clerk, then director of accounting division, Ministry of Agriculture, Commerce, and Public Works, 1874-1908. Member, and Censor, 1862-64, Conservatório Dramático Brasileiro; Founding President, Academia Brasileira de Letras, 1897-1908. Order of the Rose, 1888. *Died 29 September 1908.*

PUBLICATIONS

Collections

    Obras completas. 31 vols., 1937-42.
    Obra completa, edited by Afrânio Coutinho. 3 vols., 1959-62.

Fiction

    Contos fluminenses. 1872.
    Resurreição. 1872.
    Histórias da Meia-Noite. 1873.
    A mão e a luva. 1874; as *The Hand and the Glove*, 1970.
    Helena. 1876.
    Yayá Garcia. 1878; translated as *Yayá Garcia*, 1976.
    Memórias póstumas de Bráz Cubas. 1881; as *The Posthumous Memoirs of Braz Cubas*, 1951; as *Epitaph for a Small Winner*, 1952.
    Papéis avulsos. 1882.
    Histórias sem data. 1884.
    Quincas Borba. 1891; as *Philosopher or Dog?*, 1954; as *The Heritage of Quincas Borba*, 1954.
    Várias histórias. 1896.
    Páginas Recolhidas. 1899.
    Dom Casmurro. 1899; translated as *Dom Casmurro*, 1953.
    Esaú e Jacó. 1904; as *Esau and Jacob*, 1965.
    Relíquias de Casa Velha. 1906.
    Memorial de Ayres. 1908; as *Counselor Ayres' Memorial*, 1982.
    The Psychiatrist and Other Stories. 1963.
    Casa Velha. 1968.
    The Devil's Church and Other Stories. 1977.

Plays

    Pipelet, from the novel *Les Mystères de Paris* by Eugène Sue (produced 1859).
    As bodas de Joaninha, with Luíz Olona, music by Martin Allu (produced 1861).
    Desencantos: Phantasia dramatica. 1861.
    O caminho da porta (produced 1862). In *Teatro*, 1863.
    O protocolo (produced 1862). In *Teatro*, 1863.
    Gabriella (produced 1862).
    Quase ministro (produced 1863). 1864(?).
    Montjoye, from a play by Octave Feuillet (produced 1864).

Suplício de uma mulher, from a play by Émile de Girardin and Dumas fils (produced 1865). In *Teatro*, 1937.
Os deuses de casaca (produced 1865). 1866.
O barbeiro de Sevilha, from the play by Beaumarchais (produced 1866).
O anjo de Meia-Noite, from a play by Théodore Barrière and Edouard Plouvier (produced 1866).
A família Benoiton, from a play by Victorien Sardou (produced 1867).
Como elas são tôdas, from a play by Musset (produced 1873).
Tu só, tu, puro amor (produced 1880). 1881.
Não consultes médico (produced 1896). In *Teatro*, 1910.

Verse

Chrysálidas. 1864.
Phalenas. 1870.
Americanas. 1875.
Poesias completas. 1901.

Other

Correspondência, edited by Fernando Nery. 1932.
Adelaide ristori. 1955.

Translator, *Os trabalhadores do mar*, by Victor Hugo. 1866.

*

Bibliography: *Bibliografía de Machado de Assis* by J. Galante de Sousa, 1955.

Critical Studies: *The Brazilian Othello of Machado de Assis: A Study of Dom Casmurro*, 1960, and *Machado de Assis: The Brazilian Master and His Novels*, 1970, both by Helen Caldwell; *The Craft of an Absolute Winner: Characterization and Narratology in the Novels of Machado de Assis* by Maris Luisa Nunes, 1983; *The Deceptive Realism of Machado de Assis* by John Gledson, 1984.

*   *   *

Had Machado de Assis not written in the Portuguese language—so often described as "the cemetery of literature"—there is no doubt that he would today be universally regarded as one of the greatest 19th-century writers of prose fiction. Brazil did not possess a strong novelistic tradition—the genre developed there during Machado's own lifetime—and he therefore felt free to experiment with forms and techniques which seem far closer to Kafka or Borges than to Dickens or Flaubert. While the surface texture of Machado's novels and stories is carefully realistic, providing a Balzacian panorama of Brazilian society, the universe of his fiction is an artificial, created reality of improbabilities, of egregiously unreliable narrators who speculate at length about the process of writing, of texts layered within texts.

Machado's technically traditional early novels show his intense interest in the social and psychological effects of upward mobility. This preoccupation is understandable, for Machado's own biography—the poor and dependent mulatto who attained great prestige among a white elite which came to perceive him as equally white—represents the most extreme case of upward social mobility within the hierarchical rigidity of imperial Brazil.

With *The Posthumous Memoirs of Braz Cubas*, Machado freed himself from all constraints of tradition, although his obsessive interest in social change continued. Braz Cubas's autobiographical narrative—not merely published after his death, but composed posthumously as well—is at once hilariously funny and pathetically moving. The evasive and unreliable omniscient third-person narrator of *Quincas Borba* presents his text as the exemplification of a comprehensive theory of human behavior—in fact a brilliant parody of Positivism and Social Darwinism—which both explains and justifies the vast network of mutual aggression and humiliation Machado saw in society; the story the narrator relates, as Machado structures it, forces us instead to reject that theory and to confront our common inhumanity.

The third of Machado's major novels, *Dom Casmurro*, is the most technically complex of all. The narrator recounts his marriage to Capitu and her infidelity, marshalling all the incriminating evidence. Half hidden within Dom Casmurro's narrative, however, is another story entirely, a mirror image of the explicit text—Capitu's story of innocence and fidelity betrayed by her husband's insane jealousy; we, as readers, must write this story for ourselves, discovering and ordering the hints and details Dom Casmurro lets slip. In the final analysis, both these absolutely irreconcilable narratives are equally valid; we cannot logically choose between them. And this is, perhaps, Machado's ultimate assault upon the traditional novel and its most basic postulate: that human experience can be arranged into meaningful and comprehensible patterns.

Machado's fiction implies two quite different possible theories: either human lives and emotions are simply too complex and illogical to be understood; or the reality of human existence is so blinding in its utter amorality and meaninglessness that we cannot bear to look upon it without the tinted lenses of our pitiable and improbable illusions—one of which is the form we call the novel.

—David T. Haberly

MACHIAVELLI, Niccolò.   Born in Florence, 3 May 1469. Married Marietta Corsini in 1501; five children. Probably involved in overthrowing the Savonarolist government, 1498; appointed to head the new government's Second Chancery, 1498, and secretary of an agency concerned with warfare and diplomacy, 1498-1512: some 6000 surviving documents record his unceasing activity, including trips to visit Caterina Sforza, 1499, Cesare Borgia, 1502, Rome, 1503 and 1506, France, 1504 and 1510, and Germany, 1507-08; helped to set up a standing army (which reconquered Pisa, 1509); the Florentine Republic ended with the return to power of the Medici family (under Piero dei Medici), 1512: Machiavelli was jailed and exiled to Sant'Andrea in Percussina where he spent his remaining years in retirement, though he was given a few diplomatic or writing jobs. *Died 21 June 1527.*

PUBLICATIONS

Collections

The Chief Works and Others, translated by Allan Gilbert.   3 vols., 1965.
Opere, edited by Sergio Bertelli.   1968— .
Tutti le opere, edited by Mario Martelli.   1971.
The Portable Machiavelli, edited by Peter E. Bondanella and Mark Musa.   1979.

Fiction

Novella di Belfagor arcidiavolo.   1545; as *Belfagor*, in *The Literary Works*, 1961.

Plays

La mandragola (produced 1522).   1519(?); edited by Roberto Guicciardini, 1977; translated as *La Mandragola*, 1940; as *The Mandrake*, in *Classic Theatre 1*, edited by Eric Bentley, 1958.

La Clizia (produced 1525), edited by Guido Davico Bonino.   1977; translated as *Clizia*, in *The Literary Works*, 1961.

Teatro (includes *Andria* from the play by Terence, *Mandragola, Clizia*).   1979.

Verse

Decennale Primo.   1504(?).
Lust and Liberty, translated by Joseph Tusiani.   1963.

Other

Discorso dell'ordinare lo stato di Firenze alle armi.   1507(?).
Dell'Arte della guerra.   1521; as *The Art of War*, 1562.
Discorsi sulla prima deca di Tito Livio.   1531; as *The Discourses on Livy*, 1636, translation edited by Bernard Crick, 1971.
Discorsi.   1531; as *Discourses*, 2 vols., 1950.
Il principe.   1532; as *The Prince*, 1560.
Istorie fiorentine.   1532; as *Florentine History*, 1595; as *History of Florence and of the Affairs of Italy*, 1960.
Discorso o dialogo intorno a la nostra lingua, as *A Dialogue on Language*, in *The Literary Works*.   1961.
The Literary Works (includes *Mandragola, Clizia, Belfagor, A Dialogue on Language*), translated by John R. Hale.   1961.
Letters: A Selection, edited by Allan H. Gilbert.   1961.
Legazioni, commissarie, scritti di governo, edited by Fredi Chiappelli.   1971— .
The Prince and Other Political Writings, edited by Bruce Penman.   1981.

*

Critical Studies: *Machiavelli's Prince and Its Forerunners* by Allan H. Gilbert, 1938; *Machiavellism: The Doctrine of Raison d'Etat and Its Place in Modern History* by Friedrich Meinecke, 1957; *Thoughts on Machiavelli* by Leo Strauss, 1958; *Machiavelli and Renaissance Italy* by J.R. Hale, 1961; *The Life of Machiavelli* by Roberto Ridolfi, 1963; *The English Face of Machiavelli: A Changing Interpretation 1500-1700* by Felix Raab, 1964; *Studies on Machiavelli* edited by Myron P. Gilmore, 1965; *Discourses on Machiavelli* by J.H. Whitfield, 1969; *The Political Calculus: Essays on Machiavelli's Philosophy* by Anthony Parel, 1972; *Machiavelli and the Art of Renaissance History* by Peter E. Bondanella, 1974; *The Machiavellian Moment: Florentine Political Thought and the Atlantic Republican Tradition* by J.G.A. Pocock, 1975; *Machiavelli* by Quentin Skinner, 1981.

*   *   *

Machiavelli's talents were so varied that it is difficult to classify him. Public servant, diplomat, poet, playwright, satirist, historian, he is best known as a political theorist. Yet his most celebrated work, *Il Principe* (*The Prince*), does not fit easily into the category of political theory. It belongs rather to the literature of political practice.

Machiavelli's ideas on government are best represented in his *Discorsi sulla prima deca di Tito Livio* (*Discourses on the First Ten Books of Livy*). In 1513, out of favour with the Medici, he turned his mind to the question of stability in politics. Commenting on Livy's history of Rome, he accepts the cyclical theory of successive changes but suggests that they can be arrested by a modern form of mixed government, similar to a constitutional monarchy, the nearest possible to his ideal of a republic. A second-best solution was the absolute rule of a prince. Becoming interested in the problems of establishing and securing a principality, he broke off work on the *Discorsi* and wrote *The Prince*.

The Prince is based, the author claims, on long experience of modern affairs and a continual study of the past. In this it differs from earlier works on government, which describe ideal republics and principalities. Machiavelli intends to show how things really are. A ruler who tries to follow moral precepts instead of pragmatic considerations is bound to fail, for men are ungrateful, untrustworthy, cowardly, and greedy for gain. He admires Cesare Borgia for his ruthlessness and his ability to conquer by force or fraud. When dealing with opponents, half-measures are dangerous, but cruelty should not be used unnecessarily. If a prince cannot avoid being feared he can at least avoid being hated, above all by respecting the property of his subjects, "for men sooner forget the death of a father than the loss of their property."

Statements like these made *The Prince* notorious. Machiavelli was held to be the embodiment of guile and lack of scruple. Yet the literature of political practice (memoirs, reports of ambassadors, letters of statesmen) abounds in similar recommendations and comments. The impact made by *The Prince* was exceptional. This was due not so much to the novelty of Machiavelli's method as to his superb skill as a writer of lucid, trenchant, remorselessly logical prose.

The same skill is found in his *Istorie fiorentine* (*History of Florence*). He is at his best when relating events involving suspense, such as the Pazzi conspiracy against the Medici in 1478. His comedy, *La Mandragola* (*The Mandrake*) is a perfect combination of classical form and contemporary satire. The play is a sharp and shrewd comment on hypocrisy and corruption, with superb moments of farce. Machiavelli also wrote a short story, *Novella di Belfagor arcidiavolo* (Story of the Archdevil Belfagor), in which an archdevil is commanded to take human form on earth, choose a wife, and report back after ten years. Pretending to be a wealthy man, he chooses the most beautiful among the many women eager to marry him. He is ruined by her extravagance and takes refuge with a peasant, whom he enriches by tricks of exorcism. The peasant proves ungrateful and tricks him into believing that his wife has come to claim him. Terrified, Belfagor scuttles back to Hell. The tale, told in lively satirical style, and aimed at superstition as well as marriage, has been favourably compared to *The Decameron*.

—Barbara Reynolds

MAETERLINCK, Maurice (Mauritius Polydorus Maria Bernardus Maeterlinck). Born in Ghent, Belgium, 29 August 1862. Educated at a convent school in Ghent, age 6-7; Institut Central, Ghent, age 7-11; Jesuit Collège de Sainte-Barbe, 1874-81; studied law at University of Ghent, 1881-85, Dr. of Law, 1885, and registered as barrister, 1885. Lived with Georgette Leblanc, 1896-1918; married Renée Dahon in 1919. Practiced law in Ghent, 1886-89; writer:

lived in Paris, 1896-1906, Grasse, 1906-11, Nice, 1911-39, Portugal, 1939-40, United States, 1940-47, and Nice, after 1947. Recipient: Nobel Prize for Literature, 1911; Medal of the French Language, 1948. Honorary degrees: Glasgow University, 1919; University of Brussels, 1920; Rollins Park College, Florida, 1941. Member, Belgian Royal Academy, 1920. Grand Officier, 1912, and Grand Croix, 1920, Order of Leopold; Order of St. James of the Sword, Portugal, 1939. Created Count of Belgium, 1932. *Died 6 May 1949.*

PUBLICATIONS

Plays

La Princesse Maleine. 1889; as *The Princess Maleine,* 1890.
Les Aveugles, L'Intruse (produced 1891). 1890; as *The Blind, The Intruder,* 1891.
Les Sept Princesses. 1890; as *The Seven Princesses,* in *Plays,* 1895.
Pelléas et Mélisande (produced 1893). 1892; translated as *Pelleas and Melisande,* 1894.
Trois petits drames pour marionnettes (includes *Alladine et Palomides, Intérieur, La Mort de Tintagiles*). 1894; as *Alladine and Palomides, Interior, and The Death of Tintagiles,* 1895.
Intérieur (produced 1895). In *Trois petits drames,* 1894.
Alladine et Palomides (produced 1896). In *Trois petits drames,* 1894.
La Mort de Tintagiles (produced 1905). In *Trois petits drames,* 1894.
Annabella:'Tis Pity She's a Whore, from the play by John Ford (produced 1894). 1895.
Aglavaine et Sélysette (produced 1896). 1896; as *Aglavaine and Selysette,* 1897.
Ariane et Barbe-Bleue, music by Paul Dukas (produced 1907). In *Théâtre 2,* 1901; as *Ariane and Barbe-Bleue,* 1901.
Soeur Béatrice, in *Théâtre 2.* 1901; as *Sister Beatrice,* 1901.
Théâtre. 3 vols., 1901-02.
Monna Vanna (produced 1902). 1901; translated as *Monna Vanna,* 1903.
Joyzelle (produced 1903). 1903; translated as *Joyzelle,* 1906.
Le Miracle de Saint-Antoine (produced 1903). 1919; as *The Miracle of Saint Anthony,* 1918.
L'Oiseau bleu (produced 1908). 1909; as *The Blue Bird,* 1909.
Macbeth, from the play by Shakespeare (produced 1909). 1910.
Marie-Magdeleine (produced 1910). 1913; as *Mary Magdalene,* 1910.
Le Malheur passe (produced 1916?). 1925; as *The Cloud That Lifted,* 1923.
Le Bourgmestre de Stilmonde, suivi de Le Sel de la Vie. 1919; as *The Burgomaster of Stilmonde,* 1918.
Les Fiançailles (produced 1918). 1918; as *The Betrothal; or, The Blue Bird Chooses,* 1919.
Berniquel (produced 1923). 1929.
La Puissance des morts. 1926; as *The Power of the Dead,* 1923.
Marie-Victoire. 1927.
Juda de Kérioth. 1929.
La Princesse Isabelle (produced 1935). 1935.
L'Abbé Sétubal (produced 1941). In *Théâtre inédit,* 1959.
Jeanne d'Arc. 1948.
Théâtre inédit (includes *L'Abbé Sétubal, Les Trois Justiciers, Le Jugement dernier*). 1959.

Fiction

Deux contes: Le Massacre des innocents, Onirologie. 1918.

Verse

Serres chaudes: Poèmes. 1889; as *Poems,* 1915.
Album de douze chansons. 1896; as *XII Songs,* 1912.
Serres chaudes, suivi de quinze chansons. 1900.
Serres chaudes, quinze chansons, vers de fin. 1947.

Other

Le Trésor des humbles. 1896; as *The Treasure of the Humble,* 1897; excerpt, as *The Inner Beauty,* 1910.
La Sagesse et la destinée. 1898; as *Wisdom and Destiny,* 1898.
La Vie des abeilles. 1901; as *The Life of the Bee,* 1901; excerpt as *The Swarm,* 1906.
Le Temple enseveli. 1902; as *The Buried Temple,* 1902.
Le Double Jardin. 1904; as *The Double Garden,* 1904; as *Old-Fashioned Flowers and Other Out-of-Door Studies,* 1905; excerpt as *Our Friend the Dog,* 1904; as *My Dog,* 1906.
L'Intelligence des fleurs. 1907; as *Life and Flowers,* 1907; as *Intelligence of the Flowers,* 1907; excerpt as *Measure of the Hours,* 1907.
La Mort. 1913; as *Death,* 1911; revised edition, as *Our Eternity,* 1913.
Hours of Gladness. 1912; as *News of Spring and Other Nature Studies,* 1913.
L'Hôte inconnu. 1917; as *The Unknown Guest,* 1914.
Les Débris de la guerre. 1916; as *The Wrack of the Storm,* 1916.
Les Sentiers dans la montagne. 1919; as *Mountain Paths,* 1919.
Le Grand Secret. 1921; as *The Great Secret,* 1922.
En Égypte: Notes de voyage. 1928; as *Ancient Egypt,* 1925.
En Sicile et en Calabre. 1927.
Le Vie des termites. 1927; as *The Life of the White Ant,* 1927.
La Vie de l'espace. 1928; as *The Life of Space,* 1928.
La Grande Féerie: Immensité de l'univers, notre terre, influences sidérales. 1929; as *The Magic of the Stars,* 1930.
La Vie des fourmis. 1930; as *The Life of the Ant,* 1930.
L'Araignée de verre. 1932; excerpt as *Pigeons and Spiders (The Water Spider),* 1934.
La Grande Loi. 1933; as *The Supreme Law,* 1934.
Avant le grand silence. 1934; as *Before the Great Silence,* 1935.
Le Sablier. 1936; as *The Hour-Glass,* 1936.
L'Ombre des ailes. 1936.
Devant Dieu. 1937.
La Grande Porte. 1939.
L'Autre Monde; ou, Le Cadran stellaire. 1942.
Bulles bleues: Souvenirs heureux. 1948.
Le "Cahier bleu," edited by Joanne Wieland-Burston. 1977.

Translator, *L'Ornement des noces spirituelles,* by Jan van Ruysbroeck. 1891; as *Ruysbroeck and the Mystics,* 1894.
Translator, *Les Disciples à Saïs,* by Novalis. 1895.

*

Bibliography: *Bibliographie de Maeterlinck: Litterature, science, philosophie* by Maurice Lecat, 1939; revised edition, in *Le Maeterlinckisme,* vol. 2, 1941.

Critical Studies: *Maeterlinck and America* by Francoise Dony Cartwright, 1935; *The Magic of Maeterlinck* by P. Mahoney, 1951; *Maeterlinck: A Study of His Life and Thought* by W.D.

Halls, 1960; *Maeterlinck* by Bettina Knapp, 1975.

*   *   *

Maurice Maeterlinck's entire literary production can be seen as a life-long quest better to understand the human condition, its essential enigma being death in his view. An extraordinary sensitivity as well as thirst for liberation from a narrow and stifling reality through a greater spiritual dimension already characterize his early poetry. The title of his first collection, *Serres chaudes* (Hothouses), refers to the soul's imprisonment and indicates a revolt against the dominant Realism of the time. The poet soon chose to explore the soul's predicament in a different mode and proceeded to create a suggestive, poetic, dramatic universe where silence and absence are more eloquent than words and physical action, and in which the overwhelming forces of death and of love are presented as tragic obstacles to freedom and creative action. The so-called "second dialogue" to which the spoken one is conducive, along with "the sublime character" (Death), conveyed by reactions of fear among the real characters of the plays and thus forcefully present in its silence and invisibility, are the most innovative and effective devices in Maeterlinck's Symbolist theatre.

The setting for this metaphysical drama is often a strange fairy-tale world of princes and princesses, who are helplessly groping for light, love, and understanding within medieval castles, dark forests, and above murky waters (e.g., *The Princess Maleine, Pelleas and Melisande, The Death of Tintagiles*). Fear is here the pervasive feeling. But the mysterious unknown invades and threatens life and action also in a more modern—but always vague and indefinite—dramatic environment (*The Intruder, Interior*). Such theatrical strategies which create distance, connect Maeterlinck's drama to classical tragedy where moral and psychological forces reign supreme over everyday reality. Yet the reductive quality of his plays aims at revealing the most ordinary experience, in fact the seemingly insignificant aspects of our lives to which most are blind. The author himself refers to this essential dimension as "the quotidian tragic" and discusses it at length in an essay by the same title (in *The Treasure of the Humble*).

In spite of enthusiastic response from literary colleagues in Paris, Maeterlinck's symbolic, elusive, certainly avant-garde plays did not reach the large public. It was not until he adopted a rather naturalistic style with a historical event as dramatic plot that he won world recognition as a playwright. *Monna Vanna*, though a drama of love, can also be seen as a subtle analysis of the creative and destructive powers of language. The writer had suffered a crisis in his search for meaningful knowledge and authentic expression, evidenced by two former plays, *Aglavaine and Selysette* and *Ariane and Barbe-Bleue*, which made him relinquish—although reluctantly—the symbolic mode and accept the full reality of language.

Notwithstanding returns to dramatic symbolism as in *The Bluebird*, which also became a world success, Maeterlinck gradually relied more on prose than on poetic dialogue. His many essays, most of a philosophical nature, in which his speculations on various aspects of the human condition often take their point of departure in close observation of natural life, like that of flowers and insects, found a more positive public response than the bulk of his dramatic work. He was awarded the Nobel Prize in 1911, primarily for this genre. It should be noted, however, that he continued to write plays, and that his analyses in prose demonstrate a certain dramatic quality: they often proceed in question and answer form. Although his "philosophical" reflections constitute efforts to reject nihilism and to discover consolation for a life condemned to ignorance about its meaning and purpose, the undercurrent continues to question a tragic human destiny from which Maeterlinck could never free himself. There is therefore a solid continuity in his work. The changes from poetry, to drama, and to prose, do not constitute reversals in the author's evolution as much as decisions to explore new forms of thinking and writing, necessitated by a continual threat of despair in this heroic, wonderfully perceptive, and productive quest for certainty.

—Linn Bratteteig Konrad

MAHABHARATA.

PUBLICATIONS

Mahabharata (Sanskrit text with commentary), edited by Vishnu S. Sukthankar. 7 vols., 1933-54; translated by P.C. Roy (prose), 13 vols., 1883-90, and M.N. Dutt (prose), 1895-1905; "transcreated" by P. Lal, 1969-79; shortened versions translated by R.C. Dutt (verse), 1929, R.K. Narayan, 1978, and Kamala Subramaniam, 1980.

*

Critical Studies: *The Heroic Age of India* by N.K. Siddhantha, 1929; *The Mahabharata: An Ethnological Study* by G.J. Held, 1935; *On the Meaning of the Mahabharata* by V.S. Sukthankar, 1957; *Gods, Priests, and Warriors: The Bhrgus of the Mahabharata* by Robert P. Goldman, 1977; *Folklore in the Mahabharata* by N.B. Patil, 1983; *The Mahabharata: A Criticism* by C.V. Vaidya, 1983.

*   *   *

With a hundred thousand verses, the *Mahabharata*, the world's longest epic, is about eight times the length of the *Iliad* and the *Odyssey* put together. It had originally 18 books (a 19th was added later). Interwoven with the central story are a number of subsidiary ones, long enough to be epics by themselves. Though the *Mahabharata* is replete with philosophical passages, it is essentially a literary work. It is believed to have been written about the 4th century or perhaps earlier, and its celebrated author was the sage Vyasa. Tradition, however, assigns it a divine origin.

The central story revolves round the enmity between the Kauravas and their half-brothers, the Pandavas, consequent to Yudhishthira of the Pandavas being nominated as the heir apparent of Hastinapura. Escaping a plot hatched by the Kauravas, the Pandava brothers fled to the forest in disguise. Sometime after, Arjuna, the Pandava leader, won the hand of Draupadi, daughter of the king of the Panchalas, and the brothers came out of exile. A settlement was finally made, the Kauravas getting Hastinapura and the Pandavas, Indraprastha. But the Kauravas went on plotting against Yudhishthira, now Indraprastha's ruler, tempting him to a gambling match in which he wagered and lost everything, even his brothers, himself, and his wife. Draupadi was openly insulted, and this widened the gulf between the two clans. Yudhishthira's possessions were restored, but he again speedily gambled them away, forcing the Pandavas into exile again for 12 years. Nevertheless they resolved to regain their lost kingdom. Arjuna and Duryodhana, the Kaurava leader, both sought the assistance of Krishna, king of Dwarka. Duryodhana was given Krishna's entire army, while Arjuna wisely chose the divine Krishna himself. So Krishna became Arjuna's charioteer. In the great battle which followed the Kauravas were destroyed. But Yudhishthira and the other Pandavas were filled with remorse for causing the bloodshed of their kinsmen. Yudhishthira abdicated the throne and, along with his brothers, went away to the Himalayas to dwell in Indra's heaven on mount Meru.

The literature to which the *Mahabharata* belongs is called Akhyana and Itihasa. The work abounds in picturesque descriptions, like that of the sudden downpour while the Pandavas were in the forest in exile: "The rain poured and poured till hills, dales and rivers could not be distinguished, and all one could see was an endless sheet of water." Vyasa often uses colours as symbols, as for example when he likens the orange flames of fire to the glory of a hermit even though he just wears rags, the warrior whose ire mounts, and the fiery rage of a chaste woman approached by a licentious man.

Folk tradition is used to give keenness to language. Bhishma is like the flamingo who kept prattling about morality so that other birds trusted him with their eggs, which he promptly ate up. The inveterate gambler, Yudhishthira, who still preaches righteousness, is likened to a cat who practises austerities to entice mice. Asvatthama runs away from the battlefield and plans revenge. In the night he sees an owl who kills birds when they are asleep. Taking the cue he falls on his enemies while they are sleeping and slays them all. There are picturesque descriptions of lovely women, like those of Draupadi with eyes like the lotus leaves and waist slender as a wasp, and Urvashi, the celestial nymph, "of finely tapering breasts, looking like the slender moon amid fleecy clouds."

The *Mahabharata* represents Hindu culture at its best. Its fascinating episodes have inspired many writers to create masterpieces, for example Kalidasa's renowned play *Shakuntala*. Not without justification it has been said "What is not in the *Mahabharata*, is nowhere."

—K.P. Bahadur

MALLARMÉ, Stéphane. Born in Paris, 18 March 1842. Educated at schools in Passy, 1852-56; Lycée de Sens, 1856-60; schools in England, 1862-63. Married Maria Christina Gerhard in 1863; one daughter and one son. Taught English in Tournon, 1863-66, Besançon, 1866-67, Avignon, 1867-70, Lycée Fontanes, Paris, 1871-84, and Lycée Janson de Sailly, Paris, 1884-85; Professeur, Collège Rollin, Paris, after 1885. Also writer: Editor, *La Dernière Mode*, 1874-75. Member, French Academy, 1883. *Died 9 September 1898.*

PUBLICATIONS

Collections

Oeuvres complètes, edited by Henri Mondor and G. Jean-Aubry. 1945.

Verse

L'Après-midi d'un faune: Eglogue. 1876.
Les Poésies. 1887; augmented edition, 1899, 1913.
Un Coup de dés jamais n'abolira le hasard. 1914; edited by Mitsou Ronat, 1980.
Madrigaux. 1920.
Vers de circonstance. 1920.
Mallarmé in English Verse, translated by Arthur Ellis. 1927.
Poems, translated by Roger Fry. 1951.
Selected Poems, translated by C.F. MacIntyre. 1957.
Poems, translated by Keith Bosley. 1977.

Other

Les Mots anglais. 1877.
Les Dieux antiques. 1880.

Album de vers et de prose. 1887.
Villiers de L'Isle-Adam. 1890.
Pages. 1891.
Vers et prose. 1893.
La Musique et les lettres. 1895.
Divigations. 1897.
Igitur; ou, La Folie d'Elbehnon. 1925.
Contes indiens. 1927.
Thèmes anglais. 1937.
Correspondance, edited by Henri Mondor, J.P. Richard, and Lloyd James Austin. 4 vols., 1959-73.

Editor, *Favourite Tales for Very Young Children,* by James Stephens. 1885.

Translator, *Le Corbeau, The Raven,* by Poe. 1875.
Translator, *L'Étoile des fées,* by Mrs. W.-C. Elphinstone Hope. 1881.
Translator, *Les Poèmes d'Edgar Poe.* 1888.
Translator, *Le "Ten O'Clock,"* by J.M. Whistler. 1888.

*

Critical Studies: *Mallarmé* by Wallace Fowlie, 1953; *Mallarmé and the Symbolist Drama* by Haskell M. Block, 1963; *Towards the Poems of Mallarmé,* 1965, *Mallarmé's "Un Coup de dés,"* 1980, and *Mallarmé Igitur,* 1981, all by Robert Greer Cohn; *Mallarmé* by Guy Michaud, 1966; *Mallarmé* by Frederick C. Saint Aubyn, 1969; *The Prose of Mallarmé* by Judy Kravis, 1976; *The Anatomy of Poesis: The Prose Poems of Mallarmé* by Ursula Franklin, 1976; *The Aesthetics of Mallarmé in Relation to His Public* by Paula Gilbert Lewis, 1976; *The Early Mallarmé,* vol. 1., by Austin Gill, 1979; *Mallarmé and the Art of Being Difficult* by Malcolm Bowie, 1979.

*   *   *

Stéphane Mallarmé is a significant figure in the history of French literature, not only because his poetry is strikingly unusual and fine, but because he was a major influence on the poets of the next generation. Writers such as Paul Valéry in France, Stefan George in Germany, d'Annunzio in Italy, and Oscar Wilde in England, all acknowledge their debt to Mallarmé.

The extent of his influence seems ironic; after all, his aim to render poetry less accessible to a general readership, to "purify the language of the tribe," as the alchemist transforms dross to gold, hardly seems conducive to widespread influence. Mallarmé's poems are far from easy to read. But he was the key figure in a movement which achieved a complete transformation of French poetry. Poets such as Rimbaud and Verlaine had for some time been trying to escape the excesses of Romantic lyricism, and when, in 1883, Verlaine published *Les Poètes maudits* (The Accursed Poets), a collection which included some of Mallarmé's compositions, the public became aware for the first time that a revolution had been fermenting, and that Mallarmé was one of the leading revolutionaries. Their clarion-call was "Art for Art's sake," trumpeted most directly in Huysman's *Against Nature,* whose hero, not surprisingly, bears many of Mallarmé's own characteristics; Huysmans openly extols Mallarmé's work, calling it "...this condensed literature, this concentration of essence, this purification of art...". Mallarmé, modest and reserved though he was, found himself a literary celebrity, and hailed as the leading light of the new aesthetic movement.

His own definition of poetry, as he stated it in 1885, is that "Poetry is the expression, by means of the human language restored to its essential rhythm, of the mysterious sense of certain aspects of existence; poetry thus endows our span on earth with authenticity, and constitutes our sole spiritual task...". An investigation of Mallarmé's writings prior to this statement shows to what exent this was a summary of his own practice. As early as the year 1862 he had declared his allegiance to the new art, when he wrote in an article entitled "Hérésie artistique: l'art pour tous" that "..everything sacred that is to remain sacred is veiled in mystery." It is the poet's task to restore the sense of religious mystery to poetry, to preserve its sanctity. The notion of a task, together with the cultivation of mystery, are at the core of Mallarmé's work.

Although the poet's mission is to purify language, the ideal of absolute purity may conflict with his vocation. The poet, in Mallarmé's words, is like "a ridiculous Hamlet who can't come to terms with his own downfall." How can the poet reconcile an imperative vocation with the inaccessibility of his ideal? The conflict is clearly expressed in an image recurring throughout Mallarmé's work, namely that of *whiteness*. White is both a non-colour and the synthesis of all colours; it represents at once potential (the whiteness of a virgin page to be covered with lines of poetry), and, at the same time, sterility (the clinical whiteness of hospital curtains, the "sterile winter" imprisoning the swan).

Two longer poems, the dramatic pieces "Hérodiade" and *L'Après-midi d'un faune*, again demonstrate the complexity of the conflict. The princess Herodias refuses life and its attractions for the sake of purity. Her nurse, who tries in vain to tempt her back to life, asks the crucial question:

> For whom, devoured
> By anquish, do you reserve the unknown splendour
> And the vain mystery of your being?

The Faun is Herodias's counterpart and complement. Where Herodias is sheathed in icy reserve, the Faun is all fire and desire. He sees two nymphs asleep, united in an embrace, and, witnessing their "extase d'être deux," their ecstasy at being two, he tries to possess them, bearing them away in his arms. But they awake and flee. The Faun is left alone with his memories, pondering them in the silence. Are they real, or are they merely a figment of his imagination? He is punished for attempting to divide what was once whole, for trying to sully the purity which his alter ego, Herodias, wanted to preserve at all costs.

Mallarmé was a little puzzled that Debussy should want to set the *Afternoon of a Faun* to music—was it not already musical enough? The restoration of language "to its essential rhythm"involved the exploitation of the sound, rather than the meaning, of words, so that they would appeal, as music does, to the reader's senses before appealing to his intellect. The reader must be aware of this fact if he is to appreciate Mallarmé's poetry. In order to enhance the music of language, Mallarmé distorted conventional syntax, developed the significance of rhythm and vowel-pitch, and made extensive use of aural evocation. All these techniques present difficulties for the translator, and indeed for the reader of a translation. The sonnet *Une Dentelle s'abolit* ("A Lace curtain stands effaced") ends with the line "Filial on aurait pu naître," which has been translated as "Filial one might be born." It is inevitable that part of the richness of the French should be lost, and unfortunate that the aural evocation of "n'être," a negation of being, which adds a crucial ambiguity to Mallarmé's original French line, cannot be conveyed by a similar technique in English.

However, as Mallarmé stated during the composition of "Herodias," he was creating a "très nouvelle poétique," a very new mode of poetic expression, whose chief aim was to "peindre, non la chose mais l'effet qu'elle produit"—to paint, not the object itself, but the effect it produces. In other words, Mallarmé relies on the sensation aroused in the reader by his words rather than on any intellectual process of analysis. If the English translation is capable of arousing similar sensations, the loss of certain nuances is only of secondary importance.

In the light of Mallarmé's encouragement of intuitive response to his works, it is something of a paradox that they should be considered "obscure." He has been accused of wilfully baffling and disconcerting the reader, of practising "hermeticism" quite deliberately. This is undoubtedly true, up to a point. Yet the motive behind the "art of being difficult" is not merely mischievous pleasure in mystification, but Mallarmé's concern to endow his work with a third dimension. In order to identify with the Mallarmean universe, the reader has to become familiar with the idiom. The attempt to find a single logical pattern of meaning among the polyvalent images is doomed to failure. Mallarmé himself said of a young follower, "he is charming, but why does he always explain my poems? Anyone would think they were obscure!"

—Sally McMullen (Croft)

MALRAUX, (Georges) André. Born in Paris, 3 November 1901. Educated at a school in Bondy; Lycée Condorcet, Paris; École Turgot, Paris, 1915-18; attended lectures at Musée Guimet and École du Louvre, 1919. Served in the French Army during World War II; wounded, imprisoned, escaped, and joined resistance: Compagnon de la Libération, Medal of the Resistance, Croix de Guerre, Distinguished Order. Married Clara Goldschmidt in 1921 (divorced), one daughter; had two sons by Josette Clotis; married Marie-Madeleine Lioux Malraux in 1948, one stepson. Worked for René-Louis Doyon, booksellers, and in art department of Kra, publishers, Paris; archaeological expedition to Indochina, 1923: detained for stealing ancient sculptures, but case set aside; involved in political activities in Indochina: established opposition newspaper, *L'Indochine*, later *L'Indochine Enchainée*, 1925-26; art editor, then literary editor, and director of the Pléiade series, Gallimard publishers, Paris, after 1928. Actively engaged in political acivities: fought in Spain in the civil war: Colonel of the Spanish Republic; Minister of Information in De Gaulle's government, 1945-46; Minister of Culture in De Gaulle's cabinet, 1959-69. President, Charles De Gaulle Institute, 1971. Recipient: Prix Goncourt, 1933; Prix Louis-Delluc, for film, 1945; Asolo film festival prize, 1973; Nehru Peace Prize, 1974. Honorary degree: Oxford University, 1967; Jyvacskylae University, Finland, 1969; Rajshahi University, Bangladesh, 1973. Officer, Legion of Honor. *Died 23 November 1976.*

PUBLICATIONS

Fiction

Lunes en papier. 1921.
La Tentation de l'occident. 1926; as *The Temptation of the West*, 1961.
Les Conquérants. 1928; as *The Conquerors*, 1929.
Royaume farfelu. 1928.
La Voie royale. 1930; as *The Royal Way*, 1935.
La Condition humaine. 1933; as *Man's Fate*, 1934; as *Storm in Shanghai*, 1934; as *Man's Estate*, 1948.
Le Temps du mépris. 1935; as *Days of Wrath*, 1936; as *Days of Contempt*, 1936.
L'Espoir. 1937; as *Man's Hope*, 1938; as *Days of Hope*, 1938.
Les Noyers de l'Altenburg. 1943; as *The Walnut Trees of Altenburg*, 1952.
Et sur la terre... (unpublished chapter of *L'Espoir*). 1977.

Other

Le Démon de l'absolu. 1946.

Esquisse d'une psychologie du cinéma. 1946; translated in *Reflections on Art*, edited by Susanne Langer, 1958.

La Psychologie de l'art: Le Musée imaginaire, La Création artistique, La Monnaie de l'absolu. 3 vols., 1947-49; as *The Psychology of Art: Museum Without Walls, The Creative Act, The Twilight of the Absolute*, 3 vols., 1949-51; revised edition, as *Les Voix du silence*, 4 vols., 1951; as *The Voices of Silence*, 4 vols., 1953.

The Case for De Gaulle, with James Burnham. 1949.

Saturne: Essai sur Goya. 1949; as *Saturn: An Essay on Goya*, 1957.

La Musée imaginaire de la sculpture mondiale: Le Statuaire, Des Bas-reliefs aux grottes sacrées, Le Monde chrétien. 3 vols., 1952-54.

La Métamorphose des dieux:

L'Inaccessible. 1957; revised edition, as *Le Surnaturel*, 1977; as *The Metamorphosis of the Gods*, 1960.

L'Irréel. 1974.

L'Intemporel. 1975.

Brasilia, la capitale de l'espoir (multilingual edition). 1959.

Discours 1958-1965. 1966.

Le Miroir des limbes:

Antimémoires. 1967; revised edition, 1972; as *Anti-Memoirs*, 1968.

La Corde et les souris:

Les Hôtes de passage. 1976.

Les Chênes qu'on abat. 1971; as *Fallen Oaks*, 1972; as *Felled Oaks*, 1972.

La Tête d'obsidienne. 1974; as *Picasso's Mask*, 1976.

Lazare. 1974; translated as *Lazarus*, 1976.

Le Triangle noir. 1970.

Oraisons funèbres. 1971.

Paroles et écrits politiques 1947-1972. 1973.

L'Homme précaire et la littérature. 1977.

*

Critical Studies: *Malraux and the Tragic Imagination* by W.M. Frohock, 1952, revised edition, 1967; *Malraux* by Geoffrey H. Hartman, 1960; *Malraux, Tragic Humanist* by Charles D. Blend, 1963; *Malraux: A Collection of Critical Essays* edited by R.W.B. Lewis, 1964; *Malraux* by Denis Boak, 1968; *Malraux* by Jean Lacouture, 1975; *Malraux: Life and Work* edited by Martine de Courcel, 1976; *Malraux: A Biography* by Axel Madsen, 1977; *Imagery in the Novels of Malraux* by Ralph Tarica, 1980.

*   *   *

André Malraux's theme, running through all his works, can best be summed up by a remark made by a quite different writer in an altogether different connection. It was Gore Vidal who wrote, in *Sex, Death, and Money* (1968), that "in certain human actions, in love, in violence, [man] can communicate with others, touch and be touched, act and in the act forget his fate." This sentiment lies at the heart of Malraux's humanism also; but it is a tragic humanism, as critics have clearly perceived. W.M. Frohock, for instance, put it this way: "there inheres in man's fate, in spite of all the possibilities of defeat, the possibility of the power and glory of being a man."

Malraux's mythic explorations of men (women play only a subordinate role in his fiction) caught up in history, picked out for large action by destiny, probe our fate in a grandiose manner that is comparable in few other novels. Indeed, it is to the great epic writers like Zola, Melville, or Dostoevsky that we have to turn if we are to seek parallels. Malraux is justly admired for the way he has used adventure stories—in much the same way as Melville used a whaling narrative, or Conrad tales of the merchant navy—to convey a world-view marked by a tragic humanism which is nevertheless uniquely his own.

His individuality arises from a distinctive prose style. He uses a rhetorical manner which is elevated, imposing, even grandiloquent, on the one hand, and, on the other, a utilitarian style, modelled on Céline and the American writers of the 1920's whom he admired, which is curt, economical, and firmly action-oriented. This makes him a fine writer of stories in which men are fighting for a noble cause, especially when that cause is doomed. As a result, his best books are *Man's Estate*, a graphic narrative of the collapse of the Communist rebellion in Shanghai in 1927, and *Days of Hope*, an account of the Spanish civil war seen from the Republican standpoint as a moment of glory, sacrifice, and brotherhood.

Correspondingly there is not much to laugh about in Malraux's world, and where there is humour it tends to be other-directed rather than self-directed: at the buffoon Clappique in *Man's Estate*, for instance, or at grotesques like the worthies of French Guiana satirised in *Anti Memoirs*. His sometimes excessive fondness for aphorisms, too, can give the impression of an inflation in which the sublime teeters on the brink of the ridiculous and in which the nobility of the utterance can slide into windy rhetoric.

In politics Malraux was a kind of pessimistic radical, which accounts for his left-wing leanings before the war and his whole-hearted endorsement of Charles de Gaulle after it. All his writings—his influential art criticism and autobiographical works as well as his novels and essays—are ultimately meditations on death. In *The Temptation of the West* a Chinese intellectual indicts Western man for having given death "a tragic face." Not surprisingly, therefore, Malraux's finest book, *Man's Estate*, ends on the death of love and the death of hope. Nevertheless he has done much—not only as a writer, but also as a controversial minister for the arts in de Gaulle's administration in the 1960's—to promote a sense of human dignity, a recognition of the value of a man's life which, as he once eloquently put it, "is worth nothing, but which nothing can buy."

—John Fletcher

MANDELSTAM, Osip (Emil'evich). Born in Warsaw, Poland, 15 January 1891. Educated at Tenishev School, St. Petersburg, 1900-07; in Western Europe, 1907-10, and attended lectures at University of Heidelberg, 1909; studied philosophy, University of St. Petersburg, 1911. Married Nadezhda Yakovlevna Khazina in 1919 (formally in 1922). Writer; not involved politically in revolution, and free-lance writer in 1920's: translator of works by Upton Sinclair, Jules Romains, Charles de Coster, and others; a poem critical of Stalin in 1934 led to sentence of hard labor on White Sea canal; sentence commuted to exile in Cherdyn, later in Voronezh; exile ended in 1937, but he was again arrested, and died en route to labor camp. *Died 27 December 1938.*

PUBLICATIONS

Collections

Sobraniye sochineniy, edited by Gleb Struve and Boris Filippov.   3 vols., 1964-71; vol. 1 revised, 1967.

Complete Poetry, translated by Burton Raffel and Alla Borago. 1973.
Stikhotvoreniya [Poems], edited by A.L. Dymshitz and N.U. Khardzhiev. 1974.

Verse

Kamen'. 1913; revised edition, 1916, 1923; as *Stone*, translated by Robert Tracy, 1981.
Tristia. 1922.
Vtoraya kniga [The Second Book]. 1923.
Stikhotvoreniya [Poems]. 1928.
Selected Poems, translated by Clarence Brown and W.S. Merwin. 1973.
Selected Poems, translated by David McDuff. 1973.
Octets, translated by John Riley. 1976.
50 Poems, translated by Bernard Meares. 1977.
Poems, translated by James Greene. 1977; revised edition, 1980.

Fiction

Shum vremeni. 1925; as *The Noise of Time*, in *Prose*, 1965.
Yegipetskaya marka. 1928; as *The Egyptian Stamp*, in *Prose*, 1965.

Other

Primus (juvenile). 1925.
Dva tramvaya [Two Streetcars] (juvenile). 1926.
Shary [Balloons] (juvenile). 1926.
Kukhnia [The Kitchen] (juvenile). 1926.
O poezii [On Poetry]. 1928.
Puteshestviye v Armeniyu. 1933; as *Journey to Armenia*, 1973.
Prose, edited by Clarence Brown. 1965; revised edition, 1967.
Selected Essays, edited by Sidney Monas. 1977.
Complete Critical Prose and Letters, edited by Jane Gary Harris. 1979.
Voronezhkie tetradi [The Voronezh Notebooks]. 1980.

*

Critical Studies: *Hope Against Hope*, 1970, and *Hope Abandoned*, 1974, both by Nadezhda Mandelstam; *Mandelstam* by Clarence Brown, 1973; *Mandelstam: An Essay in Antiphon* by Arthur A. Cohen, 1974; *Mandelstam and His Age: A Commentary on the Themes of War and Revolution in the Poetry 1913-1923* by Steven Broyde, 1975; *Essays on Mandelstam* by Kiril Taranovsky, 1976; *Mandelstam: The Egyptian Stamp* by Daphne M. West, 1981.

*   *   *

Osip Mandelstam is regarded by many as the greatest Russian poet of this century. The beginning of his bɪ.ˡliant poetic career is associated with the Acmeist movement, which stood for clarity and precision and rejected the Symbolists' aesthetics. The title of Mandelstam's first book of poems, *Stone*, suggests the Acmeists' demand that verse has to be constructed like a stone edifice. Mandelstam aspired to "build" his poems like Gothic Towers (see his poems "Hagia Sophia," "Notre Dame," "The Admiralty Building"):"To build," he says, "means to conquer emptiness, to hypnotise space." For the Acmeists a poet is no longer a prophet or a theurgist, but a craftsman, a master, and "...beauty is not the fancy of a demi-god, but the predatory eye of the simple carpenter." Hence, the abundance of architectural metaphors in Mandelstam's early poetry. The balance of rhythm and imagery, the classical structural organization are the hallmarks of his second collection, *Tristia*. Like Pushkin, using both the solemn archaism and the plain colloquialism, Mandelstam "built" the most refined lyrics of 20th-century Russian poetry. But he travelled further down its path of cultural tradition: "The silver trumpet of Catullus alarms and excites us more forcefully than any Futurist riddle" ("Word and Culture"). Homer, Ovid, Virgil, and Dante gaze at us from every poem of the early Mandelstam. If *Stone* can be called his "Roman" book, *Tristia* is full of allusions to the classical world of Greece. He defined Acmeism as "the nostalgia for a world culture." World culture is given by Mandelstam its finest representation in the Russian language. "Such poetry does not exist in Russian. Yet, it must exist in Russian" he wrote in his essay "Word and Culture." His poetry reflects the wholeness of our Judean-Hellenic-Latin civilisation. J. Brodsky called him "a poet for and of civilisation," others called him a bookish, erudite poet.

Reading Mandelstam is an endless labour (as he said for Dante), but it is also an endless pleasure. His poems are powerful and haunting. He possessed an amazing ability to reconstruct an ancient cultural heritage which he interpreted as a living active force in the contemporary world. "Mandelstam was a philosopher of History," wrote the critic Berkovsky. "He had to place every bird, large or small, back into the cultural nest from which it had flown." It is precisely his historical sensitivity which enabled him to comprehend the pathos of the October Revolution, "the majesty of history in the making." As he said in one of his apocalyptic poems, "The Twilight of Freedom" (1918):

> Then let us try: enormous, cumbersome,
> one screeching turn of the wheel.
> The earth is sailing. Be manful, men.

Mandelstam hardly ever concentrated on his own personality. He preferred to confront Time, to celebrate Life, or to redefine History. He transformed the raw materials of History— the "noise of Time"—into a cultural creation. As S. Monas wrote: "Mandelstam saw a Culture marked for death, and a new barbarism terrifying yet perhaps potentially creative, waiting at the gate." In his third and last published collection of verse (1928), Hellenism has been put aside. Such poems as "The Age," "The Slate Ode," and "1 January 1924" are about the relationship between the poet and his era. Mandelstam found himself completely estranged from official Soviet literature. According to Nadezhda Mandelstam, his name was crossed out of all the Soviet periodicals after 1923. The poet was certainly aware of the increasing hostility of the new regime: "the wolf-hound age rushes onto my shoulders." Between 1925 and 1930 he wrote no poetry. Soon he fell victim to the beast. In 1934 he was arrested, imprisoned, and tortured. Although it was his "Epigram on Stalin" that cost Mandelstam his freedom and his life, he was doomed to destruction by the specific quality of his poetry and his personality. J. Brodsky said in his essay on Mandelstam: "When a man creates a world of his own, he becomes a foreign body against which all laws are aimed: gravity, compression, and annihilation. Mandelstam's world was big enough to invite all of these." He was deported to a small town in the Urals where he tried to commit suicide, then he was transferred to Voronezh. Some of his best poems were written during his second exile. They reveal the naked existential horror of his isolation and poverty. After having been allowed to return to Moscow (in 1937) he was rearrested (May, 1938). He was moved from camp to camp until he reached the very end of Soviet territory, Vladivostok, where he died a horrible death of starvation and madness (27 December 1938). "Mandelstam is one of those supreme artists who convinces you that there is such a thing as poetic immortality, and that it is at one with the simplest forces of creation, so that nothing can destroy it" (C. James).

—Valentina Polukhina

MANN, (Paul) Thomas. Born in Lübeck, Germany, 6 June 1875; brother of the writer Heinrich Mann. Educated at Dr. Bussenius's school, 1882-89; Gymnasium, Lübeck, 1889-94. Military service, 1898-99. Married Katja Pringsheim in 1905; six children, including the writers Erika and Klaus. Worked in insurance company, Munich, 1894-95, then writer; lived in Switzerland, 1933-36 (deprived of German citizenship, 1936), Princeton, New Jersey, 1938-41, Santa Monica, California, 1941-52, and Switzerland, 1952-55. Recipient: Bauernfeld Prize, 1904; Nobel Prize for Literature, 1929; Goethe Prize (Frankfurt), 1949; Feltrinelli Prize, 1952. Honorary degree: University of Bonn (rescinded, 1936). Honorary Citizen, Lübeck, 1955. *Died 12 August 1955.*

PUBLICATIONS

Collections

Gesammelte Werke. 14 vols., 1974.

Fiction

Der kleine Herr Friedemann: Novellen. 1898; augmented edition, 1909.
Buddenbrooks: Verfall einer Familie. 1900; as *Buddenbrooks: The Decline of a Family,* 1924.
Tristan: Sechs Novellen. 1903.
Königliche Hoheit. 1909; as *Royal Highness: A Novel of German Court-Life,* 1916.
Der Tod in Venedig. 1912; as *Death in Venice,* 1925.
Das Wunderkind: Novellen. 1914.
Herr und Hund: Ein Idyll. 1919; augmented edition, 1919; as *Basham and I,* 1923; as *A Man and His Dog,* 1930.
Wälsungenblut. 1921.
Bekenntnisse des Hochstaplers Felix Krull; Buch der Kindheit. 1922; additional chapter published as *Die Begegnung,* 1953; complete version, 1953; as *Confessions of Felix Krull, Confidence Man: The Early Years,* 1955.
Novellen. 2 vols., 1922.
Der Zauberberg. 1924; as *The Magic Mountain,* 1927.
Death in Venice and Other Stories. 1925.
Children and Fools. 1928.
Mario und der Zauberer: Ein tragisches Reiseerlebnis. 1930; as *Mario and the Magician,* 1930.
Joseph und seine Brüder: Die Geschichten Jaakobs, Der junge Joseph, Joseph in Ägypten, Joseph der Ernährer. 4 vols., 1933-43; as *Joseph and His Brothers (Joseph and His Brethren): The Tale of Jacob (Joseph and His Brothers), Young Joseph, Joseph in Egypt, Joseph the Provider,* 4 vols., 1934-44.
Nocturnes. 1934.
Stories of Three Decades. 1936; augmented edition, as *Stories of a Lifetime,* 1961.
Lotte in Weimar. 1939; translated as *Lotte in Weimar,* 1940; as *The Beloved Returns,* 1940.
Die vertauschten Köpfe: Eine indische Legende. 1940; as *The Transposed Heads: A Legend of India,* 1941.
Das Gesetz: Erzählung. 1944; as *The Tables of the Law,* 1945.
Ausgewählte Erzählungen. 1945.
Doktor Faustus: Das Leben des deutschen Tonsetzers Adrian Leverkühn, erzählt von einem Freunde. 1947; as *Doctor Faustus: The Life of the German Composer, Adrian Leverkuehn, as Told by a Friend,* 1948.

Der Erwählte. 1951; as *The Holy Sinner,* 1951.
Die Betrogene. 1953; as *The Black Swan,* 1954.

Play

Fiorenza. 1906.

Other

Bilse und Ich. 1908.
Friedrich und die grosse Koalition. 1915.
Betrachtungen eines Unpolitischen. 1918; as *Reflections of a Nonpolitical Man,* 1983.
Rede und Antwort: Gesammelte Abhandlungen und kleine Aufsätze. 1922.
Okkulte Erlebnisse. 1924.
Bemühungen. 1925.
Pariser Rechenschaft. 1926.
Three Essays. 1929.
Die Forderung des Tages: Reden und Aufsätze aus den Jahren 1925-1929. 1930.
A Sketch of My Life. 1930.
Goethe und Tolstoi: Zum Problem der Humanität. 1932.
Past Masters and Other Papers. 1933.
Leiden und Grösse der Meister: Neue Aufsätze. 1935.
Achtung, Europa! Aufsätze zur Zeit. 1938.
Dieser Friede. 1938; as *This Peace,* 1938.
Schopenhauer. 1938.
This War. 1940.
Order of the Day: Political Essays and Speeches of Two Decades. 1942.
Deutsche Hörer! 25 Radiosendungen nach Deutschland. 1942; as *Listen, Germany!*
   Twenty-Five Radio Messages to the German People over B.B.C., 1943; augmented
   edition (55 messages), 1945.
Adel des Geistes: Sechsehn Versuche zum Problem der Humanität. 1945; augmented
   edition, 1956.
Leiden an Deutschland: Tagebuchblätter aus den Jahren 1933 und 1934. 1946.
Essays of Three Decades. 1947.
Neue Studien. 1948.
Die Entstehung des Doktor Faustus: Roman eines Romans. 1949.
Michelangelo in seinen Dichtungen. 1950.
The Thomas Mann Reader, edited by Joseph Warner Angell. 1950.
Altes und Neues: Kleine Prosa aus fünf Jahrzehnten. 1953; revised edition, 1956.
Ansprache im Schillerjahr 1955. 1955.
Versuch über Schiller. 1955.
Zeit und Werk: Tagebücher und Schriften zum Zeitgeschehen. 1956.
Nachlese: Prosa 1951-55. 1956.
Last Essays. 1959.
Briefe an Paul Amann 1915-1952, edited by Herbert Wegener. 1959; as *Letters,* 1961.
Gespräch in Briefen, with Karl Kerenyi, edited by Kerenyi. 1960; as *Mythology and
   Humanism: Correspondence,* 1975.
Briefe an Ernst Bertram 1910-1955, edited by Inge Jens. 1960.
Briefe 1899-1955, edited by Erika Mann. 3 vols., 1961-65; as *Letters,* edited by Richard
   and Clara Winston, 2 vols., 1970.
Briefwechsel, with Robert Faesi, edited by Faesi. 1962.
Briefwechsel 1900-1949, with Heinrich Mann, edited by Hans Wysling, revised edition,
   edited by Ulrich Dietzel. 1968; revised edition, 1975.

Briefwechsel, with Hermann Hesse, edited by Anni Carlsson. 1968; revised edition, 1975; as *Letters*, 1975.
Briefwechsel im Exil, with Erich Kahler, edited by Hans Wysling. 1970; as *An Exceptional Friendship: Correspondence*, 1975.
The Letters to Caroline Newton, edited by Robert F. Cohen. 1971.
Briefwechsel 1932-1955, with Gottfried Bermann Fischer, edited by Peter de Mendelssohn. 1973.
Briefe an Otto Grautoff 1894-1901, und Ida Boy-Ed, 1903-1928, edited by Peter de Mendelssohn. 1975.
Tagebücher, edited by Peter de Mendelssohn. 1977— ; as *Diaries*, 1983— .

Editor, *The Living Thoughts of Schopenhauer*. 1939.
Editor, *The Permanent Goethe*. 1948.

*

Bibliography: *Fifty Years of Thomas Mann Studies* by Klaus Werner Jonas, 1955, and *Thomas Mann Studies* by Klaus Werner and Ilsedore B. Jonas, 1967; *Das Werk Manns: Eine Bibliographie* by Hans Bürgin, 1959; *Manns Briefwerk* by Georg Wenzel, 1969; *Die Literatur über Mann: Eine Bibliographie 1898-1969* by Harry Matter, 2 vols., 1972.

Critical Studies: *Mann*, 1952, revised edition, 1962, and *From "The Magic Mountain": Mann's Later Masterpieces*, 1979, both by Henry Hatfield; *Mann: The World as Will and Representation* by Fritz Kaufmann, 1957; *The Ironic German: A Study of Mann* by Erich Heller, 1958, revised edition, 1981; *The Two Faces of Hermes*, 1962, and *Understanding Mann*, 1966, both by Ronald D. Miller; *Mann* by J.P. Stern, 1967; *Mann* by Reginald J. Hollingdale, 1971; *Mann: The Use of Tradition* by Terence J. Reed, 1974; *Mann* by Martin Swales, 1980; *Mann: The Making of an Artist 1875-1911* by Richard Winston, 1981.

*   *   *

Thomas Mann's origins lie unmistakeably in the *fin de siècle* period of neo-romanticism and fascination with decadence. Dominating his early stories and the precocious masterpiece, *Buddenbrooks*, is the duality of *Komik und Elend*, comedy and pathos. He shares a contemporary sense of his era as a terminal one and depicts a *Spätzeit* (latter-day age) in which neurasthenic characters, especially artist-figures, find release from the world's coarse demands only in the grand life-denying pessimism of Schopenhauer or the climax of a Wagnerian *Liebestod* (love-death, death in love), as in the episode in the story "Tristan" which recreates the *Liebestod* of the second Act of Wagner's *Tristan und Isolde*, or the scene in which the young Hanno Buddenbrook, the last of his line and a doomed artist *manqué*, extemporizes a piano-fantasy whose culmination bears a strong suggestion both of death and of sexual climax. The individual is seen as incomplete, a fragment broken away from the whole, and necessarily both tragic and comic. The dualism of Life and Death which ultimately asserts its domination in "Tristan" is as remote from the tragi-comic struggles of the characters in the story as are the mountains surrounding the sanatorium which is the setting for this novella, and of the later novel *The Magic Mountain*. Decadence is the cult of beauty proclaimed against a background of decline, and Mann is certainly drawn to this cult. And yet, typically, his attitude to it was a highly ambivalent one, similar to his ambivalence towards Wagner. Although it goes without saying that he was not in sympathy with the materialist and arrogant society of pre-First World War Germany, at the same time he was prevented by his solid, north German burgher inheritance from sustaining a mood of disgust with reality or retreat into decadence. The result of ambivalence is irony. This most famous aspect of his work derives in part from the critical insight of the ousider who has taken lessons from Nietzsche in the self-deceiving motivation of human conduct; and in part from a latter-day scepticism about the function of art itself in an era when the quest for form and harmony suspiciously resembles a denial of that disturbing

Nietzschean insight. An illustration is provided by the artist figure, Gustav Aschenbach, in *Death in Venice*, who, from a highly respected position as the traditional German *Dichter* (a combination of poet and pedagogue)—a position he holds, it becomes clear, only by an effort of will to deny certain painful complexities—degenerates in the course of the story to become an old *roué* whose homoerotic fixation upon a young boy leads him to "conspire" with the Venetian authorities to conceal the facts of a cholera epidemic sweeping through the tourist city. By his immoral denial of Knowledge for the sake of the pursuit of Beauty he allegorically betrays the artist's deeper duty to society, that of portraying the truth as he sees it, even at the expense of the security of social existence.

The irony of Mann's treatment of Aschenbach characteristically includes also an element of parody of his own beautifully controlled and convoluted "master-style." Equally characteristically, Mann's political sense lagged some way behind his artistic insight (it is a familiar observation in German cultural history) and in his overgrown war-time essay, *Reflections of a Nonpolitical Man*, written as a defence of Germany's war-aims in terms of her separate cultural tradition, Mann even resurrects concepts he had already completely undermined in *Death in Venice*: for example, his desire to see the artist as a "warrior," just as his hero Aschenbach had done at the outset of the story. It is not surprising that after the war, in his final and permanent conversion to democracy in 1922, he uses very much the same language and authorities as he had called upon in his attack on democracy in the *Reflections*. As well as employing Novalis's metaphysics of the State to assert that the idea of a republic is a part of the German Romantic legacy, he now presents the Romantic "attraction of death" of the *Reflections* as a constituent part of "an interest in life." The central themes of his great post-war novel of education, *The Magic Mountain*, can be summarized as the need to break out from decadence. The question is a constant one in Mann: how is it possible to know and yet live, to be a man of your age, sharing in all its spiritual insecurity and scepticism, and yet be able to say "yes" to life? The answer to the question is not constant, but evolving. Art, which in Mann sets out in opposition to life, in the end becomes identified with life. The vast question raised by *The Magic Mountain*, "what is life?," is answered partly in terms of "life is increasing knowledge of life." Forming, writing, is a life-giving act in itself, a bulwark against chaos. It is true—as the earlier, Romantic Mann knew—that the insight into "first causes," the self-knowledge which informs the Romantic irony of consciousness spying upon consciousness, can paralyze the will to form: that this can even be a liberating discovery, however, a giving way to chaos, is shown in the experiences of Hans Castorp, hero of *The Magic Mountain*, in the early chapters of the novel. But the second wisdom goes further: to give shape to life reflecting upon life is a healthy adjunct to living it, overcoming on behalf of man in general the "sickly" temptation to doubt and introspection. Mann's own (always ironized) surrender to romantic aestheticism was the precondition for his renunciation of it; just as Hans Castorp's illness on the Magic Mountain had to be brought to light before it could be cured.

It was as well that Mann had resolved these issues before the chaos of the Weimar years and the emergence of totalitarianism gave a new urgency to the intellectual debate he had always incorporated in an interplay of "ideas" so tangible as to become almost the protagonists of his works. The reply to crude and regressive Nazi mythologizing was the tetralogy of Joseph-novels, *Joseph and His Brethren*, where the journey into the biblical past is at once a Nazi-defying homage to the Judeo-Christian humanistic tradition, and a journey into the depths of the individual unconscious, the region where myths originate and are perpetuated. His attempt to comprehend Germany's lapse into diabolism is incorporated in *Doctor Faustus*, in the story of a demonic artist, the composer Adrian Leverkühn, presented through a new version of the Faust legend. German inwardness is here brilliantly related to Germany's outward "adventures" and journey towards catastrophe. The extraordinary range of Mann's talent is apparent in his last novel, *Confessions of Felix Krull, Confidence Man*, which he took up again in 1953 where he had left off in 1910. A picaresque and superbly humorous book, it allows its autobiographical narrator to manipulate and parody a number of literary conventions and establish himself as the archetypal "unreliable narrator"; quite appropiately, since Krull is a confidence-trickster as well as an artist of life, bringing to the fore once again Mann's early perception of the "bad conscience" of the artist who manipulates his readers' response and "simulates" for their benefit emotions which he does not feel but has cold-bloodedly observed. It is an appropriate conclusion to Mann's career: a sublimated account of the ambivalence of fiction, and yet a vindication of fiction by its very existence, without which the world would be infinitely poorer.

—Alan F. Bance

MANZONI, Alessandro (Francesco Tommaso Antonio). Born in Milan, 7 March 1785. Educated at the Somaschian college at Merate, 1791-96, and at Lugano, 1796-98; Barnabite Collegio dei Nobili, Milan and Magenta, 1797-1801. Married 1) Henriette Blondel in 1808 (died, 1833), eight children survived infancy; 2) Teresa Borri in 1837. Senator of the Kingdom, 1860; Honorary Citizen, Rome, 1872. *Died 22 May 1873.*

PUBLICATIONS

Collections

Opere, edited by Riccardo Bacchelli. 1953.
Tutte le opere, edited by Alberto Chiari and Fausto Ghisalberti. 11 vols., 1957-70.

Fiction

I promessi sposi. 3 vols., 1827; revised edition, 1840-42; as *The Betrothed Lovers*, 1828; as *The Betrothed*, 1834.
Storia della colonna infame. With *I promessi sposi*, 1842; edited by Renzo Negri, 1974; as *The Column of Infamy*, 1964.

Plays

Il conte di Carmagnola (produced 1823). 1820.
Adelchi (produced 1822). 1822.
Tragedie, edited by Giulio Bollati. 1965.

Verse

Inni sacri. 1815; edited by Dino Brivio, 1973; as *The Sacred Hymns*, 1904.
Del trionfo della libertà, edited by C. Romussi. 1878.

Other

Sulla morale cattolica. 1819; revised edition, 1855; edited by R. Amerio, 1965; as *A Vindication of Catholic Morality*, 1836.
Discorso sopra alcuni punti della storia longobardica in Italia. 1822.
Opere varie. 1845-55.
La rivoluzione francese del 1789 e la rivoluzione italiana del 1859, edited by Pietro Brambilla. 1889.
Lettere, edited by Cesare Arieti. 3 vols., 1970.

*

Bibliography: *Bibliografia manzoniana* by M. Parenti, 1936; *Critica Manzoniana d'un decennio (1939-1948)* by F. Ghisalberti, 1949; *Bibliografia manzoniana 1949-1973* by Silvia Brusamolino Isella and Simonetta Usuelli Castellani, 1974.

Critical Studies: *Manzoni: Esthetics and Literary Criticism* by Joseph F. de Simone, 1946; *The Linguistic Writings of Manzoni* by Barbara Reynolds, 1950; *Manzoni and His Times* by Archibald Colquhoun, 1954; *Manzoni: The Story of a Spiritual Quest* by Stanley B. Chandler, 1974; *Manzoni's Christian Realism* by Ernesto G. Caserta, 1977.

*   *   *

The Betrothed, the work which won Manzoni lasting fame and which occupies a place of fundamental importance in the development of both the Italian language and its literature, was written and initially read in the wake of the phenomenal European success of Scott's historical novels. The link with Scott has insured continuing attention for Manzoni on the part of readers interested in the evolution of modern narrative fiction. But it has also served as a barrier to a deeper, more sensitive and unprejudiced understanding of his art. Manzoni's plumbing of the inner forces at work in individual consciences and social movements finds no parallel in Scott's lively and colorful reconstructions of a people's national past. Two early (1827) French comments on *The Betrothed* are worth noting. "All in all I prefer Manzoni to Scott. But he will not have the same success for he is religious and thoroughly Catholic," wrote Lamennais, probably France's chief Catholic apologist at the time, boldly recognizing the powerful influence of opposing beliefs and ideologies in literary judgments. As for the poet Lamartine, one of the few to praise the long historical passages (especially those on the 1630 plague in Lombardy) which most critics found prolix and digressive, he urged Manzoni "to get out of the historical novel and give us history of a new kind" instead; thus he pointed ahead to the radical solution of epistemological and aesthetic problems perceived by Manzoni himself in his attempt to reconcile the dictates of art with respect for historical truth. Indeed, Manzoni never wrote the expected second novel, but in his *The Column of Infamy*, begun as an off-shoot of *The Betrothed* and eventually published as a separate work, he created the forerunner of a new genre, today's "essay in narrative reporting" (as Solzhenitsyn has called *The Gulag Archipelago*) or "documentary novel" (as Truman Capote called *In Cold Blood*).

The choice of 17th-century Lombardy under Spanish domination as the setting for *The Betrothed* was a by-product of Manzoni's highly developed historical interests that had already found expression in the two tragedies and the essays accompanying them. He was attracted to the period (as he wrote to Fauriel) because of the "extraordinary state of society" it manifested: "the most arbitrary government combined with feudal and popular anarchy; legislation that is amazing in the way it expressed a profound, ferocious, pretentious ignorance; classes with opposed interests and maxims; some little-known anecdotes, preserved in trustworthy documents; finally a plague which gave full rein to the most consummate and shameful excesses, to the most absurd prejudices, and to the most touching virtues"—in short, enough to fill a canvas.

An episode of the Thirty Years War in Lombardy, which pitted the French against the Spanish king and the latter's liege and sovereign lord the Holy Roman Emperor, provides the time-frame (1628-31) for the novel. The foreground is occupied by the "little world" of Manzoni's fictional characters in the rural landscape of the Lecco branch of Lake Como. With an unusual twist in the storytelling tradition—be it romance, fairy tale, or even realistic novel—the courtship leading to the betrothal of Renzo and Lucia already lies in the past when the novel opens: this is not a story of love and passion but of tranquil affections and the founding of family life. Though they succeed in bettering their social and economic condition in an instance of upward mobility perhaps more typical of the century in which the book was written than of that in which it is set, neither Renzo nor Lucia has any other ambition than marriage within their class and environment. They are humble artisans who have not quite ceased being peasants: "nobody's people," Manzoni calls them, "without even a master," he adds, referring to their defenselessness in a society of well-organized, belligerent, corrupt, and wary factions and groups. They run afoul of the petty local lord, a small-time tyrant who on a whim makes a bet that he will succeed in seducing Lucia, and of the cowardly parish priest who once again forgets "the duties and noble aims" of his profession and permits himself to be intimidated by the lord's henchmen against performing the marriage. Forced to leave their native village, they are separated and reunited only three years later after the scourges of famine, war, pestilence, and death have devastated the land, cleared and cleansed it for a new beginning.

Increasing secularism and more recently the spread of schools of literary criticism averse to moral judgments have created a barrier of ambiguities between Manzoni and the contemporary reader. *The Betrothed* reflects Manzoni's religious beliefs on virtually every page. It is present in the succession of "trials," the fictional equivalent to the Christian view of life as a testing time, which the plot prepares for the characters. It is present in the judgments expressed by the author in his many different guises, from ominiscient narrator to detached observer, to mediator between the reader and the anonymous writer of the supposed manuscript from which the story derives. It is present in the "portraits," the more or less elaborate presentations of the physical, psychological, and life-history particulars of the characters, both "invented" and derived from factual reality. It is present in "the moral of the tale" with which the story ends. And it is present in a distinctly disquieting manner in the intertwining of a pessimistic view of human nature with the optimistic acceptance of the ways of God to man. The over-all design is providential; the ending is a happy one; as in comedy it brings the accommodation of a well-assorted marriage. But along the way, in passage upon passage, instances of violence abound: a veritable anatomy of acts of violence is built up, from the unbridled application of force in riots, duels, forced entry, kidnapping, and murder to more subtle forms of coercion in political manipulation or the imposition of one man's will upon another's. Again and again, sometimes directly, more often indirectly, the reader is invited to weigh the implications of an action, to arrive at a moral judgment whereby in the long run he will himself be implicitly judged.

By today's standards a conservative, Manzoni was in his own time liberal and in siding with the Romantics against the Classicists and in supporting the struggle for Italian independence and unity actually revolutionary. The most important intellectual events in Manzoni's life preceding the composition of *The Betrothed* were his two so-called "conversions": the return to the practice of Catholicism and the rejection of the neo-classical poetry of his youth. In *The Sacred Hymns* the heavily accented octosyllables of short rhyming stanzas reminiscent of popular poetry close the gap between audience and poet and make present the ever-recurrent encounter between man and God celebrated in the major festivities of the liturgical year. *Il conte di Carmagnola* and *Adelchi* mark a major innovation in the Italian theatre by breaking with the classical rules of tragedy. Their heroes are historical figures faced by problems of individual responsibility and the need to come to terms with the presence of injustice and evil. The essence of Manzoni's religious thought is found in *Vindication of Catholic Morality*, his major work in Italian prose before *The Betrothed*. (His most important work of literary criticism, the *Lettre à M. Chauvet sur l'unité de temps et de lieu dans la tragédie*, as well as most of his correspondence, was in French.) His tone is eloquent and solemn, and as with his wonted emphasis on telling particulars he details "the unity of revelation" (which is also at work in the novel): "What is and what should be; misery and lust, and the ever living idea of perfection and order that we also find in ourselves; good and evil; the words of divine wisdom and the vain talk of men; the watchful joy of the righteous, the sorrows and consolations of the repentant, the terror or unshakeable indifference of the wicked; the triumphs of justice and those of iniquity; men's plans brought to fruition amidst a thousand obstacles or overturned by the one unexpected one; disbelief itself—all is explained with the Gospel, all confirms it."

In an age of increasing violence, of its growing acceptance as a part of daily life, of its polarization into rival group struggles, and its frequent institutionalization into accepted norms of behaviour, Manzoni's message continues to be that of love and compassion, of a common destiny and burdens shared, of purpose in life, of the individual's capacity to will and effect change by transforming himself, by making or aiming to make himself more human through the education of his faculties of thought and feeling.

—Olga Ragusa

MARCUS Aurelius. *See* **AURELIUS, Marcus.**

MARIVAUX. Born Pierre Carlet in Paris, 4 February 1688. Studied law in Paris from 1710; law degree, 1721, and practiced briefly. Married Colombe Bollogne in 1717 (died 1723), one daughter; lived with Mlle. Angelique Saint—Jean from 1744. Journalist and writer. Member, 1742, Chancellor, 1750, and Director, 1759, French Academy. *Died 12 February 1763.*

PUBLICATIONS

Collections

> *Oeuvres complètes.* 12 vols., 1781.
> *Théâtre complet,* edited by Frédéric Deloffre. 2 vols., 1968.
> *Journaux et oeuvres diverses,* edited by Frédéric Deloffre and Michel Gilot. 1969.
> *Oeuvres de jeunesse,* edited by Frédéric Deloffre and Claude Rigault. 1972.

Plays

> *Le Père prudent et équitable; ou, Crispin l'heureux fourbe* (produced 1712). 1712.

L'Amour et la vérité, with Chevalier Rustaing de Saint-Jory (produced 1720). In *Théâtre complet*, 1968.

Arlequin poli par l'amour (produced 1720). 1723; as *Robin, Bachelor of Love*, in *Seven Comedies*, 1968.

Annibal (produced 1720). 1727.

La Surprise de l'amour (produced 1722). 1723.

La Double Inconstance (produced 1723). 1723; as *Double Infidelity*, in *Seven Comedies*, 1968; as *Infidelities*, 1980.

Le Prince travesti; ou, L'Illustre Aventurier (produced 1724). 1727.

La Fausse Suivante; ou, Le Fourbe puni (produced 1724). 1729.

Le Dénouement imprévu (produced 1724). 1727.

L'Île des esclaves (produced 1725). 1725.

L'Héritier du village (produced 1725). 1729.

L'Île de la raison; ou, Les Petits Hommes (produced 1727). 1727.

La (Seconde) Surprise de l'amour (produced 1727). 1728.

Le Triomphe de Plutus (produced 1728). 1739; as *Money Makes the World Go Round*, in *Seven Comedies*, 1968.

La Colonie (as *La Nouvelle Colonie*, produced 1729; revised version, produced 1750). In *Théâtre complet*, 1968.

Le Jeu de l'amour et du hasard (produced 1730). 1730; as *Love in Livery*, 1907; as *The Game of Love and Chance*, in *French Comedies of the 18th Century*, 1923, and in *Seven Comedies*, 1968.

La Réunion des amours (produced 1730). 1732.

Le Triomphe de l'amour (produced 1732). 1732.

Les Serments indiscrets (produced 1732). 1732.

L'École des mères (produced 1732). 1732.

L'Heureux Strategème (produced 1733). 1733; as *The Agreeable Surprise*, 1766; as *The Wiles of Love*, in *Seven Comedies*, 1968.

Le Méprise (produced 1734). 1739.

Le Petit-Maître corrigé (produced 1734). 1739.

La Mère confidante (produced 1735). 1735.

Le Legs (produced 1736). 1736; as *The Legacy*, 1915.

Les Fausses Confidences (produced 1737). 1738; as *The False Confessions*, in *The Classic Theatre 4*, edited by Eric Bentley, 1961; as *Sylvia Hears a Secret*, in *Seven Comedies*, 1968.

La Joie imprévue (produced 1738). 1738.

Les Sincères (produced 1739). 1739.

L'Épreuve (produced 1740). 1740; as *The Test*, in *Seven Comedies*, 1968.

La Commère (produced 1741). In *Théâtre complet*, 1968.

La Dispute (produced 1744). 1747.

Le Préjugé vaincu (produced 1746). 1747.

La Femme fidèle (produced 1755). In *Théâtre complet*, 1968.

Les Acteurs de bonne foi (produced 1947). In *Théâtre complet*, 1968.

Félicie (produced 1957). In *Théâtre complet*, 1968.

Seven Comedies, edited and translated by Oscar Mandel. 1968.

Fiction

*Les Aventures de * * * ; ou, Les Effets surprenants de la sympathie*. 1713-14.

La Voiture embourbée. 1714.

*La Vie de Marianne; ou, Les Aventures de Mme. la comtesse de * * **. 1731-41; edited by Frédéric Deloffre, 1957; as *The Life of Marianne*, 1736-42; as *The Virtuous Orphan*, 1743; as *The Life and Adventures of Indiana*, 1746; as *The Hand of Destiny*, 1889.

*Le Paysan parvenu; ou, Les Mémoires de M. * * **. 1735-36; edited by Frédéric Deloffre,

1959; as *The Fortunate Villager*, 1765; as *The Upstart Peasant*, 1974.
Le Télémaque travesti. 1736.
Pharsamon; ou, Les nouvelles folies romanesques. 1737; translated as *Pharsamond*, 1950.

Verse

L'Homère travesti; ou, L'Iliade en vers burlesques. 2 vols., 1716.

Other

Le Spectateur français. 2 vols., 1723-24; augmented edition, 1725.
L'Indigent Philosophe; ou, L'Homme sans souci. 1727.
Le Cabinet du philosophe. 1734.
Le Miroir. 1755; edited by Mario Matucci, 1958.
Journals et oeuvres diverses, edited by Frédéric Deloffre and Michel Gilot. 1969.
Oeuvres de jeunesse, edited by Frédéric Deloffre and Claude Rigault. 1972.

*

Critical Studies: *Une Préciosité nouvelle: Marivaux et le marivaudage* by Frédéric Deloffre, 1955, revised edition, 1971; *The Theatre of Marivaux* by Kenneth N. McKee, 1958; *Marivaux* by E.J.H. Greene, 1965; *The Novel of Worldliness: Crebillon, Marivaux, Laclos, and Stendhal* by Peter P. Brooks, 1969; *Love in the Theatre of Marivaux* by Valenti Papadopoulou Brady, 1970; *Marivaux* by Oscar A. Haac, 1973; *Marivaux: Un Humanisme experimental* by Henri Coulet and Michel Gilot, 1973; *Marivaux' Novels* by Ronald C. Rosbottom, 1974; *Marivaux: Le Jeu de l'amour et du hasard and Les Fausses Confidences* by Graham E. Rodmell, 1982.

*   *   *

Marivaux's comedies today are the most frequently performed in France after Molière's; his two major novels are important precursors of the psychological novel; his journals, first conceived like the *Spectator* of Addison and Steele, provide a significant commentary on man's struggle to find himself. Indeed, *The Search for Truth*, the title of a work by Malebranche that Marivaux admired, qualifies his own literary enterprise, "grounded neither in traditional morality nor the cult of passions, but in respect for the human person" (Deloffre).

Comedy arises from paradox which makes the spectator feel wiser and smile. The "reflections" of his characters often express their misapprehensions. In *La Double Inconstance* (*Double Infidelity*) Silvia, the peasant girl, will not love the Prince: better poor in my village than weeping in luxury! But later she enjoys his palace and is happy there. The lighthearted style hides seduction and cruelty, as can be seen in *The Rehearsal*, the tragic reinterpretation by Jean Anouilh of the *Double Inconstance*. Marivaux's interplay of meanings veils the truth (like Pirandello), a surprisingly modern note which lets us discover in his sparkling wit the undertones of realism or even pessimism: this is "marivaudage."

Paradox may arise also from the contrasting meanings of a single word like *honnêté* (honor; the code of a gentleman; simple politeness). The ambitious Marianne and Jacob, her male counterpart in the novel *Le Paysan parvenu* (*The Upstart Peasant*), are much beset by these implications, tor how *honnêté* must one be to make a good marriage? The Europeans, reduced to liliputian size in *L'Île de la raison* (The Isle of Reason), are required to admit their faults and prejudices to recover their stature (i.e., greatness) and this is a much harder task for gentlemen and ladies than for their less complicated servants.

Characters are placed in perspective by their servants. The idealistic masters are often entrapped by convention and illusion, in striking contrast to the more basic motivation (hunger, thirst, love) of their associates who keep them in touch with reality, as Sancho Panza does for Don Quixote. For all that they are not frozen in their social positions. Just as the peasant girl may marry the Prince, Arlequin may outwit a fairy queen (in *Arlequin poli par l'amour*; *Robin, Bachelor of Love*), or master and servant may exchange roles to bring about a more dramatic victory of love (*Le Jeu de l'amour et du hasard*; *The Game of Love and Chance*). The sharply individualized portrayal of each character is all the more remarkable because their names and roles are adapted from the stock of the Italian Comedy, the troupe for whom he wrote most of his plays.

Marivaux is a master of language who lets everyone speak in his own particular style. Marianne's self-assured rhetoric overcomes the obstacles to her ambitions very differently than Jacob's disarming frankness. Dorante attracts Silvia by his sensitivity where Arlequin repels her with his popular mind (*The Game of Love and Chance*). Here Marivaux could have gone much further, as we can see in the battle of words between Marianne's coachman and her landlady, a washer woman (critics of the time were scandalized by this vulgarity), if the pressures of society and Marivaux's ambitions to enter the French Academy had not stood in the way. Even so, it is the variety of styles that lends dramatic perspective.

—Oscar A. Haac

MARTIAL (Marcus Valerius Martialis).   Born in Bilbilis (now Calatayud), Spain, 1 March 38-41 A.D.   Educated in Spain; in Rome in 64: client of the powerful Seneca family: honorary military tribuneship; also patronized by others; his return to Spain c. 99 was subsidized by Pliny the Younger. *Died c. 104 A.D.*

PUBLICATIONS

Verse

[*Verse*], edited by W. Heraeus, revised by J. Borovskij.   1976; also edited by Ugo Carratello, 1980; as *Epigrams*, translated by W.C.A. Ker (Loeb edition), 1919-20, revised edition, 1968; also translated by A.L. Francis and H.F. Tatum, 1924, Rolfe Humphries, 1963, R. Marcellino, 1968, James Michie, 1972, and Peter Whigham, 1983.

*

Critical Studies: "Martial and the Satiric Epigram" by C.W. Mendell, in *Classical Philology 17*, 1922; *Martial and the Modern Epigram* by Paul Nixon, 1927; *Aspects of Martial's Epigrams* by A.G. Carrington, 1960; *Epigrammaton: Martial* (introduction and commentary on book 1) by Mario Citroni, 1975; *A Commentary on Book One of the Epigrams of Martial* by Peter Howell, 1980.

*   *   *

Martial commenced writing epigrams on relatively limited themes before developing a wider range of subject-matter and techniques. Earliest was his *Liber Spectaculorum* (Book of the Spectacles), a collection of about thirty brief poems written to celebrate the opening of the Colosseum by the Emperor Titus in 80 A.D. The poems reflect the extravagance of the Games staged on that occasion, describing with wonder and enthusiastic expressions of loyalty to the Emperor the "Spectacles" provided by men and beasts.

Next to appear, in around 84 A.D., were his two books of two-line poems or mottoes ostensibly designed to accompany presents, the *Xenia* (Guest-Gifts) and *Apophoreta* (Take-Away Gifts), numbered Books 13 and 14. Martial suggests that these poems may be sent in place of gifts (13.3.5).

Then from 86 A.D. onwards appeared Martial's Books of Epigrams, at a rate of approximately one per year. Books 1-9 (86-96 A.D.) were written and published under Domitian, the last of the Flavian emperors; Books 10 and 11 (97 A.D.) were produced under the new emperor Nerva, and Martial published his last book, 12, in 101 A.D., under the Emperor Trajan, after his return to Spain in 98 A.D. Whoever the emperor, Martial's voice is full of adulation; his poetry is typical, in this respect, of the poetry of court circles at this time.

The genre of epigram was lowly and minor, proclaiming no great literary pretensions. It provided light yet cultured entertainment for wealthy gentlemen of leisure, both as audience and as poets themselves. According to the convention expressed by Martial like this—"my page is lascivious, my life without rebuke" (1.4.8)—writing epigram in no way detracted from a man's moral integrity.

Among his literary forerunners and models, Martial names Catullus (Preface to Book 1): in form, matter, and manner, Catullus's influence on Martial is obvious. Martial exhibits Catullus's range of metres in his poems: elegiacs, hendecasyllables, scazons, hexameters, and iambics. His range of subject-matter is similar too. There are poems about poetry—his own and others'—and the prose prefaces (to Books 1, 2, 8, 9 and 12) contain literary apologia and polemic. Many epigrams have as their theme decorum and moderation in social and sexual behaviour; obscenity and invective abound here. Sometimes Martial attempts longer poems on non-satiric themes—the praise of places, buildings, or works of art—highly reminiscent of Statius's occasional poetry in the *Silvae*.

Finally, and most important, Martial's manner. Martial takes over Catullus's stress on *urbanitas*: polish and sophistication in the presentation of poems. Careful structure through repetition, balance, and chiasmus are intrinsic to the epigrams of both poets. But the special and most influential feature of Martial's epigrams is "point": in his poems, the reader's enjoyment frequently resides in a final pun, surprise, antithesis, or paradox to which the entire poem has been building up. With a deft word or phrase, often rude or shocking, usually witty, Martial pulls the rug from under his victim's feet: this moment of deflation is often the only rationale for the poem. At this moment, we, the audience, experience a sense of satisfaction and a sense of complicity with the author resulting from superiority over the victim. This was probably still more vivid for Martial's original audience: it seems apparent that the Books were published for an "in-crowd" of cognoscenti who were in a position to appreciate Martial's jokes, the leading intellectuals of the day, men like Silius Italicus, Valerius Flaccus, Pliny the Younger, and Quintilian. And while it may not be to the modern taste to read a Book of Martial's epigrams from start to end, yet they are arranged so as to provide maximum possible variation, of form and content and manner: quite a tour de force in a minor and limited genre.

—S.H. Braund

MAUPASSANT, (Henri René Albert) Guy de. Born in the Château de Miromesnil, near Rouen, France, 5 August 1850. Educated at Lycée Impérial Napoléon, Paris, 1859-60; Institution Ecclesiastique, Yvetot, 1863-68; Lycée Pierre Corneille, Rouen, 1868-69; studied law, University of Paris, 1869-70. Messenger, then orderly, in the army, 1870-71. Clerk in Ministry of the Navy: in library, 1872-73, and in Department for the Colonies, 1873-77; transferred to Ministry of Education, 1878-80. Also writer, especially for *Gaulois* and *Gil-Blas* newspapers. Confined to insane asylum, Passy, 1892. *Died 6 July 1893.*

PUBLICATIONS

Collections

Oeuvres complètes.   29 vols., 1925-47.
Contes et nouvelles, edited by Albert-Marie Schmidt.   2 vols., 1956-57.
Complete Works.   9 vols., 1910.
Works.   10 vols., 1923-29.

Fiction

La Maison Tellier.   1881.
Mademoiselle Fifi.   1882.
Une Vie.   1883.
Contes de la Bécasse.   1883.
Miss Harriet.   1883.
Clair de lune.   1884.
Les Soeurs Rondoli.   1884.
Yvette.   1885.
Bel-Ami.   1885; translated as *Bel-Ami,* 1891.
Contes et nouvelles.   1885.
Contes du jour et de la nuit.   1885.
Monsieur Parent.   1885.
Toine.   1886.
La Petite Roque.   1886.
Mont-Oriol.   1887; translated as *Mont-Oriol,* 1891.
Le Horla.   1887.
Pierre et Jean.   1888; as *Pierre and Jean,* 1890.
Le Rosier de Madame Husson.   1888.
La Main gauche.   1889.
Fort comme la mort.   1889; as *Strong as Death,* 1899; as *The Master Passion,* 1958.
L'Inutile Beauté.   1890.
Notre coeur.   1890; as *Notre Coeur (The Human Heart),* 1890.
88 Short Stories.   1928.
Complete Short Stories.   3 vols., 1970.

Plays

Une Répétition.   1879.
Histoire du vieux temps (produced 1879).   In *Des vers,* 1880.
Musotte, with Jacques Normand, from a story by Maupassant (produced 1891).   In *Oeuvres complètes illustrées,* 1904.
La Paix du ménage, from his own story (produced 1893).

Verse

Des vers.   1880.

Other

Au soleil. 1884.
Sur l'eau. 1888.
La Vie errante. 1890.
Correspondance, edited by J. Suffel. 3 vols., 1973.

*

Bibliography: *Maupassant Criticism in France 1880-1940* by Artine Artinian, 1941; *Maupassant Criticism: A Centennial Bibliography 1880-1979* by Robert Willard Artinian, 1982.

Critical Studies: *Maupassant: A Biographical Study* by Ernest Bond, 1928; *Maupassant: A Lion in the Path* by Francis Steegmuller, 1949; *Maupassant the Novelist*, 1954, and *Maupassant: The Short Stories*, 1962, both by Edward D. Sullivan; *The Private Life of Guy de Maupassant* by R. de L. Kirkbridge, 1961; *The Paradox of Maupassant* by Pál Ignotus, 1967; *Illusion and Reality: A Study of the Descriptive Techniques in the Works of Maupassant* by John R. Dugan, 1973; *Maupassant* by Albert H. Wallace, 1973; *Maupassant* by Michael G. Lerner, 1975.

* * *

Maupassant's literary apprenticeship ended in 1880 with the appearance of "Boule de suif" (Ball of Fat). His literary preceptor and friend, Gustave Flaubert, rightly characterized the work as evidencing the arrival of a new master of the short story. Flaubert's death that same year firmed the young writer's resolve to be, at whatever cost, a worthy disciple of his dear friend. For about eight years Maupassant dedicated himself totally to his work, a tribute to Flaubert's influence, and also possibly because of a premonition of how especially desperate was his own race with time.

The great stream of stories, novels, travel accounts, and essays that flowed from his pen is astonishing for its high quality. The mediocre offerings, substantial in number in the vast outpouring, seem proportionately insubstantial when measured against the accomplishments, and pose no threat to the high place he occupies among 19th-century writers.

He has attracted a large and appreciative audience among general readers and critics with his highly developed powers of observation. They are a result of Flaubert's insistence that the artist observe his subject until he can distinguish in it the one feature that sets it apart from all similar subjects. Then he must represent this feature with the exact language that only it calls into use. Maupassant did not approach the latter ideal as closely as did his master, but he demonstrated the ability to penetrate the meaning of his subject by observation to a degree that few other writers have.

Maupassant had little fondness for the unaccomplished individuals who are his subjects. His popularity among this group certainly does not derive from flattering suggestions of some great redeeming virtue in their kind. The privileged class was affronted that those it scorned and cast out were the very ones Maupassant depicted in a favorable light. He is saying that real virtue is something people have; it is not something they talk about. Elizabeth Rousset (Ball of Fat), Irma (Bed 29) and Rachel (*Mademoiselle Fifi*), prostitutes to whom it would never occur to define courage, have it when it alone will serve. Maupassant was contemptuous of social institutions whose product was more often than not fruitless talk; doubtless this attitude contributes to his popular following. It offended many of his contemporaries who saw it as a narrowly unfair and prejudiced attack of the system.

Heroic efforts are monopolized by women characters in Maupassant's stories. It was evident to him that conventional morality was shaped in such a way as to suppress the female and favor the male. Hers was the social struggle that would produce the dramatic and courageous defiance that he wished to portray. With considerable understanding he depicts the situation of the unhappy and unfulfilled married woman. For her, unlike her husband, the discovery of her unhappiness means the end of the prospect that her life might have meaning; she is trapped. Defiance is the only way out. Merely the courage to defy convention is not enough in the case of Madame Roland in *Pierre et Jean*—she needs, not just a lover, but one who satisfies the ideal she had hoped to find in marriage, for the severe consequences of being found out far outweigh the temporal satisfactions of a mediocre affair. Maupassant, as in other stories, depicts the husband in such a way that the reader is rather pleased to see him cuckolded: trust in one's wife is no virtue if it is merely a manifestation of vanity. Though Maupassant more generally breaks with tradition in his depiction of adulteresses and prostitutes, occasionally he presents the conventional image of her as the corrupter of the species. In his personal life he established the reputation for being a misogynist. But the real Maupassant is to be found in his writing which treats cuckoldry as a situation which is not at all amusing.

Most of his characters are Norman peasants, Parisian bureaucrats, soldiers and sailors. All have a diminished belief in a Higher Order and in their dreams. But on their holidays and weekends they resurrect them as if reality had never marked them for death. The consequences of these momentary delusions run the gamut from the amusingly petty to the soberingly tragic. He has no favorite ending, for life has none. He merely chooses one from the possible endings that reality imposes and which he has verified by observation. The presentation of a distinct image of what he has seen with his eyes is his first purpose. If what a character does cries out for a reason hidden in his mind, then, and only then, does Maupassant entangle himself in the web of psychological speculation.

Pathological behaviour calls for psychological explanations. Maupassant wrote stories about madness with tragic authority. *Le Horla*, "Lui?" (Him?), and "Qui sait?" (Who knows?), with heroes subject to autoscopic hallucinations, pathological loneliness, and suicidal tendencies, reflect some of the pain of his own struggle with the fatal malady. The anguishing conviction that existence was pointless evidences itself progressively in his work until it becomes a crushing presence. In "La Vie errante" (The Wanderer's Life) he is continually troubling himself with the question of why mind was given dominion over its own futility, just as the hero of the masterpiece, *Pierre et Jean*, troubles himself over the absurdity of being forced to accept the unacceptable. Such, for Maupassant, was the profit of giving thought to the meaning of life. That is why he preferred to observe and present what could be seen with the eye.

—Albert H. Wallace

MAURIAC, François (Charles). Born in Bordeaux, France, 11 October 1885. Educated at Collège des Marianites, Grand-Lebrun; University of Bordeaux, licence ès lettres; École Nationale des Chartes, Paris. Served as hospital orderly in Salonika, 1916-17. Married Jeanne Lafon in 1913; two sons, including the writer Claude Mauriac, and two daughters. Free-lance writer in Paris from 1906; columnist ("Bloc-Notes"), *L'Express*, 1954-61; contributor *Figaro Littéraire*, after 1961. Recipient: Heinemann Prize, 1925; French Academy Grand Prize for Novel, 1926; Nobel Prize for Literature, 1952. D.Litt.: Oxford University. President, Société des Gens de Lettres, 1932-70. Member, French Academy, 1934; Honorary Member, American Academy. Grand Cross, Legion of Honor. *Died 1 September 1970.*

PUBLICATIONS

Collections

Oeuvres romanesques et théâtrales complètes, edited by Jacques Petit.   3 vols., 1978-81.

Fiction

L'Enfant chargé de chaînes.   1913; as *Young Man in Chains,* 1963.
La Robe prétexte.   1914; as *The Stuff of Youth,* 1960.
La Chair et le sang.   1920; as *Flesh and Blood,* 1954.
Préséances.   1921; as *Questions of Precedence,* 1958.
Le Baiser au lépreux.   1922; as *The Kiss to the Leper,* 1923.
Le Fleuve de feu.   1923; as *The River of Fire,* 1954.
Génitrix.   1923; translated as *Genetrix,* in *The Family,* 1930.
Le Désert de l'amour.   1925; as *The Desert of Love,* 1929.
Fabien.   1926.
Thérèse Desqueyroux.   1927; translated as *Thérèse,* 1928.
Le Démon de la connaissance.   1928.
Destins (includes *Coups de couteau* and *Un Homme de lettres*).   1928; as *Destinies,* 1929;
    as *Lines of Life,* 1957.
La Nuit du bourreau de soi-même.   1929.
Trois récits.   1929.
Ce qui était perdu.   1930; as *Suspicion,* 1931; as *That Which Was Lost,* with *Dark
    Angels,* 1951.
Le Noeud de vipères.   1932; as *Vipers' Tangle,* 1933; as *Knot of Vipers,* 1951.
Le Mystère Frontenac.   1933; as *The Frontenac Mystery,* 1952.
La Fin de la nuit.   1935; as *The End of the Night,* in *Therese: a Portrait in Four Parts,*
    1947.
La Mal.   1935; as *The Enemy,* with *The Desert of Love,* 1949.
Les Anges noirs.   1936; as *The Dark Angels,* with *That Which Was Lost,* 1951; as *The
    Mask of Innocence,* 1953.
Plongées.   1938.
Les Chemins de la mer.   1939; as *The Unknown Sea,* 1948.
La Pharisienne.   1941; as *A Woman of the Pharisees,* 1946.
Therese: A Portrait in Four Parts.   1947.
Le Sagouin.   1951; as *The Little Misery,* 1952.
Galigaï.   1952; as *The Loved and the Unloved,* 1952.
L'Agneau.   1954; as *The Lamb,* 1955.
A Mauriac Reader, edited by Wallace Fowlie.   1968.
Un Adolescent d'autrefois.   1969; as *Maltaverne,* 1970.

Plays

Asmodée (produced 1937).   1938; as *Asmodee; or, The Intruder,* 1939.
Les Mal-aimés (produced 1945).   1945.
Passage du Malin (produced 1947).   1948.
Le Feu sur la terre (produced 1950).   1951.
Le Pain vivant.   1955.

Screenplay: *Thérèse,* with Claude Mauriac and Georges Franju, 1963.

Verse

Les Mains jointes. 1909.
L'Adieu à l'adolescence. 1911.
Orages. 1925; revised edition, 1949.
Le Sang d'Atys. 1940.

Other

De quelques coeurs inquiets: Petits essais de psychologie religieuse. 1920.
La Vie et la mort d'un poète (on André Lafon). 1924.
Le jeune homme. 1926.
Le Tourment de Jacques Rivière. 1926.
Les beaux esprits de ce temps. 1926.
Proust. 1926.
La Province. 1926.
Bordeaux. 1926.
Le Rencontre avec Pascal. 1926.
Conscience, instinct divin. 1927.
Dramaturges. 1928.
Supplément au Traité de la concupiscence de Bossuet. 1928.
Divigations sur Saint-Sulpice. 1928.
La Vie de Jean Racine. 1928.
Le Roman. 1928.
Voltaire contre Pascal. 1929.
Dieu et Mammon. 1929; as *God and Mammon,* 1936.
Mes plus lointains souvenirs. 1929.
Paroles en Espagne. 1930.
Trois grands hommes devant Dieu. 1930.
L'Affaire Favre-Bulle. 1931.
Blaise Pascal et sa soeur Jacqueline. 1931.
Le Jeudi saint. 1931; as *Maundy Thursday,* 1932; as *The Eucharist: The Mystery of Holy Thursday,* 1944.
Souffrances et bonheur du chrétien. 1931; as *Anguish and Joy of the Christian Life,* 1964.
René Bazin. 1931.
Pèlerins. 1932; as *Pèlerins de Lourdes,* 1933.
Commencements d'une vie. 1932.
Le Drôle (juvenile). 1933; as *The Holy Terror,* 1964.
Le Romancier et ses personnages. 1933; reprinted in part as *L'Education des filles,* 1936.
Journal. 5 vols., 1934-53.
Vie de Jésus. 1936; as *Life of Jesus,* 1937.
Les Maisons fugitives. 1939.
Le Cahier noir. 1943; as *The Black Note-book,* 1944.
La Nation française a une âme. 1943.
Ne pas se renier.... 1944.
Sainte Marguerite de Cortone. 1945; as *Saint Margaret of Cortona,* 1948.
La Rencontre avec Barrès. 1945.
Le Bâillon dénoué, après quatre ans de silence. 1945.
Du côté de chez Proust. 1947; as *Proust's Way,* 1950.
Mes grands hommes. 1949; as *Men I Hold Great,* 1951; as *Great Men,* 1952.
Terres franciscaines. 1950.
Oeuvres complètes. 12 vols., 1950-56.

La Pierre d'achoppement. 1951; as *The Stumbling Block,* 1952.
La Mort d'André Gide. 1952.
Lettres ouvertes. 1952; as *Letters on Art and Life,* 1953.
Écrits intimes. 1953.
Paroles catholiques. 1954; as *Words of Faith,* 1955.
Bloc-Notes 1952-1967. 5 vols., 1958-71.
Trois écrivains devant Lourdes, with others. 1958.
Le Fils de l'homme. 1958; as *The Son of Man,* 1958.
Mémoires intérieures. 1959; translated as *Mémoires Intérieures,* 1960.
Rapport sur les prix de vertu. 1960.
Second Thoughts: Reflections on Literature and Life. 1961.
Ce que je crois. 1962; as *What I Believe,* 1963.
Cain, Where Is Your Brother? 1962.
De Gaulle. 1964; translated as *De Gaulle,* 1966.
Nouveaux mémoires intérieures. 1965; as *The Inner Presence: Recollections of My Spiritual Life,* 1968.
D'autres et moi. 1966.
Mémoires politiques. 1967.
Correspondance 1912-1950, with André Gide, edited by Jacqueline Morton. 1971.
Laçordaire, edited by Keith Goesch. 1976.
Correspondance 1916-1942, with Jacques-Émile Blanche, edited by Georges-Paul Collet. 1976.
Mauriac avant Mauriac (early writings), edited by Jean Touzot. 1977.
Chroniques du Journal de Clichy, with Paul Claudel (includes Claudel-Fontaine correspondence), edited by François Morlot and Jean Touzot. 1978.
Lettres d'une vie (1904-1969), edited by Caroline Mauriac. 1981.

Editor, *Les Pages immortelles de Pascal.* 1940; as *Living Thoughts of Pascal,* 1940.
Editor, with Louise de Vilmorin, *Almanach des Lettres 1949.* 1949.

*

Bibliography: *Mauriac: Essai de bibliographie chronologique 1908-1960* by Keith Goesch, 1965.

Critical Studies: *Mauriac* by Elsie Pell, 1947; *Mauriac* by Martin Jarret-Kerr, 1954; *Faith and Fiction: Creative Process in Greene and Mauriac* by Philip Stratford, 1964; *Mauriac* by Cecil Jenkins, 1965; *Mauriac* edited by A.M. Caspary, 1968; *A Critical Commentary on Mauriac's "Le Noeud de vipères,"* 1969, and *Intention and Achievement: An Essay on the Novels of Mauriac,* 1969, both by John Flower; *Mauriac: A Study of the Writer and the Man* by Robert Speaight, 1976; *Mauriac: The Politics of a Novelist* by Malcolm Scott, 1980.

*   *   *

Saurai-je jamais rien dire des êtres ruisselants de vertu et qui ont le coeur sur la main? Les "coeurs sur la main" n'ont pas d'histoire; mais je connais celle des coeurs enfouis et tout mêlés à un corps de boue.

(Will I ever have anything to say about the virtuous and open-hearted? The open-hearted have no story. But those whose hearts are buried deep, and mingle with the vile flesh, their story I know.)

—*Thérèse Desqueyroux*

François Mauriac writes as a moralist and a Roman Catholic, the essence of whose Catholicism lies in a sense of sin. Avarice and greed, selfishness and self-congratulation, sham piety and canting respectability are the very stuff of his novels. His characters are extreme, in the grip of powerful passions. Each craves an absolute, each fashions a "religion" after his own heart—be it mysticism, sensuality, or veneration for the land and the accumulation of property.

At the centre of Mauriac's novels is the family: a sacrosanct institution which seals itself in with prejudice, casts out justice and humanity, and imprisons the indivvidual. The family ordains marriage and values procreation for the sake of inheritance, alone, and the preservation of its name: Thérèse Desqueyroux marries into a family who revere her as "a sacred vessel, the receptacle of their progeny." The majority of Mauriac's characters are so engulfed in materialism that they go through life like sleep-walkers—neither seeing, hearing, thinking, nor understanding. Lacking the ability to "go beyond themselves" in empathy or love for another human being, they are unreceptive to suffering and, therefore, hopeless of salvation.

Mauriac sees no easy way to atonement. Mere confession may not buy it, nor may mystical exaltation, tainted—as Pierre Gornac's in *Destins*—with a blind and selfish pride. Only where a human being plumbs the depths of humiliation and despair does Mauriac offer us a glimmer of hope. Solitude and emotional asphyxiation drive Thérèse Desqueyroux to commit a monstrous crime—the attempted poisoning of her husband; and yet, Thérèse, of all his many sinners, Mauriac portrays with great compassion, creating in her one of his most powerful and sympathetic figures.

Mauriac's sympathy clearly lies with his victims and his lovers. And yet the problem of sin and atonement remains a complex and ambivalent one. Had Robert Lagave in *Destins* lived, could his "simple love" have saved him from degeneracy? Should one see in his horrific death an atonement for sins committed in this life? Elisabeth Gornac wakes from moral stupour to catch a glimpse of the eternal in human love; for the first time she truly "sees" another human face. And yet she can never rise above a love of the senses, but slips back into the sluggish current of "death-in-life."

The very heat and torpor of Mauriac's Landes evoke the aridity of human passion; the fire ever threatening to consume the pines symbolises its destructiveness. Mauriac's characters are isolated, without grace, in a desert as bleak as the wind-blown dunes and marshes which stretch endlessly to the sea. Theirs is a world governed by fatality—for Mauriac is both playwright and *dramatic* novelist. Robert Lagave is doomed to debauchery by his physical beauty; lack of maternal affection drives Pierre Gornac towards a warped mysticism; Thérèse is drawn into her crime almost unconsciously—like a sleep-walker.

These psychological dramas have an extraordinary intensity, and an economy and vigour of style—the style of the dramatist. In this lies Mauriac's striking originality as a novelist, as in his powerful evocation of the landscape of his native Landes, which goes beyond realistic description to become symbol.

—Ruth Sharman

MAYAKOVSKY, Vladimir (Vladimirovich). Born in Bagdadi, now Mayakovsky, 7 July 1893. Educated at gymnasium, Kutais, 1902-06; school in Moscow, 1906-08; Stroganov School of Industrial Arts, Moscow, 1908-09; Moscow Institute of Painting and Sculpture and Architecture, 1911-14. Political activities led to his being jailed, 1909-10; in Futurists circle after 1912; Editor, *Seized* and *New Satyricon*, Petrograd; served in the army, 1917; reader at Poets Cafe, Moscow, 1918; Editor, *Futurist Gazette*, 1918; film actor and writer; associated with the magazine *Art of the Commune*, 1918-19, and *Art*, Petrograd; designed posters and wrote short propaganda plays and texts for Russian Telegraph Agency (Rosta), Moscow, 1919-21; co-founder, with Osip Brik, *Lef*, 1923-25, and *New Lef*, 1927-28. *Died (suicide) 14 April 1930.*

PUBLICATIONS

Collections

Polnoye sobraniye sochineniy, edited by V.A. Katanyan.   13 vols., 1955-61.

Verse

Oblako v shtamakh [The Cloud in Trousers].   1915; revised edition, 1918.
Fleyta pozvonochnik [The Backbone Flute].   1916.
Prostoye kak mychanie[Simple as Mooing].   1916.
Voyna i mir [War and the Universe].   1916.
Vse sochinennoye Vladimirom Mayakovskim [Everything Written by Vladimir Mayakov-sky].   1919.
150,000,000.   1921.
Pro eto [About This].   1923.
Lirika [Lyrics].   1923.
Vladimir Ilich Lenin.   1924.
Khorosho! [Good!].   1927.
Mayakovsky and His Poetry, edited by Herbert Marshall.   1942; revised edition, 1945, 1955.
(Selections), edited by Herbert Marshall.   1965.
Wi the Haill Voice (in Scots), translated by Edwin Morgan.   1972.
Poems, translated by Dorian Rottenberg.   1972.

Plays

Vladimir Mayakovsky (produced 1913).   1914; translated as *Vladimir Mayakovsky: A Tragedy*, in *Complete Plays*, 1968.
Misteriya-Buff (produced 1918; revised version, produced 1921).   1919; as *Mystery-Bouffe*, in *Complete Plays*, 1968.
Klop (produced 1929).   1929; as *The Bedbug*, 1960.
Banya (produced 1930).   1930; as *The Bathhouse*, in *Complete Plays*, 1968.
Complete Plays.   1968.

Other

Ya: Futur-almanakh vselenskoy samosti [Me: Futuro-Miscellany of Universal Selfhood].   1913.
Sobraniye sochineniy.   4 vols., 1925.
Moye otkrytiye Ameriki [My Discovery of America].   1926.
Kino.   1937.
Pis'ma [Letters], edited by Lili Brik.   1956.
The Bedbug and Selected Poetry, edited by P. Blake.   1960.
How Are Verses Made?   1970.
Essays on Paris.   1975.

*

MAYAKOVSKY

Critical Studies: *The Symbolic System of Mayakovsky* by Lawrence Leo Stahlberger, 1964;
The Life of Mayakovsky by Wiktor Woroszylski, 1971; *Mayakovsky and His Circle* by Viktor
Shklovsky, 1972; *Mayakovsky, A Poet in the Revolution* by Edward J. Brown, 1973; *I Love:
The Story of Mayakovsky and Lili Brik* by Ann and Samuel Charters, 1979; *Mayakovsky: A
Tragedy* by A.D.P. Briggs, 1979.

*   *   *

Everything in Vladimir Mayakovsky evokes either admiration or indignation: his appearance, his behaviour, his poetry. He began as a subverter of authority in life and in literature. As
a futurist he revolted against all established artistic practice. The titles of many of his works
reveal his individualistic self-assertion: from "I" (1913) and "I and Napoleon" (1913) to the very
last unfinished poem "At the Top of My Voice" (1930). Outrageous metaphors, eccentric
rhymes, rough-textured phonetics, broken sentences, and heavy inversions are the mark of his
poetic style. He expressed the essence of futuristic poetics when he said: "The word, its outline,
its phonetic property, myth, symbol are the concept of poetry." He emphasised "the word as
such" by graphic, grammatical, and rhythmical means while creating myth out of his own "I."
His whole poetry can be viewed as a huge metaphor of himself. "The poet himself is the theme of
his poetry," said Pasternak about the tragedy *Vladimir Mayakovsky*. He also entertained the
futurist's cult of big industrial cities. He said: "The city must take the place of nature." He never
was too tired to militate against all established habits of living, feeling, and thinking that is
called "byt"—a short untranslatable Russian word. Cases are two of his best long poems
Oblako v shtamakh and *Pro eto*.

Mayakovsky is often seen as a revolutionary par excellence for his innovation in poetic
language and for subordinating his talent to the "social command." "To accept or not to accept
[the Revolution]—for me is no question. It is my Revolution," stated Mayakovsky in 1917. To
be accepted himself took a little longer. After the revolution his great ambition was to become a
poet of the masses. He considerably changed his poetic manner by introducing ordinary speech,
street slang, and political slogans. But he was never able to avoid wild, emotional diction or to
resist clashing the sublime with the ridiculous in his attempt to create "a poetry for all." His
poetry remains too intricate for the masses to understand. He complained: "I must confess with
some pain, that even advanced revolutionary comrades, even they...showered us with bewildered questions: 'But what the devil is this?' 'Please explain!' " Being his own most severe
censor, he "democratized" his style even further in two of his most inferior poems, *V.I. Lenin*
and *Khorosho*. But they help to set up Lenin as a "mythical hero." In order to strengthen the
new revolutionary art he founded the highly controversial journal *Lef* (Left Front), loudly
declaring its communist and anti-aesthetic intent. Mayakovsky had always been a kind of
"anti-poet"; now with *Lef* he declared a war against poetry. The tragic end was inevitable.
Marina Tsvetaeva explained his suicide as his last revolutionary act: "For twelve years on end
Mayakovsky the man killed in himself Mayakovsky the poet, in the 13th the poet arose and
killed the man."

Mayakovsky's "I" dominates over all his principal themes: Love, God, Art, and Revolution.
He demanded the impossible from these. He has "blasphemed and screamed that there is no
God" in order to take His place. He assigned his art to serve the Revolution by "stepping on the
throat of his own song." Disillusioned with its outcome he called for "the third Revolution of
spirit." Many times a rejected lover, he shouted out in every direction and blamed God and
"byt" for love's madness and pain. This "man from the future" projected a huge image of
himself in his writing: "From the tail of the years I must resemble a long-tailed monster." He
strikes us, however, as a sad and lonely figure: "I am lonely as the last eye left to a man on his
way to join the blind." "He inflated his talent and tortured it until it burst," wrote Isaiah Berlin.
His art was forcibly propagated "like potatoes in the reign of Catherine the Great" after Stalin's
pronouncement in 1935: "Mayakovsky was and remains the most talented poet of our Soviet
epoch. Indifference to his memory and words is a crime." As Pasternak remarked: "That was
his second death."

—Valentina Polukhina

MENANDER. Born of an Athenian family, c. 342-41 B.C. Studied with the philosopher Theophrastus, and associated with Demetrius of Phalerum. First play to be produced was *Orge* [Anger], 321; won eight prizes; titles of more than 100 of his plays are known, though some might be alternative titles. *Died 293-289 B.C.*

PUBLICATIONS

Collections

[*Plays*], edited by F.H. Sandbach. 1972, revised edition, 1976; also edited by W.G. Arnott (includes translations), 1979— ; as *Plays and Fragments*, translated by Philip Vellacott, 1967; also translated, as *The Plays*, by Lionel Casson, 1971.

Plays

Dyskolos (produced 317). Edited by Eric W. Handley, 1965; also edited by H. Lloyd-Jones, 1960, revised edition, 1970, J.M. Jacques, 1963, and Warren B. Blake (includes translation), 1966; as *Dyskolos*, translated by W.G. Arnott, 1960; as *The Cross Old Devil*, translated by H.C. Fay, in *Three Classical Comedies*, 1967; as *The Grouch*, in *The Plays*, 1971.
Perikeiromene (produced c. 310). As *The Rape of the Locks*, translated by Gilbert Murray, 1942; as *She Who Was Shorn*, in *The Plays*, 1971.
Samia (produced 308). Edited by Colin Austin, 1969, and David M. Bain, 1983; as *The Samia*, translated by J.M. Edmonds, 1951; as *The Woman of Samos*, in *The Plays*, 1971; as *The Girl from Samos*, translated by Eric G. Turner, 1972.
Epitrepontes, edited by Ulrich von Wilamowitz-Moellendorf. 1925; as *The Arbitration*, translated by Gilbert Murray, 1945.
Aspis, edited by Colin Austin. 1969; as *The Shield*, in *The Plays*, 1971.
Sikyonios [The Man from Sicyon], edited by R. Kassel. 1965.

*

Critical Studies: *Studies in Menander*, 1950, revised edition, 1960, and *An Introduction to Menander*, 1974, both by T.B.L. Webster; *Menander and Plautus: A Study in Comparison* by Eric W. Handley, 1968; *Menander, Plautus, and Terence* by W.G. Arnott, 1968; *Menander: A Commentary* by F.H. Sandbach and Arnold W. Gomme, 1973; *Tragic Patterns in Menander* by A.G. Katsouris, 1975; *Menander and the Monologue* by John Blundell, 1980; *The Making of Menander's Comedy* by Sander M. Goldberg, 1980.

*   *   *

Until recently, the greatest writer of Greek New Comedy was little more than a name to us. Ancient critics had ranked Menander with Homer and found him vastly superior to Aristophanes, but a combination of changing tastes and bad luck conspired against him. Menander lost his readership in late antiquity. Without readers, his plays were neglected, and the old books eventually perished. Little remained for us save short quotations by other authors, a collection of epigrams (many of dubious authenticity), and Latin adaptations of his plays by Plautus and Terence. In 1905, however, excavators in Egypt discovered a papyrus book from the 5th century A.D. that contained large fragments of five plays, and since 1959 much further material has come to light on papyri. We now possess one play complete (*The Grouch*), one that is almost complete (*The Woman of Samos*), and substantial portions of several more. The literary appraisal of these discoveries has only just begun, but several things are rapidly becoming clear.

Though the Roman poet Ovid once claimed that there was no play of Menander without "pleasant love" (*iucundus amor*), we now see just how limited that truth is and how deliberately unfaithful were the Roman copies. All the plays do in fact have a clear romantic component, but it is rarely the true focus of the dramatist's interest. *The Woman of Samos* concentrates on the fragility of trust between a father and son, *She Who Was Shorn* on a soldier's difficulty in adjusting to civilian society. *The Arbitration* explores the foolishness and vanity of moral pretensions. Even *The Grouch*, with a plot that probably comes closest to the romantic stereotype, derives its point not from its rather foolish Lothario, but from the dilemma of an old misanthrope forced to confront his social responsibilities. Menander treats these characters with an amused and affectionate sympathy that displays not only their foibles and frailties, but also the means for their improvement. He regularly uses a divine expository prologue—the device was perhaps learned from Euripides—to tell the audience more than the characters know and to hint at divine order behind the human confusion. The audience develops true interest in the characters and comes away with a sense of good lessons well learned.

Considerable technical skill underlies the plays. Menander's iambic and trochaic verse patterns capture the freshness of colloquial speech without undue stylization. Characters regularly develop individual speech mannerisms to help create unique characterizations. Plots are carefully built around a five-act structure marked by unrelated choral interludes (labeled simply "choral song" in our manuscripts) to pace the action. They are not, however, unnecessarily complicated. Exits and entrances are carefully orchestrated, but there are no true double plots or any elaborate use of stage properties, contrived coincidence, or convoluted intrigues. The ubiquitous birth tokens are only the exception that proves the rule. The plays' richness comes more from their skillful depiction of common dilemmas than from elaborate stage action. "Menander and Life," wondered an ancient critic, "which of you really imitated which?" It is a fair question, and not easily answered.

—Sander M. Goldberg

MEUNG, Jean de. *See* **ROSE, Romance of the.**

MICKIEWICZ, Adam (Bernard). Born in Zoasie, near Nowogródek, Lithuania, 24 December 1798. Educated at a secondary school in Nowogródek, graduated 1815; University of Vilna, 1815-19. Married Celina Szymanowska; two sons and two daughters. Teacher at a gymnasium, Kovno, 1819-23; arrested for anti-Russian activities, 1823: exiled to Russia and lived in St. Petersburg, Moscow, and the Crimea, 1824-29; travelled in Europe, 1829-32; settled in Paris, 1832; Editor, *The Pilgrim*, 1833; Professor of Latin, University of Lausanne, 1839-40; Professor of Slavonic Languages and Literatures, Collège de France, Paris, 1840-44; attempted to raise a Polish military unit, 1848; Editor, *La Tribune des peuples*, Paris, 1849; Librarian, Arsenal Library, Paris, 1852; died in Constantinople attempting to help Poles in Crimean War. *Died 26 November 1855.*

PUBLICATIONS

Collections

Dziela (includes letters), edited by Leon Ploszewski. 16 vols., 1948-55.

Fiction

Konrad Wallenrod. 1828; translated as *Konrad Wallenrod*, 1841.

Play

Dziady. 2 vols., 1823-32; as *Forefathers' Eve*, edited by G.R. Noyes, 1925; as *Forefathers* in *Poems*, 1944.

Verse

Poezye 1-2 [Poetry]. 2 vols., 1822-23.
Sonety [Sonnets]. 1826.
Sonety krymskie. 1826; as *Sonnets from Crimea*, 1917.
Pan Tadeusz. 1834; as *Master Thaddeus; or, The Last Foray in Lithuania*, edited by M.A. Biggs and E.S. Naganowski, 2 vols., 1885; translated as *Pan Tadeusz*, 1917 (prose) and 1962 (verse); selection, as *The Forests of Lithuania*, translated by Donald Davie, 1959.
Mickiewicz: The National Poet of Poland (selections). 1911.
The Lilies, Twardowski's Wife, and Religious Poems. 1938.
Poems, edited by G.R. Noyes. 1944.
Mickiewicz in Music; Twenty Five Songs to Poems of Mickiewicz, edited by A. and M. Coleman. 1947.
Selected Poems and *New Selected Poems*, edited by Clark Mills. 2 vols., 1956-57.
Poems, edited by Jack Lindsay. 1957.

Other

Ksiegi narodu i pielgrzymstwa polskiego. 1832.
L'Église officielle et le Messianisme, L'Église et le Messie (lectures). 1845.
Konrad Wallenrod and Other Writings, edited by G.R. Noyes. 1925.
Selected Poetry and Prose, edited by Stanislaw Helsztynski. 1955.

Translator, *Giaour*, by Byron. 1833.

*

Bibliography: *Mickiewicz: His Life and Work in Documents, Portraits, and Illustrations* by Marie Kapuścieńska and Wanda Markowska, 1956; *Bibliografia utworów: Adama Mickiewicza* by Aleksander Semkowicz, 1958.

Critical Studies: *Mickiewicz, Poet of Poland: A Symposium* edited by Manfred Kridl, 1951; *The Poetry of Mickiewicz* by Wiktor Weintraub, 1954; *Mickiewicz 1798-1855: In Commemoration of the Centenary of His Death*, 1955; *Mickiewicz in World Literature: A Symposium* edited by Waclaw Lednicki, 1956; *Young Mickiewicz* by Marion Moore Coleman, 1956; *Literature as Prophecy: Scholarship and Martinist Poetics in Mickiewicz' Parisian Lectures* by Wiktor Weintraub, 1959; *Mickiewicz* by David Welsh, 1966.

*   *   *

Few writers have had quite the impact on their own nation as Adam Mickiewicz. Hailed after the publication of his first volume of verse in 1822 as an innovator, Mickiewicz continually surprised his readers with experiments and changes in form and content, much like Chopin, his contemporary, in another medium. Mickiewicz's legacy is not merely represented by an "oeuvre complete"—it must also include what may be termed his contribution to a nation's mentality: the association of historical past to prophetic future, patriotic cause to spiritual aspiration, and national to personal despair.

That first collection of poems, based on peasant song and local legend, is indebted to the precedents and theories of German Romanticism, and emphasizes emotionality and authenticity. Mickiewicz's next artistic success was more formal and conventional, with two sets of sonnets. One entitled simply *Sonety*, deals with lovers' emotional games, the ennuis of the fashionable salons, and impressions of nature. The other set, *Sonnets from Crimea*, are Mickiewicz's finest poetic achievement. They are intricate and delicate as miniatures; the language is inventive and captivating, and the style exotic, all intensified by the sonnet form. Mickiewicz the poet-pilgrim travels through a landscape that is wild, rich, and mystical, and momentarily finds himself a home. Yet his sense of nationality overpowers him as he ponders his isolation, and the Oriental environment only exaggerates his contradictory feelings of impotence, commitment, and spirituality.

The *Dziady (Forefathers' Eve)* series of dramatized poems, completed by 1832, and inspired by the very real but very unsuccessful November Uprising of 1830, blends history and soteriology, student plots and superstition, horror and comedy. It is a vital stage of Mickiewicz's self-revelatory voyage through the Polish national consciousness, and is still the most formative and informative source of a national historiosophy (Polish Messianism) ever written, influencing all generations that followed. Konrad, the hero of the crucial third part of *Dziady* (*Cześć III*) is portrayed as the poet-battleground for the opposing forces of Good (Poland/Catholicism) and Evil (the Tsar/Lucifer/Russia). Improvisation, ritual, visions, and historical events merge as Lucifer's Russian lackeys contrive the downfall and possession of Konrad. Exorcized of these forces, Konrad as the horseman of apocalyptic national liberation goes forth for the cause. The sequel showing how this liberation would come about was never written, but the result was that Mickiewicz had created a new stereotype: a nationalized poet with Catholicized patriotism instilled.

Pan Tadeusz, written not long after *Dziady*, seems different yet again. Mickiewicz's last significant work, it is an "autobiographical" epic poem recounting the euphoria of his adolescence, when in 1811-12 Napoleon's troops liberated Poland and Lithuania en route to Moscow. Superficially a superior satire on the life-style of the Lithuanian gentry, *Pan Tadeusz* is also a subtle compilation of most of the themes in previous works in an idealized setting. Here the "old country's" virtues and vices are paraded, highlighting the xenophobic, anarchistic attitudes that led to the Partitions of 1795, remaining at the same time a sentimental portrayal of the characters concerned. The poem charts how the bumbling gentry replaces personal concerns with national cause, and selfishness for self-sacrifice. This Catholic morality is the real tenor of the work: the blinding faith exemplified by the saint-hero in monk's clothing, Jacek Soplica (expiating before God and Country his youthful treason), is matched by the patriotic fervour of his son Tadeusz (thus abandoning the delights of adolescent innocence). As Mickiewicz bitterly admitted in his Epilogue to the work, such zeal led nowhere. In recounting his vision of the past and its Truth, the historical detail and depiction of traditional social graces alone make *Pan Tadeusz* a masterpiece. Like *Dziady* it was read by a nation in geographical exile as a true picture of its origins and aspirations, a Messianic Covenant of national identity.

Mickiewicz wrote through the prism of his own experiences. His poetic output reflects the changes in and around him, in his culture and his fellow Poles, but does not reflect the enormous contribution Mickiewicz made to that nation and its people.

—Donald Peter Alexander Pirie

MISHIMA Yukio. Pseudonym for Hiraoka Kimitake. Born in Tokyo, 14 January 1925. Educated at Peers School and College, graduated 1944; Tokyo University, degree in jurisprudence 1947. Married Sugiyama Yoko in 1958; one daughter and one son. Civil servant, Finance Ministry, 1948; then free-lance writer; also film director, designer, and stage producer and actor. Recipient: Shincho prize, 1954; Kishida Drama Prize, 1955; Yomiuri prize, 1957, 1961; Mainichi Prize, 1965. *Died 25 November 1970.*

PUBLICATIONS

Collections

 Zenshu [Collected Works], edited by Shoichi Saeki and Donald Keene, 36 vols., 1973-76.

Fiction

 Hanazakari no mori [The Forest in Full Bloom]. 1944.
 Misaki nite no monogatari [Tales at a Promontory]. 1947.
 Yoru no Shitaku [Preparations for the Night]. 1948.
 Tozoku [Thieves]. 1948.
 Shishi [Lion]. 1948.
 Kamen no Kokuhaku. 1949; as *Confessions of a Mask*, 1958.
 Hoseki Baibai [Precious-Stone Broker]. 1949.
 Magun no tsuka [Passing of a Host of Devils]. 1949.
 Ai no kawaki. 1950; as *Thirst for Love*, 1969.
 Kaibutsu [Monster]. 1950.
 Janpaku no Yoru [Snow-White Nights]. 1950.
 Ao no jidai [The Blue Period]. 1950.
 Kinjiki; Higyo. 2 vols., 1951-53; as *Forbidden Colours*, 1968.
 Natsuko no boken [Natsuko's Adventures]. 1951.
 Manatsu no shi [Death in Midsummer]. 1953.
 Nipponsei [Made in Japan]. 1953.
 Shiosai. 1954; as *The Sound of Waves*, 1956.

Shizumeru taki [The Sunken Waterfall]. 1955.
Kinkakuji. 1956; as *The Temple of the Golden Pavilion*, 1959.
Kofuku go shuppan. 1956.
Bitoku no yorimeki [The Tottering Virtue]. 1957.
Hashizukushi [A List of Bridges]. 1958.
Kyoko no Ie [Kyoko's House]. 1959.
Utage no ato. 1960; as *After the Banquet*, 1963.
Suta [Movie Star]. 1961.
Nagasugita haru [Too Long a String]. 1961.
Utsukushi hoshi [Beautiful Star]. 1962.
Gogo no eilo. 1963; as *The Sailor Who Fell from Grace with the Sea*, 1965.
Ken [The Sword]. 1963.
Nikutai no gakko [The School of Flesh]. 1964.
Kinu to meisatsu [Silk and Insight]. 1964.
Han-teijo Daigaku [College of Unchasteness]. 1966.
Eirei no Koe [Voices of the Spirits of the War Dead]. 1966.
Death in Midsummer and Other Stories. 1966.
Fukuzatsuma Kare [A Complicated Man]. 1966.
Yakaifuku [Evening Dress]. 1967.
Taiyo to tetsu. 1968; as *Sun and Steel*, 1970.
Hojo no umi; as *The Sea of Fertility*:
    1. *Haru no yuki.* 1969; as *Spring Snow*, 1972.
    2. *Homba.* 1969; as *Runaway Horses*, 1973.
    3. *Akatsuki no tera.* 1970; as *The Temple of Dawn*, 1973.
    4. *Tennin josui.* 1971; as *The Decay of the Angel*, 1974.
Kemono no tawamure [The Play of Beasts]. 1971.

Plays

Kataku [Burning Houses] (produced 1949). In *Ningen* (magazine), 1948.
Todai [Lighthouse] (produced 1950). 1950.
Kantan (produced 1950). In *Kindai Nogakushu*, 1956; translated as *Kantan*, in *Five Modern No Plays*, 1957.
Seijo [Saintess]. 1951.
Aya no tsuzumi (produced 1952). 1953; as *The Damask Drum*, in *Five Modern No Plays*, 1957.
Sotoba komachi (produced 1952). In *Kindai Nogakushu*, 1956; translated as *Sotoba komachi*, in *Five Modern No Plays*, 1957.
Yoru no himawari (produced 1953). 1953; as *Twilight Sunflower*, 1958.
Wakodo yo yomigaere [Young Man Back to Life] (produced 1955). 1954.
Aoi no ue (produced 1955). In *Kindai Nogakushu*, 1956; as *The Lady Aoi*, in *Five Modern No Plays*, 1957.
Shiroari no su [Nest of White Ants] (produced 1955). 1956.
Fuyo no Tsuyu Ouchi Jikki [True History of the House of Ouchi] (produced 1955).
Kindai Nogakushu. 1956; as *Five Modern No Plays*, 1957.
Yuya (produced 1957). In *Kindai Nogakushu*, 1956.
Rokumeikan [Rokumei Mansion] (produced 1956). 1957.
Hanjo (produced 1957); translated as *Hanjo*, in *Five Modern No Plays*, 1957.
Bara to kaizoku [Rose and Pirates] (produced 1958). 1958.
Nettaiju (produced 1961); in *Koe* (magazine), 1960; as *Tropical Tree*, in *Japanese Quarterly 11*, 1964.
Toka no kiku [Late Flowering Chrysanthemum] (produced 1961).
Kurotokage [Black Lizard], from a story by Edogawa Rampo (produced 1962).
Gikyoku zenshu [Collected Plays]. 1962.

Yorokobo no Koto [Koto of Rejoicing] (produced 1964).
Sado koshaku fujin (produced 1965). 1965; as *Madame de Sade*, 1967.
Suzaku-ke no Metsubo [Downfall of the Suzaku Family] (produced 1967). 1967.
Waga tomo Hitler [My Friend Hitler] (produced 1968). 1968.
Raio no Terasu [Terrace of the Leper King] (produced 1969). 1969.
Chinsetsu yumiharizuki [The Strange Story of Tametomo] (produced 1969). 1969.

Screenplays: *Yukoku* [Patriotism], 1965.

Other

Kari to emono [The Hunter and His Prey]. 1951.
Aporo no sakazuki [Cup of Apollo]. 1952.
Sakuhin-shu [Works]. 6 vols., 1953-54.
Koi no miyako [City of Love]. 1954.
Megami [Goddess]. 1955.
Seishun o do ikiru ka [How To Live as a Young Man]. 1955.
Senshu [Selected Works]. 19 vols., 1957-59.
Gendai shosetsu wa koten tari-uru ka [Can a Modern Novel Be a "Classic"?]. 1957.
Fudotoku kyoiku koza [Lectures on Immoralities]. 1959.
Hayashi Fusao Ron [Study of Hayashi Fusao]. 1963.
Watashi no Henreki Jidai [My Wandering Years]. 1964.
Tampen zenshu [Short Pieces]. 1964.
Mikuma no Mode [Pilgrimage to the Three Kumano Shrine]. 1965.
Hyoron zenshu [Collected Essays]. 1966.
Hagakure nyumon. 1967; as *The Way of the Samurai: Mishima on Hagakure in Modern Life*, 1977.
Taido. 1967; as *Young Samurai*, 1967.
Taidan, ningen to bungaku, with Mitsuo Nakamura. 1968.
Wakaki samurai no tame ni [Spiritual Lectures for the Young Samurai]. 1968.
Bunka boeiron [Defense of Culture]. 1969.
Yukoku no genri [The Theory of Patriotism]. 1970.
Sakkaron [Essays on Writers]. 1970.
Gensen no kanjo [The Deepest Feelings]. 1970.
Kodogaku nyumon [An Introduction to Action Philosophy]. 1970.
Shobu no kororo [Heart of Militarism]. 1970.
Waga shishunki [My Adolescence]. 1973.

Editor, *Rokusei nakamura utaemon.* 1959.
Editor, with Geoffrey Bownas, *New Writing in Japan.* 1972.

*

Critical Studies: *Mishima: A Biography* by John Nathan, 1974; *The Life and Death of Mishima* by Henry Scott-Stokes, 1974; *Accomplices of Silence: The Modern Japanese Novel* by Masao Miyoshi, 1974; *The Moon in the Water: Understanding Tanizaki, Kawabata, and Mishima* by Gwenn Boardman Petersen, 1979.

*   *   *

The brilliant literary career of Mishima was cut short by his own hands on 25 November 1970. He killed himself in a traditional "samurai" style within the compounds of the Ground Self-Defense Force (Ichigaya, Tokyo). He planned a military *coup d'état*, and put it into practice; it turned out, of course, to be a total failure. We cannot be sure how seriously devoted he was to this fantastic scheme, and it might be surmised that he had been carried away by his literary imagination and driven to realize his imaginary vision in action.

Mishima made a dazzling literary debut as a teenage prodigy. His first book, *Hanazakari no mori*, was published in 1944, when the Pacific War was approaching its dismal close. It was a genuine tour de force, in its rich evocativeness, and clever—too clever for the 19-year-old author—pastiche of decorative classical prose. Even fastidious critics could not help admiring Mishima's extraordinary talent, but the book was just too romantic and precious. His first real achievement as novelist was *Confessions of a Mask*, which was lucid in its rich details, and challenging in its theme. He described the physical and psychological process by which the hero ("I") is led to the inevitable realization that he is a homosexual; the title suggested it should be taken as a "confessional" novel. In the late 1940's, homosexuality was not a popular theme at all. Young Mishima admired Oscar Wilde, and Wildean pose and tastes were certain to have influenced him. His essay on Wilde (1950) was full of revealing insights, on both Wilde and Mishima himself. We can even get an ominous premonition of his provocative "suicide," which seems to have been a curious mixture of exhibitionism and an irresistible impulse toward self-destruction.

Mishima proved himself even more versatile than Wilde: certainly his contribution as novelist surpasses Wilde's. *Forbidden Colours, The Sound of Waves, The Temple of the Golden Pavilion, After the Banquet, The Sailor Who Fell from Grace with the Sea,* and *The Sea of Fertility* tetralogy (completed just before his death), should be sufficient to secure his position as one of the major novelists of the 20th century. His range is wide indeed: *The Sound of Waves* is an idyllic evocation of innocent love in a remote fishing village; *The Temple of the Golden Pavilion* probes the morbid impulses of a young incendiary who destroys one of the traditional treasures of Japanese architecture; *After the Banquet* provides a satirical picture of the Japanese political scene and of the amorous behaviour of an elder statesman and his new wife; *The Sailor Who Fell from Grace with the Sea* describes youthful hero-worship, which, once bitterly disappointed, turns vindictive and destructive. Mishima was amazingly prolific, and wrote short stories, plays, literary criticism, travelogues, and political articles. His modern Noh plays are remarkable for their fusion of a refined sense of form, derived from traditional Noh drama, and vulgar realistic details in contemporary scenes and characters. *Madame de Sade*, in which the real hero of the play does not appear on the stage at all, is another tour de force, which, while adhering strictly to the classical unities, is sensual and sharp in its touch.

The Sea of Fertility, Mishima's last major work, is a tantalizing achievement. Its central theme is based on the Buddhist concept of the metamorphosis of the human soul. The underlying mystic system may not be wholly convincing, but the consecutive appearances or incarnations of "the eternal spirit" as the four main characters make for fascinating stories. This tetralogy might be taken as Mishima's gigantic bid for immortality, and, at the same time, as symbolic expression of his impulse toward annihilation.

—Shoichi Saeki

MOLIÈRE. Born Jean-Baptiste Poquelin in Paris, 15 January 1622. Educated at Collège de Clermont to 1641; studied law at University of Orléans, law degree 1642. Married Armande Béjart in 1662. Joined the Béjart family in founding a theatrical company, Illustre Théâtre, 1643; toured in French provinces, 1645-58, then in hall of the Petit-Bourbon, Paris, under the protection of the Duc d'Orléans, brother of Louis XIV; some court opposition after the production of *L'École des femmes*, 1662; Louis XIV replaced the Duc d'Orléans as his patron in 1665, and the company was established at the Palais Royal. *Died 17 February 1673.*

PUBLICATIONS

Collections

Oeuvres complètes, edited by E. Despois and P. Mesnard. 14 vols., 1873-1900.
Oeuvres complètes, edited by Maurice Rat. 2 vols., 1956; revised by Georges Coutin, 2 vols., 1971.
Works, translated by A.R. Waller. 8 vols., 1926.
Comedies. 2 vols., 1929.

Plays

La Jalousie du barbouille; le Médecin volant (attributed to Molière; produced on tour before 1655). 1819.
L'Etourdi; ou, Les Contre-temps (produced 1655?). 1663; as The Blunderers, 1762.
Le Dépit amoureux (produced 1656). 1663; as The Amorous Quarrel, 1762.
Les Précieuses ridicules (produced 1659). 1660; as The Conceited Young Ladies, 1762.
Sganarelle; ou, Le Cocu imaginaire (produced 1660). 1660; as The Picture, 1745.
Don Garcie de Navarre; ou, Le Prince jaloux (produced 1661). In Oeuvres posthumes, 1684.
L'École des maris (produced 1661). 1661.
Les Facheux (produced 1661). 1662; as The Impertinents, 1732.
L'École des femmes (produced 1662). 1663; as The School for Wives, 1971.
La Critique de L'École des femmes (produced 1663). 1663.
L'Impromptu de Versailles (produced 1663). In Oeuvres posthumes, 1684.
Le Mariage forcé (produced 1664). 1664; as The Forced Marriage, 1762.
La Princesse d'Élide (produced 1664). 1674.
Tartuffe; ou, L'Imposteur (produced 1664; revised version, produced 1664, 1667). 1669; translated as Tartuffe, 1670.
Les Plaisirs de l'île enchantée (produced 1664). 1664.
Dom Juan; ou, Le Festin de Pierre (produced 1665). 1683.
L'Amour médecin (produced 1665). 1666; as The Quacks, 1705; as Doctor Love, 1915.
Le Misanthrope (produced 1666). 1667; as The Misanthrope, 1762; as The Man-Hater, 1770.
Le Médecin malgré lui (produced 1666). 1667; as The Dumb Lady, 1672; as Love's Contrivance, 1703; as The Mock Doctor, 1732; as The Doctor in Spite of Himself, 1914.
Mélicerte (produced 1666). In Oeuvres posthumes, 1684.
La Pastorale comique, music by Lully (produced 1666). In Théâtre, 1888-93.
Le Sicilien; ou, L'Amour peintre (produced 1667). 1668; as The Sicilian, 1732.
Amphitryon (produced 1668). 1668; translated as Amphitryon, 1690.
George Dandin; ou, Le Mari confondu (produced 1668). 1669; as George Dandin; or, The Husband Defeated, 1732.
L'Avare (produced 1668). 1669; as The Miser, 1672.
Monsieur de Pourceaugnac (produced 1669). 1670; as The Cornish Squire, 1734.
Les Amants magnifiques (produced 1670). In Oeuvres posthumes, 1684.
Le Bourgeois gentilhomme (produced 1670). 1670; as The Citizen Turned Gentleman, 1672.
Psyché, with Corneille and Philippe Quinault, music by Lully (produced 1671). 1671.
Les Fourberies de Scapin (produced 1671). 1671; as The Cheats of Scapin, 1677.

La Comtesse d'Escarbagnas (produced 1671).   In *Oeuvres posthumes*, 1684.

Les Femmes savantes (produced 1672).   1673; as *The Female Virtuosos*, 1693; as *Blue stockings*, 1884.

La Malade imaginaire (produced 1673).   1673-74; as *Doctor Last in His Chariot*, 1769; as *The Imaginary Invalid*, 1925.

*

Critical Studies: *Molière: A New Criticism* by W.G. Moore, 1949; *Molière and the Comedy of Intellect* by Judd Hubert, 1962; *Men and Masks: A Study of Molière* by Lionel Gossman, 1963; *Molière: The Comedy of Unreason* by F.L. Lawrence, 1968; *Molière* by Hallam Walker, 1971; *Molière as Ironic Contemplator* by Alvin Eustis, 1973; *Molière: Stage and Study* edited by W.D. Howarth and M. Thomas, 1973; *Molière: An Archetypal Approach* by Harold C. Knutson, 1976; *Molière's Tartuffe and the Traditions of Roman Satire* by Jerry Lewis Kasparek, 1977; *The Sceptical Vision of Molière* by Robert McBride, 1977; *Molière: L'École des femmes, and Le Misanthrope* by J.H. Broome, 1982; *From Gesture to Idea: Esthetics and Ethics in Molière's Comedy* by Nathan Gross, 1982; *Molière: A Playwright and His Audience* by W.D. Howarth, 1982.

*   *   *

Molière is one of the world's greatest dramatists, a man whose originality and importance puts him in the same league as Sophocles, Shakespeare, and Ibsen. He is like Shakespeare in that he was in life very much a professional man of the theatre, a busy actor-manager who wrote plays for performance by his own company, and like Ibsen in that his work translates easily and so ensures his acceptance abroad, a distinction denied, for instance, to his illustrious contemporary Racine, who has never been widely appreciated outside France.

Because neo-classical conventions under which Molière worked—and, indeed, readily accepted—insisted on the strict segregation of dramatic categories, all his works are technically comedies, which means in practice that they have happy endings and deal with ordinary middle-class people rather than the kings and princes of tragedy. His plots are usually quite conventional, featuring for the most part young star-crossed lovers whose plans for married happiness are temporarily thwarted by older people, and they derive from the Roman comedies which Molière was happy to imitate since that was expected of him by the all-powerful critics of his age. He wrote for the most part five act plays in verse, and in all other respects conformed to the tastes of his time such as a decided preference for the "three unities" of place, time, and action, and the avoidance of coarse expressions or bawdy situations on stage.

The remarkable thing, therefore, is that he was able to transcend the restrictions imposed upon him and create works of universal appeal. His early plays, produced on tour in the provinces before he found a theatre of his own in Paris, are fairly crude pieces imitated from the *commedia dell'arte*, but he found his own voice in *The Conceited Young Ladies*, a rumbustious send-up of a contemporary affectation, that of excessively refined speech reflecting impossibly exalted sentiments. This vein of social satire proved a rich one for Molière, and he made the most of it in the dozen or so years he had left to live. *The School for Wives*, his first comedy and in some respects his most characteristic, concerns a man who plans to keep his future wife faithful by bringing her up in uneducated innocence, but the scheme misfires when a much more attractive younger man enters her life and, after several hilarious setbacks, carries her off for himself. This theme was to be taken up a decade or so later by Wycherley in his much coarser version *The Country Wife*.

More complex is *Tartuffe*, a play in which things nearly go wrong and happiness is restored only by a *deus ex machina*. It was also a much more controversial play which got Molière into serious trouble. Tartuffe is a religious hypocrite who is unmasked at the eleventh hour, but not before he has nearly ruined his gullible benefactor and come close to raping the man's loyal wife. Satire of this kind cut too near the bone for many people in that still largely devout age, and Molière escaped punishment only thanks to royal protection.

The Misanthrope is usually considered his masterpiece, largely because the comedy is ambiguous, and the play even subtler than *Tartuffe*. Alceste and Célimène—the names, as so often in Molière, are purely conventional—are expected to marry soon, but his acerbic temperament and her flightiness make this an improbable match. He rails at the hypocrisy of the age; she is a normal social being for whom tact and discretion are considerable virtues. After much friction, he insists, as a test of her loyalty, that she leave Paris with him for ever. Her response is quite predictable. In Tony Harrison's inspired translation, "I'm only twenty! I'd be terrified!" she gasps: "Just you and me, and all that countryside!" Alceste storms out in embittered despair. In one sense he is an antisocial buffoon; in another, he is a penetrating critic of a corrupt and cynical milieu. Molière shrewdly leaves the question open.

An equally serious situation is explored in *The Miser*, a probing treatment of that most dismal of human vices, avarice, and in *The Citizen Turned Gentleman*, a shrewd analysis of social snobbery and human gullibility. The last two plays which Molière wrote in a way sum up his whole career. *Bluestockings* is social satire, mocking the pretentions of women who aspire to be intellectuals and whose vanity is exploited by the unscrupulous. *Doctor Last in His Chariot* takes the scalpel of comedy to hypochondria, and Molière no doubt savoured the irony which decreed that his own death took place as he acted the part of the imaginary invalid himself.

Molière exerted a considerable influence on his contemporaries, the Restoration dramatists in England, who imitated him without always understanding him, but otherwise he had few immediate followers. He has been successfully translated and produced on the modern stage and on television. His situations are so straightforward and universal that it is not difficult for directors to update him without in any way distorting his meaning. *The Misanthrope*, for instance, has been effectively staged as a satire on Paris high society under General de Gaulle's administration, and as a shrewd comment on the "jazz age" of Scott Fitzgerald's characters. As a true pro himself, Molière would be gratified by the fact that today's actors have no difficulty in bringing his characters to life in modern dress. Religious hypocrisy may no longer be a threat in our society, but Tartuffe stands for any kind of cynical deception practised on the susceptibility of human beings to flattery, just as Alceste is the eternal boor, high on the egoism of the self-righteous, the very personification of negativity and destructiveness. And the miracle is, that in spite of being so serious, it is all so helplessly funny.

—John Fletcher

MONTAIGNE, Michel (Eyquem) de. Born in 1533. Educated at home (learned Latin as native tongue); Collège de Guienne, Bordeaux, 1540-46; probably studied law, possibly in Toulouse. Married Françoise de la Chassaigne in 1565. Entered Cour des Aides of Périgueux as magistrate, 1554; transferred his magistracy to Bordeaux, 1557; at Bar-le-Duc at court of Francis II, 1559, and at Rouen for majority of Charles IX, 1560; friend of Henry of Navarre, and legal messenger for state duties; retired to country life and resigned his magistracy after his father's death, 1568; mayor of Bordeaux, 1581, and re-elected, 1583. *Died 13 September 1592.*

PUBLICATIONS

Collections

Oeuvres complètes, edited by Albert Tribaudet and Maurice Rat. 1962.

Complete Works, translated by Donald M. Frame.   1948.

Prose

Essais.   2 vols., 1580; revised edition, 1582, 1588; edited by Marie de Gournay, 1595; as *Essays*, translated by John Florio, 1603, and E.J. Trenchman, 2 vols., 1927.
Journal de voyage en Italie par la Suisse et l'Allemagne en 1580 et 1581.   1774; translated in *Complete Works*, 1842.

Editor, *Vers français*, by Étienne de la Boëtie.   1572.
Editor, *Discours sur la servitude volontaire*, by Étienne de la Boëtie.   1574.

Translator, *La Théologie naturelle*, by Raymond Sebond.   1569.

*

Critical Studies: *Montaigne's Discovery of Man*, 1955, and *Montaigne: A Biography*, 1965, both by Donald M. Frame; *The Essays of Montaigne*, by R.A. Sayce, 1972; *Montaigne's Deceits* by Margaret McGowan, 1974; *Montaigne and the Introspective Mind* by Glyn P. Norton, 1975; *The Matter of My Book: Montaigne's "Essais" as the Book of the Self* by Richard L. Rogosin, 1977; *Montaigne and His Age* edited by Keith Cameron, 1981; *Montaigne* by Peter Burke, 1981; *Lectures on Monaigne* by Jules Brody, 1982; *Essaying Montaigne: A Study of the Renaissance Institution of Writing and Reading* by John O'Neill, 1982; *Montaigne and Melancholy* by M.A. Screech, 1983.

*   *   *

The "essay" is now a well-established and flourishing literary genre in its own right, but when Montaigne coined the word in 1580 he used it to suggest that his collection of discursive musings represented little more than "try-outs" or "attempts" at reaching an understanding of things by writing about them. His short preface is disarmingly limited in its objectives; he makes it clear that the book was originally conceived for strictly private (in his words, for a few "relations and friends") use, and that it is the work of a gentleman, not of a professional philosopher. Which is why he has no qualms about making himself the "subject matter of [my] book." He goes on to imply that his true significance is in that —like most of his readers—he is ordinary and imperfect. The self-disparagement of this opening is in part a ploy (there is an element of provocation, too, in warning your reader not to waste his time on so "frivolous and vain" a subject) which allows him to refer his critics back to the unpretentiousness of his preface should his erudition or reasoning be found wanting. But throughout his writings one finds a prickly defensiveness whenever the question of academic expertise comes up, and Montaigne rarely misses an opportunity of deriding "pedants." In his chapter (I,26) on the education of children, he claims to prefer an accomplished (*habile*) man to a scholarly (*sçavant*) one, a sound head to a well-filled one. In Montaigne's eyes morals and judgement are more important than mere learning.

The getting of this wisdom is one of the major preoccupations of the *Essays*. Like the Delphic oracle, he would have us know ourselves. Our first duty is to admit the limits of our knowledge, for "to recognize one's ignorance is one of the best and surest signs of judgement I know" ("On Books", II,10). Flexibility of mind is the surest remedy for dogmatism, which he abhorred. As early as the very first chapter of the first book, we see him stressing man's inconsistency ("vain, divers et ondoyant" as he puts it) and deciding that universally binding laws of behaviour cannot be drawn up. This "relativism" inevitably weakened his early allegiance to Stoicism and made him lean towards scepticism. In 1576 he had a medallion struck with the motto "Que sçay je?" to indicate his state of uncertainty. Along with other sceptics he wonders just what he knows, or can know. It has often been said that Montaigne evolved from Stoicism to scepticism before reaching a personal variation on Epicureanism, but this categorization is nowadays considered an over-simplification. Certainly his growing affection for Sextus Empiricus did not mean that he turned his back completely on Seneca and Plutarch and, as we have seen, he possessed an innate scepticism which never left him.

Montaigne's awareness of the wide variety of men's experience sharpened his interest in the New World, and his chapter "On Cannibals" (I,31) is a fine example of open-mindedness and tolerance. He argues that the so-called cannibals are not "barbaric" or "savage," as they are usually thought, but merely different, and remarks that "everyone calls barbaric things which are not part of their habits." In an endeavour to break down what he termed elsewhere the "barrier of custom" (I,36), he himself interviewed a Brazilian Indian and tried to see his own world through their eyes. He tackles the problem of witchcraft in a similarly level-headed fashion (III,11). Unlike most commentators of his day, Montaigne gives little credence to the self-confessed witches appearing—or being made to appear—in increasing numbers, refuses to believe stories about broomsticks or people disappearing up chimneys, and proposes to treat them as sick rather than evil. He is much harsher in the event on those who presume to punish these poor wretches with the utmost severity than on the "witches" themselves. In this case doubt becomes a positive virtue and, in the later chapters in particular, Montaigne frequently exploits the potentiality of doubt as a method of thinking and being. He comes to rejoice in the very diversity of experience and opinion he sees around him. The *Essays* started out as a sort of commonplace book, not unlike the *Adages* of Erasmus or, on a more mundane level, a collection of *Memorable Sayings* such as Gilles Corrozet's, favouring topics such as sadness or the fear of death, but they developed into "essays" in self-acceptance. Revelling in polyvalence and ambiguity, Montaigne discovers that his attempts to circumscribe life's mysteries have led him to a deeper enjoyment of them. Indeed, the beautifully serene chapter which brings the *Essays* to a close, "On Experience" (III,13), is a hymn to life, kidney stones and all: "Our great and glorious masterpiece is to live properly." By "properly"—in the original "*à propos*"—he means coming to terms with ourselves as we are. At the end of the same chapter he uses *loiallement* in a similar sense, affirming that it is "absolute perfection, and almost divine, to know how to enjoy loyally one's being." Self-knowledge increases self-enjoyment and, by the end of his *Essays*, Montaigne seems able simply to be.

—Michael Freeman

MONTALE, Eugenio. Born in Genoa, Italy, 12 October 1896. Educated at schools in Genoa to age 14; studied opera singing under Ernesto Sivori. Served in the Italian Army, 1917-19: Infantry Officer. Married Drusilla Tanzi (died, 1963). Founder, with others, *Primo Tempo* literary journal, Turin, 1922; staff member, Bemporad, publishers, Florence, 1927-28; Curator, Vieusseux Book Collection, Florence, 1928-38; Poetry Critic, *La Fiera Letteraria*, 1938-48, Director, *El Mondo*, 1945-48, Literary Editor, *Corriere della Sera*, from 1948, and Music Critic, *Corriere d'Informazione*, 1955-67, all Milan. Life Member of the Italian Senate, 1967. Recipient: Antico Fattore prize, 1932; Marzotto Prize, 1956; Feltrinelli Prize, 1962; Gulbenkian prize, 1971; Nobel Prize for Literature, 1975. Honorary degrees: Cambridge University, 1967; universities of Basel, Milan, and Rome. *Died 12 September 1981.*

PUBLICATIONS

Verse

    Ossi di seppia. 1925; revised edition, 1926, 1948.
    La casa dei doganieri e altre poesie. 1932.
    Le occasioni. 1939.
    Finisterre. 1943.
    Poesie. 3 vols., 1948-57.
    La bufera e altro. 1956.
    Poems, translated by Edwin Morgan. 1959.
    Poesie di Montale (bilingual edition), translated by Robert Lowell. 1960.
    Accordi e pastelli. 1963.
    Poesie: Poems, edited by George Kay. 1964; as *Selected Poems,* 1969.
    Selected Poems, edited by Glauco Cambon. 1965.
    Il colpevole. 1966.
    Satura. 1966; revised edition, 1971; as *Satura: Five Poems,* 1969.
    Xenia. 1966; translated as *Xenia,* 1970.
    Provisional Conclusions: A Selection of the Poetry of Montale 1920-1970, translated by
        Edith Farnsworth. 1970.
    Trentadue variazioni. 1973.
    Diario del '71 e del '72. 1973.
    Mottetti (bilingual edition), translated by Lawrence Kart. 1973.
    New Poems: A Selection from Satura and Diario del '71 e del '72, translated by G.
        Singh. 1976.
    Tutte le poesie. 1977.
    Quaderno di quattro anni. 1977.
    The Storm and Other Poems, translated by Charles Wright. 1978.
    L'Opera in versi, edited by Rosanna Bettarini and Gianfranco Contini. 2 vols., 1980.
    Altre versi e poesie disperse. 1981.

Fiction

    La farfalla di Dinard. 1956; revised edition, 1960; as *The Butterfly of Dinard,* 1970.

Other

    La solitudine dell'artista. 1952.
    Lettere: Montale-Italo Svevo. 1966.
    Auto da fé: Cronache in due tempi. 1966.
    Fuori di casa. 1969.
    La poesia non esiste. 1971.
    Nel nostro tempo. 1972; as *Poet in Our Time,* 1976.
    Sulla poesia, edited by Giorgio Zampa. 1976.
    Selected Essays, edited by G. Singh. 1978.
    It Depends: A Poet's Notebook, edited by G. Singh. 1980.
    Prime alla Scala. 1981.
    The Second Life of Art: Selected Essays, edited by Jonathan Galassi. 1982.

    Translator, *La battaglia,* by John Steinbeck. 1940.
    Translator, *La storia di Billy Budd,* by Melville. 1942.
    Translator, *Il mio mundo è qui,* by Dorothy Parker. 1943.

Translator, *Strano interludio*, by Eugene O'Neill. 1943.
Translator, *Al Dio sconosciuto*, by John Steinbeck. 1946.
Translator, *La commedia degli errori, Racconto d'inverno, Timone d'Atene*, by Shakespeare. 3 vols., 1947.
Translator, with Luigi Berti, *Il volto di pietra*. 1947.
Translator, *Quaderno di traduzioni*. 1948; revised edition, 1975.
Translator, *Amleto, principe di Danimarca*, by Shakespeare. 1949.
Translator, *La tragica storia del dottor Faust*, by Marlowe. 1951.
Translator, *Proserpina e lo straniero*, by Omar Del Carlo. 1952.
Translator, *La cicuta e dopo*, by Angus Wilson. 1956.
Translator, *(Selections)*, by T.S. Eliot. 1958.
Translator, *Il Cid*, by Corneille, in *Teatro francese del grande secolo*, edited by G. Macchia. 1960.

*

Bibliography: *Bibliografia montaliana* by Laura Barile, 1977.

Critical Studies: *Montale and Dante* by Arshi Pipa, 1968; *Three Modern Italian Poets: Saba, Ungaretti, Montale* by Joseph Cary, 1969; *Montale*, 1973, and *Montale's Poetry: A Dream in Reason's Presence*, 1982, both by Glauco Cambon; *Montale: A Critical Study of His Poetry, Prose and Criticism* by G. Singh, 1973; *Montale: The Private Language of Poetry* by Guido Almansi and Bruce Merry, 1977; *Montale: Poet on the Edge* by Rebecca J. West, 1981; *Montale and the Occasions of Poetry* by Claire de L.C. Huffman, 1983.

*   *   *

Eugenio Montale is generally considered Italy's greatest poet of this century. Much admired by writers and intellectuals of a variety of ideological persuasions, he has been a kind of stabilizing force on the Italian literary scene for more than fifty years—beginning in 1925, when he signed Croce's Manifesto of anti-Fascist Intellectuals and published his first book of poetry, to 1975, when he won the Nobel Prize for Literature, to his death in 1981. This wide-spread esteem is perhaps somewhat surprising, for Montale is an austere, highly moral, and "difficult" poet whose work requires careful rereading and reflection before it will begin to yield its meaning. In part this is because for Montale poetry is a means of understanding rather than of representation. Unabashedly (and sometimes mischievously) metaphysical, his work frequently seeks to capture the conjunction of (as he puts it) the miraculous with the necessary, the transcendent with the immanent.

To the tradition of Italian verse that he inherited, Montale has brought new and more dissonant harmonies, a broader and more eclectic poetic lexicon, and—above all—a new poetic stance of doubt, skepticism, and extreme self-reflexivity. Many of his poems are concerned with the hesitations, anxieties, and small personal defeats of everyday life. At a time in Italy's political history when official rhetoric was trumpeting the mostly spurious victories of the Fascist State, his lowered, ironic, and deliberately unheroic voice seemed a singular guarantee of the authenticity that has come to be associated with his writing ever since. Much of Montale's earliest work is set in the spare, seaside landscape of Liguria; but in *Le occasioni* of 1939 and *La bufera e altro* of 1956, the focus widens to include a variety of European settings, as historical forces tragically irrupt into the poet's intimate world of metaphysical and existential meditation. There is thus a kind of dramatic progression that accompanies his poetic development. In the *Ossi di seppia* of 1925 such personal considerations as memory, identity, and the relation of the self with the outside world are paramount, while in the later volumes these same concerns are viewed in the more complex historical context of the threat to civilized values posed by the brutal forces of war and Fascism. A saving constant for the poet in this period and a compelling presence in much of his poetry is that of the woman he usually calls "Clizia," a *senhal* strikingly reminiscent of Dante's Beatrice and perhaps the most vivid and important poetic "lady" in

Italian poetry since Petrarch's Laura. Opposed by her very nature to the forces of darkness that threaten not only a lover's affection but also the survival of all the accomplishments that previous centuries of civilization have amassed, she is a numinous presence frightening in her splendor, a miraculous reminder of the potency of love, and a tantalizing hint at the existence of something more than human at large in the cosmos.

With the "fourth phase" of Montale's work after *La bufera* there is a change of tone, as the sometimes exalted language of the earlier production gives way to a more informal, even offhand manner in verse that can seem little more than wry jottings or entries in a day-book, but has sufficient resilience to treat issues of importance with wit and insight. The same gentle humor and delight in the unusual and paradoxical that characterize these poems also permeate the far from negligible prose produced mostly on commission for newspapers and other periodicals.

—Charles Klopp

MURASAKI Shikibu. Also known as Lady Murasaki. Pseudonym.   Born c. 978. Married Fujiwara no Nobutaka in 998 (died, 1001). Spent some years in close contact with the court at Kyoto; in the service of Empress Akiko from c. 1005. Date of death unknown.

PUBLICATIONS

Fiction

> *Genji Monogatari*, edited by Yamagishi Tokuhei.   5 vols., 1958-63; also edited by Abe Akio and others, 6 vols., 1970-76; as *The Tale of Genji*, translated by Arthur Waley, 6 vols., 1925-33; also translated by Edward Seidensticker, 1976.

Other

> *Murasaki Shikibu: Her Diary and Poetic Memoirs*, translated by Richard Bowring.   1982.

*

Critical Studies: *Murasaki Shikibu: The Greatest Lady Writer in Japanese Literature* by Sen'ichi Nisamatsu and others, 1970; *Ukifume: Love in The Tale of Genji* edited by Andrew Pekarik, 1982; *Iconography of The Tale of Genji* by Miyeko Murase, 1983.

*   *   *

Murasaki Shikibu, sometimes called Lady Murasaki, is the author of a "diary" which is not so much that as a discursive account of events at the Japanese court over a short expanse of time early in the 11th century; a collection of more than a hundred short lyric poems which overlaps in some measure with the diary; a scattering of poems to be found only in royally commissioned anthologies; and *The Tale of Genji*.

The last, much her most important work, is a very long romance probably finished (if it is finished—of that we cannot be sure) in the first or second decade of the 11th century. Nothing survives in her hand, and the earliest texts of the *Genji*, from almost two centuries after the probable date of composition, are fragmentary. So scholars will forever ask how close the texts of our day are to Murasaki's original, and the quest for a definitive text will be endless. The sensible view, supported by a large mass of scholarly writing, is that what we read today is essentially what came from the brush of a very remarkable Japanese court lady early in the 11th century.

Though there are sallies and sub-plots, the story is essentially simple. The first two-thirds or so are dominated by an increasingly powerful courtier known, from his family name, as "the shining Genji," and the story is of perdurable love. Genji meets the great love of his life in the fifth of the fifty-four chapters. She dies in the fortieth, and a chapter later Genji himself disappears from the scene. The remainder of the story has to do with the less vigorous affairs, also largely amorous, of Genji's grandson and of a young man reputed to be his son but actually the grandson of his best friend.

Though the story is simple the *Genji* is a complex work. Numbers of meanings can be abstracted from it, most of them deriving from the fact that the tone is melancholy and the general import pessimistic. Since the action covers almost three-quarters of a century, the earlier portions are set at a considerable though not precisely defined time in the past. An important meaning would seem to be that there once were giants, Genji pre-eminent among them, and they will not come again. The best time has passed. So the story is of social decline, and it may also be about metaphysical decline, a popular notion of the time being that the "good law" of Buddhism was about to enter the last phase before its extinction. The *Genji* is certainly about evanescence, and it may also be about retribution; and it may tell of the quest for a lost parent. Genji is drawn to the ladies most important to him by a fancied resemblance to his mother, whom he cannot remember.

It may be about all these things, but it is something more immediate, and less abstractable. The reader's attention is held through the very great length of the tale not by remarkable incident and suspense, but by character. Several hundred characters make their appearance, and among them perhaps forty or fifty may be called major. They are distinguished one from another with most remarkable skill, and each is what Forster called three-dimensional, a believable individual and not merely a type or caricature.

The *Genji* is often called the first great novel in the literature of the world. The designation is controversial, but the controversy is largely a matter of definition. If by "novel" we mean a kind of prose narrative in which character, and not plot or incident, is the most important element, then a very strong case can be made for proclaiming the *Genji* the first superior specimen of the genre. There is nothing like it, certainly, in earlier Oriental literature.

—Edward Seidensticker

MUSIL, Robert. Born in Klagenfurt, Austria, 6 November 1880. Educated at a school in Steyr; military school in Eisenstadt, 1892-94, and in Mährisch-Weisskirchen, 1895-98; studied engineering at Technische Hochschule, Brno, 1898-1901; studied philosophy, University of Berlin, 1903-05, Ph.D. 1908. Military service: 1901-02; served in Austrian army, 1914-16; hospitalized, 1916, then editor of army newspaper, 1916-18; bronze cross. Married Martha

Marcovaldi in 1911. Engineer in Stuttgart, 1902-03; in Berlin until 1911; archivist, 1911-14; in press section of Office of Foreign Affairs, Vienna, 1919-20, and consultant to Defense Ministry, 1920-23; then free-lance writer: in Berlin, 1931-33, Vienna, 1933-38, and Switzerland, 1938-42. Recipient: Kleist Prize, 1923; City of Vienna Prize, 1924. *Died 15 April 1942.*

PUBLICATIONS

Collections

    Gesammelte Werke, edited by Adolf Frisé. 3 vols., 1952-57; revised edition, 2 vols., 1978.

Fiction

    Die Verwirrungen des Zöglings Törless. 1906; as *Young Törless*, 1955.
    Vereinigungen. 1911; as *Unions*, 1965.
    Drei Frauen. 1924; as *Three Women*, 1965; as *Tonka and Other Stories*, 1965.
    Der Mann ohne Eigenschaften, completed by Martha Musil. 3 vols., 1930-43; as *The Man Without Qualities*, 3 vols., 1953-60.

Plays

    Die Schwärmer. 1921.
    Vinzenz und die Freundin bedeutender Männer. 1923.

Other

    Das hilflose Europa. 1922.
    Nachlass zu Lebzeiten. 1936.
    Theater: Kritisches und Theoretisches, edited by Marie-Louise Roth. 1965.
    Der Deutsche Mensch als Symptom, edited by Karl Corino and Elisabeth Albertsen. 1967.
    Briefe nach Prag, edited by Barbara Köpplova and Kurt Krolop. 1971.
    Tagebücher, edited by Adolf Frisé. 2 vols., 1976.
    Texte aus dem Nachlass. 1980.
    Briefe 1901-1942, edited by Adolf Frisé. 1981.

*

Bibliography: *Musil-Bibliographie* by Jürgen C. Thöming, 1968.

Critical Studies: *Musil: An Introduction to His Work* by Burton Pike, 1961; *Femininity and the Creative Imagination: A Study of Henry James, Musil, and Marcel Proust* by Lisa Appignanesi, 1973; *Musil, Master of the Hovering Life* by Frederick G. Peters, 1978; *Musil: "Die Mann ohne Eigenschaften": An Examination of the Relationship Between Author, Narrator, and Protagonist* by Alan Holmes, 1978; *Musil and the Crisis of European Culture 1880-1942* by David S. Luft, 1980; *Musil and the Ineffable: Hieroglyph, Myth, Fairy Tale, and Sign* by Ronald M. Paulson, 1982.

*   *   *

The Austrian novelist Robert Musil ranks with Thomas Mann and Franz Kafka among major German writers of the 20th century, but the highly essayistic nature of much of his writing makes him less of a story-teller than Mann and less of a pure modernist than Kafka. Nonetheless, his extraordinary intelligence and his genius for metaphor allowed him to achieve in *The Man Without Qualities* a prose that has few equals in German literature, and no one writing in German in this century has had more balanced or penetrating insight into so broad a range of issues.

The task of Musil's fiction was to invent the inner person and to extend our understanding in the realm of the soul by portraying borderline experiences of perception, sexuality, and mysticism. His first novel, *Young Törless*, established these themes when he was only 25; this portrayal of adolescent homosexuality and political conflict is the most realistic and accessible of Musil's narrative works, but even here the emphasis is on the protagonist's inner crisis and his complex feelings about sexuality and the behavior of those around him. In the stories of *Unions* Musil continued to explore sexuality and ethical experience, but now from the perspective of feminine consciousness; by this time, Musil was familiar with Freud and ready for an ambitious experiment in the metaphorical representation of inwardness. In these stories, as in the aesthetically more perfected novellas of *Three Women* and the play *Die Schwärmer* (The Visionaries), Musil was preoccupied with the unreal life of the feelings—not the lives we lead but the lives we feel.

What makes Musil a writer of such a high order is that he was able to deal with these psychological themes in relation to the problems of modern, technological society and the breakdown of traditional European ideologies. His scientific training and his dissertation on Ernst Mach (1908) not only established his high level of scientific sophistication, but provided him with the tools for criticizing outmoded ideologies and theories of human nature and history. Drawing on Nietzsche as well as Mach, Musil began to develop his critique of ideology and morality in the essays that he wrote for the *Neue Rundschau* and other liberal journals before the First World War. But it was the war that brought his characteristic themes into focus, and the major essays of the postwar period clarified his view that European civilization before 1914 had failed to create a meaningful cultural and emotional life. The realm of the spirit had failed to keep pace with the practical achievements of the age.

Musil devoted the last two decades of his life to an attempt to summarize the predicament of the individual in modern civilization. Critics differ concerning whether Musil managed to break out of the modern predicament in a decisive way, but all are agreed that his novel, *The Man Without Qualities*, is a brilliant description of the situation. Ulrich, the protagonist of Musil's masterpiece, explores the possibilities for right living in the midst of the massive scale and cultural fragmentation of life in modern civilization. The setting is Austria on the eve of the First World War, but the satire of old-fashioned ideologies leads on to more universal questions about the sources of ethical motivation. Ulrich's ironic voice emphasizes the critique of action, ego, and dead ideology, but the appearance of his sister Agathe opens the door on a more constructive attempt to think about morality and the world out of the condition of love. This novel is the purest expression of Musil's capacity to balance positivism and romanticism, thinking and feeling, masculinity and femininity, to think out a world in which human beings are likely to become in part highly efficient masters of practical reality and in part mystics.

—David S. Luft

MUSSET, (Louis Charles) Alfred de. Born in Paris, 11 December 1810. Educated at Collège Henri IV, Paris, 1820-28; studied law and medicine briefly. Lived with George Sand, 1833-34; later associated with Mlle. Aimée d'Alton and Mme. Allan-Despréaux. Librarian, Ministry of the Interior, 1838-48, and after 1851. Member, French Academy, 1852. *Died 2 May 1857.*

PUBLICATIONS

Collections

> *Oeuvres complètes*, edited by Paul de Musset. 10 vols., 1865-66.
> *Oeuvres complètes*. 8 vols., 1907-09.
> *Oeuvres complètes illustrées*. 10 vols., 1927-29.
> *Oeuvres complètes en prose*; *Théâtre complet*; *Poésies complètes*, edited by Maurice Allem. 3 vols., 1951-58.
> *Oeuvres complètes*, edited by Philippe Van Tieghem. 1963.
> *Complete Writings*. 10 vols., 1905.

Plays

> *La Nuit vénitienne* (produced 1830). In *Un Spectacle dans un fauteuil*, 1834.
> *André del Sarto* (produced 1848). In *Un Spectacle dans un fauteuil*, 1834; revised version (produced 1848), 1851.
> *Les Caprices de Marianne* (produced 1851). In *Un Spectacle dans un fauteuil*, 1834; revised version (produced 1851), 1851; edited by P.-G. Castex, 1979; as *A Good Little Wife*, n.d. (1847?).
> *On ne badine pas avec l'amour* (produced 1861). In *Un Spectacle dans un fauteuil*, 1834; edited by P.-G. Castex, 1979; as *No Trifling with Love*, in *Comedies*, 1890.
> *Fantasio* (produced 1866). In *Un Spectacle dans un fauteuil*, 1834; translated as *Fantasio*, in *Comedies*, 1890.
> *Lorenzaccio* (produced 1896). In *Un Spectacle dans un fauteuil*, 1834; edited by Paul Dimoff, in *La Genèse de Lorenzaccio*, revised edition, 1964.
> *Comédies et proverbes*. 1840; augmented and revised edition, 2 vols., 1853; edited by Pierre and Françoise Gastinel, 4 vols., 1934, 1952-57.
> *Le Chandelier*, in *Comédies et proverbes*. 1840; revised version (produced 1848), 1848.
> *Il ne faut jurer de rien* (produced 1848). In *Comédies et proverbes*, 1840.
> *Un Caprice* (produced 1847). In *Comédies et proverbes*, 1840.
> *La Quenouille de Barberine*, in *Comédies et proverbes*. 1840; revised version, as *Barberine* (produced 1882), in *Comédies et proverbes*, 1853; translated as *Barberine*, in *Comedies*, 1890.
> *Il faut qu'une porte soit ouverte ou fermée* (produced 1848). 1848; as *A Door Must Be Either Open or Shut*, in *Comedies*, 1890.
> *L'Habit vert*, with Émile Augier (produced 1849). 1849; as *The Green Coat*, 1914.
> *Louison* (produced 1849). 1849.
> *On ne saurait penser à tout* (produced 1849). In *Comédies et proverbes*, 1853.
> *Bettine* (produced 1851). 1851.
> *Carmosine* (produced 1865). In *Comédies et proverbes*, 1853; translated as *Carmosine*, n.d. (1865?).
> *L'Âne et le ruisseau* (produced 1876). In *Oeuvres posthumes*, 1860; as *All Is Fair in Love and War*, 1868.
> *La Quittance du diable* (produced 1938). 1896.

Fiction

La Confession d'un enfant du siècle. 2 vols., 1836; as *The Confession of a Child of the Century*, 1892.
Nouvelles. 1848; as *Tales from Musset*, 1888, and *The Two Mistresses, etc.*, 1900.
Contes. 1854.

Verse

Les Contes d'Espagne et d'Italie. 1830; edited by Margaret A. Rees, 1973.
Poésies complètes. 1840.
Premières poésies, Poésies nouvelles. 2 vols., 1852.
Poésies complètes. 2 vols., 1854.

Other

Un Spectacle dans un fauteuil (verse and plays). 1833; second series, 2 vols., 1834.
Mélanges de littérature et de critique (essays and criticism). 1867.
Oeuvres, Correspondance, edited by Léon Séché. 1907.
Lettres d'amour à Aimée d'Alton, edited by Léon Séché. 1910.
Oeuvres complémentaires, edited by Maurice Allem. 1911.
George Sand et Musset: Correspondance..., edited by Louis Évrard. 1956.

*

Bibliography: *Musset: A Reference Guide* by Patricia Joan Siegel, 1982.

Critical Studies: *Alfred: The Passionate Life of Musset* by Charlotte Haldane, 1960; *Stage of Dreams: The Dramatic Art of Musset* by Herbert S. Gochberg, 1967; *Musset* by Margaret A. Rees, 1971; *A Stage for Poets: Studies in the Theatre of Hugo and Musset* by Charles Affron, 1971; *Theatre of Solitude: The Drama of Musset* by David Sices, 1974.

*　　　*　　　*

Alfred de Musset is both an exemplary and a paradoxical figure of French Romanticism. The youthful disciple of Hugo and the *Cénacle* had, by the age of twenty, estranged himself from the movement. His parodic collection of narrative and dramatic poems, *Les Contes d'Espagne et d'Italie*, of Byronic inspiration, showed both his independence and a precocious mastery of form, language, and rhythm; it points toward the *Poésies nouvelles*, particularly "Rolla" (1833) and the celebrated four "Nuits" (the "Nights" of May, December, August and October, 1835-37), in which he attained the height of his lyric powers. Inspired in great part by his stormy love affair with George Sand, the "Nuits" present a repertory of Romantic poetic theory and practice. These dialogues between Poet and Muse turn upon the confrontation between poetry and love, art and life, expression and feeling, language and silence. Their exasperated individualism and exalted pathos spoke powerfully to and for several generations of readers.

Musset's dialogic imagination emerges most remarkably in four plays which he wrote during his twenty-third and twenty-fourth years: *Les Caprices de Marianne, Fantasio, On ne badine pas avec l'amour*, and *Lorenzaccio*. The author's alter-ego protagonists engage in the "game of love and death" of a Romantic Marivau, or, with his monumental Renaissance historical drama, *Lorenzaccio*, in a deadly, mocking duel of conscience and politics, ideal and reality. They are Protean—or splintered, as in the *Caprices*, where Coelio and Octave embody idealistic and disillusioned halves of Musset's personality. His lovers are often surrounded, or confronted, by uncomprehending puppet-figures. The plays' language is a supple, imaged, eloquent prose. Musset the dramatist has survived the rigors of time better than his more successful contemporaries, such as Hugo, Vigny, and Dumas père. His efforts to free dramatic form from contemporary stage practice (the works were not intended for performance) have attracted significant modern directors like Copeau, Baty, Vilar, and Krejca. His later dramas are less original and important, but several "comedy-proverbs"—*Le Chandelier*, *Il ne faut jurer de rien*, and *Il faut qu'une porte soit ouverte ou fermée*—have remained staples of the French repertory, thanks to their verbal elegance and humor.

Musset completed one novel, *La Confession d'un enfant du siècle*, a fictional treatment of the Sand affair. Conceived as an apologia for his mistress, the novel—with its over-wrought rhetoric, its tone of a *mea culpa*, and the discontinuity between its apocalyptic historical prologue and the confessions which follow—has not aged well. It had a considerable *succès de scandale* at its publication, however, and elicited passionate controversy for the remainder of the century. Musset's short fiction, collected as *Nouvelles* and *Contes*, was a major source of revenue but, aside from the transposed autobiography of "Le Fils du Titien," does not add significantly to his literary reputation.

Throughout his career, Musset published art and drama reviews and essays. These point up his growing literary conservatism—"classicism" in the terms of the period—yet do not constitute a major contribution to the genre, in comparison with such contemporaries as Gautier or Baudelaire. But the *Lettres de Dupuis et Cotonet*, 1836-7, a satire of Romantic aesthetics, and his reviews of the actress Rachel's revival of neo-classical tragedy, 1838, were influential in the French reaction to Romanticism.

Musset's greatest influence on his century may have been as a quasi-mythic *poète damné*: the portrait of the artist as suffering lover, as self-destructive genius, and ultimately as failure. It is ironic that this apologist for the classical ethos and aesthetic should be one of the models of the Romantic, confessional artist-hero.

—David Sices

NATSUME Soseki.   Born Natsume Kinnosuke in Tokyo, 9 February 1867.   Educated at schools in Tokyo; Tokyo University, 1890-93. Married Nakane Kyoko in 1896; five daughters. Taught at Tokyo Normal College, 1894-95; Middle School, Matsuyama, 1895-1900; lived in England, 1900-02; Professor of English Tokyo University, 1903-07. Member of the staff, *Tetsugaku Zasshi*, 1892; associated with *Asahi* from 1907: in charge of literary columns from 1909. Honorary doctorate: Ministry of Education (refused). *Died 9 December 1916.*

PUBLICATIONS

Collections

Zenshu [Complete Works], edited by Komiya Toyataka.   34 vols., 1956-59.
Zenshu.   16 vols., 1965-67.

Fiction

Wagahai wa Neko de aru. 1905-07; as *I Am a Cat,* 1906-09.
Yokyoshu [Seven Stories]. 1906.
Uzurakago [Three Stories]. 1906.
Botchan. 1906; as *Botchan (Master Darling),* 1918; as *Barchuk,* 1943.
Kusamakura. 1907; as *Unhuman Tour,* 1927; as *The Three-Cornered World,* 1965.
Gubijinso [The Poppy]. 1908.
Kofu [Miner]. 1908.
Sanshiro. 1909; translated as *Sanshiro,* 1977.
Yume Juya. 1910; as *Ten Nights' Dream,* 1934.
Sorekara. 1910; as *And Then,* 1978.
Mon. 1911; translated as *Mon,* 1972.
Higan Sugi made [Until the Equinox]. 1912.
Kojin. 1914; as *The Wanderer,* 1967.
Kokoro. 1914; translated as *Kokoro,* 1941.
Garasudo no Naka. 1915; as *Within My Glass Doors,* 1928.
Michikusa. 1915; as *Grass on the Wayside,* 1969.
Meian (incomplete). 1917; as *Light and Darkness,* 1971.
Ten Nights' Dream, and Our Cat's Grave. 1934.
Ten Nights of Dream, Hearing Things, The Heredity of Taste. 1974.

Other

Eibungaku Keishiki Ron [Theory of Form in English Literature]. 1903.
Bungakuron [Theory of Literature]. 1907.
Bungaku Hyoron [Literary Criticism]. 1909.
Kirinukicho Yori [Random Recollections]. 1911.
Shakai to Jibun [Society and I]. 1913.

*

Bibliography: *Ogai and Soseki* by Naruse Masakatsu and Hashimoto Yoshiichiro, 1965.

Critical Studies: *Natsume* by Beongcheon Yu, 1969; *Two Japanese Novelists: Soseki and Toson* by Edwin McClellan, 1969; *Essays on Natsume's Works,* 1970; *Accomplices of Silence: The Modern Japanese Novel* by Masao Miyoshi, 1974; *Natsume as a Critic of English Literature* by Matsui Sakuko, 1975; *The Psychological World of Natsume* by Takeo Doi, 1976.

*   *   *

One of the leading figures at the formative stage of Japan's "modern" prose fiction, Natsume Soseki is still widely read and highly revered. Acutely aware of the nation's cultural and historical fissure that resulted from the exposure to Western hegemony, he saw the problems of a rapid change everywhere. The inherited values and customs had to be re-examined in the light of new and "rational" knowledge, but this freshly acquired modern insight, too, required authentication both for its legitimacy and adaptability. His earlier studies of English literature may have led him to believe that historical discontinuity was universal, as it was in some sense. The notion of universalism and centrality of the West was, however, not unmixed with a conviction about Japan's distinctness and orientality. As has been the case with most serious Japanese writers since, the major motif of his work from beginning to end was a struggle to make the competing claims somehow compatible and to contain the incongruous and contra-dictory within the narrative form he had to forge.

Reflecting the deep cultural fracture, Soseki's form and style are both traditional and experimental. His attachment to "pre-modern" Edo culture is evident throughout his work: in the colloquialism of the dialogue, the narrator's reference to the commonplace in arts, and the choice of familiar and vulgar characters in the older quarters of Tokyo, which together serve to deflate the pompous pretentions of the newly emerging bureaucracy. Also unmistakable is his fascination with a dense verbal texture—puns, parodies, and periphrases—which he discovered in eighteenth-century *gesaku* (playful writing) books and their entertainment-hall descendants. This, together with his intimate knowledge of Chinese classics, foregrounds Soseki's writing in the art of eloquence. Especially in his earliest works such as *I Am a Cat, Botchan*, and *Three-Cornered World*, Soseki's still youthful buoyancy and energy are at times defined in the imagery and rhetoric of Edo fiction. Soseki, however, was also a "modern" intellectual obsessed with the crisis of alienation. Hero after hero in his works broods darkly and endlessly over his personal isolation and cultural insularity. Mr. Hirota ("Great Darkness") in *Sanshiro*, Daisuke in *And Then*, the Sensei in *Kokoro* are such characters confronting the blind alley of bourgeois life. And in such writing, Soseki's grammar, too, takes on the vocabulary and syntax of an unidiomatic "translation style."

The sentence in *Kokoro* (Heart) is dominated by the first-person pronoun. As in Conrad's *Heart of Darkness* (which Soseki is most likely to have read), the multiple narrators of the work are guides for the reader on a journey inward to glimpse the darkest core of the interior. Deaths abound, and the disrupted narrative sequence finally leads to the starting point that was already a dead end, and the central character's suicide silences the story at the end.

By the time of Soseki's death Japan had been embarking on its own program of expansionism into the Asian continent. His last work, *Light and Darkness*, intimates a firmer will to face the national and social issues with clarity and irony. A bourgeois critic of Imperial Japan, Soseki still remains perhaps the most thoughtful of writers produced in 20th-century Japan.

—Masao Miyoshi

NERUDA, Pablo. Born Neftalí Ricardo Reyes Basoalto in Parral, Chile, 12 July 1904; Pablo Neruda became his legal name, 1946. Educated at school for boys in Temuco, 1910-20; Instituto Pedagógico, Santiago (poetry prize, 1921), in the 1920's. Married María Antonieta Hagenaar in 1930, one daughter; lived with Delia del Carril; married Matilde Urrutia. In Chilean consular and diplomatic service: consul in Rangoon, 1927, Colombo, 1928, Batavia, 1930, Singapore, 1931, Buenos Aires, 1933, Barcelona, 1933, Madrid, 1935-36; helped Spanish refugees as consul in Paris, 1939; Consul-General, Mexico City, 1940-43; elected to Chilean Senate as communist, 1945; attacked President Gonzales Videla in print, and in exile after 1947; returned to Chile after victory of anti-Videla forces, 1952; after Allende's victory in 1970, named Ambassador to France, 1971-72 (resigned because of ill health). Editor, with Manuel Altolaguirre, *Caballo Verde*, Spain, 1935-36, and *Aurora de Chile*, 1938. Member, World Peace Council, from 1950; President, Union of Chilean Writers, 1957-73. Recipient: National Literature Prize, 1945; Stalin Peace Prize, 1953; Viareggio-Versilia Prize, 1967; Nobel Prize for Literature, 1971. Honorary doctorate: University of Michoacán, Mexico, 1941; Oxford University, 1965. Honorary Fellow, Modern Language Association (USA). *Died 23 September 1973.*

Verse

Crepusculario. 1923.
Veinte poemas de amor y una canción desesperada. 1924; as *Twenty Love Poems and a
    Song of Despair*, translated by W.S. Merwin, 1969.
Tentativa del hombre infinito. 1926.
El hondero entusiasta 1923-1924. 1933.
Residencia en la tierra. 2 vols., 1933-35.
Tres cantos materiales. 1935; as *Three Material Songs*, translated by Angel Flores, 1948.
España en el corazón: Himno a las glorias del pueblo en la guerra 1936-1937. 1937.
Las furias y las penas. 1939.
Un canto para Bolívar. 1941.
Selected Poems. 1941.
Nuevo canto de amor a Stalingrado. 1943.
Selected Poems, translated by Angel Flores. 1944.
Obra poética. 10 vols., 1947-48.
Tercera residencia 1935-1945. 1947.
Que despierte el leñador! 1948; as *Peace for Twilights to Come!*, 1950; as *Let the Rail
    Splitter Awake and Other Poems*, 1950.
Himno y regreso. 1948.
Dulce patria. 1949.
Canto general. 1950; translated in part by Nathaniel Tarn, as *The Heights of Macchu
    Picchu*, 1966; as *Poems from Canto General*, translated by Ben Belitt, 1968.
Poesías completas. 1951.
Los versos del capitán: Poemas de amor. 1952; as *The Captain's Verses*, translated by
    Donald D. Walsh, 1972.
Todo el amor (selection). 1953.
Odas elementales, Nuevas odas elementales, Tercer libro de las odas. 3 vols., 1954-57;
    translated by Carlos Lozano, as *Elementary Odes*, 1961.
Las uvas y el viento. 1954.
Oda a la tipografía. 1956.
Estravagario. 1958; translated by Alastair Reid as *Extravagaria*, 1972.
Todo lleva tu nombre. 1959.
Odas: Al libro, a las Americas, a la luz. 1959.
Navegaciones y regresos. 1959.
Cien sonetos de amor. 1959.
Algunas odas. 1959.
Toros. 1960.
Canción de gesta. 1960.
Las piedras de Chile. 1960.
Los primeros versos de amor. 1961.
Selected Poems, translated by Ben Belitt. 1961.
Cantos ceremoniales. 1961.
Plenos poderes. 1961; as *Fully Empowered*, translated by Alastair Reid, 1975.
La insepulta de Paita. 1962.
Oceana. 1962.
Memorial de Isla Negra. 5 vols., 1964; as *Isla Negra: A Notebook*, translated by Alastair
    Reid, 1981.
Bestiary/Bestiario. 1966.
Arte de pájaros. 1966.
We Are Many, translated by Alastair Reid. 1967.
La barcarola. 1967.

Twenty Poems, translated by James Wright and Robert Bly.   1968.
Las manos del día.   1968.
Aún.   1969.
Fin de mundo.   1969.
Early Poems, translated by David Ossman and Carlos B. Hagen.   1969.
A New Decade: Poems 1958-67, translated by Ben Belitt and Alastair Reid.   1969.
La espada encendida.   1970.
Maremoto.   1970.
Las piedras del cielo.   1970.
Selected Poems, edited by Nathaniel Tarn.   1970.
Neruda and Vallejo: Selected Poems, translated by Robert Bly, James Wright, and John
   Knoepfle.   1971.
Geografía infructuosa.   1972.
La rosa separada.   1972.
Incitación al nixonicidio y alabanza de la revolución chilena.   1973; as *Incitation to
   Nixoncide and Praise for the Spanish Revolution*, translated by Steve Kowit, 1973.
Residence on Earth, translated by Donald Walsh.   1973.
El mar y las campanas.   1973.
New Poems 1968-1970, translated by Ben Belitt.   1973.
Jardín de invierno.   1974.
2000.   1974.
El corazón amarillo.   1974.
Libro de las preguntas.   1974.
Elegía.   1974.
Defectos escogidos.   1974.
Five Decades: Poems 1925-1970, translated by Ben Belitt.   1974.

Plays

Romeo and Juliet, from the play by Shakespeare (produced 1964).   1964.
Fulgor y muerte de Joaquín Murieta (produced 1967).   1967; as *Splendor and Death of
   Joaquín Murieta*, translated by Ben Belitt, 1972.

Fiction

El Habitante y su esperanza.   1926.

Other

Prosas.   1926.
Anillos, with Tomas Lagos.   1926.
Neruda entre nosotros, with Emilio Oribe and Juan Marinello.   1939.
La crisis democratica de Chile.   1947; as *The Democratic Crisis of Chile*, 1948.
Cartas a Mexico.   1947.
Viajes al corazon de Quevedo y por las costas del mundo.   1947.
Pablo Neruda acusa.   1948.
Gonzales Videla, el Laval de la America Latina.   1949.
Poesía política: Discursos políticos.   2 vols., 1952.
Cuando de Chile.   1952.
Viajes.   1955.
Obras completas.   1957; 4th edition, 3 vols., 1973.
Cuba, los obispos.   1962 (?).

Una casa en la arena. 1966.
Comiendo en Hungría, with M.A. Asturias. 1968.
Confieso que he vivido. 1974; as *Memoirs,* 1977.
Cartas de amor, edited by Sergio Larrain. 1974.
Cartas a Laura, edited by Hugo Montes. 1978.
Correspondancia, with Héctor Eandi, edited by Margarita Aguirre. 1980.
Para nacer he nacido. 1980; as *Passions and Impressions,* 1982.

Editor and translator, *Páginas escogidas de Anatole France.* 1924.

Translator, *44 poetas rumanos.* 1967.

*

Bibliography: *Neruda: Bibliografía* by Horacio Jorge Becco, 1975.

Critical Studies: *The Word and the Stone: Language and Imagery in Neruda's "Canto General"* by Frank Riess, 1972; *The Poetry of Neruda* by René de Costa, 1979; *Neruda: All Poets the Poet* by Salvatore Bizzaro, 1979; *Translating Neruda: The Way to Macchu Picchu* by John Felstiner, 1981; *Earth Tones: The Poetry of Neruda* by Manuel Durán and Margery Safir, 1981; *Neruda: The Poetics of Prophecy* by Enrico Mario Santí, 1982.

*   *   *

Pablo Neruda, sometimes called the Picasso of poetry, is a writer of many styles and many voices; his vast and varied work, spanning more than half a century, is central to every major development in Spanish and Spanish American poetry between the 1920's and the 1970's. Despite his humble beginnings (born into a working-class family and raised in a rough-and-tumble frontier town in the south of Chile), by the time he turned twenty he had come to occupy a preeminent place in the literature of his country.

Twenty Love Poems and a Song of Despair was a succès de scandale when it first appeared in 1924. Judged to be shamelessly erotic and faulted for its bold departure in form and style from the genteel tradition of Hispanic lyricism the book went on to become something of a best-seller, and remains so today. Its power derives from Neruda's new and unusual treatment of the age-old subject of love. Employing a dense and almost hermetic language combining the normally unarticulated level of digressive thought and the ordered level of logical discourse, each poem is a kind of monologue in which the poet speaks as though to himself and to an absent lover. Making use of a rhetoric which is not conventionally poetic (staggered repetitions, an irregular temporal exposition, and a prosaic syntax), Neruda managed to convey a quality that was often lacking in traditional love poetry: the quality of sincerity and conviction. The result was a highly charged confessional intimacy which challenged and charmed the sensibility of its reader, creating in the process a contemporary *stil nuovo* which continues to resonate in the language of love in Spanish.

Tentativa del hombre infinito furthered the poet's experiments with form and placed him in the forefront of the Chilean avant-garde. In this long and difficult poem, organized in fifteen cantos around the idea of a nocturnal voyage in search of the absolute, he foregoes the use of rhyme, meter, capitalization and punctuation to attain a more concentrated literary language capable of conveying a maximum degree of subjectivity. The poem's seemingly unmediated discourse is similar in texture to that of Surrealist writing but differs in that it is not the outcome of "psychic automatism," but the result of a lengthy compositional process of revision and modification, pruning relator words, connectives, and punctuation so as to enhance the run-on associative power of the imagery. Neruda, in his later years, called attention to this vanguard experiment of 1926, relating it to his hermetic poetry of the *Residencia* cycle.

Residencia en la tierra I & II (translated as *Residence on Earth*), when published in Spain in 1935, was hailed by García Lorca and others as "one of the most authentic realities of poetry in the Spanish language today." At the time Neruda also felt that in this work he had achieved a kind of perfection and "had passed a literary limit" hitherto thought impossible. *Residencia*, which assured his international fame, is a work in two volumes, the first of which was originally published in Chile in a limited edition of 100 copies and contains poems written in the Far East where Neruda had served as a consular official from 1927 to 1931. These texts cover a diverse range of topics, from monsoons to marriage, and stand as individual testimonials of moments of heightened awareness. The discourse is quite free, unbound by logic, and despite the ample use of prosaic locutions utilizes an unprosaic reasoning process based on implied and generative associations. Although the basic discursive situation is soliloquial, as in the earlier poetry, the style is decidedly anti-lyrical, often jarring the reader's sensibility with references to the ordinary and the "unpoetic." In 1935 *Residencia I* was reissued with a companion volume, *Residencia II*, containing Neruda's more recent poetry and a significant change of form and style: where once the poet had been concentrated and introspective, he is now digressive and outward. Essentially, by the mid-1930's, Neruda was beginning to write a poetry to be spoken out loud, not to be read in silence, and for the first time his discourse is addressed not to an absent personage or to the poet's inner self, but to his reader. The second *Residencia*, dealing engagingly with life's random experiences substantiated a new kind of poetic realism. In a manifesto of the time ("On Impure Poetry"), Neruda explains this change, speaking out against his earlier hermetic writing and against the ultra-refined estheticism of "pure poetry." His goal henceforth was a poetry that was not only sincere but also uninvented, in a word "realistic."

Tercera residencia, a collection of post-*Residencia* poems, documents Neruda's new social and political awareness. The realities of Fascism and the Spanish Civil War provoked a shift in perspective, transforming his poetic realism to a more committed kind of writing. The idea was to use the persuading power of literature to make the reader share the writer's view of the socio-political realities of a world at war. Oral diction is enhanced and rendered poetic through a revival of traditional poetic forms: rhymed stanzas and metered verses. At this point, secure in his position as a public poet, Neruda assumed a broader role, spokesman for the continent.

Canto general, the general song of America, presenting in some 500 pages and almost 20,000 verses the theme of man's struggle for justice in the New World, is by far his most ambitious work, and caused a sensation when it first appeared in 1950. Even today critics are split into two camps over the contents of this text: those who oppose Neruda's militant politics (he joined the Communist Party in 1945) and those who share them. Politics aside, the work is masterful for its epic sweep and for the extraordinary variety and quantity of old and new poetic forms and voices employed to maintain reader interest and render persuasive the political message.

Odas elementales continues Neruda's efforts to reach the common man, to bring poetry to the people. Political without appearing to be politicized, simple without being simplistic, it appealed to an extraordinary wide range of readers through a seemingly artless, almost breezy series of compositions exalting the most basic things of daily existence, the plain and the ordinary, fruits and flowers, thread and bread. Since many of these poems were first published in the columns of a daily newspaper the style is simple and straightforward, the verses are short and direct, and the tone is intimate and conversational. *Estravagario* took the conversational mode of the odes one step further, desolemnizing poetry itself. In this book, for the first time, everything is treated irreverently, even politics—and in a sardonic tone and an everyday manner typical of what has come to be called anti-poetry.

Neruda, in his later years tried his hand at theater (*Splendor and Death of Joaquín Murieta*), and took a more direct role in politics, serving as the Communist Party's pre-candidate to the 1970 elections which brought Salvador Allende to power. He continued to cultivate a poetry concerned with the here and now: the Cuban revolution in *Canción de gesta*; Vietnam and the generally deplorable state of the world in *Fin de mundo*; and Nixon in *Incitation to Nixoncide*. Two volumes of memoirs and several volumes of posthumously published poetry cap this extraordinary career in the literature of our time.

—René de Costa

NERVAL, Gérard de. Pseudonym for Gérard Labrunie. Born in Paris, 22 May 1808. Educated at Lycée Charlemagne, Paris, 1820-28; possibly apprenticed to a printer and studied law; studied medicine to 1834. Led a life of wandering; after inheriting money from his grandfather in 1834 founded *Le Monde Dramatique*, 1835; drama critic, *La Presse*, and contributor to other journals from 1838. Hospitalized in mental clinics, 1841, 1849, 1851, 1853, 1854. *Died 26 January 1855.*

PUBLICATIONS

Collections

> *Oeuvres complètes*, edited by Aristide Marie, Jules Marsan, and Édouard Champion. 6 vols., 1926-32.
> *Oeuvres complémentaires*, edited by Jean Richer. 1959—.
> *Oeuvres*, edited by Albert Béguin and Jean Richer. 2 vols., 1960-61.

Verse

> *Élégies nationales.* 1826.
> *Les Chimères*, in *Les Filles du feu.* 1854; edited by Norma Rinsler, 1973; as *The Chimeras*, translated by Andrew Hoyem, 1966, and Derek Mahon, 1982.
> *Fortune's Fool: Thirty-Five Poems*, translated by Brian Hill. 1959.

Plays

> *Piquillo*, with Alexandre Dumas, père, music by Hippolyte Monpou (produced 1837). 1837.
> *Léo Burckart*, with Alexandre Dumas, père (produced 1839). 1839.
> *L'Alchimiste*, with Alexandre Dumas, père (produced 1839). 1839.
> *Les Monténégrins*, with E. Alboize, music by Armand Limnander (produced 1849). 1849.
> *Le Chariot d'enfant*, with Joseph Méry (produced 1850).
> *L'Imagier de Harlem*, with Joseph Méry and Bernard Lopez, music by Adolphe de Groot (produced 1851). 1852.

Fiction

> *Contes et facéties.* 1852.
> *Les Filles du feu.* 1854; as *Daughters of Fire*, 1923.
> *Aurélia.* 1855; translated as *Aurelia*, 1933; as *Dreams and Life*, 1933.
> *Le Prince des sots*, edited by Louis Ulbach. 1866.

Other

> *Voyage en Orient.* 1851; translated in part as *The Women of Cairo*, 1929; as *Journey to the Orient*, edited by Norman Glas, 1972.
> *Les Illuminés; ou, Les Précurseurs du socialisme.* 1852.
> *Lorély.* 1852.
> *Petits châteaux de Bohème: Prose et poésie.* 1853.
> *Selected Writings*, edited by G. Wagner. 1958.

Le Carnet de Dolbreuse, edited by Jean Richer.   1967.

Editor, *Choix des poésies de Ronsard.*   1830.
Editor and translator, *Choix de poésies allemandes.*   1830.

Translator, *Faust,* by Goethe.   1828; augmented edition, *Faust, et Le Second Faust,* 1840.

*

Bibliography: *Nerval: Essai de bibliographie* by Jean Senelier, 1959, supplement, 1968, 1982; *Nerval: A Critical Bibliography 1900-1967* by James Villas, 1968.

Critical Studies: *Nerval: L'Homme et l'oeuvre* by Léon Cellier, 1956; *Nerval and the German Heritage* by Alfred Dubreck, 1965; *The Disinherited: The Life of Nerval* by Benn Sowerby, 1973; *Nerval* by Norma Rinsler, 1973; *The Style of Nerval's Aurelia* by William Beauchamp, 1976.

*   *   *

Gérard de Nerval, who belonged to the generation of the younger Romantics, published his first volumes of verse while still at school, and translated Goethe's *Faust* before he was twenty. His precocious and graceful talent was threatened from his early thirties onwards by bouts of alternating depression and elation which led to several periods of treatment in clinics and to a widespread belief among his contemporaries that he was incurably mad. This reputation bedevilled criticism of his achievement for at least a century, since the more difficult of his works were labelled as incoherent or insane. More recently it has become clear that late texts such as *Dreams and Life* and "Pandora" are accounts of a mind obsessed by the search for the ideal, distracted by guilt for its human failings, but lucidly aware of the sources of its problems. Early in the 20th century, Nerval was best known as a poet; his sonnets, *Les Chimères,* were rediscovered by the French Symbolists and acclaimed in both France and England as examples of "pure" poetry. A more judicious approach to these immensely dense and complex poems may be attempted by way of the prose pieces in *Daughters of Fire,* with which they were originally published: in "Sylvie," he offers a penetrating analysis of the dilemma of the French Romantics, torn between their heritage of 18th-century rationalism, their daily experience of social and political disorder, and their frustrated idealism; the clash between religion and reason appears again in "Isis" (*Daughters of Fire*), and also in the study of "Quintus Aucler" in *Les Illuminés* (The Illuminati). *Dreams and Life* explores the role of dream as a non-rational mode of knowledge, and Nerval concludes that reason alone is not the road to salvation. "Les Chimeres" means "illusions," but illusions may be consciously preferred, may indeed be necessary; and the world of the illusory ideal is brilliantly explored in "Sylvie," where the dream-like course of the narrative mirrors the theme.

Nerval's writings are interrelated to a quite remarkable extent; almost every work finds echoes and inversions of its themes and images in other works ranging over the whole of his career. His concerns are deeply serious, but he is never solemn. Nor is he only a dreamer: fantasy, humour, and compassion are blended with sharp observation in "Les Nuits d'Octobre" (October Nights), in "Angélique," in "Promenades et Souvenirs" (Excursions and Memories), and in his travel books. The sonnets are technically very interesting, using a method of juxtaposition later much favoured by the Surrealists, but creating thereby a coherent network of musical echoes and resonant images which maps a mental landscape, engaging the reader's understanding without asking for his indulgence. Difficult poetry, in the sense that it demands very close attention to syntax and to what the words are actually saying—the sonnets are tightly organised structures which a relaxed and "lyrical" reading will fail to grasp—but dignified and approachable poetry in which Nerval believed he had managed to say what was most important to him.

—Norma Rinsler

NIBELUNGENLIED. German poem of c. 1200, probably composed in Austria; the author is possibly to be linked with the court of Wolfger von Erla, Bishop of Passau, 1191-1204.

PUBLICATIONS

Nibelungenleid

B manuscript group: edited by Karl Bartsch. 1870-80; revised by Helmut de Boor, 1963.
A manuscript: edited by Karl Lachmann. 1826; revised by Ulrich Pretzel and Willy Krogmann, 1960.
C manuscript: edited by Friedrich Zarncke. 1856; also edited by Adolf Holtzmann, 1857, and Ursula Hennig, 1977.
Nibelungenlied und Kudrun, edited by Heinz Rupp. 1982.

Translations: by A.T. Hatto, 1965, D.G. Mowatt, 1962, and Frank G. Ryder, 1962.

*

Bibliography: *The Study of the Nibelungenlied* by Mary Thorp, 1940; *Bibliographie zum Nibelungenlied und zur Klage* by Willy Krogmann and Ulrich Pretzel, 1966; *Nibelungenlied-Studien* by Werner Schroeder, 1968.

Critical Studies: *The Nibelungenlied Today* by Werner A. Mueller, 1962; *Des Nibelungenlied: Stoff, Form, Ethos* by Bert Nagel, 1965; *The Nibelungenlied: An Interpretative Commentary* by D.G. Mowatt and Hugh Sacker, 1967; *The Nibelungenlied: A Literary Analysis* by Hugo Bekker, 1971.

*   *   *

The events narrated in the *Nibelungenlied* fall into two distinct halves. In the first half, the hero Siegfried grows up in the Netherlands and moves to the Burgundian court at Worms. Here he eventually wins Kriemhilde, the King's sister, in marriage, but he is then murdered by his hosts. In the second half of the story his widow Kriemhilde marries Attila, moving to what is now Hungary. She induces the Burgundians to visit her from Worms and takes revenge for the death of Siegfried when the Burgundians are in various stages eventually massacred to the last man by their Hunnish hosts.

There are various sub-plots. The most important one is the complex theme of Kriemhilde's brother Gunther. He is married to the Icelandic queen Brunhilde, who however continually displays a relentless sexual affinity (presumably of extremely ancient origin in the development of the legend) with Kriemhilde's husband Siegfried.

It is established historical fact that the Burgundians were massacred by the Huns in 437: but Attila was not there and moreover his death in the bed of a woman of Germanic extraction did not take place until 453. In the *Nibelungenlied* she is promoted to his wife and the two events are chronologically reversed. She prompts the massacre of the Burgundians after the marriage. These and numerous similar observations show how the poem distorts history unrecognizably in the 750-year course of its development. It seems that adaptations were frequently made quite consciously in order to suit changing fashions of literary and cultural taste. The factual basis of many features of the poem must of course have been lost beyond redemption.

The version which we possess is itself unrestrained in its radical modernisation of the tradition. All the characters exhibit the most exquisite courtly taste, breeding, and self-restraint. The poem tells of many festivals and contests and of much lavish and sensitive hospitality. The warriors are capable of displaying immense courtesy to each other even as they fight to the death. In Book 37 for example Ruediger gives his shield to his enemy Hagen.

Such noble behaviour is not confined in literature to the courtly warriors of the High Middle

Ages. In this instance there is no real conflict between the traditional material and the tastes of the era in which our version was composed. But of very great interest are the numerous instances where the tradition proves incompatible with the intentions of the poet. The result is a large number of most interesting inconsistencies and evasions. The poet is reticent, for example, about the provenance of Siegfried's magical powers and about the background to Albrecht the Dwarf and his cloak of invisibility which could play no part in courtly behaviour. In a parallel version a quarrel between two queens is based on one of them dirtying the river water in which the other is washing her hair. The courtly version changes this to an essentially unconvincing argument about who should enter Church first. Furthermore why the quarrel should break out at this time rather than years earlier is never made clear.

There are countless similar weaknesses of construction of recent or less recent origin. One assumes that each one was consciously introduced because of some overriding cultural consideration valid at a given time. The work is of great length and there are parallel versions especially in Norse and German sources which must have diverged from the tradition represented in our version at different times. The events can be identified with historical events sometimes with certainty, sometimes vaguely, and sometimes not at all. These circumstances combine to make the pre-history of the *Nibelungenlied* and its gradual evolution a study of the utmost complexity and fascination.

The work also has a genuine appeal as a work of literature. The poet introduces emotional sensitivity to characters who in the hands of less gifted authors of parallel versions remain the fairly lifeless bearers of famous historical names. For all the myriad inconsistencies of detail, a powerful tragedy is told with a clear linear development in verses of sustained lucidity and power. There is not a poetically weak line in the whole poem. There are many striking effects, such as the dead and wounded bodies of the Huns being thrown out of the hall in Book 34. If the poetry lacks the truly striking originality and lyrical beauty of some other contemporary work, the *Nibelungenlied* remains a monumental achievement. It is one of the most impressive and powerful of all medieval epics and preserved for Germany its most important national legends in a form which gives them a prominent place on the stage of world literature.

—G.P. Cubbin

NOVALIS. Pseudonym for Georg Philipp Friedrich Leopold von Hardenberg. Born in Oberwiederstedt, 2 May 1772. Studied at universities of Jena, Leipzig, and Wittenberg, 1790-94; completed law studies, 1794; studied mining in Freiberg, 1797-99. Actuary for Kreisamtmann Just, Tennstedt, 1794-97; assistant in salt works, Weissenfels, 1796-97, 1799-1801; associated with Bergakademie, Freiberg, 1797-99. *Died 25 March 1801.*

PUBLICATIONS

Collections

Schriften, edited by Ludwig Tieck and Friedrich Schlegel. 2 vols., 1802.
Schriften, edited by J. Minor. 4 vols., 1907.
Sämtliche Werke, edited by Ernst Kamnitzer. 4 vols., 1924.

Werke, Briefe, Dokumente, edited by E. Wasmuth. 4 vols., 1953.
Schriften, edited by Paul Kluckholn and Richard Samuel. 4 vols., 1960-75.
Werke, edited by Gerhard Schulz. 1969.

Verse

Devotional Songs, edited by Bernard Pick. 1910.
Hymns to the Night, translated by Mabel Cotterell. 1948.
Sacred Songs, translated by Eileen Hutchins. 1956.

*

Critical Studies: *Novalis* by F. Hiebel, 1954; *Novalis: The Veil of Imagery* by Bruce Haywood, 1959; *Novalis'"Fichte Studies": The Foundation of His Aesthetics* by Geza W.E. Von Molnár, 1970; *Bifocal Vision: Novalis' Philosophy of Nature and Disease* by John Neubacher, 1971; *Blake and Novalis: A Comparison of Romanticism's High Arguments* by Joachim J. Scholz, 1978; *The Boundless Present: Space and Time in the Literary Fairy Tales of Novalis and Tieck* by Gordon Birrell, 1979; *The Fichtean Dynamic of Novalis' Poetics* by Richard W. Hannah, 1981; *The Androgyne in Early German Romanticism: Friedrich Schlegel, Novalis, and the Metaphysics of Love* by Sara Friedrichsmeyer, 1983.

*   *   *

Novalis, the central figure of early German Romanticism, combines strong philosophical leanings with his poetic gift. It was his view that "the separation of philosopher from poet is only apparent and to the disadvantage of both." The poet is for him both seer and scientist, priest and craftsman, whose ability to harmonize and unify can overcome the divisions of human knowledge. "Blütenstaub," his early contribution to the Schlegel brothers' journal *Athenäum*, takes the form of speculative "Fragments" which display novel powers of creative thinking through the use of analogue, metaphor, conceit, and paradox. His literary beginnings reflect assiduous study of contemporary Romantic thought (Fichte, Schelling) as well as of the Mystic Jacob Böhme.

A highly individual form of religious mysticism informs a great part of Novalis's writings. His essay "Die Christenheit oder Europa," which looks back nostalgically to pre-Reformation times, offers an idealized image of an undivided Church and society; it became an influential document of German Romantic attitudes to Catholicism. The *Hymns to the Night*, immediately inspired by the death of his 15-year-old fiancée, Sophie von Kühn, are mystical celebrations of a love which finds its transcendental fulfilment beyond the grave. The painful consciousness of finite existence redeemed by an assurance of eternal union through love, the inversion of life and death symbolism, the fusion of eroticism and religion, are features which give these rhythmic prose poems a complex richness of texture. The unfinished novel *Heinrich von Ofterdingen* represents the poet's vocation in terms of a symbolic journey in search of "the blue flower" (subsequently to become the representative symbol of all Romanticism). Heinrich's various encounters with dream, fairy-tale, myth, nature symbolism, and poetic art represent stages in the growth of the poet's self-awareness. The goal of fulfilment towards which he securely moves is essentially a form of self-knowledge which unites elements of erotic, spiritual, and religious experience. The *Geistliche Lieder*, based on the Pietist hymn tradition, are confessional in character, conveying intimate accents of Romantic yearning. The combination of mystical religiosity with Romantic sensibility and imagination places these devotional songs outside orthodoxy.

Novalis is a master of the aphorism, and the greater part of his oeuvre consists of fragmentary thoughts on a vast range of subjects from experimental physics to poetics, from school philosophy to magic. His plan was to bring about a unification of disparate human knowledge into a kind of encyclopedia which he called "a scientific bible." The creation of wholeness, the

NOVALIS

reconciliation of disparities, were Romantic ideals which he strove to realize in the realm of thought. The characteristic form of most of Novalis's aphorisms involves either a synthesis which attempts to bridge the dialectical divide, or an arresting analogue which forms a connection. Among his most stimulating and fruitful contributions are his ideas on literary, aesthetic, and philosophical topics. By virtue of his paramount gift of symbolic statement Novalis became of seminal importance to the Symbolist movement in France and his influence on later 19th-century neo-Romanticism was equally important.

—Alexander Stillmark

OMAR KHAYYAM. Born in Nishapur, Persia, 18 May 1048. Well-educated in geometry and astronomy. In Samarkand, worked for the chief magistrate, Abu Taher, and the ruler of Bokhara, Shamsolmolk Nasr; later entered the service of the Saljuq Sultan Malikshah (ruled 1072-92): helped in construction of an observatory and in compiling a set of astronomical tables as the basis of a new calendar era; journey in 1095 to Mecca and Baghdad, then returned to Nishapur. Contemporary reputation was as a scientist, and some mathematical works have survived. *Died 4 December 1131.*

PUBLICATIONS

Verse

Rubaiyat, edited by M.A. Forughi and Q. Ghani, 1942; also edited by B.A. Rozenfeld and A.P. Yushkevish, 1961; as *The Rubaiyat of Omar Khayyam*, translated by Edward Fitzgerald, 1859; also translated by John C.E. Bowen, 1961, Parichehr Kasra, 1975, and Peter Avery and John Heath-Stubbs, 1979

*

Bibliography: *A Bibliography of the Rubaiyat* by A.C. Potter, 1929.

Critical Studies: *Critical Studies in the Ruba'iyat* by Arthur Christensen, 1927; *The Nectar of Grace: Omar Khayyam's Life and Works* (includes translations of some scientific works) by Swami Govinda Tirtha, 1941; *The Romance of the Rubaiyat: Edward Fitzgerald's First Edition Reprinted, with Introduction and Notes* by A.J. Arberry, 1959; *In Search of Omar Khayyam* by Ali Dashti, 1971.

*   *   *

The name Omar Khayyam is more accurately transliterated from its original Persian as "Umar-i-Khayyam," Umar the son of the tent-maker, but since publication in 1859 of Edward Fitzgerald's brilliant English versions of the *rubaiyat* (literally, quatrains) attributed to this poet, he has been known to too many as Omar Khayyam for this style to be dropped. He was born in 1048 in the northeastern Iranian city of Nishapur, where he died and was buried in 1131.

His times were perilous. Saljuq Turks, tribesmen from the steppes of central Asia, an environment very different from that of the sophisticated city in which Omar was brought up, were completing their infiltration of Iran, Mesopotamia, and Asia Minor at the time of his birth, and by the year of his death near to consolidating a great empire which extended from the River Oxus to Syria, the area where they confronted the Crusaders from Europe. One of the more remarkable of the early Saljuq Sultans was Jalalu'd-Din Malikshah, who reigned from 1072 to 1092. He figured in Omar's life in the latter's capacity as astronomer and mathematician.

In fact, if we followed what Omar's contemporaries had to say of him we should be extolling him as a mathematician and one of the most eminent philosophers of his time, not as a poet, and certainly not as composer of four-part stanzas of a markedly irreligious and sceptical kind. Before he was 30 he had produced a work on algebra that established him as the pioneer of cubic equations and is still accessible to scholars both in its original Persian and in translation. Thus in 1074 Omar was among the astronomers summoned by Malikshah to revise the calendar and build a new observatory. The result was the new Jalali or Maliki Era, which dated from 16th March 1079.

This practical interest in the application of astronomy indicates a pragmatic side to the Turkish warlords by whom Omar and his contemporaries were ruled, but as recent converts to Islam and leaders who had prospered since becoming Muslim, the Saljuq Sultans showed a powerful proclivity to insist on a rigorously orthodox practice of religion, the more so since their empire was threatened by the Frankish knights from without and by serious heresies within. Omar Khayyam, the great mathematician, seems, on the other hand, to have been a man as devoutly rational as the decrees of Sultans would have had him devoutly Muhammadan. It is perhaps for this reason his contemporaries are silent about his composition of boldly irreligious quatrains, which were no doubt circulated clandestinely and anonymously. It is significant that a writer who speaks of Omar some ninety-odd years after his death and is among the first to mention the *rubaiyat* only does so to castigate their composer and the verses themselves as wholly evil and corrupt. Yet that Omar's poems should be as sceptical as they are is hardly surprising since they were the products (where genuinely his as many are probably not) of an age when assiduous government patronage of religion must have encourged a type of hypocrisy which would be repugnant to a thinker like Omar.

Materials for his biography in contemporary records are in fact sparse. One contemporary describes him somewhat unfavourably as a testy old philosopher who did not suffer fools gladly; but this description softens when the writer comes to mention the circumstances of the great teacher's death as he was quietly studying a favourite text. Another notice, by a former pupil, says that Omar did not believe in forecasts of the future but nevertheless foretold his own death and did so at a party of friends the nature of which proves him to have had a convivial side to his character. He also foretold that he would be buried in a spot outside his native city where almond blossom would fall on his grave each spring. It still does, no doubt deservedly on the grave of a man whose thoughts, expressed in pithy, word-thrifty four-lined stanzas, have found an echo as widely accepted epigrams in the minds of so many, and well may continue to do so as long as human-beings remain perplexed over the purpose of the universe and man's place in it.

—Peter Avery

OVID (Publius Ovidius Naso). Born in Sulmo (now Sulmona), Abruzzi, 20 March 43 B.C. Educated in the schools of rhetoric in Rome under Arellius Fuscus and Porcius Latro; also studied in Athens, and traveled in Greece. Married three times; one daughter, probably from second marriage. Held minor judicial posts, but abandoned public career for poetry, in circle of Messalla; banished for an unknown offence by the emperor Augustus to Tomis (now Constanta, Romania), on the Black Sea, 8 A.D.: served in the Tomis home guard during times of barbarian unrest, and wrote some poetry in the local language, Getic. *Died 17 A.D.*

PUBLICATIONS

Collections

[*Works*], edited by Rudolf Ehwald and others. 1916-78; translated by Grant Showerman and others (Loeb edition), 6 vols., 1914-31.

Verse

Amores [Loves], edited by E.J. Kenney. 1965; also edited by F. Munari, 1970; translated by Rolfe Humphries, 1957, Horace Gregory, 1964, Guy Lee, 1968, and Peter Green, 1982.
Heroides (*Epistulae heroidum*) [Heroines], edited by H. Dörrie. 1971; translated by Harold C. Cannon, 1972.
Ars Amatoria [Art of Love], edited by E.J. Kenney. 1954; also edited by F.W. Lenz, 1969; translated by Rolfe Humphries, 1957, Horace Gregory, 1964, B.P. Moore, 1965, Paul Turner, 1968, and Peter Green, 1982.
Remedia Amoris [Cures for Love], edited by E.J. Kenney. 1965; also edited by A.A.R. Henderson, 1979; translated by Rolfe Humphries, 1957, Horace Gregory, 1964, Paul Turner, 1968, and Peter Green, 1982.
Fasti [Calendar], edited by G.B. Pighi. 2 vols., 1973; also edited by Franz Bömer and H. Le Bonniec, 2 vols., 1969-71.
Metamorphoses [Transformations], edited by M. Haupt and others. 1966; as *The Metamorphoses*, translated by A.E. Watts, 1954, Rolfe Humphries, 1955, M.M. Innes, 1955, and Horace Gregory, 1958.
Tristia [Sorrows], edited by S.G. Owen. 1915; also edited by Georg Luck, 2 vols., 1967-77; translated by A.L. Wheeler, 1924, and L.R. Lind, 1975.
Epistulae ex Ponto [Letters from the Black Sea], edited by S.G. Owen. 1915; also edited by Jacques André, 1977; translated by A.L. Wheeler, 1924.

*

Critical Studies: *Ovid, A Poet Between Two Worlds* by H. Fränkel, 1945; *Ovid Recalled* by L.P. Wilkinson, 1955, shortened version as *Ovid Surveyed*, 1962; *The Mystery of Ovid's Exile* by J.C. Thibault, 1964; *Ovid as an Epic Poet* by Brooks Otis, 1966, revised edition, 1970; *Ovid* edited by J.W. Binns, 1973; *Ovid's Heroides* by Howard Jacobson, 1974; *Ovid's Metamorphoses: An Introduction to the Basic Aspects* by G. Karl Galinsky, 1975; *Ovid* by John Barsby, 1978; *History in Ovid* by Ronald Syme, 1978; *The Poetics of Exile: Program and Polemic in the Tristia and Epistulae ex Ponto of Ovid* by Betty Rose Nagle, 1980.

* * *

Among the classical Latin poets Ovid stands in the highest rank. He may be inferior to Virgil in depth of feeling and in seriousness of purpose, but as a poet of wit and sensibility and of verbal and narrative skill he has no equal.

His earliest work was the *Amores* ("Loves"), a collection of love elegies probably written between his 18th and 25th years. This has come down to us in a later edition, reduced from five books to three, but remains essentially the work of his early period. The collection is centered upon an affair with a mistress called Corinna, who must be regarded as fictitious rather than merely pseudonymous. They are poems of the intellect, not of emotional involvement. What Ovid is doing is taking the contemporary genre of love elegy and mischievously playing with its conventions. Most of the stock themes and situations occur, but always with some sort of comic twist. In Ovid's hands the traditional lover acquires a new *persona*, who regards the frustrations of the genre as a challenge rather than as a source of gloom. Beneath the fun there is perhaps a serious point: Ovid is offering the Romans a new light-hearted approach to love, which avoids both the hopeless idealism of the elegists and the moral strictures of the philosophers.

Next Ovid wrote the *Heroides* ("Heroines"), imaginary verse epistles from mythological heroines to their faithless lovers. This collection was expanded at some later date by the addition of some "paired" letters, in which the heroine's reply is set beside a letter received from her love. The *Heroides* had no precedent in Greek or Latin literature. In inventing the genre Ovid set himself the challenge of creating variety out of a potentially repetitive set of situations. He meets this by choosing heroines whose external circumstances are different and then giving each an individual character. At the same time he contrives to provide a new slant on the particular myth in the manner of the Greek poets of the Alexandrian age, often with a humanising or modernising touch. There is a certain artificiality about the exercise. But there are passages of pathos and lyricism, and beneath the rhetoric Ovid does show a sympathetic understanding of female psychology, if not the psychoanalytical powers with which some modern critics have credited him.

For his next variation on the theme of love Ovid turned to the didactic genre, with his *Ars Amatoria* ("Art of Love") and its sequel *Remedia Amoria* ("Cures for Love"). Didactic poetry had a long and honourable tradition; these poems constitute a light-hearted burlesque of the genre. The *Ars* is not a pornographic or even an erotic work. Its theme is how to catch and keep a mistress or lover (men are addressed in the first two books, and women in the third), and its tone is essentially the amused detached tone of the *Amores*, where indeed a number of the precepts here given are foreshadowed. The same tone is maintained in the *Remedia*, where Ovid neatly and ironically reverses his previous stance to advise those seeking a release from love. These are cultivated poems, enlivened with some vivid vignettes of contemporary Roman life. But unfortunately for Ovid this was not the kind of cultivation that commended itself to the emperor Augustus, who was at the time trying to revive traditional Roman morality and the institution of marriage.

Whatever the emperor may have thought, Ovid had now worked out his amatory vein, and he turned to two large-scale poems, on which he seems to have worked simultaneously. The *Fasti* ("Calendar") is a versified calendar of Roman religious observances in six books covering the first six months of the year (it was never completed). On the surface this seems to represent a conversion from irresponsible personal poetry to patriotic Roman themes, and the work does contain in passing some contemporary Augustan propaganda. But the real inspiration behind it was the Alexandrian poet Callimachus, who had written an *Aetia* ("Origins") explaining Greek customs and rites; Ovid was setting himself to write a Roman equivalent, though the spirit would still be essentially Greek. The *Fasti* incorporates a large amount of religious and antiquarian lore, which Ovid serves up with a characteristic mixture of wit and sensitivity, making the most of the opportunities it offers for extended passages of narrative and description. Many of the individual stories are brilliantly told, but the work as a whole suffers from a lack of unity and continuity.

Meanwhile Ovid was writing the *Metamorphoses* ("Transformations"), his greatest work both in size and in achievement. It is a collection of some 250 myths and legends strung together in a loosely chronological order from the Creation and Flood to the deification of Julius Caesar. As the title implies, the myths are linked by the common theme of metamorphosis; but in many cases the metamorphosis is tangential to the main story, and Ovid in fact draws on the whole corpus of Greek and Roman mythology with some near Eastern added. The incorporation of all this material into a continuous poem of epic proportions is itself a tour de force involving ingenious and often audacious transitions. The great qualities of the work are its narrative brilliance and its human interest. Ovid abandons the end-stopped elegiac couplets of his earlier works and develops a flowing narrative style which carries the reader effortlessly along. At the same time the sheer scale of the work provides scope for some exuberant rhetorical effects—in set speeches, dramatic narrative, allegory, and description. The frequency of divine intervention (often comic or cruel) and of metamorphosis itself gives the poem an air of unreality, but neither this nor the poet's irrepressible wit destroys the human interest with which the stories are invested. Its imitation by writers and painters down the centuries is eloquent testimony to the greatness of the poem.

At the age of 51 Ovid was suddenly banished by Augustus to Tomis on the shores of the Black Sea. From here he wrote two collections of verse epistles, the *Tristia* ("Sorrows") in five books and the *Epistulae ex Ponto* ("Letters from the Black Sea") in four, addressed to his wife, the emperor, and various friends at Rome, describing the hardships of exile and pleading for his recall. This poetry has to be appreciated against the situation which produced it. Tomis was a barbaric outpost of the empire, where the Latin language was not even spoken; Ovid was cut off not only from family and friends but from the whole civilised culture which was his inspiration. Some of the exile poems are immediately attractive, as pieces of narrative or description or as expressions of simple emotion. If the rest end by seeming monotonous, two qualities stand out—the degree of poetic artifice which Ovid still employs, and the note of defiance by which he appeals over Augustus's head to public opinion at Rome and asserts the overriding validity of his calling as a poet. Ovid died in exile unpardoned: it was a sad end to Rome's most brilliant poet.

—John Barsby

PASOLINI, Pier Paolo. Born in Bologna, Italy, 5 March 1922. Educated at the University of Bologna, Ph.D. Served in the Italian Army, 1943. Writer, film director, and actor. Editor, *Officina*, 1955-58; columnist, *Tempo Illustrato*. Founder, Academy of Friulan Language. Recipient (for films): Karlovy Vary Festival award, 1962; Silver Bear Award, 1971; Golden Bear Award, 1972; Cannes special jury award, 1974; (for verse): Viareggio Prize, 1958. *Died (murdered) 2 November 1975.*

PUBLICATIONS

Collections

Opere. 1978—.

Fiction

Ragazzi di vita. 1955; as *The Ragazzi*, 1968.

Una vita violenta. 1959; as *A Violent Life*, 1968.
Il sogno di una cosa. 1962.
Alì dagli occhi azzurri. 1965.
Teorema. 1968.

Plays

Accattone (screenplay). 1961.
Il Vangelo Secondo Matteo (screenplay). 1964.
Uccellacci e uccellini (screenplay). 1966.
Orgia (produced 1968). In *Porcile, Orgia, Bestia da stile*, 1979.
Affabulazione: Pilade (produced 1969). 1973.
Medea (screenplay). 1970.
Ostia (screenplay). 1970.
Oedipus Rex (translation of screenplay). 1971.
Calderon. 1973.
Trilogia della vita (screenplays; includes *Il Decamerone, I racconti di Canterbury, Il fiore delle mille e una notte*). 1975.
San Paolo (film project). 1977.
Porcile, Orgia, Bestia da stile. 1979.

Screenplays (with others): *La donna del Fiume*, 1954; *Le notti di Cabiria* (*The Nights of Cabiria*), 1956; *Marisa la civetta*, 1957; *Giovanni mariti*, 1958; *La notte brava*, 1959; *Il bell'Antonio* (*Bell'Antonio*), 1960; *Morte di un amico*, 1960; *La lunga notte del '43*, 1960; *La giornata balorda* (*From a Roman Balcony*), 1960; *Il carro armata dell'settembre*, 1960; *La ragazza in vetrina*, 1961; *La commare secca*, 1962; (by Pasolini only): *Accattone*, 1961; *Mama Roma*, 1962; "La ricotta" episode of *RoGoPag*, 1962; *Sopraluoghi in Palestina* (documentary), 1964; *Il Vangelo Secondo Matteo* (*The Gospel According to St. Matthew*), 1964; *Comizi d'amore* (documentary), 1965; *Uccellacci e uccellini* (*The Hawk and the Sparrows*), 1966; "La terra vista dalla luna" episode of *Le streghe* (*The Witches*), 1967; *Edipo Re* (*Oedipus Rex*), 1967; "Che Cosa sono le nuvole" episode of *Capriccio all'italiana*, 1968; *Appunti per un film indiano*, 1968; *Teorema*, 1968; "La sequenza del fiore di carta" episode of *Amore e rabbia* (*Vangelo 70, Love and Anger*), 1969; *Porcile* (*Pig Pen*), 1969; *Medea*, 1970; *Appunti per un' Orestiade africano*, 1970; *Il Decamerone* (*The Decameron*), 1971; *I muri di sano*, 1971; *I racconti di Canterbury* (*The Canterbury Tales*), 1972; *Il fiore delle mille e una notte* (*A Thousand and One Nights/The Arabian Nights*), 1974; *Salò; o, Le centoventi giornate di Sodoma* (*Salo: The 120 Days of Sodom*), 1975; *Orestiade africano*, 1976; *La ricotta*, 1976.

Verse

Poesia a Casarsa. 1942.
La meglio gioventù: Poesia friulane. 1954.
Il canto popolare. 1954.
Le ceneri di Gramsci. 1957; as *The Ashes of Gramsci*, 1982.
L'usignolo della chiesa cattolica. 1958.
Roma 1950: Diario. 1960.
La religione del mio tempo. 1961.
Poesia in forma di rosa 1961-1964. 1964.
Poesia dimenticate. 1965.
Potentissima signora, with Laura Betti. 1965.
Poesia. 1970.
Trasumanar e organizzar. 1971.
Tal cour di un frut: Nel cuore di un fanciullo. 1974.

La nuova gioventù: Poesie friulane 1941-1974. 1975.
Poesie e pagine ritrovate, edited by Andrea Zanzotto and Nico Naldini. 1980.
Selected Poems (bilingual edition). 1983.

Other

Passione e ideologia 1948-1958. 1960.
L'odore dell'India. 1962.
Pasolini on Pasolini, edited by Oswald Stack. 1969.
Entretiens avec Pasolini, with Jean Duflot. 1970.
Empirismo eretico. 1972.
Il padre selvaggio. 1975.
La divina mimesis. 1975.
Scritti corsari. 1975.
Lettere agli amici, edited by Luciano Serra. 1976.
Pasolini in Friuli 1943-1949. 1976.
Lettere luterane. 1976; as *Lutheran Letters*, 1983.
Con Pasolini (interview), edited by Enrico Magrelli. 1977.
La belle dandiere: Dialoghi 1960-1965, edited by Gian Carlo Ferretti. 1977.
Pasolini e "Il Setaccio" 1942-1943, edited by Mario Ricci. 1977.
I disegni 1941-1975, edited by Giuseppe Zigaina. 1978.
Il caos, edited by Gian Carlo Ferretti. 1979.

Editor, with M. dell'Arco, *Poesia dialettale del novecento.* 1952.
Editor, *La poesia popolare italiana.* 1960.
Editor, *Canzoniere italiano.* 2 vols., 1972.

Translator, *Orestiade*, by Aeschylus. 1960.
Translator, *Il vantone*, by Plautus. 1963.

*

Bibliography: *Pasolini: A Guide to References and Resources* by Ben Lawton, 1980.

Critical Studies: *Pasolini: Materiali critici* edited by Alfredo Luzi and Luigi Martellini, 1973; *Pasolini* edited by Paul Willemen, 1977; *Pasolini* by Stephen Snyder, 1980; *Pasolini* by Enzo Siciliano, 1981.

*   *   *

Some of Pier Paolo Pasolini's earliest writings are poems in the Friulan dialect and he later depicts the peasantry of this region in *Il Sogno di una cosa* (The Dream of Something). This novel describes traditional rural life as a flawed utopia: full of vitality but riddled with the political and sexual tensions that stem from oppression.

Pasolini's admiration for the Friulan peasants' protests led him to join the Italian Communist Party. Although he was expelled because of his homosexuality he retained a lifelong attachment to the party and considered himself a heretical communist. He loathed the institution of the Catholic church—although he had a keen religious sense—and the Christian Democrats who governed Italy.

His best-known poem, *The Ashes of Gramsci*, displays his ambiguous attitude towards the Communists. While applauding them as the champions of social protest, he proclaims his own attachment to working-class life as it is, to the warm human contacts that survive amid poverty. *Poesia in forma di rosa* proclaims his joyous identification with working-class boys, Third World peasants, and outsiders of all kinds. A strong erotic drive marks these poems which oscillate between loneliness and that sympathy for everything human which is Pasolini's special trait.

Two novels, *The Ragazzi* and *A Violent Life*, delve into the Rome sub-proletariat, a world left outside the new, prosperous Italy. Although Pasolini uses the slang of this world, his novels are not studies of low-life. Their complex structure allows him to depict characters who struggle against dehumanization and know moments of tenderness and of political awareness.

Outside Italy Pasolini is best known for his films. The cinema seemed to him a more direct art form than writing but his films offer a blend of realism and fantasy. Thus *Accattone* is set in the Rome slums but has a religious dimension, while *The Gospel According to St. Matthew* resets Christ's life amid the southern Italian peasantry. *A Thousand and One Nights* is a utopia of sexual liberation, but Pasolini's last film, *Salò*, based on a work by de Sade, is a gruesome depiction of cruelty.

Within Italy he was also known as a polemicist whose newspaper articles have been collected in such volumes as *Lettere luterane* (*Lutheran Letters*). The stands he took were resolutely controversial, and in his last years he denounced the young protestors of 1968 and declared his opposition to abortion. He was especially harsh on the consumer society which he saw emerge in Italy and which he considered to be, behind its false tolerance and prosperity, a form of total alienation. Frequently denounced as a reactionary but still disliked by the right, Pasolini is best seen as a scandal-bringer who chose to tell the most unpleasant truths.

—Patrick McCarthy

PASTERNAK, Boris (Leonidovich). Born in Moscow, 29 January 1890. Educated at Moscow Fifth Gymnasium, 1901-08; University of Moscow, 1909-13; also studied at University of Marburg, 1912. Married 1) Evgeniya Vladimirovna Lourie in 1922, one son; 2) Zinaida Nikolaevna Neuhaus in 1934, one son. Tutor; worked in management in chemical factories in the Urals, 1915-17; Librarian, Soviet Ministry of Education, 1918; official duties for Union of Writers from 1932, but expelled, 1958. Recipient: Medal for Valiant Labor, 1946; Nobel Prize for Literature (refused), 1958. *Died 30 May 1960.*

PUBLICATIONS

Collections

Sochineniya, edited by Gleb Struve and Boris Filippov. 3 vols., 1961.
Stikhotvoreniya i poemy, edited by L.A. Ozerov. 1965.
Stikhi, edited by Z. and E. Pasternak. 1966.

Fiction

Detstvo Lyuvers. 1922; as *Childhood*, 1941; as *The Childhood of Luvers*, in *Collected Prose Works*, 1945.
Rasskazy [Stories]. 1925; as *Vozdushnye puti* [Aerial Ways], 1933.

Povest' [A Tale]. 1934; as *The Last Summer*, 1959.
Doktor Zhivago. 1957; as *Doctor Zhivago*, 1958.
Zhenia's Childhood and Other Stories. 1982.

Plays

Slepaya krasavitsa. 1969; as *The Blind Beauty*, 1969.

Verse

Bliznets v tuchakh [Twin in the Clouds]. 1914.
Poverkh bar'erov [Above the Barriers]. 1917.
Sestra moya zhizn': Leto 1917 goda. 1922; as *Sister My Life: Summer, 1917*, 1967; complete version, as *My Sister—Life*, 1983.
Temy i variatsii [Themes and Variations]. 1923.
Devyat'sot pyaty god [Nineteen Five]. 1927.
Spektorsky. 1931.
Vtoroye rozhdeniye [Second Birth]. 1932.
Stikhotvoreniya [Verse]. 1933; revised edition, 1935-1936.
Poemy [Poems]. 1933.
Na rannikh poezdakh [On Early Trains]. 1943.
Zemnoy prostor [Earth's Vastness]. 1945.
Selected Poems. 1946.
Poems, translated by Eugene M. Kayden. 1959.
The Poetry, translated by George Reavey. 1959.
In the Interlude: Poems 1945-1960, translated by Henry Kamen. 1962.
Fifty Poems, translated by Lydia Pasternak Slater. 1963.
The Poems of Doctor Zhivago, translated by Donald Davie. 1965.
Selected Poems, translated by Jon Stallworthy and Peter France. 1983.

Other

Karusel [The Carrousel] (juvenile). 1925.
Zverinets [The Menagerie] (juvenile). 1929.
Okhrannaya gramota. 1931; as *The Safe Conduct*, in *Collected Prose Works*, 1945.
Knizhka dlya detey [Little Book for Children]. 1933.
Izbranniye perevody [Selected Translations]. 1940.
Collected Prose Works, edited by Stefan Schimanski. 1945.
Selected Writings. 1949.
Safe Conduct: An Early Autobiography, and Other Works. 1959.
Prose and Poems, edited by Stefan Schimanski. 1959.
An Essay in Autobiography. 1959; as *I Remember*, 1959; partial Russian text, as *Lyudi i polozheniya*, in *Novy Mir*, January 1967.
Letters to Georgian Friends, edited by David Magarshack. 1968.
Marina Cvetaeva, Pasternak, Rainer Maria Rilke: Lettere 1926. 1980.
Perepiska s Olga Freydenberg, edited by Elliott Mossman. 1981; as *Correspondence with Olga Freydenberg*, 1982.

Translator, *Gamlet prints datsky*, by Shakespeare. 1941.
Translator, *Romeo i Dzhuletta*, by Shakespeare. 1943.
Translator, *Antony i Kleopatra*, by Shakespeare. 1944.
Translator, *Otello, venetsy ansky maur*, by Shakespeare. 1945.

Translator, *Genrikh chetvyorty* [Henry IV, parts I and II], by Shakespeare. 1948.
Translator, *Korol'Lir* [King Lear], by Shakespeare. 1949.
Translator, *Faust* (part I), by Goethe. 1950; complete version, 1953.
Translator, *Vityaz yanoshch*, by Sándor Petofi. 1950.
Translator, *Makbet*, in *Tragedii*, by Shakespeare. 1951.
Translator, *Mariya Styuart*, by Schiller. 1958.

Editor and translator, with Nikolai Tikhonov, *Gruzinskiye liriki.* 1935.

*

Critical Studies: *Pasternak's Lyric: A Study of Sound and Imagery* by Dale L. Plank, 1966; *Pasternak's Doctor Zhivago* by Mary F. and Paul Rowland, 1967; *Pasternak: Modern Judgements* edited by Donald Davie and Angela Livingstone, 1969; *Pasternak* by J.W. Dyck, 1972; *The Poetic World of Pasternak* by Olga R. Hughes, 1974; *Themes and Variations in Pasternak's Poetics* by Krystyna Pomarska, 1975; *Pasternak: A Critical Study* by Henry Gifford, 1977; *Pasternak: A Collection of Critical Essays* edited by Victor Erlich, 1978; *Pasternak: His Life and Art* by Guy de Mallac, 1982; *Pasternak: A Biography* by Ronald Hingley, 1983.

*   *   *

For many years Boris Pasternak "held undisputed sway over Russian poetry," but remained unknown outside the literary world until October 1958, when he was awarded the Nobel Prize for Literature. In a few days' time the situation had been reversed: he was expelled from the "literary world" (the Union of Soviet Writers) and became "the story on everyone's lips." The poet who had been almost allergic to politics and publicity was turned into a public figure on the political stage. The crowning paradox in the paradox-ridden Soviet reality was that Khrushchev had succeeded where Stalin had failed in staging Pasternak's public execution. Yet, the novel (*Doctor Zhivago*) which produced such an explosion of political passion is still unavailable to the Soviet reader to whom it was addressed. Pasternak, the modernist poet of startling originality, had written a traditional novel because there was no room in his poetry for the tragic events of his age.

For him, poetry and politics were incompatible with each other. In 1917 he pictured himself shouting through the window of his study: "What millennium is it out there?" Despite the world being "turned upside down" he wrote about love, nature, and life. As Andrey Sinyavsky said: "Wonder at the miracle of existence is the attitude in which Pasternak is fixed—always bewitched by his discovery, that it is Spring again." Pasternak's love of life is the principal idea of his work, including *Doctor Zhivago*. The title of his third volume of verse, *My Sister—Life*, expresses Pasternak's credo of life and art. He made an effort to depict the revolutionary reality in his long poems (1924-31), but it is not these works which account for Pasternak's greatness as a poet. He saw himself as a vessel through which nature creates its own poems. Marina Tsvetaeva put it well: "His verse was written before the sixth day, when God created man...it lacks human beings." Pasternak felt at the time that his poems had not been written by him, but by some mysterious outside force, as if "the world became language." This feature accounts for certain obscure and impressionistic qualities in his poetry. He introduced a complex, dynamic syntax which is, in Mandelstam's words, "Poetry's circulatory system." He omits words, interrupts himself, speaks not in lines, but in whole stanzas. Conversely, he uses very brief sentences thereby creating an additional rhythmical division. All his rhythmical varieties are achieved by means of classical metrics. The wealth of the sound structure of his poetry is so great that it enables him to use imprecise rhymes which are often dazzling and unexpected. The phonetic links between the words allow a transformation of meaning, as happens with metaphors. Pasternak's imagery is notoriously difficult; it reflects his belief that the world is a "moving entirety."

Like the hero of his novel, Pasternak strived throughout his life towards Pushkinian simplicity. He rewrote half of his early poems in order to make them "clearer." He succeeded only in making them ordinary. He achieved a synthesis between simplicity and complexity in the poems of Yuri Zhivago, with which the novel ends. These poems create an inner harmony from the novel's otherwise episodic structure by comprising a vast range of ideas. In its inferiority to the poetry, the novel is far from straightforward. By telling the story of Yuri Zhivago in a highly poetic style, with especial reference to the concept of the poet as a Christ-figure, Pasternak sought to integrate history, religion, and the individual. He gives an intensely personal view of history. Like one of his characters, he "quarrels with history," focussing on those matters uppermost in his mind: love, nature, and the enigma of death. The novel is not apolitical, since it exposes the inner essence of the Revolution. Zhivago himself is not so much a man of life, as many critics think, but a man of meaning. His world is a world of bold thinking and original art. When "the iron broom" of ideology has finished with the value of personal opinions as well as with justice and the freedom to create, life has lost its meaning for Zhivago. In the suffocating atmosphere of political dogma, Zhivago is unable to immerse himself in life. In this sense, he is not Pasternak's "alter-ego," since for Pasternak everything in life preserved its depth of meaning till the very end.

—Valentina Polukhina

PAVESE, Cesare.   Born in Santo Stefano Belbro, Italy, 9 September 1908.   Educated at a Jesuit school, Turin; Ginnasio Moderno, Turin; Liceo Massimo d'Azeglio, 1924-27; University of Turin, 1927-30, degree in letters 1930. Translator and teacher in the early 1930's; Editor, *La Cultura* review, Turin, 1934-35; confined for association with communists to Brancaleone Calabro for 8 months, 1935-36; staff member, Einaudi, publishers, Turin, from 1942. Recipient: Strega Prize, 1950. *Died (suicide) 27 August 1950.*

PUBLICATIONS

Collections

Opere.   16 vols., 1960-68.

Fiction

Paesi tuoi.   1941; as *The Harvesters*, 1961.
La spiaggia.   1942; as *The Beach*, 1963.
Feria d'agosto.   1946; translated in part as *Summer Storm and Other Stories*, 1966.
Dialoghi con Leucò.   1947; as *Dialogues with Leucò*, 1965.
Il compagno.   1947; as *The Comrade*, 1959.
Prima che il gallo canti (includes *Il carcere* and *La casa in collina*).   1949; *Il carcere* as *The Political Prisoner*, 1959; *La casa in collina* as *The House on the Hill*, 1961.
La bella estate (includes *La bella estate*, *Il diavolo sulle colline*, *Tra donne sole*).   1949; *La bella estate* as *The Beautiful Summer*, in *The Political Prisoner*, 1959; *Il diavolo sulle*

colline as *The Devil in the Hills*, 1959; *Tra donne sole* as *Among Women Only*, 1953 and *For Women Only*, 1959.
La luna e i falò. 1950; as *The Moon and the Bonfires*, 1952; as *The Moon and the Bonfire*, 1952.
Notte di festa. 1953; as *Festival Night and Other Stories*, 1964.
Fuoco grande, with Bianca Garufi. 1959; as *A Great Fire*, in *The Beach*, 1963.
Racconti. 1960; as *Told in Confidence and Other Stories*, 1971.
Ciau Masino. 1969.
The Leather Jacket: Stories, edited by Margaret Crosland. 1980.

Verse

Lavorare stanca. 1936; revised edition, 1943; as *Hard Labor*, 1979.
Verrà la morte e avrà i tuoi occhi (includes *La terra e la morte*). 1951.
Poesie edite e inedite, edited by Italo Calvino. 1962.
A Mania for Solitude: Selected Poems 1930-1950, edited and translated by Margaret Crosland. 1969; as *Selected Poems*, 1971.

Other

La letteratura americana e altri saggi. 1951; as *American Literature: Essays and Opinions*, 1970.
Il mestiere di vivere: Diario 1935-1950. 1952; as *The Burning Brand: Diaries 1935-1950*, 1961; as *This Business of Living*, 1961.
8 poesie inedite e quattro lettere a un'amica. 1964.
Lettere 1924-50, edited by Lorenzo Mondo. 2 vols., 1966; as *Selected Letters 1924-1950*, edited by A.E. Murch, 1969.
Selected Works, edited by R.W. Flint. 1968.
Vita attraverso le lettere, edited by Lorenzo Mondo. 1973.

Translator, *Il nostro signor Wrenn*, by Sinclair Lewis. 1931.
Translator, *Moby Dick*, by Melville. 1932.
Translator, *Riso nero*, by Sherwood Anderson. 1932.
Translator, *Dedalus*, by Joyce. 1934.
Translator, *Il 42° parallelo*, by John Dos Passos. 1935.
Translator, *Un mucchio de quattrini*, by John Dos Passos. 1937.
Translator, *Autobiografia di Alice Toklas*, by Gertrude Stein. 1938.
Translator, *Moll Flanders*, by Defoe. 1938.
Translator, *David Copperfield*, by Dickens. 1939.
Translator, *Tre esistenze*, by Gertrude Stein. 1940.
Translator, *Benito Cereno*, by Melville. 1940.
Translator, *La rivoluzione inglese del 1688-89*, by G.M. Trevelyan. 1941.
Translator, *Il cavallo di Troia*, by Christopher Morley. 1941.
Translator, *Il borgo*, by Faulkner. 1942.
Translator, *Capitano Smith*, by R. Henriques. 1947.

*

Critical Studies: *Three Italian Novelists: Moravia, Pavese, Vittorini* by Donald W. Heiney, 1968; *The Smile of the Gods: A Thematic Study of Pavese's Works* by Gian-Paolo Biasin, 1968; *The Narrative of Realism and Myth: Verga, Lawrence, Faulkner, Pavese* by Gregory L. Lucente, 1981; *Pavese: A Study of the Major Novels and Poems* by Doug Thompson, 1982; *An*

Absurd Vice: A Biography of Pavese by Davide Lajolo, 1983.

*   *   *

Cesare Pavese was known in the 1930's as an Americanist. Having written his university thesis on Whitman, he translated works by several major American authors to whom Italians were looking because of the dearth of relevant writers in their own language. He also wrote essays on Sherwood Anderson, Gertrude Stein, and Sinclair Lewis for Leone Ginzburg's *La cultura*. Part of the attraction of American literature was that it dealt with the everyday problems of ordinary people whereas Italian literature was still remote from the man in the street or the fields, and was forced to remain so because of censorship.

Pavese was particularly attracted to the colloquial language and even slang used by American writers. His first experiment with prose fiction was a collection of short stories (published in 1969), *Ciau Masino*, about a Piedmontese tramp. At the same time he wrote poetry in which he tried to combine verse and story, capturing the rhythms of narrative and speech in long 13-syllable lines. The first poem in *Hard Labor*, "I mari del Sud," about the return of his cousin to the Langhe hills, contains nearly all the themes that Pavese explored throughout his 20 adult years: the escape of the young lad, country versus town, the return to one's roots, work, city night-life, misogyny, and solitude. Some of the poems were written in *confino*, where he was sent because of links with a Communist girlfriend. Unlike Carlo Levi (confined in Lucania) Pavese turned inwards to try to come to terms with this experience. "Lo stradduzza" ("The Morning Star") of 1936 expresses his sense of futility with this experience.

The Political Prisoner and *The Comrade* (both published after the war) also reflect his experiences in prison and in *confino*. Another product of this experience was his diary, *This Business of Living*, which he kept until his suicide in 1950. This provides striking insights into his creative processes and his states of mind. *The Harvesters*, written in 1939, describes in almost Lawrentian terms the return to the land of two prisoners. His own favourite book was *Dialogues with Leucò* which represents the culmination of his thinking about the nature of myth, and his Leopardian exploration of a number of classical myths. It is a product of Pavese's retreat into the hills during the last period of the war, when he was apolitical and preferred not to participate but turned inward again to contemplate eternal truths. After the war, with the unmuzzling of the Left, Pavese tried to commit himself to the Communist cause and wrote several articles attempting to find a more open intellectual and cultural position. These are now included in *American Literature: Essays and Opinions*, along with others that look back over the 1930's infatuation with things American.

The Moon and the Bonfires is Pavese's best novel. It tells of the return of an emigrant from America to the Langhe, where he had been fostered in a well-to-do family alongside the family's three daughters. Gradually the lives of these three girls are pieced together until one has a sense of the local community during the Fascist period. The title refers to local agricultural myths of death and renewal which finally involve in their mysteries the partisans, the German soldiers, and the youngest girl who has fallen foul of both. The whole is told in a spare but lyrical language which makes for an elegiac, distancing tone.

Pavese's last poems, *Verrà la morte e avrà i tuoi occhi* (Death Will Come and Will Have Your Eyes), were published posthumously. The collection reflects Pavese's last unhappy love for an American film star, Constance Dowling. Here, and in *La terra e la morte*, Pavese reverted to a lyrical and personal poetry, very finely chiselled and totally without hope. It is difficult to separate Pavese from his suicide, if only because it was a theme that preoccupied him throughout his life. With all his personal obsessions, however, he did give voice to the alienation and frustration felt by many of his generation in Italy.

—Judy Rawson

PAZ, Octavio. Born in Mexico City, 31 March 1914. Educated at the National University of Mexico, Mexico City. Married Marie José Tramini in 1964; one daughter. Writer: founder or editor of literary reviews *Barandal*, 1931, *El Popular*, late 1930's, *Taller*, 1938-41, *El Hijo Pródigo*, 1943-46, and since 1976, *Plural*, later called *Vuelta*. Secretary, Mexican Embassy, Paris, 1945-51; Chargé d'Affaires, 1951, later posted to Secretariat for External Affairs, Mexican Embassy, Tokyo; Mexican Ambassador to India, 1962-68 (resigned). Taught at University of Texas; Simón Bolívar Professor of Latin American Studies, 1970, and Fellow of Churchill College, 1970-71, Cambridge University; Charles Eliot Norton Professor of Poetry, Harvard University, Cambridge, Massachusetts, 1971-72. Recipient: Guggenheim Fellowship, 1944; Grand Prix International de Poésie, 1963; City of Jerusalem Prize, 1977; Neustadt International Prize for Literature, 1982. Member, American Academy. Lives in Mexico, D.F. Mexico.

Publications

Verse

Luna silvestre. 1933.
Raíz del hombre. 1937.
¡ No pasarán! 1937.
Bajo tu clara sombra y otros poemas sobre España. 1937; revised edition, 1941.
Entre la piedra y la flor. 1941.
A la orilla del mundo y primer día: Bajo tu clara sombra, Raíz del hombre, Noche de resurrecciónes. 1942.
Libertad bajo palabra. 1949.
¿Aquila o sol? 1951; as *Eagle or Sun?*, translated by Eliot Weinberger, 1970.
Semillas para un himno. 1954.
Piedra de sol. 1957; as *Sun Stone*, translated by Muriel Rukeyser, 1963; as *The Sun Stone*, translated by Donald Gardner, 1969.
La estación violenta. 1958.
Agua y viento. 1959.
Libertad bajo palabra: Obra poética 1935-1958. 1960; revised edition, 1968.
Salamandra 1958-1961. 1962.
Selected Poems, translated by Muriel Rukeyser. 1963.
Viento entero. 1965.
Vrinidiban, Madurai. 1965.
Blanco. 1967; as *Blanco*, translated by Eliot Weinberger, 1974.
Ladera este (1962-1968). 1969.
La centana: Poemas 1935-1968. 1969.
Configurations. 1971.
Renga, with others. 1971; as *Renga*, translated by Charles Tomlinson, 1972.
Early Poems 1935-1955. 1973.
Pasado en claro. 1975.
Vuelta. 1976.
A Draft of Shadows and Other Poems. 1979.
Selected Poems, translated by Charles Tomlinson. 1979.
Airborn/Hijos del aire, with Charles Tomlinson. 1981.

Play

La hija de Rappaccini, from the story by Nathaniel Hawthorne (produced, 1956). Published in *Primera antología de obras en un acto*, edited by Maruxa Vilalta, 1959.

Other

El laberinto de la soledad. 1950; revised edition, 1959; as *The Labyrinth of Solitude*, 1962.

El arco y la lire: El poema, la revelación poética, poésia e historia, 1956; revised edition, 1967; as *The Bow and the Lyre: The Poem, The Poetic Revelation, Poetry and History*, 1973.

Las peras del olmo. 1957.

Cuadrivio (on Darío, Lopez Verlarde, Pessoa, Cernuda). 1965.

Los signos en rotación. 1965.

Puertas al campo. 1966.

Claude Lévi-Strauss; o, El nuevo festín de Esopo. 1967; as *Claude Lévi-Strauss: An Introduction*, 1970; as *On Lévi-Strauss*, 1970.

Corriente alterna. 1967; as *Alternating Current*, 1973.

Marcel Duchamp; o, El castillo de la pureza. 1968; as *Marcel Duchamp; or, The Castle of Purity*, 1970.

Conjunciones y disyunciones. 1969; as *Conjunctions and Disjunctions*, 1974.

Posdata. 1970; as *The Other Mexico: Critique of the Pyramid*, 1972.

Las cosas en su sitio: Sobre la literatura espanola del siglo XX, with Juan Marichal. 1971.

Los signos en rotación y otra ensayos, edited by Carlos Fuentes. 1971.

Traducción: Literatura y literalidad. 1971.

Apariencia desnuda: la obra de Marcel Duchamp. 1973; as *Marcel Duchamp: Appearance Stripped Bare*, 1979.

El signo y el garabato. 1973.

Solo a dos voces, with Julián Ríoa. 1973.

La busqueda del comienzo. 1974.

Teatro de signos/transparencias, edited by Julián Ríos. 1974.

Versiones y diversiones (translations). 1974.

Los hijos del limo: Del romanticismo a la vanguardia (Lectures). 1974; as *Children of the Mire: Modern Poetry from Romanticism to the Avant-Garde*, 1974.

El mono gramático. 1974; as *The Monkey Grammarian*, 1981.

The Siren and the Seashells and Other Essays on Poets and Poetry. 1976.

Xavier Villaurrutia en persona y en obra. 1978.

El ogro filantrópico: Historia y política 1971-1978. 1979.

Rufino Tamayo: Myth and Magic. 1979.

Editor, *Voces de España.* 1938.

Editor, with others, *Laurel: Antología de la poésia moderna en lengua española.* 1941.

Editor, *Anthologie de la poésie mexicaine.* 1952.

Editor, *Antología poética.* 1956.

Editor, *Anthology of Mexican Poetry*, translated by Samuel Beckett. 1958.

Editor, *Tamayo en la pintura mexicana.* 1959.

Editor, *Magia de la risa.* 1962.

Editor, *Antología*, by Fernando Pessoa. 1962.

Editor, with Pedro Zekeli, *Cuatro poetas contemporáneos de Suecia: Martinson, Lundkvist, Ekelöf, y Lindegren.* 1963.

Editor, with others, *Poésia en movimiento: Mexico 1915-1966.* 1966; as *New Poetry of Mexico*, edited by Mark Strand, 1970.

Translator, with E. Hayashiya, *Sendas de Oku*, by Basho. 1957.

Translator, *Veinte poemas*, by William Carlos Williams. 1973.

Translator, *15 poemas*, by Apollinaire. 1979.

*

Bibliography: *Paz: Bibliografía crítica* by Hugo J. Verani, 1983.
Critical Studies: *The Poetic Modes of Paz* by Rachel Phillips, 1972; *The Perpetual Present: The Poetry and Prose of Paz* edited by Ivar Ivask, 1973; *Paz: A Study of His Poetics* by Jason Wilson, 1979.

*   *   *

Within the intellectual landscape of the 20th century, in an increasingly specialized and divided world, Octavio Paz is a writer of exceptional and diverse interests, of prodigious versatility, unusual erudition and imagination, recognized as one of the major poets of our time and as a lucid interpreter of modernity. His critical thought includes a bewildering number of fields of human activity—art, aesthetics, philosophy, Oriental religion, anthropology, psychology, political ideology. The preoccupations that cross the writing of Octavio Paz—the search for lost unity and the reconciliation of man with himself and the universe, the celebration of love and of freedom of thinking, the merging of contraries, the reviving of the poetic work—converge in the reflexive prose of his essays and in a poetry that assumes the form of self-criticism and incessant interrogation, two sides of an organic whole of inseparable unity in its diversity, that constitutes an uncommon and passionate testimony of humanity.

Paz is primarily a poet, considered (along with Neruda and Vallejo) as one of the truly outstanding Spanish-American poets of the century. Paz sees poetry as a path towards the revelation of man, as a means to restore authenticity. Poetic creation and erotic love are the only ways to reconcile the opposing forces of the world, the only ways to transcend solitude and reach spiritual fulfillment.

During the five years that Paz lived in France (1946-51), he participated in the surrealism movement and developed a lifelong affinity with its tenets. Paz sees surrealism as an activity of the human spirit based on the idea of rebellion, love, and freedom, as a total subversion, as a movement to recapture the natural innocence of man. The conjunction of ancient Mexican mythology and surrealism ("telluric surrealism" as termed by Benjamin Péret) guides his quest for eternal values, his desire to transcend the contradictions of humanity. "Hymn among the Ruins" and, above all, *Sun Stone* are the masterpieces of this period of his poetry. His stay in India, as Ambassador of his country (1962-68), profoundly affected his vision of the world and his approach to poetry. Many concepts of Oriental thought were incorporated into his poetics: detachment from the outside world, the illusory nature of the world, the stress on natural man, the illusion of the ego, sudden illumination, transcendence through the senses, rebellion against all systems. *Ladera este* and *Blanco* include the major poems of this period. Since the early 1960's the most significant constants of Paz's poetic work are experimentation with space and the use of visual effects. The most important poems of the 1960's ("Whole Wind," *Blanco*) are constellations of juxtaposed fragments and of voices in perpetual rotation in which the simultaneity of times and spaces is the point of confluence in an inexhaustible net of relations that enrich the analytical reading of the text. In his poetry the spatial-temporal markings disappear, and all ages converge in a privileged moment, in that evanescent and fleeting, atemporal and archetypal present. Paz liberates language from the illusion of representing an empirical reality: spaces, times, and distant cultures interweave without explicit transition and give the poem a plural meaning.

Paz is also a major essayist. Few Spanish-American writers, if any, have developed a critical system that encompasses the main intellectual currents of modern times. During almost half a century Paz has adhered to two fundamental premises: the questioning of all established truths and, above all, the passionate search for human dignity and the defense of the freedom of the human being, principles whose aim is always in Paz a recovery of the essential values of humanism.

—Hugo J. Verani

PÉREZ GALDÓS, Benito. Born in Las Palmas, Grand Canary Island, 10 May 1843. Educated at an English school, Las Palmas; Colegio de San Agustín, 1856-62; studied law at the University of Madrid, 1862-65. Staff member, *La Nación* from 1865, and associated with *La Revista de España* from 1870; abandoned journalism for writing and travel, 1873; Liberal deputy for Puerto Rico, 1886-90; Republican deputy for Madrid, from 1907. Blind after about 1912. Member, Spanish Academy, 1897. *Died 4 January 1920.*

PUBLICATIONS

Collections

> *Obras inéditas*, edited by Alberto Ghiraldo. 11 vols., 1923-33.
> *Obras completas*, edited by F.C. Sainz de Robles. 6 vols., 1942-45.

Fiction

> *La fontana de oro.* 1870.
> *La sombra.* 1871; as *The Shadow*, 1980.
> *El audaz: Historia de un radical de antaño.* 1871.
> *Doña Perfecta.* 1876; translated as *Lady Perfecta*, 1883.
> *Gloria.* 1876-77; translated as *Gloria*, 1879.
> *Marianela.* 1878; translated as *Marianela*, 1883.
> *La familia de León Roche.* 1878; as *The Family of Leon Roche*, 1888.
> *La desheredada.* 1881; as *The Disinherited Lady*, 1957.
> *El amigo Manso.* 1882.
> *El doctor Centeno.* 1883.
> *Tormento.* 1884; as *Torment*, 1952.
> *La de Bringas.* 1884; as *The Spendthrifts*, 1951.
> *Lo prohibido.* 1884-85.
> *Fortunata y Jacinta.* 1886-87; as *Fortunata and Jacinta*, 1973.
> *Miau.* 1888; translated as *Miau*, 1963.
> *La incógnita.* 1889.
> *Torquemada en la hoguera, Torquemada en la cruz, Torquemada en el Purgatorio, Torquemada y San Pedro.* 4 vols., 1889-95.
> *Realidad.* 1889.
> *Ángel Guerra.* 1890-91.
> *Tristana.* 1892.
> *La loca de la casa.* 1892.
> *Nazarín.* 1895.
> *Halma.* 1895.
> *Misericordia.* 1897; as *Compassion*, 1962.
> *El abuelo.* 1897.
> *Casandra.* 1905.
> *El caballero encantado.* 1909.
> *La razón de la sinrazón.* 1915.

Fiction: *Episodios Nacionales* series

> *Trafalgar.* 1873; translated as *Trafalgar*, 1884.
> *La Corte de Carlos IV.* 1873.
> *El 19 de marzo y el 2 de mayo.* 1873.

Bailén.   1873.
Napoleón en Chamartín.   1874.
Zaragoza.   1874; translated as *Zaragoza,* 1899.
Gerona.   1874.
Cádiz.   1874.
Juan Martín, el Empecinado.   1874.
La batalla de los Arapiles.   1875; as *The Battle of the Arapiles,* 1895.
El equipaje del Rey José.   1875.
Memorias de un cortesano de 1815.   1875.
La segunda casaca.   1876.
El Grande Oriente.   1876.
El 7 de julio.   1876.
Los cien mil hijos de San Luís.   1877.
El terror de 1824.   1877.
Un voluntario realista.   1878.
Los apostólicos.   1879.
Un faccioso más y algunos frailes menos.   1879.
Zumalacárregui.   1898.
Mendizábal.   1898.
De Oñate a La Granja.   1898.
Luchana.   1899.
La campaña del Maestrazgo.   1899.
La estafeta romántica.   1899.
Vergara.   1899.
Montes de Oca.   1900.
Los ayacuchos.   1900.
Bodas reales.   1900.
Las tormentas del 48.   1902.
Narváez.   1902.
Los duendes de la camarilla.   1903.
La revolución de julio.   1904.
O'Donnell.   1904.
Aita Tettauen.   1905.
Carlos VI en La Rápita.   1905.
La vuelta al mundo en la Numancia.   1906.
Prim.   1906.
La de los tristes destinos.   1907.
España sin rey.   1908.
España trágica.   1909.
Amadeo I.   1910.
La primera República.   1911.
De Cartago a Sagunto.   1911.
Cánovas.   1912.

Plays

Realidad, from his own novel (produced 1892).   1892.
Gerona, from his own novel (produced 1893).   1893.
La loca de la casa, from his own novel (produced 1893).   1893.
La de San Quintín (produced 1894).   1894.
Las condenados.   1894.
Voluntad (produced 1895).   1895.
Doña Perfecta, from his own novel (produced 1896).   1896.

La fiera. 1896.
Electra (produced 1901). 1901; translated as *Electra*, 1901.
Alma y vida (produced 1902). 1902.
Mariucha (produced 1903). 1903.
El abuelo, from his own novel (produced 1904). 1904.
Bárbara (produced 1905). 1905.
Amor y ciencia. 1905.
Pedro Minio. 1908.
Casandra, from his own novel (produced 1910). 1910.
Celia en los infiernos (produced 1913). 1913.
Alceste. 1914.
Sor Simona (produced 1915). 1915.
El tacaño Salomón. 1916.
Santa Juana de Castilla (produced 1918). 1918.
Un joven de provecho, edited by H.C. Berkowitz, in *Publications of the Modern Language Association*, September 1935.

Other

Memoranda. 1906.
Cartas a Mesonero Romanos, edited by E. Varela Hervías. 1943.
Madrid, edited by J. Pérez Vidal. 1955.
Cartas a Galdós, edited by Soledad Ortega. 1964.
Cartas del archivo de Galdós, edited by Sebastián de la Nuer and Joseph Schraibman. 1967.
Las cartas desconocidas in "La Prensa" de Buenos Aires, edited by William H. Shoemaker. 1973.
Los artículos políticos en la "Revista de España," 1871-1872, edited by Brian J. Dendle and Joseph Schraibman. 1982.

*

Bibliography: *Pérez Galdós: An Annotated Bibliography* by Theodore A. Sackett, 1968; *Bibliografía de Galdós I* by Manuel Hernández Suárez, 1972; *Pérez Galdós: A Selective Annotated Bibliography* by Hensley C. Woodbridge, 1975.

Critical Studies: *Pérez Galdós, Spanish Liberal Crusader* by H.C. Berkowitz, 1948; *The Novels of Pérez Galdós* by S.H. Eoff, 1954; *An Introduction to the "Episodios nacionales" of Galdós* by Alfredo Rodríguez, 1967; *Galdós Studies I* edited by J.E. Varey, 1970, and *Doña Perfecta* by Varey, 1971; *Galdós Studies II* edited by Robert J. Weber, 1974; *Pérez Galdós* by Walter T. Pattison, 1975; *Fortunata y Jacinto* by Geoffrey Ribbans, 1977; *Miau* by Eamonn Rodgers, 1978; *Galdós: The Mature Thought* by Brian J. Dendle, 1980; *La de Bringas*, 1981, and *Galdós's Novel of the Historical Imagination*, 1983, both by Peter A. Bly; *Galdós and the Art of the European Novel 1867-1887* by Stephen Gilman, 1981; *Galdós and the Irony of Language* by Diane F. Urey, 1982.

*   *   *

As he began his literary career, around 1870, Galdós was uncomfortably aware that Spain, the country of Cervantes, had produced, in the 19th century, no works of prose fiction to rival the achievements of Dickens and Balzac. The remedy, however, could not consist merely in a slavish imitation of foreign models, for although Galdós was more open to European trends than his conservative Catholic contemporaries, he was still influenced by the cultural nationalism which was one of the keynotes of Spanish literary life. In seeking, therefore, to provide a counterpart to Balzac's encyclopaedic view of French society in the *Comédie humaine*, Galdós preferred to choose as models Spanish writers such as Cervantes and Quevedo, who represent a tradition of realism which was humorous, satirical, and moralistic.

This moralistic element sometimes gives rise to a certain polemical quality, especially in novels like *Doña Perfecta*, which portrays contemporary religious and political conflict. However, the novels of the 1870's do not represent Galdós's most characteristic mode. By 1881, some of the tensions in post-revolutionary society had become less acute, and this is reflected in a more sober, complex, and detached presentation of contemporary reality in Galdós's novels. Nevertheless, the primary focus of interest in his work remains ethical: his major themes are social pretence, self-deception, vanity, and egoism. The treatment of these themes, however, is by no means schematic or theoretical, for Galdós's depiction of the context in which moral choices have to be made gives rise to a vivid and detailed re-creation of the atmosphere of Madrid society in the last quarter of the century. For example, *El amigo Manso* is the story of a professor of philosophy who, at the very beginning of the novel, asserts that he only exists as a fictional being, and who spends his life unsuccessfully pursuing the ideal of perfect balance between reason and feeling, and between abstract principle and concrete action. Yet by portraying in detail the various social relationships in which Manso is involved, the novel also immerses the reader in the spheres of politics, fashion, the theatre, family life, and amorous intrigue. In one very characteristic scene, for instance, the philosopher is shown trying to assess the qualifications of various peasant women for the position of wet-nurse to his nephew.

This vivid quotidian realism places Galdós firmly within the broad tradition of the 19th-century European novel. At the same time, however, his links with his native literary traditions give his writings a characteristically Spanish flavour which goes beyond mere local colour. Moreover, his work is informed throughout by the desire to re-educate his contemporaries to a true understanding of their experience. This is particularly obvious in the series of historical novels, the *Episodios nacionales*, which Galdós composed at various times between 1873 and 1912, and which trace the history of Spain from the Battle of Trafalgar (1805) to the restoration of the Bourbon monarchy (1875). This sense of educational and moral mission gives his work a tone of civic seriousness tempered by humour which is perhaps his most characteristic contribution to world literature.

—Eamonn Rodgers

PERSE, Saint-John. *See* **SAINT-JOHN PERSE.**

PESSOA, Fernando (António Nogueira). Born in Lisbon, 13 June 1888. Educated at an Irish convent school in Durban, South Africa; Durban High School, 1899-1905; University of Lisbon, 1906-07. Owner, Emprêsa Ibis, publishers, Lisbon, 1907; free-lance translator, into French and English, for commercial firms, Lisbon, 1907-34; involved in several literary movements, especially *Renascença portuguêsa*; co-founder, *Orfeu* magazine, 1915. Wrote in Portuguese, English, and French. *Died 30 November 1935.*

PUBLICATIONS

Collections

Obras completas. 1952— .
Obra Poética, edited by Maria Aliete Galhoz. 1960.

Verse

Antinous, 35 Sonnets (in English). 2 vols., 1918.
English Poems: Antinous, 35 Sonnets, Epithalamium. 3 vols., 1921.
Mensagem. 1934.
Alberto Caeiro, Ricardo Reis, Álvaro de Campos, Fernando Pessoa, edited and translated by Jonathan Griffin. 4 vols., 1971.
Selected Poems, edited and translated by Peter Rickard. 1971.
Selected Poems, edited and translated by Edwin Honig. 1971.
Sixty Portuguese Poems, edited and translated by F.E.G.Q. 1971.
Selected Poems, edited and translated by Jonathan Griffin. 1974.

Other

Cartas a Armando Côrtez-Rodrigues, edited by Joel Serrão. 1945; revised edition, 1959.
Páginas de doutrina estética, edited by Jorge de Sena. 1946.
Cartas a João Gaspar Sinões, edited by Simões. 1957.
Cartas a Fernando Pessoa (includes some works by Pessoa), by Mário Sá-Carneiro, edited by Helena Cidade Moura. 2 vols., 1958-59.
Páginas íntimas e de auto-interpretação, edited by J. do Prado Coelho and G.R. Lind. 1966.
Textos filosóficos, edited by A. de Pina Coelho. 2 vols., 1968.
Obras em prosa, edited by J. Bernardinelli. 1974.

*

Critical Studies: *Three Twentieth-Century Portuguese Poets* by J.M. Parker, 1960; *Cuadrivio* (on Darío, Lopez Verlarde, Pessoa, Cernuda) by Octavio Paz, 1965; *The Man Who Never Was: Essays on Pessoa* edited by George Monteiro, 1982.

*   *   *

Fernando Pessoa is the greatest Portuguese poet since Camões, and one of the most complex and astonishing figures of 20th-century literature. At the time of his death at the age of 47, Pessoa had published very little; his reputation, even within Portuguese literary circles, was quite limited. Pessoa left behind a vast collection of unpublished works—some 25,000 texts and fragments. As these works have been organized and edited, a process which is still underway, Pessoa's uniqueness has been revealed; his posthumous influence on Portuguese and Brazilian letters has been profound, and numerous translations into other European languages have begun to establish his international reputation as a major writer and as an icon of the modern crisis of identity.

Pessoa's crisis of identity was at once personal and literary. Most of his poetry before 1909 was written in English; at that point, just as Pessoa began to shift into Portuguese, he became aware of a very broad range of foreign literary movements—everything from French Symbolism to Italian Futurism—which arrived almost simultaneously in Lisbon. Pessoa, like his contemporaries, struggled to make sense of these new and discordant voices; unlike his contemporaries, he was also obsessed with doubts about his own sanity, about his sexual orientation, and about the meaning of what now appears to have been a strongly repressed tendency towards multiple personalities.

Pessoa's solution to these crises began to take form in 1914: the creation, or liberation, of a number of distinct and separate literary personalities he called heteronyms. These are not pseudonyms, but discrete individuals—possessed of biographies and coherent and independent philosophies and literary styles. We now know of at least twenty heteronyms and semi-heteronyms. The four most complete identities, however, are Alberto Caeiro, Álvaro de Campos, Ricardo Reis, and the orthonym, Fernando Pessoa, whom the poet insisted was neither more nor less real than the others. Fernando Pessoa is an esoteric neo-Symbolist poet of traditional forms, preoccupied with religious and patriotic myths. Caeiro, the happy survivor of a lost Golden Age, is a pastoralist whose forms and diction reflect his relative lack of education; he believes only in the simple objects which surround him and the simple joys his senses perceive. Reis, Caeiro's disciple, is also within the classical tradition; but Reis is Horace to Caeiro's bucolic Virgil, and his complex and perfect formal odes are intensely intellectual creations designed to communicate his weariness of emotion and mortality. Álvaro de Campos, Reis's mirror image, is a passionate, dynamic child of our own century—the creature of Whitman and of Marinetti, delightedly obsessed with the machines he tends as first engineer on a tanker; his formless free verse is violent and exclamatory, filled with a dead-end existentialism born before its time.

Taken as a whole, the writings of Pessoa and his heteronyms and semi-heteronyms form a document, unique to literature if not to psychoanalysis, which is also a vibrant one-man show that simultaneously exhibits a full range of literary reactions to the human condition from Theocritus to Sartre.

—David T. Haberly

PETRARCH (Francesco Petrarca). Born in Arezzo (where his father was in political exile from Florence), 20 July 1304. Educated in Carpentras, France, from 1312; studied law in Montpellier, 1316-20, and Bologna, 1320-26. Had two illegitimate children. Lived in Avignon from 1326; possibly took minor orders; in service of the Colonna family, 1330-37; held several canonries from 1335; diplomat and traveller: lived in Vaucluse, 1337-47, Milan, 1353-61, Venice, 1362-68, and Arquà, near Padua, 1369-74. Crowned poet laureate in Rome, 1341. *Died 18 July 1374.*

PUBLICATIONS

Collections

Opera omnia. 1544.

Rime, trionfi, e poesia latine, edited by F. Neri and others.   1951.
Prose, edited by G. Martellotti and others.   1955.
Opere, edited by Giovanni Ponte.   1968.

Verse

Rerum vulgarium fragmenta [Fragments of Vulgar THings] (includes *Rime in vita di Laura* and *Rime in morte di Laura*; also known as *Canzoniere* or *Rime*), edited by F. Neri, in *Rime*.   1951; also edited by Ezio Chiorboli, 1924; translated by C.B. Cayley as *Sonnets and Stanzas*, 1879, by A.M. Armi as *Sonnets and Songs*, 1946, and by R.M. Durling as *Lyric Poems*, 1976; selections translated by Joseph Auslander as *Sonnets*, 1931, by Morris Bishop as *Love Rhymes*, 1932, in *Selected Sonnets, Odes, and Letters* edited by Thomas G. Bergin, 1966, and by A. Mortimer as *Selected Poems*, 1977.
Epistolae metricae [Metrical Letters], in *Poemata minora*, edited by D. Rossetti.   1829-34; translated in part in *Petrarch at Vaucluse* by E.H. Wilkins, 1958.
I Trionfi, edited by F. Neri, in *Rime, trionfi, e poesia latine*.   1951; as *Triumphs*, translated by Lord Morley, 1554, and by E.H. Wilkins, 1962.
Bucolicum carmen [Eclogues], edited by A. Avena.   1906; as *Bucolicum carmen*, translated by Thomas G. Bergin, 1974.
Africa (in Latin), edited by N. Festa.   1926; as *Africa*, translated by Thomas G. Bergin and A.S. Wilson, 1977.

Other

De remediis contra utriusque fortunae, as *Physic Against Fortune*.   1579.
De sui ipsius et multorum ignorantia, as *On His Own Ignorance and That of Many Others*, in *The Renaissance Philosophy of Man*, edited by Ernst Cassirer.   1948.
Secretum meum, as *Petrarch's Secret*.   1911.
De vita solitaria, as *The Life of Solitude*.   1924.
Epistolae familiarium, edited by V. Rossi and U. Bosco.   4 vols., 1933-42; translated as *Rerum familiarium* and *Letters on Familiar Matters*, 2 vols., 1975-82; as *Letters* (selection), 1966.
Invectiva contra quendam magni status hominem..., edited by P.G. Ricci.   1949.
Invectivarum contra medicum [Invective Against a Doctor], edited by P.G. Ricci and D. Silvestri.   1950.
Petrarch's Testament, edited and translated by Theodor E. Mommsen.   1957.
De otio religioso [On Religious Idleness], edited by G. Rotondi.   1958.
Liber sine nomine, as *Book Without a Name*, 1973.

*

Bibliography: *Catalogue of the Petrarch Collection Bequeathed by Willard Fiske* edited by Mary Fowler, 1916, supplement, 1973; *The Present State of Scholarship in Fourteenth Century Literature* by Thomas D. Cooke, 1982.

Critical Studies: *The Making of the "Canzoniere" and Other Petrarchan Studies*, 1951, *Studies in the life and Works of Petrarch*, 1955, *Petrarch's Eight Years in Milan*, 1958, *Petrarch's Later Years*, 1959, and *The Life of Petrarch*, 1961, all by Ernest H. Wilkins; *Petrarch, Scipio, and the "Africa,"* 1962, *Petrarch, Laura, and the "Triumphs,"* 1974, and *Petrarch, Citizen of the World*, 1980, all by Aldo S. Bernardo; *Petrarch and His World* by Morris Bishop, 1963; *Petrarch* by Thomas G. Bergin, 1970; *Petrarch: Six Centuries Later* edited by Aldo Scaglione, 1975; *Petrarch's Visions and Their Renaissance Analogues* by J.C. Bondanella, 1978; *The Poet as Philosopher: Petrarch and the Formation of Renaissance Consciousness* by C. Trinkaus, 1979;

Petrarch's Poetics and Literary History by Marguerite R. Waller, 1980.

*   *   *

By the time he had reached middle age Petrarch had attained to a state of eminence unique for a man of letters in the Europe of his times, and indeed unparalleled in all the centuries that had followed the collapse of the Roman Empire. He has been well called "the first modern man of letters." His fame was assured by his works as a scholar and a poet, but it is apparent too that his personality, outgoing, affable, and winning, had much to do with it. He made friends easily, as he admits with some complacency in his autobiographical "Letter to Posterity"—and useful friends for the most part. Rich and powerful patrons sought him out and willingly subsidized him. By the end of his life he had reached a point where he no longer needed patronage and was able to own his own house and to enjoy the library which he had collected with persistent zeal. Such an achievement for a man of letters was unheard of before the invention of printing. To his credit, the poet-scholar had won his independence without seriously compromising his principles, although his acceptance of the hospitality of the Visconti, despots of Milan, disturbed his younger friend Boccaccio.

Petrarch made good use of the comfortable life and leisure provided for him by his protectors. His works are numerous and substantial, and reveal an alert and inquiring mind and keen interest in the world around him and in his own personality. In the vernacular he composed only two works: the *Trionfi* and the collection of lyrics (mostly sonnets, a form to which he brought a new and unsurpassed grace), which with affected modesty he called *Rerum vulgarium fragmenta* (Fragments of Vulgar Matters) but which is commonly known as the *Canzoniere*. This lyric account of a lifetime's unrequited love has had an enduring resonance. It is divided into two parts, the first consisting of items written during Laura's life and the second made of poems of mourning for her death. It is uncertain whether Laura really existed or is merely a creation of the poet's wistful fancy; the tone of the second part at least suggests that his grief is real and his tears are shed for a woman of flesh and blood. For many years critics have been in general content to identify her with the Avignon lady Laurette de Sade, who died in the plague of 1348. Except to record the date and place of his enamorment Petrarch tells us little about her, save that she had golden hair—and never yielded to his entreaties. But his verses in praise of her are so skillfully woven, so musical in tone and elegant in style, that they charm a reader of today as compellingly as they did the poet's contemporaries. Not all the items in the *Canzoniere* deal with the beloved; occasionally the poet puts aside his obsession and writes on other topics, addressing his words to friends or patrons. The short sequence on the corruption of the Avignon Papacy is notable for its scorching invective, and his ode to the discordant Italian princes has a convincing patriotic fervor. But it is Laura to whom his thoughts and his longings constantly return. The worship of the unattainable lady is hardly new in European letters; it had been the central motif of the Provençal lyric. One might even see in Laura a kind of regression; unlike Dante's Beatrice she carries no evident suggestion of ethical or theological nature though the poet himself hints that her name is suggestive of the laurel wreath signifying fame. On the literal level twenty years of unrequited courtship might seem a little absurd (Gibbon has his fun with it), but if the background is contrived and the posturing sometimes tedious, yet the drama is real, for it is evident that Petrarch is recording and analyzing a spiritual-emotional condition which is truly human and very moving. In this sense the sincerity of the *Canzoniere* is beyond question. The tension within the poet's heart cannot be doubted; it becomes especially clear in the poems written after Laura's death that whatever the beloved signifies (carnal love, thirst for fame, earthly pleasures) it is something at war with what should be the first concern of a Christian, the salvation of his soul. To this unending conflict, which is of the essence of our earthly pilgrimage, Petrarch gave eloquent and convincing expression. The forms—sonnets, odes, sestinas—he employs are no more his invention than the substance of his song, but with his mastery of cadence, rhyme, and musical verbal patterns he endowed them with a grace and polish never known before and hardly rivaled since.

If the vernacular Petrarch reveals new areas of sensibility and new secrets of technique to poets yet to come, the Latin Petrarch is no less significant in the field of letters. Collectively the Latin works display the same range of conflicting concerns that we find in the *Canzoniere*. The *Letters*, whether in prose or verse, are at once a shrewd commentary on the passing scene and the *autoritratto* of a man of sincere faith, aware of the transience of the things of this fascinating world and uneasy about his spiritual condition. Both aspects of this articulate man are apparent in other Latin writings. The *Secretum* is a moving if somewhat stylized examination of conscience, the essay on *The Life of Solitude* exemplifies the author's penchant for meditation and seclusion, while the record of *Memorable Matters* shows us an avid "sight-seer." (Petrarch loved travel and enjoyed meeting people.) The *Bucolicum Carmen*, with its description of wars and plagues and its concomitant strain of melancholy, offers, in not contemptible hexameters, the same very human melange that we find in the *Letters* and to some degree in the *Canzoniere*. Much of Petrarch's Latin is mannered, patently in emulation of Latin authors, particularly Cicero, yet it is *au fond* effective and often vivid (witness for example the uninhibited mordancy of his *Invectives*). But more important for western culture than the Latin works themselves is Petrarch's fresh and sympathetic approach to the classics; he saw the Latin writers not as remote prophets but as men like himself, greater perhaps in stature but recognizably kin. In this sense he is rightly called the father of humanism. A century later scholars would learn how to write smoother Latin than Petrarch's, and his Latin works were overshadowed. In the days of the High Renaissance "Petrarch" meant the *Canzoniere* and "petrarchismo." But in more recent times the role of the Latin Petrarch has won perceptive appreciation, as is attested by the number of editions, translations, and studies that have appeared. Conceding that the Latin works lack the compelling emotional appeal of the *Canzoniere*, they yet remain an invaluable legacy. It is difficult to imagine the course of European letters without the contribution of Laura's lover—and likewise without the labors of Cicero's disciple.

—Thomas G. Bergin

PETRONIUS. Identified by most scholars with Titus Petronius Niger, a close associate of Nero who called him "arbiter elegantiae" (director of elegance): proconsul of province of Bithynia; consul, 62 A.D.; denounced as being involved in an assassination conspiracy against Nero, he committed suicide. *Died 66 A.D.*

PUBLICATIONS

Fiction

[*Satyricon*], edited by K. Müller. 1961; revised edition by K. Müller and W. Ehlers, 1965; also edited by Alfred Ernout, 4th edition, 1958, and Carlo Pellegrino, 1975; as *The Satyricon*, translated by Jack Lindsay, 1927, Paul Dinnage, 1953, revised edition, 1971, William Arrowsmith, 1959, John Sullivan, 1965, and Paul Gillette, 1970.

*

Bibliography: *A Bibliography of Petronius* by Gareth L. Schmeling, 1977.

Critical Studies: *The Satyricon of Petronius* by John Sullivan, 1968; *Aspects of the Ancient Romance and Its Heritage: Essays on Apuleius, Petronius, and the Greek Romances* edited by

Alexander Scobie, 1969; *The Roman Novel: The "Satyricon" of Petronius and the "Metamorphoses" of Apuleius* by P.G. Walsh, 1970; *Petronius* by Philip B. Corbett, 1970; *The Date and Author of the Satyricon* by Kenneth C. Rose, 1971; *Petronius the Artist* by Herbert D. Rankin, 1971.

*　　*　　*

Scholars are generally agreed that the fragments we possess of the *Satyricon* were written by the Petronius who served during the period of Nero's emperorship as proconsul in Bithynia and also as Nero's "arbiter elegantiae." Most of the obvious features of the work are appropriate to a dating during the middle third of the 1st century A.D.

The overall form of the work as it can be reconstructed suggests that it takes the form of a parody of Homer's *Odyssey*—with the wrath of the god Priapus parodying the wrath of Poseidon directed towards Odysseus, the various travels of the hero, Encolpius, parodying Odysseus's travels, and the various persons and adventures met and experienced by Encolpius relating to similar experiences of Odysseus. (There is, however, no indication that Petronius applied such a strict program to his work as James Joyce did in writing his novel *Ulysses*.) Suggestions that the work originated as a parody of the sentimental Greek novel are less accepted: the emotional "romance" elements, heightened rhetoric, separation of lovers, and other motifs used in this sort of argument either all apply to the work's being an epic parody or are misplaced. The episode of the banquet of Trimalchio—the only complete section of the original work to survive—finds parallels in previous banquet or symposium literature (especially that of Plato and Horace). The use of alternating verse and prose (in the traditional arrangement of Menippean satire) naturally leads to explicit discussion of literary forms, a constant occurrence in the *Satyricon*, as well as the insertion of short tales (the stories of the Woman of Ephesus and the Boy from Pergamum—both, incidentally, concerned with sexual themes).

The sexual nature of much of the work has led until recently to the *Satyricon* being largely ignored—except for the section devoted to the banquet of Trimalchio. The plot follows the adventures—in picaresque fashion—of the narrator, Encolpius, a young bisexual who, when we first meet him, has teamed up with the effeminate Giton. Rivals for Giton's affections include another young homosexual, Asclytos, and two older men, Agamemnon and Eumolpus. The extant fragments can plausibly be arranged into a series of episodes (though their exact arrangement is unclear and it is apparent that a large proportion of the original work is missing): 1) Encolpius is the victim of a punishment for having defiled the ritual observances of Priapus—during which both Encolpius and Giton are sexually abused; 2) a series of rough and tumble adventures of the three young men in their sexual rivalry; 3) the banquet at Trimalchio's villa; 4) an elaborate adventure on shipboard when Encolpius, Giton, and Eumolpus flee the region around Puteoli, with some new characters (though perhaps they had appeared in earlier, now lost, episodes); 5) the last double adventure: Eumolpus pretends to be dying in order to encourage the gifts of the fortune-hunters of Croton, and Encolpius, having fallen in love with Circe, proves impotent, and various methods are tried to restore his sexual vigor.

What emerges is a very modern-seeming story, with the added piquancy (for modern readers) of sexual explicitness and abnormality. Because of the fame of the section devoted to Trimalchio, and Petronius's obvious link to the satiric tradition of ridiculing the rich, vulgar freedman—and also because of many other satiric targets, such as lecherous women, superstition, religion, legacy hunting, etc.—Petronius has often been seen as a satirist. But Petronius's own view of his material is difficult to ascertain, both because of its fragmentary nature, and because the story is told in the first person by a character who is himself satirized. Older views of Petronius as a vicious pornographer or as a strictly moral satirist have generally given way to a view of him as a detached observer of the silliness and barbarism of life around him—probably for the amusement of Nero's court.

—George Walsh

PINDAR. Born in Cynoscephalae, Boeotia, in 518 (or possibly 522) B.C. Studied in Athens. Married. Earliest known poem dates from 498. In Sicily at courts of Theron of Acragas and Hieron I of Syracuse, 476-74. *Died 438 (or possibly 446) B.C.*

PUBLICATIONS

Verse

[*Verse*], edited by Bruno Snell. 2 vols., 1953-64; Snell's edition revised by Hervicus Maehler, 1971—; also edited by O. Schroeder, 1923, C.M. Bowra, 1947, and Alexander Turyn, 1948; translated by J.E. Sandys (Loeb edition), 1915; also translated by L.R. Farnell, 1930-32, Richmond Lattimore, 1947, revised edition, 1976, C.M.Bowra, 1969, Geoffrey Conway, 1972, R.A. Swanson, 1974, and Frank J. Nisetich, 1980; *Selected Odes* translated by Carl A.P. Ruck and William H. Matheson, 1968.

*

Bibliography: *A Bibliography of Pindar 1513-1966* by Douglas E. Gerber, 1969.

Critical Studies: *Studia Pindarica I* and *II* by E.L. Bundy, 1962; *Pindar's Pythian Odes* by Reginald W.B. Burton,1962; *Pindar* by C.M. Bowra, 1964; *Critical Commentary to the Works of Pindar* by L.R. Farnell, 1967; *Folktale Motifs in the Odes of Pindar* by Mary A. Grant, 1967; *Studies in Pindar with Particular Reference to Paean VI and Nemean VII* by Staffan Fogelmark, 1972; *Epinikion: General Form in the Odes of Pindar* by Richard Hamilton, 1974; *The Victory Ode* by Mary R. Lefkowitz, 1976; *The Structure of Pindar's Epinician Odes* by Carola Greengard, 1980; *Choreia: Pindar and Dance* by William Mullen, 1982; *Song and Action: The Victory Odes of Pindar* by Kevin Crotty, 1982.

*   *   *

For the ancients, Pindar was the greatest of the lyric poets; for us, he is the only Greek lyric poet whose work survives in something more than fragments. We have a total of 45 complete poems from 4 of his books, along with numerous fragments from 13 books that were lost.

The surviving poems are choral odes written to be sung and danced by a chorus in celebration of victory in the Greek athletic festivals. The choreography and musical accompaniment Pindar devised for them have perished. Worse still, the principles governing the meters in which the odes are composed were forgotten even in antiquity, with the result that Pindar, whose lines we now know obey rigorous rules, came to be regarded as an exponent of free verse. But the greatest distortion of all resulted from loss of appreciation for the conventions of the genre in which Pindar worked.

The main business of Pindar's poetry is praise, but praise is difficult to carry off. It was especially difficult in Pindar's day, when men believed that happiness was a divine prerogative, something the gods would resent seeing mortal men claim for themselves. The poet must praise his patron, but he must also secure divine favor for him and for himself. He must balance enthusiasm with caution. These conflicting needs resulted in the creation of a complex poetic genre that reached its highest development in Pindar and ceased to be cultivated almost immediately after; its unique conventions, the special devices evolved for the task of praise, were rapidly misunderstood. Until Bundy's work began the process of recovering their meaning, we have had to take Pindar's greatness on authority.

Several factors contribute to that greatness, not least the prestige that poetry enjoyed in Pindar's day. His poems do not in the first instance express his personal feelings and opinions, as was thought before; they speak rather to and for an entire society that looks upon him as the representative of Apollo and the Muses. "Prophesy, Muse, and I will be your voice," he says in one of his fragments (150 Snell). This confidence in his divine mission and genius is one of his most noticeable traits; it exerted a major influence on the creation of Pindar's traditional image as the poet *par excellence*, who owes allegiance only to the spirit that moves him and who often soars where he cannot be followed. So Horace pictured him in Odes IV.2, and so also he appears in Longinus's treatise *On The Sublime*. The careful reader, however, will perceive that Pindar's celebrations of poetic genius, like the brilliant myths that he tells, are closely bound up with the execution of his task. His poems do not for that matter amount to a simple hurrah; on the contrary, they are shot through with gleams of a tragic vision.

It has been said that Pindar's art cannot be appreciated at all in translation. This would be true if it had no theme of universal interest and importance, but it does: it deals with the springs of human motivation. Measuring hope, effort, and achievement against the ultimate failure of death, it ends by affirming the individual's longing for distinction: "Creatures of a day! What is someone? What is no one? Man: a shadow's dream. But when godgiven glory comes, a bright light shines upon us and our life is sweet" (*Pythian* 8, end).

—Frank J. Nisetich

PIRANDELLO, Luigi. Born in Agrigento, Sicily, 28 June 1867. Educated at schools in Agrigento to 1882, and Palermo to 1886; University of Palermo, 1886-87; University of Rome, 1887-89; University of Bonn, 1889-91, received doctorate. Married Antonietta Portulano in 1894 (she was committed to a mental clinic from 1919); two sons and one daughter. Writer in Rome from 1891; teacher, Regio Istituto Superiore di Magistero Femminile, 1897-1922; Co-Editor, *Ariel*, 1898; financial disaster in 1903 forced him to increase his income by tutoring and working as traveling examination commissioner; became involved in the theatre during World War I; Director, with Nino Martoglio, Teatro Mediterraneo troupe, Rome, 1919; Co-Founder, Teatro d'Arte di Roma, 1924-28; joined Fascist party, 1924, but his relations with it were strained; lived outside Italy, mainly in Berlin and Paris, 1928-33. Recipient: Nobel Prize for Literature, 1934. Member, Italian Academy; Legion of Honor (France). *Died 10 December 1936.*

PUBLICATIONS

Collections

Opere. 6 vols., 1956-60.

Plays

L'epilogo. 1898; as *La morsa* (produced 1910), 1926; as *The Vise*, in *One-Act Plays*, 1928.
Samandro (produced 1928). 1909.
Lumie di Sicilia (produced 1910). 1911; as *Sicilian Limes*, in *One-Act Plays*, 1928.

Il dovere di medico. 1912; as *The Doctor's Duty*, in *One-Act Plays*, 1928.

Se non cosi (produced 1915). 1915; revised version, as *La ragione degli altri*, 1921.

L'aria del continente, with Nino Martoglio (produced 1916).

Pensaci Giacomino! (produced 1916). 1917.

La giara (produced 1916). 1925; as *The Jar*, in *One-Act Plays*, 1928.

Il berretto a sonagli (produced 1916). 1918.

Liolà (produced 1916). 1917; translated as *Liola*, in *Naked Masks*, 1952; revised version, music by Giuseppe Mule (produced 1935).

'A vilanza, with Nino Martoglio (produced 1917).

Cosi e (si vi pare) (produced 1917). 1918; as *Right You Are (If You Think So)*, in *Three Plays*, 1922; as *It Is So (If You Think So)*, in *Naked Masks*, 1952.

Il piacere dell'onesta (produced 1918). 1918; as *The Pleasure of Honesty*, in *Each in His Own Way and Two Other Plays*, 1923.

Il giuoco delle parti (produced 1918). 1919; as *The Rules of the Game*, in *Three Plays*, 1959.

Ma non e una cosa seria (produced 1918). 1919.

La patente (produced 1919). 1918; as *By Judgment of the Court*, in *One-Act Plays*, 1928.

L'uomo, la bestia, e la virtu (produced 1919). 1922.

'U ciclopu, from *Cyclops* by Euripides (produced 1919). 1967.

L'innesto (produced 1919). 1921.

Come prima, meglio di prima (produced 1920). 1921.

Tutto per bene (produced 1920). 1920; as *All for the Best*, 1960.

La signora Morli, una e due (produced 1920). 1922.

Cece (produced 1920). 1926; as *Chee-Chee*, in *One-Act Plays*, 1928.

Sei personaggi in cerca d'autore (produced 1921). 1921; as *Six Characters in Search of an Author*, in *Three Plays*, 1922.

Vestire gl'ignudi (produced 1922). 1923; as *Naked*, in *Each In His Own Way and Two Other Plays*, 1923; as *To Clothe the Naked*, 1962.

Enrico IV (produced 1922). 1922; as *Henry IV*, in *Three Plays*, 1922.

L'imbecille (produced 1922). 1926; as *The Imbecile*, in *One-Act Plays*, 1928.

All'uscita (produced 1922). 1926; as *At the Gate*, in *One-Act Plays*, 1928.

La vita che ti diedi (produced 1923). 1924; as *The Life I Gave You*, in *Three Plays*, 1959.

L'altro figlio (produced 1923). 1925; as *The House with the Column*, in *One-Act Plays*, 1928.

L'uomo dal fiore in bocca (produced 1923). 1926; as *The Man with the Flower in His Mouth*, in *One-Act Plays*, 1928.

Ciascuno a suo modo (produced 1924). 1924; as *Each In His Own Way*, 1923.

La sagra del signore della nave (produced 1925). 1925; as *Our Lord of the Ship*, in *One-Act Plays*, 1928.

Diana e la Tuda (produced 1926). 1927; as *Diana and Tuda*, 1950.

L'amica delle mogli (produced 1927). 1927; as *The Wives' Friend*, 1960.

La nuova colonia (produced 1928). 1928; as *The New Colony*, in *The Mountain Giants and Other Plays*, 1958.

Lazzaro (produced 1928). 1929; as *Lazarus*, 1952.

La salamandra, music by Massimo Bontempelli (produced 1928).

Bellavita (produced 1928?). 1937.

O di uno o di nessuno (produced 1929?). 1929.

Questa sera si recita a soggetto (produced 1930). 1930; as *Tonight We Improvise*, 1932.

Come tu mi vuoi. 1930; as *As You Desire Me*, 1931.

Sogno (ma forse no) (produced 1931). 1936.

Trovarsi. 1932; as *To Find Oneself*, 1960.

Quando si e qualcuno (produced 1933). 1933; as *When Someone Is Somebody*, in *The Mountain Giants and Other Plays*, 1958.

La favola del figlio cambiato, music by Malpiero (produced 1933). 1938.

Non si sa come (produced 1934). 1935; as *No One Knows How*, 1963.
I giganti della montagna (unfinished). 1938; as *The Mountain Giants*, 1958.
Naked Masks: Five Plays, edited by Eric Bentley. 1952.

Screenplays: *Pantera nera*, with Arnaldo Frateili, 1920; *Acciaio*, with Stefano Landi, 1933; *Pensaci Giacomino!*, with others, 1935.

Fiction

Amori senza amore. 1894.
L'esclusa. 1901; as *The Outcast*, 1925.
Beffe della morte e della vita. 2 vols., 1902-03.
Quand'ero matto.... 1902.
Il turno. 1902.
Il fu Mattia Pascal. 1904; revised edition, 1921; as *The Late Mattia Pascal*, 1923.
Bianche e nere. 1904.
Erma bifronte. 1906.
La vita nuda. 1910; as *The Naked Truth*, 1934.
Suo marito. 1911; as *Giustino Roncella nato Boggiolo*, 1953.
Terzetti. 1912.
I vecchi e i giovani. 2 vols., 1913; as *The Old and the Young*, 2 vols., 1928.
Le due maschere. 1914; as *Tu Ridi*, 1920.
La trappola. 1915.
Erba del nostro orto. 1915.
Si gira.... 1916; as *Quaderni di Serafino Gubbio, operatore*, 1925; as *Shoot!*, 1926.
E domani, lunedi. 1917.
Un cavallo nella luna. 1918; as *The Horse in the Moon*, 1932.
Berecche e la guerra. 1919.
Il carnevale dei morti. 1919.
Novelle per un anno. 15 vols., 1922-37(?).
Uno, nessuno, e centomila. 1926; as *One, None and a Hundred Thousand*, 1933.
Better Think Twice about It. 1933.
A Character in Distress. 1938.
Four Tales. 1939; as *Limes from Sicily and Other Stories*, 1942.
Short Stories, edited by Frederick May. 1965.

Verse

Mal giocondo. 1889.
Pasqua di Gea. 1891.
Pier Gudrò. 1894.
Elegie renane. 1895.
Zampogna. 1901.
Fuori di chiave. 1912.

Other

Laute und Lautentwicklung der Mundart von Girgenti. 1891.
Arte e Scienza. 1908.
L'umorismo. 1908; as *On Humor*, edited and translated by Antonio Illiano and Daniel P. Testa, 1974.

Translator, *La filologia romanza*, by Fed. Neumann.   1893.
Translator, *Elegie romane*, by Goethe.   1896.

*

Bibliography: *Bibliografia di Pirandello* by Manlio Lo Vecchio-Musti, 1952; *Bibliografia della critica pirandelliana 1889-1961* by Alfredo Barbina, 1967.

Critical Studies: *The Drama of Pirandello* by D. Vittorini, 1935; *The Age of Pirandello* by Lander McClintock, 1951; *Pirandello and the French Theatre* by Thomas Bishop, 1960; *Pirandello* by Oscar Büdel, 1966; *Pirandello: A Collection of Critical Essays* edited by Glauco Cambon, 1967; *Pirandello 1867-1936* by Walter Starkie, 4th edition, 1967; *Pirandello's Theatre: The Recovery of the Modern Stage for Dramatic Art* by Anne Paolucci, 1974; *Pirandello: A Biography* by Gaspare Giudici, 1975; *The Mirror of Our Anguish: A Study of Pirandello's Narrative Writings* by Douglas Radcliff-Umstead, 1978; *Pirandello: An Approach to His Theatre* by Olga Ragusa, 1980; *Pirandello, Director: The Playwright in the Theatre* by A. Richard Sogliuzzo, 1982; *Pirandello* by Susan Basnett-McGuire, 1983.

*   *   *

Pirandello is one of the most distinguished authors in the history of modern Italian literature. Outside of Italy he is known primarily for his drama, but by the time Pirandello received the Nobel Prize in 1934, he had also written poetry, essays, and novels as well as several hundred short stories. Like most European writers who came of age in the late 19th century, Pirandello's early work was heavily influenced by the aesthetics of realism (an influence that was perhaps heightened by his friendship in Rome with his fellow Sicilian, Luigi Capuana, one of the original standard-bearers of Italian *verismo*). This realist slant is especially apparent in Pirandello's early stories and in his historical novel set in 19th-century Sicily, *The Old and the Young*. It is evident, too, in many of the one-act plays of the period 1910-20 that were drawn from previous short stories, such as *Sicilian Limes*, *Pensaci Giacomino!*, and *The Jar*.

As Pirandello's thought developed, however, he moved away from the realist depiction of the surface of everyday life toward examination of the turbulent phenomena underneath. In Pirandello's theater, this shift in interest and this increasing complexity can be detected as early as *Liolà* (1916), in which society's dependence on passion and fantasy as well as on order and control is examined through the play's presentation of the sexual intrigues of its clever but feckless title character. Pirandello's concern for the truth lying beneath the mask of reality—a truth that is, however, always relative and that therefore cannot be totally understood or explained—is even clearer in *It Is So (If You Think So)* (1917). By means of a series of dramatic discussions, Pirandello reveals the emotional trials that have made up the lives of a seemingly ordinary middle-class family. At the play's conclusion, the group of questioners on stage is challenged to choose between competing versions of the family's story and at the same time cautioned against making any such choice. Because the audience, by implication, participates in this same challenge and warning, *It Is So* serves as a transition from Pirandello's dramas of bourgeois life to his trilogy of plays dealing with one of his favorite topics, the "theater in the theater."

The trilogy comprises three of Pirandello's most highly regarded plays, *Six Characters in Search of an Author*, *Each in His Own Way*, and *Tonight We Improvise*. The first and most innovative piece among them, *Six Characters*, is also the best known of all of Pirandello's works. The play portrays a family of characters who are looking for an author to write out the events of their lives. Through their story of familial jealousy, competition, lust, and tragic violence—and the characters' presentation of the story before the uncomprehending stage company and director—Pirandello probes both the relation between art and life and that between appearance and reality. Together with *Henry IV*, Pirandello's forceful drama of rivalry, madness, and aggression, the trilogy demonstrates Pirandello's concern, one might also say his obsession, with self-reflection in art and with the limitations of reason in coming to terms with human nature, which, by definition, contains irrational as well as rational components.

These questions of human perception, will, and understanding, all of which are basic to Pirandello's developing view of individual and social life, were already at work in his first mature novel, *The Late Mattia Pascal*. These and related issues are treated in expository fashion, moreover, in one of Pirandello's roughly contemporaneous essays, *L'umorismo (On Humor)*. For Pirandello, *umorismo* is more than an attribute solely of wit or of emotion; rather, it is an all-encompassing perspective on life. According to the essay, the primary characteristics of this typically Pirandellian perspective are: first, the individual's "perception" of the comic, that something runs contrary to the normal expectations of daily life; second, the individual's emotional reaction to this perception, or the internal "sentiment" of the comic, experienced in the characteristic passage from perception to sentiment; third, the ever-present activity of reflection—including self-reflection—from which this sentiment arises and which it then further stimulates; and fourth, the constant tendency to decompose ("scomporre") the form of experience into its constituent elements so that they may be considered both separately and in relation to one another and, if possible (though for the full-fledged *umorista* such a feat is never really possible), reassembled in a workable and more liveable fashion, in a new fusion of what the essay terms life and form, "vita" and "forma."

The story of the "late" Mattia Pascal is in many respects the story of his development as an *umorista*. In essence, the plot of the novel is based on the standard anecdote of the man who dies (complicated here by a crucial instance of mistaken identity) and who then returns to this world from beyond with the uncanny knowledge of his own death. It is this special knowledge, the peculiarly distanced view of life, that lends Mattia's story the characteristic perspective of *umorismo*. That Mattia's narrative is told in the first-person by the mature, or literally "late," narrator only heightens its self-reflexive quality.

This perspective is also fundamental to one of Pirandello's novels of his middle period, *Shoot!*; but its fullest expression is contained in Pirandello's last and in many respects his most problematic novel, *One, None, and a Hundred Thousand*. Whereas *The Late Mattia Pascal* represents the *discovery* of psychological and artistic reflexivity, *One, None, and a Hundred Thousand* is a programmatic exposition not only of the process but also of the *consequence* of such discoveries. The novel's plot is made up of Vitangelo Moscarda's attempts to see himself as others see him. He carries out this project by gradually discarding all of those particular attributes (his wife, his reputation, his profession as a banker) that have come together to compose his identity in society. Vitangelo's social "suicide" eventually leads to a critical impasse, at which point he gives up on his project and leaves life in society altogether. At the novel's conclusion, disgusted with his former existence and with all those who were part of it, Vitangelo retires from the town in which he has spent his life in order to establish a new, totally non-reflective form of day-to-day existence at a hospice in the countryside.

Although at the beginning of the novel Vitangelo sounds a good deal like Pirandello's other highly rationalistic, skeptical, and self-involved characters, the novel's conclusion shows him in a very different light. Vitangelo's story was Piirandello's most extreme statement of the philosophy of *umorismo*, which derived both from earlier European intellectual philosophy and from the then influential views of Henri Bergson. But the novel also represented a turning point in Pirandello's thought, the completion of one line of investigation and the beginning of another. This new set of interests had been implicit in Pirandello's work for some time, but it became dominant only in such later, socially oriented plays as *The New Colony*, *Lazarus*, and the unfinished (and pointedly pessimistic) *The Mountain Giants*. Generally speaking, this final shift in Pirandello's interests was from the rational powers of the self-reflective, alienated individual to the communal truth of myth. Although Pirandello did not live to carry this line of artistic and social inquiry to its conclusion, his last plays indicate that, even at his death, Pirandello had once again found the pulse of the future.

In the decades since his death, and particularly since the close of World War II, there have been many studies of Pirandello's relationship with the Fascist government in Rome. It should be noted, however, that even though Pirandello's ties with the regime were close until the very end of his career, in all of the various phases of his thought—whether realistic, rationally self-reflexive, or mythic—his work regularly manifested an iconoclastic aversion to absolute authority that set it apart from the standard political doctrines of the time in Italian social and intellectual life (and perhaps most distinctly from the work of his well-known contemporary, Gabriele D'Annunzio). The body of criticism dealing with Pirandello continues to grow at an exceptional rate in America as well as in Europe, but despite the extraordinary variety of critical treatments that his work has received, Pirandello's importance and his influence on subsequent writers both inside and outside Italy have remained beyond dispute.

—Gregory L. Lucente

PLATO.   Born in Athens (possibly in Aegina), c.429-27 B.C. A disciple of Socrates: when Socrates was executed in 399, Plato retired with other Socratics to Megara, then traveled for the next 12 years: visited Egypt, Sicily, 390-88, where he met Dionysius I of Syracuse, and Italy, where he met Archytas of Tarentum; began teaching near the grove of Academus outside Athens in 388, and continued for his remaining 40 years; visited Dionysius II of Syracuse, 366-65, and again in Syracuse, 362-61. *Died 347 B.C.*

PUBLICATIONS

Collections

[*Dialogues*], edited by J. Burnet.   5 vols., 1900-07; as *Dialogues*, translated by Benjamin Jowett, revised edition, 1953; also translated by H.N. Fowler and others (Loeb edition), 1914-29; *Collected Dialogues* (various translators), edited by Edith Hamilton and Huntington Cairns, 1961.

Dialogues (in chronological order)

Hippias Minor
Laches, edited by M.T. Tatham.   1966; as *Laches*, translated by Rosamund Kent Sprague, 1973.
Charmides: as *Charmides*, translated by Rosamund Kent Sprague, 1973.
Ion: as *Ion*, translated by W.H.D. Rouse, 1956.
Protagoras: as *Protagoras*, translated by W.K.C. Guthrie, 1956, and C.C.W. Taylor, 1976.
Euthyphro, edited by T.R. Mills.   1927; as *Euthyphro*, translated by J. Warrington, in *The Trial and Death of Socrates*, 1963; also translated by R.E. Allen, 1970.
Apologia (not a dialogue), edited by Edward Henry Blakeney.   1929; as *The Apology*, translated by H. Tredennick, in *The Last Days of Socrates*, 1954; also translated by W.H.D. Rouse, 1956, and Thomas G. West, 1979; in *The Trial and Death of Socrates*, translated by J. Warrington, 1963.
Crito: as *Crito*, translated by H. Tredennick, in *The Last Days of Socrates*, 1954; also

translated by W.H.D Rouse, 1956; in *The Trial and Death of Socrates*, translated by J. Warrington, 1963.

Gorgias, edited by E.R. Dodds. 1959; as *Gorgias*, translated by W. Hamilton, 1960, and Terence Irwin, 1980.

Meno, edited by R.S. Bluck. 1961; also edited by A. Sesonske and N. Fleming, 1965; as *Meno*, translated by W.H.D. Rouse, 1956, and W.K.C. Guthrie, 1956.

Lysis, translated in *Plato's Dialogue on Friendship* by David Bolotin. 1979.

Menexenus.

Euthydemus: as *Euthydemus*, translated by Rosamund Kent Sprague, 1972.

Cratylus.

Symposium, edited by R.G. Bury. 1973; also edited by K.J. Dover, 1980; as *The Symposium*, translated by W. Hamilton, 1951, W.H.D. Rouse, 1956, and S.Q. Groden, 1970.

Republic, edited by James Adam, revised by D.A. Rees. 2 vols., 1963; as *The Republic*, translated by F.M. Cornford, 1941, H.D.P. Lee, 1955, W.H.D. Rouse, 1956, and I.A. Richards, 1966.

Parmenides: as *Parmenides*, translated by A.E. Taylor, 1934, F.M. Cornford, 1939, J. Warrington, 1961, and R.E. Allen, 1983.

Theaetetus: as *Theaetetus*, translated by J. Warrington, 1961, Tayler Lewis, 1963, and John McDowell, 1973; as *Plato's Theory of Knowledge*, translated by F.M. Cornford, 1935.

Phaedrus: as *Phaedrus*, translated by R. Hackforth, 1952, W. Hamilton, 1973, and A.H. Waterfield, 1982.

Sophist: as *Sophist*, translated by A.E. Taylor, 1961, and J. Warrington, 1961.

Statesman: as *Politicus*, translated by J.B. Skemb, 1952; as *Statesman*, translated by A.E. Taylor, 1961, and J. Warrington, 1961.

Philebus: as *Philebus*, translated by R. Hackforth, in *Plato's Examination of Pleasure*, 1945, A.E. Taylor, 1956, and J.C.B. Gosling, 1975.

Timaeus: as *Timaeus*, translated by A.E. Taylor, 1929, H.D.P. Lee, 1956, and J. Warrington, 1965.

Critias: as *Critias*, translated by H.D.P. Lee, 1971.

Laws, edited by E.B. England. 2 vols., 1921; as *Laws*, translated by A.E. Taylor, 1934, and Trevor S. Saunders, 1970.

Doubtful works:

Hippias Major, edited by Paul Woodruff (includes translation). 1983.

Clitopho.

Epinomis: as *Epinomis*, translated by J. Harward, 1928, and A.E. Taylor, 1956.

Letters: as *Epistles*, translated by L.A. Post, 1925, J. Harward, 1932, and Glenn R. Morrow, 1935.

*

Critical Studies: *What Plato Said* by Paul Shorey, 1933; *The Open City: The Spell of Plato* by Karl Popper, 1957; *Plato* by Paul Friedlander, 3 vols., 1958-69; *Plato's Cretan City* by Glenn R. Morrow, 1960; *An Examination of Plato's Doctrines* by I.M. Crombie, 2 vols., 1962-63; *Preface to Plato* by E.A. Havelock, 1963; *New Essays on Plato and Aristotle* edited by R. Bambrough, 1965; *Plato's Progress* by Gilbert Ryle, 1966; *Plato: A Collection of Critical Essays* edited by Gregory Vlastos, 1971, and *Platonic Studies*, 1973, and *Plato's Universe*, 1975, both by Vlastos; *Plato and Modern Morality* by P.M. Huby, 1972; *The Unity of the Platonic Dialogue* by R.H. Weingartner, 1973; *Plato* by J.C.B. Gosling, 1973; *Plato: The Written and Unwritten Doctrine*, 1974, and *Plato and Platonism: An Introduction*, 1978, both by J.N. Findlay; *Plato's Ideas on Art and Education* by E.J.F. James, 1975; *Plato* by J.B. Skemp, 1976;

PLATO

The Fire and the Sun: Why Plato Banished the Artists by Iris Murdoch, 1977; *Plato's Moral Theory: The Early and Middle Dialogues* by Terence Irwin, 1977; *Plato's Trilogy: Theaetetus, the Sophist, and the Statesman* by Jacob Klein, 1977; *Plato* by R.M. Hare, 1982.

*　　*　　*

Plato is not, as Sir Karl Popper taught the 20th century to believe in *The Open Society and Its Enemies*, the father of modern totalitarian political ideology. No writer has ever condemned the tyrant more powerfully than Plato did in *The Republic*, not even the Greek tragic dramatists with their scathing indictments of the rule of the "great men." Nor was Plato an enemy to toleration. He recommended the reading of Aristophanes to his pupil Dionysius, even though the comic dramatist had handled his master Socrates roughly, and might have been held indirectly responsible for his later trial and death. "It is never required of us that we know the truth, only that we never knowingly accept error." Popper, speaking for modern "realism," assumes that all idealists must be intolerant. But *Areopagitica* was written by Plato's greatest disciple in English, John Milton, and not by Bacon or Hobbes, precursors of modern skepticism.

Alfred North Whitehead once described western philosophy as "a series of footnotes to Plato." Plato has suffered the fate of being assigned to the domain of university departments of philosophy. Renaissance neoplatonists were probably more correct in viewing him as the Poet whose philosophical ideas were secondary to his imaginative creations. And any appraisal of Plato must transcend his contribution to the epistemological debate, started by his pupil Aristotle, as to whether there is laid up in heaven the perfect ideal of any earthly chair. Plato was far more concerned with achieving justice in human society, and whether or not there is an ideal for the just society is a far more important, and more practical, question than that concerning the chair.

The Republic is the first, and probably the greatest, of all contributions to political thought. As the word itself indicates, politics is as much a Greek invention as philosophy. Humans can only find their fulfillment as members of a *polis*. One who is not a member of such a community is either a wild beast or a god. This idea was subsequently Christianized; the person found salvation as member of the *ecclesia* (the assembly of citizens of the *polis*). But by divorcing the *ecclesia* from time and space, in effect morality was divorced from politics, to the damage of both. No task of modern thought is more urgent than to again unite politics and morality.

The crisis event in Plato's life was the trial and death of Socrates, analogous in every respect to the crucifixion for the disciples. With one great difference: Plato did not believe in a personal resurrection, and for him the task was to build a human society that would not execute those who should be the moral leaders. This was not a problem for Christian thought, since Jesus was historically unique. There could be a future Socrates. In Christian thought justice would be achieved by the return to earth of the triumphant Messiah. Plato had to take a more earthly route. *The Republic* is Plato's attempt to build a society that will honor its moral leaders, not destroy them. Plato never expected that such a society would exist, but he knew that humanity must never cease trying to build it. It is a foolish modern error to equate idealism with optimism. The great idealists have been great pessimists. Plato understood the terrible effects of power: "Power must never be given to those who want power." No modern political treatise recognizes that problem, let alone resolves it. Plato was profoundly doubtful that democracy would solve the problem, and his doubts seem justified. The "Great Beast" (the state) rewards those who flatter it; it will destroy those who oppose it. Each democracy has executed its own Socrates. Nor does *The Republic* ignore economic issues. "You cannot have a society with great extremes of wealth and poverty. For then you will have two societies, and they will be at war with each other." Modern political theory, descending from Machiavelli and Hobbes, simply ignores the problems Plato raised. We are farther than ever from solving them.

As Werner Jaeger recognized in his *Paideia*, Plato also originated theology. When he exiled the poets from the Republic because they did not tell the truth about the gods, he began the study of the nature of those gods. From Plato these speculations migrated to the early Christian thinkers, who proceeded to turn the Jewish Jehovah into the Christian *Deus* (simply Latin for ZEUS). It is worth noting that the early Christians, including Jesus himself, lived in bilingual areas and were drenched in Greek thought. The New Testament is a work in Greek literature.

As the Renaissance Platonists realized, Plato is the father of love. Every modern treatment descends from his *Symposium* and *Phaedrus*. All love poetry is Platonist. Interestingly in its origin love is homosexual. Modern notions of heterosexual love are perversions of homosexual love. Testimony to this fact is provided by the unsuccessful attempt to link romantic love with marriage. The resulting mix would have brought smiles to Plato, who discussed the two incompatible horses to which the human chariot was yoked.

Plato is also the inventor of the university. His Academy was the prototype of all others. He admitted women as full equals, an achievement not again duplicated until Oberlin College was founded as a coeducational institution in the 19th century. Plato was also the first to call for full sexual equality. Women trained with men on terms of total equality as guardians of the *Republic*, and w⌐uld in turn become the philosopher-kings. Plato's idealism was to dominate the university until in modern times Bacon turned its interests in the direction of research. Plato's Academy was to train the leadership for his ideal *polis*. Only those with an ideal of justice could hope to move the human city in the direction of achieving it.

But Plato's greatest contribution was a poetic one, the creating of his Socrates. Philip Sidney in the Renaissance had said that the essential function of the poet was "to feign notable images of virtues," and only the Jesus of the New Testament writers has rivalled Plato's Socrates as the ideal of virtue. That this was Plato's creation and not just the historical Socrates is demonstrated by the different figure in Xenophon. Prior to Plato the Greek ideal had been the *arete* of Achilles in the *Iliad*, or the shrewdness of Odysseus, the man "never without an apt word or a clever plan." Odysseus might be clever like the fox; the wisdom of Socrates was of an altogether higher order. The world after Plato could never go back to Homer; it had no choice but to go on to Christianity. To the extent that the world has been able to admire those who suffer for truth's sake, and to turn away from the "destroyers of cities," that debt in great measure is owed to Plato. Not one of the problems he raised has been solved, or will be solved. But once he had written, there was hope, and no reason for the best to lack all conviction. That is his legacy to us.

—Myron Taylor

PLAUTUS (Titus Maccius Plautus).   Born, possibly in Sarsina, Umbria, c. 254 B.C. Active c. 195-184; associated with the actor-impresario T. Publilius Phellio on the plays *Stichus* and *Epidicus*; more than 130 scripts of plays were passed under his name, but Varro listed only 21 plays as genuine. *Died c. 184 B.C.*

PUBLICATIONS

Collections

[*Plays*], edited by Friedrich Leo.   1895-96; also edited by W.M. Lindsay, 1904-05, Alfred Ernout, 7 vols., 1932-40, G. Augello, 1968-72, and Ettore Paratore, 5 vols., 1976;

translation (Loeb edition), 5 vols., 1916-38; also translated in *Complete Roman Drama*, edited by George Duckworth, 1942.

Plays

Amphitryo, edited by W.B. Sedgwick.   1960; also edited by Thomas Cutt, 1970; as *Amphitryon*, translated by Lionel Casson, 1963, E.F. Watling, 1964, and Paul Roche, 1968.
Asinaria [Asses' Tale], edited by F. Bertini.   2 vols., 1968.
Aulularia, as *The Pot of Gold*, translated by Lionel Casson, 1963, and E.F. Watling, 1965.
Bacchides [The Two Bacchises], edited by C. Questa.   1975; translated by James Tatum, in *The Darker Comedies*, 1983, and John Barsby, 1984.
Captivi, edited by W.M. Lindsay, revised edition.   1921; as *The Prisoners*, translated by E.F. Watling, 1965, Paul Roche, 1968, and A.G. Gillingham, 1968.
Casina, edited by W.T. MacCary and M.M. Willcock.   1976, translated by Lionel Casson, 1963, and by James Tatum, in *The Darker Comedies*, 1983.
Cistellaria [The Casket Comedy].
Curculio, edited by G. Monaco.   1969; also edited by John Wright, 1981; as *The Weevil*, translated by A.G. Gillingham, 1968.
Epidicus [Legally Liable], edited by George Duckworth.   1940.
Menaechmi, edited by J. Brix, O. Niemeyer, and F. Conrad.   1929; also edited by N. Moseley and Mason Hammond, 1959, and Gilbert Lawall and Betty Nye Quinn, 1978; as *The Brothers Menaechmus*, translated by Erich Segal, 1963, Lionel Casson, 1963, and E.F. Watling, 1965.
Mercator [Merchant], edited by P.J. Enk.   2 vols., 1966.
Miles gloriosus [The Braggart Soldier], edited by Mason Hammond, Arthur W. Mack, and Walter Moskalew.   1970; translated by Erich Segal, 1965, E.F. Watling, 1965, S. Allot, 1967, and Paul Roche, 1968.
Mostellaria [Ghost or Haunted House], edited by J. Collart.   1970; also edited by F. Bertini, 1970; translated by E.F. Watling, 1965, Erich Segal, 1965, S. Allot, 1967, and A.G. Gillingham, 1968.
Persa [Persian], edited by Erich Woytek.   1982.
Poenulus [The Little Carthaginian], edited by G. Maurach.   1975.
Pseudolus [Trickster], edited by Edgar H. Sturtevant.   1932; translated by Lionel Casson, 1963, and E.F. Watling, 1965.
Rudens [Rope], edited by F. Marx.   1928; also edited by H.C. Fay, 1969; translated by Lionel Casson, 1963, E.F. Watling, 1964, and S. Allot, 1967.
Stichus [Row], edited by H. Petersmann.   1973.
Trinummus [Threepence], edited by J. Brix and O. Niemeyer.   1907; translated by E.F. Watling, 1964.
Truculentus [Churl], edited by P.J. Enk.   2 vols., 1953; translated by James Tatum, in *The Darker Comedies*, 1983.
Vidularia [The Rucksack Play] (fragment).

*

Bibliography: *A Bibliography of Scholarship on Plautus* by J. David Hughes, 1975; "Scholarship on Plautus 1965-76" by Erich Segal, in *Classical World 74*, no. 7, 1981.

Critical Studies: *A Chronology of the Plays of Plautus* by Charles H. Buck, 1940; *The Nature of Roman Comedy* by George Duckworth, 1952; *Roman Laughter: The Comedy of Plautus*, by Erich Segal, 1968; *Menander, Plautus, and Terence* by W.G. Arnott, 1968; *Menander and Plautus: A Study in Comparison* by Eric W. Handley, 1968; *Dancing in Chains: The Stylistic Unity of the Comoedia Palliata* by John H. Wright, 1974; *Roman Comedy* by Kenneth

McLeish, 1976; *Tradition and Originality in Plautus* by Netta Zagagi, 1980; *Roman Comedy* by David Konstan, 1983.

*   *   *

Plautus, whose comedies are much the earliest works of Latin literature that have survived entire, began producing in the later years of the Hannibalic war, when the number of festivals at which dramas were presented had increased to seven or eight each year. Plautus probably wrote original plots situated in Italian towns, but the plays we have are all adaptations of Greek originals by Menander and his contemporaries, the composers of Greek New Comedy. New Comedy was domestic drama, concentrating largely on the vicissitudes of young men's romantic infatuation with modest girls or clever courtesans. The style was one of artful naturalism, and this Plautus transformed into an exuberant dazzle of puns, neologisms, strings of alliteration so dear to Roman taste, fanciful figures and tropes like oxymoron and the unexpected twist at the end of a phrase, and an operatic variety of rhythms in the *cantica*, or songs, for which there was no counterpart in his models. This vivacity of style and diction was matched by Plautus's handling of plot, where he trimmed or expanded or at times conflated his models with a view to enlivening the action and emphasizing the roles of pert and farcical characters like the wily slaves who engineer liaisons and the greedy brothelkeepers or pompous mercenaries who obstruct them.

While Plautus delighted in the comic license of representing slaves riding piggy-back on their young masters (*Asinaria*), or taunting their elder masters as they sputter gruesome but quite realistic threats of punishment (*Mostellaria*), he was sensitive as well to the themes of the comedies he adapted, sometimes highlighting them by reference to a Roman practice or by the use of significant names for his characters. The twin courtesans who seduce a pair of friends and their fathers are called Bacchis in a play that is liberal with allusions to the worship of Dionysus, which was at the time a matter of concern to the Roman senate; a miser who refuses all commerce with his neighbors in order to hoard his gold prohibits his housekeeper from lending anyone fire or water, an interdiction reminiscent of the Roman formula for banishment (*Aulularia*). The miser is duly humbled. A father who unwittingly holds his own son hostage as a prisoner of war affords a glimpse into the paradoxes of strife and enslavement among the Greek city-states which may have had special meaning to the Romans as they reconquered Italy from the retreating Carthaginian armies (*Captivi*). An old man, in exile from Athens, is reunited with his daughter on a distant shore in a kind of pastoral affirmation of the community of men, gods, and nature (*Rudens*). With its limited cast of characters and conventional narrative repertory of outwitted parents and improbable recognitions, New Comedy touched the anxious issues of class, status, authority, and community in Hellenistic civic life. Plautus developed the spirit of farce or vaudeville in these performances without entirely sacrificing their seriousness and refinement. With the recovery of the New Comic tradition in the Renaissance, both sides of Plautus were there to be imitated and exploited (e.g. *Ralph Roister Doister* and *The Comedy of Errors*). Their coexistence in the theater of Plautus endows his best comedies with the permanent appeal of high entertainment.

—David Konstan

PLUTARCH (Lucius? Mestrius Plutarchus).   Born in Chaeronea, Boeotia, c. 46 A.D. Studied in Athens in mid-60's. Married Timoxena; at least four sons and one daughter. Lectured in Rome and visited Egypt; a priest at Delphi, and helped revive the shrine there; held numerous municipal posts in Chaeronea; possibly made a procurator by the emperor Hadrian. *Died after 120 A.D.*

PUBLICATIONS

Collections

[*Works*], edited by D. Wyttenbach.   1795-1830.

Prose

Moralia, edited by H. Wegehaupt and others.   1925— ; translated by Frank G. Babbitt and others (Loeb edition), 1927— ; *Selected Essays* translated by T.G. Tucker and A.O. Prickard, 2 vols., 1913-18; *Moral Essays* (selection), translated by Rex Warner, 1971.
Vitae parallelae [Parallel Lives], edited by K. Ziegler and others.   1914-39, revision in progress, 1957-80; also edited by Robert Flacelière and others, 1957— ; as *Lives*, translated by Thomas North, 1579; also translated in an edition edited by Dryden, 1683-86; also translated by Bernadotte Perrin (Loeb edition), 11 vols., 1914-26; *Fall of the Roman Republic* (6 lives) translated by Rex Warner, 1958, revised edition, 1972; *The Rise of Athens* (9 lives), 1960, *Makers of Rome* (9 lives), 1965, and *The Age of Alexander* (9 lives), 1973 all translated by Ian Scott-Kilvert.

*

Critical Studies: *Plutarchos von Chaironeia* by Konrat Ziegler, revised edition, 1964; *Plutarch's Historical Method* by P.A. Stadter, 1965; *Plutarch and His Times* by Reginald H. Barrow, 1967; *Plutarch* by Constantine C. Gianakaris, 1970; *Plutarch and Rome* by Christopher P. Jones, 1971; *Plutarch* by Donald Russell, 1972; *Plutarch's Lives* by Alan Wardman, 1974; *Plutarch's Ethical writings and Early Christian Literature* by Hans Dieter Betz, 1975; *In Mist Appareled: Religious Themes in Plutarch's Moralia and Lives* by F.E. Brenk, 1977; *Plutarch's Themistocles* by Frank J. Frost, 1980.

*   *   *

Plutarch has left us the second largest corpus of works to have been preserved from classical antiquity. The prize goes to the philosopher-physician Galen, but while Galen's books slumber peaceably on the shelves of the few libraries that possess the only complete edition, Plutarch has been eagerly read by everyone with an interest in the ancient world since his works were rediscovered during the Renaissance. It would be difficult to imagine a writer better qualified to reflect every aspect of the culture of the Graeco-Roman world during the *Pax Romana*. His education was the finest a wealthy family could provide, as measured by the thousands of citations from the entire legacy of classical literature scattered throughout his works, many from authors now lost. Although he trifled with rhetoric as a young man (*Fame of the Athenians, Fortune of Alexander*, etc.), he developed quickly into a philosopher in the literal sense: a lover of all wisdom. He claimed Plato and the Academy as his school, but his writings show his personal philosophical outlook to have been quite eclectic, being in general positive, optimistic, humanist, and philanthropic. He was convinced of the possibility of human progress and believed that reason was the best guide to such progress. The *Parallel Lives* of notable Greeks and Romans were designed to educate; he never seems to have doubted that if young men were shown good examples they would follow them.

Plutarch was not a brilliant scientist, an elegant stylist, a critical historian, or a profound thinker, but he had read and absorbed the works of those who were and was able, with an easy familiarity, to convey their wisdom to a larger audience. "He had that universal sympathy with genius which makes all its victories his own," said Emerson in the introduction to the complete Boston edition of 1870. Plutarch was a popularizer of scientific and religious thought, even the most complex (*On the Face in the Moon, Isis and Osiris*). As an essayist he was fluent and productive, if sometimes verbose and perfunctory. He wrote on a surprising variety of topics— *On Superstition, On Fate, On Exile*; the *Cleverness of Animals* and the advantages of a mature wife (*Amatorius*); even a curious attack on the Father of History himself (*Malignity of Herodotus*), just to name a few examples. The popularity of Plutarch's biographies rests neither on literary style nor on historical insight but on his skill as a superb storyteller, whether describing epic battles (*Aristeides, Fabius*), thrilling escapades (*Aratus, Demetrius, Sulla*), virtue triumphan† (*Timoleon, Pericles*), or the tragedy of thwarted idealism (*Cleomenes, Sertorius*). His sense of plot and narrative did not escape later writers, as Shakespeare's *Coriolanus, Julius Caesar*, and *Antony and Cleopatra* remind us.

Higher criticism, particularly German, in the late 19th century attempted to portray Plutarch as a second-rate compiler, stitching together his essays and biographies from the real scholarship of creative predecessors (whose works have conveniently disappeared). But since World War II there has been a revival of appreciation for Plutarch as writer and thinker. The originality of his scholarship is now generally accepted and his liberal humanism makes him one of the more attractive and illuminating spokesmen for all of Graeco-Roman antiquity.

—Frank J. Frost

PRÉVOST, Abbé (Antoine-François Prévost d'Exiles).   Born in Hesdin, France, 1 April 1697. Probably educated at a college in Hesdin; Collège d'Harcourt, Paris; studied for the priesthood at La Flèche: novice, Society of Jesus, 1713, but soon joined the army and led a dissolute life for 5 years; joined community of Benedictines at Saint-Maur, 1719; ordained a priest, 1721, and preacher and teacher until 1728; another spell of worldly life, often in exile in Holland and London: founded periodical *Le Pour et le contre* in London, 1733-40; again reconciled with the Benedictines: almoner and secretary, 1736; then lived the rest of his life as a writer and journalist: Editor, *Le Journal Étranger*, 1755. *Died 23 November 1763.*

PUBLICATIONS

Collections

    Oeuvres choisies.   39 vols., 1783-85.
    Oeuvres, edited by Pierre Berthiaume and Jean Sgard.   1978— .

Fiction

    Les Aventures de Pomponius, chevalier romain; ou, L'Histoire de notre temps.   1724.

Mémoires et aventures d'un homme de qualité qui s'est retiré du monde. 1728-31; revised edition, 1756; as *Memoirs of a Man of Quality*, 1938.

Histoire du chevalier Des Grieux et de Manon Lescaut. 1733 (originally constituted the last volume of *Mémoires et aventures d'un homme de qualité*); edited by Frédéric Deloffre and Raymond Picard, 1965; translated as *Manon Lescaut*, 1738.

Le Philosophe anglais; ou, Histoire de Monsieur Cleveland, fils naturel de Cromwell. 1731-39; as *The Life and Adventures of Mr. Cleveland*, 1734.

Le Doyen de Killerine: Histoire morale composée sur les mémoires d'une illustre famille d'Irlande. 1735-40; as *The Dean of Coleraine*, 1742-43.

Histoire d'une grecque moderne. 1740; as *The History of a Fair Greek*, 1755.

Histoire de Marguerite d'Anjou, Reine d'Angleterre. 1740; as *The History of Margaret of Anjou, Queen of England*, 1755.

Campagnes philosophiques; ou, Mémoires de M. de Monteal. 1741.

Mémoires pour servir à l'histoire de Malte; ou, Histoire de la jeunesse du commandeur de * * *. 1741.

Histoire de Guillaume le Conquérant, duc de Normandie, et roi d'Angleterre. 1741-42.

Voyages de capitaine Robert Lade. 1744.

Mémoires d'un honnête homme. 1745.

Le Monde moral; ou, Mémoires pour servir à l'histoire du coeur humain. 1760-64.

Other

Le Pour et le contre. 20 vols., 1733-40.

Le Critique français. 1734.

Histoire générale des voyages. 15 vols., 1746-59.

Manuel lexique; ou, Dictionnaire portatif des mots français. 2 vols., 1750.

Editor, *Histoire metallique des XVII provinces des Pays-Bas*, by Gerard Van Loon. 2 vols., 1732.

Editor and translator, *Lettres de Cicéron à M. Brutus et de M. Brutus à Cicéron.* 1744.

Editor and translator, *Lettres de Cicéron.* 5 vols., 1745-47.

Translator, with others, *Histoire universelle*, by J.—A. de Thou. 1733-34.

Translator, *Tout pour l'amour; ou, Le Monde bien perdu*, by Dryden. 1735.

Translator, *Histoire de Cicéron*, by Conyers Middleton. 4 vols., 1743-44.

Translator, *Lettres anglaises; ou, Histoire de Miss Clarisse Harlove*, by Richardson. 1751.

Translator, *Nouvelles lettres anglaises; ou, Histoire de Chevalier Grandisson*, by Richardson. 1755-58.

Translator, *Histoire de la maison de Stuart sur la trône d'Angleterre*, by Hume. 3 vols., 1760.

Translator, *Almoran et Hamet: Anecdote orientale*, by J. Hawkesworth. 1763.

Translator, *Lettres de Mentor à un jeune seigneur.* 1764.

*

Critical Studies: *The Abbé Prévost and English Literature* by G.R. Havens, 1921; *The Art of French Fiction* by Martin Turnell, 1959; *Prévost, romancier* by Jean Sgard, 1968; *Prévost: Manon Lescaut* by Vivienne Mylne, 1972; *Structuralist Perspectives in Criticism of Fiction: Essays on "Manon Lescaut" and "La Vie de Marianne"* by Patrick Brady, 1978.

* * *

Like Choderlos de Laclos, l'Abbé Prévost is a man known to the modern reader for only one book, though for very different reasons than the author of *Les Liaisons dangereuses*. For although the book that has ensured literary immortality for Prévost, *Histoire du Chevalier des Grieux et de Manon Lescaut* (*The History of the Chevalier des Grieux and of Manon Lescaut*), contains no more than 300 pages, it is part of a very much longer but now rarely read novel entitled *Mémoires d'un homme de qualité* (*Memoirs of a Gentleman of Quality*). Prévost continued to occupy himself during his long life with a series of other compositions, but never again encountered the success immediately won for him by this account of how a young man of 17 falls in love with a girl of 16 and proceeds to ruin all his chances of future happiness by his devotion to someone who, in spite of her love for him, is totally incapable of fidelity the moment she runs short of money. This devotion is indeed the central theme of a novel which is generally if inappropriately shortened to *Manon Lescaut* or even, in the case of Massenet's opera, to *Manon*. For although the attention of readers has always gone to the irresistible Manon, it is the paradox of the moralistic and monogamous man attached to the polygamous and amoral woman which gives the book its originality and inexhaustible fascination. For although Des Grieux loves Manon with an exclusive and all-devouring passion, he rapidly learns that there is nothing he can do to prevent her from going to bed with the nearest rich admirer as soon as he can no longer support her in the luxurious style of living without which she cannot be happy. Yet he is never able to move away from this knowledge to a position where he can do without Manon and her charms, and one result of this has been to lead critics to see Des Grieux—and, through him, his creator—as continuing the Jansenist theme of "Video meliora proboque; deteriora sequor" (I see the best and approve of it; but I follow the worst) which informs the tragic vision of Racine.

Yet there is nothing of the tragic grandeur of Racine in this story of what one hostile contemporary critic referred to as "the adventures of a crook and his whore," and Prévost's account of Paris in the Regency of Louis XV, with its tricksters, gambling dens, prostitutes, shady financiers, and cheap lodging houses looks forward to the realist novel of the 19th and even of the 20th century. Indeed, in 1950, the story was made into an interesting film in which the Paris of the 1720's was replaced by the comparably sordid and ambiguous period of the German Occupation of the 1940's, and the final shipping off of Manon to the Louisiana of the early 18th century was replaced by her being sent to Israel at the difficult time of the 1948 war. In both novel and film she dies in the desert and is buried by Des Grieux, who then returns to tell the story to the "Homme de Qualité," who adopts towards him the same moralising and moralistic tone which characterises Prévost's Preface to the novel. Yet it is very difficult to accept Prévost's claim that the story of Manon and Des Grieux is "a moral treatise agreeably reduced to an exercise." Neither Prévost nor the narrator has any real set of values to set by the side of the "world well lost for love" theme which inspires the two principals, and Prévost shows such a lack of awareness of how amoral society is in general that Manon's sexual infidelities seem relatively venial sins in comparison.

—Philip Thody

PROUST, Marcel. Born in Auteuil, Paris, 10 July 1871. Educated at Lycée Condorcet, Paris, 1882-89; the Sorbonne, Paris, 1891-93. Military service, 1889-90. Active in society in the 1890's, but gradually became a recluse. Recipient: Goncourt Prize, 1919. *Died 18 November 1922.*

PUBLICATIONS

Fiction

À la recherche du temps perdu.   1913-27; as *Remembrance of Things Past*, 1922-31; revised translation, 1981.
Du côté de chez Swann.   1913; as *Swann's Way*, 1922.
À l'ombre des jeunes filles en fleurs.   1919; as *Within a Budding Grove*, 1924.
Le Côté de Guermantes.   1920-21; as *The Guermantes Way*, 1925.
Sodome et Gomorrhe.   1921-22; as *Cities of the Plain*, 1927.
La Prisonnière.   1923; as *The Captive*, 1929.
Albertine disparue.   1925; as *The Sweet Cheat Gone*, 1930.
Le Temps retrouvé.   1927; as *Time Regained*, 1931; as *The Past Recaptured*, 1932.
Jean Santeuil.   1952; translated as *Jean Santeuil*, 1955.

Other

Les Plaisirs et les jours.   1896; as *Pleasures and Regrets*, 1948.
Pastiches et mélanges.   1919.
Chroniques.   1927.
Correspondance générale.   6 vols., 1930-36; selection, as *Letters*, edited by Mina Curtiss, 1950.
A Selection, edited by Gerald Hopkins.   1948.
Contre Sainte-Beuve.   1954; as *On Art and Literature 1896-1919*, 1958; as *By Way of Sainte-Beuve*, 1958.
Letters to His Mother, edited by George D. Painter.   1957.
Textes rétrouvés, edited by Philip Kolb and Larkin B. Price.   1968.
Correspondance, edited by Philip Kolb.   1970— .
Le Carnet de 1908, edited by Philip Kolb.   1976.
Selected Letters 1880-1903, edited by Philip Kolb.   1983.

Translator, *La Bible d'Amiens*, by Ruskin.   1904.
Translator, *Sésame et le lys*, by Ruskin.   1906; Proust's preface as *On Reading*, edited by Jean Autret and William Burford, 1972.

*

Bibliography: *Bibliographie des études sur Proust et son oeuvre* by Victor E. Graham, 1976.

Critical Studies: *Proust: A Biography* by George D. Painter, 2 vols., 1959-65; *A Reading of Proust* by Wallace Fowlie, revised edition, 1975; *A Reader's Handbook to Proust: An Index Guide to Remembrance of Things Past* by P.A. Spalding, revised by R.H. Cortie, 1975; *Proust's Additions: The Making of "À la recherche du temps perdu"* by Alison Winton, 2 vols., 1977; *Proust* by Patrick Brady, 1977; *Proust and the Art of Love: The Aesthetics of Sexuality in the Life, Times, and Art of Proust* by J.E. Rivers, 1980; *Proust's Recherche: A Psychoanalytic Interpretation* by Randolph Splitter, 1981; *A Proust Dictionary* by Maxine Arnold Vogely, 1981; *Proust* by J.M. Cocking, 1982; *A Guide to Proust* by Terence Kilmartin, 1983; *The Reading of Proust* by David R. Ellison 1984.

*   *   *

To some of his earliest critics, Proust appeared as the novelist-heir of Balzac, as the artist bent upon painting the huge fresco of an age in French history. Today the literary ancestors appear more numerous, and the critics are beginning to estimate how much he owes to Chateaubriand, Nerval, Baudelaire, and Mallarmé. These would seem to be the writers who taught Proust something concerning the art of transfiguring objects and human beings, the art of selecting and magnifying, which is the art of transfiguration.

By comparison with the traditional 19th-century novel, *À la recherche du temps perdu* (*Remembrance of Things Past*) seems a new form in which the psychological analysis is far more developed, but is not conclusive, not dogmatic. The patterns of human existence are not clear in Proust. So many mysteries remain after the psychological exploration of the characters, that they end by bearing some resemblance to allegories. Proust is a secretive writer. Despite the elaborate analysis of scenes and characters, we never learn his complete thought about the significance of a scene or his complete understanding of a personality. The novel as a whole is esoteric, and the countless critics of Proust tend to be exegetes in their effort to explain the allegory, to pierce the secret of Proust and of his work.

Proust believed that the self a man exhibits in his daily habits, in his social life, in his vices, is artificial and even false. His real self is not easily exhibited. It is inner and concealed. If the man is a writer, it will be exhibited in his books. Far more than in the laborious and repetitious biographies of Marcel Proust, he is visible in his own novel. His real self is meticulously described in the three major cycles of the novel, all of which engage in different ways the personality of the protagonist Marcel: the cycle of Swann, first, where we see the boy as an admirer of Swann the esthete, the connoisseur of art, and the father of Gilberte. Marcel the social being is portrayed in the cycle of the Guermantes, especially in his relationship with the duchesse Oriane and the baron Charlus. The third cycle, that of Albertine, is Marcel in love, going through all the tortured phases of love we associate with Proust.

Through the years of more than a half century, the main character of Proust, this Marcel, has taken on the dimensions of a hero, of an initiate whom we watch being submitted to trials and to tests. The hierarchy of society, the various circles of the Guermantes world, are temptations of social power, tests of endurance and skill, related to all the pleasures of worldliness. One after the other, Marcel savors each, is disillusioned, and passes on to the next. Before he leaves it, he sees its moral defects and its trivialities. In his quest for love, Marcel also passes through a series of tests and disillusionments. His love as a boy for the young girl Gilberte, his love as an adolescent for the older woman Oriane, his infatuation for Mlle. Stermaria, and finally his long painful suffering and jealousy over Albertine, represent initiatory degrees of love and passion. Here there is no real triumph for the initiate. The Proustian hero in love is either vanquished, or simply outlives his love, as in the case of Gilberte.

These tests, the initiations to the world and to love, are the great scenes in Proust's novel, when Marcel discovers the key to the one blessing in which he can believe. The title of the last volume, *Le Temps retrouvé* (*Time Regained*), is in reality the recapturing of a lost vocation. It is the writer's vocation we learned of in "Combray," when Marcel's father discouraged his son from thinking of such a vocation, when Norpois, his father's dinner guest, encouraged him, and when Bergotte, encountered a bit later at Mme. Swann's luncheon, incited him to reconsider the vocation.

In the careful choice he made of themes and episodes, Proust was able to construct an entire world, namely the world encompassed by the sentiments of Marcel. We are present at the genesis of a sentiment and then we watch it rise up and develop, slowly diminish, and finally die. The ego of Marcel is a series of successive egos: Marcel in love with Gilberte is one self; Marcel infatuated with the duchesse de Guermantes is another being. He is a son, a grandson, a friend of Bergotte, an admirer of Mme. Swann, a friend of Elstir, a friend of Robert de Saint-Loup, a young friend of Charlus, an intimate friend of the duc and duchesse de Guermantes. He is especially described as the unhappy lover of Albertine. Time is consumed and lost as Marcel plays each of these roles.

Through him we watch the disappearance of love and social intercourse and time. In Marcel's sentimental life we feel the uselessness of everything that time stamps with its death. A sentiment, by its very nature, cannot be fixed outside of time. It is characterized by an inexplicable beginning, by development, and by dissolution.

The universe of Proust is the analysis of these sentiments, of Marcel living through various states of being, of enacting a series of selves in which as hero he is despondent. He is unable to hold on to any sentiment or any being because of whom the sentiment has deepened. In this sense, Marcel is the victim of an abiding pessimism. But this pessimism about life in the deaths and resurrections of its metamorphoses, is contradicted by the optimism of Marcel the narrator and by Proust the writer. The narration of the book is a transfiguration. It is the immobilization of what changes. Life, as described by Marcel, is proliferation, both continuous and mortal. But this proliferation, in the hands of a artist, has a second life.

The temperament of Proust is everywhere visible in his book: the man's intensity of feeling, his subjectivism, his own personal adventure on this earth. But Proust the writer was the technician who adapted all of that to the laws and the architecture of the work. His depiction of society and his analysis of the heart were revealed to him not as the man living in society and suffering from his sentiments, but as the writer who, alone in his room, filled the large *cahiers* with the writing which constituted his search for the absolute beyond time.

—Wallace Fowlie

PUSHKIN, Alexander (Sergeyevich). Born in Moscow, 26 May 1799. Educated at home, and at lycée in Tsarskoye Selo, 1811-17. Married Natalya Goncharova in 1831. Civil servant, St. Petersburg, 1817-20; exiled in southern Russia and Pskov province, 1820-26; Editor, *Contemporary*, 1836-37. *Died (in duel) 29 January 1837.*

P<small>UBLICATIONS</small>

Collections

Polnoye sobraniye sochineniy, edited by B.V. Tomachevskim. 10 vols., 1977-79.
Complete Prose Fiction, edited by Paul Debreczeny. 1983.

Verse

Stikhotvoreniya. 1826; revised edition, 4 vols., 1829-35, and later editions.
Evgeny Onegin. 1833; translated as *Eugene Onegin*, 1881; also translated by Vladimir Nabokov, 1964, revised, 1981, and by Charles Johnston, 1977.
Selections from the Poems, edited by Ivan Panin. 1888; as *Poems*, 1888.
Pushkin Threefold: Narrative, Lyric, Polemic, and Ribald Verse, translated by W. Arndt. 1972.
The Bronze Horseman: Selected Poems, translated by D.M. Thomas. 1982.
Narrative Poems by Pushkin and Lermontov, translated by Charles Johnston, 1983.

Plays

Boris Godunov. 1831; translated as *Boris Godunov*, in *Translations from Pushkin*, 1899.

Motsart i Sal'eri. 1831; as *Mozart and Salieri*, in *Translations from Pushkin*, 1899.
Pir vo vremya chumy. 1832; as *The Feast During the Plague*, in *The Little Tragedies*, 1946.
Skupoy rytsar'. 1836; as *The Covetous Knight*, in *The Works*, 1939.
Kamenny gost'. 1839; as *The Statue Guest*, in *Translations from Pushkin*, 1899; as *The Stone Guest*, in *The Works*, 1939.

Fiction

Povesti pokoynovo I.P. Belkina. 1830; as *Tales of P. Bielkin*, 1947; as *The Tales of Belkin, and The History of Goryukhino*, 1983.
Pikovaya dama. 1834; as *The Queen of Spades*, with *The Captain's Daughter*, 1858.
Kapitanskaya dochka. 1836; as *The Captain's Daughter*, 1846; as *Marie: A Story of Russian Love*, 1877.
Dubrovsky (fragment). 1841.
Russian Romances. 1875.
Complete Prose Tales. 1966.

Other

Puteshestviye v Arzrum [The Journey to Arzrum]. 1836.
The Works: Lyrics, Narrative Poems, Folk Tales, Prose, edited by A. Yarmolinsky. 1939.
Letters. 1964.
Pushkin in Literature, edited by Tatiana Wolff. 1971.

*

Critical Studies: *Pushkin and Russian Literature* by Janko Lavrin, 1947; *Pushkin's Bronze Horseman: The Story of a Masterpiece* by W. Lednecki, 1955; *Pushkin* by E.J. Simmons, 1964; *Pushkin: A Biography* by David Magarshack, 1967; *Pushkin* by Walter Vickery, 1970; *Pushkin: A Comparative Commentary* by John Bayley, 1971; *Pushkin* by Henri Troyat, 1974; *Pushkin and His Sculptural Myth* by Roman Jakobson, 1975; *Russian Views of Pushkin* edited by D.J. Richards and C.R.S. Cockrell, 1976; *Pushkin: A Critical Study* by A.D.P. Briggs, 1982; *The Other Pushkin: A Study of Pushkin's Prose Fiction* by Paul Debreczeny, 1983.

* * *

The Protean talent of Alexander Pushkin gave Russian literature its first firm foothold in the wider arena of European letters. Pushkin developed and refined the literary language into a graceful, economical vehicle of expression, putting it on display in a broad range of genres. The innovations he brought to poetry, drama, fiction, and journalism were so varied and fruitful that at least a century of Russian literature was occupied with developing the forms which he had introduced.

Pushkin's writing career began early while he was still a schoolboy at Tsarskoye Selo, Alexander I's newly established lycée for aristocratic youth. His early poems, though hardly memorable for their themes, exhibited the clarity and concision that became the hallmark of his later verse. Pushkin's nascent talent was well-known among his close friends and fellow writers, but he first won wide acclaim with the publication in 1820 of his narrative poem *Ruslan and Lyudmila*. A light romance sprinkled with folk motifs, *Ruslan and Lyudmila* is at once a move away from the stylistic strictures of classicism and a parodic poke at German Romanticism and its chief Russian practitioner, Alexander Zhukovsky. The transcendental ideals and lofty language of the romantic ballad are replaced in Pushkin's poem by a gutsy earthiness and more colloquial diction.

The artistic playfulness of *Ruslan and Lyudmila* is counterbalanced in these post-lycée years by more-serious political verses that circulated among educated circles in Petersburg. Having been nurtured at Tsarskoye Selo on the values of the 18th-century French Enlightenment, Pushkin's political views were at best questionable in the eyes of the government authorities. His liberal perspective was clear in such works as the ode "Freedom" (1817), in which he admonishes emperors to remember that their rule is grounded in law, not divine right; the elegy "The Village" (1819), which decries serfdom; and a number of epigrams mocking some of the leaders of the Tsarist regime. Eager to be rid of this brilliant gadfly, Alexander I exiled Pushkin to the south of Russia.

Inspired by the exotic landscapes of Bessarabia and the Crimea and a new enthusiasm for Byron, Pushkin essayed a number of narrative poems in the Byronic style. *The Captive of the Caucasus* (1823) and *The Fountain of Bakhchiseray* (1823) were completed in the South, while *The Gypsies* (1824) (given special attention by Dostoevsky in his famous "Pushkin Speech"), was completed after arriving at his family's estate at Mikhailovskoye, where his exile continued until 1826. Like Byron, Pushkin situates his dramatic action in an exotic region, but, unlike the English bard, he brings those landscapes more sharply into focus. Pushkin's style is more controlled and less flamboyant than is Byron's, and his heroes have none of the demonic dimensions of their English prototypes. While the two earlier works became models for the Russian romantic narrative poem, *The Gypsies* remains the most memorable of the "Southern poems." Lacking the consistent lyricism of the earlier works, its portrayal of the Hero's abortive search for absolute freedom among the gypsies presents a philosophical problem with power and grace.

Pushkin began his most original and influential work, *Eugene Onegin*, in the South, but completed it eight years later, in 1831. From the outset Pushkin distinguished *Eugene Onegin* from his other narrative poems by declaring it a "novel-in-verse," an apt designation for the work that prepared the way for his transition to prose. In fact, the work is a microcosm of Pushkin's artistic development during the eight years of its genesis. In *Eugene Onegin* Pushkin parodies Byronism as a worldview and a literary style and announces the passing of his youthful romanticism. His descriptions of Petersburg high society as well as the gentry on their provincial estates introduced details of everyday life that heralded a new realism in Russian literature. But Pushkin was never a naive realist. The touchstone of his complex vision is the figure of the narrator: beginning as an enthusiastic participant in the Petersburg world in which his hero travels, he becomes by the end of *Eugene Onegin* separated from his fictive world—the self-conscious author who frustrates any simple identification of art and life.

Both hero and heroine became prototypes for later fiction. Onegin is a vivid exemplar of the "superfluous men," a type that figured prominently not only in the literary but also in the sociological imagination of 19th-century Russia: upon finding that the world fails to respond to his talents, the "superfluous man" retreats into inertia or dilettantism. Tatyana provides the model for the strong-willed heroines who grace the pages of Turgenev, Tolstoy, and Dostoevsky, among others.

By the time Pushkin completed *Eugene Onegin*, he had already published his first complete prose work, *The Tales of Belkin*. Ironically, Pushkin's style displays more flexibility in his novel-in-verse, where the demands of versification would seem to militate against this very quality than in his prose, a model of classical restraint. *The Tales of Belkin* are lighthearted parodies of some of the popular genres of the time, and as such are formal experiments through which Pushkin tested the limits of the early prose tradition in Russia.

After returning from exile, Pushkin turned his attention increasingly to prose fiction, which was becoming popular with the reading public. He also busied himself with journalism, carrying on heated literary polemics on the pages of *The Literary Gazette* and later editing and writing articles for his own journal, *The Contemporary*, which began publication in 1836. His journalistic prose reflects his lucid and energetic habit of mind, and was often laced by his characteristic wit.

The list of Pushkin's completed prose works is brief, but numerous fragments were quite developed. They bear witness to a lively quest into a variety of forms, from the society tale to the epistolary novel. Of his completed works, *The Queen of Spades* and *The Captain's Daughter* are the most famous. The former is a masterly short story, whose contemporary Petersburg setting and monomaniacal hero influenced Dostoevsky when he set out to create the ultra-rational hero verging on madness. Its style is terse and bare despite the romantic trappings of its subject. *The Captain's Daughter*, a historical novel in the style of Scott, is a fast-moving adventure that examines the meaning of honor in a world confused by partisan allegiances. Published posthumously, the novel grew out of Pushkin's historical treatise on the Pugachev rebellion, the 18th-century peasant revolt.

The fascination with history which dominated the last years of Pushkin's life had in fact surfaced earlier, most notably in *Boris Godunov*. In that play, written in the style of Shakespeare's historical drama, Pushkin relied on Karamzin's *History of the Russian State* for his interpretation of the Time of Troubles; his later historical works were products of his own research in the State Archives. He never completed his first project, a study of Peter the Great, but his developing historical insight powerfully informs the narrative poem *The Bronze Horseman*. Juxtaposed to the encomium to Peter and his accomplishmentss which opens the poem is the story of how an autocratic vision, no matter how glorious, can oppress the average Russian's dreams. The Petersburg clerk Eugene loses his fiancée and finally his mind in the aftermath of the 1824 flood that is nature's revenge on Peter's hubristic plan to introduce a note of modernity into an inhospitable cultural and physical landscape. When Dostoevsky referred to Petersburg as "the most rational city in the world," or when the Symbolist writer Andrey Bely built an entire novel on the "Petersburg myth," they traced their understanding back to Pushkin's blend of history and imagination.

While experimenting with prose and historical topics, Pushkin never ceased writing in the traditional poetic genres with which he began his writing career. The period of his most fruitful poetic activity was from 1825 to 1831, when he wrote some of the most beautiful and memorable lyrics in the language. The subjects of the poems are varied; many were written in response to specific incidents in Pushkin's life, but all rise above the purely personal to make statements that are universal in their appeal. Friendship, nature, and the role of the poet are recurring topics, but it is love that inspired a good number of Pushkin's best-known verses. The inimitable style of Pushkin's poetry resists both classification and translation; its classical precision, measure, and fine sense of cadence finally derive from an exquisite understanding of all the potentialities of the Russian language. Pushkin stands at the center of Russia's Golden Age of poetry, developing and perfecting the power of poetic expression to a level often aspired to but rarely equalled.

—Nancy Kanach Fehsenfeld

QUENEAU, Raymond. Born in Le Havre, France, 21 February 1903. Educated at a lycée in Le Havre; the Sorbonne, Paris, from 1920, degree in philosophy. Military service, 1925-27; served in World War II, 1939-40. Married Janine Kahn in 1928; one son. Worked in a bank in Paris, from 1927; columnist ("Connaissez-vous Paris?"), *L'Intransigeant*, 1936-38; Reader, 1938-39, Secretary-General from 1941, and Director of the *Encyclopédie de la Pléiade*, 1955-75, Gallimard, publishers, Paris. Also a painter. Member, Goncourt Academy, 1951. *Died 25 October 1976.*

PUBLICATIONS

Fiction

Le Chiendent. 1933; as *The Bark-Tree*, 1968.
Gueule de Pierre. 1934.
Les derniers jours. 1935.
Odile. 1937.
Les Enfants du Limon. 1938.
Un rude hiver. 1939; as *A Hard Winter*, 1948.
Les Temps mêlés. 1941.
Pierrot mon ami. 1942; translated as *Pierrot*, 1950.
Loin de Rueil. 1944; as *The Skin of Dreams*, 1948.
On est toujours trop bon avec les femmes (as Sally Mara). 1947; as *We Always Treat Women Too Well*, 1981.
Une Trouille verte. 1947.
À la limite de la forêt. 1947; as *At the Edge of the Forest* (with *The Trojan Horse*), 1954.
Le Cheval troyen. 1948; as *The Trojan Horse* (with *At the Edge of the Forest*), 1954.
Saint-Glinglin (includes revised versions of *Gueule de Pierre* and *Les Temps mêlés*). 1948.
Journal intime (as Sally Mara). 1950.
Le Dimanche de la vie. 1951; as *The Sunday of Life*, 1976.
Zazie dans le métro. 1959; as *Zazie*, 1960.
Les Oeuvres complètes de Sally Mara. 1962.
Les Fleurs bleues. 1965; edited by Barbara Wright, 1971; as *Between Blue and Blue*, 1967; as *The Blue Flowers*, 1967.
Un conte à votre façon. 1967; as *Yours for the Telling*, 1983.
Le Vol d'Icare. 1968; as *The Flight of Icarus*, 1973.
Contes et propos. 1981.

Plays

En passant. 1944.

Screenplays: *Monsieur Ripois* (*Knave of Hearts*; *Lovers, Happy Lovers*), with René Clement and Hugh Mills, 1954; *La Mort en ce Jardin* (*Gina*; *Death in the Garden*), with Luis Buñuel and Luis Alcoriza, 1956; *Un Couple*, with others, 1960.

Verse

Chêne et chien (novel in verse). 1937.
Les Ziaux. 1943.
Bucoliques. 1947.
L'Instant fatal. 1948.
Petite cosmogonie portative. 1950.
Si tu t'imagines 1920-1951. 1952.
Sonnets. 1958.
Le chien à la mandoline. 1958; revised edition, 1965.
Cent mille milliards de poèmes. 1961; as *One Hundred Million Million Poems*, 1983.
Courir les rues. 1967.
Battre la campagne. 1968.
Fendre les flots. 1969.
Poems, translated by Teo Savory. 1970.

Bonjour, Monsieur Prassinos. 1972.
Morale élémentaire. 1975.

Other

Exercices de style. 1947; as *Exercises in Style*, 1958.
Monuments. 1948.
Bâtons, chiffres, et lettres. 1950; revised edition, 1965.
Lorsque l'esprit. 1956.
Le Declin du romantisme: Edgar Poe. 1957.
Entretiens, with Georges Charbonnier. 1962.
Bords: Mathématiciens, précurseurs, encyclopédistes. 1963.
Une histoire modèle. 1966.
Queneau en verve, edited by Jacques Bens. 1970.
De quelques langages animaux imaginaires.... 1971.
Le Voyage en Grèce. 1973.
La Littérature potentielle. 1973.
Correspondance, with Elie Lascaux. 1979.

Editor, *Anthologie des jeunes auteurs.* 1955.
Editor, *Histoires des littératures.* 3 vols., 1955-58.

Translator of works by Maurice O'Sullivan, Sinclair Lewis, George du Maurier, and Amos Tutuola.

*

Bibliography: *Queneau: Bibliographie des études sur l'homme et son oeuvre* by Wolfgang Hillen, 1981.

Critical Studies: *Queneau* (in French) by Jacques Bens, 1962; *Queneau* (in French) by Andrée Bergens, 1963; *Queneau* (in French) by Jacques Guicharnaud, 1965; *Les poèmes de Queneau* by Renée Baligand, 1972; *Queneau* by Richard Charles Cobb, 1976; *Queneau: Zazie dans le métro* by W.D. Redfern, 1980.

*   *   *

Not long before Raymond Queneau's death, *Le Monde* referred to him as "one of the most universal minds of our time." A justified accolade. Though primarily a novelist and poet, Queneau also wrote on philosophy, science, history, and mathematics. He was also the General Editor of the Gallimard *Encyclopédie de la Pléiade.*

In the field of "pure" literature, Queneau always said he could see no difference between poetry and prose, and all his novels are infused with poetry—taking the word in its widest sense. They are also infused with humour, and for long this prevented critics from regarding Queneau as anything but a joker. This was particularly the case with *Pierrot* and *Zazie*. Martin Esslin, however, in *The Novelist as Philosopher* (1962), said of *Pierrot*: "It is only the effortless simplicity of the telling of the story that hides the delicacy of its construction and the depth of its thought. *Pierrot mon ami* is a poem on chance and destiny...." And of *Zazie* he said: "Critics did not notice the brilliant philosopher-poet behind the clowning."

Queneau's novels are all highly structured, none more so than his first, *Le Chiendent* (*The Bark-Tree*), which was actually based on mathematical principles. Robbe-Grillet called *Le Chiendent* "the new novel twenty years ahead of its time." Queneau said he hoped no one would notice its structure, its "scaffolding," and no one did, until he himself wrote about it. This first book contains all the elements that preoccupied Queneau throughout his lifetime: his predilection for humble characters and for the unacknowledged philosophical implications of their everyday lives; his humour (sometimes sardonic); his surrealistic inclinations; and, very particularly, his love of language. James Joyce, Faulkner, and Conrad were the only literary influences Queneau recognized. Anglo-Saxon writers, he said, were free to write as they chose, whereas French writers were strait-jacketed by what the French Academy decreed to be "correct."

In liberating the French language, Queneau used poetically heightened representations of the speech of the ordinary Frenchman, he interwove puns and word play with classical references, he ran words together, he coined neologisms. Thus he created books which can be read—and reread—on many levels, and always with enjoyment.

This approach, these elements, also permeate Queneau's poetry. Even at its most serious-or melancholy—it is often playful. Many of his poems were made famous during the heyday of the cabarets in St-Germain-des-Prés by artists like Juliette Greco. His extraordinary *Cent mille milliards de poèmes* is a supreme example of the fusion of mathematics with poetry. Ten sonnets are printed on pages consisting of 14 loose strips, making it possible for the reader to construct 10^{14} intelligible poems.

A further extension of such experimentation is to be found in the *OuLiPo*, or *Ouvroir de Littérature Potentielle (Workshop of Potential Literature)*, of which Raymond Queneau was a co-founder. *Time* wrote that this "lunatic fringework" is "yet another proof that the gap between science and art can still be bridged."

—Barbara Wright

RABELAIS, François. Born in 1483 (?). Possibly studied law, 1500-10, in Bourges, Angers, or Poitiers; became a Franciscan in 1520's, but later studied medicine, possibly in Paris, later in Montpellier, Bachelor of medicine 1530, Doctor of medicine, 1537. Had three illegitimate children (two surviving children later formally legitimated). Lectured in medicine, Montpellier, 1531, and practiced in southern France: physician at Hôtel-Dieu, Lyons, 1532; visited Italy as personal doctor of Bishop, later Cardinal, Jean Du Bellay, 1534, and later visits with Guillaume Du Bellay; Canon at Benedictine Abbey of Saint Maur-les-Fossés, 1536; given benefices at Meudon and Jambet, 1551 (resigned them, 1553). *Died 9 April (?) 1553.*

PUBLICATIONS

Collections

> *Oeuvres*, edited by Abel Lefranc and others. 6 vols., 1912-55.
> *Oeuvres complètes*, edited by P. Jourda. 2 vols., 1962.
> *The Works*, edited by Albert Jay Nock and Catherine Rose Wilson. 2 vols., 1931.

Fiction

> *Gargantua and Pantagruel*, translated by Thomas Urquhart, 1653, continuation by P.A. Motteux, 1694; also translated by J.M. Cohen, 1955.
> *Pantagruel*. 1532; edited by V.L. Saulnier, 1965.
> *Gargantua*. 1534 (?) (now usually printed as first book); edited by R.M. Calder and M.A. Screech, 1970.
> *Tiers Livre...Pantagruel*. 1546; edited by M.A. Screech, 1944.

Quatre Livre...Pantagruel.   1552; edited by R. Marichal, 1947.

Other

Pantagruéline prognostication.   1533; edited by M.A Screech, 1974.

Editor, [*Works*], by Hippocrates and Galen.   1532.
Editor, *Aphorismorum*, by Hippocrates.   1532.
Editor, *Typographia antiquae Romae*, by J.B. Marlianus.   1534.

*

Critical Studies: *The Rabelaisian Marriage: Aspects of Rabelais's Religion, Ethics, and Cosmic Philosophy*, 1958, and *Rabelais*, 1979, both by M.A. Screech; *Rabelais: A Critical Study in Prose Fiction* by Dorothy Gabe Coleman, 1971; *The Age of Bluff: Paradox and Ambiguity in Rabelais and Montaigne* by B.C. Bowen, 1972; *The Wine and the Will: Rabelais's Bacchic Christianity* by F.M. Weinberg, 1972; *Rabelais: A Study* by Donald M. Frame, 1977; *The Countervoyage of Rabelais and Ariosto* by Elizabeth A. Chesney, 1982.

*   *   *

Rabelais's reputation has been largely fashioned by people who have never read a word he wrote. "Rabelaisian" is often used as a synonym for smutty, while many who have never thought to read the book like to pride themselves on their gargantuan appetites. The image goes back a long way: as early as the middle of the 16th century, Ronsard wrote an epitaph to Rabelais in which he asked passers-by to throw sausages and sides of ham on the dead author's grave instead of flowers. But practitioners of learned wit from Swift to Joyce and Robertson Davies have read and admired him, and Laurence Sterne swore by the "ashes of my dear Rabelais."

Rabelais is unique. His particular brand of encyclopedic humour has its origins in his theological training, his vast erudition (he was perfectly at home in Latin and Greek and conversant with most of the major classical authors), and in his expertise in the spheres of medicine, law, and popular culture. To say that he is an Evangelical Christian humanist of Neo-Platonic and Stoic inclinations is to provide the prospective reader with a map of Rabelais country; to get the feel of the landscape you have to plunge into the works themselves with as open a mind as you can. The going will never be easy, for the way is strewn with private jokes and a network of allusions which only a reader armed with a fully annotated edition can hope to understand, but the reward for perseverance will be not only a good deal of healthy laughter but admission to a world imagined by a wordsmith and story-teller of genius.

Recent years have seen Rabelais rescued from the writers of wine catalogues and restored to his rightful place as a great creative writer living in an age dominated by ideas. Yet generalisations (however complimentary) about him are rarely helpful, for the four books of *Gargantua and Pantagruel* (the posthumous fifth book is probably only partly by him) were written at different dates and in very different circumstances, when the world around him and his reaction to it had undergone great changes.

When Rabelais wrote *Pantagruel* in 1532, he was in his late forties with a couple of quite separate careers already behind him. This first excursion into prose fiction may well have been written for money (he himself suggests as much in his prologue), but it also released a side of his personality which the learned doctor had hitherto kept in check. Using the easily decipherable pseudonym of Alcofrybas Nasier, he lets the genie out of the bottle and indulges in that archetypal lord of misrule Panurge.

Whereas *Pantagruel* is a chronicle of mischief, its sequel, *Gargantua*, has a very different tone, even though the structure and subject-matter are similar. The doings of the family of giants become less important than the ideas they embody. Gargantua's mother eats vast quantities of tripe, the young giant urinates over 274,418 Parisians, steals the bells of Notre-Dame, but, notwithstanding these episodes, one senses that he is increasingly the vehicle for Rabelais's ideas. The book divides conveniently into three distinct sections. In the first 24 chapters, devoted to the childhood of Gargantua, he expounds the sort of ideas of education which had been current for some years among "progressive" educationalists. Rabelais's debt to Erasmus and Vivès is obvious, and he is swimming with the same tide as Sir Thomas Elyot and, in his praise of discreet elegance, Castiglione. With its emphasis on courtly attributes, this part of the book is very much a "mirror for princes" and, despite the jokes, quite removed from the spirit of much of *Pantagruel*. The narrative abruptly switches to the countryside around the author's native Chinon in which he sets the Picrocholean War between the giants and an irascible neighbour. This "war" allows Rabelais to air his views (once again strongly influenced by Erasmus) on the moral limits of military might, and the need for Christians to outlaw wars of aggression. Finally, in the third section of the book, Rabelais builds for his conquering heroes an abbey to their liking, an anti-monastery very different from any existing religious institution. This "Abbey of Thelema" (New Testament Greek for "will") is a palatial refuge from an imperfect world where those whose lives are guided by selflessness and a sense of honour learn to live together, in preparation perhaps for carrying their message beyond the abbey's walls. The famous motto "Do as you wish" must be seen in context: it is definitely not a recipe for a free-for-all.

This reflective mood continues in the *Third Book*, published in 1546. Panurge, who had not figured in the *Gargantua*, returns—almost, one feels, by popular demand—to overshadow the giants themselves, but is now portrayed as less a frolicsome hero than a confused and somewhat pathetic figure, an ageing lecher who is unable to make up his mind as to whether or not he should marry. Attracted by marriage for its physical benefits, he is nevertheless haunted by the fear of being made a cuckold. The book provides Rabelais with an excuse for making a contribution to the topical "*querelle des amies,*" a variation on the ever-popular "battle of the sexes" theme, and one to which, one would have thought, the ecclesiastical authorities could not have taken exception. But they had their man in their sights, and, like its predecessors, the *Third Book* was banned. For this reason perhaps Rabelais returns to his old hobby-horses in the *Fourth Book*, the final version of which came out in 1552. It contains a streak of bitter satire which was not much in evidence before, and some of his attacks (on Calvin, for example) are a treat for connoisseurs of invective. Of all Rabelais's works, the *Fourth Book* is the most linguistically inventive, and a high proportion of the jokes and anecdotes still come off. The delightfully ambiguous Brother John, who had been so important in *Gargantua*, is once more playfully to the fore, his muscular Christianity contrasting with Panurge's pusillanimity. As our heroes sail in search of the oracle of the bottle, each port of call represents them with a different aspect of human life. The model for this technique was Lucian's *True History*, but Rabelais's vision is his own. It is summed up by that *mediocrité*, his version of Horace's *aurea mediocritas* or golden mean, which came to dominate his thinking in these last years of his life. He speaks out against sectarianism, rails at being caught between the "hammer and the anvil," and makes great play with human folly in all its variety. But parts of the *Fourth Book* lead one to suspect that the author's spirits were low, and that his advice to his reader to keep a "certain gaiety of mind full of contempt for the accidents of life" was meant as much for himself. While some episodes are pure fun, others—notably the moving chapter on the death of heroes—are tinged with sadness. Taken as a whole, though, Rabelais's work stands out as one of the great comic masterpieces of world literature. Rabelais is indeed a doctor of laughter whose books remain, in our very different world, a perfect cure of melancholy.

—Michael Freeman

RACINE, Jean.   Born in La Ferté-Milon, France 22 December 1639.   Educated by Jansenists at Convent of Port Royal, Paris; Collège d'Harcourt, Paris, 1658-59; studied theology with his uncle at Uzès 1661-63. Married Cathérine de Romanet in 1677; five daughters and two sons. Molière's troupe performed his first play, but he broke with him; wrote no plays 1677-89; wrote his last two plays for the girls school at St. Cyr, patronized by Madame de Maintenon. Appointed Historiographer (with Boileau) by the King, 1677. *Died 21 April 1699.*

PUBLICATIONS

Collections

> *Oeuvres complètes*, edited by P. Mesnard.   8 vols., 1865-73.
> *Oeuvres complètes*, edited by Raymond Picard.   2 vols., 1960.
> *Oeuvres complètes*, edited by Jacques Morel and Alain Viala.   1980.
> *Complete Plays.*   2 vols., 1967.

Plays

> *La Thébaïde; ou, Les Frères ennemis* (produced 1664).   1664; edited by Michael Edwards, 1965; as *The Fatal Legacy*, 1723.
> *Alexandre le grand* (produced 1665).   1666; as *Alexander the Great*, 1714.
> *Andromaque* (produced 1667).   1668; edited by R.C. Knight and H.T. Barnwell, 1977; translated as *Andromache*, 1675; as *The Distressed Mother*, 1712.
> *Les Plaideurs* (produced 1668).   1669; as *The Litigants*, 1715; as *The Suitors*, 1862.
> *Britannicus* (produced 1669).   1670; edited by Philip Butler, 1967; translated as *Britannicus*, 1714.
> *Bérénice* (produced 1670).   1671; edited by C.L. Walton, 1965; as *Titus and Berenice*, 1701.
> *Bajazet* (produced 1672).   1672; as *The Sultaness*, 1717.
> *Mithridate* (produced 1673).   1673; translated as *Mithridates*, 1926.
> *Iphigénie* (produced 1674).   1675; as *Achilles; or, Iphigenia in Aulis*, 1700; as *The Victim*, 1714; as *Iphigenia*, 1861.
> *Phèdre et Hippolyte* (produced 1677).   1677; translated as *Phaedre and Hippolytus*, 1756; also translated as *Phaedra.*
> *L'Idylle de la paix*, music by Lully.   1685.
> *Esther* (produced 1689).   1689; translated as *Esther*, 1715.
> *Athalie* (produced 1691).   1691; edited by Peter France, 1966; translated as *Athaliah*, 1722.

Verse

> *La Nymphe de la Seine.*   1660.
> *Ode sur la convalescence du Roi.*   1663.
> *Cantiques spirituels.*   1694.
> *Campagne de Louis XIV*, with Boileau.   1730; as *Éloge historique du Roi, Louis XIV*, 1784.

Other

> *Abrégé de l'histoire de Port-Royal.*   1742.

*

Critical Studies: *The Classical Moment*, 1947, and *Racine, Dramatist*, 1972, both by Martin Turnell; *Aspects of Racinian Tragedy* by John C. Lapp, 1955; *The Art of Racine* by Bernard Weinberg, 1963; *Racine's Rhetoric*, 1965, and *Racine: Andromaque*, 1977, both by Peter France; *Racine* by Odette de Mourgues, 1967; *Racine: Modern Judgements* edited by R.C. Knight, 1969; *Racine: Myths and Renewal in Modern Theatre* by Bettina Knapp, 1971; *Corneille and Racine: Problems of Tragic Form* by Gordon Pocock, 1973; *Racine* by Lucien Goldman, 1973; *Racine* by Philip Butler, 1974; *Racine* by Philip John Yarrow, 1978; *The Tragic Drama of Corneille and Racine* by H.T. Barnwell, 1982.

*   *   *

Probably France's greatest tragic playwright, arguably its best dramatic poet, and certainly the writer who observed the rules of the neo-classical drama with the greatest ease and success, Jean Racine is rightly regarded as the most perfect embodiment of the French genius for psychological analysis and the accurate use of language. He solved the problem of how to write a play which conformed to the three unities of time, place, and action by the simple device of taking an emotional situation at the very moment it is about to explode. In his first great success, *Andromaque*, it is the arrival of Orestes to demand that Pyrrhus hand over Hector's son Astyanax to the Greeks which sets the tragedy into motion, and it is wholly convincing that, within 24 hours, Orestes himself should then kill Pyrrhus at the instigation of Hermione and go mad, while Hermione herself commits suicide, and the widowed Andromache is left in sole command at Epirus. For beneath the perfect finish of his 12-syllable Alexandrines—Racine wrote out his plays in prose before putting the final version into verse—there is an immensely powerful world of violent, passionate emotions, and it is the contrast between this primitive world and the classical form of his plays which has made Racine one of the most admired and studied of all French 17th-century authors.

Like the mathematician and philosopher Blaise Pascal, Racine had strong links with the heresy known as Jansenism, and shared the neo-Augustinian view that man was an irredeemably fallen creature who was doomed to damnation unless saved by the gratuitous intervention of a Divine Grace which he could do nothing to deserve by his own efforts. The eponymous heroine of his most famous play, *Phèdre*, seems in this respect almost the epitome of the sinner who wishes to be virtuous but is refused the Grace which alone makes this possible, and the fact that Racine gave up writing for the profane theatre after 1677 has been interpreted as a sign that it was his own spiritual anguish and feelings of guilt which inspired this play. The continuity and intensity of his appeal to a 20th-century audience nevertheles lies more in the wider metaphysical overtones of Jansenist theology, and the edifying Christian plays which he wrote on his return to the theatre, *Esther* and *Athalie*, strike a rather strange note on the modern stage. His vision of mankind as unable to control or escape its destiny, doomed to destruction in an absurd universe in which the only sign of the Gods is their remorseless cruelty, has obvious associations with Sartre or Beckett, though his plays are far superior theatrically to anything in French other than the very best of Corneille or Molière. His female roles, especially, offer some of the best acting parts in the whole classical repertory, and Aldous Huxley's remark about the "somewhat featureless males who serve as a pretext to their anguish" does not really fit the demands and potentialities of roles such as Pyrrhus in *Andromaque*, Acomat in *Bajazet*, or Thésée in *Phèdre*.

As a man, Racine seems to have had little of the humanity and generosity of spirit which make Molière so attractive, and he was as ruthless in promoting his own career as he was scathing in his remarks about his rivals. There is also something odd about a man who created the most passionate tragic heroines in French literature but who married a woman who never went to the theatre and is said never to have read a single one of his plays. The apparently effortless perfection of Racine's versification is partially explicable by the fact that he wrote the second line of each rhyming couplet first in order to avoid any impression of artificiality, but may also be linked to his excellence as a classical scholar. He was unusual among French 17th-century writers in reading the Greek dramatists in the original, and the atmosphere of "Jansenist perdition" so frequently detected in his plays might equally well stem from the influence of Euripides, the classical playwright whom he most admired. His own aesthetic was very much based on classical models, and only one of his tragedies—*Bajazet*, which takes place in Turkey—has a contemporary setting. He himself justified this by arguing that distance in space could compensate for proximity in time. Among his other plays, only the comedy *Les Plaideurs* (*The Litigants*) takes place in the 17th century, and he fully accepted the classical notion that we "see the heroes of tragedy with a different eye" because they are so far away from us in time.

The celebrated parallel with Corneille enshrined in La Bruyère's comment that "Corneille depicts men as they should be, Racine as they are" can also be explained by historical reasons. By the time Racine began his career, the self-confident and turbulent nobility depicted in Corneille's earlier tragedies had been defeated in the civil war of the 1650's known as *La Fronde* and domesticated into the court life at Versailles. There, they tended to fill their enforced leisure by the analysis of their own amorous intrigues, and were thus ready to appreciate the detailed account which Racine provided of political impotence coupled with intense if frustrated passion. Much of the 19th century's enthusiasm for Racine stemmed from this view of him as a superb analyst of the human heart, though he was naturally also used in the defence of Classicism against Romanticism as the embodiment of the classical writers of moderation, rationality, and verisimilitude as contrasted with "vigorous barbarism" of Shakespeare. The vision of Racine as a periwig-pated practitioner of the duller literary virtues did much to hinder an appreciation of his work in England and America, though it should be said that no other great French writer loses more in translation. From a deliberately limited, conventional vocabulary, less than 2000 words, he produces the most extraordinary poetic effects, and no playwright has depicted sexual aggression and sexual jealousy with greater accuracy and force. While the English reader will find him inferior to Shakespeare in the narrowness of his range, abstention from speculation, and reluctance to depict the complexity of human life, compensation can nevertheless be found in the concentration of his vision, unity of aesthetic creation, and constant attention to the emotions immediately under analysis.

—Philip Thody

RAMAYANA.

PUBLICATIONS

Ramayana, edited by R. Pandey. 1956; also edited by G.H. Bhatt, 7 vols., 1958-67, and S.K. Mudholakara, 1983; translated by R.T.H. Griffith, 5 vols., 1870-75; condensed versions translated by R.C. Dutt, 1899, Aubrey Menen, 1954, and R.K. Narayan, 1972.

*

Critical Studies: *Studies in the Ramayana* by K.S. Ramaswami Sastri, 1948; *Lectures on the Ramayana* by V.S.S. Sastri, 1952; *The Ramayana: A Linguistic Study* by S. Vrat, 1964; *The Concept of Dharma in Valmiki's Ramayana* by B. Khan, 1964; *India in the Ramayana Age* by S.N. Vyas, 1967.

*   *   *

RAMAYANA

The version of the *Ramayana* which is best known internationally is the Sanskrit one of Valmiki, of the 1st or 2nd century. But the ones popular in India are those of Tulsidasa (Hindi, Avadhi dialect) in the north, the Kamban (Tamil) in the south, and the Krittibasa Ramayana (Bengali) in the east. All of them are based on the story of Rama. Rama, son of Dashrath, king of Ayodhya (in northern India), was banished due to the intrigue of his step-mother, Kaikeyi. The kingdom went to Bharata his half-brother. Along with his brother Lakshmana, and his wife Sita, who insisted on accompanying him, Rama roamed the forest. Ravana, the demon king of Lanka, carried away his wife in his absence, and so he had to fight a war to get her back. Recovering Sita, he returned to Ayodhya in triumph, after his 14-year exile, and took over the kingdom from Bharata who had held it in trusteeship for him.

According to Sir William Jones the *Ramayana* was composed in the year 2029 B.C. Tradition has it that it was inspired when Valmiki heard the anguished cry of a bird whose mate had been shot by a hunter. The epic has seven books (24,000 stanzas or 96,000 lines). The seventh book is believed to be a later addition. The metre used is largely the *anushtup*, a tetrastich containing four feet. The fifth syllable of each line is short, the sixth long, the seventh alternately long and short, while the first four syllables and the eighth follow an arbitrary pattern.

The *Ramayana* excels in rich imagery, expressive descriptions, and brilliant characterization. After his night of debauchery, Ravana, decked in all his jewels, lying spent on his couch, is like a huge thundercloud streaked with flashes of lightning. The sleeping women of his harem look like lotuses in a pond, or like flowers in a garland, or stars fallen from heaven. When Sita is by Rama's side, the forest seems to him lovely in the rains. The breeze is cool as camphor. The grassy slopes gleam and peacocks dance with glee. But after her abduction the sky looks like one wounded and the clouds stained red with the dim glow of the setting sun. The golden thongs of lightning appear to whip the clouds so that they thunder out their agony. "It seems," says Rama, "that the lightning leaping from the clouds is like Sita struggling in Ravana's hold." When Sita is away from Rama, the south wind seems to waft to him her caress. The lovely scarlet flowers of the Pampa lake set his heart afire. The gleaming sandy banks of the river, exposed as the water in it gradually recedes, are like the alabaster thighs of shy girls, bared as they move up their dress when prevailed upon to make love. When the erotic-minded Ravana camps on the Narmada bank, the river seems to him like a timid girl, the foaming waves her dress, the flowering trees by the riverside her diadem, the lotuses her eyes, the pair of ruddy geese her breasts, the gleaming sandbanks her thighs and the swans flying in the air her shining girdle.

Valmiki's characters are exemplary in their conduct, but they are also human in their shortcomings. Rama is the embodiment of calm and serenity. At times, however, he can be wrathful or maudlin. He threatens the ocean god for not getting his army across the ocean, and when Sita has been abducted by Ravana he goes about piteously asking the trees where she has gone. The sagacious Janaka breaks down with grief when his daughter, Sita, leaves for her husband's home. Lakshmana, Rama's brother, is by nature impetuous and excitable, but he doesn't say a word when he learns of Rama's banishment. The self-controlled and restrained Bharat cannot hold himself back when he learns his mother had asked for Rama's exile and reviles not only her, but also his dead father. There are touches of humour, too, as when Rama, assisting Sita to get dressed in barks for going to the forest, has trouble putting the pieces in place, and between the two of them they make a clumsy job of it.

The *Ramayana* is known in China, and from Cambodia to Java. It has been translated into Hindi and Indian regional languages like Bengali, Tamil, Kannada, Kashmiri, Telugu and Malayalam. There are versions in English, Latin, French and Italian. It is one of those world classics whose place is not so much on bookshelves as in the hearts of people.

—K.P. Bahadur

RILKE, Rainer Maria. Born René Karl Wilhelm Johann Josef Maria Rilke, in Prague, 4 December 1875. Educated at Piarist School, Prague, 1882-84; military schools of St. Pölten and Mährisch-Weisskirchen, 1886-91; gymnasium, Linz; a period of study preparing for university studies in Prague, 1895-96, Munich, 1896-97, and Berlin, 1897-98. Served in Military Records Office, Vienna, 1916. Married Clara Westhoff in 1901; one daughter. Traveller in most of Europe during his life: in a painters colony at Worpswede, 1901-02; associated with Rodin in Paris, 1902-03, 1905-06; residence in Italy and Sweden; friendships with a series of wealthy patrons; happy relationship with the generous publisher Kippenberg from 1908; patronized particularly by Princess Marie von Thurn und Taxis from 1910; lived in Chateau de Muzot, Switzerland, after 1921. *Died 29 December 1926.*

PUBLICATIONS

Collections

Sämtliche Werke, edited by Ernst Zinn. 6 vols., 1955-66.

Verse

Leben und Lieder. 1894.
Larenopfer. 1896.
Traumgekrönt. 1897.
Advent. 1898.
Mir zur Feier. 1899; revised edition, as *Die frühen Gedichte*, 1909.
Das Buch der Bilder. 1902; revised edition, 1906.
Das Stunden-Buch. 1905; as *Poems from the Book of Hours*, translated by Babette Deutsch, 1941.
Die Weise von Liebe und Tod des Cornets Christoph Rilke. 1906; edited by Walter Simon, 1974; as *The Story of the Love and Death of Cornet Christopher Rilke*, translated by B.J. Morse, 1927; as *The Cornet*, translated by Constantine FitzGibbon, 1958.
Neue Gedichte. 2 vols., 1907-08; as *New Poems*, translated by J.B. Leishman, 1964.
Requiem. 1909.
Das Marien-Leben. 1913; as *The Life of the Virgin Mary*, translated by R.G.L. Barrett, 1921; also translated by C.F. MacIntyre, 1947, Stephen Spender, 1951, and N.K. Cruickshank, 1952.
Fünf Gesänge. 1915.
Duineser Elegien. 1923; as *Duino Elegies*, translated by J.B. Leishman and Stephen Spender, 1939, revised edition, 1948, 1963; also translated by Nora Wydenbruck, 1948, Stephen Garmey and Jay Wilson, 1972, Elaine E. Boney, 1975, and David Young, 1978.
Die Sonette an Orpheus. 1923; as *Sonnets to Orpheus*, translated by J.B. Leishman, 1936; also translated by M.D. Herter Norton, 1942.
Späte Gedichte. 1934; as *Later Poems*, translated by J.B. Leishman, 1938.
Requiem and Other Poems, translated by J.B. Leishman. 1935.
Fifty Selected Poems, translated by C.F. MacIntyre. 1940.
Poems 1906-1926, translated by J.B. Leishman, 1957.
Angel Songs, translated by Rhoda Coghill. 1958.
Poems, translated by G.W. McKay. 1965.
Visions of Christ: A Posthumous Cycle of Poems, translated by Siegfried Mandel. 1967.
Holding Out, translated by Rita Lesser. 1975.
Possibility of Being, translated by J.B. Leishman. 1977.
Selected Poems, translated by Robert Bly. 1981.

An Unofficial Rilke: Poems 1912-1926, translated by Michael Hamburger. 1981.

Plays

Im Fruhfrost (produced 1897). In *Aus der Frühzeit*, 1921; as *Early Frost*, in *Nine Plays*,
   1979.
Ohne Gegenwart. 1898; as *Not Present*, in *Nine Plays*, 1979.
Die Weisse Fürstin. 1899; revised version, in *Die Frühen Gedichte*, 1909; as *The White
   Princess*, in *Nine Plays*, 1979.
Das tägliche Leben (produced 1901). 1902; as *Everyday Life*, in *Nine Plays*, 1979.
Nine Plays. 1979.

Fiction

Am Leben hin. 1898.
Zwei Prager Geschichten. 1899.
Vom lieben Gott und Anderes. 1900; revised edition, as *Geschichten vom lieben Gott*,
   1904; as *Stories of God*, 1931.
Die Letzten. 1902.
Die Aufzeichnungen des Malte Laurids Brigge. 1910; as *Journal of My Other Self*, 1930;
   as *The Notebooks of Malte Laurids Brigge*, 1958.
Ewald Tragy. 1929; translated as *Ewald Tragy*, 1929.

Other

Worpswede. 1903.
Auguste Rodin. 1903; revised edition, 1907; translated as *August Rodin*, 1919.
Aus der Frühzeit: Vers, Prosa, Drama 1894-1899. 1921.
Briefe an Auguste Rodin. 1928.
Briefe an einen jungen Dichter. 1929; as *Letters to a Young Poet*, 1945.
Briefe und Tagebücher, edited by Ruth Sieber-Rilke and Carl Sieber. 7 vols., 1929-37;
   revised edition of *Briefe*, as *Gesammelte Briefe*, 6 vols., 1936-39.
Tagebücher aus der Frühzeit, edited by Ruth Sieber-Rilke and Carl Sieber. 1942.
Letters 1892-1926. 2 vols., 1945; *Selected Letters, 1902-1926*, 1946.
Freundschaft mit Rilke, by Elya Maria Nevar. 1946.
La dernière amitié: Lettres à Madame Eloui Bey, edited by Edmond Jaloux. 1949; as
   Unpublished Letters, 1952.
Briefe an Gräfin Sizzo 1921-1926, edited by Ingeborg Schnack. 1950; revised edition,
   1977.
Briefwechsel in Gedichte, with Erika Mitterer. 1950; as *Correspondence in Verse*, 1953.
Briefwechsel, with Benvenuta, edited by Magda von Hattingberg. 1954; as *Letters to
   Benvenuta*, 1951.
Briefwechsel, with Marie von Thurn und Taxis, edited by Ernest Zinn. 2 vols., 1951; as
   Letters, 1958.
Briefe über Cézanne, edited by Clara Rilke. 1952.
Briefwechsel, with Lou Andreas-Salome, edited by Ernst Pfeiffer. 1952.
Correspondance 1909-1926, with André Gide, edited by Renée Lang. 1952.
Briefe an Frau Gudi Nölke, edited by Paul Obermüller. 1953; as *Letters*, 1955.
Briefwechsel, with Katharina Kippenberg, edited by Bettina von Bomhard. 1954.
Correspodance 1920-1926, with Merline, edited by Dieter Bassermann. 1954; as *Letters
   to Merline*, 1951.
Selected Works, translated by G. Craig Houston and J.B. Leishman. 2 vols., 1954-60.

Rilke, Gide, et Verhaeren: Correspondance inédite, edited by C. Bronne. 1955.
Lettres milanaises 1921-1926, edited by Renée Lang. 1956.
Briefwechsel, with Inga Junghanns, edited by Wolfgang Herwig. 1959.
Briefe an Sidonie Nadherny von Borutin, edited by Bernhard Blume. 1973.
Übertragungen, edited by Ernst Zinn and Karin Wais. 1975.
Rilke on Love and Other Difficulties, edited by John J.L. Mood. 1975.
Briefwechsel 1910-1925, with Helene von Nostitz, edited by Oswalt von Nostitz. 1976.
Briefe an Nanny Wunderly-Volkart, edited by Nikjlaus Bigler and Rätus Luck. 2 vols.,
1977.
Briefwechsel 1899-1925, with Hugo von Hofmannsthal, edited by Rudolf Hirsch and
Ingeborg Schnack. 1978.
Briefe an Axel Juncker, edited by Renate Scharffenberg. 1979.
Briefwechsel, with Rolf Freiherrn von Ungern-Sternberg, edited by Konrad Kratzsch. 1980.
Briefwechsel, with Anita Forrer, edited by Magda Kerényi. 1982.

Translator, *Sonette nach dem Portugiesischen*, by Elizabeth Barrett Browning. 1908.
Translator, *Der Kentauer*, by Maurice de Guérin. 1911.
Translator, *Die Liebe der Magdalena*. 1912.
Translator, *Portugiesische Briefe*, by Marianna Alcoforado. 1913.
Translator, *Die Rückkehr des verlorenen Sohnes*, by André Gide. 1914.
Translator, *Die vierundzwanzig Sonette der Louïze Labé*. 1918.
Translator, *Gedichte*, by Paul Valéry. 1925.

*

Bibliography: *Rilke Bibliographie* by Walter Ritzer, 1951.

Critical Studies: *Rilke: A Study of His Later Poetry*, 1952, and *Portrait of Rilke*, 1971, both by
H.E. Holthusen; *Rilke: The Ring of Forms* by F.H. Wood, 1958; *Phases of Rilke* by Norbert
Fuerst, 1958; *Rilke: Masks and the Man* by H.F. Peters, 1960; *Rilke, Europe, and the
English-Speaking World*, 1961, and *Rilke*, 1963, both by Eudo C. Mason; *Creativity: A Theme
from Faust and the Duino Elegies* by E.L. Stahl, 1961; *Rilke in Transition: An Exploration of
His Earliest Poetry* by James Rolleston, 1970; *Rilke* by Arnold Bauer, 1972; *The Symbolism of
Space and Motion in the Works of Rilke* by Richard Jayne, 1972; "Rilke and Nietzsche" in *The
Disinherited Mind* by Erich Heller, revised edition, 1975; *Stone into Poetry: The Cathedral
Cycle in Rilke's "Neue Gedichte"* by Ernest M. Wolf, 1978; *Rilke and Jugendstil* by K.E. Webb,
1978; *Landscape and Landscape Imagery in Rilke* by John Sandford, 1981; *The Sacred
Threshold: A Life of Rilke* by J.F. Hendry, 1983.

*   *   *

Rainer Maria Rilke is unquestionably one of the greatest individualists among poets of the
German language; his internationally wide appeal might seem incompatible with his oblique
poetic diction, which resists translation, his frequently idiosyncratic turn of mind, and a
generally unyielding attitude towards his reader. His work has been subjected to every conceiv-
able treatment, from the manifestly uncritical admiration of many biographies and personal
reminiscences, through every shade of theological, ethical, and philosophical interpretation, to
claims that his aesthetic aristocratism was but thinly veiled Fascism.
    Rilke made little attempt to maintain any clear distinction between his public and his private
persona and was disinclined to commit himself to any particular allegiances. His copious
correspondence can justifiably be considered part of his creative production; read with due
circumspection, the letters illuminate many aspects of his literary works, though scattered
comments on social and political affairs are too non-committal and self-contradictory to be of
any great relevance to his poetry.

One of the greatest cosmopolitans of modern literature, Rilke continually assimilated and processed material from his ceaseless travels. Above all, the homelessness which characterised his life (his marriage was "suspended" in the interests of the freedom and solitude he considered essential to his art)—that loneliness among men which he shared with Nietzsche—became the supreme metaphor for the rootlessness and transitoriness which are major themes of his work.

From a posture of inward exile—Hölderlin was his poetic ancestor—Rilke's work gives utterance, not simply to private agonies of spirit, but to the spiritual and intellectual impoverishment of his age: to the crisis of idioms and values which threatened Western culture as a whole, exposing man in all his vulnerability to the plurality, disjunction, and fortuitousness of a universe no longer structured around reliable concepts of religious faith, moral principle, or historical relevance. The cry of the poet *in extremis* is simultaneously a lament for an entire generation of "Enterbten" (disinherited), defenceless on the outer frontiers of human experience. The "City of Pain" of the Tenth Duino Elegy forms a counterpart to T.S. Eliot's "Waste Land."

The derivative, *fin de siècle* sentimentality of Rilke's earliest verse reveals nothing of the poet's ultimate stature, though various themes of the later work are adumbrated. His abortive essays at the dramatic form are interesting primarily for their Neo-Romantic and *Jugendstil* characteristics; Maeterlinck's influence is apparent here. The quasi-mystical religiosity which marks the *Poems from the Book of Hours* has prompted some over-confident "theological" interpretations; the association of the divine with the sphere of darkness is an early example of the dramatic "reversals" that were to figure in later works, while the glorification of poverty pre-figures the presentation of social outcasts as "aristocrats of inwardness" in *The Notebooks of Malte Laurids Brigge*.

The *New Poems*, product of his Paris years, represent the first real peak of Rilke's artistic development. Inspired by the techniques of Rodin and Cézanne, he developed the concept of the *Dinggedicht*: each poem represents a separate object in such total self-sufficiency that its intangible qualities become concrete, its outward features interiorised—its essence is made visible. However, the perfect self-containment of the object exposes the existential inadequacy of the onlooker-poet: much later, in "Turning-Point" (1914), Rilke wrote "For looking, you see, has a limit./ And the more looked-at world/ wants to be nourished by love./...now practise heart-work...."

The reciprocity of inwardness and outwardness is central to the *Notebooks*. This episodic journal-novel is of seminal importance in the development of the modern novel, inviting comparisons with Proust, Kafka, Musil, and Sartre (*La Nausée*). The reader is powerfully aware of the presence of Baudelaire in Malte's quest for authentic experience amid the soulless, materialistic horror of urban existence. The theme of a "personal death" is taken from the Danish poet and novelist J.P. Jacobsen, whose work greatly influenced Rilke. Invaded by impressions of his physical surroundings, the hypersensitive narrative persona becomes as much object as subject: the inner world breaks out into the outer world. Besides the themes of Angst, loneliness, death, and the poet's struggle for authenticity of expression, the novel develops the idea of "intransitive love," ending with a reversal of the parable of the Prodigal Son, in which all hope of salvaging an authentic individual existence is seen to lie in immunity from the love of others.

The 12 silent years which elapsed between the completion of the *Notebooks* and the publication of the *Duino Elegies* were not as barren as is often implied, although it was no coincidence that Rilke's "crisis years" were years of cultural and political upheaval in Europe as a whole. Rich in ambiguities and contradictions, the *Elegies* are open to radical objections and infinite misinterpretations. They can ultimately be interpreted only in Rilke's own terms, and in his consciousness "that we don't feel very securely at home in this interpreted world." It is in the *Elegies* that the most radical reversal (*Umschlag*) occurs: the transition from negation to affirmation. Acute awareness of the irrevocability of human existence becomes a positive incentive to the creation of a new order of existence. Through *Verwandlung* (transformation) a final, radical revision of the frontiers within human experience is achieved, and the antitheses of life/death, joy/suffering, love/separation, terror/bliss, immanence/transcendence are resolved into "pure contradiction." The Angel to whom the Elegies are addressed is not that of the Christian heaven, but a symbolic transcendental being "who vouches for the recognition of a higher degree of reality in the invisible."

Only in the *Sonnets to Orpheus*, however, does the artist emerge as the ultimate agent of re-integration, poetry as a means of salvation from the impossibility of living with the truth— another echo of Nietzsche. The final transformation, from *Klage* (Lament) to *Rühmung* (Praise) is accomplished: "Song Is Existence," and man can pass into "the other relation."

The *Sonnets*, with their serene tone and structural formality, were not Rilke's final word. The poetry of his last years continued to challenge the fundamental contradictions of human destiny and thus to reinforce the timeless pertinence of his message.

—Andrea C. Cervi

RIMBAUD, (Jean Nicolas) Arthur. Born in Charleville, France, 20 October 1854. Educated at local schools to age 16. Ran away from home several times, 1870-71; left to join Paul Verlaine in Paris, with whom he had a fiery relationship in France, Belgium, and England, to 1873: Verlaine jailed for 2 years for shooting him, 1873; taught briefly in Reading, Berkshire, 1874, then lived and worked in various parts of Europe to 1878; from 1878, in Cyprus, Egypt, and, as a trader, in Aden and Abyssinia: illness caused his return to France, 1891: Leg amputated, May 1891. *Died 10 November 1891.*

PUBLICATIONS

Collections

> *Oeuvres complètes*, edited by Antoine Adam. 1972.
> *Oeuvres*, edited by Suzanne Bernard and André Guyaux. 1981.
> *Complete Works, Selected Letters*, edited by Wallace Fowlie. 1966.

Verse and Prose

> *Une Saison en enfer.* 1873; as *A Season in Hell*, translated by Delmore Schwartz, 1939, Louise Varese, 1945, Norman Cameron, 1950, and Enid Rhodes Peschel, 1973.
> *Illuminations*, edited by Paul Verlaine. 1886; edited by A. Py, 1967, and Nick Osmond, 1976; as *Les Illuminations*, translated by Enid Rhodes Peschel, 1973.
> *Le Reliquaire*, edited by L. Genonceaux. 1891.
> *Poésies complètes*, edited by Paul Verlaine. 1895.
> *Les Stupra.* 1923.
> *Selected Verse Poems*, translated by Norman Cameron. 1942.
> *Selected Verse*, translated by O. Bernard. 1962.

*

Critical Studies: *Rimbaud* by Wallace Fowlie, 1946, revised edition, 1965; *The Time of the Assassins: A Study of Rimbaud* by Henry V. Miller, 1956; *Rimbaud*, 1957, and *Rimbaud: A Critical Introduction*, 1981, both by C.A. Hackett; *Rimbaud* by Enid Starkie, 1961; *The Design of Rimbaud's Poetry* by J.P. Houston, 1963; *Rimbaud's Poetic Practice* by W.M. Frohock, 1963; *The Poetry of Rimbaud* by Robert Greer Cohn, 1973; *Rimbaud* by Frederic C. Saint Aubyn, 1975; *Rimbaud* by C. Chadwick, 1979; *Rimbaud: Visions and Hesitations* by Edward J. Ahearn, 1984.

*   *   *

Rimbaud's career as a poet began early in 1870, shortly after his 15th birthday, and was over by 1875, before he was 21, and yet, in the space of those few adolescent years, he produced work of a quite exceptional power and originality.

Although his earliest poems were orthodox enough, his poetry soon began to reveal the first stirrings of his revolutionary ideas as regards both content and form. A vehemently anti-Christian attitude is apparent in such poems as "Soleil et Chair," "Le Mal," and "Les Premières Communions," and a no less vehement political commitment in his fiercely pro-Republican poems such as "Le Forgeron" and in his vicious attacks on Napoleon III in "L'éclatante victoire de Sarrebruck" and "Rages de Césars." Even in its minor manifestations authoritarianism was intolerable to Rimbaud with the result that customs officers, librarians, and his domineering mother provoked his contempt and derision in "Les Douaniers," "Les Assis," and "Les Poètes de sept ans." But, as an alternative reaction to his refusal to conform, Rimbaud also sought refuge with equal fervour in the consoling world of his imagination and it was this that gave rise to what is no doubt his best-known poem, "Le Bateau ivre," in which the drunken boat of the title revels in the exhilarating experience of drifting wildly out of control through fantastic seas.

This rebellion against all authority and desire for total freedom soon spread to the form as well as the content of Rimbaud's poetry. In May 1871 he wrote his celebrated "lettre du voyant" in which he contended that the poet's function is simply to note down his disordered sensations without exercising any conscious control over their presentation. "Je est un autre," he wrote, amplifying this statement by comparing the poet to a violin or a trumpet on which some outside force plays. To thus act merely as a passive instrument was easier said than done for an inexperienced poet of 16, but even in such conventionally structured poems as "Le Bateau ivre" and "Les Voyelles" the way in which images are piled pell-mell one on top of the other suggests that the balance between the orderly control of the intellect and the free play of the imagination is already shifting towards the latter.

This balance was to shift still further once Rimbaud, after several abortive attempts, finally escaped from the provincial backwater of his home town of Charleville to Paris in September 1871. There he came under the influence of a poet ten years his senior, Paul Verlaine, who had already experimented with unconventional versification. In a group of poems written in the summer of 1872 Rimbaud soon outdistanced his mentor in freedom of form, and in such poems as "Larme" and "Bonne Pensée du matin" he dispensed with rhyme in places and departed from a regular rhythmic pattern. He was soon to take the final step of moving from verse to prose in the *Illuminations* which he began to write later in 1872 and from which almost all trace of regular rhyme and uniform rhythm has disappeared. Instead, Rimbaud achieves his poetic effects by piling brilliant and unexpected images one on top of the other even more so than he had done in "Le Bateau ivre" and "Les Voyelles" and by creating flexible rhythmic patterns that extend much further the relatively modest innovations of "Larme" and "Bonne Pensée du matin."

The encounter with Verlaine had a similar liberating effect on Rimbaud's ideas. Both of them had a homosexual element in their make-up and Rimbaud gave to the intense emotional relationship that grew up between them in 1872 and the first half of 1873 an intellectual justification by seeing it as a rebellion against yet another constraint imposed by society. So along with the continuing themes of the destruction of the real world and the creation of a different, fantasy world, the theme of "le nouvel amour" is introduced into the *Illuminations* in such passages as "Conte" and "Royauté," as well as the wider theme, in "Matinée d'ivresse" and "Génie," for example, of the creation of an amoral society in which the Christian concepts of good and evil will no longer exist.

Many of the 42 passages of the *Illuminations* dealing with these themes are full of optimistic fervour, but there are others, such as "Angoisse" and "Barbare," in which a sense of disappointment and disillusion can be detected, heralding the tone which prevails throughout Rimbaud's next and probably last work, *Une Saison en enfer*, which he wrote between April and August 1873. The significance of the title resides in the fact that Rimbaud had at first viewed his months with Verlaine as a season in heaven when, with the help of his disciple, he was to achieve his goal of total freedom. But instead of complementing each other, their widely different temperaments soon became a source of conflict and the final painful break-up of their relationship in July 1873 led Rimbaud to doubt the validity of the concepts that their union was to have expressed and furthered. "Délires," the central chapter of *Une Saison en enfer*, is divided into two sections, the first of which is a disenchanted account of what is now dismissed as a "drôle de ménage" and the second an equally disenchanted account of what he now regards as a foolish excursion into "verbal alchemy," as he describes it. The remaining chapters of *Une Saison en enfer* acknowledge the failure of other aspects of Rimbaud's revolt. "Nous sommes à l'Occident," he writes, "je suis escalve de mon baptême," recognising that if one is born into Christian, western society one can neither refuse to adapt to its values nor erase those values from one's mind.

Some critics believe that immediately after *Une Saison en enfer* Rimbaud abandoned poetry. This certainly seems the logical consequence of his changed ideas, but other critics nonetheless believe that some of the *Illuminations* date from 1874 and were written as a kind of post-script to *Une Saison en enfer*. But, whatever the precise date, Rimbaud certainly did give up writing poetry by 1875 and thereafter opted out of society not through the medium of his imagination but in reality. He turned his back on Europe and, like his own "bateau ivre," drifted first out to the Far East and then to the Middle East and finally down the Red Sea to live from 1880 until his death in 1891 as a trader first in Aden and then in Abyssinia, totally uninterested in his growing reputation as one of the major figures in late 19th-century French literature.

—C. Chadwick

ROBBE-GRILLET, Alain. Born in Brest, France, 18 August 1922. Educated at Lycée de Brest, and lycées Buffon and St. Louis, Paris; National Institute of Agronomy, Paris, diploma 1944. Sent to work in German tank factory during World War II. Married Catherine Rstakian in 1957. Engineer, National Statistical Institute, Paris, 1945-49, and Institute of Colonial Fruits and Crops, Morocco, French Guinea, and Martinique, 1949-51; then full-time writer: since 1955, literary consultant, Éditions de Minuit, Paris. Recipient: Feneon Prize, 1954; Critics Prize, 1955; Louis Delluc Prize, 1963. Lives in Neuilly-sur-Seine, France.

PUBLICATIONS

Fiction

Les Gommes. 1953; as *The Erasers*, 1964.

Le Voyeur. 1955; as *The Voyeur*, 1958.
La Jalousie. 1957; as *Jealousy*, 1959.
Dans le labyrinthe. 1959; as *In the Labyrinth*, 1960.
L'Année dernière à Marienbad. 1961; as *Last Year at Marienbad*, 1962.
Instantanés. 1962; as *Snapshots*, with *Towards a New Novel*, 1965.
L'Immortelle. 1963; as *The Immortal One*, 1971.
La Maison de rendez-vous. 1965; translated as *La Maison de Rendez-vous*, 1966; as *The House of Assignation*, 1970.
Projet pour une révolution à New York. 1970; as *Project for a Revolution in New York*, 1972.
Glissements progressifs du plaisir. 1974.
Topologie d'une cité fantôme. 1976; as *Topology of a Phantom City*, 1977.
Souvenirs du triangle d'or. 1978; as *Memories of the Golden Triangle*, 1984.
Un Régicide. 1978.
Djinn. 1981; translated as *Djinn*, 1982.

Plays

Screenplays: *L'Année dernière à Marienbad* (*Last Year at Marienbad*), 1961; *L'Immortelle*, 1963; *Trans-Europ-Express*, 1967; *L'Homme qui ment* (*The Man Who Lies*), 1968; *L'Eden et après*, 1970; *Glissements progressifs du plaisir*, 1973; *Le Jeu avec le feu*, 1975; *La Belle Captive*, 1983.

Other

Pour un nouveau roman. 1963; revised edition, 1970; as *Towards a New Novel*, with *Snapshots*, 1965; as *For a New Novel: Essays on Fiction*, 1966.
Rêves de jeunes filles, photographs by David Hamilton. 1971; as *Dreams of a Young Girl*, 1971; as *Dreams of Young Girls*, 1971.
Les Demoiselles d'Hamilton, photographs by David Hamilton. 1972; as *Sisters*, 1973.
La Belle Captive, with René Magritte. 1976.
Temple aux miroirs, with Irina Ionesco. 1977.

*

Bibliography: *Robbe-Grillet: An Annotated Bibliography of Critical Studies 1953-1972* by Dale W. Fraizer, 1973.

Critical Studies: *Robbe-Grillet and the New French Novel* by Ben Frank Stoltzfus, 1964; *The French New Novel: Claude Simon, Michel Butor, Robbe-Grillet* by John Sturrock, 1969; *Les Gommes* edited by J.S. Wood, 1970; *Narrative Consciousness: Structure and Perception in the Fiction of Kafka, Beckett, and Robbe-Grillet* by G.H. Szanto, 1972; *The Novels of Robbe-Grillet* by Bruce Morrissette, 1975; *The Film Career of Robbe-Grillet* by William F. Van Wert, 1977; *The Films of Robbe-Grillet* by Roy Armes, 1981; *Robbe-Grillet* by John Fletcher, 1983.

*   *   *

The best-known of the so-called *nouveaux romanciers* in France, Alain Robbe-Grillet began life as an agricultural scientist, and turned to literature only after illness brought his research career to an end. He thus comes from a background which is different to that of the normal French person of letters, and explains to some extent the iconoclastic impact he made on the literary scene when his second novel, *Les Gommes*, was published in Paris in 1953 (his first novel, *Un Régicide*, appeared only in 1978).

Les Gommes is a detective story based on the legend of Oedipus, a complex, enigmatic novel.

In *Le Voyeur*, the next book, a travelling salesman visits the offshore island of his birth and (perhaps) commits a sadistic rape and murder before leaving scot-free some days later; but the crime may have been enacted in the protagonist's sick mind only. In *La Jalousie*, the workings of the sick mind of the protagonist now actually become the text, so that the novel itself constitutes a fit of jealousy in which the narrator watches his wife obsessively as she plans (or so he believes) a night away from home in the company of a neighbouring planter. The jealous frenzy subsides—and the novel ends—only with the return of the (errant?) wife and the (apparent) discomfiture of the neighbour.

Robbe-Grillet has declared on a number of occasions how much he owes to Kafka, and so it is not surprising that *Dans le labyrinthe* should be Kafkaesque in inspiration. A soldier is wandering in a snow-covered town looking for a man to whom he wants to deliver the effects of a dead comrade after a major military disaster, and he ends up dying from wounds himself. What is not clear is how far the whole story is elaborated by the narrator on the basis of a picture called "The Defeat at Reichenfels," that is to what extent, like jealousy in the previous novel, it is a construct of the fantasising consciousness.

During the next few years Robbe-Grillet concentrated on making or helping to make a number of films, of which the best-known is *Marienbad* (directed by Alain Resnais), the story of a man who succeeds in persuading a woman that she agreed, the year before in Marienbad, to meet him in the resort where they presently are staying and leave her husband for him. He returned to the novel in *La Maison de rendez-vous*, a witty parody of James Bond stories set in an exotic Hong Kong where women's flesh "plays a large part" in the protagonist's dreams, and *Projet pour une révolution à New York*, a more self-indulgently sadistic fantasy about an imaginary wave of terrorism in Manhattan. Since then the preoccupation with sadism and voyeurism has become almost totally obsessive. It is now clear that his best work is contained in the three mature novels of his middle period, *Le Voyeur*, *La Jalousie*, and *Dans le labyrinthe*, works which will remain important in the history of 20th-century literature long after the polemics which surrounded their publication have been forgotten.

—John Fletcher

ROJAS, Fernando de. Born in La Puebla de Montalbán, Spain, c. 1475. Received Bachelor of Law degree from University of Salamanca, c. 1498. Married Leonor Alvarez; four sons and three daughters. Practiced law in Talavera de la Reina from c. 1507, and served as mayor of the town. *Died in April 1541.*

PUBLICATIONS

Play

> *Comedia de Calisto y Melibea* (16 acts). 1499; as *Tragicomedia* (21 acts), 1502; as *La Celestina*, edited by M. Criado de Val and G.D. Trotter, 1958, 3rd edition, 1970; manuscript edited by Guadalupe Martinez Lacalle, 1972; as *The Spanish Bawd*, translated by James Mabbe, 1631; also translated by L.B. Simpson, 1954, M.H. Singleton, 1958, Phyllis Hartnoll, 1959, and J.M. Cohen, 1964.

*

Critical Studies: *The Art of La Celestina*, 1956, and *The Spain of Fernando de Rojas*, 1972, both by Stephen Gilman; *The Petrarchan Sources of La Celestina* by Alan D. Deyermond, 1961; *Two Spanish Masterpieces: The Book of Good Love and the Celestina* by Maria R. Lida de Malkiel, 1961; *Memory in La Celestina* by Dorothy S. Severin, 1970; *Love's Fools: Aucassin, Troilus, Calisto, and the Parody of the Courtly Lover* by June H. Martin, 1972.

*   *   *

The facts surrounding the creation of the book called *Celestina* present the critical reader with mystery at almost every point. Fernando de Rojas states in a prefatory "letter to a friend" that he read the anonymous first act of a play which circulated in the university ambience of Salamanca and decided to spend a short vacation from his studies of the law in completing it. The statement may be artistic subterfuge, but internal evidence suggests that it is true. The result of Rojas's work is the 16-act *Comedia*. Some three years later a new version in 21 acts appeared, renamed *Tragicomedia*, with a prologue that only partially justifies an extensive amplification of the original text. Thus a new question arises: Are the additions really the work of Rojas? Opinion is far from unanimous.

The plot is not strikingly original, but its elements are combined in a new and remarkable balance to achieve vivid characterization and intense dramatic movement. Calisto, a young nobleman, falls in love with Melibea, a maiden of equally high birth. On her furious rejection of his proposal of "illicit love," one of his servants recommends the intervention of Celestina, an avaricious old bawd who has great ability in arranging these matters. Celestina achieves a second meeting for the two, and on the following night Calisto scales the wall of Melibea's garden to become her lover. Celestina's services have been rewarded with a gold chain of great value which she refuses to share with her accomplices, Calisto's servants. Enraged, they murder the old lady and are summarily executed as they attempt to flee.

The *Comedia* allows the lovers only one meeting; as Calisto leaves Melibea's garden, he falls from its high wall to his death. Melibea feels that she must follow her lover in death and finds the opportunity to climb to a tower of her father's house. There she reveals the history of her seduction and bereavement and leaps to her death, leaving her father to lament the loss of his only child. "For whom did I build towers, for whom did I acquire honors, for whom did I plant trees, for whom did I build ships?" The play ends in silence and the eternal, unanswerable questions of human aspiration and grief. The *Tragicomedia* ends in the same way, but adds a month in time for the lovers' meetings and a gloriously lyrical night-scene in Melibea's garden.

The plot alone does not account for the astonishing growth of critical interest in *Celestina* in the last thirty years. Well over five hundred editions, translations, theatrical adaptations, monographs, and studies of various aspects of the work have been published in that period and scholarly and popular interest continues to grow. It is above all a work of enormous innovation in language, character, and literary style. All is dialogue, monologue, or soliloquy, and yet it is not theatre in any practical sense. The nearest approximation to its genre would be the Latin humanistic comedies of the renaissance or English closet drama. Character, movement, action and reaction, love and death: all are communicated through speech, ranging from the sublimely lyrical to the popular, vulgar, and obscene. The characters lie, scheme, deceive, cheat, and reward each other, all in incessant and remarkably realistic dialogue, very different from the medieval didactic *dialogus* or the nascent theatre, with its stereotyped figures and limited range.

Celestina marks, in a very literal sense, the frontier between the medieval and the modern world in the literature of Spain, with its crossing of social barriers—old meet with young, rich with poor, nobility with servants and prostitutes—and its successful search for a linguistic procedure which allows us to know the characters even more intimately than they know themselves, to see them as others see them. Several direct imitations of *Celestina* were of poor quality and soon forgotten, but Rojas's work has survived as one of the four or five true masterworks of Spanish literature, and his presence is felt strongly in the work of Cervantes and

Lope de Vega; *Celestina* was a major influence in the creation of the Golden Age novel and theatre.

—James R. Stamm

ROLAND, Song of. Epic poem based on an historical event of 778, written c. 1100, possibly by Turoldus; of the many surviving manuscripts, that in the Bodleian Library, Oxford, is considered the oldest and best.

<small>PUBLICATIONS</small>

Verse

> *Le Chanson de Roland*, edited and translated by Joseph Bédier.   1921; revised edition, 1937; also edited by F. Whitehead, 1946.
> *Le Chanson de Roland: Oxford Version*, edited by T. Atkinson Jenkins.   1929 (revised edition).
> *Les Textes de la Chanson de Roland*, edited by Raoul Mortier.   10 vols., 1940-44.
> *The Song of Roland: An Analytical Edition*, edited and translated by Gerard J. Brault.   2 vols., 1978; also translated by Dorothy L. Sayers, 1957, W.S. Merwin (in *Medieval Epics*), 1963, Robert Harrison, 1970, D.D.R. Owen, 1972, Howard S. Robertson, 1972, and C.H. Sisson, 1983.

*

Bibliography: *A Guide to Studies on the "Chanson de Roland"* by Joseph John Duggan, 1976.

Critical Studies: see the above editions; also: *Le Chanson de Roland commentée* by Joseph Bédier, 1927; *The Ethos of the Song of Roland* by George Fenwick Jones, 1963; *The Chanson de Roland* by Pierre Le Gentil, 1969; *Reading the Song of Roland* by Eugene Vance, 1970.

*   *   *

About the year 1100, an anonymous French author recreated an event that had occurred more than three centuries earlier. The poem not only recalls the exploits of the legendary hero Roland but also provides a wealth of information about contemporary society.

The *Song of Roland* is based on an incident that took place on August 15, 778. After a short and indecisive campaign in Muslim-held Spain, Charlemagne sustained a crushing defeat in the Pyrenees while returning to his capital at Aachen. Basque (or Gascon) marauders ambushed and destroyed the army's rearguard, looted the baggage train, and dispersed before the Franks could retaliate. Only sketchy information is available but one chronicler, Einhard (d. 840), mentions Roland, prefect of the Breton march, as having been among the fallen. Roncesvalles (Roncevaux, in French) is first identified at the end of the 11th century as the pass where the action happened but the exact site of the battle remains uncertain.

In the poem, Saracens led by King Marsile of Saragossa are responsible for the attack upon the rearguard and the traitor Ganelon, who hates his stepson Roland, secretly plans the ambush with the enemy. At Roncevaux, Roland, who heads the rearguard, refuses to sound the oliphant to call Charlemagne to the rescue, this despite the urgent entreaty of his companion-in-arms Oliver. The Emperor avenges Roland's heroic death by defeating the remnants of Marsile's army, then another vast Saracen force led by the Emir Baligant. Later, at Aix, Ganelon admits that he caused Roland's death but denies that he committed treason. A judicial combat determines that this defense has no validity and the traitor is executed.

One of the earliest works in French literature, this epic is believed to portray in fairly accurate fashion the behavior and mores of the aristocratic warrior class in France at the time of the First Crusade. Members of the upper nobility valued courage, strength, ability to give sound advice, and loyalty based on family and feudal ties. The *Song of Roland* is a profoundly Christian poem that exalts righteousness and martyrdom but also depicts violent individuals at times motivated by bloodthirstiness, greed, racial prejudice, and revenge. A warlike prelate, Archbishop Turpin, fights by the hero's side. Many details are provided about armor, weapons, and tactics but a good deal of epic exaggeration is also apparent in battle scenes.

The poem has some of the characteristics of the formulaic style of oral tradition but also other features usually associated with written literature. The author was familiar with the Bible; it is not clear that he was influenced by the classics. The entire work is constructed on a series of oppositions and parallels, and effective use is made of such narrative devices as foreshadowing, irony, repetition, and understatement. Gestures and symbols play an important role. Charlemagne is an idealized monarch but, though forewarned by dreams, is powerless to stay the course of events. Roland is surpassingly brave, loyal, and strong; however, some scholars believe the poet may have suggested that one can carry these virtues too far.

The oldest and best version of the poem, written in Anglo-Norman dialect, is found in a 12th-century manuscript preserved in the Bodleian Library at Oxford. When emended, this text has 4,002 decasyllabic verses arranged in assonanced strophes of varying length called *laisses*. A rhymed French version appeared in the 13th century. The poem was translated into several languages during the Middle Ages and a 12th-century Latin prose adaptation, the *Pseudo-Turpin Chronicle*, had a great influence on the literature and art of the period.

—Gerard J. Brault

RONSARD, Pierre de. Born in Château de la Possonière, near Couture, France, 10/11 September 1524. Educated at Collège de Navarre, Paris, 1533-34; Royal Riding School, Paris 1539. Page at French Court, 1536: accompanied Madeleine (the daughter of Francis I) to Scotland on her marriage to James V, 1537, and again in Scotland, 1538-39; in service of the diplomat Lazare de Baïf, 1540; lived on his family estate to recover his health, 1540-43; took minor orders, 1543; studied under Jean Dorat, 1544-47, with Du Bellay at Collège du Coqueret, Paris, 1547, and at the Collège de Boncourt, Paris; given ecclesiastical appointment, Evaillé, 1555; named almoner and counsellor to the king, 1559; Canon of St. Julien, Le Mans, 1560; Prior of St. Cosme des Tours, 1565; exchanged Evaillé appointment for prebendary of St. Martin, Tours, 1566; Prior of Croixval, 1566. *Died 27/28 December 1585.*

Collections

Oeuvres complètes, edited by Paul Laumonier, completed by Raymond Lebègue and
Isidore Silver. 18 vols., 1914-67.
Oeuvres complètes (text of 1584), edited by Gustave Cohen. 2 vols., 1950.
Oeuvres (text of 1587), edited by Isidore Silver. 4 vols., 1966-70.

Verse

Quatre premiers livres des odes. 1550; *Odes*, 1550; augmented edition, 1553, revised
edition, 1555; complete edition, as *Les Odes*, edited by Charles Guerin, 1952.
Le Premier Livre des amours, le Cinquième des Odes. 1552; revised edition, 1553;
Continuation des amours, 1555; *La Nouvelle continuation des amours*, 1556; complete
edition, as *Les Amours*, edited by Albert-Marie Schmidt, 1974.
Livret de folastries. 1553.
Mélanges. 1555; *Second Livre de mélanges*, 1559.
Hymnes. 2 vols., 1555-56; edited by Albert Py, 1978.
Sonets à Sinope. 1559.
Mélanges et Chansons. 1560.
Oeuvres. 1560; revised edition, 1567, 1571, 1573, 1578, 1584, 1587.
Institution pour l'adolescence du Roy Charles IX. 1562.
Discours sur les misères de ce temps. 1562.
Remonstrance au peuple de France. 1563.
Recueil de trois livres de nouvelles poésies. 1563.
Réponse aux injures et calomnies. 1563.
Elégies, mascarades, et bergerie. 1565.
VIe et VIIe Livres des poèmes. 1569.
Franciade. 1572.
Tombeau de Charles IX. 1574.
Tombeau de Marguerite de France. 1575.
Derniers vers. 1586.
Lyrics, translated by W. Stirling. 1956.
(Selections), translated by Grahame Castor and Terence Cave. 2 vols., 1975-77.
Poems, translated by Nicholas Kilmer. 1979.

Other

Abrégé de l'art poétique francais. 1565.

*

Critical Studies: *Spenser, Ronsard, and Du Bellay* by Alfred W. Satterthwaite, 1960; *Ronsard, Poet of Nature* by D.B. Wilson, 1961; *Ronsard and the Hellenic Renaissance in France*, 1961, *The Intellectual Evolution of Ronsard: The Formative Influences*, 1969, *Three Ronsard Studies*, 1978, and *Ronsard and the Grecian Lyre*, 1981, all by Isidore Silver; *Ronsard's Sonnet Cycles* by Donald Stone, Jr., 1966; *Ronsard and the Age of Gold* by Elizabeth Armstrong, 1968; *Ronsard* by K.R.W. Jones, 1970; *Ronsard the Poet* edited by Terence Cave, 1973; *Love Elegies of the Renaissance: Marot, Louise Labé, and Ronsard* by Gertrude S. Hanisch, 1979;

Ronsard's Ordered Chaos: Visions of Flux and Stability in the Poetry of Ronsard by Malcolm Quainton, 1980; *Ronsard and the Biblical Tradition* by Joyce Main Hanks, 1982.

*   *   *

The undisputed "prince of poets" in 16th-century France, Ronsard achieved what he and Joachim Du Bellay had set out to do in their early theoretical writings, namely change the whole course of French poetry. Insisting on the need to create a distinctly poetic language and make a complete break with the "monstrous error" of the past, he was a considerable innovator, bringing into the French tradition the ode and the "hymne" and making the love sonnet more widely accepted.

His range was both deep and wide. He is now known to the poetry-reading public mainly as a poet of love—unrequited and intellectualized in the Petrarchist sonnets to Cassandre and to Hélène, joyful and uncomplicated in those to Marie—but his stylistic register goes from the Rabelaisian frolics of the *Livret de folastries* to the serious and sometimes pedantic erudition of his Pindaric odes. What is more, he accustomed his public to the notion of the poem as a vehicle for ideas. Ronsard was never shy of philosophizing in verse. He wrote consciously (occasionally arrogantly) for a social and intellectual elite but he was not above involving himself in bruising conflicts with other poets on religious and political issues. His apotheosis as a poet—the publication of his collected works in 1560—coincided with the outbreak of the Wars of Religion, and his later life was overshadowed as much by the political upheavals of the time as by the ill-health which dogged him and of which he complained in his verses. A poet through and through, Ronsard felt to the very end of his life the need to write about even his most intimate experiences; lying on his death-bed and physically unable to put pen to paper, he managed to dictate nine final poems, published posthumously as the *Derniers vers*, in which he describes in poignant detail his sufferings and calls for release through death. The thought of his imminent demise is made more bearable by the certainty of that immortality which alone justifies the poet's vocation. Already, in a famous sonnet to Hélène de Surgères reminding her that she will grow old ("Quand vous serez bien vieille, au soir à la chandelle"), he had remarked that one day she will marvel at the fact that no less a poet than Ronsard had admired her youthful beauty. Thanks to his genius, he implies, the name of an otherwise unexceptional young woman will thus live as long as men have pen and ink.

Enormously prolific, immensely learned, and endowed with enviable facility, Ronsard was without doubt the colossus his contemporaries acclaimed. Today, when much of his philosophical and religious poetry has inevitably lost its accessibility, he remains the greatest French exponent of the theme of *carpe diem* and the transience of life, and at a distance of more than four centuries he is still able to make the reader delight in the freshness of a May morning and shed a tear for the dying of a rose.

—Michael Freeman

ROSE, Romance of the.   First 4000 lines written by Guillaume de Lorris, c. 1225-37; remaining 18,000 lines written by Jean de Meung, in the 1270's.   **LORRIS, Guillaume de:** Born c. 1200 in Lorris, near Orléans. Brother of a canon of the church in Orléans; possibly educated as a cleric. *Died c.1237.*   **MEUNG, Jean (Clopinel or Chopinel) de:** Born in Meun-sur-Loire, c.1260.   Educated as a cleric, possibly in Paris; closely associated with the court; translated works by Vegetius, Boethius, Aelred of Rievaulx, and Giraldus Cambrensis, and the letters of Abelard and Heloise. *Died c. 1315.*

PUBLICATIONS

Verse

Le Roman de la Rose, edited by Félix Lecoy. 3 vols., 1965-70; also edited by E. Langlois, 5 vols., 1914-24; translated, as *The Romaunt of the Rose*, by Chaucer, in *Works*, 1532 (translation edited by R. Sutherland, 1967); also translated, as *The Romance of the Rose*, by F.S. Ellis, 3 vols., 1900, H.W. Robbins, 1962, and Charles Dahlberg, 1971.

*

Critical Studies: *The Allegory of Love* by C.S. Lewis, 1936; *The Mirror of Love: A Reinterpretation of The Romance of the Rose* by Alan M.F. Gunn, 1952; *The Roman de la Rose: A Study in Allegory and Iconography* by John V. Fleming, 1969.

* * *

The *Romance of the Rose* was without doubt the most important work of the late Middle Ages in France; until a shift of sensibility occurred in the middle of the 16th century which robbed it of an audience which shared its cultural points of reference it was read and re-read by generation after generation. A vast work of some 22,000 lines, it is by two different authors, and the two parts of the poem have little in common but the bare bones of their subject matter.

The first part (4,028 lines in length) was written around 1230 by Guillaume de Lorris. As the author himself makes clear, it is an "art of love" in which the difficulties facing a would-be lover and the strategies he must adopt if he is to overcome them are set out. The object of the hero's affections is portrayed as a rose (hence the title of the work) growing in a Garden of Love. This search for sexual gratification is, however, couched in metaphorical language. The young man's state of mind, the hurdles he must surmount, and the lady's feelings are expressed by means of allegorical personifications such as Jealousy, Danger, Shame, etc. It is shown how they help or hinder him in his quest. On the other hand, this first part of the romance is a guide to seduction in the manner of Ovid, on the other a manual for the perfect courtier. A considerable leap of the imagination is required if a modern reader is to grasp the psychological and metaphysical refinements of this intellectually and emotionally subtle work, and one is made constantly aware of the fact that it is the product of a society which deliberately blurred the distinction between dream and reality, fact and fiction.

Jean de Meung, unlike Guillaume de Lorris, was no admirer of the code of chivalry. Taking up the unfinished work some forty years after it first appeared, he consciously subverts his predecessor's values and assumptions. His "continuation" is in fact more than four times the length of the original and is a vehicle for the author's caustic wit at the expense of particular targets such as monks and women and the more general ones of hypocrisy and falsehood. Against the artificiality of "society," Jean de Meung extols the virtues of "Nature," using the allegorical figure of Genius for a plea for honesty and simplicity, loyalty, and compassion. Jean de Meung was a moralist steeped in classical and clerical culture, a reader of Boethius and Plato, who saw the life of the courts as a world of illusion and *fin amour* as a game of dalliance in which ladies were flattered only to be seduced and who was unconcerned by the sweet sufferings of courtly lovers. His literary style is of a piece with his views. The extraordinary figure of the Old Woman is symptomatic of the difference between the two authors. In a bitter, cynical speech, she describes the reality of sexual love, and throughout the work of Jean de Meung makes love subservient to Nature and to Reason. The significance of this debunking of courtly behaviour was not lost upon Jean de Meung's critics such as Jean Gerson and Christine de Pisan who were quick to realize and rebut the consequences of his attack upon court etiquette and the role it gave women.

But more than a mere misogynistic tract, Jean de Meung's *Romance of the Rose* is a "summa" in which his rationalism is brought to bear on a variety of social, theological, and philosophical questions. Indeed, his influence as a thinker remained so great that no understanding of French literature of the 14th and 15th centuries can be had without a knowledge of the *Romance of the Rose*, and especially of his contribution to it.

—Michael Freeman

ROUSSEAU, Jean-Jacques. Born in Geneva, Switzerland, 28 June 1712. Married Thérèse Levasseur in 1768; several children. Apprenticed at age 13 to a clerk, and for five years to an engraver: ran away to Annecy, 1728, and converted to Catholicism; had various occupations, often as a teacher or copyist of music; tutor in the early 1740's; secretary to French Ambassador to Venice, 1743-44; readmitted to Calvinism, 1754; settled at Montmorency, 1756, then in Neuchâtel to 1765; renounced Geneva citizenship, 1763; lived in Bienne, Switzerland, 1765; visited England, 1766; lived near Lyons, and in Paris from 1770; moved to Ermenonville, 1778. *Died 2 July 1778.*

PUBLICATIONS

Collections

The Works. 10 vols., 1773-74.
Oeuvres complètes, edited by Bernard Gagnebin and Marcel Raymond. 4 vols., 1959-69.
The Indispensable Rousseau, edited by John Hope Mason. 1979.

Fiction

La Reine fantasque: Conte cacouac. 1758.
Julie; ou, La Nouvelle Héloïse. 1761; translated as *Eloisa*, 1761.
Émile; ou, De l'éducation. 1762; as *Emilius and Sophia; or, A New System of Education*, 1762-63.

Plays

Les Muses galantes (ballet), music by the author (produced 1745). In *Oeuvres*, 1826.
Le Devin du village (opera), music by the author (produced 1752). 1753; as *The Cunning Man*, 1766.
Narcisse; ou, L'Amant de lui-même (produced 1753). 1753.
Pygmalion, incidental music by the author (produced 1770). 1771.

Other

Dissertation sur la musique moderne. 1743.
Discours sur les sciences et des arts. 1750; as *A Discourse on the Arts and Sciences,* 1752.
Discours sur l'origine et les fondements de l'inégalité parmi les hommes. 1755.
Oeuvres diverses. 2 vols., 1756 (and later editions).
Lettre à d'Alembert sur les spectacles. 1758; as *A Letter to M. d'Alembert,* 1759.
Lettre à Voltaire. 1759.
Du Contrat social; ou, Principes du droit politique. 1762; as *A Treatise on the Social Compact,* 1764.
À Christophe de Beaumont (letter). 1763.
Lettres écrites de la montagne. 1764.
Dictionnaire de musique. 1767; as *A Dictionary of Music,* 1770.
Rousseau juge de Jean-Jacques: Dialogues. 1780.
Considérations sur le gouvernement de la Pologne. 1782; as *The Government of Poland,* 1972.
Les Rêveries du promeneur solitaire. 1782; as *The Reveries of a Solitary,* 1927.
Les Confessions. 2 vols., 1782-89; as *The Confessions,* 1783-91.
Botanique des enfants. 1800; as *Letters on the Elements of Botany,* 1785; revised edition, 1800.
Correspondance, edited by R.-P. Plan. 20 vols., 1924-34.
Correspondance, edited by R.A. Leigh. 1965— .
Essai sur l'origine des langues, edited by Charles Porset. 1976.

*

Bibliography: *Bibliographie générale des oeuvres de Rousseau* by Jean Senelier, 1949.

Critical Studies: *Rousseau and the French Revolution 1762-1791* by Joan McDonald, 1965; *Rousseau* by Jean Guéhenno, 1966; *Rousseau in Staffordshire* by J.H. Broome, 1966; *Rousseau in America 1760-1809* by Paul Merrill Spurlin, 1969; *Rousseau and His Reader* by Robert J. Ellrich, 1969; *Rousseau: A Study in Self-Awareness* by Ronald Grimsley, 1969; *Rousseau and His World* by Sir Gavin de Beer, 1972; *The Extravagant Shepherd: A Study of the Pastoral Vision in Rousseau's Nouvelle Héloise* by Christie M. Vance, 1973; *Rousseau's Political Philosophy: An Interpretation from Within* by Stephen Ellenburg, 1976; *The Political Philosophy of Rousseau* by Roger Davis Masters, 1976; *Rousseau's Political Philosophy: An Exposition and Interpretation* by Ramon M. Lemos, 1977; *Rousseau's Socratic Aemilian Myths* by Madeleine B. Ellis, 1977; *Rousseau's State of Nature* by Marc F. Plattner, 1979; *Rousseau in England* by Edward Duffy, 1979; *Rousseau's Theory of Literature* by James F. Hamilton, 1979; *Reappraisals of Rousseau* edited by Simon Harvey and others, 1980; *Jean-Jacques: The Early Life of Rousseau 1712-1754* by Maurice Cranston, 1983.

*   *   *

Among the intellectuals of the French Enlightenment, Rousseau is the one whose writings have had the greatest influence outside his country and period. He was a profound and in many respects original and contentious thinker, and his major works raised fundamental questions in the fields of ethics, education, politics, and aesthetics.

Rousseau's literary career began in the 1740's with a series of minor works, now largely forgotten, which earned him a reputation principally as a composer and writer on music. In 1750 his *Discourse on the Arts and Sciences* won a prize offered by the Dijon Academy on the topic "Has the restoration of the Arts and Sciences had a purifying effect upon morals?" The view Rousseau took was that, on the evidence he saw around him, the renascence of culture had enfeebled and depraved man. Rousseau's thesis was singularly at variance with the views of the time, and especially with Voltaire's, whose "Le Mondain," a poem in praise of luxury, had appeared in 1736. Rousseau submitted his second *Discourse* (*On the origin of inequality*) for the 1755 Dijon prize, which it did not win—for one thing, it exceeded the required length. Here, he developed the view that contemporary civilization had denatured man, and he saw the institution of property as mainly responsible for this. The gradual development of the differential possession of property had, he argued, brought with it social and legal inequality. Men had come to be socially valued in consequence of what they possessed rather than of their moral worth. Civil law, which protects property, had therefore usurped the place of Natural Law. While Rousseau was not so naive as to propose a return to "primitive nature," he assumed that human nature, having changed once, for the worse, could therefore be changed again for the better. In order to reform the social machine, a new type of man, with a different moral outlook, was needed.

It was in this belief that Rousseau composed his treatise on education, *Emile*. Though Rousseau's practical experience as a tutor was limited and unsuccessful, the theoretical basis of *Emile* has made it one of the most influential works in the history of educational theory. Emile is brought up in a one-to-one relationship with his tutor, who introduces him to experience in carefully calculated steps which correspond to the increasing capacity of Emile, as he grows up, to respond and use it. Thus he will develop the moral and intellectual self-reliance which would enable him, as an adult, to fit into virtually any society. The education Rousseau proposed was essentially child-based, and, though the programme followed by the fictitious Emile would be impossible to put into practice, it was this *conception* of the educational process that influenced subsequent educationalists including Froebel and Dewey. *Emile* was banned in France and Switzerland, largely because of the emotional deism of the Savoyard curate's profession of faith, included in the fourth book.

There is a conceptual link between the type of self-disciplined and self-reliant individual whom Rousseau seeks to form in *Emile* and the nature of the political institution envisaged in the *Social Contract*, published a month or so previously (April 1762), and banned in Geneva shortly afterwards. Taking men as they are, Rousseau sought to define a political system which would restore to them the freedom which they had lost in the way he had outlined in his two early discourses. In Rousseau's scheme, each citizen is under an obligation to enhance the welfare of the state. When he acts with that obligation in mind, he contributes to the General Will of that society. The General Will is seen as taking into account only the common interest of the citizens, not private interests, and it is this that distinguishes it, Rousseau argues, from what he calls the Will of All. If a man acts selfishly or in the interest of a faction within the state, he contributes nothing to the General Will. The General Will, according to Rousseau, constitutes real sovereignty and cannot be relinquished or delegated. Since it emanates from the *whole* community, the *whole* community is sovereign. It is this formulation that has, in the view of some commentators, made Rousseau a great democratic theorist. But Rousseau believed that the General Will of the whole community could more easily find expression, unimpaired by the effects of sectional interests, if partial societies within the state did not exist and if each citizen thought independently. This monolithic political structure, lacking the pluralism which western societies see as a fundamental prerequisite of a free state, and incorporating a religious system based on the requirement that citizens should have "social sentiments without which a man could not be a good citizen or a faithful subject" (on pain of banishment), has also been seen as a totalitarian nightmare.

In 1757 D'Alembert's article "Geneva" appeared in volume VII of Diderot's *Encyclopedia*. Although drama figured in Rousseau's works, he reacted against D'Alembert's suggestion, prompted by Voltaire, that a theatre should be allowed in Geneva, where it was at the time forbidden. Rousseau's reaction was the *Letter to M. d'Alembert*, in which he argued that plays were immoral and useless, encouraged the passions and led people into temptation. (The age-old argument over the moral value of the theatre had intensified since the writings of Caffaro in 1694.) Rousseau's *Letter* marks the final breakdown in the already strained relations between himself and Voltaire, Diderot and D'Alembert.

Early in 1761 Rousseau published *Julie; ou La Nouvelle Héloïse* translating into a novel of passion and duty his thwarted love for Mme. D'Houdetot. Its success was instantaneous, and it ran into more editions than any other 18th-century French novel. It tells the story of Julie d'Etanges, who falls passionately in love with her tutor, Saint-Preux. Her father refuses to let her marry him, and instead she is married to M. de Wolmar. A model wife and mother, she tells her husband of her love for Saint-Preux, and he invites the former tutor to stay with them. Julie and Saint-Preux realise their love still exists, but, with much agonising, duty and virtue prevail. Julie eventually dies of a chill, contracted while rescuing her son from drowning. Though the slow unfolding of the digressive and improbable plot hardly appeals to the modern reader, the importance of the work lies in its new Romantic sensibility and the appeal of virtue discovered in a simple, rural life lived in a natural and harmonious environment.

By 1760 Rousseau had parted company with most of the influential French intellectuals of the day. His social clumsiness, his rejection of polite society, his austerity and eccentricity, as well as his differing views on many important topics, all served to isolate him. Those with whom he came into contact saw him as quarrelsome and discerned what they took for hypocrisy. He had written plays and operas, and he had written a treatise condemning the theatre. He had denigrated culture and deplored intellectualism, and yet he had published a novel and submitted philosophical treatises for academic prizes. A failed tutor, he had put his five children in a foundlings' home, and gone on to publish a treatise on education. Rousseau, for his part, came increasingly to see others' indifference or dislike as evidence of a universal plot to blacken and ostracise him. From 1767 Rousseau, who could not understand why he, who saw himself as basically good and well-meaning, should be the object of hostility, devoted most of his energies as a writer to works of self-justification. By making himself vulnerable, showing himself in detail in an often unfavourable light, he hoped that the world would come to pardon him and accept him as a good man, and thus he would be able finally to forgive himself for all the actions which had imposed on him a lifelong burden of guilt. The best-known and most readable of these late works is the *Confessions*, which give an account of Rousseau's life from 1712 to 1765. They contain, as one would expect, errors of detail, but their importance lies in their recording of the author's feelings and in the novelty of the frank self-examination they contain. New of their kind, they were to influence later generations of writers throughout Europe.

A more insistent attempt at self-justification marks the *Dialogues*, written between 1772 and 1776. This period was followed by one of calm resignation to being misunderstood, recorded by the *Reveries of a Solitary*. Rousseau claimed that these essays were written in order to enable him to recall and reactivate past pleasures, and to console him in his isolation. From then on, he was to be self-sufficient. However, the elegant and harmonious prose in which they are written, and the frequent references to the injustice of Rousseau's enemies raise doubts both about his psychic self-sufficiency and about his intention never to publish them.

A widespread cult of sensibility, inspired by Rousseau's work, arose during the writer's lifetime and characterizes much late 18th-century French literature.

—John Dunkley

ROY, Gabrielle.   Born in St. Boniface, Manitoba, Canada, 22 March 1909.   Educated at St. Joseph Academy, St. Boniface; Teachers Training School, Winnipeg, Manitoba. Married Marcel Carbotte in 1947. Teacher in a village school, 1928-29, and in St. Boniface, 1929-37;

associated with newspapers and magazines in Quebec and France, especially *Le Jour*, 1939-40, and *Bulletin des Agriculteurs*, 1940-45. Recipient: Académie Canadienne-Francaise award, 1946; Prix Fémina, 1947; Lorne Pierce Medal, 1948; Governor-General's award, 1948, 1958, 1977; Prix Duvernay, 1956; Canada Council Medal, 1968; Prix David, 1971; Molson Award, 1977. Fellow, Royal Society of Canada, 1947. Honorary Doctorate: University of Laval, Quebec, 1968. Companion, Order of Canada, 1967. *Died 13 July 1983.*

PUBLICATIONS

Fiction

    Bonheur d'occasion.   1945; as *The Tin Flute*, 1947.
    La Petite Poule d'eau.   1950; as *Where Nests the Water Hen*, 1951.
    Alexandre Chenevert, caissier.   1954; as *The Cashier*, 1955.
    Rue Deschambault.   1955; as *Street of Riches*, 1957.
    La Montagne secrète.   1961; as *The Hidden Mountain*, 1972.
    La Route d'Altamont.   1966; as *The Road Past Altamont*, 1966.
    La Rivière sans repos.   1970; as *Wildflower*, 1970.
    Cet été qui chantait.   1972; as *Enchanted Summer*, 1976.
    Un Jardin au bout du monde.   1975; as *Garden in the Night*, 1977.
    Ces enfants de ma vie.   1977.

Other

    Ma vache Bossie (juvenile).   1976.
    Fragiles lumières de la terre: Écrits divers 1942-1970.   1978.

*

Bibliography: by Paul Socken, in *The Annotated Bibliography of Canada's Major Authors 1* edited by Robert Lecker and Jack David, 1979.

Critical Studies: *La Création romanesque chez Roy* by Monique Genuist, 1966; *Roy* by Phyllis M. Grosskurth, 1969; *Visages de Roy* by Marc Gagné, 1973; *Roy* (in French) by Francois Ricard, 1975; *Three Voices: The Lives of Margaret Laurence, Roy, and Frederick Philip Grove* by Joan Hind-Smith, 1975.

*   *   *

Gabrielle Roy is perhaps the first truly *Canadian* author. Her novels and short stories, written in French, render not only the complex reality of her adopted province of Quebec (*Bonheur d'occasion, The Tin Flute*, which earned her the prestigious French Prix Fémina in 1947, and *Alexandre Chenevert, The Cashier*), as well as of her native St. Boniface in Manitoba (among others, *La Petite Poule d'eau, Where Nests the Water Hen*, but also the world of the Inuit (*La Rivière sans repos, Wildflower*), and of some of the typical immigrant groups that make up the rich texture of Canadian life, such as the Doukhobors, the Chinese, the Poles (*Un Jardin au bout du monde, Garden in the Night*).

The Tin Flute is very traditional in form, a characteristic it may owe to Roy's previous career as a journalist; it is an excellent social document and the first novel in French to chart a major crisis in the history of Quebec: the transition from a rural to an urban society—Montreal—dominated by an English-speaking Establishment, during the great economic upheaval preceding the Second World War.

Although Roy was never again to tackle this kind of large-scale endeavour, the loving sympathy with which she here portrays even her weakest characters and this same theme of change, of its impact on ordinary people, particularly women, are characteristic of almost all her writing. Roy's own constant oscillation between stories of her early years in Manitoba and portrayals of life elsewhere reflects not only the changes she herself knew but also her need to "touch base" periodically in order to accept new challenges, a need with which she could then sympathize in others.

Indeed, there is, in her writing, a clear division between those who can go back to their roots, however temporarily, and those who are condemned to a complete break with the past. The latter are the immigrants, the Chinese, the Poles, and the Doukhobors of *Garden in the Night*. The former are the natives of Canada like Elsa in *Wildflower* who, when threatened by the white man's power, retreats into the Inuit traditions, or Alexander Chenevert, a victim of the social and spiritual upheavals of 1940's, who undertakes a pilgrimage into the past of Quebec. But change, however unpleasant, is inevitable; there can be no permanent return, no stopping the clock. Stasis is death, as Alexandre Chenevert suspects during his journey in *The Cashier* and as Pierre, the artist, discovers at the end of his in *La Montagne secrète* (*The Hidden Mountain*).

There are those who regret Gabrielle Roy's progressive abandoning of the major in favour of the minor key. In so doing, however, she developed a clarity of style and a mastery of the cameo that are missing from her early writings.

—Maïr Verthuy

SADE, Marquis de (Donatien Alphonse-François, Comte de Sade).   Born in Paris, 2 June 1740.   Educated at Collège d'Harcourt, Paris, 1750-54; at a military school for light cavalry, 1754: 2nd Lieutenant, 1755. Served in the French Army during the Seven Years' War: Captain, 1759; resigned commission, 1763. Married Renée Pélagie Cordier de Launay de Montreuil in 1763; two sons and one daughter. Succeeded to the title Comte, 1767; condemned to death for sex offences, 1772, but reprieved; convicted again and imprisoned in Vincennes, 1778-84, Paris, 1784-89, and Charenton, 1789-90; liberated and joined Section des Piques, 1790: organized cavalry and served as hospital inspector, but condemned for moderation; arrested for obscene work (*Justine*), and imprisoned, 1801; in Charenton from 1803. *Died 2 December 1814.*

PUBLICATIONS

Collections

Oeuvres.   35 vols., 1953-70.

Fiction

Justine; ou, Les Malheurs de la vertu.   1791; as *Justine; or, The Misfortunes of Virtue*, 1953.
Aline et Valcour; ou, Le Roman philosophique.   1795.

La Philosophie dan le boudoir. 1795; as *The Bedroom Philosophers*, 1965.

La Nouvelle Justine. 1797; second part, *Juliette; ou, Les Prospérités du Vice*, translated as *Juliette*, 1968.

Pauline et Belval; ou, Les Victimes d'un amour criminel: Anecdote parisienne du XVIIIe siècle. 1798.

Les Crimes de l'amour: Nouvelles héroïques et tragiques. 1800; as *Historiettes, contes, et fabliaux*, edited by Maurice Heine, 1926; selection, as *Quartet*, 1963.

Zoloé et ses deux acolytes; ou, Quelques décades de la vie de trois jolies femmes: Histoire véritable du siècle dernier. 1800.

Le marquise Gange. 1813.

Dorci; ou, La Bizarrerie du sort. 1881.

Les 120 jours de Sodome; ou, L'École du libertinage. 1904; edited by Maurice Heine, 3 vols., 1931-35; as *The 120 Days of Sodom*, 1954.

Dialogue entre un prêtre et un moribund, edited by Maurice Heine. 1926.

Les Infortunes de la vertu, edited by Maurice Heine. 1930.

Histoire secrète d'Isabelle de Bavière, reine de France, edited by Gilbert Lély. 1953.

Adelaide of Brunswick. 1954.

Nouvelles exemplaires, edited by Gilbert Lély. 1958.

The Crimes of Love (short stories). 1964.

Play

Oxtiern; ou, Les Malheurs du libertinage (produced 1791). 1800.

Other

Correspondance inédite, edited by Paul Bourdin. 1929.

Cahiers personnels (1803-04), edited by Gilbert Lély. 1953.

Selected Writings, edited by Margaret Crosland. 1953.

Lettres inédites 1778-1784, edited by Gilbert Lély. 1954.

Écrits politiques (includes *Oxtiern*). 1957.

Mon arrestation du 26 août: Lettre inédite, suivie des Étrennes philosophiques, edited by G. Lély. 1959.

Selections, edited by Paul Dinnage. 1962.

Selected Letters, edited by Margaret Crosland. 1965.

Journal inédit, edited by Georges Daumas. 1970.

*

Bibliography: *The Marquis de Sade: A Bibliography* by E. Pierre Chanover, 1973.

Critical Studies: *The Marquis de Sade* by Donald Thomas, 1976; *De Sade: A Critical Biography* by Ronald Hayman, 1978; *The Sadeian Woman* by Angela Carter, 1979; *Intersections: A Reading of Sade with Bataille, Blanchot, and Klossowski* by Jane Gallop, 1981.

*   *   *

Sade, like Edgar Allan Poe, is one of those writers whose importance is out of all proportion to the actual literary quality of his compositions. As a novelist Sade is a hopeless amateur: his plots are underdeveloped, his characterisation is perfunctory, his settings are purely conventional, and his prose style is undistinguished. Judged solely as a writer of fiction Sade is stolidly third rate, and even the sensational nature of his subject-matter would not have ensured his survival as anything but a moderately competent pornographer were it not for the manic lucidity of his vision of man as a creature of intrinsic and irredeemable evil who—Sade argues at tedious length—must cast aside the last shreds or morality if he is to be true to himself.

In fact, Sade is a sort of inverted *philosophe*, a monstrous child of his time. Where the Encyclopedists, Voltaire, Rousseau, and others urged the basic goodness and perfectibility of mankind and advanced a faith in reason and sensibility, Sade turned their views on their head. For him, human beings are fundamentally evil and any goodness is purely apparent or calculatedly feigned; if genuinely guided by reason and not a watered-down deism, people would be true to their basic nature and deceive, humiliate, and exploit their fellow human beings in the quest for the only thing of true value, sensual gratification of the cruellest imaginable kind. To call him a pessimist is to do Sade an injustice: far from lamenting this state of affairs, he welcomed it and celebrated it in his voluminous writings; and to a certain extent, indeed, he fulfilled his own preaching in his personal lifestyle, although whether he was actually more scandalous than the average petty libertine of the period is open to question. The evidence, such as it is, would seem to indicate that the man whose name gave rise to the term was a rather pathetic sadist in real life.

Of course, Sade did not invent sadism, but he was the first to demonstrate with graphic precision that human beings can and do draw intense erotic pleasure from making others suffer. Most of his wicked torturers are men (although not always so: Juliette is no phallocrat, for instance); since men were socially dominant in his day he tends to present them as sexually dominant too. A typical situation in his novels is that of men who can only attain orgasm when stimulated manually by one woman as they watch another being flogged with vicious cruelty so that each stroke of the whip literally brings their ejaculation to bursting point. This is unsavoury stuff, and it is not to uphold but to betray liberal values to gloss over the sheer nastiness of Sade's vision. Simone de Beauvoir once asked rhetorically whether we should burn Sade's books, and naturally one agrees with her that we should not, so long as we recognise that he catalogues and glorifies behaviour which not only the Nazis but ordinary criminals like the British "moors murderers" have indulged in in real earnest. Sade saw, and described, what people are capable of; therefore in a paradoxical way we owe him a debt of gratitude, but this does not mean that his books, like Hitler's *Mein Kampf*, are anything more than frightening abortions of the human spirit.

—John Fletcher

SAINT-JOHN PERSE. Pseudonym for Marie-René Aléxis Saint-Léger Léger. Born near Point-à-Pitre, Guadeloupe, French West Indies, 31 May 1887. Educated at lycée in Pau; University of Bordeaux; University of Paris; degrees in law, diploma from École des Hautes Études Commerciales. Married Dorothy Milburn Russell in 1958. Deputy Diplomat in political and commercial division, French Foreign Office, Paris, 1914-16; Secretary, French Embassy, Peking, 1916-21; worked with Foreign Minister Aristide Briand, 1921-32; with Ministry of Foreign Affairs: Counsellor, 1925, Chef de Cabinet, 1925-33, Minister, 1927, Ambassador and Secretary-General, 1933-40; deprived of citizenship and left France, 1940; moved to Washington, D.C., 1941: Consultant on French Poetry, Library of Congress, 1941-45; citizenship restored, 1945; returned to France, 1957. Recipient: American Academy Award of Merit Medal, 1950; National Grand Prize, 1959; International Grand Prize for Poetry (Belgium), 1959; Nobel Prize for Literature, 1960. Honorary Member or Fellow:

American Academy of Arts and Sciences; American Academy; Modern Language Association; Bavarian Academy. Honorary degree: Yale University, New Haven, Connecticut. Commander of Arts and Letters; Grand Officer, Legion of Honor. K.C.V.O. (Knight Commander, Royal Victorian Order), 1927; G.B.E. (Knight Grand Cross, Order of the British Empire), 1938; K.C.B. (Knight Commander of the Bath), 1940. *Died 20 September 1975.*

PUBLICATIONS

Verse

Éloges (as Saint-Léger Léger).   1911; bilingual edition, as *Eloges and Other Poems*, 1944; revised edition, 1956.
Anabase.   1924; translated by T.S. Eliot as *Anabasis*, 1930; revised edition, 1938, 1949, 1959.
Exil.   1942; edited by Roger Little, 1973.
Pluies.   1944.
Quatre poèmes 1941-1944.   1944; as *Exil, suivi de Poème à l'étrangère, Pluies, Neiges*, 1945; revised edition, 1946; as *Exile and Other Poems*, translated by Denis Devlin, 1949.
Vents.   1946; as *Winds*, translated by Hugh Chisholm, 1953.
Oeuvre poétique.   2 vols., 1953; revised edition, 1960.
Etroits sont les vaisseaux.   1956.
Amers.   1957; as *Seamarks*, translated by Wallace Fowlie, 1958.
Chronique.   1960; translated by Robert Fitzgerald as *Chronique*, 1961.
L'ordre des oiseaux.   1962; as *Oiseaux*, 1963; as *Birds*, translated by Robert Fitzgerald, 1966.
Éloges, suivi de la Gloire de rois, Anabase, Exil.   1967.
Chante par celle qui fut la...(bilingual edition).   1970.
Collected Poems.   1971.
Chant pour un équinoxe.   1975; as *Song for an Equinox*, translated by Richard Howard, 1977.
Amitiés du prince, edited by Albert Henry.   1979.
Selected Poems, edited and translated by Mary Ann Caws.   1982.

Other

A Selection of Works for an Understanding of World Affairs since 1914.   1943.
Briand (in English).   1943.
La Publication française pendant la guerre: Bibliographie restreinte 1940-1945.   4 vols., n.d..
On Poetry (Nobel Prize acceptance speech; bilingual).   1961.
Oeuvres complètes (includes letters).   1972.
Letters, edited by Arthur J. Knodel.   1979.

*

Bibliography: *Saint-John Perse: A Bibliography for Students of His Poetry* by Roger Little, 1971; revised edition, 1982.

Critical Studies: *Saint-John Perse: A Study of His Poetry* by Arthur Knodel, 1966; *Paul Claudel and Saint-John Perse* by Ruth N. Horry, 1971; *Saint-John Perse* by René M. Galand, 1972; *Saint-John Perse* by Roger Little, 1973; *Worlds Apart: Structural Parallels in the Poetry of Paul Valéry, Saint-John Perse, Benjamin Peret, and René Char* by Elizabeth R. Jackson, 1976.

*   *   *

From his earliest poems, published under the title *Éloges* in 1911, through *Anabase, Exil, Seamarks* and *Oiseaux*, Saint-John Perse continued to describe and analyze the condition of man in our time, the fate of man at this moment in history.

In *Anabase*, in *Vents*, in *Amers*, the poet seeks to express the wholeness of man, the integral forces of his life and his memory. Even more than that, he seeks to project man ahead into the uncharted and the new, into a future that was impatient to live. There is a dramatic movement everywhere in these poems where man, in his historical and natural environment, is playing the role of his existence.

This poet's work relates the secular and the spiritual efforts of man to see himself as a part of the natural world, to tame the hostile powers of the world, to worship the endlessly renewed beauty of the world, to conjugate his ambitions and dreams with the changes and modifications of time. This becomes clear in his last long work, *Amers*, a massive ceremonial poem that revealed an extraordinary sensibility to historic man.

The manner of *Amers* is a fuller development of the manner characteristic of the earlier poems. It involves all the diverse activities of man and states them in successive gestures. The world of this poem has the freshness of a new creation. Whatever legendary elements remain are actualized in this poetry, which is always praise, as the title of the first volume, *Éloges*, revealed.

Amers is a poem that moves far beyond the violence of man's history in order to exalt the drama of his fate which is looked upon as a *march*, the march of all humanity. The poet himself, in a brief statement about his poem, calls it the march toward the sea, *La marche vers la mer*. The word sea, *la mer*, is in the title *amers* ("seamarks"), those signs on the land, both natural and man-made, that guide navigators as they approach the coastline.

The work of Saint-John Perse seems to be consecrated to pointing out a way to reconcile man with nature, and hence with himself. In *Anabase* man is seen confronting the burning of the desert sands; in *Vents* man confronts the violence of the winds, as he confronts the violence of the sea in *Amers*. Not only in *Éloges* but in all the subsequent poems, he praises the sky and sea, the earth and the winds, the snow and the rains.

In his speech at Stockholm, on the occasion of the Nobel prize award in 1960, Saint-John Perse emphasized the power of the adventure called poetry and claimed it is not inferior to the great dramatic adventures of science. The poet's purpose is to consecrate the alliance between man and the creation, and he needs the seamarks to show that the alliance takes place when the land recognizes its relationship of vassal to the sea.

—Wallace Fowlie

SAND, George. Born Amantine Aurore Lucile Dupin in Paris, 1 July 1804. Educated at Nohant, her grandmother's estate, and at Couvent des Anglaises, Paris, 1817-20. Married Casimir Dudevant in 1822 (judicially separated, 1836; died, 1871), one son and one daughter; had liaisons with Jules Sandeau, Alfred de Musset, 1833-34, Chopin, 1838-47, Alexandre Manceau, 1849-65, and others. Inherited Nohant, 1821; left her husband to live in Paris, 1831: journalist, *Le Figaro*, 1831; adopted pseudonym George (briefly Georges) Sand, 1832; contributor, *Revue des Deux Mondes*, 1832-41; co-editor, *Revue Indépendente*, 1841; contributor, *La République*, 1848; settled at Nohant, 1848; lived in Palaiseau, near Versailles, 1864-67. *Died 8 June 1876.*

Collections

Oeuvres autobiographiques, edited by Georges Lubin.   2 vols., 1970.

Fiction

Rose et Blanche, with Jules Sandeau.   1831.
Indiana.   1832; translated as *Indiana*, 1850.
Valentine.   1832; translated as *Valentine*, in *Masterpieces*, 1900-02.
Lélia.   1833; revised edition, 1839; translated as *Lélia*, 1978.
Le Secrétaire intime (includes *Métella*, *La Marquise*, *Lavinia*).   1834; *Lavinia* translated
    as *Lady Blake's Love-Letters*, 1884.
Jacques.   1834; translated as *Jacques*, 1847.
Leone Leoni.   1835; translated as *Leone Leoni*, in *Masterpieces*, 1900-02.
André.   1835; translated as *André*, 1847.
Simon.   1836.
Mauprat.   1837; translated as *Mauprat*, 1847.
Les Maîtres mosaïstes.   1838; as *The Mosaic Workers*, 1844; as *The Mosaic Masters*,
    1847; as *The Master Mosaic Workers*, 1895.
La Dernière Aldini.   1838; as *The Last Aldini*, 1847.
L'Uscoque.   1838; as *The Uscoque*, 1850.
Spiridion.   1839; translated as *Spiridion*, 1842.
Gabriel.   1839.
Pauline.   1840.
Le Compagnon du tour de France.   1841; as *The Companion of the Tour of France*,
    1847; as *The Journeyman Joiner*, 1847.
Horace.   1842.
Consuelo.   1842-43; translated as *Consuelo*, 1846.
La Comtesse de Rudolstadt.   1843-44; as *The Countess of Rudolstadt*, 1847.
Jeanne.   1844; edited by Simone Viernne, 1978.
Le Meunier d'Angibault.   1845; as *The Miller of Angibault*, 1847.
Isidora.   1845.
Teverino.   1845; translated as *Teverino*, 1855; as *Jealousy; or, Teverino*, 1855.
Le Péché de Monsieur Antoine.   1846; as *The Sin of M. Antoine*, in *Masterpieces*,
    1900-02.
La Mare au diable.   1846; as *The Haunted Marsh*, 1848; as *The Enchanted Lake*, 1850; as
    The Devil's Pool, 1861; as *Germaine's Marriage*, 1892.
Lucrezia Floriani.   1846.
Fanchette (in English).   1847.
Le Piccinino.   1847; as *The Piccinino*, 1900.
François le Champi.   1848; as *Francis the Waif*, 1889; as *The Country Waif*, 1930.
La Petite Fadette.   1849; as *Little Fadette*, 1850; as *Fadette*, 1851; as *Fanchon the
    Cricket*, 1863.
Le Château des Déserts.   1851; as *The Castle in the Wilderness*, 1856.
Mont-Revêche.   1853.
La Filleule.   1853.
Les Maîtres sonneurs.   1853; as *The Bagpipers*, 1890.
Le Diable aux champs.   1856.
Évenor et Leucippe.   1856; as *Les Amours de l'âge d'or*, in *Oeuvres*, 1871.
La Daniella.   1857.
Les Dames vertes.   1857.

Les beaux messieurs de Bois-Doré. 1858; as *The Gallant Lords of Bois-Doré*, 1890.
L'Homme de neige. 1858; as *The Snow Man*, 1871.
Narcisse. 1859.
Elle et lui. 1859; as *He and She*, in *Masterpieces*, 1900-02; as *She and He*, 1902.
Flavie. 1859.
Jean de la Roche. 1860.
Constance Verrier. 1860.
La Ville noire. 1860; edited by Jean Courrier, 1978.
Le Marquis de Villemer. 1860-61; as *The Marquis of Villemer*, 1871.
Valvèdre. 1861.
La Famille de Germandre. 1861; as *The Germandre Family*, in *Masterpieces*, 1900-02.
Tamaris. 1862.
Antonia. 1863; translated as *Antonia*, 1870.
Mademoiselle la Quintinie. 1863.
Laura. 1864.
La Confession d'une Jeune fille. 1864.
Monsieur Sylvestre. 1865; translated as *M. Sylvestre*, 1870.
Le Dernier Amour. 1867.
Cadio. 1868.
Mademoiselle Merquem. 1868; edited by Raymond Rheault, 1981; translated as *Mademoiselle Merquem*, 1868.
Pierre qui roule; Le beau Laurence. 1870; as *A Rolling Stone*, 1871 and *Handsome Laurence*, 1871.
Malgrétout. 1870.
Césarine Dietrich. 1871; translated as *Césarine Dietrich*, 1871.
Francia. 1872.
Nanon. 1872; translated as *Nanon*, 1890.
Ma soeur Jeanne. 1874; as *My Sister Jeannie*, 1874.
Flamarande; Les Deux Frères. 1875.
La Tour de Percemont; Marianne. 1876; translated as *The Tower of Percemont*, 1877, and *Marianne*, 1880.

Plays

Les Sept Cordes de la lyre. 1839.
Cosima (produced 1840). 1840.
François le Champi, from her own novel (produced 1849). 1856.
Claudie (produced 1851). 1851.
Le Mariage de Victorine (produced 1851). 1851.
Molière (produced 1851). 1851.
Le Démon du foyer (produced 1852). 1852.
Mauprat, from her own novel (produced 1853). 1854.
Maitre Favilla (produced 1855). 1855; as *La Baronnie de Muhldorf*, n.d.
Lucie (produced 1856). 1856.
Les Beaux Messieurs de Bois-Doré, with Paul Meurice, from the novel by Sand. 1862.
Le Marquis de Villemer, with Dumas fils, from the novel by Sand (produced 1864). 1864.
Le Drac, with Paul Meurice (produced 1864). 1865.
Cadio, with Paul Meurice (produced 1868). 1868.
Théâtre complet. 3 vols., 1879.

Other

Lettres d'un voyageur. 1837; as *Letters of a Traveller*, 1847.

Oeuvres. 27 vols., 1837-42 (and later editions).
Un Hiver à Majorque. 1842; as *Winter in Majorca,* 1956.
Histoire de France écrite sous la dictée de Blaise Bonnin. 1848.
Adriani. 1853.
Histoire de ma vie. 20 vols., 1854-55.
La Guerre. 1859.
Journal d'un voyageur pendant la guerre. 1871.
Impressions et souvenirs. 1873; as *Recollections,* 1874; as *Impressions and Reminiscences,* 1876.
Contes d'une grand'mère (juvenile). 2 vols., 1873-76; as *Tales of a Grandmother,* 1930.
Questions d'art et de littérature. 1878.
Questions politiques et sociales. 1879.
Journal intime, edited by Aurore Sand. 1926; as *Intimate Journal,* edited by Marie Howe Jenney, 1929.
Letters, edited by Veronica Lucas. 1930.
Correspondance inédit, with Marie Dorval, edited by Simone André-Maurois. 1953.
Sand et Alfred de Musset: Correspondance..., edited by Louis Évrard. 1956.
Lettres inédites de Sand et de Pauline Viardot 1839-1849, edited by Thérèse Marix-Spire. 1959.
Lettres à Sainte-Beuve, edited by Östen Södergård. 1964.
Correspondance, edited by Georges Lubin. 10 vols., 1964-72.
Correspondance, with Flaubert, edited by Alphonse Jacobs. 1981.

*

Bibliography: *Bibliographie des premières publications des Romans de Sand* by Georges Colin, 1965.

Critical Studies: *Lélia: The Life of Sand* by André Maurois, 1953; *Sand: A Biography* by Curtis Cate, 1975; *Sand: A Biography* by Ruth Jordan, 1976; *Sand and the Victorians* by Patricia Thomson, 1977; *The Double Life of Sand: Woman and Writer* by Renée Winegarten, 1978; *Sand and the Victorian World* by Paul G. Blount, 1979; *Turgenev and Sand* by Patrick Waddington, 1981.

*   *   *

Like her eighteenth century predecessor, Germaine de Staël, and her twentieth century equivalent, Simone de Beauvoir, George Sand (the English spelling of her assumed Christian name was her choice) showed how indissoluble the link has always been so far in Western culture between feminism and political ideas which are advanced to the point of being revolutionary by contemporary standards. Her tempestuous life-style, involving as it did the break-up of her early marriage with Casimir Dudevant and a series of rather ostentatious *affaires* with Alfred de Musset, Fréderic Chopin, and several others, was reflected in the subject-matter of her early novels. These, and especially *Lélia,* probably her best, developed the Romantic theme of the incompatibility between sexual passion and conventional family life, were much read in her day, and are not wholly devoid of interest for the modern reader. She identified herself closely and fervently with the early socialist movement, and described working conditions in the France of her time in *Le Compagnon du tour de France.*

Like Victor Hugo, she strongly disapproved of the military *coup d'état* whereby Napoleon III put an end to the existence and hopes of the 1848 revolution in December 1851, and retired into private life. She lived in her native Berry, in the West of France, which she had already described in idyllic tones in *La Mare au Diable* (*The Devil's Pool*) and *François le Champi.*

These pastoral novels are still admired and read today, and provided consolation for the narrator in the first volume of Proust's *À la recherche du temps perdu* on that memorable evening when his mother was allowed—and allowed herself—to calm his anguish by spending the night in his bedroom. While strongly disapproving of her progressive ideas, Gustave Flaubert kept up a long and interesting correspondence with George Sand, and she wrote voluminously to other intellectuals and men of letters of her day. Although Charles Baudelaire regarded her as the epitome of all that was most obnoxious in the optimistic humanitarianism of mid-19th-century France, her sense of human and humane values is in many ways preferable to the misanthropic pessimism which informs *Les Fleurs du Mal* and *Madame Bovary*. Yet one only needs to compare her novels to those of the English 19th-century writer whom she most resembles, George Eliot, to see that the woman who was *née* Amantine Aurore Lucile Dupin lacked both the initial intelligence and the understanding of society which make *Middlemarch* a masterpiece.

—Philip Thody

SAPPHO. Born in Eresos, Lesbos, c. 612 B.C. Married; one daughter. Spent part of her life in exile in Sicily; lived most of her life in Mytilene.

PUBLICATIONS

[*Verse*], edited by Edgar Lobel and Denys Page. 1955; also edited with works of Alcaeus by Denys Page, 1955 (includes translation), and by Eva-Maria Voigt, 1971; translated by David A. Campbell (Loeb edition), 1983; also translated by Mary Barnard, 1958, Willis Barnstone, 1965, Guy Davenport, 1965, and S.G. Groden, 1966.

*

Critical Studies: *Sappho and Her Influence* by D.M. Robinson, 1924; *Sappho and Alcaeus: An Introduction to the Study of Ancient Lesbian Poetry* by Denys Page, 1955; *Three Classical Poets: Sappho, Catullus, and Juvenal* by Richard Jenkyns, 1982; *Three Archaic Poets: Archilochus, Alcaeus, Sappho* by Anne Pippin Burnett, 1983; *The Golden Lyre: The Themes of the Greek Lyric Poets* by David A. Campbell, 1983.

*   *   *

The nine books of Sappho's poems edited at Alexandria did not survive the Middle Ages. All that remained of them were 120 quotations made by various writers. These were not collected into a single volume until 1733 and it was not until 1885 that all were translated and published together in English. In the past century the amount of surviving Sappho has almost doubled with the recovery of fragments of her poems preserved on papyri. In 1955 Lobel and Page edited the new together with the older fragments and produced the standard text (LP). For all the achievements of modern scholarship, the fragmentary state of Sappho's poems remains the most powerful factor conditioning our appreciation of her.

A second factor is the nature of her eroticism. Her most famous poem, imitated by Catullus and quoted in part by Longinus, describes her feelings on seeing a girl she loves seated beside a man (31 LP). The hymn to Aphrodite, Sappho's only poem to survive in its entirety, calls on the goddess to help her win the love of an unnamed girl (1 LP). The situation, unambiguous in the Greek, so embarrassed English translators that they substituted a young man for the girl; it was not until 1883, in Symonds's version, that the girl was allowed back onto the page. A similar, possibly worse distortion results from the opposite tendency, overemphasis on Sappho's sexual orientation. Only one of the new (and none of the older) fragments contains a hint of physical contact between Sappho and a girl or between two girls of Sappho's circle (94 LP, 21-23).

Most of Sappho's poems address someone specific; others belong to a specific occasion, such as a wedding. Portions of her wedding songs, for which she was famous in antiquity, survived in quotation, but the longest specimen we now have is papyrus fragment 44 LP, a poem in which Sappho apparently compared the bride and groom to Andromache and Hektor on their wedding day. Another poem in which she uses myth to highlight the present is fragment 16 LP, which opens by declaring that beauty is for each person not what others call beautiful but what each desires for himself; the point is then illustrated by the myth of Helen, who abandoned husband, home, and daughter for love of Paris. The last surviving stanza draws a parallel between Helen's ruinous passion and Sappho's own longing for Anaktoria. In 94 LP we find Sappho consoling a girl for a loss she no doubt feels herself. The objectification of her emotions is the most striking feature of her art.

Sappho's reputation, high in antiquity, is so high in modern times that new discoveries can hardly enhance it. The papyrus fragments, however, have given us a fuller view of her work. We can tell that she employed a more traditional diction in her wedding poems. Her love songs cleave to the vernacular of Lesbos, combining directness of expression with rigorous metrical control. Comparison of 34 and 96 LP shows that she was not averse to using the same image twice. The word "again" recurs with remarkable frequency in her love poems, suggesting a conventionality that we could not detect before because we had so few examples. But for all the qualities that make her appealing to a contemporary audience, her conviction of her own immortality is quintessentially Greek. When she admonishes her daughter not to mourn for her death because "it is not right that there should be lamentation in the house of those who serve the Muses" (130 LP), she is looking back to Hesiod and forward to Pindar.

—Frank J. Nisetich

SARTRE, Jean-Paul (-Charles-Aymard). Born in Paris, 21 June 1905. Educated at Lycée Montaigne and Lycée Henri-IV, Paris; École Normale Supérieure, Paris, agrégation in philosophy 1929. Served in the French Army 1929-31, and World War II: captured, 1940; escaped, 1941. Began lifelong relationship with the writer Simone de Beauvoir in 1929; Sartre had one adopted daughter. Professor, Lycée du Havre, 1931-32 and 1934-36; Lycée de Laon, 1936-37; Lycée Pasteur, Paris, 1937-39; Lycée Condorcet, Paris, 1941-44; traveled and lectured extensively during the 1950's and 1960's: member of Bertrand Russell's International War Crimes Tribunal, 1966. Founding Editor, with de Beauvoir, *Les Temps Modernes*, from 1945; Editor, *La Cause du Peuple*, from 1970, *Tout*, 1970-74, *Révolution*, 1971-74, and *Libération*, 1973-74; Founder, with Maurice Clavel, Liberation news service, 1971. Recipient: French Institute Research grant, 1933; Popular Novel prize, 1940; New York Drama Critics Circle award, 1947;

Grand Novel prize, 1950; Omegna Prize (Italy), 1960; Nobel Prize for Literature, 1964 (refused). Foreign Member, American Academy of Arts and Sciences. *Died 15 April 1980.*

PUBLICATIONS

Fiction

La Nausée. 1938; as *The Diary of Antoine Roquentin*, 1949; as *Nausea*, 1949.
Le Mur. 1939; as *The Wall and Other Stories*, 1949; as *Intimacy and Other Stories*, 1949.
Les Chemins de la liberté (Paths of Freedom):
    L'Âge de raison. 1945; as *The Age of Reason*, 1947.
    Le Sursis. 1945; as *The Reprieve*, 1947.
    La Mort dans l'âme. 1949; as *Iron in the Soul*, 1950; as *Troubled Sleep*, 1951.
Oeuvres romanesques, edited by Michel Contat and Michel Rybalka. 1981.

Plays

Bariona; ou, Le Fils du tonnerre (produced 1940). 1962; as *Bariona; or, The Son of Thunder*, in *The Writings 2*, 1974.
Les Mouches (produced 1943). 1943; as *The Flies*, in *The Flies and In Camera*, 1946.
Huis clos (produced 1944). 1945; as *In Camera*, in *The Flies and In Camera*, 1946; as *No Exit*, in *No Exit and The Flies*, 1947.
The Flies and In Camera. 1946.
Morts sans sépulture (produced 1946). 1946; as *Men Without Shadows*, in *Three Plays* (UK), 1949; as *The Victors*, in *Three Plays* (USA), 1949.
La Putain respectueuse (produced 1946). 1946; as *The Respectable Prostitute*, in *Three Plays* (UK), 1949; as *The Respectful Prostitute*, in *Three Plays* (USA), 1949.
No Exit and The Flies. 1947.
Les Jeux sont faits (screenplay). 1947; as *The Chips Are Down*, 1948.
Les Mains sales (produced 1948). 1948; as *Crime Passionnel*, in *Three Plays* (UK), 1949; as *Dirty Hands*, in *Three Plays* (USA), 1949.
L'Engrenage (screenplay). 1948; as *In the Mesh*, 1954.
Three Plays (UK; includes *Men Without Shadows, The Respectable Prostitute, Crime Passionnel*). 1949.
Three Plays (USA; includes *The Victors, The Respectful Prostitute, Dirty Hands*). 1949.
Le Diable et le bon dieu (produced 1951). 1951; as *Lucifer and the Lord*, 1953; as *The Devil and the Good Lord*, in *The Devil and the Good Lord and Two Other Plays*, 1960.
Kean, from the play by Dumas père (produced 1953). 1954; translated as *Kean*, 1954.
Nekrassov (produced 1955). 1956; translated as *Nekrassov*, 1956.
Les Séquestrés d'Altona (produced 1959). 1960; as *Loser Wins*, 1960; as *The Condemned of Altona*, 1961.
The Devil and the Good Lord and Two Other Plays (includes *Kean* and *Nekrassov*). 1960.
Les Troyennes, from a play by Euripides (produced 1965). 1965; as *The Trojan Women*, 1967.

    Screenplays: *Les Jeux sont faits (The Chips Are Down)*, 1947; *L'Engrenage*, 1948; *Les Sorcières de Salem (Witches of Salem)*, 1957.

Other

L'Imagination. 1936; as *Imagination: A Psychological Critique*, 1962.

Esquisse d'une théorie des émotions. 1939; as *The Emotions: Outline of a Theory*, 1948; as *Sketch for a Theory of the Emotions*, 1962.

L'Imaginaire: Psychologie phénoménologique de l'imagination. 1940; as *Psychology of the Imagination*, 1949.

L'Être et le néant: Essai d'ontologie phénoménologique. 1943; as *Being and Nothingness*, 1956.

L'Existentialisme est un humanisme. 1946; as *Existentialism*, 1947; as *Existentialism and Humanism*, 1948.

Explication de "L'Etranger." 1946.

Réflexions sur la question juive. 1947; as *Anti-Semite and Jew*, 1948; as *Portrait of an Anti-Semite*, 1948.

Baudelaire. 1947; translated as *Baudelaire*, 1949.

Situations 1-10. 10 vols., 1947-76; selections as *What Is Literature?*, 1949; *Literary and Philosophical Essays*, 1955; *Situations*, 1965; *The Communists and Peace*, 1965; *The Ghost of Stalin*, 1968 (as *The Spectre of Stalin*, 1969); *Between Existentialism and Marxism*, 1974; *Life/Situations*, 1977; *Sartre in the Seventies*, 1978.

Entretiens sur la politique, with others. 1949.

Saint Genet, Comédien et martyr. 1952; as *Saint Genet, Actor and Martyr*, 1963.

L'Affaire Henri Martin, with others. 1953.

The Transcendence of the Ego: An Existentialist Theory of Consciousness. 1957.

Critique de la raison dialectique: Théorie des ensembles pratiques. 1960; as *Critique of Dialectical Reason: Theory of Practical Ensembles*, 1976.

On Cuba. 1961.

Les Mots (autobiography). 1963; as *Words*, 1964; as *The Words*, 1964.

Essays in Aesthetics, edited by Wade Baskin. 1963.

Que peut la littérature?, with others. 1965.

The Philosophy of Sartre, edited by Robert Denoon Cumming. 1966.

Of Human Freedom, edited by Wade Baskin. 1967.

Essays in Existentialism, edited by Wade Baskin. 1967.

On Genocide. 1968.

Les Communistes ont peur de la révolution. 1969.

L'Idiot de la famille: Gustave Flaubert de 1821 à 1857. 3 vols., 1971-72; as *The Family Idiot: Gustave Flaubert 1821-1857*, 1981— .

War Crimes in Vietnam, with others. 1971.

Un théâtre de situations, edited by Michel Contat and Michel Rybalka. 1973; as *On Theatre*, 1976.

Politics and Literature. 1973.

The Writings 2: Selected Prose, edited by Michel Contat and Michel Rybalka. 1974.

On a raison de se révolter, with others. 1974.

*

Bibliography: *The Writings 1: A Bibliographical Life* by Michel Contat and Michel Rybalka, 1974; *Sartre: A Bibliography of International Criticism* by Robert Wilcocks, 1975; *Sartre and His Critics: An International Bibliography 1938-1980* by François and Claire Lapointe, 1981.

Critical Studies: *Sartre, Romantic Rationalist* by Iris Murdoch, 1953; *Sartre: a Literary and Political Study*, 1960, and *Sartre: A Biographical Introduction*, 1971, both by Philip Thody; *Sartre: A Collection of Critical Essays* edited by Mary Warnock, 1971; *From Sartre to the New Novel* by Betty T. Rahv, 1974; *Critical Fictions: The Literary Criticism of Sartre* by Joseph Halpern, 1976; *Sartre* by Peter Caws, 1979; *Sartre and Surrealism* by Marius Perrin, 1980; *Sartre as Biographer* by Douglas Collins, 1980; *Sartre and Flaubert* by Hazel E. Barnes, 1981; *The Philosophy of Sartre* edited by Paul Arthur Schilpp, 1981.

*   *   *

Jean-Paul Sartre can be said to have made a profession of being the gadfly of France and of a sizeable portion of the western world for some three decades following the second World War. His moral authority extended far beyond the actual readership of his literary, philosophical, and political writings, although these were quite numerous and varied. Among intellectuals in the English-speaking world, only Bertrand Russell was his equal as a force in marshalling opinion on the left, and together they created the International War Crimes Tribunal in 1966 to condemn the American war in Vietnam. Sartre's career as a writer and thinker traces a long, rather tortuous route from the radical individualism of his beginnings to spokesman for all wars of national liberation, and for proletarian causes of every sort, from the 1950's onward.

On the eve of World War II, Sartre began to emerge as a redoubtable if impetuous critic of the previous generation of French writers, in articles (on Giraudoux and Mauriac, most notably) that he contributed to the *Nouvelle Revue Française*. At the same time he published a first novel, *Nausea*, that presents an atheist intellectual hero, seriously at odds with society, who undergoes a psychological crisis that threatens his very identity. He ultimately concludes that salvation is to be found only in the making of art. Antoine Roquentin, the hero of this pre-existentialist *Kunstlerroman*, thus bears a marked resemblance to Proust's Marcel, and the novel has frequently been taken to represent a critical phase of development within European Modernism. An early collection of short stories evidencing numerous naturalistic and ironic features (*The Wall*) dates from this same period, which antedates the Sartrean notion of the writer's commitment to his time and to changing the world.

His experiences in a German prisoner of war camp from June 1940 to March 1941 had a determining effect on Sartre's notion of ethical choice. For Christmas 1940 he wrote a play on the massacre of the Innocents entitled *Bariona; or, The Son of Thunder*, which he produced in the prison camp. The effect of the play on his fellow prisoners moved Sartre deeply, as he was to relate much later to Jean Genet. From this experience derives a central feature of his early theater: the conversion of a protagonist to responsible action in the name of a community with whom he henceforth recognizes a bond. This was to be the treatment he would give the Orestes myth in his first play produced commercially in occupied Paris, *The Flies*. His second play, *No Exit*, produced a year later, in 1944, has provided two of the most memorble catch phrases of Sartrean existentialism: "You are—your life, and nothing else"; and: "Hell is—other people!"

Sartre's optimism concerning the creative writer's ability to influence others and, in particular, to jar them from complacency to a recognition that all mankind is doomed to freedom—reliance upon exterior moral values and trust in an inner life being equally reprehensible forms of "bad faith," in his view—stimulated him to formulate an austere, yet exhilarating form of the writer's commitment (*engagement*) in *L'Existentialisme est un humanisme* early in the postwar years. This existentialist ethos, in which the individual is obliged to make choices as though he were choosing for all mankind, owes much to Kant's categorical imperative, and possibly more to the Alsatian Protestant values of Sartre's grandfather Schweitzer, who reared him. (Despite the obvious differences in their professed thought and in their careers, Jean-Paul Sartre and his second cousin, Albert Schweitzer, had this important element of their formative years in common.) This difficult and restless version of ethics represents Sartre's first major effort to overcome the individualist ontology of *Being and Nothingness*, which belongs conceptually to Sartre's prewar period.

Sartre had high hopes for a novelistic tetralogy published under the programmatic title, *Paths of Freedom*, from 1945 to 1949. As a formal experiment, it is a modification of techniques developed by the prewar American novel. In it Sartre intended to align his notion of individual freedom with responsible political action. Possibly because Sartre wished to maintain that a fictional character is "free" of the author, the proposed synthesis of the work, projected for the fourth novel, was never completed. It is probably for a similar reason that Sartre never wrote the formal treatise on ethics that he had promised as an accompaniment to *Being and Nothingness*. Sartre was to write several more plays between 1951 (*The Devil and the Good Lord*) and 1965 (*The Trojan Women*), as well as three screenplays.

Les Temps Modernes, a magazine of contemporary commentary co-founded by Sartre with Simone de Beauvoir and Maurice Merleau-Ponty in 1945, rapidly took its place as the foremost moulder of opinion among readers of the non-Communist left. From the early 1950's onward, Sartre's evolution as a writer is inseparable from his relations with the French Communist Party. A series of essays prompted by the Cold War and published in English as *The Communists and Peace* appeared in *Les Temps Modernes* from July 1952. At the same time Sartre had a noisy falling-out with Camus. Seen from a sufficient distance, Sartre's political articles resemble many other pro-Soviet, anti-Atlantic Alliance positions. Their real interest, however, lies in Sartre's efforts to establish a position independent of the Party, while defending it against its enemies. The same decade of the 1950's again found Sartre thinking against a former self, the author of *Being and Nothingness*. Whereas he had initially refused Marxist historical determinism as well as the Freudian unconscious, the methodological preface to his *Critique of Dialectical Reason* (1960) attempted to conciliate the two.

Still another activity that spans his existentialist and Marxist periods is that of biographer, in a series of existential psychoanalyses of Baudelaire, Genet, and, eventually, himself. The least interesting of these books is *Baudelaire*, which on existentialist principles indicts Baudelaire for making the wrong choices in his life. *Saint Genet, Actor and Martyr* is richer, more sympathetic, and, although characteristically turgid at times, a better piece of writing. *The Words* may well stand as Sartre's literary masterwork.

Sartre enjoyed a lifelong love-hate relationship with Flaubert, and, had he been able to complete the promised study of *Madame Bovary* (yet another unfinished major project), he might have given the world the most thorough critical study any major writer ever devoted to another. As it stands, in three volumes, *The Family Idiot* is rather the most extensive application of Sartre's new critical method as set forth in the *Critique of Dialectical Reason*.

By the time he published his autobiography, Sartre had completely lost confidence in the ability of writers to change anything in the world through their writing. Never one to avoid taking a stand, however, he refused the Nobel Prize for Literature that same year, on the grounds that it rewarded anti-Soviet writers. From the mid-1960's until his death, Sartre published nothing literary, aside from his work on Flaubert, and even his political writing tended progressively toward journalism. In 1969 he signed the pamphlet *Les Communistes ont peur de la révolution*, accusing the French Communist Party of conservatism. The student revolt of 1968 finally provided him with an opportunity to mount the barricades, at age 63, and exhort youth to bring about the Revolution. In 1970, consistent with these principles and to the chagrin of many former admirers, Sartre assumed the editorship of the rabble-rousing Maoist paper, *La Cause du Peuple*. Sartre's last decade was marked by ruined health and near-blindness. On the eve of his death, near the end of his seventy-fifth year, he was arguably the best-known living writer in the world.

—A. James Arnold

SCHILLER, (Johann Christoph) Friedrich von. Born in Marbach am Neckar, 10 November 1759. Educated at village school in Lorch; Latin school, Ludwigsburg, 1766-72. Married Charlotte von Lengefeld in 1790; two sons and two daughters. Conscripted in 1773, and studied law, later medicine, in military academy of Duke Karl August of Württemberg: regimental surgeon, 1780; his writing displeased the Duke, so he left Württemberg, 1782: contract as writer for Mannheim theatre, 1783-84, then journalist: Editor, *Rheinische Thalia*, 1785-93; joined the Körner circle, in Leipzig, then in Dresden; in Weimar, 1787: through Goethe's help, obtained professorship of history at University of Jena, 1789-91 (resigned because of illness); lived in

Weimar after 1799, and several plays produced under Goethe's direction. Raised to nobility by Emperor Franz II, 1802. *Died 9 May 1805.*

PUBLICATIONS

Collections

Sämtliche Werke (Säkular-Ausgabe), edited by Eduard von der Hellen. 16 vols., 1904-05.
Sämtliche Werke, edited by Otto Güntter and Georg Witkowski. 20 vols., 1910-11.
Werke [Nationalausgabe], edited by Julius Petersen and Gerhard Fricke. 1943— .
Sämtliche Werke, edited by G. Fricke, H.G. Cröpfert, and H. Stubenrauch. 5 vols., 1958-59.
Works (Bohn Standard Library). 4 vols., 1846-49.

Plays

Die Räuber (produced 1782). 1781; as The Robbers, 1792; also translated by F.J. Lamport, 1979.
Die Verschwörung des Fiesko zu Genua (produced 1784). 1783; as Fiesco; or, The Genoese Conspiracy, 1796.
Kabale und Liebe (produced 1784). 1784; as Cabal and Love, 1795; as The Minister, 1798; as The Harper's Daughter, 1813.
Don Carlos (produced 1787). 1787; translated as Don Carlos, 1798; also translated by James Kirkup, in The Classic Theatre, edited by Eric Bentley, 1959.
Egmont, from the play by Goethe (produced 1796). 1857.
Wallenstein: Wallensteins Lager, Die Piccolomini, Wallensteins Tod (produced 1798-99). 1798-99; translated as Wallenstein, by Coleridge, 1800; also translated by Charles E. Passage, 1958, and F.J. Lamport, 1979.
Maria Stuart (produced 1800). 1801; translated as Mary Stuart, 1801; also translated by Stephen Spender, 1959, and F.J. Lamport, in Five German Tragedies, 1969.
Macbeth, from the play by Shakespeare (produced 1800). 1801.
Nathan der Weise, from the play by Lessing (produced 1801).
Die Jungfrau von Orleans (produced 1801). 1801; as The Maid of Orleans, 1835.
Turandot, from the play by Gozzi (produced 1802). 1802.
Der Neffe als Onkel, from a play by Louis-Benoit Picard (produced 1803). 1842; as The Nephew as Uncle, 1856.
Der Parasit, from a play by Louis-Benoit Picard (produced 1803). 1806; as The Parasite, 1856.
Die Braut von Messina (produced 1803). 1803; as The Bride of Messina, 1837.
Wilhelm Tell (produced 1804). 1804; translated as William Tell, 1825; also translated by William F. Mainland, 1972.
Die Huldigung der Künste (produced 1804). 1805.
Phädra, from the play by Racine (produced 1805). 1805.
Iphigenie in Aulis, from the play by Euripides. 1807.

Fiction

Der Verbrecher aus Infamie. 1786; as Der Verbrecher aus verlorener Ehre, 1792; as The Dishonoured Irreclaimable, 1826.
Der Geisterseher. 1787-89; as The Ghost Seer, or Apparitionist, 1795; as The Armenian, 1800.

Spiel des Schicksals. 1789.

Verse

Anthologie auf das Jahr 1782. 1782.
Gedichte. 2 vols., 1800-03.

Other

*Die Geschichte des Abfalls der vereinigten Niederlande von der spanischen Regie-
rung.* 1788; as *History of the Rise and Progress of the Belgian Republic,* 1807.
Geschichte des dreissigjährigen Krieges. 1793; as *The History of the Thirty Years' War
in Germany,* 1799.
Über naive und sentimentalische Dichtung. 1795-96; as *On Simple and Sentimental
Poetry,* in *Essays Aesthetical and Philosophical,* 1884; as *On the Naive and Sentimental
in Literature,* 1981.
Briefe über die ästhetische Erziehung des Menschen. 1795; as *Upon the Aesthetic
Culture of Man,* in *Philosophical and Aesthetic Letters and Essays,* 1845; as *On the
Aesthetic Education of Man,* 1954.
Briefwechsel, with Cotta, edited by W. Vollmer. 1876.
Briefwechsel, with Goethe, edited by F. Muncker. 4 vols., 1892.
Briefe, edited by Fritz Jonas. 7 vols., 1892-96.
Briefwechsel, with Körner, edited by L. Gaiger. 4 vols., 1893; edited by Klaus Berghahn,
1973.
Briefwechsel, with Wilhelm von Humboldt, edited by A. Leitzmann. 1900.
Briefe 1776-1789, edited by Karl Pörnbacher. 1969.

*

Bibliography: *Schiller-Bibliographie 1893-1958* by W. Vulpius, 1959; supplements in *Jahrbuch
der Deutschen Schillergesellschaft.*

Critical Studies: *Schiller's Drama: Theory and Practice* by E.L. Stahl, 1954; *Schiller and the
Ideal of Freedom,* 1959, and *The Drama of Schiller,* 1963, both by Ronald D. Miller; *Schiller's
Writings on Aesthetics* by Stanley S. Kerry, 1961; *Schiller* by Bernt von Heiseler, 1962; *Schiller,
The Poet as Historian* by Walter M. Simon, 1966; *Schiller, The Dramatic Writer* by H.B.
Garland, 1969; *The Theatre of Goethe and Schiller* by John E. Prudhoe, 1973; *Schiller, A
Master of the Tragic Form* by Ilse Graham, 1975; *Schiller* by Charles E. Passage, 1975;
Schiller: Medicine, Psychology, and Literature by Kenneth Dewhurst and Nigel Reeves, 1978;
Schiller by John D. Simons, 1981; *Schiller and the Historical Character* by Lesley Sharpe,
1982.

*   *   *

Schiller is the principal writer, after Goethe, first of the "Sturm und Drang," then of the
Classical movement in German literature. Goethe observed in 1827 that "the idea of freedom
dominates all Schiller's work...in his youth it was physical, in his later years ideal freedom that
concerned him." The three early prose plays, *Die Räuber, Fiesko,* and *Kabale und Liebe,* all
depict heroes who rebel against physical and social confinement, who seek to be the architects
of their own and others' earthly destinies, and who fail tragically because they seek to fly too
high, to transcend the limits inherent in human nature. All begin as idealists, but Karl Moor in
Die Räuber turns into a criminal, Fiesko and on a smaller scale Ferdinand (in *Kabale und
Liebe*) into tyrants like the corrupt rulers they oppose. Their rebellion is expressed in a dramatic
style of extreme forcefulness, even violence, which is also found in Schiller's early poetry. *Don*

Carlos marks the beginning of a transition. It is still concerned with "physical"—in this case social and political—freedom, and it evokes this ideal in language recalling what is probably (thanks to Beethoven) Schiller's best-known poem, the Ode to Joy (*An die Freude*), which dates from the same period. It also shows how idealism may verge upon fanaticism (Schiller's verdict on the political idealist Marquis Posa remains ambiguous and disputed); and the nominal hero and his friend Posa appear scarcely more tragic than their tyrannical adversary, Philip II of Spain, seen as the prisoner of history, of the Inquisition, and of the despotic system of which he himself is the head. *Don Carlos* anticipates Schiller's mature dramas in its adoption of blank verse and elevated diction, in contrast to the prose of the early plays, with their often uneasy mixture of earthy realism and exaggerated rhetoric. But it is an over long and unwieldy play, and did not satisfy its creator, who after it completed no more dramatic work for thirteen years.

Those years were principally devoted to aesthetic, historiographical, and philosophical studies. The instinctive playwright now yielded to the theorist, concerned to define the nature and function of his own art and of art in general, the role of art and culture in human society and history. The idealistic champion of freedom and progress was shocked by the excesses of the French Revolution (though on the strength of *Die Räuber* he was made an honorary citizen of the French Republic) and now sought to understand the nature of the historical process and to relate to it the ultimate freedom of the human will in which he still strove to believe. He grappled intensively with the philosophy of Kant, and sought to understand the human and artistic character of his friend Goethe, so different from his own. The great essay *Über naive und sentimentalische Dichtung* sums up all these speculative concerns. Schiller's collaboration with Goethe extended to joint authorship in the case of the *Xenien*, satirical epigrams on the state of contemporary German culture, and friendly rivalry in the ballads of which both men produced notable examples in 1797.

The *Wallenstein* trilogy ushers in Schiller's dramatic maturity. The themes of self-determination, of idealism, of personal and political freedom take on new significance against a background of war and of harsh political necessity, and Schiller hints at parallels between the Thirty Years' War and the revolutionary wars of his own day. True freedom is now seen to be "ideal" in the sense that it cannot be achieved in the real world, or measured by any kind of material success, but is only to be found in the acceptance of moral responsibility. This is also the theme of *Maria Stuart*, embodied in the contrast between the physical and political freedom achieved by Elizabeth of England at the price of her moral dignity, and the spiritual freedom achieved by Mary Queen of Scots at the price of her own death and the defeat of her political cause. These two works mark the summit of Schiller's classical phase, combining a rich and complex historical subject-matter and lofty philosophical themes with a high degree of dramatic concentration and formal discipline—a synthesis, as Schiller himself defined his aim, of Shakespearian and Sophoclean drama.

His later plays are more experimental, tending in *Die Braut von Messina* to further classical concentration, in *Die Jungfrau von Orleans* and *Wilhelm Tell* to a more Romantic expansiveness, with large casts and colourful spectacle. All three again show freedom to be found not in self-assertion but in the acceptance of responsibility, though in *Die Jungfrau* and particularly in *Wilhelm Tell* this moral autonomy appears as the guarantee of the ultimate possibility of national and political liberation. But if in these works Schiller appears to oppose an optimistic vision of history to the chaos of his own times, the unfinished *Demetrius*, on which he was working when he died, seems to revert to the grimmer realism of *Wallenstein*.

Schiller's later plays established the historical drama as the major serious dramatic form in German; this prestige the form still to some extent enjoys. The plays themselves, with their elevated sentiments and elevated language, have fallen somewhat out of theatrical fashion in recent years: modern taste has tended to prefer the rawness and vigour and the more direct political engagement of his earlier works. The idealism of *Die Jungfrau von Orleans* was parodied by Brecht in his *Die heilige Johanna der Schlachthöfe* (1930), and more recently *Wilhelm Tell* and *Maria Stuart* have similarly been irreverently "demythologised" by Max Frisch and Wolfgang Hildesheimer respectively. Latterly a number of German academic critics have drawn attention to the complexity and subtlety of Schiller's vision of history; but it remains doubtful whether his mature works will receive appropriate productions in a theatre still largely dominated by the Brechtian tradition, so resolutely opposed to the view of art which he and Goethe in their classical collaboration propounded.

—F.J. Lamport

SCHNITZLER, Arthur. Born in Vienna, 15 May 1862. Educated at Akademisches Gymnasium, Vienna, 1871-79; University of Vienna, 1879-85, M.D. 1885. Married Olga Gussmann in 1903 (separated, 1921); one son and one daughter. Medical intern, 1885-88; Assistant at Allgemeine Poliklinik, 1888-93, then in private practice. Recipient: Bauernfeld Prize, 1899, 1903; Grillparzer Prize, 1908; Raimund Prize, 1910; Vienna Volkstheater Prize, 1914. *Died 21 October 1931.*

PUBLICATIONS

Collections

> *Gesammelte Werke: Die erzählenden Schriften, Die dramatischen Werke, Aphorismen und Betrachtungen.* 5 vols., 1961-67.

Plays

> *Anatol.* 1893; edited by Ernst L. Offermann, 1964; as *Anatol: A Sequence of Dialogues,* 1911; as *The Affairs of Anatol,* 1933; as *Anatol,* in *The Round Dance and Other Plays,* 1982.
> *Das Märchen* (produced 1893). 1894.
> *Liebelei* (produced 1895). 1896; as *Light-o'-Love,* 1912; as *Playing with Love,* 1914; as *Love Games,* in *The Round Dance and Other Plays,* 1982.
> *Freiwild.* 1898; as *Free Game,* 1913.
> *Das Vermächtnis.* 1899; as *The Legacy,* in *Poet Lore,* July-August 1911.
> *Der grüne Kakadu, Paracelsus, Die Gefährtin.* 1899; as *The Green Cockatoo and Other Plays* (includes *Paracelsus, The Mate*), 1913; *Der grüne Kakadu* also translated as *The Duke and the Actress,* 1910.
> *Reigen* (produced 1920). 1900; as *Hands Around,* 1920; as *Couples,* 1927; as *Round Dance,* in *From the Modern Repertoire,* edited by Eric Bentley, 1949; as *Merry-Go-Round,* 1953; as *La Ronde,* 1959; as *Dance of Love,* 1965; as *The Round Dance,* in *The Round Dance and Other Plays,* 1982.
> *Der Schleier der Beatrice.* 1901.
> *Lebendige Stunden* (includes *Die Frau mit dem Dolche, Die letzten Masken, Literatur, Lebendige Stunden*). 1902; as *Living Hours* (includes *The Lady with the Dagger, Last Masks, Literature, Living Hours*), 1913.
> *Der einsame Weg.* 1904; as *The Lonely Way,* 1904.
> *Marionetten* (includes *Der Puppenspieler, Der tapfere Cassian, Zum grossen Wurstel*). 1906; revised version of *Der tapfere Cassian,* music by Oscar Straus, 1909;

translated as *Gallant Cassian*, 1914.
Der Ruf des Lebens. 1906.
Zwischenspiel. 1906; as *Intermezzo*, in *Three Plays*, 1915.
Komtesse Mizzi; oder, Der Familientag. 1909; as *Countess Mizzie*, 1907.
Der Schleier der Pierrette, music by Ernst von Dohnanyi. 1910.
Der junge Medardus. 1910.
Das weite Land. 1911; as *Undiscovered Country*, 1980.
Professor Bernhardi. 1912; translated as *Professor Bernhardi*, 1913.
Komödie der Worte (includes *Stunde des Erkennens, Grosse Szene, Das Bacchus-fest*). 1915; as *The Hour of Recognition, The Big Scene, The Festival of Bacchus*, in *Comedies of Words and Other Plays*, 1917.
Fink und Fliederbusch. 1917.
Die Schwestern; oder, Casanova in Spa. 1919.
Komödie der Verführung. 1924.
Der Gang zum Weiher. 1926.
Im Spiel der Sommerlüfte. 1930.
Zug der Schatten, edited by Françoise Derre. 1970.

Fiction

Sterben. 1895.
Die Frau des Weisen: Novelletten. 1898.
Leutnant Gustl. 1901; as *None But the Brave*, 1926.
Frau Bertha Garlan. 1901; translated as *Bertha Garlan*, 1913.
Die griechische Tänzerin: Novellen. 1905.
Dämmerseelen: Novellen. 1907.
Der Weg ins Freie. 1908; as *The Road to the Open*, 1923.
Die Hirtenflöte. 1912.
Masken und Wunder: Novellen. 1912.
Frau Beate und ihr Sohn. 1913; translated as *Beatrice*, 1926.
Viennese Idylls. 1913.
Doktor Gräsler, Badearzt. 1917; translated as *Dr. Graesler*, 1923.
Casanovas Heimfahrt. 1918; as *Casanova's Homecoming*, 1921.
Der Mörder. 1922.
The Shepherd's Pipe and Other Stories. 1922.
Fräulein Else. 1924; translated as *Fräulein Else*, 1925.
Die dreifache Warning: Novellen. 1924.
Die Frau des Richters. 1925.
Traumnovelle. 1926; as *Rhapsody: A Dream Novel*, 1927.
Beatrice and Other Stories. 1926.
Spiel im Morgengrauen. 1927; as *Daybreak*, 1927.
Therese: Chronik eines Frauenlebens. 1928; as *Theresa: The Chronicle of a Woman's Life*, 1928.
Little Novels. 1929.
Flucht in die Finsternis. 1931; as *Flight into Darkness*, 1931.
Viennese Novelettes. 1931.
Abenteuernovelle. 1937.
Vienna 1900: Games with Love and Death. 1973.

Other

Buch der Sprüche und Bedenken: Aphorismen und Fragmente. 1927.
Der Geist im Wort und der Geist in der Tat. 1927.

Über Krieg und Frieden. 1939.
Breifwechsel, with Otto Brahm, edited by Oskar Seidlin. 1953; revised edition, 1964.
Briefwechsel, with Georg Brandes, edited by Kurt Bergel. 1956.
Briefwechsel, with Hugo von Hofmannsthal, edited by Therese Nickl and Heinrich Schnitzler. 1964.
Jugend in Wien: Eine Autobiographie, edited by Therese Nickl and Heinrich Schnitzler. 1968; as *My Youth in Vienna,* 1971.
Liebe, die starb vor der Zeit: Ein Briefwechsel, with Olga Waissnix, edited by Therese Nickl and Heinrich Schnitzler. 1970.
Briefwechsel, with Max Reinhardt, edited by Renate Wagner. 1971.
Correspondence, with Raoul Auernheimer, edited by David G. Daviau and Jorun B. Johns. 1972.
Briefe 1875-1912, edited by Therese Nickl and Heinrich Schnitzler. 1981.
Tagebuch 1909-1912, edited by Peter M. Braunworth and others. 1981.

*

Bibliography: *An Annotated Schnitzler Bibliography* by Richard H. Allen, 1966; supplement by Jeffrey B. Berlin, 1978.

Critical Studies: *Schnitzler* by Sol Liptzin, 1932; *Studies in Schnitzler* by H.W. Reichart and Herman Salinger, 1963; *Schnitzler: Die späte Prosa als Gipfel seines Schaffens* by William H. Rey, 1968; *Schnitzler: A Critical Study* by Martin Swales, 1971; *Schnitzler* by R. Urbach, 1971.

*   *   *

Arthur Schnitzler's reputation stood high in the Austria and Germany of his day, but until its reinstatement in the 1950's it was diminished by his close identification with one time and place, turn-of-the-century Vienna (also recently "rediscovered"), and by the Nazis' suppression of his works. Even now, it is probable that he is best known for one play, *Reigen* (*Hands Around, La Ronde, The Round Dance*), a sexually explicit series of ten seduction scenes forming a "coital circle" linking all Vienna, high and low. The subject of considerable scandal (its premiere had to wait for some years) it has found its way into more than one film version; and its notoriety never ceased to depress its author. A reputation for lack of seriousness was compounded by the limitation of his range, and by a facile association of his work with the myth of "gay Vienna," encouraged by his penchant for idle young aristocrats and their dalliance with actresses or touchingly vulnerable shop-girls (the "süsses Mädel" of, e.g., *Liebelei, Light-o'-Love*). It is true that Schnitzler's range is limited. He wrote only about the period that ended in August 1914; and for him the city of his birth, from which he never moved away, was a sufficient mirror of the world. Critics are agreed, too, that his limitations are most apparent in his larger works, the longer plays like *Professor Bernhardi* or the one attempt at a full-scale novel of society; *Der Weg ins Freie* (*The Road to the Open*). But the other side of the critical coin is that he is a master of the short form. He wrote some forty novellas and about the same number of one-act plays, and within their narrow compass he evokes the existential confrontations of his characters with the basic crises of love, isolation, or death (especially death), bringing to the fore their whole mentality and psychological complexity. Freud's envy of Schnitzler's apparently effortless grasp of psychological processes is well known.

Schnitzler was, in fact, the product of a highly cultivated, almost over-refined milieu, and a member of a brilliant circle centering upon the Viennese coffee-house culture epitomized by the famous Café Griensteidl, a meeting place of literati such as Hugo von Hofmannsthal, Hermann Bahr, Peter Altenberg, and Schnitzler himself. His medical training and practice gave him the stock of experience he needed to act as the vehicle for his sensitive insight. As a Jew he was well placed to explore the pathology of a society in many ways atrophied, whose upper middle class had failed to liberalize the moribund Austrian Empire and had taken refuge in a cult of aestheticism, nuances, and ambiguities, inclining to reject all that presented itself in too uncomfortably distinct a form. If, as Schnitzler saw it, casual sex reflected the identity crisis of the individual, then anti-Semitism was the social embodiment of this crisis. He considered it a symptom of a universal spiritual malaise, and presented its morphology, with the professional restraint of the medical man, in both *Der Weg ins Freie* and *Professor Bernhardi*. But the play typically moves beyond anti-Semitism to become an exposure of the very Austrian theme of the way the world distorts the individual's intentions even as he gives utterance to them. Out of Bernhardi's professional stand against religious and political interference in the running of his hospital a *cause célèbre* is created; and out of Bernhardi himself, an unwilling and, in the end, inadequate martyr. The victim of anti-Semitism and dishonest politics appears just as much the victim of himself. Not that Schnitzler is inclined to pass judgement, for, as he said: "I see it as my profession to create characters, and I am out to prove nothing except the world's variety." In that variety is included, however, a good deal of Ibsen-style relation of the "lie of life," as for example in the masterly, pioneering stream-of-conscious narrative *Leutnant Gustl* (*None But the Brave*)—published 21 years before Joyce's *Ulysses*—where the inner monologue takes us into the world of a young army officer confronted with a personal conflict in which a false concept of honour is exposed for what it is by a healthy instinct for self-preservation. (The Imperial Army took umbrage, and Schnitzler lost his reserve officer's rank.) There is no element of caricature in the portrait of Gustl, and we are even enabled to enter his world with a degree of sympathy. Schnitzler's variety also has room for a *fin de siècle* fascination with abnormal states (e.g., his last story, *Flucht in die Finsternis*, *Flight into Darkness*, a case of incipient insanity which becomes total), with sickness as more interesting than health; and he is very much a modern in his exploration of "the whole crisis of man's erotic experience as symptomatic of a total philosophical revaluation of the world and man's place in it" (Martin Swales).

Yet he is a Janus-faced phenomenon in that he also looks back to the Austrian baroque tradition of the *Theatrum Mundi*, or notion of the world as spectacle, a view which was influential, as he said, in "developing that basic motif of the intermingling of seriousness and playacting, of life and theatre, of truth and mendacity...that moved and preoccupied me again and again, beyond any concern for the theatre and acting, indeed to a point beyond the realm of art". The seriousness of his intentions has long ceased to be in dispute, but any lingering doubts should be dispelled by his "Sprüche und Aphorismen," the collection of aphorisms which was slow to see the light of publication, but contains penetrating observations on art, religion, philosophy, and the issues of his day.

—Alan Bance

SCHULZ, Bruno. Born in Drohobycz, Poland, in 1892. Educated at schools in Drohobycz; studied architecture in Lvov, and fine arts in Vienna. Art teacher in gymnasium, Drohobycz, 1924-39; shot in Drohobycz ghetto by German officer, 1942. Recipient: Golden Laurel Award, 1938. *Died in 1942.*

PUBLICATIONS

Collections

Proza, edited by Artur Sandauer and Jerzy Ficowski. 1964; revised edition, 1973.

Fiction

> *Sklepy cynamonowe.* 1934; as *The Street of Crocodiles*, 1963; as *Cinnamon Shops and Other Stories*, 1963.
> *Sanatorium pod klepsydra.* 1937; as *Sanatorium under the Sign of the Hourglass*, 1978.

Other

> *Ksiega Listow* [A Book of Letters], edited by Jerzy Ficowski. 1975.

*

Critical Study: *Die Prosa von Schulz* by Elisabeth Baur, 1975.

* * *

Bruno Schulz was a shy teacher, whose life in an obscure corner of Europe camouflaged an extraordinary imagination. His stories magnify the provincial characters of the predominantly Jewish town of Drohobycz to the status of epic heroes involved in magical and surreal events.

Two separate collections of stories were published in his lifetime, *Sklepy cynamonowe* and *Sanatorium pod klepsydra*. On first reading, they seem to tell of a young man's path to maturity, but experiences that should lead the author's alter ego, Joseph N., to greater understanding instead confirm his naivety and remoteness from truth. The universe first revealed to him by his wily Magus-like father Jacob, the "incorrigible improvisor," is one that has forms but no Form (Creation after the Fall?). Like his Biblical forebear, Joseph remains trusting, innocent, and blessed by Providence.

Decomposition and decay are the main elements of a Schulz story, as the mannequin-like characters, the village, the plot, and the time materialize, merge, and melt away again. Though sequential in written form, the stories occur in parallel as alternative readings of the same elements in the same space. In the anti-world of the Sanatorium run by Dr. Gothard, the clock is put back to postpone the father's imminent death so he can set up business one last time in that dimension. In another dimension the father's metamorphosis into a crab surprises no one in the family, indeed he is even served up for supper. Joseph's uncanny influence over reality is shown particularly in the story "Wiosna" (Spring), when he is shown a stamp album by his cousin Rudolf. The stamps' portraits and countries suggest to him a perilous adventure set in the romantic Mexico of the Emperor Maximilian, though its events seem to take place on the very edge of the town where Joseph lives. His passion for a Bianca, imprisoned by a wicked uncle, disintegrates into faithful duty as Joseph becomes a minister when a coup d'état is staged in her name. As the plot crumbles further, and the waxworks dummies of a travelling show get involved, Joseph is arrested and sacrificed for the cause.

The schizophrenic character of Joseph's many manifestations and experiences and the unstable nature of everything around him are balanced by Creation itself: it assures that each dimension is self-contained, and as declared by Joseph in "Wiosna," "it was a spring that took its text seriously." Here is the sense of Schulz's writing: not self-discovery, but discovery itself is the objective, the quest for the "Authentic," for the "Book," and thus God Himself. The multiple dimensions of Schulz's stories are the environments lent to facilitate or hinder that search. Thus Schulz gives no conclusive definitions, but a finite number of readings of Creation, expressed as highly metaphorically charged writing. Just as Jehovah's written Word is an approximation of Him, so too the stories are permutations of God's Creativity. The final effect is magical, timeless, and intensely claustrophobic.

In effect, Schulz's worlds are a constantly shifting set of conversions of his adolescent memory. Runaway similes and metaphors create infinite numbers of unpredictable texts. Joseph's mission to isolate the "Authentic," much like his father's definitive "Grammar of Autumn," is closely linked to the Cabbalistic transliteration of the correspondences between physical objects, mental states, and Divine inspiration, but could equally be seen as a case history of sublimated hysteria. Yet his multi-dimensional world is not one of the struggle between Good and Evil: Jewish moralism plays no part at all—it is rather a complex metaphor for his own creativeness, and repudiation of the bleak reality around him, the one in which he was shot by an SS-officer in 1942.

—Donald Peter Alexander Pirie

SEFERIS, George. Pseudonym for Giorgos Stylianou Seferiades. Born in Smyrna (now Izmir), Turkey, 29 February 1900; emigrated to Athens in 1914. Educated at Protypon Classical Gymnasium, Athens; University of Athens; the Sorbonne, Law degree 1924; studied English in London, 1924-25. Married Maria Zannos in 1941. Entered Royal Greek Ministry of Foreign Affairs, 1926: vice-consul, later consul, in London, 1931-34; in Athens, 1934-36; consul, Korytsa, Albania, 1936-38; press officer, Athens, 1938-41; worked for Free Greek Government in Crete, 1941, South Africa, 1941-42, Egypt, 1942-44, and Italy, 1944; in Athens, 1944-48, Ankara, 1948-50, and London, 1951-52; Ambassador to Lebanon and Minister to Syria, Iraq, and Jordan, 1953-56; Ambassador to Great Britain, 1957-62; retired, 1962. Full-time writer from 1962. Recipient: Kostis Palamas Prize, 1947; Foyle Poetry Prize (UK), 1961; Nobel Prize for Literature, 1963. Litt.D.: Cambridge University, 1960; Oxford University, 1964; Princeton University, New Jersey, 1965; D.Phil.: University of Thessaloniki, 1964. Member, Institute for Advanced Study, Princeton, 1968; Honorary Member, American Academy of Arts and Sciences, and American Academy, 1971. Knight Commander of Order of George I; Grand Cross of Order of Phoenix; Order of Holy Sepulchre; Grand Cross of the Cedar; Grand Cross of Order of Merit (Syria). *Died 20 September 1971.*

PUBLICATIONS

Verse

Strophe [Turning Point]. 1931.
I sterna [The Cistern]. 1932.
Mythistorema. 1935.
Gymnopedia. 1936.
Imerologio katastromatos A, B, C. 3 vols., 1940-55.
Tetradio gymnasmaton [Exercise Book]. 1940.
Poiemata I [Poems]. 1940.
Six Poems from the Greek of Sikelianos and Seferis, translated by Lawrence Durrell. 1946.
Kichli [The Thrush]. 1947.
The King of Asine and Other Poems. 1948.
Poiemata 1924-1946 [Poems]. 1950; 6th edition, 1974; as *Collected Poems 1924-1955,* edited and translated by Edmund Keeley and Philip Sherrard, 1967; revised edition, 1982.

Poems, translated by Rex Warner. 1960.
Tria kryfa poiemata. 1966; as *Three Secret Poems*, translated by Walter Kaiser, 1969.

Fiction

Eksi nychtes sten Akropole [Six Nights on the Acropolis], edited by G.P. Savidis. 1974.

Other

Dokimes [Essays]. 1944; revised edition, 1962; edited by G.P. Savidis, 2 vols., 1974.
Antigraphes [Copies] (translations). 1965.
On the Greek Style: Selected Essays in Poetry and Hellenism. 1966.
Cheirographo Sep. '41 [Manuscript Sept. '41]. 1972.
Meres tou 1945-1951. 1973; as *A Poet's Journal: Days of 1945-1951*, 1974.
Politiko imerologio [Political Diary], edited by Alexandrou Hyde. 1979.
Metagraphes, edited by Giorges Giatromanolakes. 1980.

Translator, *T.S. Eliot* (selection). 1936; revised edition, as *The Waste Land and Other Poems*, 1949.
Translator, *Phoniko oten Ekklesia* [Murder in the Cathedral], by T.S. Eliot. 1963.
Translator, *Asma asmaton* [Song of Songs]. 1965.
Translator, *E apokalypse tou Ioanne* [The Apocalypse of St. John]. 1966.

*

Critical Studies: "Seferis and the 'Mythical Method' " by Edmund Keeley, in *Comparative Literature Studies 6*, 1969; *Seferis* (by National Book League and British Council), 1975.

*   *   *

It can be said with hindsight that George Seferis was the foremost of a generation of Greek poets and prose writers who in different ways introduced modernism into Greek letters, the so-called "Generation of the Thirties." His early career developed under the influence of French symbolism, but additional formative influences on him were an urgent awareness of the Greek cultural tradition stretching back to antiquity, and, from 1931 on, the poetry and critical ideas of T.S. Eliot.

These three strands first come together in an integrated, and highly innovative, work *Mythistorema* (the title, which means 'a novel' also alludes to the poem's main theme, the juxtaposition of ancient myth and contemporary history). In this sequence of 24 short poems Seferis attempts, through the mouthpieces of different, anonymous characters and through the evocation of their changing moods—heroic aspiration, frustrated love, fear, resignation—to come to terms as a modern Greek with the past tradition of his country, which he sees as both an inspiration and a burden. The poem alludes to the mythical voyage of the Argonauts in search of the Golden Fleece, a quest which Seferis sees repeated throughout history up to the present, and for the most part futile thanks to man's inadequacy and weakness.

Mythistorema portrays modern man, and more particularly the modern Greek, as cut off from the creative power that inspired the artistic achievements of the classical past, but weighed down by the burden of the relics it has left behind, represented by the worn statues and the "old stones." This theme continues to be prominent throughout his poetry of the 1930's and 1940's, culminating in the longer poem *Kichli*, (1946), in which he imagines a modern Odysseus striving to return, not to Ithaca, but to a symbolic home which he calls merely "the light."

New refinements and differences of emphasis appear in Seferis's collections of poems of the 1950's and 1960's, respectively "Logbook III" based on his experience of Cyprus in 1953 and

1954, and *Three Secret Poems*, in which the poet retreats into a fragmented world, a world that "must burn/This noon when the sun is nailed/To the heart of the centifoliate rose." The poems of Seferis's last decade show a new pessimism, and an even sparser style that almost literally fades out into silence in the posthumously published late poems and fragments.

Seferis was not only a poet but also one of Greece's most lucid essayists and critics. Many of his essays on older figures in modern Greek literature (essays on Kalvos, Makriyannis, *Erotókritos*) have become classics and have helped to shape the contemporary perspective on modern Greek literary history, while others deal perceptively with the issues of tradition and modernism which also preoccupied him in his poetry. Poetry and essays alike are permeated by Seferis's deeply held humanist convictions.

Seferis was largely responsible for introducing modern English poetry to Greece, through his acclaimed translations of Eliot, Pound, and Yeats. He also translated the Apocalypse into modern Greek.

Before embarking on his career as a poet, he wrote a novel, *Eksi nychtes sten Akropole*, which was substantially complete and posthumously published. In this novel, written chiefly in 1928 and re-worked in 1954, Seferis first tried to work out many of the themes which came to dominate his poetry, but without the novelist's grasp of narration and character *Eksi nychtes* is a failure, though a remarkable literary experiment.

—Roderick Beaton

SENECA (Lucius Annaeus Seneca).   Born in Corduba (now Cordoba), Spain, c. 4 B.C.; son of the writer and teacher of rhetoric Lucius Annaeus Seneca.   Studied philosophy in Rome. Married Pompeia Paulina; one son. Spent some time in Egypt for his health; returned to Rome, c. 31; elected quaestor in 30's; exiled to Corsica by Caligula, 41-49; tutor to Nero, and designated praetor, 50; with Burrus, adviser and minister to Nero, 54-62: consul, 56; on Burrus's death in 62, Seneca asked to retire, and did so; forced to commit suicide for supposed participation in Pisonian conspiracy, 65 A.D.

PUBLICATIONS

Collections

> *Opera*, edited by F. Haase.   1884-87; translated by J.W. Basore and others (Loeb edition), 10 vols., 1917-72.
> [*Tragedies*], edited by G.C. Giardina.   2 vols., 1966.

Plays

> *Hercules furens*, edited by Franco Caviglia.   1979.
> *Troades*, edited by Elaine Fantham.   1982; as *Trojan Women*, translated by E.F. Watling, 1966.

Phoenissae

Medea, edited by C.D.N. Costa.   1973; translated by Moses Hadas, 1955.

Phaedra [also called *Hippolytus*], edited by Pierre Grimal.   1965; translated by E.F. Watling, 1966.

Oedipus: translated by Moses Hadas, 1956, E.F. Watling, 1966, and Ted Hughes, 1969.

Agamemnon, edited by R.J. Tarrant.   1976.

Thyestes: translated by Moses Hadas, 1957, E.F. Watling, 1966, and Jane Elder, 1982.

Octavia [not by Seneca], edited by Lucile Yow Whitman.   1978; translated by E.F. Watling, 1966.

Hercules oetaeus [probably not by Seneca].

Verse

Apocolocyntosis divi Claudii [Pumpkinification of the Divine Claudius] [possibly not by Seneca], edited by C.F. Russo.   1964.

Other

Dialogorum, edited by E. Hermes and others.   3 vols., 1898-1907; also edited by L.D. Reynolds, 1977.

De beneficiis and De clementia, edited by C. Hosius.   1914.

Naturales quaestiones, edited by P. Oltramare.   1929.

Ad Lucilium epistulae morales, edited by L.D. Reynolds.   2 vols., 1965; as *Letters from a Stoic*, translated by Robin Campbell, 1969.

*

Critical Studies: *Seneca and Elizabethan Tragedy* by F.L. Lucas, 1922; *Discourses upon Seneca the Tragedian* by W. Cornwallis, 1952; *Seneca the Philosopher and His Modern Message* by R.M. Gummere, 1963; *Anger in Juvenal and Seneca* by William S. Anderson, 1964; *The Medieval Tradition of Seneca's Letters* by L.D. Reynolds 1965; *Seneca Sourcebook*, 1971, and *Seneca*, 1973, both by A.L. Motto; *Racine and Seneca* by Ronald W. Tobin, 1971; *Seneca* edited by C.D.N. Costa, 1974; *Seneca, A Philosopher in Politics* by Miriam Tamara Griffin, 1976.

*   *   *

Seneca's influence and importance have been enduring and twofold, as a thinker and as a stylist. Though he was by no means an original philosopher his prose works are a major source for the history of Stoicism as developed and modified at Rome. Most of these (the *Dialogues*) are ethical treatises, strongly hortatory in tone and including traditional moralising topics—the shortness of life, tranquillity of mind, the self-sufficiency of the wise man—and three "consolations" (addresses to afflicted individuals with conventional advice on coping with distress and bereavement). These treatises are not so much exercises in speculative philosophy as practical moral teaching, and though there are dull stretches in them the style overall is brilliant, and the arguments skilfully highlighted by anecdote and wit. His 124 *Letters to Lucilius* have a similar aim of ethical instruction. Though ostensibly addressed to a younger friend in public life they are not genuine private letters but clearly look to a general readership. With their variety of tone and wide-ranging subject matter they have always been Seneca's most attractive and popular works, and were one of the most widely read classical texts in the Middle Ages. Another side of his omnivorous learning is seen in the seven books of *Natural Questions*, which consist largely of surveys and assessments of existing theories on natural phenomena, and are of considerable interest to the history of scientific speculation. The *Apocolocyntosis* is an interesting literary survival: a moderately funny skit on the deification of the dead emperor Claudius, written in an early style of satire which mingled prose and verse.

Seneca's *Tragedies* have a unique place in classical literature. Their themes are taken from Greek legend, and most of them have detectable links with surviving Greek tragedies, but the treatment is very different. They were almost certainly not written for full stage performance but recited or declaimed by a solo performer. Seneca is not interested in plots or character-development but in exploring strongly opposed attitudes and the conflict of violent emotions. This is done usually in a succession of virtually self-contained scenes of dialogue or self-debating soliloquy, with little regard for dramatic continuity between them. The tragedies were enormously popular in the Renaissance and were the models for innumerable imitations in both Latin and vernacular languages in Italy, France, and England: tragedians in 16th-century England and 17th-century France were particularly indebted to them, and the influence of the Latin declamatory style can be traced in Shakespeare.

Both the plays and the prose works illustrate very markedly the rhetorical use of language and verbal ingenuity which was always to some extent characteristic of Latin literature, but which was brought to a high degree of refinement in the first century A.D., and notably by Seneca himself. This brilliant, pointed, and strongly epigrammatic style was in strong contrast with Ciceronian Latin, and the popularity of Seneca's works in the Middle Ages and Renaissance led in turn to the fashion of imitating his prose style. Thus by the late 16th century, when Latin was still the language of learned communication, there was a reaction against Ciceronianism and the Senecan style became overwhelmingly popular.

—C.D.N. Costa

SIENKIEWICZ, Henryk (Adam Aleksander Pius). Born in Wola Okrzejska, Poland, 5 May 1846. Educated at Warsaw Gymnasium, 1858-65; Polish University, Warsaw, 1866-71. Married 1) Maria Szetkiewicz (died, 1885), one son and one daughter; 2) Maria Wolodkowicz (marriage annulled); 3) Maria Babska in 1904. Journalist and free-lance writer; visited the United States to search for site for a California settlement, 1876-78; Co-Editor, *Slowo* [The Word] newspaper, 1882-87. Given an estate by the Polish government at Oblegorek, near Kielce, 1900. Recipient: Nobel Prize for Literature, 1905. *Died 15 November 1916.*

PUBLICATIONS

Collections

Dziela [Works], edited by Julian Krzyzanowski. 60 vols., 1948-55.
Pisma wybrane [Selected Works]. 1976— .

Fiction

Na marne. 1872; as *In Vain*, 1899.

Stary sluga [The Old Servants]. 1875.

Hania. 1876; translated as *Hania,* 1897; in part as *Let Us Follow Him,* 1897.

Za chlebem. 1880; as *After Bread,* 1897; as *For Daily Bread,* 1898; as *Peasants in Exile,* 1898; as *Her Tragic Fate,* 1899; as *In the New Promised Land,* 1900.

Trilogy

    Ogniem i mieczem. 1884; as *With Fire and Sword,* 1890.

    Potop. 1886; as *The Deluge: An Historical Novel of Poland, Sweden, and Russia,* 1892.

    Pan Wolodyjowski. 1887-88; as *Pan Michael,* 1895.

On the Sunny Shore. 1886; as *On the Bright Shore,* 1898.

Bez dogmatu. 1889-90; as *Without Dogma,* 1893.

Yanko the Musician and Other Stories. 1893.

Lillian Morris and Other Stories. 1894.

Rodzina Polanieckich. 1894; as *Children of the Soil,* 1895; as *The Irony of Life,* 1900.

Quo vadis? 1896; translated as *Quo Vadis?,* 1896.

The Third Woman. 1897.

Na jasnym brzegu. 1897; as *In Monte Carlo,* 1899.

Sielanka, A Forest Picture, and Other Stories. 1898.

So Runs the World: Stories. 1898.

The Fate of a Soldier. 1898.

Tales. 1899.

Where Worlds Meet. 1899.

Krzyzacy. 1900; as *The Knights of the Cross,* 1900; as *Danusia,* 1900; as *The Teutonic Knights,* 1943.

Life and Death and Other Legends and Stories. 1904.

Na polu chwaly. 1906; as *On the Field of Glory,* 1906.

Wiry. 1910; as *Whirlpools: A Novel of Modern Poland,* 1910.

Legiony [Legions] (unfinished). 1914.

Western Septet: Seven Stories of the American West, edited by Marion Moore Coleman. 1973.

Other

Listy z podrózy do Ameryki. 1876-78; as *Portrait of America: Letters of Sienkiewicz,* edited by Charles Morley, 1959.

Listy z Afryki [Letters from Africa]. 1891-92.

W pustyni i w puszczy (juvenile). 1911; as *In Desert and Wilderness,* 1912; as *Through the Desert,* 1912.

Listy [Letters], edited by Julian Krzyzanowski and others, 1977— .

*

Critical Studies: *The Patriotic Novelist of Poland, Sienkiewicz* by Monica M. Gardner, 1926; *Sienkiewicz: A Retrospective Synthesis* by Waclaw Lednicki, 1960; *Wanderers Twain: Modjeska and Sienkiewicz: A View from California* by Arthur Prudden and Marion Moore Coleman, 1964; *Sienkiewicz* by M. Giergielewicz, 1968.

*   *   *

Sienkiewicz's historical novels comprising his *Trilogy* (*With Fire and Sword, The Deluge,* and *Pan Michael*) and *Quo vadis?,* brought him celebrity in Poland and abroad. The historical novel had a special place in 19th-century Polish literature, when Poland was partitioned between Russia, Prussia, and Austro-Hungary, and was used by a number of novelists as a metaphor, in which the Polish reader could see contemporary reality "masked" by historical events. Too much can be made of this, of course: did Sienkiewicz intend the early Christians in *Quo vadis?* to represent the early Socialists in 19th-century Russia? He never said so.

His popularity was due largely to his narrative power: from his early fiction, he reveals himself as a self-conscious literary artist, not a mere "story-teller," stringing together striking incidents. He gained his effects from the manner in which he tells the tale: scenes are scupulously dramatised for maximum effect, and the various elements—dialogue, description, auctorial comment, analysis—are balanced, and he used sophisticated literary devices such as "represented discourse" to produce dramatic presence. The dominant element in his narrative is the extended scene, following a character or group of characters intently for many pages at a time—a device frequently used by other major novelists, from Dickens to Tolstoy and Dostoevsky. The fact that all his novels were originally written as serials for Warsaw newspapers had an essential bearing on their structure: Sienkiewicz learned early on the necessity of careful planning in advance. His use of historical source materials for *The Trilogy* (17th-century) and *Quo vadis?* (Rome under Nero) was scrupulous, and is reflected in his prose style. When he turned to novels of psychological analysis (fashionable in Western Europe in the 1890's), Sienkiewicz was less successful, although both *Without Dogma* and *Children of the Soil* are still of interest to literary people, as are the novels of Henry James, read not so much for what happens next, as "how the thing is done."

—David Welsh

SIKELIANOS, Angelos. Born on island of Levkas, Greece, 28 March 1884. Educated at home; studied law at the University of Athens, 1900. Married Eva Palmer in 1907; also married a second time. Writer; attempted to revive the Delphic drama festivals, 1927-30. *Died 6 June 1951.*

PUBLICATIONS

Collections

Apanta [Collected Works], edited by G.P.Savidis. 6 vols., 1965-69.

Verse

Alafroiskiotos [The Visionary]. 1909.
Prologos sti zoi [Prologue to Life]. 4 vols., 1915-17; 5th vol., 1947.
Mitir theou [Mother of God]. 1917-19.
The Delphic Word, translated by Alma Reed. 1928.
Ho dithyrambos tou Rhodou. 1934; as *The Dithyramb of the Rose*, translated by Frances Sikelianos, 1939.
Akritan Songs (bilingual edition), translated by Paul Nord. 1944.
Six Poems from the Greek of Sikelianos and Seferis, translated by Lawrence Durrell. 1946.

To Pascha ton Ellinon [Easter of the Greeks].   1947.
Selected Poems, translated by Edmund Keeley and Philip Sherrard.   1979.

Plays

O Daidalos stin Criti [Daedalus in Crete].   1943.
Sivylla [Sibyl].   1944.
Ho Christos ste Rome [Christ at Rome].   1946.
Thymele [Collected Plays].   2 vols., 1950.

Other

Grammata sten Anna [Letters to Anna].   1980.

*

Critical Studies: *The Marble Threshing Floor* by Philip Sherrard, 1956.

*   *   *

Angelos Sikelianos was something very unusual in the 20th-century—an uncompromising Romantic. This does not make him an anachronism: the world of his poetry was enhanced by what he knew of Einstein, and by 20th-century discoveries in archaeology and comparative mythology, as well as by the events through which he lived. But Sikelianos's larger-than-life personality, both in his life and his poetry, the boundless confidence with which he expounded his vision of a greater reality beyond the visible world, and the ponderous, sculpted rhetoric of his verse, seem almost incongruous in a poet who had fought in the First World War, lived through the Greek defeat in Anatolia in 1922, with its disastrous repercussions for the Greek sense of identity, the political polarization of the 1930's, and then the German occupation of the early 1940's. In fact Sikelianos was the kind of visionary poet who might appear in any age; but the roots of his poetry lie in the final stage of Greek and European Romanticism in which he grew up.

The poem *Alafroiskiotos* (The Visionary), was written in 1907 and in many respects belongs to its time, with its "profound *logos*" that "We are but images and shadows." But the exultant lyricism of the poem, and the breathless rhythms of its free verse, reveal that even then Sikelianos was a poet with a voice very much his own. And it is this same voice, tempered but never deflected by the events of his times, that Sikelianos developed over the next 40 years. It is above all a lyrical voice: and it is appropriate that the title he later gave to his collected poems was *Lyrikós Víos* (Lyrical Life). *Alafroiskiotos* anticipates the themes and mood of much that was to follow, in its celebration of the joy of life, of the unity of man with nature, and in weaving together myths from ancient Greece with modern folk legends and a rich evocation of the Greek landscape.

In later poems Sikelianos began to introduce a synthesis of Christian and pagan mythology, and also, in defiance of the trend among his contemporaries, moved steadily away from free verse to more formal verse patterns. After the long poems of the second decade of the century, we find Sikelianos in the 1920's writing some of his finest short lyrical poems. But to many readers his greatest achievement consists in the poems, written in a form of blank verse with long flowing periods, that began in 1935 with "Iera Odos" (Sacred Way). In this poem a chance encounter with a gypsy and two performing bears, mother and child, on the sacred way that led in classical times from Athens to Eleusis, provides both a re-enactment of the ancient myth of Demeter and Persephone, and a symbol, in the bears brutally forced by their master to dance for a few coppers, of human exploitation and suffering.

Sikelianos had the conviction that poetry includes and unifies everything in the universe, and he linked it with the primitive capacity for myth-making, in opposition to science and rational philosophy. His ideas on the almost supernatural powers of poetry, as he saw it, and on myth, are expressed in his few prose works, which are vitiated by a diffuse and bombastic style. Sikelianos also wrote a number of verse dramas from which, however, the element in drama is largely lacking. This is probably due to the very gift for synthesis and a perception of the hidden sameness underlying opposites, that make him one of Europe's most remarkable lyric poets.

—Roderick Beaton

SILONE, Ignazio. Born Secondo Tranquilli in Pescina dei Marsi, Abruzzi, Italy, 1 May 1900. Educated at Jesuit and other Catholic schools in Abruzzi and Rome. Married Darina Laracy in 1944. Secretary, Federation of Land Workers of the Abruzzi, 1917, and a leader of the Italian Socialist Youth Movement, 1917-21; member, Central Committee of Italian Communist Party 1921-29, and editor of several party newspapers, including *L'Avanguardia*, Rome, *Il Lavoratore*, Trieste, 1921-22, and *L'Unità*; imprisoned in Spain, 1923; left Communist Party, 1930; worked in anti-fascist underground and when warrants were issued against him by Fascist Special Tribunal he left Italy to live in Switzerland, 1931-43: Political Secretary, Foreign Center of the Italian Socialists, Zurich; Member of the Executive Committee, Italian Socialist Party, 1941-47; Editor, *Avanti*, a socialist daily paper, after World War II; Founding President, Teatro del Popolo, 1945; Socialist Party Deputy, Italian Constituent Assembly, 1946-48; mainly a writer from 1950; Co-Editor, *Tempo Presente* magazine, Rome, 1956-68. President, Italian P.E.N. Club, 1945-59; Chairman, Italian Committee for Cultural Freedom. Recipient: Salento Prize, 1957; Marzotto Prize, 1965; Campiello Prize, 1968; Jerusalem Prize, 1969; Cino del Duca Prize, 1971; Golden Pen Prize, 1971; Keller Prize, 1973. D.Litt.: Yale University, New Haven, Connecticut, 1965; University of Warwick; University of Toulouse, 1969. Commander, Legion of Honor (France). *Died 22 August 1978.*

PUBLICATIONS

Fiction

> *Fontamara.* 1934; revised edition, 1958; translated as *Fontamara*, 1934; revised edition, 1960.
> *Un viaggio a Parigi* (short story). 1934.
> *Mr. Aristotle.* 1935.
> *Pane e vino.* 1937; revised edition, as *Vino e pane*, 1955; as *Bread and Wine*, 1936; revised edition, 1962.
> *Il seme sotto la neve.* 1942; as *The Seed Beneath the Snow*, 1942.
> *Una manciato di more.* 1952; as *A Handful of Blackberries*, 1953.
> *Il segreto di Luca.* 1956; as *The Secret of Luca*, 1959.
> *La volpe e le camelie.* 1960; as *The Fox and the Camellias*, 1961.
> *Severina.* 1982.

Plays

Ed egli si nascose, from his novel Pane e vino. 1944; revised edition, 1966; as And He Did Hide Himself, 1946; as And He Hid Himself, 1946.
L'avventura di un povero cristiano. 1968; as The Story of a Humble Christian, 1970.

Other

Der Fascismus: Seine Entstehung und seine Entwicklung. 1934.
La scuola dei dittatori. 1962; as The School for Dictators, 1938.
Un dialogo difficile: Sono liberi gli scrittori russi?, with Ivan Anissimov. 1950; as An Impossible Dialogue Between Ivan Anissimov and Silone, 1957.
Uscita di sicurezza. 1951; as Emergency Exit, 1968.
La scelta dei compagni. 1954.
Mi paso por el comunismo. 1959.
Per una legge sull'obiezione di coscienza, with others. 1962.
Paese dell'anima, edited by Maria Letizia Cassata. 1968.
Memoriale dal carcere svizzero, edited by Lamberto Mercuri. 1979.

Editor, Mazzini. 1939; as The Living Thoughts of Mazzini, 1939.
Editor, A trent'anni dal concordata. 1959.

*

Critical Studies: The God That Failed: Six Studies in Communism edited by Richard Crossman, 1950; Silone (in Italian) Ferdinando Virdia, 1967; Silone: Un amore religioso per la giustizia by Alessandro Scurani, 1969; Invito alla lettura di Silone by Carlo Annoni, 1974; A Need to Testify: Portraits of Lauro de Bosis, Ruth Draper, Gaetano Salvemini, and Silone by Iris Origo, 1983.

*　　*　　*

Ignazio Silone's origins were humble and his early life was spent in active politics. His father was a day-labourer and his mother a weaver. He was left an orphan after the 1915 earthquake that destroyed large areas of central Abruzzi and his consciousness was first raised, as he describes in Emergency Exit, by the misappropriation of relief funds. His first articles for Avanti in 1917 were on this subject.

Under Fascism, books by known Communists and Socialists were not published in Italy. Silone wrote his first and most famous novel, Fontamara, in Switzerland just after he left the Communist Party. It describes the plight of the peasants, the Abruzzese cafoni, struggling under the abuse that Fascism had added to their eternal sufferings. The story of the rape and destruction of the village of Fontamara is told by three people, father, mother, and son, who have escaped and come to the author with their tale. Silone simply sets it down. This novel device may have been suggested to him by a Tolstoy tract, "What's to Be Done," which describes Tolstoy in a similar situation after the 1905 revolution in Russia. Silone thus manages to communicate the immediacy of the peasants' plight, their limited knowledge of the world, and yet their clear understanding of what has been done to them. And he avoids the very real difficulty of trying to make peasants speak in "standard" Italian. The end of the novel describes the foundation of a newspaper at Fontamara called Che fare, a name which echoes the Russian revolutionary call of Chernyshevsky, Tolstoy, and Lenin. It rings through the ending of the novel challenging the tragic events of the plot. The sacrificial death of the hero, Berardo, in a Fascist gaol in Rome may well parallel the death of Romolo, Silone's brother, at the hands of his jailers on Procida.

In Bread and Wine (later dramatised as And He Hid Himself) and The Seed Beneath the

Snow a third-person narrator describes the clandestine wanderings of the returned political exile, Pietro Spina, who tries to raise the consciousness of the *cafoni* and to span the enormous gap between the official propaganda of the Left and the peasants' understanding. He is disguised as a priest, which emphasises Silone's continual use of Christian symbolism, liturgy, and language. He frequently said that before Socialism the only movement to have stirred the primaeval consciousness of the Abruzzi was the 13th-century Franciscan movement. Both novels end with a sacrifice, and in *The Seed Beneath the Snow*, Silone's favourite novel, the legendary Abruzzi figure of the dying Christ who is still on the Cross is likened to the suffering peasants.

Silone's post-war writing faces the problem of the individual at the mercy of political machines invented ostensibly for his good. *A Handful of Blackberries* tackles post-war problems and the position of the ex-Communists. *The Secret of Luca* concerns the integrity of one *cafone* falsely imprisoned for murder. *The Fox and the Camellias*, the only work set outside the Abruzzi, in Switzerland, allows for some good in a Fascist character for the first time. *The Story of a Humble Christian* sees the 13th-century Pope Celestine V as an idealist who prefers to abdicate rather than compromise. *Severina* is a figure similarly committed to "truth" who falls against the background of the militancy of the 1960's. The message is still one of hope, however, despite all institutions which menace the integrity of the individual.

—Judy Rawson

SNORRI STURLUSON. *See* **STURLUSON, Snorri.**

SOLZHENITSYN, Alexander (Isayevich). Born in Kislovodsk, 11 December 1918. Educated at school in Rostov-on-Don; University of Rostov, 1936-41, degree in mathematics and physics 1941; correspondence course in philology, Moscow University, 1939-41. Served in the Soviet Army, 1941-45: captain; decorated twice; arrested and stripped of rank, 1945. Married 1) Natalya Alexeevna Reshetovskaya in 1940 (divorced), remarried in 1957 (divorced, 1973), three sons; 2) Natalya Svetlova in 1973, one stepson. Physics teacher, secondary school, Morozovka, 1941; sentenced to 8 years imprisonment for anti-Soviet agitation, 1945: in prisons in Moscow, 1945-50, and labor camp in Kazakhstan, 1950-53; released from prison, and exiled to Kok-Terek: mathematics teacher, 1953-56; released from exile, 1956, and settled in Ryazan, 1957, as teacher, then fulltime writer; unable to publish from 1966; expelled from USSR, 1974; lived in Zurich, 1974-76, and in Vermont since 1976. Recipient: Prix du Meilleur Livre Etranger, 1969; Nobel Prize for Literature, 1970. Member, American Academy of Arts and Sciences, 1969; Honorary Fellow, Hoover Institution on War, Revolution, and Peace, 1975.

SOLZHENITSYN

PUBLICATIONS

Fiction

Odin den' Ivana Denisovicha. 1962; as *One Day in the Life of Ivan Denisovich*, 1963.
Dlya pol'zy dela. 1963; as *For the Good of the Cause*, 1964.
Sluchay na stantsii Krechetvoka; Matryonin dvor. 1963; as *We Never Make Mistakes*, 1963.
Etudy i krokhotnye rasskazy. 1964; as *Stories and Prose Poems*, 1971; as *Prose Poems*, 1971; as *Matryona's House and Other Stories*, 1975.
V kruge pervom. 1968; complete version as *The First Circle*, 1968.
Rakovy korpus. 1968; complete version, 1968; as *Cancer Ward*, 2 vols., 1968-69; as *The Cancer Ward*, 1969.
Six Etudes. 1971.
Avgust chetyrnadtsatovo. 1971; expanded version, as *Krasnoe koleso 1* [The Red Wheel], in *Sobraniye sochineniy 11-12*, 1983; as *August 1914*, 1972.

Plays

Olen i shalashovka. 1968; as *Respublika truda*, in *Sobraniye sochineniy 8*, 1981; as *The Love-Girl and the Innocent*, 1969.
Svecha na vetru. 1968; as *Svet, koroty, v tebe*, in *Sobraniye sochineniy 8*, 1981; as *Candle in the Wind*, 1973.
Pir podebiteley, in *Sobraniye sochineniy 8*. 1981; as *Victory Celebrations*, 1983.
Plenniki, in *Sobraniye sochineniy 8*. 1981; as *Prisoners*, 1983.

Verse

Prusskiye nochi: Poema napisannaya v lagere v 1950. 1974; as *Prussian Nights*, 1977.

Other

Sobraniye sochineniy [Collected Works]. 6 vols., 1969-1970.
Les Droits de l'écrivain. 1969.
Nobelevskaya lektsiya po literature. 1972; as *Nobel Lecture*, edited by F.D. Reeve, 1972.
Arkhipelag Gulag. 3 vols., 1973-76; as *The Gulag Archipelago*, 3 vols., 1974-78.
Mir i nasiliye [Peace and Violence]. 1974.
Pis'mo vozhdyam Sovetskovo soyuza. 1974; as *Letter to the Soviet Leaders*, 1974.
A Pictorial Autobiography. 1974.
Bodalsya telyonok s dubom (autobiography). 1975; as *The Oak and the Calf*, 1980.
Lenin v Tsyurikhe. 1975; as *Lenin in Zurich*, 1976.
Detente: Prospects for Democracy and Dictatorship. 1975.
Warning to the Western World (interview). 1976.
A World Split Apart (address). 1978.
The Mortal Danger: How Misconceptions about Russia Imperil the West. 1980.
Sobraniye sochineniy [Collected Works]. 1978— .
East and West (miscellany). 1980.

Bibliography: *Solzhenitsyn: An International Bibliography of Writings by and about Him* by Donald M. Fiene, 1973.

Critical Studies: *Solzhenitsyn: The Major Novels* by Abraham Rothberg, 1971; *Solzhenitsyn* by David Burg and George Feifer, 1973; *Solzhenitsyn: Critical Essays and Documentary Materials* edited by John B. Dunlop and others, 1973, revised edition, 1975; *Solzhenitsyn* by Christopher Moody, 1973, revised edition, 1976; *Solzhenitsyn: Politics and Form* by Francis Barker, 1977; *Solzhenitsyn* by Steven Allaback, 1978; *Solzhenitsyn and the Secret Circle* by Olga Andreyev Carlisle, 1978; *Solzhenitsyn and Dostoevsky: A Study in the Polyphonic Novel* by Vladislav Krasnov, 1980.

*   *   *

Solzhenitsyn's literary ambitions were already manifested in 1937 when he conceived the idea of creating a long novel about the Russian revolution and wrote several chapters of it. At that time Solzhenitsyn believed in Leninism, approving of the October Revolution. His experience in Soviet prisons and forced labor camps made him change his political orientation, and he took upon himself the messianic task of exposing the brutality, the mendacity, and the illegitimacy of the Communist rule in Russia.

One Day in the Life of Ivan Denisovich, called a novel in the West but a short story by Solzhenitsyn, was his first published work. Written tersely and effectively, it presents a Soviet camp through the eyes of a peasant prisoner who manages to preserve his integrity in dehumanizing conditions. The story came out only because Khrushchev considered it useful for his anti-Stalin campaign. This fact facilitated the publication of "An Incident at Krechetovka Station," "Matryona's House," and "For the Good of the Cause." The first story demonstrates how a young lieutenant is corrupted by the intense propaganda of vigilance designed to justify domestic repression. In the second story Solzhenitsyn draws an impressive portrait of a kind and unselfish peasant woman, a type of the righteous person that forms Russia's moral foundation. The third story, showing a callous bureaucratic disregard for ordinary Soviet citizens, lacks depth and poignancy. Solzhenitsyn's fifth, and last, work published in his homeland is the short story "Zakhar the Pouch" concerned with the preservation of historic monuments. No Soviet publisher could be found for "The Right Hand," "Kak zhal" (What a Pity), "The Easter Procession," and some fifteen poems in prose—tiny masterpieces containing Solzhenitsyn's philosophical observations.

The novels *The First Circle* and *Cancer Ward* draw much upon Solzhenitsyn's personal experiences—the one upon his life in a special prison for scientists and the other upon his stay in a cancer clinic. In both novels Solzhenitsyn raises questions of human destiny, morality, freedom, happiness, love, death, faith, social injustice, and the political purges. Man is seen in non-materialist terms as a repository of the image of eternity. He must guide himself by his own conscience. The full 96-chapter version of *The First Circle*, published for the first time in Russian in 1978, has a stronger political coloration than its 87-chapter version which was translated into many languages.

As in all of Solzhenitsyn's fiction, the action in both novels takes place within a very brief period of time. The characters are well individualized. In transmitting different viewpoints, Solzhenitsyn relies heavily on heated dialogues, enhancing their dynamism by the use of short interrogative and exclamatory sentences and by references to the characters' gestures, eyes, tone of voice, and facial expressions. Solzhenitsyn is fond of refreshing the Russian literary language with racy folk locutions, sayings, and proverbs. The novels are rich in metaphors, notably *Cancer Ward*, in which the animal imagery takes on symbolic significance. At the end of the novels the reader is left in the dark about the ultimate fate of the characters. But this does not matter much for Solzhenitsyn. What counts is the moral behavior of a character at the critical point in his life, where he reveals his true value.

August 1914 is the first published "knot" in what should be a multi-volume cycle of novels entitled *Krasnoe koleso* (The Red Wheel) and intended to depict the history of the Russian revolution by focusing on its crucial events. In *August 1914* such an event is the defeat of the Russian troops in East Prussia, which, in Solzhenitsyn's view, was the first in a series of military disasters that eventually led to the revolution. Solzhenitsyn equates the revolution with the senseless destruction of Russia, whose salvation lay in a gradual socio-economic evolution with the emphasis on individual morality.

Outside the imaginative literature Solzhenitsyn's unique achievement is *The Gulag Archipelago*, a comprehensive picture of the Soviet penal system from its inception to the mid-1960's. Resorting to metaphors and irony, Solzhenitsyn tells the story of arrests, interrogations, executions, camps, and exile. He rejects the principle of survival at any price. Moral decline caused by materialism and the appeasement of the Soviet Union by the West are the dominant themes of his speeches and journalistic writings. His literary autobiography, *The Oak and the Calf*, is essential for an understanding of his personality.

—Herman Ermolaev

SOPHOCLES. Born in Colonus, near Athens, c. 496 B.C. Married Nicostrate, one son; also had one son by his concubine Theoris. Won his first playwriting prize in 468: won a total of 18 victories at the Great Dionysia, and 6 at the Lenaea; actor in his early plays; we know 122 titles (though some may be sub-titles). Served as imperial treasurer, 443-42; elected general twice, the first time in 440 when he was a colleague with Pericles in suppressing the Samian revolt; advisory commissioner for recovery after defeat at Syracuse, 413. Also served as priest of the hero Halon (?), a cult associated with that of Asclepius, and founded a literary club. *Died in late 406 B.C.*

PUBLICATIONS

Collections

[*Plays*], edited by A.C. Pearson. 1924; also edited by A. Dain, 1955-58, and R.D. Dawe, 2 vols., 1975-79; translated in *Complete Greek Tragedies* edited by David Grene and Richmond Lattimore, 1959; also translated by R.C. Jebb (includes text and commentary), 1883-96, F. Storr (Loeb edition), 1912-13, and E.F. Watling, 1947-53.

Plays

Ajax (produced before 441?). Edited by W.B. Stanford, 1963; as *Ajax*, translated by John Moore, in *Complete Greek Tragedies*, 1959; also translated by T.H. Banks, 1966.
Antigone (produced 441?). As *Antigone*, translated by Elizabeth Wyckoff, in *Complete Greek Tragedies*, 1959; also translated by T.H. Banks, in *Three Theban Plays*, 1956, Paul Roche, 1958, H.D.F. Kitto, 1962, Richard Emil Braun, 1973, Kenneth McLeish, 1979, and Robert Fagles, in *The Three Theban Plays*, 1982.
Oedipus Tyrannus (produced after 430?). Edited by R.D. Dawe, 1979; as *Oedipus the King*, translated by David Grene, in *Complete Greek Tragedies*, 1959; also translated by T.H. Banks, in *Three Theban Plays*, 1956, Albert Cook (as *Oedipus Rex*), 1957, Paul Roche, 1958, H.D.F. Kitto, 1962, T. Gould, 1970, Philip Vellacott, 1971, Anthony Burgess, 1972, and Robert Fagles, in *The Three Theban Plays*, 1982.
Trachiniae (produced in 420's?). Edited by P.E. Easterling, 1982; as *Women of Trachis*,

translated by Michael Jameson, in *Complete Greek Tragedies*, 1959; also translated by T.H. Banks, 1966, R. Torrance, 1966, and C.K. Williams and Gregory W. Dickerson, 1978.

Electra (produced ?).   Edited by J.H. Kells, 1973; as *Electra*, translated by David Grene, in *Complete Greek Tragedies*, 1959; also translated by H.D.F. Kitto, 1962, T.H. Banks, 1966, William Sale, 1973, and Kenneth McLeish, 1979.

Philoctetes (produced 409).   Edited by T.B.L. Webster, 1970; as *Philoctetes*, translated by David Grene, in *Complete Greek Tragedies*, 1959; also translated by Kathleen Freeman, 1949, T.H. Banks, 1966, R. Torrance, 1966, Douglas Brown, 1969, and Kenneth McLeish, 1979.

Oedipus Coloneus (produced 401).   As *Oedipus at Colonus*, translated by Robert Fitzgerald, in *Complete Greek Tragedies*, 1959; also translated by T.H. Banks, in *Three Theban Plays*, 1956, Paul Roche, 1958, and Robert Fagles, in *The Three Theban Plays*, 1982.

Ichneutae [Trackers; fragment of satyr play], as *The Searching Satyrs*, translated by Roger Lancelyn Green, in *Two Satyr Plays*.   1957.

[*Fragments*], edited by S. Radt.   1977.

*

Critical Studies: *An Introduction to Sophocles* by T.B.L. Webster, 1936; *Sophoclean Tragedy* by C.M. Bowra, 1944; *Sophocles: A Study of Heroic Humanism* by C.H. Whitman, 1951; *Sophocles the Dramatist* by A.J.A. Waldock, 1951; *A Study of Sophoclean Drama* by G.M. Kirkwood, 1958; *Sophocles, Dramatist and Philosopher*, 1958, and *Poiesis: Structure and Thought*, 1966, both by H.D.F. Kitto; *Oedipus Rex: A Mirror for Greek Drama* edited by Albert Cook, 1963; *The Heroic Temper: Studies in Sophoclean Tragedy* by B.M.W. Knox, 1964; *Sophocles: A Collection of Critical Essays* edited by T.M. Woodard, 1966; *Sophocles* by K. Reinhardt, 1979; *The Chorus in Sophocles' Tragedies* by R.W.B. Burton, 1980; *Sophocles: An Interpretation* by R.P. Winnington-Ingram, 1980; *Tragedy and Civilization: An Interpretation of Sophocles* by G. Segal, 1981.

*   *   *

Very little of Sophocles's large output survives, and only his last two plays can be dated with certainty. We are not in a position to trace stylistic or ideological development in his work. Since the seven tragedies we possess display a considerable unity of theme and style, it is possible that their composition may not have spanned a very long period.

Sophocles began his dramatic career in competition with Aeschylus. For most of his life, however, his most distinguished rival was his younger contemporary Euripides whom he briefly survived. Antiquity often treats these playwrights as polar opposites and modern criticism has tended to follow suit. The pious, traditional, "Homeric," conservative craftsman, Sophocles, is set against the free-thinking, materialistic, artistic innovator, Euripides. This contrast is not wholly convincing when applied to stagecraft since a strong case can be made for regarding Sophocles as at least as daring in some aspects of dramatic technique as Euripides. Even regarding ideology and belief it requires considerable qualification (in any case not many would now accept the traditional picture of Euripides as committed rationalist). Euripides allows the world of 5th-century Athens and the advanced thought of his time to intrude anachronistically into his plays, but Sophocles's restraint in this matter need not imply a lack of interest in or total alienation from the time in which he lived. It may be questioned whether either of the tragedians' apparent criticism of the Olympian gods is anything more than effective articulation of the feelings of characters reacting to exceptional and terrible sufferings, but it should be pointed out in any case that there are occasions in Sophocles when complaints about the divine dispensation are voiced which are just as strong as those to be found in the plays of Euripides. *Trachiniae*, a play which has seen the destruction of the great hero and benefactor of mankind,

Heracles, brought about unwittingly by his long-suffering wife, ends with the chorus's bitter assertion "and nothing of what has happened is not [the work] of Zeus."

Sophoclean "heroism" has been the subject of much study in modern times and, although some critics have attacked the approach to his work by way of "the hero," it cannot be denied that the recalcitrant, isolated individual at odds with the world in which he lives is a prominent feature of the seven tragedies. Heracles, Ajax, Antigone, Electra, Philoctetes, and Oedipus are alike in that they operate on a level different from their more comfortable and less-demanding fellows. Sometimes we can actually observe Sophocles changing the details of a particular heroic legend in order to enhance the isolation and suffering of the central character of the play. It happens that the treatment of the story of the return of Orestes and the avenging of Agamemnon is extant in the plays of all three tragedians. Where Sophocles is seen to differ from the other two in his *Electra*, almost all the divergences are calculated to make the heroine more isolated and her condition more pitiable. She is given a sister Chrysothemis—a replica of Antigone's timid sister Ismene—whose pusillanimity serves to make Electra even more alone and helpless. In the other versions brother and sister are reunited before the intrigue against their enemies is set in motion and in Euripides's play Electra takes an active part in it. In Sophocles's play she is excluded. Her final desolation comes when she is confronted by her disguised brother (whom she does not recognise until he reveals himself to her) carrying an urn supposed to contain the ashes of the dead Orestes.

We also happen to know how Aeschylus and Euripides treated the story of the Greeks' embassy to the great archer Philoctetes who at the beginning of their campaign against Troy had been deposited by them on the island of Lemnos after a snake-bite had rendered his presence among them physically repellent. Sophocles's reshaping of the legend in his *Philoctetes* is radical. Lemnos is transformed into a desert island and Philoctetes becomes a virtual Robinson Crusoe. Instructed by the villainous Odysseus, Philoctetes's mortal enemy, the young Neoptolemus, son of the great Achilles, deceitfully ingratiates himself with Philoctetes and wins possession of the famous bow without which it is prophesied the Greeks will never take Troy. When Philoctetes realises he has been betrayed (the betrayal is redeemed since Neoptolemus, temperamentally and by heredity a stranger to deceit, eventually breaks with Odysseus and returns the bow) his despair and sense of isolation are all the greater because, thinking that after ten solitary years he had found a true friend, he has been cruelly deceived.

In late antiquity and during the middle ages the three Sophoclean tragedies most read and studied were *Ajax*, *Oedipus Tyrannus*, and *Electra*. In the modern era attention has concentrated perhaps most upon two plays, *Antigone* and *Oedipus Tyrannus*.

For many the attraction of *Antigone* is the conflict between the rebellious heroine and her uncle Creon. Antigone goes against his decree and buries her traitor brother, justifying her action by appeal to the "unwritten laws" which are not man's laws. The conflict has been seen as a kind of clash between two sorts of right, the right of the individual against the right of the state, the demands of conscience opposed to the constraints of legitimate authority. However that may be, the issue is settled decisively in favour of Antigone. Total calamity befalls Creon and his family. That does not, however, save Antigone from death. The second half of the play arouses less enthusiasm than the first as it is hard to feel moved by the downfall of a man as undistinguished as Creon.

Oedipus Tyrannus, regarded as the model tragedy by Aristotle, has certainly become the most famous of all Greek tragedies. When real events are compared to "a Greek tragedy" it is almost always this play which lurks behind the comparison. In fact there are many respects in which the play is not at all typical of its genre. The investigative nature of the plot with the hero as detective eventually uncovering his own identity and at the same time the terrible crimes he has unknowingly committed is unique. Devastating in its effect and constantly fascinating (by reason of the myth it retails) as the play is, it would be a pity if it were to eclipse all other Sophoclean tragedies, particularly the two great plays of Sophocles's final years, *Philoctetes* and *Oedipus Coloneus*.

"The other Oedipus play" contains some of Sophocles's finest choral poetry, odes which evoke the beauties of the Athenian landscape and reflect with extreme pessimism on the afflictions of man's existence and the burdens of old age. Oedipus about to confront his final destiny now a blind beggar attended only by his daughters, abandoned by the sons he hates, arrives in the Athenian suburb of Colonus where Apollo has told him he will end his life. Another oracle makes him the object of pursuit by warring parties. Whoever has him on his side will win the coming battle for Thebes. An attempted kidnap by the Thebans is thwarted by the Athenian king Theseus. Eventually Oedipus answers a sign from heaven and walks unaided into the sacred grove where he is to meet his end. The account of his disappearance is one of the most remarkable and enthralling passages in all Greek tragedy. Although the play brings an end for Oedipus, general harmony and resolution of conflict are not attained. One son, dismissed with a father's curse, has departed to certain death. He will kill his brother and be killed by him. The curse is not retracted, and Oedipus leaves the world implacable and irreconcilable. His faithful daughters have nothing but ill to contemplate in the future. It is something of a paradox, though perhaps only an apparent one, that Sophocles, renowned throughout his life for piety and serenity of temperament and praised by critics for the harmony and moderation of his creations, was capable of writing such emotionally disturbing and harrowing plays. Whatever Aristotle said about the matter, it is Sophocles, not Euripides, who seems to the modern reader the "most tragic" of the three tragedians if we define "tragic" with reference to the ability to depict human suffering at its harshest and human emotions at their most deep.

—David M. Bain

STENDHAL. Pseudonym for Marie-Henri Beyle. Born in Grenoble, France, 23 January 1783. Educated by tutors at home, and at École Centrale, Grenoble, 1796-99. Served as a clerk in the war office, then in French Army in Italy, 1800: Second Lieutenant of Dragoons; invalided to Paris, 1801; resigned, 1802. Lived in Paris, 1802-06; Civil Servant: Provisional Deputy, Deputy, and Intendant to Commissariat of Wars at Brunswick, 1806-09; in Vienna, 1809; Commissioner for Council of State and Inspector of Crown Furnishings and Buildings, Paris, 1810; courier to Russia, 1812; administrator in Silesia and Dauphiné; returned to Paris and left governmnet service, 1814; lived in Milan, 1814-21, and in Paris, doing much free-lance journalism for French and English papers, 1821-30; French Consul, Trieste, 1830-31, and Civitavecchia, from 1831; in Paris on extended leave, 1836-39, and on sick leave from 1841. *Died 23 March 1842.*

PUBLICATIONS

Collections

[Works], edited by Henri Martineau. 6 vols., 1952-68.
Oeuvres complètes, edited by Victor del Litto and Ernest Abravanel. 18 vols., 1961-62.

Fiction

Armance; ou, Quelques scènes d'un salon de Paris en 1827. 1827; translated as *Armance,* 1928.

Le Rouge et le noir: Chronique du XIXe siècle. 1830; as *Red and Black,* 1900 as *The Red and the Black,* 1914; as *Scarlet and Black,* 1938.

La Chartreuse de Parme. 1839; translated as *La Chartreuse de Parme,* 1895; as *The Charterhouse of Parma,* 1925.

L'Abbesse de Castro (includes *Vittoria Accoramboni* and *Les Cenci*). 1839.

Nouvelles inédites. 1855.

Lucien Leuwen, in *Nouvelles inédites.* 1855; published separately, 1894; translated as *Lucien Leuwen,* 1951.

Lamiel, edited by Casimir Stryienski. 1889; edited by Victor del Litto, 1971; translated as *Lamiel,* 1951.

Feder; or, The Moneyed Husband. 1960.

Other

Lettres écrites de Vienne...sur...Haydn,...Mozart et...Métastase. 1814; as *Vies de Haydn, de Mozart, et de Métastase,* 1817; translated as *Haydn, Mozart, Métastase,* 1817.

Histoire de la peinture en Italie. 1817.

Rome, Naples, et Florence en 1817. 1817; revised edition, 1826; as *Rome, Naples, and Florence,* 1818.

De l'amour. 1822; edited by Victor del Litto, 1980; as *On Love,* 1928; as *Love,* 1957.

Racine et Shakespeare. 2 vols., 1823-25; as *Racine and Shakespeare,* 1962.

La Vie de Rossini. 1823; as *The Memoirs of Rossini,* 1824; as *Life of Rossini,* 1970.

Promenades dans Rome. 1829; as *A Roman Journal,* edited by Haakon Chevalier, 1959.

Vie de Napoléon, in *Oeuvres complètes.* 1876; as *A Life of Napoleon,* 1956.

Vie de Henry Brulard, edited by Casimir Stryienski. 1890; revised edition, edited by Henry Debraye, 2 vols., 1913; edited by Beatrice Didier, 1978; as *The Life of Henry Brulard,* 1925.

Souvenirs d'égotisme, edited by Casimir Stryienski. 1892; edited by Henri Martineau, 1927; as *Memoirs of an Egotist,* 1949.

Journal, edited by Henry Debraye and Louis Royer. 5 vols., 1923-34; edited by Henri Martineau, 5 vols., 1937; selection, as *Private Diaries,* edited by Robert Sage, 1955.

To the Happy Few (selected letters), edited by Norman Cameron. 1952.

En marge des manuscripts de Stendhal, edited by Victor del Litto. 1955.

Feuillets inédits (journal of 1837-38), edited by Marcel A. Ruff. 1957.

Selected Journalism from the English Reviews, edited by Geoffrey Strickland. 1959.

Correspondance, edited by Henri Martineau and Victor del Litto. 3 vols., 1962-68.

Stendhal and the Arts, edited by David Wakefield. 1973.

Voyages en Italie, edited by Victor del Litto. 1973.

Oeuvres intimes, edited by Victor del Litto. 2 vols., 1981-82.

*

Bibliography: *Bibliographie stendhalienne 1938-1946* by Victor del Litto, 1948 (and supplements).

Critical Studies: *Stendhal: Notes on a Novelist* by Robert Martin Adams, 1959; *Stendhal: A Collection of Critical Essays* edited by Victor Brombert, 1962, and *Stendhal: Fiction and the Themes of Freedom* by Brombert, 1968; *Stendhal: A Study of His Novels* by F.W.J. Hemmings, 1964; *The Masked Citadel: The Significance of the Title of Stendhal's Chartreuse de*

Parme, 1968, and *The Romantic Prison*, 1978, both by Herbert Morris; *Stendhal* by Michael Wood, 1971; *Stendhal* by Marcel M. Gutwirth, 1971; *Stendhal: The Background of the Novels* by Margaret G. Tillett, 1971; *The Unhappy Few: A Psychological Study of the Novels of Stendhal* by Gilbert D. Chaitin, 1972; *Stendhal: Le Rouge et le Noir* by John Mitchell, 1973; *The Education of a Novelist* by Geoffrey Strickland, 1974; *Stendhal and the Age of Napoleon* by Gita May, 1977; *Stendhal: A Biography* by Robert Alter, 1979; *Stendhal: La Chartreuse de Parme* by Alison Finch, 1983.

*   *   *

Stendhal belongs to that small and privileged group of writers whose modernity has grown with the passage of time. An eminently self-conscious and self-critical author, he nevertheless did not consider art above and apart from the business of living. He expected and demanded a relation of art to life.

Stendhal's position among French Romantics is crucial by virtue of several factors. His life span embraced an era marked by swift and momentous changes, ranging from the French Revolution through the Empire, Bourbon Restoration and July Monarchy. He maintained strong intellectual, ideological, and esthetic ties with the 18th century, especially the Enlightenment and the French Revolution, which he considered the logical extension of the principles and ideals set forth by the *philosophes*. This commitment to the political and intellectual ideals of the 18th century is repeatedly attested by Stendhal's steadfast devotion to libertarian principles and by the hostility and scorn he heaped upon Restoration and Orleanist France.

Non-conformist by temperamental inclination as well as by ideological conviction, for he remained deeply convinced that marginality is the fate of any writer or artist sincerely committed to his calling, Stendhal nevertheless had strong opinions which he was always prepared to defend at great personal risk. Unlike a Flaubert, he eagerly accepted the challenges and even absurdities of life and did not regard his calling as a writer as a sufficient reason for retiring to the isolation of an ivory tower. Yet, even in the most heated moments of personal involvement, enthusiasm, or physical danger, something always held him back from total commitment.

Intellectual clear-sightedness, a sense of humor and of the grotesque, a healthy skepticism in the 18th-century tradition which his contemporaries only too willingly identified with outright cynicism prevented him from becoming the docile follower of a cause, no matter how compelling. Unquestioning admiration was not Stendhal's forte. In this respect, as in so many others, he remains the supreme individualist. Hence his sense of alienation and growing estrangement from his contemporaries.

Nothing was more alien to Stendhal's temperament than a fixed, rigid course and set ways. The variegated and colorful pattern of his own life and career amply testify to his openness of mind and heart: the precociously rebellious and lonely boy of Grenoble, the bookish and solitary young philosopher, the enthusiastic yet solitary dragoon of Milan, the passionate and quixotic lover, the fearless soldier and ambitious administrator closely involved in Napoleon's campaigns across Europe, the avid theater-goer and witty conversationalist, the incisive and provocative critic, the tirelessly inquisitive traveler and tourist, and, finally, the disillusioned yet tender-hearted diplomat belatedly and reluctantly turned novelist.

Stendhal's apprenticeship as a novelist was a long and roundabout one, and he came to it almost by accident and afterthought. Yet having at last come to the realization that writing fiction was his true calling, he turned to it with immense zest and enthusiasm. But because he would frequently use actual events and cases, as in *The Red and the Black*, or historical sources, as in the *Charterhouse of Parma*, he has been accused of lacking the powers of invention and imagination.

If it is true that Stendhal is not, like Balzac, the creator of a host of fictional characters, and that his main protagonists either reflect aspects of himself or of the men and women who had made a strong impact upon him, his originality and creativity lie elsewhere. Always fascinated with cases exemplifying the conflict between the energetic, strong-willed individual and social institutions, Stendhal came to the realization that contemporary France, as well as Italian folk history, mores, and legends, could provide him with stunning insights into human behavior under unusual stress. If Julien Sorel, the hero of *The Red and the Black*, is like his real-life counterpart, a social misfit, endowed with a lively intelligence but soon embittered by life, he embodies, more than anything else, the conflict between passionate impulsiveness and opportunistic hypocrisy.

Fabrice del Dongo, the hero of *The Charterhouse of Parma*, is much more open to the tender, gentle feelings of life than the somber, ambitious, and calculating Julien Sorel. The Italian background confers on *The Charterhouse of Parma* a particularly poetic and lyrical aura, and the presence of mountains, lakes, and high towers adds special color to the narrative. But these external features are not merely meant to introduce a note of exoticism for its own sake; they are the symbols of Stendhal's inner ideal landscape. The prison theme, present in both novels, is also an integral part of this symbolic language of sacrifice and exaltation through suffering and love.

If Fabrice is Stendhal's fictional projection of his young, idealistic self, Count Mosca, minister and man of experience and of the world, is Fabrice's dramatic counterpart. He might well be, as has been suggested, a recreation of Stendhal, the mature, disillusioned, yet still generous man.

In *The Red and the Black*, two dissimilar yet complementary feminine figures vie for the hero's affections. Mme. de Rênal and Mathilde de La Mole may be envisioned as two facets of the feminine dilemma: compliance and tenderness on the part of Mme. de Renal, and rebellion as well as headstrong action on the part of Mathilde de La Mole. Similarly, in *The Charterhouse of Parma* the touching and innocent young Clelia Conti contrasts with the fiery, knowledgeable, and willful Duchess Sanseverina. All Stendhalian heroines are strongly individualized and have the capacity to seek and define their own identity and to assert their will and freedom of choice as individuals. Lamiel, the main protagonist of Stendhal's last and unfinished novel by that name, is perhaps the most striking example of Stendhal's willingness to endow a female character with those qualities of boldness and recklessness generally reserved for heroes.

Stendhal's interest in the novel and in autobiography developed simultaneously; and this is no mere accident. But the relationship between autobiography and fiction is never a simple linear one with Stendhal. Having reached his fifties and faced with his own mortality, Stendhal embarked upon *The Life of Henry Brulard*, which was to retrace his spiritual development more fully than his other autobiographical essays and furnish some sort of an answer to a question that had long haunted him: "What kind of a man have I been?"

The Life of Henry Brulard was never finished. But if it does not go beyond the author's 17th year, it offers us a world of intimate details revealing the circumstances of his early life, but more importantly his reaction to the big and small events that contributed to shaping his mental and emotional outlook. It combines tenderness and humor, sincerity and reticence, candor and discretion, but while it evidently owes much of its inspiration to Rousseau's *Confessions*, it resolutely rejects self-justification. There is always an element of self-deprecatory humor and irony in Stendhal's most solemn declarations.

Stendhal's loyalty to the ideals of the Enlightenment produced among his contemporaries the mistaken impression that he was not moving with the times. He emerged from the revolutionary era with his faith in its accomplishments wholly intact, and his desolation after Waterloo knew no bounds, especially when he saw legitimist France foster a narrow conformism and hypocrisy in many ways even more repressive than the Old Regime.

Stendhal's youthful admiration for Bonaparte and his nostalgic cult of Napoleon after Waterloo can best be understood in light of his lifelong belief in the spirit of adventure and in his willingness to take risks, to gamble on uncertain stakes. When he undertook to write, not to please his contemporaries but in order to appeal to future yet unborn generations of readers, he could only hope that posterity would vindicate his daring act of faith. His tentative expectation was fulfilled beyond his fondest dreams, for the *happy few* for whom he wrote have multiplied into a vast reading public and teams of scholars and critics scrutinize his every printed word and scrap of manuscript.

—Gita May

STIFTER, Adalbert. Born in Oberplan, Bohemia, Austria (now Horní Planá, Czechoslovakia), 23 October 1805. Educated at village school; Benedictine monastery school, Kremsmünster, 1818-26; studied law at University of Vienna, 1828-30. Married Amalia Mohaupt in 1837; one adopted daughter. Tutor, painter, writer: Editor, *Der Wiener Bote*, 1849-50; school inspector, Vienna, 1850, and in Linz, 1851-65; art critic, *Linzer Zeitung*, 1852-57. Curator of Monuments for Upper Austria, 1853, Vice-President, Linzer Kunstverein. Order of Franz Joseph, 1854; Ritterkreuz des Weissen Falkenordens, 1867. *Died 28 January 1868.*

PUBLICATIONS

Collections

> *Sämtliche Werke*, edited by August Sauer. 25 vols., 1904-79.
> *Werke*, edited by Gustav Wilhelm. 5 vols., 1926.
> *Gesammelte Werke*, edited by Max Stefl. 6 vols., 1939.
> *Werke*, edited by Max Stefl. 9 vols., 1950-60.
> *Werke und Briefe*, edited by Alfred Doppler and Wolfgang Frühwald. 1978— .

Fiction

> *Studien.* 6 vols., 1844-50; augmented edition, 1855.
> *Rural Life in Austria and Hungary.* 3 vols., 1850.
> *Pictures of Life.* 1852.
> *Der Hagelstolz.* 1852; as *The Recluse*, 1968.
> *Bunte Steine: Ein Festgeschenk.* 1853; translated in part as *Mount Gars; or, Marie's Christmas Eve*, 1857; as *Rock Crystal*, 1945.
> *Der Nachsommer.* 1857.
> *Witiko.* 1865-67.
> *Erzählungen*, edited by Johannes Aprent. 2 vols., 1869.
> *Der Waldsteig* (in English translation). 1942.
> *The Condor.* 1946.
> *Die Mappe meines Urgrossvaters* (Letzte Fassung). 1946.
> *Erzählungen in der Urfassung*, edited by Max Stefl. 3 vols., 1950-52.
> *Limestone and Other Stories.* 1968.

Other

> *Briefe*, edited by Johannes Aprent. 3 vols., 1869.
> *Stifter: Sein Leben in Selbtzeugnissen, Briefen, und Berichten*, edited by Karl Privat. 1946.
> *Jugendbriefe (1822-1839)* edited by Gustav Wilhelm. 1954.
> *Leben und Werk in Briefen und Dokumenten*, edited by K.G. Fischer. 1962.
> *Briefwechsel*, edited by Josef Buchowiecki. 1965.

> Editor, with Johannes Aprent, *Lesebuch zur Förderung humaner Bildung.* 1854.

*

Bibliography: *Stifter: Bibliographie* by Eduard Eisenmeier, 3 vols., 1964-78.

Critical Studies: *Stifter: A Critical Study* by E.A. Blackall, 1948; *Natural Science in the Work of Stifter* by W.E. Umbach, 1950; *The Marble Statue as Idea: Collected Essays on Stifter's "Der*

Nachsommer" by Christine O. Sjögren, 1972; *Stifter* by Margaret Gump, 1974. *Stifter Heute* edited by Johann Lachinger, Alexander Stillmark, and Martin Swales, 1984.

*   *   *

The publication of Adalbert Stifter's narrative prose, consisting of some 30 stories and novellas and three novels, broadly coincides with the end of the Biedermeier era and extends into the so-called Poetic Realism of the 1850's and 1860's. The temper of the age, which was moderate, contemplative, and reverential, is ostensibly reflected in the restrained, measured prose of this meticulous stylist. At a submerged level, Stifter's language expresses profound existential tensions and conflicts. The subjects of his fiction are set very largely within the landscapes of his native Bohemia. His masterly descriptions of forest and mountain scenery early gained him the reputation of being a painter in words (he was, in fact, also a gifted landscape painter). From his earliest stories, an unusual prominence is ascribed to the presence of nature: man is continually seen in his relationship to nature and a subtle parallelism of meaning is insinuated largely through symbolic suggestion but also by means of juxtaposition and contrast. The trials and griefs of fallible humanity are set beside the flawless model of a natural order which expresses constancy, innocence, and beauty. Though he suppresses overt representation of violent passions and the darker aspects of life, Stifter often achieves an increased intensity by narrative devices which exploit concealment and intimation. Underlying his descriptions of even the smallest detail of a world minutely explored and fastidiously recorded is the grandeur of a universal design. However, the protective "gentle law" active in nature and in human society which Stifter acknowledges in his famous "Preface" to the collection *Bunte Steine*, is not readily discernible in all his works. The proximity of the sublime to the terrible, of beauty to pain, repeatedly asserts itself.

From his *Studien* onwards, the attention Stifter lavishes on objects, whether natural or domestic, conveys an almost obsessional interest, which dignifies "things" with ontological import. (His influence on Rilke and Kafka has not gone unnoticed.) The human figures he draws are not so much psychologically explored as externally observed and related to their physical environment. An heir to the legacy of Weimar classicism and dedicated to the humanist ideals of enlightenment and self-cultivation, Stifter wrote his first novel in the genre of the German novel of education. *Der Nachsommer* is a monumental tribute to that tradition, while in another sense it presents, in transfiguring light, the archetypal heart-break situation of a love that failed in youth, yet finds propitiation and fulfilment in maturity. The historical novel *Witiko* is an ambitious and original attempt to depict the founding of a society on premises of morality and justice. In his last, unfinished novel, *Die Mappe meines Urgrossvaters*, Stifter offers the moving story of a country doctor who attains to self-mastery and wholeness through the dire trials of renunciation, bereavement, and service to others. In his late style Stifter develops an austere simplicity of expression, a stylized manner which is defiantly contrary to contemporary realism. His later fiction puzzled and alienated his readership and it fell to Nietzsche to discover his importance.

—Alexander Stillmark

STONE, Story of the.   *See* **DREAM OF THE RED CHAMBER.**

STRINDBERG, August. Born in Stockholm, 22 January 1849. Educated at Uppsala University, 1867, 1870-72, no degree. Married 1) Baroness Siri von Essen in 1877 (divorced, 1891), four children; 2) Frida Uhl in 1893 (divorced, 1897), one daughter; 3) Harriet Bosse in 1901 (divorced, 1904), one daughter. Teacher, tutor, actor, journalist; trained as telegraph-clerk, 1873; assistant librarian, Royal Library, Stockholm, 1874-79; center of a group of radical writers in 1880's; tried for blasphemy, but acquitted, 1884; also a painter; lived in Berlin, 1892-94, Paris, 1894-96, Lund, 1896-99, and Stockholm after 1899; organized his own Intimate Theatre, 1907. *Died 14 May 1912.*

PUBLICATIONS

Collections

> *Samlede skrifter,* edited by J. Landqvist. 55 vols., 1912-20.
> *Dramer,* edited by C.R. Smedmark. 1962— .
> *Samlede verk,* edited by Lars Dahlbäck and others. 1980— .
> *The Washington Strindberg,* edited and translated by Walter Johnson. 1955— .

Plays

> *I Rom* [In Rome] (produced 1870). 1870.
> *Hermione.* 1871.
> *Den fredlöse* (produced 1871). 1881; as *The Outlaw,* in *Plays,* 1912.
> *Mäster Olof* (prose version; produced 1872). 1872; revised version (verse, produced 1881), 1878; as *Master Olof,* 1915.
> *Gillets hemlighet* [The Secret of the Guild] (produced 1880). 1880.
> *Anno fyrtioåtta* [Anno Forty-Eight]. 1881.
> *Lycko-Pers resa* (produced 1883). 1882; as *Lucky Pehr,* 1912; as *Lucky Peter's Travels,* 1930.
> *Herr Bengts husfru* [Sir Bengt's Wife]. 1882.
> *Kamraterna* (produced 1905). 1885; as *Comrades,* in *Plays,* 1913.
> *Fadren* (produced 1887). 1887; as *The Father,* 1889.
> *Fröken Julie* (produced 1889). 1888; as *Countess Julia,* 1912; as *Miss Julie,* 1918.
> *Paria* (produced 1889). 1890; as *Pariah,* 1913.
> *Den starkare* (produced 1889). 1890; as *The Stronger,* in *Plays,* 1912.
> *Samum* (produced 1889). 1890; as *Simoon,* in *Plays,* 1913.
> *Hemsöborna* [The Natives of Hemsö], from his own novel (produced 1889).
> *Fordringsägare* (produced 1890). 1890; as *The Creditors,* 1909.
> *Bandet* (produced 1902). 1892; as *The Link,* in *Plays,* 1912; as *The Bond,* 1930.
> *Leka med elden* (produced 1908). 1892; as *Playing with Fire,* 1930.
> *Debet ock kredit* (produced 1900). 1892; as *Debit and Credit,* in *Plays,* 1913.
> *Moderskärlek* (produced 1894). 1892; as *Motherlove,* 1910.
> *Första varningen* (produced 1892). 1892; as *The First Warning,* in *Plays,* 1916.
> *Inför döden* (produced 1893). 1892; as *Facing Death,* 1915; as *In the Face of Death,* in *Eight Expressionist Plays,* 1965.
> *Advent* (produced 1915). 1898; translated as *Advent,* in *Plays,* 1913.
> *Till Damaskus* (trilogy) (produced 1900-16). 1898-1904; edited by G. Lindström, 1964; as *To Damascus,* 1913.
> *Folkungasagan* (produced 1901). 1899; as *The Saga of the Folkungs,* in *Master Olof and Other Plays,* 1931.
> *Gustav Vasa* (produced 1899). 1899; translated as *Gustavus Vasa,* in *Plays,* 1916.
> *Erik XIV* (produced 1899). 1899; translated as *Erik XIV,* in *Master Olof and Other*

Plays, 1931.
Brott och brott (produced 1900). 1899; as *There Are Crimes and Crimes*, 1912.
Påsk (produced 1901). 1900; as *Easter*, in *Easter and Stories*, 1912.
Gustav Adolf (produced 1903). 1900; translated as *Gustav Adolf*, in *Plays*, 1912.
Svanevit (produced 1908). 1901; as *Swanwhite*, 1909.
Karl XII (produced 1902). 1901; translated as *Charles XII*, 1955.
Dödsdansen (produced 1905). 1901; as *The Dance of Death*, in *Plays*, 1912.
Engelbrekt (produced 1901). 1901; translated as *Engelbrekt*, 1955.
Midsommar (produced 1901). 1901.
Kronbruden (produced 1906). 1902; as *The Bridal Crown*, in *Plays*, 1912; as *The Virgin Bride*, in *Plays*, 1975.
Gustav III (produced 1902). 1902; translated as *Gustav III*, 1955.
Ett drömspel (produced 1907). 1902; as *The Dream Play*, in *Plays*, 1912.
Näktergalen i Wittenberg (produced 1914). 1903; as *The Nightingale of Wittenberg*, in *World Historical Plays*, 1970.
Himmelrikets nycklar, in *Samlede dramatiska arbeten*. 1903-04; as *The Keys of Heaven*, in *Eight Expressionist Plays*, 1965.
Kristina (produced 1908). 1904; as *Queen Christina*, 1955.
Spöksonaten (produced 1908). 1907; edited by G. Lindström, 1963; as *The Spook Sonata*, in *Plays*, 1916; as *The Ghost Sonata*, in *Easter and Other Plays*, 1929.
Oväder (produced 1907). 1907; as *The Storm*, in *Plays*, 1912.
Brända tomten (produced 1907). 1907; as *After the Fire*, in *Plays*, 1913; as *The Burned House*, 1962.
Pelikanen (produced 1907). 1907; as *The Pelican*, in *Plays*, 1916.
Abu Casems tofflor [Abu Casem's Slippers] (produced 1908). 1908.
Siste riddaren (produced 1909). 1908; as *The Last of the Knights*, 1956.
Riksföreståndaren (produced 1911). 1908; as *The Regent*, 1956.
Bjälbo-Jarlen (produced 1909). 1908; as *Earl Birger of Bjälbo*, 1956.
Svarta handsken (produced 1909). 1909; as *The Black Glove*, in *Plays*, 1916.
Stora landsvägen (produced 1910). 1909; as *The Great Highway*, 1945.
Genom öknar till arvland; eller, Moses (produced 1922). In *Samlede otryckta skrifter*, 1918-19; as *Moses*, in *Plays*, 1916; as *Through Deserts to Ancestral Lands*, in *World Historical Plays*, 1970.
Toten-Insel, in *Samlede skrifter*. 1918; as *Isle of the Dead*, in *Modern Drama 3*, 1962.
Hellas; eller, Sokrates (produced 1922). In *Samlede otryckta skrifter*, 1918-19; as *Hellas*, in *World Historical Plays*, 1970.
Lammet och vilddjuret; eller, Kristus (produced 1922). In *Samlede otryckta skrifter*, 1918-19; as *The Lamb and the Beast*, in *World Historical Plays*, 1970.

Fiction

Röda rummet. 1879; as *The Red Room*, 1913.
Giftas. 1884-85; as *Married*, 1913; complete version, as *Getting Married*, 1972.
Hemsöborna. 1887; as *The Natives of Hemsö*, 1959.
Skärkarlsliv [Life in the Skerries]. 1888.
Tschandala (in Danish). 1889.
I havsbandet. 1890; as *By the Open Sea*, 1913.
Fagervik och skamsund. 1902; as *Fair Haven and Foul Strand*, 1913.
Sagor. 1903; as *Tales*, 1930.
Gotiska rummen [The Gothic Rooms]. 1903.
Historiska miniatyrer. 1905; as *Historical Miniatures*, 1913.
Svarta fanor [Black Banners]. 1907.

Taklagsöl [Topping Out]. 1907.
Syndabocken. 1907; as *The Scapegoat*, 1967.

Other

Svenska folket [The Swedish People]. 2 vols., 1881-82.
Det nya riket [The New Kingdom]. 1882.
Utopier i verkligheten [Utopias in Reality]. 1884.
Tjästekvinnans son. 4 vols., 1886-87; translated in part as *The Son of a Servant*, 1967.
Le Plaidoyer d'un fou. 1888; revised edition, 1893; as *En dåres försvarstal*, 1920; as *The Confessions of a Fool*, 1912; as *A Madman's Defense*, 1967.
Inferno. 1897; translated as *Inferno*, 1967.
Legender [Legends]. 1898.
Ensam. 1903; as *Alone*, 1968.
En blå bok. 4 vols., 1907-12; translated in part as *Zones of the Spirit*, 1913.
Öppna brev till Intima Teatern. 1908; as *Letters to the Intimate Theatre*, edited by Walter Johnson, 1967.
Tal till svenska nationen [Speeches to the Swedish Nation]. 1910.
Easter and Stories (miscellany). 1912.
Samlede otryckta skrifter. 2 vols., 1918-19.
Brev, edited by Torsten Eklund. 1948— .
Vivisektioner, edited by Torsten Eklund. 1958.
Letters to Harriet Bosse, edited by Arvid Paulson. 1959.
Brev till min dotter Kerstin, edited by Karin Boye and Åke Thulstrup. 1961.
Ur ockulta dagboken, edited by Torsten Eklund. 1963; complete version, 1977; translated in part as *From an Occult Diary*, 1965.
Klostret. 1966; as *The Cloister*, 1969.

*

Bibliography: "Strindberg's Reception in England and America" by Esther H. Rapp, in *Scandinavian Studies 23*, 1951, supplemented by Jackson R. Bryer in *Modern Drama 5*, 1962, and Birgitta Steene in *Structures of Influence: A Comparative Approach to Strindberg* edited by Marilyn John Blackwell, 1981; *Illustrerad svensk litteraturhistoria 4* by Sven Rinman, 1967.

Critical Studies: *The Strange Life of Strindberg* by Elizabeth Sprigge, 1949; *Strindberg's Naturalistic Theatre* by B.G. Madsen, 1962; *Strindberg and the Historical Drama*, 1963, and *Strindberg*, 1976, both by Walter Johnson; *The Novels of Strindberg* by Eric O. Johannesson, 1968; *Strindberg* by M. Lamm, 1971; *The Greatest Fire: A Study of Strindberg* by Birgitta Steene, 1973; *Strindberg in Inferno* by Gunnar Brandell, 1974; *The Social and Religious Plays of Strindberg* by John Ward, 1980; *Strindberg and the Poetry of Myth* by Harry G. Carlson, 1982; *Strindbergian Drama* by Egil Törnqvist, 1982; *Strindberg as Dramatist* by Evert Sprinchorn, 1982; *Strindberg* by Olof Lagercrantz, 1983.

*   *   *

August Strindberg's achievement as an immensely productive dramatist, poet, novelist, essayist, painter, historian, autobiographer, and speculator in the natural sciences, alchemy, and linguistics is so various as almost to preclude summary. His international reputation, however, undoubtedly rests upon his plays. Strindberg experimented with many theatrical forms, fairy-tale comedy in *Lucky Peter's Travels*, the folk play in *The Virgin Bride*, and, beginning with his first major work, *Master Olof*, in 1872, a cycle of 12 history plays which represent the most important contribution to the genre since Shakespeare. Indeed, *Gustav Vasa*, *Erik XIV*, *Charles XII*, and *Queen Christina* combine a Shakespearean response to the sweep and detail of history with an acute and personal insight into historical characters, but they have been unduly neglected abroad because their material is taken from Swedish history.

This is certainly not the case with the two sets of plays which Strindberg wrote with his sights already trained on the theatres of France and Germany, two countries where, after his attack on Swedish society in the satirical pamphlet *Det nya riket* (The New Kingdom) in 1882, and his trial for blasphemy arising from the collection of stories *Getting Married* in 1884, he was to spend several important years of his life. The first set consists of the naturalist plays which Strindberg wrote between 1887 and 1892 as if in response to Zola's plea for someone to abandon the contrived formula of the contemporary well-made play and "put a man of flesh and bones on the stage, taken from reality scientifically analysed, and described without one lie." Building upon extensive reading in current psychology and cultivating a remarkable propensity for self-analysis that he owed in part to his pietist upbringing, Strindberg developed an intense and concentrated form for the portrayal on stage of what he called "the harsh, cynical and heartless drama that life presents." At the heart of this drama is an elemental struggle between man and woman, which he explores tragically in *The Father* and *Miss Julie* and sardonically in *Creditors*. Conflict, however, is no longer physical but what Strindberg termed a "battle of the brains" in which one character seeks through suggestion to impose its will upon another. His ideas are outlined in the volume of essays, *Vivisektioner*, whose title implies the kind of analysis to which the naturalist writer aspired, and the preface to *Miss Julie*, which is the major theoretical statement of theatrical naturalism, where Strindberg describes his characters as not only the products of environmental and inherited forces but also as "split and vacillating...agglomerations of past and present cultures, scraps from books and newspapers, fragments of humanity, torn shreds of once-fine clothing that has become rags, in just the way that a human soul is patched together."

Miss Julie itself may not fully realise Strindberg's intentions, but in his next major group of plays, begun after an interval of six years, he effected a radical break with prevailing dramatic conventions and produced the key works in the development of theatrical modernism. In *To Damascus*, a sequence of three plays in which Strindberg projects his inner life through the figure of his protagonist, The Unknown, the picture-frame stage of the naturalists, with its abundance of realistic detail, gives way to the interior stage of the mind, a landscape through which The Unknown journeys as he delves into the past and encounters characters who are either aspects of his own personality or the product of his anxious imagination. In *The Dream Play*, meanwhile, which is generally regarded as Strindberg's major achievement, he seeks "to imitate the inconsequent yet transparently logical shape of a dream" where time and place do not exist and everything is possible and probable. The similarity of Strindberg's concerns with those of his contemporary, Freud, have often, and rightly, been observed, but the dramatic presentation of life as a dream and the world as a stage also occurs in earlier drama, for example in Shakespeare, Calderón, and Ibsen's *Peer Gynt*. Nevertheless, *The Dream Play* inititates a succession of metatheatrical plays and marks the transition from a drama centred on plot and character to a theme-centred drama. In their use of concrete theatrical images enlisting all the resources of the stage, and in their apparently fluid structure, it is often easier to grasp the nature of these plays in terms of music, an affinity Strindberg underlined by calling his last important collection of plays, the Chamber Plays (*Storm*, *The Burned House*, *The Ghost Sonata*, and *The Pelican*) written in 1907, his "last sonatas."

That Strindberg could make this remarkable transition from naturalism to modernism was largely a consequence of what is known as his "Inferno crisis." This was a period of acute mental suffering which verged upon psychological breakdown, during which he was largely unproductive as an imaginative writer. Between 1892 and 1898 he spent much time on scientific studies which, in accord with the spirit of *fin de siècle* Paris where he lived for long periods, gravitated towards alchemy and magic. Behind his apparently aimless experiments, however, lay the need to renew himself by the discovery of fresh ways of seeing and apprehending both the visible and invisible world. At a time when Freud was similarly engaged on the self-analysis which led to *The Interpretation of Dreams* (1900), Strindberg also sought and found access to the unconscious life of the mind, employing techniques, outlined in the essay "The New Arts;

or, The Role of Chance in Artistic Creation," which anticipate Surrealism, and which he first applied in his paintings. A friend of Gauguin and Munch, Strindberg was a considerable artist, and the way in which he approaches a non-representational art in his paintings marks a parallel development to his move away from plot and character in drama.

A partial account of these years is provided by the auto-biographical novel, *Inferno*, and his *Occult Diary*, two in a sequence of autobiographical works which Strindberg saw as the core of his life's work. Employing various narrative techniques he traces the stages of an existence during which, both in life and literature, he experimented in a Kierkegaardian manner with a succession of different points of view, including an anarchism penetrated by the thought of Rousseau, an uneasy accommodation with Darwinism, atheism, Nietzschean individualism, and, after 1896, the discovery of a fruitful perspective for his writing in a personal syncretic religion that owed much to the Swedish scientist and mystic Emanuel Swedenborg (1688-1772). In *The Son of a Servant*, which stresses his lifelong identification with his mother, a former servant girl and waitress, rather than with his middle-class father, he undertakes a naturalist investigation into his childhood and youth. This is followed by *A Madman's Defense*, the savage and exuberant vivisection of the first of his three turbulent marriages, *The Cloister*, *Inferno*, *Legender*, and finally *Alone*, an evocative portrayal of loneliness and the artistic process. Strindberg wished these works to be published as a single book, together with the *Occult Diary* and his letters, an unwieldy project since the letters alone (and Strindberg was a formidable correspondent) fill over 15 volumes.

Inevitably the problem of subjectivity is one that Strindberg's work frequently raises. He regarded his life as literary capital and can often be discovered provoking experience in order to obtain material for further books. The real point, however, is not whether it is possible to correlate what is known of his life with the matter of his writing, but the transformation this material undergoes as it is turned into literature to enter into a complex set of relationships with all his other works. And if Strindberg appears to lack both imagination and humour, the reproach is belied by yet another portion of his work, again little known abroad, his novels and stories. *The Red Room*, for example, with which he first made his reputation in Sweden, is an iridescent novel of Stockholm life, by turns comic, pathetic, and satiric, in which the influence of Dickens and Balzac is adroitly balanced. The humour of *The Natives of Hemsö* is rich, even ribald, and like its successor, *By the Open Sea*, it demonstrates Strindberg's passionate feeling for nature, particularly the landscape of the Stockholm archipelago; *Getting Married* is amusing as well as acerbic in its treatment of the woman question; *Taklagsöl* (Topping Out) is a finely judged experiment in the stream-of-consciousness technique; and *Gotiska Rummen* and *Svarta fanor* are both lively as well as bitter attacks on contemporary society. In all these books, as well as in his many essays on natural history, his historical studies *Gamla Stockholm* (Old Stockholm) and *Svenska folket* (The Swedish People), his historical fiction, and the political polemics in which he was engaged at the end of his life, Strindberg displays a multi-faceted response to experience which is consistently envigorated by a virtuoso command of his native language.

—Michael Robinson

STURLUSON, Snorri. Born on estate of Hvamm, Iceland, in 1179. Grew up in the cultivated household of Jón Loptsson at Oddi, 1181-97. Married Herdís Bersadóttir in 1199

(separated, 1206 or 1207); had children by several other women. Lived in Reykholt after his separation from his wife, and became leading chieftain in Iceland; served as Law-Speaker of the Althing, 1215-18, 1222-31; visited Norway and Sweden, 1218-20, and made a later visit to Norway under political threat, 1237-39; murdered by political rival in 1241. Collector of earlier court poetry. *Died 23 September 1241.*

PUBLICATIONS

Fiction

Heimskringla [The Orb of the World], edited by Bjarni Adalbjarnarson.2 vols., 1941-51; as *Chronicle of the Kings of Norway*, translated by Samuel Laing, 3 vols., 1844, revised by Peter Foote, 1961; also translated by William Morris and Eiríkr Magnússon as *The Stories of the Kings of Norway, called The Round World*, 4 vols., 1893-1905, by Erling Monsen and A.H. Smith, 1932, and by Lee M. Hollander, 1964; translated in part as *King Harald's Saga* by Magnus Magnusson and Hermann Pálsson, 1966.

Other

Edda (prose), edited by Finnur Jónsson, 1900; revised edition, 1931; translated by G.W. Dasent, 1842, Arthur G. Brodeur, 1916, and Jean I. Young, 1954.

*

Bibliography: in *Islandica*, 1908—.

Critical Studies: *Snorri Sturluson* (in Icelandic) by Sigurdur Nordal, 1920; *The Meaning of Snorri's Categories* by Arthur G. Brodeur, 1952; *Origins of Icelandic Literature* by G. Turville-Petre, 1953.

*   *   *

Snorri Sturluson lived during the great age of saga-writing in Iceland, the 13th century; and his name has survived where the names of most other saga-writers have long been forgotten. He was a child of his time, combining a love of learning and intellectual pursuits with greed for wealth and power, and participation in the political machinations of the power struggle between Iceland and Norway, which at first brought him royal patronage, but finally a violent end. However, it is for his historical and imaginative writings, composed during the period 1222-35, that he is now remembered, and still read in Scandinavia as is no other medieval writer.

Snorri's major achievement as a historical writer is *Heimskringla* (The Orb of the World), a history of the kings of Norway from the earliest days (based on semi-mythical tales) to 1177. It is actually a collection of 17 sagas, of which one—the saga of King Olaf the Saint—dominates over all the others. Although Olaf ruled for only 15 years, his saga takes up one-third of the work; the Christian warrior-king was a figure who fascinated Snorri, and there is evidence that his saga was written first and then incorporated into the longer work. Snorri was a painstaking and meticulous historian, who used all the available source material, including written histories, earlier sagas, verbal reports, and scaldic poetry, in order to arrive at as accurate a version as possible of past events. He was, however, not merely a scientific recorder; his aim was rather to give a personal interpretation of events, to reconstruct the past. History was in his view formed by great men—a view with which many modern historians would disagree; yet his skilful reconstructions of the lives of the kings, combining fact with imagination and inventiveness, bring the atmosphere of the age vividly before us.

The other work which Snorri is known to have composed, the *Prose Edda*, gave full scope to his creative literary talents. It fulfils several aims, but its most important function is as a preserver of literary and mythological tradition. It contains a mythology of the old Norse gods and the heathen world-view, ostensibly as an aid to poets who needed to know the origins of the myths from which scaldic poetry drew its images—material which was in danger of being forgotten in the new Christian era. But is is also clearly a story which Snorri relishes telling; his enthusiasm for the myths turns the text-book into a lively and humorous re-creation. The *Edda* further records and gives examples of all the different forms of scaldic verse, of which it provides an invaluable collection; and it explains and exemplifies the use of poetic imagery in scaldic verse. Thus in several areas it has preserved material which would otherwise have been lost.

In addition to these two works, Snorri wrote other poems—mainly to wealthy patrons; and there is a large body of scholarly opinion which attributes to him the authorship of *Egil's Saga*, the life-story of the poet Egill Skalla-Grímsson.

—Janet Garton

SVEVO, Italo. Pseudonym for Ettore Schmitz. Born in Trieste (then part of Austro-Hungary), 19 December 1861. Educated at Jewish schools in Trieste to 1873; Brüsselische Handels- und Erziehunginstitut, Segnitz-am-Main, 1873-78; Istituto Revoltella, Trieste, 1878-80. Married Livia Veneziani in 1896. Clerk, Trieste branch of Unionbank of Vienna, 1880-99; partner in his wife's family's manufacturing firm from 1899. Took English lessons from James Joyce in Trieste from 1907. *Died 13 September 1928.*

PUBLICATIONS

Collections

Opera omnia, edited by Bruno Maier. 4 vols., 1966-69.

Fiction

Una vita. 1892; as *A Life*, 1963.
Senilità. 1898; as *As a Man Grows Older*, 1932.
La coscienza di Zeno. 1923; as *The Confessions of Zeno*, 1930.
The Hoax. 1929.
La novella del buon vecchio e della bella fanciulla. 1930; as *The Nice Old Man and the Pretty Girl and Other Stories*, 1930.
Corto viaggio sentimentale e altri racconti inedite. 1949; as *Short Sentimental Journey and Other Stories*, 1967.
The Further Confessions of Zeno. 1969.

Plays

Terzetta spezzato (produced 1927). In *Commedie*, 1960.
Commedie (includes *Terzetta spezzato, Un marito, L'avventura di Maria, Una commedia inedita, La verità, Inferiorità, Le ire di Giuliano, Le teorie del conte Alberto, Il ladro in casa, Primo del ballo, Atto unico, Con la penna d'oro, La regenerazione*), edited by Umbro Apollonio. 1960.
Un marito (produced 1961). In *Commedie*, 1960.
L'avventura di Maria (produced 1966). In *Commedie*, 1960.
Una commedia inedita, La verità, Inferiorità (produced 1967). In *Commedie*, 1960.

Other

Saggi e pagine sparse. 1954.
Lettere alla moglie, edited by Anita Pittoni. 1963.
Lettere: Eugenio Montale-Svevo. 1966.

*

Bibliography: by Bruno Maier, in *Opera omnia 2*, 1969; "Criticism of Svevo: A Selected Checklist" by J.W. Van Voorhis, in *Modern Fiction Studies 18*, 1972.

Critical Studies: *Svevo: The Man and the Writer* by P.N. Furbank, 1966; *Essays on Svevo* edited by Thomas F. Staley, 1969; *Svevo: A Critical Introduction* by Brian Moloney, 1974; *Svevo* by Naomi Lebowitz, 1978; *Svevo, The Writer from Trieste* by Charles C. Russell, 1978.

*   *   *

The first Italian novelist who tackled such typical 20th-century themes as psychoanalysis and investigation into the self-obsessed modern anti-hero, Italo Svevo makes telling use of autobiography in order to depict the problems faced by his anti-heroes. His experience as a clerk in his father's bank in Trieste provided him with the raw material for his first interesting, though artistically uneven novel, *A Life*. The protagonist, Alfonso Nitti, is an inept young man unable to come to grips with the reality around him which does not match his grandiose dreams. This inability leads to an increasingly irreconcilable hiatus between his meaningless existence and his lofty aspirations, as a result of which he commits suicide.

Svevo's second novel, *As a Man Grows Older*, has as protagonist Emilio Brentani, a rather older version of Alfonso Nitti, who in spite of a minor literary success, finds himself at the age of 35 essentially a failure in art as well as in life. His senility is depicted as a psychological condition which, as in the case of Alfonso Nitti, prevents him from coming to terms with the reality of everyday life. His abortive attempt at self-fulfilment through a relationship with an exuberantly sexual working-class girl, Angiolina, merely serves to bring out his basic inability to cope with the most vital aspects of human experience. He ultimately renounces life and takes refuge in a self-contained dream world of his own making in which even the memory of his sister, neglected by Emilio in life and abandoned by him on her death (she dies of alcoholism), becomes distorted and merges with his idealized memory of Angiolina.

Svevo's reputation as a major Italian novelist depends on *The Confessions of Zeno*, the novel of his maturity. Zeno Cosini, the protagonist, is an older and wiser Brentani who has come to terms with his basic ineptitude and lack of direction in life. With the help of psychoanalysis he learned to diagnose his own weakness and "sickness" and to face the challenges of the "healthy" everyday life of the generally corrupt and unthinking bourgeoisie of which he is a member. Thus he can look forward to a relatively comfortable old-age—the reward of an almost Darwinian struggle to survive. The originality of Svevo's view of the survival of the fittest lies in the fact that his anti-hero Zeno, although to all intents and purposes a perfect example of a vacillating, weak-willed, inept man, survives and prospers precisely because of his ability to cope with his shortcomings, and even to exploit them to his own advantage. His account of his efforts to overcome his fear of illness (deriving, according to him, from his addiction to cigarettes), his sense of guilt (for having desired the death of his father and for his infidelity to his wife), his feelings of jealousy (provoked by the manifestly virile behaviour of his initially successful brother-in-law) are recounted and analysed with an unfailing sense of humour and irony which elicit from the reader something like the indulgent sympathy one shows to a naughty but endearing child. It is, perhaps a mark of Svevo's originality that he was long neglected in Italy as a writer. Part of the reason for this neglect was undoubtedly his rather unstylistic Italian; and part was possibly due to the fact that his anti-heroes were too far removed from the cult and ideal of the superman that a writer like D'Annunzio had done so much to propogate in Fascist Italy.

—Gabrielle Barfoot

TACITUS (Publius, or Gaius, Cornelius Tacitus).   Born, perhaps in Gaul, c. 56 A.D.   Studied law in Rome. Entered public life under Vespasian; married the daughter of Agricola, 77; quaestor, 81, praetor, 88, consul, 97; prosecuted Marius Priscus for extortion, 100; proconsul of Asia, c. 112-13. *Died 116 A.D. or later.*

<small>PUBLICATIONS</small>

Works

De vita Iulii Agricolae, edited by R.M. Ogilvie.   1973; also edited by J. Delz, 1983; edited
   with comentary by R.M. Ogilvie and I.A. Richmond, 1967; as *Agricola*, translated by
   G.J. Acheson, 1938, and H. Mattingly, revised by S.A. Handford, 1970.
De origine et situ Germanorum, edited by M. Winterbottom.   1973; also edited by A.
   Önnerford, 1983; edited with commentary by J.G.C. Anderson, 1938; as *Germania*,
   translated by H. Mattingly, revised by S.A. Handford, 1970.
Dialogus de oratoribus, edited by M. Winterbottom.   1973; also edited by H. Heubner,
   1983; edited with commentary by R. Güngerich, 1980; translated by M. Winterbottom,
   1972.
Historiae, edited by C.D. Fisher.   1911; also edited by H. Heubner, 1978; edited with
   commentary by H. Heubner, 1963-82; as *Histories*, translated by Kenneth Wellesley,
   1964, revised edition, 1972.
Annales, edited by C.D. Fisher.   1906; also edited by H. Heubner, 1983; edited with
   commentary by E. Koestermann, 1963-68; as *Annals*, translated by Michael Grant,
   1952, revised edition, 1971, and D.R. Dudley, 1966.

*

Critical Studies: *Tacitus* by Clarence W. Mendell, 1957; *Tacitus*, 1958, and *Ten Studies in*

TACITUS

Tacitus, 1970, both by Ronald Syme; *The Annals of Tacitus* by B. Walker, 1960; *Religion and Philosophy in the Histories of Tacitus* by Russell T. Scott, 1968; *Tacitus* edited by T.A. Dorey, 1969; *The World of Tacitus* by D.R. Dudley, 1969; *Tacitus* by F.R.D. Goodyear, 1970; *An Introduction to Tacitus* by H.W. Benario, 1975; *Tacitus* by Ronald Martin, 1981.

*   *   *

Tacitus began his literary career with the publication in A.D. 98 of a biography of his father-in-law, Julius Agricola, who governed Britain between A.D. 78 and 84. He capitalised on ancient literary convention, which dictated that biography should be eulogistic, by contrasting the work's eponymous hero with the evil emperor Domitian, thus throwing the former's virtues into greater relief. In his next work, *Germania* (Germany), published in the same year, Tacitus again took advantage of literary tradition. Ethnographical works had always included discussion of the morality of races and peoples, and Tacitus suggested that the more primitive Germans displayed qualities which were lacking from the more advanced society of contemporary Rome. Such disillusionment with Roman politics in general, and with emperors in particular, emerges also in Tacitus's work on the decline of oratory, *Dialogus* (Dialogue), and blossoms forth in the two principal works for which he is most famous.

The *Histories*, published c. A.D. 106 and covering the years A.D. 69-96, and the *Annals*, published almost a decade later and covering the years A.D. 14-68, together amounted to thirty volumes, of which more than half are now lost. This ambitious treatment of the emperors of the first century A.D. from Tiberius to Domitian was composed on a large scale and in the annalistic manner, thereby recalling the outstanding history of the republic, that of Livy (c. 59 B.C.-A.D. 17), whom Tacitus clearly wished to rival. But whereas Livy had portrayed the republic in largely sympathetic terms and in the fullness and elegance of a Ciceronian style, Tacitus chose to present the early empire in dissenting terms and in the abbreviated and disjointed style of Sallust (c. 86-35 B.C.). Tacitus' choice of Sallust as his chief stylistic inspiration is likely to have represented a radical departure from his immediate predecessors since most first-century A.D. historians seem, despite the almost total loss of their works, to have emulated Livy's style rather than Sallust's. Moreover, since Sallust charted the disintegration of society at the end of the republic, Tacitus's adoption of his style suggests also an affinity of subject-matter: the crises of the new autocracy are presented as the crises of the dying republic, and the new emperors and their henchmen appear as reincarnations of the villains of the past.

On account of his dissenting attitude Tacitus has been praised as an anti-imperialist by the opponents or victims of dictatorship, and as a forerunner of modern historiography by those who confuse cynicism with criticism. The reality is perhaps somewhat different. In his writing Tacitus reveals not only an admiration for Sallust which is itself idiosyncratic, but also an almost obsessive aversion to the normal conventions of language and style: he is the writer who literally refused to call a spade a spade ("the tools with which soil is dug out and turf cut,"*Annals* 1.65.7). This characteristic is so pervasive that we may legitimately infer that Tacitus was a dissenter by nature rather than by conviction. Indeed, he himself prospered and held high office under the political system which his writings so vigorously attack. But none of this is to deny him his superb merits as a dramatic story-teller. Ancient historiography was aimed primarily at entertaining its readers, as Tacitus himself was naturally well aware (*Histories* 1.2-3); his typically perverse claim that the *Annals* do not meet this requirement (*Annals* 4.32-3) has been rightly disbelieved by generations of readers, for whom his works symbolise everything that was wrong about the Roman empire.

—A.J. Woodman

TANIZAKI Jun'ichiro. Born in Tokyo, 24 July 1886. Attended Tokyo University, 1908-10. Married 1) Chiyoko Ishikawa in 1915 (divorced, 1930); 2) Furukawa Tomiko in 1931 (divorced); 3) Nezu Matsuko in 1935. Recipient: Mainichi Prize, 1947; Asahi Culture Prize, 1949; Imperial Cultural Medal, 1949. Member, Japan Academy of Arts, 1957; Honorary Member, American Academy, 1964. *Died 30 July 1965.*

PUBLICATIONS

Collections

Zenshu [Collected Works]. 28 vols., 1966-70.

Fiction

Shisei [Tattoo] (includes plays). 1911.
Akuma [Demon]. 1913.
Osai to Minosuke [Osai and Minosuke]. 1915.
Otsuya-goroshi. 1915; as *A Spring-Time Case,* 1927.
Ningyo no Nageki [Mermaid's Grief]. 1917.
Kin to Gin [Gold and Silver]. 1918.
Chijin no ai [A Fool's Love]. 1925.
Kojin [Shark-Man]. 1926.
Tade kuu mushi. 1929; as *Some Prefer Nettles,* 1955.
Manji [A Swastika]. 1931.
Momoku monogatari [A Blind Man's Tale]. 1932.
Ashikari. 1933; translated as *Ashikari,* with *The Story of Shunkin,* 1936.
Shunkin Sho. 1933; as *The Story of Shunkin,* with *Ashikari,* 1936.
Bushuko hiwa. 1935; as *The Secret History of the Lord of Musashi,* with *Arrowroot,* 1982.
Setsuyo Zuihitsu. 1935.
Yoshino Kuzu. 1937; as *Arrowroot,* with *The Secret History of the Lord of Musashi,* 1982.
Neko to Shozo to Futari no Onna [A Cat and Shozo and His Two Women]. 1937.
Sasameyuki. 1948; as *The Makioka Sisters,* 1957.
Rangiku monogatari [Story of Tangled Chrysanthemums]. 1949.
Shoso Shigemoto no Haha [The Mother of Captain Shigemoto]. 1950.
Kagi. 1956; as *The Key,* 1960.
Yume no ukihashi [Floating Bridge of Dreams]. 1960.
Futen Rojin Nikki. 1962; as *Diary of a Mad Old Man,* 1965.
Seven Japanese Tales. 1963.

Plays

Hosshoji Monogatari [Story of Hosso Temple] (produced 1915).
Okuni to Gohei [Okuni and Gohei] (produced 1922).
Alsureba koso [Because of Love]. 1923.
The White Fox, in *Eminent Authors of Contemporary Japan,* edited by E.S. Bell and E. Ukai. 1930.
Shinzei [Lord Shinzei]. 1949.

Other

Zenshu [Collected Works]. 12 vols., 1930; and later editions.
In' ei raisan [In Praise of Shadows]. 1933.
Bunshu tokuhon [On Style]. 1936.
Yosho-jidai [Boyhood]. 1957.
Setsugoan yawa [Reminiscences]. 1968.

Translator (into modern Japanese), *Genji monogatari*, by Murasaki Shikibu. 26 vols., 1939-41.

*

Critical Studies: *The Search for Authenticity in Modern Japanese Literature* by Hisaaki Yamanouchi, 1978; *The Moon in the Water: Understanding Tanizaki, Kawabata, and Mishima* by Gwenn Boardman Petersen, 1979.

*   *   *

Tanizaki is better regarded as a narrative artist or story-teller than as a novelist—narrative artistry is something broader, more basic, even primitive. He was a born narrator, remarkable for his spontaneity and versatility, and many of his writings do not conform to the general concept of or rules for the "modern novel." He could be both realistic and fabulous at the same time, so factually detailed in his description of the daily lives of his characters, and yet so unconventional, so fantastic in his plots and themes. Tanizaki made a brilliant literary debut in 1910 with *Shisei*, in which a beautiful but modest girl is turned into a different personality by being tattooed. Young Tanizaki was intensely interested in Western aestheticism of the fin de siècle brand, but this story was something native and his own. Mishima Yukio was an ardent admirer of Tanizaki, and they obviously had much in common. They were committed aesthetes, and pursued and developed an ideal of a beauty highly coloured with sensuality. Each could be called both modern and classical at the same time, being susceptible to Western literature and yet well versed in traditional Japanese literature. Both were, at least when young, flamboyant personalities, notorious "bad boys" of the rather closed literary world of Japan, and their behaviour and life-styles often shocked conservative readers. However, Tanizaki turned out more consistent as an aesthete, keeping himself quite aloof from politics throughout his unusually long literary career of more than a half century, a stormy period for modern Japan.

Tanizaki was one of the few Japanese writers who passed through the turbulent war years almost unscathed. Of course, there was a censorship problem, and *The Makioka Sisters*, serialized in a literary magazine, was stopped by the militaristic censors. But he continued to write consistently, and this marvelous novel of manners was completed three years after the war. Having successfully preserved the pre-war mores and nuances of an upper-middle-class family in Osaka, he struck readers as a master of the "art of survival." In the early 1930's there was a sudden upsurge of "proletarian literature" and quite a number of the established writers turned "left." Tanizaki's *Some Prefer Nettles* (1929) suffered from the hostility of leftist critics, being condemned as "bourgeois, decadent, reactionary." But his next novel, *Manji* turned out even more decadent, dealing with Lesbian characters and promiscuity. Literary concession or conformity was out of the question for him, and it was not Tanizaki but the "proletarian" writers who were soon submerged. He proved as bold and challenging in his technique of narration, though he was neither avant garde nor experimental. His literary innovations were accomplished in a far more subtle way. In *Some Prefer Nettles*, he managed to keep a delicate balance between the psycho-sexual analysis of domestic crisis and the theme of the central character's cultural conversion from West to East. *Manji* is another triumph for this born narrator with its subtle blend of female confessions in Osaka dialect, badly written letters, and town gossip.

Tanizaki proved himself a marvellous impersonator in narrative. He liked to use first-person narrative, which seemed apparently naive, but the range of adopted voices was very wide and rich in variety. The narrator in *Chijin no ai* was a middle-aged engineer, who fell into love with a very young girl (anticipating Nabokov's *Lolita*), and tried hard to "educate" her into his "ideal woman," a highly Westernized type both in dress and manner. This plan turned out too successfully. The girl became independent, and began to tease and even tyrannize him. The whole story could be taken as an allegory, or even a moral lesson, concerning the folly of hasty Westernization, but the confessional voice of the protagonist provides a curious mixture of bitter self-mockery and sensual intoxication—he is both grieved and satisfied with the reversal of his plan. This masochistic element was discernible in many of Tanizaki's stories, and probably rooted deeply in his personality. First-person narration was also used in "Story of a Blind Masseur," in which the blind protagonist reminisces about the attractive ladies whom he had adored and massaged. *The Key* and *Diary of a Mad Old Man* are minor masterpieces from Tanizaki's last period, with the dotage and ecstasy of old age for common themes. Tanizaki should assuredly be counted among the narrative masters of this century.

—Shoichi Saeki

TASSO, Torquato. Born in Sorrento, 11 March 1544; son of the poet Bernardo Tasso. Educated at a Jesuit school in Naples; at Court of Urbino with his father, 1557-60; studied law at University of Padua, 1560-62, and in Bologna, 1562-64; joined Accademia degli Eterei (under Scipione Gonzaga), Padua, 1564-65. In household of Cardinal Luigi d'Este, Ferrara, 1565-70, and Paris, 1570-71; in Duke Alfonso d'Este's household, 1572-78; fearful of persecution, fled to Sorrento, 1577, but returned to Ferrara for medical treatment; confined as insane to hospital of Sant'Anna, 1579-86: released into care of Duke of Mantua, and spent remaining years wandering through Italy, to Naples, Rome, Florence, and Mantua; granted pension by Pope Clement VIII, 1595. *Died 25 April 1595.*

PUBLICATIONS

Collections

Opere. 1722-36.

Verse

Rinaldo. 1562; edited by Luigi Bonfigli, 1936; translated as *Rinaldo*, 1792.
Gerusalemme liberata. 1580 (as *Il Goffredo*); complete version, 1581; revised edition, 1581; edited by Lanfranco Caretti, in *Tutte le Poesie*, 1957; translated by Edward Fairfax as *Godfrey of Bouillon: The Recovery of Jerusalem*, 1600, and by Joseph Tusiani as *Jerusalem Delivered*, 1970.
Gerusalemme conquistata. 1593; edited by Luigi Bonfigli, 1934.
Le sette giornate del mondo creato. 1607; edited by Giorgio Petrocchi, 1951.

Opere minori in versi, edited by Angelo Solerti.   3 vols., 1891-95.
Rime, edited by Angelo Solerti.   3 vols., 1898-1902.

Plays

Aminta (produced 1573).   1581; edited by C.E.J. Griffiths, 1972; translated in *The Countess of Pembroke's Ivychurch*, 1591; translated as *Aminta*, 1628.
Il Re Torrismondo.   1586; edited by Bartolo T. Sozzi, in *Opere 2*, 1956.
Intrichi d'amore (produced 1598).   1604; edited by Enrico Malato, 1976.

Other

Rime e prose. 1581.
Discorsi dell'arte poetica (lecture).   1587; revised version, as *Discorsi del poema eroico*, 1594; both versions edited by Luigi Poma, 1964; as *Discourses on the Heroic Poem*, 1973.
Lettere, edited by Cesare Guasti.   5 vols., 1852-55.
Prose diverse, edited by Cesare Guasti.   2 vols., 1875.
Dialoghi, edited by Ezio Raimondi.   3 vols., 1958; as *Tasso's Dialogues: A Selection, with Discourse on the Art of the Dialogue*, edited by Carnes Lord and Dain A. Trafton, 1983.

*

Bibliography: *Bibliografia analitica tassiana* by A. Tortoreto and J.G. Fucilla, 1935; in *Aevum 20*, 1946, and in *Studi tassiani*, from 1952.

Critical Studies: *Tasso and His Times* by William Boulting, 1907; *From Virgil to Milton* by C.M. Bowra, 1945; *Tasso: A Study of the Poet and of His Contribution to English Literature* by C.P. Brand, 1965; *The Textual Problems of Tasso's "Gerusalemme conquistata"* by Anthony Oldcorn, 1976; *Trials of Desire: Renaissance Defenses of Poetry* by Margaret W. Ferguson, 1983.

*   *   *

Although best known for his epic poem *Jerusalem Delivered*, Torquato Tasso was a typical man of his age in that he wrote important works in virtually all of the literary genres practised in Italy during the late Renaissance. Like his father Bernardo, who was also a poet of some prominence, Tasso spent most of his adult life as a courtier. It was in this capacity that he wrote the lyric, religious, and occasional verse, epic poetry, plays, dialogues, letters, and literary criticism that poured from his pen throughout a productive but unhappy life. Though clearly not the misunderstood, persecuted, and consequently mad poet his 19th-century admirers thought him, Tasso was certainly neurotic, in today's terms, and in certain periods of his life severely unbalanced. Indeed, there were times when his extreme susceptibility and the fears of persecution that plagued him for much of his adulthood led him to behavior so politically injudicious that his worried patron had him placed in protective custody and eventually imprisoned. Tasso was a man of great learning and sophistication who at the same time was emotionally torn by doubts of his own worth and orthodoxy. Misgivings of this sort help explain his sometimes aberrant behavior and were behind his incessant request that his religious views be examined by the Inquisition. They were also responsible for his insistence that the text of his poem be scrutinized by the leading literary arbiters of the day for traces of possible offense to linguistic, literary, or moral propriety.

The tensions and contradictions that made Tasso's life a legend even in his own time give his poetry its unmistakable aura of high drama and intensity. In the *Jerusalem Delivered*, discipline and indulgence, piety and sensuality, jealousy and magnanimity, hope and disillusionment, love and solitude, cowardice and valor, calculation and ingenuousness, history and invention, theatricality and simplicity, the epic and the lyric all combine in an impassioned poetic texture that is unique in the tradition of chivalric epic. In this work, Tasso's characters excite admiration not so much for their virtues or heroic accomplishments as for their capacities for intense feeling. Some of the most celebrated moments in the poem—the combat of Tancredi and Clorinda, for example, or the episode of Erminia and the shepherds—find their true dynamic in a barely repressed eroticism pulsing beneath an ostensibly heroic or idyllic surface. Partly from temperament, partly because of the uncertainties of the age in which he lived, Tasso was acutely aware of the fragility of virtue, the evanescence of even the best of human emotions, and the potential insidiousness of an imperfectly understood natural environment. The importance allotted to magic in his poem is indicative of his belief in the fundamental mysteriousness of life and the universe in which the human drama unfolds. Tasso is a poet of desire rather than satisfaction, and his best writing is characterized by anxiety and melancholy, a longing for liberation from the contingencies to which the human condition is subject.

Jerusalem Delivered is an epic poem in twenty cantos of *ottava rima*. Much of its action concerns the fall of Jerusalem in 1099 to Godfrey of Boulogne and his European allies during the First Crusade. Unlike the previous chivalrous epics written for the Ferrarese court by Boiardo and Ariosto, Tasso's poem is an overtly serious work, stoutly Christian and explicitly moralistic, and deeply concerned from its inception with such theoretical matters as the relation of truth to invention and the problem of historical authenticity. Its subject matter, a protracted military contest between Christians and Moslems, was not without contemporary significance in a time of continuing struggle between the Italian states and the Ottoman Empire for commercial domination of the eastern Mediterranean. Moreover, the themes of loyalty and treachery and the conflicting claims of public and private obligation, so important for Renaissance epic in general, were still pertinent to the court ethos and interstate political rivalry characteristic of the age in which Tasso lived. In the poem, the blood and gore of antique epic (the "aspra tragedia dello stato umano," as Tasso called it) are mitigated by idyllic and lyric passages which derive more from Petrarch and the Greek and Latin elegiac and erotic poets than from Homer or Tasso's own sometimes rough-hewn epic forbears. The women of Tasso's poetry, in particular, and the love interests they give rise to provide a more complex foil to the traditional military skirmishing and bravado, in part because all of Tasso's characters are more fully realized and psychologically developed than those of his predecessors.

Second in importance to Tasso's epic poetry are his plays. They too come at the end of a long and glorious Ferrarese tradition. There are three of these: *Aminta*, a pastoral; *Torrismondo*, a tragedy on the Aristotelian-Sophoclean model; and *Intrichi d'amore*, a comedy whose authorship has only recently been securely attributed to Tasso. Of the three, the most important and influential is the *Aminta*. An only apparently naive story of a shepherd in love with a reluctant nymph, this "woodland fable" was first produced in 1573 for the delectation of the Ferrarese court, many of whose members are alluded to or depicted in it. The play is permeated by a kind of Counter-Reformation *weltschmerz* that gives it its special sweetness; its charm derives in part from Tasso's indulgent smile at the simplicity of his rustic characters and the impossible world of innocence and fantasy they inhabit.

Tasso wrote over fifteen hundred occasional poems or *Rime* on a very wide variety of subjects. In addition to the sonnets, ballads, *canzoni*, and *sestine* of tradition, these include a large number of madrigals, a relatively new form that was particularly well suited to his sensual and musical poetic imagination. In these lyrics one finds not the chaste introspection of Petrarch, but rather an unabashed though sometimes bittersweet delight in amorous attraction and the physical world.

Tasso's prose works include letters, dialogues, and literary discourses. These last are elegant examples of the neo-Aristotelian theory of the day and deal primarily with epic poetry; first composed in the late 1560's and published as the *Discorsi dell'arte poetica*, they were then reworked and expanded and in 1594 republished as the *Discorsi del poema eroico*. The *Dialoghi* are part of a long Renaissance tradition and treat such fashionable subjects as nobility, courtesy, jealousy, dignity, and piety. The letters, especially those from confinement, are often extremely moving. Generally lucid and elegant, Tasso's prose works are considered by many to be among the most accomplished that the century produced. Tasso also wrote devotional verse, especially at the end of his life, including *Il mondo creato*, which was known and admired by John Milton. Tasso belongs to the end of the Renaissance, a time when many were inclined to agree with Dafne's remark in the *Aminta*, "Il mondo invecchia, / E invecchiando intristisce" ("the world grows old and growing old grows sad"). His personal inquietude and problematic character both mark his own peculiar genius and herald a succeeding age that would quickly claim him as the dawn of a new, baroque era.

—Charles Klopp

TERENCE (Publius Terentius Afer).   Born c. 194 or 190 or 186-85 B.C. Had a daughter. Possibly a freed slave in household of Terentius Lucanus; his plays were produced in the 160's. *Died 159 B.C.*

PUBLICATIONS

Collections

[*Plays*], edited by W.M. Lindsay and R. Kauer, revised by O. Skutsch.   1958; also edited by J. Marouzeau, 1947-56, and R. Ranzato and R. Cantarella, 1971—; translated by George Colman the Elder, 1765, Betty Radice, 2 vols., 1965-67, and Frank Copley, 1967; also in *Complete Roman Drama* edited by George Duckworth, 1942, and *Complete Comedies* edited by S.P. Bovie, 1974.

Plays

Andria [The Girl from Andros] (produced 166). Edited by G.P. Shipp, 1960.
Hecyra [The Mother-in-Law] (produced 165). Edited by T.F. Carney, 1968.
Heauton timorumenos [Self-Tormentor] (produced 163). Edited by K.I. Lietzmann, 2 vols., 1974.
Eunuchus [The Eunuch] (produced 161). Edited by P. Fabia, 1895.
Phormio (produced 161). Edited by R.H. Martin, 1959.
Adelphoe [The Brothers] (produced 160). Edited by R.H. Martin, 1976.

*

Critical Studies: *The Nature of Roman Comedy* by George Duckworth, 1952; *Menander, Plautus, and Terence* by W.G. Arnott, 1968; *Roman Comedy* by Kenneth McLeish, 1976; "Scholarship on Terence and the Fragments of Roman Comedy" by Sander M. Goldberg, in

Classical World 75, 1981; *Roman Comedy* by David Konstan, 1983.

*   *   *

The plays of Terence read like close adaptations of Greek New Comedy, an effect both innovative and deceptive. The innovation lies in Terence's rebellion against the popular aesthetic of his time. Where traditional Roman comedy—well represented to us in the plays of Plautus—delighted in the broad effects of stock characters and situations, elaborate songs, and extravagant, highly stylized diction, Terence sought instead to reproduce the more subtle effects of the later Greek comedy. He based four of his six plays upon works of Menander, the most literary of the Greek dramatists, and two upon Apollodorus of Carystos, himself said to have been a particular admirer of Menander. The result was a set of Latin plays with more sophisticated characterizations, a more sedate and elegant diction, and a more refined humor than Roman audiences had previously witnessed. The plays are also deceptive, however, because they are not in fact faithful copies of Greek models. Terence avoided the expository divine prologues of Greek drama so that his audiences can rarely feel superior to his characters. The dramatic action takes place purely on the human level. He also borrowed elements freely from one Greek play to enrich the action of another, a process modern scholars call *contaminatio.* Terence's *Eunuch,* for example, which is based on a play of that name by Menander, nevertheless features a soldier and parasite borrowed from a second play called *The Flatterer.* In *The Brothers,* a slap-stick scene from Diphilus is woven into a Menandrean plot. Yet even more striking is the change in outlook between Menander and Terence. Menander treats human frailties with great sympathy. His characters learn from their mistakes, and we share in that process of growth. Terence is the consummate ironist. In his plays, a correct course of action is not always easy to see, a character's virtue is not easily defined, and rewards are thus more difficult to imagine. His wry view of human capabilities has more in common with the later Roman genres of satire and elegy than with his Greek dramatic predecessors.

The Romans themselves, however, were slow to appreciate Terence, and they never really admired him as a dramatist. Though *The Eunuch* won him a record fee and an encore performance, two audiences walked out on *The Mother-in-Law,* and his successors reverted to the broader, more traditional style of Plautus. Yet in the first century B.C., by which time stage comedy at Rome was all but dead, Terence took on new life. His elegant diction and simple vocabulary made him an ideal school text. Both Cicero and Caesar praised his style. Cicero quoted him often and cited him as an example of correct Latin usage. By the 4th century A.D. grammarians had produced copiously annotated editions of his plays, and Terence acquired a fame second only to Vergil's. The 10th-century nun Hrotswitha of Gandersheim claimed him as the stylistic model for her own martyr plays, and the Latin comedies themselves were never forgotten. Many manuscripts, some with beautiful illustrations, survive. During the 15th and 16th centuries the plays were widely studied and translated and became a seminal influence on Renaissance, and thus modern comedy.

—Sander M. Goldberg

THEOCRITUS.   Little is certain about his life: probably born in Syracuse, Sicily, before 300, associated with the poetic circle in Cos under Philetas's patronage, and active in Alexandria under the patronage of Ptolemy II Philadelphus in 270's.

THEOCRITUS

PUBLICATIONS

[*Verse*], edited by A.S.F. Gow (includes translation). 1952; *Selected Poems* edited by K.J. Dover, 1971; translated by Anna Rist, 1978, Thelma Sargent, 1982, and Daryl Hine, 1982.

*

Critical Studies: "Landscape in Greek Poetry" by Adam Parry, in *Yale Classical Studies 15*, 1957; *Theocritus' Coan Pastorals: A Poetry Book* by Gilbert Lawall, 1967; *The Green Cabinet: Theocritus and the European Pastoral Lyric* by Thomas G. Rosenmeyer, 1969; "Fluctuation in Theocritus' Style" by Gianfranco Fabiano, in *Greek Roman and Byzantine Studies 12*, 1971; *Theocritus at Court* by Frederick T. Griffiths, 1979; *Poetry and Myth in Ancient Pastoral: Essays on Theocritus and Virgil* by Charles Segal, 1981; *Before Pastoral: Theocritus and the Ancient Tradition of Bucolic Poetry* by David M. Halperin, 1983.

*   *   *

Theocritus wrote most of the poems for which we remember him in Alexandria, the capital of Hellenistic Egypt, during the second quarter of the 3rd century B.C. His work—like that of Callimachus of Cyrene and Apollonius of Rhodes, Theocritus's contemporaries and fellow Alexandrians—owes its heightened consciousness of poetic artifice and almost painful awareness of the overshadowing presence of accumulated literary tradition to the temper of the post-classical, pre-Roman era in which it was composed. In an age whose sophistication made it difficult for writers to treat personal experience with a sense of immediacy, Theocritus strives to recover for poetry a measure of freshness and emotional power. He accomplishes his purpose without vulgar displays of feeling or explicit literary polemics; rather, his best effects are typically achieved through a complex combination of irony, allusiveness, detachment, wit, total control, and subtle manipulation of lexical and linguistic nuance.

Theocritus's reputation rests chiefly upon ten of the thirty preserved poems, commonly called Idylls (though few are in fact idyllic), which antiquity has transmitted to us under his name together with two dozen epigrams and a few fragments. The poems numbered 1 and 3-11 in the conventional arrangement (8 and 9 are probably spurious) furnished the model for the major portion of Virgil's Eclogues and so became in time the ultimate if indirect source of the European pastoral tradition. Although the pastoral Idylls exploit many of the literary conventions familiar to us from later pastoral poetry in order to express the outlook or set of attitudes we currently recognize as distinctive to the pastoral genre, it is not certain that Theocritus considered them a separate sub-group within his larger oeuvre or conceived his own invention, which he termed bucolic poetry, according to the same criteria we use to define pastoral. At any rate, poems 1, 3-11 contain rustic dialogues and serenades which celebrate, with pointed naivety, the enamored Cyclops, the sorrows of Daphnis, and other piquant, faintly absurd subjects from the lives and loves of Greek herdsmen. Adapting a technique previously employed by Homer in the *Odyssey*'s rural interludes, by Euripides in certain choral odes, and by Plato in the *Phaedrus*, Theocritus transforms his country settings by means of an aesthetic illusion and thereby creates a landscape halfway between the sensuous descriptions of the classical poets and the sentimental metaphors of the Romantics. Within such a landscape at once realistic and artificial, distant and familiar, the cultivated reader and the passionate shepherd are equally at home. Their encounter is one of the triumphs of Hellenistic poetry.

Although the pastoral Idylls include some minor masterpieces (1, 7, 11), the majority of Theocritus's best works are to be found outside the pastoral corpus (2, 13, 16, 24; also of considerable interest are 12, 14, 15, and 22). They feature unsentimental tales of love, impertinent reworkings of mythological episodes, and humorous scenes of daily life among housewives or mercenaries. With the exception of Idylls 28-31, composed in Aeolic dialect and in lyric meters, all of Theocritus's genuine Idylls are set in dactylic hexameter, the form of versification used by Homer, Hesiod, and the Greek epicists for heroic or didactic poetry. If there is unity in the works of Theocritus as they have come down to us, perhaps it can be found in a shared programme of epic revisionism spanning both the pastoral and non-pastoral works and utilizing a variety of artistic strategies to a common end. Theocritus replaces princes with paupers, tragic sympathy with comic irony, and heroic themes with erotic ones, thereby reversing traditional epic society, tone, and subject-matter. In this way he was able to prolong and to renew the life of the Greek epic.

—David M. Halperin

THOUSAND AND ONE NIGHTS (*Arabian Nights*).

PUBLICATIONS

Alf layla wa-layla (Calcutta edition), edited by William Hay Macnaghten. 4 vols., 1839-42; Bulaq edition, 1835; Zotenberg edition, 1888; as *The Thousand and One Nights*, translated by E.W. Lane, 3 vols., 1838-42; as *The Book of the Thousand Nights and One Night*, translated by John Payne, 9 vols., 1882-84; as *The Arabian Nights' Entertainment*, translated by Richard Burton, 16 vols., 1885-88; selection as *Scheherazade: Tales from the Thousand and One Nights*, translated by A.J. Arberry, 1953; selection as *The Thousand and One Nights*, 1954, and *Aladdin and Other Tales*, 1957, combined version as *Tales from the Thousand and One Nights*, 1973, all translated by N.J. Dawood; and many other selections under various titles.

*

Critical Studies: *The Minstrelsy of "The Arabian Nights": A Study of Music and Musicians in the Arabic "Alf Laila wa Laila"* by Henry George Farmer, 1945; *Thèmes et motifs des Mille et une nuits: Essai de classification* by Nikita Elisséeff, 1949; *The Art of Story-Telling: A Literary Study of the Thousand and One Nights* by Mia I. Gerhardt, 1963.

*   *   *

The fictional characters of Aladdin, Sindbad, and Ali Baba have become part of western culture, even though they are characters from the large collection of tales from the far and near east known in the west as the *Thousand and One Nights* or the *Arabian Nights*. The general interest in oriental tales in western Europe, particularly in France and England in the 18th century, can be traced back to the first French translation of the work in 1704-1717 (this was, in fact, the first printed version of the collection in any language), and the almost immediate translation into English of the French version (1706-08). Fabulous palaces and cities, decorated with jewels and peopled with slaves and dancing girls, poor fishermen and porters who through the accidental finding of an enchanted fish or a magic ring or lamp are given fabulous riches, meditative caliphs and envious viziers—these things have entered the western consciousness through a multitude of translated versions, often written for children. That Aladdin has become the subject of a popular Christmas pantomime suggests both the strength of the appeal of his story and its gradual loss of exoticism.

The nucleus of the collection that became the *Thousand and One Nights* derives from a lost

Persian book of fairy tales called *Hazar Adsanah* (A Thousand Legends), translated into Arabic by 1000 A.D. The Persian version itself reflected a background of Indian as well as Persian folklore and popular tales. Gradually more and more stories were added to it; scholars, in fact, are able to determine a series of layers of agglomerative material, though complicated by the insertion of local details into earlier material. The framework story itself—Scheherazade telling King Shahriyar a succession of stories, never quite finished—is Indian, though the characters in the tale are Persian and the largest proportion of names is Arabic. The Persian and Indian stories and folk tales form a substantial group in the collection, but in addition there are stories associated with Baghdad (including the Sindbad story and the 50-odd stories centering on Harun al-Rashid and his court), probably dating from c. 1000-1200, stories from Egypt (including the Aladdin story), from c. 1000-1400, and stories from Iraq, Turkey, and possibly Greece. The agglomerative motif associated with Scheherazade is also used in many of the individual stories (so the Hunchback's tale encloses a series of tales by the Tailor, the Barber, and the Barber's six brothers). The number of nights being set at 1001 was probably conventional, but as the collection grew an effort was made to extend the number of tales (about 180) to accomodate that many evenings.

The Arabic version of the work is written in a simple style—often colloquial and idiomatic, reflecting oral transmission—and this has tended to make it relatively disregarded by Arabic scholars. It is not deemed a typical Arabic work, and even now there is no standard edited Arabic text. But the general reader, and especially the child, has always responded to mere story-telling, and that is indeed the pattern of the entire work—will the king become bored by Scheherazade's story and have her killed, or will dawn come again before she has finished and give her another day of life? The stories cover the entire range of human life—from love and demons and magic and crime to bawdy anecdotes (e.g., "The Historic Fart")—and under the fantasy and exoticism lies an awareness of human nature and its simplest needs and desires that has never failed to find an audience.

—George Walsh

THUCYDIDES. Born c. 460 B.C. Owned property in Thrace. Plague victim in Athens 430-427, but recovered; elected military magistrate (*strategos*) in 424 with task of protecting the Thracian coast, but he lost Athenian colony of Amphipolis to the Spartans, was condemned in his absence, and went into exile until the end of the Peloponnesian war, 404. *Died c. 399 B.C.*

PUBLICATIONS

[*History*], edited by H. Stuart Jones, revised by Enoch Powell. 2 vols., 1942; also edited by Jacqueline de Romilly and others, 1953-72; commentary by A.W. Gomme, A. Andrewes, and K.J. Dover, 1945-81; as *History of the Peloponnesian War*, translated by C.F. Smith (Loeb edition), 4 vols., 1919-23; also translated in part by Thomas Hobbes, 1629 (this edition, *Eight Books of the Peloponnesian War*, edited by David Grene, 1959), Benjamin Jowett, 2 vols., 1881, and Rex Warner, 1954, revised edition, 1972.

*

Critical Studies: *Thucydides*, 1942, and *Three Essays on Thucydides*, 1967, both by John H. Finley, Jr.; *Man in His Pride: A Study in the Political Philosophy of Thucydides and Plato* by David Grene, 1950; *Thucydides and His History* by F.E. Adcock, 1963; *Poiesis* by H.D.F. Kitto, 1966; *Individuals in Thucydides* by H.D. Westlake, 1968; *Thucydides on the Nature of Power* by A.G. Woodhead, 1970; *Thucydides* by K.J. Dover, 1973; *The Speeches in Thucydides: A Collection of Original Studies and a Bibliography* edited by Philip A. Stadter, 1973; *Thucydides, The Artful Reporter*, 1973, and *Past and Process in Herodotus and Thucydides*, 1982, both by Virginia J. Hunter; *Chance and Intelligence in Thucydides* by Lowell Edmunds, 1975; *The Necessities of War: A Study of Thucydides' Pessimism* by Peter R. Pouncey, 1980; *Logos and Ergon in Thucydides* by A.M. Parry, 1981; *The Structure of Thucydides' History* by H.R. Rawlings III, 1981; *The Human Thing: The Speeches and Principles of Thucydides' History* by M. Cogan, 1981; *The Experience of Thucydides* by D. Proctor, 1981; *Collected Essays* by Colin Macleod, 1983; *Thucydides* by S. Hornblower, 1984.

*　　　*　　　*

Thucydides's plan was to write the history of the Peloponnesian War between Athens and Sparta (431-04 B.C.), but his narrative breaks off at 8.109 in the year 411 and it is generally agreed that substantial parts of the extant work are unfinished. His history has nevertheless been immensely influential.

Thucydides states (1.1.1) that he began writing in the expectation that the war would be a great one and more worthy of record than any in the past. This statement will have raised eyebrows among his contemporaries, who would not only have remembered the wars with Persia and Herodotus's recent account of them but would also have regarded with reverence the presentation of the Trojan War given by Homer in the *Iliad*. Yet it was Thucydides's intention precisely to challenge his predecessors, and Homer in particular. The whole of his preface is devoted to an elaborate depreciation of earlier history (1.1-21.1), especially of the Trojan War (1.9-11), and a corresponding magnification of his own subject (1.21.2, 23.1-3). Moreover, it is clear from 1.23.1-3, which constitutes a beautifully written programme for the work as a whole, that Thucydides saw his own war principally in terms of the sufferings which it entailed (and which were "without parallel over a similar period") and of the disasters which it brought (and among which he mentions an unprecedented number of sacked cities, refugees, deaths, earthquakes, droughts, famines—and also "that which caused very great damage and significant destruction: the plague"). As we know from the beginnings of the *Iliad* and *Odyssey*, this is the perspective of epic poetry, in which war and its attendant sufferings are the staple ingredients.

The greatest disaster was that which overtook Thucydides's native city, Athens; the greatest sufferings those which afflicted her inhabitants. Thucydides's treatment of both is analogous to that of a tragic poet, as a classic section of Book 2 demonstrates. In the famous Funeral Speech early in that book (34-46) the leading Athenian, Pericles, is made to describe the city as an oasis of sunlight and civilisation, his fellow citizens as models of virtue and culture. No sooner has he finished speaking (or so it seems) than the plague strikes Athens. The symptoms are described in all their medical detail (49-50), and the consequent collapse of morale gives rise to the kind of *peripeteia* (reversal) associated with Greek tragedy: Thucydides relates (51-3) the vices to which the citizens now succumbed in place of the virtues which Pericles had previously been made to catalogue. The effect is all the more dramatic because Thucydides characteristically makes no personal comment but appears to let the events speak for themselves; in fact, he has imposed a structure on the narrative which brings the plague into dramatic contrast with all that has gone before. The relationship of speech to action, the suggestion that reality is different from appearances and from the protestations of men, the transition from joy to despair, the combination of the inflated and the understated—all these are typical of Thucydides's technique and are used with almost equal effectiveness throughout his work.

Thucydides is traditionally seen as little different from a modern historian: he, uniquely among ancient historians, took the trouble to acquire multiple sources of evidence, evaluated them with painstaking care, and from them compiled a narrative which is unrivalled in its accuracy and objectivity. Unfortunately, through lack of comparative material, we are almost always unable to check Thucydides's statements; so the traditional view of his achievement rests almost entirely on the magisterial assurance of his narrative and on the unverifiable assumption that he consistently adhered to the methodology which he famously outlines in Book 1 (22). His ancient readers saw him quite differently. According to Plutarch (*Moralia* 347a-c) he "is always struggling for vivid representation, eager to turn his readers into eyewitnesses and to engender in them the emotional disturbances actually experienced by the real eyewitnesses"; and to Dionysius of Halicarnassus (*On Thucydides* 15) he "sometimes makes the sufferings appear so cruel, so terrible, so piteous, as to leave no room for historians or poets to surpass him." With their references to emotional disturbances and emulation by poets, these verdicts would have pleased the historian who employed tragic techniques in his ambition to rival the work of Homer.

—A.J. Woodman

TIRSO de Molina. Pseudonym for Gabriel Téllez. Born in Madrid, in 1580 or 1581(?). Educated at the universities of Alcalá and Guadalajara. Entered the Order of Mercy, 1601: novitiate, then friar: probably in Toledo, 1605-15; in Santo Domingo, West Indies, 1616-18; the Order opposed his play-writing in 1625; Prior of a friary in Trujillo, 1626-29; official chronicler of the Order, 1632; in Barcelona, 1632-39; another controversy about his plays, 1640; Prior of the Soria friary, 1645-47; in Almazán, 1647. *Died in 1648.*

PUBLICATIONS

Collections

 Comedias, edited by Francisco de Ávila. 5 vols., 1627-36.
 Obras dramaticas completas, edited by Blanca de los Ríos. 3 vols., 1946-58.

Plays (selection: plays translated into English or recently edited)

 Antona García, edited by Margaret Wilson. 1957.
 El burlador de Sevilla, edited by G.E. Wade. 1969; as *The Playboy of Seville*, in *The Theatre of Don Juan*, edited by Oscar Mandel, 1963; as *The Trickster of Seville*, in *The Classic Theatre*, edited by Eric Bentley, 1959; as *The Joker of Seville*, 1979.
 El castigo del penséque, as *The Opportunity*. 1640.
 El condenado por desconfiado, edited by Daniel Rogers. 1974.
 Don Gil de las calzas verdes, edited by Everett W. Hesse and Charles J. Moolick. 1971.
 Marta la piadosa, edited by Elvira E. García. 1972.
 El melancólico, edited by Jacomé Delgado Varela. 1967.
 Por el sótano y el torno, edited by A. Zamora Vicente. 1949.
 Privar contra su gusto, edited by Battista J. Galassi. 1971.
 La prudencia en la mujer, edited by R.R. MacCurdy. 1965; as *Prudence in Women*, in

The Genius of the Spanish Theatre, edited by Robert O'Brien, 1964.
La Santa Juana, edited by A. del Campo. 1948.
La venganza de Tamar, edited by A.K.G. Paterson. 1969.
La villana de Vallecas, edited by Sherman W. Brown. 1948.

Fiction

El bandolero, edited by Luis Carlos Viada y Lluch. 1915.

Verse

Acto de contricion. 1630.
Poesías líricas, edited by Ernesto Jareño. 1969.

Other

Cigarrales de Toledo (miscellany). 1621; edited by Victor Said Armesto, 1913; translated in part as *Three Husbands Hoaxed*, 1955.
Deleitar aprovechando. 1635.
Una obra inédita [La vida de la santa Madre doña María de Cervellón], edited by M. Menéndez y Pelayo. 1908.
Historia general de la Orden de Nuestra Señora de las Mercedes, edited by Manuel Penedo Rey. 2 vols., 1974.

*

Bibliography: *An Annotated, Analytical Bibliography of Tirso Studies 1627-1977* by Vern G. Williamsen and Walter Poesse, 1979.

Critical Studies: *Tirso: Studies in Dramatic Realism* by Ivy L. McClelland, 1948; *The Situational Drama of Tirso* by Ion T. Agheana, 1972; *Studies in Tirso: The Dramatist and His Contemporaries 1620-26* by Ruth Lee Kennedy, 1974; *Tirso and the Drama of the Counter Reformation* by Henry W. Sullivan, 1976; *Tirso: El burlador de Sevilla* by Daniel Rogers, 1977.

*   *   *

Tirso de Molina is the pseudonym of the Mercedarian priest and Spanish Golden-Age playwright Fray Gabriel Téllez. Best known to posterity as the creator of the defiant seducer Don Juan Tenorio (or Don Giovanni), Tirso wrote 80-odd extant, full-length dramas and one-act allegories which place him, with Lope de Vega and Calderón, in the forefront of Spanish Classical drama. He was more aggressive and intelligent in his defense of the *comedia nueva* ("new drama") than his master Lope, however, and in prose miscellanies such as *Los cigarrales de Toledo* he justified his non-Classical methods by using arguments derived from mimesis and pragmatic didacticism *against* the neo-Aristotelians, as well as by advancing revolutionary theories of his own invoking the freedom of the artistic will and expressiveness in the act of creation.

After priestly ordainment in 1601, Tirso began writing for the Madrid theatres (1605-10). He produced his comic masterpiece *Don Gil de las calzas verdes* in 1615. This uses his favourite device of the resolute heroine who, dressed as a man, pursues the fickle lover who has seduced and abandoned her. The heroine's successful wooing of the rival woman gives an erotic and perversely tantalizing effect to the 20 or so works built around this situation. Tirso presents striking female characters of a different kind in his *El amor médico*, where Jerónima, in an anticipation of modern feminism, adopts male attire to pursue her lover and her career as a doctor. The heroine of *Marta la piadosa* is an early, but engaging, stage hypocrite, who feigns a religious vocation in order to avoid an arranged marriage and to receive her lover under her father's roof. The eponymous heroines of *Antona García* and *Mari-Hernández la gallega* embody another favourite type: the virile superwoman or *mujer hombruna*. Tirso's uncanny insight into male and female psychology and his championing of women over the tyrannies and conventions of the male-dominated Spanish society of his time have helped to make him the greatest dramatist of character in the Golden Age.

Tirso also wrote a number of fine Old-Testament plays, such as *La mujer que manda en casa* treating the career of the orgiastic, power-driven and bloody Queen Jezabel, and *La mejor espigadera*, a moving, insightful account of the lives of Ruth and Naomi, and Ruth's ambiguous stance towards marriage and her destiny. His Old-Testament masterpiece, *La venganza de Tamar*, is a gripping tragedy concerning Amnon's incestuous rape of his half-sister, and the dynastic chaos this unleashes in the House of David. Tirso dealt with mediaeval Spanish history in *La prudencia en la mujer*, the finest chronicle-drama of the Golden Age, where Queen María de Molina saves her bloodline by her astute political wisdom. Tirso also contributed a vivid historical trilogy on his near-contemporaries, the Pizarros, conquerors of Peru.

Tirso displayed great gifts of social and political satire (*El vergonzoso en palacio*; *Tanto es lo de más como lo de menos*), which eventually led to his official suppression (1625) under the régime of Philip IV's first minister, Olivares. But he reserved his greatest genius for two theological plays: one of them, *El condenado por desconfiado*, treating the theme of free-will and predestination in paradoxical fashion. The other was his ultimate masterpiece, *El burlador de Sevilla*, and the first Don Juan play. The flippant libertine and homicide Don Juan is dragged into Hell by the stone Comendador not for his social misconduct, but for his defiance of the day of reckoning with God. Tirso also wrote a didactic miscellany in prose, *Deleitar aprovechando*, and a bulky History of the Mercedarian Order (MS, 1637-39). He resembles Molière in his arresting felicity of rhyme, as well as in the creation of comic lead parts; his stress on butts and wits, and the rigid predictability of his gullible personages, places him closer to Ben Jonson. Tirso is well loved in Germany and Austria, and his Don Juan has become a property of the Western tradition. He died in obscurity at Almazán (Soria) in 1648.

—Henry W. Sullivan

TOLSTOY, Leo (Count Lev Nikolayevich Tolstoy). Born at Yasnaya Polyana, near Tula, 28 August 1828. Educated at home, in Moscow, 1837-41, and in Kazan, 1841-44; Kazan University, 1844-47. Marrried Sofiya Andreyevna Bers in 1862; 13 children; also one illegitimate son. Landowner on his inherited estate, 1847-48; in Moscow, 1848-51; visited his brother's military unit in Caucasus, and joined artillery battery as non-commissioned officer, 1851-54, then transferred to a unit near Bucharest, 1854, and, as sub-lieutenant, in Sevastopol, 1854-55: resigned as lieutenant, 1855; after some travel, a serious landowner: set up school, and edited the school journal *Yasnaya Polyana*, 1862-63 (and member of local educational committee, 1870's); social and religious views widely disseminated in last decades of his life, and religious views excluded him from church, 1901; because of censorship, many works first published abroad. *Died 7 November 1910.*

Collections

Polnoye sobraniye sochineniy.   90 vols., 1928-58.
Centenary Edition (in English), translated by Aylmer Maude.   21 vols., 1929-37.

Fiction

Sevastopolskiye rasskazy.   1855-56; as *Sebastopol, 1887.*
Semeynoye schast'e.   1859; as *Katia,* 1887; as *Family Happiness,* 1888; as *My Husband and I,* 1888; as *The Romance of Marriage,* 1890.
Kazaki.   1863; as *The Cossacks,* 1878.
Voyna i mir.   1863-69; as *War and Peace,* 1886.
Anna Karenina.   1875-77; translated as *Anna Karenina,* 1886.
Kreytserova sonata.   1891; as *The Kreutzer Sonata,* 1890.
Khozyain i rabotnik.   1895; as *Master and Man,* 1895.
Voskreseniye.   1899; as *Resurrection,* 1899.

Plays

Vlast' t'my (produced 1888).   1887; as *The Dominion of Darkness,* 1888.
Plody prosveshcheniya (produced 1889).   1889; as *The Fruits of Enlightenment,* 1891.

Other

Detstvo, Otrochestvo, Yunost'.   3 vols., 1852-57; as *Childhood, Boyhood, Youth,* 1886.
Azbuka [An ABC Book].   1872; revised edition, 1875.
Ispoved'.   1884; as *A Confession,* 1885.
V chom moya vera?   1884; as *My Religion,* 1885; as *What I Believe,* 1885.
Tak chtozhe nam delat'?   1902; as *What to Do,* 1887; uncensored edition, 1888.
The Long Exile and Other Stories for Children.   1888.
O zhizni.   1888; uncensored edition, 1891; as *Life,* 1888; as *On Life,* 1902.
Gospel Stories.   1890.
Kritika dogmaticheskovo bogosloviya [An Examination of Dogmatic Theology].   1891.
Soyedineniye i perevod chetyryokh evangelii.   3 vols., 1892-94; as *The Four Gospels Harmonized and Translated,* 1895-96; shortened version, 1890; as *The Gospel in Brief,* 1896.
Tsarstvo Bozhye vnutri vas.   2 vols., 1893-94; as *The Kingdom of God Is Within You,* 2 vols., 1894.
Pis'ma o Genre Dzhorzhe [Letters on Henry George].   1897.
Kristianskoye ucheniye.   1898; as *The Christian Teaching,* 1898.
Chto takoye iskusstvo?   1898; as *What Is Art?,* 1898.
Rabstvo nashevo vremeni.   1900; as *The Slavery of Our Times,* 1900.
Letters, edited by R.F. Christian.   2 vols., 1978.

*

Bibliography: "Tolstoy Studies in Great Britain: A Bibliographical Survey" by Garth M. Terry, in *New Essays on Tolstoy* by Malcolm Jones, 1978.

Critical Studies: *Tolstoy,* 1946, *Introduction to Tolstoy's Writings,* 1968, and *Tolstoy,* 1973, all by Ernest H. Simmons; *The Hedgehog and the Fox: An Essay on Tolstoy's View of History* by

TOLSTOY

Isaiah Berlin, 1953; *Tolstoy or Dostoevsky* by George Steiner, 1959; *Tolstoy's "War and Peace,"* 1962, and *Tolstoy: A Critical Introduction*, 1969, both by R.F. Christian; *Tolstoy and the Novel* by John Bayley, 1966; *Tolstoy: A Collection of Critical Essays* edited by R.E. Matlaw, 1967; *Tolstoy: A Critical Anthology* edited by Henry Gifford, 1971, and *Tolstoy* by Gifford, 1982; *Tolstoy and Chekhov* by Logan Spiers, 1971; *Tolstoy: The Making of a Novelist* by Edward Crankshaw, 1974; *Tolstoy: The Comprehensive Vision* by E.B. Greenwood, 1975; *Tolstoy* by T.G.S. Cain, 1977; *Tolstoy's Major Fiction* by Edward Wasiolek, 1978; *New Essays on Tolstoy* by Malcolm Jones, 1978.

*　　*　　*

The name of Tolstoy is indissolubly linked to Russian literature and the great tradition of the prose novel. Yet these associations, if taken alone, diminish the standing of this unique figure. Tolstoy, the creed of Tolstoyanism, and the legend of the man were among the principal intellectual and spiritual influences in Russia for the last four decades of the 19th century.

From the beginning Tolstoy's literature was never just fiction. His experiences of childhood and youth, military adventure and war, education and land-owning, foreign travel, courtship and marriage, history and philosophy, religion and art, the fear of death and the love of life are transformed into a uniquely personal body of literature. Tolstoy's search for moral codes and values, the discipline to hold himself to them and a new, simple, "real" vision of the Christian faith, all this is played out as a national and even cosmic experience on the broad Russian canvas of his writings. This striving for a presumed "truth," the whole, unified system of being he desired is pursued through works dominated almost exclusively by the only two social groups he really knew, the aristocracy to which he belonged and the peasantry who belonged to him, and his kind. Rarely do the inconveniently modern faces of the middle classes and the urban poor, so illuminated by Dostoevsky, intrude into Tolstoy's attempt to recapture a "natural" world.

Tolstoy's early series of autobiographical works, *Childhood, Boyhood,* and *Youth,* establish his interest in the loss and retrieval of innocence and the life of the family. Other essential lines of development are laid down by his military stories, including his Caucasian tales (such as "The Raid" and "The Wood Felling") and the grimmer *Sebastopol.* The tensions and contradictions within Tolstoy's practice and beliefs are revealed in the interplay between spontaneous comradeship and conflict on the one hand and loneliness, sadness, and death on the other. The Caucasian stories also initiate that Rousseauesque confrontation between "civilized" man (the Russian military) and the natural man (the Caucasian tribespeople) which Tolstoy was to continue in *The Cossacks* and "Hadji Murat" and which manifested itself elsewhere in his work in the oppositions between town and country, Petersburg and Moscow, Europe and Russia, the rulers and the people, Church dogma and popular faith. In the distinctly unromantic *Sebastopol* Tolstoy grasps the bitterness of war with pitiless documentary detail: here war is folly, an insane, drab routine of destruction and butchery, and death no gallant moment, but an inexorable process of disintegration through violence and fear.

Between 1856 and 1863 Tolstoy's educational work on his estate at Yasnaya Polyana, his European travels, his courtships and marriage provided the rest of the background for *War and Peace.* This is Tolstoy's extraordinary attempt to capture the wholeness of life in his "comprehensive vision" of the fates of the Rostov and Bolkonsky families and the Russia which they represent, in the period of the Napoleonic Wars. In the fiction, the historical documentary, and the philosophy of history that is *War and Peace* Tolstoy pursues his truth: the truth of real life for Natasha Rostov, the truth of the meaning of life for the "God-seekers" Pierre Bezukhov and Andrei Bolkonsky, the truth of traditional Russia and the truth of historical reality, in which "great men" are found to be merely appearances and history is seen to move under the impetus of an impossibly complex network of causes.

Whereas in *War and Peace* the newly married Tolstoy had seen the constancy of the family as a unifying force in society and the gradual willing surrender of the individual's freedom to that greater whole as the true course, the unfolding of *Anna Karenina* reflects very different experiences. Heroic, historical Russia gives way to the contemporary scene. The family, important though it is as an abstract concept, remains just that: everywhere it is incomplete, displaced, or disrupted. The society of *Anna Karenina* is one of alienated and restless individuals, frustrated by and yet dependent on the conventions of a duplicitous society. The ordeal of the doomed Anna, who forsakes a sterile marriage for the transient happiness of a passionate liaison, is paralleled by the attempts of Levin, Tolstoy's autobiographical representative, to find both happiness and meaning within the bounds of lawful existence. While Anna gradually loses self-mastery, Levin gradually acquires it. Anna's surrender to the flesh, her disruption of her family and the fated course of her life, and, finally, her desire to retain the good opinion of society draw her down to death; while Levin's gradual submission to the natural rhythms of life, his creation of a family, and his measured disregard for the opinion of society raise him to life.

In his remaining years Tolstoy sought certainties with a furious, self-imposed rigour. To do so, he purged himself, rejected his past, sundered his family, and gave himself away to his Tolstoyan followers and a demanding humanity. The route towards the demystification of Christianity, its reduction to simple, child-like yet meaningful precepts such as those revealed to Pierre Bezukhov and Levin, is described in *A Confession*. While Tolstoy's devotion to life as the medium of discovery is evinced in his quietly appalling picture of illness and death in "The Death of Ivan Ilich," his desire for a moral revolution in sexual relations results in works such as "Father Sergei," "The Devil," and *The Kreutzer Sonata*. Two fictional evocations of moral transformation, the short novel *Master and Man* and the novel *Resurrection*, together with two daunting dramas of good and evil, *The Dominion of Darkness* and *The Fruits of Enlightenment*, are also of note in this period, which is otherwise characterised by the extensive essay *What Is Art?*, an articulate rejection of all art which is not accessible to the people and of positive moral purpose.

Even as Tolstoy devoted himself to the Tolstoyan cause, scriptural revision, and the writing of simple fables, he could not exorcise his artistic gift. That gift is fundamentally simple. It is that of the pre-eminent realist, the ability to articulate to us our unformed feelings and perceptions of life with such accuracy and reality that we are held entranced. At the same time, this realism, whether in the fleeting detail of a character's facial expression or the abiding evocation of a natural scene, is never an end in itself for Tolstoy. Harnessed to sweeping narrative command and relentless moral scrutiny, it promotes the natural, positive movement of life entailed in Tolstoy's reflection—"Pitiful are those who do not seek, or who think that they have found."

—Christopher R. Pike

TRAKL, Georg. Born in Salzburg, Austria, 3 February 1887. Educated at Catholic school, Salzburg; Gymnasium, Salzburg, 1899-1905; apprenticeship at pharmacy in Salzburg, 1905-08; University of Salzburg, 1908-10, graduated as pharmacist. Military service in Vienna, 1910-11, 1914. Pharmacist in Salzburg, 1911, and several short stints as military pharmacist and other military jobs; regular contributor to *Der Brenner*, 1912-14. *Died 7 November 1914.*

<small>PUBLICATIONS</small>

Collections

Gesamtausgabe, edited by Wolfgang Schneditz. 3 vols, 1938-49.

Dichtungen und Briefe, edited by Walther Killy and Hans Szklenar. 2 vols., 1969.

Verse

Gedichte. 1913.
Sebastian im Traum. 1915.
Die Dichtungen, edited by Karl Röck. 1918.
Aus goldenem Kelch: Die Jugenddichtungen, edited by Erhard Buschbeck. 1939.
Decline: Twelve Poems, translated by Michael Hamburger. 1952.
Twenty Poems, translated by James Wright and Robert Bly. 1961.
Selected Poems, edited by Christopher Middleton. 1968.
Poems, translated by Lucia Getsi. 1973.
Georg Trakl in the Red Forest, translated by Johannes Kaebitzsch. 1973.

Other

Erinnerungen an Trakl: Zeugnisse und Briefe, edited by Ludwig von Ficker. 1926; 3rd
edition, 1966.

*

Bibliography: *Trakl-Bibliographie*, 1956, and *Neue Trakl Bibliographie*, 1983, both by W.
Ritzer.

Critical Studies: *Manshape That Shone: An Interpretation of Trakl* by Timothy J. Casey,
1964; *Trakl* by Herbert Lindenberger, 1971; *Trakl* by Maire Jaanus Kurrik, 1974; *Dimensions
of Style and Meaning in the Language of Trakl and Rilke* by Joseph P. Colbert, 1974; *The
Poet's Madness: A Reading of Trakl* by Francis Michael Sharp, 1981; *Trakl's Poetry: Toward
a Union of Opposites* by Richard Detsch, 1983.

*   *   *

The poet Georg Trakl was a dedicated perfectionist for whom the craft of poetry meant
striving for absolute truth of expression, purity, and precision of language. His relatively small
and cohesive oeuvre is remarkable for the extant number of variant versions of the poems.
Though Rimbaud, Verlaine, and Baudelaire variously influenced his development and he
showed a partial affinity with German Expressionism, Trakl early established a pronounced
personal style. This is distinguished by great linguistic concentration, recurrent patterns in
diction and imagery, individual use of colour symbolism, and a fine lyricism, which set him
apart as a distinctive new voice in poetry. Like Hölderlin, to whom he owes something of his
elliptical conciseness and hymnic intensity, Trakl was essentially a visionary poet in whom the
inner vision, the image-making faculty, takes precedence over the mimetic function of creative
imagination.

His early poetry is written in rhyming and mellifluous verse which still owes much to *fin de
siècle* influence. In one sense, it represents a development out of Decadence in its rejection of
the classical ideal of beauty, its preoccupation with disease, corruption, death, and the
aesthetic of the ugly. (Trakl wrote in 1910: "one does well to resist perfect beauty.") In another,
it wholly overcomes art for art's sake and fashions necessary connections between the aesthetic
and the moral, an existential aspect which owes much to the idealistic influence of Dostoevsky
and Tolstoy. The persistent religious registers of his poetic language also owe something to this
moral orientation as well as to a highly individualized use of traditional biblical and devotional
vocabulary.

In Trakl the melancholy and elegiac moods predominate and his poetry heralds the calamity of the Great War. (His most frequent adjectives are: dark, blue, black, quiet, silent.)The principal subject of this poetry is a darkened world of pain, death, and decay in which man is the passive, suffering victim. The poet's self is repeatedly projected into mythical poetic personas (Elis, Sebastian, Helian, Kaspar Hauser) who represent pure vessels of violated humanity, yet not without an ethereal strength and some redemptive significance.

The privacy of Trakl's poetic language derives from the solitariness of his self-centered world which is nonetheless registered in deeply sensuous terms. His poems achieve their vividness because the urgency of meaning, however complex or suggestive, unerringly finds its objective correlative in glowing images. Though his poetic language appears, on early acquaintance, to consist of autonomous meanings and to have a hermetic quality, the repeated verbal patterns, poetic ciphers, symbols, and distinctive tonalities combine into a coherent vision of life. His supreme economy of verbal means is largely a result of the conscious aim to achieve a high degree of objectivism in composition, to evolve a mode of lyrical utterance which depends upon a wholly impersonal form. The effect produced, however, is that of a personal tone of great intimacy. A sparseness and simplicity of diction result which render the full stress of subjective experience. Strong incantatory elements and energetic rhythms constantly assert themselves in Trakl's language and these serve both to counterbalance and to heighten the tragic tone.

—Alexander Stillmark

TS'AO Hsueh-ch'n. *See* **DREAM OF THE RED CHAMBER.**

TSVETAYEVA, Marina (Ivanovna). Born in Moscow, 26 September 1892. Educated at schools in Switzerland and Germany, and at the Sorbonne, Paris. Married Sergey Efron in 1912 (died, 1939); two daughters and one son. Emigrated in 1922 to Berlin, then Prague and Paris; returned to the USSR in 1939, but ostracized and unable to publish. *Died (suicide) 31 August 1941.*

PUBLICATIONS

Collections

Izbrannoye, edited by V. Orlov. 1961; revised edition, as *Izbrannye proizvedeniya*, 1965.
Stikhotvoreniya i poemy, edited by A.A. Saakyants. 1980.
Izbrannoye proza v dvukh tomakh 1917-1937. 1980.
Stikhotvoreniya i poemy v piati tomakh. 1980-83.

Verse

Vecherny al'bom [Evening Album].   1910.
Volshebny fonar' [Magic Lantern].   1912.
Iz dvukh knig [From Two Books] (selections).   1913.
Vorsty [Versts].   1921.
Vorsty I [Versts].   1922.
Razluka [Parting].   1922.
Stikhi k Bloku [Poems to Blok].   1922.
Tsar'-devitsa [Tsar-Maiden].   1922.
Remeslo [Craft].   1923.
Psikheya [Psyche].   1923.
Molodets [Brave].   1924.
Posle Rossii [After Russia].   1928.
Lebediny stan.   1957; as *The Demesne of the Swan*, edited and translated by Robin Kemball, 1980.
Selected Poems, translated by Elaine Feinstein.   1971; revised edition, 1981.
Three Russian Women Poets (with Akhmatova and Akhmadulina), edited and translated by Mary Maddock.   1983.

Play

Konets Kazanovy [Casanova's End].   1922.

Other

Proza.   1953.
Pis'ma k Anne Teskovoy [Letters to Anna Teskovy].   1969.
Pis'ma k raznym litsam [Letters to Various Persons].   1969.
Neizdannye pis'ma [Unpublished Letters].   1972.
A Captive Spirit: Selected Prose, edited by J. Marin King.   1980.
Cvetaeva, Boris Pasternak, Rainer Maria Rilke: Lettere 1926.   1980.

*

Bibliography: *Bibliographie des oeuvres de Tsvetayeva* by Tatiana Gladkova and Lev Mnukhin, 1982.

Critical Studies: *Cvetaeva: Her Life and Art* by Simon Karlinsky, 1966; *Cvetaeva: Studien und Materialien* edited by Horst Lampl and Aage A. Hansen-Löve, 1981.

*   *   *

Marina Tsvetayeva, who was called "the most Russian of poets," "a poet's poet," and "a poet of sacrifice," died virtually forgotten: nobody attended her funeral and the location of her grave is not known. Today she enjoys international fame and respect. Her life was a tragedy; but she is a triumph. She had gone "beyond and above" her fellow poets, including the most outstanding. Her poetry offers in many ways the culmination of modern poetry's concern with language. With her, language assumes an importance far greater than we might ever have imagined: she marks its concern with the creation and maintenance of existential orders. Tsvetayeva's poetry plays a part in what constitutes an enormous intellectual challenge for the reader: "The rediscovery of the pun," i.e., the rediscovery of the vital interconnections of language and reality, that we find in Shakespeare. Her mystical belief in the power of poetry was expressed in one of her earliest poems, dated 1913:

> Thrown carelessly about the dusty shelves of bookshops,
> Untouched, then, now, by any reader's thumb,
> My poems, stored deep like wines of precious vintage,
> I know their time will come.

Throughout her life she was forced to speak not only across space, but also across time. It took so long for her to be accepted as among the great, not only because of her life and her character, but because of the very nature of her poetry. Her first collection of verse, privately printed, was noticed only by the poets. Her next two books of lyrics had mixed reviews, although Pasternak praised her "tremendous, uniquely powerful language." Both in Russia and in exile she had failed to find a reading public. As she said: "For those on the Right it [her poetry] is Left in form. For those on the Left it is Right in content." Her loyalty to all the "old oaths" was out of fashion in post-revolutionary Russia. Outcast by fellow émigrés, she proclaimed the absolute, unsullied concepts of honour, duty, and justice: "I have two foes in the world, twins inextricably interrelated—the hunger of the hungry and the glut of the glutted." This "calvinistic spirit of personal responsibility," as Brodsky called it, is felt in all her works. "A single one—from everyone—for everyone—against everyone," she stated her place in life and in poetry.

Her ethics are in many ways determined by her aesthetics. Her massive self-confidence was based on her idealistic cult of the Poet: "...there are not poets, there is one single poet, one and the same from the beginning of creation to the end." In Russia at that time the Poet's name was Marina Tsvetayeva. A keen, poetic, and fertile intelligence is revealed in Tsvetayeva's innovative treatment of language and in her profound meditation on Time and the tragedy of human existence. She demonstrated that language itself is interested in tragic content: by using dactylic rhymes, for instance, she created an intonation of lament. With her, the density of the sentence is often achieved by omission of the verbs "compensated by a brilliant and characteristic use of inflection, especially dative and instrumental case endings, a tactic beyond the scope of any translator," wrote John Bayley. Forceful alliteration and internal rhymes allow her to expand the formal and semantic possibilities of the end-rhyme. She was a master of enjambment, a device she used to attack "the most inhumanely senseless of words: se-pa-ration." This insane, unnatural state of being was, in fact, her fate. Separated from her country, from her family, from her readers, she wrote shortly before her suicide, "I don't want to die. I want not to be":

> I refuse to be. In the mad house of inhuman.
> I refuse to live. With the wolves
> of the market place. I refuse to howl...

She saw even death in linguistic terms, -"tot svet...ne bez—a vse—yazychen" [The other world is not without language, it is multi-lingual]. There is a constant awareness of the power of language to shape and explode perception of the world. She commemorated all her love affairs, real and imaginary, in her poetry. Again and again, language takes her to such heights and with such speed that neither experience nor imagination can compete with it. She had written the finest love poems ever addressed to a man. All her lovers, even those "who can stand the sunlight," wither under Tsvetayeva's gaze. Her "emotional superiority" was equal to her linguistic capacity to surprise. In her numerous letters, in her brilliant prose, and in theoretical essays she displayed the same degree of dependence on language as in her poetry. She did an enormous service to Russian poetry by creating a new linguistic space. She influenced a whole new generation of poets, including Joseph Brodsky, who has written the most penetrating appreciation of her poetry and prose.

—Valentina Polukhina

TU FU. Born in Hsiang-yang, China, in 712. Brought up by an aunt, and given a traditional Confucian education. Married; had children. Celebrated locally as a poet by age 15; traveler by 731; failed imperial examinations, 735, but finally got a minor official post, 751, and another minor post, 757, but often in poverty and unable to support his family; patronized by an old friend in Chengtu, 760-65, then traveled again, and died in Hengchow. *Died in 770.*

PUBLICATIONS

Collections

(*Complete Works*), in *A Concordance to the Poems of Tu Fu* (Harvard-Yenching Institute Sinological Series, Supplement 14). 3 vols., 1967 (reprint).
Tu shih hsiang-chu [Annotated Complete Works]. 5 vols., 1979.

Verse

The Autobiography of a Chinese Poet; The Travels of a Chinese Poet, translated by Florence Ayscough. 2 vols., 1929.
Selected Poems, translated by Rewi Alley. 1962.
A Little Primer of Tu Fu (Chinese and English texts), edited and translated by David Hawkes. 1967.
Poems (with Li Po), translated by Arthur Cooper. 1973.

*

Critical Studies: *Tu Fu, China's Greatest Poet* (includes translations) by William Hung, 1952; *Tu Fu* by A.R. Davis, 1971.

*   *   *

Honoured as a "saint poet," Tu Fu is considered one of the greatest poets not only of the T'ang dynasty but also in the history of Chinese literature. Indeed, he has remained one of the best-loved, most widely read poets in China. His poems have always been studied by writers and critics, and many have been translated into foreign languages.

He travelled across the country for more than ten years when he was young. But judging from his extant poems, he did not write much during this happy period of time. He is best remembered for his later works. He lived in an age when the feudal rulers became decadent and corrupt, when the T'ang dynasty went downhill after it had enjoyed prosperity for more than a hundred years. Through various ways he tried hard to get an official position, but without success. He was only given low positions for brief periods. He began to wander once again and lived in poverty till his death. The misery of his life and his bitter experiences gave him a chance to see with his own eyes the chaos, poverty, and tragedy of the war-worn nation. His poems, which are filled with social themes which mirror that period of Chinese history, are thus often called "poetic history."

He was a realist poet. His poems explicitly express his concern for the common people and lament their sufferings, while implicitly satirizing the extravagant and licentious life of the emperor and his imperial concubines. His poem "A Ballad of Beautiful Women" exposes the decadence and cruelty of the imperial prime minister. In his often-quoted lines "Meat and wine behind the doors of the powerful rich are becoming stinking, while in the streets corpses of the miserable people frozen to death are lying" he makes a striking contrast between the extravagant rich and the suffering poor.

Corruption and war were the root cause of the misery he described. The cruel and corrupt officials robbed the people, leaving them destitute. And the successive wars threw the people into the abyss of sufferings. His poems reflect the heavy burden of misery, the grief of lovers separated by war, and, above all, the desolate scene all over the war-torn country. Poems like "The Song of Chariots," "Farewell of the Newlyweds," and "Husband on an Expedition," epitomize the bitter and tragic state during the war: "Grass smells of the lying corpses, The vast plains are flooded with blood." In many poems he expressed the hope that the war would soon come to an end and people could live in peace. He used his poems to show sympathy with people, comment on state affairs, and reproach the wrong-doings of the rulers.

Tu Fu was more than a political poet, however. His poems cover a wide range of subjects and use various forms including pastoral, narrative and lyric poetry, folk songs and ballads (*yueh-fu*). His genius for diction, excellent mastery of rhythm and rhyme, and astonishing skill at creating images gave such beauty to his poetry and won him so much renown that no poet in the history of Chinese literature has attracted so many followers and influenced so much later poetry.

—Binghong Lu

TURGENEV, Ivan (Sergeyevich). Born in Orel, 28 October 1818. Educated at home; briefly at Armenian Institute and Weidenhammer's boarding school in Moscow; University of Moscow, 1833-34; University of St. Petersburg, 1834-37; University of Berlin, 1838-41; completed master's exam in St. Petersburg, 1842. Civil servant in Ministry of the Interior, 1843-45; then mainly interested in country pursuits, especially hunting; went to France with the singer Pauline Viardot and her husband, 1845-46, and again in 1847-50; exiled to his country estate for a "faulty" obituary of Gogol, 1852-53; in Western Europe again for long spells after 1856, often in Baden-Baden after 1863, and in Paris with the Viardots, 1871-83. Corresponding Member, Imperial Academy of Sciences, 1860. Dr. of Civil Laws: Oxford University, 1879. *Died 3 September 1883.*

PUBLICATIONS

Collections

> *Novels,* translated by Constance Garnett. 15 vols., 1894-99.
> *Polnoye sobraniye sochineniy i pisem.* 28 vols., 1960-68.

Fiction

> *Zapiski okhotnika.* 1852; as *Russian Life in the Interior,* 1855; as *Annals of a Sportsman,* 1885; as *A Sportsman's Sketches,* 1932.
> *Povesti i rasskazy* [Tales and Stories]. 1856.
> *Rudin.* 1856; as *Dmitri Roudine,* 1873.
> *Asya.* 1858; as *Annouchka,* 1884.
> *Dvoryanskoye gnezdo.* 1859; as *A Nest of Gentlefolk,* 1869; as *Lisa,* 1872; as *Home of*

the Gentry, 1970.
Pervaya lyubov'. 1860; as *First Love*, 1884.
Nakanune. 1860; as *On the Eve*, 1871.
Ottsy i dety. 1862; as *Fathers and Sons*, 1867.
Dym. 1867; as *Smoke*, 1868.
Neschastnaya. 1869; as *An Unfortunate Woman*, 1886.
Stepnoy Korol' Lir. 1870; as *A Lear of the Steppe*, with *Spring Floods*, 1874.
Veshniye vody. 1872; as *Spring Floods*, with *A Lear of the Steppe*, 1874.
Nov'. 1877; as *Virgin Soil*, 1877.
Klara Milich. 1883.

Plays

Neostorozhrost' [Carelessness]. 1843.
Bezdenezh'e [Lack of Money]. 1846.
Gde tonko, tam i rvyotsya (produced 1851). 1848; as *Where It's Thin, There It Tears*, in *Plays*, 1924.
Zavtrak s predvoditelya [Lunch with the Marshal of the Nobility] (produced 1849). 1856.
Kholostyak (produced 1849). 1849; as *The Bachelor*, in *Plays*, 1924.
Razgovor na bolshoy doroge (produced 1850). 1851; as *A Conversation on the Highway*, in *Plays*, 1924.
Provintsialka (produced 1851). 1851; as *The Provincial Lady*, in *Plays*, 1924.
Mesyats v derevne (produced 1872). 1855; as *A Month in the Country*, in *Plays*, 1924.
Nakhlebnik (produced 1857). 1857; as *The Family Charge*, in *Plays*, 1924.
Vecher v Sorrente (produced 1884). 1891; as *An Evening in Sorrento*, in *Plays*, 1924.
Plays. 1924.

Verse

Parasha. 1843.
Razgovor [The Conversation]. 1845.
Andrey. 1846.
Pomeshchik [The Landowner]. 1846.
Senilia. 1878; as *Stikhotvoreniya v proze*, 1882; as *Poems in Prose*, 1883; as *Senilia: Poems in Prose*, 1890.

Other

Sobraniye sochineniy. 5 vols., 1860-61, and later editions.
Literaturnye i zhiteyskiye vospominaniya. 1874; revised edition, 1880; as *Literary Reminiscences and Autobiographical Fragments*, 1958.
Nouvelle correspondance inédite, edited by A. Zviguilsky. 2 vols., 1971-72.
Lettres inédites à Pauline Viardot et à sa famille, edited by A. Zviguilsky. 1972.
Letters (selection), edited by A.V. Knowles. 1983.
Letters (selection), edited by David Lowe. 2 vols., 1983.

*

Bibliography: *Turgenev in English: A Checklist of Works by and about Him* by Rissa Yachnin and David H. Stam, 1962.

Critical Studies: *Turgenev: The Man, His Art, and His Age* by A. Yarmolinsky, 1959;

Turgenev, The Novelist's Novelist: A Study by Richard Freeborn, 1963; *Turgenev: The Portrait Game* edited by Marion Mainwaring, 1973; *Hamlet and Don Quixote: Turgenev's Ambivalent Vision* by Eva Kagan-Kans, 1975; *The Clement Vision: Poetic Realism in Turgenev and James* by Dale E. Peterson, 1976; *The Gentle Barbarian: The Life and Work of Turgenev* by V.S. Pritchett, 1977; *Turgenev: His Life and Times* by Leonard Schàpiro, 1978; *Turgenev's Russia: From "Notes of a Hunter" to "Fathers and Sons"* by Victor Ripp, 1980; *Turgenev and England,* 1980, and *Turgenev and George Sand,* 1981, both by Patrick Waddington.

*   *   *

Ivan Turgenev is indisputably in the pantheon of 19th-century Russian literature, but he stands apart from many of the other authors, and especially from his two great contemporaries, Tolstoy and Dostoevsky. He had little taste for confronting the ultimate questions of life, for wrestling with philosophical issues as they visited themselves on the Slavic soul—indeed he doubted that an abstraction like "Slavic soul" was meaningful. The scope of Turgenev's works is narrow, often confined to the cares of a small group of gentry gathered on a remote estate, and his style was geared to capture the half-spoken phrase and the tremor of emotion. He was a miniaturist; but a miniaturist who produced some of the most politically telling fiction of the century.

It took some time for Turgenev to find his distinctive voice. He began his career arguing with German Romanticism, whose influences he had felt during his years as a student at the University of Berlin. His early works, notably the long story "Andrei Kolosov," were attempts to deflate Romantic pretensions, but they were partially contaminated by the disease they attacked. In these early works, Turgenev's language is occasionally pompous and his sense of character vague.

With the *Sportsman's Sketches* cycle, Turgenev hit his stride. Begun almost off-handedly as a favor to some friends who needed material to fill their journal, it comprised 22 sketches when it was published to great acclaim in 1852. The sketches relate the events that befall a nobleman from Orel as he wanders through the countryside. With the creation of this character—much like himself, yet slightly distanced—Turgenev found the means to control his tendency toward high-flown sentiments. Though there are many descriptions about the futility of life and the indifference of nature, the overall effect is bracing, the view of a man coolly contemplating the social landscape of mid-19th-century Russia.

The sense of control is most evident in Turgenev's treatment of the peasantry, which in fact represented an innovation in the Russian tradition. Previously, peasants were treated as stock characters or aspects of an undifferentiated mass, the *narod.* From the first paragraph of the first sketch, "Khor and Kalinych," where the traits of the peasants of one district are contrasted with those of another, Turgenev shows that the peasantry was variegated and individualized. Obviously deeply felt, this perspective also fit into the program of the group with which Turgenev was allied, the Westernizers, who argued that the self-conscious individual was the most important element of a society, on all its levels. As Turgenev himself put it, "Let me be an atom, but my own matter; I do not want salvation but truth, and I expect it from reason not grace."

Whether or not *A Sportsman's Sketches* was instrumental in Alexander II's decision to abolish serfdom (and Turgenev always believed it was), there is no question that it was a key part of the quickening political atmosphere. It was a tenet of the times, however, that only the novel could adequately capture social reality, and in the early 1850's Turgenev turned to that genre. His first, never-completed effort, entitled *Two Generations,* served mainly to show how unsuited his temperament was for complicated plot construction and pyschological development.

He solved many of these technical problems in *Rudin.* Though essentially composed of one incident with an extended preamble and epilogue, and set among a small group of gentry on their provincial estate, the book has novelistic scope because the concerns of the characters parallel the nation's concerns. Most of all this applies to the treatment of the eponymous hero (based in part on Turgenev's old friend the anarchist Michael Bakunin). The question asked of Rudin—can he match his idealistic phrases with action?—was a question that many educated Russians in the 1850's asked themselves.

In his next two novels, *Home of the Gentry* and *On the Eve*, Turgenev continued his investigation of the moral life of the nation. Though these works confirmed his status as the pre-eminent author of the period, the themes he chose also made him a likely target of criticism, especially from the group of radical critics who were at that time acquiring new influence. Men like Chernyshevsky and Dobrolyubov, both of whom served on the leading journal *The Contemporary*, agreed that the questions the novels put were pertinent, but they insisted that Turgenev was too restrained, too moderate in his answers. The tone of this quarrel is summed up by Dobrolyubov's review of *On the Eve*. Significantly entitled "When Will the Real Day Come?," it drew out all the revolutionary implications of the novel, as well as several that were not there.

Such instances tended to strengthen a side of Turgenev which had always despised politics. he wrote numerous works, such as "Faust" (1856) and "Journey to the Forest" (1857), stories that announce the omnipotence of transcendental, ahistorical forces. As it happens, this view of the world also accounts for one of Turgenev's masterpieces, *First Love*. This story, which was his own favorite, is one of the great accounts of the universal relations between father and son.

But for all his reservations about politics, Turgenev never ignored the subject for very long, and was capable of remarkable perspicacity and broadness of vision. Thus, though he intensely disagreed with the utilitarian ethics of the radicals, he showed a remarkable understanding for their political program, even to the extent of sympathetically comparing it with his own liberalism. He defined this contrast in his landmark essay "Don Quixote and Hamlet" (1860), in which he posited two political personalities: one jousts singlemindedly at windmills, ignoring adverse odds, the other understands these odds so acutely that even the first step toward action seems not worth taking. Turgenev saw the heroism and shortcomings of each type.

His most notable acknowledgement of the radical position, however, was the creation of the character Bazarov, in *Fathers and Sons*. Written just as the emancipation of the serfs was becoming a reality, the novel underscores the extreme handicaps confronting a progressive political movement in mid-19th-century Russia. Bazarov, who has grown up watching the fumblings of a generation committed to the spiritual and idealistic aspects of man, puts his faith in science and reason, even though that means totally ignoring many of the humanistic values that the "fathers" embraced. Turgenev shows the historical logic of Bazarov's position; but he also depicts its fatal flaw, the inability to comprehend emotion. Indeed, at the climax of the novel, Bazarov, the powerful representative of radical politics, is brought low by unrequited love.

The novel provoked a maelstrom of controversy. To conservatives, it appeared an apotheosis of Bazarov, to radicals, it was a calumny against one of their kind. In fact, the character is so richly depicted that no simple political definition is possible. Some years later, Turgenev announced that he sympathized with most of Bazarov's views, but this afterthought did not quiet the dispute, which indeed continues to this day.

The reaction to *Fathers and Sons* proved a turning point for Turgenev. Though he had spent much of his adult life abroad, in order to be near his great love, Pauline Viardot, he now settled himself still more firmly in Europe, first in Baden-Baden and then in the estate he purchased jointly with Viardot and her husband in Bougival, outside Paris. He returned to Russia only rarely thereafter, and when he did felt out of touch with the direction of events there—even though it was his Bazarov that had inspired some of the more radical members of the political opposition.

Turgenev's work also became distant from Russia's problems. Two later novels, *Smoke* and *Virgin Soil*, both suffer from a caricaturing of the radical mentality, a striking flaw in view of Turgenev's earlier ability to depict sympathetically political types he disagreed with. A more compelling strain in Turgenev's later work is a philosophical pessimism derived from Schopenhauer. This melancholic mood, which is on display in *Poems in Prose*, prompted some powerful writing, though still not comparable to his early work. In fact, the greatest achievement of the final two decades of his life was the introduction of Russian culture to Europe, through translations he made or through the medium of the many literary friends he acquired abroad.

—Nancy Kanach Fehsenfeld

UNAMUNO (y Jugo), Miguel de.   Born in Bilbao, Spain, 29 September 1864.   Educated at Colegio de San Nicolás, and Instituto Vizacaíno, both Bilbao; University of Madrid, 1880-84, Ph.D. 1884. Married Concepción Lizárraga Ecénarro in 1891; nine children. Professor of Greek, 1891-1924, 1930-34, and Rector, 1901-14, 1934-36, University of Salamanca. Exiled to Canary Islands for criticism of Primo de Rivera government, 1924, then lived in Paris, 1924, and Hendaye, 1925-30; under house arrest for criticism of Franco government, 1936. Cross of the Order of Alfonso XII, 1905. *Died 31 December 1936.*

PUBLICATIONS

Collections

> *Obras completas,* edited by Manuel García Blanco.   16 vols., 1966-71.
> *Selected Works,* edited by Anthony Kerrigan.   1967— .

Fiction

> *Paz en la guerra.*   1897.
> *Amor y pedagogía.*   1902.
> *El espejo de la muerte.*   1913.
> *Niebla.*   1914; as *Mist,* 1928.
> *Abel Sánchez: Una historia de pasión.*   1917; translated as *Abel Sanchez,* 1947.
> *Tulio Montalban y Julio Macedo.*   1920.
> *Tres novelas ejemplares y un prólogo.*   1920; as *Three Exemplary Novels,* 1930.
> *La tía Tula.*   1921.
> *San Manuel Bueno, mártir y tres historias más.*   1933.
> *Abel Sanchez and Other Stories.*   1956.

Plays

> *La Venda, La princesa, Doña Lambra.*   1913.
> *Fedra.*   1924.
> *Sombras de sueño.*   1931.
> *El otro.*   1932; as *The Others,* in *Selected Works,* 1976.

Raquel. 1933.
El hermano Juan; o, El mundo es teatro. 1934.
La esfinge. 1934.
Teatro completo, edited by Manuel García Blanco. 1959.

Verse

Poesías. 1907.
Rosario de sonetos líricos. 1911.
El Cristo de Velázquez. 1920; as *The Christ of Velazquez*, 1951.
Rimas de dentro. 1923.
Teresa. 1923.
De Fuerteventura a París. 1925.
Romancero del destierro. 1928.
Poems, translated by Eleanor L. Turnbull. 1952.
Cancionero: Diario poético. 1953.
Cincuenta poesías inéditas, edited by Manuel García Blanco. 1958.
Last Poems, translated by Edita Mas-López. 1974.

Other

De la enseñanza superior en España. 1899.
Tres ensayos. 1900.
En torno al casticismo. 1902.
Paisajes. 1902.
De mi país. 1903.
Vida de Don Quijote y Sancho. 1905; as *The Life of Don Quixote and Sancho*, 1927.
Recuerdos de niñez y de mocedad. 1908.
Mi religión y otros ensayos breves. 1910; as *Perplexities and Paradoxes*, 1945.
Por tierras de Portugal y de España. 1911.
Soliloquios y conversaciones. 1911.
Contra esto y aquello. 1912.
El porvenir de España, with Angel Ganivet. 1912.
Del sentimiento trágico de la vida en los hombres y en los pueblos. 1913; as *The Tragic Sense of Life in Men and in Peoples*, 1926.
Ensayos. 8 vols., 1916-18; revised edition, 2 vols., 1942.
Andanzas y visiones españolas. 1922.
La agonía del cristianismo. 1925; as *The Agony of Christianity*, 1928.
Essays and Soliloquies. 1925.
Cómo se hace una novela. 1927; as *How to Make a Novel*, in *Selected Works*, 1976.
Dos artículos y dos discursos. 1930.
La ciudad de Henoc: Comentario 1933. 1941.
Paisajes del alma. 1944.
Algunas consideraciones sobre la literatura hispano-americana. 1947.
Madrid. 1950.
Mi Salamanca. 1950.
Epistolario, with Juan Maragall. 1951; revised edition, 1976.
Autodiálogos. 1959.
Pensamiento político, edited by Elías Diaz. 1965.
Our Lord Don Quixote and Sancho with Related Essays. 1967.
Diario íntimo, edited by P. Félix García. 1970.
Epistolario, with Alonso Quesada, edited by Lázaro Santana. 1970.
Cartas 1903-1933. 1972.

The Agony of Christianity and Essays on Faith. 1974.
Escritos socialistas. 1976.
Unamuno "agitador de espíritus" y Giner: Correspondencia inédita, edited by D. Gómez Molleda. 1976.
Artículos olvidados sobre España y la primera guerra mundial, edited by Christopher Cobb. 1976.
Gramática y glosario del Poema del Cid, edited by Barbara D. Huntley and Pilar Liria. 1977.

Translator, *Etica de las prisiones, Exceso de legislación, De las leyes en general,* by Herbert Spencer. 3 vols., 1895.
Translator, *Historia de la economica política,* by J.K. Ingram. 1895(?).
Translator, *Historia de las literaturas castellana y portuguesa,* by Ferdinand J. Wolf. 2 vols., 1895-96.

*

Bibliography: *Bibliografía crítica de Unamuno 1888-1975* by Pelayo H. Fernández, 1976.

Critical Studies: *Unamuno* by José Ferrater-Mora, 1962; *The Lone Heretic: A Biography of Unamuno* by Margaret Thomas Rudd, 1963; *Death in the Literature of Unamuno* by Mario J. Valdés, 1964; *Unamuno: The Rhetoric of Existence* by Allen Lacy, 1967; *Unamuno: An Existential View of Self and Society* by Paul Ilie, 1967; *Unamuno* by Martin Nozick, 1971; *Unamuno's Webs of Fatality* by David G. Turner, 1974; *Unamuno: Abel Sánchez* by Nicholas G. Round, 1974; *Unamuno: The Contrary Self* by Frances Wyers, 1976; *Unamuno: San Manuel Bueno, Mártir* by John Butt, 1981.

*   *   *

Miguel de Unamuno strove very consciously to be the voice and conscience of Spain for his generation, to give form to a timeless and metaphysical "Spanishness" that he felt as part of his flesh and bone. The Basque, educated in Madrid, found the roots of his life in the ancient university town of Salamanca as professor of Greek and Romance philology, later as rector of the university. His academic profession served as a secure base for Unamuno, as did his marriage and the family it produced. Yet his unquiet spirit drove him to incessant travel throughout the peninsula in his attempt to know Spain in its most intimate historical, linguistic, and geographical detail. His travels are recorded in two collections of short articles, *Por tierras de Portugal y de España* and *Andanzas y visiones españolas.* Their language is not that of the Baedeker, but a subjective, often intellectual, reaction to provincial cities and towns, rivers, mountains, and plains. Indeed, Unamuno lacked the painter's eye for color and detail; everywhere he finds literary and historical associations. A stripped cork-oak brings to his mind the martyrdom of St. Bartholomew; a group of shepherds he encounters are the very ones Don Quixote engaged in his "eternal discourse"; Trujillo is the cradle of the conquistadores; Avila, of course, is St. Theresa.

Unamuno is one of the most difficult writers to classify in a generation of extreme individualists—the Generation of 1898. This loosely defined group included poets, novelists, playwrights, and essayists of outstanding quality. Unamuno wrote in all of these forms, but in one field he was unique: he was the only theologian of the literary group. He was a troubled, anguished, declamative doubter whose quest for God was basic to all of his mature work. Like Pascal and Kierkegaard, whose writing he knew and revered, the Basque could accept no religious panaceas or compromises. Following a religious crisis in 1897, he was deeply shaken to an agonizing awareness of his own mortality and the horrendous void of non-being. He could no longer accept the traditional comforts of Catholic doctrine nor accomodate himself to the facile, intellectualized atheism of some rationalist currents. He read widely in contemporary Protestant theologians, but Unamuno was not looking for answers; he was looking for the core questions that would serve him to find his own answers, his personal faith that could never be enshrined in doctrine or dogma. Years later this desperate search would be externalized in his great philosophical analysis, *Del sentimiento trágico de la vida en los hombres y en los pueblos.* Faith was never a serene gift to Unamuno. It had to be constantly re-examined, explored, doubted, denied, and revindicated. This is the sense of a second treatise, *La agonía del cristianismo.*

Unamuno had written an early historical, loosely autobiographical novel, *Paz en la guerra,* dealing with the impact of the Carlist wars on Bilbao, where he had spent his childhood. He would not repeat this exercise of writing within the typical framework of 19th-century historical fiction. He sought a totally different approach, a more reduced and intimate way of creating fictional beings and examining their reactions to life. His first *nivola*—as he baptized this new form—was *Mist*; it has come to be one of his most widely translated and universally known creations. Augusto Pérez, a rich young man of no talent, no convictions, and no overriding interests, wanders through life as a series of relationships grow around him. He decides to be in love, and when the girl he has chosen, a piano teacher who detests music, dupes him and runs off with her lover, Augusto determines to kill himself. First, however, he wants to discuss his decision with Unamuno, and he makes the journey to Salamanca to consult the sage. Unamuno informs Augusto that suicide is impossible for him, since Augusto is merely a character in a novel that Unamuno is writing. The author tells his creation that he will, indeed, kill him in the novel. Now, Augusto, threatened with death from outside himself, wants desperately to live. He begs for his life, but the author rather testily replies that he can't carry Augusto about with him indefinitely. Augusto points out that Unamuno, too, will die, that God will run out of ideas for him, and he, too, will return to nothingness, as will the readers as well. Unamuno is obdurate with the death sentence and Augusto, terribly shaken, returns to Madrid, orders an almost endless meal, and dies that night of a heart attack induced by overeating.

The situation of the character appealing to his author, of confrontation between creator and created, broke totally with 19th-century novelistic procedure and provided Unamuno with a means to examine his own existence as well as his creative instinct. His next novel, *Abel Sánchez,* is a chilling study of envy and hatred: the Cain/Abel theme which obsessed Unamuno and was later given theatrical form in his play *The Others.* Between 1898 and 1929 Unamuno wrote a half dozen short plays. All are talky, muddled, undramatic, serving as clumsy go-carts to parade the ideas he had already examined more effectively in his essays and novels.

The political dimension of Unamuno's thought parallels his religious quest. He was outspoken in the extreme on questions of government. An early attraction to Socialism and the nascent workers' movements in Spain, along with wide reading in the social philosophy of the late 19th century, especially German, inspired him for a while in the 1890's, but was soon rejected. He quickly came to feel that the progressive doctrines of a workers' state were fundamentally deceptive and served only to mask the true problems of Man's existence in the world. As he found no panaceas in organized religion, he found none in organized or organizational politics. His severe criticism of the Spanish monarchy and the ineptitude of its ministers during World War I grew ever more volatile with the disaster of Spain's African policy and the dictatorship of Primo de Rivera in the 1920's, and finally led to his exile, 1924-30. The establishment of the Republic in 1931 restored Unamuno to the rectorship of the university of Salamanca, but the chaotic politics of Spanish liberalism pleased him no more than the repressive regime of Alfonso XIII. He continued to criticize both left and right of the new government in the most acerbic tones, a Socratic gadfly in every area of public faith.

It was perhaps primarily as a poet that Unamuno sought the immortality of literary fame. His production was voluminous, from the early *Poesías* to the *Romancero del destierro* and a posthumous collection, *Cancionero.* His major work of poetry is the massive *The Christ of Velazquez,* a long and complex meditation on the figure of the crucified Christ painted by the Spanish baroque master. This fervent Christology has all the thunder and bombast of evangelical certainty, but with the peculiar and personal insight of Unamuno, of "religious, not theological faith, free of dogma." As a poet, Unamuno lacked tone and sensibility; he had little ear for the rhythms and subtleties of verse. As he resorts to declamation and repetition in his essays, so he does in his poetry, rejecting the refinements of language and the sensuality of metaphor typical of Modernism, the movement that had influenced both the poetry and the prose of many of his contemporaries. In his frequently tortured lines, Unamuno gives us little music, little that might be called lyric beauty. He tries to open our eyes to see his own despairing vision of reality, and this severe honesty gives unmatched force and intensity of spirit to the best of his work.

One short novel that may stand as a recapitulation of Unamuno's thought and style, perhaps his last *nivola*, is *San Manuel Bueno, mártir*. Revealed here is the tragedy of a village priest who is denied the gift—or the blindfold—of faith. His life is spent in the martyrdom of leading a village of simple folk in a faith that he cannot personally accept, in the "pious fraud" of giving temporal peace and the hope of eternal life to those who must never feel the agony of Christian doubt. The author raises the question, Does faith make the martyr, or does the martyr, in his own heroic act, make the faith?

Unamuno had very real shortcomings as a poet, novelist, and dramatist, yet through all his work the originality of his mind and the sincerity and magnitude of his philosophic and religious quest elevate the text and smooth the sometimes belicose harshness of his language, often as gritty as the clay of the Castilian highlands he so loved.

—James Russell Stamm

UNDSET, Sigrid. Born in Kalundborg, Norway, 20 May 1882; brought up in Oslo. Attended Commercial College, graduated 1898. Married the painter Anders C. Svarstad in 1912 (marriage annulled, 1924); two sons and one daughter. Worked in office of electrical firm, Oslo, 1899-1909; then writer; lived in the United States during World War II. Recipient: Nobel Prize for Literature, 1928. Honorary degrees: Rollins College, Winter Park, Florida, 1942; Smith College, Northampton, Massachusetts, 1943. Grand Cross of Order of St. Olav, 1947. *Died 10 June 1949.*

PUBLICATIONS

Collections

    Middelalder-romaner [Historical Novels].   10 vols., 1959.
    Romaner og fortellinger fra nutiden [Contemporary Novels and Stories].   10 vols., 1964-65.

Fiction

    Fru Marta Oulie [Mrs. Martha Oulie].   1907.
    Den lykkelige alder [The Happy Age].   1908.
    Fortaellingen om Viga-Ljot og Vigdis.   1909; as *Gunnar's Daughter*, 1936.
    Jenny.   1911; translated as *Jenny*, 1920.

Fattige skjaebner [Miserable Fates]. 1912.
Vaaren [Spring]. 1914.
Splinten av troldspeilet. 1917; as *Images in a Mirror*, 1938.
De kloke jomfruer [The Wise Virgins]. 1918.
Kristin Lavransdatter. 3 vols., 1920-22; translated as *Kristin Lavransdatter*, 3 vols., 1923-27.
Olav Audunssøn. 4 vols., 1925-27; as *The Master of Hestviken*, 4 vols., 1928-30.
Gymnadenia. 1929; as *The Wild Orchid*, 1931.
Den braendende busk. 1930; as *The Burning Bush*, 1932.
Ida Elisabeth. 1932; translated as *Ida Elisabeth*, 1933.
Elleve år. 1934; as *The Longest Years*, 1935.
Den trofaste hustru. 1936; as *The Faithful Wife*, 1937.
Madame Dorthea. 1939; translated as *Madame Dorothea*, 1941.

Plays

Østenfor sol og vestenfor maane [East of the Sun and West of the Moon]. 1960.

Verse

Ungdom [Youth]. 1910.

Other

Fortaellinger om Kong Artur og ridderne av Det runde Bord [Tales of King Arthur and the Knights of the Round Table]. 1915.
Tre søstre [Three Sisters]. 1917.
Et kvindesynpunkt [A Woman's Point of View]. 1919.
Katholsk propaganda [Catholic Propaganda]. 1927.
Etapper. 2 vols., 1929-33; as *Stages on the Road*, 1934.
Hellig Olav, Norges Konge [St. Olav, King of Norway]. 1930.
Christmas and Twelfth Night. 1932.
Fortschritt, Rasse, Religion (written in German). 1935.
Norske helgener. 1937; as *Saga of Saints*, 1934.
Selvportretter og landskapsbilleder. 1938; as *Men, Women, and Places*, 1939.
Lykkelige dager—. 1947; as *Happy Times in Norway*, 1942.
Tilbake til fremtiden. 1945; as *Return to the Future*, 1942.
Die Saga von Vilmund Vidutan und seinen Gefährten (written in German), as *Sigurd and His Brave Companions.* 1943.
Caterina av Siena. 1951; as *Catherine of Siena*, 1954.
Artikler og taler fra krigstiden [Articles and Speeches from the War]. 1952.
Steen Steensen Blicher. 1957; as *Diary of a Parish Clerk*, 1976.
I grålysningen [At Dawn]. 1968.

*

Bibliography: *Undset bibliografi* by Ida Packness, in *Norsk Bibliografisk Bibliotek*, 1963.

Critical Studies: *Three Ways of Modern Man* by Harry Slochower, 1937; *Undset: A Study in Christian Realism* by A.H. Winsnes, 1953; *Six Scandinavian Novelists* by Alrik Gustafson, 1966; *Undset* by Carl F. Bayerschmidt, 1970.

*   *   *

Thirst for knowledge and wide reading, particularly in the fields of history and archeology, disposed Sigrid Undset early in life for a career as a researcher into and chronicler of past ages. Coming from an academic background, she used her intimate knowledge of Norwegian history as a foundation for a number of medieval historical novels, of which the most successful were the trilogy *Kristin Lavransdatter*, set in the 14th century, and the two novels about Olav Audunssøn, from the 13th century.

Kristin Lavransdatter is usually classed as Sigrid Undset's finest achievement. It is the story of a young girl, Kristin, and her development through maturity, marriage, and motherhood, to old age and death, the whole set against a panoramic backdrop of medieval Norway, involving the political jockeyings between the Scandinavian kingdoms, and the struggles between an emergent Christianity and a still tenacious paganism. The illusion of realism is sustained by a wealth of detail about the minutiae of daily life; yet the greatest strength of the trilogy lies in the timeless and sympathetic portrayal of the central character. Kristin as a young woman is torn between submission to the patriarchal tradition and the desire to follow the dictates of her own heart; she chooses the latter, but pays a heavy price of guilt and self-recrimination throughout her life.

Not all of Sigrid Undset's fiction is historical; in fact the majority of her novels and short stories deal with contemporary society. She was herself forced to earn her own living as a young woman, and many of the women in her novels and stories are modern working girls, faced with the dilemmas created by the clash between newly won independence and traditional expectations. The central characters of *Fattige skjaebner* ("Miserable Fates") are low-paid workers who suffer from both physical and emotional deprivation, finding that the struggle to survive takes all their strength. The eponymous heroine of *Jenny* is an artist who stakes her life on fulfilment both in art and in love, and is defeated—but because of forces within herself rather than external social or moral pressures. Sigrid Undset's relationship to women's liberation was always an ambivalent one; her heroines have ambition and ability which demand to be realised, and yet many of them, like Marta in *Fru Marta Oulie*, conclude with the insight that home, husband, and family represent the ultimate goal of female self-fulfilment.

Religious themes are central to many of Sigrid Undset's novels, particularly her medieval ones (for which she won the Nobel prize in 1928). In 1925 she became a Catholic. Yet she was never a dogmatic one; on religious as on many other matters she kept an open mind. In the political crisis of the 1930's, however, she took a determined stand, speaking out and writing against nazism from the start. With the outbreak of the war she had to flee to the United States, and her fictional career came to an abrupt end in the middle of a planned series; but she continued writing essays and memoirs until the end of her life.

—Janet Garton

UNGARETTI, Giuseppe. Born in Alexandria, Egypt, 10 February 1888. Educated at École Suisse Jacot, Alexandria, until 1905; Collège de France, Paris, 1912; the Sorbonne, Paris. Served in the Italian Army infantry, 1915-18. Married Anne Jeanne Dupoix in 1920 (died, 1958); one daughter and one son. Paris correspondent, *Popolo d'Italia*, 1919-20; journalist, Ministry of Foreign Affairs, Rome, 1921-30; travel writer, *Gazzetta del Popolo*, Turin, 1931-35; Joint Managing Editor, *Mesures*, Paris, 1935-36; Professor of Italian Literature, University of São Paulo, Brazil, 1936-42; Professor of Modern Italian Literature, University of Rome, 1942-59. Visiting Professor, Columbia University, New York, 1964;

Lecturer, Harvard University, Cambridge, Massachusetts, 1968. President, European Community of Writers, 1962-63. Recipient: Premio del Gonfaloniere, 1932; Premio Roma, 1949; International Grand Prize for Poetry, 1956; Etna-Taormina International Prize, 1967; Neustadt International Prize, 1970. Member, Bavarian Academy; Chevalier, Legion of Honor (France); Honorary Fellow, Modern Language Association (USA). *Died 1/2 June 1970.*

PUBLICATIONS

Verse

Il porto sepolto. 1916.
La Guerre (in French). 1919.
Allegria di naufragi. 1919; revised edition, as *L'Allegria*, 1931; edited by Annalisa Cima, 1967.
Sentimento del tempo. 1933.
La Vita d'un Uomo:
  L'Allegria. 1942.
  Sentimento del tempo. 1943.
  Poesie disperse. 1945.
  Il dolore (1937-1946). 1947.
  La terra promessa. 1954.
  Un grido e paesaggi. 1954.
  Il taccuino del vecchio. 1961.
  Tutte le poesie, edited by Leone Piccione. 1969; revised edition, 1972.
Frammenti per la terra promessa. 1945.
Derniers jours 1919, edited by Enrico Falqui. 1947.
La terra promessa. 1950.
Gridasti: Soffoco.... 1951.
Un grido e paesaggi. 1952.
The Promised Land and Other Poems: An Anthology of Four Contemporary Poets, edited by Sergio Pacifici. 1957.
Life of a Man, edited and translated by Allen Mandelbaum. 1958; revised edition, as *Selected Poems,* 1975.
Il taccuino del vecchio. 1960.
Quattro poesie. 1960.
75° compleanno: Il taccuino del vecchio, Apocalissi. 1963.
Poesie, edited by Elio Felippo Accrocca. 1964.
Apocalissi e sedici traduzioni. 1965.
Morte delle stagioni, edited by Leone Piccioni. 1967.
Dialogo, with Bruna Bianco. 1968.
Croazia segreta. 1969.
L'impietrito e il velluto. 1970.
Selected Poems, edited by Patrick Creagh. 1971.

Other

Piccola Roma. 1944.
La Vita d'un Uomo (translations):
  40 Sonetti di Shakespeare. 1946.
  Da Góngora e da Mallarmé. 1948.
  Fedra di Jean Racine (includes critical study). 1950.
  Visioni di William Blake. 1965.

Il povero nella città (essays).   1949.
Pittori italiani contemporanei.   1950.
La Vita d'un Uomo (prose):
    Il deserto e dopo: Prose di viaggio e saggi.   1961.
    Saggi e interventi, edited by Mario Discono and Luciano Rebay.   1974.
Viagetto in Etruria.   1965.
Il Carso mon è più un inferno, edited by Vanni Scheiwiller.   1966.
Innocence et mémoire.   1969.
Propos improvisés, with J. Amrouche.   1972.
Lettere a un fenomenologo.   1972.

Editor, with David Lajolo, *I poeti scelti.*   1949.
Editor, *Le voci tragiche di Guido Gonzato.*   1952.

Translator, *Traduzioni.*   1936.
Translator, *XXII Sonetti di Shakespeare.*   1944.
Translator, *L'Après-Midi et le Monologue d'un Faune*, by Mallarmé.   1947.
Translator, *Finestra del caos*, by Murilo Mendes.   1961.
Translator, *Anabase*, by Saint-John Perse.   1967 (trilingual edition, with English translation by T.S. Eliot).
Translator, *Cinque poesie di Vinicius de Moraes.*   1969.

*

Critical Studies: *Ungaretti* by Glauco Cambon, 1967; *Three Modern Italian Poets: Saba, Ungaretti, Montale* by Joseph Cary, 1969; "Ungaretti Issue" of *Books Abroad 44*, 1970; *Ungaretti Poet and Critic* by Frederic J. Jones, 1977.

*   *   *

Together with Montale, Ungaretti is regarded as the most important modern Italian poet. This, however, does not mean that there is any fundamental affinity between the two, nor, for that matter, any comparison in terms of influence. Montale's has no doubt been a greater and more enduring influence than that of Ungaretti. But it was Ungaretti who, with his first volume of poems, *Il porto sepolto* (1916), which came out 9 years before Montale's *Ossi di seppia*, signalled a crucial as well as creatively important reaction against D'Annunzianism and made the impact that only a major poet could have made. Pinpointing what was original in his poetry, the Italian critic Francesco Flora characterized it as hermetic, thereby indicating the succinct, epigrammatic, and pictorially graphic character of Ungaretti's lyricism and particularly of his poetic imagery. In fact, in Ungaretti's best and most characteristic lyrics imagery and sentiment, moral intensity and artistic self-control, verbal economy and evocative richness are so interfused as to form an accomplished pattern that serves as its own objective correlative. Another characteristic of Ungaretti's poetry, which he shares with Saba, is his habit of taking the depth and tumult of a personal sentiment as a sufficient guarantee that even a simple and unelaborated linguistic transcription of it can stand by itself as poetry. Thus what is subjective about Ungaretti's lyricism is rooted in what one might call psychological innocence or naive psychologism.

The volumes *Allegria di naufragi*, *Sentimento del tempo*, and *Il dolore* represent Ungaretti's art and technique at their best—an art in which, by discarding the use of punctuation, traditional syntax, and metre, and by introducing the pauses or the so-called "spazi bianchi" (blank spaces), Ungaretti not only forges the accents and idiom of modern poetry, but also achieves a peculiar kind of unity and autonomy that reminds one of Imagistic poetry. (Not for nothing was Ungaretti an admirer of Pound and translated some of his poems.) In the poems dealing with the theme of his brother's and his son's deaths—the most poignantly personal Ungaretti ever wrote—while giving vent to his sense of bereavement, he shows a degree of self-control and moral maturity that determined the form and structure as well as the style and imagery of his best poetry. In such poems each and every detail—a memory, an image, or an association—serves to transmute the pain of a personal tragedy into something objective and impersonal and mould it into the sharply chiselled contours of art. From the anguished yet ennobling intensity of personal tragedy Ungaretti derived a strength, and—more importantly—a relentless austerity of form and diction, which enabled him to deal with the explosive force of emotion with impressive mastery over the imaginative resources of the language as well as over his own experience.

Ungaretti subsequently published other volumes of poetry in which the theme of bereavement gives way to the theme of love—love which, "mentre arrivo vicino al gran silenzio" (while I approach the great silence), reasserts its hold on the poet and makes him experience all its frenzy, and all its grandeur and cruelty once more. For under the duress of the race against time and of the relentless tug-of-war between age and desire, reason and emotion, the poet finds himself in the grip of what Thomas Hardy called "the strongest passion known to humanity" which shakes, to quote Hardy again, "this fragile frame at eve/With throbbings of noontide."

—G. Singh

UPANISHADS

PUBLICATIONS

Collections

> *The Upanishads,* edited by S.C. Vasu (includes translation). 3 vols., 1909-16; also edited by S. Radhakrishnan, 1953, T.M.P. Mahadevan, 1977, and Jagdish Shastri, 1980; translated by N.K. Aiyar, 1914, R.E. Hume, 1921, revised edition, 1931, Swami Nikhilananda, 4 vols., 1949-59, Swami Prabhavananda and Frederick Manchester, 1957, and Juan Mascaro, 1965.

Individual *Upanishads*

> *Brihadaranyaka,* translated by E. Roer, 1865, and S.C. Vasu, 1913-16.
> *Chhandogya,* translated by R. Mitra, 1848.
> *Aitareya,* translated by Bhadkamkar, 1899.
> *Taittiriya,* translated by A.M. Shastri, S.C. Vidyarnava, and M.L. Sandal, 1925.
> *Kena,* translated by S.C. Vasu and A.C. Thirlwall, 1902, M. Hiriyanna, 1912, and D.K. Das, 1969.
> *Katha,* translated by W.D. Whitney, 1890, S.C. Vasu, 1905, and R.L. Pelly, 1924.
> *Isha,* translated by William Jones, 1799, S.C. Vasu and A.C. Thirlwall, 1902, and P. Lal, 1969.
> *Mandukya,* translated by M.N. Dvivedi, 1894.
> *Kaushitaki,* translated by E.B. Cowell, 1861, and S.C. Vidyarnava and M.L. Sandal, 1925.

Maitri, translated by E.B. Cowell, 1870.
Ayvakta, translated by P. Lal, 1969.
Mahanarayana, translated by P. Lal, 1971.
Brhadaranyaka, translated by P. Lal, 1974.
Jabala, translated by D.K. Das, 1979.
Paingala, translated by D.K. Das, 1979.

*

Critical Studies: *The Philosophy of the Upanishads* by A.E. Gouch, 1882-84; *Philosophy of the Upanishads* by Paul Deussen, 1906; *The Religion and Philosophy of the Vedas and the Upanishads* by A.B. Keith, 1925; *A Constructive Survey of the Upanishadic Philosophy* by R.D. Ranade, 1926; *Upanishads, Gita, and the Bible* by Geoffrey Parrinder, 1962.

*   *   *

The word "Upanishad" is from *upa* "near," *ni* "down," and *sad* "to sit." It literally means "sitting down near." The pupils who wished to know about the *Upanishads* sat by their teachers and learnt it from them. Going back to 800 B.C., the books are believed to be of divine origin, and revealed by god to inspired sages. Though some put the number of the *Upanishads* at 150, the genuine ones are believed to be 108. Of these the classical ones on which Shankaracharya commented are 11, the Chhandogya, Brihadaranyaka, Kena, Aitareya, Mandukya, Isha, Katha, Mundaka, Taittiriya, Svetashvatara, and Prashna. Most of the *Upanishads* are in Sanskrit prose (with occasional verse), but five of them are in verse alone.

The spiritual wisdom contained in the *Upanishads* is, as Paul Deussen says, "unequalled in India or perhaps anywhere else in the world." The soul, they believe, is of the same nature as the Cosmic Absolute known as Brahman. It is changeless and eternal, and transmigrates from a body at death into another body, the circumstances being determined by the man's actions in his previous life or lives. The soul is only apparently associated with the body it dwells in like the "redness" of transparent glass when placed over red cloth. The concept that it is the soul which acts and suffers is due to ignorance. When this ignorance is removed, Brahman, which is the only truth, is realized; and this can be in one's lifetime itself. Then actions become desireless and, like burnt seed, will not sprout into results. The circle of births and rebirths is broken for such a man, and he has achieved emancipation.

Although there is a great deal of repetition, prolixity, and sometimes even obscurity in the *Upanishads,* and the Sanskrit is often terse, abundant compensation is made by their vivid comparisons and rich imagery. The nature of Brahman is described as "without limit, as when we drop a lump of salt in water the whole solution is salty from wherever you might taste it." The soul and Brahman are like "two birds sitting on the same tree. One eats the fruits of the tree with relish, the other looks on without eating." The soul taking a new body is like "a caterpillar leaving one blade of grass and grasping another," or as though "a goldsmith may take a piece of gold and fashion it into a lovelier form." In a beautiful verse the sage Yajnavalkya compares man to a mighty tree. The simile of the chariot is used to explain the nature of the soul: "The soul is the rider, the body the chariot, the intellect the charioteer, the mind the reins. The senses are the horses, their objects the roads." The path of emancipation is "sharp as a razor's edge." There is the lighter side too, as when the hypocrisy of priests is exposed: "The priests who move along chanting a hymn, are like dogs going together, and what they say is 'may the gods bring us more food; let us eat and drink!'"

The *Upanishads* do not take a gloomy view of life. They are for hard work and a full existence. "One should live a hundred years," one of them says, "and carry out the tasks allotted to him." If one is patient with the *Upanishads,* he will be rewarded as the man "seeking goodly pearls, who when he had found one pearl of good price, went and sold all that he had, and bought it." Schopenhauer had the *Upanishads* on his table and read through some of it daily before going to bed. "They are the products of the highest wisdom," he said, "destined sooner or later to become the faith of the people."

—K.P. Bahadur

VALÉRY, (Ambroise) Paul (Toussaint Jules). Born in Cette (now Sète), France, 30 October 1871. Educated at a school in Sète to 1884, and a lycée in Montpellier, 1884; University of Montpellier, licence in law 1892. Military service: 1889-90. Married Jeannie Gobillard in 1900; three children. Worked for the War Office, 1897-99; private secretary to Edouard Lebey, Director of the press association Agence Havas, Paris, 1900-22; Editor, with Valéry Larbaud and Léon-Paul Fargue, *Commerce* literary review, 1924-32; Administrator, Centre Universitaire Mediterranéen, Nice, from 1933; held Chair of Poetics, Collège de France, Paris, 1937-45. Member, French Academy. Honorary Doctorate: Oxford University. Chevalier, 1923, Officer, 1926, and Commander, 1931, Legion of Honor. *Died 20 July 1945.*

PUBLICATIONS

Collections

Oeuvres, edited by Jean Hytier. 2 vols., 1957-60.
Collected Works, edited by Jackson Mathews. 15 vols., 1956-75.

Verse (includes prose poems)

La Jeune Parque. 1917; edited by Octave Nadal, 1957.
Album de vers anciens 1890-1900. 1920.
Charmes ou poèmes. 1922.
Poésies. 1933; augmented edition, 1942.
Paraboles. 1935.
Mélange (includes prose). 1941.
L'Ange. 1946.
Agathe; ou, La Sainte du sommeil. 1956.

Plays

Amphion: Mélodrame, music by Arthur Honegger (produced 1931). 1931.
Sémiramis: Mélodrame, music by Arthur Honegger (produced 1934). 1934.

Other

La Soirée avec Monsieur Teste. 1919; revised edition, as *Monsieur Teste,* 1946; as *An Evening with Mr. Teste,* 1925; translated as *Monsieur Teste,* 1947.

Introduction à la méthode de Léonard de Vinci. 1919; as *Introduction to the Method of Leonardo da Vinci,* 1929.
Eupalinos ou l'architecte, L'Âme et la danse. 1923; as *Eupalinos; or, The Architect,* 1932, and *Dance and the Soul,* 1951.
Fragments sur Mallarmé. 1924.
Variété 1-5. 5 vols., 1924-44; first 2 vols., as *Variety,* 1927-38.
Une conquête méthodique. 1924.
Durtal. 1925.
Études et fragments sur le rêve. 1925.
Le Retour de Hollande: Descartes et Rembrandt. 1926.
Petit recueil de paroles de circonstance. 1926.
De la diction des vers. 1926.
Propos sur l'intelligence. 1926.
Analecta. 1926.
Rhumbs. 1926.
Quinze lettres à Pierre Louÿs (1916-17). 1926.
Autre Rhumbs. 1927.
Maîtres et amis. 1927.
Quatre lettres sur Nietzsche. 1927.
Essai sur Stendhal. 1927.
Lettre à Madame C.... 1928.
Poésie: Essais sur la poétique et le poète. 1928.
Variation sur une "Pensée." 1930.
Propos sur la poésie. 1930.
Cahiers B. 1930.
Littérature. 1930.
Oeuvres. 12 vols., 1931-50.
Discours de l'histoire. 1932.
Choses tues. 1932.
Moralités. 1932.
Discours en l'honneur de Goethe. 1932.
Calepin d'un poète: Essais sur la poétique et le poète. 1933.
L'Idée fixe. 1934.
Pièces sur l'art. 1934.
Suite. 1934.
Hommage à Albert Thibaudet. 1936.
Villon et Verlaine. 1937.
L'Homme et la coquille. 1937.
Technique au service de la pensée. 1938.
Discours aux chirurgiens. 1938.
Introduction à la poétique. 1938.
Degas, Danse, Dessin. 1938; as *Degas, Dance, Drawing,* 1948.
Existence du symbolisme. 1939.
Conférences. 1939.
Tel quel. 2 vols., 1941-43.
Mauvaises Pensées et autres. 1942.
Eupalinos ou l'architecte, L'Âme et la danse, Dialogue de l'arbre. 1944.
Au sujet de Nerval. 1944.
Regards sur le monde actuel et autre essais. 1945.
Henri Bergson. 1945.
Mon Faust: Ébauches. 1946.
Souvenirs poétiques. 1947.
Vues. 1948.
Écrits divers sur Stéphane Mallarmé. 1950.

Histoires brisées. 1950.
Lettres à quelques-uns. 1952.
Correspondance 1890-1942, with André Gide, edited by Robert Mallet. 1955; as *Self-Portrait: The Gide/Valéry Letters,* 1966.
Correspondance 1887-1933, with Gustave Fourment, edited by Octave Nadal. 1957.
Cahiers. 29 vols., 1957-61.

Translator, *Les Bucoliques,* by Virgil. 1953.

*

Bibliography: *Bibliographie des oeuvres de Valéry 1895-1925* by Ronald Davis and Raoul Simonson, 1926.

Critical Studies: *Valéry* by Theodora Bosanquet, 1935; *Valéry* by Elizabeth Sewell, 1952; *The Art of Valéry* by Francis Scarfe, 1954; *The Universal Self: A Study of Valéry* by Agnes Ethel Mackay, 1961; *Valéry* by Henry Grubbs, 1968; *Worlds Apart: Structural Parallels in the Poetry of Valéry, Saint-John Perse, Benjamin Peret, and René Char* by Elizabeth R. Jackson, 1976; *Valéry* by Charles Gammons Whiting, 1978; *Figures of Transformation: Rilke and the Example of Valéry* by Richard Cox, 1979; *Valéry and the Poetry of Voice* by Christine M. Crow, 1982; *Valéry's "Album de vers anciens"* by Suzanne Nash, 1983.

*   *   *

After 20 years of solitude and study (1897-1917), Valéry broke his silence in 1917 with a five-hundred-line poem, *La Jeune Parque.* His early poems were collected in *Album de vers anciens,* and in 1922 his major collection, *Charmes,* appeared; this contains "Le Cimetière Marin," "Fragments du Narcisse," "Ebauche d'un serpent," "Palme," and other poems. *Charmes* (meaning "incantations" or "poems") placed Valéry in company with the purest of the French poets—with Mallarmé, in particular, and with Chénier, La Fontaine, and Racine.

After *Charmes,* Valéry wrote two Platonic dialogues: *L'Âme et la danse,* a meditation on the movement of a dancer that transforms her from an ordinary woman into a supernatural being; and *Eupalinos,* a discussion on the genius of the architect and, more generally, any artist who is able to create out of his chosen materials a masterpiece. In a series of five volumes of collected essays, *Variété,* Valéry discussed several problems of his age and analyzed various literary problems, especially those related to poets with whom he felt close affinity: Mallarmé, Verlaine, Baudelaire, Poe, La Fontaine.

For Valéry, the poet is the artist who does not stifle any of his inner voices or any of the hidden desires of his nature. His particular vocation forces him to translate and interpret those voices and desires. To do this, he must remain lucid and fully rational. He is not a man inspired by the Muse, but one who must cultivate a universal intelligence and thus not close himself off from any reality. *La Jeune Parque* describes the successive stages of consciousness in a young girl as she moves from sleep to a full awakening. "La Pythie" is the oracle (Pythoness), convulsed before she can deliver herself of the divine message (or the poem). In composing sonnets ("L'Abeille," "Les Grenades") or odes ("Aurore") or the long poems of "Le Cimetière Marin" and *La Jeune Parque,* Valéry accepted all the discipline of the classical style, all the demanding rules of vocabulary, rhythm, and rhyme. He used metaphors, alliteration, and harmonious effects to sustain the mystery and the enchantment of the poem.

Charmes is the last landmark of French symbolism. From the time of its publication until his death, Valéry was an almost official representative of his country's culture. In today's language Valéry's mind and attitude would be called that of a *contestataire.* He decried any doctrine that named literature something sacred and, like his master Mallarmé, pointed out the discrepancy between the thought of a man and the words in which he tries to express the thought. The composition of a poem interrupts and distorts the purity of the inner dialogue the poet carries on with himself.

Valéry ushered in a moment in French literature in which the poem was preferred to the poet, the study of poetics preferred to the study of the poem, and a literary work studied in its relationship to the general power of language. He treated poetry as something comparable to architecture and music. All three of these arts were for Valéry the offspring of the science of numbers. Almost in spite of himself, his work was expressed in words, in poetry, and in accord with that "inspiration" (a word he disliked) which the contemplation of the sea offered him.

"Le Cimetière Marin," not his greatest poem perhaps, but the one that has received the greatest attention, restored the forgotten resources of the decasyllabic line of French poetry. The long poem is a monologue in which the poet's voice speaks of the most basic and constant themes of his emotional and intellectual life associated with the sea and the sunlight as it strikes certain parts of the land bordering on the Mediterranean.

No thinker has considered this age with greater perspicacity and penetration than Valéry. And no thinker has demolished it more thoroughly. His fame has been built upon fragments—upon poems, aphorisms, dialogues, brief essays. He was the supreme example of a writer indifferent to his public, detached from any need to please his public. The actual "subjects" of his pages are varied: the beauty of a shell, the prose of Bossuet, the method of Stendhal. He tells us that *le moi pur* is unique and monotonous. Yet it is the deepest note of existence that dominates all the "varieties" of existence. To hear this note clearly was the goal and the ecstasy of Valéry's intellectual search.

With each essay, with each fragment of prose writing and each poem, Paul Valéry extended the hegemony of his thought over most of the intellectual problems facing man today. But the subtlety and suppleness of his writing were such that he never reached, nor wished to reach, the creation of a philosophical system.

It has often been claimed that all of French literature, more than other national literatures, is of a social origin. It seems to come into its own under the stimulation of debate, in an atmosphere of worldliness and *mondanité*. Paul Valéry was for many years, and particularly during the decade of the 1930's, looked upon as an esoteric poet, as a difficult thinker who never left the realm of abstractions, and hence as a writer who stood apart from the central tradition of French letters. But he was in reality a fervent observer of humanity and a man who always strove to express himself in the most meaningful and the most "social" way. The conquest of *le moi pur* led Valéry through a labyrinth of human experience and human sentiment, from the seeming indifference of M. Teste to the tenderness of the character Lust in the posthumously published volume, *Mon Faust*. Our entire historical period is in his work—the gravest problems that worry us and the oldest myths that enchant us.

—Wallace Fowlie

VALLEJO, César (Abraham). Born in Santiago de Chuco, Peru, 16 March 1892. Educated at a secondary school in Huamachuco, 1905-08; Trujillo University, 1910-11, 1913-17, B.A. 1915, also law degree; studied medicine in Lima, 1911. Married Georgette Phillipart. Worked in his father's notary office, in mine offices, as a tutor, and in an estate accounts office; taught at Centro Escolar du Verones and Colegio Nacional de San Juan while at Trujillo University; lived in Lima, 1917-23: teacher at Colegio Barrós, 1918-19, and another school, 1920; involved in political riot at Santiago de Chuco and imprisoned, 1920-21; teacher, Colegio Guadalupe,

1921-23; lived in Europe after 1923; Secretary, Iberoamerican press agency, 1925; free-lance writer: Founder, with Juan Larrea, *Favorables-Paris-Poema* (two issues), 1926; visited Russia several times; expelled from France and lived in Spain, 1930-32; lived in Paris from 1932; helped publish *Nuestra España* during Spanish Civil War. *Died 15 April 1938.*

PUBLICATIONS

Collections

> *Obras completas.* 3 vols., 1973-74.

Verse

> *Los heraldos negros.* 1919.
> *Trilce.* 1922; translated by David Smith as *Trilce*, 1973.
> *Poemas humanos.* 1939; as *Human Poems*, translated by Clayton Eshleman, 1969.
> *España, aparta de mí este cáliz.* 1940; as *Spain, Take This Cup from Me*, translated by Clayton Eshleman, 1974.
> *Twenty Poems*, translated by Robert Bly, James Wright, and John Knoepfle. 1962.
> *Obra poética completa*, edited by Georgette de Vallejo. 1968.
> [*Selected Poems*] (in Spanish), edited by James Higgins. 1970.
> *Neruda and Vallejo: Selected Poems*, translated by Robert Bly, James Wright, and John Knoepfle. 1971.
> *Selected Poems*, edited by Gordon Brotherston and Ed Dorn. 1976.
> *The Complete Posthumous Poetry*, translated by Clayton Eshleman and José Rubia Barcia. 1978.
> *Poesía completa*, edited by Juan Larrea. 1978.

Fiction

> *Escalas melografiadas.* 1923.
> *Fabla salvaje.* 1923.
> *El tungsteno.* 1931.
> *Novelas y cuentos completos.* 1970.

Other

> *Rusia en 1931.* 1931.
> *El romanticismo en la poesía castellana.* 1954.
> *Reflexiones al pie del Kremlin.* 1959.
> *Aula Vallejo 1-3.* 1959-67.
> *Artículos olvidados*, edited by Luis Alberto Sánchez. 1960.
> *Rusia ante el segundo plan quinquenal.* 1965.
> *Literatura y arte.* 1966.
> *Desde Europa*, edited by Jorge Puccinelli. 1969.
> *Cartas a Pablo Abril.* 1971.

> Translator, *L'Élévation*, by Henri Barbusse. 1931.

*

Critical Studies: *Aproximaciones a Vallejo* edited by Angel Flores, 2 vols., 1971; *Vallejo: Héroe y mártir indo-hispano*, 1973, and *Vallejo y el surrealismo*, 1976, both by Juan Larrea; *Vallejo* edited by Julio Ortega, 1975; *Vallejo: The Dialectics of Poetry and Silence* by Jean Franco, 1976.

*   *   *

A man of a profound and complex sensibility who could not express himself in the commonly accepted patterns of poetic communication, César Vallejo transformed the Spanish lyrical language so dramatically that his works have had a definite influence on contemporary poetry. The intensity of his feelings finds expression in a simple but highly concentrated style in which everyday language, and the extremely personal images of his own views on the world, create a very effective tension supported by the broken rhythm of free verse.

When reading Vallejo's poetry it is important to take into consideration his being a *mestizo* from the Peruvian Andes. His outlook on life was greatly affected by his early formation in the traditionally Catholic and economically poor circumstances of his boyhood. Although early in his life he ceased to be a practicing Catholic, he was imbued by religious values and made constant use of religious images and references in his poetry. Most of his life he suffered from poverty and from a feeling of bereavement as he confronted a world characterized by human injustice.

Suffering is a main motive in Vallejo's writing. At the beginning it is mainly a self-centered preoccupation as he encounters the injustices of Peruvian society, and longs for the lost world of the Andes, the family, and his religious beliefs. His first two books of verse, both published in Peru before he left for Europe, deal with this personal anguish. The first one, *Los heraldos negros*, is very much a continuation of Latin American modernism. *Trilce*, on the contrary, represents a break with tradition and constitutes one of the best examples in Spanish of contemporary vanguardist poetry. A very difficult book because of its peculiar syntax and hermetic images, *Trilce* is the result of Vallejo's desperate effort to express his very painful and complex intimate feelings and emotions.

The poems he wrote in Europe are much more influenced by his political views, and they are the result of his involvement in political activity as a Left Wing writer. Thus *Human Poems* and *Spain, Take This Cup from Me*, both published posthumously, are concerned mostly with social matters, and with the political developments of socialism in the world. Suffering has become now a communal feeling and the poet develops a new language which, in spite of retaining many peculiarly personal elements, is highly communicative. The colloquialisms and common expressions used by Vallejo in all of his books have in these two a more direct effect in making the poem an expression of the common man, of the basic needs and dreams of the working classes. The poet has made of his own suffering a redeeming force, taking upon himself the duty to save the poor and the defenseless. As such, Vallejo became one of the first writers to develop in Spanish a politically committed lyric poetry. The rest of his literary works seem much less valuable than his poems.

—Santiago Daydi-Tolson

VEDAS.

PUBLICATIONS

Collections

Vedas, edited by Lakshmana Swarup. 4 vols., 1939-55; also edited by Ramagovinda Trivedi, 8 vols., 1963, and Dayanda Sansthan, 4 vols., 1973.

Individual *Vedas*

Rig Veda, translated by R.T.H. Griffith, 4 vols., 1889-91, Max Muller, 1892, and R. Trivedi, 1945; *Hymns from the Rig Veda* translated by Jean Le Mee, 1975.
Sama Veda, translated by S. Samasrami, 1874-78, and R.T.H. Griffith, 1898.
Atharva Veda, translated by M.A. Bloomfield, 1899.

*

Critical Studies: *Vedic Culture* by M. Giri, 1921; *Religion in Vedic Literature* by P.S. Deshmukh, 1933; *Vedic Religion and Philosophy* Swami Prabhavananda, 1940; *Rigvedic India* by A.C. Das, 1947; *The Heart of the Rigveda* by M.R. Gopalacharya, 1971; *Poetry and Speculation of the Rig Veda* by Willard Johnson, 1980.

*   *   *

The word "Veda," from *vid* "to know," means sacred knowledge. The *Vedas* are four in number—Rig, Yajur, Sama, and Atharva—and are believed to have been revealed by divine agency to the rishis (sages) whose names they bear. According to popular belief the *Rig Veda* was compiled by Vyasa in four collections (samhitas) and addressed to various gods, chiefly to Agni the god of fire, and Indra the god of the firmament. The *Vedas* are revered as *apaurusheya* "not of human origin." The *Rig Veda* is the oldest and most widely known. It dates back to 3,000 B.C. The *Atharva Veda* is comparatively recent. Except for Egyptian and Mesopotamian literature, that of the Vedas is the oldest in the world.

The *Rig Veda* (*rik* meaning "a verse") has 11,000 hymns spread over ten books. The stanzas have four lines each having usually eight, eleven or twelve syllables, and sometimes five or four. The metre is not uniform, and there is no rhyme. The Vedic poets were expert craftsmen, and their Sanskrit is simple, spontaneous, and rich in figures of speech, particularly comparisons. The bow pressed close to a warrior's ear is like a loved woman held in his embrace, and the twang of the bowstring like the secrets she whispers to him.

The *Vedas* did not exult in Asceticism. They were for a full life of learning, domestic bliss, and finally renunciation. Lopamudra, a sage, says "one does not break his penance if he has children." They are a mirror of their age. The acts of generous kings, legends of heroes, social manners and customs like marriage and funeral ceremonies, drinking and gambling, black magic spells and incantations, and village life are all vividly described in them. A lover casts a spell on his girl to make her "desire my body, my feet, love my eyes and lips, and hasten to lie on my bosom." A man who lost his fortune gambling bemoans "My mother-in-law hates me, and no one pities me. They all say they find no more use in a gambler than in an aged horse that's for sale!" Nonetheless emphasis was on character. The goddess of learning tells a teacher not to bring her one who is envious of others, crooked, discontented, and licentious, but he who is pure, attentive, intelligent, and chaste. Hard work on the fields was the way to prosperity, and a farmer says, "The land I plough with my sharp-pointed smooth-handled plough, making neat furrows, enables me to possess a sheep, a horse to draw my cart, and a plump lass!"

The *Sama Veda* and the *Yajur Veda* use the hymns of the *Rig Veda*, merely rearranging them for purposes of ritual. The *Atharva Veda* has neither the sanctity nor the importance of the *Rig Veda*. The old Buddhist texts omit them altogether.

The *Vedas* advocated ideals which were to become the basis of Hindu culture. They have survived the war-filled strife-torn centuries, and one may still hear them chanted in a deep voice by Hindu priests in temples or by devout Hindu worshippers in their homes. To the world of today they have a particular message—that of friendly coexistence. There should be unity not only in the country, they say, but throughout the world. The *Atharva Veda* goes even further: "Varuna belongs not to our land only," it declares, "but to foreign lands too." What the United Nations has thought up now, the Vedas conceived more than three thousand years before Christ.

—K.P. Bahadur

VEGA Carpio, Lope (Felix) de. Born in Madrid, 25 November 1562. Educated at Jesuit Imperial College, 1574-75; Universidad Complutense, 1577. Married 1) Isabel de Urbina in 1588 (died, 1595); 2) Juana de Guarda c. 1602 (died), several children; also had children by Micaela de Luján and Marta de Nevares, and another illegitimate son. Went to Madrid after leaving the university: writer and traveller; patronized by Marqués de Las Navas, 1583-87, and Marqués de Malpica; love affair led to libel, and jail and exile from Castille; joined the Spanish Armada against England in 1588; then lived in Valencia and Toledo; Secretary to the Duke of Alba, 1590-95; in household of Marqués de Sarría, 1598-1600; secretary and counsellor to the Duke of Sessa from 1605; also "familiar of the Inquisition," 1608, and prosecutor of Apostolic Chamber; lived in Madrid after 1610; ordained priest, 1614. Order of Malta, 1627. *Died 27 August 1635.*

PUBLICATIONS

Collections

Las Comedias. 29 vols., 1604-45(?).
Fiestas des Santíssimo Sacramento. 1644.
Colección de las obras sueltas así en prosa, come en verso, edited by F. Cerdá y Rico. 21 vols., 1776-79.
Obras, edited by M. Menéndez y Pelayo. 15 vols., 1890-1913; revised edition, edited by E. Cotarelo y Mori, 13 vols., 1916-30.
Poemas, edited by L. Guarner. 1935.
Epistolario, edited by Agustín González de Amezúa. 4 vols., 1935-43.
Obras escogidas, edited by F.C. Sainz de Robles. 3 vols., 1946-55.
Cartas completas, edited by Ángel Rosenblatt. 2 vols., 1948.

Plays (selection)

El acero de Madrid, edited by Jean Lemartinel and others. 1971.
Las almenas de toro, edited by Thomas E. Case. 1971.

Amar sin saber a quién, edited by Carmen Bravo-Villasante. 1967.
El amor desatinado, edited by J. García Morales. 1968.
El amor enamorado, edited by J.B. Wooldridge. 1978.
El arauco domado, edited by A. de Lezama. 1953.
Arminda celosa.
Barlaán y Josafat, edited by José F. Montesinos. 1935.
Las bizarrías de Belisa, edited by Alonso Zamora Vicente (with *El Villano en su rincón*). 1963.
El Brasil restituido, edited by José Maria Viqueira Barreiro. 1950.
Las burlas de amor.
Las burlas veras, edited by S.L.M. Rosenberg. 1912.
El caballero de Olmedo, edited by Francisco Rico. 1970; as *The Knight from Olmedo*, in *Five Plays*, edited by R.D.F. Pring-Mill, 1961.
El cardenal de Belén, edited by Elisa Aragone. 1957.
Carlos V en Francia, edited by Arnold G. Reichenberger. 1962.
Castelvines y Monteses.
El castigo del discreto, edited by William L. Fichter. 1925.
El castigo sin vengenza, edited by A.D. Kossoff. 1970; as *Justice Without Revenge*, in *Five Plays*, edited by R.D.F. Pring-Mill, 1961.
La corona de Hungría, edited by R.W. Tyler. 1972.
La corona merecida, edited by José F. Montesinos. 1923.
El cuerdo loco, edited by José F. Montesinos. 1922.
La dama boba, edited by E.R. Hesse (with *Fuenteovejuna*). 1964; as *The Lady Nit-Wit*, 1958.
El desdén vengado, edited by M.M. Harlan. 1930.
La desdichada Estefania, edited by J.H. Arjona. 1967.
Dineros son calidad, edited by Klaus Wagner. 1966.
El doctor simple, as *Doctors All*. 1937.
El duque de Viseo, edited by F. Ruiz Ramón. 1966.
Los embustes de Celauro, edited by Joaquín de Entrambasaguas. 1942.
La estrella de Sevilla, edited by William M. Whitley and Robert Roland Anderson. 1971; as *The Star of Castille*, 1950.
Las ferias de Madrid, edited by Alva V. Ebersole (with *La vitoria de la honra*). 1977.
La fianza satisfecha, edited by William M. Whitley and Robert Roland Anderson. 1971; as *A Bond Honoured*, 1966.
Fuenteovejuna, edited by E.R. Hesse (with *La dama boba*). 1964; as *Fuente Ovejuna*, in *Four Plays*, 1936; as *All Citizens Are Soldiers*, 1969.
El galán de la membrilla, edited by Diego Marín and Evelyn Rugg. 1962.
Lo que hay que fiar del mundo, edited by A.L. Gasparetti. 1931.
El Marqués de las Navas, edited by José F. Montesinos. 1925.
El mayordomo de la duquesa de Amalfi.
El mejor alcalde, el rey, as *The King the Greatest Alcalde*, in *Four Plays*. 1936.
El mejor mozo de España, edited by W.T. McCready. 1967.
Los melindres de Belisa, edited by Henriette C. Barrau. 1933.
La moza de cántaro, edited by C. Gonzalez Echegaray. 1968.
La noche de San Juan, edited by H. Serís. 1935.
La nueva victoria de don Gonzalo de Córdoba, edited by Henryk Ziomek. 1962.
El nuevo mundo descubierto por Cristóbal Colón, edited by J. Martinel and Charles Minguet. 1980; as *The Discovery of the New World by Christopher Columbus*, 1950.
Las paces de los reyes y judía de Toledo, edited by James A. Castañeda. 1962.
El padre engañado, as *The Father Outwitted*. 1805.
El palacio confuso, edited by Charles Henry Stevens. 1939.
Pedro Carbonero, edited by José F. Montesinos. 1929.
Peribáñez y el Comendador de Ocaña, edited by J.M. Ruano and J.E. Varey. 1980;

translated as *Peribanez*, 1938; as *The Commander of Ocaña*, 1958.

El perro del hortelano, edited by Victor Dixon.   1981; as *The Gardener's Dog*, in *Four Plays*, 1936; as *The Dog in the Manger*, in *Five Plays*, edited by R.D.F. Pring-Mill, 1961.

Il piadoso aragonés, edited by James N. Greer.   1951.

El príncipe despeñado, edited by Henry H. Hoge.   1955.

La prueba de los amigos, edited by L.B. Simpson.   1934.

Los Ramírez de Arellano, edited by Diana Ramírez de Arellano.   1954.

El remedio en la desdicha, edited by J.W. Barker.   1931.

Santiago el Verde, edited by Jean Lemartinel and others.   1974.

El secretario de sí mismo.

El sembar en buena tierra, edited by William L. Fichter.   1944.

Servir a señor discreto, edited by F. Weber de Kurlat.   1975.

La siega, edited by José Fradejas Lebrero.   1958.

El sufrimiento premiado, edited by Victor Dixon.   1967.

El villano en su rincón, edited by Alonso Zamora Vicente (with *Las bizarrías de Belisa*).   1963; as *The King and the Farmer*, 1948.

La vitoria de la honra, edited by Alva V. Ebersole (with *Las ferias de Madrid*).   1977.

Ya anda la de Mazagatos, edited by S.G. Morley.   1924.

Verse

La Dragontea.   1598.

Isidro: Poema castellano.   1599.

La hermosura de Angélica, con otras diversas rimas.   1602.

Rimas.   1604.

La Jerusalém conquistada.   1609; edited by Joaquín de Entrambasaguas, 3 vols., 1951-54.

Arte nuevo de hacer comedias en este tiempo.   1609.

Rimas sacras.   1614; edited by Luis Guarner (with *Romancero espiritual*), 1949.

Triunfo de la fee en los reynos del Japón.   1618; edited by J.S. Cummins, 1965.

La Filomena con otras diversas rimas, prosas, y versos.   1621.

La Circe, con otras rimas y prosas.   1624; edited by Charles V. Aubrun and Manuel Muñoz Cortés, 1962.

Romancero espiritual.   1624; edited by Luis Guarner, 1941.

Triunfos divinos con otras rimas sacras.   1625.

Corona trágica: Vida y muerte de la Sereníssima Reyna de Escocia María Estuarda.   1627.

Laurel de Apolo, con otras rimas.   1630.

Amarilis: Égloga.   1633.

Rimas humanas y divinas.   1634.

La Gatomaquia.   1807; edited by Agustín del Campo, 1948.

Ultimos amores.   1876.

Sonetos, edited by Manuel Arce.   1960.

Fiction

La Arcadia: Prosas y verso.   1598; edited by Edwin S. Morby, 1975.

El peregrino en su patria.   1604; edited by M.A. Peyton, 1971; as *The Pilgrim; or, The Stranger in His Own Country*, 1738.

Pastores de Belén: prosas y versos divinos.   1612.

La Dorotea: Accion en prosa.   1632; edited by Edwin S. Morby, 1958.

Other

Fiestas de Denia al Rey Cathólico Felipe III. 1599.
Iusta poética y alabanzas iustas. 1620.

Translator, *Soliloquios amorosos de un alma a Dios.* 1626; edited by María Antonia
Sanz Cuadrado, 1948.

*

Bibliography: *The Chronology of the Lope de Vega Comedias* by S. Griswold Morley and
Courtney Bruerton, 1940, addenda in *Hispanic Review 15,* 1947; *Ensayo de una bibliografía de
las obras y artículos sobre la vida y escritos de Lope de Vega Carpio* by I. Simón Díaz and J. de
José Prades, 1955, and *Nuevos estudios,* 1961; *Bibliografía de las comedias históricas de Lope
de Vega* by R.B. Brown, 1958; *Lope de Vega Studies 1937-1962* by Jack H. Parker and Arthur
M. Fox, 1964; *Bibliografía del teatro de Lope de Vega* by María Cruz Pérez y Pérez, 1973.

Critical Studies: *The "Romancero" in the Chronicle-Legend Plays of Lope de Vega* by Jerome
Aaron Moore, 1940; *The Internal Line-Structure of Thirty Autograph Plays of Lope de Vega*
by Walter Poesse, 1949; *Physical Aspects of the Spanish Stage in the Time of Lope de Vega* by
Ruth Lundelius, 1961; *Lope de Vega* by Francis C. Hayes, 1967; *Lope de Vega: El Caballero de
Olmedo* by Jack W. Sage, 1974; *The Metamorphosis of Lope de Vega's King Pedro* by Frances
Exum, 1974; *Experience and Artistic Expression in Lope de Vega: The Making of La Dorotea*
by A.S. Trueblood, 1974; *Songs in the Plays of Lope de Vega* by Gustavo Umpierre, 1975; *The
Honor Plays of Lope de Vega* by Donald R. Larson, 1977.

*   *   *

Lope de Vega fashioned the *comedia* the distinctive drama that prevailed in the popular
theatres (the *corrales de comedias*) of 17th-century Spain. His copious output gave contemporaries and successors such as Tirso de Molina, Ruiz de Alarcón and Calderón de la Barca
influential models for the *arte nuevo,* the "new art," of dramatic composition. But Lope's
literary activity went beyond the theatre. His poetic works are varied and prolific, even by the
standards of his own times. His prose writings are substantial and represent a wide range of
genres (the picaresque excluded). He acted as "secretario de señor" to several noble masters.
For these activities as much as for the social figure he cut (he was a skilled dancer) and his
love-life, the man was a legend in his own time. Lope's complex self and rich experience stand at
the centre of much of his literary activity. His youthful affair with Elena Osorio, of scandalous
consequence, took on many guises in the ensuing years, eventually to reach an elegant synthesis
of mature wisdom, regretful melancholy, and compassionate humour in a last major work (*La
Dorotea*) by the then septuagenarian writer; from many points of view, this is the most
remarkable piece of fiction of its century, inside and outside Spain. The intricate weaving of
experience and fiction over a great span of years that culminates in *La Dorotea* is traced in the
masterful study by A.S. Trueblood. As one literary persona replaces another in this process,
Lope's sincerity ceases to be a clear-cut issue. Even his memorable confession, "I was born into
two extremes, to love and to hate; I have never had a middle way," is adapted from a verse by
Publius Sirus. The interaction between life and poeisis is often signalled in his works by familiar
pseudonyms (Belardo, Fernando, Dorotea, Amarilis). But not always. Lope's major contribution to the pastoral, *La Arcadia,* though ostensibly recording the loves of his patron the Duke
of Alba, must owe its pessimism and suffering—unusual even for pastoral—to its author's own
emotional mood. By way of contrast, Lope's great poem on personal tribulation, "Huerto
deshecho," the central image of which—the poet's garden laid waste by storm—has often been
related to the abduction of the poet's daughter, appeals simultaneously to our own humanity
and for our intellectual engagement on several levels; the biographical circumstances add little
to our enjoyment. Lope could stand above the traditions of poetry, while yet absorbing them;

in *Rimas humanas y divinas del licenciado Tomé de Burquillos*, the eponymous sonneteer, in hapless love with a washerwoman, turns Petrarchism to warm mockery; in *La Gatomaquia*, an epic battle between Madrid cats, Lope genially sends up the devices of his own poetry.

Lope claimed to have written a total of 1500 plays; a modest third survive, including Corpus Christi playlets and palace plays. The temptation to see his theatre as carelessly composed should be resisted. His art was born of and made for a popular theatre. He recognised that his true capital as a dramatist lay in his audience. That is the burden of his single excursion into dramatic aesthetics, the *Arte nuevo de hacer comedias*, an apologia for a type of play that defied rules for dramatic excellence revered in academic circles; "the art of plays and poetry," Lope claimed, "is the invention of the princes among poets, for great minds are not bound by rules." His theatre mirrors life, without forfeiting imagination and fantasy. Its issues can range from the values and customs of gentrified Madrid (e.g., *The Lady Nit-Wit*, an urban satire, with an elegant peripety that turns its heroine from *boba* to *discreta*) to deep issues concerning the individual and social order. His theatre contains generic sub-groups. *Fuente Ovejuna*, *Peribanez*, *The King the Greatest Alcalde*, and *The King and the Farmer* have a common interest in the peasant. They combine a rich poetical evocation of authentic, rural existence with a rigorous, even realistic analysis of conflict in society. Lope was fascinated by how passion can disrupt social order. The privileged maintainers of order (typically a *comendador*, a local lord) betray the values that give their social role credence and purpose. Lope has been disparaged as an "idealist" in his view of society, especially for ending social conflict with the "restoration of harmony." Yet he has a realistic sense that a community seeks, after suffering, deliverance into a new order (not a restored one) that can contain turbulence in a way that a past system of authority could not. These plays are complex compositions. They draw local events and national events into one coherent dramatic structure. What happens at the level of a village community is sensed as being part of the great forces at work in a nation's evolution. The passage from an old and flawed order to a new and whole one is willed by those who are ruled as much as by their rulers. They are history plays, their plots frequently drawn from chronicles and ballads. Yet they engage with contemporary issues concerning the sovereign state that much exercised political philosophers of Lope's time and the previous century as they applied themselves to defining the moral identity of a modern state. How centralised monarchy is based on a divinely entrusted and just exercise of power and how hierarchy is justified in terms of morally informed relationships between its lowly and privileged are key issues in these plays. Lope was a brilliant apologist for the centralised Habsburg authority under which he and his audience lived, and his theatre can be seen as an epic celebration of their common values. Yet he was not afraid of confronting the violence and disorientation caused when social restraints are broken; witness the fury of the womenfolk of *Fuente Ovejuna* who hold aloft the severed head of their *comendador*, or the lethal rage of Peribanez in defense of his wife Casilda. *The King and the Farmer* deals with these issues in a comic vein; the humorously presented rivalry between countryside and court is resolved in a solemn, even sacramental banquet at which the king invites the peasant to partake of the species of power with his ruler.

In another sub-group, that has plays such as *The Gardener's Dog*, *Arminda celosa*, *Las burlas de amor* and *El secretario de sí mismo*, Lope explores another area of social turbulence, caused by the social climber who confuses established roles. In *El mayordomo de la duquesa de Amalfi*, he adapts for a similar end, but in sombre key, the well-known tale from Bandello. And in another adaptation from Bandello's *novelle*, he offers his most disturbed tragic vision of passion and disorder, *Justice Without Revenge*; there, the Duke of Ferrara, driven by a lethal combination of pride and sexual humiliation, wreaks vengeance on his bastard son and adulteress duchess in a double murder which he chillingly justifies as an act of divine and human justice. It may be wondered why the same Bandello tale that provided Shakespeare with the plot of *Romeo and Juliet* should end happily in Lope's version, *Castelvines y Monteses*; but the lovers' cheeky trouncing of the rival elders together with the casual appearance of a Fernando and a Dorotea in the last act are a reminder not only of Lope's sympathy for the young and distrust of the old, but also of the imperious influence exerted by his youthful love for Elena Osorio. In *The Knight from Olmedo*, however, Lope confronts the tragedy of youth, and in an intensely lyrical play offers his moving account of romantic love, jealousy, and death.

—Alan K.G. Paterson

VERGA, Giovanni. Born in Catania, Sicily, 2 September 1840. Educated at home, and privately, 1851-60; studied law at University of Catania, 1860-65. Lived in Florence, 1865-70, and Milan, 1870-85; then returned to Catania. Made a senator, 1920. *Died 27 January 1922.*

PUBLICATIONS

Collections

> *Le Opere*, edited by Lina and Vito Perroni. 2 vols., 1945.
> *Opere*, edited by Luigi Russo. 1955.

Fiction

> *I carbonari della montagna.* 4 vols., 1861-62.
> *Una peccatrice.* 1867.
> *Storia di una capinera.* 1873.
> *Eva.* 1874.
> *Nedda.* 1874; translated as *Nedda*, 1888.
> *Tigre reale.* 1875.
> *Eros.* 1875.
> *Primavera ed altri racconti.* 1876.
> *Vita dei campi.* 1880; as *Cavalleria Rusticana and Other Tales of Sicilian Life*, 1893; as *Under the Shadow of Etna*, 1896.
> *I vinti:*
> > *I Malavoglia.* 1881; as *The House by the Medlar Tree*, 1890.
> > *Mastro-don Gesualdo.* 1889; edited by Carla Riccardi, 1979; as *Master Don Gesualdo*, 1893.
> *Il marito di Elena.* 1882.
> *Novelle rusticane.* 1882; as *Little Novels of Sicily*, 1925.
> *Per le vie.* 1883.
> *Drammi intimi.* 1884.
> *Vagabondaggio.* 1887.
> *I ricordi del Capitano d'Arce.* 1891.
> *Don Candeloro e c.^{i}.* 1894.
> *The She-Wolf and Other Stories.* 1958.

Plays

> *Cavalleria rusticana*, from his own story (produced 1884). 1884.

La lupa; In portineria, from his own stories.   1896.
La caccia al lupo; La caccia alla volpe.   1902.
Dal tuo al mio.   1906.
Teatro (includes *Cavalleria rusticana, La lupa, In portineria, La caccia al lupo, La caccia alla volpe*).   1912.
The Wolf-Hunt, in *Plays of the Italian Theatre*, edited by Isaac Goldberg.   1921.
Rose caduche, in *Maschere 1.*   1929.

Other

Lettere a suo traduttore (correspondence with Édouard Rod), edited by Fredi Chiappelli. 1954.
Lettere a Dina (correspondence with Dina Castellazzi di Sordevolo), edited by Gino Raya.   1962.
Lettere a Luigi Capuana, edited by Gino Raya.   1975.
Lettere sparse, edited by Giovanna Finocchiaro Chimirri.   1980.
*

Bibliography: *Un secolo di bibliografia verghiana* by Gino Raya, 1960; revised edition, as *Bibliografia verghiana*, 1972.

Critical Studies: *Verga* by Thomas G. Bergin, 1931; *Verga's Milanese Tales* by Olga Ragusa, 1964; *Verga: A Great Writer and His World* by Alfred Alexander, 1972; *Language in Verga's Early Novels* by Nicholas Patruno, 1977; *The Narrative of Realism and Myth: Verga, Lawrence, Faulkner, Pavese* by Gregory L. Lucente, 1981.

*   *   *

Verga, along with his fellow Sicilian Luigi Capuana, was one of the founding fathers of the Italian realist movement known as *verismo*. Although Verga began his literary career writing elegantly stylized novels of romance, illicit desire, and adventure, both the interests and the manner of presentation of his narratives changed markedly with the appearance in the mid-1870's of his first work in the new realist mode, *Nedda* (1874, subtitled "A Sicilian Sketch"). Verga's subsequent literary output was substantial, including various plays and a large number of short stories, but his literary reputation rests predominantly on four works published in the 1880's, including two collections of stories, *Vita dei campi* (Life in the Fields) and *Little Novels of Sicily*, and two novels, *The House by the Medlar Tree*, and *Mastro-don Gesualdo*, all of which are masterpieces of realist prose.

In common with such other authors writing in the age of Darwin as Dickens, Zola, and Galdós, Verga focused on the day-to-day events and struggles of human society, and especially on those of the lower classes. Verga's narratives concentrated, moreover, on the customs and characteristics of the region he knew best, Sicily. However, because the everyday language of the Sicilian populace is a regional dialect quite different from Italian, Verga was faced with a particularly intricate linguistic problem. To solve it, he transposed the locutions, rhythms, and syntax peculiar to the dialect into standard Italian both in dialogue and in descriptive passages. At the same time, he made extensive use of free indirect discourse, in which the distinctions between the narrator and the characters are blurred to such an extent that the work of art, in Verga's own words in the introduction to the story "Gramigna's Mistress," seems "to have made itself." The dual effects of Verga's linguistic mastery are, therefore, immediacy and objectivity. Since Verga's narrative is told from what appears in part to be the perspectives of the characters themselves, furthermore, his stories seem to bear the stamp of authenticity in their very narration, as though the world created by the fiction were indeed "real."

These characteristics are shared by all of Verga's realist narratives, even though their characters and subject matter vary considerably. *Nedda* is the story of a young farm worker whose child (fathered by Janu, who has died of malaria) is born out of wedlock. When Nedda refuses to give up her baby, she is ostracized, and the child dies of starvation shortly thereafter. Although Nedda suffers from her situation, she does not seem finally to understand it. If there is to be understanding, therefore, it must come from the reader. This sort of implicit appeal to the reader is typical of Verga's works, and it accounts both for the power of their starkly objective presentation and for the surprisingly consistent sympathy that they elicit for the plight of their protagonists.

Among the short stories of *Vita dei campi* and *Little Novels of Sicily*, four in particular deserve special mention. "Cavalleria Rusticana" is the story of temptation, jealousy, and violence amid Sicily's rural peasantry that furnished the characters and plot for Mascagni's opera of the same name. "The She-Wolf" uses a distinctive mixture of realistic effects and mythic background to portray the superhuman powers and sexual enticements of its title character. "Rosso Malpelo" describes the unconscionable conditions of child labor in the period of Sicily's incipient industrialization, and it shows the local populace's pathetically uncomprehending view of its own role in contributing to such conditions. "Property" tells the story of the vast holdings of the successful and avaricious proprietor, Mazzarò, and of his fetishistic obsession with what he owns. Indeed, his obsession is so strong that even at his death he is unwilling to leave his belongings behind, as he goes about his courtyard killing the animals like a madman, screaming, "Roba mia, vientene con me!" ("My property, come with me!").

Verga's first full novel in the realist mode, *The House by the Medlar Tree*, is the story of the Malavoglia family of Aci Trezza, a fishing village not far from Catania. Padron 'Ntoni, the head of the family, contracts to use his boat, the *Provvidenza*, to transport a cargo of lupins to be sold on the mainland. When the *Provvidenza* goes down in stormy seas off the Sicilian coast, the family not only loses several of its members but also forfeits the familial house by the medlar tree because of failure to repay the sum borrowed to make the contract. Even more clearly than the short story "Property," *The House by the Medlar Tree* demonstrates Verga's condemnation of the economic system then on the rise in Italy, which brought with it, in his view, the destruction of the social order of the family and the end of the old codes of honor and labor that the family had always sustained.

Mastro-don Gesualdo carries Verga's critique a step further by concentrating on the main character's economic and social advancement from "Mastro," or "Journeyman," to "Don," or "Lord." Mastro-don Gesualdo uses both his wits and an advantageous marriage to gain fabulous wealth. But his social and economic success is matched by the nearly total deterioration of his emotional life, until at the end of the novel, in a scene reminiscent of the conclusion of Balzac's *Père Goriot*, Gesualdo suffers the agonies of the deathbed completely alone, with only the uncaring servants to notice his passage. These two novels were originally planned as the first and second entries in a five-part series entitled "I vinti," or "The Defeated," which was to move up the social scale until it reached the Sicilian aristocracy, Verga's own class. It is probably impossible to establish beyond doubt whether Verga stopped with *Mastro-don Gesualdo* because his inspiration failed him, because of unresolvable stylistic problems, or because his view of Italian historical development was simply too pessimistic to permit him to continue. What is certain, however, is that before Verga gave up on the rest of the cycle, he had created several of the most memorable and most enduring narratives in all of 19th-century European literature.

—Gregory L. Lucente

VERLAINE, Paul (-Marie). Born in Metz, France, 30 March 1844. Educated at Institution Landry, Paris; Lycée Bonaparte (now Condorcet), Paris, 1855-62, baccalauréat, 1862; École de Droit, Paris, 1862-63. Married Mathilde Mauté in 1870 (judicially separated, 1874; divorced, 1884); one son. Clerk for insurance company, 1864, 1872, and at the Hôtel de Ville, Paris, 1864-71; associated with Arthur Rimbaud in France, Brussels, and London, 1871-73: shot Rimbaud in Brussels and served term in Petits-Carmes prison, Brussels, and in Mons, 1873-75; teacher, Stickney, Lincolnshire, 1875-76, St. Aloysius' School, Bournemouth, 1876-77, Collège Notre-Dame, Rethel, France, 1877-79, and Solent School, Lymington, Hampshire, 1879; made two attempts at farming in northeastern France, then returned to Paris; served short prison term for threatening his mother, 1884; hospitalized for much of the time from 1886. *Died 8 January 1896.*

PUBLICATIONS

Collections

Oeuvres complètes, edited by H. de Bouillane de Lacoste and Jacques Borel. 2 vols., 1959-60.
Oeuvres poétiques complètes, Oeuvres en prose complètes, edited by Jacques Borel. 2 vols., 1962-72.

Verse

Poèmes saturniens. 1866.
Les Amies. 1868.
Fêtes galantes. 1869; as Gallant Parties, 1912.
La Bonne Chanson. 1870.
Romances sans paroles. 1874; edited by D. Hillery, 1976; as Romances Without Words, 1921.
Sagesse. 1880; revised edition, 1889; edited by C. Chadwick, 1973.
Jadis et naguère. 1884.
Amour. 1888.
Parallèlement. 1889.
Dédicaces. 1890; revised edition, 1894.
Femmes. 1890.
Bonheur. 1891.
Chansons pour elle. 1891; translated as Chansons pour elle, 1926.
Choix de poésies. 1891.
Liturgies intimes. 1892.
Élégies. 1893.
Odes en son honneur. 1893.
Dans les limbes. 1894.
Épigrammes. 1894.
Poems, translated by Gertrude Hall. 1895.
Invectives. 1896.
Chair. 1896.
Hombres. 1903 or 1904; edited by Huber Juin, 1977.
Biblio-sonnets. 1913.
Hashish and Incense, translated by François Pirou. 1925.
Selected Poems, translated by C.F. MacIntyre. 1948.
The Sky above the Roof: Fifty-six Poems, translated by Brian Hill. 1957.

Selected Poems, translated by Joanna Richardson. 1974.
Femmes/Hombres, edited and translated by William Packard and John D. Mitchell. 1977; also translated as Women, Men by Alistair Elliot, 1979.

Other

Les Poètes maudits. 1884; revised edition, 1888.
Mémoires d'un veuf. 1886.
Louise Leclercq (short stories and play, Madame Aubin). 1886.
Mes hôpitaux. 1891.
Mes prisons. 1893.
Confessions. 1895; as Confessions of a Poet, 1950.
Oeuvres posthumes. 1903.
Correspondance, edited by A. van Bever. 3 vols., 1922-29.
Oeuvres oubliées. 2 vols., 1926-29.
Lettres inédites à Cazals, edited by Georges Zayed. 1957.
Lettres inédites à Charles Morice, edited by Georges Zayed. 1964.
Lettres inédites à divers correspondants, edited by Georges Zayed. 1976.

Editor, Illuminations, by Rimbaud. 1886.
Editor, Poésies complètes, by Rimbaud. 1895.

*

Critical Studies: The Art of Paul Verlaine by Antoine Adam, 1963; Verlaine: A Study in Parallels by Alfred E. Carter, 1969; Verlaine by Joanna Richardson, 1971; Verlaine by C. Chadwick, 1973; Verlaine and the Decadence 1882-1890 by Phillip Stephan, 1974.

*   *   *

"Verlaine," wrote the French critic Jules Lemaître in 1889, "c'est un enfant, seulement cet enfant a une musique dans l'âme". Ten years later the English critic Arthur Symons made the same points when he talked of Verlaine's "simplicity of language which is the direct outcome of a simplicity of temperament" and contended that some of his poems "go as far as verse can go to become pure music." Verlaine himself, in his "Art poétique" of 1874, recognised that his genius did indeed lie in simplicity and musicality. "De la musique avant toute chose," he commanded in the poem's opening line and he went on to condemn eloquence and to plead instead for a certain casual quality that had been lacking in French poetry up to that time.

In point of fact it was only during the ten years from 1865 to 1875 that Verlaine's poetry achieved this simplicity and musicality. Before 1865, as a young poet barely twenty years old, he imitated the classical grandeur of the Parnassian poets who were then in vogue, preaching the virtue of industry rather than inspiration and claiming that poetry is analogous not to music but to sculpture in that it must be slowly and carefully shaped. It was he who formulated one of the best known statements of the Parnassian doctrine when, in the prologue to his first volume of verse, Poèmes saturniens, in 1866, he asked: "Est-elle en marbre ou non, la Vénus de Milo?" Not surprisingly the volume often practises what it preaches in, for example, a description of a portrait of Caesar Borgia and an account of the death of Philippe II, both of them in sonorous 12-syllable alexandrines richly rhymed. But in the same volume there are, in contrast, a number of poems such as "Soleils couchants," "Chanson d'automne," and "Le Rossignol" which have an intimate rather than an oratorical note, achieved through the use of short lines rather than alexandrines, and lines with an uneven number of syllables creating an unstable rhythm, plus extensive "enjambement" in which one line frequently runs into the next, thus further disturbing any fixed rhythmic pattern, and weak rather than rich rhymes so that the verse is not too far removed from everyday prose. These are poems of an intensely personal kind inspired by Verlaine's emotional problems and their hesitant, murmuring rhythms are matched by the blurred, ill-defined landscapes he uses to symbolise his vague feelings of unhappiness—setting suns, waning moons, falling leaves, weeping willows, misty horizons.

His second volume of poetry, *Fêtes galantes*, in 1869, may appear to mark a backward step in his development in so far as it is the transposition into poetry of paintings by Watteau and other 18th-century artists of life during the Regency. But behind the façade of costumed figures, "quasi tristes sous leurs déguisements fantasques" can be perceived the lonely, moody figure of the "poète saturnien" himself still searching for the "femme inconnue, et que j'aime, et qui m'aime," of whom he had written in his first volume. Not only does *Fêtes galantes* despite its 18th-century setting thus continue the note of personal sadness that had made its appearance in *Poèmes saturniens*, it also continues the trend noted in the earlier poems as regards imagery and versification. Verlaine is more than ever the poet of twilight and moonlight, of autumn leaves and fading flowers, and he is more than ever the poet of short lines with weak rhymes and a fluid rhythm.

His third volume of verse, *La Bonne Chanson*, does however, save for one or two poems, mark a backward step in the development of his poetry. His forthcoming marriage in August 1870 made life seem less gloomy and the future more stable. The vague melancholy and inexplicable sadness of the earlier volumes is therefore replaced by a joyful certainty, the blurred imagery by sunlit scenes, and changing, hesitant rhythms by firm and measured lines. But despite the solemn promises made in *La Bonne Chanson*, before the marriage was much more than a year old Verlaine found himself once more in that state of emotional uncertainty that seems to have been essential for the flowering of his poetic genius. The arrival in Paris in September 1871 of Arthur Rimbaud meant that Verlaine fell increasingly under his spell over the course of the next two years and in his fourth volume, *Romances sans paroles*, whose very title suggests that it is the music of the lines that matters more than their meaning, there is the same note of indecision, reflected in the same kind of twilit scenes and uncertain rhythms as in *Poèmes saturniens* and *Fêtes galantes*.

Perhaps predictably, Verlaine's relationship with Rimbaud lasted scarcely longer than his marriage had done and it ended in a violent quarrel in July 1873 as a consequence of which he was sentenced to two years imprisonment. The devastating effect of these two related events plunged him even deeper into gloom and despondency and in such poems as "Je ne sais pourquoi," "Un grand sommeil noir," "L'espoit luit," and "Le ciel est, par-dessus le toit," written in the last half of 1873 and later incorporated into *Sagesse*, the simple vocabulary, the uncomplicated syntax, the undeveloped images, the tenuous rhymes, and the intimate rhythms transcribe his distress with telling directness.

Verlaine had one final supreme emotional crisis in his life when, after his wife rejected his attempt at reconciliation, he turned instead towards God for comfort and consolation. The initial ardour of his conversion in 1874 inspired some of his finest poems, such as "Mon Dieu m'a dit: Mon fils, il faut m'aimer," "Bon chevalier masqué qui chevauche en silence," and "Les faux beaux jours ont lui tout le jour." But all too soon, as in *La Bonne Chanson*, his new found optimism and stability led him to lapse into wordy platitudes and to adopt the more composed kind of style that makes so many of the poems of *Sagesse* as disappointing as the vast majority of those in *La Bonne Chanson*.

The remainder of Verlaine's considerable output, after this crucial decade from 1865 to 1875, is equally disappointing. Lacking any further emotional impulse to write but driven to do so by the necessity to earn a living, he simply used up old poems that he had not thought worthy of publication at an earlier stage and then lapsed permanently into a verbose, descriptive, platitudinous style that renders fifteen of his twenty volumes of verse virtually unreadable. But, despite this long, sad decline over the last twenty years of his life, Verlaine remains for posterity the poet who, in his first five volumes of poetry, displayed in a number of memorable poems his unique gift for subtly conveying the infinite sadness of things.

—C. Chadwick

VICENTE, Gil. Born c. 1465. Married 1) Branca Bezerra (died, 1512-14); 2) Melicia Rodrigues, c. 1517; had children by both wives. Dramatist and actor at Portuguese court, 1502-36: wrote plays in both Spanish and Portuguese. *Died c. 1536.*

PUBLICATIONS

Collections

    Copilaçam de todalas obras. 1562.
    Lyrics, edited and translated by Aubrey F.G. Bell. 1914.
    Obras completas, edited by Marques Braga. 6 vols., 1942-44.
    Obras completas, edited by Júlio da Costa Pimpão. 1956; revised edition, 1962, 1979.
    Obras dramáticas castellanas, edited by Thomas R. Hart. 1962.
    Obras completas, edited by Reis Brasil. 1966— .

Plays (Selection; plays translated English or recently edited)

    Auto da Alma, edited and translated, as *The Soul's Journey*, by Aubrey F.G. Bell, in *Four Plays.* 1920; edited by Reis Brasil, 1956, and Manuel dos Santos Alves, 1964.
    Os autos das barcas, edited by Luiz Francisco Rebello. 1975; as *The Ship of Hell*, 1929.
    Auto da Barca do Inferno, edited by I.S. Révah. 1951.
    Auto da Barca do Purgatório, edited by Maria da Conceição Gonçalves. 1970.
    Auto da Barca da Gloria, edited by Paulo Quintela. 1956.
    Auto da Cananeia, edited by Agostinho de Campos. 1938.
    Auto da Índia, edited by Thomas R. Hart, in *Farces and Festival Plays.* 1972; as *The Sailor's Wife*, in *Early Spanish Plays*, edited by Robert O'Brien, 1964.
    Auto da Lusitânia, edited by Segismundo Spina, in *Obras-primas do teatro vicentino.* 1970.
    Auto da sibila Cassandra, as *Cassandra the Sibyl*, in *Early Spanish Plays*, edited by Robert O'Brien, 1964.
    Auto das ciganas, edited by Thomas R. Hart, in *Obras dramáticas castellanas.* 1962.
    Auto de Deus Padre e justiça e misericórdia (attributed to Vicente), edited by I.S. Révah, in *Deux "autos" méconnus.* 1948.
    Auto de Mofina Mendes, edited by Segismundo Spina, in *Obras-primas do teatro vicentino.* 1970.
    Auto dos reis magos, edited by Sebastião Pestana. 1979; as *Three Wise Men*, in *Early Spanish Plays*, edited by Robert O'Brien, 1964.
    Auto pastoril castelhano, edited by Sebastião Pestana. 1978.
    Breve sumário da história de Deus, edited by João de Almeida Lucas. 1943.
    Comédia de Rubena, edited by Giuseppe Tavani. 1965.
    Comédia do viúvo, edited by Alonso Zamora Vicente. 1962; as *The Widower's Comedy*, in *Early Spanish Plays*, edited by Robert O'Brien, 1964.
    Comédia sobre a divisa da cidade de Coimbra, edited by Daniel Rangel-Guerrero. 1980.
    Côrtes de Júpiter, edited by Thomas R. Hart, in *Farces and Festival Plays.* 1972.
    Exortação da guerra, edited and translated as *Exhortation to War*, by Aubrey F.G. Bell, in *Four Plays.* 1920.
    Farsa dos almocreves, edited and translated as *The Carriers*, by Aubrey F.G. Bell, in *Four Plays.* 1920; edited by Segismundo Spina, in *Obras-primas do teatro vicentino*, 1970.
    Farsa dos físicos, edited by Alberto da Rocha Brito. 1946.
    Farsa de Inês Pereira, edited by Albano Monteiro Soares. 1975.
    Floresta de enganos, edited by C.C. Stathatos. 1972.

Frágua de Amor, edited by Thomas R. Hart, in *Farces and Festival Plays*. 1972.
O Juiz da Beira, edited by Maria de Lourdes Saraiva, in *Sátiras sociais*. 1975.
Obra da geração, (attributed to Vicente), edited by I.S. Révah, in *Deux "autos méconnus."* 1948.
Quem tem farelos?, edited by Ernesto de Campos de Andrada. 1938; as *The Serenade*, in *Early Spanish Plays*, edited by Robert O'Brien, 1964.
Romagem de agravados, edited by Paul Teyssier. 1975.
Tragicomédia de Amadis de Gaula, edited by T.P. Waldron. 1959.
Tragicomédia de Dom Duardos, edited by Thomas R. Hart, in *Obras dramáticas castellanas*. 1962; translated as *Don Duardos*, 1976.
Tragicomédia pastoril da Serra da Estrêla, edited and translated, as *Pastoral Tragicomedy of the Serra da Estrella*, by Aubrey F.G. Bell, in *Four Plays*. 1920; edited by Júlio da Costa Pimpão, 1963.
O triunfo do inverno, edited by Thomas R. Hart, in *Farces and Festival Plays*. 1972.
O velho da horta, edited by João de Almeida Lucas. 1943.

Verse

Pranto de Maria Parda, edited by Sebastião Pestana. 1975.

*

Bibliography: *Bibliografia vicentina* by Luísa Maria de Castro e Azevedo, 1942; *A Gil Vicente Bibliography (1940-1975)* by C.C. Stathatos, 1980, supplement, 1982.

Critical Studies: *Gil Vicente* by Aubrey F.G. Bell, 1921; *The Court Theatre of Gil Vicente* by Laurence Keates, 1962; *Gil Vicente* by Jack Horace Parker, 1967; *The Farces of Gil Vicente: A Study in the Stylistics of Satire* by Hope Hamilton-Faria, 1976; *Gil Vicente: Cassandra and Don Duardos* by Thomas R. Hart, 1981.

*   *   *

From 1502 to 1536, Gil Vicente served as purveyor of entertainment for the Portuguese royal court under two successive sovereigns, Manuel I and John III. In that capacity, he composed plays expressly designed to celebrate specific occasions in the life of the Court. Writing to order does not seem to have stifled his creative genius, especially since his patrons encouraged artistic endeavors.

His dramatic production, as we know it today, consists of 44 plays, 15 of which are entirely in his native Portuguese, 11 in Spanish, and the remaining 18 in both languages. His Spanish has its own idiosyncrasies and is typical of one who had never been in Spain. His mastery of it was not such that would allow him to delineate some of the delightful types which appear in his Portuguese plays. With few exceptions, Vicente's plays were compiled and published for the first time posthumously in 1562. Unfortunately, the text of this edition is corrupt, a fact which has been attributed primarily to the incompetence of his son and editor Luís.

In his work Vicente blended the most diverse and unpredictable ingredients, so that a good portion of it defies categorization under a single genre. Of the several attempts to classify his plays in terms of content, the most widely accepted is that of T.P. Waldron, who, in his edition of *Amadís de Gaula* (1959), has devised the following categories: (1) early plays in the rustic style of Juan del Encina's *églogas*, (2) moralities, (3) farces, (4) allegorical fantasies, (5) romantic comedies.

A distinctive feature of Vicente's career as a dramatist is that he tends to be cyclic: he takes up a certain theme and then abandons it, only to come back to it later on. The motif of the lecherous old man, for instance, which first appeared in the *Velho da horta* (Old Man of the Orchard), reappears in the *Comédia de Rubena* (Play of Rubena) and, once again, in his last play, *Floresta de enganos* (Forest of Deceits). Since he keeps experimenting with new possibilities, there is no clear pattern of development in his work.

Several of Vicente's plays are characterized by a lack of dramatic unity, as we understand it today. The fact, however, that his pieces were composed on command to form integral parts of court festivals may account for their structure. In all likelihood, theatricality was the playwright's main concern. A play like *The Serenade* may not be dramatically significant but it is eminently theatrical.

Vicente's work is permeated by a profound lyricism, which has exerted a considerable influence on even 20th-century poets (e.g., Federico García Lorca and Rafael Alberti) and reaches a climax in *Don Duardos*, one of the finest poetic dramas in Hispanic literature. Apart from this overall lyricism, all his plays are veritable mines of songs, whether his own compositions or borrowed from popular tradition. As a rule, they are well integrated into the dramatic action, as is the case with the *Play of the Sibyl Cassandra* which abounds in delightful songs (the most frequently translated and anthologized).

In general, Vicente's plays are plays of character rather than intrigue. In this respect, they are more akin to those of Molière than those of the Spanish Golden Age. Although types (the peasant, the negro, the Jew, the gypsy, the fool, the braggart, the corrupt judge, the impoverished squire, the maid, etc.), some of his characters are so well drawn that they become three-dimensional. This is particularly true of female characters in farces as well as serious plays: Constança and Inês, the unfaithful wives of the *Sailor's Wife* and *Inês Pereira*, respectively, the presumptuous Cassandra, of the *Play of the Sibyl Cassandra*, who expects to become the mother of God. Even though the plays are crowded with figures from literary tradition, the Bible, and the classical pantheon and mythology, it is Vicente's contemporary Portuguese society which supplied most of his characters.

As a believer in a well-structured society, he was disturbed by the rampant social abuse and the decline of mores and reacted forcefully against them, not only in his farces and comedies but also in his allegorical plays. The principal butts of his satire were the two major parasitic classes, the nobility and the clergy. Noblemen, judges, and clerics are ridiculed in the trilogy of the *Ship of Hell*, the *Frágua de amor* (Forge of Love), and the *Floresta de enganos* (Forest of Deceits). No member of the clerical hierarchy was immune to his caustic wit, although it was the friar who was ridiculed most vehemently for his improper conduct and his absurd aspirations, like Frei Narciso in the *Romagem de agravados* (Pilgrimage of the Aggrieved).

Considering that he had no access to an established literary dramatic tradition on which to rely, Vicente succeeded admirably in shaping Portuguese theater and in creating a poetic cosmos that delighted his audience and can still delight his reader. The prominent place he occupies in Peninsular literature is well deserved, as is the critical attention accorded him.

—C.C. Stathatos

VIGNY, Alfred de. Born in Loches, France, 27 March 1797. Educated at Pension Hix, 1807-11; Lycée Condorcet, Paris, 1811-14. Sub-Lieutenant, 1st Regiment of Gendarmes du Roi, 1814-15; in Garde Royale, 1815; Captain in an infantry regiment, 1816-27 (frequently on leave after 1822). Married Lydia Bunbury in 1825 (died, 1862). Member, French Academy, 1845. *Died 16 September 1863.*

PUBLICATIONS

Collections

Oeuvres complètes, edited by F. Baldensperger. 7 vols., 1914-35.
Oeuvres complètes, edited by F. Baldensperger. 2 vols., 1948.

Verse

Poèmes. 1822.
Eloa; ou, La Soeur des anges. 1824.
Poèmes antiques et modernes. 1826; augmented edition, 1829; revised edition, 1837; edited by E. Estève, 1931.
Les Destinées, edited by Louis Ratisbonne. 1864; edited by V.L. Saulnier, 1947, and Paul Viallaneix, 1983.

Plays

Le More de Venise, from *Othello* by Shakespeare (produced 1829). 1839 (with *Le Marchand de Venise*).
La Maréchale d'Ancre (produced 1831).
Quitte pour la peur (produced 1833).
Chatterton (produced 1835). 1835; edited by L. Petroni, 1962, and A.H. Diverres, 1967; translated as *Chatterton*, 1847.
Le Marchand de Venise, from *The Merchant of Venice* by Shakespeare. 1839 (with *Le More de Venise*); revised version, as *Shylock* (produced 1905), in *Oeuvres complètes*, 1914-35.

Fiction

Cinq-Mars. 1825; translated as *Cinq-Mars*, 1847; as *The Conspirators*, 1877; as *The Spider and the Fly*, 1925.
Stello; ou, Les Diables bleus. 1832.
Servitude et grandeur militaires (short stories). 1835; as *Military Servitude and Grandeur*, 1919; as *The Military Necessity*, 1953.
Daphné. 1912.

Other

Journal d'un poète, edited by Louis Ratisbonne. 1867.
Mémoires inédites, fragments, et projets, edited by Jean Sangnier. 1958.

*

Critical Studies: *La Pensée rel'gieuse et morale de Vigny* by G. Bonnefoy, 1946; *L'Imagination de Vigny* by F. Germain, 1961; *Vigny* by James Doolittle, 1967; *Les Destinées d'un style* by J.P. Saint-Gérand, 1979.

*   *   *

Alfred de Vigny was the most philosophically minded and the most pessimistic of the French romantic poets, and the one whose works have perhaps remained the most readable in the 20th century. Indeed, his vision of humanity as condemned to inexplicable physical suffering in an absurd and godless world has strong similarities with the world view of Albert Camus, and his poem "Le Mont des Oliviers" (The Agony in the Garden) could well be read as a commentary on certain chapters of Camus's *La Peste* (*The Plague*). His view that the poet, like all men of genius, can never be understood or appreciated by ordinary people nevertheless strikes a more dated note, though it may have contributed to Vigny's early recognition of Charles Baudelaire as the greatest and most original of all French lyric poets. Some of Vigny's own poems, especially "La Maison du Berger" (The Shepherd's Hut), have a Baudelairean touch to their poetic rhythm, though the extent of Vigny's achievement and appeal in a different direction can be judged from the fact that he was the first non-classical French author to be included on the syllabus at Eton. The high strain of stoic morality which informs the closing stanza of "La Mort du Loup" (The Death of the Wolf) is certainly assimilable within the tradition that gave rise to Henry Newbolt's "Vitae Lampada" ("Play-up, Play-up, and Play the Game"), and Vigny was very fond of England. He was married to an English woman, Lydia Bunbury, who was unfortunately unable to have children to carry on the family name, and who became a life-long invalid. Vigny, true to his principles and to the genuine affection he felt for her, cared for her devotedly, though he found consolation with the actress Marie Dorval. He was disappointed when she left him for, *inter alia*, George Sand, and wrote a very bad poem called "La Colère de Samson" (The Anger of Samson). Marie Dorval had, however, added considerably to Vigny's reputation as a dramatist by sliding to her death down a banister in the appalling drama *Chatterton*. Vigny shared the desire of other Romantics such as Victor Hugo to revolutionize the French theatre, often by following what they thought of as the example of Shakespeare.

Vigny's best work of fiction, *Servitude et grandeur militaires*, presents the soldier as the model of stoic self-denial in modern society, and has considerable value as an account of certain aspects of French society in the early 19th century. His historical novel, *Cinq-Mars*, is an indictment of Richelieu's policy of domesticating the hereditary nobility to make way for the absolutism of Louis XIV, and Vigny's sense of personal isolation was heightened by his awareness that the aristocracy to which he was so conscious of belonging had no further role to play in contemporary society. His pessimism was thus social as well as religious and metaphysical, and he also differed from the majority of the romantic poets, in France as well as in England, in totally rejecting the "Pathetic Fallacy" and seeing Nature as not so much hostile as indifferent to man. The reactionary nature of his political views revealed itself towards the end of his life when he showed himself ready to collaborate with the government of Napoleon III in providing information on anyone in his area holding political views unpopular with the government.

—Philip Thody

VILLON, François. Born François de Montcorbier in Paris c. 1430; adopted when very young by Guillaume de Villon. Educated at the University of Paris, baccalauréate 1449, M.A. 1452. Fled Paris after killing a priest in a brawl; pardoned six months later, but then involved in a theft and again left Paris; led a wandering life in the provinces and was imprisoned at Meung-sur-Loire, 1461; probably returned to Paris, but condemned to death for involvement in a street brawl, 1462: sentence commuted to 10-year banishment, after which the record ends. Villon's works—about 3000 lines—were first published in 1489.

PUBLICATIONS

Verse

Complete Poems, edited by John Fox, translated by Beram Saklatvala.   1968.
The Legacy and Other Poems, translated by Peter Dale.   1971; revised edition, as *The Legacy, The Testament, and Other Poems,* 1973; as *Selected Poems,* 1978.
La Testament Villon, edited by Jean Rychner and Albert Henry.   2 vols., 1974.
The Poems, translated by Galway Kinnell.   1977.
Les Lais Villon et les poèmes variés, edited by Jean Rychner and Albert Henry.   2 vols., 1977.

*

Critical Studies: *Villon: A Documented Survey* by D.B. Wyndham Lewis, 1928; *Lexique de la langue de Villon* by A. Burger, 1957; *The Poetry of Villon* by John Fox, 1962; *Recherches sur le Testament de Villon* by Jean Dufournet, 2 vols., 1971-73; *Villon: Un Testament ambigu* by Pierre Demarolle, 1973; *The Otherness Within: Gnostic Readings in Marcel Proust, Flannery O'Connor, and Villon* by Jefferson Humphries, 1983.

*   *   *

Swinburne called Villon the last medieval and first modern poet but, although there is a kernel of truth in this, he was in fact neither. François Villon was very much a man of his time and, for that matter, place. His works were so firmly rooted in the France—the Paris even—of the 1450's and 1460's that much of their meaning had become obscure by the time they were first printed in 1489.

For Villon's work is topical in the extreme, and he wrote not for posterity but for a small audience who might not only understand but also be prompted into helping him. He is not above a certain obsequiousness (notably towards the King of France, Louis XI), and most of the targets of his jibes had skeletons in their cupboards which the present-day reader can only guess at but which were probably more or less open secrets. His major work, the *Testament,* is probably an anthology collected and revised some time between his release from prison in October 1461 and the following summer. Its function was to amuse, dazzle, flatter, and move, and also to signal his continued existence and myriad talents to an audience of friends and potential patrons. A false impression can be gained of his work as a whole by wrenching the more accessible parts of the *Testament* from their context. Nevertheless it is these anthology pieces which have earned him his reputation and inspired dozens of imitators and translators (from Rossetti to Lowell). The deservedly famous "Ballade des dames du temps jadis" is a disquisition on time and its treachery to women, the harshness of the sentiments wonderfully softened by the haunting refrain which likens the passing of beauty to the melting of last year's snows. What is sometimes overlooked, though, is that it is part of a verse triptych describing the inevitability of death and the vanity of human wishes. He fatalistically remarks that this world is but illusion and points out—not without a hint of grim satisfaction perhaps—that even princes are ruled by death.

Critical opinion has learned not to take the author at face value and it is now widely agreed that poems such as the prayer on his mother's behalf to the Virgin are less altruistic than they might at first appear. This ballade's refrain, "In this faith I wish to live and die," should not necessarily be taken as proof of Villon's repentance or religious sincerity. By the same token, the ballade to "Fat Margot" does not represent so much a slice of the poet's life as a very successful literary exercise in the tradition of the *sotte chanson,* in which the traditions of courtly poetry were deliberately turned on their head.

Not all Villon's compositions could be fitted into the framework of the *Testament.* Among them are two of his finest poems: in the "Debat" or dialogue with his heart he publicly examines his conscience and (predictably?) regrets the errors of his ways, and in the magnificent ballade about the hanged criminals among whom he seems to count himself by implication he graphically describes the rotting corpses on the Paris gibbet and makes a plea for absolution.

Villon has become known almost as much for his life—about which we know little, despite the fantasizings of later poets and critics—as for his work, but as a writer he has become the archetypal outsider, the spokesman for the misfit and the failure, the poet of lost love and lost youth, bemoaning the power of Fortune over men's lives and our impotence in the face of Time. His frequent obscenities and scurrilous jokes are a useful antidote to over-seriousness, and the cup of strong red wine which he downs at the end of his fictitious *Testament* is both an act of poetic bravado and a form of courage.

—Michael Freeman

VIRGIL (Publius Vergilius Maro).   Born in Andes, near Mantua, 15 October 70 B.C.   Educated at Cremona, Milan, Rome, and Naples. Associated with C. Asinius Pollio, then with the patron Maecenas; took no part in public life, though he had the friendship of many important men. *Died 20 September 19 B.C.*

PUBLICATIONS

Collections

[*Works*], edited by R.A.B. Mynors.   1969; also edited by R.D. WIlliams, 3 vols., 1972-79,   and M. Geymonat, 1973; translated by C. Day Lewis, 3 vols., 1940-63.

Verse

Aeneis, edited by J.W. Mackail.   1930; as *The Aeneid*, translated by Rolfe Humphries, 1951, Michael Oakley, 1957, Patric Dickinson, 1961, T.H. Delabere May, 1961, L.R. Lind, 1963, Frank Copley, 1965, Kevin Guinagh, 1970, Allen Mandelbaum, 1971, and Robert Fitzgerald, 1983.
Eclogae [Eclogues or Bucolics or Pastorals], edited by Robert Coleman.   1977; translated by E.V. Rieu (prose), 1949, Geoffrey Johnson, 1960, W. Berg, in *Early Virgil*, 1974, A.J. Boyle, 1976, Paul Joel Alpers, in *The Singer of the Eclogues*, 1979, and Guy Lee, 1980.
Georgica [Georgics], edited by W. Richter.   1957; translated by S.P. Bovie, 1956, Nigel Lambourne, 1969, Robert Wells, 1982, and L.P. Wilkinson, 1982.

*

Critical Studies: *The Art of Virgil* by Viktor Poschl, 1962; *Virgil: A Study in Civilized Poetry* by Brooks Otis, 1963; *The Poetry of the Aeneid*, 1965, *Virgil's Pastoral Art*, 1970, and *Virgil's Poem of the Earth*, 1979, all by Michael C.J. Putnam; *Roman Vergil* by W.F. Jackson Knight, 2nd edition, 1966; *Virgil: A Collection of Critical Essays* edited by Steele Commager, 1966; *Virgil's Aeneid* by Kenneth Quinn, 1968; *Virgil* edited by D.R. Dudley, 1969; *The Georgics of Virgil* L.P. Wilkinson, 1969; *The Art of the Aeneid* by William S. Anderson, 1969; *The*

Speeches in Vergil's Aeneid by Gilbert A. Highet, 1972; *Darkness Visible: A Study of Virgil's Aeneid* by W.R. Johnson, 1976; *The Design of Virgil's Bucolics* by John Van Sickle, 1978; *The Singer of the Eclogues: A Study of Virgilian Pastoral* by Paul Joel Alpers, 1979; *Virgil's Georgics* by Gary B. Miles, 1980; *Poetry and Myth in Ancient Pastoral: Essays on Theocritus and Virgil* by Charles Segal, 1981; *Technique and Ideas in the Aeneid* by Gordon Williams, 1983.

*   *   *

The reputation of Virgil's poetry and the meaning ascribed to it have varied greatly through the ages. He was highly respected during his own lifetime. His *Aeneid*, published posthumously and contrary to his dying wishes, quickly established itself as the Romans' national epic. Later generations of school teachers praised his rhetorical accomplishment. During the middle ages, a change in the spelling of his name from *Vergilius* to *Virgilius* reflected his role for some as master of the occult with his magic wand (*virga*); for others that same change underlined his role as the pagan of virginal purity who foresaw the birth of Christ. Dante cast Virgil as his guide in the *Inferno*; Milton chose his *Aeneid* as the model for *Paradise Lost*; Addison honored his *Georgics* as "the best poem by the best poet." But with the 19th century Virgil's reputation suffered a decline. His poetry was thought to lack the spontaneity that was rather naively attributed to his Greek models: Theocritus for the *Eclogues*, Hesiod for the *Georgics*, and Homer for the *Aeneid*. His great epic was regarded as a rather mannered celebration of the Augustan Principate and Roman imperialism.

Modern interest in Virgil, particularly since the 1950's, may be seen partly as a reaction against 19th-century assessments of his works. Stylistic and thematic studies have sought to establish the full measure to which Virgil transformed the raw material of his Greek sources in accordance with a vision distinctively Roman and distinctively his own. In particular, his relation to the Augustan regime has come into question. Early debates about whether Virgil was pro- or anti-Augustan have generally given way to more nuanced attempts to discover the depth of Virgil's ambivalence and the subtlety of his judgments both about the course of Roman politics in his own age and about the human condition itself.

Not surprisingly for one who began writing in the midst of civil war and died before the Augustan Principate could be felt to have attained stability, the problems of achieving order and of coping with disorder are close to the surface of all Virgil's works and thematically at their core. Throughout his life Virgil explored those problems on two levels, the political and the psychological. In his earliest works those two themes are developed as complementary parallels. The first eclogue introduces shepherds who represent the innumerable Italians caught up by forces vastly beyond their power to control or even adequately to comprehend during the Roman civil wars. Against that harsh reality Virgil contrasts the modest satisfactions of a way of life in jeopardy and the longed-for escape of a Golden age. He also shows the disturbing power of human passion, whether in the self-dramatizing laments of a young love-sick shepherd, in the madness of an unrequited lover, even in the melancholy of one of his own fellow-poets whose longing for an absent lover finds no solace in the countryside and its divinities.

The *Georgics*, leaving behind interest in an ideal of pastoral ease, turns instead to the national myth of the Roman Republic, an ideal of rustic life as the austere school of Roman excellence. The poem juxtaposes the fruitful orderliness of this and other idealized versions of rustic life with contrasting scenes of urban decadence and civil war. Such disorders are now viewed as analogous to disorder inherent in nature itself: Virgil introduces the civil wars as a kind of storm accompanied by heavenly signs, just as other storms; description of the wars parallels description of a plague against which all efforts are helpless. Human passion is presented as actually part of an elemental vitality that operates in all creatures. Comparing humans and animals, Virgil observes that "love is the same for all." In animals it is the necessary basis for procreation, but also a dangerous force that leads to violence; in the moving story of Orpheus and Eurydice that dominates the poem's conclusion it is the force that inspires

Orpheus to brave Hades and win permission for his wife's return to the living, but it is also the force that compels him to look back at her as they approach the upper world and so to violate the one condition on which her return depended.

In the *Aeneid* Virgil contrasts the high promise of Augustus's new Golden Age, which is presented as the final goal of Roman civilization, with the terrible suffering and sense of personal loss that must be experienced in the pursuit of that goal. Here for the first time, he shows a close interrelation between the two types of disorder that were complementary themes in his previous works: political disorder emanates from the passions of individuals. The desperate rage of Dido, queen of Carthage, when she is abandoned by Aeneas, and her curse against his descendants through eternity prepare for the fierce and protracted rivalry between Carthage and Rome; the resentment of the Latin hero, Turnus, when Aeneas usurps both his bride and his political position, gives rise to bitter warfare that implicates all of Italy—warfare that anticipates later wars between Rome and her Italian allies and the civil wars of Virgil's own age.

True to the underlying vision of man and nature developed in the *Georgics*, Virgil continues to present violent disorder as inherent in the very order of nature itself. The *Aeneid* begins with the wrath of the goddess Juno, jealous and quick to anger, who sets herself against the Trojans; Dido compromises her personal and her political integrity under the influence of a love that has been arranged through the intrigues of Juno and Venus; Turnus is attacked by Juno's agents, who enter secretly into his breast and drive him mad; the poem ends with Juno and Jupiter reaching an accomodation: no people will honor Juno more than the Romans. The actors of the *Aeneid* are at the mercy of overpowering forces—the gods, Roman destiny, their own passions—whose influence on themselves they perceive only occasionally and then only fleetingly and imperfectly, and whose meaning is never certain and clear: when the destiny of Rome is laid out before Aeneas by his father in the Underworld and again on a shield made for him by Vulcan, the hero responds with awe but without full understanding.

Of the many qualities that have impressed Virgil's readers, the richness of his language, the vividness of his narrative, the magnitude of the events he describes, two perhaps deserve special attention. The first is the range of his human sympathies. Without losing sight of values to which we should aspire and by which we must be measured, Virgil nonetheless refrains from making simple judgments. In his vision we are all subject to the same forces of nature; none of us is capable of resisting their influence. In the *Eclogues* and *Georgics* he acknowledges explicitly his own susceptibility to *amor*. In the *Aeneid* Dido and Turnus, the unwitting agents of opposition to Roman destiny, are as much the victims of the divine powers arrayed against Aeneas and his followers as are those heroes of Roman destiny themselves. In the final books of the *Aeneid*, Turnus achieves a kind of nobility, despite his madness, while Aeneas becomes increasingly a victim of his passions until he, too, acts not from a sense of misssion, but "inflamed with rage."

Related to this complexity of viewpoint is a second distinguishing characteristic, Virgil's restraint. He interprets events from the perspective of the shepherd or the farmer or, in the *Aeneid*, of a hero who is by disposition modest in his aspirations, moderate in his behavior. It is in the intimate, often mundane details of private existence that Virgil locates the ultimate measure of significance and value. And it is in terms of those details that he is able to acknowledge both the powerlessness of humankind to resist the pervasive forces of disorder in nature, in society, and in the individual, and simultaneously the awesome capacity to persist in the face of uncertainty, repeatedly to start anew in the face of disaster. Virgil conveys both respect for the cost that such continual effort requires and also a conviction that the effort is necessary.

—Gary B. Miles

VITTORINI, Elio. Born in Syracuse, Sicily, 23 July 1908. Worked in a road-building gang, Gorizia, 1925; proofreader and journalist, Florence, 1929-35; translator and editor for Bompiani, Einaudi, and Mondadori publishers, Milan, from 1936; imprisoned by the Fascists, 1943; founded the periodicals *Il politecnico*, 1945-47, and *Il menabò*, 1959-67; Founding Editor of the "I gettoni" series, 1951, and the "Nuovo politecnico" series, 1965, both for Einaudi, and of the "Nuovi scritteri stranieri" series, 1964, for Mondadori. Recipient: Salento Prize, 1956. *Died 12/13 February 1966.*

Publications

Collections

Le opere narrative, edited by Maria Certi. 2 vols., 1974.

Fiction

Piccola Borghesia. 1931.
Nei Morlacchi—Viaggio in Sardegna. 1936; as *Sardegna come un'infanzia*, 1952.
Conversazione in Sicilia. 1941; edited by Giovanni Falaschi, 1975; as *In Sicily*, 1949; as *Conversation in Sicily*, 1949.
Nome e lagrime. 1941.
Uomini e no. 1945; edited by Edoardo Esposito, 1977.
Il garofano rosso. 1948; as *The Red Carnation*, 1952.
Il sempione strizza l'occhio al Fréjus. 1949; as *The Twilight of the Elephant*, 1951; as *June for an Elephant*, 1955.
Le donne di Messina. 1949; revised edition, 1964; as *Women of Messina*, 1973.
Erica e i suoi fratelli; La garibaldina. 1956; as *The Dark and the Light: Erica and La Garibaldina*, 1961.
Women on the Road: Three Short Novels. 1961.
Le città del mondo. 1969.
Nome e lagrime e altri racconti, edited by Raffaella Rodondi. 1972.
The Twilight of the Elephant and Other Novels. 1974.

Play

Le città del mondo: Una sceneggiatura (screenplay). 1975.

Other

La tragica vicenda di Carlo III, with Giansiro Ferrata. 1939; as *Sangue a Parma*, 1967.
Guttuso. 1942.
Diario in pubblico 1929-1956. 1957; revised edition, 1970.
Storia di Renato Guttuso e nota congiunta sulla pittura contemporanea. 1960.
Le due tensioni: Appunti per una ideologia della letterature, edited by Dante Isella. 1967.
Vittorini: Progettazione e letteratura, edited by Italo Calvino. 1968.

Editor, with Enrico Falqui, *Scrittori nuovi.* 1930.
Editor, *Teatro spagnolo.* 1941.
Editor, *Americana.* 1942.
Editor, *Orlando Furioso*, by Ariosto. 1950.

Editor, *Commedie*, by Goldoni. 1952.

Translator, *Il purosangue*, by D.H. Lawrence. 1933.
Translator, *La vergine e lo zingaro*, by D.H. Lawrence. 1935.
Translator, *Il serpente piumato*, by D.H. Lawrence. 1935.
Translator, with Delfino Cinelli, *Racconti e arabeschi*, by Poe. 1936.
Translator, with Delfino Cinelli, *Gordon Pym e altre storie*, by Poe. 1937.
Translator, *Luce d'agosto*, by Faulkner. 1939.
Translator, *Il mietitore di Dodder*, by T.F. Powys. 1939.
Translator, *Pian della Tortilla*, by John Steinbeck. 1939.
Translator, *Che ve se sembra dell'America?*, by William Saroyan. 1940.
Translator, *La peste di Londra*, by Defoe. 1940.
Translator, *I pascoli del cielo*, by John Steinbeck. 1940.
Translator, *Piccolo campo*, by Erskine Caldwell. 1940.
Translator, *Il cammino nella polvere*, by John Fante. 1941.
Translator, *Nozze di sangue*, by García Lorca, in *Teatro spagnolo*. 1942.
Translator, *Pagine di viaggio*, by D.H. Lawrence. 1942.
Translator, *Tito Andronico*, by Shakespeare, in *Teatro*. 1943.
Translator, *Il potere e la gloria*, by Graham Greene. 1945.

*

Critical Studies: *Three Italian Novelists: Moravia, Pavese, Vittorini* by Donald W. Heiney, 1968; *Vittorini* (in Italian) by Sandro Briosi, 1970; *Vittorini* (in Italian) by Folco Zanobini, 1974; *Guida a Vittorini* by Sergio Pautasso, 1977.

*   *   *

Elio Vittorini's origins were humble. His father was a Sicilian station master. He ran away to the north, and in Milan and Florence turned himself into a powerful intellectual who for the rest of his life was ready to take his stand in the area where literature and politics overlap. The stories of *Piccola borghesia* (Petty Bourgeoisie) turn a sharp eye on the middle classes under fascism. *Viaggio in Sardegna* combines the factual with childhood memories and was written in the spirit of the Florentine magazine *Solaria*, for which he worked as a proofreader. It was in this capacity that he "discovered" Pavese's early poetry. In 1933-34 *Solaria* published the first eight instalments of *The Red Carnation* which portrays the attitudes of adolescents to fascism in the early 1930's. Censorship intervened and the book did not appear in full until 1948 when a very important preface described how in both *The Red Carnation* and *Conversation in Sicily* Vittorini had invented a new style that would incorporate into "poetry" (in the sense of creative writing) the essay material that had accrued to the genre of the novel during the last century.

Having learned English by reading *Robinson Crusoe*, Vittorini had gone on to translate Poe, Faulkner, Steinbeck, and Saroyan. He read Hemingway, and became friendly with him. From Saroyan and Hemingway he picked up and perfected a style based on rhythm and repetition which went a long way to achieving his ambitions for the novel. *Conversation in Sicily*, first published in *Letteratura* (the successor to *Solaria*) in 1938-39, is his most famous work. It describes a journey back to his childhood roots by an autobiographical, near-Dantesque, figure who is trying to make positive sense of his past and his present. The reality of today is superimposed on the past in symbolical and even allegorical terms. For instance much importance is given to food: the bitter oranges of returning fruit pickers, his mother's herring, and the childhood memories of melons—a basic reality and yet symbolic of poverty, oppression, and resilience. The language used to recreate this experience is lyrical but sometimes unorthodox, and yet through the rhythmic repetition of certain key phrases such as "reale due volte" (twice real) and "l'in più d'ora" (the extra now) the theme is raised to the level of the universal. Speaking of poetry in his post-war magazine *Il politecnico* in 1945, Vittorini said, "Poetry is poetry because it does not stay bound to its origins and if it is born of sorrow it can be linked to all sorrow."

Il politecnico was his contribution to the polemics of the culture of the left after the war. The final struggle of the Milan Resistance is depicted in *Uomini e no*; the social problems of the immediate post-war period are the subject of *June for an Elephant* with the apotheosis of the Vittorinian worker-grandfather figure as the elephant preparing himself for death. *Erica* (written in 1936) deals with women's suffering when the heroine is forced into prostitution in order to buy food. *Women of Messina, La garibaldina,* and *Le città del mondo* (which was never finished) all return to Sicily with some hope of renewal despite inertia. During the 1950's and 1960's Vittorini presided over the later period of neo-realism, discovering Sciascia, Cassola, and Fenoglio, while rejecting Lampedusa's *The Leopard* as too old-fashioned. The journal *Il Menabò* (on which Calvino also worked) was meant to tackle the new problems of industrialisation.

Vittorini's greatest contributions are his raising of the consciousness of his readers and his work as cultural impresario for Italian letters during the mid-20th century.

—Judy Rawson

VOLTAIRE. Pseudonym for François-Marie Arouet. Born in Paris, 21 November 1694. Educated at Collège Louis-le-Grand, Paris, 1704-11; studied law, 1711-13. Articled by his father to a lawyer, 1714; exiled from Paris for 5 months, 1716, and imprisoned in Bastille, 1717-18, for satiric writings; quarrel with a nobleman led to another term in the Bastille and exile in England, 1726-28; retired to Château de Cirey with Madame Du Châtelet, 1734 (she died, 1749); Chamberlain for Frederick of Prussia, Berlin, 1750-53; lived in Colmar, 1753-54, at Les Délices, near Geneva, 1755-59, and at Ferney, 1759-78; visited Paris and received triumphant welcome, 1778. Member, Royal Society (London); Royal Society of Edinburgh, 1745; French Academy, 1746; and Academy of St. Petersburg, 1746; Royal Historiographer of France, 1745-50; Gentleman of the Bedchamber, 1746. *Died 30 May 1778.*

PUBLICATIONS

Collections

Oeuvres complètes (Kehl Edition). 70 vols., 1785-89.
Oeuvres complètes, edited by L. Moland. 52 vols., 1877-85.
Complete Works (includes *Correspondence,* 51 vols., 1968-77), edited by Theodore Besterman. 1968— .

Fiction

Zadig; ou, La Destinée. 1748; edited by G. Ascoli and J. Fabre, 1962.
Micromégas. 1752; edited by Ira O. Wade, 1950; translated as *Micromegas,* 1753.

Candide; ou, L'Optimisme. 1759; edited by René Pomeau, in *Complete Works 48*, 1980; translated as *Candid*, 1759; also translated as *Candide*.
L'Ingénu. 1767; edited by W.R. Jones, 1957; as *Le Huron; ou, L'Ingénu*, 1767; as *The Pupil of Nature*, 1771; as *The Sincere Huron*, 1786.
La Princesse de Babylone. 1768; as *The Princess of Babylon*, 1927.
L'Homme aux quarante écus. 1768; edited by N. Kotta, 1966; as *The Man of Forty Crowns*, 1768.
Les Lettres d'Amabed. 1769.
Le Taureau blanc. 1774; edited by René Pomeau, 1957; as *The White Bull*, 1774.
Histoire de Jenni; ou, Le Sage et l'athée. 1775; as *Young James; or, The Sage and the Atheist*, 1776.
Zadig and Other Stories, edited by Haydn T. Mason. 1971.
Romans et contes, edited by Frédéric Deloffre and Jacques Van den Heuvel. 2 vols., 1978.

Plays

Oedipe (produced 1718). 1719.
Artémire (produced 1720). Fragments published in *Oeuvres 1*, 1784.
Mariamne (produced 1724; as *Hérode et Mariamne*, produced 1725). 1725.
L'Indiscret (produced 1725). 1725.
Brutus (produced 1730). 1731.
Ériphile (produced 1732). 1732.
Zaïre (produced 1732). 1733; edited by E. Jacobs, 1975; translated as *Zara*, 1736.
Les Originaux (produced 1732). In *Oeuvres 9*, 1820.
Adélaïde du Guesclin (produced 1734). In *Oeuvres 6*, 1745.
La Mort de César (produced 1735). 1736; edited by A.-M. Rousseau, 1964.
Alzire; ou, Les Américains (produced 1736). 1736; translated as *Alzira*, 1736.
L'Enfant prodigue (produced 1736). 1738.
L'Échange (produced 1736; revised version, as *Quand est-ce qu'on me marie?*, produced 1761). 1761; as *Le Comte de Boursoufle*, in *Oeuvres 7*, 1819.
Zulime (produced 1740). 1761.
Mahomet (produced 1741). 1742; as *Le Fanatisme; ou, Mahomet le prophète*, 1743; as *Mohamet the Imposter*, 1744.
Mérope (produced 1743). 1744; translated as *Merope*, 1744.
La Princesse de Navarre (produced 1745). 1745.
Le Temple de la Gloire, music by Rameau (produced 1745). 1745.
La Prude; ou, La Gardeuse de cassette, from *The Plain-Dealer* by Wycherley (produced 1747). In *Oeuvres 8*, 1748.
Sémiramis (produced 1748). 1749; translated as *Semiramis*, 1760.
Nanine (produced 1749). 1749.
Oreste (produced 1750). 1750.
Rome sauvée (produced 1750). 1752; as *Catilina; ou, Rome sauvée*, 1753; as *Rome Preserved*, 1760.
Le Duc de Foix (produced 1752). 1752; as *Amélie; ou, Le Duc de Foix*, in *Collection complète des oeuvres 11*, 1756.
L'Orpheline de la Chine (produced 1755). 1755; as *The Orphan of China*, 1756.
Saül. 1755; translated as *Saul*, 1820.
La Femme qui a raison (produced 1758). 1759.
Socrate. 1759; translated as *Socrates*, 1760.
Tancrède (produced 1759). 1760; translated as *Almida*, 1771.
L'Écossaise (produced 1760). 1760; as *The Coffee House*, 1760.
Le Droit de seigneur (as *L'Écueil du sage*, produced 1762). 1763; as *L'Écueil du sage*,

1764.
Olympie (produced 1764).   1763.
Le Triumvirat (produced 1764).   1766.
Les Scythes (produced 1767).   1767.
Charlot; ou, La Comtesse de Givri (produced 1767).   1767.
Les Guèbres; ou, La Tolérance.   1769.
Sophonisbe (produced 1774).   1770.
Le Dépositaire (produced 1772).   1772.
Les Lois de Minos.   1773.
Don Pèdre.   1775.
Agathocle (produced 1777).   In *Oeuvres 6*, 1784.
Irène (produced 1778).   1779.
Le Duc d'Alençon; ou, Les Frères ennemis, edited by M.L. Dubois.   1821.

Verse

La Ligue; ou, Henri le Grand: Poème epique.   1723; as *La Henriade*, 1728; edited by
   O.R. Taylor, in *Complete Works 2*, 1970; translated as *Henriade*, 1732.
Le Temple du Goût.   1733; revised edition, as *Le Temple de l'amitié et le temple du goût*,
   1733; as *The Temple of Taste*, 1734.
La Pucelle d'Orléans.   1755; augmented edition, 1762, 1780; edited by J. Vereruysse, in
   Complete Works 7, 1970; as *La Pucelle; or, The Maid of Orleans*, 2 vols., 1785-86.
Poème sur le désastre de Lisbonne.   1756.
Poème sur la loi naturelle.   1756.
Précis de l'Ecclésiaste en vers.   1759.
La Cantique des cantiques en vers.   1759.
Contes de Guillaume Vadé.   1764.
La Guerre civile de Genève.   1767; as *The Civil War of Geneva*, 1769.
Épîtres, satires, contes, odes, et pièces fugitives.   1771.
Poèmes, épîtres, et autres poésies.   1777.

Other

Essai sur les guerres civiles de France.   1729; as *Essay upon the Civil Wars in France*,
   1727.
Histoire de Charles XII, roi de Suède.   2 vols., 1731.
Lettres écrites de Londres sur les Anglais.   1734; as *Lettres philosophiques*, 1734; edited
   by G. Lanson and A.-M. Rousseau, 1964; as *Letters Concerning the English Nation*,
   1733; as *Letters on England*, 1980.
Eléments de la philosophie de Newton.   1738; as *The Elements of Newton's Philosophy*,
   1738.
Oeuvres.   8 vols., 1739 (and many later editions).
Histoire de la guerre de mil sept cent quarante et un.   2 vols., 1745; as *The History of the
   War of Seventeen Hundred and Forty One*, 1756.
Le Siècle de Louis XIV.   2 vols., 1751; *Supplément*, 1753; as *The Age of Louis XIV*, 2
   vols., 1752; revised edition, 1753.
Annales de l'Empire depuis Charlemagne.   2 vols., 1753.
Essai sur l'histoire générale et sur les moeurs et l'esprit des nations.   7 vols., 1756; revised
   edition, 8 vols., 1761-63; as *The General History and State of Europe*, 1754; as *An Essay
   on Universal History*, 1759.
Histoire de l'empire de Russie sous Pierre le Grand.   2 vols., 1759-63; as *The History of
   the Russian Empire under Peter the Great*, 1763.

Appel à toutes les nations de l'Europe. 1761.

Traité sur la tolérance. 1763; as *A Treatise of Religious Tolerance,* 1764.

Dictionnaire philosophique portatif. 1764; revised edition, 1765 (and later editions): revisions include *La Raison par Alphabet,* 2 vols., 1769, and *Questions sur l'Encyclopédie,* 9 vols., 1770-72; as *The Philosophical Dictionary for the Pocket,* 1765.

La Philosophie de l'histoire. 1765; edited by J.H. Brumfitt, in *Complete Works 59,* 1969.

Collection des lettres sur les miracles. 1765; 20 letters also published separately, 1765.

Le Philosophe ignorant. 1766; edited by J.L. Carr, 1965; as *The Ignorant Philosopher,* 1767.

Commentaire sur le livre Des Délits et des peines. 1766.

Les Honnêtetés littéraires. 1767.

Examen important de milord Bolingbroke. 1767.

Lettres sur Rabelais. 1767.

Homélies prononcées à Londres en 1765. 1767; *Cinquième homélie,* 1769.

Le Dîner du comte de Boulainvilliers. 1767.

Les Singularités de la nature. 1768.

ABC. 1768.

Histoire du Parlement de Paris. 2 vols., 1769.

Collections d'anciens évangiles. 1769.

Dieu et les hommes: Oeuvre theologique, mais raisonnable. 1769.

Précis du siècle de Louis XV. 2 vols., 1769; as *The Age of Louis XV,* 2 vols., 1774.

Fragments sur l'Inde. 1773; augmented edition, with *Fragments l'histoire générale, et sur la France,* 1774.

Commentaire historique sur les oeuvres de l'auteur de la Henriade (autobiography). 1776; as *Historical Memoirs of the Author of the Henriade,* 1977.

Le Bible enfin expliquée. 2 vols., 1776.

Dialogue d'Evhémère. 1777.

Commentaire sur L'Esprit des Lois de Montesquieu. 1778.

Prix de la justice et de l'humanité. 1778.

Traité de métaphysique. 1784; edited by H. Temple Petterson, 1937.

Oeuvres historiques, edited by René Pomeau. 1957.

The Portable Voltaire, edited by Ben Ray Redman. 1968.

Notebooks, edited by Theodore Besterman, in *Complete Works 81-82.* 1968.

Editor, *Anti-Machiavel; ou, Essais critiques sur Le Prince de Machiavel,* by Frederick II. 1740.

Editor, *Testament de Jean Meslier.* 1762.

Editor, *Théâtre de Pierre Corneille avec des commentaires.* 12 vols., 1764; *Commentaires* edited by D. Williams, in *Complete Works 53-55,* 1974-75.

Editor, *Journal de la cour de Louis XIV,* by the Marquis de Dangeau. 1769.

Editor, *Les Souvenirs de Mme. de Caylus.* 1770.

Editor, *Éloge et pensées de Pascal.* 1778.

Translator, *Jules César,* by Shakespeare, in *Théâtre de Pierre Corneille 2.* 1764.

Translator, *L'Héraclius espagnol; ou, Dans cette vie tout est verité et tout mensonge,* by Calderón, in *Théâtre de Pierre Corneille 5.* 1764.

*

Bibliography: *Voltaire: Bibliographie de ses oeuvres* by Georges Bengesco, 4 vols., 1882-90 (index by Jean Malcolm, 1953); *A Bibliography of Writings on Voltaire 1825-1926* by Mary Margaret Barr, 1929 (supplements in *Modern Language Notes,* 1933, 1941).

Critical Studies: *Voltaire Historian* by J.H. Brumfitt, 1958; *Voltaire and "Candide,"* 1959, and *The Intellectual Development of Voltaire,* 1969, both by Ira O. Wade; *Voltaire* by V.W.

Topazio, 1967; *Voltaire dans ses contes* by Jacques Van den Heuvel, 1967; *Voltaire*, 1975, and *Voltaire: A Biography*, 1981, both by Haydn Mason; *Voltaire and the Century of Light* by A.O. Aldridge, 1975; *Voltaire* by Theodore Besterman, 1976.

* * *

Voltaire was the universal genius of the French Enlightenment: dramatist, poet, philosopher, scientist, novelist, moralist, satirist, polemicist, historian, letter-writer. He established his credentials in the literary world at an early age, laying claim to pre-eminence in two of the most exalted domains of letters: tragedy and the epic. His very first play, *Oedipe* (1718), on a theme where he rivalled Sophocles and Corneille, was an immediate success, placing him at once in the front rank of tragic dramatists. His epic poem *La Ligue* (1723—later called *La Henriade*) triumphed likewise, bringing heroic verse back into fashion. But this early brilliance was checked by the quarrel with the chevalier de Rohan that led to his years in England. From them emerged on his return the *Lettres philosophiques* (1734) which, based on the superior example of English life, worked out a programme for a whole civilisation, where the French might learn to use experimental enquiry, avoid matters of faith in science and philosophy, encourage trade, literature, and the arts.

The scandal caused by these Letters forced him into retreat at Cirey, where began the career of unremitting hard work that was to characterise the rest of his life. Poetry, plays, *contes*, historical and philosophical works poured forth: like the *Traité de métaphysique* (1734-7), the tragedy *Zaïre* (1733), the worldly poems "Le Mondain" and "Défense du Mondain" (1736-7), and most notably of all the *Eléments de Newton* (1736-40), where a popular account of the great Englishman's thought becomes a major vehicle in spreading enlightenment. By contrast, the 1740's are less prolific, but they include his first-published important *conte, Zadig*, where the problem of evil is evoked, without any reassuring answers being found. After the fiasco of his stay at Frederick the Great's court, Voltaire eventually found an ever-precarious but growing stability in and later near Geneva. Shock at the catastrophic earthquake in Lisbon led within weeks to the *Poème sur le désastre de Lisbonne* (1756), an anguished exploration of the meaning of such suffering. In *Candide* (1759), the same theme is revisited, but in a more profound form and expanded into an attack on philosophical Optimism and, through it, all philosophical systems which claim falsely to justify the presence of evil in the world. It is, however, by its style above all that *Candide* is superior to the poem about Lisbon. Brilliantly ironic where the latter is but sombre, satirical of human pretensions and malice alike, expressing at the same time both a horror of evil and an unquenchable vitality, it conveys a unique tone that makes it Voltaire's masterpiece. Every illusion is betrayed, even the belief (held by the Manichean Martin) that everything is evil. The human lot is not to make sense of the universe, nor yet to abandon hope and commit suicide; it is to survive, to work, to put together a few fragments as a flimsy structure against total despair. Experience is a better teacher than metaphysical systems: "il faut cultiver notre jardin." That final phrase appears to represent a counsel of positive endeavour and courage.

Such a spirit animates the multitudinous writings of the Ferney years (1759-78), in which Voltaire makes an all-out assault on man-made injustice. Crusades in real life on behalf of persecuted victims like Calas, Sirven, and La Barre find their literary counterpart in such works as the *Traité sur la tolérance* (1763), the *Dictionnaire philosophique* (1764), *contes* like *L'Ingénu* (1767) and innumerable pamphlets, dialogues, satires, sermons. *L'Ingénu* seeks to heighten the reader's awareness of the reality of persecution in France, whether the target be Protestants or Jansenists or innocent maidens, by a sentimental tale that makes the injustices all the more horrible for being viewed through the reactions of the simple and natural hero who gives the story its title. More polemically, the *Examen important de milord Bolingbroke* (1767) is a comprehensive attack on the follies of the Christian faith, first as found in the Old and New Testament and then as seen in the history of the Catholic Church; the tone is one of high indignation at the massacres and barbarities which absurdities of dogma have caused ever since the time of Christ. Everything about Christianity is false: founder, scriptures, doctrines, morality. Enlightened men should quit Catholicism and turn to the only true religion, deism, which consists simply of worshipping God and being just to one's fellow-men.

How to represent fairly in a thousand words a man whose extant works alone run to fifteen million? The scale of Voltaire's prestige overwhelms all attempts to convey comprehensively his writings as his life. For sixty years he dominated the French intellectual and literary world. The greatest tragedian and epic-writer of his day, he has come since then to be seen as unparalleled *conteur philosophique*. His historical works, especially the *Siècle de Louis XIV* (1751) and the universal *Essai sur les moeurs* (1756), are major items in the development of historiography as the study of civilisation. Latterly, now that his correspondence is at last available in the great Besterman edition, containing some 17,000 surviving letters by him with some 1,200 correspondents and on a vast range of subjects, it is coming to be seen that here too is a literary masterpiece. His comprehensive commitment to secular values in the defence of intellectual and judicial freedom, arrayed against a Church-dominated society, allied to his love of classical ideals—reason and lucidity—expressed in brilliant irony and wit, assure him a dominance in the history of French literature that is unlikely ever to be surpassed.

—Haydn Mason

WALTHER von der Vogelweide. Born in Austria, possibly in the Tyrol, probably about 1170. Active at the ducal court in Vienna and influenced there by Reinmar, before 1198; worked in numerous princely courts of southern and central Germany in the next twenty years; mentioned in the household accounts of Bishop Wolfger of Passau in 1203; sought the patronage of Emperor Frederick II after 1212 and received a grant of land near Würzburg a few years later; last datable poem c.1227.

PUBLICATIONS

Verse

Gedichte, edited by P. Wapnewski, with modern German translations. 1962.
Die Gedichte, edited by K. Lachmann, revised by Hugo Kuhn. 1965.
Die Lieder, edited by Friedrich Maurer. 2 vols., 1967-74.
The Poems, translated by Edwin H. Zeydel and Bayard Q. Morgan. 1952.

*

Bibliography: *Bibliographie zu Walther von der Vogelweide* by Manfred Scholz, 1969.

Critical Studies: *Walther von der Vogelweide* by George F. Jones, 1968.

*   *   *

Walther von der Vogelweide still holds the leading position among medieval German lyric poets which contemporaries accorded him—both for his original development of the *Minne-*

sang (courtly love lyric), and for his striking songs of social commentary. As poetic interpreter of the social scene Walther was not merely the first but the greatest German, if not indeed medieval, political poet. His career spanned the four decades from the 1190's to the 1220's.

Walther's love poetry ranges from juvenilia, somewhat laboured in style and strongly imitative, to superbly composed lyrics which bestow upon traditional themes and motifs startling simplicity and spontaneity. *Minnesang* derived largely from French *trouvère* lyric; the poet extols the courtly lady in a love which ennobles him although—or rather because—it lacks the prospect of consummation. The genre involves speculation about the nature of love and the emotions of the lovers, in a kaleidoscope of stock motifs and epithets. Faced with conventional treatments of emotional aesthetic experiences Walther evolved a stimulating, critical, personal ideal: the girl of humble station embodying the purest type of womanly grace. (Here Walther broke with Reinmar, the mentor of his youth in Vienna.) Reciprocity plays a major role in his love poems; so, too, does humour, and above all direct, frank self-assertion, qualities central to his political poetry, too. Walther's lyric embraces the range of the Troubadours, then, but also that of the Latin Wandering Scholars, to whom he shows close affinities.

Walther was active as political poet in the troubled decades of German affairs after the accession of Pope Innocent III. In the struggle between Staufen and Welf for the Imperial crown after 1198 he worked for various royal and princely patrons including the monarchs Philipp, Otto, and Frederick. His propaganda poems reflect the conflicts which the need for patronage imposed, and his frequent changes of patron invite the charge of opportunism. In fact, it is clear that Walther campaigned consistently for the unity and stability of Germany, seeing the prestige of the emperor as the best guarantor of peace at home and as the sole effective check on papal power without and princely pretension within. His political poems contain pregnant theoretical statements on the nature and duties of kingship, couched in striking and vigorous language: the imperial crown occurs repeatedly as embodiment of the imperial ideal, the monarch is frequently extolled in Christological or Trinitarian terms. As overriding goal Walther posits the order embodied in God's creation: German disorder he contrasts to the ordered ranks of the animal kingdoms; papal interference in the sphere of the monarchy he repudiates as abuse of the pope's very blessing in the imperial coronation. In a host of religious and didactic poems Walther appeals for ordered balance in individual conduct (*mâze*), and stresses the manly virtues of *triuwe* ("keeping faith with others") and *staete* ("steadfastness").

Perhaps Walther's most startling facet is his enormous self-assertion: while showing solidarity with professional itinerant poets he claims for himself extreme respect which his powerful art justified. Repeatedly he addresses himself directly to princes, pope, and emperors alike; on occasion he adopts the biblical prophet's pose as *"penseur"*; once he even claims the title of *vrônebote* ("messenger of the Lord"). For his expressive enrichment of the fledgeling genres of love lyric and political verse in Germany Walther stands justified in his high poetic pretension.

—Lewis Jillings

WATER MARGIN (also translated as *All Men Are Brothers* and *Outlaws of the Marsh*).

PUBLICATIONS

Fiction

I-pai-erh-shih-hui ti Shui-hu [The 120-Chapter Shui-hu], preface by Hu Shih. 20 vols., 1929.
Chin Sheng-t'an ch'i-shih-i-hui-pen Shui-hu-chuan [The Chin Sheng-t'an Version of Shui-hu-chuan in 71 Chapters]. 24 vols., 1934.
Shui-hu ch'üan-chuan [The Complete Shui-hu-chuan], edited by Cheng Chen-to, Wang Li-ch'i, and others. 4 vols., 1954.
All Men Are Brothers, translated by Pearl S. Buck. 2 vols., 1933.
Water Margin, translated by J.H. Jackson. 2 vols., 1937.

*

Critical Studies: *The Evolution of a Chinese Novel: Shui-hu-chuan* by Richard G. Irwin, 1953; *The Classic Chinese Novel* by C.T. Hsia, 1968.

*   *   *

The novel *Shui-hu Chuan*, variously translated as *Water Margin*, *All Men Are Brothers*, or *Outlaws of the Marsh*, has been popular with Chinese readers for almost four centuries. Its authorship is traditionally assigned to a 14th-century writer of fiction and drama, Lo Kuan-chung (c. 1330-1400), and also jointly to him and to a more obscure figure named Shih Nai-an. The novel as it is read now is almost certainly a later redaction, perhaps dating from the early to mid-16th century, and has been published in editions of different lengths, from 71 (the most popular), to 100, 110, 115, and 124 chapters.

The story derives its source material from oral tales which originated in historical fact. The central legend is about a 12th-century band of outlaw-rebels who occupied a mountain in northern China, eventually made peace with the Sung dynasty emperor, and helped him conquer another rebel group in the South. The novel tells of the gradual gathering and dissolution of the band: in the early days one "hao-han" ("good fellow" or "stalwart," as they are generally called) after another is forced by unjust circumstances to seek refuge from the law and to join with others as bandits who live off the land. Soon the numbers grow; a hierarchy develops; and the outlaws reach an apogee of strength and prosperity. However, the leader, Sung Chiang, has always wanted to serve the emperor in a legitimate way, and finally achieves his wish, though he thus puts an end to the life style of the rebel utopia. In the service of the emperor the band wins great honor but steadily loses members in battle until only a handful remain. In the end Sung Chiang commits suicide along with his closest companion, Li K'uei.

The novel divides into units consisting of either a single hero's evolution from common citizen to outlaw or of some mission in which many participate. These units are sometimes interspersed with unrelated sub-plots, but all weave together to lead into and out of the central scene of action in the text, the mountain fortress which is a more or less self-sufficient society of its own.

Early on, the novelist presents character types and themes that are treated throughout. Of these types there are the coarse, swarthy men who combine naive heartiness with a tendency to be cold-blooded (Li K'uei, Lu Ta, and Wu Sung); the clean-shaven and valiant heroes who embody the values of honesty and civility (Lin Ch'ung, Lu Chun-i); and the magicians and masterminds who advise on strategy (Wu Yung, Kung-sun Sheng). Thematic issues include such things as the requital of official injustice, the definition of true leadership, and the mutual recognition of what it takes to be a "hao-han."

Perhaps not surprisingly, one of the singular undercurrents of the book is misogyny. Women frequently appear as adulteresses who must be ruthlessly exterminated; few of the major heroes are married; and lustful behavior is frowned upon. Sung Chiang, for example, "not very interested in women," marries but neglects his wife and drives her to adultery. When she threatens to reveal his connections with outlaws, he murders her. He is led to such an act neither because of her mockery of his sexual inadequacy (in one of the most humorous scenes of the novel) nor her adultery itself, but because of the possibility of breaking the code of honor with his friends.

It is significant that in the latter half of the novel, when Sung Chiang's band is already declining, a figure enters who subtly eclipses the other male heroes. He is Yen Ch'ing, a handsome and physically adept young man who is at the same time more socially versatile. He symbolizes the eclipse of the band most pointedly when he shoots at a flock of geese in the sky: this is interpreted as an ill omen since he thus disturbs the integrity of a naturally formed group.

At first reading *Water Margin* will perhaps seem episodic and unorganized, a situation that is partly due to the nature of the source material and partly to the lengthy evolution of the text as we have it now. However, like *Golden Lotus*, though to a lesser extent, *Water Margin* achieves cohesiveness by means of what may be called correlative patterning, that is, multiple levels of textual or figural recurrence. From minute to large scale, such repetition at times merely provides a sense of linkage, at others it creates an ironic contrast between parallel elements. These patterns of meaning have been celebrated in a famous commentary on the novel by Chin Sheng-t'an of the 17th century.

In general *Water Margin* is written in an extremely lively, colloquial style, and is filled with proverbs, folk idioms, and comic obscenity. Unfortunately putting this flavor into English has proved difficult so that at times the reader must bear with somewhat wooden and naive-sounding translations.

—Keith McMahon

WEDEKIND, (Benjamin) Frank(lin). Born in Hanover, 24 July 1864. Educated at Gemeindeknabenschule and Bezirksschule, Lenzburg; Kantonsschule, Aarau; universities of Lausanne, 1884, Munich, 1884-85, and Zurich, 1888. Married the actress Tilly Newes (died, 1917); two daughters. Journalist and actor; visited Paris, London, Zurich, Berlin; lived mainly in Munich. *Died 9 March 1918.*

PUBLICATIONS

Collections

Ausgewählte Werke, edited by Fritz Strich. 5 vols., 1924.
Prosa, Dramen, Verse, edited by Hans-Georg Maier. 2 vols., 1954-60.

Werke, edited by Manfred Hahn.   3 vols., 1969.

Plays

Der Schnellmaler (produced 1916).   1889.
Kinder und Narren.   1891; revised version, as *Die junge Welt* (produced 1908), 1897.
Frühlings Erwachen (produced 1906).   1891; as *The Awakening of Spring*, 1909; as
    Spring Awakening, 1980.
Lulu.   1913; translated as *Lulu*, 1971.
    Der Erdgeist (produced 1898).   1895; as *Earth Spirit*, 1914.
    Die Büchse der Pandora (produced 1904).   1904; as *Pandora's Box*, 1918.
Der Kammersänger (produced 1899).   1899; as *Heart of a Tenor*, 1913; as *The Tenor*,
    1927.
Der Liebestrank (produced 1900).   1899.
Der Marquis von Keith (produced 1901).   1901; edited by Wolfgang Hartwig, 1965; as
    The Marquis of Keith, in *From the Modern Repertoire 2*, edited by Eric Bentley, 1952.
So ist der Leben (produced 1902).   1902; as *König Nicolo*, 1911; as *King Nicolo; or,
    Such Is Life*, 1912.
Die Kaiserin von Neufundland (pantomime; produced 1902).
Hidalla; oder, Sein und Haben (produced 1905).   1904; as *Karl Hetmann, der Zwer-
    griese*,   in *Gesammelte Werke*, 1913.
Totentanz (produced 1906).   1906; as *Tod und Teufel*, 1909; as *Death and Devil*, 1952.
Musik (produced 1908).   1908.
Die Zensur (produced 1909).   1908.
Oaha (produced 1911).   1908; as *Till Eulenspiegel*, 1916.
Der Stein der Weisen (produced 1911).   1909.
In allen Sätteln gerecht.   1910.
Mit allen Hunden gehetzt.   1910.
In allen Wassern gewaschen.   1910.
Schloss Wetterstein (produced 1917).   1912; as *Castle Wetterstein*, 1952.
Franziska (produced 1912).   1912.
Simson; oder, Scham und Eifersucht (produced 1914).   1914.
Bismarck (produced 1926).   1916.
Überfürchtenichts (produced 1919).   1917.
Herakles (produced 1919).   1917.
Das Sonnen spektrum (produced 1922).   As *The Solar Spectrum*, 1959.
Ein Genussmensch, edited by Fritz Strich.   1924.

Fiction

Die Fürstin Russalka.   1897.
Mine-Haha; oder, Über die körperliche Erziehung der jüngen Mädchen.   1901.
Feuerwerk.   1905.

Verse

Lautenlieder.   1920.
Ich hab meine Tante geschlachtet: Lautenlieder und "Simplizissimus"-Gedichte, edited by
    Manfred Hahn.   1967.

Other

Schauspielkunst: Ein Glossarium. 1910.
Gesammelte Briefe, edited by Fritz Strich. 2 vols., 1924.
Selbstdarstellung, edited by Willi Reich. 1954.
Der vernummte Herr: Briefe 1881-1917, edited by Wolfdietrich Rasch. 1967.

*

Critical Studies: *Wedekind* by S. Gittleman, 1969; *Wedekind in Selbstzeugnissen und Bilddokumenten* by Günter Seehaus, 1974; *Wedekind* by Alan Best, 1975.

*   *   *

Few writers have ever aroused as much controversy as did Frank Wedekind during the Wilhelmine era in Germany. Celebrated in literary circles, he held views and used methods of expressing them that were bound—and often calculated—to antagonise the establishment and shock the general public. As a result he was frequently censored and banned on grounds of immorality, and once imprisoned for offences against the majesty of the Emperor.

In his plays, stories, and essays, as well as his satirical sketches, poems, and ballads—many of which he published in the magazine *Simplizissimus* or sang in the cabaret "Die elf Scharfrichter" (The Eleven Executioners) in Munich—Wedekind violently attacked the moral, spiritual, and political beliefs of the bourgeoisie, and particularly its attitude to sex. Inspired by Nietzsche, and sharing some ideas with Freud, he set out to liberate primitive irrational instinct from the constraints of rational civilisation.

As a playwright Wedekind disowned both the Classical tradition and contemporary Naturalism. Drawing on various types of popular entertainment—circus, funfair, pantomime, vaudeville, grand-guignol—he replaced the "closed" form, which dominated the mainstream theatre, with "open" structures involving disjointed episodic actions, puppet-like characters moved by the dramatist's idiosyncrasies regardless of psychological or circumstantial motivation, and distorted dialogues incongruously combining rhetorical and poetic devices with trite colloquialisms, evoking a sense of non-communication, and displaying a brutally cynical wit. Set in a demi-monde of bohemians, adventurers, prostitutes, deviants, and criminals, culminating in sexual excesses and death by murder or suicide, mixing melodrama and slapstick, revelling in lurid sensations and steeped in black humour, his grotesque tragicomedies—for which he demanded, and at times personally demonstrated, a harshly stylised technique of acting—are outstanding examples of "anti-Aristotelian" drama. Influenced by Büchner and Grabbe, he became in his turn a decisive influence on Expressionism, Dadaism, the Epic Theatre of Brecht, and the Theatres of Cruelty and the Absurd.

Wedekind's most successful plays include *The Tenor, The Marquis of Keith, King Nicolo, or, Such Is Life,* and *Hidalla* (also known as *Karl Hetmann,der Zwergriese,* Karl Hetmann, the Dwarf-Giant), all of which dramatise, ironically and more or less autobiographically, the plight of artistically inclined non-conformists in a middle-class environmment that they reject and that rejects them. His masterpieces, however, are two tragicomedies concerned mainly with sexual themes. The first, *Spring Awakening,* juxtaposes the sympathetic portrayal of teenagers in the throes of adolescence—some of whom die while others emerge into a life of pleasure— with vicious caricatures of prudish or authoritarian adults. The second, comprising *Earth Spirit* and *Pandora's Box*—also famous as Alban Berg's opera *Lulu*—chronicles the escapades of a demonic vamp, praised as "the true animal, the wild beautiful animal," who ruins a succession of bizarre lovers before she is reduced to a cheap streetwalker and killed by a sadistic pervert. In both works Wedekind glorifies his concept of uninhibited natrual impulses, pitted against a repressed and repressive society bent on corrupting and destroying them.

It is debatable whether Wedekind reverses the accepted social and aesthetic norms in order to indulge in his notorious "Satanism" or to make an oblique case for a genuine morality. What is certain is that he will long be remembered as the author of some remarkably original plays and as one of the great innovators of European drama.

—Ladislaus Löb

WEISS, Peter (Ulrich). Born in Nowawes, Germany, 8 November 1916; naturalized Swedish citizen, 1945. Lived in England, 1934-36; attended Art Academy, Prague, 1936-38. Married the artist and designer Gunilla Palmstierna in 1964. Painter, writer, and film producer; lived in Sweden after 1939; one-man shows of his paintings after 1935: retrospective, Zurich, 1979. Recipient: Charles Veillon prize, 1963; Lessing Prize (Hamburg), 1965; Heinrich Mann Prize (East Berlin), 1966; Tony Award (USA), 1966; New York Drama Critics Circle Award, 1966; Thomas Dehler Prize, 1978. *Died 10 May 1982.*

PUBLICATIONS

Plays

Der Turm (broadcast, 1949; produced on stage, 1950). 1963; as *The Tower*, 1966.
Die Versicherung (produced 1971). 1952.
Ein Traumspiel, from the play by Strindberg. 1963.
Nacht mit Gästen (produced 1963). 1963; as *Night with Guests*, 1968.
Die Verfolgung und Ermordung Jean Paul Marats, dargestellt durch die Schauspiel-gruppe des Hospizes zu Charenton unter Anleitung des Herrn de Sade (produced 1964). 1964; as *The Persecution and Assassination of Jean-Paul Marat as Performed by the Inmates of the Asylum of Charenton under the Direction of the Marquis de Sade*, 1965.
Die Ermittlung: Oratorium in elf Gesängen (produced 1965). 1965; as *The Investigation: Oratorio in Eleven Cantos*, 1966.
Gesang vom lusitanischen Popanz (produced 1967). 1968; as *Song of the Lusitanian Bogey*, in *Two Plays*, 1970.
Diskurs über die Vorgeschichte und den Verlauf des lang andauernden Befreiungskrieges in Viet Nam als Beispiel für die Notwendigkeit des bewaffneten Kampfes der Unter-drückten gegen ihre Unterdrücker, sowie über die Versuche der Vereinigten Staaten von Amerika die Grundlagen der Revolution zu vernichten (produced 1968). 1967; as *Discourse on the Progress of the Prolonged War of Liberation in Viet Nam*, in *Two Plays*, 1970.
Wie dem Herrn Mockinpott das Leiden ausgetrieben wird (produced 1968). In *Dramen*, 1968; as *How Mr. Mockinpott Was Cured of His Sufferings*, 1971.
Dramen. 2 vols., 1968.
Trotzki im Exil (produced 1970). 1970; as *Trotsky in Exile*, 1971.
Hölderlin (produced 1971). 1971.
Der Prozess, from the novel by Kafka (produced 1975).
Der neue Prozess (produced 1982).

Fiction

> *Duellen* (in Swedish). 1953.
> *Der Schatten des Körpers des Kutschers.* 1960; as *The Shadow of the Coachman's Body,* in *Bodies and Shadows,* 1970.
> *Abschied von den Eltern.* 1961; as *The Leavetaking,* 1962.
> *Fluchtpunkt.* 1962; as *Vanishing Point,* 1966.
> *Das Gespräch der drei Gehenden.* 1963; as *Conversations of the Three Wayfarers,* in *Bodies and Shadows,* 1970.
> *Exile* (includes *The Leavetaking* and *Vanishing Point*). 1968.
> *Die Ästhetik des Widerstandes.* 3 vols., 1975-81.

Verse

> *Från ö till ö* [From Island to Island] (in Swedish). 1947.
> *De besegrade* [The Vanquished] (in Swedish). 1948.

Other

> *Dokument I.* 1949.
> *Avantgardefilm.* 1956.
> *10 Arbeitspunkte eines Autors in der geteilten Welt.* 1965.
> *Notizen zum kulturellen Leben der Demokratischen Republik Viet Nam.* 1968; as *Notes on the Cultural Life of the Democratic Republic of Vietnam,* 1970.
> *Das Material und die Modelle: Notizen zum dokumentarischen Theater.* 1968.
> *Rapporte.* 2 vols., 1968-71.
> *Aufsätze, Journale, Arbeitspunkte: Schriften zu Kunst und Literatur,* edited by Manfred Haiduk. 1979.
> *Der Maler Peter Weiss: Bilder, Zeichnungen, Collagen, Filme.* 1980.
> *Notizbücher 1971-1980.* 2 vols., 1981.

*

Critical Studies: *Weiss: A Search for Affinities* by Ian Hilton, 1970; *Der Dramatiker Weiss* by Manfred Haiduk, 1977; *The Theme of Alienation in the Prose of Weiss* by Kathleen A. Vance, 1981.

*   *   *

When Bertolt Brecht died in East Berlin in 1956, Peter Weiss was already 40. His own unexpected death in 1982 at the age of 66 robbed the world of the legitimate successor to the great Marxist dramatist from whom, Weiss had said, he had learned "clarity...., the necessity of making clear the social quesion in a play."

"Change the world, it needs it," Brecht had demanded; Weiss likewise believed that it was absolutely necessary "to write with the point of trying to influence or change society," and in his last novel, *Die Ästhetik des Widerstandes* (The Aesthetics of Resistance) he wrote that "we should never be in a position to change our situation as long as we remained prisoners of our incompleteness [*Halbheit*] and our alienation."

Brecht died in a country which he believed was at least *trying* to bring about the changes for which he yearned; Weiss, a German writer, but resident in Stockholm since 1939, could claim that he had seen changes in western society—the anti-authoritarian students' revolts of 1968 and the advance in the cause of feminism, for example—which might just herald the dawn of that juster, socialist society.

The three prose works—the "micro-novel" *The Shadow of the Coachman's Body, Leavetaking*, and *Vanishing Point*, the last two in particular describing in autobiographical manner a young man's search for an identity—brought Weiss international recognition in the early 1960's. His move from novel-writing to the stage began with the premiere in 1964 of his best-known play, usually shortened to *The Marat-Sade*, a famous example of "total theatre" in Artaud's then modish "Theatre-of-Cruelty" style.

The imagined confrontation of the individualist, authoritarian Marquis de Sade with the demagogic, revolutionary Marat, set against the background of the frightening, obscene gyrations of the demented inmates, was Weiss's attempt to show why society must be changed. Marat's "socialist" solution was mirrored in the next important plays—*The Investigation* and *The Viet Nam Discourse*—which coincided with the growing anti-American trend in world opinion, in particular of the younger generation. *The Investigation*, a documentary play based on the transcripts of the Auschwitz Concentration Camp trials, castigated the world of the students' fathers who had "permitted" these atrocities, while the Viet Nam play fuelled that discontent at the massive USA involvement in a war against what was termed a "peasant population." (The angry critical reception of his next plays, *Trotsky in Exile* and *Hölderlin*, led to Weiss's first serious heart-attack.)

His last important work, the three-volume novel *The Aesthetics of Resistance*, which dealt with the important international crises and wars during Weiss's life-time, shows the progressive (and, for Weiss, depressing) de-humanization of mankind to which "resistance" must be offered.

This gifted literary artist, painter and film-buff made a major contribution to European culture and has an honoured place among those European intellectuals who have sought to make the world a better place to live in.

—Kenneth S. Whitton

WITKIEWICZ, Stanislaw (Ignacy). Pseudonym: Witkacy. Born in Warsaw, 24 February 1885; son of the writer and painter Stanislaw Witkiewicz (used pseudonym to distinguish himself from his father). Educated at the Academy of Fine Arts, Cracow, 1905-06, and in Italy, France, and Germany. Served in the Tsarist forces in Russia during World War I; elected political commissar by his regiment, 1917. Married Jadwiga Unrug in 1923. Accompanied Bronislaw Malinowski on an anthropological expedition to Australia, 1914; painter from 1918: one-man show, Cracow, 1967; founder, Formist Theatre, an amateur group, Zakopane, 1925-27. *Died (suicide) 18 September 1939.*

PUBLICATIONS

Plays

> *Pragmatysci* (produced 1921). In *Dramaty*, 1962; as *The Pragmatists*, in *Tropical Madness*, 1972.
> *Tumor Mózgowicz* [Tumor Brainiowicz] (produced 1921). In *Dramaty*, 1962.

Kurka wodna (produced 1922). In *Dramaty*, 1962; as *The Water Hen*, in *The Madman and the Nun*, 1968.

W malym dworku [In a Small Country House] (produced 1923). In *W malym dworku i Szewcy*, 1948.

Wariat i zakonnica (produced 1924). In *Dramaty*, 1962; as *The Madman and the Nun*, in *The Madman and the Nun*, 1968.

Nowe Wyzwolenie (produced 1925). In *Dramaty*, 1962; as *The New Deliverance*, 1974.

Jan Maciej Karol Wścieklica [Jan Maciej Karol Hellcat] (produced 1925). In *Dramaty*, 1962.

Mister Price; czyli, Bzik tropikalny, with Eugenia Dunin-Borkowska (produced 1926). In *Dramaty*, 1962; as *Mr. Price; or, Tropical Madness*, in *Tropical Madness*, 1972.

Persy Zwierzatkowskaja [Persy Bestialskaya] (produced 1927).

Metafizyka dwuglowego cielecia (produced 1928). In *Dramaty*, 1962; as *Metaphysics of a Two-Headed Calf*, in *Tropical Madness*, 1972.

Matwa (produced 1933). In *Dramaty*, 1962; as *The Cuttlefish*, in *Treasury of the Theatre 2*, edited by Bernard F. Dukore and John Gassner, 1969.

Straszliwy wychowawca [The Frightful Tutor] (produced 1935).

W malym dworku i Szewcy [In a Small Country House and the Shoemakers]. 1948.

Szewcy (produced 1957). In *W malym dworku i Szewcy*, 1948; as *The Shoemakers*, in *The Madman and the Nun*, 1968.

Dramaty [Plays], edited by K. Puzyna. 2 vols., 1962; revised edition, 1972.

Oni (produced 1963). In *Dramaty*, 1962; as *They*, in *The Madman and the Nun*, 1968.

Matka (produced 1964)., In *Dramaty*, 1962; as *The Mother*, in *The Madman and the Nun*, 1968.

Szalona lokomotywa (produced 1965). In *Dramaty*, 1962; as *The Crazy Locomotive*, in *The Madman and the Nun*, 1968.

Gyubal Wahazar (produced 1966). In *Dramaty*, 1962; translated as *Gyubal Wahazar*, in *Tropical Madness*, 1972.

Sonata Belzebuba [The Beelzebub Sonata] (produced 1966). In *Dramaty*, 1962.

Bezimienne dzielo (produced 1967). In *Dramaty*, 1962; as *The Anonymous Work*, in *Twentieth-Century Polish Avant-Garde Drama*, edited by Daniel Gerould, 1977.

Nabobnisie i koczkodany [Dainty Shapes and Hairy Apes] (produced 1967). In *Dramaty*, 1962.

Janulka, córka Fizdejki [Janulka, Daughter of Fizdejko] (produced 1974). In *Dramaty*, 1962.

The Madman and the Nun and Other Plays (includes *The Water Hen*, *The Crazy Locomotive*, *The Mother*, *They*, *The Shoemakers*). 1968.

Tropical Madness: Four Plays (includes *The Pragmatists*; *Mr. Price, or Tropical Madness*; *Gyubal Wahazar*; *Metaphysics of a Two-Headed Calf*). 1972.

Panna Tutli-Putli [Miss Tootli-Pootli] (produced 1975). 1974.

Fiction

Pozegnanie jesieni [Farewell to Autumn]. 1927.

Nienasycenie. 1930; as *Insatiability*, 1977.

Jedyne wyjscie [The Only Way Out], edited by Tomasz Jodelka-Burzecki. 1968.

622 upadki Bunga [622 Downfalls of Bung]. 1972.

Other

Nowe formy w malarstwie i wynikajace stad nieporozumienia [New Forms in Painting and the Resulting Misunderstandings]. 1919.

Teatr: Wstep do teorii czystej formy w teatrze [Theatre: Introduction to the Theory of

Pure Form in the Theatre]. 1923; as *Czysta forma w teatrze*, edited by J. Degler, 1977.
Nikotyna, alkohol, kokaina, peyotl, morfina, eter [Nicotine, Alcohol, Cocaine, Peyote, Morphine, Ether]. 1932.
Pojecia i twierdzenia implikowane przez pojecie istnienia [The Concepts and Principles Implied by the Concept of Existence]. 1935.
Pisma filozoficzne i estetyczne [Philosophical and Aesthetic Writings], edited by J. Leszczyński. 2 vols., 1974-76.
Bez kompromisu: Pisma krytyczne i publicystyczne [No Compromise: Critical and Journalistic Writings], edited by J. Degler. 1976.
Poza rzeczywistościa [Outside Reality]. 1977.
Marzenia improduktywne: Dywagacja metafizyczna [Improductive Daydreams: Metaphysical Palaver]. 1977.
Zagadnienie psychofizyczne [A Psychophysical Problem], edited by B. Michalski. 1978.
Listy do Bronislawa Malinowskiego [Letters to Bronislaw Malinowski]. 1981.

*

Critical Studies: *Witkiewicz: Aux sources d'un théâtre nouveau* by Alain von Crugten, 1971; "Witkiewicz Issue" of *Polish Review 18*, 1973; *Witkacy: Witkiewicz as an Imaginative Writer* by Daniel Gerould, 1981.

*   *   *

Stanislaw Witkiewicz (also known as Witkacy) was an artist of many sides: in his lifetime his reputation as a painter easily superseded his literary fame, and within the domain of literature he cultivated three such different fields as the theatre, the novel, and art criticism. All his literary works to some extent illustrated his philosophical and aesthetic theories which were first expounded in *Nowe formy w malarstwie* (New Forms in Painting) and in *Teatr: Wstep do teorii czystej formy w teatrze* (Theatre: Introduction to the Theory of Pure Form in the Theatre). According to Witkiewicz nothing can be asserted about Being except that it predicates "particular existences" and that these "monads" experience the strangeness of separate existence. It is only through metaphysical feelings that the mystery of the Universe can be grasped, and the significance of art lies in its unique capacity (with the decline of religious feeling) to induce "metaphysical thrills." In art Witkiewicz was an advocate of Pure Form ("The form of the work of art is its only essential content") but he realized that it was attainable only in music and perhaps in painting, so in the theatre he suggested bold deformations and illogical, irrational, purely "scenic" constructions. Though for a while he was associated with the Formists, a group of painters and poets in Cracow, Witkiewicz's aesthetic views differed from those of the so-called "Cracow Vanguard" showing more affinity with such similarly lonely precursors of the modern theatre as Antonin Artaud.

Most of Witkiewicz's plays were written in the 1920's though his best political satire, *The Shoemakers*, dates from 1931-34. His plays do not fit into traditional categories: they are grotesque and eclectic mixtures of sex, philosophy, politics, and art in which sudden outbursts of private passion alternate with lengthy expositions of new creeds and ideologies. The characters, as Milosz puts it in his *The History of Polish Literature*, 1969, are mainly "madmen, misfits and maniacs" moving in a cosmopolitan upper-class and intellectual milieu; they usually include a tyrannical leader, a disillusioned Artist or Philosopher, and a Demonic Woman who all undergo shattering changes during the play, even death (often reversed) or moral degradation. Some of Witkiewicz's plays can be read as parables on history and society. In *The Shoemakers*, for example, we witness the fall of the *ancien régime* and the victory of the shoemakers' revolution which is then followed by the murder of Sajetan Tempe, their leader, by the shoemakers themselves and by the imposition of military and bureaucratic rule upon the people, with the gigantic figure of the Hyperworkoid (Hiper-Robociarz) serving as a convenient facade.

Witkiewicz's plays achieved popularity only after 1956, when with the advent of the theatre of the absurd and the theatre of cruelty his dramatized fantasies struck the public as thoroughly modern. As for his novels only two of these were published in his lifetime and of these *Insatiability* was the more ambitious. It is an anti-Utopian novel on one level, evoking the image of a decadent and semi-Fascistic Polish state of the future ruled by a popular dictator, a Poland which is a buffer-zone between the superficially Communistic states of the West and the radical Communist Chinese who have by now taken over Russia. On another level, it is the story of a young hero's initiation in sex, art, drugs, and politics: a novel of adventure. *Insatiability* ends with the collapse of Western civilization—the Chinese take over Poland without war, thanks to the widespread use of the excellent drug *Murti-Bing*, not unlike Aldous Huxley's *soma*. In fact, Witkiewicz experimented with drugs many years before Huxley and described his experiences in *Nikotyna, alkohol, kokaina, peyotl, morfina, eter* (Nicotine, Alcohol, Cocaine, Peyote, Ether, 1932).

Insatiability makes interesting though difficult reading; although Witkiewicz often parodied the style of the modernist writers of "Young Poland," his own roots lie in *art nouveau* and his style suffers from an excess of metaphors and adjectives. Story-telling is often interrupted by digressions and debates on the merits of modern philosophical theories, while important political events are told in small print in the form of "information bulletins." The style of *Insatiability* can be described as "psycho-expressionistic"—it represents an expressionism with much psychological insight but sometimes steering perilously close to psychotic phenomena. Witkiewicz's fear of a collectivized, mechanized, herd-like society turning its back on art for the sake of advanced technology is well-nigh prophetic; according to his English translator, Louis Iribarne, Witkiewicz's main concern was "the threat posed to human consciousness by a process that is beyond man's capacity to control."

—George Gömöri

WOLFRAM von Eschenbach. Fl. 1195-1220. Possibly in the service of the counts of Wertheim, and of the Landgrave Hermann of Thuringia at Wartburg.

PUBLICATIONS

Collections

[*Works*], edited by Albert Leitzmann, revised edition.   3 vols., 1933-48.
[*Works*], edited by Karl Lachmann, revised by Eduard Hartl.   1952.

Verse

Parzifal, und Titurel, edited by Karl Bartsch, revised by Marta Marti.   3 vols., 1929-35;
   Parzifal translated by Jessie L. Weston, 2 vols., 1894; also translated by Helen M.
   Mustard and Charles E. Passage, 1961, and A.T. Hatto, 1980; translated in part by
   Margaret F. Richey, as *Schionatulander and Sigune*, 1960.
Die Lyrik, edited by Peter Wapnewski.   1972.

*

Bibliography: *Bibliographie zu Wolfram von Eschenbach* by Willy Krogmann and Ulrich Pretzel, 1963, revised edition, 1968.

Critical Studies: *Studies of Wolfram von Eschenbach* by Margaret F. Richey, 1957; *An Introduction to Wolfram's "Parzifal"* by Hugh Sacker, 1963; *Wolfram's "Parzifal"* by H.J. Wiegand, edited by Ursula Joffman, 1969; *Wolfram von Eschenbach* by James F. Poag, 1972; *Wolfram's Parzifal: An Attempt at a Total Evaluation* by Henry Kratz, 1973; *Approaches to Wolfram von Eschenbach* by D.H. Green, 1978.

*   *   *

Wolfram is best known for his epic poems, but eight short poems composed by him have also been preserved. These display great lyricism, passion, and control. They are also notable for certain features of striking originality such as his praise of marital love.

His only completed epic is *Parzival* (25,000 lines), loosely based on a similar epic by Chrétien de Troyes. Through very many connected and unconnected episodes the hero progresses from a state of complete innocence and naivety brought about by his secluded infancy to a state of readiness to be Grail King. He is the epitome of the Knight in the service of ladies, humanity, and God.

The Holy Grail is a central feature of this poem, and Wolfram's conception of the Grail bears close similarities in its gnosticism to the Cathar heresy which prevailed in the area of the Pyrenees at the beginning of the 13th century. Wolfram himself tells us that he was supplied with additional material by one Kyot, who has been, albeit problematically, identified with Guiot of Provence. Moreover, Wolfram displays a genuine ethical and religious seriousness which is not in any conventional ecclesiastical tradition.

Parzival is a very rich development of the material which he took from his basic sources, and show signs of constant re-editing over the period (1200-10 approximately), in which it was composed, with immense elaboration of detail.

Parzival's progress is illustrated in the very numerous incidents of the epic. He first follows the advice of others in obtaining the trappings of chivalry, such as knightly weapons and tactful avoidance of being over-inquisitive. He later discovers that it is necessary to transcend formal etiquette when the dictates of humanity require this. A knight who serves humanity and is at one with God will sense when it is right to show sympathetic interest in another's suffering despite the rules enjoining discretion. The rules of chivalry are in these scenes depicted as a guide to those who seek to serve humanity and God, but not as the epitome of such service.

An excellent example of the unceasing development of his ideas is given by the Titurel fragments (c. 1210-20). In this, characters associated with *Parzival* recur in a work dealing with a hunt. In these fragments Wolfram's mastery of form combines magnificently with immense profundity of feeling in a work of striking maturity. *Parzival* and *Willehalm* are in rhyming couplets, but *Titurel* is composed in complex strophes.

Willehalm (14,000 lines; from c. 1210-12) is unfinished and is again the work of a mature writer displaying a sure mastery of form. The central pillars of the work are the two battles of Aliscans against the Saracens. One of these battles results in the tragic death of the model knight Vivianz. In the other the mighty hero Renewart plays a notable part in the successful quest for revenge.

Wolfram is an unconventional and strikingly confident poet with strong powers of imagination and humor. He displays a genuine piety and belief in the possibility of a direct knowledge of God by man. Realistic detail suffuses the idealistic knightly world, and his characters are brought lovingly to life. Even in his own lifetime, the richness of his language was the subject of comment (albeit unfavourable comment by Gottfried von Strassburg). He himself showed an awareness that his love of detail (foreign words are an example) was human or antiquarian rather than scholarly. It may be true that his love of detail, the sheer mass of his work, its depth and richness, the eccentricities and difficulties of his style, conspire occcasionally to give an impression of excessive weight. Yet this is a minor misgiving when placed beside Wolfram's truly monumental achievements. When material of such richness and complexity is contained with sure control in works of masterly form which are suffused throughout with life and interest, the resulting impact is unambiguously great literature of the very first rank.

—G.P. Cubbin

XENOPHON. Born in Athens, c. 431 or 428-27 B.C. Married to Philesia; two sons. Associated with the Socratics as a young man; served in Athenian cavalry in latter stages of Peloponnesian War; left Athens in 410, and joined the army of the Persian prince Cyrus in Asia Minor in his unsuccessful attempt to gain the Persian throne; after the failure of the expedition, Xenophon was elected general by the army, and led the army from Persia to the Greek city of Trapezus (now Trabzon) on the Black Sea, 400; hired out the army as a mercenary to a Thracian prince in present-day Bulgaria and to Spartan generals in Asia Minor, 399; probably formally exiled from Athens in 399; served with the Spartan forces under general Agesilaus in war with Persia, 396-94, and the Corinthian War against Athens, 394; lived in Sparta, then granted an estate at Scillus, near Olympia: served as local representative (*proxenos*); forced to leave Scillus for Corinth, 371; his Athenian exile was rescinded, c. 368, when Athens and Sparta became allies against Thebes, and he probably returned to Athens, c. 366. *Died c. 354 B.C.*

PUBLICATIONS

Collections

> [*Works*], edited by E.C. Marchant.   5 vols., 1900-21; translated by C.L. Brownson and others (Loeb edition), 7 vols., 1914-68.
> *Opuscula* [Small Works], edited by G. Pierleoni.   1937.

Prose

> *Hellenica*, edited by Carl Hude.   1969; also edited by Gisela Strasburger, 1970; as *History of My Times*, translated by Rex Warner, 1966.
> *Anabasis*, edited by Carl Hude, revised by J. Peters.   1972; as *The March Upcountry*, translated by W.H.D. Rouse, 1947; as *The Persian Expedition*, translated by Rex Warner, 1949.
> *Respublica Lacedaemoniorum* [Spartan Constitution]: translated by J.M. Moore, in *Aristotle and Xenophon on Democracy and Oligarchy*, 1975.
> *Apologia:* as *Socrates' Defence Before the Jury*, translated by A.S. Benjamin, 1965.
> *Symposium*, translated by H. Tredennick.   1970.
> *Memorabilia*, edited by Carl Hude.   1969; as *Recollections of Socrates*, translated by A.S. Benjamin, 1965; as *Memoirs of Socrates*, translated by H. Tredennick, 1970.
> *Oeconomicus:* translated by Carnes Lord, in *Xenophon's Socratic Discourse: An Interpretation of the "Oeconomicus"* by Leo Strauss, 1970.
> *Cyropaedia*, edited by W. Genoll.   1968; as *The Story of Cyrus*, 1900; as *The Education of Cyrus*, 1914.

XENOPHON

Hiero: translated by Leo Strauss, in *On Tyranny*.   1948; revised edition, 1963.

*

Critical Studies: *On Tyranny: An Interpretation of Xenophon's Hiero*, 1948, revised edition, 1963, *Xenophon's Socratic Discourse: An Interpretation of the "Oeconomicus,"* 1970, and *Xenophon's Socrates*, 1972, all by Leo Strauss; *The Ten Thousand: A Study of Social Organization and Action in Xenophon's Anabasis* by Gerald B. Nussbaum, 1967; *Military Theory and Practice in the Age of Xenophon*, 1970, and *Xenophon*, 1974, both by J.K. Anderson; *Xenophon and Thucydides* by E.M. Soulis, 1972; *Aristotle and Xenophon on Democracy and Oligarchy* by J.M. Moore, 1975; *Xenophon the Athenian* by W.E. Higgins, 1977; *Xenophon* by Rainer Nickel, 1979.

*   *   *

Xenophon's distinguished military career fitted him to deal with practical details rather than with philosophical abstractions or broad historical questions. His *Memorabilia* consist of short conversations in which Socrates, while constantly reminding his hearers of their duty to the city and its gods, instructs them on such matters as the qualifications of a speaker in the Assembly, the duties of a general or of a cavalry officer, and even table manners. These conversations recall the openings of some of the Platonic dialogues, but break off at the point where Plato's Socrates begins to develop some abstract question, such as the nature of justice or the aims of education. Even when, in the *Oeconomicus*, Xenophon does make Socrates discuss a matter at some length, the subject is practical—the detailed management of a rich man's house and estate—and the "Socratic method" of cross-examination is turned upon its inventor, not in order to elicit abstract principles but to show that the science of agriculture is based on common-sense observations that are within the power of the average townsman. The work is of great interest to the social historian rather than to the philosopher.

To what extent Xenophon's Socrates resembles the historical man is debated. Xenophon certainly used the "Socratic dialogue" as a vehicle for his own opinions; put into Socrates's mouth, in the *Oeconomicus*, an account of the younger Cyrus which he could not possibly have heard Socrates utter, and which is based on facts reported in his own *Anabasis*; and offered in his *Apologia* a defence of Socrates which is unlikely to bear any resemblance to the philosopher's own speech in court. But there is insufficient reason to doubt Xenophon's testimony in the *Anabasis* that he was sufficiently close to Socrates to rely on his advice. Socrates may be supposed to have known young men whom he considered capable of moral improvement, though not of metaphysics. Recent attempts to read profound subtleties into Xenophon's philosophy have demonstrated their authors' own intellectual ability, rather than Xenophon's.

Xenophon's chief historical work, the *Hellenica*, picks up the story of the Peloponnesian War where the unfinished history of Thucydides breaks off in 411 B.C., covers the end of the war and its aftermath down to the restoration of democracy in 403 B.C., neglects the next four years, during much of which Xenophon was campaigning in Asia, and resumes as a somewhat rambling chronicle ending with the battle of Mantinea in 362 B.C. It reports vividly a number of events which Xenophon may have witnessed or heard described by eye-witnesses, but lacks Thucydides' power of analysis and ability to draw general conclusions. Its supposed Spartan bias seems to reflect the one-sidedness of Xenophon's sources rather than intentional prejudice.

In the *Anabasis* Xenophon's abilities as a first-hand reporter show at their best. It is a pity that most students first come to this brilliant and exciting narrative when their knowledge of Greek only allows them to struggle slowly through its opening chapters. The clarity and purity of Xenophon's style make his work an excellent text-book.

The *Cyropaedia*, a historical romance based on the career of the founder of the Persian empire, sums up Xenophon's practical and moral teachings, and was formerly regarded as his masterpiece. It continued to influence political thought until the 18th century, but is now little read.

Of Xenophon's instructional handbooks, that on the *Art of Horsemanship* retains its freshness, and something of practical value, to the present day.

—J.K. Anderson

ZAMYATIN, Evgeny (Ivanovich). Born in Lebedyan', 20 January 1884. Educated at Progymnasium, Lebedyan', 1892-96; gymnasium in Voronezh 1896-1902; studied naval engineering at St. Petersburg Polytechnic Institute, 1902-08; arrested and exiled for student political activity, 1906 and 1911. Naval engineer, 1908-11, and lecturer from 1911, St. Petersburg Polytechnic Institute; supervised the construction of ice-breakers in England, 1916-17; associated with the Serapion Brothers literary group, from 1921; Editor, *Dom Iskusstva* [House of the Arts], 1921, *Sovremenny zapad* [Contemporary West], 1922-24, and *Russky Sovremennik* [Russian Contemporary], 1924; Editor, with Kornei Chukovsky, English section of World Literature series; victimized from the late 1920's, and removed from the leadership of Soviet Writers Union; left Soviet Union, 1931; settled in Paris, 1932. *Died 10 March 1937.*

PUBLICATIONS

Collections

> *Povesti i rasskazy* [Tales and Stories]. 1963.
> *Sochineniya* [Works]. 2 vols., 1970-72.

Fiction

> *Uyezdnoye* [A Provincial Tale]. 1916.
> *Istrovityane.* 1922; title story translated as *The Islanders*, 1978.
> *Bolshim detyam skazki* [Fairy Tales for Grown-Up Children]. 1922.
> *Na kulichkakh* [At the World's End]. 1923.
> *My.* 1952; translated as *We*, 1924.
> *Nechstivye rasskazy* [Impious Tales]. 1927.
> *Zhitiyo Blokhi ot dnya chudesnogo yeyo rozhdeniya...*[The Life of a Flea from the Day of Its Miraculous Birth...]. 1929.
> *Navodneniye* [The Flood]. 1930.
> *Bich Bozhy* [The Scourge of God] (unfinished). 1939.
> *The Dragon: Fifteen Stories.* 1967; as *The Dragon and Other Stories*, 1975.

Plays

> *Ogni svyatogo Doninika* [The Fires of St. Dominic]. 1922.
> *Blokha* [The Flea] (produced 1925). 1926.
> *Obshchestvo pochotnykh zvonarey* [The Society of Honorable Bellringers] (produced 1925). 1926.

Sensatsiya, from the play *The Front Page* by Ben Hecht and Charles MacArthur (produced 1930).
Atilla, and *Afrikansky gost'* [The African Guest], in *Novy zhurnal 24* and *73*, 1950, 1963.

Screenplays: *Severnaya lyubov'* [Northern Love], 1928; *Les Bas-Fonds* (*The Lower Depths*), 1936.

Other

Robert Mayer.   1922.
Gerbert Uells [H.G. Wells].   1922.
Sobraniye sochineniy [Collected Works].   4 vols., 1929.
Litsa [Faces].   1955; as *A Soviet Heretic: Essays*, edited by Mirra Ginsburg, 1969.

*

Critical Studies: *Zamyatin: A Russian Heretic* by David J. Richards, 1962; *The Life and Works of Evgeny Zamjatin* by Alex M. Shane, 1968 (includes bibliography); *Zamjatin: An Interpretative Study* by Christopher Collins, 1973; "Literature and Revolution in *We*" by Robert Russell, in *Slavonic and East European Review*, 1973; *Brave New World, 1984, and We: An Essay on Anti-Utopia* by Edward J. Brown, 1976; "The Imagination and the 'I' in Zamjatin's *We*" by Gary Rosenshield, in *Slavic and East European Journal*, 1979; *Three Russian Writers and the Irrational: Zamyatin, Pil'nyak, and Bulgakov* by T.R.N. Edwards, 1982; "Adam and the Ark of Ice: Man and Revolution in Zamyatin's *The Cave*" by Andrew Barratt, in *Irish Slavonic Studies 4*, 1983.

*   *   *

Evgeny Zamyatin published his first short story as early as 1908, but the best known of his early works was *Uyezdnoye*, which illustrates many of the features of his "neorealist" innovative style (elements of the grotesque, distortive imagery, satire, primitivism, and distinctive characterization and linguistic effects). He saw this development in literature as a dialectical synthesis of the two dominant trends of the turn of the century—Symbolism and naturalism— which would superimpose the stylistic flights of the one upon the materialist base of the other. He developed in his stories systems of imagery which at times almost dominated the narrative, as in "Mamay" and "Peshchera," and are a prominent feature of his only completed novel, *We*. His sojourn in England produced two satirical depictions of bourgeois English life: *The Islanders*, set in the North East, and "Lovets chelovekov" ("A Fisher of Men"), set in London. Zamyatin turned again to satire and renewed experimentation, and to the theatre, in his work of the 1920's. His later stories, notably *Navodneniye*, achieved a greater structural unity in a style which may best be described as mature primitivism. Zamyatin himself remarked: "all the complexities through which I passed turned out to be necessary in order to achieve simplicity."
Returning to Russia between the two revolutions of 1917, Zamyatin, a convinced revolutionary, proceeded to question the direction of the revolution from the standpoint of his philosophy of heresy (a kind of renegade Marxism): there must always be "a voice in the wilderness" inveighing against the status quo, in order to maintain a dialectical progression of history which recognizes no final revolution. These views, expressed in a number of pungent stories and essays and in the futuristic novel *We*, aroused the antipathy of the new Soviet literary establishment, who did not take kindly, to his concern for the future of literature. *We* was denounced as "a malicious pamphlet" and has never been published in the Soviet Union. Branded an "inner émigré" by Trotsky, Zamyatin was hounded from Soviet literature after the "Pil'nyak-Zamyatin affair" of 1929 (see Vera Reck's account in her book *Boris Pil'niak*, 1975).

We, Zamyatin's best-known work, depicts an apparently unsuccessful uprising against a totalitarian, glass-enclosed city-state of the distant future. Built on extreme mathematical and collectivist principles, "The Single [or "One"] State," having reduced its populace to the status of "numbers," determines to eradicate all remaining individuality by imposing an operation of "fantasiectomy," to remove the imagination. Narrated in diary form, *We* shows Zamyatin's innovative style at its most developed (notably its image systems built on mathematical terminology and colour symbolism), as well as providing an imaginative psychological view of a virtually alien society. It is also the principal fictional statement of his philosophical preoccupations: the role of the heretic, inevitable conflict with the stagnation and philistinism of whatever the status quo, and the cosmic struggle between energy and entropy. Influenced stylistically by Andrey Bely, in its promotion of the irrational by Dostoevsky and in its futurism by H.G. Wells, *We* can be read as: a prophetic warning against tyranny (of whatever complexion); an unusually advanced work of science fiction (for 1920); and a penetrating study of alienation and schizophrenia. Its assumed influence upon Huxley's *Brave New World* (1932) is probably erroneous; Orwell, however, acknowledged its impact on *1984* (1949). There are also parallels to be seen with near-contemporaneous works by Karel Capek and Georg Kaiser, and with Fritz Lang's film *Metropolis*.

Zamyatin was a leading figure of Russian modernism and an important influence on the prose of the 1920's. Yet he is far better known today in the West than in the Soviet Union where, unlike most of his disgraced contemporaries, he remains totally unpublished and has only recently begun to be discussed.

—Neil Cornwell

ZOLA, Émile. Born in Paris, 2 April 1840, of Italian father; naturalized French citizen, 1862. Educated at Collège d'Aix; Lycée Bourbon, Aix; Lycée Saint-Louis, Paris, 1858-59. Married Alexandrine-Gabrielle Meley in 1870; had two children by Jeanne Rozerot. Worked briefly as a clerk in the Excise Office; worked in the dispatch office, then in sales promotion, Hachette, publishers, Paris, 1862-66; art critic (as "Claude"), *L'Événement* newspaper, 1866; staff member, *Le Globe* and *L'Événement Illustré*, 1868, and staff member or contributor to other papers until 1900; made accusations of false trial during the Dreyfus affair: tried and convicted of libel, 1898: in England, 1898-99. *Died 29 September 1902.*

PUBLICATIONS

Collections

> *Oeuvres complètes*, edited by Eugène Fasquelle and Maurice Le Blond. 50 vols., 1927-29.
> *Oeuvres complètes*, edited by Henri Mitterand. 15 vols., 1966-69.

Fiction

> *Contes à Ninon.* 1864; as *Stories for Ninon*, 1895.

La Confession de Claude. 1865; as *Claude's Confession*, 1888.
Le Voeu d'une morte. 1866; as *A Dead Woman's Wish*, 1902.
Les Mystères de Marseille. 1867; as *The Mysteries of Marseilles*, 1895.
Thérèse Raquin. 1867; translated as *Thérèse Raquin*, 1887; as *Theresa*, 1952.
Madeleine Férat. 1868; translated as *Madeleine Férat*, 1888; as *Shame*, 1954.
Les Rougon-Macquart, edited by Henri Mitterand. 5 vols., 1960-67.
  1. *La Fortune des Rougon.* 1871; as *The Fortune of the Rougons*, 1886.
  2. *La Curée.* 1872; as *The Rush for the Spoil*, 1886; as *The Kill*, 1895.
  3. *Le Ventre de Paris.* 1873; as *La Belle Lisa; or, The Paris Market Girls*, 1882; as *The Fat and the Thin*, 1888; as *Savage Paris*, 1955.
  4. *La Conquête de Plassans.* 1874; as *The Conquest of Plassans*, 1887; as *A Priest in the House*, 1957.
  5. *La Faute de l'Abbé Mouret.* 1875; as *Abbé Mouret's Transgression*, 1886; as *The Sin of the Abbé Mouret*, 1904.
  6. *Son Excellence Eugène Rougon.* 1876; as *Clorinda; or, The Rise and Reign of His Excellency Eugène Rougon*, 1880; as *His Excellency Eugène Rougon*, 1886; as *His Excellency*, 1958.
  7. *L'Assommoir.* 1877; translated as *L'Assommoir*, 1879; as *Gervaise*, 1879; as *The Dram-Shop*, 1897; as *Drink*, 1903; as *The Gin Palace*, 1952.
  8. *Une Page d'amour.* 1878; as *Hélène: A Love Episode*, 1878; as *A Page of Love*, 1897; as *A Love Affair*, 1957.
  9. *Nana.* 1880; translated as *Nana*, 1884.
 10. *Pot-Bouille.* 1882; as *Piping Hot!*, 1885; translated as *Pot-Bouille*, 1895; as *Lesson in Love*, 1953; as *Restless House*, 1953.
 11. *Au Bonheur des Dames.* 1883; edited by Henri Mitterand, 1980; as *Shop Girls of Paris*, 1883; as *The Ladies' Paradise*, 1883; as *Ladies' Delight*, 1957.
 12. *Le Joie de vivre.* 1884; as *How Jolly Life Is!*, 1886; as *The Joy of Life*, 1901; as *Zest for Life*, 1955.
 13. *Germinal.* 1885; translated as *Germinal*, 1885.
 14. *L'Oeuvre.* 1886, as *The Masterpiece*, 1886; as *His Masterpiece*, 1886.
 15. *La Terre.* 1887; edited by Henri Mitterand, 1980; as *The Soil*, 1888; translated as *La Terre*, 1895; as *Earth*, 1954.
 16. *Le Rêve.* 1888; as *The Dream*, 1893.
 17. *La Bête humaine.* 1890; as *The Human Beast*, 1891(?); as *The Monomaniac*, 1901; as *The Beast in Man*, 1958.
 18. *L'Argent.* 1891; as *Money*, 1894.
 19. *La Débâcle.* 1892; as *The Downfall*, 1892; as *The Debacle*, 1968.
 20. *Le Docteur Pascal.* 1893; as *Doctor Pascal*, 1893.
Nouveaux contes à Ninon. 1874.
Le Capitaine Burle. 1882.
Naïs Micoulin. 1884.
A Soldier's Honour (short stories). 1888.
The Attack on the Mill (short stories). 1892.
Les Trois villes:
  Lourdes. 1894; translated as *Lourdes*, 1894.
  Rome. 1896; translated as *Rome*, 1896.
  Paris. 1898; translated as *Paris*, 1898.
Les Quatres Évangiles (incomplete):
  Fécondité. 1899; as *Fruitfulness*, 1900.
  Travail. 1901; as *Labor*, 1901; as *Work*, 1901.
  Vérité. 1903; as *Truth*, 1903.
Madame Sourdis. 1929.
Stories. 1935.

Plays

Les Mystères de Marseille, with Marius Roux (produced 1867).
Thérèse Raquin, from his own novel (produced 1873). 1873; as *Seeds*, in *Modern Drama*, 1966.
Les Héritiers Rabourdin (produced 1874). 1874; as *The Heirs of Rabourdin*, 1893.
Le Bouton de Rose (produced 1878). In *Théâtre*, 1878.
Nana, with William Busnach, from the novel by Zola (produced 1881). In *Trois pièces*, 1885.
Pot-Bouille, with William Busnach, from the novel by Zola (produced 1883). In *Trois pièces*, 1885.
Le Ventre de Paris, with William Busnach, from the novel by Zola (produced 1887).
Renée (produced 1887). 1887.
Germinal, with William Busnach, from the novel by Zola (produced 1888).
Madeleine (produced 1889). In *Oeuvres complètes*, 1927-29.
Messidor, music by Alfred Bruneau (produced 1897). 1897.
L'Ouragan, music by Alfred Bruneau (produced 1901). 1901.
L'Enfant-Roi, music by Alfred Bruneau (produced 1905). 1905.
Poèmes lyriques (opera librettos; includes *Messidor, L'Ouragan, L'Enfant-Roi, Lazare, Violaine la chevelue, Sylvanire*). 1921.

Other

Mes haines. 1866.
Le Roman expérimental. 1880.
Les Romanciers naturalistes. 1881.
Documents littéraires. 1881.
Le Naturalisme au théâtre. 1881.
Nos auteurs dramatiques. 1881.
Une Campagne. 1882.
The Experimental Novel and Other Essays. 1893.
Nouvelle campagne. 1897.
La Vérité en marche. 1901.
Letters to J. Van Santen Kolff, edited by Robert J. Niess. 1940.
La République en marche: Chroniques parlementaires, edited by Jacques Kayser. 2 vols., 1956.
Mes voyages: Lourdes, Rome: Journaux inédits, edited by René Ternois. 1958.
Salons (art criticism), edited by F.W.J. Hemmings and Robert J. Niess. 1959.
Lettres inédites à Henry Céard, edited by A.J. Salvan. 1959.
Vingt messages inédits de Zola à Céard, edited by A.J. Salvan. 1961.
L'Atelier de Zola: Textes de journaux 1865-1870, edited by Martin Kanes. 1963.
Lettres de Paris (articles from *Vestnik Europy*), edited by P.A. Duncan and Vera Erdely. 1963.
Correspondance, edited by B.H. Bakker. 1978—.

*

Bibliography: *Zola, Journaliste: Bibliographie chronologique et analytique* by Henri Mitterand and Halina Suwala, 2 vols., 1968-72; *Zola: A Selective Analytical Bibliography* by Brian Nelson, 1982.

Critical Studies: *Zola: An Introductory Study of His Novels* by Angus Wilson, 1952; *Zola's "Son Excellence Eugène Rougon"* by Richard B. Grant, 1960; *Zola* by Marc Bernard, 1960; *Zola's "Germinal": A Critical and Historical Study*, 1962, and *Zola*, 1967, both by Elliott M.

Grant; *Zola and the Theatre* by Lawson A. Carter, 1963; *Zola Before the "Rougon-Macquart"* by John C. Lapp, 1964; *Zola*, 1966, and *The Life and Times of Zola*, 1977, both by F.W.J. Hemmings; *Zola* by Philip Walker, 1968; *Zola, Cézanne, and Manet: A Study of "L'Oeuvre"* by Robert J. Niess, 1968; *Through Those Living Pillars: Man and Nature in the Works of Zola* by Winston Hewitt, 1974; *Zola* by Joanna Richardson, 1978; *Garden of Zola: Zola and His Novels for English Readers* by Graham King, 1978; *Zola and the Bourgeoisie: A Study of Themes and Techniques in "Les Rougon-Macquart"* by Brian Nelson, 1983.

* * *

With the death of Victor Hugo in 1885, Émile Zola became the dominant literary figure in France. That year saw the publication of *Germinal*, generally recognized as his masterpiece, but he had already achieved fame, indeed notoriety, by some twenty novels, including *L'Assommoir* (1877) and *Nana* (1880).

At the centre of Zola's work stands the twenty-volume cycle of novels entitled *Les Rougon-Macquart* (1871-1893), which contains all his best work. It represents an attempt to "study" the effects of hereditary flaws (neurosis, alcoholism, violence) and various environments on the members of two families during the Second Empire (1851-70).

Zola developed an aesthetic that combined Hugo's epic breadth and imaginative power with Balzac's stress on the material setting and Flaubert's relative detachment and objectivity. In order to emphasize its originality, he dubbed it "Naturalism" and underlined its supposedly scientific character. This strategy was successful in drawing attention to his work, but it was ultimately to mislead many critics into neglecting the poetic and Romantic character of much of his output. In the epic treatment of crowd scenes such as the miners' rampage in *Germinal*, and the mythical atmosphere that transforms key scenes of novels like *Nana*, Zola succeeded brilliantly in creating a world that owed much to tendencies quite foreign to the scientific pretentions of Naturalism. Zola's greatest works owe little or nothing to the Naturalist theories he propagated in his volumes of criticism.

Sex was a central element in Zola's novels, and this undoubtedly helped to make them best-sellers because at that period such a topic was considered scandalous. But his treatment of sex was no cynical exploitation, for he saw in it a dark but magnificent force of almost mystical character on which man was dependent not only for reproduction but for all creativity.

Although he became wealthy from the sale of his novels, Zola never forgot the poverty of his youth, and he remained a convinced democrat and socialist all his life, with a deep sympathy for the lower classes—workers (*L'Assommoir*), miners (*Germinal*), peasants (*La Terre*)—which he specialized in portraying, and a bitter contempt for the corruption and cynicism of the bourgeoisie, which he castigated in vitriolic portraits in *La Curée, Son Excellence Eugène Rougon, L'Argent*.

Zola was a class-mate and particular friend of Paul Cézanne, and wrote much art criticism supporting the struggle of Edouard Manet and Impressionists like Claude Monet to develop and impose a revolutionary new style and vision in painting. Manet thanked him with a now well-known portrait.

In 1898, Zola's scandalous anti-establishment reputation (he was rejected by the French Academy thirty-one times) took on a new dimension when he wrote an open letter to the President of France denouncing the racism that had led to the framing of Dreyfus, a Jewish army man, as a spy by fellow officers. For his role in this affair, Zola was convicted and forced to flee the country until the courts recognized the truth of his accusations and released Dreyfus from Devil's Island.

—Patrick Brady

TITLE
INDEX

The following list of titles cites all works included in the fiction, play, and verse sections of the individual entries in the book, and uncategorized titles for some entrants. The name(s) in parenthesis is meant to direct the reader to the appropriate entry, and not necessarily to give complete information about the work. The date given is that of first publication (or production of a play, if earlier). The following abbreviations are used:

f   fiction

p   play

v   verse

These should refer the reader to the appropriate sections of the entry. The lack of one of the three abbreviations indicates that the publications of the entrant are not divided into categories. Revised and translated titles, if different from the original title, are listed with their appropriate dates.

A csodafurulyás juhász (v Illyés), 1954
A família Benoiton (p Machado de Assis), 1867
À la limite de la forêt (f Queneau), 1947
A la orilla del mundo y primer día (v Paz), 1942
À la recherche du temps perdu (f Proust), 1913
À l'ombre des jeunes filles en fleurs (f Proust), 1919
A María el corazón (p Claderón)
A secreto agravio, secreta vengenza (p Calderón)
A semmi közelit (v Illyés), 1983
A tú foka (p Illyés), 1944
A vilanza (p Pirandello), 1917
Abbé Mouret's Transgression (f Zola), 1886
Abbé Sétubal (p Maeterlinck), 1941
Abbesse de Castro (f Stendhal), 1839
Abel Sánchez (f Unamuno), 1917
Abendstunde im Spätherbst (p Dürrenmatt), 1959
Abenteuerliche Simplicissimus Teutsch (f Grimmelshausen)
Abenteurer und die Sängerin (p Hofmannsthal), 1898
Abrojos (v Darío), 1887
Abscheid von den Eltern (f Weiss), 1961
Absent Without Leave (f Böll), 1965
Absolute at Large (f Capek), 1927
Abu Casems tofflor (p Strindberg), 1908
Abuelo (f Pérez Galdós), 1897
Accattone (p Pasolini), 1961
Acciaio (p Pirandello), 1933
Accomplished Maid (p Goldoni)
Accordi e pastelli (v Montale), 1963

Acero de Madrid (p Vega)
Acharneis (p Aristophanes)
Acharnians (p Aristophanes)
Achilles (p Racine)
Achilles auf Skyros (p Hofmannsthal), 1926
Achterloo (p Dürrenmatt), 1983
Acoso (f Carpentier), 1956
Acquainted with the Night (f Böll), 1954
Acté (f Dumas), 1839
Acteurs de bonne foi (p Marivaux), 1947
Acto de contricion (v Tirso)
Ad Heinah (f Agnon), 1952
Ad Pyrhham (v Horace)
Adam and Eve (p Bulgakov), 1971
Adam i Eva (p Bulgakov), 1971
Adam i Eva (p Krleža), 1925
Adam Stvořitel (p Capek), 1927
Adam the Creator (p Capek), 1929
Adam, Where Art Thou? (f Böll), 1955
'Adame Miroir (p Genet), 1948
Adélaïde du Guesclin (p Voltaire), 1734
Adelaide of Brunswick (f Sade), 1954
Adelchi (p Manzoni), 1822
Adelphoe (p Terence)
Aderfofades (p Kazantzakis), 1963
Adieu (f Balzac), 1839
Adieu à l'adolescence (v Mauriac), 1911
Adolescent d'autrefois (f Mauriac), 1969
Adorable Clio (f Giraudoux), 1920
Adultera (f Fontane), 1882
Advantages and Disadvantages of a Name (p Calderón)
Advent (v Rilke), 1898
Advent (p Sprindberg), 1898
Adventures of a Simpleton (f Grimmelshausen), 1962

Adventurous Simplicissimus (f Grimmel-shausen), 1912
Aeneid (v Virgil)
Aeneis (v Virgil)
Affabulazione: Pilade (p Pasolini), 1969
Africa (v Petrarch)
Afrikansky gost' (p Zamyatin), 1963
Aftenrøde (p Hamsun), 1898
After the Banquet (f Mishima), 1963
After the Fire (p Strindberg), 1913
Aftonland (v Lagerkvist), 1953
Agadat ha-Sofer (f Agnon), 1929
Agamemnon (p Aeschylus)
Agamemnon (p Claudel), 1896
Agamemnon (p Seneca)
Agamemnons Tod (p Hauptmann), 1941
Agathe (v Valéry), 1956
Agathocle (p Voltaire), 1777
Âge de raison (f Sartre), 1945
Age of Reason (f Sartre), 1947
Age of the Fish (f Horváth), 1939
Agenor de Mauleon (f Dumas), 1897
Agésilas (p Corneille), 1666
Aglavaine et Sélysette (p Maeterlinck), 1896
Agneau (f Mauriac), 1954
Agnes Bernauer (p Hebbel), 1852
Agnete of Havmanden (p Andersen), 1833
Agreeable Surprise (p Marivaux)
Agua y viento (v Paz), 1959
Ägyptische Helena (p Hofmannsthal), 1928
Ah Q (f Lu Hsun)
Ahasverus' död (f Lagerkvist), 1960
Ahnfrau (p Grillparzer), 1817
Ährenlese (v Hauptmann), 1939
Ai no kawaki (f Mishima), 1950
Aigle a deux têtes (p Cocteau), 1946
Air de l'eau (v Breton), 1934
Airborn (v Paz), 1981
Aisuru (f Kawabata), 1941
Aita Tettauen (f Pérez Galdós), 1905
Ajax (p Sophocles)
Akatsuki no tera (f Mishima), 1970
Akritan Songs (v Sikelianos), 1944
Akuma (f Tanizaki), 1913
Al Kapot ha-Man'ul (f Agnon), 1922
Alafroiskiotos (v Sikelianos), 1909
Albert Savarus (f Balzac), 1842
Albertine disparue (f Proust), 1925
Albine (f Dumas), 1843
Album des vers anciens (v Valéry), 1920
Alcaic Poems (v Hölderlin)
Alcalde de Zalamea (p Calderón)
Alceste (p Pérez Galdós), 1914
Alcestis (p Euripides)

Alchemist (f Balzac), 1861
Alchimiste (p Dumas, Nerval), 1839
Alcools (v Apollinaire), 1913
Alcyone (v D'Annunzio), 1904
Aleph (f Borges), 1949
Alexander the Great (p Racine)
Alexandre Chenevert, caissier (f Roy), 1954
Alexandre le grand (p Racine), 1665
Algavaine and Selysette (p Maeterlinck), 1897
Alì dagli occhi azzurri (f Pasolini), 1965
Aline et Valcour (f Sade), 1795
Alkestis (p Hofmannsthal), 1911
All Citizens Are Soldiers (p Vega)
All for the Best (p Pirandello), 1960
All Is Fair in Love and War (p Musset), 1868
Alladine and Palomides (p Maeterlinck), 1895
Alladine et Palomides (p Maeterlinck), 1894
Allegoria dell'autunno (v D' Annunzio), 1895
Allégories (v Cocteau), 1941
Allegria di naufragi (v Ungaretti), 1919
All'uscita (p Pirandello), 1922
Alma y vida (p Pérez Galdós), 1902
Almas de violeta (v Jiménez), 1900
Almenas de toro (p Vega)
Almida (p Voltaire), 1771
Als der Krieg ausbrach, Als der Krieg zu Ende war (f Böll), 1962
Als der Krieg zu Ende war (p Frisch), 1948
Als vom Butt nur die Gräte geblieben war (v Grass), 1977
Alsureba koso (p Tanizaki), 1923
Alte Geschichten (f Hesse), 1918
Alte Jungfer (p Lessing), 1749
Altro figlio (p Pirandello), 1923
Alzira (p Voltaire), 1736
Alzire (p Voltaire), 1736
Am Leben hin (f Rilke), 1898
Am Weg (f Hesse), 1915
Amadeo I (f Pérez Galdós), 1910
Amal (p Gide), 1922
Amants magnifiques (p Molière), 1670
Amar después de la muerta (p Calderón)
Amar sin saber a quién (p Vega)
Amarilis (v Vega), 1633
Amaury (f Dumas), 1844
Âme à naître (f Dumas), 1844
Amédée (p Ionesco), 1954
Amélie (p Voltaire), 1856
America libera (v Alfieri), 1784
America the Free (v Alfieri), 1975

Americanas (v Machado de Assis), 1875
Amerika (f Kafka), 1927
Amers (v Saint-John Perse), 1957
Âmes mortes (p Adamov), 1960
Ameto (p Boccaccio)
Amica delle mogli (p Pirandello), 1927
Amies (v Verlaine), 1868
Amigo Manso (f Pérez Galdós), 1882
Aminta (p Tasso), 1573
Amita und das Existenzminimum (p Böll), 1955
Amitiés du prince (v Saint-John Perse), 1982
Ammalet Beg (f Dumas), 1859
Amor de Don Perlimpín (p García Lorca), 1933
Amor desatinado (p Vega)
Amor enamorado (p Vega)
Amor y ciencia (p Pérez Galdós), 1905
Amor y oedagogia (f Unamuno), 1902
Amore artigiano (p Goldoni)
Amore e rabbia (p Pasolini), 1969
Amores (v Ovid)
Amori senza amore (f Pirandello), 1894
Amorosa visione (v Boccaccio)
Amorous Fiammetta (f Boccaccio)
Amorous Quarrel (p Molière)
Amour (v Verlaine), 1888
Amour absolu (f Jarry), 1899
Amour en visites (v Jarry), 1898
Amour et la vérité (p Marivaux), 1720
Amour médecin (p Molière), 1665
Amours de l'âge d'or (f Sand), 1871
Amours de Psyché et Cupidon (f La Fontaine), 1669
Amphion (p Valéry), 1931
Amphitryo (p Plautus)
Amphitryon (p Kleist), 1807
Amphitryon (p Molière), 1668
Amphitryon (p Plautus)
Amphitryon 38 (p Giraudoux), 1929
Amy Robsart (p Hugo), 1827
Anabase (v Saint-John Perse), 1924
Anabasis (v Saint-John Perse), 1930
And He Did Hide Himself (p Silone), 1946
And He Hid Himself (p Silone), 1946
And Never Said a Word (f Böll), 1978
And Pippa Dances (p Hauptmann), 1907
And So ad Infinitivum (p Capek), 1923
And Then (f Natsume), 1978
And Where Were You Adam? (f Böll), 1974
Andorra (p Frisch), 1961
André (f Sand), 1835
André del Sarto (p Musset), 1834

Andreas (f Hofmannsthal), 1932
Andrey (v Turgenev), 1846
Andria (p Machiavelli)
Andria (p Terence)
Andromache (p Euripides)
Andromache (p Racine)
Andromaque (p Racine), 1667
Andromède (p Corneille), 1649
Âne (v Hugo), 1880
Âne et le ruisseau (p Musset), 1860
Anecdotes of Destiny (f Dinesen), 1958
Ange (v Valéry), 1946
Ange Heurtebise (v Cocteau), 1926
Ange Pitou (f Dumas), 1853
Angel Comes to Babylon (p Dürrenmatt), 1964
Ángel Guerra (f Pérez Galdós), 1890
Angel Songs (v Rilke), 1958
Angèle (p Dumas), 1833
Angelic Avengers (f Dinesen), 1946
Angelica y Medoro (v Góngora)
Angelo (p Hugo), 1835
Anger (p Ionesco), 1968
Anger of Achilles (v Homer)
Anges du péché (p Giraudoux), 1943
Anges noirs (f Mauriac), 1936
Ångest (v Lagerkvist), 1916
Anikina vremena (f Andrić), 1967
Animal de fondo (v Jiménez), 1949
Anjo de Meia-Noite (p Machado de Assis), 1866
Anna (v Hauptmann), 1921
Anna Karenina (f Tolstoy), 1875
Anna Svärd (f Lagerlöf), 1928
Annabella (p Maeterlinck), 1894
Annals of a Sportsman (f Turgenev)
Année dernière à Marienbad (p Robbe-Grillet), 1961
Année terrible (v Hugo), 1872
Annette et le criminel (f Balzac), 1824
Annibal (p Marivaux), 1720
Anno Domini MCMXXI (v Akhmatova), 1922
Anno fyrtioåtta (p Strindberg), 1881
Annoce faite à Marie (p Claudel), 1912
Annouchka (f Turgenev)
Anonymous Work (p Witkiewicz), 1977
Ansichten eines Clowns (f Böll), 1963
Antérotique (v Du Bellay), 1549
Antigone (p Brecht), 1948
Antigone (p Cocteau), 1922
Antigone (p Sophocles)
Antikrists mirakler (f Lagerlöf), 1897
Antinous (v Pessoa), 1918

(p Brecht), 1957
Aufsteig und Fall der Stadt Mahagonny (p Brecht), 1929
Aufzeichnungen des Malte Laurids Brigge (f Rilke), 1910
August (f Hamsum), 1930
August 1914 (f Solzhenitsyn), 1972
Aulularia (p Plautus)
Aún (v Neruda), 1969
Aurélia (f Nerval), 1855
Aurora en Copacabana (p Calderón)
Aus dem Tagebuch einer Schnecke (f Grass), 1972
Aus goldenem Kelch (v Trakl), 1939
Aus Kinderzeiten (f Hesse), 1968
Ausgefragt (v Grass) 1967
Ausnahme und die Regel (p Brecht), 1938
Aussatz (p Böll), 1969
Autre Tartuffe (p Beaumarchais), 1792
Autumn (f Hamsum), 1922
Auto da Alma (p Vicente)
Auto de Barca da Gloria (p Vicente)
Auto da Barca do Inferno (p Vicente)
Auto da Barca do Purgatório (p Vicente)
Auto da Cananeia (p Vicente)
Auto da Índia (p Vicente)
Auto da Lusitânia (p Vicente)
Auto da sibila Cassandra (p Vicente)
Auto das ciganas (p Vicente)
Auto de Deus Padre e justiça e misericórdia (p Vicente)
Auto de Filodemo (p Camões), 1587
Auto de Monfina Mendes (p Vicente)
Auto dos Enfatriões (p Camões), 1587
Auto dos reis magos (p Vicente)
Auto pastoril castelhano (p Vicente)
Auto-da-Fé (f Canetti), 1946
Autos das barcas (p Vicente)
Avare (p Molière), 1668
Avare fastueux (p Goldoni)
Avaro (p Goldoni)
Avenir est dans les oeufs (p Ionesco), 1957
Aventure d'amour (f Dumas), 1860
Aventures de *** (f Marivaux), 1713
Aventures du dernier Abencérage (f Chateaubriand), 1826
Aveugle de Smyrne (p Corneille), 1637
Aveugles (p Maeterlinck), 1890
Avgust chetyrnadtsatovo (f Solzhenitsyn), 1971
Avventura di Maria (p Svevo), 1960
Avventura di un povero cristiano (p Silone), 1968
Awakening of Spring (p Wedekind), 1909

Axur, King of Ormus (p Beaumarchais), 1813
Aya no tsuzumi (p Mishima), 1952
Ayucuchos (f Pérez Galdós), 1900
Az éden elvesztése (p Illyés), 1967
Azul (v Darío), 1888

Baal (p Brecht), 1922
Bacchae (p Euripides)
Bacchante (p Dumas), 1858
Bacchides (p Plautus)
Bacchus (p Cocteau), 1951
Bachelor (p Turgenev)
Bachelor's Establishment (f Balzac)
Back Roads to Far Towns (v Basho)
Badener Lehrstück vom Einverständnis (p Brecht), 1929
Bagpipers (f Sand), 1890
Bagrovy ostrov (p Bulgakov), 1928
Bahnhof von Zimpren (f Böll), 1959
Bahnwärter Thiel (f Hauptmann), 1888
Bailén (f Pérez Galdós), 1873
Baiser au lépreux (f Mauriac), 1922
Bajazet (p Rachine), 1672
Bajo tu clara sombra (v Paz), 1937
Bál a pusztán (p Illyés), 1972
Baladas de primavera (v Jiménez), 1910
Balade Petrice Kerempuha (v Krleža), 1936
Balaganchik (p Blok), 1906
Balcon (p Genet), 1956
Balcony (p Genet), 1957
Bald Soprano (p Ionesco), 1958
Balthazar (f Balzac), 1859
Ball of Snow (f Dumas), 1895
Bandet (p Strindberg), 1892
Bandlyst (f Lagerlöf), 1918
Bandolero (f Tirso)
Banket u Blitvi (f Krleža), 1938
Bankrupt (f Balzac)
Bannen (f Dazai), 1936
Banqueiro anarquista (f Pessoa), 1964
Banya (p Mayakovsky), 1930
Bara to kaizoku (p Mishima), 1958
Barabbas (f Lagerkvist), 1950
Bárbara (p Pérez Galdós), 1905
Barbarians (p Gorky), 1945
Barbeiro de Sevilha (p Machado de Assis), 1866
Barber of Seville (p Beaumarchais), 1776
Barberine (p Musset), 1853
Barbier de Séville (p Beaumarchais), 1775
Barcarola (v Neruda), 1967
Barchuk (f Natsume), 1943
Bariona (p Sartre), 1940

Bark-Tree (f Queneau), 1968
Barlaán u Josafat (p Vega)
Baron fantôme (p Cocteau), 1943
Baronnie de Muhldorf (p Sand)
Barriére de Clichy (p Dumas), 1851
Baruffe chiozzote (p Goldoni)
Bas-Fonds (p Zamyatin), 1936
Basham and I (f Mann), 1923
Bastard of Mauleon (f Dumas), 1849
Batalla de los Arapiles (f Pérez Galdós),
  1875
Bâtard de Mauléon (f Dumas), 1846
Bathhouse (p Mayakovsky), 1968
Bathilde (p Dumas), 1839
Bathsheba (p Gide), 1951
Batrachoi (p Aristophanes)
Battle of the Arapiles (f Pérez Galdós), 1895
Battre la campagne (v Queneau), 1968
Bear (p Chekhov)
Beast in Man (f Zola)
Beatrix (f Balzac), 1839
Beau Laurence (f Sand), 1870
Beau Tancrede (f Dumas), 1861
Beauty and Sadness (f Kawabata), 1975
Beaux Messieurs de Bois-Doré (f Sand),
  1858
Beaver Coat (p Hauptmann), 1912
Bedbug (p Mayakovsky), 1960
Bednye Lyudi (f Dostoevsky), 1846
Bedroom Philosophers (f Sade), 1965
Beffe della morte e della vita (f Pirandello),
  1902
Before Dawn (p Hauptmann), 1909
Befristeten (p Canetti), 1964
Beg (p Bulgakov), 1957
Beg vremeni (v Akhmatova), 1965
Begegnung (f Mann), 1953
Beim Bau der chinesischen Mauer (f Kafka),
  1931
Bekenntnisse des Hochstaplers Felix Krull
  (f Mann), 1922
Bel-Ami (f Maupassant), 1885
Belaya gvardiya (f Bulgakov), 1927
Belaya staya (v Akhmatova), 1917
Belfagor arcidiavolo (f Machiavelli), 1545
Bella (f Giraudoux), 1926
Bell'Antonio (p Pasolini), 1960
Bella-Vista (f Colette), 1937
Bellavita (p Pirandello), 1928
Belle Captive (p Robbe-Grillet), 1983
Belle et la bête (p Cocteau), 1946
Belle Lisa (f Zola), 1882
Belleza (v Jiménez), 1923
Beloved Returns (f Mann), 1940

Beneath the Wheel (f Hesse), 1968
Beneficent Bear (p Goldoni)
Benia Krik (f Babel), 1935
Benoni (f Hamsum), 1908
Benya Krik (f Babel), 1926
Berecche e la guerra (f Pirandello), 1919
Bérénice (p Racine), 1670
Bergbahn (p Horváth), 1928
Bergroman (f Broch), 1969
Bergwerk zu Falun (p Hofmannsthal), 1899
Berichte an die Freunde (v Hesse), 1961
Berniquel (p Maeterlinck), 1923
Berretto a sonagli (p Pirandello), 1916
Berthold (f Hesse), 1945
Besegrade (v Weiss), 1948
Be-Shuva u-ve-Nahat (f Agnon), 1935
Be-Sod Yesharim (f Agnon), 1921
Bestiare (v Apollinaire), 1911
Bestiario (v Neruda) 1965
Bestiary (v Nerusa), 1965
Besuch der alten Dame (p Dürrenmatt),
  1956
Besy (f Dostoevsky), 1872
Bête humaine (f Zola), 1890
Bethsabé (p Gide), 1912
Betrachtung (f Kafka), 1913
Betrogene (f Mann), 1953
Betrothal (p Maeterlinck), 1919
Betrothed (f Agnon), 1966
Betrothed (f Manzoni), 1834
Betrothed Lovers (f Manzoni), 1828
Better Think Twice about It (f Pirandello),
  1933
Bettine (p Musset), 1851
Between Blue and Blue (f Queneau), 1967
Beware of Smooth Water (p Calderón)
Beyond Recall (f Fontane), 1964
Bez dogmatu (f Sienkiewicz), 1889
Bezdenezh'e (p Turgenev), 1846
Bezimienne dzielo (p Witkiewicz), 1962
Bianche e nere (f Pirandello), 1904
Biberpelz (p Hauptmann), 1893
Biblio-sonnets (v Verlaine), 1913
Bich Bozhy (f Zamyatin), 1939
Biedermann und die Brandstifter (p Frisch),
  1953
Bijoux indiscrets (f Diderot), 1748
Bilá nemoc (p Capek), 1937
Bilanz (p Böll), 1957
Bi-levav Yamin (f Agnon), 1935
Billard um Halbzehn (f Böll), 1959
Billedbog uden Billeder (f Andersen), 1838
Billiards at Half Past Nine (f Böll), 1961
Billy-Club Puppets (p García Lorca), 1963

Bin (f Frisch), 1945
Biografie (p Frisch), 1967
Biography (p Frisch), 1969
Bird of Fate (f Dumas), 1906
Birds (p Aristophanes)
Birds (v Saint-John Perse), 1966
Bismarck (p Wedekind), 1916
Bitoku no yorimeki (f Mishima), 1957
Bitvy (Khlebnikov), 1915
Biyon No Tsuma (f Dazai), 1947
Bizarrías de Belisa (p Vega)
Bjälbo-Jarlen (p Strindberg), 1908
Black (f Dumas), 1858
Black Glove (p Strindberg), 1916
Black Sheep (f Balzac), 1970
Black Snow (f Bulgakov), 1967
Black Swan (f Mann), 1954
Black Tulip (f Dumas), 1854
Blacks (p Genet), 1960
Blanco (v Paz), 1967
Blancs et les bleus (f Dumas), 1867
Blaubart (f Frisch), 1982
Blaue Blume (v Hauptmann), 1924
Blé en herbe (f Colette), 1923
Blechtrommel (f Grass), 1959
Blendung (f Canetti), 1936
Blind (p Maeterlinck), 1891
Blind Beauty (p Pasternak), 1969
Blind Man's Boy, see Lazarillo de Tormes
Blinde (p Dürrenmatt), 1948
Blaznets v tuchakh (v Pasternak), 1914
Blokha (p Zamyatin), 1925
Blood Wedding (p García Lorca), 1947
Blue Bird (p Maeterlinck), 1909
Blue Flowers (f Queneau), 1967
Blue-Apron Statesman (p Holberg), 1885
Bluebeard (f Frisch), 1983
Bluestockings (p Molière)
Blunderers (p Molière)
Blütenzweig (v Hesse), 1945
Bluzhdaiushchiye zvezdy (f Babel), 1926
Bodas de sangre (p García Lorca), 1933
Bodas reales (f Pérez Galdós), 1900
Bödeln (f Lagerkvist), 1933
Bodies and Shadows (f Weiss), 1970
Boeuf sur le toit (p Cocteau), 1920
Bogen des Odysseus (p Hauptmann), 1914
Bölcsek a fán (p Illyés), 1972
Bolhabál (p Illyés), 1962
Bolshim detyam skazki (f Zamyatin), 1922
Bond (p Strindberg), 1930
Bond Honoured (p Vega)
Bonheur (v Verlaine), 1891
Bonheur d'occasion (f Roy), 1945

Bonjour, Monsieur Prassinos (v Queneau), 1972
Bonne Chanson (v Verlaine), 1870
Bonnes (p Genet), 1946
Book of Christopher Columbus (p Claudel), 1930
Book of Sand (f Borges), 1977
Book of Theseus (v Boccaccio)
Boor (p Chekhov)
Boors (p Goldoni)
Boris Godunov (p Pushkin), 1831
Børn av Tiden (f Hamsun), 1913
Bösen Köche (p Grass), 1961
Bosnian Chronicle (f Andrić), 1963
Bosnian Story (f Andrić), 1958
Botchan (f Natsume), 1906
Bottle de sept lieues (p Beaumarchais)
Boule de neige (f Dumas), 1859
Bourgeois gentilhomme (p Molière), 1670
Bourgmestre de Stilmonde (p Maeterlinck), 1919
Bourru bienfaisant (p Goldoni)
Bouton de Rose (p Zola), 1878
Bouvard et Pécuchet (f Flaubert), 1881
Bow of Ulysses (p Hauptmann), 1919
Boy and the Magic (p Colette), 1964
Boži muka (f Capek), 1917
Braendende busk (f Undset), 1930
Braggart Soldier (p Plautus)
Brand (p Ibsen), 1866
Brända tomten (p Strindberg), 1907
Brasil restituido (p Vega), 1950
Brat'ya Karamazovy (f Dostoevsky), 1880
Braut von Messina (p Schiller), 1803
Bread and Wine (f Silone), 1936
Bread of Our Early Years (f Böll), 1957
Bread of Those Early Years (f Böll), 1976
Break of Day (f Colette), 1961
Break of Noon (p Claudel), 1960
Breve sumário da história de Deus (p Vicente)
Bridal Canopy (f Agnon), 1937
Bridal Crown (p Strindberg), 1912
Bride of Messina (p Schiller), 1837
Bridge on the Drina (f Andrić), 1959
Brigand (f Dumas), 1897
Britannicus (p Racine), 1669
Broken Pitcher (p Kleist), 1961
Bronze Horesman (v Pushkin)
Brot der frühen Jahre (f Böll), 1955
Brothers (p Terence)
Brothers Karamazov (f Dostoevsky), 1912
Brothers Menaechmus (p Plautus)
Brotladen (p Brecht), 1967
Brott och brott (p Strindberg), 1899

Brücke von Berczaba (p Böll), 1952
Bruden fra Lammermoor (p Andersen), 1832
Bruderzwist in Habsburg (p Grillparzer) 1872
Brutus (p Voltaire), 1730
Brylluppet ved Como-søen (p Andersen), 1849
Buch der Bilder (v Rilke), 1902
Buch der Leidenschaft (f Hauptmann), 1930
Büchse der Pandora (p Wedekind), 1904
Bucolics (v Virgil)
Bucoliques (v Queneau), 1947
Buddenbrooks (f Mann), 1900
Buddha (p Kazantzakis), 1983
Bufera e altro (v Montale), 1956
Bugiardo (p Goldoni)
Bug-Jargal (f Hugo), 1826
Bunte Buch (v Hauptmann), 1888
Bunte Steine (f Stifter), 1853
Buona famiglia (p Goldoni)
Buona figliuola (p Goldoni)
Burburo benefico (p Goldoni)
Bureaucracy (f Balzac), 1889
Bürger als Edelmann (p Hofmannsthal), 1918
Bürgergeneral (p Goethe), 1793
Burgomaster of Stilmonde (p Maeterlinck), 1918
Burgraves (p Hugo), 1943
Burlador de Sevilla (p Tirso)
Burlas veras (p Vega)
Burned House (p Strindberg), 1961
Burning Bush (f Undset), 1932
Bushuko hiwa (f Tanizaki), 1935
Butterfly of Dinard (f Montale), 1970
Butterfly's Evil Spell (p García Lorca), 1963
By Judgment of the Court (p Pirandello), 1928
By Order of the King (f Hugo), 1870
By the Open Sea (f Strindberg), 1913
Bygmester Solness (p Ibsen), 1892
Bystander (f Gorky), 1938

Cabal and Love (p Schiller), 1795
Cabal of Hypocrites (p Bulgakov), 1972
Caballero encantado (f Pérez Galdós), 1909
Caballero de Olmedo (p Vega)
Cabellos de Absalón (p Calderón)
Cabinet des antiques (f Balzac), 1839
Cabiria (p D'Annunzio), 1914
Caccia al lupo (p Verga), 1902
Caccia alla volpe (p Verga), 1902
Caccia di Diana (v Boccaccio)

Cachemire vert (p Dumas), 1849
Cada uno para si (p Calderón)
Cadio (f Sand), 1868
Cádiz (f Pérez Galdós), 1874
Cahiers d'André Walter (f Gide), 1891
Calderon (p Pasolini), 1973
Caligula (p Dumas), 1944
Caligula (p Dumas), 1837
Calisto y Melibea, Comedia (p Rojas), 1499
Calligrammes (v Apollinaire), 1918
Caminho da porta (p Machado de Assis), 1862
Camino de Santiago (f Carpentier), 1958
Campagne de Louis XIV (v Racine), 1730
Campagnes philosophiques (f Prévost), 1741
Campaña del Maestrazgo (f Pérez Galdós), 1899
Campiello (p Goldoni)
Cancer Ward (f Solzhenitsyn), 1968
Canción de gesta (v Neruda), 1960
Cancionero: Diario poético (v Unamuno), 1942
Canciones (v García Lorca), 1927
Candidat (p Flaubert), 1874
Candide (f Voltaire), 1759
Candle in the Wind (p Solzhenitsyn), 1973
Cánovas (f Pérez Galdós), 1912
Cantate à trois voix (v Claudel), 1931
Cantatrice chauve (p Ionesco), 1950
Canterbury Tales (p Pasolini), 1972
Cantique des cantiques (p Giraudoux), 1939
Cantique des cantiques (v Voltaire), 1759
Cantiques spirituels (v Racine), 1694
Canto a la Argentina (v Darío), 1914
Canto errante (v Darío), 1907
Canto general (v Neruda), 1950
Canto para Bolívar (v Neruda), 1941
Canto popolare (v Pasolini), 1954
Cantos ceremoniales (v Neruda), 1961
Cantos de vida y esperanza (v Darío), 1905
Canzone ad Angelo Mai (v Leopardi), 1820
Canzone di Garibaldi (v D'Annunzio), 1901
Cap de Bonne-espérance (v Cocteau), 1919
Capitaine Burle (f Zola), 1882
Capitaine Paul (f Dumas), 1838
Capitaine Richard (f Dumas), 1858
Capriccio all'italiana (p Pasolini), 1968
Caprice (p Musset), 1840
Caprices de Marianne (p Musset), 1834
Captain Bombastes Thunderton (p Holberg)
Captain Paul (f Dumas), 1848
Captain's Daughter (f Pushkin)
Captain's Verses (v Neruda), 1972
Captive (f Proust), 1929

Captivi (p Plautus)
Carbonari della montagna (f Verga), 1861
Cardenal de Belén (p Vega)
Carlos V en Francia (p Vega)
Carlos VI en La Rápita (f Pérez Galdós), 1905
Carmosine (p Musset), 1853
Carnevale dei morti (f Pirandello), 1919
Carnival (f Dinesen), 1977
Carriers (p Vicente)
Carro armata dell'settembre (p Pasolini), 1960
Cas intéressant (p Camus), 1955
Casa con dos puertas malas es de guardar (p Caderón)
Casa de Bernarda Albu (p García Lorca), 1945
Casa dei doganieri (v Montale), 1932
Casa nova (p Goldoni)
Casa Velha (v Machado de Assis), 1968
Cassandra the Sibyl (p Vicente)
Cassaria (p Ariosto), 1508
Castigo del discreto (p Vega)
Cashier (f Roy), 1955
Casina (p Plautus)
Casket Comedy (p Plautus)
Cassandra the Sibyl (p Vicente)
Cassiria (p Ariosto), 1508
Castigo del discreto (p Vega)
Castigo del penséque (p Tirso)
Castigo sin vengenza (p Vega)
Castle (f Kafka), 1930
Castle in the Wilderness (f Sand), 1856
Castle of Eppstein (f Dumas), 1903
Castle to Castle (f Céline), 1968
Castle Wetterstein (p Wedekind), 1952
Cat (f Colette), 1936
Cat and Mouse (f Grass), 1963
Catalina (p Dumas), 1848
Catalina (p Ibsen), 1850
Cataline (p Ibsen), 1921
Catherine Blum (f Dumas), 1854
Catherine de Médicis expliquée (f Balzac), 1845
Catherine Howard (p Dumas), 1834
Catilina (p Voltaire), 1753
Caucasian Chalk Circle (p Brecht), 1948
Cavalier of the Rose (p Hofmannsthal), 1963
Cavaliere e la dama (p Goldoni)
Cavalleria rusticana (p Verga), 1884
Cavallo nella luna (f Pirandello), 1918
Caves du Vatican (f Gide), 1914
Ce formidable bordel (p Ionesco), 1973

Ce qui était perdu (f Mauriac), 1930
Cece (p Pirandello), 1920
Cécile (f Dumas), 1844
Cecile (f Fontane), 1887
Celebrated Crimes (f Dumas), 1896
Celestina (p Rojas)
Celia en los infiernos (p Pérez Galdós) 1913
Celos aún de aire matan (p Calderón)
Celos aún de aire matan (p Calderón)
Cena de Baltazar (p Calderón)
Cenci (p Artaud), 1935
Cenci (f Stendhal), 1839
Ceneri di Gramsci (v Pasolini), 1957
Cent mille milliards de poèmes (v Queneau), 1961
Centana (v Paz), 1969
Centenaire (f Balzac), 1822
Cérémonial espagnol du phénix (v Cocteau), 1961
Ces enfants de ma vie (f Roy), 1977
César-Antéchrist (p Jarry), 1895
Césarine Dietrich (f Sand), 1871
Cet été qui chantait (f Roy), 1972
Cette heure qui est entre le printemps et l'été (v Claudel), 1913
Chair (v Verlaine), 1896
Chair et le sang (f Mauriac), 1920
Chairs (p Ionesco), 1958
Chaises (p Ionesco), 1952
Chambre d'hôtel (f Colette), 1940
Chambre éclairée (f Colette), 1920
Champs magnétiques (v Breton), 1920
Chandelier (p Musset), 1840
Changed Bridgegroom (p Holberg), 1950
Chansons des rues et des bois (v Hugo), 1865
Chansons pour elle (v Verlaine), 1891
Chant d'amour (p Genet), 1950
Chant pour un équinoxe (v Saint-John Perse), 1975
Chante par celle qui fut la... (v Saint-John Perse), 1970
Chants du crépuscule (v Hugo), 1835
Chants secrets (v Genet), 1947
Chapter the Last (f Hamsum), 1929
Character in Distress (f Pirandello), 1938
Chariot d'enfant (p Nerval), 1850
Charlemagne's Hostage (p Hauptmann) 1919
Charles le téméraire (f Dumas), 1857
Charles VII chez ses grands vassaux (p Dumas), 1831
Charles the Bold (f Dumas), 1860
Charles XII (p Strindberg), 1955
Charlot (p Voltaire), 1767

Charlotte Löwensköld (f Lagerlöf), 1925
Charme ou poèmes (v Valéry), 1922
Charmides (Plato)
Charterhouse of Parma (f Stendhal), 1925
Chartreuse de Parme (f Stendhal), 1839
Chasse au Chastre (f Dumas), 1841
Chasse et l'amour (p Dumas), 1825
Chasseur de Sauvagine (f Dumas), 1859
Château d'Eppstein (f Dumas), 1844
Château des coeurs (p Flaubert), 1874
Château des Désertes (f Sand), 1851
Château étoilé (v Breton), 1937
Chateau-Rouge (f Dumas), 1859
Châtiments (v Hugo), 1853
Chatte (f Colette), 1933
Chatterton (p Vigny), 1835
Chayka (p Chekhov), 1896
Cheat (f Capek), 1941
Cheats of Scapin (p Molière)
Chee-Chee (p Pirandello), 1928
Chelovek (v Gorky), 1902
Chemins de la liberté (f Sartre), 1945
Chemins de la mer (f Mauriac), 1939
Chêne et chien (v Queneau), 1937
Cher Menteur (p Cocteau), 1960
Chéri series (f Colette)
Cherry Orchard (p Chekhov)
Cheval troyen (f Queneau), 1948
Chevalier de la charrette (v Chrétien)
Chevalier de Maison—Rouge (f Dumas),
  1846
Chevalier Des Grieux et de Manon Lescaut,
  Histoire du (f Prévost), 1733
Chevalier d'Harmental (f Dumas), 1843
Chevalier d'Olmedo (p Camus), 1957
Chevalier du Lansquenet (p Dumas), 1850
Chevalier du Lion (v Chrétien)
Chevaliers de la table ronde (p Cocteau),
  1937
Chicot the Jester (f Dumas), 1857
Chien à la mandoline (v Queneau), 1958
Chiendent (f Queneau), 1933
Chiffre (v Cocteau), 1952
Chijin no ai (f Tanizaki), 1925
Child of Our Time (f Horváth), 1938
Child of Pleasure (f D'Annunzio), 1898
Childhood (f Pasternak), 1941
Childhood of Luvers (f Pasternak), 1945
Childhood's Dreams (p Dumas), 1881
Children and Fools (f Mann), 1928
Children Are Civilians Too (f Böll), 1970
Children of Heracles (p Euripides)
Children of the Age (f Hamsun), 1924
Children of the Game (f Cocteau), 1955

Children of the Soil (f Sienkiewicz), 1895
Children of the Sun (p Gorky), 1912
Chimera (v D'Annunzio), 1890
Chimeras (v Nerval), 1966
Chimères (v Nerval), 1854
Chinese Wall (p Frisch), 1961
Chinesische Mauer (p Frisch), 1946
Chinsetsu yumiharizuki (p Mishima), 1969
Chips Are Down (p Sartre), 1947
Choéphores (p Claudel), 1920
Choerophoroi (p Aeschylus)
Choix des élues (f Giraudoux), 1938
Chotki (v Akhmatova), 1913
Chouans (f Balzac), 1834
Christ Legends (f Lagerlöf), 1908
Christ of Velazquez (v Unamuno), 1951
Christ Recrucified (f Kazantzakis), 1954
Christinas Heimreise (p Hofmannsthal), 1910
Christine (p Dumas), 1830
Christmas Party (p Holberg), 1950
Christoforos Kolomvos (p Kazantzakis),
  1955
Christopher Columbus (p Kazantzakis), 1969
Christos (p Kazantzakis), 1928
Christos voskres (v Bely), 1918
Christos Xanastavronetai (f Kazantzakis),
  1954
Chronicles of Bustos Domecq (f Borges),
  1979
Chronique (v Saint-John Perse), 1960
Chrysalidas (v Machado de Assis), 1864
Chudaki (p Gorky), 1910
Churl (p Plautus)
Chute (f Camus), 1956
Ciascuno a suo modo (p Pirandello), 1924
Ciclopu (p Pirandello), 1919
Cid (p Corneille), 1637
Cien mil hijos de San Luís (f Pérez Gladós),
  1877
Ci-gîtt (v Artaud), 1947
Cinna (p Corneille), 1640
Cinnamon Shops (f Schulz), 1963
Cinna's Conspiracy (p Corneille)
Cinq grandes odes (v Claudel), 1910
Cinq-Mars (f Vigny), 1825
Circassian Boy (v Lermontov)
Circe (v Vega), 1624
Cistellaria (p Plautus)
Cities of the Plain (f Proust), 1927
Citizen Turned Gentleman (p Molière)
Città del mondo (f Vittorini), 1969
Città del silenzio (v D'Annunzio), 1926
Città morta (p D'Annunzio), 1898
Civil War of Geneva (v Voltaire), 1769

Clair de lune (f Maupassant), 1884
Clair de terre (v Breton), 1923
Clair-obscur (v Cocteau), 1954
Claude's Confession (f Zola), 1888
Claudie (p Sand), 1851
Claudine series (f Colette)
Claudine von Villa Bella (p Goethe), 1780
Clavigo (p Goethe), 1774
Cligès (v Chrétien)
Clitandre (p Corneille), 1630
Clitopho (Plato)
Clizia (p Machiavelli), 1525
Clorinda (f Zola), 1880
Clothes Maketh Man (f Keller)
Clotilde de Lusignan (f Balzac), 1822
Cloud That Lifted (p Maeterlinck), 1923
Clouds (p Aristophanes)
Clown (f Böll), 1965
Coffee House (p Voltaire), 1760
Coffer (p Ariosto)
Coiners (f Gide), 1950
Colère (p Ionesco), 1962
Colin et Colette (p Beaumarchais)
Colleague Crampton (p Hauptmann), 1914
Collier de la Reine (f Dumas), 1849
Colombe (f Dumas), 1851
Colonel's Photograph (f Ionesco), 1967
Colonie (p Marivaux), 1729
Colpevole (v Montale), 1966
Column of Infamy (f Manzoni), 1964
Combat avec l'ange (f Giraudoux), 1934
Come prima, meglio di prima (p Pirandello), 1920
Come tu mi vuoi (p Pirandello), 1930
Comédia de Rubena (p Vicente)
Comédia do viúvo (p Vicente)
Comédia sin título (p García Lorca), 1978
Comédia sobre a divisa da cidade de Coimbra (p Vicente)
Comédie des Tuileries (p Corneille), 1635
Comédie du bonheur (p Cocteau), 1940
Comédie humaine (f Balzac)
Comedie i det Grønne (p Andersen), 1840
Comédiens sans le savoir (f Balzac), 1846
Comedy of Vanities (p Canetti), 1982
Comic Theatre (p Goldoni)
Coming of Peace (p Hauptmann), 1900
Comizi d'amore (p Pasolini), 1965
Commander of Ocaña (p Vega)
Commare secca (p Pasolini), 1962
Comme nous avons été (p Adamov), 1953
Commedia (v Dante)
Commemoration Masque (p Hauptmann), 1919

Commère (p Marivaux), 1741
Common Story (f Goncharov), 1894
Como elas são tôdas (p Machado de Assis), 1873
Compagnon du tour de France (f Sand), 1841
Compagnons de Jéhu (f Dumas), 1857
Companion of the Tour of France (f Sand), 1847
Company of Jehu (f Dumas), 1894
Compassion (f Pérez Galdós), 1962
Complaintes (v Laforgue), 1885
Comrades (f Gorky), 1907
Comrades (p Strindberg), 1913
Comte de Monte-Cristo (f Dumas), 1844
Comte de Morcerf (p Dumas), 1851
Comte de Moret (f Dumas), 1866
Comte Hermann (p Dumas), 1849
Comtesse de Charny (f Dumas), 1852
Comtesse de Rudolstadt (f Sand), 1843
Comtesse de Salisbury (f Dumas), 1839
Comtesse de Tende (f Lafayette), 1724
Comtesse d'Escarbagnas (p Molière), 1672
Con la penna d'oro (p Svevo), 1960
Conceited Young Ladies (p Molière)
Concierto barroco (f Carpentier), 1974
Concile féerique (v Laforgue), 1886
Condemned of Altona (p Sartre), 1961
Condenado por desconfiado (p Tirso)
Condenados (p Pérez Galdós), 1894
Condition humaine (f Malraux), 1933
Condor (f Stifter), 1946
Condor et le morpion (v Apollinaire), 1931
Confession (f Gorky), 1909
Confession de Claude (f Zola), 1865
Confession d'un enfant du siècle (f Musset), 1836
Confession d'un jeune fille (f Sand), 1864
Confession of a Child of the Century (f Musset), 1892
Confessions (Augustine)
Confession of a Mask (f Mishima), 1958
Confessions of Felix Krull (f Mann), 1955
Confessions of Zeno (f Svevo), 1930
Configurations (v Paz), 1971
Conflagration (p Hauptmann), 1913
Congreso (f Borges), 1970
Congress (f Borges), 1974
Congresswomen (p Aristophanes)
Connaissance du temps (v Claudel), 1904
Connétable de Bourbon (p Dumas), 1849
Conquérants (f Malraux), 1928
Conquerors (f Malraux), 1929
Conquest of Plassans (f Zola), 1887

Crónicas de Bustos Domecq (f Borges), 1967
Crop-Ear Jacquot (f Dumas), 1903
Cross Old Devil (p Menander)
Cross Purpose (p Camus), 1947
Crucifixion (v Cocteau), 1946
Crusts (p Claudel), 1945
Cuaderno San Martin (v Borges), 1929
Cuerdo loco (p Vega)
Curculio (p Plautus)
Curé de village (f Balzac), 1841
Curée (f Zola), 1872
Curioso accidente (p Goldoni)
Cuttlefish (p Witkiewicz), 1969
Cyclops (p Euripides)

Da Spanierne var her (p Andersen), 1865
Dachniki (p Gorky), 1904
Daidalos stin Criti (p Sikelianos), 1943
Dal tuo al mio (p Verga), 1906
Dama boba (p Vega)
Dama duende (p Calderón)
Damask Drum (p Mishima), 1957
Dame à la licorne (p Cocteau), 1953
Dame de Monsoreau (f Dumas), 1846
Dame Kobold (p Hofmannsthal), 1920
Dames du Bois du Boulogne (p Cocteau), 1945
Dames vertes (f Sand), 1857
Danae (p Hofmannsthal), 1952
Dance of Death (p Strindberg) 1912
Dangerous Acquaintances (f Laclos)
Dangerous Connections (f Laclos)
Dangerous Game (f Dürrenmatt), 1960
Dániel az övei közt (p Illyés), 1976
Daniella (f Sand), 1857
Dans la foule (f Colette), 1918
Dans le labyrinthe (f Robbe-Grillet), 1959
Dans les limbes (v Verlaine), 1894
Dans de Sophocle (v Cocteau), 1912
Danton's Death (p Büchner)
Dantons Tod (p Büchner), 1835
Danusia (f Sienkiewicz), 1900
Daphné (f Vigny), 1912
Dark and the Light (f Vittorini), 1961
Dark Angels (f Mauriac), 1951
Dasu Gemaine (f Dazai), 1940
Daughter of Eve (f Balzac)
Daughter of Jorio (p D'Annunzio), 1907
Daughters of Fire (f Nerval), 1923
Davor (p Grass), 1969
Day of the Turbins (f Bulgakov), 1934
Days of Hope (f Malraux), 1938
Days of the Commune (p Brecht), 1971

De Cartago a Sagunto (f Pérez Galdós), 1911
De Fuerteventura a París (v Unamuno), 1925
De Rerum Natura (v Lucretius)
Dead City (p D'Annunzio), 1900
Dead Souls (f Gogol), 1887
Dead Woman's Wish (f Zola), 1902
Deadly Game (p Dürrenmatt), 1966
Dean of Coleraine (f Prévost)
Dearest Father (f Kafka), 1954
Death and Devil (p Wedekind), 1952
Death and the Fool (p Hofmannsthal), 1914
Death and the Lover (f Hesse), 1932
Death in Midsummer (f Mishima), 1966
Death in the Garden (p Queneau), 1956
Death in Venice (f Mann), 1925
Death of Ahasuerus (f Lagerkvist), 1962
Death of Tintagiles (p Maeterlinck), 1895
Death of Titian (p Hofmannsthal), 1920
Death of Vergil (f Broch), 1945
Death on the Installment Plan (f Céline), 1938
Deathwatch (p Genet), 1954
Débâcle (f Zola), 1892
Debauched Hospodar (f Apollinaire), 1958
Debet ock kredit (p Strindberg), 1892
Debit and Credit (p Strindberg), 1913
Début dans la vie (f Balzac), 1844
Decadence (f Gorky), 1927
Decameron (f Boccaccio)
Decameron (p Pasolini), 1971
Décapitée (p Colette), 1941
Decay of the Angel (f Mishima), 1974
Decline (v Trakl), 1952
Dédicaces (v Verlaine), 1890
Del trionfi della libertà (v Manzoni), 1878
Délire à deux (p Ionesco), 1962
Delo Artamonvykh (f Gorky), 1925
Delphic Word (v Sikelianos), 1928
Deluge (f Sienkiewicz), 1892
Demesne of the Swan (v Tsvetayeva), 1980
Demian (f Hesse), 1919
Demoiselles de Saint-Cyr (p Dumas), 1843
Demon (v Lermontov), 1842
Démon de la connaissance (f Mauriac), 1928
Démon du foyer (p Sand), 1852
Dénouement imprévu (p Marivaux), 1724
Dentelle d'éternité (v Cocteau), 1953
Dépit amoureux (p Molière), 1656
Dépositaire (p Voltaire), 1772
Député d'Arcis (f Balzac), 1854
Députés de la Halle (p Beaumarchais)

Deputy of Arcis (f Balzac), 1896
Derecho de asilo (f Carpentier) 1972
Dernier Amour (f Sand), 1867
Dernier Chouan (f Balzac), 1829
Dernier Jour d'un condamné (f Hugo), 1829
Dernière Aldini (f Sand), 1838
Dernière Fée (f Balzac), 1823
Dernière Incarnation de Vautrin (f Balzac), 1848
Derniers jours (f Queneau), 1935
Derniers jours 1919 (v Ungaretti), 1947
Desdén vengado (p Vega)
Desdicha de la voz (p Calderón)
Desdichada Estefania (p Vega)
Desencantos (p Machado de Assis), 1861
Désert de l'amour (f Mauriac), 1925
Desert of Love (f Mauriac), 1929
Desheredada (f Pérez Galdós), 1881
Destinées (v Vigny), 1864
Destinies (f Mauriac), 1929
Destins (f Mauriac), 1928
Destvo (f Babel)
Deti solntsa (p Gorky), 1905
Detstvo Lyuvers (f Pasternak), 1922
Deuses de casaca (p Machado de Assis), 1865
Deutschland (v Heine), 1844
Deux Amis (p Beaumarchais), 1770
Deux Frères (f Balzac), 1842
Deux Frères (f Sand), 1875
Deux poètes (f Balzac), 1837
Devil and the Good Lord (p Sartre), 1960
Devils (f Dostoevsky), 1953
Devil's Church (f Machado de Assis), 1977
Devil's Pool (f Sand), 1861
Devil's Yard (f Andrić), 1962
Devin du village (p Rousseau), 1752
Devoción de la cruz (p Calderón)
Dévotion à la croix (p Camus), 1953
Devotion of the Cross (p Calderón)
Devotional Songs (v Novalis)
Devushka i smert (v Gorky), 1917
Devyat'sot pyaty (v Pasternak), 1927
Diable aux champs (f Sand), 1856
Diable et le bon dieu (p Sartre), 1951
Diaboliad (f Bulgakov), 1972
Dialogue entre un prêtre et un moribund (f Sade), 1926
Diamant (p Hebbel), 1847
Diana and Tuda (p Pirandello), 1950
Diana e la Tuda (p Pirandello), 1926
Diane (f Dumas), 1901
Diario de un poeta recién casado (v Jiménez), 1917

Diario de poeta y mar (v Jiménez), 1948
Diario del '71 e del '72 (v Montale), 1973
Diary of a Mad Old Man (f Tanizaki), 1965
Diary of Antoine Roquentin (f Sartre), 1949
Dicha y desdicha del nombre (p Calderón)
Dictionary of Accepted Ideas (f Flaubert), 1954
Dictionnaire des ideés reçues (f Flaubert), 1966
Didactic Play of Baden-Baden on Consent (p Brecht), 1960
Diderich Menschenschreck (p Holberg)
Diderich the Terrible (p Holberg)
Diesseits (f Hesse), 1907
Dieu (v Hugo), 1891
Dieu bleu (p Cocteau), 1912
Dieu dispose (f Dumas), 1851
Difficult Man (p Hofmannsthal), 1963
Dimanche de la vie (f Queneau), 1951
Dineros son calidad (p Vega)
Dirty Hands (p Sartre), 1949
Disbanded Officer (p Lessing)
Discours du grand sommeil (v Cocteau), 1920
Discours sur les misères de ce temps (v Ronsard), 1562
Discourse on... Viet Nam (p Weiss), 1970
Discovery of the New World by Christopher Columbus (p Vega)
Dishonoured Irreclaimable (f Schiller), 1826
Disinherited Lady (f Pérez Galdós), 1957
Diskurs über...Viet Nam (p Weiss), 1967
Dismissal of the Greek Envoys (p Kochanowski), 1918
Dispute (p Marivaux), 1744
Disputed Inheritance (f Dumas), 1847
Distance, The Shadows (v Hugo), 1981
Distressed Mother (p Racine)
Dithyramb of the Rose (v Sikelianos), 1939
Dithyrambos tou Rhodou (v Sikelianos), 1934
Divan (v Garcia Lorca), 1974
Divina Filotea (p Calderón)
Divine (p Colette), 1935
Divine Comedy (v Dante)
Djinn (f Robbe-Grillet), 1981
Dlya pol'zy dela (f Solzhenitsyn), 1963
Dmitri Roudine (f Turgenev)
Dni Turbinykh (f Bulgakov), 1927
Dobrý voják Švejk (f Hašek), 1912
Docteur mystérieux (f Dumas), 1872
Docteur Pascal (f Zola), 1893
Doctor Basilius (f Dumas), 1860

Dr. Brodie's Report (f Borges), 1972
Doctor Centeno (f Pérez Galdós), 1883
Doctor Faustus (f Mann), 1948
Doctor in Spite of Himself (p Molière)
Doctor Last in His Chariot (p Molière)
Doctor Love (p Molière)
Doctor Pascal (f Zola), 1893
Doctor Simple (p Vega)
Doctor Zhivago (f Pasternak), 1958
Doctors All (p Vega)
Doctor's Duty (p Pirandello), 1928
Dödsdansen (p Strindberg), 1901
Dog in the Manger (p Vega)
Dog Years (f Grass), 1965
Doke No Hana (f Dazai), 1937
Doktor Faustus (f Mann), 1947
Doktor Murkes gesammeltes Schweigen
  (f Böll), 1958
Doktor Zhivago (f Pasternak), 1957
Dolore (v Ungaretti), 1947
Dölt vitorla (v Illyés), 1965
Doll's House (p Ibsen), 1890
Dom Casmurro (f Machado de Assis), 1899
Dom Juan (p Molière), 1665
Dominion of Darkness (p Tolstoy)
Don Candeloro e c.i (f Verga), 1894
Don Carlos (p Schiller), 1787
Don Duardos (p Vicente)
Don Garcie de Navarre (p Molière), 1661
Don Gil de las calzas verdes (p Tirso)
Don Juan (p Brecht), 1953
Don Juan (p Frisch), 1953
Don Juan Comes Back from the Wars
  (p Horváth), 1978
Don Juan de Marana (p Dumas), 1836
Don Juan (in the Russian Manner)
  (p Chekhov)
Don Juan kommt dem Krieg (p Horváth),
  1952
Don Kikhot (p Bulgakov), 1940
Don Pèdre (p Voltaire), 1775
Don Quixote de la Mancha (f Cervantes),
  1605
Don Sanche d'Aragon (p Corneille), 1649
Doña Lambra (p Unamuno), 1913
Doña Perfecta (f Pérez Galdós), 1876
Doña Rosita la soltera (p García Lorca),
  1935
Doña Rosita the Spinster (p García Lorca),
  1963
Donna del Fiume (p Pasolini), 1954
Donne di Messina (f Vittorini), 1949
Donne gelose (p Goldoni)
Door Must Be Either Open or Shut

(p Musset)
Doppelgänger (p Dürrenmatt), 1960
Dorci (f Sade), 1881
Dorf ohne Männer (p Horváth), 1937
Dorotea (f Vega), 1632
Dorothea Angermann (p Hauptmann), 1926
Dorval (p Diderot)
Dos poemas afrocubanos (v Carpentier),
  1929
Dostigaeff and the Others (p Gorky), 1937
Dostigayev i drugiye (p Gorky), 1933
Double (f Dostoevsky), 1917
Double Act (p Ionesco), 1979
Double Inconstance (p Marivaux), 1723
Double Infidelity (p Marivaux)
Dove (f Dumas), 1906
Dovere di medico (p Pirandello), 1912
Downfall (f Zola), 1892
Doyen de Killerine (f Prévost), 1735
Dózsa György (p Illyés), 1954
Drac (p Sand), 1864
Draft of Shadows (v Paz), 1979
Dragon (f Zamyatin), 1967
Dragonne (f Jarry), 1943
Dragontea (v Vega), 1598
Drame au bord de la mer (f Balzac), 1835
Drame dans les prisons (f Balzac), 1847
Drames galants (f Dumas), 1860
Drammi intimi (f Verga), 1884
Dram-Shop (f Zola), 1897
Drayman Henschel (p Hauptmann), 1913
Dream (f Zola), 1893
Dream Is Life (p Grillparzer), 1946
Dream of a Spring Morning (p D'Annun-
  zio), 1911
Dream of an Autumn Sunset (p D'Annun-
  zio), 1903
Dream Play (p Strindberg), 1912
Dreamers (f Hamsun), 1921
Dreams and Life (f Nerval), 1933
Dreamtigers (v Borges), 1963
Drei Frauen (f Musil), 1924
Dreigroschenoper (p Brecht), 1928
Dreigroschenroman (f Brecht), 1934
Drink (f Zola), 1903
Droit de seigneur (p Voltaire), 1763
Drömspel (p Strindberg), 1907
Dronning Tamara (p Hamsun), 1903
Dronningen paa 16 aar (p Andersen), 1844
Drottningar i Kungahälla (f Lagerlöf), 1899
Drums in the Night (p Brecht), 1966
Du côté de chez Swann (f Proust), 1913
Du fährst zu oft nach Heidelberg (f Böll),
  1979

Dubrovsky (f Pushkin), 1841
Duc d'Alençon (p Voltaire), 1821
Duc de Foix (p Voltaire), 1752
Duchess of Langeais (f Balzac), 1946
Due gemelli veneziani (p Goldoni)
Due maschere (f Pirandello), 1914
Duel (f Chekhov), 1892
Duel (p Ionesco), 1979
Duel of Angels (p Giraudoux), 1958
Duellen (f Weiss), 1953
Duendes de la camarilla (f Pérez Galdós), 1903
Duineser Elegien (v Rilke), 1923
Duino Elegies (v Rilke), 1939
Dukkehjem (p Ibsen), 1879
Dumb Lady (p Molière)
D'un château à l'autre (f Céline), 1957
Dunungen (p Lagerlöf), 1914
Duo (f Colette), 1934
Duque de Viseo (p Vega)
Dvärgen (f Lagerkvist), 1944
Dvenadtsat (v Blok), 1918
Dvoryanskoye gnezdo (f Turgenev), 1859
Dvoynik (f Dostoevsky), 1846
Dwarf (f Lagerkvist), 1945
Dyadya Vanya (p Chekhov) 1896
D'yavoliada (f Bulgakov), 1925
Dym (f Turgenev), 1867
Dyskolos (p Menander)
Dziady (p Mickiewicz), 1823

E domani, lunedi (f Pirandello), 1917
Each in His Own Way (p Pirandello), 1923
Eagle Has Two Heads (p Cocteau), 1948
Eagle or Sun? (v Paz), 1970
Earl Birger of Bjälbo (p Strindberg), 1956
Early Frost (p Rilke), 1979
Earth (f Zola)
Earth Spirit (p Wedekind), 1914
Easter (p Strindberg), 1912
Échange (p Claudel), 1901
Échange (p Voltaire), 1736
Echec et Mat (p Dumas), 1846
Eclogae (v Virgil)
Eclogues (v Virgil)
Eco y Narciso (p Calderón)
École des femmes (f Gide), 1929
École des femmes (p Molière), 1662
École des indifférents (f Giraudoux), 1934
École des maris (p Molière), 1661
École des ménages (p Balzac), 1907
École des mères (p Marivaux), 1732
Écossaise (p Voltaire), 1760
Écoute, ma fille (v Claudel), 1934

Écueil du sage (p Voltaire), 1762
Écue-yamba-Ó! (f Carpentier), 1933
Ed ogli si nascose (p Silone), 1944
Edelmira (f Darío)
Eden et après (p Robbe-Grillet), 1970
Edipo Re (p Pasolini), 1967
Edo and Enam (f Agnon), 1966
Education sentimentale (f Flaubert), 1869
Edward II (p Brecht), 1966
Effi Briest (f Fontane), 1895
Eglantine (f Giraudoux), 1927
Église (p Céline), 1933
Egmont (p Goethe), 1784
Egmont (p Schiller), 1796
Egy év (v Illyés), 1945
Egyptian Stamp (f Mandelstam), 1965
Ehe des Herrn Mississippi (p Dürrenmatt), 1952
Ehrengard (f Dinesen), 1963
Eiffel Tower Wedding Party (p Cocteau), 1963
Einsame Menschen (p Hauptmann), 1891
Eirei no Koe (f Mishima), 1966
Eirene (p Aristophanes)
Ekklesiazousai (p Aristophanes)
Eksi nychtes sten Akropole (f Seferis), 1974
Elective Affinities (f Goethe)
Electra (p Euripides)
Electra (p Giraudoux), 1957
Electra (p Hofmannsthal), 1963
Electra (p Pérez Galdós), 1901
Electra (p Sophocles)
Electra (p Giraudoux), 1937
Elegía (v Neruda), 1974
Elegia di Madonna Fiammetta (f Boccaccio)
Elegías (v Jiménez), 1908
Elégie aux nymphes de Vaux (v La Fontaine), 1661
Elegie renane (v Pirandello), 1895
Elegie romane (v D'Annunzio), 1892
Élégies (v Verlaine), 1893
Élégies nationales (v Nerval), 1826
Elegio de sombra (v Borges), 1969
Elektra (p Hauptmann), 1941
Elektra (p Hofmannsthal), 1903
Elementary Odes (v Neruda), 1961
Elephant Calf (p Brecht), 1964
Elephantenkalb (p Brecht), 1926
Elettra (v D'Annunzio), 1904
Elga (p Hauptmann), 1905
Elixiere des Teufels (f Hoffmann), 1815
Elle et lui (f Sand), 1859
Ellernklipp (f Fontane), 1881
Elleve år (f Undset), 1934

Farfalla di Dinard (f Montale), 1956
Farsa de Inês Pereira (p Vicente)
Farsa dos almocreves (p Vicente)
Farsa dos físicos (p Vicente)
Fasching (f Hauptmann), 1887
Fasti (v Ovid)
Fat and the Thin (f Zola), 1888
Fata morgana (v Breton), 1941
Fatal Legacy (p Racine)
Fate of a Soldier (f Sienkiewicz), 1898
Father (p Diderot)
Father (p Strindberg), 1889
Father of a Family (p Goldoni)
Father Outwitted (p Vega)
Fathers and Sons (f Turgenev)
Fattige skjarbner (f Undset), 1912
Fause Maîtresse (f Balzac), 1844
Fausse Suivante (p Marivaux), 1724
Fausses Confidences (p Marivaux), 1737
Faust (p Goethe), 1808
Faute de l'Abbé Mouret (f Zola), 1875
Faux-monnayeurs (f Gide), 1926
Favola del figlio cambiato (p Pirandello), 1933
Feast During the Plague (p Pushkin)
Fécondité (f Zola), 1899
Feder (f Stendhal), 1960
Fedra (p D'Annunzio), 1909
Fedra (p Unamuno), 1924
Féerie pour une autre fois (f Céline), 1952
Fekete-feher (v Illyés), 1968
Félicie (p Marivaux), 1957
Fellow Culprits (p Goethe)
Female Virtuosos (p Molière)
Femme abandonnée (f Balzac), 1833
Femme assise (f Apollinaire), 1920
Femme auteur (f Balzac), 1950
Femme cachée (p Colette), 1919
Femme et son ombre (p Claudel), 1923
Femme fidèle (p Marivaux), 1755
Femme qui a raison (p Voltaire), 1758
Femme supérieure (f Balzac), 1837
Femmes (v Verlaine), 1890
Femmes savantes (p Molière), 1672
Fencing-Master (f Dumas), 1850
Fendre les flots (v Queneau), 1969
Ferdydurke (f Gombrowicz), 1937
Ferias de Madrid (p Vega)
Fernande (f Dumas), 1844
Ferro (p D'Annunzio), 1913
Fervor de Buenos Aires (v Borges), 1923
Festen paa Kenilworth (p Andersen), 1836
Festspiel in deutschen Reimen (p Hauptmann), 1913

Fêtes galantes (v Verlaine), 1869
Feu sur la terre (p Mauriac), 1950
Feud of the Schroffensteins (p Kleist), 1916
Feuerwerk (f Wedekind), 1905
Feuilles d'automne (v Hugo), 1831
Feuilles de saints (v Claudel), 1925
Fiaccola sotto il moggio (p D'Annunzio), 1905
Fiançailles (p Maeterlinck), 1918
Fianza satisfecha (p Vega)
Ficciones (f Borges), 1944
Fictions (f Borges), 1965
Fiera (p Pérez Galdós), 1896
Fiesco (p Schiller), 1796
Fiesque de Lavagna (p Dumas), 1974
Figaro lässt sich scheiden (p Horváth), 1937
Figlia di Iorio (p D'Annunzio), 1904
Figlia obbediente (p Goldoni)
Fille de régent (f Dumas), 1844
Fille d'Eve (f Balzac), 1839
Fille du marquis (f Dumas), 1872
Filles du feu (f Nerval), 1852
Filleule (f Sand), 1853
Filocolo (f Boccaccio)
Filomena (v Vega), 1621
Filosofo di campagna (p Goldoni)
Filostrato (v Boccaccio)
Fils de Forçat (f Dumas), 1864
Fils de l'émigré (p Dumas), 1832
Fils naturel (p Diderot), 1757
Fin de Babylone (p Apollinaire), 1914
Fin de la nuit (f Mauriac), 1935
Fin de mundo (v Neruda), 1969
Fin de Potomak (f Cocteau), 1940
Fin de Satan (v Hugo), 1886
Fin de Siegfried (p Giraudoux), 1934
Finisterre (v Montale), 1943
Finsternisse (p Hauptmann), 1947
Fiore delle mille e una notte (p Pasolini), 1974
Fiorenza (p Mann), 1906
Fire Raisers (p Frisch), 1962
Firebugs (p Frisch), 1963
First Circle (f Solzhenitsyn), 1968
First Encounter (v Bely), 1979
First Love (f Turgenev)
First Republic (f Dumas), 1894
First Rescue Party (f Capek), 1939
First Warning (p Strindberg), 1916
Fischerin (p Goethe), 1782
Five Great Odes (v Claudel), 1967
Five Modern No Plays (p Mishima), 1957
Flamarande (f Sand), 1875
Flame of Life (f D'Annunzio), 1900

Flavie (f Sand), 1859
Flesh and Blood (f Mauriac), 1954
Fleur des pois (f Balzac), 1834
Fleurs bleues (f Queneau), 1965
Fleurs du mal (v Baudelaire), 1861
Fleuve de feu (f Mauriac), 1923
Fleyta pozvonochnik (v Mayakovsky), 1916
Flies (p Sartre), 1946
Flight (p Bulgakov), 1970
Flight of Icarus (f Queneau), 1973
Flood (p Grass), 1967
Floresta de enganos (p Vicente)
Florian Geyer (p Hauptmann), 1896
Florindo (p Hofmannsthal), 1923
Flowers of Evil (v Baudelaire)
Fluchtpunkt (f Weiss), 1962
Flug der Lindberghs (p Brecht), 1929
Folkefiende (p Ibsen), 1882
Folkungasagan (p Strindberg), 1899
Folle de Chaillot (p Giraudoux), 1945
Folle Journée (p Beaumarchais), 1783
Follies of a Day (p Beaumarchais), 1785
Foma Gordeyev (f Gorky), 1899
Fontamara (f Silone), 1933
Fontana de oro (f Pérez Galdós), 1870
Fool in Christ, Emanuel Quint (f Hauptmann), 1911
Foot of the Wall (p Ionesco), 1971
For Daily Bread (f Sienkiewicz), 1898
For the Good of the Cause (f Solzhenitsyn), 1964
Forbidden Colours (f Mishima), 1968
Forced Marriage (p Molière)
Fordringsägare (p Strindberg), 1890
Forefathers (p Mickiewicz), 1944
Forefathers' Eve (p Mickiewicz), 1925
Forest Picture (f Sienkiewicz), 1898
Foresters (f Dumas), 1854
Forestiers (p Dumas) 1858
Forests of Lithuania (v Mickiewicz), 1959
Forse che si, forse che no (f D'Annunzio), 1910
Första varningen (p Strindberg), 1892
Fort comme la mort (f Maupassant), 1889
Fortaellingen om Viga-Ljot og Vigdis (f Undset), 1909
Fortunata and Jacinta (f Pérez Galdós), 1973
Fortunata y Jacinta (f Pérez Galdós), 1886
Fortunate Villager (f Marivaux)
Fortune des Rougon (f Zola), 1871
Fortune of the Rougons (f Zola), 1886
Fortune's Fool (v Nerval), 1959
Forty-Five Guardsmen (f Dumas), 1847

Forvandlede Brudgom (p Holberg)
Fourberies de Scapin (p Molière), 1671
Foursome (p Ionesco), 1959
Fox and the Camellias (f Silone), 1961
Frágua de Amor (p Vicente)
Frailty and Hypocrisy (p Beaumarchais), 1804
Från ö till ö (v Weiss), 1947
Francesca da Rimini (p D'Annunzio), 1901
Francia (f Sand), 1872
Franciade (v Ronsard), 1572
Francis I (f Dumas), 1849
Francis the Waif (f Sand), 1889
François le Champi (f Sand), 1848
Frank V (p Dürrenmatt), 1959
Franziska (p Wedekind), 1912
Fraszki (v Kochanowski), 1584
Fratricides (f Kazantzakis), 1964
Frai im Fenster (p Hofmannsthal), 1898
Frau Jenny Treibel (f Fontane), 1892
Frau ohne Schatten (p Hofmannsthal), 1916
Fredlöse (p Strindberg), 1871
Freedom and Death (f Kazantzakis), 1956
Freedom or Death (f Kazantzakis), 1955
Frenzy for Two (p Ionesco), 1965
Frenzy of Orlando (v Ariosto)
Freunde (f Hesse), 1957
Friedenfest (p Hauptmann), 1890
Frist (p Dürrenmatt), 1977
Fritiofs saga (p Lagerlöf), 1899
Frogs (p Aristophanes)
Fröken Julie (p Strindberg), 1888
From a Roman Balcony (p Pasolini), 1960
From a Swedish Homestead (f Lagerlöf), 1901
From Bad to Worse (p Calderón)
From the Diary of a Snail (f Grass), 1973
Frontenac Mystery (f Mauriac), 1952
Fru Inger til Østråt (p Ibsen), 1855
Fru Marta Oulie (f Undset), 1907
Fruen fra havet (p Ibsen), 1888
Frühlings Erwachen (p Wedekind), 1891
Fruitfulness (f Zola), 1900
Fruits of Enlightenment (p Tolstoy)
Fruits of the Earth (f Gide), 1949
Ftochoulis tou Theou (f Kazantzakis), 1956
Fu Mattia Pascal (f Pirandello), 1904
Fuente ovejuna (p Vega)
Fuglen i Paeretraeet (p Andersen), 1842
Fuhrmann Henschel (p Hauptmann), 1898
Fukuzatsuma Kare (f Mishima), 1966
Fulgor y muerte de Joaquín Murieta (p Neruda), 1967

Fully Empowered (v Neruda), 1975
Funeral Rites (f Genet), 1969
Fuoco (f D'Annunzio), 1900
Fuori di chiave (v Pirandello), 1912
Furcht und Elend des Dritten Reiches (p Brecht), 1937
Furias y las penas (v Neruda), 1939
Fürsorgliche Belagerung (f Böll), 1979
Fürstin Russalka (f Wedekind), 1897
Further Confessions of Zeno (f Svevo), 1969
Fussy Man (p Holberg), 1946
Futen Tojin Nikki (f Tanizaki), 1962
Future Is in Eggs (p Ionesco), 1960
Fuyo no Tsuyu (p Mishima), 1955

Gaadefulde (f Hamsun), 1878
Gabriel (f Sand), 1839
Gabriel Lambert (f Dumas), 1844
Gabriel Le Faussaire (p Dumas), 1868
Gabriel Schilling's Flight (p Hauptmann), 1919
Gabriel Schillings Flucht (p Hauptmann), 1912
Gabriella (p Machado de Assis), 1862
Galán de la membrilla (p Vega)
Galatea (f Cervantes), 1585
Galère (v Genet), 1947
Galerie du Palais (p Corneille), 1632
Galigaï (f Mauriac), 1952
Galileo (p Brecht), 1943
Gallant Lords of Bois-Doré (f Sand), 1890
Gallant Parties (v Verlaine), 1912
Galley Slave (f Dumas), 1849
Gambara (f Balzac), 1839
Gambler (f Dostoevsky), 1887
Gamblers (p Gogol), 1927
Game of Love and Chance (p Marivaux)
Gantenbein (f Frisch), 1982
Garasudo no Naka (f Natsume), 1915
Garde-Forestier (p Dumas), 1845
Garden in the Night (f Roy), 1977
Garden of Priapus (f Jarry), 1936
Gardener's Dog (p Vega)
Gargantua and Pantagruel (f Rabelais)
Garibaldina (f Vittorini), 1956
Garofano rosso (f Vittorini), 1948
Gäst hos verkligheten (p Lagerkvist), 1925
Gatomaquia (v Vega), 1807
Gde tonko, tam i rvyotsya (p Turgenev), 1848
Gedichte des Malers (v Hesse), 1920
Geheimnisse (f Hesse), 1964
Geisterseher (f Schiller), 1787

General's Ring (f Langerlöf), 1928
Geneviève (p Gide), 1936
Gengaeldeslens Veje (f Dinesen), 1944
Gengangere (p Ibsen), 1881
Génitrix (f Mauriac), 1923
Genius (v Langerkvist), 1937
Genji Monogatari (f Murasaki)
Genom öknar till arvland (p Strindberg), 1918
Genoveva (p Hebbel), 1843
Gentilhomme de la montagne (p Dumas), 1860
Gentle Libertine (f Colette), 1931
Genussmensch (p Wedekind), 1924
Geografia infructuosa (v Neruda), 1972
George (f Dumas), 1846
George Dandin (p Molière), 1668
Georges (f Dumas), 1843
Georgica (v Virgil)
Georgics (v Virgil)
Gerettete Venedig (p Hofmannsthal), 1905
Germaine's Marriage (f Sand), 1892
Germandre Family (f Sand)
Germany (v Heine)
Germinal (f Zola), 1885
Gerona (f Pérez Galdós), 1874
Geroy nashevo vremeni (f Lermontov), 1840
Gertrud (f Hesse), 1910
Gertrude (f Hesse), 1955
Gertrude and I (f Hesse), 1915
Gerusalemme conquistata (v Tasso), 1593
Gerusalemme liberata (v Tasso), 1580
Gervaise (f Zola), 1879
Gesang vom lusitanischen Popanz (p Weiss), 1967
Geschichten aus dem Wiener Wald (p Horváth), 1931
Geschichten Jaakobx (f Mann), 1933
Geschwister (p Goethe), 1776
Gesetz (f Mann), 1944
Gesichte der Simone Machard (p Brecht), 1957
Gespräch der drei Gehenden (f Weiss), 1963
Gestern (p Hofmannsthal), 1896
Gestes et opinions du docteur Faustroll, Pataphysicien (f Jarry), 1911
Getting Married (f Strindberg), 1972
Gewehre der Frau Carrar (p Brecht), 1937
Ghost (p Plautus)
Ghost Seer (f Schiller), 1795
Ghost Sonata (p Strindberg), 1929
Ghosts (p Ibsen), 1888
Giara (p Pirandello), 1916
Giftas (f Strindberg), 1884

Giganti della montagna (p Pirandello), 1938
Gigi (f Colette), 1944
Gil Pérez the Galician (p Calderón)
Gil-Blas en Californie (f Dumas), 1852
Gillers hemlighet (p Strindberg), 1880
Gillette (f Balzac), 1847
Gin Palace (f Zola)
Gina (p Queneau), 1956
Gioconda (p D'Annunzio), 1898
Giornata balorda (p Pasolini), 1960
Giovanni mariti (p Pasolini), 1958
Girl from Andros (p Terence)
Girl from Samos (p Menander)
Girl from the Marsh Croft (f Lagerlöf), 1911
Girl with the Golden Eyes (f Balzac), 1928
Giuoco delle parti (p Pirandello), 1918
Giustino Roncella nato Boggiolo (p Pirandello), 1953
Givat ha-Hol (f Agnon), 1920
Glasperlenspiel (f Hesse), 1943
Glass Bead Game (f Hesse), 1969
Glaube, Liebe, Hoffnung (p Horváth), 1932
Gleisdreieck (v Grass), 1960
Glissements progressifs du plaisir (p Robbe-Grillet), 1973
Gloria (p D'Annunzio), 1899
Gloria (f Pérez Galdós), 1876
Glück (f Hesse), 1952
Go sei-gen kidan (f Kawabata), 1954
Godfrey of Bouillon (v Tasso)
God's Pauper (f Kazantzakis), 1962
God's Will Be Done (f Dumas), 1909
Goetz of Berlichingen (p Goethe)
Goffredo (v Tasso), 1580
Gogo no eilo (f Mishima), 1963
Golden Ass (f Apuleius)
Golden Fleece (p Grillparzer), 1942
Goldene Harfe (p Hauptmann), 1933
Goldene Vlies (p Grillparzer), 1821
Golgota (p Krleža), 1922
Goldmund (f Hesse), 1959
Gommes (f Robbe-Grillet), 1953
Gondole des morts (v Cocteau), 1959
Gondreville Mystery (f Balzac) 1898
Good Girl (p Goldoni)
Good Little Wife (p Musset)
Good Soldier Schweik (f Hašek), 1930
Good Woman of Setzuan (p Brecht), 1948
Good-Humoured Ladies (p Goldoni)
Gorgias (Plato)
Gorodok Okurov (f Gorky), 1909
Gospel According to St. Matthew (p Pasolini), 1964
Gospoda Glembajevi (p Krleža), 1928
Gospodjica (f Andrić), 1945

Gösta Berlings Saga (f Lagerlöf), 1891
Gostiska rummen (f Strindberg), 1903
Götter, Helden, und Wieland (p Goethe), 1774
Götz von Berlichingen (p Goethe), 1772
Goubbiah (p Genet), 1955
Government Inspector (p Gogol), 1927
Gracques (p Giraudoux), 1958
Graf Öderland (p Frisch), 1951
Graf Petöfy (f Fontane), 1884
Gran duque de Gandia (p Calderón)
Gran teatro del mundo (p Calderón)
Grand Écart (f Cocteau), 1923
Grand Homme de province à Paris (f Balzac), 1839
Grande et la petite manoeuvre (p Adamov), 1950
Grande Oriente (p Pérez Galdós), 1876
Grandes Chaleurs (p Ionesco), 1953
Grass on the Wayside (f Natsume), 1969
Great Fury of Philipp Hotz (p Frisch), 1967
Great Highway (p Strindberg), 1945
Great Lover (p Dumas)
Great Man of the Provinces in Paris (f Balzac), 1893
Great Stage of the World (p Calderón)
Grecque moderne, Histoire d'une (f Prévost), 1740
Greek Passion (f Kazantzakis), 1954
Green Coat (p Musset), 1914
Green Henry (f Keller), 1960
Grenadière (f Balzac), 1833
Grete Minde (f Fontane), 1880
Gridasti: Soffoco... (v Ungaretti), 1951
Grido e paesaggi (v Ungaretti), 1952
Grieche sucht Griechin (f Dürrenmatt), 1955
Griselda (p Hauptmann), 1909
Gross-Cophta (p Goethe), 1791
Grosse Traum (v Hauptmann), 1942
Grosse Wut des Philipp Hotz (p Frisch), 1958
Grouch (p Menander)
Group Portrait with Lady (f Böll), 1973
Growth of the Soil (f Hamsun), 1920
Grüne Flöte (p Hofmannsthal), 1923
Grüne Heinrich (f Keller), 1853
Gruppenbild mit Dame (f Böll), 1971
Guardate del agua mansa (p Calderón)
Gubijinso (f Natsume), 1908
Guèbres (p Voltaire), 1769
Guelfes et Gibelins (f Dumas), 1836
Guelphs and Ghibellines (f Dumas), 1905
Guermantes Way (f Proust), 1922
Guerra del tiempo (f Carpentier), 1958
Guerre (v Ungaretti), 1919

Guerre civile de Genève (v Voltaire), 1767
Guerre de Troie n'aura pas lieu (p Giraudoux), 1935
Guerre des femmes (f Dumas), 1845
Guest of Reality (p Lagerkvist), 1936
Guest-Friend (p Grillparzer), 1947
Guetteur mélancolique (v Apollinaire), 1952
Gueule de Pierre (f Queneau), 1934
Guignol's Band (f Céline), 1944
Guillaume le Conquérant, Histoire de (f Prévost), 1741
Guiltless (f Broch), 1974
Gunnar's Daughter (f Undset), 1936
Guns of Carrar (p Brecht), 1971
Gustav Adolf (p Strindberg), 1900
Gustav III (p Strindberg), 1902
Gustav Vasa (p Strindberg), 1899
Gustavus Vasa (p Strindberg), 1916
Gute Mensch von Sezuan (p Brecht), 1943
Gutter in the Sky (f Genet), 1956
Gyges and His Ring (p Hebbel), 1914
Gyges und sein Ring (p Hebbel), 1856
Gymnadenia (f Undset), 1929
Gymnopedia (v Seferis), 1936
Gypsy Ballads (v García Lorca), 1963
Gyubal Wahazar (p Witkiewicz), 1962

Habit vert (p Musset), 1849
Habitante y su esperanza (f Neruda), 1926
Hacedor (v Borges), 1960
Haermaendene på Helgeland (p Ibsen), 1857
Hagelstolz (f Stifter), 1852
Hakhnasath Kallah (f Agnon), 1931
Half Brothers (f Dumas), 1858
Halifax (p Dumas), 1842
Halma (f Pérez Galdós), 1895
Hamlet (p Dumas), 1847
Hamlet (p Gide), 1946
Hamlet in Wittenberg (p Hauptmann), 1935
Han d'Islande (f Hugo), 1823
Han er ikke født (p Andersen), 1864
Han of Iceland (f Hugo), 1825
Han som fick leva om sitt liv (p Lagerkvist), 1928
Hana no warutsu (f Kawabata), 1936
Hanazakari no mori (f Mishima), 1944
Hand and the Glove (f Machado de Assis), 1970
Hand of Destiny (f Marivaux)
Handful of Blackberries (f Silone), 1953
Handsome Laurence (f Sand), 1871
Hangman (f Lagerkvist), 1936
Hangmen Also Die (p Brecht), 1943
Hania (f Sienkiewicz), 1876
Hanjo (p Mishima), 1957

Hannele (p Hauptmann), 1894
Hanneles Himmelfahrt (p Hauptmann), 1893
Hans Dierlamms Lehrzeit (f Hesse), 1916
Han-teijo Daigaku (f Mishima), 1966
Happy Death (f Camus), 1973
Happy End (p Brecht), 1929
Hard Winter (f Queneau), 1948
Hard-Boiled Egg (p Ionesco), 1976
Harlot High and Low (f Balzac), 1970
Harlot's Progress (f Balzac)
Három öreg (v Illyés), 1931
Harper's Daughter (p Schiller), 1813
Haru no yuki (f Mishima), 1969
Hashish and Incense (v Verlaine), 1925
Hashire Merosu (f Dazai), 1940
Hashizukushi (f Mishima), 1958
Haunted House (p Plautus)
Haunted Marsh (f Sand), 1848
Haus der Träume (v Hesse), 1936
Haus ohne Hüter (f Böll), 1954
Hausfriedensbruch (p Böll), 1969
Hausierer (f Hesse), 1914
Hauspostille (v Brecht), 1927
Haute surveillance (p Genet), 1949
Hawk and the Sparrows (p Pasolini), 1966
Haza a magasban (v Illyés), 1972
He and She (f Sand)
Headbirths (f Grass), 1982
Healing Spring (p Holberg), 1957
Hearing Things (f Natsume), 1974
Heart of a Dog (f Bulgakov), 1968
Heart of a Russian (f Lermontov)
Heart of a Tenor (p Wedekind), 1913
Heauton timorumenos (p Terence)
Hecabe (p Euripides)
Hecuba (p Euripides)
Hacyra (p Terence)
Hedda Gabler (p Ibsen), 1890
Heights of Macchu Picchu (v Neruda), 1966
Heilige Johanna der Schlachthöfe (p Brecht), 1932
Heilige und der Räuber (p Böll), 1953
Heimskringla (f Sturluson)
Heinrich and Pernille (p Holberg), 1912
Heirs of Rabourdin (p Zola), 1893
Heizer (f Kafka), 1916
Helen (p Eupidides)
Helena (p Euripides)
Helena (f Machado de Assis), 1876
Hélène (f Zola), 1878
Heliga Landet (f Lagerkvist), 1964
Hell of a Mess (p Ionesco), 1975
Hellas (p Strindberg), 1918
Hemmet och stjärnan (v Lagerkvist), 1942
Hemsöborna (f Strindberg), 1887

Henri III et sa cour (p Dumas), 1829
Henriade (v Voltaire), 1728
Henrik of Pernille (p Holberg)
Henry IV (p Pirandello), 1922
Henry of Auë (p Hauptmann), 1914
Her Tragic Fate (f Sienkiewicz), 1899
Heracleidae (p Euripides)
Heracles (p Euripides)
Héraclius (p Corneille), 1646
Herakles (p Wedekind), 1917
Heraldos negros (v Vallejo), 1919
Herbert Engelmann (p Hauptmann), 1952
Hercules and the Augean Stable (p Dür-
renmatt)
Hercules furens (p Seneca)
Hercules oetaeus (p Seneca)
Here Comes a Chopper (p Ionesco), 1971
Heredity of Taste (f Natsume), 1974
Heresiarch and Company (f Apollinaire),
1965
Hérésiarque et cie (f Apollinaire), 1909
Heretic of Soana (f Hauptmann), 1923
Héritage de Birague (f Balzac), 1822
Heritage of Quincas Borba (f Machado de
Assis), 1954
Héritier du village (p Marivaux), 1725
Héritiers Rabourdin (p Zola), 1874
Herkules und der Stall der Augias (p Dür-
renmatt), 1960
Herman and Dorothea (v Goethe)
Hermann und Dorothea (v Goethe)
Hermannsschlacht (p Kleist), 1821
Hermano Juan (p Unamuno), 1934
Herminie (f Dumas), 1858
Hermione (p Strindberg), 1871
Hermit (f Ionesco), 1974
Hermosura de Angélica (v Vega), 1602
Hernani (p Hugo), 1830
Hero and Leander (p Grillparzer), 1938
Hero of Our Times (f Lermontov)
Herod and Mariamne (p Hebbel), 1914
Herod and Mariamne (f Lagerkvist), 1968
Hérode et Mariamne (p Voltaire), 1725
Herodes und Mariamne (p Hebbel), 1849
Heroides (v Ovid)
Herr Arne's Hoard (f Lagerlöf), 1923
Herr Arnes Penningar (f Lagerlöf), 1903
Herr Bengts husfru (p Strindberg), 1882
Herr Puntila und sein Knecht Matti
(p Brecht), 1948
Herr Rasmussen (p Andersen), 1846
Herr und Hund (f Mann), 1919
Herrnburger Bericht (p Brecht), 1951
Heureux Strategème (p Marivaux), 1733
Hi mo tsuki mo (f Kawabata), 1953

Hidalga del Valle (p Calderón)
Hidalla (p Wedekind), 1904
Hidden Mountain (f Roy), 1972
Higan Sugi made (f Natsume), 1912
Higyo (f Mishima), 1951
Hiji de Rappaccini (p Paz), 1956
Hija del aire (p Calderón)
Hijos del aire (v Paz), 1981
Hiljadu i jedna smrt (f Krleža), 1933
Himlens hemlighet (p Lagerkvist), 1919
Himmelrikets nycklar (p Strindberg), 1903
Himmelwärts (p Horváth), 1950
Himno y regreso (v Neruda), 1948
Him und Her (p Horváth), 1934
Hippeis (p Aristophanes)
Hippias Major (Plato)
Hippias Minor (Plato)
Hippolytus (p Euripides)
Hippolytus (p Seneca)
His Excellency Eugène Rougon (f Zola),
1886
His Masterpiece (f Zola), 1886
Histoire de César Birotteau (f Balzac), 1838
Histoire de Jenni (v Voltaire), 1775
Histoire de Tobie et de Sara (p Claudel),
1947
Histoire des treize (f Balzac), 1834
Histoire du vieux temps (p Maupassant),
1879
Histoire d'un Cabanon et d'un chalet
(f Dumas), 1859
Histoire d'un mort (f Dumas), 1844
Histoire d'une âme (f Dumas), 1844
Histoire secrète d'Isabelle de Bavière
(f Sade), 1953
Historia (p Gombrowicz), 1975
Historia universal de la infamia (f Borges),
1935
Histórias da Meia-Noite (f Machado de
Assis), 1873
Histórias sem data (f Machado de Assis),
1884
Historical Miniatures (f Strindberg), 1913
Historiska miniatyrer (f Strindberg), 1905
History of Goryukhino (f Pushkin)
History of the Grandeur and Downfall of
Cesar Birotteau (f Balzac), 1860
History of the Thirteen (f Balzac), 1974
Ho Christos ste Rome (p Sikelianos), 1946
Hjärtats sånger (v Lagerkvist), 1926
Hoax (f Svevo), 1929
Hochwasser (p Grass), 1957
Hochzeit (p Brecht), 1926
Hochzeit (p Canetti), 1932
Hochzeit auf Buchenhorst (f Hauptmann),

1931
Hochzeit der Sobeide (p Hofmannsthal), 1899
Hofmeister (p Brecht), 1950
Hojo no umi (f Mishima), 1969
Hölderlin (p Weiss), 1971
Holding Out (v Rilke), 1975
Holy City (f Lagerlöf), 1918
Holy Land (f Lagerkvist), 1966
Holy Sinner (f Mann), 1951
Holy Terrors (f Cocteau), 1957
Homba (f Mishima), 1969
Hombres (v Verlaine), 1903
Home Life in Russia (f Gogol), 1854
Home of the Gentry (f Turgenev)
Homère travesti (v Marivaux), 1716
Homme aux quarante écus (f Voltaire), 1768
Homme aux valises (p Ionesco), 1975
Homme de lettres (f Mauriac), 1928
Homme de qualité, Mémoires d'un (f Prévost), 1728
Homme et son désir (p Claudel), 1921
Homme qui ment (p Robbe-Grillet), 1968
Homme qui rit (f Hugo), 1869
Hommes de fer (f Dumas), 1867
Homo Faber (f Frisch), 1957
Hondero entusiasta (v Neruda), 1933
Honeysuckle (p D'Annunzio), 1911
Honnête homme, Mémoires d'un (f Prévost), 1745
Honneur est satisfait (p Dumas), 1858
Honorine (f Balzac), 1845
Horace (p Corneille), 1640
Horace (f Sand), 1842
Horatians and the Curatians (p Brecht), 1947
Horatier und die Kuriatier (p Brecht), 1938
Horatius (p Corneille)
Hordubal (f Capek), 1933
Horla (f Maupassant), 1887
Horoscope (f Dumas), 1858
Horse in the Moon (f Pirandello), 1932
Hoseki Baibai (f Mishima), 1949
Hosökröl beszélek (v Illyés), 1933
Hosshoji Monogatari (p Tanizaki), 1915
Hostage (p Claudel), 1917
Hours in the Garden (v Hesse), 1979
House by the Medlar Tree (f Verga), 1890
House of Assignation (f Robbe-Grillet), 1970
House of Atreus (p Aeschylus)
House of the Sleeping Beauties (f Kawabata), 1969
House with the Column (p Pirandello),

1928
House with Two Doors Is Difficult to Guard (p Calderón)
How Jolly Life Is! (f Zola), 1886
How Mr. Mockinpott Was Cured of His Suffering (p Weiss), 1971
Hrvatska rapsodija (f Krleža), 1918
Hrvatski bog Mars (f Krleža), 1922
Hugenau (f Broch), 1932
Huis clos (p Sartre), 1944
Huldingung der Künste (p Schiller), 1804
Human Beast (f Zola), 1891
Human Comedy (f Balzac)
Human Heart (f Maupassant), 1890
Human Poems (v Vallejo), 1969
Human Voice (p Cocteau), 1951
Humiliation of the Father (p Claudel), 1945
Hunchback of Notre-Dame (f Hugo), 1833
Hundejahre (f Grass), 1963
Hundred Thousand Billion Poems (v Queneau), 1979
Hunger (f Hamsun), 1899
Hunger and Thirst (p Ionesco), 1968
Hungerkünstler (f Kafka), 1924
Húnok Párizsban (f Illyés), 1946
Huron (f Voltaire), 1767
Hyldemoer (p Andersen), 1851
Hymnes (v Du Bellay), 1555
Hymns to the Night (v Novalis)
Hyperion (f Hölderlin), 1797
Hypsipyle (p Euripides)

I Am a Cat (f Natsume), 1906
I den tiden (f Lagerkvist), 1935
I havsbandet (f Strindberg), 1890
I promessi sposi (f Manzoni), 1827
I Rom (p Strindberg), 1870
I sterna (v Seferis), 1932
Iaiá Garcia (f Machado de Assis)
Ich hab meine Tante geschlachtet (v Wedekind), 1967
Ich habe nichts gene Tiere (p Böll), 1958
Ichneutae (p Sophocles)
Ida Elisabeth (f Undset), 1932
Idiot (f Dostoevsky), 1869
Idylle de la paix (p Racine), 1685
Ifjúság (v Illyés), 1934
Igra v adu (Khlebnikov), 1912
Igrok (f Dostoevsky), 1866
Igroki (p Gogol), 1842
Il faut qu'une porte soit ouverte ou fermée (p Musset), 1848
Il ne faut jurer de rien (p Musset), 1840
Île de feu (f Dumas), 1870

Île de la raison (p Marivaux), 1727
Île des esclaves (p Marivaux), 1725
Iliad (v Homer)
Illuminations (Rimbaud), 1886
Illusion comique (p Corneille), 1635
Illusions perdues (f Balzac)
Illustre Gaudissart (f Balzac), 1833
Im dickicht der Städte (p Brecht), 1927
Im Fruhfrost (p Rilke), 1897
I'm Not Stiller (f Frisch), 1958
Im Pressel'schen Gartenhaus (f Hesse), 1920
Im Tal der donnernden Hufe (f Böll), 1957
Im Wirbel der Berufung (f Hauptmann), 1936
Images in a Mirror (f Undset), 1938
Imagier de Harlem (p Nerval), 1951
Imaginary Invalid (p Molière)
Imbecile (p Pirandello), 1928
Imbecille (p Pirandello), 1922
Imerologio katastromatos (v Seferis) 1940
Imitation de Notre-Dame la Lune (v Laforgue), 1886
Immoralist (f Gide), 1930
Immoraliste (f Gide), 1902
Immortal One (f Robbe-Grillet), 1971
Immortelle (f Robbe-Grillet), 1963
Impertinents (p Molière)
Impietrito e il velluto (v Ungaretti), 1970
Imposter (f Cocteau), 1957
Impresario delle Smirne (p Goldoni)
Impressario from Smyrna (p Goldoni)
Impromptu de l'Alma (p Ionesco), 1956
Impromptu de Versailles (p Molière), 1663
Impromptu du Palais-Royal (p Cocteau), 1962
Impromptu du Paris (p Giraudoux), 1937
Impromptu pour la Duchesse de Windsor (p Ionesco), 1957
Improvisation (p Ionesco), 1960
Improvisatore (f Andersen), 1845
Improvisatoren (f Andersen), 1835
In allen Sätteln gerecht (p Wedekind), 1910
In allen Wassern gewaschen (p Wedekind), 1910
In Camera (p Sartre), 1946
In der Strafkolonie (f Kafka), 1919
In Monte Carlo (f Sienkiewicz), 1899
In portineria (p Verga), 1896
In Praise of Darkness (v Borges), 1974
In Sicily (f Vittorini), 1949
In the Egg (v Grass), 1977
In the Face of Death (p Strindberg), 1965
In the Grip of Life (p Hamsun), 1924
In the Heart of the Seas (f Agnon), 1948

In the Mesh (p Sartre), 1948
In the Interlude (v Pasternak), 1962
In the Labyrinth (f Robbe-Grillet), 1960
In the New Promised Land (f Sienkiewicz), 1900
In the Swamp (p Brecht), 1961
In Vain (f Sienkiewicz), 1899
Incitación al nixonicidio... (v Neruda), 1973
Incitation to Nixoncide... (v Neruda), 1973
Incógnita (f Pérez Galdós), 1889
Indiana (f Sand) 1832
Indipohdi (p Hauptmann), 1920
Indiscret (p Voltaire), 1725
Indiscreet Toys (f Diderot)
Indulgent Husband (f Colette), 1935
Inferiorità (p Svevo), 1960
Infernal Machine (p Cocteau), 1936
Infidelities (p Marivaux)
Inför döden (p Strindberg), 1892
Informe de Brodie (f Borges), 1970
Infortunes de la vertu (f Sade), 1930
Ingénu (v Voltaire), 1767
Ingénue (f Dumas), 1854
Ingénue libertine (f Colette), 1909
Inmarypraise (v Grass), 1973
Innamorati (p Goldoni)
Innesto (p Pirandello), 1919
Inni sacri (v Manzoni), 1815
Innocent Wife (f Colette), 1934
Innocente (f D'Annunzio), 1892
Insatiability (f Witkiewicz), 1977
Insect Play (p Capek), 1923
Insel der grossen Mutter (f Hauptmann), 1924
Insepulta de Paita (v Neruda), 1962
Inspector-General (p Gogol), 1891
Instant fatal (v Queneau), 1948
Instantanés (f Robbe-Grillet), 1962
Institution pour l'adolescence du Roy Charles IX (v Ronsard), 1562
Interdiction (f Balzac), 1836
Intérieur (p Maeterlinck), 1894
Interior (p Maeterlinck), 1895
Intermezzo (p Giraudoux), 1933
Intermezzo di rime (v D'Annunzio), 1883
Intimacy (f Sartre), 1949
Intimate Relations (p Cocteau), 1962
Intrichi d'amore (p Tasso), 1598
Intrigue et amour (p Dumas), 1847
Intruder (f D'Annunzio), 1898
Intruder (p Maeterlinck), 1891
Intruse (p Maeterlinck), 1890
Inutile Beauté (f Maupassant), 1890
Invasion (p Adamov), 1950

Invectives (v Verlaine), 1896
Investigation (p Weiss), 1966
Invisible Links (f Lagerlöf), 1899
Invitation à la valse (p Dumas), 1857
Invraisemblance (f Dumas), 1844
Ion (p Euripides)
Ion (Plato)
Ioulianos (p Kazantzakis), 1945
Iphigeneia Aulidensis (p Euripides)
Iphigeneia Taurica (p Euripides)
Iphigenia (p Racine)
Iphigenia among the Taurians (p Euripides)
Iphigenia in Aulis (p Euripides)
Iphigenia in Tauris (p Goethe)
Iphigenia (p Goethe), 1779
Iphigénie (p Racine), 1674
Iphigenie auf Tauris (p Goethe), 1787
Iphigenie in Aulis (p Hauptmann), 1941
Iphigenie in Aulis (p Schiller), 1807
Iphigenie in Delphi (p Hauptmann), 1941
Ire di Giuliano (p Svevo), 1960
Irène (p Voltaire), 1778
Iron in the Soul (f Sartre), 1950
Ironhand (p Goethe)
Irony of Life (f Sienkiewicz), 1900
Irrungen, Wirrungen (f Fontane), 1888
Isaac Laquedem (f Dumas), 1852
Isabelle (f Gide), 1911
Isabelle de Bavière (f Dumas), 1836
Isaotta Guttadàuro (v D'Annunzio), 1886
Isidora (f Sand), 1845
Isidro (v Vega), 1599
Isla Negra (v Neruda), 1981
Island of the Great Mother (f Hauptmann), 1925
Islanders (f Zamyatin), 1978
Isle of the Dead (p Strindberg), 1962
Isottèo (v D'Annunzio), 1890
Ispoved' (f Gorky), 1908
Istoriya moey golubyatni (f Babel), 1926
Istrovityane (f Zamyatin), 1922
It Happened in Venice (p Goldoni)
It Is So (If You Think So) (p Pirandello), 1952
Italienische Nacht (p Horváth), 1930
Ivan Vasil'evich (p Bulgakov), 1964
Ivanhoë (p Dumas), 1974
Ivanov (p Chekhov), 1887
Ivona, Princess of Burgundy (p Gombrowicz), 1969
Iwona, Ksiezniczka Burgunda (p Gombrowicz), 1957
Iz dvukh knig (v Tsvetayeva), 1913
Izbor (f Andrić), 1961

Izu Dancer (f Kawabata), 1964
Izu no odoriko (f Kawabata), 1926

Jack (p Ionesco), 1958
Jacques (p Ionesco), 1954
Jacques (f Sand), 1834
Jacques le fataliste (f Diderot)
Jacquot sans oreilles (f Dumas), 1860
Jadis e naguère (v Verlaine), 1884
J'adore ce qui me brûle (f Frisch), 1943
Jahrmarktsfest zu Plundersweilern (p Goethe), 1778
Jalousie (f Robbe-Grillet), 1957
Jalousie du barbouille (p Molière)
James the Fatalist (f Diderot)
Jan Maciej Karol Wścienklica (p Witkiewicz), 1925
Jane (f Dumas), 1859
Jane la pâle (f Balzac), 1836
Janpaku no Yoru (f Mishima), 1950
Janulka, córka Fizdejki (p Witkiewicz), 1962
Jar (p Pirandello), 1928
Jardin au bout du monde (f Roy), 1975
Jardín de invierno (v Neruda), 1974
Jardín de senderos que se bifurcan (f Borges), 1942
Jardin des rochers (f Kazantzakis), 1959
Jardines lejanos (v Jiménez), 1904
Jargal (f Hugo), 1840
Järn och människor (f Lagerkvist), 1915
Jarvis l'honnête homme (p Dumas), 1840
Jasager (p Brecht), 1930
Je...ils... (f Adamov), 1969
Jealousies of the Country Town (f Balzac)
Jealousy (f Robbe-Grillet), 1959
Jealousy (f Sand), 1855
Jean Bête à la foire (p Beaumarchais)
Jean de la Roche (f Sand), 1860
Jean Santeuil (f Proust), 1952
Jean-Louis (f Balzac), 1822
Jeanne d'Arc (p Maeterlinck), 1948
Jeanne d'Arc au bucher (p Claudel), 1938
Jeannic le Breton (p Dumas), 1841
Jedermann (p Hofmannsthal), 1911
Jedyne wyjscie (f Witkiewicz), 1968
Jehanne la Pucelle (f Dumas), 1842
Jenny (f Undset), 1911
Jeppe of the Hill (p Holberg), 1914
Jeppe paa Bjerget (p Holberg)
Jérôme Bardini, Aventures de (f Giraudoux), 1930
Jerusalem (f Lagerlöf), 1901
Jerusálem conquistada (v Vega), 1609

1955
Karl Hetmann, der Zwergriese (p Wedekind), 1913
Karl XII (p Strindberg), 1901
Kasimir und Karoline (p Horváth), 1932
Kataku (p Mishima), 1948
Kata-ude (f Kawabata), 1965
Käthchen von Heilbronn (p Kleist), 1810
Katia (f Tolstoy)
Katz und Maus (f Grass), 1961
Kaukasische Kreiderkreis (p Brecht), 1947
Kavaljersnoveller (f Lagerlöf), 1918
Kazaki (f Tolstoy), 1863
Kean (p Dumas), 1836
Kean (p Sartre), 1953
Keep your Own Secret (p Calderón)
Kegyenc (p Illyés), 1963
Kejsarn av Portugallien (f Lagerlöf), 1914
Kejser og Galilaeer (p Ibsen), 1873
Kelev Hutsot (f Agnon), 1950
Kemono no tawamure (f Mishima), 1971
Ken (f Mishima), 1963
Képi (f Colette), 1943
Két férfi (f Illyés), 1950
Két kéz (v Illyés), 1950
Ketzer von Soana (f Hauptmann), 1918
Key (f Tanizaki), 1960
Keys of Heaven (p Strindberg), 1965
Kezfogások (v Illyés), 1956
Kháron Ladikján (f Illyés), 1969
Khmurye Lyudi (f Chekhov), 1890
Kholostyak (p Turgenev), 1849
Khorosho! (v Mayakovsky), 1927
Khozyain i rabotnik (f Tolstoy), 1895
Kichli (v Seferis), 1947
Kilderejsen (p Holberg)
Kill (f Zola), 1895
Killer (p Ionesco), 1960
Killing Game (p Ionesco), 1974
Kin to Gin (f Tanizaki), 1918
Kind unserer Zeit (f Horváth), 1938
Kindai Nogakushu (p Mishima), 1956
Kinder und Narren (p Wedekind), 1891
Kindred by Choice (f Goethe)
King (p Lagerkvist), 1966
King and the Farmer (p Vega)
King Candaules (p Gide), 1951
King Harald's Saga (f Sturluson)
King Nicolo (p Wedekind), 1912
King of Asine (v Seferis), 1948
King Ottokar, His Rise and Fall (p Grillparzer), 1932
King the Greatest Alcalde (p Vega)
Kingdom of This World (f Carpentier),

1957
King's Edict (p Hugo), 1872
King's Favorite (f Dumas), 1906
Kinjiki (f Mishima), 1951
Kinju (f Kawabata), 1935
Kinkakuji (f Mishima), 1956
Kinu to meisatsu (f Mishima), 1964
Kiss to the Leper (f Mauriac), 1923
Kjaempehøjen (p Ibsen), 1850
Kjaerlighed paa Nicolar Taarn (p Andersen), 1829
Klara Milich (f Turgenev), 1883
Klein Zaches genannt Zinnober (f Hoffmann), 1819
Kleinbürgerhochzeit (p Brecht), 1966
Kleine Herr Friedemann (f Mann), 1898
Kleine Welt (f Hesse), 1933
Kleine Welttheater (p Hofmannsthal), 1903
Klingsor's Last Summer (f Hesse), 1970
Klingsors Letzter Sommer (f Hesse), 1920
Kloke jomfruer (f Undset), 1918
Klop (p Mayakovsky), 1929
Klopfzeichen (p Böll), 1960
Knave of Hearts (p Queneau), 1954
Knight from Olmedo (p Vega)
Knights (p Aristophanes)
Knights of the Cross (f Sienkiewicz), 1900
Knights of the Round Table (p Cocteau), 1963
Knot of Vipers (f Mauriac), 1951
Knulp (f Hesse), 1915
Kofu (f Natsume), 1908
Kofuku go shuppan (f Mishima), 1956
Kojiki Gakusei (f Dazai), 1941
Kojin (f Natsume), 1914
Kojin (f Tanizaki), 1926
Kokoro (f Natsume), 1914
Kollege Crampton (p Hauptmann), 1892
Komödie der Eitelkeit (p Canetti), 1950
Konarmiya (f Babel), 1926
Konerne ved Vandposten (f Hamsun), 1920
Konetz Kazanovy (v Tsvetayeva), 1922
Kongen Drømmer (p Andersen), 1844
Kongs-Emnerne (p Ibsen), 1863
König Johann (p Dürrenmatt), 1968
König Nicolo (p Wedekind), 1911
König Ödipus (p Hofmannsthal), 1910
König Ottokars Glück und Ende (p Grillparzer), 1825
Königliche Hoheit (f Mann), 1909
Konrad Wallenrod (f Mickiewicz), 1828
Konstantinos o Paleaologos (p Kazantzakis), 1955
Konungen (p Lagerkvist), 1932

Konzert für vier Stimmen (p Böll)
Kopfgeburten (f Grass), 1980
Kora tavasz (f Illyés), 1941
Körkarlen (f Lagerlöf), 1912
Korol' (f Babel), 1926
Kosmos (f Gombrowicz), 1965
Kotik Letaev (f Bely), 1971
Kotik Letayev (f Bely), 1922
Közügy (v Illyés), 1981
Krakatit (f Capek), 1924
Krakonošova zahrada (f Capek), 1918
Kraljevo (p Krleža), 1955
Krasnoe koleso (f Solzhenitsyn), 1973
Kratskrog (f Hamsun), 1903
Kreshchony kitayets (f Bely), 1927
Kreutzer Sonata (f Tolstoy)
Kreytserova sonata (f Tolstoy), 1891
Kristin Lavransdatter (f Undset), 1920
Kristina (p Strindberg), 1904
Kristofor Kolumbo (p Krleža), 1955
Kristus (p Strindberg), 1918
Kristuslegender (f Lagerlöf), 1904
Kronbruden (p Strindberg), 1902
Krzyzacy (f Sienkiewicz), 1900
Kuhle Wampe (p Brecht), 1932
Külön világban (v Illyés), 1939
Különc (p Illyés), 1963
Különös testamentum (v Illyés), 1977
Kun en Spillemand (f Andersen), 1837
Kunstens Dannevirke (p Andersen), 1848
Kurgast (f Hesse), 1925
Kurka wodna (p Witkiewicz), 1922
Kurotokage (p Mishima), 1962
Kusamakura (f Natsume), 1907
Kvoko no Ie (f Mishima), 1959

La de bringas (f Pérez Galdós), 1884
La de los tristes destinos (f Pérez Galdós), 1907
La de San Quintín (p Pérez Galdós), 1894
Laberinto (v Jiménez), 1913
Labor (f Zola), 1901
Lac aux dames (p Colette), 1934
Laches (Plato)
Lacune (p Ionesco), 1965
Ladera est (v Paz), 1969
Ladies Day (p Aristophanes)
Ladies' Delight (f Zola)
Ladies of Saint-Cry (p Dumas), 1870
Ladies' Paradise (f Zola), 1883
Ladomir (Khlebnikov), 1920
Ladro in casa (p Svevo), 1960
Lady Aoi (p Mishima), 1957
Lady Blake's Love-Letters (f Sand)

Lady from the Sea (p Ibsen), 1890
Lady Inger of Ostraat (p Ibsen)
Lady Nit-Wit (p Vega)
Lady of Belle Isle (p Dumas), 1872
Lady Perfecta (f Pérez Galdós), 1883
Lafcadio's Adventures (f Gide), 1927
Laird de Dumbicky (p Dumas), 1843
Lais (v Villon)
Lake (f Kawabata), 1974
Lamb (f Mauriac), 1955
Lamb and the Beast (p Strindberg), 1970
Lament for the Death of a Bullfighter (v García Lorca), 1937
Laments (v Kochanowski), 1920
Lamiel (f Stendhal), 1889
Lammet och vilddjuret (p Strindberg), 1918
Lampe d'Aladin (v Cocteau), 1909
Lancelot (v Chrétien)
Landarzt (f Kafka), 1919
Landstrykere (f Hamsun), 1927
Larenopfer (v Rilke), 1896
Lásky hra osudná (p Capek), 1910
Last Aldini (f Sand), 1847
Last Day of a Condemned (f Hugo), 1840
Last Days of Socrates (Plato)
Last Days (Pushkin) (p Bulgakov), 1976
Last of the Abencérages (f Chateaubriand), 1826
Last of the Knights (p Strindberg), 1956
Last Summer (f Pasternak), 1959
Last Temptation of Christ (f Kazantzakis), 1960
Last Vendee (f Dumas), 1894
Last Year at Marienbad (p Robbe-Grillet), 1961
Lästigen (p Hofmannsthal), 1916
Lat människan leva (p Lagerkvist), 1949
Late Mattia Pascal (f Pirandello), 1923
Laudi del cielo... (v D'Annunzio), 1903
Laughing Man (f Hugo), 1887
Laune des Verliebten (p Goethe), 1779
Laura (f Sand), 1864
Laurel de Apolo (v Vega), 1630
Lautenlieder (v Wedekind), 1920
Lavinia (f Sand), 1834
Laws (Plato)
Lazare (p Zola), 1921
Lazarus (p Pirandello), 1952
Lazzaro (p Pirandello), 1928
Le connaissez-vous? (p Ionesco), 1953
Le là (v Breton), 1961
Leader (p Ionesco), 1960
League of Youth (p Ibsen), 1890
Léandre (p Beaumarchais)

Lear of the Steppe (f Turgenev)
Learning to Walk (p Ionesco), 1973
Leavetaking (f Weiss), 1962
Lebedinaya pesnya (p Chekhov), 1888
Lebediny stan (v Tsvetayeva), 1957
Leben Eduards des Zweiten von England
(p Brecht), 1924
Leben und Lieder (v Rilke), 1894
Lebens-Ansichten des Katers Murr (f Hoff-
mann), 1820
Leçon (p Ionesco), 1951
Leda (p Krleža), 1930
Leda senza cigno (f D'Annunzio), 1916
Legacy (p Marivaux)
Legacy (v Villon)
Legally Liable (p Plautus)
Legende (p Krleža), 1933
Légende de Prakriti (v Claudel), 1934
Légende des siecles (v Hugo), 1859
Legender (f Lagerlöf), 1904
Legiony (f Sienkiewicz), 1914
Legs (p Marivaux), 1736
Leiden des jungen Werthers (f Goethe),
1774
Leka med elden (p Strindberg), 1892
Lélekbúvár (p Illyés), 1948
Lélia (f Sand), 1833
Lena (p Ariosto), 1528
Léo Burckart (p Dumas, Nerval), 1839
Leonce and Lena (p Büchner)
Leonce und Lena (p Büchner), 1842
Léone (v Cocteau), 1945
Leone Leoni (f Sand), 1835
Leoun (v Cocteau), 1960
Leshy (p Chekhov), 1889
Lesser Bourgeoisie (f Balzac), 1890
Lesson (p Ionesco), 1958
Lesson in Love (f Colette), 1932
Lesson in Love (f Zola)
Let Man Live (p Lagerkvist), 1951
Let the Rail Splitter Awake (v Neruda),
1950
Let Us Follow Him (f Sienkiewicz), 1897
Leto (f Gorky), 1909
Letters from the Underworld (f Dostoevsky),
1915
Lettres d'Amabed (f Voltaire), 1769
Letzten (f Rilke), 1902
Leute von Seldwyla (f Keller), 1856
Leyenda (v Jiménez), 1978
Liaisons dangereuses (f Laclos), 1782
Liar (p Goldoni)
Libertad bajo palabra (v Paz), 1949
Libro de arena (f Borges), 1975

Libro de las preguntas (v Neruda), 1974
Libro delle vergina (f D'Annunzio), 1884
Libussa (p Grillparzer), 1872
Lichtzwang (v Celan), 1970
Liden Kirsten (p Andersen), 1846
Liebe geprüft (v Grass), 1974
Liebestrank (p Wedekind), 1899
Life (f Svevo), 1963
Life and Adventures of Indiana (f Marivaux)
Life and Death (f Sienkiewicz), 1904
Life I Gave You (p Pirandello), 1959
Life of a Man (v Ungaretti), 1958
Life of a Useless Man (f Gorky), 1971
Life of Galileo (p Brecht), 1960
Life of Marianne (f Marivaux)
Life of Matvei Kozhemyakin (f Gorky),
1959
Life of the Insects (p Capek), 1923
Life of the Virgin Mary (v Rilke), 1921
Life's a Dream (p Calderón)
Life-Terms (p Canetti), 1982
Light and Darkness (f Natsume), 1971
Lighting of the Christmas Tree (p Lagerlöf),
1921
Ligue (v Voltaire), 1723
Lila (p Goethe), 1777
Liliecrona's Home (f Lagerlöf), 1913
Lilies (v Mickiewicz), 1938
Liljecronas hem (f Lagerlöf), 1911
Lille Eyolf (p Ibsen), 1894
Lillian Morris (f Sienkiewicz), 1894
Lily of the Valley (f Balzac), 1891
Limes from Sicily (f Pirandello), 1942
Limestone (f Stifter), 1968
Lines of Life (f Mauriac), 1957
Link (p Strindberg), 1912
Liolà (p Pirandello), 1917
Lisa (f Turgenev)
Litigants (p Racine)
Little Carthaginian (p Plautus)
Little Eyolf (p Ibsen)
Little Fadette (f Sand), 1850
Little Misery (f Mauriac), 1952
Little Novels of Sicily (f Verga), 1925
Little Theatre of the World (p Hofmann-
sthal), 1961
Liturgies intimes (v Verlaine), 1892
Livet i vold (p Hamsun), 1910
Livets Spil (p Hamsun), 1896
Livre de Christophe Colomb (p Claudel),
1929
Livre mystique (f Balzac), 1835
Livret de folastries (v Ronsard), 1553
Ljubav u Kasabi (f Andrić), 1963

1949
Magic Mountain (f Mann), 1927
Magic Skin (f Balzac), 1888
Magico prodigioso (p Calderón)
Magister Ludi (f Hesse), 1949
Magnet (f Gorky), 1938
Magnus Garbe (p Hauptmann), 1942
Magun no tsuka (f Mishima), 1949
Magyar királyi honvéd novela (f Krleža),
 1921
Mahomet (p Goethe), 1799
Mahomet (p Voltaire), 1741
Maia (v D'Annunzio), 1903
Maid of Orleans (p Schiller), 1835
Maid to Marry (p Ionesco), 1960
Maidens of the Mount (p Hauptmann),
 1919
Maidens of the Rocks (f D'Annunzio), 1898
Maids (p Genet), 1954
Maihime (f Kawabata), 1951
Main droite du Sire de Giac (f Dumas),
 1838
Main gauche (f Maupassant), 1889
Mains jointes (v Mauriac), 1909
Mains sales (p Sartre), 1948
Maison de glace (f Dumas), 1860
Maison de Rendez-vous (f Robbe-Grillet),
 1965
Maison Nucingen (f Balzac), 1838
Maison Tellier (f Maupassant), 1881
Maître Favilla (p Sand), 1855
Maîtres mosaïstes (f Sand), 1838
Maîtres sonneurs (f Sand), 1853
Makioka Sisters (f Tanizaki), 1957
Mal (f Mauriac), 1935
Mal giocondo (v Pirandello), 1889
Malade imaginaire (p Molière), 1673
Mal-aimés (p Mauriac), 1945
Malavoglia (f Verga), 1881
Maleficio de la mariposa (p García Lorca),
 1920
Malentendu (p Camus), 1944
Malgrétout (f Sand), 1871
Malheur passe (p Maeterlinck), 1916
Malom a Séden (p Illyés), 1960
Maltaverne (f Mauriac), 1970
Mama Roma (p Pasolini), 1962
Mamelles de Tirésias (p Apollinaire), 1917
Man and His Dog (f Mann), 1930
Man in the Holocene (f Frisch), 1980
Man in the Iron Mask (f Dumas), 1893
Man of Forty Crowns (f Voltaire), 1768
Man of Honor (f Fontane), 1975
Man of Quality, Memoirs of a (f Prévost)

Man Who Lies (p Robbe-Grillet), 1968
Man Who Lived His Life Over (p Lager-
 kvist), 1971
Man Who Was Afraid (f Gorky), 1905
Man with Bags (p Ionesco), 1977
Man with the Flower in His Mouth
 (p Pirandello), 1928
Man with the Luggage (p Ionesco), 1979
Man Without a Soul (p Lagerkvist), 1944
Man Without Qualities (f Musil), 1953
Manatsu no shi (f Mishima), 1953
Manciata di more (f Silone), 1952
Mandragola (p Machiavelli), 1519
Mandrake (p Machiavelli)
Man-Hater (p Molière)
Manji (f Tanizaki), 1931
Mann ist Mann (p Brecht), 1926
Mann mit den Messern (f Böll), 1958
Mann ohne Eigenschaften (f Musil), 1930
Mannen utan själ (p Lagerkvist), 1936
Männer und Helden (v Fontane), 1850
Människor (f Lagerkvist), 1912
Manon Lescaut (f Prévost)
Manos del día (v Neruda), 1968
Man's a Man (p Brecht), 1964
Man's Estate (f Malraux), 1948
Man's Fate (f Malraux), 1934
Man's Hope (f Malraux), 1938
Manual of Piety (v Brecht), 1966
Mão e a luva (f Machado de Assis), 1874
Mappe meines Urgrossvaters (f Stifter),
 1946
Mar y las campanas (v Neruda), 1973
Marana (f Balzac), 1834
Marâtre (p Balzac), 1848
Marat-Sade (p Weiss)
Marbrier (p Dumas), 1854
Marcas (f Balzac), 1846
Marchand d'Agnus (p Beaumarchais)
Marchand de Venise (p Vigny), 1839
Märchen (f Hauptmann), 1941
Märchen der 672. Nacht (f Hofmannsthal),
 1905
Mare au diable (f Sand), 1846
Maréchale d'Ancre (p Vigny), 1831
Maremoto (v Neruda), 1970
Margaret de Navarre (f Dumas), 1845
Margaret of Anjou, History of (f Prévost)
Marguerite d'Anjou, Histoire de (f Pré-
 vost), 1740
Marguerite de Valois (f Dumas), 1846
Mari de la veuve (p Dumas), 1832
Maria Magdalena (p Hebbel), 1846
Maria Stuart (p Schiller), 1800

Mariage de Figaro (p Beaumarchais), 1783
Mariage de Victorine (p Sand), 1851
Mariage forcé (p Molière), 1664
Mariage sous Louis XV (p Dumas), 1841
Mariamne (f Lagerkvist), 1967
Mariamne (p Voltaire), 1724
Mariana Pineda (p García Lorca), 1927
Marianela (p Pérez Galdós), 1878
Marianne (f Sand), 1876
Mariazuehren (v Grass), 1973
Marie (f Pushkin)
Marie Antoinette (f Dumas), 1846
Marie Tudor (p Hugo), 1833
Marie-Magdeleine (p Maeterlinck), 1910
Marien-Leben (v Rilke), 1913
Mariés de la Tour Eiffel (p Cocteau), 1921
Marie-Victoire (p Maeterlinck), 1927
Mario and the Magician (f Mann), 1930
Mario und der Zauberer (f Mann), 1930
Marion Delorme (p Hugo), 1831
Marion und die Marionotten (f Frisch), 1946
Marisa la civetta (p Pasolini), 1957
Marito (p Svevo), 1960
Marito di Elena (f Verga), 1882
Mariucha (p Pérez Galdós), 1903
Mariya (p Babel), 1935
Markens Grøde (f Hamsun), 1917
Marqués de las Navas (p Vega)
Marquis de Brunoy (p Dumas), 1836
Marquis de Villemer (f Sand), 1860
Marquis of Villemer (f Sand), 1871
Marquis of Keith (p Wedekind), 1952
Marquis von Keith (p Wedekind), 1901
Marquise (f Sand), 1834
Marquise d'Escoman (f Dumas), 1860
Marquise Gange (f Sade), 1881
Marquise of O. (f Kleist), 1960
Marriage (p Gogol), 1927
Marriage (p Gombrowicz), 1969
Marriage Feast (f Lagerkvist), 1955
Marriage of Convenience (p Dumas), 1899
Marriage of Figaro (p Beaumarchais), 1785
Marriage of Mr. Mississippi (p Dürrenmatt), 1966
Marriage of Zobeide (p Hofmannsthal), 1961
Marriage Proposal (p Chekhov)
Married (f Strindberg), 1913
Married Lover (f Colette), 1935
Marshlands (f Gide), 1953
Marta la piadosa (p Tirso)
Martin Salander (f Keller), 1886
Martinique charmeuse de serpents (v Bre-

ton), 1948
Martyr calviniste (f Balzac), 1845
Martyre de Saint Sébastien (p D'Annunzio), 1911
Martyrs (f Chateaubriand), 1809
Martyrs ignorés (f Balzac), 1837
Mary Magdalene (p Maeterlinck), 1910
Mary Stuart (p Schiller), 1801
Marya (p Babel)
Mascarade (p Holberg)
Mask of Innocence (f Mauriac), 1953
Maskarad (p Lermontov)
Maske (p Hoffmann), 1923
Masked Ladies (p Holberg), 1946
Maskerata (p Krleža), 1955
Maski (f Bely), 1933
Masquerade (p Holberg), 1946
Masquerade of Souls (f Lagerkvist), 1954
Massacre des innocents (f Maeterlinck), 1918
Massimilla Doni (f Balzac), 1839
Massnahme (p Brecht), 1930
Master and Man (f Tolstoy)
Master and Margarite (f Bulgakov), 1967
Master Builder (p Ibsen), 1893
Master Darling (f Natsume), 1918
Master Don Gesualdo (f Verga), 1893
Master i Margarita (f Bulgakov), 1967
Master Mosaic Workers (f Sand), 1895
Master of Go (f Kawabata), 1972
Mäster Olof (p Strindberg), 1872
Master Passion (f Maupassant), 1958
Master Thaddeus (v Mickiewicz), 1885
Masterpiece (f Zola), 1886
Mastro-don Gesualdo (f Verga), 1889
Mat' (f Gorky), 1906
Mathilde Möhring (f Fontane), 1906
Matka (p Capek), 1938
Matka (p Witkiewicz), 1962
Matryona's House (f Solzhenitsyn), 1975
Matryonin dvor (f Solzhenitsyn), 1963
Matwa (p Witkiewicz), 1933
Mauprat (f Sand), 1837
Maurerpigen (p Andersen), 1840
Max (p Grass), 1972
Mayor monstruo los celos (p Calderón)
Mayor of Zalamea (p Calderón)
Measures Taken (p Brecht), 1965
Me-Az une-Ata (f Agnon), 1931
Medea (p Euripides)
Medea (p Grillparzer), 1879
Medea (p Pasolini), 1970
Medea (p Seneca)
Médecin de campagne (f Balzac), 1833

Médecin de Java (f Dumas), 1859
Médecin malgré lui (p Molière), 1666
Médecin volant (p Molière)
Médée (p Corneille), 1635
Medico de su honra (p Calderón)
Medved' (p Chekhov), 1888
Meer end Perler og Guld (p Andersen), 1849
Meeres und der Liebe Wellen (p Grillparzer), 1831
Meerwunder (f Hauptmann), 1934
Meeting at Telgte (f Grass), 1971
Meglio gioventù (v Pasolini), 1954
Me-Hamat ha-Metsik (f Agnon), 1921
Meian (f Natsume), 1917
Mein Name sei Gantenbein (f Frisch), 1964
Mejor alcalde, el rey (p Vega)
Mejor mozo de España (p Vega)
Melancolia (v Jiménez), 1912
Melancólico (p Tirso)
Meli (f Lagerlöf), 1909
Mélicerte (p Molière), 1666
Melindres de Belisa (p Vega)
Melissa (p Kazantzakis), 1939
Mélite (p Corneille), 1629
Melmoth réconcilié (f Balzac), 1836
Melusina (p Grillparzer), 1833
Mémoires de deux jeunes mariées (f Balzac), 1842
Mémoires d'un jeune Don Juan (f Apollinaire), 1907
Mémoires d'un maître d'armes (f Dumas), 1840
Mémoires d'un médecin (f Dumas), 1846
Mémoires pour servir à l'histoire de la révolution française (f Balzac), 1829
Mémoires pour servir à l'histoire de Malte (f Prévost), 1741
Memoirs of a Physician (f Dumas), 1847
Memoirs of the Golden Triangle (f Robbe-Grillet), 1984
Memoirs of Two Young Married Women (f Balzac), 1894
Memorial de Ayres (f Machado de Assis), 1908
Memorial de Isla Negra (v Neruda), 1964
Memorias de un cortesano de 1815 (f Pérez Galdós), 1875
Memórias póstumas de Bráz Cubas (f Machado de Assis), 1881
Men Livet Lever (f Hamsun), 1933
Men Without Shadows (p Sartre), 1949
Menaechmi (p Plautus)
Ménage de garçon en province (f Balzac), 1843

Mendizábal (f Pérez Galdós), 1898
Meneur de loups (f Dumas), 1857
Menexenus (Plato)
Meno (Plato)
Mensagem (v Pessoa), 1934
Mensch erscheint im Holozän (f Frisch), 1979
Menteur (p Corneille), 1643
Menteuse (f Giraudoux), 1958
Méprise (p Marivaux), 1734
Mercadet (p Balzac)
Mercator (Plautus)
Merchant (p Plautus)
Mère confidante (p Marivaux), 1735
Mère coupable (p Beaumarchais), 1792
Merope (v D'Annunzio), 1912
Mérope (p Voltaire), 1743
Meshchane (p Gorky), 1902
Mesiter Floh (f Hoffmann), 1822
Messaline (f Jarry), 1900
Messe de l'Athée (f Balzac), 1837
Messe là-bas (v Claudel), 1919
Messidor (p Zola), 1897
Mester Gert Westphaler (p Holberg)
Mesyats v derevne (p Turgenev), 1857
Metafizyka dwuglowego cielecia (p Witkiewicz), 1928
Metamorphoses (f Apuleius)
Metamorphoses (v Ovid)
Metamorphosis (f Kafka), 1961
Metaphysics of a Two-Headed Calf (p Witkiewicz), 1972
Métella (f Sand), 1834
Meteor (f Capek), 1935
Meteor (p Dürrenmatt), 1966
Meunier d'Angibault (f Sand), 1845
Miau (f Pérez Galdós), 1888
Michael Kramer (p Hauptmann), 1900
Michel Angelo (p Hebbel), 1851
Michelangelo Buonarroti (p Krleža), 1925
Michikusa (f Natsume), 1915
Micromégas (f Voltaire), 1752
Middle Classes (f Balzac), 1898
Midsommar (p Strindberg), 1901
Midsommardröm i fattighuset (p Lagerkvist), 1941
Midsummer Dream in the Workhouse (p Lagerkvist), 1953
Mignon (f Hauptmann), 1944
Mikkels kjaerligheds Historier i Paris (p Andersen), 1840
Miles Gloriosus (p Plautus)
Military Necessity (f Vigny), 1953
Military Servitude and Grandeur (f Vigny),

1919
Mille et un fantômes (f Dumas), 1848
Miller of Angibault (f Sand), 1847
Minden lehet (v Illyés), 1973
Mine at Falun (p Hofmannsthal), 1961
Mine Hostess (p Goldoni)
Mine-Haha (f Wedekind), 1901
Minin i Pozharski (p Bulgakov), 1976
Minister (p Schiller), 1798
Minna von Barnhelm (p Lessing), 1767
Minne (f Colette), 1903
Mir zur Feier (v Rilke), 1899
Miracle de la rose (f Genet), 1946
Miracle de Saint-Antoine (p Maeterlinck),
 1903
Miracle of Saint Anthony (p Maeterlinck),
 1918
Miracle of the Rose (f Genet), 1965
Miracles of Antichrist (f Lagerlöf), 1899
Mirandolina (p Goldoni)
Mire (p Ionesco), 1973
Mirgorod (f Gogol), 1835
Mirova Konference (f Hašek), 1922
Misaki nite no monogatari (f Mishima),
 1947
Misanthrope (p Molière), 1666
Miscreant (f Cocteau), 1958
Miser (p Molière)
Misérables (f Hugo), 1862
Misericordia (f Pérez Galdós), 1897
Miss Harriet (f Maupassant), 1883
Miss Julie (p Strindberg), 1918
Miss Sara Sampson (p Lessing), 1755
Mist (f Unamuno), 1928
Mistaken Beauty (p Corneille)
Mr. Aristotle (f Silone), 1935
Mr. Cleveland, Life and Adventures of
 (f Prévost)
Mister Price (p Witkiewicz), 1926
Mr. Puntila and His Man Matti (p Brecht),
 1977
Misteriya-Buff (p Mayakovsky), 1918
Mistress of the Inn (p Goldoni)
Mit allen Hunden gehetzt (p Wedekind),
 1910
Mit dem Kopf (p Horváth), 1934
Mit Sophie in die pilze Gegangen (v Grass),
 1976
Mithridate (p Racine), 1673
Mithridates (p Racine)
Mitir theou (v Sikelianos), 1917
Mitmacher (p Dürrenmatt), 1973
Mitschuldigen (p Goethe), 1777
Mitsou (f Colette), 1918

Mizuumi (f Kawabata), 1955
Mock Doctor (p Molière)
Modelo para la muerte (f Borges), 1946
Moderskärlek (p Strindberg), 1892
Mohamet the Imposter (p Voltaire), 1744
Mohicans de Paris (f Dumas), 1854
Mohn und Gedächtnis (v Celan), 1952
Mol'er (p Bulgakov), 1936
Molière (p Bulgakov), 1983
Molière (p Sand), 1851
Molodets (v Tsvetayeva), 1924
Momoku monogatari (f Tanizaki), 1932
Mon (f Natsume), 1911
Mönch und Räuber (p Böll)
Monde moral (f Prévost), 1760
Money (f Capek), 1929
Money (f Zola), 1894
Money Makes the World Go Round
 (p Marivaux)
Monna Vanna (p Maeterlinck), 1901
Monomaniac (f Zola), 1901
Monseigneur Gaston Phoebus (f Dumas),
 1839
Monsieur Coumbes (f Dumas), 1860
Monsieur de Pourceaugnac (p Molière),
 1669
M. le Modéré (p Adamov), 1968
Monsieur Parent (f Maupassant), 1885
Monsieur Ripois (p Queneau), 1954
Monsieur Tête (p Ionesco), 1970
Monstres sacrés (p Cocteau), 1940
Mont de piété (v Breton), 1919
Montagne secrète (f Roy), 1961
Montauk (f Frisch), 1975
Monte-Cristo (p Dumas), 1848
Monténégrins (p Nerval), 1849
Montes de Oca (f Pérez Galdós), 1900
Month in the Country (p Turgenev)
Montjoye (p Machado de Assis), 1864
Mont-Oriol (f Maupassant), 1887
Mont-Revêche (f Sand), 1853
Morale élémentaire (v Queneau), 1975
Moralités légendaires (f Laforgue), 1887
More de Venise (p Vigny), 1829
Morgenlandfahrt (f Hesse), 1932
Morning Glory (f Colette), 1932
Mors porträtt (f Lagerlöf), 1930
Morsa (p Pirandello), 1910
Mort à crédit (f Céline), 1936
Mort dans l'âme (f Sartre), 1949
Mort de César (p Voltaire), 1735
Mort de Pompée (p Corneille), 1643
Mort de Tintagiles (p Maeterlinck), 1894
Mort en ce Jardin (p Queneau), 1956

Mort heureuse (f Camus), 1971
Morte delle stagioni (v Ungaretti), 1967
Morte di un amico (p Pasolini), 1960
Morts sans sepulture (p Sartre), 1946
Mosaic Masters (f Sand), 1847
Mosaic Workers (f Sand), 1844
Moses (p Strindberg), 1916
Moskva (f Bely), 1926
Mostellaria (p Plautus)
Mother (p Brecht), 1965
Mother (p Capek), 1939
Mother (f Gorky), 1907
Mother (p Witkiewicz), 1968
Mother Courage (f Grimmelshausen), 1965
Mother Courage and Her Children
  (p Brecht), 1961
Mother-in-Law (p Terence)
Motherlove (p Strindberg), 1910
Mother's Guilt (p Beaumarchais), 1983
Mothwise (f Hamsun), 1921
Motiv (v Lagerkvist), 1914
Motor Show (p Ionesco), 1963
Motsart i Sal'eri (p Pushkin), 1831
Mottetti (v Montale), 1973
Mouches (p Sartre), 1943
Mount Gars (f Stifter), 1857
Mountain Giants (p Pirandello), 1958
Mousquetaires (p Dumas), 1845
Moutardier du pape (p Jarry), 1907
Mouth of Hell (f Dumas), 1906
Moza de cántaro (p Vega)
Mozart and Salieri (p Pushkin)
Mtsyri (v Lermontov)
Muerte y la brújala (f Borges), 1951
Muj obchod se psy (f Hašek), 1915
Mulatten (p Andersen), 1840
Munken Vendt (p Hamsun), 1902
Mur (f Sartre), 1939
Murat (f Dumas), 1838
Muri di sano (p Pasolini), 1971
Murky Business (f Balzac), 1972
Muses galantes (p Rousseau), 1745
Musik (p Wedekind), 1908
Musik des Einsamen (v Hesse), 1915
Musketeers (p Dumas), 1898
Musotte (p Maupassant), 1891
Mutter (p Brecht), 1932
Mutter Courage und ihre Kinder (p Brecht),
  1941
Mutter und Kind (v Hebbel), 1859
My (f Zamyatin), 1952
My Husband and I (f Tolstoy)
My Sister Jeannie (f Sand), 1874
My Sister—Life (v Pasternak), 1983

Myortvye dushi (p Bulgakov), 1932
Myortvye dushi (f Gogol), 1842
Mystère Frontenac (f Mauriac), 1933
Mystères de Marseille (f Zola), 1867
Mysterier (f Hamsun), 1892
Mysteries (f Hamsun), 1927
Mysteries of Marseilles (f Zola), 1895
Mystery of the Rue Soly (f Balzac), 1894
Mystery-Bouffe (p Mayakovsky), 1968
Mythistorema (v Seferis), 1935
Mythologie (v Cocteau), 1934

Na dne (p Gorky), 1902
Na Drini ćupriji (f Andrić), 1945
Na Han (f Lu Hsun), 1923
Na jasnym brzegu (f Sienkiewicz), 1897
Na kulichkakh (f Zamyatin), 1923
Na marne (f Sienkiewicz), 1872
Na polu chwaly (f Sienkiewicz), 1906
Na rannikh poezdakh (v Pasternak), 1943
Na ruba pameti (f Krleža), 1938
Nabobnisie i koczkodany (p Witkiewicz),
  1962
Nachsommer (f Stifter), 1857
Nacht mit Gästen (p Weiss), 1963
Nächtliches Gespräch mit einem verach-
  teten Menschen (p Dürrenmatt), 1957
Nachtstücke (f Hoffmann), 1817
Nadia fie su secreto (p Calderón)
Nagasugita haru (f Mishima), 1961
Naïs Micoulin (f Zola), 1884
Naissance d'une fée (p Céline), 1959
Naissance du jour (f Colette), 1928
Nakanune (f Turgenev), 1860
Naked (p Pirandello), 1923
Naked Masks (p Pirandello), 1952
Naked Truth (f Pirandello), 1934
Nakhlebnik (p Turgenev), 1857
Näktergalen i Wittenberg (p Strindberg),
  1903
Nana (f Zola), 1880
Nanine (p Voltaire) 1749
Nanon (f Dumas), 1847
Nanon (f Sand) 1872
Não consultes médico (p Machado de Assis),
  1896
Napoléon Bonaparte (p Dumas), 1831
Napoleón en Chamartín (f Pérez Galdós),
  1874
Når vi døde vågner (p Ibsen), 1899
Narcisse (p Rousseau), 1753
Narcisse (f Sand), 1859
Narcissus and Goldmund (f Hesse), 1968
Narr in Christo, Emanuel Quint (f Haupt-

North (f Céline), 1972
Not Present (p Rilke), 1979
Notebook of Andre Walter (f Gide), 1968
Notebooks of Malte Laurids Brigge (f Rilke), 1958
Notes from Underground (f Dostoevsky), 1918
Notre Coeur (f Maupassant), 1890
Notre-Dame de Paris (f Hugo), 1831
Notre-Dame des Fleurs (f Genet), 1944
Notte brava (p Pasolini) 1959
Notti di Cabiria (p Pasolini), 1956
Nourritures terrestres (f Gide), 1897
Nouveau Locataire (p Ionesco), 1955
Nouvelle Colonie (p Marivaux), 1729
Nouvelle Héloïse (f Rousseau), 1761
Nouvelle Justine (f Sade), 1797
Nov' (f Turgenev), 1877
Novella del buon vecchio e della bella fanciulla (f Svevo), 1930
Novelle della Pescare (f D'Annunzio), 1902
Novelle rusticane (f Verga), 1882
Nowe Wyzwolenie (p Witkiewicz), 1925
Noyers de l'Altenburg (f Malraux), 1943
Nueva victoria de don Gonzalo de Córdoba (p Vega)
Nuevo canto de amor a Stalingrado (v Neruda), 1943
Nuevo mundo descubierto por Cristóbal Colón (p Vega)
Nuit à Florence (f Dumas), 1861
Nuit de Noël 1914 (p Claudel), 1915
Nuit du bourreau de soi-même (f Mauriac), 1929
Nuit vénitienne (p Musset), 1830
Numancia (p Cervantes)
Nun (f Diderot)
Nun singen sie wieder (p Frisch), 1945
Nuova colonia (p Pirandello), 1928
Nuova giovento (v Pasolini), 1975
Ny Jord (f Hamsun), 1893
Nye Barselstue (p Andersen), 1845
Nyitott ajtó (v Illyés), 1963
Nymph of Fiesole (v Boccaccio)
Nymphe de la Seine (v Racine), 1660
Nymphs of Fiesole (v Boccaccio)

O.T. (f Andersen), 1836
O di uno o di nessuno (p Pirandello), 1929
Oaha (p Wedekind), 1908
Objet aimé (p Jarry), 1953
Oblako v shtamakh (v Mayakovsky), 1915
Oblomov (f Goncharov), 1859
Obra da geração (p Vicente)

Obryv (f Goncharov), 1870
Obshchestvo pochotnykh zvonarey (p Zamyatin), 1925
Obyčejny život (f Capek), 1934
Obyknovennaya istoriya (f Goncharov), 1848
Occasioni (v Montale), 1939
Oceana (v Neruda), 1962
Octavia (p Seneca)
Octets (v Mandelstam), 1976
Oda a la tipografía (v Neruda), 1956
Oda a Walt Whitman (v García Lorca), 1933
Odas elementales (v Neruda), 1954
Ode à Charles Fourier (v Breton), 1947
Ode à Picasso (v Cocteau), 1920
Ode sur la convalescence du Roi (v Racine), 1663
Ode to Charles Fourier (v Breton), 1969
Odes en son honneur (v Verlaine), 1893
Odesskie rasskazy (f Babel), 1931
Odei navali (v D'Annunzio), 1893
Odin den' Ivana Denisovicha (f Solzhenitsyn), 1962
Ödipus und die Sphinx (p Hofmannsthal) 1905
Odile (f Queneau), 1937
O'Donnell (f Pérez Galdós), 1904
Odprawa prolów greklich (p Kochanowski), 1578
Odyseia (v Kazantzakis), 1938
Odysseas (p Kazantzakis), 1928
Odyssey (v Homer)
Odyssey (v Kazantzakis), 1958
Oedipe (p Corneille), 1659
Oedipe (p Gide), 1931
Oedipe (p Voltaire), 1718
Oedipe-Roi (p Cocteau), 1928
Oedipus (p Seneca)
Oedipus at Colonus (p Sophocles)
Oedipus Coloneus (p Sophocles)
Oedipus Rex (p Cocteau), 1927
Oedipus Rex (p Pasolini), 1967
Oedipus Rex (p Sophocles)
Oedipus the King (p Sophocles)
Oedipus Tyrannus (p Sophocles)
Oeuf dur (p Ionesco), 1966
Oeuvre (f Zola), 1886
Oeuvres complètes de Sally Mara (f Queneau), 1962
Off Limits (p Adamov), 1969
Ogni svyatogo Doninika (p Zamyatin), 1922
Ogniem i mieczem (f Sienkiewicz), 1884
Oh What a Bloody Circus (p Ionesco), 1976
Ohne Gegenwart (p Rilke), 1898

Ouragan (p Zola), 1901
Ours de la lune (p Claudel), 1919
Outcast (f Lagerlöf), 1920
Outcast (f Pirandello), 1925
Outcasts (f Gorky), 1902
Outlaw (p Strindberg), 1912
Outlaw of Iceland (f Hugo), 1885
Outsider (f Camus), 1946
Ováder (p Strindberg), 1907
Oversight (p Ionesco), 1971
Oxtiern (p Sade), 1791
Ozorai példa (p Illyés), 1952

Paa gjengrodde Stier (f Hamsun) 1949
Paa Langebro (p Andersen), 1864
Paces de los reyes y judía de Toledo (p Vega)
Padre di famiglia (p Goldoni)
Padre engañado (p Vega)
Page d'amour (f Zola), 1878
Page du duc de Savoie (f Dumas), 1855
Page of Love (f Zola), 1897
Pain dur (p Claudel), 1941
Pain vivant (p Mauriac), 1955
Painter of His Own Dishonour (p Calderón)
Paix du ménage (p Maupassant), 1893
Palacio confuso (p Vega)
Paläophron und Neoterpe (p Goethe), 1800
Palata No. 6 (f Chekhov), 1893
Paludes (f Gide), 1895
Pamela (p Goldoni)
Paméla Giraud (p Balzac), 1843
Pamietnik z okresu dojrzeqanie (f Gombrowicz), 1933
Pan (f Hamsun), 1894
Pan (v Krleža), 1917
Pan Michael (f Sienkiewicz), 1895
Pan Tadeusz (v Mickiewicz), 1834
Pan Wolodyjowski (f Sienkiewicz), 1887
Pandora no Hako (f Dazai), 1946
Pandora's Box (p Wedekind), 1918
Pane e vino (f Silone), 1937
P'ang-huang (f Lu Hsun), 1926
Panna Tutli-Putli (p Witkiewicz), 1974
Panne (f Dürrenmatt), 1960
Pantagruel (p Jarry), 1911
Pantagruel (f Rabelais)
Pantera nera (p Pirandello), 1920
Pantsatte bondedreng (p Holberg)
Paolo Paoli (p Adamov), 1957
Pape (v Hugo), 1878
Papéis avulsos (f Machado de Assis), 1882
Papesse Jeanne (p Jarry), 1981
Para las seis cuerdas (v Borges), 1965
Parables for the Theatre (p Brecht), 1948

Paraboles (v Valéry), 1935
Parade (p Cocteau), 1917
Paradises terrestres (f Colette), 1932
Paraíso de los creyentes (f Borges), 1955
Paralipomeni della Batracomiomachia (v Leopardi), 1842
Parallelement (v Verlaine), 1889
Parasha (v Turgenev), 1843
Parasit (p Schiller), 1803
Parasite (p Schiller), 1856
Paravents (p Genet), 1961
Parents pauvres (f Balzac), 1847
Parents terribles (p Cocteau), 1938
Paria (p Strindberg), 1889
Pariah (p Strindberg), 1913
Parigi sbastigliata (v Alfieri), 1789
Paris (f Zola), 1898
Paris Spleen (v Baudelaire)
Parisiens et provinciaux (f Dumas), 1868
Parisina (p D'Annunzio), 1913
Parmenides (Plato)
Pariodie (p Adamov), 1950
Parsival (f Hauptmann), 1914
Partage de midi (p Claudel), 1906
Partie d'echecs (v Cocteau), 1961
Parzifal (v Wolfram)
Pasado en claro (v Paz), 1975
Pascal Bruno (f Dumas), 1838
Pascha tom Ellinon (v Sikelianos), 1947
Pasenow (f Broch), 1931
Pasha's Concubine (f Andrić), 1968
Påsk (p Strindberg), 1901
Pasos perdidos (f Carpentier), 1953
Pasqua di Gea (v Pirandello), 1891
Passage du Malin (p Mauriac), 1947
Passion dans le désert (f Balzac), 1837
Passion noire (p Carpentier), 1932
Passions and Ancient Days (v Cavafy), 1972
Past Recaptured (f Proust), 1932
Pasteur d'Ashbourne (f Dumas), 1853
Pastoral Symphony (f Gide), 1931
Pastoral Tragedy of the Serra da Estrella (p Vicente)
Pastorale comique (p Molière), 1666
Pastorales (p Jiménez), 1911
Pastorals (v Virgil)
Pastores de Belén (f Vega), 1612
Patente (p Pirandello), 1918
Paths of Freedom (f Sartre), 1947
Pauken und Trompeten (p Brecht), 1956
Paul Jones (p Dumas), 1838
Pauline (f Dumas), 1838
Pauline (f Sand), 1840
Pauline et Belval (f Sade), 1798

Pauvre Matelot (p Cocteau), 1927
Paysan parvenu (f Marivaux), 1735
Paysans (f Balzac), 1855
Paz en la guerra (f Unamuno), 1897
Peace (p Aristophanes)
Peace for Twilights to Come! (v Neruda), 1950
Peasant in Pawn (p Holberg), 1950
Peasantry (f Balzac)
Peasants in Exile (f Sienkiewicz), 1898
Peau de chagrin (f Balzac), 1831
Peccatrice (f Verga), 1867
Pêche aux filets (f Dumas), 1864
Péché de Monsieur Antoine (f Sand), 1846
Pedro Carbonero (p Vega)
Pedro Minio (p Pérez Galdós), 1908
Peer Gynt (p Ibsen), 1867
Pelican (p Strindberg), 1916
Pelikanen (p Strindberg), 1907
Pelléas et Mélisande (p Maeterlinck), 1892
Penny for the Poor (f Brecht), 1937
Pensaci Giacomino! (p Pirandello), 1916
Pensya o Burevestnike (v Gorky), 1901
Penthesilea (p Kleist), 1808
People from the Puszta (f Illyés), 1967
People of Seldwyla (f Keller), 1929
Peor está que estaba (p Calderón)
Pepel (v Bely), 1908
Pepíček Nový (f Hašek), 1921
Per le vie (f Verga), 1883
Perceval (v Chretien)
Père de famille (p Diderot), 1758
Père Goriot (f Balzac), 1835
Père humilié (p Claudel), 1920
Père la Ruine (f Dumas), 1860
Père prudent et équitable (p Marivaux), 1712
Peregrino en su patria (f Vega), 1604
Peribáñez y el Comendador de Ocaña (p Vega)
Perikeriomene (p Menander)
Permanent Husband (f Dostoevsky), 1888
Perro del hortelano (p Vega)
Persa (p Plautus)
Persae (p Aeschylus), 472
Persecution and Assassination of Jean-Paul Marat... (p Weiss), 1965
Perséphone (p Gide), 1934
Persian (p Plautus)
Persians (p Aeschylus)
Persy Zwierzatkowskaja (p Witkiewicz), 1927
Pertharite (p Corneille), 1651
Pervaya lyubov' (f Turgenev), 1860

Pervoye svidanie (v Bely), 1921
Pesnya pro tsarya Ivana Vasil'evicha (v Lermontov), 1837
Pesnya sud'by (p Blok), 1919
Peste (f Camus), 1947
Peter Bauer (p Hauptmann), 1921
Peter Camenzind (f Hesse), 1904
Peterburg (f Bely), 1916
Peterburg (f Bely), 1978
Petite cosmogonie portative (v Queneau), 1950
Petite Fadette (f Sand), 1849
Petite Poule d'eau (f Roy), 1950
Petite Roque (f Maupassant), 1886
Petites misères de la vie conjugale (f Balzac), 1845
Petit-Maître corrigé (p Marivaux), 1734
Petits Bourgeois (f Balzac), 1856
Pettegolezzi della donne (p Goldoni)
Petty Annoyances of Married Life (f Balzac), 1861
Petty Bourgeois (p Gorky), 1979
Pfirsichbaum (f Hesse), 1945
Phädra (p Schiller), 1805
Phaedra (p Racine)
Phaedra (p Seneca)
Phaedre and Hippolytus (p Racine)
Phaedrus (Plato)
Phaethon (p Euripides)
Phalenas (v Machado de Assis), 1870
Phantom (f Hauptmann), 1922
Phantom Lady (Calderón)
Pharisienne (f Mauriac), 1941
Pharsamon (f Marivaux), 1737
Pharsamond (f Marivaux)
Phèdre et Hippolyte (p Racine), 1677
Philebus (Plato)
Philoctète (p Gide), 1919
Philoctetes (p Gide), 1951
Philoctetes (p, Sophocles)
Philomena (v Chrétien)
Philosophe anglais (f Prévost), 1731
Philosopher or Dog? (f Machado de Assis), 1954
Philosopher's Stone (p Lagerkvist), 1966
Philosophie dans le boudoir (f Sade), 1795
Philotas (p Lessing), 1759
Phoenician Women (p Euripides)
Phoenissae (p Euripides)
Phoenissae (p Seneca)
Phormio (p Terence)
Photo du Colonel (f Ionesco), 1962
Physicists (p Dürrenmatt), 1963
Physiker (p Dürrenmatt), 1962

Poharaim (v Illyés), 1967
Polifemo (v Góngora)
Polin (f Agnon), 1925
Polish Spy (f Dumas), 1869
Political Tinker (p Holberg), 1914
Politicus (Plato)
Politique des restes (p Adamov), 1963
Politiske Kandestøber (p Holberg)
Poloumnyi Zhurden (p Bulgakov), 1965
Polyeucte, Martyr (p Corneille), 1642
Polyeuctes (p Corneille)
Polyphemus and Galatea (v Góngora)
Pomeshchik (v Turgenev), 1846
Pompeji (p Horváth), 1959
Pompes funèbres (f Genet), 1947
Pompey the Great (p Corneille)
Pomponius, Aventures de (f Prévost), 1724
Pont de Londres (f Céline), 1963
Poor Folk (f Dostoevsky), 1887
Poor Relations (f Balzac), 1880
Por el sótano y el torno (p Tirso)
Porcile (p Pasolini), 1969
Pornografia (f Gombrowicz), 1960
Porte étroite (f Gide), 1909
Porto sepolto (v Ungaretti), 1916
Porträt eines Planeten (p Dürrenmatt), 1970
Posle razluki (v Bely), 1922
Posle Rossii (v Tsvetayeva), 1928
Posledniye dni (Pushkin) (p Bulgakov), 1943
Possédés (p Camus), 1959
Possessed (p Camus), 1960
Possessed (f Dostoevsky), 1913
Possessed (f Gombrowicz), 1980
Possibility of Being (v Rilke), 1977
Posthumous Memoirs of Craz Cubas (f Machado de Assis), 1951
Post-Inn (p Goldoni)
Postrer duelo de España (p Calderón)
Pot of Gold (p Plautus)
Pot-Bouille (f Zola), 1882
Potentissima signora (v Pasolini), 1965
Potomak (f Cocteau), 1919
Potop (f Sienkiewicz), 1886
Pour en finir avec le jugement de Dieu (p Artaud), 1948
Pour Lucrèce (p Giraudoux), 1953
Pour préparer un oeuf dur (p Ionesco), 1966
Poverkh bar'erov (v Pasternak), 1917
Povesti pokoynovo I.P. Belkina (p Pushkin), 1830
Povětrón (f Capek), 1934
Povídny z druhé kapsy (f Capek), 1929
Povídny z jedné kapsy (f Capek), 1929

Povratak Filipa Latinovicza (f Krleža), 1932
Power and Glory (p Capek), 1938
Power of the Dead (p Maeterlinck), 1923
Pozegnanie jesieni (f Witkiewicz), 1927
Pragmatists (p Witkiewicz), 1972
Pragmatysci (p Witkiewicz), 1921
Praise of Folly (Erasmus)
Praxède (f Dumas), 1841
Précieuses ridicules (p Molière), 1659
Precipice (f Goncharov), 1916
Précis de l'Ecclésiaste (v Voltaire), 1759
Predlozheniye (p Chekhov), 1889
Préséances (f Mauriac), 1921
Prestupleniye i nakazaniye (f Dostoevsky), 1867
Pretenders (p Ariosto)
Pretenders (p Ibsen), 1890
Prica o kmeta Simanu (f Andrić), 1950
Prica o vezirovam slonu (f Andrić), 1948
Prière mutilée (v Cocteau), 1925
Priest in the House (f Zola)
Prim (f Pérez Galdós), 1906
Prima Ballerina (p Hofmannsthal), 1923
Primavera (f Verga), 1876
Primer romancero gitano (v García Lorca), 1928
Primera República (f Pérez Galdós), 1911
Primo del ballo (p Svevo), 1960
Primo vere (v D'Annunzio), 1879
Prince de la Bohéme (f Balzac), 1845
Prince des sots (f Nerval), 1866
Prince frivole (v Cocteau), 1910
Prince of Homburg (p Kleist), 1959
Prince travesti (p Marivaux), 1724
Princesa (p Unamuno), 1913
Princess Ivona (p Gombrowicz), 1969
Princess Maleine (p Maeterlinck), 1890
Princess Monpensier (f Lafayette)
Princess of Babylon (f Voltaire)
Princess of Cleves (f Lafayette)
Princesse de Babylone (f Voltaire), 1768
Princesse de Clèves (p Cocteau), 1961
Princesse de Clèves (f Lafayette), 1678
Princesse de Montpensier (f Lafayette), 1662
Princesse de Navarre (p Voltaire), 1745
Princesse d'Élide (p Molière), 1664
Princesse Flora (f Dumas), 1859
Princesse Isabelle (p Maeterlinck), 1935
Princesse Maleine (p Maeterlinck), 1889
Principe constante (p Calderón)
Príncipe despeñado (p Vega)
Printemps 71 (p Adamov), 1961
Prinz Eugen der edle Ritter (f Hofmann-

Quitt (f Fontane), 1890
Quittance du diable (p Musset), 1896
Quitte pour la peur (p Vigny), 1833
Quo vadis? (f Sienkiewicz), 1896

R.U.R. (p Capek), 1920
Rabouilleuse (f Balzac), 1912
Racconti di Canterbury (p Pasolini), 1972
Ragazza in vetrina (p Pasolini), 1961
Ragazzi di vita (f Pasolini), 1955
Ragione degli altri (p Pirandello), 1921
Raio no Terasu (p Mishima), 1969
Raíz del hombre (v Paz), 1937
Rakhel (p Bulgahov), 1943
Rakovy korpus (f Solzhenitsyn), 1968
Ralentir travaux (v Breton), 1930
Rameau's Nephew (f Diderot)
Ramírez e Arellano (p Vega)
Rangiku monogatari (f Tanizaki), 1949
Rape of the Locks (p Menander)
Raquel (p Unamuno), 1933
Rats (p Hauptmann), 1913
Ratten (p Hauptmann), 1911
Räuber (p Schiller), 1781
Ravnen (p Andersen), 1832
Raw Youth (f Dostoevsky), 1916
Rayons et les ombres (v Hugo), 1840
Razgovor (v Turgenev), 1845
Razgovor na bolshoy doroge (p Turgenev), 1850
Razluka (v Tsvetayeva), 1922
Razón de la sinrazón (f Pérez Galdós), 1915
Re Torrismondo (p Tasso), 1586
Realidad (f Pérez Galdós), 1889
Reasons of State (f Carpentier), 1976
Recaptured (f Colette), 1931
Recherche de l'absolu (f Balzac), 1834
Recluse (f Stifter), 1968
Reconciliation (p Hauptmann), 1914
Recurso del método (f Carpentier), 1974
Red and Black (f Stendhal), 1900
Red Carnation (f Vittorini), 1952
Red Commissar (f Hašek), 1981
Red Room (f Strindberg), 1913
Redaktør Lynge (f Hamsun), 1893
Regenerazione (p Svevo), 1960
Regent (p Strindberg), 1956
Regent's Daughter (f Dumas), 1847
Régicide (f Robbe-Grillet), 1978
Regrets (v Du Bellay), 1558
Reine fantasque (f Rousseau), 1758
Reine Margot (f Dumas), 1845
Reineke Fuchs (v Goethe), 1794

Reino de este mundo (f Carpentier), 1949
Rei-Seleuco (p Camões), 1645
Rekviem (v Akhmatova), 1964
Religieuse (f Diderot)
Religione del mio tempo (v Pasolini), 1961
Religions et religion (v Hugo), 1880
Relíquias de Casa Velha (f Machado de Assis), 1906
Remedia Amoris (v Ovid)
Remedio en la desdicha (p Vega)
Remeslo (v Tsvetayeva), 1923
Remembrance of Things Past (f Proust), 1922
Reminiscences of Antony (f Dumas), 1905
Renaud et Arminde (p Cocteau), 1943
Rend a romokban (v Illyés), 1937
René (f Chateaubriand), 1802
Renée (p Zola), 1887
Renée la vagabonde (f Colette), 1931
Renga (v Paz), 1971
Rentier (f Balzac), 1847
Répétition (p Maupassant), 1879
Repos du septième jour (p Claudel), 1901
Reprieve (f Sartre), 1947
Republic (Plato)
Requiem (v Akhmatova), 1976
Requiem (v Cocteau), 1961
Requiem (v Rilke), 1909
Requiem pour une nonne (p Camus), 1956
Residence on Earth (v Neruda), 1973
Residencia en la tierra (v Neruda), 1933
Resistible Rise of Arturo Ui (p Brecht), 1976
Resources of Quinola (p Balzac)
Respectable Prostitute (p Sartre), 1949
Respectable Wedding (p Brecht), 1970
Respectful Prostitute (p Sartre), 1949
Respublika truda (p Solzhenitsyn), 1981
Ressources de Quinola (p Balzac), 1842
Restless House (f Zola)
Resurrection (f Tolstoy)
Resurreição (f Machado de Assis), 1872
"Retablillo" de Don Cristóbal (p García Lorca), 1935
Retour de l'enfant prodigue (f Gide), 1907
Retraite sentimentale (f Colette), 1907
Retreat from Love (f Colette), 1974
Retrouvailles (p Adamov), 1955
Return of Philip Latinovicz (f Krleža), 1959
Réunion des amours (p Marivaux), 1730
Revanche de la nuit (v Jarry), 1949
Rêve (f Zola), 1888
Revenge of Truth (p Dinesen), 1971
Revizor (p Gogol), 1836

Revolte auf Cote 3018 (p Horváth), 1927
Revolución de julio (f Pérez Galdós), 1904
Révolver à cheveux blancs (v Breton), 1932
Reynard the Fox (v Goethe)
Rhesos (p Euripides)
Rhesus (p Euripides)
Rhin (v Hugo), 1842
Rhinocéros (p Ionesco), 1959
Rhume onirique (p Ionesco), 1953
Richard Darlington (p Dumas), 1831
Richter und sein Henker (f Dürrenmatt), 1952
Ricordi del Capitano d'Arce (f Verga), 1891
Ricotta (p Pasolini), 1976
Rieurs de Beau-Richard (p La Fontaine), 1659
Rigadon (f Céline), 1969
Rigadoon (f Céline), 1974
Right You Are (If You Think So) (p Pirandello), 1922
Riksföreståndaren (p Strindberg), 1908
Rimas de dentro (v Unamuno), 1923
Rinaldo (v Tasso), 1562
Ring Is Closed (f Hamsun), 1937
Ring of the Löwenskölds (f Lagerlöf), 1931
Ringen sluttet (f Hamsun), 1936
Rip van Winkle (p Frisch), 1953
Ripening Corn (f Colette), 1931
Ripening Seed (f Colette), 1959
Rise and Fall of the City of Mahagonny (p Brecht), 1976
Rivalités en province (f Balzac), 1838
River of Fire (f Mauriac), 1954
Rivière sans repos (f Roy), 1970
Road Leads On (f Hamsun), 1934
Road Past Altamont (f Roy), 1966
Robbers (p Schiller), 1792
Robe de noces (f Dumas), 1844
Robe prétexte (f Mauriac), 1914
Robert (p Gide), 1930
Robert Guiskard (p Kleist), 1826
Robin, Bachelor of Love (p Marivaux)
Rock Crystal (f Stifter), 1945
Rock Garden (f Kazantzakis), 1963
Röda rummet (f Strindberg), 1879
Rodogune (p Corneille), 1644
Rodzina Polanieckich (f Sienkiewicz), 1894
RoGoPaG (p Pasolini), 1962
Roi Candaule (p Gide), 1901
Roi s'amuse (p Hugo), 1832
Roi se meurt (p Ionesco), 1962
Rokumeikan (p Mishima), 1956
Rokvyye yaytsa (f Bulgakov), 1928
Roland of Montreval (f Dumas), 1860

Rolling Stone (f Sand), 1871
Roma 1950: Diario (v Pasolini), 1960
Romagem de agravados (p Vicente)
Roman d'Elvire (p Dumas), 1860
Roman Elegies (v Goethe)
Romance of Marriage (f Tolstoy)
Romancero (v Heine)
Romancero del destierro (v Unamuno), 1928
Romancero espiritual (v Vega), 1624
Romances de Coral Gables (v Jiménez), 1948
Romances sans paroles (v Verlaine), 1874
Romances Without Words (v Verlaine), 1921
Romantische Lieder (v Hesse), 1899
Romanzero (v Heine), 1851
Rome (f Zola), 1896
Rome Preserved (p Voltaire), 1760
Rome sauvée (p Voltaire), 1750
Romeo and Juliet (p Neruda), 1964
Roméo et Juliette (p Cocteau), 1924
Romeo und Juliet (p Goethe), 1812
Römische Elegien (v Goethe), 1789
Romulus (p Dumas), 1854
Romulus der Gross (p Dürrenmatt), 1949
Rope (p Plautus)
Rosa (f Dumas), 1854
Rosa (f Hamsun), 1908
Rosa separada (v Neruda), 1972
Rosario de sonetos líricos (v Unamuno), 1911
Rosas andinas (v Darío), 1888
Rose Bernd (p Hauptmann), 1903
Rose caduche (p Verga), 1929
Rose de François (v Cocteau), 1923
Rose et Blanche (f Sand), 1831
Rosenkavalier (p Hofmannsthal), 1911
Rosier de Madame Husson (f Maupassant), 1888
Rosmersholm (p Ibsen), 1886
Rosshalde (f Hesse), 1914
Rossum's Universal Robots (p Capek), 1923
Rote Hahn (p Hauptmann), 1901
Rouge et le noir (f Stendhal), 1830
Rougon-Macquart (f Zola)
Round World (f Sturluson)
Roundheads and Peakheads (p Brecht), 1966
Route d'Altamont (f Roy), 1966
Row (p Plautus)
Royal Highness (f Mann), 1916
Royal Way (f Malraux), 1935
Royaume farfelu (f Malraux), 1928

Rubin (p Hebbel), 1849
Rucksack Play (p Plautus)
Rude hiver (f Queneau), 1939
Rudens (p Plautus)
Rudin (f Turgenev), 1856
Rue Deschambault (f Roy), 1955
Ruinen von Athen (p Hofmannsthal) 1925
Ruins of Rome (v Du Bellay)
Rules of the Game (p Pirandello), 1959
Runaway Horses (f Mishima), 1973
Rund um den Kongress (p Horváth), 1929
Rundköpfe und die Spitzköpfe (p Brecht), 1936
Rural Life in Austria and Hungary (f Stifter), 1850
Rush for the Spoil (f Zola), 1886
Russian Gipsy (f Dumas), 1860
Russian Life in the Interior (f Turgenev), 1855
Rusteghi (p Goldoni)
Ruy Blas (p Cocteau), 1947
Ruy Blas (p Hugo), 1838
Ryav! (Khlebnikov), 1913

Sacred Hymns (v Manzoni), 1904
Sacred Songs (v Novalis)
Sado koshaku fujin (p Mishima), 1965
Safety Net (f Böll), 1982
Saga of the Folkungs (p Strindberg), 1931
Sagesse (p Claudel), 1939
Sagesse (v Verlaine), 1880
Sagouin (f Mauriac), 1951
Sagra del signore della nave (p Pirandello), 1925
Saha the Cat (f Colette), 1936
Sailor Who Fell from Grace with the Sea (f Mishima), 1965
Sailor's Wife (p Vicente)
Saint Francis (f Kazantzakis), 1962
St. Joan of the Stockyards (p Brecht), 1956
St. John's Eve (f Gogol), 1886
St. John's Night (p Ibsen)
St. Petersburg (f Bely), 1959
Sainte Agnès (v Claudel), 1963
Saint-Glinglin (f Queneau), 1948
Saison en enfer (Rimbaud), 1873
Salamandra (v Paz), 1962
Salamandra (p Pirandello), 1928
Salammbô (f Flaubert), 1862
Salle d'Armes (f Dumas), 1838
Salmigondis (f Balzac), 1832
Salo (p Pasolini), 1975
Saloma (p Krleža), 1963
Salon de l'automobile (p Ionesco), 1953

Salteador (f Dumas), 1854
Salutations (p Ionesco), 1963
Salvator le Commissionnaire (f Dumas), 1854
Salzburg Everyman (p Hofmannsthal), 1930
Salzburger Grosse Welttheater (p Hofmannsthal), 1922
Samandro (p Pirandello), 1909
Same Old Story (f Goncharov), 1957
Samfundets støtter (p Ibsen), 1877
Samia (p Menander)
Samukh ve-Nireh (f Agnon), 1951
Samum (p Strindberg), 1889
San Manuel Bueno, mártir (f Unamuno), 1933
San Pantaleone (v D'Annunzio), 1886
San Paolo (p Pasolini), 1977
Sanatorium pod klepsydra (f Schulz), 1937
Sanatorium under the Sign of the Hourglass (f Schulz), 1978
Sand aus den Urnen (v Celan), 1948
Sandhedens Haevn (p Dinesen), 1936
San-Felice (f Dumas), 1864
Sang d'Atys (v Mauriac), 1940
Sang d'un poète (p Cocteau), 1930
Sang och strid (v Lagerkvist), 1940
Sankthansnatten (p Ibsen), 1852
Sanshiro (f Natsume), 1909
Santa Cruz (p Frisch), 1946
Santa Juana (p Tirso)
Santa Juana de Castilla (p Pérez Galdós), 1918
Santiago el Verde (p Vega)
Sappho (p Grillparzer), 1818
Sardegna come un'infanzia (f Vittorini), 1952
Sarjúrendek (v Illyés), 1931
Sasameyuki (f Tanizaki), 1948
Satin Slipper (p Claudel), 1931
Satura (v Montale), 1966
Satyr (v Kochanowski), 1564
Satyricon (f Petronius)
Saül (p Voltaire), 1755
Savage Paris (f Zola)
Scapegoat (f Strindberg), 1967
Scatterbrains (p Holberg), 1912
Scène à quatre (p Ionesco), 1959
Scènes de la vie privée (f Balzac), 1832
Scènes de la vie privée et publique des animaux (f Balzac), 1842
Schach von Wulthenow (f Fontane), 1883
Schatten des Körpers des Kutschers (f Weiss), 1960
Schionatulander and Sigune (v Wolfram)

Schlafwandler (f Broch)
Schloss (f Kafka), 1926
Schloss Wetterstein (p Wedekind), 1912
Schluck Erde (p Böll), 1961
Schluck und Jau (p Hauptmann), 1900
Schneepart (v Celan), 1971
Schnellmaler (p Wedekind), 1889
Scholastica (p Ariosto), 1547
Schön ist die Jugend (f Hesse), 1916
School for Honor (p Lessing)
School for Rakes (p Beaumarchais), 1769
School for Wives (f Gide), 1929
School for Wives (p Molière)
Schuldlosen (f Broch), 1950
Schuss im Park (f Hauptmann), 1939
Schwärmer (p Musil), 1921
Schwarzen Schafe (f Böll), 1951
Schweik im zweiten Weltkrieg (p Brecht), 1957
Schweyk in the Second World War (p Brecht), 1976
Schwierige (p Hofmannsthal), 1921
Screens (p Genet), 1962
Scythes (p Voltaire), 1767
Sea of Fertility (f Mishima), 1972
Seagull (p Chekhov)
Seamarks (v Saint-John Perse), 1958
Searching Satyrs (p Sophocles)
Season in Hell (Rimbaud)
Sebastian im Traum (v Trakl), 1915
Sebastopol (f Tolstoy)
Seconde (f Colette), 1929
Seconde Surprise de l'amour (p Marivaux), 1727
Secret des Ruggieri (f Balzac), 1837
Secret History of the Lord of Musashi (f Tanizaki), 1982
Secret of Heaven (p Lagerkvist), 1966
Secret of Luca (f Silone), 1959
Secret Spoken Aloud (p Calderón)
Secret Vengeance for Secret Insult (p Calderón)
Secrétaire intime (f Sand), 1834
Secreto a voces (p Calderón)
Sedoye utro (v Blok), 1920
Séducteur et le mari (p Dumas), 1842
Seed Beneath the Snow (f Silone), 1942
Segelfoss By (f Hamsun), 1915
Segelfoss Town (f Hamsun), 1925
Seger i mörker (p Lagerkvist), 1939
Segreto di Luca (f Silone), 1956
Segunda casaca (f Pérez Galdós), 1876
Sei personaggi in cerca d'autore (p Piranello), 1921

Seigi to Bisho (f Dazai), 1942
Seijo (p Mishimo), 1951
Seis problemas para don Isidro Parodi (f Borges), 1942
Sel de la Vie (p Maeterlinck), 1919
Self-Tormentor (p Terence)
Seltsame Leiden eines Theater-Direktors (f Hoffmann), 1819
Seltsame Springinsfeld (f Grimmelshausen)
Sembazuru (f Kawabata), 1952
Sembler en buena tierra (p Vega)
Seme sotto la neve (f Silone), 1942
Semejante a la noche (f Carpentier), 1958
Semeynoye schast'e (f Tolstoy), 1859
Semillas para un himno (v Paz), 1954
Semiramis (p Hofmannsthal), 1933
Sémiramis (p Valéry), 1934
Sémiramis (p Voltaire), 1749
Sempione strizza l'occhio al Fréjus (f Vittorini), 1949
Senilia (v Turgenev), 1878
Senilità (f Svevo), 1898
Sens de la marche (p Adamov), 1953
Sensatsiya (p Zamyatin), 1930
Sentimental Education (f Flaubert), 1896
Sentimento del tempo (v Ungaretti), 1933
Sept Cordes de la lyre (p Sand), 1839
Sept Pêchés capitaux (p Ionesco), 1962
Sept Princesses (p Maeterlinck), 1890
Septem contra Thebas (p Aeschylus), 467
Séquestrés d'Altona (p Sartre), 1959
Serephita (f Balzac), 1889
Serapion Brethren (f Hoffmann), 1886
Serapions-Brüder (f Hoffmann), 1819
Serebryany golub' (f Bely), 1909
Serenade (p Vicente)
Serments indiscrets (p Marivaux), 1732
Serpent and Lily (f Kazantzakis), 1980
Serres chaudes (v Maeterlinck), 1889
Sertorius (p Corneille), 1662
Servant of Two Masters (p Goldoni)
Servir a señor discreto (p Vega)
Servitore di due padroni (p Goldoni)
Servitude et grandeur militaires (f Vigny), 1835
Sestra mota zhizn' (v Pasternak), 1922
Setsuyo Zuihitsu (f Tanizaki), 1935
Sette giornate del mondo creato (v Tasso), 1607
Setting Sun (f Dazai), 1956
Sevastopolskiye rasskazy (f Tolstoy), 1855
Seven Against Thebes (p Aeschylus)
7 de julio (f Pérez Galdós), 1876
Seven Deadly Sins of the Petty Bourgeoisie

Skin of Dreams (f Queneau), 1948
Sklepy cynamonowe (f Schulz), 1934
Skrizhal sbornik (v Akhmatova), 1921
Skupoy (p Bulgakov), 1939
Skupoy rytsar' (p Pushkin), 1836
Sky above the Roof (v Verlaine), 1957
Sladek (p Horváth), 1928
Slave King (f Hugo), 1833
Sleepwalkers (f Broch), 1932
Slepaya krasavitsa (p Pasternak), 1969
Ślub (p Gombrowicz), 1963
Sluchay na stantsii Krechetvoka (f Solzhe-
nitsyn), 1963
Smanie della villeggiatura (p Goldoni)
Smoke (f Turgenev)
Smug Citizens (p Gorky), 1906
Snake Train (Khlebnikov), 1976
Snapshots (f Robbe-Grillet), 1965
Snezhnaya maska (v Blok), 1907
Snow Country (f Kawabata), 1957
So ist der Leben (p Wedekind), 1902
So non così (p Pirandello), 1915
So Runs the World (f Sienkiewicz), 1898
So ward Abend und Morgen (f Böll), 1955
Sobach'e serdtsa (f Bulgakov), 1969
Sobeide, Abenteurer (p Hofmannsthal), 1899
Socrate (p Voltaire), 1759
Socrates (p Voltaire), 1760
Sodoma kai Gomorra (p Kazantzakis), 1955
Sodome et Gomorrhe (p Giraudoux), 1943
Sodome et Gomorrhe (f Proust), 1921
Soeur Béatrice (p Maeterlinck), 1901
Soeurs Rondoli (f Maupassant), 1884
Sogno di un tramonto d'autunno (p D'An-
nunzio), 1898
Sogno di una cosa (f Pasolini), 1962
Sogno d'un mattino di primavera (p D'An-
nunzio), 1897
Sogno (ma forse no) (p Pirandello), 1931
Soif et la faim (p Ionesco), 1964
Soil (f Zola), 1888
Sokrates (p Strindberg), 1918
Sol del domingo (v Darío), 1917
Solar Spectrum (p Wedekind), 1959
Soldier's Honour (f Zola), 1884
Soledad sonora (v Jiménez), 1911
Soledades (v Góngora)
Solitaire (f Ionesco), 1973
Solitudes (v Góngora)
Solov'iny sad (v Blok), 1918
Sombra (f Pérez Galdós), 1871
Sombras de sueño (p Unamuno), 1931
Some Prefer Nettles (f Tanizaki), 1955
Somov i drugiye (p Gorky), 1931

Son Excellence Eugène Rougon (f Zola),
1876
Sonata Belzebuba (p Witkiewicz), 1962
Sonetos espirituales (v Jiménez), 1917
Sonets à Sinope (v Ronsard), 1559
Sonette an Orpheus (v Rilke), 1923
Sonety krymskie (v Mickiewicz), 1826
Song about Tsar Ivan Vasilyecivh (v Ler-
montov)
Song for an Equinox (v Saint-John Perse),
1977
Song of the Lusitanian Bogey (p Weiss),
1970
Songs of Twilight (v Hugo), 1836
Sonnen spektrum (p Wedekind), 1922
Sonnets from Crimea (v Mickiewicz), 1917
Sonnets to Orpheus (v Rilke), 1936
Sons of Heracles (p Euripides)
Sons of the Soil (f Balzac), 1890
Sophist (Plato)
Sophonisbe (p Corneille), 1663
Sophonisbe (p Voltaire), 1770
Sopraluoghi in Palestina (p Pasolini), 1964
Sor Simona (p Pérez Galdós), 1915
Sorcier (f Balzac), 1837
Sorcières de Salem (p Sartre), 1957
Sorekara (f Natsume), 1910
Sorrows of Werter (f Goethe)
Sotoba komachi (p Mishima), 1952
Soul Shall Bear Witness (f Lagerlöf), 1921
Soulier de satin (p Claudel), 1929
Soul's Journey (p Vicente)
Sound of the Mountain (f Kawabata), 1970
Sound of Waves (f Mishima), 1956
Sous le rempart d'Athènes (p Claudel), 1927
Souvenirs d'Antony (f Dumas), 1835
Souvenirs du triangle d'or (f Robbe-Grillet),
1978
Souvenirs d'un favorite (f Dumas), 1865
Spain, Take This Cup From Me (v Valeljo),
1974
Spanish Bawd (p Rojas)
Spectre (f Gorky), 1938
Spectre Mother (f Dumas), 1864
Speech-Grille (v Celan), 1971
Spektorsky (v Pasternak), 1931
Spendthrifts (f Pérez Galdós), 1951
Sphekes (p Aristophanes)
Spider and the Fly (f Vigny), 1925
Spiel des Schicksals (f Schiller), 1789
Spiridion (f Sand), 1839
Splendeurs et misères des courtisanes
(f Balzac), 1845
Splendor and Death of Joaquín Murieta

(p Neruda), 1972
Splinten av troldspeilet (f Undset), 1917
Spöksonaten (p Strindberg), 1907
Spook Sonata (p Strindberg), 1916
Sportsman's Sketches (f Turgenev)
Sprachgitter (v Celan), 1959
Sprechanlage (p Böll)
Spring Awakening (p Wedekind), 1980
Spring Floods (f Turgenev)
Spring Snow (f Mishima), 1972
Spring-Time Case (f Tanizaki), 1927
Spuk (p Hauptmann), 1928
Spurlosen (p Böll), 1957
Spy (f Gorky), 1908
Squabbles of Chioggia (p Goldoni)
Stadt (f Dürrenmatt), 1952
Star of Castille (p Vega)
Starik (p Gorky), 1915
Starkare (p Strindberg), 1889
Stary sluga (f Sienkiewicz), 1875
State of Siege (p Camus), 1958
Statesman (Plato)
Statue Guest (p Pushkin)
Stechlin (f Fontane), 1899
Stein der Weisen (p Wedekind), 1909
Steinwurf (p Hebbel), 1883
Stella (p Goethe), 1776
Stello (f Vigny), 1832
Sténie (f Balzac), 1936
Stepmother (p Balzac)
Stepnoy Korol' Lir (f Turgenev), 1870
Steppenwolf (f Hesse), 1927
Stichus (p Plautus)
Stikhi k Bloku (v Tsvetayeva), 1922
Stikhi o Prekrasnoy Dame (v Blok), 1905
Stikhi o Rossii (v Bely), 1922
Stikhi o Rossii (v Blok), 1915
Stiller (f Frisch), 1954
Stine (f Fontane), 1890
Stoffreste (p Grass), 1957
Stone (v Mandelstam), 1981
Stone Guest (p Pushkin)
Stora landsvägen (p Strindberg), 1909
Storia della colonna infame (f Monzoni), 1842
Storia di una capinera (f Verga), 1873
Stories for Ninon (f Zola), 1895
Stories of God (f Rilke), 1931
Stories of the Kings of Norway (f Sturluson)
Storm (v Montale), 1978
Storm (p Strindberg), 1912
Storm in Shanghai (f Malraux), 1934
Stormyrtösen (p Lagerlöf), 1913
Story of a Humble Christian (p Silone),

1970
Story of Gösta Berling (f Lagerlöf), 1898
Story of Shunkin (f Tanizaki), 1936
Story of the Love and Death of Cornet
  Christopher Rilke (v Rilke), 1927
Strait Is the Gate (f Gide), 1924
Strange News from Another Star (f Hesse),
  1972
Stranger (f Camus), 1946
Stranitzky und der Nationalheld (p Dür-
  renmatt), 1959
Straszliwy wychowawca (p Witkiewicz), 1935
Street of Crocodiles (f Schulz), 1963
Street of Riches (f Roy), 1957
Streghe (p Pasolini), 1967
Stridende Liv (f Hamsun), 1905
Stroll in the Air (p Ionesco), 1965
Strong as Death (f Maupassant), 1899
Stronger (p Strindberg), 1912
Strophe (v Seferis), 1931
Students (p Ariosto)
Studien (f Stifter), 1844
Stuff of Youth (f Mauriac), 1960
Stunde aufenthalt (p Böll), 1957
Stunde der Wahrheit (p Böll), 1958
Stundeløse (p Holberg)
Stunden im Garten (v Hesse), 1936
Stunden-Buch (v Rilke), 1905
Stupra (Rimbaud), 1923
Sturz (f Dürrenmatt), 1971
Submerged (p Gorky), 1914
Sufrimiento premiado (p Vega)
Suigetsu (f Kawabata), 1953
Suitable Match (f Fontane), 1968
Suite du Menteur (p Corneille), 1644
Suitors (p Racine)
Suivante (p Corneille), 1633
Sulce patria (v Neruda), 1949
Sult (f Hamsun), 1890
Sultaness (p Racine)
Sultanetta (f Dumas), 1895
Summerfolk (p Gorky), 1975
Sun and Steel (f Mishima), 1970
Sun Stone (v Paz), 1963
Sunday of Life (f Queneau), 1976
Sunken Bell (p Hauptmann), 1898
Suo marito (f Pirandello), 1911
Superior Residence (p Goldoni)
Supermale (f Jarry), 1968
Suplício de uma mulher (p Machado de
  Assis), 1865
Supplément au voyage de Cook (p Girau-
  doux), 1935
Suppliant Maidens (p Aeschylus)

Suppliant Women (p Euripides)
Suppliants (p Aeschylus)
Suppliants (p Euripides)
Supplices (p Aeschylus)
Supplices (p Euripides)
Suppositi (p Ariosto), 1509
Suréna (p Corneille), 1674
Surenas (p Corneille), 1969
Surgeon of His Honour (p Calderón)
Surmâle (f Jarry), 1902
Surprise de l'amour (p Marivaux), 1722
Sursis (f Sartre), 1945
Suspicion (f Mauriac), 1931
Suta (f Mishima), 1961
Suzaku-ke no Metsubo (p Mishima), 1967
Suzanne and the Pacific (f Giraudoux), 1923
Suzanne et le Pacifique (f Giraudoux), 1921
Svad'ba (p Chekhov), 1889
Svaermere (f Hamsun), 1904
Svanevit (p Strindberg), 1901
Svåra stunden (p Lagerkvist), 1918
Svarta fanor (f Strindberg), 1907
Svarta handsken (p Strindberg), 1909
Svecha na vetru (p Solzhenitsyn), 1968
Svendborger Gedichte (v Brecht), 1939
Svet, koroty, v tebe (p Solzhenitsyn), 1981
Swan Song (p Chekhov)
Swann's Way (f Proust), 1922
Swanwhite (p Strindberg), 1909
Sweet Cheat Gone (f Proust), 1930
Sylvandire (f Dumas), 1844
Sylvanire (p Zola), 1921
Sylvia Hears a Secret (p Marivaux)
Symphonie pastorale (f Gide), 1919
Symposium (Plato)
Syndabocken (f Strindberg), 1907
Syv fantastiske Fortaellinger (f Dinesen), 1935
Szachy (v Kochanowski), 1562
Szálló egek alatt (v Illyés), 1935
Szalona lokomotywa (p Witkiewicz), 1962
Szembenézve (v Illyés), 1947
Szewcy (p Witkiewicz), 1948

Tableau (p Ionesco), 1955
Tables of the Law (f Mann), 1945
Tacaño Salomón (p Pérez Galdós), 1916
Taccuino del vecchio (v Ungaretti), 1960
Tade kuu mushi (f Tanizaki), 1929
Tag wie sonst (p Böll), 1953
Tage des Kommune (p Brecht), 1956
Tägliche Leben (p Rilke), 1901
Taiyo to tetsu (f Mishima), 1968

Taking the Bastille (f Dumas)
Taklagsöl (f Strindberg), 1907
Tal cour di un frut (v Pasolini), 1974
Tale of a Manor (f Lagerlöf), 1922
Tale of Genji (f Murasaki)
Tale of Jacob (f Mann), 1934
Tale of the Argonauts (v Apolonnius)
Tales from the Calendar (f Brecht), 1961
Tales from the Vienna Woods (p Horváth), 1977
Tales from Two Pockets (f Capek), 1932
Tales of Belkin (f Pushkin)
Tales of My Native Town (f D'Annunzio), 1920
Tales of P. Bielkin (f Pushkin)
Tales of the Caucasus (f Dumas), 1895
Tales the Moon Can Tell (f Andersen), 1955
Talkative Barber (p Holberg), 1950
Tamaris (f Sand), 1862
Tampopo (f Kawabata), 1972
Tancred (p Goethe), 1801
Tancrède (p Voltaire), 1759
Tarare (p Beaumarchais), 1787
Taras Bulba (f Gogol), 1887
Tartuffe (p Molière), 1664
Taschenpostille (v Brecht), 1926
Taureau blanc (f Voltaire), 1774
Tchitchikoff's Journeys (f Gogol), 1886
Teatralny roman (f Bulgakov), 1966
Teatro comico (p Goldoni)
Tehilla (f Agnon), 1956
Teleftaios Peirasmos (f Kazantzakis), 1955
Télémaque travesti (f Marivaux), 1736
Température (p Apollinaire), 1975
Temple de la Gloire (p Voltaire), 1745
Temple de l'amitié et le temple du goût (v Voltaire), 1733
Temple du Goût (v Voltaire), 1733
Temple of Dawn (f Mishima), 1973
Temple of Taste (v Voltaire), 1734
Temple of the Golden Pavilion (f Mishima), 1959
Temps mêlés (f Queneau), 1941
Temps retrouvé (f Proust), 1927
Temptation of Saint Anthony (f Flaubert), 1895
Temptation of the West (f Malraux), 1961
Temy i variatsii (v Pasternak), 1923
Ten Nights' Dream (f Natsume), 1934
Tendre comme le souvenir (v Apollinaire), 1952
Tenebreuse Affaire (f Balzac), 1842
Tennin josui (f Mishima), 1971
Tenohira no shosetsu (f Kawabata), 1926

Tenor (p Wedekind), 1927
Tentation de l'occident (f Malraux), 1926
Tentation de Saint Antoine (f Flaubert), 1874
Tentative Amoureuse (f Gide), 1893
Tentative del hombre infinito (v Neruda), 1926
Teorema (p Pasolini), 1968
Teorie del conte Alberto (p Svevo), 1960
Teremteni (v Illyés), 1972
Térésa (p Dumas), 1832
Teresa (v Unamuno), 1923
Terje Viken (v Ibsen), 1918
Terra promessa (v Ungaretti), 1950
Terra vergine (f D'Annunzio), 1882
Terre (f Zola), 1887
Terreur prussienne (f Dumas), 1867
Terror de 1824 (f Pérez Galdós), 1877
Tertsines (v Kazantzakis), 1960
Terzetta spezzato (p Svevo), 1927
Terzetti (f Pirandello), 1912
Tesedia (v Boccaccio)
Tessa (p Giraudoux), 1934
Test (p Marivaux)
Testament (v Villon)
Testament de César (p Dumas), 1849
Testament d'Orphée (p Cocteau), 1960
Testament of Orpheus (p Cocteau), 1968
Testvérek (p Illyés), 1972
Tête d'or (p Claudel), 1890
Tetradio gymnasmaton (v Seferis), 1940
Teutonic Knights (f Sienkiewicz), 1943
Teutscher Michel (f Grimmelshausen)
Teverino (f Sand), 1845
Thaïs (p Dumas), 1858
That Which Was Lost (f Mauriac), 1951
That Worthless Fellow Platonov (p Chekhov)
Theaetetus (Plato)
Theatrical Illusion (p Corneille), 1975
Thébaïde (p Racine), 1664
Théodore (p Corneille), 1645
Theogonia (v Hesiod)
Theogony (v Hesiod)
There Are Crimes and Crimes (p Strindberg), 1912
Theresa (f Zola)
Thérèse Desqueyroux (f Mauriac), 1927
Thérèse Raquin (f Zola), 1867
Thésée (f Gide), 1946
Theseus (f Gide), 1948
Thesmophoriazusae (p Aristophanes)
They (p Witkiewicz), 1968
Third Woman (f Sienkiewicz), 1897
Thirst for Love (f Mishima), 1969

Thirteen Questions of Love (f Boccaccio)
Thomas l'imposteur (f Cocteau), 1923
Thomas the Imposter (f Cocteau), 1925
Thor und der Tod (p Hofmannsthal), 1900
Thou Shalt Not Lie (p Grillparzer), 1939
Thousand and One Nights (p Pasolini), 1974
Thousand Cranes (f Kawabata), 1959
Three (f Gorky), 1958
Three Judgments at a Blow (p Calderón)
Three Material Songs (v Neruda), 1948
Three Men (f Gorky), 1902
Three Musketeers (f Dumas), 1846
Three of Them (f Gorky), 1902
Three Secret Poems (v Seferis), 1969
Three Sisters (p Chekhov)
Three Wise Men (p Vicente)
Three Women (f Musil), 1965
Three-Cornered World (f Natsume), 1965
Threepence (p Plautus)
Threepenny Novel (f Brecht), 1956
Threepenny Opera (p Brecht), 1958
Through Deserts to Ancestral Lands (p Strindberg), 1970
Thyestes (p Seneca)
Thymele (p Sikelianos), 1950
Tía Tula (f Unamuno), 1921
Tidings Brought to Mary (p Claudel), 1916
Tiger at the Gates (p Giraudoux), 1955
Tigre reale (f Verga), 1875
Till Damaskus (p Strindberg), 1898
Till Eulenspiegel (v Hauptmann), 1928
Till Eulenspiegel (p Wedekind) 1916
Timaeus (Plato)
Times (p Goldoni)
Tin Drum (f Grass), 1962
Tin Flute (f Roy), 1947
Tiszták (p Illyés), 1969
Tite et Bérénice (p Corneille), 1670
Títeres de Cachiporra (p García Lorca), 1923
Titurel (v Wolfram)
Titus and Berenice (p Racine)
Titus Andronicus (p Dürrenmatt), 1970
Tizenkét nap Bulgáriában (v Illyés), 1947
Tmol Shilshom (f Agnon), 1945
To Baronesser (f Andersen), 1848
To Be, or Not To Be (f Andersen), 1857
To Clothe the Naked (p Pirandello), 1962
To Find Oneself (p Pirandello), 1960
To Damascus (p Strindberg), 1913
To Have Done with the Judgment of God (p Artaud), 1976
Tochter der Kathedrale (p Hauptmann),

Trionfi (v Petrarch)
Trionfo della morte (f D'Annunzio), 1894
Triptych (p Frisch), 1981
Triptychon (p Frisch), 1978
Tristan (v Gottfried)
Tristan (f Mann), 1903
Tristan und Isolde (v Gottfried)
Tristana (f Pérez Galdós), 1892
Tristia (v Mandelstam), 1922
Tristia (v Ovid)
Triumph der Empfindsamkeit (p Goethe), 1778
Triumph of Death (f D'Annunzio), 1896
Triumph of Death (p Ionesco), 1971
Triumvirat (p Voltaire), 1764
Triunfo de la fee en los reynos del Japón (v Vega), 1618
Triunfo do inverno (p Vicente)
Triunfos divinos (v Vega), 1625
Troades (p Euripides)
Troades (p Seneca)
Trofaste hustru (f Undset), 1936
Trois Don Juan (f Apollinaire), 1915
Trois Justiciers (p Maeterlinck), 1959
Trois maîtres (f Dumas), 1844
Trois Mousquetaires (f Dumas), 1844
Trois villes (f Zola)
Trojan Horse (f Queneau), 1954
Trojan War Will Not Take Place (p Giraudoux), 1983
Trojan Women (p Euripides)
Trojan Women (p Sartre), 1967
Trojan Women (p Seneca)
Troll och människor (f Lagerlöf), 1915
Trommeln in der Nacht (p Brecht), 1922
Tropical Madness (p Witkiewicz), 1972
Tropical Tree (p Mishima), 1964
Trotsky in Exile (p Weiss), 1971
Trotzki im Exil (p Weiss), 1970
Trou de l'enfer (f Dumas), 1850
Troubled Sleep (f Sartre), 1951
Trouille verte (f Queneau), 1947
Trovarsi (p Pirandello), 1932
Troye (f Gorky), 1900
Troyennes (p Sartre), 1965
Truba marsian (Khlebnikov), 1916
Truculentus (p Plautus)
Truth (f Zola), 1903
Trutz Simplex (Grimmelshausen)
Tsar'-devitsa (v Tsvetayeva), 1922
Tschandala (f Strindberg), 1889
Tsugaru (f Dazai), 1944
Tu Ridi (f Pirandello), 1920
Tu só, tu, puro amor (p Machado de Assis), 1880

Tueur sans gages (p Ionesco), 1958
Tulio Montalban y Julio Macedo (f Unamuno), 1920
Tulipe noire (f Dumas), 1850
Tumor Mózgowicz (p Witkiewicz), 1921
Tungsteno (f Vallejo), 1931
Turandot (p Schiller), 1802
Turm (p Hofmannsthal), 1925
Turm (p Weiss), 1749
Turno (f Pirandello), 1902
Tutto per bene (p Pirandello), 1920
Tüvé-tevök (p Illyés), 1953
Tüz-víz (p Illyés), 1952
Två sagor om livet (f Lagerkvist), 1913
Tvoreniya (Khlebnikov), 1914
Twenty Love Poems and a Song of Despair (v Neruda), 1969
Twenty Years After (f Dumas), 1846
Twenty-Six Men and a Girl (f Gorky), 1902
Twilight of the Elephant (f Vittorini), 1951
Twilight Sunflower (p Mishima), 1958
Twin Captains (f Dumas), 1861
Two Bacchises (p Plautus)
Two Baronesses (f Andersen), 1848
Two Brothers (f Balzac), 1887
Two Friends (p Beaumarchais), 1800
Two Martyrs (f Chateaubriand), 1819
Two Mistresses (f Musset), 1900
Two Symphonies (f Gide), 1931
2000 (v Neruda), 1974
Tyette (f Maupassant), 1885
Typewriter (p Cocteau), 1947

U agoniji (p Krleža), 1928
U logoru (p Krleža), 1934
U samogo moria (v Akhmatova), 1914
Überfürchtenichts (p Wedekind), 1917
Ubu series (p Jarry)
Uccellacci e uccellini (p Pasolini), 1966
Uchitel' i uchenik (Khlebnikov), 1912
Udaijin Sanetomo (f Dazai), 1943
Ulrich von Lichtenstein (p Hauptmann), 1939
Umwege (f Hesse), 1912
Unbekannte aus der Seine (p Horváth), 1933
Unbekannte Grösse (f Broch), 1933
Unberechenbare Gäste (f Böll), 1956
Unbestechliche (p Hofmannsthal), 1923
Uncle Vanya (p Chekhov)
Und Pippa tanzt (p Hauptmann), 1906
Und sagte kein einziges Wort (f Böll), 1953
Under Høststjaernen (f Hamsun), 1906

Under the Autumn Stars (f Hamsun), 1975
Under the Shadow of Etna (f Verga), 1896
Unfortunate Woman (f Turgenev)
Ungdom (v Undset), 1910
Unges forbund (p Ibsen), 1869
Unguarded House (f Böll), 1957
Unhuman Tour (f Natsume), 1927
Union Libre (v Breton), 1931
Unions (f Musil), 1965
Universal History of Infamy (f Borges), 1971
Unknown Quantity (f Broch), 1935
Unknown Sea (f Mauriac), 1948
Uno, nessuno, e centomila (f Pirandello), 1926
Unrequited Love (f Gorky), 1949
Unterm Birnbaum (f Fontane), 1885
Unterm Rad (f Hesse), 1906
Unternehmen der Wega (p Dürrenmatt), 1958
Unterwegs (v Hesse), 1911
Unwiederbringlich (f Fontane), 1891
Uomini e no (f Vittorini), 1945
Uomo dal fiore in bocca (p Pirandello), 1923
Uomo, la bestia, e la virtù (p Pirandello), 1919
Upstart Peasant (f Marivaux)
Urbain Grandier (p Dumas), 1850
Urfaust (p Dürrenmatt), 1970
Urien's Voyage (f Gide), 1964
Urna (v Bely), 1909
Ursula (f Balzac), 1891
Ursule Mirouët (f Balzac), 1842
Urteil (f Kafka), 1916
Uscoque (f Sand), 1838
Usignolo della chiesa cattolica (v Pasolini), 1958
Usynlige (p Holberg)
Usynlige paa Sprogø (p Andersen), 1839
Utage no ato (f Mishima), 1960
Utsukushi hoshi (f Mishima), 1962
Utsukushii tabi (f Kawabata), 1947
Utsukushisa to kanashimi to (f Kawabata), 1965
Uyezdnoye (f Zamyatin), 1916
Uzurakago (f Natsume), 1906

V kruge pervom (f Solzhenitsyn), 1968
V sumerkakh (f Chekhov), 1887
Vaaren (f Undset), 1914
Vagabondaggio (f Verga), 1887
Vagabonde (f Colette), 1911
Vagabonds (f Hamsun), 1931

Vagrant (f Colette), 1912
Valentine (f Sand), 1832
Válka s mloky (f Capek), 1936
Valvèdre (f Sand), 1861
Vampire (p Dumas), 1851
Vangelo Secondo Matteo (p Pasolini), 1964
Vangelo 70 (ϝ Pasolini), 1969
Vanishing Point (f Weiss), 1966
Varvary (p Gorky), 1905
Vase (p Ionesco), 1974
Vassa Zheleznova (p Gorky), 1910
Vatican Cellars (f Gide), 1952
Vatican Swindle (f Gide), 1925
Vautrin (p Balzac), 1840
Věc Makropulos (p Capek), 1922
Vecchi e i giovani (f Pirandello), 1913
Vecher (v Akhmatova), 1912
Vecher v Sorrente (p Turgenev), 1884
Vechera na khutore bliz Dikanki (f Gogol), 1831
Vecherny al'bom (v Tsvetayeva), 1910
Vechny muzh (f Dostoevsky), 1870
Ved rigets port (p Hamsun), 1895
Vedova scaltra (p Goldoni)
Veinte poemas de amor y una cancion desesperada (v Neruda), 1924
Veland (p Hauptmann), 1925
Velho da horta (p Vicente)
Venda (p Unamuno), 1913
Venetian Twins (p Goldini)
Venitienne (p Dumas), 1834
Ventaglio (p Goldoni)
Ventre de Paris (f Zola), 1873
Vents (v Saint-John Perse), 1946
Verbrecher aus Infamie (f Schiller), 1786
Verbrecher aus verlorener Ehre (f Schiller), 1792
Verdacht (f Dürrenmatt), 1953
Verdadero dios Pan (p Calderón)
Verdugo (f Balzac), 1840
Vereinigungen (f Musil), 1911
Verfolgung und Ermordung Jean Paul Marats... (p Weiss), 1964
Vergara (f Pérez Galdós), 1899
Vergine delle rocce (f D'Annunzio), 1896
Verhör des Lukullus (p Brecht), 1940
Verità (p Svevo), 1960
Vérité (f Zola), 1903
Verlogung (f Hesse), 1924
Verlorene Ehre der Katharina Blum (f Böll), 1974
Verrou de la reine (p Dumas), 1856
Vers d'exile (v Claudel), 1895
Verschollene (f Kafka), 1983

Verschwörung des Fiesko zu Genua (p
 Schiller), 1783
Versicherung (p Weiss), 1952
Versos del capitán (v Neruda), 1952
Versprechen (f Dürrenmatt), 1958
Versucher (f Broch), 1953
Versunkene Glocke (p Hauptmann), 1896
Vertauschten Köpfe (f Mann), 1940
Verwandlung (f Kafka), 1915
Verwirrungen des Zöglings Törless (f Musil),
 1906
Veshniye vody (f Turgenev), 1872
Vestire gl'ignudi (p Pirandello), 1922
Vestnik (Khlebnikov), 1922
Veuve (p Corneille), 1631
Viage al Parnaso (v Cervantes), 1614
Viaggio a Parigi (f Silone), 1934
Viaje a la semilla (f Carpentier), 1944
Vicaire des Ardennes (f Balzac), 1822
Vicomte de Bragelonne (f Dumas), 1848
Victim (f D'Annunzio), 1915
Victim (p Racine)
Victimes du devoir (p Ionesco), 1953
Victims of Duty (p Ionesco), 1958
Victoria (f Hamsun), 1898
Victors (p Sartre), 1949
Victory Celebrations (p Solzhenitsyn), 1983
Vid Lägereld (v Lagerkvist), 1932
Vida es sueño (p Calderón)
Vidularia (p Plautus)
Vie (f Maupassant), 1883
Vie de Marianne (f Marivaux), 1731
Vieille Fille (f Balzac), 1837
Viento entero (v Paz), 1965
Vikings at Helgeland (p Ibsen), 1890
Vildanden (p Ibsen), 1884
Vilde Kor (v Hamsun), 1904
Villa Santo-Sospiro (p Cocteau), 1952
Villana de Vallecas (p Tirso)
Villano en su rincón (p Vega)
Ville (p Claudel), 1893
Ville Noire (f Sand), 1860
Villefort (p Dumas), 1851
Villeggiatura (p Goldoni)
Vingt ans après (f Dumas), 1845
Vingt-quatre fevrier (p Dumas), 1850
Vinter Eventry (f Dinesen), 1942
Vinterballaden (p Lagerlöf), 1919
Vinti (f Verga), 1881
Vinzenz und die Freundin bedeutender
 Männer (p Musil), 1923
Violaine la chevelue (p Zola), 1921
Violent Life (f Pasolini), 1968
Vios kai Politeia tou Alexi Zorba (f

Kazantzakis), 1946
Vipers' Tangle (f Mauriac), 1933
Virgin Bride (p Strindberg), 1975
Virgin Soil (f Turgenev)
Virgins of the Rocks (f D'Annunzio), 1899
Virtuous Island (p Giraudoux), 1956
Virtuous Orphan (f Marivaux)
Visages radieux (v Claudel), 1946
Vise (p Pirandello), 1928
Vises sten (p Lagerkvist), 1947
Vishnyovy sad (p Chekhov), 1904
Visions of Christ (v Rilke), 1967
Visions of Simone Machard (p Brecht),
 1965
Visit (p Dürrenmatt), 1958
Vita (f Svevo), 1892
Vita che ti diedi (p Pirandello), 1923
Vita dei campi (f Verga), 1880
Vita d'un Uomo (Ungaretti)
Vita nuda (f Pirandello), 1910
Vita Nuova (v Dante)
Vita violenta (f Pasolini), 1959
Vitam impendere amori (v Apollinaire),
 1917
Vitoria de la honra (p Vega)
Vittoria Accoramboni (f Stendhal), 1839
Vizier's Elephant (f Andrić), 1962
Vladimir Ilich Lenin (v Mayakovsky), 1924
Vladimir Mayakvosky (p Mayakovsky), 1913
Vlast' t'my (p Tolstoy), 1887
Vocabulaire (v Cocteau), 1922
Voces de mi copla (v Jiménez), 1945
Voegelsindede (p Holberg)
Voeu d'une morte (f Zola), 1866
Vögel (p Goethe), 1780
Vogelscheuchen (p Grass), 1970
Voie royale (f Malraux), 1930
Voiture embourbée (f Marivaux), 1714
Voix humaine (p Cocteau), 1930
Voix intérieures (v Hugo), 1837
Vol d'Icare (f Queneau), 1968
Volpe e le camelie (f Silone), 1960
Volshebny fonar' (v Tsvetayeva), 1912
Voluntad (p Pérez Galdós), 1895
Voluntario realista (f Pérez Galdós), 1878
Vom Baum des Lebens (v Hesse), 1934
Vom Lieben Gott (f Rilke), 1900
Von der schönen Rosamunde (v Fontane),
 1850
Von Schwelle zu Schwelle (v Celan), 1955
Vor dem Sturm (f Fontane), 1878
Vor Sonnenaufgang (p Hauptmann), 1889
Vor Sonnenuntergang (p Hauptmann), 1932
Vorsty (v Tsvetayeva), 1921

Vorzüge der Windhühner (v Grass), 1956
Voskreseniye (f Tolstoy), 1899
Voudos (p Kazantzakis), 1955
Voyage au bout de la nuit (f Céline), 1932
Voyage d'Urien (f Gide), 1893
Voyage of the Argo (v Apollonius)
Voyages chez les morts (p Ionesco), 1981
Voyages de capitaine Robert Lade (f Prevost), 1744
Voyeur (f Robbe-Grillet), 1955
Voyna i mir (p Bulgakov), 1981
Voyna i mir (v Mayakovsky), 1916
Voyna i mir (f Tolstoy), 1863
Voyou Paul, Pauvre Virginie (p Céline), 1959
Vozdushyne puti (f Pasternak), 1933
Vozvrashchen'e na rodinu (v Bely), 1922
Vragi (p Gorky), 1907
Vraži otok (f Krleža), 1924
Vremya Mera mira (Khlebnikov), 1916
Vrilles de la vigne (f Colette), 1908
Vrinidiban, Madurai (v Paz), 1965
Vse sochinennoye V.Mayakovskim (v Mayakovsky), 1919
Vsem (Khlebnikov), 1927
Vstrechna (p Gorky), 1910
Vtoraya kniga (v Mandelstam), 1923
Vtoroye rozhdeniye (v Pasternak), 1932
Vucjak (p Krleža), 1922
Vuelta (v Paz), 1976
Vuelta al mundo en la Numancia (f Pérez Galdós), 1906

W malym dworku (p Witkiewicz), 1923
Waage der Baleks (f Böll), 1958
Waga tomo Hitler (p Mishima), 1968
Wagahai wa Neko de aru (f Natsume), 1905
Wahlverwandtschaften (f Goethe), 1809
Wakodo yo yomigaere (p Mishima), 1954
Waldstein (f Stifter), 1942
Wall (f Sartre), 1949
Wallenstein (p Schiller), 1798
Walnut Trees of Altenburg (f Malraux), 1952
Wälsundenblut (f Mann), 1921
Wanda (f Hauptmann), 1928
Wanderer (f Hamsun), 1975
Wanderer (f Natsume), 1967
Wanderer, kommst du nach Spa... (f Böll), 1950
Wanderers (f Hamsun), 1922
Wandering Jew (f Apollinaire), 1965
Wann-Chlore (f Balzac), 1825
War and Peace (f Tolstoy)

War of the Mice and the Crabs (v Leopardi)
War of Women (f Dumas), 1895
War with the Newts (f Capek), 1937
Wariat i zakonnica (p Witkiewicz), 1924
Warren Hastings (p Brecht), 1929
Warrior's Barrow (p Ibsen), 1921
Wasps (p Aristophanes)
Water Hen (p Witkiewicz), 1968
Waves of Sea and Love (p Grillparzer), 1969
Way of All the Earth (v Akhmatova), 1979
Way Things Are (v Lucretius)
Wayfarers (f Hamsun), 1980
We (f Zamyatin), 1924
We Always Treat Women Too Well (f Queneau), 1981
We Are Many (v Neruda), 1967
We Never Make Mistakes (f Solzhenitsyn), 1963
Weathercock (p Holberg), 1946
Weavers (p Hauptmann), 1899
Weber (p Hauptmann), 1892
Wedding (p Chekhov)
Wedding Preparations in the Country (f Kafka), 1953
Wedding Ring (p Goldoni)
Weevil (p Plautus)
Weh dem, der lügt (p Grillparzer), 1838
Weise von Liebe und Tod des Cornets Christoph Rilke (v Rilke), 1906
Weisse Fächer (p Hofmannsthal), 1898
Weisse Fürstin (p Rilke), 1899
Weisse Heiland (p Hauptmann), 1920
Western Septet (f Sienkiewicz), 1973
West-östlicher Divan (v Goethe), 1819
When Someone Is Somebody (p Pirandello), 1958
When the War Was Over (p Frisch), 1967
When We Dead Awaken (p Ibsen)
Where It's Thin, There It Tears (p Turgenev)
Where Nests the Water Hen (f Roy), 1951
Where Worlds Meet (f Sienkiewicz), 1899
Whirlpools (f Sienkiewicz), 1910
White Bull (f Voltaire), 1774
White Fox (p Tanizaki), 1930
White Guard (f Bulgakov), 1971
White Notebook (f Gide), 1965
White Princess (p Rilke), 1979
White Savior (p Hauptmann), 1925
Whites and the Blues (f Dumas), 1895
Wicked Cooks (p Grass), 1967
Widower's Comedy (p Vicente)
Wie dem Herrn Mockinpott das Leiden ausgetrieben wird (p Weiss), 1968
Wiedertäufer (p Dürrenmatt), 1967

Wild Ass's Skin (f Balzac)
Wild Duck (p Ibsen), 1890
Wild Duck Shooter (f Dumas), 1906
Wild Grass (f Lu Hsun)
Wild Orchid (f Undset), 1931
Wilderness of Mirrors (f Frisch), 1965
Wildflower (f Roy), 1970
Wiles of Love (p Marivaux)
Wilhelm Meister series (f Goethe)
Wilhelm Tell (p Schiller), 1804
Wilhelm Tell für die Schule (f Frisch), 1971
William Tell (p Schiller), 1825
Winds (v Saint-John Perse), 1953
Winter Ballad (p Hauptmann), 1925
Winterballade (p Hauptmann), 1917
Winter's Tales (f Dinesen), 1942
Wiry (f Sienkiewicz), 1910
Witches (p Pasolini), 1967
Witches of Salem (p Sartre), 1957
With Fire and Sword (f Sienkiewicz), 1890
With Muted Strings (f Hamsun), 1922
Within a Budding Grove (f Proust), 1924
Within My Glass Doors (f Natsume), 1928
Without Dogma (f Sienkiewicz), 1893
Witiko (f Stifter), 1865
Wives' Friend (p Pirandello), 1960
Wo warst du, Adam? (f Böll), 1951
Wolf Leader (f Dumas), 1904
Wolf-Hunt (p Verga), 1921
Woman from Sarajevo (f Andrić), 1963
Woman of Samos (p Menander)
Woman of the Pharisees (f Mauriac), 1946
Woman Taken in Adultery (f Fontane), 1979
Women at the Pump (f Hamsun), 1928
Women in Parliament (p Aristophanes)
Women, Men (v Verlaine), 1979
Women of Messina (f Vittorini), 1973
Women of Trachis (p Sophocles)
Women of Troy (p Euripides)
Women on the Road (f Vittorini), 1961
Wonderworking Magician (p Calderón)
Wood Demon (p Chekhov)
Work (f Zola), 1901
Works and Days (v Hesiod)
World We Live In (p Capek), 1933
Worst Is Not Always Certain (p Calderón)
Woyzeck (p Büchner)
Wozzeck (p Büchner), 1879
Wunderbarliche Vogelnest (f Grimmelshausen)
Wunderkind (f Mann), 1914

Xenia (v Du Bellay), 1569

Xenia (v Montale), 1966

Ya anda la de Mazagatos (p Vega)
Yakaifuku (f Mishima), 1967
Yama no oto (f Kawabata), 1954
Yamba-O (p Carpentier), 1928
Yamby (v Blok), 1919
Yanko the Magician (f Sienkiewicz), 1893
Yayá Garcia (f Machado de Assis), 1878
Yegipetskaya marka (f Mandelstam), 1928
Yegor Bulichoff and the Others (p Gorky), 1937
Yegor Bulychov i drugiye (p Gorky), 1932
Yerma (p García Lorca), 1934
Yokyoshu (f Natsume), 1906
Yorokobo no Koto (p Mishima), 1964
Yoru no himawari (p Mishima), 1953
Yoru no Shitaku (f Mishima), 1948
You Must Know Everything (f Babel), 1969
Young Captain (f Dumas), 1870
Young Cherry Trees Secured Against Hares (v Breton), 1946
Young James (f Voltaire), 1776
Young Joseph (f Mann), 1934
Young King Louis (p Dumas), 1979
Young Lady of Paris (f Colette), 1931
Young Man in Chains (f Mauriac), 1963
Young Törless (f Musil), 1955
Yours for the Telling (f Queneau), 1983
Yukiguni (f Kawabata), 1937
Yukoku (p Mishima), 1965
Yume Juya (f Natsume), 1910
Yume no ukihashi (f Tanizaki), 1960
Yuya (p Mishima), 1956
Yvain (v Chrétien)

Z (f Balzac), 1846
Za chlebem (f Sienkiewicz), 1880
Za gran'yu proshlykh dney (v Blok), 1920
Zadig (f Voltaire), 1748
Zaïde (f Lafayette), 1669
Zaïre (p Voltaire), 1732
Zakat (p Babel), 1927
Zampogna (v Pirandello), 1901
Zangezi (Khlebnikov), 1922
Zapatera prodigiosa (p García Lorca), 1930
Zapiski iz podpol'ya (f Dostoevsky), 1864
Zapiski okhotnika (f Turgenev), 1852
Zapiski yunogo vracha (f Bulgakov), 1963
Zara (p Voltaire), 1736
Zaragoza (f Pérez Galdós), 1874
Zářivé hlubiny (f Capek), 1916
Zastave (f Krleža), 1967
Zauberberg (f Mann), 1924

NOTES
ON
ADVISERS
AND
CONTRIBUTORS

ANDERSEN, Hans Christian. Lector in Danish, University of Newcastle upon Tyne. **Essay:** Hans Christian Andersen.

ANDERSON, J.K. Professor of Classical Archaeology, University of California, Berkeley. Author of *Ancient Greek Horsemanship*, 1961, *Military Theory and Practice in the Age of Xenophon*, 1970, and *Xenophon*, 1974. **Essay:** Xenophon.

ARNOLD, A. James. Professor of French, University of Virginia, Charlottesville. Author of *Paul Valéry and His Critics: A Bibliography*, 1970, *"Les Mots" de Sartre*, 1973, *Modernism and Negritude: The Poetry and Poetics of Aimé Césaire*, 1981, and the entry on Valéry in *A Critical Bibliography of French Literature*, vi, 2, 1980. Editor of *Caligula (1941)* by Camus, 1984. **Essays:** Albert Camus; Jean-Paul Sartre.

ARROWSMITH, William. Former Professor of Classics at University of Texas, Austin, Boston University, Yale University, New Haven, Connecticut, Johns Hopkins University, Baltimore, New York University, and Emory University, Atlanta; General Editor of *The Greek Tragedy in New Translation*. Translator of works by Petronius, Euripides, Aristophanes, and Cesare Pavese. Editor of *Image of Italy*, 1961, *The Craft and Context of Translation* (with Roger Shattuck), 1962, and *Five Modern Italian Novels*, 1964.

AVERY, Peter. University Lecturer, Cambridge University; Director of the Cambridge Faculty of Oriental Studies Middle East Centre. Author of *Modern Iran*, 1965. Translator, with John Heath-Stubbs, of *Thirty Poems of Hafiz of Shiraz*, 1952, and *The Rubaiyat of Omar Khayyam*, 1979. **Essay:** Omar Khayyam.

BAHADUR, K.P. Administrator with the Uttar Pradesh government, India. Author of more than 50 books including works on philosophy, sociology, and history, and novels, books for children, and translations. **Essays:** *Bhagavad Gita*; *Mahabharata*; *Ramayana*; *Upanishads*; *The Vedas*.

BAILEY, D.R. Shackleton. Pope Professor of Latin Language and Literature, Harvard University, Cambridge, Massachusetts; Editor of *Harvard Studies in Classical Philology*. Author of *Propertiana*, 1956, *Cicero*, 1971, *Two Studies in Roman Nomenclature*, 1976, and *Profile of Horace*, 1982. Editor or translator of several volumes of Cicero's correspondence. **Essay:** Cicero.

BAIN, David M. Reader in Greek, University of Manchester. Author of *Actors and Audience*, 1977, and *Masters, Servants, and Orders in Greek Tragedy*, 1982. Editor and Translator of *Samia* by Menander, 1983. **Essay:** Sophocles.

BALDWIN, Barry. Professor of Classics, University of Calgary, Alberta. Author of *Studies in Lucian*, 1973, *Studies in Aulus Gellius*, 1975, *The Roman Emperors*, 1980, *Suetonius*, 1983, and many chapters, monographs, articles, and reviews of Greek, Roman, and Byzantine history, language, and literature. Translator (with commentary), of *Philogelos*, 1983, and *Timarion*, 1984. **Essay:** Lucian.

BANCE, Alan. Professor and Head of the Department of German, University of Keele, Staffordshire. Author of *The German Novel 1945-1960*, 1980, and *Theodor Fontane: The Major Novels*, 1982. Editor of *Die Kapuzinergruft* by Joseph Roth, 1972, *Weimar Germany: Writers and Politics*, 1982, and co-editor and contributor, *The Second World War in Fiction*, 1984. Translator of *Art of the Nineteenth Century* by A.M. Vogt, 1973. **Essays:** Theodor Fontane; Thomas Mann; Arthur Schnitzler.

BARFOOT, Gabrielle. Lecturer in Italian, Queen's University, Belfast. Author of "Dante in T.S. Eliot's Criticism" in *English Miscellany*, 1973, and "The Theme of Usury in Dante and

Pound" in *Rivista di Letterature Moderne e Comparate*, 1977. **Essay:** Italo Svevo.

BARSBY, John. Professor of Classics, University of Otago, New Zealand. Author of *Ovid*, 1978. Translator (with commentary) of *Amores, Book One* by Ovid, 1973, and *Bacchides* by Plautus, 1984. **Essay:** Ovid.

BEATON, Roderick. Lecturer in Modern Greek Language and Literature, King's College, University of London. Author of *Folk Poetry of Modern Greece*, 1980, and articles on modern and medieval Greek literature, oral poetry, and traditional music. **Essays:** C.P. Cavafy; George Seferis; Angelos Sikelianos.

BERGIN, Thomas G. Sterling Professor of Romance Languages Emeritus, Yale University, New Haven, Connecticut. Author of many books, including *Giovanni Verga*, 1931, *Dante*, 1965 (as *An Approach to Dante*, 1965), *A Diversity of Dante*, 1969, *Petrarch*, 1970, and *Boccaccio*, 1981. Editor or translator of works by Dante, Petrarch, Vico, Shakespeare, William of Poitou, Quasimodo, and editor of collections of Italian and French literature. **Essays:** Giovanni Boccaccio; Dante Alighieri; Petrarch.

BINGHONG LU. Associate Professor and Department Director, Peking Languages Institute Author of *Stylized Intonation in English and Chinese*, 1982, *A Concise Chinese-English Dictionary* (with others), 1982, and *Reader for Language Teaching and Studies*. Translator of the Chinese stories *Kite Streamers*, 1983, and *The Fascinating Sea*, 1984. **Essays:** Li Po; Tu Fu.

BRADY, Patrick. Favrot Professor of French, Rice University, Houston. Author of two books in French on Zola, and *Marcel Proust*, 1977, *Structuralist Perspectives in Criticism of Fiction*, 1978, and *Rococo Style Versus Enlightenment Novel*, 1983. **Essay:** Émile Zola.

BRAULT, Gerard J. Professor of French, Pennsylvania State University, University Park. Author of *Early Blazon: Heraldic Terminology in the Twelfth and Thirteenth Centuries*, 1972, and *Eight Thirteenth-Century Rolls of Arms in French and Anglo-Norman Blazon*, 1973. Editor of *Celestine:...the First French Translation (1527) of the Spanish Classic La Celestina*, 1963, and editor and translator of *The Song of Roland*, 2 vols., 1978. **Essays:** Chrétien de Troyes; *Song of Roland*.

BRAUND, S.H. Lecturer in Classics, University of Exeter, Devon. Author of articles on Juvenal in *Liverpool Classical Monthly*, 1981, *Greece and Rome*, 1982, and other journals. **Essays:** Juvenal; Martial.

BROTHERSTON, Gordon. Professor of Literature, University of Essex, Wivenhoe. Author of *Manuel Machado: A Revaluation*, 1968, *Latin American Poetry: Origins and Presence*, 1975, *The Emergence of the Latin American Novel*, 1977, and *Image of the New World*, 1979. Editor or co-editor of *Selected Poems* by César Vallejo, 1976, *Ficciones* by Borges, 1976, and collections of Spanish American fiction and poetry. **Essay:** Rubén Darío.

BULLOCH, A.W. Associate Professor of Classics, University of California, Berkeley. Author of *Callimachus: The Fifth Hymn*, 1984, and the chapter on Hellenistic poetry in *Cambridge History of Classical Literature I: Greek Literature*, 1984. **Essays:** Apollonius of Rhodes; Callimachus.

CAWS, Mary Ann. Distinguished Professor of French and Comparative Literature, City University of New York Graduate Center. Author of many books, including *Surrealism and the Literary Imagination*, 1966, *The Poetry of Dada and Surrealism*, 1970, *The Inner Theatre of Recent French Poetry*, 1972, *The Eye in the Text*, 1981, *A Metapoetics of the Passage*, 1981, *Yves Bonnefoy*, 1984, two books on André Breton, two books on René Char, and books on

Robert Desnos and Pierre Reverdy. Editor or translator of works by Tristan Tzara, Char, Reverdy, Mallarmé, Breton, and Saint-John Perse, and editor of critical collections on French writing. **Essay:** André Breton.

CERVI, Andrea C. Research Student, Newnham College, Cambridge. **Essays:** Paul Celan; Rainer Maria Rilke.

CHADWICK, C. Professor of French, University of Aberdeen. Author of *Études sur Rimbaud*, 1959, *Mallarmé, sa pensée dans sa poésie*, 1962, *Symbolism*, 1971, *Verlaine*, 1973, and *Rimbaud*, 1979. Editor of *Sagesse* by Verlaine, 1973. **Essays:** Arthur Rimbaud; Paul Verlaine.

COHN, Ruby. Professor of Comparative Drama, University of California, Davis. Author of *Samuel Beckett: The Comic Gamut*, 1962, *Currents in Contemporary Drama*, 1969, *Edward Albee*, 1969, *Dialogue in American Drama*, 1971, *Back to Beckett*, 1974, *Modern Shakespeare Offshoots*, 1976, *Just Play: Beckett's Theatre*, 1980, and *New American Dramatists 1960-1980*, 1982. **Essay:** Antonin Artaud.

COLLIE, Michael. Professor of English, York University, Downsview, Ontario. Author of two books on Jules Laforgue, *George Gissing: A Biography*, 1977, *The Alien Art: A Critical Study of George Gissing's Novels*, 1979, a bibliography of Gissing, and *George Borrow, Eccentric*, 1982. Editor of *Les Derniers Vers* (with J.M. L'Heureux), 1965, and *Les Complaintes*, 1977, both by Laforgue. **Essay:** Jules Laforgue.

CONACHER, Desmond J. Professor of Classics, Trinity College, University of Toronto. Author of *Euripidean Drama: Myth, Theme and Structure*, 1967, *Aeschylus: Prometheus Bound: A Literary Commentary*, 1980, and articles on Greek tragedy. **Essays:** Aeschylus; Euripides.

CONSTANTINE, David. Lecturer in German, Queen's College, Oxford. Author of *The Significance of Locality in the Poetry of Friedrich Hölderlin*, 1979. Editor of *German Short Stories*, 1976. **Essays:** Hans Jakob Christoffel von Grimmelshausen; Friedrich Hölderlin.

COOKE, Ray. Author of "Image and Symbol in Khlebnikov's 'Night Search,'" in *Russian Triquarterly 12*, 1975, and "Magic in the Poetry of Velimir Khlebnikov," in *Essays in Poetics 5*, 1980. **Essay:** Velimir Khlebnikov.

CORNWELL, Neil. Lecturer in Slavonic Studies, Queen's University, Belfast; Founding Editor, *Irish Slavonic Studies*. Author of a forthcoming book on V.F. Odoyevsky, and of articles, reviews, and translations of 19th- and 20th-century Russian literature. **Essays:** Isaak Babel; Evgeny Zamyatin.

COSTA, C.D.N. Senior Lecturer in Classics, University of Birmingham. Editor of *Medea* by Seneca, 1973, and of the collections *Horace*, 1973, and *Seneca*, 1974. **Essay:** Seneca.

(CROFT), Sally McMullen. Ph.D. student, Cambridge University. **Essays:** Hugo von Hofmannsthal; Stéphane Mallarmé.

CUBBIN, G.P. University Lecturer in German, Cambridge University. Author of numerous articles on German literature. **Essays:** *Nibelungenlied*; Wolfram von Eschenbach.

DAYDI-TOLSON, Santiago. Assistant Professor of Spanish, University of Virginia, Charlottesville. Author of *The Post-Civil War Spanish Social Poets*, 1983, and articles on Gabriel Mistral, José Angel Valente, and other writers. Editor of *Vicente Aleixandre: A Critical Appraisal*, 1981, and *Five Poets of Aztlán* (forthcoming). **Essay:** César Vallejo.

de COSTA, René. Professor of Romance Languages and Director of the Center for Latin American Studies, University of Chicago. Author of *The Poetry of Pablo Neruda*, 1979, *En pos de Huidobro*, 1980, *Vicente Huidobro: The Careers of a Poet*, 1984, and many articles on Neruda, Borges, Huidobro, Reverdy, and other writers. Editor of works by Huidobro and Pedro Prado, and of a collection of articles on Huidobro. **Essay:** Pablo Neruda.

DOWDEN, Ken. Lecturer in Classics, University College, Cardiff. Author of articles on Greek religion and on Apuleius, including "Psyche on the Rock," in *Latomus 41*, 1982, and "Apuleius and the Art of Narration," in *Classical Quarterly 32*, 1982. **Essay:** Apuleius.

DRIVER, Sam. Professor and Chairman of the Department of Slavic Languages, Brown University, Providence, Rhode Island. Author of *Anna Akhmatova*, 1972. **Essay:** Anna Akhmatova.

DUNKLEY, John. Lecturer in French, University of Aberdeen. Author of *Gambling: A Social and Moral Problem in France 1684-1792* (forthcoming). Editor of *Amusements sérieux et comiques* by Dufresny, 1976, *Electre* by Crébillon père, 1980, and *Le Joueur* by Regnard (forthcoming). **Essays:** Denis Diderot; Jean-Jacques Rousseau.

ERMOLAEV, Herman. Professor of Russian Literature, Princeton University, New Jersey. Author of *Soviet Literary Theories 1917-1934: The Genesis of Socialist Realism*, 1963, and *Mikhail Sholokhov and His Art*, 1982. Editor and translator of *Untimely Thoughts* by Gorky, 1968. **Essay:** Alexander Solzhenitsyn.

FEHSENFELD, Nancy Kanach. Director of Studies and Lecturer, Princeton University, New Jersey. **Essays:** Alexander Pushkin; Ivan Turgenev.

FLETCHER, John. Professor of Comparative Literature, University of East Anglia, Norwich. Author of *The Novels of Samuel Beckett*, 1964, *Samuel Beckett's Art*, 1967, *New Directions in Literature*, 1968, *Claude Simon and Fiction Now*, 1975, *Novel and Reader*, 1980, and *Alain Robbe-Grillet*, 1983. **Essays:** Colette; Eugène Ionesco; Madame de Lafayette; André Malraux; Molière; Alain Robbe-Grillet; Marquis de Sade.

FOULKES, A.P. Professor of German, University College, Cardiff. Author of *The Reluctant Pessimist: A Study of Franz Kafka*, 1967, *The Search for Literary Meaning*, 1975, and *Literature and Propaganda*, 1983. Editor of *Das deutsche Drama von Kleist bis Hauptmann* (with others), 1973, and *The Uses of Criticism*, 1976. **Essays:** Gerhart Hauptmann; Kafka; Gottfried Keller.

FOWLIE, Wallace. Professor Emeritus of French, Duke University, Durham, North Carolina. Author of many books, including poetry, a novel, studies of Villon, Mallarmé, Rimbaud, Claudel, Proust, Gide, Cocteau, Stendhal, and Lautréamont, general books on French literature, and autobiographical works. Editor or translator of works by Maurice Scève, Balzac, Saint-John Perse, Cocteau, Claudel, Baudelaire, Molière, Mauriac, Rimbaud, and of several anthologies. **Essays:** Guillaume Apollinaire; Paul Claudel; Jean Cocteau; Jean Genet; André Gide; Marcel Proust; Saint-John Perse; Paul Valéry.

FREEMAN, Michael. Lecturer in French, University of Leicester. Author of articles on Pierre de Larivey, Guillaume Coquillart, and the *sottie*. Editor of *Oeuvres* by Coquillart, 1975, and *Les Esprits* by Larrivey, 1979. **Essays:** Joachim Du Bellay; Michel de Montaigne; François Rabelais; Pierre de Ronsard; *Romance of the Rose*; François Villon.

FROST, Frank J. Professor of Greek History, University of California, Santa Barbara; Associate Editor, *American Journal of Ancient History*. Author of *Greek Society*, 2nd edition 1980, *Plutarch's Themistocles*, 1980, and many articles on Greek history and archaeology. **Essay:** Plutarch.

GARTON, Janet. Lecturer in Scandinavian Studies, University of East Anglia, Norwich; Assistant Editor, *Scandinavica.* Author of *Writers and Politics in Modern Scandinavia,* 1978, and several articles on modern Scandinavian literature. **Essays:** Knut Hamsun; Henrik Ibsen; Snorri Sturluson; Sigrid Undset.

GIBSON, Margaret. Reader in Medieval History, University of Liverpool. Author of *Lanfranc of Bec,* 1978. Editor of *The Letters of Lanfranc,* 1980, and *Boethius: His Life, Thought and Influence,* 1981. **Essay:** Boethius.

GLATZER, Nahum N. University Professor of Judaica, Boston University; Chief Editorial Adviser, Schocken Books, New York. Author of books in German on the Talmud and Leopold Zunz, and of *Franz Rosenzweig: His Life and Thought,* 1953, and *Essays in Jewish Thought,* 1978. Editor of *The Complete Stories* by Kafka, 1971, *Twenty-One Stories* by S.Y. Agnon, 1970, and, with others, *Schriften, Tagebücher, Briefe* by Kafka, from 1983. **Essay:** S.Y. Agnon.

GOLDBERG, Sandor M. Assistant Professor of Classics, University of Colorado, Boulder. Author of *The Making of Menander's Comedy,* 1980, *The Problem of Terence* (forthcoming), "Scholarship on Terence and the Fragments of Roman Comedy," in *Classical World 75,* 1981, and many other articles and reviews. **Essays:** Menander; Terence.

GÖMÖRI, George. Lecturer in Slavonic Studies, Cambridge University. Author of *Polish and Hungarian Poetry 1945 to 1956,* 1966, and *Cyprian Norwid,* 1974. Editor, with others, of *Love of the Scorching Wind* by László Nagy, 1973, and *Forced March* by Miklós Radnóti, 1979. **Essays:** Witold Gombrowicz; Gyula Illyés; Stanislaw Witkiewicz.

GREEN, Roger. Modern Greek Librarian, Taylor Institution, Oxford. Author of *Notes from Overground* (as Tiresias), 1984. **Essay:** Nikos Kazantzakis.

GRUZELIER, Claire E. D.Phil. Research Student, Balliol College, Oxford. **Essays:** St. Augustine; Marcus Aurelius.

HAAC, Oscar A. Professor of French, State University of New York, Stony Brook. Author of *Les Principes Inspirateurs de Michelet,* 1951, *Marivaux,* 1973, and *Jules Michelet,* 1982. Editor of works by Michelet and Ballanche. **Essay:** Marivaux.

HABERLY, David T. Associate Professor of Portuguese, University of Virginia, Charlottesville. Author of *Three Sad Races: Racial Identity and National Consciousness in Brazilian Literature,* 1983, and numerous articles on Brazilian, Portuguese, Spanish American, and comparative literature. **Essays:** Joaquim Maria Machado de Assis; Fernando Pessoa.

HÁJEK, Igor. Lecturer in Slavonic Languages and Literatures, University of Glasgow. Co-Editor and contributor, *Modern Slavic Literatures 2,* 1976, and *Dictionary of Czech Writers 1948-1979,* 1982; author of numerous articles and reviews.

HALPERIN, David M. Associate Professor of Literature, Massachusetts Institute of Technology, Cambridge. Author of *Before Pastoral: Theocritus and the Ancient Tradition of Bucolic Poetry,* 1983, "Solzhenitsyn, Epicurus, and the Ethics of Stalinism," in *Critical Inquiry 7,* 1980, "The Forebears of Daphnis," in *Transactions of the American Philological Association 113,* 1983, and "Plato and Erotic Reciprocity," in *Journal of the History of Ideas 45,* 1983. **Essay:** Theocritus.

HARRIES, P.T. Lecturer in Japanese, School of Oriental and African Studies, University of London; Editor of *Bulletin of the European Association for Japanese Studies.* Author of *The*

Poetic Memoirs of Lady Daibu, 1980, and "Personal Poetry Collections," in *Monumenta Nipponica 36*, 1980. **Essay:** Basho.

HART, John. Senior Classics Master, Malvern College, Worcestershire. Author of *Herodotus and Greek History*, 1982. Winner of BBC Television's "Mastermind" competition, 1975. **Essay:** Herodotus.

HART, Thomas R. Professor of Romance Languages, University of Oregon, Eugene; Editor of *Comparative Literature*. Author of *Gil Vicente: Casandra and Don Duardos*, 1981, and many articles on Spanish and Portuguese literature. Editor of *Obras dramáticas castellanas*, 1962, and *Farces and Festival Plays*, 1972, both by Gil Vicente. **Essay:** Luís de Camoẽs.

HAWKESWORTH, E.C. Lecturer in Serbo-Croat, University of London. Author of *Ivo Andrić: A Bridge Between East and West*, 1984. **Essay:** Ivo Andrić.

HUTCHINSON, Peter. Fellow of Selwyn College, Cambridge. Author of *Literary Presentations of Divided Germany*, 1977, and *Games Authors Play*, 1983.

HYSLOP, Lois Boe. Professor Emerita of Romance Languages, Pennsylvania State University, University Park. Author of *Henry Becque*, 1972, and *Baudelaire, Man of His Time*, 1980. Editor, with F.E. Hyslop, of *Baudelaire on Poe*, 1952, *Baudelaire: A Self-Portrait*, 1957, *Baudelaire as a Literary Critic*, 1964, and *Baudelaire as a Love Poet and Other Essays*, 1969. **Essay:** Charles Baudelaire.

JANES, Regina. Associate Professor of English, Skidmore College, Saratoga Springs, New York. Author of *Gabriel García Márquez: Revolutions in Wonderland*, 1981, articles on Carlos Fuentes, Mary Wollstonecraft in *Journal of the History of Ideas*, 1978, and Edmund Burke in *Bulletin of Research in the Humanities*, 1979, and interviews with Guillermo Cabrera Infante and Carlos Fuentes in *Salmagundi*, 1978 and 1981. **Essay:** Alejo Carpentier.

JILLINGS, Lewis. Senior Lecturer in German, University of Stirling. Author of *"Diu Crone" of Heinrich von dem Türlein: The Attempted Emancipation of Secular Lyric*, 1980. **Essays:** Gottfried von Strassburg; Martin Luther; Walther von der Vogelweide.

KIRTON, W.J.S. Lecturer in French, University of Aberdeen. Author of plays for radio and stage. **Essay:** Victor Hugo.

KLOPP, Charles. Associate Professor of Romance Languages, Ohio State University, Columbus. Author of " 'Peregrino' and 'Errante' in the *Gerusalemme liberata*," in *Modern Language Notes*, 1979, the entry on Giosuè Carducci in *European Writers: The Romantic Century* (forthcoming), and articles on Italian literature. **Essays:** Eugenio Montale; Torquato Tasso.

KONRAD, Linn Bratteteig. Assistant Professor of French, Rice University, Houston. Author of "Modern Hieratic Ideas on Theatre: Maurice Maeterlinck and Antonin Artaud," in *Modern Drama 22*, 1979, "Symbolic Action in Modern Drama: Maurice Maeterlinck," in *Themes in Drama 4*, 1982, and "Maurice Maeterlinck in the 'Pharmaceutical Tradition,' " in *Romanic Review 73*, 1982. **Essay:** Maurice Maeterlinck.

KONSTAN, David. Jane A. Seney Professor of Greek, Wesleyan University, Middletown, Connecticut. Author of *Some Aspects of Epicurean Psychology*, 1973, *Catullus' Indictment of Rome: The Meaning of Catullus 64*, 1977, *Roman Comedy*, 1983, and a commentary on *Dyskolos* by Menander, 1983. **Essay:** Plautus.

LaBELLE, Maurice Marc. Professor of English and Comparative Literature, Drake University, Des Moines, Iowa. Author of *Alfred Jarry: Nihilism and the Theatre of the Absurd*,

1980, and of articles on Artaud and Céline. **Essay:** Alfred Jarry.

LAMPORT, F.J. Fellow of Worcester College, Oxford. Author of *A Student's Guide to Goethe*, 1971, and *Lessing and the Drama*, 1981. Translator of *Five German Tragedies*, 1969, and *The Robbers* and *Wallenstein* by Schiller, 1979. **Essays:** Johann Wolfgang von Goethe; Gotthold Ephraim Lessing; Friedrich von Schiller.

LEVIN, Harry. Irving Babbitt Professor of Comparative Literature, Harvard University, Cambridge, Massachusetts. Author of many critical books, the most recent being *The Myth of the Golden Age in the Renaissance, Grounds for Comparison, Shakespeare and the Revolution of the Times*, and *Memories of the Moderns*. Editor of works by Jonson, Rochester, Joyce, Shakespeare, and Hawthorne, and of anthologies.

LÖB, Ladislaus. Reader in German, University of Sussex, Brighton. Author of *Mensch und Gesellschaft bei J.B. Priestley*, 1962, *From Lessing to Hauptmann: Studies in German Drama*, 1974, a textbook on German, and articles on German drama for journals and anthologies. **Essays:** Friedrich Hebbel; Heinrich von Kleist; Frank Wedekind.

LUCENTE, Gregory L. Associate Professor of Romance Languages, Johns Hopkins Univesity, Baltimore. Author of *The Narrative of Realism and Myth: Verga, Lawrence, Faulkner, Pavese*, 1981, and of articles on D'Annunzio, Joyce, Silone, and *verismo*. **Essays:** Luigi Pirandello; Giovanni Verga.

LUFT, David S. Associate Professor of History, University of California at San Diego, La Jolla. Author of *Robert Musil and the Crisis of European Culture 1880-1942*, 1980, "Schopenhauer, Austria, and the Generation of 1905," in *Central European History*, March 1983, and a forthcoming essay on Otto Weininger. **Essay:** Robert Musil.

MASON, Haydn T. Professor of French, University of Bristol. Author of *Pierre Bayle and Voltaire*, 1963, *Voltaire*, 1975, *Voltaire: A Biography*, 1981, *French Writers and Their Society 1715-1800*, 1982, and *Cyrano de Bergerac: L'Autre Monde*, 1984. Editor of *Les Fausses Confidences* by Marivaux, 1964, *The Leibniz-Arnauld Correspondence*, 1967, and *Zadig and Other Stories* by Voltaire, 1971. **Essay:** Voltaire.

MAY, Gita. Professor and Chairman of the Department of French and Romance Philology, Columbia University, New York. Author of *Diderot et Baudelaire, critiques d'art*, 1957 (3rd edition, 1973), *De Jean-Jacques Rousseau à Madame Roland*, 1964 (2nd edition, 1974), *Madame Roland and the Age of Revolution*, 1970, *Stendhal and the Age of Napoleon*, 1977, essays on Diderot and George Sand in *European Writers* (forthcoming), and many articles and reviews. Editor, with Otis Fellows, of *Diderot Studies III*, 1961, and of works for the Paris edition of Diderot's *Oeuvres complètes*. **Essay:** Stendhal.

McCARTHY, Patrick. Member of the Department of French, Haverford College, Pennsylvania. Author of *Céline*, 1975, and *Camus: A Critical Study of His Life and Work*, 1982. **Essays:** Louis-Ferdinand Céline; Pier Paolo Pasolini.

McMAHON, Keith. Member of the Faculty, Princeton University, New Jersey. **Essays:** *Chin P'ing Mei*; Lu Hsun; *Water Margin*.

MILES, Gary B. Associate Professor of History, University of California, Santa Cruz. Author of *Virgil's Georgics*, 1980, and of articles on Virgil, Theocritus, the Bible, and other subjects in *California Studies in Classical Antiquity, Ramus, Harvard Theological Review*, and other journals. **Essay:** Virgil.

MINER, Earl. Townsend Martin Professor of English and Comparative Literature, Princeton University, New Jersey. Author of *Dryden's Poetry*, 1967, *An Introduction to Japanese Court Poetry*, 1968, *The Metaphysical Mode from Donne to Cowley*, 1969, *The Cavalier Mode from Jonson to Cotton*, 1971, *Seventeenth-Century Imagery*, 1971, *The Restoration Mode from Milton to Dryden*, 1974, *Literary Uses of Typology*, 1977, and *Japanese Linked Poetry*, 1979. Translator, with Hiroko Odagiri, of *The Monkey's Straw Raincoat and Other Poetry of the Basho School*, 1981. Editor of *A History of Japanese Literature* by Jin'ichi Konishi, from 1984.

MINYARD, John Douglas. Associate Professor of Classical Civilization, University of North Carolina, Greensboro. Author of *Mode and Value in the De Rerum Natura: A Study in Lucretius's Metrical Language*, 1978, and of articles on Catullus. **Essay:** Lucretius.

MIYOSHI, Masao. Professor of English, University of California, Berkeley. Author of *The Divided Self: A Perspective on the Literature of the Victorians*, 1969, *Accomplices of Silence: The Modern Japanese Novel*, 1974, and *As We Saw Them: The First Japanese Embassy to the United States (1860)*, 1979. **Essays:** Kawabata Yasunari; Natsume Soseki.

MIZENKO, Matthew. Assistant Professor of Asian Languages and Literatures, Amherst College, Massachusetts. **Essay:** Dazai Osamu.

MUIR, Kenneth. Emeritus Professor and Honorary Fellow, Liverpool University. Author of many books, including *Shakespeare's Tragic Sequence*, 1972, *Shakespeare the Professional*, 1973, *The Singularity of Shakespeare*, 1977, *The Sources of Shakespeare's Plays*, 1977, *Shakespeare's Comic Sequence*, 1979, and studies of Milton, Elizabethan literature, and the comedy of manners. Editor of five plays by Shakespeare, and works by Thomas Wyatt, Keats, and Middleton, and of anthologies. Translator of *Five Plays* by Racine, 1960, and *Four Comedies* by Calderón, 1980. **Essay:** Pedro Calderón de la Barca.

NISETICH, Frank J. Associate Professor of Classics, University of Massachusetts, Boston. Translator of *Victory Songs* by Pindar, 1980. **Essays:** Pindar, Sappho.

PARROTT, (Sir) Cecil. Professor Emeritus in Central and South-Eastern European Studies, University of Lancaster; British Ambassador to Czechoslovakia, 1960-66. Author of *Czechslovakia: Its Heritage and Future*, 1968, two volumes of memoirs—*The Tightrope*, 1975, and *The Serpent and the Nightingale*, 1977—, *The Bad Bohemian: The Life of Jaroslav Hašek*, 1978, and *Jaroslav Hašek: A Study of Svejk and the Short Stories*, 1982. Translator of *The Good Soldier Svejk* (complete version), 1973, and *The Red Commissar and Other Stories*, 1981, both by Hašek. **Essays:** Karel Capek; Jaroslav Hašek.

PATERSON, Alan K.G. Professor of Spanish, St. Andrews University, Fife, Scotland. Author of numerous articles on Spanish Golden Age poetry and drama, including "The Traffic of the Stage in Calderón's *La vida es sueño*," in *Renaissance Drama 4*, 1971, and "The Alchemical Marriage in Calderón's *El médico de su honra*," in *Romanistisches Jahrbuch 30*, 1979. Editor of *La venganza de Tamar* by Tirso de Molina, 1969. **Essay:** Lope de Vega Carpio.

PETERKIEWICZ, Jerzy. Author of many books, including novels (*Future to Let, Isolation, Green Flows the Bile*), plays (*The Third Adam*), verse, and critical books (*The Other Side of Silence: The Poet at the Limits of Language*, 1975). Editor and translator of *Polish Prose and Verse*, 1956, *Five Centuries of Polish Poetry 1450-1970* (with Burns Singer), 1970, and *Easter Vigil and Other Poems*, 1979, and *Collected Poems*, 1982, both by Karol Wojtyla (Pope John Paul II). Formerly, Professor of Polish Language and Literature, University of London.

PIKE, Christopher R. Lecturer in Russian Studies, University of Keele, Staffordshire; Editor of the journal *Essays in Poetics*. Author of "Formalist and Structuralist Approaches to

Dostoevsky," in *New Essays on Dostoevsky* edited by Malcolm V. Jones and Garth M. Terry, 1983. Editor of *The Futurists, The Formalists and the Marxist Critique*, 1980. **Essays:** Anton Chekhov; Fyodor Dostoevsky; Leo Tolstoy.

PIRIE, Donald Peter Alexander. Writer and teacher. **Essays:** Jan Kochanowski; Adam Mickiewicz; Bruno Schulz.

POCOCK, Gordon. Author of *Corneille and Racine: Problems of Tragic Form*, 1973, and *Boileau and the Nature of Neo-Classicism*, 1980. **Essays:** Nicolas Boileau; Pierre Corneille.

POLUKHINA, Valentina. Lecturer in Russian, University of Keele, Staffordshire. Author of an article and a forthcoming monograph on Joseph Brodsky's poetry, and of entries on Russian and Soviet writers for *The Fontana Biographical Companion to Modern Thought*, 1983. **Essays:** Andrey Bely; Alexander Blok; Osip Mandelstam; Vladimir Mayakovsky; Boris Pasternak; Marina Tsvetayeva.

PORTER, Charles A. Professor of French, Yale University, New Haven, Connecticut. Author of *Restif's Novels; or, An Autobiography in Search of an Author*, 1967, and *Chateaubriand: Composition, Imagination, and Poetry*, 1978. **Essay:** Chateaubriand.

PUVAČIĆ, Dušan. Lecturer in Yugoslav Studies, University of Lancaster. Contributor to Yugoslav literary journals. Editor of *Kritički radovi Branka Lazarevića*, 1975, and translator into Serbo-Croat of many works of English and American literature. **Essay:** Miroslav Krleža.

RAGUSA, Olga. Da Ponte Professor and Chairman of the Department of Italian, Columbia University, New York; Editor of the journal *Italica*. Author of *Mallarmé in Italy: A Study in Literary Influence and Critical Response*, 1957, *Verga's Milanese Tales*, 1964, *Narrative and Drama: Essays in Modern Italian Literature from Verga to Pasolini*, 1976, *Luigi Pirandello: An Approach to His Theatre*, 1980, and an essay in *"Romantic" and Its Cognates: The European History of a Word* edited by H. Eichner, 1972. **Essays:** Vittorio Alfieri; Alessandro Manzoni.

RAWSON, Judy. Senior Lecturer and Chairman of the Department of Italian, University of Warwick, Coventry. Editor of *Fontamara* by Ignazio Silone, 1972. **Essays:** Cesare Pavese; Ignazio Silone; Elio Vittorini.

REID, J.H. Senior Lecturer in German, University of Nottingham. Author of *Critical Strategies: German Fiction in the Twentieth Century* (with E. Boa), 1972, *Heinrich Böll: Withdrawal and Re-Emergence*, 1973, and articles in *Modern Langage Review, German Life and Letters, Renaissance and Modern Studies, Forum for Modern Language Studies*, and other periodicals. **Essays:** Heinrich Böll.

REID, Robert. Lecturer in Slavonic Studies, Queen's University, Belfast. Author of articles on Lermontov in *New Zealand Slavonic Journal 1*, 1977, *The Slavonic and East European Review 60*, 1982, and *Essays in Poetics 7*, 1982. Editor and contributor, *Problems of Russian Romanticism* (forthcoming). **Essays:** Ivan Goncharov; Mikhail Lermontov.

REILLY, John H. Professor of French, Queens College, City University of New York. Author of *Arthur Adamov*, 1974, and *Jean Giraudoux*, 1978. Editor of *Intermezzo* by Giraudoux, 1967. **Essays:** Arthur Adamov; Jean Giraudoux.

REYNOLDS, Barbara. Reader in Italian, Nottingham University, now retired; General Editor of the *Cambridge Italian Dictionary*. Author of *The Linguistic Writings of Manzoni*, 1950. Translator with Dorothy L. Sayers, of *Paradise* by Dante, 1962, and of *Vita Nuova* by Dante, 1969, and *The Frenzy of Orlando* by Ariosto, 2 vols., 1975. **Essays:** Ludovico Ariosto;

Niccolò Machiavelli.

RINSLER, Norma. Professor of French Language and Literature, King's College, University of London. Author of *Gérard de Nerval*, 1973, and of many articles on Nerval, Hugo, Aragon, Valéry, Apollinaire, Gide, and other writers. Editor of *Les Chimères* by Nerval, 1973. **Essay:** Gérard de Nerval.

ROBINSON, Michael. Lecturer in the Department of English and Drama, Loughborough University, Leicestershire. Author of *The Long Sonata of the Dead: A Study of Samuel Beckett*, 1969, *Sven Delblanc: Åminne*, 1981, and essays on Ibsen, Strindberg, and Beckett. **Essay:** August Strindberg.

RODGERS, Eamonn. Senior Lecturer in Spanish, Trinity College, Dublin. Author of articles in *Bulletin of Hispanic Studies*, *Forum for Modern Language Studies*, *Anales Galdosianos*, and *Cuadernos Hispano-amricanos*. Editor of *Tormento* by Pérez Galdós, 1977. **Essay:** Benito Pérez Galdós.

RORRISON, Hugh. Lecturer in the Department of German, University of Leeds, Yorkshire. Author of essays in the collections *Modern Austrian Writing*, 1980, and *Brecht in Perspective*, 1982, and of "Kroetz Checklist" in *Theatrefacts 3*, 1976. Editor of *Erwin Piscator: The Political Theatre* (also translator), 1978, and *Mother Courage* by Brecht, 1983; adviser on German theatre for *Oxford Companion to the Theatre*, 1983. **Essays:** Georg Büchner; Franz Grillparzer.

SHOICHI SAEKI. Professor at Chuo University, Tokyo. Author of *In Search of the Japanese Self*, 1974, *Japanese Autobiographies*, 1974, and *Mishima Yukio: A Critical Biography*, 1978 (all in Japanese). Editor, with Donald Keene, of *Zenshu* [Collected Works] by Mishima, 36 vols., 1973-76. **Essays:** Mishima Yukio; Tanizaki Jun'ichiro.

SALE, William Merritt, III. Professor of Classics and Comparative Literature, Washington University, St. Louis. Author of *Existentialism and Euripides*, 1977. Editor and translator, *Electra* by Sophocles, 1973. **Essays:** Hesiod; Homer.

SAMMONS, Jeffrey L. Leavenworth Professor of German, Yale University, New Haven, Connecticut. Author of *The Nachtwachen von Bonaventura: A Structural Interpretation*, 1965, *Angelus Silesius*, 1967, *Heinrich Heine, The Elusive Poet*, 1969, *Six Essays on the Young German Novel*, 1972, *Literary Sociology and Practical Criticism: An Inquiry*, 1977, *Heinrich Heine: A Modern Biography*, 1979, and *Heinrich Heine: A Critical Bibliography of the Secondary Literature 1956-1980*, 1982. **Essay:** Heinrich Heine.

SANDARS, N.K. Author of *Prehistoric Art in Europe*, 1967 (revised edition, 1984), and *The Sea-Peoples, Warriors of the Ancient Mediterranean 1250-1150 B.C.*, 1978. Translator of *The Epic of Gilgamesh*, 1960 (revised edition, 1972), and *Poems of Heaven and Hell from Ancient Mesopotamia*, 1971. **Essay:** Gilgamesh.

SAUNDERS, Barbara. Social worker. Author of *Contemporary German Autobiography: Literary Approaches to the Problem of Identity* (forthcoming), "Christa Wolf's *Kindheitsmuster*: An East German Experiment in Political Autobiography" (with Neil Jackson), in *German Life and Letters*, July 1980, and an article on Max Frisch in *Forum for Modern Language Studies 18*, 1982. **Essay:** Elias Canetti.

SCHERR, Barry P. Associate Professor of Russian, Dartmouth College, Hanover, New Hampshire. Author of "Notes on Literary Life in Petrograd, 1918-1922: A Tale of Three Houses," 1977, "Gor'kij's *Childhood*: The Autobiography as Fiction," 1979, and "Russian and English Versification: Similarities, Differences, Analysis," 1980; co-author of "Russian Verse

Theory since 1974: A Commentary and Bibliography," 1980. **Essay:** Maxim Gorky.

SCOBBIE, Irene. Reader in Scandinavian Studies, University of Aberdeen. Author of *Pär Lagerkvist: An Introduction*, 1963, *Sweden: Nation of the Modern World*, 1972, *Pär Lagerkvist's Gäst hos verkligheten*, 1974, and articles on Lagerkvist, Strindberg, P.O. Sundman, Stig Claesson, and other writers. Editor and contributor, *Essays on Swedish Literature from 1880 to the Present Day*, 1978. **Essays:** Pär Lagerkvist; Selma Lagerlöf.

SCOTT, Mary. Assistant Professor of Asian Studies, University of Puget Sound, Tacoma, Washington. **Essay:** *Dream of the Red Chamber*.

SEIDENSTICKER, Edward. Professor of Japanese, Columbia University, New York. Author of *Kafu the Scribbler*, 1965, and *Low City, High City*, 1983. Translator of *The Tale of Genji* by Murasaki Shikibu, 1976, and works by Tanizaki Jun'ichiro, Kawabati Yasunari, Mishima Yukio, and other modern and classical Japanese writers. **Essay:** Murasaki Shikibu.

SHARMAN, Ruth. Press Officer, Fontana Paperbacks, London. Author of an article on Giraut de Borneil in *Medium Aevum*, 1982, and reviews in *French Studies* and *Romance Philology*. Editor of *The Poems of Giraut de Borneil*, 1984. **Essay:** François Mauriac.

SHAW, Barnett. Playwright and actor. Translator of several plays by Feydeau, Labiche, and Dumas père. **Essay:** Alexandre Dumas, père.

SICES, David. Professor of French and Italian, Dartmouth College, Hanover, New Hampshire; Assistant Editor of *French Review*. Author of *Harmony of Contrasts: Music and the Musician in Jean-Christophe*, 1968, *Theatre of Solitude: The Drama of Alfred de Musset*, 1974, *2001 French Idioms*, 1982, and the Musset entry in *European Writers*, 1984. **Essay:** Alfred de Musset.

SINGH, G. Professor of Italian, Queen's University, Belfast. Author of *Leopardi and the Theory of Poetry*, 1964, *Leopardi e l'Inghilterra*, 1968, *Montale: A Critical Study of His Poetry, Prose and Criticism*, 1973, and *Ezra Pound*, 1979. Editor of *It Depends: A Poet's Notebook* by Montale, 1980, and *Collected Essays of Q.D. Leavis*, vol. 1, 1983. Translator of *New Poems* by Montale, 1976. **Essays:** Guido Cavalcanti; Gabriele D'Annunzio; Giacomo Leopardi; Giuseppe Ungaretti.

SMITH, C.N. Senior Lecturer, School of Modern Languages and European History, University of East Anglia, Norwich; Editor of *Seventeenth-Century French Studies*. Author of many articles and of reviews of the performing arts. Editor of works by Antoine de Montchrestien, Jacques de la Taille, and Pierre Matthieu. **Essay:** Honoré de Balzac.

SOWARDS, J. Kelley. Distinguished Professor of Humanities and History, Wichita State University, Kansas. Co-author of *The Julius exclusus of Erasmus*, 1968, and author of *Desiderius Erasmus*, 1975. Member of the Editorial Board of *The Collected Works of Erasmus*, and editor of vols. 25 and 26, 1984. **Essay:** Desiderius Erasmus.

STAMM, James Russell. Associate Professor of Spanish and Portuguese, New York University. Author of *A Short History of Spanish Literature*, 1966 (revised edition, 1979), and numerous articles on the early Spanish novel and theatre. Editor, with Herbert E. Isar, of *Dos novelas cortas: Miguel de Unamuno*, 1967. **Essays:** Miguel de Cervantes; Fernando de Rojas; Miguel de Unamuno.

STATHATOS, C.C. Associate Professor of Spanish, University of Wisconsin—Parkside, Kenosha. Author of *A Gil Vicente Bibliography (1940-1975)*, 1980 (supplement, 1982). Editor of *Floresta de enganos* by Gil Vicente, 1972. **Essay:** Gil Vicente.

ADVISERS AND CONTRIBUTORS

STEWART, Mary E. Fellow and Lecturer in German, Robinson College, Cambridge. Author of numerous articles on the German novel since 1880 in *Modern Language Review*, *German Life and Letters*, *Journal of European Studies*, and other periodicals. **Essays:** Max Frisch; Hermann Hesse.

STILLMARK, Alexander. Lecturer in German, University College, London. Author of "Stifter's Symbolism of Beauty," in *Oxford German Studies*, 1971, "Stifter's Early Portraits of the Artist," in *Forum for Modern Language Studies*, 1975, and "The Poet and His Public: Hofmannsthal's 'idealer Zuhörer,' " in *London German Studies 1*, 1980. Joint Editor of *Adalbert Stifter Heute*, 1984. **Essays:** Ödön von Horváth; Novalis; Adalbert Stifter; Georg Trakl.

STOREY, Ian C. Associate Professor of Classical Studies, Trent University, Peterborough, Ontario. **Essay:** Aristophanes.

SUBIOTTO, Arrigo V. Professor and Head of the Department of German, University of Birmingham. Author of *Bertolt Brecht's Adaptations for the Berliner Ensemble*, 1975, and of many articles on Brecht, Grass, Hochhuth, Dürrenmatt, Frisch, Müller, and other writers. **Essays:** Bertolt Brecht; Günter Grass.

SULLIVAN, Henry W. Professor of Spanish and Chairman of the Department of Modern Languages and Literatures, University of Ottawa. Author of *Tirso de Molina and the Drama of the Counter Reformation*, 1976, *Juan del Encina*, 1976, *Calderón in the German Lands and the Low Countries: His Reception and Influence 1654-1780*, 1983, and many articles on Spanish Golden Age drama and the theory of tragedy. **Essay:** Tirso de Molina.

SZÉPE, Helena. Free-lance writer; author of many articles on German literature. Former Associate Professor of German, Roosevelt University, Chicago. **Essay:** Hermann Broch.

TAYLOR, Myron. Associate Professor of English, State University of New York, Albany. Author of articles on Shakespeare in *The Christian Scholar*, *Studies in English*, and *Shakespeare Quarterly*. **Essays:** *Bible*; Plato.

THODY, Philip. Professor of French Literature, University of Leeds, Yorkshire. Author of two books on Camus and two books on Sartre, books on Genet, Anouilh, Laclos, Aldous Huxley, and Barthes, and a novel, *Dog Days in Babel*, 1979. Editor of works by Camus and Sartre. **Essays:** Beaumarchais; Gustave Flaubert; Choderlos de Laclos; Jean de La Fontaine; Abbé Prévost; Jean Racine; George Sand; Alfred de Vigny.

THOMAS, David. Lecturer in Drama, University of Bristol. Author of *Henrik Ibsen*, 1983. Editor of volume 8 (on the Restoration and 18th Century) of *Theatre in Europe: Sources and Documents* (forthcoming). **Essay:** Ludvig Holberg.

THURMAN, Judith. Author of *Isak Dinesen: The Life of a Storyteller*, 1982. **Essay:** Isak Dinesen.

TORRANCE, Robert M. Professor of Comparative Literature, University of California, Davis. Author of *The Comic Hero*, 1978. Translator of *The Women of Trachis* and *Philoctetes* by Sophocles, 1966.

VERANI, Hugo J. Professor of Spanish-American Literature, University of California, Davis. Author of *Narrativa contemporánea*, 1979, *Onetti: El ritual de la impostura*, 1981, and *Octavio Paz: Bibliografía crítica*, 1983. **Essays:** Jorge Luis Borges; Octavio Paz.

VERTHUY, Maïr. Associate Professor of French, and Fellow of the Simone de Beauvoir

Institute, Concordia University, Montreal; Editor of *Canadian Women's Studies*. Author of articles on Hélène Parmelin, Christiane Rochefort, Roger Vailland, Michèle Mailhot, and other writers. Editor of *Femme*, 1984. **Essay:** Gabrielle Roy.

WALLACE, Albert H. Professor of Romance Languages, University of Tennessee, Knoxville. Author of *Guy de Maupassant*, 1973, and articles on Maupassant and Flaubert. **Essay:** Guy de Maupassant.

WALSH, George. Publisher and free-lance writer. **Essays:** Carlo Goldoni; Petronius; *Thousand and One Nights*.

WEISSBORT, Daniel. Professor of Comparative Literature, and Director of the Translation Workshop, University of Iowa, Iowa City; Co-Founding Editor, with Ted Hughes, *Modern Poetry in Translation*. Author of three books of poetry, *The Leaseholder*, 1971, *In an Emergency*, 1972, and *Soundings*, 1977. Editor and translator of many books, including works by Gorbanevskaya, Vinokurov, Evtushenko, and Claude Simon, and of collections of Russian poetry.

WELSH, David. Professor Emeritus, University of Michigan, Ann Arbor. Author of *Russian Comedy*, 1966, *Adam Mickiewicz*, 1966, *Ignacy Krasicki*, 1969, and *Jan Kochanowski*, 1974. **Essay:** Henryk Sienkiewicz.

WHITTON, Kenneth S. Chairman of the School of European Studies, University of Bradford, Yorkshire. Author of *The Theatre of Friedrich Dürrenmatt: A Study in the Possibility of Freedom*, 1980, *Dietrich Fischer-Dieskau: Mastersinger*, 1981, *Lieder for the Layman: An Introduction to German Song*, 1984, several textbooks, and *Wir waren vier*, a series for British television. Translator of *Schubert's Songs* by Fischer-Dieskau, 1977. **Essays:** Friedrich Dürrenmatt; Peter Weiss.

WOODMAN, A.J. Professor of Latin, University of Leeds, Yorkshire. Author of *Velleius Paterculus: The Tiberian Narrative*, 1977, and *Valleius Paterculus: The Caesarian and Augustan Narrative*, 1983. Editor, with David West, of *Quality and Pleasure in Latin Poetry*, 1974, *Creative Imitation and Latin Literature*, 1979, and *Poetry and Politics in the Age of Augustus*, 1984. **Essays:** Catullus; Horace; Livy; Tacitus; Thucydides.

WOODS, M.J. Lecturer in Spanish, King's College, University of London. Author of *The Poet and the Natural World in the Age of Góngora*, 1978, and "Pitfalls for the Moralizer in *Lazarillo de Tormes*," in *Modern Language Review 74*, 1979. **Essays:** Luis de Góngora; *Lazarillo de Tormes*.

WOODWARD, James B. Professor of Russian, University College, Swansea. Author of *Leonid Andreyev: A Study*, 1969, *Gogol's "Dead Souls"*, 1978, *Ivan Bunin: A Study of His Fiction*, 1980, and *The Symbolic Art of Gogol: Essays on His Short Fiction*, 1982. Editor of *Selected Poems* by Alexander Blok, 1968. **Essay:** Nikolai Gogol.

WRIGHT, A. Colin. Professor of Russian, Queen's University, Kingston, Ontario. Author of *Mikhail Bulgakov: Life and Interpretations*, 1978, and articles in *PMLA*, *Canadian-American Slavic Studies*, and *Canadian Slavonic Papers*. Editor of *Rakhel*, 1972, and *Minin i Pozharski*, 1976, both by Bulgakov. **Essay:** Mikhail Bulgakov.

WRIGHT, Barbara. Free-lance translator. Translator of works by Queneau, Robbe-Grillet, Sarraute, Pinget, and Tournier; contributor to the *Times Literary Supplement*. **Essay:** Raymond Queneau.

WRIGHT, Elizabeth. Fellow in German, Girton College, Cambridge.. Author of *Hoff-*

mann and the Rhetoric of Terror, 1978, and *Psychoanalytic Criticism: Theory in Practice* (forthcoming). **Essay:** E.T.A. Hoffmann.

YOHANNAN, John D. Professor Emeritus, City College of New York. Author of *A Treasury of Asian Literature*, 1956, *Joseph and Potiphar's Wife in World Literature*, 1968, and *Persian Poetry in England and America: A Two-Hundred Year History*, 1977. Editor, with Leo Hamalian, of *New Writing from the Middle East*, 1978. **Essay:** Hafiz.

YOUNG, Howard T. Professor of Romance Languages, Pomona College, Claremont, California. Author of *The Victorian Expression*, 1964, *Juan Ramón Jiménez*, 1967, and *The Line in the Margin: Jiménez and His Readings in Blake, Shelley, and Yeats*, 1980. **Essays:** Federico García Lorca; Juan Ramón Jiménez; Saint John of the Cross.